CW00722987

A History of the Study of Grammar among the Syrians

Perspectives on Linguistics and Ancient Languages

13

Perspectives on Linguistics and Ancient Languages (PLAL) contains peer-reviewed essays, monographs, and reference works. It focuses on the theory and practice of ancient-language research and lexicography that is informed by modern linguistics.

A History of the Study of Grammar among the Syrians

An English translation of
Historia artis grammaticae apud Syros

By

Adalbert Merx

Translated by

Daniel King

2023

Gorgias Press LLC, 954 River Road, Piscataway, NJ, 08854, USA

www.gorgiaspress.com

2023  

ISBN 978-1-4632-4197-1 **ISSN 2165-2600**

Library of Congress Cataloging-in-Publication Data

A Cataloging-in-Publication is available from the Library of Congress.

Printed and bound by CPI Group (UK) Ltd, Croydon, CR0 4YY

Table of Contents

Editorial Introduction

I. Adalbert Merx, his Life and Work[1]

Adalbert Merx was born in 1838. His mother, Eulalia, was a novelist of some repute, though not as (in)famous as her sister Louise Aston, a notorious and irrepressible radical, whose views hardly coincided with the far more conservative Protestant tastes of her sister, and of her brother-in-law, Friedrich Wilhelm Merx.

Adalbert studied in a variety of locations (Pforta, Marburg, Halle, Breslau), picking up a number of 'oriental' languages along the way (including Sanskrit, Persian and Ethiopic). After *Habilitation* in Jena in 1865 and an appointment as professor in the same place in 1869, he was invited in the same year to Tübingen to a position as professor of Semitic languages. After a brief stint at Giessen (1873-5), Merx finally became professor of theology at Heidelberg, the university with which he and his family would be associated for many years to come (his mother moved there and died only a year before her son). He made several journeys to the Near East in connection with his developing expertise as an all-round Orientalist, and this in the days of such figures as Theodor Nöldeke. In Heidelberg he was considered something of a polymath and linguistic genius.

Here he came into contact with both Ernst Troeltsch and the latter's close friend and colleague Max Weber. Troeltsch's account of his time in Heidelberg does not present us with a particularly flattering portrait of Merx, calling him vain and pedantic,[2] al it was during the 1890s that the faculty there grew into a significant international establishment. Merx himself must have been a rather stern and unsympathetic figure, perhaps not readily sympathetic to the ideas of the younger sociologists of his day. Despite the breadth of his research and the thoroughness of his arguments, Merx hardly engenders in the reader that same admiration elicited by the ever-relevant and pointed insights of his contemporary Nöldeke.

Besides publishing extensively in Old Testament studies, he was also actively engaged in epigraphy and Targumic studies. His interest in

---

[1] For further details and bio-bibliography, see the article by Klaus Breuer in the *Neue Deutsche Biographie*, vol. 17, 194-5.

[2] H. Libersohn, *Fate and Utopia in German Sociology 1870-1923* (MIT Pres 1989), p.51

linguistics stemmed from his early textbook on Syriac grammar (1st part, 1867) and was brought to full fruition in the present monumental monograph (1889). Towards the end of his career, Merx devoted himself to consideration of the Old Syriac Gospels in the Sinaitic palimpsest, which had been discovered in 1892. His initial results were published in *Die vier kanonischen Evangelien* (1897-1905), with further work completed by his student Julius Ruska. The last work published in his lifetime was a layman's commentary on the Hexateuch. He died suddenly at Heidelberg on the 6th of August 1909 while attending the funeral of a colleague.

As mentioned, Merx's work on the Sinai manuscript was completed by his principal student Julius Ruska, whose principal contribution to Syriac studies was an 1896 edition of part of Jacob Bar Šakko's *Dialogues*. The pupil married the professor's daughter, Elizabeth, and their son Ernst Ruska became somewhat more widely celebrated than his Syriacist father and grandfather on account of his inventing the electron microscope in 1931, for which he was eventually awarded a Nobel Prize in 1986.[1] His brother Helmut also pioneered the use of electron optics in medicine. Merx's other daughter married the Heidelberg astronomer Max Wolf, whose respect for his theologian father-in-law extended to naming a couple of minor planets after him, generally still known as 330 Adalberta and 808 Merxia! Perhaps Wolf held Merx in higher esteem than did Max Weber.

II. A Select Bibliography of Merx's writings

Meletemata Ignatiana. Critica de epistolarum Ignatiarum versione syriaca commentatio (Halle, 1861). This was Merx's Doctoral dissertation, completed under the arabist F.A. Arnold in Breslau. It demonstrated the importance of the Syriac version of the Ignatian correspondence in establishing the authentic letters.

Archiv für wissenschaftliche Erforschung des Alten Testamentes (Halle, 1869-72) was a short-lived journal founded and edited by Merx, to which he also contributed a number of items. It was the first real attempt at a journal dedicated to Old Testament studies.

[1] See the account in Ruska's Nobel Prize Lecture, "The development of the electron microscope and of electron microscopy," *Reviews of Modern Physics* 59 (1987), 627–638, and L. Lambert & T. Mulvey, "Ernst Ruska (1906–1988), Designer Extraordinaire of the Electron Microscope: A Memoir" *Advances in Imaging and Electron Physics* 95 (1996), 2-62.

"Kritische Untersuchung über die Opfergesetze Lev 1 bis 7," *Zeitschrift für wissenscaftliche Theologie* 6,1 (1863), 41-84; 6,2 (1863), 164-82.

Bardesanes von Edessa. Nebst einer Untersuchung über das Verhältniss der clementinischen Recognitionen zu dem Buche der Gesetze der Länder (Halle, 1863).

Cur in libro Danielis iuxta Hebraeam Aramea adhibita sit dialectus explicatur (Halle, 1865). Merx's *Habilitation,* which attempts to demonstrate that the Aramaic portions of Daniel were written for the uneducated, whereas the Hebrew parts were meant for the learned.

Grammatica Syriaca. 2 parts (Halle, 1867-70). This was in fact a new edition of Andreas Gottlieb Hoffmann's Syriac Grammar.

"Die Inschrift von Umm el Awamid I" *ZDMG* 21 (1867), 476-87. Note also the response by M. A. Levy, "Einige Bemerkungen zu des Herrn Dr. Merx Erklärung der Inschrift von Umm-el-Awamid I," *ZDMG* 22 (1868), 538-41.

C.M. Von Beurmann, *Vocabulary of the Tigré language, with a grammatical sketch by* A. Merx (London, 1868).

"Miscellen zur semitischen Lautlehre. Bemerkunden zu Nöldeke's Beiträgen zur Kenntnis der aramäischen Dialekte," *ZDMG* 22 (1868), 271-8.

"Bemerkungen über bis jetzt bekannte aramäische Inschriften," *ZDMG* 22 (1868), 674-99.

Das Gedicht von Hiob. Hebräischer Text, kritisch bearbeitet und übersetzt (Jena, 1871).

Neusyrisches Lesebuch. Texte im Dialecte von Urmia (Breslau, 1873).

Zur Religionsphilosophie: Zwei akademische Reden. Offprints from *Philosophischen Monatsheften* vols. IV and VII (Giessen, 1875). These offprints may be found in the Bensley library collection in the Cambridge University Library.

Türkische Sprichwörter ins Deutsche übersetzt (Venice, 1877; 2nd ed. 1893). A collection of 355 Turkish proverbs presented in no particular order and with no accompanying notes or list of sources. Turkish is printed in Armenian characters.

Die Prophetie des Joel und ihre Ausleger von den ältesten Zeiten bis zu den Reformatoren (Halle, 1879). Established Joel as post-exilic and developed a theory of the apocalyptic genre and its association with prophecy.

Eine Rede vom Auslegen insbesondere des Alten Testaments. Vortrag gehalten am 3 Juli 1878 (Halle, 1879).

Specimina targumica e codicibus Londinensibus et Caroliruhensibus selegit (Heidelberg, 1881).

Die Saadjanische Uebersetzung des Hohen Liedes ins Arabische (Heidelberg, 1882).

"Eröffnungsrede das Präsidenten. Generalversammlung zu Carlsruhe der Deutschen Mogenländischen Gesellschaft," *ZDMG* 36 (1882), xxxi-xxxix.

"Proben der syrischen Uebersetzung von Galenus' Schrift über die einfachen Heilmittel," *ZDMG* 39 (1885), 237-305. See aso the response by I. Löw, "Bemerkungen zu Merx, Proben der syrischen Übersetzung von Galenus' Schrift über die einfachen Heilmittel," *ZDMG* 40 (1886), 763-5.

"De artis Dionysianae interpretatione Armeniaca," in G. Uhlig, ed., *Dionysii Thracis ars grammatical. Grammatici Graeci 1.1* (Leipzig, 1883), lvii-lxxiii.

"Johannes Buxtorf's des Vaters Targumcommentar Babylonia," *Zeitschrift für wissenschaftliche Theologie* 30 (1887), 280-99, 462-71; 31 (1888), 42-8.

"Bemerkungen über die Vocalization der Targume," in *Verhandlungen des fünften internationalen Orientalisten-Congresses II, Abhandlungen und Vorträge* (Berlin, 1881-2), 142-88.

Chrestomathia Targumica quam collatis libris manuscriptis antiquissmimis tiberiensibusque impressis celeberrimis. E codicibus ad codices vocalibus babylonicis instructis (Berlin, 1888).

Historia artis grammaticae apud Syros (Leipzig, 1889).

Über die heutigen Aufgaben des Evangelischen Bundes. Rede, zu Mannheim 1892 gehalten (Leipzig, 1892).

Die Ideen von Staat und Staatsmann im Zusammenhange mit der geschichtlichen Entwicklung der Menschheit. Festrede zur Feier des vierzigjährigen Regierungsjubiläums Seiner Königlichen Hoheit des Grossherzogs Friedrich von Baden gehalten in der Aula der Universität Heidelberg am 28. April 1892 (Heidelberg, 1892).

Idee und Grundlinien einer allgemeinen Geschichte der Mystik. Akademische Rede zum Geburtsfeste des höchstseligen Grossherzogs Karl Friedrich am 22. November 1892 beim Vortrage des Jahresberichtes und der Verkündung der akademischen Preise gehalten (Heidelberg, 1893).

Documents de paléographie hébraïque et arabe (Leiden, 1894).

"Die in der Peschito fehlenden Briefe des Neuen Testamentes in arabischer der Philoxeniana entstammender Uebersetzung," *Zeitschrift für Assyriologie und Vorderasiatische Archäologie* 12 (1897), 348–381.

Die vier kanonischen Evangelien nach ihrem ältesten bekannten Texte. Übersetzung und Erläuterung der syrischen im Sinaikloster gefundenen

Palimpsesthandschriften (Berlin, 1897-1911). Each gospel was published in its own fascicle which are sometimes found separately. See the comments on Merx's work in L. Vaganay, *L'évangile de Pierre*, 2nd ed. (Paris, 1930), 268-71.

Aus Muallim Nadschi's Sünbüle : die Geschichte seiner Kindheit (trans.) (Berlin, 1898).

"Collation of the Armenian Text," in *The Ecclesiastical History of Eusebius in Syriac*, ed. W. Wright and N. McLean (Cambridge, 1898).

"Die Schlussmassora aus dem Cairiner Codex vom Jahre 1028," *Zeitschrift für Assyriologie und Vorderasiatische Archäologie* 14, 293–330.

Die morgenländischen Studien und Professuren an der Universität Heidelberg vor und besonders im 19. Jahrhundert (Heidelberg, 1903).

Die Bücher Moses und Josua. Eine Einführung für Laien. Religionsgeschichtliche Volksbücher für die deutsche christliche Gegenwart (Tübingen, 1907).

Der Messias oder Ta'eb der Samaritaner (Giessen, 1909).

"Le rôle du foie dans la littérature des peuples sémitiques," in *Florilegium, ou recueil de travaux d'érudition dédiés a Monsieur le Marquis Melchior de Vogüé* (Paris, 1909).

III. THE *HISTORIA ARTIS GRAMMATICAE* IN SUBSEQUENT RESEARCH

Theodor Nöldeke praised Merx's monograph as "eine wirkliche Förderung der Wissenschaft."[1] Although he was not averse to suggesting a number of improvements on matters of detail, the great orientalist concurred with the basic direction and burden of Merx's research. Nöldeke's comments, as well as specific remarks or criticism voiced by other scholars over the years are mentioned as they arise in the endnotes of the current edition. It may be useful at this point, however, to describe and survey briefly the directions taken by the post-Merx discussion on a few key issues raised by the book. Especially in view here is the question of various cultural influences in the area of language and grammar. The possible influence of Greek grammar upon its Syriac counterpart; the (suggested) influence of the Syriac system of accentuation and vocalisation upon the Hebrew masoretic traditions; and perhaps above all the question of the origins of Arabic grammar and Merx's claim to have uncovered its *Grundlage* in late antique Aristotelian logic.

[1] Nöldeke, Review, 1220.

Seeing as any assertion of the influence of one cultural sphere upon another seems to attract a more than representative quantity of suspicion, it may be as well to set out for the modern reader at least a broad overview of these questions as they have developed since 1889, only partly of course in response to Merx, who was hardly the first to have broached these sometimes sensitive topics.

The influence of Greek upon Syriac points and accents

Merx believed firmly that Syriac accentuation (those points in the text that mark sense division and rhetorical features) was but an offshoot of the late antique system of Greek punctuation. This theory of origins is set out as follows: Merx begins by explaining the Greek system of three types of basic 'point' used for the internal division of the sentence, making use of Dionysius Thrax's *Technē* and its scholia (p.63-4).[1] He then proceeds to show that this is exactly the same system that one sees in the earliest dated Syriac manuscript (p.65-6). From these basic beginnings there developed (on internal impulses) the rather better known system of four logical accents for dividing a verse, namely šewāyā, taḥtāyā, ʿalāyā, and pasōqā, a pattern of which he gives an example taken from a manuscript of John of Ephesus, dated 688 (p.67). Joseph Huzaya, the sixth century master from the School of Nisibis, further elaborated this system by adding to these 'logical' accents what Merx calls 'rhetorical' accents (i.e. those designed to indicate kinds of sentences, e.g. questions or commands). This again was an inner-Syriac development. After an excursus on Hebrew pointing (p.69-77, for which see below), he goes on to detail (p.77-81) how Jacob of Edessa added a number of further rhetorical accents to those of Joseph, thereby creating an even more sophisticated system. This was not an internal development, however, for Jacob was also heavily indebted to the Greek tradition—in the first place to the *Technē* again, to which we owe the distinction of mimetic and temporal accents, but also to later Greek grammarians, especially Nicanor, whose specific influence upon Jacob is worked out (p.81-8). The Greek elements in Jacob's system include such features as giving different temporal accents precise quantities for indicating different pausal lengths, the use of the Greek hyphen (Syriac *garōra*), further precision amongst different types of the basic point, and

[1] Page nos. refer to the original edition, which are marked with a bar, as e.g. |[54]

points for marking unexpected inversions of word order. This lengthy discussion is followed by a reconstruction (p.89-100) of the section in Jacob's *Grammar* that dealt with accents, on the basis of his other works (especially the *Letter on Orthography*) and from Jacob Bar Šakko, who seems to be dependent upon his namesake of Edessa.

The theory as explained by Merx is neither simple nor unilinear. It is important above all to note that he postulates two major moments of Greek influence, an original one which gave rise to the very earliest system of Syriac pointing, and a later, rather more sophisticated, one in which Jacob of Edessa used his knowledge of the later Greek grammatical tradition to 'update' the native system which he had inherited from Joseph Huzaya. Merx further alludes (p.101) to the Greek influence upon the intermediate system of Thomas the Deacon, which is especially notable in the latter's discussion of the *garōra* (p.73,84).

On the basis of a thoroughgoing analysis of Barhebraeus's *Grammar*, Axel Moberg staged a point-by-point refutation of Merx's argument.[1] According to Moberg, who went on to edit and translate Barhebraeus's *Grammar*, the main problems with Merx's discussion about the development and origins of the Syriac accentuation system are as follows:

- The derivation of the pointing system contained in the earliest dated Syriac manuscript from Dionysius's *Technē* requires that the latter's 'mid-point' developed into the Syriac pasōqā. Yet the former is clearly a type of 'rhetorical' accent in Dionysius rather than a piece of punctuation. It is thus far-fetched to imagine that this less significant mark developed into the most fundamental Syriac accent.
- Merx fails to demonstrate any clear parallel between Nicanor and Jacob. Why, for instance, does Jacob not adopt Nicanor's other symbols, and why does Jacob have a series of accents that have no parallel at all in Nicanor? In essence, Nicanor cannot account for the basic structure of Jacob's system.
- The distinction among the rhetorical accents between those that are mimetic (sense accents) and those that indicate pauses (temporal accents) is apparently based on the Dionysian expressions καθ' ὑπόκρισιν and κατὰ διαστολήν. The latter, however, has already

[1] A. Moberg, "Über den griechischen Ursprung der syrischen Akzentuation," *Le Monde oriental* 1 (1906), 87-99.

been used (p.63) to refer to the logical, as distinct from the rhetorical, accents.

- The supposed distinction (in Joseph's system) between ܡܥܠܝܢܐ and ܦܩܘܕܐ (two accents indicated by the same symbol) makes no sense. Here Moberg hit upon an important issue which becomes central for Segal's *Diacritical Points*, namely that one can really only start with the points and their actual use in the manuscripts, rather than, as Merx and others, with the lists provided by so-called theorists.

Moberg does not reject the hypothesis of Greek influence. He merely sees it coming from another direction. Barhebraeus, after all, makes it clear, especially as regards his comment about the doctor of Melitene (Merx, p.85f.), that we should seek the origins of the system among the Greeks.

Moberg argues that there is no need to go into details of this or that system or to compare Eastern and Western systems, as Merx does, since the general purpose of accentuation is evident from Barhebraeus (see the citation at Merx, 264-5 = Barhebraeus, *Gramm*, 246f.), namely what Moberg calls 'declamatory-rhetorical'. Accents were simply designed to provide the correct modulations of the voice for the reading of the Scriptures—this is universal to every variation among the 'systems' (Merx himself recognised this, of course, but does not draw from it the straightforward conclusion that Moberg finds inevitable). The simple conclusion that Moberg draws is that the Syrian system is the same as the Greek *neuma* system of using points in the lectionary to indicate vocal modulation—this was not designed for chanting as such but rather for a type of reading that comes close to it in which the tones and modulations of the voice are carefully specified (his understanding of the *neuma* system is based on the earlier work of Fleischer and Praetorius).[1]

In order to try to make the two systems (Greek and Syriac) match closely, he analyses the accents according to their visual nature, considering all other developments to be mere complications, and notes that the complete system is virtually already present in Joseph Huzaya and that this parallels an early form of the Greek *neuma* system. The latter goes back to the fifth century (according to Fleischer, even though the earliest testimony is in the seventh) and so the priority must be given to the Greek,

---

[1] O. Fleischer, *Neumen-studien, Abhandlungen über mittelalterliche Gesangs-Tonschriften*, 3 vols. (Leipzig, 1895-1904); F.Praetorius, *Über die Herkunft der hebräischen Accente* (Berlin, 1901).

which therefore influenced the Syriac, since Huzaya belongs to the mid/late sixth century.

Once Moberg enters into the details of the two systems (97-8) he finds the evidence rather less conclusive. Undeterred by such details, however, he maintains that 'es ist die prinzipielle identität, auf welche es hier ankommt' (98). Although he refers to two Syriac mss which have Greek musical notation written onto them (one mentioned by J. Thibaut, "Étude de musique Byzantine" *Byzantinische Zeitschrift* 8 (1899), 145; the other by Merx, 82), these are most likely the result of late combinations of Syriac language and Byzantine notation, and prove nothing about the origins of either.[1]

Moving on from Moberg's critique of Merx and his alternative thesis, we encounter Weiss's study, *Zur ostsyrischen Laut- und Akzentlehre*. This offers a useful overview, with plenty of examples provided, of the accentual system used in the famous East Syriac Masorah (Add. 12138), but adds nothing to the discussion of origins.

The next landmark is Segal's seminal work of 1953, *The diacritical point and the accents in Syriac*, deviates in a number of ways from previous scholarship. Firstly, he insists that the study of the accents must begin from the mss themselves and "what the reader sees," rather than with the lists produced by grammarians (p.61). In fact, Moberg had already made this point in his 1908 article, but Segal carries it through with greater rigour and success.

On the subject of Greek influence, Segal made the important point that the Syrians themselves regularly attributed the invention of the accents to the Greeks and that this in itself should not be taken seriously.[2] For instance, when Barhebraeus says that Syriac and Greek are the only languages to have accents (a well-known citation used by Merx, Duval, and Moberg), he is so clearly in the wrong (by omitting Hebrew) that one can hardly accept what he, or anyone else, says about the origins of Syriac accents.

In response to the arguments put forward by Merx and Moberg in support of Greek origins, however, Segal simply states rather (p.63) that

[1] The first of the mss Moberg never saw – it is a facsimile of an unidentified ms still in the Middle East, the other is a ms in Dresden.

[2] Both Epiphanius and Aristotle were claimed as the originators of the idea, although other traditions, especially in the East, preferred to ascribe them to Joseph Huzaya.

"we may assume a native Syrian origin for the accents," on the basis that the system is straightforward and, as it were, required by the nature of things, such that it would have occurred without external prompting. The parallels demonstrated by Moberg between the Syriac accents and the Greek *neuma* system are, he says, "no greater than might be expected from their common *raison d'être*."

Segal thus raises the possibility of the self-origination of the system on the basis that external influence is not a *necessity*. Of course, this falls well short of demonstrating that Merx and Moberg were wrong. The argument, for instance, that the pasōqā must be a native development because it appears in other Semitic languages, begs the question since these other systems are most likely derived from Syriac in any case. Segal does suggest in a footnote, however, that if there is a relationship between Greek and Syriac it may be the other way.

The question of the origin and the development of Greek *ekphonetic* notation should probably be brought into the centre of this discussion. Its similarity to the earlier Syriac accentuation system is clear for all to see—both grew out of basic Greek prose punctuation and were designed for the semi-chanted reading of the scriptures.[1] Whether the dating of the oldest Greek *ekphonetic* system allows for it to have exerted any influence upon the Syriac remains to be seen.[2] The earliest manuscripts bearing these symbols belong to the ninth century, although the names and functions of the *ekphonetic* symbols imply that their origin lies much further back as a development from Greek prosodic punctuation as it is described in the late antique handbooks.

Greek musical notation from the Roman imperial era has been discovered in a number of papyri. The notes tend to consist of letter-like symbols for the most part, though in a number of cases points are also used to indicate rhythm rather than melody. Similar systems were in use for

[1] E. Wellesz, *Byzantine Music and Hymnography* (Oxford, 1961), 249-60, describes the system with examples. He backs a fourth century dating for their invention (p.246), although the mss are of course considerably younger, not pre-dating the eleventh century. The *ekphonetic* system is to be distinguished from the *neumes* proper, which really refer to the fully melodic Byzantine system of notation used from about the ninth or tenth century.

[2] G. Engberg, art. "Ekphonetic Notation," in *The New Grove Dictionary of Music and Musicians*, 2nd ed., vol.8, 47-51.

traditional religions and for Christian hymns.[1] It was thus reasonably common among Greek-speaking Christian groups to mark up their manuscripts with a basic musical notation. It has been suggested that an unusual pointing system found on some Greek papyri (including a Psalter) are in reality a basic (pre-*ekphonetic*) form of musical notation and that the patterns of points used are so similar to the Syriac as to make a genetic relationship more than likely.[2] If correct, this thesis, although as yet not fully worked out, would clinch the argument for Hellenogenesis. On the other hand, a careful comparative study of the Greek *ekphonetic* system with the Hebrew accentuation has shown no necessary genetic relationship, but rather suggests that Greek, Hebrew, and Syriac systems all arose out of a basic chanting system for the scriptures which developed independently in each case.[3] Knowledge of the very earliest Greek systems is probably insufficiently detailed to allow a clear answer to emerge at present. Given the constant interaction between Greek and Syriac literary and religious spheres in the two to three centuries before Islam, we may well have to do here with an ongoing relationship between related phenomena.

Merx's theory of the influence of Greek interpunction upon the earliest stages of the Syriac tradition was later upheld against Segal's scepticism, on the basis of a fresh and more nuanced reading of the earliest dated Syriac manuscript.[4] Furthermore, the influence of Greek theory upon Jacob of Edessa, and probably also upon Thomas the Deacon and others, is admitted even by Segal (p.120f., at least for the West Syrian 'rhetorical' accents; the East followed its own, more 'musical' course, p.80f.), whether this came directly by way of Nicanor (as Merx) or from elsewhere. On the

---

[1] For the former see P.Oxy 2436; for the latter P. Oxy 1786. Further examples may be found in *Symbolae Osloenses* xxxi (1955), 1-98, and in O.M. Pearl and R.P. Winnington-Ingram, "A Michigan Papyrus with musical notation," *J. of Egyptian Archaeology* 51 (1965), 179-95.

[2] D. Jourdan-Hemmerdinger, "Nouvaux fragments musicaux sur papyrus (une notation antique par points)," in M. Velimirovic, ed., *Studies in Eastern Chant*, vol.IV (London, 1979), 81-111.

[3] E. J. Revell, "Hebrew Accents and Greek Ekphonetic Neumes," in Velimirovic, op.cit., 140-70.

[4] F. Stanley Jones, "Early Syriac Pointing in and behind British Museum Additional Manuscript 12,150," in R. Lavenant, ed., *Symposium Syriacum VII* (Rome, 1998), 429-444.

most significant question, however, namely that of the absolute origin of Syriac accentuation, the balance still seems to lie with Hellenogenesis, especially in light of the above-noted observations of Stanley Jones. The strongest argument to the contrary remains Moberg's point that the Syriac system was always about declamatory-rhetorical effects rather than interpunction as such, and Merx's reading of the early Edessan manuscript relies on interpunction being the original purpose of the points.

The influence of Syriac upon Hebrew points and accents

While the idea that Syriac accents may have been an influence upon Greek systems remains a rather remote possibility, the thesis of Syriac influence upon Hebrew is almost a matter of dogma. Such a theory was first propounded by Ewald, and to this day basic textbooks still repeat Merx's assertion that the Hebrew vocalisations and accents took their origin from the Syrians.[1] Even in Merx's day, however, not all were so certain.[2] More recently one of the most prominent experts on the Hebrew Masorah has shown a great deal of scepticism by demonstrating how the Hebrew accentual system is a separate beast from the system used for its vowel signs;[3] moreover, the internal evidence of Hebrew literature provides us with no firm *terminus post quem* for the former, which may have been mentioned in the Talmud and have originated significantly earlier. Dotan prefers to attribute the Hebrew system to internal impulses and sees no need to postulate a Syriac influence, which in some specific cases at least

[1] E. Tov, *Textual Criticism of the Hebrew Bible* (Minneapolis, 2001), 40, following Gesenius-Kautzsch §7h, who in turn is following the orthodoxy of Geiger and Merx, and ultimately of Ewald. The dictum is even incorporated into wider accounts of Semitics, e.g. E. Lipinski, *Semitic Languages. Outline of a Comparative Grammar* (Leuven, 2001), 164 (also for Arabic, 169). Other accounts are more descriptive and do not dare venture into the issue of historical origins, e.g. S. Morag, *The Vocalization Systems of Arabic, Hebrew and Aramaic: their phonetic and phonemic principles* ('s-Gravenhage, 1962).

[2] Phillips, *Accents*, 222-3.

[3] A. Dotan, "The relative chronology of the Hebrew vocalization and accentuation," *Proceedings of the American Academy for Jewish Research* 48 (1981), 87-99; id., "Masorah," in *Encyclopedia Judaica* (Jerusalem, 1972), Vol.16, col.1415-6, §2.1.3 (reprinted in 2nd ed., 2007, Vol.13, 613).

the evidence appears to refute.[1] On the basis of Segal's reconstruction of the history of the East Syrian vowel notation, he suggests influence rather in the opposite direction.[2] As the author concedes, however, a much fuller investigation is required if a firm solution to the problem is to be found. On the question of dating, he is at least on the same ground as Merx; it seems certain that the Hebrew system did not develop until after c.500 and was largely accomplished by c.700. This period does of course coincide with the formative age of the Syriac Masorah (and possibly of the Greek *ekphonetic* system, see above). The Hebrew Masorah as an oral tradition of recitation, on the other hand, is of much greater antiquity than this. It should be borne in mind that the question of influence concerns only the notation and not the chanting itself. The latter was in existence in a form broadly anticipating its later developments already in the second century BC.[3]

Merx's own argument for mutual dependence in general and for Syriac priority in particular is found in the midst of his discussion of Syriac pointing (p.69-77). In line with most scholars of his day, Merx believed that Hebrew accentuation was primarily designed for logical verse division and that melodic considerations were secondary. He attempts to demonstrate, however, that within the constraints of the logical system, choice was exercised on a melodic basis. He goes on to parallel the Hebrew and Syriac systems, starting from such basic observations as the similarity of names among the key accents (pasōqā = pasōq; athnaḥ = taḥtāyā). Once he has dealt with the broad similarity of the logical accents in both systems, he goes on to show that there are some traces even of rhetorical accents in Hebrew. As Dotan, Merx believes that the Hebrew accents preceded the Hebrew vowel notation (p.76). He concludes that the Hebrews borrowed the older form of the Syriac system before it was developed by Thomas the Deacon (c.600) and Jacob of Edessa.

---

[1] Ibid., §4.1.1.2, §4.3.2.

[2] Ibid., §5.2.1.1.2.

[3] E.J. Revell, "The Oldest Evidence for the Hebrew Accent System," *Bulletin of the John Rylands Library* 54 (1971/2), 214-22.

The Greek and Syriac influences upon Arabic grammar

In the ninth chapter of his work, Merx deals with a subject only tangentially related to his main theme but which has become a focal point for controversy and debate to the present day, namely the question of the origins of Arabic grammar. Merx raises this question at this point in his monograph at just the point when he is about to embark upon the work of Elias of Ṭirhan, the first Syriac grammarian who sought to use Arabic grammatical theory to underpin his analysis of Syriac.

In the first instance, Merx quickly dismisses the notion that Arabic grammar was itself derivative from the Syriac. There are parallels, but these arise merely from the common problems with which both traditions were faced. Similarly, the influence of the Greek grammatical tradition is also ultimately of little value as an explanatory factor due to the general discontinuity between the two theories, their terminology, basic principles etc. It is, however, in the field of Greek logic that Merx finds the antecedents he seeks. He argues that the elaborate Aristotelian commentary tradition of late antiquity was adopted by the Arabs, and its principles were applied to the study of language, giving rise to the great edifice we know as the Arabic grammatical tradition. Merx especially demonstrates (p.141-8) this genetic relationship through a study of Arabic grammatical terminology, in particular 1) the use of the three parts of speech (noun, verb, particle; here he adds pertinent observations about Sībawayhi's analysis of tense); 2) the derivation of the notion of *ʿirāb* from *hellenismos*; 3) the odd Arabic way of explaining gender in nouns; 4) the origin and meaning of the term *ẓarf*, related to aspects of Aristotle's *Physics*;[1] 5) the same for *ḥāl*, related to Greek *diathesis* in its philosophical sense; 6) the use of logical predicate for grammatical subject. He goes on to show that much of the developed Arabic grammar was *not* based on Greek equivalents, whether in Aristotle's *Poetics* or elsewhere (e.g. the names for the cases are unrelated). In this, then, the Arab genius was its own.

The debate over this hypothesis variously moved back and forth over the next century, its most significant opponent being Josef Weiss, whereas

[1] A suggestion that is 'unverifiable' according to Michael Carter, EI^2, XI,459a, though this may be true of most theories of origins that have to work with limited evidence.

Nöldeke was a supporter.[1] It also received a stout defence in an article by Rundgren, who defended the older idea that Arabic grammar might have derived from Greek philosophy, calling especially upon the form of the logical tradition that is found in the Syriac commentators Proba and Paul the Persian.[2] This elicited a lengthy rejoinder from Elamrani-Jamal, who took on the Merx theory in full debate in his 1983 monograph, *Logique aristotélicienne et Grammaire arabe*, in which he argued that the hypothesis of Greek origins was grounded in colonialist prejudice against the capacity of Semitic cultures to produce science or philosophy by their own momentum.[3] Elamrani-Jamal interacts directly with many of Merx's arguments, although his work does suffer from its interacting almost exclusively with a summary article that Merx wrote on the subject in 1892 rather than with the fuller exposition in the *Historia Artis Grammaticae*. He also misunderstands Merx in at least one respect, viz. he takes Merx to be arguing that Arab grammarians took their ideas from Aristotle, to which Elamrani-Jamal objects that the Arabic translations of Aristotle had not yet begun in Sībawayhi's day. Merx is quite clear, however, that it is the Alexandrian commentary tradition through which such knowledge was transmitted to Arabic thinkers (Merx, 141). Nonetheless, his substantive criticisms of the Merx thesis stand as a vital contribution to the debate.

Elamrani-Jamal also included within his broader critique of this stream of scholarship, a number of other works which, while not suffering from all of Merx's faults, were nevertheless inheritors of his basic thesis, chief among these being Versteegh's 1977 work, *Greek Elements in Arabic Linguistic Thinking*, which took hold of the Merx thesis and developed some of its stronger aspects in a number of directions.[4]

In more recent years, Versteegh has significantly advanced the whole subject by a much more thorough consideration of the importance of Qurʾānic exegesis in early Arabic grammar (a point that Merx did himself make quite forcefully). His more balanced assessment can therefore be

---

[1] J. Weiss, "Die arabische Nationalgrammatik und die Lateiner," *ZDMG* 64 (1910), 349-90; for Nöldeke's mature opinion, *ZDMG* 59 (1905), 414.

[2] F. Rundgren, *Über den griechischen Einfluss auf die arabische Nationalgrammatik*, Acta Societatis Linguisticae Upsaliensis, Nova series 2,5 (1976): 119-44.

[3] A. Elamrani-Jamal, *Logique aristotélicienne et Grammaire arabe*. Paris: Vrin, 1983.

[4] K. Versteegh, *Greek Elements in Arabic Linguistic Thinking*. Studies in Semitic Language and Linguistics VII. Leiden: Brill, 1977.

found in his *Arabic Grammar and Quranic Exegesis in Early Islam* of 1997,[1] which also incorporates other important work done in the meantime, such as Talmon's research on the pre-Sībawayhi era and the possible links between the early Kufan school and Greek logic.[2] Talmon has also made a number of suggestions of influence from the Syriac side, especially in the field of punctuation and orthography.[3] In addition, Michael Carter has highlighted the close resemblances between the realms of grammar and law in Arabic literature and suggests the legal realm as the locus in which grammar arose,[4] and Troupeau has argued against Merx on the ground that the language of the first Arabic philosophers does not match that of the grammarians,[5] though it must be borne in mind that the former rediscovered Aristotle and Alexander of Aphrodisias whereas the grammarians, if they were indebted at all to Greek logic, were rather part of the late antique pedagogical commentary tradition.

This remains a very difficult area in which to arrive at any firm conclusion, partly due to a lack of edited or extant texts (in both Syriac and Arabic) and partly due to the issues of cultural colonialism which underlie much of the debate. I have discussed all this elsewhere,[6] and the reader is referred to that article for further bibliographic details and a consideration of what research in the Syriac grammatical tradition might be able to contribute.

[1] id. *Arabic Grammar and Qur'anic Exegesis in Early Islam*. Studies in Semitic Languages and Linguistics XIX. Leiden: Brill, 1997.

[2] Through a number of his articles, and the monographs *Arabic grammar in its formative age* (Leiden, 1994), and *Eighth-century Iraqi grammar* (Eisenbrauns, 2003).

[3] See the articles mentioned in the bibliography below.

[4] M.G. Carter, "The Origins of Arabic Grammar," in R. Baalbaki (ed.), *The Early Islamic Grammatical Tradition* (Ashgate, 2007), 1-26.

[5] G. Troupeau, "La logique d'Ibn al-Muqaffaʿ et les origines de la grammaire arabe," *Arabica* 28 (1981), 242-50.

[6] D. King, "Elements of the Syriac Grammatical Tradition as these Relate to the Origins of Arabic Grammar," in A. Marogy (ed.), *The Foundations of Arabic Linguistics: Sībawayhi and Early Arabic Grammatical Theory* (Brill: Leiden, 2012), 189-209.

The Interaction of Logic and Grammar in Syriac Tradition[1]

The crossover and mutual influence between logic and grammar has a long history in Semitic literature. Ever since Porphyry saved Aristotle from appearing un-platonic by interpreting his *Categories* as being about 'words' rather than 'things', the commentary tradition began to take special notice of the *De Interpretatione* as being a book apparently about sentences and how they are constructed, i.e. as a sort of grammar. Proba was the main conduit by which the commentary tradition on the *De Interpretatione* was transmitted into Syriac. He is a rather shadowy figure but belongs to the sixth century and may have written in both Greek and Syriac.[2] At any rate, his Syriac commentary on the *De Interpretatione* was well known to Syriac readers of a later age—both Bar Zo'bi and Barhebraeus open their grammars with quotes from the De Interpretatione and from Proba's commentary thereon.

For Proba, Aristotle's aim in this work is to teach us about 'speech' and he goes on to subdivide 'speech' into its five categories, question, vocative, request, command, statement (ܡܫܐܠܢܐ. ܩܪܝܢܐ. ܡܦܝܣܢܐ. ܦܘܩܕܢܐ. ܦܣܘܩܐ). Proba was evidently read by the earliest Syriac grammarians, for whom these categories of speech corresponded with the mimetic (or sense) accents which they had developed.[3] They thus attributed to Aristotle the invention of these same accents.[4] However, the traditional Aristotelian five parts-of-speech did not match the alternative tradition of ten accents, taught

[1] This is an extensive topic, only mentioned here in passing. I have outlined the issues in D. King, "Grammar and Logic in Syriac (and Arabic)," *Journal of Semitic Studies* 58 (2013), 101-120, and an analysis of examples in Paul the Persian, Proba, and Athanasius of Balad, has been carried out by H. Hugonnard-Roche, "La tradition du Peri hermeneias d'Aristote en syriaque, entre logique et grammaire," in M. Farina (ed.), *Les auteurs syriaques et leur langue*. Études syriaques 15. Paris: Geuthner, 2018, 55-94.

[2] S.P. Brock, "The Commentator Probus: Problems of Date and Identity," in J.W. Watt and J. Lössl (edd.), *Interpreting the Bible and Aristotle in Late Antiquity* (Ashgate, 2011), 195-206; H. Hugonnard-Roche, "Le commentaire syriaque de Probus sur l'Isagoge de Porphyre. Une étude préliminaire," *Studia Graeco-Arabica* 2 (2012): 227-43.

[3] Hoffmann, *Herm*, 66. Merx calls these accents 'mimetic'; Revell calls them 'sense accents'. For this, and the following remarks, see his "Aristotle and the Accents: The Categories of Speech in Jewish and other authors," *Journal of Semitic Studies* 19 (1974), 19-35.

[4] Add 12178, f.232a-234b (Anon A in our list above).

probably in the School of Nisibis and which went back to Joseph Huzaya. Hence we can see here already that eagerness typical of many West Syrian thinkers to attribute all matters pertaining to philosophy and grammar to Greek innovations even when the evidence seems to suggest otherwise.

However, as Revell has shown, this was not merely a matter of imagining Greek antecedents.[1] Rather, the actual elaboration of the accentual system depended upon the commentary tradition of the *De Interpretatione*. For Thomas the Deacon's system introduced, among its numerous new accents, the two Aristotelian categories of speech as yet unrepresented, and furthermore appears to make a fundamental visual distinction between the 'statement' on the one side and all other types on the other.[2] Segal was right to analyse the accents from the evidence of the manuscripts rather than from the theorising of the grammarians—the latter represents a strong attempt to force the practice into a preconceived theory of Aristotelian logic.

There is a great deal to be said under this head, which it is not needful to repeat here. Further research should take as a starting point the analyses of Hugonnard-Roche 2018 and King 2013, mentioned above (n.33).

IV. Texts of the Syriac Grammatical Tradition

While the foregoing notes represent some of the more heated discussions that have arisen within the field, all areas of the Syriac grammatical tradition have been subject to a certain amount of work, albeit much of it now in the increasingly distant past. Unsurprisingly, much of this research has focused on unravelling the problems of accentuation or have been connected with studies of individual authors (Jacob of Edessa, Barhebraeus). The following is a list (probably not as exhaustive as was hoped) of known texts relating to Syriac grammar up to the time of Barhebraeus. It is hoped that this may be of use to those wishing to gain an overview of this field and to pursue some part of it in the future.

---

[1] E. J. Revell, "Aristotle and the Accents: The Categories of Speech in Jewish and other authors," *Journal of Semitic Studies* 19 (1974), 19-35

[2] For this basic distinction in Proba, see the table there used (Hoffmann, *Herm.*, 67)

The West Syrian Tradition

1. The Syriac translation of ps-Dionysius Thrax, *Technē Grammatikē*. **Text I in the present volume (Eng. Tr., ch.2).**
    - BL Add.14620, Add. 14658, Berlin Syr. 89 (=Sachau 226). Ed. Merx, *Artis Grammatica*, Appendix, and ch.2.
    - Attributed to Joseph Huzaya in some copies.

2. Joseph Huzaya, *On Synonyms* (mentioned by Barhebraeus in his work on the same: Martin, *Œuvres* II,77).

3. Thomas the Deacon, *The names of the points*
    - Vat Syr. 152, f.191; BL Add. 12178, f.240a-241b (Wright I,110B, nos.1&2); Borgia K.VIII.6, no.5; Mingana Syr. 104, f.46b; Paris Syr. 64, f.212. Ed. Martin, *Ad Georgium*, text III. Also extracts in Phillips, *Letter*, Appendix II, 83 [text]; 83-4 [trans.].
    - This text, explicitly attributed to one Thomas the Deacon, is a shorter, and at times more corrupt version of no.4 (below). Mingana Syr. 104 appears to include elements from the next item as well, further establishing their relationship, which needs to be worked out in detail.
    - Thomas the Deacon was identified with the well-known Bible translator Thomas of Harkel by Phillips (*Letter*, 90-3) on the firm authority of Barhebraeus, whose testimony about the text matches data in the text itself (unless, of course, Barhebraeus was himself conjecturing the identification for the same reason).

4. School of Thomas the Deacon, *On the Signs of Punctuation*
    - BL Add. 12178, f.232a-234b (Wright I,110A); Mingana 104, f.46b ff. (Ca) (see comment above). Ed. Phillips, *Letter*, Appendix I, 68-74 [text]; 74-83 [trans.].
    - This text is much fuller and more detailed than the foregoing. A number of passages within it have also been lifted wholesale into the other, underlining the very close connection between them. The evidence adduced by Phillips (*Letter*, 93) to show this relationship (the equation of ܡܦܣܩܢܐ with ܣܘܡ ܬܠܐ, also mentioned by Barhebraeus, further establishes it) is thus hardly necessary.
    - The text is to be dated late sixth or perhaps early seventh century.

- Besides mentioning the traditions about Epiphanius and Aristotle, this text is useful in interpreting Jacob of Edessa's grammar, since the latter does not describe the actual positions of the accents as this does.

5. Anon., *Tract on the Syriac Conjunctions*
    - BL Add. 7183, f.126b-127 (Rosen & Forshall, *Catalogue*, 70). BL Add. 12178, f.242a-b; Berlin Syr. 174 (Sachau 70), no.X; Paris Syr. 64, f.213 (prob.); Mingana Syr. 104 (Cc); Vat. Syr. 152, f.192a (following, Gottheil rather than Assemani's catalogue). Ed. R.J.H. Gottheil, "A Tract on the Syriac Conjunctions," *Hebraica* 4 (1888), 167-178, principally on the basis of Berlin Syr. 174.
    - The full significance of this text remains to be ascertained. There are important Aristotelian antecedents to the definitions found here which make their way also into the later tradition (Bar Zuʿbi, Barhebraeus). The material here is a developed form of John the Stylite's (see Moberg, *Johannes Estonaja*, 29).

6. Ps-Epiphanius, *Names of the Greek Accents*
    - Mss as above.
    - This text is really a list of just two lines (Gottheil, p.168), which has been prefixed to the *Tract* (no.5).

7. Anon., *The various forms of the points arranged alphabetically*
    - BL Add. 12178, f.242b; Paris Syr. 64, f.213, and ?again f.222. Another text in BL Add. 7183, f.132a (Rosen & Forshall, 71a) may be identical.

8. Ramišoʿ
    - Best known for his contribution to the Syrian Masorah (Merx, ch.8). Ramišoʿ's father Sabroy is credited with the invention of the accents by David Bar Paulos (in his letter 14; Rahmani, *Studia syriaca I* [Lebanon, 1904], 44-46). If Bar Paulos is right (Vööbus, *School*, 202, doubts it, but Loopstra, *Add 12138*, vol.II, §4.7, raises it again) then the origin of the Masorah lies with a westerner from Mar Mattai who must have influenced the eastern tradition heavily (perhaps through the school of Nisibis). For further biographical data on Ramišoʿ and

his family, see Barsoum, *Scattered Pearls*, 329-30, 358-9. See Merx, ch.3, endnote iv.
- A *Grammar* is attributed to him by Joseph/Išoʿyabh Bar Malkon et al. (GSL, 246; Vööbus, *School*, 201; Barhebraeus, cited at Merx, 179).

9. Jacob of Edessa, *Grammar* (ܬܘܪܨ ܡܡܠܠܐ) **TEXT II in the present volume**
- Reconstructed from frags. in BL Add. 17217, f.37-8; BL Add. 14665, f.28; Oxford Bodl. Ms. 159, f.1. Ed. W. Wright, *Fragments of the Turras mamlla nahraya or Syriac Grammar of Jacob of Edessa. Edited from MSS. in the British Museum and the Bodleian Library* (London, 1871). Repr. in Merx, *Historia*, Appendix.
- Translation in the present volume, together with digital reproduction of Wright's 1871 edition, which was the basis of Merx's own.
- Revell, *Jacob of Edessa*, 366, n.2, gives a different reconstruction of the fragments and questions Merx's argument about the Greek origin of the material. Moberg, *Buch der Strahlen* II, 103, disagrees with Merx on some points and questions the inclusion of the Bodleian fragment.
- Talmon, *Jacob of Edessa*, offers an excellent up-to-date analysis with a useful glossary of terms to supplement Moberg's.

10. Jacob of Edessa, *Letter to George of Sarug 'On Syriac Orthography'*
- BL Add. 12178, f.223b-228a ; Add.7183, f.122b ; Vat.Syr. 152, f.185; Berlin Syr. 174 (Sachau 70); Borgia K.VIII.6; Mingana Syr. 104, f.1-26a; Paris Syr.64, f.206; St Mark's, Jerusalem, 1-5. Ed. Martin, *Ad Georgium*, text I (from Vat. ms, with Latin translation); also Phillips, *Letter*, ܐ-ܝܒ (tr., 1-12), from the London copies.
- This is the letter in which Jacob rebukes the scribes of his day for carelessness and gives instructions concerning certain words, spellings and pointings. The letter was to be bound up with the middle book of Jacob's translation of Severus of Antioch's *Cathedral Homilies*.

11. Jacob of Edessa, *On Forms and Genders* (or, *On Persons and Genders*)
- BL Add. 12178, f.228a-232a; Add. 7183, f.125a; Vat. Syr. 152, f.188; Borgia K.VIII.6; Mingana Syr. 104, f.1-26a; Berlin Syr. 174 (Sachau 70), no.IX; frag. also in BL Add. 17125, f.79b at the end of a Psalter. Ed. Martin, *Ad Georgium*, text II; also Phillips, *Letter*, ܝܓ-ܠܓ (tr., 13-33).

- Also Merx ed. based on copy apud Jacob bar Šakko.
- 'Persons' in the title does not refer to what the term means in current grammatical jargon, but perhaps refers to different vowel shapes placed onto the consonantal skeleton. See Farina, "La linguistique syriaque selon Jacques d'Édesse," 184; or to 'homographs,' see Balzaretti, "Ancient Treatises on Syriac Homonyms."

12. Western 'Masoretic' material.
    - The following are the principal manuscripts containing traditions of the West Syrian Masorah: BL Add. 7183; BL Add. 12178; Borgia K.VIII.6; Vat. Syr. 152; Paris Syr. 64; Mingana Syr. 104; St Mark's, Jerusalem, 1-5. Some also in Berlin Syr. 174 (Sachau 70).

The East Syrian Tradition

This is wholly represented by BL Add. 12138 (date: 899), a ms used extensively by Merx (a facsimile is now published).[1] For our purposes, it includes the following noteworthy pieces:

13. The Joseph Huzaya notice
    - BL Add 12138, f.312a. Translation and text-critical discussion in Segal, *Diacritical Points*, 66. The end of the codex is filled with notes by the scribe, some on grammatical issues. This is one of a group entitled 'traditions of the masters of the schools.' It tells how Joseph Huzaya (sixth century, see item 1 above) invented the accents for the purpose of Bible translation; the text connects this with the work of Theodore of Mopsuestia and Ibas of Edessa.

14. A series of four short grammatical tracts on the use of certain morphemes
    - Add. 12138, f.308a-309b.

[1] J. Loopstra, ed., *An East Syrian Manuscript of the "Syriac Masora" Dated to 899 CE. A Facsimile Reproduction of British Library, Add. MS 12138*. 2 vols. Gorgias Press, 2014.

Other pre-ʿAbbāsid writers

15. Aḥudemmeh
    - Late sixth century. Work not extant, but cited by Bar Zuʿbi (see Merx, 33). Probably not to be identified with the well-known metropolitan and martyr of the same name (J.M. Fiey, "Aḥoudemmeh," *Le Muséon* 81 [1968], 155-159), nor with the author of *Man as Microcosm.*

16. ʿEnanišoʿ, *Glossary*
    - Late seventh century. Ed. Hoffmann, *Opuscula Nestoriana*, 2-49. There are now other mss of the combined ʿEnanišoʿ/Ḥunain text (e.g. NDS 290 = Scher 139). See Merx ch.7, and further references there.
    - There are mss in Berlin (Berlin Syr. 69, no.XV) and New York (Union Seminary) containing a longer version of the treatise edited in Hoffmann's *Opuscula.* See Gottheil, *Elias*, 61*-67* (appendix); and id., "A Syriac Lexicographical Tract," *Hebraica* 5 (1889), 215-29.

17. Athanasius of Balad, *Introduction to Logic*
    - The section on *De Interpretatione* includes some grammatical definitions.
    - Ed. G. Furlani, "Contributi alla storia della filosofia greca in Oriente, Testi siriaci, VI, Una introduzione alla logica aristotelica di Atanasio di Balad," *Rendiconti della Reale Accademia dei Lincei, Classe di scienze morali, storiche e filologiche*, serie quinta, vol.25 (1916), 717-778. English translation forthcoming, Daniel King.

ʿAbbāsid Period onwards (Easterners)

18. John Bar Penkaye (late seventh century), *On the particles*
    - BO III,I,189. See Merx, 136.

19. Timothy I (Catholicos 780-823), *Letter 19*
    - Ed. O. Braun, *Timothei patriarchae I: Epistulae I* (CSCO 74, Louvain, 1914), 126-30, trans., 84-6.
    - For discussion, V. Berti, *Vita e Studi di Timoteo I Patriarca Cristiano di Baghdad* (Paris, 2009), 309-21, and King, "Elements of the Syriac Grammatical Tradition."

20. Išoʿ Bar Nūn (Catholicos 824-8), *On Synonyms*
    - Mosul 109, no.1; NDS 138; Seert 108, no.5.
    - Mentioned by Barhebraeus in his own work on the same subject (Martin, *Œuvres* II,77); also Mingana, *Catalogue*, 938. Obviously of the same type as ʿEnanišoʿ's treatise (no.17 above).
    - Also note the *Grammar* written by the same, of which extracts are extant in Cambridge Add. 2812, f.25.

21. Išoʿdenaḥ
    - Cited by Bar Zuʿbi (though with some uncertainty; see Merx, 34). See J.-M. Fiey, "Ichoʿdnah, Métropolite de Basra et son œuvre," *Orient Syrien* 11 (1966), 431-50.

22. Ḥunain ibn Isḥaq, *On Points*
    - Quoted in Elias of Nisibis (no. 24 below). Also mentioned by Barhebraeus; *ZDMG* 32 (1878), 741.
    - It should be noted that Ḥunain also composed an enlargement of ʿEnanišoʿ's treatise (no.17 above). Ed. Hoffmann, *Opuscula Nestoriana*, 2-49. See Merx ch7, and further references there; and also a work on Arabic syntax which sometimes made comparisons with Syriac. It is quoted by Elias of Nisibis (no. 24 below).

23. Elias of Nisibis (aka Elias bar Šinaya, d.c.1050), *Grammar*
    - Ed. & tr. Gottheil, *Elias.* Discussion in Merx ch8, and further references there.

24. Elias of Nisibis, Sixth Dialogue of his *Book of Sessions* (Arabic)
    - Ed. K. Samir, "Deux cultures qui s'affrontent: une controverse sur l'iʿrāb au XI siècle entre Élie de Nisibe et le vizier Abū al-Qāsim," *Mélanges de l'Université Saint-Joseph* 49 (1975/6), 619-49.
    - Discussion with translated extracts in D. Bertaina, "Science, syntax, and superiority in eleventh-century Christian-Muslim discussion: Elias of Nisibis on the Arabic and Syriac languages," *Islam and Christian-Muslim Relations* 22 (2011), 197-207.
    - Of this well-known series of debates between Elias and the vizier Abū al-Qāsim, the sixth concerns the relative merits of Syriac and

Arabic grammar and thus tells us something of the state of the former in Elias's day.
- Elias also composed a thematic glossary, which was the foundation of Tommaso Obicino's *Thesaurus Arabico-syro-latinus*. See Weninger, "Das Übersetzungsbuch," and McCollum, "Prolegomena."

25. Elias of Ṭirhan, *Grammar*,
- Ed. Baethgen, *Elias*. Discussion in Merx ch9.
- See also the anonymous treatises on accents below.

26. Joseph bar Malkon (later known as Išōʿyabh bar Malkon; 12th cent.), *Net of Points*
- For mss see GSL, 309 n13, to which now add Mingana Syr. 94, 244a-255a. Unedited. Selections are quoted in Merx, ch.8.
- A metrical grammar based partly on Elias of Nisibis.

27. Joseph bar Malkon, *Prose Grammar*
- BO III,I,295, under the name Išōʿyabh Bar Malkon. The text was discovered by Scher in three Mosul mss and Išōʿyabh was identified with Joseph bar Malkon by Martin, confirmed in GSL, 309 (see n11 for mss). Merx 111-12.
- Text in Arabic, with Syriac used for examples and sometimes for expressing rules that are commented upon in Arabic.
- At least two mss of this text are available online: BnF Syr. 370, and BML Or.419.

28. Four anonymous treatises on accents
- Berlin Syr. 88 (Petermann 9), nos.7,8,9,36 (Sachau, *Verzeichniss*, 323,333b)
- Edited in Merx, 194-197; 197-200; 189-194; 183-189 respectively.
- One of these may be by Elias of Ṭirhan (attributed by Merx, 179-82).
- Like the Western masoretic mss, Petermann 9 also has lexicographical lists (explanations of Greek words etc., this from a later Nestorian source, though the purpose is clearly the same).

29. John Bar Kamis (12th cent.)
    - BO III,I,296. See Merx, 136.

30. John Bar Zuʿbi (fl. c.1210), *Grammar*
    - Partial eds. by J.P.P. Martin, *Traité sur accentuation chez les Syriens orientaux par Jean bar Zuʿbi (Syriac Text)* (Paris, 1877), and G. Bohas, *Les bgdkpt en syriaque* (Toulouse, 2005).
    - For mss, GSL 310n12. To which add now Mingana Syr. 94, 29a-212a and Cambridge Or.1303 (Jenks Collection).
    - Extensive discussion, Merx ch10. Merx calls him "the greatest of the East Syrian grammarians." Despite the many oddities of his grammatical work, Bar Zuʿbi remains the most important witness to the earlier traditions among the East Syrians in matters of accentuation etc.
    - See especially the various works by George Bohas on Bar Zuʿbi, together with the pair of articles by Farina (details in the bibliography below).

31. John Bar Zuʿbi, *Metrical Grammar*
    - Numerous mss (GSL 311n5). Unedited. Short extracts are offered by Merx, 158,161.

32. John Bar Zuʿbi, Various other grammatical tracts
    - GSL 311n6,7,8,9.
    - A good idea of the variety of Bar Zuʿbi's as yet unedited works may be gauged from a perusal of the catalogue entries for BL Add. 25876 (Wright, *Cat.*, III,1175ff.) and Cambridge Add. 2013.

ʿAbbāsid Period onwards (Westerners)

33. John the Stylite (eighth or ninth century?), *Grammar*
    - This text was known to Merx via the note in Bar Zuʿbi, but was later discovered by Addai Scher in a manuscript at Notre Dame des Semences. It was described in some detail by Moberg, *Johannes Estonaja*. The text remains unedited.
    - There is some confusion over the identification of the ms. Vosté includes it under his ms no.293, which is not in Scher's older

catalogue. The latter's no.139, which Moberg cites as his source, is possibly equivalent to Vosté's 290. It seems that Scher has amalgamated the contents of at least two separate mss into his no.139.

- Date could be mid-ninth cent (Assemani, Moberg), early eighth by identifying the author with a correspondent of Jacob of Edessa (Schröter, Baumstark), or earlier than Jacob (Merx, arguing on evolutionary grounds, but he only had Bar Zuʿbi's comment to go on).
- Moberg also uses this grammar to reconstruct some elements of the teaching of Jacob of Edessa.

34. David Bar Paulos (late eighth cent.), *Letter on the origins of pointing*
   - I. Rahmani, *Studia Syriaca* I, ܡܘ-ܣܐ (Latin tr., 44-6).
   - This letter is significant in particular for the light it sheds on Ramišoʿ and the origins of accentuation (s.v. above).

A Note on David Bar Paulos

The information on this figure found in Baumstark (*GSL*, 272-3) is based upon the discussion in Rahmani, *Studia Syriaca* I, 43-6, 67-9. Rahmani's texts are only excerpts, however, from a ms containing a collection of David's letters. There are also fragments of information about David in Bar Ṣalibi and Barhebraeus, picked up already in *BO*. The *letter on the origins of pointing* is unfortunately missing its middle section in the Šarfeh ms used by Rahmani. It is also extant, however, in the similar collection of more than sixty of David's letters in a ms at Deir Zaʿfaran. This ms was numbered Mardin Orth. 158 by Vööbus ("Entdeckung des Briefkorpus des Dawid bar Paulos," *Oriens Christianus* 58 [1974], 45-80), but Deir Zaʿfaran 248 by Ignatius Barsoum (*Scattered Pearls*, 2nd ed. trans. M. Moosa [Gorgias Press, 2003], 373). The latter gives an extended description of the contents of some of these letters. His biographical information (p.372) seems to derive wholly from this letter (no.13 in Vööbus's listing). Mingana Syr.29 is a modern copy of the Deir Zaʿfaran codex (our letter at f.19a-21a).

The letter appears to imply that David is himself a descendent of Sabroy (both are"of Beth Rabban"), although "to the fifth generation" not as a grandson (as Barsoum).[1] The letters provide other fragments of biographical information, such as that David studied Greek at the monastery of Khanushia in Sinjar (one of his letters attributes all wisdom to the Greeks). He was also a poet and liturgist of some renown. Although everyone now seems to agree on dating David to the middle or end of the eighth century, there is a dislocated (possibly inauthentic) sentence attributed to him which quotes the ninth-century Ḥunain (Gottheil, "Dawidh bar Paulos," cxviii).

35. David Bar Paulos, *On the Definition of Speech*

- Mss: India Office 9; Mosul 109, no.3; Mosul 111, no.4; Seert 108, no.4. Possibly also Mingana 420, H. Ed: R. J. H. Gottheil, "Dawidh bar Paulos, a Syriac Grammarian," *Journal of the American Oriental Society* 15 (1893): cxii-cxiii.
- A French translation by Margherita Farina is forthcoming.
- This piece, together with those on the alphabet and the noun (next two items) are found together in India Office 9, and probably Mosul 109 and Mingana 420 (the headings in the latter suggest that it is the same three texts in question there), together forming a sort of 'grammar'.

36. David Bar Paulos, *On the division of nouns*

- Mss: India Office 9; Petermann 9, no.7 (=Berlin Syr 88); Mosul 111, no.5; Seert 108, no.4; Mingana 420, 63b. Ed: Gottheil, cxiii,10-cxv,4, Sachau, *Verzeichniss*, 330; Hoffmann, *Herm*, 129-30.
- A French translation by Margherita Farina is forthcoming

37. David Bar Paulos, *On the Letters of the alphabet*

- Ms: India Office 9; Seert 108, no.4. Possibly also Mingana, H. Ed: Gottheil, *op.cit.*, cxv,5-cxviii,6.
- A French translation by Margherita Farina is forthcoming
- The text describes the purported origins of the alphabet and some of its mysteries. David also wrote various poems dealing with the

[1] Some of the letters of David were published in I. Armalet, *Lettres de Josué, fils de David, surnommé Bar-Kilo, de Sévère Jacques de Bartelli, surnommé Bar-Chacaco, et de David de Beit-Rabban* (1929); and Dolapönü, *Egratheh d-Dawid bar Paulos* (Mardin, 1953) – non vidi.

mysteries of the alphabet as well as numerous acrostic poems, about which he had some typical, if to us rather strange, ideas (*GSL*, 273 n2)

38. David bar Paulos, *On the changeable letters* (i.e. bgdkpt)
    - Mingana 475, f.164b-166a; Paris Syr. 276, no.14e; St Mark's, Jerusalem 2-12.
    - A French translation by Margherita Farina is forthcoming

39. David Bar Paulos, *On Pointing*
    - (Known only from a Damascus ms mentioned by Baumstark, GSL, 272, n.10). This is significant in light of the contents of the letter.

40. David Bar Paulos, Other fragments
    - Lexicographical comments are sometimes picked up by Bar ʿAlī (*Thesaurus*, 464 etc.)

41. ʾEbdochus, *On Synonyms* (probably 12th cent.)
    - For the various recensions of ʾEbdochus's glossary, see *GSL*, 294-5, to which add Mingana 475 (St Mark's, Jerusalem 30* = 2-12 Macomber Catalogue), Deir el-Zafaran 192, and plenty of other copies in eastern collections.
    - Mentioned by Barhebraeus (Martin, *Œuvres* II,77). Date unknown. See chapter 4, endnote xxviii below.

42. Jacob Bar Šakko (d.1241), *Dialogues*. **Text III in the present volume.**
    - Only one part of one dialogue dealt with grammar. Ed. Merx, Appendix. Extensive discussion, Merx ch 11.
    - Before Barhebraeus, the most important exponent of the Western traditions (although Bar Zuʿbi was among his teachers).

43. Jacob Bar Šakko, *Harmonia* (Metrical Grammar). **Text IV in the present volume.**
    - Partial ed. Merx, Appendix. Since then see also Mingana Syr. 501, f.61b-79b.

44. Barhebraeus (1226-86), *Book of Splendours (Buch der Strahlen)* (ܟܬܒܐ ܕܨ̈ܡܚܐ)
   - Ed. Martin, *Œuvres* I; and Moberg, *Livre des Splendeurs*. For full ms listings see Takahashi, *Barhebraeus: A Biobibliography* (Gorgias Press, 2005), 375-84.
   - German trans. Moberg, *Buch der Strahlen*; English trans. of extracts (with Syriac text) in Phillips, *Letter*, and Martin, *Ad Georgium*. Other bibliography by Farina (see listings below).
   - This is the principal grammatical output of Barhebraeus and is the most important and extensive of all ancient Syriac grammars, especially for the reconstruction of the work of Jacob of Edessa.

45. Barhebraeus, *Metrical Grammar* (ܟܬܒܐ ܕܓܪ̈ܡܛܝܩܝ)
   - Ed. E. Bertheau, *Gregorii bar Hebraei, Grammatica linguae Syriacae in metro Ephraemeo* (Göttingen, 1843)—reprint, *The Metrical Grammar of Gregory Bar Hebraeus* (Gorgias Press, 2009); Martin, *Œuvres* II, 1-76. Mss in Takahashi, 359-72.

46. Barhebraeus, *De Aequilitteris* (ܟܬܒܐ ܕ̈ܡܚܠܐ)
   - Ed. Martin, *Œuvres* II, 77-127. Mss in Takahashi, 359-73.
   - See also Balzaretti, *Homonymns*.

V. Bibliography of subsequent research

Much of the most important work on Syriac grammar is to be found within the various editions mentioned above, especially their introductions, notes etc. The following list notes a number of other pieces of modern research.

Balzaretti, C., "Ancient Treatises on Syriac Homonyms," *Oriens Christianus* 89 (1997), 73-81.

Bohas, G., "Les 'états du nom' en syriaque," *Études sémitiques et samaritaines offertes à Jean Margain* (Lausanne, 1998), 109-15.

___, "Les accidents du verbe dans la grammaire de Bar Zo'bi ou, une adaptation de la *Techne*," *Langues et littératures du monde arabe* 4 (2003), 55-86.

___, "Radical ou racine/schème, l'organisation de la conjugaison syriaque avant l'adoption de la racine," *Le Muséon* 116 (2003), 343-76.

___, "Sur l'hypothèse de la racine triconsonantique en syriaque," *Langues et littératures du monde arabe* 5 (2004), 135-58.

___, *Les bgdkpt en syriaque* (Toulouse, 2005).

___, "Barhebraeus et la tradition grammaticale syriaque," *Parole de L'Orient* 33 (2008), 145-58.

___, "Définition du substantif et catégorisation des choses qui sont dans l'univers chez Bar Zo'bī," *Mélanges de l'Université Saint-Joseph* 66, 2015-2016, 21-40.

___, "La morphologie dans la Grande grammaire de Barhebraeus, à travers l'étude des verbes défectueux," in M. Farina (ed.), *Les auteurs syriaques et leur langue* (Paris, Geuthner, 2018), 189-206.

___, "La ressemblance (muḍāraʿa), de Zamaḫšarî à Bar Hebraeus," *The Arabist: Budapest Studies in Arabic* 39 (2018), 1-10.

___, "Transitivité et intransitivité dans la grammaire de Bar Hebraeus," *Histoire Epistémologie Langage*. Forthcoming.

___, "La formation de l'impératif dans la grammaire de Bar Hebraeus ," *The Arabist: Budapest Studies in Arabic*. Forthcoming.

___, "La définition du mot et des parties de la phrase dans la tradition grammaticale syriaque," *Parole de l'Orient* 45. Forthcoming

Coakley, J. F., "When were the five Greek vowel-signs introduced into Syriac writing?" *Journal of Semitic Studies* 56 (2011), 307-25.

Conti, S. E., "Les sources grecques des textes grammaticaux syriaques," in M. Farina (ed.), *Les auteurs syriaques et leur langue* (Paris, Geuthner, 2018), 27-54.

Contini, R., "Gli inizi della linguistica siriaca nell' 'Europa rinascimentale,'" *Rivista di Studi Orientali* 68 (1994), 15-30.

___, "Greek linguistic thinking and the Syriac linguistic tradition," *Sprawozdania z posiedzen komisji naukowych, Polska Akadema Nauk* 40/1 (1996), 45-9.

___, "Considerazioni interlinguistiche sull'adattamento siriaco della 'Technē Grammatikē' di Dionisio Trace," in B. M. Finazzi and A. Valvo (edd.), *La diffusione dell'eredità classica nell'età tardoantica e medievale. Il Romanzo di Alessandro e altri scritti* (Alessandria: Edizioni dell'Orso, 1998), 95-111.

___, "The role of linguistics in Syrian society," in S. Auroux et al. (edd.), *History of the language sciences, vol. 1: An International Handbook on the Evolution of the Study of Language from the Beginnings to the Present* (New York: de Gruyter, 2000), 341-4.

___, "Storia della scienza siriaca. III. Le scienze del linguaggio," *Storia della scienza, vol. IV: Medioevo - Rinascimento* (Roma: Istituto dell'Enciclopedia Italiana, 2001), 26-36, 68-9.

___, "Aspects of linguistic thought in the Syriac exegetical tradition," in M. Doerfler, E. Fiano and K. Smith (edd.), *Syriac Encounters: Papers from the Sixth North American Syriac Symposium* (Leuven, 2015), 91-117.

Daniels, Peter T., "The Native Syriac Linguistic Tradition: Resources Ancient and Modern," *Historiographia Linguistica* 39 (2012), 327-340.

Ewald, H., "Über das syrische Punctationssystem, nach syrischen Handschriften," *Abhandlungen zur orientalischen und biblischen Literatur* (Göttingen: Dieterrich, 1832), 53–129.

___, "Weitre Erläuterungen der syrischen Punctation, aus syrischen Handschriften," *Zeitschrift für die Kunde des Morgenlandes* 1 (1837), 204-12.

Farina, M., "Diathesis and Middle Voice in the Syriac Ancient Grammatical Tradition: The Translations and Adaptations of the *Techne Grammatike* and the Arabic Model," *Aramaic Studies* 6/2 (2008), 175-93.

___, "The Accidents of the Verb in Some Medieval Syriac Grammars," in S. E. Conti and M. Farina, *Comparing Ancient Grammars: The Greek, Syriac and Arabic Traditions* (Pisa: Edizioni della Normale, 2013), 131-53.

___, "La Grammatica Metrica di Barhebraeus (XIII sec.) e le sue glosse. Siriaco, greco e arabo in contatto," in Marina Benedetti (ed.), *Rappresentazioni linguistiche dell'identità* (Università degli Studi di Napoli "L'Orientale," 2015), 107-25.

___, "Barhebraeus' Metrical Grammar and Ms. BML Or. 298: Codicological and Linguistic Remarks," *Studi classici e orientali* 62 (2016): 345-60.

___, "The Syro-Arabic Glosses to Barhebraeus' Metrical Grammar," in Piera Molinelli (ed.), *Language and Identity in Multilingual Mediterranean Settings: Challenges for Historical Sociolinguistics*. Trends in Linguistics. Studies and Monographs 310 (Berlin / New York: Walter de Gruyter, 2017), 157-70.

___, ed. *Les auteurs syriaques et leur langue*. Études syriaques 15. Paris: Geuthner, 2018.

___,"La linguistique syriaque selon Jacques d'Édesse," in *Les auteurs syriaques et leur langue* (as above), 167-87.

___, "Manuscrits de grammaires et lexiques syriaques," in *Les auteurs syriaques et leur langue* (as above), 243-54.

___, "Le traitement des noms composés par les grammairiens syriaques," *Semitica et Classica* 12 (2019): 209-23.

___, "Bar Zobi's Grammar and the Texture of Knowledge in 13th Century," in Z. Paša and S. Rassi, edd., *The Impact of ʿAbdīshōʿ bar Brīkhā. Papers Collected on His 700th Anniversary* (Rome, Pontificio Istituto Orientale). In press.

___, "Amira's Grammatica Syriaca: Genesis, Structure and Perspectives," in E. Leuschner and G. Wolf, edd., *Proceedings of the workshop Typographia Linguarum Externarum—The Medici Oriental Press. Knowledge and Cultural Transfer around 1600.* In press.

___, "La tradition grammaticale syriaque comme 'extension' de la grammaire grecque : les parties du discours et le participe," in *Histoire épistémologie langage.* In press.

Gottheil, R. J. H., "Dawidh bar Paulos, a Syriac Grammarian," *Journal of the American Oriental Society* 15 (1893), cxi-cxviii.

Hugonnard-Roche, H., "Du commentaire à la reconstruction: Paul le Perse interprète d'Aristote (sur une lecture du Peri Hermeneias, à propos des modes et des adverbes selon Paul, Ammonius et Boèce)," in John W. Watt and J. Lössl (edd.), *Interpreting the Bible and Aristotle* (Ashgate, 2011), 207-24.

___, "La tradition du *Peri hermeneias* d'Aristote en syriaque, entre logique et grammaire," in M. Farina (ed.), *Les auteurs syriaques et leur langue.* Études syriaques 15. Paris: Geuthner, 2018, 55-94.

Jones, F. S., "Early Syriac Pointing in and behind British Museum Additional Manuscript 12,150," in R. Lavenant (ed.), *Symposium Syriacum VII* (Rome: Pontificio Istituto Orientale, 1998), 429-44.

Kessel, G., and Bamballi, N., "Field Notes on Syriac Manuscripts II: A Philosophical Manuscript *olim* Mosul 35 rediscovered," *Hugoye* 21.1 (2018), 21-42.

King, D., "Elements of the Syriac Grammatical Tradition as these relate to the origins of Arabic grammar," in A. Marogy (ed.), *The Foundations of Arabic Linguistics. Sibawayhi and the Earliest Arabic Grammatical Theory* (Leiden: Brill, 2012), 189-209.

___, "Grammar and Logic in Syriac (and Arabic)," *Journal of Semitic Studies* 58 (2013), 101-20.

Loopstra, J., " 'School Texts' for Reading the Bible and the Greek Fathers in Ninth- Through Thirteenth-Century Miaphysite Pedagogy," *Scriptura. Nouvelle série. Patristic Exegesis: the Fathers of the Church and the Bible* 10.1 (2008), 87-97.

___, *Patristic Selections in the 'Masoretic' Handbooks of the Qarqaptā Tradition.* CSCO Subsidia (Leuven, Forthcoming).

McCollum, Adam, "Prolegomena to a New Edition of Eliya of Nisibis's Kitāb al-turjumān fī taʿlīm luġat al-suryān," *Journal of Semitic Studies* 58 (2013), 297-322.

Martin, J. P. P., "Jacques d'Édesse et les voyelles syriennes," *Journal Asiatique* 6,13 (1869), 447-82.

___, "Tradition karkaphienne, ou la massore chez les Syriens," *Journal Asiatique* 6,14 (1869), 245-379.

___, "Syriens orientaux et occidentaux. Essai sur les deux principaux dialectes araméens," *Journal Asiatique* 6,19 (1872), 305-483.

___, "Histoire de la ponctuation, ou de la massore chez les Syriens," *Journal Asiatique* 7,5 (1875), 81-208.

___, *Traité sur l'accentuation chez les Syriens orientaux par Jean bar Zuʿbi (Syriac Text)* (Paris, 1877).

___, *De la métrique chez les Syriens* (Leipzig, 1879).

___, "La massore chez les Syriens," *Introduction à la Critique Textuelle du Nouveau Testament* (Paris, 1882-6).

Merx, A., *Historia artis grammaticae apud Syros* (Leipzig, 1889).

Moberg, A., "Über den griechischen Ursprung der syrischen Akzentuation," *Le monde oriental* 1 (1906), 87-99.

___, "Die syrische grammatik des Johannes Estonaja," *Le monde oriental* 3 (1909), 24-33.

___, *Eine syrische Massora-Handschrift in der Universitäts-Bibliothek zu Lund* (Lund, 1928).

Nestle, E., "Zur Geschichte der syrischen Punctation," *Zeitschrift der Deutschen Morgenländischen Gesellschaft* 30 (1876), 525-33.

Revell, E. J., "The Grammar of Jacob of Edessa and the Other Near Eastern Grammatical Traditions," *Parole d'Orient* 3 (1972), 365-74.

___, "Aristotle and the Accents: The Categories of Speech in Jewish and other authors," *Journal of Semitic Studies* 19/1 (1974), 19-35.

Rosenthal, F., "Das Syrische," *Die aramaistische Forschung : seit Th. Nöldeke's veröffentlichungen* (Leiden: Brill, 1939/1964), 179-93.

Segal, J. B., *The Diacritical Point and the Accents in Syriac* (London, 1953).

___, "Qussaya and Rukkaka: a historical introduction," *Journal of Semitic Studies* 34 (1989), 483-91.

Talmon, R., "Foreign Influence in the Syriac Grammatical Tradition," in S. Auroux et al. (edd.), *History of the language sciences, vol. 1: An International*

Handbook on the Evolution of the Study of Language from the Beginnings to the Present (Berlin: De Gruyter, 2000), 337-41.

___, "Jacob of Edessa the Grammarian," in B.T.H. Romeny (ed.), *Jacob of Edessa and the Syriac Culture of His Day* (Leiden: Brill, 2008), 159-87.

Voigt, R., "Das Vokalsystem des Syrischen nach Barhebraeus," *Oriens Christianus* 81 (1997), 36-72.

___, "Das emphatische P des Syrischen," in R. Lavenant (ed.), *Symposium Syriacum VII* (Rome, 1998), 527-37.

___, "Die metrische Struktur im *Buch der Strahlen,*" in H. Preissler and H. Stern (edd.), *Annäherung an das Fremde: XXVI Deutscher Orientalistentag* (Stuttgart, 1998), 132-44.

___, "Zu Barhebraeus' syrischer Metrik im Buch der Strahlen," in R. M. Voigt (ed.), *Akten des 5. Symposiums zur Sprache, Geschichte, Theologie und Gegenwartslage der syrischen Kirchen* (Berlin, 2006), 267-297.

Watt, J. W., "Grammar, Rhetoric, and the Enkyklios Paideia in Syriac," *Zeitschrift der Deutschen Morgenländischen Gesellschaft* 143 (1993), 45-71.

Weiss, T., *Zur ostsyrischen Laut- und Akzentlehre: auf Grund der ostsyrischen Massorah-Handschrift des British Museum.* Bonner orientalistische Studien 5 (Stuttgart, 1933).

Weninger, S., "Das 'Übersetzungsbuch' des Elias von Nisibis 10./11. Jh. im Zusammenhang der syrischen und arabischen Lexikographie," in W. Hüllen (ed.), *The World in a List of Words* (Tübingen: Niemeyer, 1994), 55-66.

VI. Summary of the Historia artis grammaticae

To enable the reader the more readily to navigate their way around Merx's work, what follows offers brief summaries to each chapter, outlining the arguments presented and the most important points that arise.

Chapter 1 Prolegomena

Merx here stresses the importance of grammar for the preservation and teaching of the higher arts of classical antiquity. It was the continuation of grammatical studies in the West that paved the way for the mediaeval return to philosophy. The Syriac pattern was different and was focused rather on their own language and on the scriptures. The Syriac method of studying grammar was motivated by their particular school curriculum.

Because grammars were written initially to teach pronunciation (scriptural recitation), the theory of pointing and accentuation was particularly significant. Apart from this, however, the Syrians tended to construct their grammars on the basis of Greek models, though there was change over time in how these different approaches were reconciled. The writing of Syriac grammars was closely associated with the translation of Greek philosophy and the collection of philosophical glossaries. Foremost among early Syriac philosophers was Sergius of Rešʿaina, but he was probably not the author of the first Syriac grammatical treatise, which was a translation of (ps) Dionysius Thrax's *Technē Grammatikē*. This text is introduced in its manuscript transmission and the possibility that Joseph Huzaya was the translator is raised, but rejected.

Chapter 2 Translation of an ancient Syriac Grammar (Dionysius Thrax)

This chapter consists of a translation of the Syriac version of the *Technē Grammatikē*, together with notes on the similarities and dissimilarities as compared to the original. Note that whereas the Syriac text in the appendix contains all the variants from mss B and C, the translation in this chapter is based on ms A, even where, as often towards the end, C fills up the gaps and corruptions in A. We have provided a translation based directly on the Syriac, only occasionally giving the Greek original as Merx does.

Chapter 3 Orthoepy, or Accurate Recitation

Joseph Huzaya may not have been the translator of Dionysius Thrax, but to him is correctly attributed a change in the system of 'reading'. This latter term is defined as the positioning of points to distinguish parts of speech. The 'Maqreyane' were those Masoretic masters from the School of Nisibis who systematised the reading of the scriptures using Greek grammatical theory as their model. This process began in the sixth century and took its lead from the work of translators of Greek philosophy and theology. The East Syrian Masoretic codex (BL Add. 12138) provides a great deal of evidence for the teachings of the Maqreyane. The development of grammar was based not just on the 'reading' of scripture, but equally on the Greek Church Fathers. Aḥūdemmēh and his (non-extant) schematisation of the verbal system is briefly mentioned.

Chapter 4 The Life and Work of Jacob of Edessa

The biography of Jacob is introduced, also his knowledge of Hebrew. His concern for church hymnography is first raised and demonstrates his philological accuracy in transposing the Greek metrical system into Syriac. The autograph manuscript of Jacob's translation of Severus's *Hymns* is discussed. His education of the clergy led him to a concern for grammar, beginning with his scholia on the Biblical text; then his work on chronology; his enforcement of the canons in his church; his teaching of Greek and the scriptures after his abdication of the episcopacy. His philological comments on the Hebrew text are briefly introduced, as is his recensional work, which leads on to the discussion of his *Letter on Orthography*. The rules laid down in this letter are summarised and his *Grammar* itself introduced.

Chapter 5 The Syriac Grammar of Jacob of Edessa

This chapter gleans as much as possible from the remaining fragments of Jacob's *Grammar*. Merx begins by pointing out that it is essentially a translation of the Greek grammatical tradition. Jacob follows the Greek ordering of each subject and he is ever comparing the Greek and Syriac languages. He begins with orthography and Jacob's vowel symbols—the later system of dotted vowels cannot have been fully developed already in his day. Jacob had nine vowels in his system. Merx reconstructs as far as possible this part of the Grammar.

After vowels, he dealt with consonants, categorising them according to the Greek sequences. He explains, using this system, the changes in consonants that occur in Syriac. He even tried to explain *bgdkpt* by means of Greek phonological classes. He shows how Bar Šakko and Barhebraeus are both dependent on Jacob for this subject.

Next comes the syllable, a subject not taken up by later grammarians. Jacob must have included it because his system of noun classification depends upon first classifying different kinds of syllables.

In classifying the noun, he seems to have used Dionysius's five attributes of the noun. Jacob lists these noun types by form, using a system derived from Theodosius's Canons. Merx proves Jacob's close borrowing from Theodosius by a number of comparisons.

Finally, there is evidence that Jacob must have treated the verb next, although this is not extant. However, the numerous parallels between Jacob and Barhebraeus show that the latter can be used to reconstruct the outline of Jacob's *Grammar* where this is not extant.

Chapter 6 Jacob's improvements to the Syriac accents and the Relationships between Greek, Syriac, and Hebrew punctuation

The Grammar has been dealt with, but the enormously important subject of pointing/accentuation has not yet been touched upon. Accentuation was dealt with by Jacob at the end of his grammar (following Dionysius) and the later giants (Bar Šakko and Barhebraeus) followed Jacob.

Merx's principal argument is that the Syriac system is based upon the Greek theorising about the use of points for providing a logical division of sentences. The Syriac adoption of this Greek approach may be seen in the earliest Syriac mss, which display a very simple system of internal sentence division. The fifth century masters developed this into the system better known today (i.e. with four logical accents: šewāyā, taḥtāyā, ʿalāyā, pasōqā). Joseph Huzaya was responsible for adding to this six further 'rhetorical' accents. These latter developments were 'native' rather than Greek-inspired.

The Hebrew accentuation system, by contrast, was logical only. Its major sentence dividers were derived from the Syriac system of disjunctive logical accents as known to Joseph Huzaya, as can easily be seen by their positions and usage. They even took from Syriac its single conjunctive accent (garōrā), which the Syrians in turn had taken from Greek. This Syriac-Hebrew borrowing took place between the middle of the sixth and the middle of the seventh century in three stages (greater accents—vowels—lesser accents).

Jacob of Edessa made significant additions to Joseph Huzaya's system, particularly in adding many new rhetorical accents by combining previously existing ones. His system for the rhetorical accents divided them into mimetic and temporal categories (even this distinction is derived from Dionysius Thrax). These rhetorical accents are then set out and described; it is suggested that the precise definitions of the temporal rhetorical accents was derived by Jacob from the Greek system of Nicanor. The process by which this is supposed to have happened is laid out in detail.

The basis for all this is a reconstructed 'list' of Jacob's accents which makes use of his letter on orthography together with the borrowings in Bar Šakko and Barhebraeus. This reconstructed text is provided after the above discussions.

The chapter closes with a notice of Thomas the Deacon's accent system, which appears to be half-way between those of Joseph Huzaya and Jacob of Edessa. It too draws independently on Greek traditions.

Chapter 7 The East Syrian Grammarians ʿEnanišoʿ and Ḥunain

After Jacob's time, the Syrians stopped writing grammars but did start writing lexica. The first of these is ʿEnanišoʿ. The nature and identity of his extant work is discussed. The outline of the work and some of its characteristics are described, including unusual terminology. Išoʿ Bar Nun also wrote in this genre but his work is lost. Ḥunain ibn Isḥāq was well known for his grammars but all that remains is his recension of ʿEnanišoʿ's list of homonyms. Its terminology is discussed. John the Stylite is also mentioned. Syriac grammar became, in Jacob of Edessa and afterwards, a synthesis of the masoretic traditions (pointing and vowels) and the translated Greek grammar (morphology).

Chapter 8 Elias of Nisibis, Jospeh Bar Malkon, and the Masoretic Manuscripts

This chapter covers the Syriac grammatical tradition between 900 until the time of John Bar Zuʿbi. It begins with a description of the life and work (Arabic and Syriac) of Elias of Nisibis, emphasising that his work has its context in the real life situations and challenges of his church. We are also introduced to Joseph Bar Malkon's *Net of Points*, the first metrical grammar, which is based in part on Elias and represents the Nisibene tradition.

Selected parts of Elias are detailed. Firstly, his list of vowels; then servile and radical consonants (including a discussion of Elias's odd story about the translation of the Syriac Bible); the cases (i.e. ܦܘܢܝ̈ܐ), including an extended section on the rules for *bgdkpt* aspiration in the presence of the cases (Bar Malkon is compared); the suppressed letters (as in Bar Šakko); the phonological effects of consonant combinations (compared to Bar Malkon); and the accents, especially ܦܣܘܩܐ.

This leads to a digression on the state of accentual theory at this time in the different schools, esp. in the Masoretic manuscript Add 12138. The differences between these traditions and that of Bar Malkon and Bar Zuʿbi is detailed, especially the system for the use of ܥܨܘܪܐ and ܡܗܓܝܢܐ.

The last part of Elias to be discussed is his appendix, on the topic of inflection, which is Greek-based; although Bar Malkon's equivalent is more native. The categorisations of both are described. The overall layout of both Elias and Bar Malkon are compared.

Finally, a few other names are mentioned and the first beginnings of Arabic influence upon Syriac grammatical teaching are introduced.

Chapter 9 Elias of Ṭirhan and the Beginnings of the Arabising School

Denial of Syriac influence on the beginnings of the Arabic grammatical tradition. The latter can be explained on internal grounds, though there are parallels with the Syriac experience. This leads to a lengthy digression on the origins of Arabic grammar. The conclusions broadly are: that religious commentary was the principal motivating factor in its genesis; that, orthoepy and orthography aside, Arabic grammar took its lead from Greek logic, channelled primarily through the Aristotelian commentary tradition; that the nomenclature, and to some extent the theories, of Greek grammar had only a minimal influence on the Arabic; and that there is therefore no need to hypothesise that Greek grammar (rather than logic) had any influence on Arabic grammar.

The subject of the influence of logical principles on Arabic grammar is dealt with at some length and has been the subject of controversy since (see Introduction). The Arabic preference for logical explanations rather than strictly grammatical ones led to shortcomings in Arabic morphological and syntactical theory. Following Ibn Chaldun, the Arabs are criticised for this faulty approach. They are praised, however, for not having slavishly copied Greek models but for having successfully developed a grammar well-suited to the Semitic language group.

This account throws a better light, according to Merx, on those Syrian grammarians who chose to base their work on Arabic rather than Greek sources. The Catholicos Elias I of Ṭirhan was the first of these. He wanted to modernise Syriac grammar by analysing it according to the Arabic system, but as a pioneer he made many mistakes and was unable to achieve his objective. A number of the confused passages from Elias's grammar are briefly discussed in relation to Arabic grammar, as well as those aspects of it that derive from traditional Syriac models and from logic.

Chapter 10 John Bar Zuʿbi

Dubbed the greatest of the East Syrian grammarians, Bar Zuʿbi was more indebted to philosophy than to Arabic grammar. His indebtedness to the Syriac Aristotelian tradition is demonstrated. The first half of his grammar follows the outline of Dionysius Thrax and owes much of its detail to the Greek tradition as well. His categorisations of the noun are based on logical rather than grammatical considerations. His analysis of the accents is again dependent on logic but is also in part derived from Elias of Ṭirhan. His classification of the verbal system comes from Joseph Bar Malkon and may go back to Jacob of Edessa, whose work lies behind much in Bar Zuʿbi.

The second half of the grammar is more 'native', dealing with accentuation, aspiration etc. after the manner of his Syriac predecessors.

Appendix I Three Treatises on East Syrian Accentuation

Merx here summarizes all that has been said about the Eastern accentual system, elucidating in particular what we know about it from the famous masoretic codex Add 12138. He then presents three texts illustrating varieties of the Eastern system of accentuation, the third of which he argues to have been authored by Elias of Ṭirhan and used by Bar Zuʿbi.

Appendix II Observations from the Reuchlian manuscript on Aramaic and Hebrew orthoepy

The principal contribution of the East Syrians in accentuation was the use of the lines of conjunction and separation (ܡܗܓܝܢܐ and ܡܒܗܠܢܐ). These were the most crucial for purposes of recitation and they are by no means unique to Syriac, for they are shown here to function in the same manner as the dagesh point in the Reuchlian manuscript of the Aramaic Targum to the Prophets.

The rules for the use of these two marks in Syriac are laid out in some detail. Numerous examples from the Reuchlian manuscript are used to illuminate the true nature of the Syriac system (which is somewhat confused in Bar Zuʿbi's account).

There follow short digressions of the so-called 'neutral dagesh' of the Hebrew text in the Reuchlian manuscript, and on the variety of theories among Syrians on the exact use of these marks.

Chapter 11 Jacob of Tagrit, otherwise known as Severus Bar Šakko

This Jacob was a son of the renowned West Syrian monastery of Mar Mattai. He wrote a series of dialogues on the liberal arts, which probably formed the curriculum at Mar Mattai. After a very cursory description of the contents and arrangement of the dialogue on grammar, there is a discussion of the ms base for the edition in the appendix. There is also a short metrical grammar, parts of which are published in the appendix.

Although a student of Bar Zuʿbi, Jacob did not follow his tecaher's method. He amalgamates Greek philosophy and Syriac grammar more thoroughly, and is indebted to Jacob of Edessa and Joseph Bar Malkon.

Chapter 12 The Grammar of Barhebraeus

Barhebraeus is announced as the foremost grammarian of Syriac. It is only from the published grammatical works that his literary achievement can be truly appreciated. His synthesis was achieved by importing the traditions of Syriac grammar (especially Jacob of Edessa) into the framework of the Arabic tradition (especially that of Az-Zamaḫšarī) rather more effectively and thoroughly than was managed by Elias of Ṭirhan.

Merx then proceeds to a detailed description and discussion of the *Book of Rays*. Its basic arrangement follows the tripartite division of Arabic grammars. His mingling of the Greek and Arabic systems is everywhere in evidence, especially in the arrangement of the nouns. The section on general nouns (IV) includes some important comments on the changing notions of 'species' and 'shapes' as applied to the noun. The section on the final book (IX) describes some of Barhebraeus's best achievements in the field.

Conclusion

Traces the history of Syriac grammar as practised in the West in the sixteenth century, starting with Teseo Ambrogio who in 1539 published the first book to deal with, and print, Syriac. The story is told of how Teseo became involved in Syriac and also how he later passed on his interest and knowledge to Widmanstetter, the editor of the first Syriac New Testament. It was Masius who really founded Syriac grammar in the west by writing a grammatical treatise as part of his contribution to the Antwerp polyglot and he was soon followed by a Syrian speaker, George Amira. These, and a few other early grammarians, are briefly noted.

VII. Abbreviations used in the footnotes and endnotes

Anec. Syr.	J.P.N. Land, *Anecdota Syriaca*, 4 vols. (Leiden, 1862-75)
Assemani, *Catalogus*	G.S. and S.E. Assmemani, *Bibliothecae Apostolicae Vaticanae codicum manuscriptorum catalogus*, vol.1 (Oriental mss) (Rome, 1756)
Baethgen, *Elias*	F. Baethgen, ed. & tr., ܬܘܪܨ ܡܡܠܠܐ ܣܘܪܝܝܐ oder *syrische Grammatik des Mar Elias von Tirhan* (Leipzig, 1880)
Barhebraeus, *Chron. Eccl.*	J.B. Abbeloos & T.J. Lamy, *Gregorii Barhebraei Chronicon Ecclesiasticum*, 3 vols. (Louvain & Paris, 1872-8)
Barhebraeus, *Gramm.*	The *Book of Rays*, in J.P.P. Martin, ed., *Œuvres grammaticales d'Abou'lfaradj dit Bar Hebreus,*

	vol.I (Paris, 1872), re-edited and translated by Moberg (s.v.)
Bekker, *Anecdota*	I. Bekker, *Anecdota Graeca* (Berlin, 1814)
BO	G.S. Assemani, *Bibliotheca Orientalis Clementino-Vaticana*, 3 vols. (Rome, 1719-28)
Busse, Ammonius De Int.	A. Busse, ed., *Ammonius in Aristotelis de interpretatione commentaria*, CAG IV,5 (Berlin, 1897)
CAG	Commentaria in Aristotelem Graeca
De Sacy, *Anthologie*	A.I. Silvestre de Sacy, *Anthologie grammaticale arabe* (Paris, 1829)
De Sacy, *Grammaire*	id., *Grammaire arabe*, 1st ed. (Paris, 1810)
EI	Encyclopaedia of Islam
Elamrani-Jamal, *Logique*	A. Elamrani-Jamal, *Logique aristotélicienne et grammaire arabe : étude et documents* (Paris, 1983)
GAP	Helmut Gätje, ed., *Grundriss der Arabischen Philologie* vol.2: Literaturwissenschaft (Wiesbaden, 1987)
GAS	F. Sezgin, ed., *Geschichte des arabischen Schrifttums* (Leiden, 1967-)
GSL	A. Baumstark, *Geschichte der syrischen Literatur* (Bonn, 1922)
Goldziher, *History*	I. Goldziher, *On the History of Grammar among the Arabs: an essay in literary history,* Studies in the History of the Language Sciences 73 (Amsterdam, 1994)
Gottheil, *Elias*	R.J.H. Gottheil, *A treatise on Syriac grammar by Mar Elia of Sobha* (Berlin, 1887), Reprint, Gorgias Press, 2003
Hoffmann, *Herm.*	J.G.E. Hoffmann, *De Hermeneuticis apud Syros Aristotelis* (Leipzig, 1869)
Hoffmann, *Opuscula*	id., *Opuscula Nestoriana* (Kiel, 1880)
King, *Syriac Categories*	D. King, *The Earliest Syriac Translation of Aristotle's Categories* (Leiden, 2010)
Martin, *Accentuation*	J.P.P Martin, ed., *Traité sur l'accentuation chez les Syriens orientaux par Jean bar Zuʿbi* (Paris, 1877)

Martin, *Ad Georgium*	id., *Jacobi Episcopi Edesseni Epistola ad Georgium Episcopum Sarugensem de orthographia syriaca* (Paris, 1869)
Martin, *De la métrique*	id., *De la métrique chez les Syriens* (Leipzig, 1879)
Martin, *Deux dialectes*	id., "Syriens orientaux et occidentaux. Essai sur les deux principaux dialectes araméens" *Journal Asiatique* 6,19 (1872), 305-483
Martin, *La Massore*	id., *La massore chez les Syriens. Introduction à la Critique Textuelle du Nouveau Testament* (Paris, 1882-6)
Martin, *Œuvres*	id., *Œuvres grammaticales d'Abou' lfaradj dit Bar Hebreus*, 2 vols. (Paris, 1872)
Martin, *karkaphienne*	id., "Tradition karkaphienne, ou la massore chez les Syriens" *Journal Asiatique* 6,14 (1869), 245-379
Merx, *Grammatica*	A. Merx, *Grammatica Syriaca.* 2 parts (Halle, 1867-70)
Moberg, *Akzentuation*	A. Moberg, "Über den griechischen Ursprung der syrischen Akzentuation" *Le monde oriental* 1 (1906), 87-99
Moberg, *Buch der Strahlen*	id., *Buch der Strahlen, die grössere Grammatik des Barhebräus*, 2 vols. (Leipzig, 1907,1913)
Moberg, *Livre des Spendeurs*	id., *Le livre des splendeurs, la grande grammaire de Grégoire Barhebraeus (texte syriaque)* (Lund, 1922)
Nestle, *Gramm.*	*Brevis linguae Syriacae Grammatica, litteratura, chrestomathia cum glossario* (Karlsruhe, 1881)
Phillips, *Accents*	G. Phillips, "Syriac Accents," *Journal of Philology* 9 (1880), 221-9
Phillips, *Letter*	id., *A Letter by Mar Jacob, Bishop of Edessa, on Syriac orthography* (London, 1869)
Revell, *Aristotle*	E.J. Revell, "Aristotle and the Accents: The Categories of Speech in Jewish and other authors," *Journal of Semitic Studies* 19 (1974), 19-35
Revell, *Grammar*	E.J. Revell, "The Grammar of Jacob of Edessa and the Other Near Eastern Grammatical Traditions," *Parole de L'Orient* 3 (1972), 365-374

Sachau, *Verzeichniss*	E. Sachau, *Verzeichniss der syrischen Handschriften der Königlichen Bibliothek zu Berlin* (Berlin, 1899)
Segal	J.B. Segal, *The Diacritical Point and the Accents in Syriac*, (London, 1953)
Segal, Quššaya	J.B. Segal, "Quššaya and Rukkaka: a historical introduction" *Journal of Semitic Studies* 34 (1989), 483-491
Sokoloff, *Syriac Lexicon*	*A Syriac lexicon : a translation from the Latin; correction, expansion, and update of C. Brockelmann's Lexicon syriacum* (Gorgias Press, 2009)
Talmon, *Jacob of Edessa*	R. Talmon, "Jacob of Edessa the Grammarian," in B.Ter Haar Romeny, ed., *Jacob of Edessa and the Syriac Culture of His Day,* Monographs of the Peshitta Institute 18 (Leiden, 2008), 159-187
Thesaurus	R. Payne-Smith, *Thesaurus Syriacus* (Oxford, 1879-1901)
Uhlig	G. Uhlig, ed., *Dionysii Thracis Artis Grammaticae*, Grammatici Graeci I (Leipzig, 1883)
Versteegh, *Elements*	Kees Versteegh, *Greek Elements in Arabic Linguistic Thinking* (Leiden, 1977)
Versteegh, *Grammar*	id., "Grammar and Exegesis : The Origins of Kufan Grammar and the Tafsir Muqatil," *Der Islam* 67 (1990), 206-42
Voigt, *Vokalsystem*	R. Voigt, "Das Vokalsystem des Syrischen nach Barhebraeus," *Oriens Christianus* 81 (1997), 36-72
Vööbus, *School*	A. Vööbus, *History of the School of Nisibis* (Louvain, 1965)
Weiss, *Laut- und Akzentlehre*	T. Weiss, *Zur ostsyrischen Laut- und Akzentlehre: auf Grund der ostsyrischen Massorah-Handschrift des British Museum*, Bonner orientalistische Studien 5 (Stuttgart, 1933)
Wright, *Syriac Literature*	W. Wright, *A Short History of Syriac Literature* (London, 1894)
ZDMG	Zeitschift der Deutschen Morgenländischen Gesellschaft

VIII. NOTE ON TRANSLATING THE HISTORIA ARTIS GRAMMATICAE

In general, Greek quotations from the original have been translated in the main text with the original Greek consigned to an endnote. This has not as a rule been done for Syriac quotations, most of which have been left in the text, with English translation provided in brackets where it was felt that this might be helpful to the general readership.

References to page and line numbers in the appended texts have been left as they were in Merx's monograph. These page and line numbers have also been included in the margins of the appended texts themselves as reprinted here, so that a single referencing system for these can be maintained.

Similarly, Merx's references to his own page numbers have been left intact. These pages are noted throughout in superscript, e.g. |[23].

Throughout his text, Merx uses both Syriac fonts and Roman-type transliterations in roughly equal proportions and without any apparent or thoroughgoing principle. Nöldeke (Review, 1219) slated Merx's transliterations for applying vowel changes that were both anachronistic and inconsistent. Rather than second guess certain vocalisations, which would anyway have differed across time and space, we have used Syriac script for all Syriac words, and only added vowel signs where this seemed either necessary or helpful.

The attentive reader will note that I have taken more liberties in translating Merx's more florid passages than with the bare technical sections, which naturally constitute the bulk of the material.

An important work on the Syriac grammatical tradition was published in 2018 (*Les auteurs syriaques et leur langue.* Études syriaques 15). The annotations to Merx in this volume were written prior to this publication, hence future researchers need to be aware that bibliographical "updates" contained in these annotations may not always contain all the most necessary references to the important chapters of that volume.

THE AUTHOR WISHES THIS WORK TO BE DEDICATED

TO THE SACRED MEMORY OF

WILLIAM WRIGHT OF CAMBRIDGE

THE PRE-EMINENT JEWEL OF OUR COMMUNITY

Editorial Note: Fate decreed that the very day after Merx signed off the preface to his book, the famous orientalist William Wright passed away, at the age of 59 (22nd May 1889). It seems that Merx received the news in time to insert this dedication page in his memory.

Preface

|[vii] The state in which the study of Syriac literature finds itself today being what it is, I believe the most necessary first stage to be simply the straightforward cataloguing of manuscripts and the accumulation of individual observations, and only thence can progress be made step by step towards the task of drawing up of a picture of the whole subject. This ought to be done in such a way that each individual subject be comprehensively surveyed in turn—their first beginnings, their rise and fall, and their current state. The whole course of each subject needs first to be mapped out; fields such as historiography, poetry, philosophy, theology, medicine, etc. Then, an even larger and more difficult enterprise, the lives of the authors themselves need to be explored, their manners, their literary qualities, their purposes and designs. Only thus, with the fog cleared away, will their personalities stand out, as if they were still with us. Which of them will turn out to be fellow spirits? Which will charm us with their delights, or affect us with their sorrows? Until all this is done, we shall never have anything but a pile of bits and pieces, much-rifled by the learned hands of careless scholars, the fruit of whose great labours will be of no general value.

Furthermore, until the history of literature is brought into close juxtaposition with social and cultural history, the goal of Syriac philology will never be truly achieved. Without just such a general sense of the whole, young students asking which subject to adopt for a dissertation will merely be advised to look into the life, character and judgment of some writer or other, in the hope that a history of literature worthy of the name can be composed bit by bit from such individual studies. The Syrian people, never having been under the constraints of statehood, lived out a great literary existence and, as the heirs to the Greek legacy, occupied for ten centuries a central position between Greek and Arabic literature. They thus played a vital part in the history of literary culture. To investigate and accurately to describe such a history as this will doubtless be a great labour whose usefulness more than adequately repays its effort.

From this great task I have picked out just one small section. I intend in the present work to describe the history of grammatical studies, a subject which seemed fairly manageable, since the material is both very limited and relatively straightforward. The only primary material in this field to have been published are the works of Barhebraeus, Elias of Ṭirhan and Elias of Nisibis—beyond this there is nothing. Hence it seemed worthwhile to add to my account (as appendices) certain unedited documents, specifically the grammar of Dionysius Thrax and the dialogue of Jacob Bar Šakko. These I decided to write out in my own hand on account of the great difficulty that the extensive punctuation in the latter text afforded to the typesetting. Finally,|viii I have reproduced, with Prof. W. Wright's permission, his edition of the fragments of Jacob of Edessa, fifty copies of which were distributed by him amongst a select few, especially also as those citations which the Oxford codex threw up have not been included in Wright's catalogue of Syriac manuscripts in the British Museum. Therefore I have reproduced the whole of Wright's edition and at the same time I have added (with great difficulty) a photolithographic table in which Jacob's vowels may be examined rather better than in the codex itself. I have come to the conclusion that the lengthy *Net of Points* by Joseph Bar Malkon and the grammatical work of John Bar Zuʿbi are not in need of being published separately, since I have quoted everything of any importance from these texts in my account. On the other hand, I have included three complete treatises on East Syrian pointing (appendix to chapter 10), since these shed some light on Barhebraeus's work, and at the same time show how the latter's sources relate to the various systems of pointing.

Adalbert Merx, Heidelberg, 21st May 1889

Chapter 1

Prolegomena

ܐܝܟܐ ܕܐܬܘܬܗ ܚܛܬܐ ܢܦܩ ܡܢ ܠܒܗ ܐܦ ܐܣܛܘܟܣܐ
ܡܘܟܝܢ ܠܗܘܢ ܡܠܘܬܐ ܠܟܬܒܐ ܚܠܠ ܕܡܬܪܟܒܢ
ܐܝܟܐ ܕܠܐ ܫܦܝܪ ܠܪܘܚܐ. ܐܝܟ ܢܫܡܐ ܕܠܐ ܦܓܪܐ ܘܠܐ
ܢܦܠܘܢ ܠܚܝܐ ܘܢܦܫ ܕܡܠܟܐ. ܘܟܕ ܗܘܝܢ ܠܟܬܒܐ.

Ḥunain ibn Isḥāq

Those who praise to the skies the fruitfulness of the Greek mind generally focus upon the gracefulness, matched by the seriousness, of their poetry, the gorgeous beauty of their statues, the wonderful majesty of their temples and public buildings, and above all the sheer depth of their philosophy which plumbed humanity and attained to divinity. Who indeed would take anything away from their outstanding achievements in such matters? But if they had not also excelled in one other sphere, one that may seem rather insignificant and feeble to those whose eyes are transfixed only upon the splendour of the finer arts and who thus deride whatever cannot compare with *them*, then the Greeks would never have become the teachers of all nations in the fine arts, which is what everyone usually praises them for.

You see, from the time when Roman power began to decline, nobody in the West actually continued to read Homer, Pindar or Sophocles; nobody wondered at the beauty of all that Greek sculpture which the Romans themselves famously removed from their original locations and then neglected and abandoned; nobody cared for the magnificence of the Greek temples, whose pillars the Christians ripped out and used to build their own basilicas; above all, nobody delved into the deepest recesses of philosophy to complete what the Greeks had left unfinished.

Nonetheless it was interest in philosophy that particularly engaged the early mediaeval scholars. The ever resourceful Minerva preserved her flickering light within the safe walls of the monasteries, ensuring that it would never be finally extinguished. But of course these young scholars were unable to steep themselves in the mysteries of logic and dialectic directly; rather, a route had to be prepared along which they could proceed, and that route was grammar—that science which the Stoics had developed out of logic and which now in the Middle Ages opened up in turn the path back to logic. Cassiodorus and Isidore of Seville thought very highly of the study of grammar, |[2] by which one could move on to philosophy, the gateway to theology, although in keeping with the general opinions of their day they kept well away from studying the ancient poets. Their contemporary, Pope Gregory the Great, wrote that, although the praises of Christ are not weakened by coming from the same mouth as the praises of Jupiter, a bishop ought not to sing of what does not edify the faithful.

That learning—unknown in the sixth and seventh centuries among the monastic clergy of Italy and Spain—was soon brought to a high level of sophistication by the Irish. Archbishop Theodore of Canterbury, first raised in Tarsus, was the first to establish schools in Britain, and in his footsteps followed closely the great luminaries of that age—the venerable Bede, Egbert, Alcuin, and later Rabanus. All of these educated their students in secular literature so that, once they had been refined by it, they might better proceed to the study of sacred literature. What is more, every secular institution used to include the seven liberal arts, both the trivium (which included grammar, metrics, dialectic and rhetoric) and the *quadrivium* of arithmetic, geometry, music and astronomy. Grammar was generally taken to be the most necessary and fundamental of these subjects—for without it books could not even be written correctly (Rabanus, *de clericorum institut.* III,18). Grammar was thus the key vehicle by which at least some sparks of Greek learning could be scattered amongst the storms of the early Middle Ages. It was the Greek grammarians who became the teachers of the whole of the western world during those centuries when the study of the fine arts went cold.

But matters were different among the Syrian people. Their young men were accustomed to begin their schooling not with grammar but with the reading of the Psalms. This pattern was possible for the simple reason that they read the Scriptures in their own language, while in the West vernacular translations were not accepted in the churches of the Germans, the French, the English or the Irish. The curriculum found both among the West Syrians (Jacobites) and the East Syrians (Nestorians) was first to read the Psalms all the way through, then to unpack the New and Old

Testaments, followed by reading the Doctors of the Church, and then finally the commentaries.[1]

The Doctors that were read by the West Syrians were Dionysius the Areopagite, Basil, Gregory Nazianzen, Severus, Ephrem, Mar Isaac, Jacob of Serug, Chrysostom, Cyril, Theodotus, and Architheus (Arcadius). To the writings of these were also added the Lives of the Fathers, Doctors, and Martyrs, the Paradise of Palladius, the Hexaemeron of Basil, seven orations of Jacob of Edessa, and an oration *On Theology* by the same, together with many letters. Of the commentators, Ephrem, Chrysostom, Mose bar Kepha, and Dionysius Bar Ṣalibi were the ones that were read.

The Doctors whose books the East Syrians read were Theodore of Mopsuestia, Ḥenanisho (whose homilies were read through the whole year), Išoʿ bar Nūn, Paul, and Barsauma. The mystical and ascetical books were reserved for men of maturer years.

|[3] The non-Christian texts in use in West Syrian schools included a book of Antony of Tagrit (which must, I think, be his book *On Rhetoric*),[2] and Aristotle's *Organon* (consisting of the Categories, On Interpretation, Analytics, Apodeictics, Topics, and Sophistical Refutations), to which were added the lecture notes on Poetics, Rhetoric, and Physics. They avoided the Metaphysics, however, of which they learnt only an outline.[3] Assemani has not recorded which profane books the East Syrians held to, but it is certain that they were well acquainted with the works of Aristotle.[4] [i]

We see then that there appears to be no trace of the study of grammar amongst these regulations for the education of the clergy. Assemani claimed that Babai of Nisibis re-established music and grammar;[5] but this is not certain, for in the Life of Babai, although music and the order of songs are mentioned, there is nothing about grammar.[6] On reflection it should come as no surprise that in the West, grammar books were always written for the use of students learning the language in question, while this was clearly not the case amongst the Syrians, for whom there was no need to

---

[1] Cf. BO III, II p.937f.

[2] Wright, *Cat.* II,614.

[3] The citation at BO I,I,938 is confused. The word ܡܛܘܠܬܐ should be deleted, and instead of ܡܢ ܦܣܩܐ ܟܝܢܐ read ܘܡܢ ܦܣܩܐ etc.

[4] BO III,I,85; Hoffmann, *Herm.*, p.141.

[5] BO III,II,941.

[6] BO III,I,178.

learn a foreign language since the Scriptures had been translated into their own tongue.

The explanation, then, as to why grammar was not much of a concern during the formative period of Syriac literature is to be found in the general nature of their schools. It is in the context of the schools that we should also seek to understand the particular method of dealing with grammar that they did, in fact, value.

For the Syrians, the basic subject of all study was the reading of the Scriptures. Now for students to become proficient in this they had first to become thoroughly acquainted with the correct method of pronunciation, then with the explanation of obscure words, and also of words that have the same consonants but differ in pronunciation and meaning (*aequilitterae*). The first of these requirements led to the development of the theory of pointing, the second in glossaries, once lists of explanations had been brought together into a single volume. Thus it was orthoepy and glossography in the Scriptures that formed the basic concerns of grammar.[ii]

Now as soon as someone wanted to try putting this medley of individual ideas and explanations into some sort of order, there were Greek grammatical treatises lying ready at hand to serve as models and the Syrians, just like the Latins and the Armenians, were able to establish their own grammars on the basis of Greek examples. The very first Syriac grammars thus normalised in the direction of the Greek models the types and forms that were natural to their own language—the rules of orthoepy being the obvious exception, since these were about expressing the vowels that should be pronounced in Syriac. Now if I started looking in a *Grammar* for an explanation of difficult words, rather than in a *Lexicon*, then in so doing I would be following the Greek method, which was after all the model for the Syrians. For according to the Greeks |[4] the parts of grammar are

1) Reading with due attention to prosody;[1]

2) The explanation of poetical figures of speech;

3) A ready explanation of glosses (i.e. obsolete or dialectal words) and allusions;

4) The discovery of etymologies;

5) The working-out of analogy (i.e. grammatical patterns);

---

[1] This is where the Syriac laws of orthoepy come in.

6) The criticism of poetry.[iii]

However, these collections of glossaries were gradually built up into full lexica and so grammar was freed from having to deal with subject matter that really belonged elsewhere. The theory of the usage and meaning of points was connected with the first part listed above (reading with attention to prosody). Because the accurate distinction of the parts of speech (which affects what is called a 'point' and what an 'accent') was connected with the same 'reading', the earliest grammarians dealt with vowel signs, aspirations, and accents (or punctuation) at the very beginning of their grammars. Later on, grammarians changed their approach. Barhebraeus, following the work of others, placed the laws about pointing at the very end of his treatment, so very adverse was he to the earlier system. One can conclude from the appendices to Dionysius Thrax's Grammar that the Greeks too had altogether rejected the earlier system.

We have so far attempted to explain everything from the standpoint of education. These same matters now need to be evidenced from historical testimony. We shall therefore move on to summarise everything we can glean about the oldest Syriac grammars themselves.

Any reader who looks carefully at the extant remains of the oldest Syriac grammars will easily be persuaded of what we argued above, namely that the Syrians read the Greek grammars and that it was for the most part the latter that provided the exemplars for the Syrians to follow. Everything that was done in this field was attempted by men steeped in Greek philosophy, since Greek texts had been translated and absorbed so eagerly. This fact needs to be recognised all the more as being the very reason why collections of words (or Syro-Greek vocabularies) which contained the technical terms of philosophy were established in the first place.

An understanding of how these translators worked is of importance in assessing the state of the Syriac version of Dionysius Thrax. We can gain some idea of this from a very interesting fragment found at the end of the Syriac version of Dionysius in BL Add. 14620 (f.25b). It reads as follows: ܐܘܟܝ. ܣܘܡܐ. ܠܡܬܡܘܗܝ. ܡܟܠܠ. ܐܝܟܢ ܡܫܘܐ. ܢܬܘܒ ܡܡܟܠܢܐ. ܐܦܝܣܛܡܣܝܣ ܕܗܘܐ. ܕܡܫܡܠܘ. ܘܕܒܟܠܗ܀ ܐܦܝܢ ܡܬܚܡܐ܀ ܐܘܦܪܣܝܣ ܡܐܡܪ ܬܐܘܐ܀ ܡܬܪܘܢ ܡܪܕܝܬܐ܀ ܘܡܠܝܢ. ܕܢܘܐ܀ ܦܫܝܛܝܣ ܦܫܝܛܐ܀ ܐܪܘܗ. ܠܣܘܡܐ܀ ܐܪܘ. ܠܣܘܡܐ܀ ܗܘܦܣܛܣܝܣ ܣܘܡܐ܀

What we have here is simply an interlinear Syriac translation, with the order of the Syriac words preserved, then copied again after the order had become mixed up. Such a confusion arose from the simple fact that the Syriac word order |[5] is different from the Greek. It starts with the common definition of a man: ἄνθρωπός ἐστι—ζῷον λογικὸν θνητὸν νοῦ καὶ ἐπιστήμης δεκτικόν (*man is a reasoning mortal creature endowed with mind and understanding*). Initially, the separate Greek and Syriac sentences were written out and the definition was accurately translated as, ܚܝܘܬܐ ܡܠܝܠܬܐ ܡܝܘܬܐ ܡܩܒܠܢܝܬܐ ܕܗܘܢܐ ܘܝܕܥܬܐ. Later, some student placed these words together with the Greek ones according to their order, 1 ζῷον 2 λογικὸν 3 θνητὸν 4 νοῦ καὶ 5 ἐπιστήμης 6 δεκτικόν, whence the following set of equivalents, 1 ζῷον = ܚܝܘܬܐ 2 λογικὸν = ܡܠܝܠܬܐ 3 θνητὸν = ܡܝܘܬܐ 4 νοῦ καὶ = ܡܩܒܠܢܝܬܐ 5 ἐπιστήμης = ܕܗܘܢܐ 6 δεκτικόν = ܘܝܕܥܬܐ. The whole was then written out in Syriac transcription (including the corruption of ܠܝܛܘܢ to ܐܝܛܘܢ) leaving the following text: .ܙܘܢ ܚܝܘܬܐ. ܠܘܓܝܩܘܢ. ܡܠܝܠܬܐ. ܠܝܛܘܢ[ܐܝܛܘܢ] ܡܝܘܬܐ. ܢܘܣܩܐ ܡܩܒܠܢܝܬܐ. ܐܦܣܛܝܡܝܣ ܕܗܘܢܐ. ܕܩܛܝܩܘܢ. ܘܝܕܥܬܐ. We shall note similar confusions here and there even in Dionysius.

The next part (of the above quotation) consists of some Greek nouns, those of the first declension being given in the accusative case, thus: ܐܦܛܝܢ = ἀπάτην, ܡܛܥܝܢܐ ; ܗܘܦܘܩܪܝܣܝܣ = ὑπόκρισις, ܡ̈ܚܠܦܬ ܟ̈ܐܦܐ ; ܡܝܛܪܘܢ = μήτραν, ܡܪܚܡܐ ; ܩܘܠܝܢ = κοιλίαν, ܟܪܣܐ ; ܦܣܝܠܝܣ = ψιλός, ܦܫܝܛܐ ; ܐܘܪܘܣ = ὅρος, ܬܚܘܡܐ ; ܐܘܪܘ = ὅροι, ܬܚܘܡܐ (sic!) ; ܗܘܦܘܣܛܐܣܝܣ = ὑπόστασις, ܩܢܘܡܐ. We have, therefore, a specimen of an ancient Greek-Syriac vocabulary, in which we find the accusatives of Greek nouns of the first declension together with the plurals of second declensions in 'u', as was the custom in later works.

When the Syriac scholars of the earliest period were translating Greek texts, they would first render word-for-word, and then rearrange the word order according to the Syriac idiom.[iv] However, if the Greek order (which was retained in the first translation and then changed during the revision as they smartened up the translation) was preserved, then confusion could arise. We shall see an example of this below in the paradigm of the verb τύπτω (ch.2). From this technique of translating word-for-word arose not only Graecisms but also translations that are incomprehensible without knowledge of the underlying Greek words, e.g. ܫܘ̈ܝ ܫܡܐ = ὁμώνυμα and ܫܡܐ ܕܒܠܚܘܕ ܕܓܘܐ = ὧν ὄνομα μόνον κοινόν.[1] [v]

|[6] Among these first translators of Greek philosophy into Syriac, particular note should be taken of Sergius of Reshʿaina,[2] [vi] a contemporary

[1] Hoffmann, *Herm.*, p.17.

[2] So Barhebraeus (BO II,315). However, the theological works of Diodore were already translated by about 470 (J.P.P Martin, "Lettres de Jacques de Saroug," *ZDMG* 30 [1876], 217-75, esp. p.224) and the books of Theodore of Mopsuestia were translated even earlier than that (Hoffmann, *Herm.*, p.142).

of Pope Agapetus (d. 536), who died shortly after him.[1] Sergius was sent to Rome by the archenemy of the Miaphysites, Patriarch Ephrem of Antioch (527-545),[2] whence he accompanied Agapetus on the journey from Rome to Constantinople. It is suggested that he was a learned man but of immoral character, much given to women and money. Among the Syrians, however, he was called an *archiatros* (i.e. one especially skilled in medicine), and he was also raised to the dignity of the priesthood.[vii]

Some of Sergius's treatises are extant in BL Add.14658, namely *On Logic, On the causes of the universe, On genus, species and individuality*, and *On the effect produced by the moon according to the opinion of astronomers*, together with an appendix *On the action of the sun*. Some of these are dedicated to Theodore of Merv (sic).[3] [viii] There is also elsewhere a scholion on the meaning of the term *schema*, a translation of Aristotle's *De Mundo*,[4] and a translation of the part of Galen's book *On the mixtures of basic medicines* which pertains to plants (books VI-VIII), which appears to have been written at the request of the same priest Theodore.[5]

To these works of philosophy and medicine he added a theological work, an introduction to Dionysius the Areopagite, whose corpus he had also translated into Syriac.[6] [ix] By doing this he demonstrated his own piety as surely as if he had written a treatise on the faith. Zacharias Rhetor claimed that he had polluted this piety by his way of life, but others recall him as reverent and modest.[7] These different judgments on the life of Sergius are to be explained by the fact that he appears to have been highly

---

[1] Zacharias Rhetor, *Ecclesiastical History* (ed. Land, *Anec. Syr.* III), p.289f., which should be compared with Barhebraeus, *Chron.Eccl.* I,207f. Barhebraeus follows Zacharias but the text of the latter is full of errors.

[2] After the patriarch Severus was expelled from Antioch in 518 (Barhebraeus, *Chron.Eccl.*, I,193) he was followed by Paul for one year, then by Euphrasius from 521-7, and finally by Ephrem of Amid from 527-545 (*Chron.Eccl.*, I,195f.).

[3] BO III,I,147.

[4] Wright, *Cat.* III,1162,1157.

[5] I have read through the whole of this translation and have given some necessary emendations in "Proben der syrischen Übersetzung von Galenus' Schrift über die einfachen Heilmittel," *ZDMG* 39 (1885), 237-305. For a description of the ms, Wright, *Cat.*, 1187.

[6] Wright, *Cat.* II,500,494.

[7] Land, *Anec. Syr.* III,289. Wright, *Cat.* II,494.

regarded as a genius of his time by the orthodox party (Agapetus, Ephrem) but was roundly hated by the miaphysites. The latter thought so badly of him that in one codex which expounds and defends miaphysite doctrine, they made sure to include the story of his death.[1]

Since we see our Sergius engaged in these squabbles between the orthodox and the miaphysites, it might not be too rash to conjecture that he is the same Sergius with whom Severus of Antioch corresponded and argued about the question of the two natures of Christ. Some unedited Greek fragments of this correspondence are extant in the Coislian collection,|[7] and some in Photius.[2] These same letters are also preserved in Syriac in a London manuscript in which he is called 'grammaticus', the title also given him in Photius.[3] [x] A Sergius Grammaticus is moreover also cited by Choeroboscos and in the *Etymologicum Magnum*,[4] which Zonaras repeats under the term Γαῖα. While one may justly question whether Sergius the doctor-priest is one and the same as Sergius grammaticus, it is at least clear that the grammatical treatise which Wright attributed to him, albeit hesitantly, was in fact neither composed nor translated by him. We shall see shortly that in fact this treatise is a translation of Dionysius Thrax.

BL Add. 14658, besides the works of Sergius already mentioned, contains several treatises on philosophy, as well as translations of Greek works on philosophy which Renan,[5] following Wright, conjecturally attributed to Sergius, perhaps with some justification. It was on this basis that Wright suggested that Sergius may also have translated Porphyry's *Eisagoge*, Aristotle's *Categories*, and the ps-Aristotelian *On the Soul*, and composed a treatise *On the Parts of Speech* and *On negation and affirmation*. None of this is self-evident, however, since there are only six works in the codex that are explicitly attributed to Sergius, 1) *On Logic*; 2) *On the universe*; 3) (ps-Aristotle) *De Mundo*; 4) *On genus, species and individuality*; 5) *On the effect of the moon*; 6) *On the effect of the sun*, and we should probably conclude

[1] Wright, *Cat.* II,983; *Anec. Syr.* II,289.

[2] B. de Montfaucon, *Bibliotheca Coisliniana sive Segueriana* (Paris, 1715), 44,55,56,57 ; I. Bekker, ed., *Photii Bibliotheca* (Berlin, 1824-5), 283b,28.

[3] Wright, *Cat.* II,557.

[4] T. Gaisford, ed., *Etymologicon magnum* (Oxford, 1848; repr. Amsterdam, 1962), 223,1.

[5] E. Renan, "Lettre à M. Reinaud, sur quelques manuscrits syriaques du Musée britannique, contenant des traductions d'auteurs grecs profanes et des traités philosophiques," *Journal Asiatique* 19 (1852), 293-333, see p.320.

from this that the rest, given that his name does not appear in their inscriptions, do not belong to him.[xi] Even if we cannot here prove this with regard to the translation of the philosophical books, it should be an easy matter to show it to be so in the case of the aforementioned grammatical treatise.

This treatise is extant both in BL Add. 14658 and in BL Add. 14620.[1] The former, which also contains Sergius's other works and which we shall designate B, has preserved only the part of the treatise that deals with the noun. In Add. 14620, which we shall call A, the whole work is extant.

The state of these exemplars is such that A (Add. 14620), despite being attributed to the ninth century, offers an older text than does B. The latter is a more worked-up version. The text of A is the one based on the original translation, in which not everything is fully worked out and the whole is schematic rather than developed and refined. It was copied by a scribe who misread words that were sometimes placed on the page in a confused order, resulting in various lacunae and incorrect sequences of words. The forms of the verb τύπτω, found at the end, will provide plenty of examples; others will be found in the notes which we have added to the translation.

|[8] By contrast, codex B (Add. 14658), of the seventh century, although older than A, offers a text which derives from the schematisation preserved in A. In doing this, however, the redactor has restored and refined only the part on the noun and left out all the rest.

If we are looking for the origin of the translation, we must therefore return to A, for the translator explains in the subscription (which has been made rather unclear by a number of lacunae) just what he wanted to do. Everything that he discovered about grammar (he says) he found neatly summarised for the use of students within a single book, although in fact all he had found was a truncated text of Dionysius Thrax's *Technē Grammatikē*. Now a Syrian living in a city far away from the world of culture might indeed say something like that, but surely not someone like Sergius, who had been educated at Alexandria. Zacharias Rhetor affirms that Sergius was very well read in Greek literature and was especially learned in the theology of Origen. When we recall that Sergius called himself a 'grammaticus'—if indeed the grammaticus and the archiatros are one and the same—it becomes altogether impossible to reckon that a grammarian who is actually quoted and used by Choeroboscos was unable to find any

---

[1] Wright, *Cat.* III,1156; II,802,809.

work of Greek grammar save that of Dionysius Thrax! Therefore, just as in the matter of the anonymous translations and philosophical treatises preserved in Add. 14658, we must conclude, if we were left in any doubt, that the translation of Dionysius cannot be attributed to Sergius.

I had already come to this very conclusion (and indeed written all the above) when Prof. Richard Gottheil presented me with a copy of the Berlin codex Sachau 226 (dated 1881), which contains our translation of Dionysius and which is there said to be by Joseph Huzaya.[xii] I have included the most important readings of this codex in the following chapter and all variants are noted in the edition of the Syriac text (Appendix 3). However, it did not make sense to me that Joseph could have written it, even though there is nothing in the text as such to prevent the attribution, for if he was the author why is his name absent from the London codices of the seventh and ninth centuries?[xiii] In another Berlin codex from the year 1825, the name Jacob of Tagrit was altered to Jacob of Edessa—it was common for a famous name to be added to an anonymous treatise by a later scribe. The Berlin codex offers a polished text, in which the hand of a later redactor can be readily recognised. The 'B' redaction must have been already known to him.

The time has now come to give the text itself, which we have transcribed directly from A, adding variants from B, a version that has been corrected and refined by later concerns. However, this makes no difference to the question whether it was the translator himself or some other corrector who did this.

It is better that we should only provide here a translation and not also a commentary. In the translation, words which were transliterated straight from the Greek are given in Greek while those that were altered and adapted to Syriac idiom are rendered into English.[xiv] By using this approach the reader can see at a glance how the translator has gone about his task of producing the first ever Syriac grammar on the basis of a Greek model. In fact, he went about his work in just the same way as did the Armenian translator of Dionysius when he wrote the first ever Armenian grammar.[xv]

---

[i] The question of the place of Aristotle in Syriac curricula has been much advanced in recent years. To name just a few, see John W. Watt, "From Sergius to Matta. Commentary and Translation in Syriac Aristotelian and Monastic Tradition," in *Interpreting the Bible and Aristotle in Late Antiquity* (ed. John W. Watt and J. Lössl, Ashgate, 2011), 239-58; id., "Grammar, Rhetoric, and the Enkyklios Paideia in Syriac," *ZDMG* 143 (1993), 45-71; H. Hugonnard-Roche, "Le corpus philosophique syriaque au VIe-VIIe siècles.," in *The Libraries of the Neoplatonists* (ed. Christina D'Ancona Costa, Leiden: Brill, 2007), 279-91.

[ii] 'Orthoepy', a term we shall meet a few times, means correctness of diction (as opposed to orthography, the correctness of writing). It was much discussed by Protagoras and was a standard feature of the Greek linguistic tradition thereafter.

[iii] 1) ἀνάγνωσις ἐντριβὴς κατὰ προσῳδίαν; 2) ἐξήγησις κατὰ τοὺς ἐνυπάρχοντας ποιητικοὺς τρόπους; 3) γλωσσῶν τε καὶ ἱστοριῶν πρόχειρος ἀπόδοσις; 4) ἐτυμολογίας εὕρεσις; 5) ἀναλογίας ἐκλογισμός; 6) κρίσις ποιημάτων.

[iv] While Merx's analysis of what went wrong with this text may be true, the generalisation about early translators is not accurate. For a more considered typology, Sebastian P. Brock, "Towards a History of Syriac Translation Technique" In René Lavenant, ed., *III Symposium Syriacum* (Rome, 1983), 1-14, and id., "Changing Fashions in Syriac Translation Technique: The Background to Syriac translations under the Abbasids" *Journal of the Canadian Society for Syriac Studies* 4 (2004), 3-14.

[v] Discussion of these terms in Daniel King, *The Earliest Translation of Aristotle's Categories in Syriac*. Aristoteles Semitico-Latinus 21 (Leiden: Brill, 2010), 170-71.

[vi] The history of Graeco-Syriac translations is now much better known. Even earlier than Diodore or Theodore was the Syriac version of Titus of Bostra and various works of Eusebius of Caesarea, which are extant in a ms of 412 (BL Add. 12150)

[vii] On Sergius: H. Hugonnard-Roche, "Note sur Sergius de Reshʿaina , traducteur du grec en syriaque et commentateur d'Aristote," in *The Ancient Tradition in Christian and Islamic Hellenism* (ed G. Endress & R. Kruk. Leiden: Brill, 1997), 121-43 [repr. ch.VI in Hugonnard-Roche, *La Logique d'Aristote* (Paris, 2004)]; Emiliano Fiori, "Un intellectuel alexandrin en Mésopotamie. Essai d'une interprétation d'ensemble de l'œuvre de Sergius de Rēšʿaynā," in *De l'Antiquité tardive au Moyen Âge. Études de logique aristotélicienne et de philosophie grecque, syriaque, arabe et latine offertes à Henri Hugonnard-Roche* (ed. Elisa Coda & Cecilia Martini Bonadeo. Paris: Vrin, 2014), 59-90; John W. Watt, "Sergius von Reschaina," in *Grundriss der Geschichte der Philosophie, begründet von Friedrich Ueberweg. Die Philosophie der Antike. Band 5: Philosophie der Kaiserzeit und der Spätantike.* Teilband 3 (ed. C. Horn et al. Basel: Schwabe, 2018).

[viii] This Theodore was not the well-known Theodore of Merv, rather a certain Theodore of Karḫ Ǧuddān east of the Tigris—see H. Hugonnard-Roche, *La Logique d'Aristote* (Paris, 2004), 126n2.

[ix] Now partially edited E. Fiori, *Dionigi Areopagita Nomi Divini, Teologia Mistica, Epistole*. CSCO 656/657. Leuven, 2014. Sergius's theological introduction to Dionysius was edited in three parts with French translation by P. Sherwood, "Mimro de Serge de Resayna sur la vie spirituelle," *L'Orient Syrien* 5 (1960), 433-457; 6 (1961), 95-115, 122-156; to be used together with the more accurate Italian translation by E. Fiori, *Sergio di Reshʿayna. Trattato sulla Vita Spirituale*. Testi dei Padri della Chiesa 93 (Monastero di Bose, 2008). See also I. Perczel, "The Earliest Syriac Reception of Dionysius" in S. Coakley and C. Stang, eds., *Rethinking Dionysius the Areopagite* (Oxford, 2009), 27-41, including much earlier work by this scholar; and E. Fiori, "Sergius of Reshaina and Dionysius: A Dialectical Fidelity," in John W. Watt and J. Lössl (eds.), *Interpreting the Bible and Aristotle* (Ashgate, 2011), 179-94.

[x] The Syriac version of Severus's letters to Sergius 'the doctor' is edited in E.W. Brooks, ed., *A Collection of Letters of Severus of Antioch : from numerous Syriac Manuscripts*, Patrologia Orientalis 12,14 (Paris, 1915-20), nos.31,85,86. The Syriac version of the correspondence between Severus and Sergius Grammaticus (the London ms of which is mentioned here by Merx) was edited by J. Lebon, ed., *Severi Antiocheni Orationes ad Nephalium. Euisdem ac Sergii Grammatici Epistulae Mutuae*, CSCO 119/120 (Leuven, 1949), with translations and studies in I.R. Torrance, *Christology after Chalcedon : Severus of Antioch and Sergius the Monophysite* (Norwich, 1988). The identity of the Sergii was also debated, on the basis of these suggestions of Merx's, by A. Baumstark, "Lucubrationes Syro-Graecae" *Jahrbücher für classische Philologie* 21 (1894), 352-524, see p.369ff. Baumstark finds the identification likely (Severus and Sergius would have been contemporaries at Alexandria), although he is less sure about the Sergius mentioned by Choeroboscus. Indeed the close knowledge of Aristotle evidenced by Sergius Grammaticus also speaks in favour of the identification (both Sergii knew Aristotle through the texts themselves rather than through the superficial summaries known and used by most). The doctrinal issue is hardly a serious barrier, for Sergius Grammaticus is not a hardliner himself, rather he simply points out the logical conclusions to which the Severan line ought to lead when seen within the context of Aristotelian physical theory.

[xi] Merx's doubts about Sergius's authorship of these texts is confirmed in the abovementioned chapter by Hugonnard-Roche (n.iv above). On the contents of this see also, D. King, "Origenism in Sixth century Syria. The Case of a Syriac Manuscript of Pagan Philosophy," in A. Fürst, ed., *Origenes und seine Bedeutung für die Theologie- und Geistesgeschichte Europas und des Vorderen Orients*. Adamantiana. Texte und Studien zu Origenes und seinem Erbe, I (Münster, 2011), 180-212

[xii] This Berlin ms Sachau 226 (now Berlin Syr.89) offers a much fuller version, probably revised according to the Greek at a later time. As he notes, Merx uses this ms in his edition printed in the Appendix (where it is designated C), and sometimes in the notes to the translation (ch.2 below), though he had evidently written both this chapter and the next before he had seen the Berlin ms, and he did not himself fully revise his work in accordance with his new find.

[xiii] The fact that Joseph's name appears in the headings to further mss of Dionysius that were unknown to Merx, namely those in Mosul and Baghdad (see Notes to the Appended Texts), does not add to the support for the attribution since these copies are most likely closely related to the Sachau ms, which may itself have been copied from the Mosul ms, with which it shares a number of texts in the field of Aristotelian logic.

[xiv] The current translation takes a different approach. See the first endnote to the next chapter.

[xv] Before writing the present work, Merx had already made a close study of the Armenian translation of Dionysius Thrax, published as a separate essay in Uhlig's edition (Uhlig, ed., *Dionysii Thracis Ars Grammatica*, Grammatici Graeci I [Leipzig 1883], lvii-lxxiii).

Chapter 2

TRANSLATION OF AN ANCIENT SYRIAC GRAMMAR BASED ON THE *TECHNĒ GRAMMATIKĒ* OF DIONYSIUS THRAX[i]

|[9] Again a grammatical treatise concerning the parts of speech[1]

Therefore the Greeks scholars say that a word[2] is the smallest part of the composition[3] of speech. Speech is a series[4] of a combination of words conveying a complete meaning. There are eight parts of speech;[5] these are noun, verb,[6] participle, article, pronoun, preposition,[7] adverb, conjunction.

But the Greeks say that an appellative[8] is like a species of noun. A noun, so they say, is a part of speech signifying either a body or a concept, a body [is, e.g.] man, horse, stone; a concept [is, e.g.] education, wisdom, prudence;

[1] Again a philosophical oration B; Again a treatise of the reverend and wholly excellent Rabban Mar Joseph Huzaya concerning the matter of grammar C.

[2] AC have ܡܬܐܡܪܢܘܬܐ for λέξις (*word*), which is the usual equivalent in this text. B's ܕܡܠܬܐ ܕܡܬܐܡܪܢܘܬܐ seems to have come about as a result of two translations being combined.

[3] ܕܪܘܟܒܐ AC, which is improved in B as ܕܪܘܟܒܗ.

[4] ܪܗܛܐ (ABC) seems to mean here a *series*, but although this seems to correspond to the Greek πεζῆς (*in prose*), I am doubtful as to whether there was an earlier translation in which ܪܗܛܐ was used to render πεζός since the present sense is perfectly acceptable, even though it does disagree with the Greek without good cause.

[5] A also adds the Greek words for these, both in Syriac letters and in Greek letters, marked by numbers corresponding to the Syriac words.

[6] ܡܐܡܪܐ = ῥῆμα, for which the later writers generally used ܡܠܬܐ, the Syriac term used here for λόγος. Because the first generations of translators had no received set of terminology to hand, there is some variety of usage, of which Hoffmann gives some examples (*Herm.*, 18). The point after ܡܐܡܪܐ is correct, for ܕܡܫܘܬܦܘܬܐ = μετοχὴ, and does not depend upon ܡܐܡܪܐ.

[7] In A ܡܩܕܡܘܬ ܣܝܡܐ = πρόθεσις. B separates these two words with a point, which cannot be right. C has ܡܩܕܡܘܬ ܣܝ̈ܡܬܐ.

[8] AB omit a term corresponding to προσηγορία. C adds ܢܦܠ = ὑποβέβληται (*it turns out*).

it can be said both commonly[1] and specifically, commonly [is, e.g.] |[10] man, horse, ox; specifically [is, e.g.] Plato, Aristotle, Socrates.[2]

These five [attributes] belong to the noun: gender, species, shapes, numbers, cases.

There are three genders, then, in the Greek language: masculine, feminine and the other besides these, which is neither masculine nor feminine, as being particular to the Greek language. In Syriac, however, there are two genders, masculine and feminine. Some people add to these two more; one they call the 'common' noun, the other the 'extra-common' noun.[ii] So the 'common' noun is e.g. camel, eagle—we speak of them as masculine in the case of both males and females; 'extra-common', however, is [e.g.] what swallows and sparrows are, and other things of this sort, for we speak of them as feminine in the case of both males and females.[3]

There are two species, in both Greek and Syriac, the 'prototype' and the 'derived-from-the-prototype'.[iii] Prototype is the [noun] spoken according to its primary form, as e.g. heaven, land, fire, air;[4] and that which is derived and spoken on the basis of the prototype is,[5] e.g., the heavenly, earthly, firey.

And there are seven species that acquire their existence from the prototype,[iv] and they are named: patronymic, possessive,[6] comparative, positional, diminutive,[1] denominal,[2] deverbal.

---

[1] B adds ܕܝܢ which makes the sentence smoother. There is no δὲ in the Greek, hence A lacks ܕܝܢ. B can thus be shown to have been worked over by a second hand, as is also clear from the names that follow at the end of this paragraph. C is corrupt here.

[2] Instead of these names, B has *Paul, Peter, John;* C *Peter, Paul, John.*

[3] B has: *'extra-common', however, is that which a swallow is, and other things like these, but we speak of them as feminine in the case of both males and females.* However in reality ܢܫܪܐ (*eagle*) is masculine, ܓܡܠܐ (*camel*) common, and ܣܢܘܢܝܬܐ (*swallow*) and ܦܪܕܐ (*sparrow*) feminine; in Greek the two examples of 'common' nouns are ἵππος and κύων (*horse* and *dog*), for which the Syriac has substituted *camel* and *eagle*, while the 'extra-common' ones are χελιδὼν and ἀετός (*swallow* and *eagle*).

[4] Only A has 'air', with no corresponding item in the second list, so there must be a corruption in one or other of the lists.

[5] The words used in the Greek to define the 'derivative' species, namely 'they take their origin from another word', are missing in the Syriac, for the words ܗܘ ܕܡܢ ܛܘܦܣܐ ܩܕܡܝܐ ܕܡܬܐܡܪ correspond simply to the word παράγωγον (*derivative*) itself. From this concept come the later theories of ܐܦ̈ܩܐ, ܒܒܢ̈ܝܬܐ and ܡܬܚ̈ܡܝܬܐ.

[6] A has 'numerative' for 'possessive'.

|[11] Patronymics [lit: from the name of the fathers], then, is that which is properly[3] formed[4] [v] from fathers, e.g. Levi, Judah; but equally also from fathers of fathers,[5] e.g. Israelites, Ammonites, Edomites.

In Greek this [type of] noun has three [sub]types, but in Syriac there is one, e.g. ܗܘܕܝܐ, ܥܡܠܩܝܐ, ܡܨܪܝܐ (Israelite, Amalekite, Egyptian). Thus also the feminine noun [of this type] in Greek has three [sub]types, but in Syriac one only, e.g. ܐܝܣܪܝܠܝܬܐ, ܗܘܕܝܬܐ, ܥܒܪܝܬܐ (Israelite, Jewish, Hebrew), but this type of noun is not formed from women's names.

Possessive[6] is named after that which comes under possession and brings together both the object possessed and its possessor, e.g. Joseph's coat, Aaron's staff, Goliath's sword.[7]

Comparative is when one thing is compared with another of the same kind, e.g. 'behold, a greater than Solomon is here' [Mt 12.42], or else one thing [is compared with] many things of a different kind, e.g. 'Solomon was much wiser than all the Sons of the East' [1 Kings 5.10/4.30]. Of the comparatives there are, in both Greek and Syriac, three [sub]types,[8] i.e., more than someone, better than someone, more than everyone.

Positional[vi] is when one thing is set down and compared with many things.[9] There are two [sub]types in both Greek and Syriac, one of these is,

---

[1] A has ܡܥܒܪܢܘܬܐ, which is altered in BC to ܡܥܒܪܢܝܘܬܐ.

[2] ܡܢ ܠܒܪ ܡܢ ܥܡܐ, where ܡܢ ܠܒܪ = παρά. Those who think it a simple business to use the Syriac as a way of reconstructing the Greek text should look to this example, for who would have understood these words without knowing the Greek behind them!

[3] ܡܪܝܐܝܬ translates literally κύριως.

[4] Reading ܡܬܩܛܡ for ܡܬܐܩܛܡ.

[5] A's expression 'fathers of fathers' renders the Greek πρόγονοι (forefathers). B has 'as if from fathers of fathers' and then inverts the order of the list, 'Israelites, Edomites, Ammonites'.

[6] B ܡܢ ܩܢܝܐ ܕܩܢܝܢܐ; A ܡܢ ܗܢܐ ܕܩܢܝܢܐ, which is more correct but hard to translate. The Greek is ἀπὸ τοῦ τῆς κτήσεως. A has ܡܢ ܗܢܐ ܕܩܢܝܢܐ ܡܬܩܪܐ ܠܬܚܬ ܗܘ ܕ (*from this possessive, it is called 'below', that which...*). I do not know whether ܠܬܚܬ has come about from a scribe's imagination or is some idle interpretation.

[7] A inexplicably has a negative particle before this sentence: 'possessive...does not bring together'.

[8] The three Greek examples are different forms, in τερος, ιων, and ων. The Syriac translates the examples.

[9] B: 'one is placed over many, [and] is compared with many'.

e.g., vanity of vanities; song of songs; the other is, e.g., largest of the large; most praised of the praised.[1]

|[12] Diminutive[2] is when it indicates a lessening of the prototype without comparison with something else, e.g., a little boy, a little man.

Denominal is,[3] e.g., Judas Maccabaeus and Antiochus Epiphanes.

Deverbal is that which takes its noun from a verb,[4] e.g., discerning, enlightened, beloved.

There are three shapes of nouns, simple, compound and derived-from-a-compound. Simple is, e.g., father (*ab*); compound is, e.g., Ab-ram; derived-from-a-compound is, e.g., Ab-ra-ham.[5] Of the compounds, there are three varieties: those which are [formed from] two complete [parts] that become one;[6] those that are from two incomplete parts, e.g., Moses;[7] those that are from an incomplete part followed by a complete part, e.g.,[8] king of kings; and those that are from a complete part followed by an incomplete part, e.g., Bar-dadeh (*cousin*, Lev 25.49, Jdg 10.1).[9]

---

[1] The Syriac version makes no sense, since it gives two subtypes, but there is really just one. For the two different Greek forms in τατος and τος it substitutes two Syriac forms, that using the Genitive relation and that using ܕ.

[2] A has ܡܒܨܪܘܬܐ (*diminution*), BC ܕܡܦܢܩܘܬܐ (*blandishment*). Hence also for μείωσις (*lessening*) A has ܒܨܝܪܘܬܐ, but B ܡܦܢܩܘܬܐ (C now agreeing with A).

[3] The words 'that which is formed from a noun' have been omitted in the Syriac, either by homoeoteleuton or else by a translator abridging the sentence.

[4] B here translates ῥηματικόν as ܡܠܐ instead of ܡܠܬܐ, against his normal usage which is ܡܠܬܐ = λόγος. AC's ܡܢ ܡܐܡܪܐ is correct. But for ἀπὸ ῥήματος A is inconsistent, since it has ܡܢ ܡܡܠܠܐ, C ܡܢ ܡܐܡܪܐ. In the Greek text the two examples are Νοήμων and Φιλήμων, which the Syriac has imitated.

[5] He uses a Biblical example to try to explain this distinction which is otherwise useless in Semitic languages. The examples used in the Greek are Μέμνων, Ἀγαμέμνων, Ἀγαμεμνονίδης. AB have the erroneous ܐܒܐ for ܐܒ, A has ܐܒܪܗܡ for the second example, where BC correctly have ܐܒܪܡ.

[6] There is no example given for this first type after the words ܐܝܟ ܗܢ ܕܗܘܐ ܚܕ, which B has altered to ܐܝܟ ܕܗܘܘ ܚܕ.

[7] The example of Moses is taken from an assumed etymology from משה and מים.

[8] A omits all the words from 'Moses' to this point. If ܡܠܟ is considered to be an 'imperfect part', then one can understand why the ܐ of the emphatic state is called ܚܠܦ ܕܫܘܡܠܝܐ (Jacob Bar Šakko , p.ܣܗ).

[9] AC Bar-hadad (1 Kings 15.18). The confusion in the Syriac text of this paragraph probably arose through the early drafts of the work. Initially, three types are mentioned

|[13] In the Greek language there are three numbers, singular, dual, and plural,[1] but in the Syriac language there are two, singular and plural, as in 'man' and 'men'. But there are other nouns that are singular but signify a plural, e.g., a people, an assembly, a company. Again, there are other nouns which are called plural but which signify either a singular or a dual, e.g., ܫܡܝ̈ܐ (*heavens*), ܡܝ̈ܐ (*waters*), ܪ̈ܟܫܐ (*horses*).[2] Again, there are other nouns which are called singular and signify something dual, e.g., ܐܘܟܠܐ, ܦܕܢܐ (*yoke*).[3]

In the Greek language, there are five cases of nouns, which are nominative, genitive, dative, accusative, vocative.[4] [vii]

Nominative is what is named, as when someone says 'man'.[5] Genitive is [something that is] owned or to do with one's father, that is, 'of a man',[6] 'of a horse'. The dative is what is given, that is, 'to a man'.[7] The accusative is the causative, that is 'by means of a man' (sic).[8] The vocative is the called, e.g., 'O man'. But in Syriac this species is confused and indistinct.

With respect to the noun,[9] these [following types] are made, which are also called[1] species: 1 proper, 2 appellative, 3 attached, 4 relative,[viii] 5 quasi-

---

but then four are given (two complete parts; two incomplete parts; an incomplete part followed by a complete part; and a complete part followed by a incomplete part). He then goes on to use two examples (the 'king of kings' and 'Bar-dadeh'), both of which are formed of an incomplete and a complete part. Although A lacks the words 'Moses...' (as in previous note) and does therefore give three types, the reading is still wrong, for 'Moses' actually consists of two incomplete parts.

[1] A omits the comment about the Greek language having three numbers.

[2] B has ܪ̈ܚܫܐ (*reptiles*). In A ܪ̈ܟܫܐ has the points which in later grammars would be removed.

[3] This paragraph has a corresponding Greek section which reads, Εἰσὶ δέ τινες ἑνικοὶ χαρακτῆρες καὶ κατὰ πολλῶν λεγόμενοι, οἷον δῆμος χορός ὄχλος· καὶ πληθυντικοὶ κατὰ ἑνικῶν τε καὶ δυϊκῶν, ἑνικῶν μὲν ὡς Ἀθῆναι Θῆβαι, δυϊκῶν δὲ ὡς ἀμφότεροι (*there are some singular forms which are applied to a plurality, such as people, chorus, crowd; and some plural forms which are applied to singulars or duals, e.g., for singulars, Athens, Thebes; for duals, 'both'*).

[4] These are expressed in Syriac by adverbs as if ὀρθῶς, γενικῶς etc. Similarly in what follows.

[5] The corresponding Greek is λέγεται δὲ ἡ μὲν ὀρθὴ ὀνομαστικὴ, omitting καὶ εὐθεῖα.

[6] There is an erasure in A after 'of a man'.

[7] The Syriac uses the same root for the name 'dative' (δοτική = ܡܫܠܡܢܝܬܐ) and the explanation (ἐπισταλτική = ܡܫܠܡܢܐ).

[8] The translator is here following a scholiast, see Uhlig, 32.

[9] The plural is found in B, together with syāmē, due to scribal error.

quasi-relative, 6 homonymous,[ix] 7 synonymous,[x] 8 name-bearing, 9 doubly-named,[2] 10 eponymous, 11 ethnic, 12 interrogative, |[14] 13 indefinite, 14 ... which is similative and correlative and demonstrative,[3] 15 collective, 16 distributive, 17 inclusive, 18 onomatopoeic,[xi] 19 generic, 20 specific, 21 ordinal, 22 numeral, 23 absolute.[4] [xii]

1. Proper is that which signifies its own substance, e.g., Joseph, Benjamin, Jacob.
2. Appellative is that which signifies a shared substance, e.g. man, horse, ox.[xiii]
3. Attached is that which is placed next to a proper or appellative [noun] and signifies praise or blame. It is understood in three ways, either from the soul, or from the body, or from external things. From the soul, therefore, is, e.g., prudent or licentious; from the body is, e.g., heavy or light; from externals is, e.g., rich or poor.
4. That which is relative is, e.g., as a father to a son,[5] a friend to a friend, right to left.
5. That which is quasi-relative[6] is, e.g., night and day.
6. A homonym is one that is placed next to many things equally, e.g., Joseph son of Jacob, Joseph son of Eli, Joseph of Ramta. Homonym is also, e.g., sea-dog (the seal), land-dog (domestic dog), Dog-Star (Sirius).[7] [xiv]

---

[1] ܡܬܩܪܐ = προσηγορεύεται, just as below προσηγορικὸν = ܡܬܩܪܝܢܐ. C has ܡܬܩܪܐ for ܐܬܩܪܝ in both places.

[2] B's ܠܬܪܝܢ ܫܡܐ makes no sense. A has ܠܬܪܝ with an erasure mark, C ܠܬܪܝ ܫܡܗܐ, I suggest ܠܬܪ̈ܝܢ ܫܡܗܐ.

[3] The Greek reads ἀναφορικόν, ὃ καὶ..., hence it is just the first word that is missing in the Syriac text, since ܗܘ ܕܐܦ ܡܕܡܝܢܐ corresponds to ὃ καὶ ὁμοιωματικόν.

[4] This list shows us just how difficult it can sometimes be to see the Greek words underlying Syriac terms—how would we understand these terms without a knowledge of the Greek original!

[5] B has 'a son to a father', AC (as text) 'a father to a son'. It seems that each ms has preserved a different portion of the original Greek, πατήρ, υἱός, φίλος, δεξιός.

[6] B omits the 'quasi'!

[7] This mimics the Greek example, which is μῦς θαλάσσιος and μῦς γηγενής (*sea mouse*, i.e. the Grey Triggerfish, and *land mouse*). See Wright, *Cat.* III,1019a, and *Thes.*, 1742.

7. [Synonyms][xv] are those which signify the same appellation[1] [xvi] by means of different nouns, e.g., a knife, a blade, a dagger.[xvii]
8. Name-bearing[2] are those names that are given from the things which are accidental to them, e.g., Benjamin and Jokebar.[3]
9. |[15] Doubly-named[4] is when two names are given, properly [referring] to one [individual], e.g., Azariah and Uzziah. This [type of] noun does not reciprocate upon itself, not everyone that is called Uzziah is also Azariah.[5]
10. Eponymous is...that which is together with another proper noun, e.g. they also call Egyptian the single name of the dragon Pharaoh.[6]
11. Ethnic is that which signifies a people, e.g. Canaanites, Perizzites, Jebusites.
12. Interrogative is that which is said as a question, e.g. 'who is' 'what kind', 'where', 'how much', 'how great'?[7]
13. Indefinite is that which is called opposite to the interrogative, e.g. whoever, whatever kind, however much, in whatever way.
14. Similative[8] is that which is also called correlative and signifies some kind of similarity, e.g., 'this' 'that' and 'like all of this'.[xviii]
15. Collective is, e.g., people, assembly, company.[9]

---

[1] C has ܣܘܥܪܢܐ (*thing*).

[2] ܩܢܝܢ ܫܡ̈ܗܐ.

[3] A also adds Zeraḥ.

[4] B has ܬܚܝܢ ܫܡ̈ܗܐ, as in the foregoing list; A ܬܝܢ with an erasure mark. As before, I suggest ܬܪܝܢ ܫܡ̈ܗܐ.

[5] For the Greek example of Alexander, also called Paris, the translator substitutes the example of the Judaean king Uzziah who is also called Azariah.

[6] The words ὃ καὶ διώνυμον καλεῖται (*which is also called name-bearing*) are missing from the Syriac. The allusion is to the dragon of Ezekiel 29.3, 32.2, which is called 'Pharaoh' and which is used to refer to Egypt at Isa 51.9.

[7] The item 'where' is added by A through dittography from the foregoing ܐܝܢܐ, and does not belong.

[8] A rightly ܡܦܚܡܢܝܐ, whence B's ܡܪܝܐ (usually for κύριον). Note that ܡܕܡܝܢܐܝܬ is used below (no.18) for μιμητικῶς, although ܡܕܡܝܢܐ is ὁμοιωματικόν.

[9] There is quite a difference from the Greek here, which has περιληπτικὸν δέ ἐστι τὸ τῷ ἑνικῷ ἀριθμῷ πλῆθος σημαῖνον, οἷον δῆμος....(*collective is that which signifies a plural although it is singular, such as people...*).

16. Distributive is that which has a reference[1] to one thing from two or more things, e.g. 'one of the two' or 'each one of them all'.[2]
17. |[16] Inclusive is that which signifies that one thing is contained in it, e.g., maidenhood and widowhood.[3]
18. Onomatopoeic is that which is named by imitation from the characteristics of the words, e.g., a 'roaring' of the sea and a 'rumbling' of the ground.
19. Generic is that which is divided into many species, e.g., animal, plant.
20. Specific is that which is subdivided from the generic, e.g. ox and horse and lion and vine and olive.
21. Ordered[4] is that which signifies an order, e.g., first, second, third.
22. Numeral is that which signifies a number, e.g., one, two, three.
23. Absolute[5] is, e.g., God, reason.

There are two states of rational things,[6] active and passive. Active is, e.g., 'judge' and 'judging'; passive is, e.g. 'the judged one' and 'being judged'.

These are the things that are said about the noun, which is the first part of speech.[7] So let us speak next about the verb, which is the second part of speech.

---

[1] AC's ܡܣܩܢܐ is correct, being derived from the causative of ܣܠܩ and an etymological equivalent for ἀναφορά. The redactor of B did not understand the term and wrote ܡܬܦܣܩܢܐ (*cut off*), since he wrongly believed that ܦܣܩ was similar to ܦܠܓ in the sense of 'to divide'.

[2] ܡܢ ܬܪܝܗܘܢ ܚܕ is for ἑκάτερος (*each, of two*), ܡܢ ܟܠ ܚܕ ܡܢܗܘܢ for ἕκαστος (*each—of many*).

[3] We have translated ܒܬܘܠܘܬܐ ܘܐܪܡܠܘܬܐ as *maidenhood and widowhood*, although the first of these is a translation of παρθενών (*a place where maidens live*) and the latter refers to a place for widows, which is called a χηρεία in *Didascalia Apostolorum syriace* (ed., P. de Lagarde [Göttingen, 1911]) 62,2. C has elaborated the whole paragraph.

[4] B has ܡܣܬܟܠܢܐ wrongly. A's ܕܛܟܣܐ is also right, the erasure mark over ܟܠ not referring to this. C has ܗܘ ܕܟܠ ܛܟܣܐ.

[5] ܫܪܝܐ (*solution*), corresponding to the Greek ἀπολελυμένον (*absolute*). The words ὃ καθ' ἑαυτὸ νοεῖται (*one which is conceived on its own*) are omitted.

[6] For the Greek τοῦ δὲ ὀνόματος (*of the noun*), BC have ܕܡܠܬܐ, which also means τοῦ λόγου (*of the word*). Hence A reads ܕܡܠܝܠܐ (*of rational things*).

[7] Add 14658 (B) ends the text here with the words, ܫܠܡ ܡܐܡܪܐ ܦܝܠܘܣܘܦܝܐ (*the end of the philosophical discourse*).

On the Verb

The verb is an utterance that is without case, possessing tense[1] and persons and numbers, and displaying active and passive. Eight [parts] are attributed to the verb: readings,[2] states, species, shapes, numbers,|[17] persons, tenses, conjugations. For in the Greek language there are eight, but in Syriac there are seven.[xix]

There are five 'readings', defining,[xx] imperative, optative, subjunctive,[3] infinitive.[4]

There are three states, active, passive, and middle. Active is, e.g., I strike, I make, I write; passive is, e.g., I am struck, I am made, I am written; middle is that which sometimes arises from the active, sometimes from the passive,[xxi] e.g., I have proceeded, I have walked, I have sat, I have run, I have crossed.[5]

There are two species, prototype and derived-from-the-prototype. The prototype is, e.g., I am perfecting; derived is, e.g., I am being made perfect.[6]

There are three shapes, simple, compound, derived-from-a-compound; simple is, e.g., I am feeding; compound is, e.g., I am thinking; derived-from-a-compound is, e.g., I am thinking hard.[xxii]

There are three numbers in the Greek language, that is singular, dual, and plural,[7] but in Syriac two, singular and plural. Singular is, e.g., I strike, I make, I write; plural is, e.g., we strike, we make, we write.

---

[1] Reading ܙܒ̈ܢܐ for ܙܒܢܐ.

[2] The expression 'readings' (ܩܪ̈ܝܬܐ) is used because the different verbal forms arise from different pronunciations signified by the points. This explains why later grammarians deal with inflection and pointing together (e.g. Joseph Bar Malkon, see ch.8 below). See also the comments on p.250.

[3] Lit. 'receiving' (ܡܩܒܠܢܐ). The reading of C (ܡܩܒܠܢܝܐ) is an alternative translation of ὑποτακτική.

[4] ܡܠܐܡܪܢܘܬܐ ܡܢ ܡܠܬܐ = lit. λέξις ῥήματος, which is probably to be read here too (cf. p.28 below). The Greek for infinitive is ἀπαρέμφατος.

[5] The mss have ܥܒܕܬ and ܟܬܒܬ where ܥܒܕܬ and ܟܬܒܬ are clearly meant and I have made the emendation, although the Greek reads ἐποιησάμην, ἐγραψάμην (*I made for myself, I wrote for myself*)!

[6] See concerning Aḥūd'emmēh's theory (see p.33) which harmonises equally with both the species and the shapes.

[7] The Syriac uses adverbs for these terms, as if ἑνικῶς, δυϊκῶς, πληθυντικῶς.

There are three persons, the first, the second, and the third. The first is the one *from* whom the statement is, the second is the one *to* whom the statement is, the third is the one *concerning* whom the statement is.

There are three tenses, present, past, future. The past tense, then, has four varieties and they are called opposite, close, complete, and indefinite.[xxiii]

There are three [relationships],[1] namely |[18] the present with the imperfect, the perfect with the pluperfect,[2] the aorist[3] with the future.

And these are the things said about the third part of speech.[4]

On the Participle

The participle is an utterance that arises from the characteristics of verbs and nouns. The things that are attributed to verbs and nouns are attributed to it also, save for persons and readings.[5]

On the Article

The article is the fourth part of speech, that which is placed in front of the readings of the nouns, and is placed at the beginning in the Greek language, and at the end in the Syriac language,[6] ...[lacuna]..., e.g. the creator, the creating, the being created by the creator.[7] There are two numbers, singular and plural; singular is, e.g., man; plural, men. The case, or completion,[8] is very common in the Syriac language, but it is otherwise in Greek. This is also all that can be said about the article. Let us speak also of the pronoun, which is the fifth part of speech.

---

[1] Mss have ܠܐ ܡܬܚܡܢܐ (*aorist*) which does not belong here—see apparatus. The Greek is συγγένειαι.

[2] Syr ܗܘ ܕܝܘܡ ܕܘܗ ܥܒܪ (*that which has now passed*). The term is not the same as used previously, there being as yet no consistency of terminology.

[3] ܠܐ ܡܬܚܡܢܐ should be restored.

[4] This is really the inscription for the next section. The Syrian translator has to omit the whole section on conjugations.

[5] Again we have ܡܬܢܝܬܐ for ἔγκλισις, as shortly also for κλίσις.

[6] Our grammarian was the first to try to identify the alaph of the emphatic state with the Greek article.

[7] The final word here has been erased.

[8] ܫܘܠܡܐ denotes both the alaph of the emphatic state and the suffix (see Jacob Bar Šakko, App.I, ܦܗ). I do not think that it is original here.

ON THE PRONOUN

The pronoun is a word, [or] an utterance[1] used in place of a noun, and is a signifier of definite persons. Its attributes are these:[2] persons, genders, |[19] numbers, cases, shapes,[3] species.

The persons of the prototype [pronouns] are these, I, you, he; those of the derived [pronouns][4] are mine, yours, his. The gender of the prototype [pronouns] are none of them distinguished by the [form of the] word, but they are distinguished by what is written [i.e. the context], e.g., I, you.[5] But in the Syriac language there are those distinguished by both the [form of the] word and by what is written, e.g. to me, to you (f.), over me, over you (f.), that (m.), that (f.), to her, to him, and things that are like these. Those that are derived from the prototypes are, e.g., mine, yours, hers.

The numbers of the prototypes are singular: I, you, he; and plural: we, you, they. Those which are derived from the prototypes are singular: mine, yours, his;[6] and plural: ours, yours, theirs.

The cases, or completion,[7] of the prototypes are nominative:[8] I, you, he; genitive: mine,[9] yours, his; dative: to me, to you, to him; accusative: by me, by you, by him.[10] Those that are from the derivatives are mine, yours, his, to me, to you, to him, by me, by you, by him.

The simple shapes are mine, yours, his; the compounds are of me myself, of you yourself, of him himself.

---

[1] The Syriac seems to have a doublet, with both ܡܠܐ and ܡܬܐܡܪܢܘܬܐ for λέξις. Perhaps for ܡܠܐ we should read ܒܪ ܡܠܐ.

[2] Greek reads 'six things'.

[3] A has ܣܝ̈ܡܬܐ (*positions*), which is clearly a corruption of ܐܣܟܝ̈ܡܐ, as in C.

[4] ܕܡܢ ܦܘܫܩܐ ܩܕܡܝܐ ܡܬܦܫܩܝܢ.

[5] What is said about the Syriac pronouns ܐܢܐ and ܚܢܢ is correct, but still needs emending in line with the Greek, since he adds to the text the word ܟܬܒܘܗܝ, and what he says about *what is written* refers to ܐܢܬ and ܐܢܬܝ. Hence instead of ܐܟܘܬ ܗܘ ܕܐܢܐ ܘܐܢܬ we should read ܐܟܘܬ ܗܘ ܕܐܢܬ ܘܐܢܬܝ, (*e.g. you [m.], you [f.]*).

[6] Read ܕܗܘ.

[7] See p.12 and 18 above.

[8] Again the Syriac uses adverbs for these terms.

[9] A has ܕܝܠܢ (*ours*) but C's ܕܝܠܝ (for ἐμοῦ) must be right.

[10] See p.13 above for this definition of the accusative, which is not really distinguished from the dative and genitive.

There are species, some of them are prototype, e.g., I, you, he; others are, so to speak, from the derivatives, |[20] as are all the possessives, and all those that are called 'bipersonal'.[1]...[The next part is corrupt].[2]

Of the pronouns some are with the article and some are without the article. Those with the article are, e.g., that which is mine, that which is yours;[3] those without the article are, e.g., I, you, he. These are the things that are said about the pronoun. Let us speak also about the preposition, which is the sixth part of speech.

On the Preposition

The preposition is an utterance that is placed at the beginning of all the parts of the statement, both in their compounds and in their constructions.[xxiv] In the Greek language there are eighteen altogether, six simple ones and twelve compounds, but it is not possible in Syriac to preserve this order, and on account of this they are confused. For this reason I have placed them, as far as possible, such that their general sense might be understood by discerning readers.

Therefore, the simple ones are these:[xxv] from, within, with, before, towards, e.g., from the house, within the house, with the house, before the house, towards the house. These do not reciprocate back to themselves.[xxvi] And these are the compounds: over-above, down-below, in it, with it, outside of, instead of, upon,[4] upon it, between, under, more, from it. This is as much as can be said about these. Let us speak also about the adverb,[5] which is the seventh part of speech.

---

[1] 'Possessives' = ܡܩܢ̈ܝܢܝܬܐ (κτητικαί); the correct reading for what follows is ܐܦ ܕܬܪܝܢ ܦܪ̈ܨܘܦܐ ܡܬܩܪܝܢ (διπρόσωπα).

[2] The words that appear here in the mss deal with nouns and do not belong here. They are as follows: *There are, however, others, which signify a single word, e.g. 'old', and the compounds are 'oldest of the old'.* There then follows a comment about possessives, as follows: *Some of these are, e.g., of me, of you, of him; and plural, as from many, e.g. we, ours.* The last part of this (from *and plural*) is extant also in the Greek (ἡμεῖς, ἡμέτερος).

[3] For ܗܿܘ ܕܝܠܟ, read ܗܘ ܕܗܿܘ ܕܝܠܟ.

[4] This item is out of place.

[5] Read ܥܠ ܥܠ ܡܐܡܪܐ.

On the Adverb[1]

The philosophers say that the adverb is an uninflected[2] part of speech that is said together with a verb or is next to a verb. Of the adverbs, then, there are some that are simple, some that are compound, and some that are in between these.

|[21] Simple is, e.g., old; compound is, e.g., oldest of old.[3]

1. Some of them are signifiers of time, e.g., now, then, afterwards. To these we should add [subspecies][4] that designate [specific] times, e.g., today, tomorrow, the day-after-tomorrow, yesterday, the day-before-yesterday.[5]
2. Some are of the middle kind, e.g., nobly, clearly, wisely.
3. Some are [adverbs] of quality,[6] e.g., he hit,[7] he kicked, in clusters, in groups, culpably.[8]
4. Some are of quantity, e.g. much, a little.
5. Some are signifiers of the numeral nouns, e.g., one, two, three.
6. Some are signifiers of places, e.g., in a place, to a place;[9] some are locational, e.g., up above, down below, of which there are three senses, i.e., to the place, in the place, from the place, e.g., to a house, in a house, from a house.
7. Some are signifiers of desire, e.g., pity me, answer me, help me.[10]

---

[1] Reading ܥܠ ܥܠ ܡܐܡܪܐ again instead of just ܥܠ ܡܐܡܪܐ.

[2] ܠܐ ܡܬܦܢܝܢܐ for ἄκλιτος, hence ܡܬܦܢܝܢܐ for κλιτός.

[3] The examples are omitted in A, but C makes up the gap.

[4] Mss. om. εἴδη.

[5] The last three replace the Greek examples: up to that time, up to this time, at what time.

[6] A ܕܥܒܘܕܘܬܐ ; C ܕܐܝܟܝܘܬܐ. See the scholion to this paragraph in Uhlig, 75, in which the term ποιότης is explained incorrectly on the basis of the meaning of ποιεῖν. This explains ܕܥܒܘܕܘܬܐ. Simplicius, commenting on *Categories* 8b26, also says εἰσὶ μὲν αἱ ποιότητες δυνάμεις, καὶ διὰ τοῦτο ποιητικαί etc. (*the qualities are faculties and because of this they are also causes*).

[7] See Cureton, *Ancient Syriac Documents*, 2.

[8] C ܡܥܪܩܠ (*complicated*).

[9] This superfluous statement shows that the translator never went back to finish off his work.

[10] The examples are either biblical or liturgical.

8. Some declare amazement, e.g., oo!, ah![1]
9. Some are of wonderment, e.g. How amazing![xxvii]
10. Some are signifiers of negation or prohibition, e.g., no, not, not then, certainly not, not at all.
11. Some are signifiers of profession [or] agreement,[2] e.g., if, yes, even if, but if.[3]
12. Some declare the opposite of persuasion, e.g., altogether, end.[4]
13. |[22] Some are as a similarity and likeness, e.g., as, for as, but as.[5]
14. Some are [of] supposition, e.g., maybe, perhaps, how often.[xxviii]
15. Some are signifiers of a sort of collection, e.g., completely, altogether, partly altogether (!).[6]
16. Some are signifiers of types,[7] e.g., beyond, afar off, from here and beyond.[8]
17. Some are commanding, e.g., let go, bring, carry, go, come, do.
18. Some are comparative, e.g., more, less.
19. Some are interrogative, e.g., whence, when, how, where, what sort.
20. Some declare the force [of something], e.g. really good, very good.
21. Some signify [something] to do with oaths, e.g., such and such a yes.[9]

---

[1] The first example, παπαί is missing.

[2] The doublet shows the scribe's negligence.

[3] The last two compound forms hardly belong here. Perhaps there is here some hebraic oath formula?

[4] The three times repeated negative particle is clearly missing here. Read ܠܐ, ܠܐܡܟܝܠ, ܠܐ ܗܘ for μή, μηδῆτα, μηδαμῶς.

[5] The first two are for ὡς, ὥσπερ. The other examples, ἠΰτε, καθάπερ, are omitted.

[6] For the last, C has ܡܫܠܡܐܝܬ ܐܚܝܕ (*fully altogether*).

[7] This should probably read 'places', i.e. τοπικοί for τύποι, an easy error in Syriac script. C has ܛܘܡܣܐ, another error from ܛܘܦܣܐ.

[8] In the Scholia Erotemata to Dionysius Thrax, πόρρω and ἐπέκεινα (which lie behind the last two examples here) are added to the examples ἄνω and κάτω of adverbs of place (item no.6 above). These examples have been transposed here and thereby created this strange group (not present in the original). The Syriac term ܡܢܗ ܘܠܗܠ is taken from Isa 18.2.

[9] I.e. this indicates the affirmation of an oath. The Greek has the adverbs of denial before the adverbs of assertion.

22. [Some are denials of oaths, e.g., such and such a no].[xxix]
23. Some are assurances, e.g., it is clear, it is well known.
24. Some are of goings, e.g., let him go, let them go.[1]
25. Some contain a signifying of praise, e.g., excellently, greatly, wonderfully.

Concerning this seventh part of speech we have spoken briefly. Let us speak also about the conjunction, which is the eighth part of speech, and then let us have done with 'speech' lest we exceed the length of a letter and make the reader sick.

|[23] On the Conjunction

The conjunction is an utterance that binds together the thought with the construction and gathers together the diffuseness and scattering of an indicative statement. Some conjunctions are conjunctive, some are disjunctive, some are affixing, some are more-than-affixing, some are aetiological, some are syllogistic,[2] some are reckoning, some are fulfilling.[3]

1. Conjunctive, then, gather together and join together statements that are dispersed without any limit, e.g., ܡܢ, ܕܝܢ, ܐܦ, ܐܠܐ, ܐܘ ܡܢ, ܐܘ ܕܝܢ, ܐܘ ܐܕܝܢ.[4]
2. Disjunctives are those that bind discourse together and also displace[5] one thing from another thing, e.g. ܐܘ, ܐܘܟܝ, ܐܘܟܝܬ,[6] ܐܘܐܢ.
3. Affixing[7] [conjunctions] are all those which do not signify any existence, but show a certain consequence,[1] e.g., ܐܢ, ܐܢܗܘ, ܐܕܝܢ, ܐܕܝܢ ܗܘ.[2]

[1] C has been revised to the Greek since its addition of ܢܙܕܘܓܘܢ corresponds to γαμητέον, which Dionysius counts among the θετικά. However, ܕܐܘܣܢܐ (C's name for this variety) is simply a false correction of A's ܕܐܘܪܚܬܐ (see Uhlig, 85).

[2] ܡܣܬܐܕܢܐ, an otherwise unknown equivalent for συλλογιστικός. C's reading (ܡܬܡܕܢܐ) would correspond to ἀπορηματικοῖς.

[3] The list in A is much truncated (see apparatus to text).

[4] The Greek correspondents are μὲν δὲ καὶ ἀλλὰ ἠμὲν ἠδὲ, there being no equivalent for the last unless it be one of the other missing examples, τέ, ἀτάρ, αὐτάρ, ἤτοι.

[5] ܡܫܢܐ which in the NT is used for μεθίστημι.

[6] ܐܘܟܝܬ = ἤτοι, for which see Payne-Smith. For this, and the other particles, it would be instructive to compare the Harclean version of the NT.

[7] A ܡܣܬܡܟܢܐ; C ܡܫܡܠܝܢܐ (also for the next item). A's reading is derived from ܡܣܬܡܟܢܐ, but ܠܝܬ ܡܣܬܡܟܢܐ is in the first hand. C's reading indicates that it should be considered as its own recension

4. More-than-affixing are all those which signify existence[xxx] and also an order, e.g., ܡܛܠ, ܡܛܠ ܕܗܘ,[3] ܡܛܠ ܕܝܢ, ܡܛܠ ܕܗܘ ܕܝܢ.
5. Aetiological are those that make a declaration concerning an apodosis on account of hatred,[4] and because of this they are taken causatively, e.g., ܐܝܟ, ܐܝܟܢܐ.[5]
6. |[24] [Doubting conjunctions] are those which we usually use to link them, when we are unsure of an answer.[xxxi]
7. Syllogistic[6] are all those that are used in connection with conclusions[xxxii] and collections of demonstrations, e.g., ܐܪܐ, ܐܠܐ.[7] [xxxiii]
8. Fulfilling are all that are used on account of metre or embellishment, e.g., ܐܡ,[8] ܐܪܐ ܗܟܝܠ,[9] ܐܘ ܕܝܢ, ܐܘ ܠܐ ܡܢ, ܐܘ ܡܢ, ܐܘ ܗܟܢ.

Again, some people add to these others that are adversative, ܒܪܡ, ܒܪܡ ܕܝܢ. This is also what we have said about the conjunctions.[1]

---

in which the names of the classes of conjunctions have been altered. So those groups mentioned in the introductory paragraph above which are from C were probably not extant in A.

[1] ܢܩܝܦܘܬܐ actually denotes adherence.

[2] εἰ, εἴπερ, εἰδή. The final example εἰδήπερ is found in C only.

[3] To be read thus, emended on the basis of the last example.

[4] This obvious corruption is a mistranslation (C's ܡܬܚܫܒܠ is an emendation). αἰτία can have the sense of *blame* or *accusation* (hence αἰτιατική became the English *accusative*). This squares well with an alternative meaning of ἀπόδοσις as *retribution.*

[5] A omits ܡܛܠ. ܡܛܠܬܗ. ܡܛܠ ܗܕܐ. ܡܛܠ ܕܝܢ. ܡܛܠ ܗܘ. ܡܛܠ ܗܘ ܕܝܢ. ܡܛܠ ܗܝܕܐ. ܡܛܠ ܗܕܐ ܕܝܢ. (added in C, for ὅπως ἕνεκα οὕκενα διό διότι καθό καθότι καθόσον). The two examples that the translator has retained, ܐܝܟ and ܐܝܟܢܐ, are comparable to καθό, καθότι, or καθόσον.

[6] A ܡܟܐܡܬܢܝܐ, C ܣܘܡܟܢܝܐ.

[7] The Greek equivalents are: ἄρα, ἀλλά, ἀλλαμήν, τοίνυν, τοιγάρτοι, and nothing for the last.

[8] The Greek is δή. The Syriac should read ܐܡ, ܐܘ ܗܘ. However, Jacob of Edessa (Wright, *Cat.* II,544b) translates δή with ܗܐ. For ܐܡ, cf. Jacob Bar Šakko, Syriac text, p.31, where I have emended ܐܢ. But that ܐܡ does correspond to δή is indicated by the expression ܐܢ ܐܡ ܗܘܝܢ ܠܗܘܢ ܚܬܢܐ = εἰ δὴ ἔσονται (BO III,I,135a).

[9] Read thus for ܐܠܐ ܗܟܘܢ, see *Thesaurus*, s.v. The Greek is νύ. The rest of the terms have no obvious one-to-one correspondence with the Greek terms, which are ποῦ, τοί, θήν, ἄρ, δῆτα, πέρ, πώ, μήν, ἄν, αὖ, νῦν, οὖν, κέν, γέ.

***

To this point the Syriac translator has followed Dionysius's text closely. The condition of the rest, however, is very poor and littered with lacunae, such that it is hardly worth translating every word of it. We shall therefore proceed rather more freely, placing in quotation marks what is worth citing in full and correcting the Syriac when necessary. Quite a few things fall somewhere in between the two extremes.

The following is the subscription, written by the translator of the text who was himself a grammarian. We have retroverted it into Greek, since the scribe was learned in that language. In C the text was corrupted by over-emendation.

"I have not found anything else in the [Greek] language,[2] and whatever I have found I have, so I believe, briefly [or, accurately] set forth,|[25] for the instruction and education of future readers. I have produced this discourse in a single work so as to increase understanding and I also give occasion to those whose judgments are harsh, so that from now on they may have as much opportunity as they can, that they might thoughtfully make corrections [to some things] without ill will through what they appropriately write, that they might confirm [other things] by their agreements, and so render to the one who gathered all this material the reward of their prayers,[3] that the Lord may [thereby] escort me to the throne of grace, forgive me what is lacking, that he may count us worthy of his mercies to worship at your holy feet, and that he may take delight in the company of that holy assembly."[xxxiv]

***

What follows next is just a few fragmentary pieces of a paradigm of the verb τύπτω (*I strike*), which is preserved in a much fuller form in a Greek ms, Monacensis Graecus 310, and in the Armenian version of Dionysius

[1] On the basis of the state of the text of this list of conjunctions, we conclude that the text as a whole was written up by an author who never gave it a final revision. In C, however, everything is smoother and more uniform, having been revised.

[2] For 'in the Greek language', C has *in the Syriac language*, clearly wrong.

[3] C is wanting the rest of the passage.

Thrax.[1] Some of the words have altered position and quite a few are lacking in the Syriac, either because a scribe was only able to work from the drafts he had to hand and these were not readily legible, or else because the translator who tried to turn this paradigm into Syriac himself never went back to revise his work. However, given the agreement of the Armenian and Syriac versions we can be quite sure at least that in the fifth century an appendix was added to the *Technē Grammatikē* in which these verbal paradigms were drawn up for students (and unless I am mistaken also paradigms of nouns, as there are some traces of these in the Armenian). These Greek paradigms were copied into Latin, Armenian, and Syriac; among later grammarians those who worked in modern western languages always had a good knowledge of Latin, but in the East the Syrian Christians first of all took their inflectional scheme from the Greeks and then adapted it to the characteristics of their own language. In doing this they set a trend for the rest of the East. Indeed, nobody would deny the Greek grammarians the honourable title of the 'international masters' (οἰκουμενίκοι διδάσκαλοι). The influence of their system and method stretched from the Tigris and Euphrates (I had better not say anything about India!) to the far West where we see them spread over the very farthest lands, beyond the shores of Cadiz and Farthest Thule [i.e. Greenland], to countries the very names of which were unknown even to the Greek themselves.

But now to the paradigm itself. We have set out below the various fragmentary parts of it according to the layout of the Greek text:[xxxv]

|26

Ρῆμα	ὁριστικὸν	ἐνεργητικὸν,	ἁπλοῦν	συζυγίας	πρώτης
ܡܐܡܪܐ	ܡܚܫܚܐ	ܡܥܒܕܢܐ [ܕܡܥܒܕܢܘܬܐ][2]	...	...	...

τῶν	βαρυτόνων	ῥημάτων,	ἐγκλίσεως	ὁριστικῆς
...	...	...	...	...

χρόνου	ἐνεστῶτος	[is]	(see below)
ܕܙܒܢܐ	[ܕܩܐܡ][3]	ܐܝܬܘܗܝ	ܕܡܚܝܢܐ[1]

[1] See Uhlig, 125, xvi.

[2] This word has been missplaced from further down. For examples of this sort of confusion, see p.4-5 above.

[3] Moved from below.

τῶν τριῶν προσώπων τε καὶ ἀριθμῶν
ܕܬܠܬܐ ... ܕܩܐܡ[2] ܕܡܢܝܢܐ[3]

ἑνικὰ τύπτω τύπτεις τύπτει
ܚܕܝܐܝܬ ܡܚܐ ܐܢܐ ܡܚܐ ܐܢܬ ܡܚܐ

πληθυντικὰ τύπτομεν τύπτετε τύπτουσι
ܣܓܝܐܝܬ ܡܚܝܢ ܡܚܝܬܘܢ ܡܚܝܢ

ἐνεργητικὸν [χρόνου παρεληλυθότος][4]
ܕܡܥܒܕܢܘܬܐ[5] ܕܙܒܢܐ ܕܥܒܪ

ἑνικὰ ἔτυπτον ἔτυπτες ἔτυπτε
ܚܕܝܐܝܬ ܡܚܐ ܗܘܝܬ ܡܚܐ ܗܘܝܬ ܡܚܐ ܗܘܐ

πληθυντικὰ ἐτύπτομεν ἐτύπτετε ἔτυπτον
ܣܓܝܐܝܬ ܡܚܝܢ ܗܘܝܢ[6] ܡܚܝܢ ܗܘܝܬܘܢ ܡܚܝܢ ܗܘܘ

[ἐνηργητικὸν] μέλλοντος ἑνικὰ τύψω τύψεις
ܕܡܥܒܕܢܘܬܐ ܕܙܒܢܐ ܕܥܬܝܕ ܚܕܝܐܝܬ ܐܡܚܐ ܬܡܚܐ

τύψει πληθυντικὰ τίψομεν τίψετε
ܢܡܚܐ ܣܓܝܐܝܬ ܢܡܚܐ[7] ܬܡܚܘܢ

τίψουσι.
ܢܡܚܘܢ.

...[Verb] ὁριστικὰ παθητικὰ [of persons]
ܡܠܬܐ ... ܡܫܘܕܥܢܐ ܕܚܫܐ ܕܦܪܨܘܦܐ

---

[1] Moved from below.

[2] Reinserted from above (see note).

[3] Reinserted from above (see note).

[4] Properly παρατατικοῦ—see p.17 under χρόνοι.

[5] Reinserted from above (see note).

[6] Ms ܡܚܐ ܝܢ.

[7] Restored. The word fell out due to similarity with the preceding item.

...	ἐνεστῶτος [παρακειμένου]	[Lacuna]	
ܬܠܬܐ	ܙܒܢܐ ܕܩܝܡ[1]		...

|[27]

τέτυμμαι	τέτυψαι	τέτυπται	[Lacuna]
ܐܬܡܚܝܬ	ܐܬܡܚܝܬ	ܐܬܡܚܝ	

ἐτετύμμεθα	ἐτέτυφθε	τετυμμένοι ἦσαν
ܐܬܡܚܝܢ ܗܘܝܢ	...	ܐܬܡܚܝܘ ܗܘܘ

καὶ	ἰακῶς	ἐτετύψατο.	μέλλοντος
...	...	ܐܬܡܚܝܘ ܗܘܝܬܘܢ[2]	ܙܒܢܐ ܕܥܬܝܕ
ἑνικὰ	τυφθήσομαι	τυφθήσῃ	τυφθήσεται
ܚܕܢܝܬ	ܐܬܡܚܐ	ܬܬܡܚܐ	ܢܬܡܚܐ
πληθυντικὰ	τυφθησόμεθα	τυφθήσεσθε	τυφθήσονται
ܣܓܝܐܝܬ	...	ܬܬܡܚܘܢ	ܢܬܡܚܘܢ[3]

There then follow the forms in which the Infinitive is included with the finite verb. The Syriac name for the Infinitive, ܡܐܡܪܐ ܠܐ ܡܣܬܝܟܢܐ, seems to me to be a calque on ῥῆμα ἀπαρέμφατον (*undefined verb*), comparable to ܙܒܢܐ ܠܐ ܡܣܬܝܟܢܐ, the aorist tense. It continues:[xxxvi]

---

[1] Thus the ms. where ܕܩܕܡ is expected, as C has. But it is possible also that this term refers to the perfect (which is the tense that follows in the examples) although after three forms of the perfect are given they are immediately followed by three persons of the pluperfect.

[2] The second person form is here completely out of place. If I reckon that it may have been invented for the Ionic form in Greek, it is the Armenian that suggests such a judgment. See my dissertation on the Armenian version in Uhlig's edition. It is clear in C, which has the list correctly.

[3] The order is confused due to the similarity of the forms ܢܬܡܚܐ (which has fallen out) and ܢܬܡܚܘܢ.

[ῥῆμα ἀόριστον] χρόνου ἀορίστου
ܡܐܡܪܐ ܠܐ ܡܬܚܡܢܐ ܕܙܒܢܐ ܠܐ ܡܬܚܡܢܐ

ἐνεργητικοῦ ἑνικὰ ἔτυψα
ܡܘܪܟܒܐ ܕܡܥܒܕܢܘܬܐ[1] ܚܕܢܝܬ ܡܡܚܐ ܡܚܐ ܐܢܐ

ἔτυψας ἔτυψε πληθυντικὰ ἐτύψαμεν
ܡܡܚܐ ܡܚܐ ܐܢܬ ܡܡܚܐ ܡܚܐ ܣܓܝܐܐܝܬ ܡܡܚܐ ܡܚܝܢ

ἐτύψατε ἔτυψαν. ῥῆμα ἀόριστον
ܡܡܚܐ ܡܚܝܢ ܐܢܬܘܢ ܡܡܚܐ ܡܚܝܢ[2] ܡܐܡܪܐ ܠܐ ܡܬܚܡܢܐ

παθητικὸν ἑνικὰ ἐτύφθην ἐτύφθης
ܡܘܪܟܒܐ ܕܚܫܐ ܚܕܢܝܬ ܡܡܚܐ ܡܚܐ ܐܢܐ ܡܡܚܐ ܡܚܐ ܐܢܬ

|28

ἐτύφθη πληθυντικὰ ἐτύφθημεν ἐτύφθητε ἐτύφθησαν
ܡܡܚܐ ܡܚܐ ܣܓܝܐܐܝܬ ܡܡܚܐ ܡܚܝܢ ܡܡܚܐ ܡܚܝܢ ܐܢܬܘܢ ܡܡܚܐ ܡܚܝܢ

What comes next has to do with infinitives with the name λέξις ἐκ ῥήματος (*word from a verb*),[3] but is not taken from Dionysius. Retroverted into Greek it reads as follows: "A word that is [taken] from a verb shows neither tenses not persons nor numbers, nor active nor passive, but is written correctly thus ܠܡܡܚܐ ܠܡܥܒܕ ܠܡܟܬܒ ܠܡܐܡܪ, and anything else like this I have been able to bring forth...." [There is a little more preserved in C].[xxxvii]

The subscription of A is: "Here ends the letter of the grammarians." In C a brief prefatory notice is placed before the paradigms and afterwards there is a subscription in which Joseph Huzaya is named as the author of the work.

---

[1] Because of this term, the following active ἔτυψα should be read. But if a lacuna is rather admitted here then the verb should be the passive ἐτύφθην, which the forms as given in the ms favour. But since the same forms are repeated in the passive sense it would seem that the points in the Syriac text have been wrongly applied.

[2] Thus corrected from the ms.

[3] For the expression, see the note on p.17 above.

---

[i] This chapter is an English translation of the Syriac text printed at the back of the volume (Text III). Merx's Latin translation is liberally interspersed with the original Greek terms wherever he felt that the Syriac follows the Greek sufficiently closely to justify it. The advantage of this approach (as he explains at the end of the previous chapter) is that the reader may readily see where the Syriac translator is following his source and where he is departing from it. Since the aim of the present reprint is to make a book on Syriac grammar available to a wider public, it would make no sense to follow this procedure here. Therefore, both Greek and Latin have been rendered into English (using the standardised terms for the jargon of Greek grammar as used in the translation by Alan Kemp, "The *Tekhne Grammatike* of Dionysius Thrax translated into English" in D.J. Taylor, ed., *The History of Linguistics in the Classical Period* [Amsterdam, 1987], 343-363). Those who wish to know in greater detail how the Syriac relates to its original ought to inspect Merx's original chapter. Merx's readings from the Syriac were also included in Uhlig's 1883 edition of the *Tekhne Grammatike*, p. lxx-c.

[ii] 'Extra common' = epicene (ἐπίκοινος). This rather untranslatable term refers to nouns which can only be grammatically masculine or feminine, regardless of the gender of the particular animal being referred to; whereas the nouns of 'common' gender are those which can be grammatically masculine or feminine as appropriate. As can be seen, the Syriac translator has wholly misunderstood this distinction.

[iii] On Al-Fārābī's borrowing, apparently via calqueing the Syriac, of this classification, F.W. Zimmermann, *Al-Farabi's Commentary and Short Treatise on Aristotle's* De Interpretatione (Oxford, 1981), xxxi.

[iv] I.e. there are seven subspecies of the species called 'derived-from-the-prototype'.

[v] Merx reads ܡܬܚܫܡ (footnote), but this must be a misprint (Nöldeke, Review, 1220). The text has been corrected.

[vi] The Syriac has translated the second element of the Greek ὑπερθετικόν, usually 'superlative'.

[vii] I have used the regular English terms, though that nomenclature comes through Latin and the etymologies are different from the five Syriac terms, ܐܘܪܝܬܐ. ܟܘܫܠܬܐ. ܡܬܩܘܒܠܬܐ. ܡܬܡܢܝܬܐ. ܟܠܟܠܬܬܐ.

[viii] ܠܘܬ ܡܕܡ became the standard philosophical term for this Aristotelian expression (πρός τι).

[ix] The term ܫܘܝܐ ܫܡܐ is close to the renderings of ὁμώνυμα in the Syriac versions of Aristotle's *Categories*, where it is ܫܘܝ ܫܡܐ (King, *Syriac Categories*, 96,6). The precise term ܫܘܝܐ ܫܡܐ, however, is used by the Syriac commentator Proba (Hoffmann, *Herm.*, 75,31 etc.). Sergius of Rešʿaina, however, calls them ܕܡܢܝܢ ܫܡܗܘܬܐ (see next note).

[x] ܕܩܢܝܢ ܫܡܗܘܬܐ. At this early stage in technical grammtico-logical translations, there was not yet a firm lexicon. Sergius of Rešʿaina, in his commentary on Aristotle's logic, and the

---

early anonymous translator of Porphyry's *Eisagoge* both use ܕܫܡ̈ܗܐ ܡܫܘܬܦܬܐ instead to render ὁμώνυμα (see previous note), whereas ܕܫܡ̈ܗܐ ܚܕ means συνώνυμα, and ܕܫܡ̈ܗܐ ܐܪ̈ܒܐ is πολυώνυμα. In the translations of the *Categories* a variety of different terms are used for συνώνυμα, none of which involve ܕܫܡܗܐ. In using ܕܫܡ̈ܗܐ ܡܫܘܬܦܬܐ for synonyms, this translator is therefore confusing the meanings of these terms.

[xi] Again, the same term is found in the Syriac versions of the *Categories*, 7a6, b12.

[xii] Merx gives the Greek terms for this list of 23 types, which are as follows: κύριον, προσηγορικόν, ἐπίθετον, πρός τι ἔχον, ὡς πρός τι ἔχον, ὁμώνυμον, συνώνυμον, διώνυμον, ἐπώνυμον, ἐθνικόν, ἐρωτηματικόν, ἀόριστον, ἀναφορικόν ὃ καὶ ὁμοιωματικὸν καὶ δεικτικὸν καὶ ἀνταποδοτικὸν

καλεῖται, περιληπτικόν, ἐπιμεριζόμενον, περιεκτικόν, πεποιημένον, γενικόν, ἰδικόν, τακτικόν, ἀριθμητικόν, ἀπολελυμένον. The English equivalents used here are those of Kemp's translation (see note i above) save for those which do not have an obvious sense.

[xiii] The Greek has man and horse only. The addition of the ox again indicates the translator's familiarity with Aristotle's *Categories*, in which horse and ox are both used as examples of general substances. We can therefore see again here the interaction between grammar and logic, which is anyway lurking behind these 'species' in Dionysius.

[xiv] The same example of the homonym, namely the three types of dog (plus the further instance of the dog-philosopher, the Cynic), is also used by Sergius of Reshʿaina (BL Add. 14658, f.10ra) on the basis of Ammonius (*In Isagogen*, ed. Busse, CAG IV,3), 48,18–49,6. The translator's term ܫܘܬܦܘܬ ܫܡܐ, however, comes from the Syriac commentator Probus (Hoffmann, *Herm.*, 75,31 etc.), and is comparable to the earlier translator of the *Categories* (King, *Syriac Categories*, 96,6). However, as noted above, Sergius calls them ܕܫܡ̈ܗܐ ܡܫܘܬܦܬܐ. In using ܕܫܡ̈ܗܐ ܡܫܘܬܦܬܐ for synonyms, this translator is therefore confusing the meanings of these terms.

[xv] See previous note.

[xvi] ܟܘܢܝܐ = προσηγορία here, though the sense is not far from that of an Aristotelian κατηγορία. Sergius coined the use of ܟܘܢܝܐ for the latter and was followed in this by the earliest translator of the *Categories*. The translator of Dionysius may well have this tradition in mind (see previous note).

[xvii] This is really comparable to Sergius's ܕܫܡܗܐ ܐܪ̈ܒܐ, for which his example, very similar to the present one, involves 'stone, rock, flint' (Add. 14658, f.10rb).

[xviii] The Greek and Syriac actually have the masculine and the feminine forms of 'this'.

[xix] The one that does not apply in Syriac is 'conjugations'. These constitute a whole extra section in Dionysius Thrax, coming at the end of the chapter on the verb, which the translator has omitted.

[xx] ܡܚܘܝܢܝܬܐ = ὁριστική. The functional equivalent in English is 'indicative' but this Latinate form is a calque on a different Greek term, ἀποφαντική.

xxi On this aspect of the translation, see M. Farina, "Diathesis and Middle Voice in the Syriac Ancient Grammatical Tradition: The Translations and Adaptations of the *Techne Grammatike* and the Arabic Model" *Aramaic Studies* 6 (2008), 175-93.

xxii In the last example, the translator uses an infinitive to give emphasis of meaning.

xxiii These correspond respectively to παρατατικόν (*imperfect*), παρακείμενον (*perfect*), ὑπερσυντέλικον (*pluperfect*), ἀόριστον (*aorist*).

xxiv I.e., both in compounded verbs and in larger grammatical constructions.

xxv The list of the simple prepositions was omitted in A, the ms upon which Merx based his translation, yet his text clearly shows that C gives the list, including the comment about reciprocation (anastrophe); hence his translation here has been expanded to include this.

xxvi The Greek term is 'anastrophe' and refers here to the ability for some prepositions (generally those of two or more syllables) to follow their governing nouns as well as precede them. This is meaningless in Syriac.

xxvii ܒܒܝ is also a Greek term, βαβαῖ. It is item no.13 in the Greek list, but has here been moved earlier.

xxviii The next item, adverbs of order, is missing. Merx's comment under this item (which reads: *an example is given which corresponds to this [missing] group, namely* ܠܒܪ *(χωρίς); the second example,* ܛܟܐ *(τάχα) belongs to the preceding group, and the third example* ܟܡܐ ܙܒܢܝܢ *(ποσάκις) I would reckon is taken from a biblical citation. These words are missing in C*) is negated by his comment in the apparatus to the text, which recognizes that A's ܠܒܪ is simply a corruption of ܟܒܪ. Hence these comments all belong to the group of adverbs of supposition, the adverbs of order being omitted in the Syriac text.

xxix This item is in C only and is not included in Merx's reconstruction of the original from A.

xxx Or 'becoming', following the reading of A, which is also that preferred by Nöldeke, Review, 1216.

xxxi Again only C provides the full set of examples (ܒܗܘܢ, ܐܝܟ ܗ̇ܢ, ܕܐܪܐ, ܟܠܡܐ, ܕܟܠܡܐ, ܟܠܡܐܢ, ܕܟܠܡܐܢ, ܐܪܐܢ, ܡܕܡ.) that is missing in A (the Greek has only three here, ἆρα, κᾶτα, μῶν). This item is called ܡܡܠܠܢܐ (*to do with speech*) in C and is unnamed in A. Although here it clearly equates to the Greek item ἀπορηματικοί (*matters of doubt*), it was used in C's earlier list to designate the syllogistic group (A's ܡܬܐܡܪܢܐ).

xxxii A sympathetic translation of ܣܠܩܐ, which is a loan translation from ἐπιφορά, lit. *an attack*, but also meaning *conclusion to a syllogism*.

xxxiii C adds the rest again, such that ἄρα=ܐܪܐ; ܐܠܐ = ἀλλά; ܐܠܐ ܡܢ = ἀλλαμήν; ܗܫܐ ܗܟܝܠ = τοίνυν; ܗܫܐ ܡܢ ܗܟܝܠ = τοιγάρτοι; nothing for τοιγαροῦν.

xxxiv This subscription is that of A (Syriac text, p.ܦܛ). C's version can be found also in the Syriac text beneath that of A. Merx's Greek retroversion of A's subscription is as

---

follows: περὶ ἑτέρου τινὸς οὐχ εὗρον (οὐδὲν) ἐν τῇ [τῶν Ἑλλήνων] γλώσσῃ, ὅσα δὲ εὗρον, ὡς οἴομαι, συντόμως (C ἀκριβῶς) τέθεικα εἰς διατριβήν τε καὶ παιδείαν τῶν ἀναγιγνώσκειν μελλόντων. εἰς δὲ πλείονα γνῶσιν ἐποίησα (ܦܠܚܬ) τὸν λόγον μιᾷ λέξει καὶ δίδωμι αἰτίαν τοῖς τὴν γνώμην δεινοῖς, ὅταν φέρωνται ἐντεῦθεν αἰτίαν κατὰ τὴν δύναμιν αὐτῶν,...καλῶς διορθώσασι ἀφθόνως δι' ὧν εὐπρεπῶς συνέγραψαν...διὰ τῆς ὁμολογίας αὐτῶν καταβεβαιῶσι καὶ τῷ συναγαγόντι αὐτὰ ἀποδῶσι τὸν μισθὸν τῶν προσευχῶν αὐτῶν, ἵνα ὁ κύριος διὰ τῶν αὐτῶν προσευχῶν ἀνάγῃ με πρὸς τὸν θρόνον τῆς χάριτος, καὶ ἀφῇ μου τὰ ὑστερήματα, καὶ ἀξιώσῃ ἡμᾶς τοῦ ἐλέους αὐτοῦ τοῦ προσκυνεῖν τοῖς ποσὶν ὑμῶν τοῖς ἁγίοις...καὶ εὐφρανθῇ τῇ ὁμιλίᾳ ἐκείνης τῆς θείας συναγωγῆς. The scribe of C then added a further subscription of his own (p.ܟܒ -ܦܛ), which Merx does not discuss.

[xxxv] The headings in the Greek text in the table below is to be translated: *The indicative active verb. Simple [forms] of the first conjugation of barytone [i.e. non-oxytone] verbs, of the indicative mood, present tense, is of three persons and numbers: singular is τύπτω...plural is...; imperfect active, singular...plural...; future active, singular...plural...; passive indicative, of three persons, of present tense..., and an ionic form...; the future, singular...plural....*

[xxxvi] The Greek parts of this section of the paradigms read as follows: *the aorist verb; of the aorist active, singular is...plural is...; of the aorist passive verb, singular is...plural is....*

[xxxvii] λέξις δὲ ἡ ἐκ τοῦ ῥήματος οὐ δηλοῖ οὔτε χρόνους οὔτε πρόσωπα οὔτε ἀριθμούς, οὔτε ἐνέργειαν οὔτε πάθος, ἀλλ' ἀληθῶς λέγεται οὕτως τύπτειν, ποιεῖν, γράψειν, ἰέναι· καὶ τὰ τούτοις ὅμοια δυναίμην ἂν προφέρειν.

Chapter 3

ORTHOEPY, OR ACCURATE RECITATION

The translator of Dionysius's compendium omitted the first part of it, that dealing with letters and syllables, since he was unable easily to draw any close comparison between his own language and the Greek in this particular area. However, Joseph Huzaya, the priest who followed Narsai as head of the school of Nisibis sometime after the latter's death post-500,[i] did tackle this subject separately (and of course he may have been the translator too). This makes sense, for the business of correct reading (ἀνάγνωσις, the first of Dionysius's parts of grammar, see p.4) as well as the 'ready explanation of glosses' (the third part of the same) both depend upon this subject.

Barhebraeus credits Joseph with making an alteration in the system of reading,[1] which we shall now consider. Assemani has already pointed out that this was not a matter of changing the pronunciation of vowels—a matter in which the work of a single man could hardly have been brought to bear upon a whole populace—but rather that it means placing points around the letters in order to make distinctions between different parts of speech (we generally call such points 'accents', following the usage of the Hebrew grammarians). The London Masoretic codex (Add. 12138)[ii] makes this clear at the end, where among the 'traditions of the teachers of the school' (ܡܫ̈ܠܡܢܘܬܐ ܕܪ̈ܒܢܐ ܕܐܣܟܘܠܐ) the following is found:[2]

> ܘܠܗܘܢ ܕܝܢ ܕܣܡ̈ܟܐ ܘܥܨ̈ܝܢܐ ܘܙܘ̈ܓܐ ܘܦܩܘ̈ܕܐ. ܘܡܢܝ̈ܚܢܐ ܘܡܫܐ̈ܠܢܐ ܗܘ ܕܡܬܪܟܒ ܡܢ ܬܪܝܢ ܙܘ̈ܓܝܢ
> ܘܬܚ̈ܬܝܐ ܘܥ̈ܠܝܐ ܕܐܝܬ ܒܪܘܙܐ ܚܕܐ. ܘܟܠܗܘܢ ܟܠܗܘܢ ܠܡܘܣܦ ܗܘܝܐ ܣܡܝܟܝܢ ܠܗܠܝܢ ܕܡܢ ܗܘܘ.
> ܘܗܘܝܐ ܥܕܡܐ ܐܢܘܢ ܠܫܡ̈ܥܝܐ. ܟܠ ܓܒܪܐ ܕܡܠܦ ܐܘ ܦܫܝܛܐ ܒܝܘܠܦܢܗ. ܥܡܗܠܐ ܕܡܦܫܩ ܡܢܝ
> ܠܐܘܪܘܪܘܣ ܢܘܗܕܪܐ ܦܩܥ ܠܡ̈ܠܬܐ ܘܡܠܐ ܡܢ ܢܘܚܐ ܠܫܘܪܢܐ ܡܕܝ ܐܝܟܢܐ ܐܦܣܩܘܦܐ
> ܕܐܘܪܗܝ. ܥܡ ܐܝܟܐ ܐܚܪ̈ܢܐ ܡܕܪ̈ܫܐ ܒܡ̈ܠܬܐ ܠܟܠܝܗ.
>
> And be sure of this, that the (points) that are in the scriptures are: sāmkē and ʿeṣyānē, zaugē and pāqodē, menīḥānē and mešayyelānē (which is made up from two zaugē), ʿellāyē and

[1] *Chron.Eccl.*III, p.78. BO II,407. G. Hoffmann, *Auszüge aus syrischen Acten persischer Märtyrer* (Leipzig, 1880), 117.

[2] Wright, *Cat.* I,107b.

> taḥtāyē. All of these were laid down by Joseph Huzaya—for there are nine. Thus he made the points according to the judgment of a word-for-word translator (or *expositor*). This was because the holy Mar Theodore |[29] expounded the Scriptures in Greek and Mar Ibas, Bishop of Edessa, translated [his works] from Greek into Syriac, along with other men well-versed in the divine Scriptures.[1]

This definition of the accents, at that stage only nine in number, constitutes that very alteration in 'reading' mentioned by Barhebraeus.[iii] The term 'readings' (ܡܩܪ̈ܝܢܘܬܐ) refers to the rules for reading which the teachers had laid down for the use of pupils. This is what is meant by the heading of the Masoretic codex, "a collection of obscure words and 'readings' found in Genesis, Exodus etc." For example, one may note that among these explanations of obscure words ܐܘܪܝܬܐ is explained as ܢܘܗܪܐ ܐܬܐ (i.e. אור אתא), and the river Gihon as the Nile.[2] On the basis of such examples, it should be clear that the term 'readings' includes such matters as the appearance or disappearance of alaph and ḥeth, or the refined pronunciation of kaf as gamal or of tau as dalath—examples of this include pronouncing ܐܟܒܪܬܗ as *ʾagbarteh*; and ܠܡܬܒܪ as *lᵉmeḏbar*. I believe that the motivation behind such rules was a desire to approach the perceived elegance of the Greek language.[iv] The whole theory of heavy, smooth, and intermediate letters in Jacob Bar Šakko (p.ܩܠ in the present volume) is also directed towards this aim. They are merely Masoretic observations condensed into the form of principles.

Since the proper distinction of the different parts of speech is a prerequisite for this 'correct reading', the placing of points was also considered to belong to the field of ܩܪܝܢܘܬܐ (*art of reading*), which Joseph Huzaya is thought to have altered. Before Joseph, and throughout the time when Narsai presided over the school of Nisibis, the Easterns had always read in the same manner as 'we Westerns', as Barhebraeus puts it.[3] In fact,

---

[1] Since Joseph appears explicitly to say that there are nine accents, I cannot but suppose that ܗܘ ܕܡܢܩܦ ܡܢ ܠܘܩܒܠ ܪܘܩܝ refers to the name of an accent.

[2] Wright, *Cat.* I,104a.

[3] The citation from Barhebraeus runs: ܘܐܚܝܕ ܕܘܟܬܗ ܒܢܨܝܒܝܢ ܝܘܣܦ ܗܘܙܝܐ ܬܠܡܝܕܗ ܘܗܘ ܫܚܠܦ ܡܩܪܝܢܘܬܐ ܐܘܪܗܝܬܐ ܠܘܬ ܡܕܢܚܝܬܐ ܘܐܣܝܡ ܢܩܘܙܘܢܝܐ ܘܐܠܐ ܩܕܡܘܗܝ ܐܝܟ ܕܐܢܚܢܢ ܡܥܪ̈ܒܝܐ ܩܪܝܢ ܗܘܘ. *Joseph Huzaya, a pupil of his [i.e. Narsai's], held his post in Nisibis. He altered the Edessene [method of] reading to the Eastern*

when he set down rules to govern pointing, Joseph Huzaya—who as we saw above was following the exegesis of Theodore of Mopsuestia—was dealing not just in grammar but actually in theology. It would appear that the Nisibene 'way of reading' that he developed |[30] was associated with that 'Nestorianism' that had been rejected by the Edessenes. It must have been in this context that the Nisibene 'tradition' arose, the tradition that was the subject of the so-called Masoretic texts.[1] Books of this latter sort, what the Syrians called ܡܗܓܝܢܐ ܕܩܠܐ,[2] were composed and used in the schools from the time of Narsai and his successors Abraham and John of Beth-Rabban. To this earliest collection of Masoretic apparatus was then afterwards added the readings of the learned Ramišoʿ, who must have lived a little later since he was among the disciples of Mar Aba, the Catholicus who died in 552; he also became head of the school of Seleuceia.[3] In this way two layers of 'readings' can be distinguished—the older readings are those of the 'masters', the later ones are those from Ramišoʿ onwards. This fact becomes much clearer in the light of the heading to part of the Masoretic codex (printed in Wright's catalogue) in which the accents that are found in the books of the ܡܗܓܝܢܐ are distinguished from those found in the work of Rabban Ramišoʿ.[4] [v]

Joseph Huzaya should himself be reckoned among the older group, who expressed the exegesis of Theodore as best they could with their own pointing. He was the founder of the Masoretic school of Nisibis, which was then developed by the ܡܗܓܝܢܐ. Joseph was one of Narsai's successors as head of the school and the books of the ܡܗܓܝܢܐ had begun to be composed from Narsai's time, as well as under his immediate successors and disciples Abraham and John. Thus all these studies concerning the reading of the Scriptures flourished at Nisibis at the turn of the sixth century.[5]

[method] which the Nestorians hold to, even though throughout the whole time of Narsai they read just as we Westerns [do].

[1] Wright, *Cat.* I,104b.

[2] I.e. *The books of the masters who teach the 'reading.* Later these books are referred to simply as ܒܡܗܓܝܢܐ, or even just 'in these books'.

[3] BO II,412; III,I,86.

[4] Wright, *Cat.* I,105b. The inscription runs: ܠܘܬ ܟܬܒ ܟܠܗ ܠܡܟܬܒ ܚܕܐ ܕܦܘܣܩܐ ܕܩܠܐ ܕܡܗܓܝܢܐ ܘܪܒܢ ܪܡܝܫܘܥ.

[5] Barhebraeus recounts certain characteristics of the school of Nisibis in his larger grammar (*Gramm.*, 153,9; 154,13; 199,11; 200,2).

Now it was the translators of Greek philosophy who—by making use of Dionysius Thrax—introduced Greek grammatical theory into the Syriac schools. They thereby brought some sort of order to material (itself gathered by the ܡܩܪ̈ܝܢܐ) that otherwise remained an unarranged mass of observations and, by a system of analogy, they rationalised them according to certain principles. This explains why all the material among the later grammarians is taken from theology and philosophy rather than from the common language—it was the literary rather than the spoken tongue that they described. We ought also to acknowledge that the Masoretes had in fact themselves already begun to arrange their observations according to systematic principles. There is thus a two-fold foundation for the writing of Syriac grammar: the matter, which was the various observations of the masters upon the Scriptures, and the form, which was drawn from Greek grammatical theory.

The codex BL Add. 12138, from which we have drawn much of the foregoing, offers examples of the grammatical idiosyncrasies of the Masoretic masters. |[31] It contains four very brief grammatical tractates, which the subscription itself claims to have been composed by teachers for the use of their charges.[1] The first one deals with how to combine the particles ܠ ܘ ܕ ܒ together with nouns and verbs. Traces of this manner of treating these particles (in which the principal question concerns whether or not they ought to be constructed with an *a* vowel) can still be found among the later grammarians. Since the treatment was all about pronunciation rather than semantics, laws naturally developed regarding their separate placement before nouns and before verbs. As a result, Jacob Bar Šakko was able to distinguish between two questions:[2] how these particles, which he calls ܡܦ̈ܠܬܐ (i.e. cases), are prefixed to nouns, and then how they are prefixed to verbs.[3] Furthermore, the following words of Bar Šakko—"we say that the ܡܦ̈ܠܬܐ are the letters that are placed before nouns and if they come up against letters that carry aspiration then they cause the first letter of the noun to become ܪܘܟܟܐ;"[4] —demonstrate that this discussion was drawn from the Masoretic books, for where else than among

[1] The subscriptions runs: ܫܠܡ...ܛܘܟܣܐ ܚܕ ܕܫܦܝܪ ܐܬܛܟܣ ܡܢ ܡܠܦ̈ܢܐ ܪ̈ܒܢܝ ܠܡܪܕܘܬܐ ܕ̈ܬܠܡܝܕܐ ܚܢܢ ܒ̈ܢܝܗܘܢ, i.e. *[here] ends a certain work beautifully composed by the teachers, our masters, for the instruction of us pupils, their sons.*

[2] Jacob Bar Šakko, Syriac text, ܝ,6.

[3] Ibid. ܝܚ,18.

[4] Ibid. ܝ,7-8.

teachers of accurate and elegant reading can we imagine that there were people who conducted discussions about these particles yet without advancing beyond the question of their effects upon aspiration? What is more, the second tractate in Add. 12138 deals with exactly this question, viz. which aspiration ought the letters ܬ ܦ ܟ ܕ ܓ ܒ take when preceded by the particles ܠ ܘ ܕ ܒ.

Similar again is the discussion of the so-called letters of completion (ܐܬܘ̈ܬܐ ܕܡܫܡܠܝܢ), viz. ܡܢ ܬ ܝ ܢ ܘ ܗ ܐ, and here again nouns and verbs are dealt with separately.[1] This evidently derives from the Masoretic books, for the very same letters are discussed as a unit in the fourth tractate in this manuscript. Its most important question for discussion concerns the use of alaph as a marker of state at the end of a noun. Finally, the third dissertation of the codex discusses the consonants ܬ ܝ ܢ ܐ in the context of the tenses and persons of the verb. It comes as no surprise that this discussion, even when it crops up again later in Jacob Bar Šakko,[2] is actually about the vocalisation of the consonants that signify the future tense (ܢ ܝ ܬ), and the fourth one, ܐ, is therefore not mentioned. It is of some interest that the prefix ܢ is included here since it does not really have anything to do with the future tense proper (ܙܒܢܐ ܕܥܬܝܕ) but rather with the participle, which ought to be called ܙܒܢܐ ܕܩܐܡ (i.e. for the Greek ἐνεστώς). When Jacob of Edessa was dealing with the future tense he also included the prefix ܢ, unthinkingly following the practice of these previous masters, as they were discussing all tenses together and not just the future tense in isolation.

|[32] From this it seems quite evident that the grammarians drew heavily upon the work of the masoretes who had worked before them. However, the comments of the latter were added not so much for the scriptural books as for the correct reading of the works of the Fathers that had to be read in the schools. Wright (*Cat.*, 114) has described just such a book which contains an edition of the sacred scriptures and of the works of the Fathers prepared as a school textbook. After the New Testament is found a list of books, together with excerpts, of the Greek Fathers that were read in the Miaphysite schools: Dionysius the Areopagite, Basil of Caesarea, Gregory Nazianzen, Severus of Antioch, with a few others interspersed among them.[3] [vi]

---

[1] Ibid. ܟܗ. The letter ܘ, which is lacking after ܗ at ܟܗ,1, is present in the London ms.

[2] Ibid. ܫ,3

[3] Cf. BO III,II,937 and p.2 above.

Another consequence of this evidence is that we can now see clearly that Barhebraeus demonstrates the various arguments put forward in his larger grammar by citing key authorities who are almost entirely drawn from the list of the authorities which were read in the schools (see above, p.2). Only three of the names mentioned are not cited in the masoretic ms (Wright, *Cat.*, 114), namely Severus, Theodotus and Architheus[vii]—and even these omissions are likely to be accidental since all the others from that earlier list are cited (at least insofar as they are enumerated in the index to Martin's edition of Barhebraeus): Dionysius, Basil, Gregory Nazianzen, Ephrem, Mar Isaac, Jacob of Serug, Chrysostom (hidden under the name of Mar Iwannis), Cyril, Palladius (author of the *Book of Paradise*),[1] [viii] Jacob of Edessa, Antony Rhetor, and Aristotle. Besides these named authors, and leaving aside grammarians, Barhebraeus barely mentions any others—only Narsai and Theodore of Mopsuestia. This agreement (between Barhebraeus and the masora) is the firm basis upon which we may conclude that the whole field of grammatical studies developed within the context of theological school-learning.

The next important grammarian after Joseph Huzaya, the founder of the masoretic technique in the school of Nisibis, was Aḥūdemmēh. He was consecrated West Syrian Metropolitan of Tagrit by Jacob Bar-Addai in 559, after he had earlier been ordained bishop of the region of Beth ʿArbaye, between Nisibis and the Tigris, by the Armenian Catholicus Christopher. He

[1] Assemani III,I,287 says the following concerning the *Paradise*: "There were two works among the Syrians and Chaldaeans bearing the title *Paradise*: the monastic history written by Palladius and Jerome, which was the *Paradise* properly so called, and also the book of David of Beth Rabban, to which the author prefixed the title of the *Lesser Paradise*. Furthermore, it was not only the works of Palladius, Jerome and David that were called *Paradise* by the Orientals, but in addition the *Meadow* of John Moschus and of Anastasius of Sinai. In fact it should be noted that there are several such collections, both Syriac and Arabic, and that they differ somewhat from those other texts just mentioned which were usually called the *Paradise*. Such are i) The *Paradise of the Monks*, or *Book of the sayings and doings of the Fathers*, divided into 313 chapters, which include almost all the 'Sayings' that Cotelerius edited (Cod. Arab. Amid 17; cf. BO I,584); ii) The *Sayings of the Fathers* in 897 chapters which are different from those in Cotelerius (Arab. Cod. Beroeensis 2; BO I,585); iii) *Excerpts from the Paradise of our monastic Fathers* (Cod. Arab. Vat. 152). For more on the *Paradise* see Wright, *Cat.* III,1070-1080, who discusses ʿEnanišoʿ's *Book of Paradise* (cf. BO III,I,145).

founded two monasteries, whose names |[33] are not known for certain,[1] although one of them was near Tagrit. He also educated many Persian magi in Christian doctrine, one of whom was a young man of the royal family, whom he baptised as George. When King Chosroes I Anoshirwan discovered this he ordered the metropolitan's execution. The Christians buried his body in the church of Mahuza. Aḥūdemmēh died on the sixth day of the second month in the year of the Greeks 886 = AD 575.[ix]

It is clear from the titles of the books he wrote that Aḥūdemmēh was something of an expert in Greek philosophy. He wrote a book *Against the Philosophers*, one *Against the Magi*, then a *Definitions of Every Kind* (ܬܘܚܡܐ ܕܟܠ ܙܢ̈ܝܢ), a book *On Logic*, and *Orations on the Composition of Humans*, the last of which is extant in a British Library ms.[2] Besides these, he was also famous in his day for producing very well-written works *On Free Will, On the Soul, On Man in Microcosm*, etc.[3]

In the British Library, there is a ms containing a life of Aḥūdemmēh.[4] Wright also mentions a church that was dedicated to him in the monastery of Beth Qube near Harran, where there was a congregation of Tagritans, among whom he was treated as an apostle and a martyr.[5] Clearly the cult of Aḥūdemmēh was maintained by the people of Tagrit.

Of the works of Aḥūdemmēh, one in particular is still noted today, theܡܐܡܪܐ ܕܥܠ ܪܘܟܒܗ ܕܒܪܢܫܐ. Wright edited the beginning of it and conjectured that this was the same as that which ʿAbdīšōʿ called the ܡܐܡܪܐ ܕܥܠ ܪܘܟܒ ܡܘܡܐ. I read this little work in manuscript and saw that the writer was a well-educated and intelligent man.[x]

John Bar Zuʿbi mentions Aḥūdemmēh's grammar. A citation that he gives from it on the subject of verbal derivation indicates that the grammar had been written according to the Greek model.[6] It is well known that a threefold scheme was applied to Greek verbs: i) simple (ἁπλοῦν), such as

---

1 Barhebraeus (*Chron.Eccl.* III,101) and Assemani (BO III,I,192) do not agree on the matter.

2 Wright, *Cat.* II,802b.

3 BO III,I,192f.

4 Wright, *Cat.* III,1113. It is preceded by the *Life of Marutha* written by Denḥā at the urging of the Tagritan faithful. Marutha, metropolitan of Tagrit, died in 649 and Denḥā, his successor, in 659. To these two Tagritans is added a third, Aḥūdʾemmēh , the third metropolitan before Marutha.

5 Wright, *Cat.* I,151b, 153a, 147b.

6 BL Add. 25876, f.107b.

φρονῶ; ii) compound (σύνθετον), such as καταφρονῶ; iii) derived-from-a-compound (παρασύνθετον), such as ἀντιγονίζω and φιλιππίζω.[1] Aḥūdemmēh followed this arrangement, about which Bar Zuʿbi says the following: ܐܣܟܝܡܐ ܕܝܢ ܐܝܟ ܕܚܝܠܐ ܕܡܕܡ ܐܝܬܘܗܝ ܕܐܝܬܘܗܝ: ܘܐܣܬܪܐ ܥܡܗ. ܠܚܕܐ ܐܬܝܠܕܘ. ܦܫܝܛܐ ܘܡܪܟܒܐ ܘܡܢ ܡܪܟܒܐ. ܐܝܟ ܕܚܝܠܐ ܕܝܠ ܕܡܕܡ ܠܟܠܐ ܘܐܣܬܪܐ ܥܡܗ. ܐܘܟܝܬ ܐܬܝܠܕܘ ܦܪܣܘܢܬܐ ܡܬܬܐܡܪܢܐ |34 Aḥūdemmēh thus distinguished a threefold scheme: i) the simple is ܪܳܕܶܐ ܐܢܐ or ܡܦܝܣ ܐܢܐ, i.e. active participle with the pronoun, which together result in the ἐνεστῶτα or ܙܒܢܐ ܕܩܐܡ, i.e. the present tense; ii) the compound, ܡܬܕܒܪ ܐܢܐ or ܡܬܠܒܫ ܐܢܐ, i.e. the passive participle, the ܡܬ of which was taken as a compound element; iii) derived-from-a-compound, ܡܬܕܒܪܢܘ ܡܬܕܒܪ ܐܢܐ or ܡܬܡܫܪܢܘ ܡܬܡܫܪܐ ܐܢܐ, i.e. joining together an infinitive with the present tense. What Elias said on this topic will be explained later.

Besides giving us this information on Aḥūdemmēh's grammar, Bar Zuʿbi also calls Bishop Īšōʿdenaḥ a grammarian, a fact which Assemani derives from Cod. Ecchellensis 17,[2] although as I have not found his name in the London codex I think it not present there.[xi] I have found no other trace of a grammarian of this name. There is just one Īšōʿdenaḥ mentioned in ʿAbdīšōʿ's long list of Syriac writers, namely an Īšōʿdenaḥ of Qasra, so it may be that this latter individual is our grammarian.[3] Qasra was an episcopal city, and is surely the same Mata d-Qasra near Zabum, which Badger visited.[4] Īšō'denaḥ lived after 695.[xii]

[1] As above in Dionysius, p.17.

[2] BO III,I,308.

[3] BO III,I,195.

[4] G.P.Badger, *The Nestorians and their Rituals* (London, 1852) I,394,38.

---

[i] Joseph was almost certainly never the head of the School of Nisibis. He was merely a teacher there, as we can see from the heading to one of the mss unknown to Merx, Mosul 35 (Vööbus, *School of Nisibis*, 160f., 223).

[ii] This ms has now been published, J. Loopstra, *An East Syrian manuscript of the Syriac 'Masora' dated to 899 CE : a facsimile reproduction of British Library, Add. MS 12138*, 2 vols. (Piscataway, NJ, 2014).

[iii] There is further corroboration that Joseph Huzaya introduced these nine accents, namely in the *De Patriarchis* of Mari (quoted in Vööbus, *School of Nisibis*, 199).

[iv] Nöldeke says that Merx takes this too far and that such pronunciations were more likely part of everyday life (Review, 1216).

[v] That the Ramišoʿ of the Masorah was also the Ramišoʿ who was the pupil of Mar Aba is an understandable error based on the list of the latter's students given in the Chronicle of Seert (*GSL*, 122). Duval repeated the identification in the first edition of his *Littérature Syriaque* (p.70), but updated this information in the second edition (p.56) in light of the fascinating letters of Dawidh bar Paulos published in the meantime (1904) by Rahmani (*Studia Syriaca* I, ܡܗ-ܡܛ). Here it becomes clear that Ramišoʿ was the son of a seventh century Jacobite teacher Sabroy who, according to Dawidh, was responsible for the invention of masoretic pointing (by which we can understand at least its elaboration rather than its true origination, which may lie much earlier) and its acceptance among the learned scribes of the West Syrian monastery of Mar Mattai. Since the manuscript in which the masoretic labours of Ramišoʿ have been preserved undoubtedly represents the Eastern tradition, we can only assume that among the monasteries in the eastern regions (Ramišoʿ worked at western Mar Mattai) there was a good deal of cross-fertilisation between the sects. On Sabroy and his sons, *GSL*, 245f. Barhebraeus also mentions Ramišoʿ (Segal, *Diacritical Point*, 150n.). Vööbus (*School of Nisibis*, 202) dispenses with the testimony of Dawidh bar Paulos for no very cogent reason. The Ramišoʿ described by Dawidh is so similar to what we see in the Eastern Masorah that the identity is hard to refute unless one insists that there can have been no intellectual interaction between western and eastern sects in the seventh century. Dawidh himself clearly knows the tradition well (he was himself a descendent of Sabroy) and was a respected grammarian and lexicographer.

[vi] On this 'patristic Masorah', see J. Loopstra, "Patristic Selections in the 'Masoretic' Handbooks of the Qarqaptā Tradition." Doctoral dissertation, The Catholic University of America, 2009; id., "Patristic Collections in the 'Syriac Masora,'" *The Harp* 23 (2008), 113-122.

[vii] Merx appears to have made an error here. Severus is found in the ms in question, but Chrysostom and Cyril (along with Theodotus and Architheus) are not. The overall point still stands, however.

[viii] On the textual history of this material, see R. Draguet, *Les formes syriaques de la matière de l'Histoire lausiaque*. CSCO 389/390, 398/399 (Louvain: Secrétariat du CorpusSCO, 1978).

[ix] Published and translated by F. Nau, *Histoires d'Ahoudemmeh et de Marouta*, Patrologia Orientalis 3,1 (Paris, 1909).

[x] Merx follows Assemani in identifying the author Aḥūdemmēh with the Miaphysite metropolitan. This identification was maintained by the editor of the ancient biography of Aḥūdemmēh (previous endnote). J.M. Fiey, "Aḥoudemmeh," *Le Muséon* 81 (1968), 155-159, however, argues that there was both a Miaphysite metropolitan Aḥūdemmēh and another who was the Nestorian bishop of Nineveh. The author of the *On the Composition of Man* may be different again from the grammarian , or else he may be identified with the Nestorian bishop, but certainly not with the Miaphysite metropolitan. None of this materially affects Merx's analysis of the possible contents of the grammar in question.

[xi] The reference in BO is to the ms now known as Vat. Syr. 194 (olim Echellensis 27; 17 being a misprint in BO). Bar Zuʿbi's list of grammarians can be found therefore also in Assemani's Catalogue of Vatican mss, vol.3, p.411. The London copy of the same codex, to which Merx refers, is BL Add. 25876 (Wright, *Cat.* III,1175ff.).

[xii] Qasra is an error of Assemani's, the correct location of Īšōʿdenaḥ's episcopacy being Basra. Īšōʿdenaḥ of Basra was the ninth century author of the so-called *Book of Chastity*, a collection of histories relating to ascetics and monastic founders. He is known to have written on logic, but there is nowhere any knowledge of him as a grammarian. Bar Zuʿbi's Īšōʿdenaḥ is probably not, then, to be identified with the metropolitan of Basra. See J.-M. Fiey, "Ichoʿdnah, Métropolite de Basra et son œuvre," *Orient Syrien* 11 (1966), 431-50, esp. p.432,4; and more briefly Joel Walker, *The Legend of Mar Qardagh: Narrative and Christian Heroism in Late Antique Iraq* (Berkeley, 2006), 257-59.

Chapter 4

THE LIFE AND WORK OF JACOB OF EDESSA

All the grammarians so far mentioned were quite surpassed by Mar Jacob of Edessa, whom they called the ܡܦܫܩܢܐ ܕܟܬܒܐ, the translator/interpreter of books. Ordained bishop of Edessa in 679 (others say 677) he died in 708 (1019 of the Greeks), or 710 as Assemani derives from Dionysius of Tell-Mahre and Barhebraeus, but this is not widely accepted.[1] [i]

|[35] Jacob was born in the town of ܥܝܢܕܒܐ (*Spring of the wolf*) in the locality of Gumia in the hinterland of Antioch. He later learnt Greek at the monastery of Qenneshre, whence he left for Alexandria and studied philosophy (ܚܟܡܬܐ) before returning to Syria. The journey to Alexandria cannot have been accomplished before 640, for even if he had managed to live a full 80 years, and hence born in 628, he would have been only 12 years old when studying in Alexandria. It seems rather more likely that it happened after 640, a fact that is worthy of some note since even after the Muslim capture of Alexandria in that year the school evidently continued

[1] BO II,336,104; I,426. These two historians are uncertain even as to the succession of Ḥabib. Dionysius gives it as 1021 of the Greeks, while Barhebraeus thinks that Ḥabib took his place after Jacob's fourth year, when he left Edessa. He was then recalled to Edessa twenty years later after Ḥabib's death and discharged his episcopal duty for a further four months until his own death (*Chron.Eccl.* I,290; BO II,336). If, however, Pohlmann is right in ascribing to Jacob the book *To all the peoples*, whose author claims that he was bishop of Edessa for 30 years and had all sorts of troubles and disasters, then the information provided by Barhebraeus and Dionysius must for the most part be incorrect. For how could he have claimed to have been bishop there for 30 years if he left after four? Otherwise we agree with Pohlmann's conjecture on the grounds that Jacob was bishop for thirty years, from 677-709, or as he himself says: ܟܠܗܘܐ ܠܡܫܡܫܢܘܬܐ ܗܘܐ ܕܢܦܫ ܟܡܐ ܕܟܠ ܐܝܟ ܠܬܠܬܝܢ ܫܢܝܢ (L.A. Pohlmann, "Über die syrische Schrift: Liber Generalis ad omnes gentes in einer Hdschr. der Bibliothek der Propaganda zu Rom," *ZDMG* 15 (1861), 648-63, esp. p.655f.; BO I, 462). Even if Jacob was not born in Edessa but rather near Antioch—for the writer of the above-mentioned book calls himself ܐܢܐ ܡܣܟܢܐ ܕܡܢ ܐܘܪܗܝ etc.—it makes no difference, for he was speaking of his place of residence and not his place of birth.

to flourish and young men flocked to it even from distant lands. Had the Muslims indeed destroyed the library, the very treasure-house of the city, there would have been no reason for anyone to study literature there any longer. The life of Jacob is therefore a very strong testimony, though not generally given its due weight, against the story of the burning of the Alexandrian library by Omar.[1]

Anyone who buried himself in literary studies at Alexandria, would naturally became conversant in the fields of with grammar, literature, and philosophy. It is thus no surprise that Jacob translated into Syriac Porphyry's *Introduction* and furnished it with a commentary, and that he also produced Syriac translations of Aristotle's *Categories*, *On Interpretation*, and *Analytics*, prefaced by a *Life of the Philosopher.*[2] [ii] He frequently made use of the philosophical method—trying to move logically from one question to the next. We see, for instance, that when he is discussing the Greek term ΠΙΠΙ, he enquires into the origins of vowel symbols, and he shows himself fully acquainted with the opposing Greek schools of thought which argued for the origin of language κατὰ φύσιν and κατὰ θέσιν respectively.[3] [iii] Elsewhere we again see him given over to philosophical musings, such as the question about the various aspects of creation—which should be assigned to God, which to nature and intellect—or when he discusses the matter of how to distinguish soul, spirit and intellect.[4] It was because he was so steeped in philosophy that he claimed himself to be hostile to the foolishness of the ascetical lifestyle, writing candidly that

> since I am endowed with a body and also with a spirit, with senses and an intellect, and since the spirit is at once swallowed up with the mud, I am thus at once both angel and man. Given that I have been created such that, while I cannot fully encapsulate anything merely by my intellect, I am myself wholly limited within this flesh that I inhabit, affected as I am by everyday activities—both |[36] those I carry out myself and

[1] See L. Krehl, "Über die Sage von der Verbrennung der alexandrinischen Bibliothek durch die Araber" in *Atti del IV Congresso internazionale degli Orientalisti a Firenze* (Florence, 1880-1), I, 433-54.

[2] BO I,493.

[3] E. Nestle, "Jakob von Edessa über den Schem hammephorasch und andere Gottesnamen. Ein Beitrag zur Geschichte des Tetragrammaton," *ZDMG* 32 (1878), 465-508 [addenda 735-6], esp. p.481f.

[4] Respectively Wright, *Cat.* II,592a, 604b.

> those that I endure—how then can I impose upon myself a rule by which I should follow one or other of those ways that are commonly known as the 'heavenly' and the 'earthly'?

He discusses the end of life at some length, not allowing that God should predetermine its limits. In so doing he does not even reject the testimony of the pagan philosopher Porphyry.[1] Finally, he was a man of charming character, although to a friend who asked to see him Jacob once described his appearance as being pitifully beardless, with large teeth, a long face, short in stature, and bald-headed (which he calls the ignominy of Elisha), his head having been thus disfigured since he was 42 years old. He judged his own literary merits neither too boastfully nor too modestly, for while he calls a friend of his an eagle, he refers to himself merely as a magpie (ܩܩܘܬܐ), adorned with feathers not his own.[2]

However, Jacob's judgment upon himself is surely too harsh for one who had acquired such exceptional learning. For Barhebraeus has already made clear when he praises him in the introduction to his *Ecclesiastical Chronicle* that Jacob had Hebrew in addition to Syriac and Greek.[iv] He rightly understood its closeness to Aramaic and so was able to distinguish the Hebrew vowel sounds, for instance when he wrote עֵבֶר = ܥܶܒܰܪ, אִישׁ = ܐܺܝܫ, אִשָּׁה = ܐܰܢܬܬܐ, and especially when he correctly distinguishes אדנִי from אדֹנָי.[3] He was also probably aware of the particle נא, which he distinguishes from the suffix, and when discussing the Behemoth he understands that it is a plural form.[4] If this is evidence for Jacob as a Hebraist then it also shows that he had some knowledge of Samaritan too, for in his scholion on Joshua 8.33 he mentions that, at Deut 27.4, the Samaritan version reads Mount Ebal (the ܥܝܒܠ of the Syrians) rather than Gerizim.[5]

---

[1] Ibid. 599b.

[2] Ibid. 593b.

[3] E. Nestle, op.cit., 479f., 491.

[4] Wright, *Cat.* II,544b; R. Schröter, "Erster Brief Jakob's von Edessa an Johannes den Styliten," *ZDMG* 24 (1870), 261-300, ref. p.290. These are his own words: "Although the 'na' in 'Hosianna' is similar to the conjunction (ܐܶܢܳܐ), they are not the same for the Hebrews." Before this he gave various words derived from the root ישע, such as ישעיהו, ישוע, ישועת. He also refers to the word סבך (Gen 22.13) and discusses the meaning of the word אדם which he reckons to be a collective—Assemani, ed., *Ephraemi Syri Opera* (Rome, 1732-46), I,131,172. He adds various words derived from the root פרץ—ibid., II,211.

[5] BO I,489.

There cannot be any doubt at all, therefore, that Jacob excelled in his own day in all manner of spheres of learning and we can easily understand why it was that his friends, in their correspondence, used to question him upon a whole range of issues. However, we can also see that his overriding concern was not with gaining knowledge but in governing the church, over which he held sway with such vigor—as we know from the responses he gave to Addai.[1] This is not the place to go through all these individually, but everywhere his responses show his gentleness, wisely moderated by severity. He strenuously opposed popular superstitions concerning things such as the power of the consecrated host, the relics of the martyrs, and the spells and crafts of magicians. He produced rules for the interaction of his priests with heretics, Jews, and Muslims, |[37] his concern being above all that the dignity of the church should be preserved and not forgotten. He said that open confession before a priest was indeed an effective cure, but he did not believe that sins were left unforgiven by God simply because the sinner had not confessed them. For he said that there was no sin whose punishment was so great that salvation should be denied to a man, so long as he flees his sins and carries out penitence, since God does not desire the destruction of a man whom he has created.[2]

Jacob's profound concern for church business led him to write many letters to friends who had queries. In these he discusses a whole range of issues relating to ecclesiastical rites. Included is the aforementioned letter to Addai in which he deals with the new and solemn right of the blessing of the water which he had instituted.[3] Another to John the Stylite concerns the feast of the finding of the cross celebrated on the 14th day of Ilul, on the origin of which he confesses himself ignorant.[4] He wrote also to the same individual on the blessing of the water.[5] In a letter written to a certain priest Thomas, Jacob shows himself an experienced investigator into these rites, suggesting that the Mass observed by the Syrians (and by himself) is different from that found in other churches, and he even goes into the history of the order of baptism as received by the Maronite, the Jacobite,

[1] P. Lagarde, *Reliquiae iuris ecclesiastici* (London, 1856), 117. Cf. Wright, *Cat.* I,223a, 388b, 815a, while others of his canons remain unedited, ibid., 221a. Cf. BO I,486.

[2] Lagarde, *op.cit.*, 143,9.

[3] BO I,486. Cf. Wright, *Cat.* I,224b.

[4] Ibid., II,597a.

[5] BO I,486.

and the Melkite churches.[1] In his *Book of Treasures* he provides a mystical explanation of the sacred rites.[2] Lastly he composed a letter, addressed to John the Stylite, dealing with the authenticity of two homilies ascribed to Jacob of Serug.[3] [v]

For one who gave himself so much to the discipline and rites of the church, it is hardly surprising that Jacob also took a keen interest in ecclesiastical singing. He took great pains over the preservation and explanation of hymns, as is amply testified by a British Library ms.[4] Another codex contains the same hymn collection, and Assemani mentions this side of his work too.[5] For the benefit of the reader, the following is a brief introduction to the Greek system of chanting.[vi]

Greek church hymns, while not being restricted by metre, rhythm, or end-rhyme, usually followed a rule for the syllable count of each verse. The result is that however many syllables and accents there are in the individual lines of the first strophe, the same number will be found in the corresponding lines of the following strophes. Thus where the first line of the first strophe has twelve syllables, the second fifteen and the third six etc., then in the remaining strophes the lines in the same positions will have the same number of syllables as in the first, once the accentuation has been observed. Pitra recognised and expounded this previously long unrecognised rule of late Greek prosody, and Christ and |[38] Paranikas have given numerous examples of it.[6] When hymns thus composed, along with their modes of singing, were taken over by the Syrians, they needed to be constructed so that the Syriac contained just the same number of syllables in each line as the corresponding Greek line. The hymns of Severus of Antioch, John bar Aphthonia of Qenneshre, another John of Qenneshre, and various other anonymous poets, upon whom Jacob lavished critical attention in the aforementioned works, all follow this rule. Let us now hear what Jacob himself says of his own method (BL Add. 17134, f.75r = Wright,

---

[1] BO I,479,477; Wright, *Cat.* I,224a.

[2] BO I,487.

[3] Edited in Schröter, *op. cit.*

[4] Wright, *Cat.* I,330.

[5] Ibid., 339; BO I,487, II,47.

[6] J.-P. Pitra, *Hymnographie de l'Église grecque* (Rome, 1867); W. Christ and M. Paranikas, *Anthologia Graeca* (Leipzig, 1871). It was the latter pair who established the rule of accentuation.

Cat. I,336, with an example of the method illustrated in vol.III, Plate V in Wright):[vii]

> The hymns have been translated from the Greek tongue into the Edessene, i.e. the Syriac, by Mar Paul, who was bishop of Edessa, although he resided in Cyprus after fleeing from the Persian persecution. Firstly they were prepared and collated from Greek exemplars, and then, with great care and hard work, and with all the detailed attention that I could manage, I myself, Jacob 'the labourer', in the 986th year of the Greeks according to the calculation made from the reign of King Seleucus Nicator of Syria (=AD675), in the third indiction, I carried out the task of separating those words that originated with the (learned) poet himself from those that were added at the discretion of Mar Paul. He had had to make these additions in order that the poem (ܡܐܠܐ) should flow with the same total number of words, given the relative brevity and conciseness (ܦܣܝܩܘܬܐ) of Syriac diction as compared to that of Greek. The original words of the poet I have written in black ink, those that have been added are in red, while where the translator has altered something (i.e. put one word instead of another, usually so as to preserve the Greek metre in Syriac), I have indicated this for you in symbols written between the lines. This way you can easily tell, wherever you may wish to, which words correspond to the Greek original.

Jacob further explains that at the end he has given all the biblical citations referred to by the hymn writers. From all of this we can conclude that Jacob had made a recension of hymns that had already been translated from Greek into Syriac and that he strove to separate out the Greek from the Syriac additions as neatly as possible. This work of Jacob's now finally opens up the textual study of the Greek hymns, if we place alongside them the Syriac additions—since nearly all the Greek hymns are, as far as I am aware, lost. However, this codex (Add. 17134) also contains the angelic hymn *Gloria in excelsis*, which Mar Paul translated according to the tradition of Qenneshre.[viii] The individual lines may therefore be compared with their Greek equivalents. Where Jacob wrote out words in red we have indicated this here by underlining the word(s) in question; where he has written words in between the lines, these we have left in place [and printed them in a smaller typeface]. The following is the *Gloria*, the Greek being taken from Lagarde's edition of the *Apostolic Constitutions* and the *Anthologia Graeca* of Christ and Paranikas [abbv. CP in the text below]. |[39]

ܫܘܒܚܐ ܠܐܠܗܐ ܒܡܪ̈ܘܡܐ.	Δόξα ἐν ὑψίστοις θεῷ
ܫܝܢܐ ܘܥܠ ܐܪܥܐ ܫܠܡܐ.	Καὶ ἐπὶ γῆς εἰρήνη,
ܫܦܪܘܬܐ ܕܨܒܝܢܐ ܒ ܣܒܪܐ ܛܒܐ ܠܒܢ̈ܝܢܫܐ.	Ἐν ἀνθρώποις εὐδοκία
ܡܫܒܚܝܢ ܠܟ.	Αἰνοῦμέν σε [ὑμνοῦμέν σε om. CP]
ܡܒܪܟܝܢ ܠܟ.	Εὐλογοῦμέν σε [εὐχαριστοῦμέν σοι δοξολογοῦμέν σε]
ܣܓܕܝܢ ܠܟ.	Προσκυνοῦμέν σε [διὰ τοῦ μεγάλου ἀρχιερέως σὲ τὸν ὄντα θεὸν ἀγέννητον ἕνα ἀπρόσιτον μόνον CP om.]
ܡܡܠܠܘܬܐ ܫܘܒܚܐ ܦܫܩܝܢ ܠܟ.	Δοξολογοῦμέν σε
ܡܘܕܝܢ ܠܟ.	Εὐχαριστοῦμέν σοι[1]
ܫܘܒܚܐ ܪܒܐ ܡܛܠ ܪܒܘܬܐ ܕܫܘܒܚܐ ܕܝܠܟ.	Διὰ τὴν μεγάλην σου δόξαν
ܡܪܝܐ ܟܪܘܝܐ ܘܡܠܟܐ ܫܡܝܢܐ.	Κύριε βασιλεῦ ἐπουράνιε
ܐܠܗܐ ܐܒܐ ܐܚܝܕ ܟܠ.	Θεὲ, πατὴρ παντοκράτωρ,

[1] The words are read in CP in an order different from that found in the Syriac text and in the *Apostolic Constitutions*. On the matter of δοξάζειν and εὐχαριστεῖν cf. Peshiṭta Romans 1.21. Here ܡܡܠܠܘܬܐ ܫܘܒܚܐ is equivalent to δοξολογία just as ܡܡܠܠܘܬܐ ܫܪ̈ܒܬܐ is equivalent to γενεαλογίαι at Wright, *Cat.* II,541a.

ܡܪܝܐ ܐܠܗܐ ܒܪܐ ܝܚܝܕܝܐ.	Κύριε υἱὲ μονογενῆ (νές)
ܝܫܘܥ ܡܫܝܚܐ.	Ἰησοῦ χριστέ
ܘܪܘܚܐ ܩܕܝܫܐ.	Καὶ ἅγιον πνεῦμα
ܡܪܝܐ ܐܠܗܐ.	Κύριε ὁ θεὸς,
ܐ ܐܡܪܗ ܕܐܠܗܐ.	Ὁ ἀμνὸς τοῦ θεοῦ,
ܒܪܐ ܘܡܠܬܐ ܕܐܒܐ.	ὁ υἱὸς τοῦ πατρὸς,
ܚܛܗܐ ܐ ܗܘ ܕܫܩܠ ܐܘܟܝܬ ܫܩܠ ܚܛܗܝܗ ܕܥܠܡܐ.	ὁ αἴρων τὰς ἁμαρτίας τοῦ κόσμου,
ܚܘܣ ܘ ܐܬܪܚܡ ܥܠܝܢ.|40	ἐλέησον ἡμᾶς.
ܐ ܗܘ ܕܫܩܠ ܐܘܟܝܬ ܫܩܠ ܚܛܗܝܗ ܕܥܠܡܐ.	ὁ αἴρων τὰς ἁμαρτίας τοῦ κόσμου,
ܩܒܠ ܠܡ ܐܘܕܝ ܘܩܒܠ ܒܥܘܬܢ.	πρόσδεξαι τὴν δέησιν ἡμῖν,
ܒ ܗܘ ܕܝܬܒ ܒܝܡܝܢܐ ܡܢ ܝܡܝܢܐ ܕܐܒܘܗܝ.	ὁ καθήμενος ἐν δεξιᾷ τοῦ πατρὸς
ܚܘܣ ܘ ܐܬܪܚܡ ܥܠܝܢ.	ἐλέησον ἡμᾶς·
ܐܠܚܘܕܝ ܡܛܠ ܕܐܢܬ ܗܘ ܒܠܚܘܕܝܟ ܩܕܝܫܐ.	ὅτι σύ εἶ μόνος ἅγιος,
ܐܠܚܘܕܝ ܐܢܬ ܗܘ ܒܠܚܘܕܝܟ ܡܪܝܐ.	σὺ εἶ μόνος κύριος,
ܝܫܘܥ ܡܫܝܚܐ.	Ἰησοῦς χριστός,
ܥܡ ܪܘܚܐ ܕܝܠܟ ܩܕܝܫܐ.	[with your Holy Spirit]

ܠܫܘܒܚܐ ܕܐܠܗܐ ܐܒܐ ܐܡܝܢ.	εἰς δόξαν θεοῦ πατρός· ἀμήν.
ܟܠ ܝܘܡ ܒܟܠܝܘܡ ܒܟܠܗܘܢ ܝ̈ܘܡܬܐ ܕܚܝ̈ܝ ܐܒܪܟܟ.	Καθ' ἑκάστην ἡμέραν εὐλογίσω σε[1]
ܐܦ ܐܫܒܚ ܠܫܡܐ ܩܕܝܫܐ ܘܡܒܪܟܐ ܠܥܠܡ.	καὶ αἰνέσω τὸ ὄνομά σου εἰς τὸν αἰῶνα
ܗܘ ܕܐܬܘܗܝ ܘܡܩܘܐ ܠܥܠܡ ܥܠܡܝܢ.	καὶ εἰς τὸν αἰῶνα τοῦ αἰῶνος [καταξίωσον κύριε καὶ τὴν ἡμέραν ταύτην ἀναμαρτήτους φυλαχθῆναι ἡμᾶς CP add.]
ܐ ܐܬܒܪܟ ܡܒܪܟ ܐܢܬ ܡܪܝܐ ܐܚܝܕ ܟܠ.	Εὐλογήτος εἶ κύριε
ܐܠܗܐ ܕܐܒܗ̈ܬܐ ܕܝܠܢ.	ὁ θεὸς τῶν πατέρων ἡμῶν
ܐ ܐ ܘܡܫܒܚ ܫܡܟ ܘܡܦܐܪ ܒܬܫܒܘܚܬܐ	καὶ αἰνετὸν καὶ δεδοξασμένον τὸ ὄνομά σου
ܠܥܠܡܝܢ ܠܥܠܡ ܥܠܡܝܢ ܐܡܝܢ.	εἰς τοὺς αἰῶνας. ἀμήν.
ܠܟ ܝܐܐ ܬܫܒܘܚܬܐ. |41	Σοὶ πρέπει αἶνος[2]
ܠܟ ܦܐܐ ܠܬܫܒܘܚܬܐ.	σοὶ πρέπει ὕμνος
ܠܟ ܦܐܐ ܫܘܒܚܐ.	σοὶ δόξα πρέπει
ܠܐܠܗܐ ܕܗܘ ܐܒܐ.	[τῷ πατρὶ

[1] Lines 29-34 from CP only.

[2] Lines 35-41 from *Apostolic Constitutions* only.

ܠܐܒܐ ܕܫܪܪܐ ܥܡ ܒܪܐ ܡܫܝܚܐ.	καὶ τῷ υἱῷ]
ܐܦ ܠܪܘܚܐ ܩܕܝܫ ܒܟܠ.	καὶ τῷ ἁγίῳ πνεύματι
ܗܫܐ ܘܒܟܠܙܒܢ ܘܠܥܠܡ ܥܠܡܝܢ ܐܡܝܢ.	εἰς τοὺς αἰῶνας τῶν αἰώνων.

It is clear that the Syriac formula is taken from a Greek recension different from those which we have printed from the *Apostolic Constitutions* and the *Anthologia Graeca*. However, where the Syriac does accurately reflect the Greek, the number of syllables in each is almost identical, especially if words such as ἁγίος and κύριος are counted as disyllablic on account of their later pronunciation 'hagyos' and 'kuryos'.[1] Some Syriac words, such as ܘܟܠ and ܥܠܡܝܢ must also be counted as disyllabic, as the method of singing appears to demand.[2] However, by adding extra interlinear words where he deemed that these accurately reflected the Greek *Vorlage*, Jacob showed himself to be aping the Greeks and he cast aside the native character of his own language in a misplaced admiration for a foreign one, even to the extent of replacing the translation ܣܒܪܐ ܛܒܐ for εὐδοκία with the unfortunate ܫܦܝܪܘܬ ܨܒܝܢܐ and again he made a poor emendation when placing an ܐ over the words ܕܐܠܗܐ, ܐܡܪܗ, on the grounds that the Greek read simply ὁ ἀμνὸς τοῦ θεοῦ.[ix]

We again come across this unthinking and slavish imitation of the Greek in the case of the homilies of Severus.[3] [x] In his translation of these homilies Jacob deals with the term κατήχησις (*catechesis*) in a remarkable manner, for having translated ἦχος (*a musical register*) by ܪܘܡܚܐ, he then wants to express κατήχησις by coining a neologism derived from this, ܡܪܘܡܚܘܬܐ, which is totally unheard of in Syriac with such a meaning.[4] [xi] Jacob himself was certainly not shy of boasting about his translation of the

[1] One cannot be quite sure about the number of syllables here, unless one takes into account the system of contractions in use in the modern language. For how far such things can be taken, see the modern Greek poetry in A. Boltz, *Der hellenische Sprache der Gegenwart* (Darmstadt, 1882), 19,56.

[2] Cf. the Syriac songs complete with musical notation edited by M. Villoteau, "De la musique des Syriens" in *Déscription de l'Égypte*, (2nd ed., Paris, 1826) XIV, 310-23.

[3] Wright has described the codex (*Cat.* II,534, cf. BO I,494; II,46). J.P.P. Martin has edited a part of Homily 82 from a codex in Rome (Martin, *Ad Georgium*)—on p.16 the words ܚܫܐ ܕܫܘܒܚܐ ܣܪܝܩܐ, represent quite literally the Greek πάθος κενοδοξίας.

[4] Cf. Nestle, *Gramm.*, 79f.

homilies, by which the Syriac Miaphysite church was much enriched, |[42] even though it hardly outlasted his own lifetime. It seems that he preferred to remain in the shadows, passing on his different ideas to other clerics rather than being energised to proclaim them out loud himself. We therefore see him fully occupied in the business of educating the clergy which, being the weightiest part of his episcopal duty, naturally led him onto writing on grammatical subjects. For despite the fact that he had infused new life into the Scriptures with his many commentaries, he was never satisfied that he had done enough—and so he decided to lay the foundations of an even sounder learning.

In countless scholia he elucidated both the themes and the language of Scripture, struggling through all the great difficulties which such a task naturally involves. Of the two tasks that he set himself, the first he entitled ܦܘܫܩܐ, i.e. 'commentary', and the other 'scholia'.[1] In his letters too he considered problems in the criticism of the Scriptures, such as that of the genealogy of Jesus, where he even goes so far as to talk about the legend of Pantera.[2] [xii] It should be noted that a certain monk Severus collected Jacob's scholia together with the commentaries of Ephrem and others. Much of this may be found in the first two volumes of the Roman edition of Ephrem, while others have been edited elsewhere.[3] [xiii] He is especially interested in the physical and geographical aspects of the text, although he is by no means averse to mystical exegesis as well. In the scholia he declaims on topics such as the various seas, the nature of air, solar eclipses, the moon and its relationship to the sun, and about the problem of whether the mountains came crashing down at the time of the flood. On this latter, he points out that the waters did not reach the very tops of the mountains and by this explanation (which we still recommend even to modern interpreters) he proves that the surface of the earth is still the same today as it was before the flood.[4] He goes into great depth in explicating

[1] BO I,488-92; Wright, *Cat.* II,591,910.

[2] Wright, *Cat.* II,597.

[3] G. Phillips, *Scholia on Passages of the Old Testament by Mar Jacob* (London 1864); W. Wright, "Two Epistles of Mar Jacob, Bishop of Edessa, edited from BM Add. 12172," *Journal of Sacred Literature* X (1867), 430-60; R. Schröter, *op.cit.*; Nestle, *Gramm.*, 32.

[4] Assemani, ed., *Ephraemi Syri Opera* (Rome, 1732-46) I,123,118,125,126.

historical questions such as the names of Esau's wives, the Rechabites, the Ethiopian wife of Numbers 12, Susanna and Joachim, etc.[1]

Chronology was another of his great interests. Because of the way that he explained the reference to the 70 weeks in the Book of Daniel, he asserted that the year of Jesus' nativity was 309 of the Greeks and Edessenes.[2] This differed so much from Eusebius's conclusions that, at a friend's request, he undertook to tackle the problem again.[3] In the end he was moved by this outstanding chronological investigation to write a whole chronicle, fragments of which are extant in a London ms.[4] [xiv] In his Chronicle he discussed the error of three years in Eusebius's calculations and he continued the latter's work from the 276th Olympiad, rather as Jerome did, embellished it and took it on beyond the time of the Caliph Abu Bakr, even though |[43] its final Olympiad is the 352nd, which began in 627—we do not know exactly in which year it ceased since the work is incomplete. Jacob was so committed to the investigation of all history that when including in his Chronicle the activities of various learned men he felt unable to suppress information on the lives of heretics such as Peter the Fuller, Timothy Aeluros, and the Shabbtāyē.[5] [xv] He also dealt with the history of Syriac literature, distinguishing between three individuals called Isaac, and he spoke of the name and origin of the hymns which the *quqaye* (ܩܘܩܝܐ) listened to.[6] He also had an opinion on the apocrypha and the canon, although he was aware that the Syrians did not much care for the apocryphal books. He seems to have approved of the Book of Enoch, if by this he is referring to one and the same as our *Ethiopic Enoch.* He argued that there were just three books of Solomon and not five, and he excluded from the canon the books of Ben Sirah, Tobit, Maccabees and the books of the women (i.e. Esther, Susanna, Thecla, and Judith).[7]

---

[1] Ibid. I,175; II,144; Wright, *Cat.* II,601a. Cf. Lagarde, *Materialien zur Kritik cet. des Pentateuch* (Leipzig, 1867) I, xvi.

[2] *Ephraemi Syri Opera* II,221.

[3] Wright, *Cat.* II,598.

[4] Wright, *Cat.* III,1062. The book finishes at the year 692. Cf. Rosen and Forshall, *Catalogus codicum manuscriptorum orientalium qui in Museo Britannico asservantur* (London, 1838), 88, col.1.

[5] Wright, *Cat.* II,600,603.

[6] Barhebraeus is making use of Jacob's Chronicle here. BO II,310.

[7] Wright, *Cat.* II,598b,601. Also on Thecla, ibid., 98.

Jacob's life coincided with the rapid expansion of the Arab empire, including the Arab conquest of Edessa and its environs. There is a tradition that the bishop of Edessa converted to Islam in the 18th year of the Hijra.[1] If so, this explains why the clergy were so concerned with the problem of how they should interact with Muslims. Traces of this debate can be found in the canons which Jacob gave to Addai, who had asked whether an abbot of a monastery was allowed to take food from the same bowl as a Muslim governor, and whether a Christian priest was permitted to educate the sons of Muslims.[2] In neither case does Jacob forbid these things. Although it seems that he acted without any great strictness in such matters, there were some bishops who were still dissatisfied and who advised him to withdraw from such a harsh observance of the ecclesiastical canons, given the demands of the situation.[3] Once those bishops that were tending towards excessive leniency had reduced the canons to a mockery, Jacob had no choice but to retire, initially to the monastery of Mar Jacob of Kaisum, afterwards to that of Eusebona,[4] [xvi] where for eleven years he taught the Psalms and the readings of the books (i.e. ܕܩ̈ܠܐ, ܡܙ̈ܡܪܐ), and where he introduced the study of the Greek language which had all but vanished. He was thus fully occupied throughout this period with the education of boys, who generally began with reading the Psalms (cf.p2). When the Greek monks there became hostile and took exception to him, he sought out the great monastery of Tell ʿAdda in the diocese of Antioch, |44 where he edited the Old Testament (and not solely on the basis of the Septuagint).[5] He lived there for another seven years and so fulfilled the role of a teacher for twenty in total.[6]

Every inch of Jacob's critical acumen was required for the scholarly work on the Scriptures to which he was at this time committed, and some

---

[1] Al-Balāḏurī (d.892), *Futūḥ al-buldān* (ed. M. J. de Goeje, *Liber expugnationis regionum*, Leiden, 1866), 174.

[2] Lagarde, *Reliquiae iuris ecclesiastici*, 140. Quastio 47,48.

[3] BO II,336 = Barhebraeus, *Chron. Eccl.* I,289: ܠܐ ܐܢܫ ܗܘ ܡܫܬܡܥ. ܐܠܐ ܠܟܠܗܘܢ ܕܟܢܘܢܐ ܐܝܟ ܠܡܫܬܪܝܘ̈ܬܐ ܢܚܬ ܡܠܟܝܢ ܗܘܘ ܠܗ.

[4] Assemani (*ibid.*) has written ܐܘܣܒܘܢܐ, ܕܒܢ̈ܝܐ. I do not know whether this is the famous Convent of Eusebius near Apamea. Kaisum was near Samosata.

[5] Scholarship flourished in this monastery even after Jacob's time, cf. Wright, *Cat.* II,498b. Tell ʿAdda was at that time largely populated by Greek monks, which was perhaps the reason why Jacob had gone there in the first place.

[6] On the chronology, see p.34 above; also Wright, *Syriac Literature*, 141-3.

fragments of his work in this field are still extant. He commented upon the Psalter and made a recension of its text, researching thoroughly both the Greek and Hebrew traditions.[1] He says, for instance, that Psalm 2 was read by the Hebrews without a title. Concerning the term *Selah* which is found in the Hebrew at the end of Psalm 9 he said the following, "those translators who were sent to Palestine by the apostle Addai and Abgar, King of Edessa, in order to translate the Holy Scriptures, although they found the term *diapsalma* after the words *'that the people may know that they are but men'* they thought that this was part of the tenth Psalm. In some Hebrew exemplars the word *forever* is written in place of *diapsalma.* The explanation of this is that, whenever the singers who praise God with a Psalm leave a break in their words, the people who are listening are meant to respond with the words *'forever,'* meaning that God is praised and blessed at all times in these Psalms. This is just the same as when in our own churches, after the words *'now and forever and for all ages to come'* the people respond as an affirmation, *'Amen.'* " The reader who wants to follow up this question should look at Sommer's research on the term *Selah.*[2] [xvii]

Although he looked to the Hebrew in these examples, in general he pedantically followed the Greek: thus in Ps 5.10 he replaced ܓܓܪܬܐ with ܩܕܠܐ for λάρυγξ (*throat*), and in Ps 4.1 he wrote ܫܡܥܢܝ for ܥܢܝܢܝ to express εἰσακούειν (*to hearken*); again at Ps 22.28, where the Peshiṭta has ܫܪ̈ܒܬܐ, the LXX reads πατρίαι (*families*), and hence Jacob ܐܒܗ̈ܬܐ.

Besides these examples, and also a few other fragments of his Psalter recension preserved in Barhebraeus's *Storehouse of the Mysteries*, there are also extant the books of Samuel that he revised according to the Syriac and various Greek editions.[xviii] The subscription to this work reveals that it was composed in the great monastery of Tell ʿAdda in the year 705.[3] To the same period we most likely ought also to attribute his recension of Isaiah, a fragment of which Wright has edited,[4] for although it is very brief it demonstrates how Jacob went about revising the Peshiṭta according to the LXX. Hence the following from the Peshiṭta [Isa 28.14-5]: ܡܛܠ ܗܢܐ ܫܡܥܘ ܡܠܬܗ ܕܡܪܝܐ. ܓܒܪ̈ܐ ܡܒܣܪ̈ܢܐ: ܘܫܠܝܛܢܘܗܝ ܕܥܡܐ ܗܢܐ ܕܒܐܘܪܫܠܡ. ܡܛܠ ܕܐܡܪܬܘܢ. ܐܩܝܡܢ. ܩܝܡܐ ܥܡ ܡܘܬܐ:

[1] BO I,493.

[2] J.G. Sommer, *Biblische Abhandlungen* (Bonn, 1846); the cited texts can be found in P. de Lagarde, *Praetermissorum libri duo* (Göttingen 1879), 102,82; 109,92.

[3] Wright, *Cat.* I,38.

[4] Ibid., 28.

ܗܢܐ] LXX τοῦτο, Jacob ܗܕܐ.
ܡܠܬܗ] LXX λόγον, Jacob ܦܬܓܡܗ.[xix]
ܡܩܛܡܢܐ] LXX τεθλιμμένοι, whence Syrohexapla's ܐܠܝܨܐ, but Jacob follows the Peshiṭta.[xx]
ܡܟܬܫܘܗܝ] Jacob ܘܡܥܒܕܢܗ.[xxi]
ܐܩܝܡܢ ܩܝܡܐ] LXX ἐποιήσαμεν διαθήκην, Jacob [45]| ܓܙܪܢ ܥܡ ܕܡܘܬܐ.
ܫܝܘܠ] LXX τοῦ ᾅδου, Jacob ܫܝܘܠ.

The fact that he retained ܡܩܛܡܢܐ for τεθλιμμένοι implies that he probably had seen Aquila's χλευασμοῦ or Symmachus's χλευασταί, unless he actually compared the Hebrew text itself.[xxii]

[Note should also be made of Jacob's work on the Pentateuch.] [xxiii]

The scholar who carried out this minute and painstaking work was able to do no more than to hope that the fruits of his labour would be preserved and passed on. We can see from his famous letter to bishop George that this is just what the dying Jacob desired above all, for in this letter he explains exactly how he wants his books to be copied. At the end of the letter it becomes clear that he enclosed with it one part, or perhaps he means one volume, of his translation of Severus's *Cathedral Homilies*. He advises George to warn the scribes not to alter anything relating to the orthography, the punctuation, or the critical and exegetical notes, since nothing he has written was done without good reason.

The letter as a whole is not really about grammar. It is in fact a set of instructions for scribes on the best way of copying the translation of the *Homilies*. It would not be far from the truth to say that Jacob's intention was that the scribes should work with the same attention to detail as he himself showed in making his own copies—as we saw in the case of the *Hymns*.[xxiv] Jacob made clear to George that both the middle part of the *Homilies* and the letter itself should be copied by Abba Julian with the utmost accuracy and that he should take care to arrange it just as if it were the original. Things seem to have turned out just as Jacob had hoped, for in the manuscript Vat. Syr. 141 (= Echellensis 30) this letter precedes the middle volume of the *Homilies*.[1] Although it seemed to Martin that the first folio, which contains the fragment of the letter, was stitched on at a later date, it is nevertheless to be understood from the end of the letter itself

[1] BO I, 570.

that this folio must have been substituted in place of an older one. If we concede this then it becomes quite evident what the letter means. Its final part reads as follows:[1] [xxv]

> Making supplication before your holy brotherhood I say: order the scribes to copy down this writing which I have dedicated to your sanctity (i.e. the letter) before the middle volume of this book of Cathedral Homilies (i.e. the one that was sent together with the letter). You must leave alone even the lemnisci[2] [xxvi] in the aforementioned volume, which in truth I myself collated for the most part and furnished with lemnisci (ܦܗܡܝܬܐ) both for love of you and so that my intention (ܣܘܟܐ ܕܝܠܝ) might be thoroughly transparent, and do not erase even one of them from the volume before it has been fully transcribed by someone so that, when scribes see[3] which items |[46] have been marked out with lemnisci (ܐܝܠܝܢ ܕܦܗܡܝܡܝܢ) and what variants have been offered for them,[4] they might understand what I was talking about when I wrote a letter to you about those points (lit. 'my aim concerning those points which are in my letter to you').
>
> Finally I ask your brotherhood: Set your signet ring (i.e. your seal) before my letter (i.e. at its beginning);[5] when you write to Abba Julian and greet him also in the name of my poverty, send him both the letter[6] and the middle volume, that he might be the first to copy it and attend to the placing of those points, to those places that are marked out with lemnisci as well as the variants offered for them; finally [that he may

[1] Syriac text in Martin, *Ad Georgium*, p.ܗ, l.3.

[2] If indeed the expression ܢܘܩܙܐ ܦܗܡܝܡܐ (*bound points*) refers to the symbol ~, the lemniscus. Concerning ܦܗܡ, cf. Barhebraeus, *Gramm.*, 248,49, and elsewhere.

[3] Martin has printed this as ܚܙܐ ܠܗܘܢ ܟܬܘܒܐ, but the following verb is ܢܣܬܟܠܘܢ, and so it should be read as ܚܙܝܢ ܠܗܘܢ ܟܬܘ̈ܒܐ.

[4] Field, *Hexapla*, p.LV, n.14: "The form ~ in a codex is simply a mark placed over the line which connects marginal readings with the text." To this end the scribe of the *Cathedral Homilies* has indeed made good use of this symbol, wherever marginal notes needed to be connected with the words of the text. This codex is thus truly faithful to Jacob's intention.

[5] Martin has ܕܝܠܝ, but Assemani (BO I,478) has ܕܝܠܟ. The latter cannot be right. It is Jacob's letter, sent on to Julian, that is being authorised by George's authentic seal.

[6] To be read with Assemani as ܫܕܪܘܗ ܠܗ ܠܐܓܪܬܐ, where Martin has ܫܕܪܘܗ ܘܠܐܓܪܬܐ.

attend] to those notations that I wrote, but which a scribe has marked up with the lemniscus incorrectly (ܣܡܝܡ, or according to a variant reading ܣܝܡ, 'placed'), not putting them in the most suitable positions.[1]

I ask also that you pass on my love to that excellent saint whom I mentioned [i.e. Abba Julian], that he might learn what it is I want. I want him to take and copy down [the middle volume of the Homilies] for his own tranquility. Moreover, he is one there who knows what he is looking at rather more than anyone else who may come across the things that we have been speaking of.[2]

Finally (ܠܘܝܦܢ = λοιπὸν) may you, above all others who may happen upon the things that have been spoken of, [xxvii] be kept safe by the Lord, holy brother, while you yet pray for my poverty and seek God's grace for me. Amen."

Therefore, after the complaint at the beginning of the letter about the scribes, who he deems to be discharging their duty poorly in a noble and dignified enterprise, he then warns them that they must transcribe his books with great accuracy even where he deviates from normal usage. He enumerates these characteristic traits of his that he wants left unaltered:

1. He has written the Greek, Hebrew and Latin names as they properly ought to be, rather than in the customary way. Thus it should be ܦܝܠܝܦܘܣ and not ܦܠܝܦܘܣ. Even the letters Alaph, Waw and Yudh must be left as Jacob has written them.

2. |[47] Words derived from ܪܝܫܐ (head) should not be written without the yudh, nor should ܒܪܫܝܬ be written for ܒܪܝܫܝܬ.[3]

3. The words ܪܘܡܝܐ, ܪܘܡܝ, ܣܘܩܪܘܣ, ܦܐܪܪܣܝܐ and the like should be written without a ܗ, although this is contrary to traditional usage. Jacob Bar Šakko also refers to this (ܡܚ,8).

---

[1] According to the readings in Assemani, this should be translated: "which a scribe has placed incorrectly as if they had been placed in the upper margin, and not in the most suitable places." Here I propose a variant reading but I make no judgment as to its genuineness since it makes no difference for our purposes.

[2] Martin has ܕܗܘ ܐܠܗܘܢ, but I think it should be read as ܕܗܘ, ܐܠܗܘܢ. These words refer to another of Jacob's books.

[3] This usage does not seem to have been taken into account in BL Add. 12178 (the codex in which this letter is contained), since there Genesis begins with ܒܪܫܝܬ (Wright, *Cat.* I,108).

4. The particle of time ܗܝܕܝܢ, written as one word, is to be distinguished from ܗܘ̇ ܕܝܢ, which must be written separately and must have a point above it.

5. A distinction must be made between ܐܬܬܦܝܣ (rt. ܦܝܣ) and ܐܬܬܓܡܣ (spelt from the Greek).[1] xxviii

6. The words ܐܬܡܠ and ܡܢܬܡܠ should be written without a yudh at the end to distinguish them from derivations of the root ܡܠܐ. Jacob Bar Šakko refers to this as well (ܡܠ,10).

7. Bar Šakko also repeats what Jacob says about ܣܡ. He wants, for instance, ܪܚܡ ܣܡ to be written rather than ܪ̈ܚܣܡ so that it can be distinguished from ܪܚܣܡ. Again ܡܛܠܛܠܡܐ written as one word must be distinguished from ܡܛܠܛܠܡ ܐܢܐ.[2]

8. Finally he warns the scribes not to alter neologisms unknown to earlier writers, such as ܗܘܝܢܘܬܐ (*identity*), ܬܪܝܢܐ (*second*), ܕܝܠܝܬܐ (*a property*), ܕܝܠܝܘܬܐ (*peculiarity*).

Jacob was here simply instructing the scribes about whatever he could think of at the time, for he says that there were other matters that he also ought to warn them about, if only he could remember them all. After this, he warns them about the proper and accurate placing of the points, neither adding nor subtracting from them as they see fit.[3] This part does not deal with vowels as such but with one particular type of pointing, namely, those that differentiate homographs. This type of pointing, he says, is used "in this Mesopotamian writing, or [we should call it] Edessene, or even, to be precise, Syriac." These points are ܦܪ̈ܘܫܐ ܘܡܦܫܩܢܐ ܕܡܕܡ ܡܕܡ, i.e. "distinguishing and explanatory of various things."

Because there is a total silence here both about points that designate vowels and also about the use of Greek vowels (which we see developing

[1] Martin called the passage unclear. It should be understood as follows: "They should not write ܓ in ܐܬܬܦܝܣܬ or in words derived from the same root, because there is a distinction between ܐܬܬܓܡܣܬ ܐܢܐ ܥܡ ܐܢܫ (with ܓ) and ܦܟܕܬ ܦܝܣܬܗ ܘܐܬܬܦܝܣܬ ܕܐܡܪ ܠܗ, such that whatever is derived from ܦܝܣܬܐ, i.e. obedience, should not have a ܓ." In short, ܥܡ needs to be read for ܥܡ in the phrase ܐܢܐ ܕܐܬܠܗ ܥܡ ܦܝܣܬܐ. For the other being written with a ܓ, cf. Eusebius, *Theophania* (S. Lee, ed., *Eusebius on the Theophania* [London, 1842]) I, 49.

[2] The text is here corrupt, but the general sense is quite clear.

[3] This passage can be read in Wright, *Cat.* III, Plate VI.

gradually during Jacob's era)[1] |[48] we must conclude that neither of these systems of writing was being practiced by Jacob, a fact that his own *Grammar* itself bears out.

The precious fragments of this *Grammar* were discovered and published, together with Martin's annotations, by Wright and Neubauer.[2] It will be discussed in the next chapter. It is an especially important text for our research, for the simple reason that Jacob was the true founder of grammatical study of Syriac. In fact, he is the first name we have of someone who took the requisite care, necessary for accomplishing the monumental task of founding grammatical scholarship in any Semitic language. The Masoretic teachers (discussed in the last chapter) did indeed collect some material, but it was rather disparate and was more in the way of individual observations than anything systematic. The philosopher who translated Dionysius Thrax into Syriac tried to infuse his people with some grammatical notions, but nobody had written a *Grammar* as such. This is just what Jacob did and he is thus the original founder of Semitic grammar.

---

[1] Wright, *Cat.* I,38a,337b; III,Tab VI,VII. In Tab VII there are two examples, in which ī is expressed with the Greek iota, wholly alien to native custom. From this it follows that the scribe of this codex from the year 719, which contains Jacob's recension of the books of Samuel, was not yet accustomed to the later usage. We moreover agree with Martin who has traced the origin of the use of Greek vowels to the time when Greek names were themselves written in the margin, thereby causing Greek vowels to be added into the text on Syriac words.

[2] W. Wright, ed., *Fragments of the* ܬܘܪܨ ܡܡܠܠܐ ܣܘܪܝܝܐ *or Syriac Grammar of Jacob of Edessa. Edited from MSS. in the British Museum and the Bodleian Library* (London, 1871). Only fifty copies were printed for private circulation. A large part was edited in his *Cat.* III,1169 [the whole is reprinted in the current volume from Wright's private edition, Text 4].

---

[i] Now see O.J. Schrier, "Chronological Problems Concerning the Lives of Severus bar Mashqa, Athanasius of Balad, Julianus Romaya, Yoḥannan Saba, George of the Arabs and Jacob of Edessa," *Oriens Christianus* 75 (1991), 62-90. There has of course been a great deal written on Jacob since the current chapter. For recent scholarship and further bibliography, B.Ter Haar Romeny, ed., *Jacob of Edessa and the Syriac Culture of his Day*. Monographs of the Peshiṭta Institute 18 (Leiden, 2008), and G. Ibrahim and G. Kiraz, eds., *Studies on Jacob of Edessa* (Piscataway, NJ, 2010).

[ii] Merx is basing himself here wholly on Assemani, who attributes all these texts to Jacob because they appear together in the same ms (Vat. Syr. 158). In fact, only the *Categories* was translated by him. See the introduction to D. King, *The Earliest Translation of Aristotle's Categories in Syriac*. Aristoteles Semitico-Latinus 21. (Leiden, 2011), and H. Hugonnard-Roche, *La Logique d'Aristote*, esp. chs 1-2.

[iii] ΠΙΠΙ—the letters erroneously used in Greek manuscripts of the Old Testament to signify the divine name יהוה, which Aquila in his translation had transcribed in Hebrew. The Hebrew letters were misread by later scribes as the Greek letters ΠΙΠΙ. κατὰ φύσιν and κατὰ θέσιν, or 'by nature' and 'by rule/decision' represented the two schools of thought in Greek philosophy regarding the origins of language. Plato's dialogue the *Cratylus* is the most famous discussion of this debate which continued throughout antiquity.

[iv] See now A. Salvesen, 'Did Jacob of Edessa know Hebrew?' in A. Rapoport-Albert and G. Greenberg, *Biblical Hebrew, Biblical Texts. Essays in Memory of Michael P. Weitzmann* (Sheffield, 2001), 457-67.

[v] Many of these have since been edited—for details see J. J. Van Ginkel, 'Greetings to a Virtuous Man: The Correspondence of Jacob of Edessa,' in *Jacob of Edessa and the Syriac Culture of His Day*, 67-82.

[vi] For a detailed treatment, E. Wellesz, *A History of Byzantine Music and Hymnography* (2nd ed., Oxford, 1961), and relevant articles in the *New Grove Dictionary of Music and Musicians*.

[vii] Published in E.W. Brooks, *The Hymns of Severus and others in the Syriac Version of Paul of Edessa as revised by James of Edessa*. Patrologia Orientalis 6/1 (1909), 1-179; 7/5 (1911), 593-802.

[viii] This is found on f.74b (Wright, *Cat.* I,336).

[ix] In fact, it was not Jacob who replaced the Peshiṭta's ܣܒܪܐ ܛܒܐ with ܡܣܒܪܢܘܬܐ ܕܛܒܐ, but Thomas of Harkel who used it in his revision of the New Testament at Lk 2.14, published in c.616.

[x] All homilies now available with French translation, M. Brière and F. Graffion, eds., *Les Homiliae Cathedrales de Sévère d'Antioche; traduction syriaque de Jacques d'Edesse*. Patrologia Orientalis 4/1, 8/2, 12/1, 16/5, 20/2, 22/2, 23/1, 25/1, 25/4, 26/3, 29/1, 35/3, 36/1, 36/3, 36/4, 37/1, 38/2.

[xi] This technique of deriving new nouns from the Pael and Aphel forms of roots was actually common already well before Jacob's day and should not be disparaged as foolish usage. See esp. Sebastian Brock, "Diachronic Aspects of Syriac Word Formation : An Aid for Dating Anonymous Texts," in René Lavenant, ed., *V Symposium Syriacum* (Rome, 1990), 321-330; and *id.*, "Some Diachronic Features of Classical Syriac," in M.F.J. Baasten and W. Th van Peursen, eds., *Hamlet on a Hill : Semitic and Greek Studies Presented to Professor T. Muraoka* (Leuven, 2003), 95-111.

[xii] Pantera was the Roman legionary supposed to have been the father of Jesus, according to Jewish anti-Christian polemic—see Origen, *Contra Celsum*, 1,32.

[xiii] Much further research has since been carried out on these *Catena Severi*—see part IIIA to the bibliography in *Jacob of Edessa and the Syriac Culture of His Day.*

[xiv] See now W. Witakowski, "The Chronicle of Jacob of Edessa," in *Jacob of Edessa and the Syriac Culture of His Day*, 25-47, and further bibliography in the Clavis in the same volume.

[xv] In Jacob's letters 12 and 14. Peter and Timothy would not have been considered heretical by Jacob, however.

[xvi] Since Jacob moved from Eusebona to Tell ʿAdda, we can assume that by the former is meant the monastery near Apamea which was itself a satellite of Tell ʿAdda.

[xvii] The text is more easily accessed via R. Schröter, "Scholien des Bar-Hebraeus : zu Psalm III. IV. VI. VII. IX.-XV. XXIII. LIII., nebst dessen Vorrede zum Neuen Testamente," *ZDMG* 29 (1875), 247-303 (text of Jacob's comment to Ps 10 on p.262; also the comment on p.293). The term here translated as 'forever' is ܠܥܠܡ. Note also the discussion in antiquity on the matter, above all in Jerome, *Ep.28,5-7*. Jacob's solution is remarkably close to the conclusions of modern scholarship—see N.H. Snaith, "Selah," *Vetus Testamentum* 2 (1952), 43-56.

[xviii] A. Salvesen, *The Books of Samuel in the Syriac Version of Jacob of Edessa* (Leiden, 1999).

[xix] It is odd that Merx gives ܡܒܠܗ as the reading of the Peshiṭta. The only reading known to the Leiden edition of Isaiah is ܦܠܓܘܗ, the reading that Jacob accepted.

[xx] The Hebrew reads אַנְשֵׁי לָצוֹן, i.e. *men who scoff/mock*, a meaning which the Peshiṭta has retained. After the LXX's variant τεθλιμμένοι (*afflicted ones*), Aquila and Symmachus returned to the meaning of the Hebrew/Syriac and Jacob deliberately retains the Peshiṭta's word for the same reason.

[xxi] The term ܪܡܘܣ (which Merx has in the main citation of the verse) is not found in the Peshiṭta—it appears to be a glossed alternative for ܡܬܟܫܘܣ.

[xxii] Compare these brief comments with the results of A. Juckel, "Septuaginta and Peshiṭta. Jacob of Edessa quoting the Old Testament in Ms BL Add 17134," in *Hugoye: Journal of Syriac Studies* 8.2, 155-77.

[xxiii] See Merx's Corrigenda (p.viii) where he references Martin, *La Massore*, 115, which is not a correct reference. He could have mentioned other earlier work on Jacob's

Pentateuchal studies including, on the translation, A.I. Silvestre de Sacy, "Notice d'un manuscrit syriaque, contenant les livres de Moïse," *Notices et extraits des manuscrits de la Bibliothèque Nationale* 4 (1798-9), 648-668; and on the scholia, G. Phillips, *Scholia on Passages of the Old Testament by Mar Jacob Bishop of Edessa* (London 1864). See now D. Kruisheer, "Reconstructing Jacob of Edessa's Scholia," in J. Frishman & L. Van Rompay (eds.), *The Book of Genesis in Jewish and Oriental Christian Interpretation. A Collection of Essays*, Traditio Exegetica Graeca 5 (Louvain, 1997), 187-196. The latter scholar is working on a full edition of this valuable material (Romeny, *Jacob of Edessa*, 273).

[xxiv] The allusion is to BL Add. 17134 (Wright, *Cat.* I,330,338-9), which Wright believed to be an autograph of Jacob's.

[xxv] In addition to Martin's Syriac text of Jacob's Letter, Phillips in the very same year published the same text with an English translation, *A Letter by Mār Jacob, Bishop of Edessa on Syriac Orthography* etc. (London, 1869). The text may be found on p.ܟܒ-ܠܐ.

[xxvi] The lemniscus was a critical symbol used by Origen in his edition of the Septuagint (the fifth column), although its meaning is disputed. It may well have referred the reader to a note elsewhere which enumerated textual variants at that point (as per Field, *Hexapla*, lv). Epiphanius (*De Ponderibus*) tells us that it indicated a place where there were synonymous variants (Migne, *Patrologia Graeca* 43,248f.). The former seems the more likely usage here. The relevant passage from Epiphanius describing this and similar notations was extant in a Syriac version by at least the seventh century (J.E. Dean, *Epiphanius' Treatise on Weights and Measures, the Syriac Version* [Chicago, 1935], 22) which was known to the compilers of the Qarqaphensian Masorah (*ibid.*, 9) who were, as we have seen, a central part of the Syriac grammatical tradition and took their lead from Jacob of Edessa.

[xxvii] Merx's translation from the Syriac is not quite right here. Surely the words 'ceterum...sunt' belong with the foregoing paragraph, the closing remarks then starting with 'salvus'. This is how Phillips understands the text. We have also followed Nöldeke's point about the meaning here (Review, 1220).

[xxviii] The text as it stands is problematic, as Phillips's nonsensical translation and Martin's evident confusion amply attest. That Jacob was making a distinction between words for 'he obeyed' and 'he was requested' was a point already made by the lexicographer Ebdokus/Eudochos (Phillips, p.6n—Ebdokus [?Eudochos] is a little known author of ?12/13 cent. lexica (*GSL*, 294f., to whose list of mss, add St. Mark's 219 and Bib. Med. Laur. Or. 441. See J. Loopstra's forthcoming edition of the *Patristic Masora*, Ch3, n11). Ebdokus was used as an authority in Quatremère's lexicon which was an important base for Payne Smith's *Thesaurus*; whether Phillips had direct access to Quatremère's notes or to the Sachau mss, I cannot tell). Merx's slight textual alteration makes good sense. But ܦܝܣܬܐ means request, not obedience, and ܢܣܒܬ ܦܝܣܬܐ (*I have received a request*) looks very much like the explanation of ܐܬܬܦܝܣ. Maybe Jacob means: "I make a distinction between

on the one hand ܐܬܬܦܝܣܬ ܐܢܐ ܡܢ ܐܢܫ [*I am requested by someone*] and (the related) ܦܝܣܬ ܦܝܣܬܗ̇ [*I received a request*] and on the other, ܐܬܬܦܝܣܬ ܕܐܥܒܕ ܠܗ [*I am obedient to do it*]. So both in the case of ܦܝܣܬܐ and where the word means 'obedience' we should not use a ܓ̣." Since Jacob was rarely followed in this (see *Thes.*, 3116), we cannot be sure what he wanted to do.

Chapter 5

THE SYRIAC GRAMMAR OF JACOB OF EDESSA[i]

We have seen that Jacob was thoroughly learned in Greek literature. He could not help but draw on its legacy. The Greeks had cultivated the study of grammar to the point where they seem to have truly perfected the foundations of the whole subject—the rules of phonology, of the parts of speech, of inflexion, of analogy and anomaly, and of syntax.[1] Jacob translated into the East this Greek approach to treating the language, as is evidenced by the remains of his *Grammar*, both in terms of its general outline and many of its individual points.[ii]

Greek grammar used to begin, after some prolegomena, with an exposition of the basic sounds (τοῦ στοιχείου) and their |[49] classification. Jacob starts off his own attempt in just the same way and we can see at once that, in describing the Syriac language and vocabulary, he has compared everything with the Greek usage. Thus in the very first fragment, which certainly comes from the early part of the *Grammar*, he speaks about the defects of the Syriac script as compared with the Greek.

The Syrians[iii] had not been accustomed to writing vowels, a defect which Jacob deems on a par with the defects of the pre-classical Greek letters, for he asserts, relying on the authority of a certain grammarian, that there were once seventeen Greek letters.[2] The Greeks [according to Jacob] then gradually added to the number of letters, such that their script became complete and was able to express all the sounds (ܐܬܡܠܝܘ ܣܦܪܐ ܡܫܡܥܢܐ). "However," he continues, "since I know the reason why those men (the Syrian doctors are clearly meant) were themselves reticent to add further letters—namely so that all those books that have been written to date with

[1] If one wishes to understand what the Greek philosophical debate concerning analogy and anomaly brought to the study of grammar, one should read H. Steinthal, *Geschichte der Sprachwissenschaft bei den Griechen und Römern* (Berlin, 1863), 522. For out of this dispute over analogy and anomaly arose the custom of drawing up rules of inflection, from which eventually emerged the system of setting out the declensions and conjugations, which has been handed on to us and which we generally still use.

[2] The majority reckoned it as sixteen letters (Bekker, *Anecdota*, 780). So why then does Jacob make it seventeen? Cf. Bekker, *Anecdota*, 777.

this imperfect writing system might not perish—and since I want to preserve the work of my predecessors, I am in a great dilemma as to whether I should [satisfy] this petition of yours, [by which you seek from me that I should add vowel symbols to the Syriac letters in my own work.]"[1] On the other hand it has been suggested to me [i.e. to Jacob, the flow of ideas implies that Jacob wrote this part almost immediately after the foregoing] that I should make a description of the language itself according to firm rules, "so that sure (ܡܫܪ̈ܪܐ) rules for this language should be instituted without actually adding to the script the vowel symbols that it lacks, although with those symbols one can demonstrate the application of the rules, as well as the correct writing (ܬܘܪ̈ܨܐ) of nouns and verbs which results from those same rules. So because I am assailed from both sides—both by your request and also by the danger of destroying the older books, which was also what motivated my predecessors—I have come to the decision that, while I shall add (vowel) letters only on the basis of sense and the establishment of rules, so as to clarify matters of inflection and phonology,[2] and not for the sake of establishing a perfect script, I shall nevertheless fulfil your request because it is love that makes the demand and because it is written, 'to him that knows to do good, and does it not, to him it is sin.'"[3]

There are two points of real significance in all this:

1. Jacob did not devise his own symbols for indicating vowels for common usage and neither did he want them to be observed by everyone, but...

2. He devised them to illustrate the rules of inflexion for nouns and verbs, and to this end alone were they directed.[iv]

|[50] From all this I think we can safely conclude that neither the Greek forms of the vowels nor the vowel signs that consist of double points were in use in Jacob's day.[v] Furthermore it seems evident that Jacob did take over and use the Greek system of describing inflexions, known as 'canons', invented by the grammarian Theodosius.

---

[1] The lacuna ought clearly to be made good on the basis of Barhebraeus, *Gramm.*, 194. The square brackets mark the addenda.

[2] The expression ܒ̈ܢܬ ܩܠܐ, which we will see used in Jacob's treatise, means not *words* but *sounds*, which may appropriately be called the 'daughters of a word'.

[3] James 4.17.

We also ought to point out that Greek vowels were beginning here and there to be written in the manuscripts of Jacob's day, although there is no trace to be found of the double points. If Jacob had known of the latter, he would hardly have devised new signs, since the double points are so naturally suited to the Syriac script.

There is one other reason that prevents us from thinking that Jacob had any knowledge of the system of double points. What he himself introduced was quite different; he also included a sound that was unknown to that system. This can be shown from Barhebraeus, although the latter did not describe the matter very accurately and his text stands in need of correction on the basis of Jacob's fragments. For of the eight vowels which Barhebraeus gives (*Gramm.*, 3), *ā, ă, ē, ě, ī, ĭ, ū, o*, he says that one, *ě*, was rejected by Jacob and that another, *u* (i.e. the middle *u*), he introduced. But then, when he later (*Gramm.*, 194) lists the forms invented by Jacob he includes *ě* (ܪܒܨܐ) but omits the middle *u* (ܥܨܨܐ ܡܨܥܝܐ). In addition he does not mention *ā* (ܙܩܦܐ), which Jacob expressed with an alaph, perhaps because the alaph was not a new symbol. So if to the seven symbols described by Barhebraeus (*Gramm.*, 194: *ă, ē, ě, ī, ĭ, ū, o*) we add both alaph, as the sign of the vowel *ā*, and the ܥܨܨܐ ܡܨܥܝܐ then we arrive at nine for Jacob, although Barhebraeus had incorrectly said that he had mentioned only eight.[vi]

Moreover Barhebraeus included (*Gramm.*, 194) the ܪܒܨܐ ܟܪܝܐ *(ě)* which he earlier asserted that Jacob had rejected (*Gramm.*, 3), and we cannot conjecture that ܚܒܨܐ ܟܪܝܐ *(ĭ)* (a vowel which does not appear in the fragments) should be read instead of ܪܒܨܐ ܟܪܝܐ *(ě)*, for the vowel is not mentioned by Barhebraeus and the addition of the example ܐܢܫ proves it. So the vowels of the Edessene dialect as enumerated by Jacob must have been as follows:

1 ă ܦܬܚܐ
2 ā ܙܩܦܐ
3 ē ܪܒܨܐ ܐܪܝܟܐ
4 ě ܪܒܨܐ ܟܪܝܐ
5 ī ܚܒܨܐ ܐܪܝܟܐ
6 ĭ ܚܒܨܐ ܟܪܝܐ
7 ū ܥܨܨܐ ܐܪܝܟܐ
8 u? ܥܨܨܐ ܡܨܥܝܐ (actually ō)
9 o ܥܨܨܐ ܟܪܝܐ (actually ŏ)

Examples of the eighth[vii] vowel show that it was marked by the East Syrians with a point over the waw—such as in ܟܘܪܬܐ, ܕܘܟܬܐ, ܐܘܪܗܣ,|[51] ܣܘܪܬܐ. Thus this vowel must be [o].[1] The seventh is the *ū*, as the example of ܣܘܡ proves. What then is the ܥܨܨܐ ܦܬܝܐ?

Examples of this latter vowel are found in such words as ܣܦܘܓܐ = σπόγγος (*sponge*), ܐܛܪܘܓܐ = אֶטְרוֹגָא (*orange*), arabised as أُتْرُجّ, and in place-names such as ܗܡܘܓܐ and ܣܠܘܓܐ. Its form is ◌݁, the very form that Barhebraeus calls the ܥܨܨܐ ܐܠܝܨܐ, and which he seemed to have found in ܣܘܡ = ܣܘܡ. Although you would expect to find this same vowel (which is in the word ܣܘܡ) also in ܙܒܘܢܬܐ, ܡܘܬܐ, ܚܒܘܪܐ, the remains of the grammar actually claim the contrary, for these words are written with the (vowel) symbol ◌ܘ, which Barhebraeus called the ܥܨܨܐ ܦܬܝܐ. There is clearly some confusion in Barhebraeus here, which if not his own might be attributed to those who copied his work. For the symbol ◌ܘ is certainly not the ܥܨܨܐ ܦܬܝܐ, which in Jacob is indicated by ◌݁, while ◌ is omitted by Barhebraeus.[viii] Thus, once we have discarded the mistakes of Barhebraeus, to whom we owe the first full (if rather confused) treatment of this matter, what we are left with (on the basis of Jacob's fragments only) is as follows:

ܥܨܨܐ ܐܠܝܨܐ = ◌ܘ,[2] as in ܡܘܬܐ = ܡܘܬܐ (ū)
ܥܨܨܐ ܦܬܝܐ = ◌݁,[3] as in ܣܦܘܓܐ = ܣܦܘܓܐ (σπόγγος, ŏ)
ܥܨܨܐ ܡܨܥܝܐ = ◌,[4] as in ܙܒܘܢܬܐ = ܙܒܘܢܬܐ (ō, ω)

Once we have sorted out the sounds that belong to each kind of symbol, we can make a judgment also on their forms, for ◌ܘ (ū) is simply *oY* contracted, with the *Y* being placed sideways and the *o* added underneath. The ◌݁ is the Greek omicron placed above the line and joined onto the line. Finally I would venture to suggest that ◌ is simply a mutated ω. For this ω in the word ܐܘܪܗܝ Barhebraeus (*Gramm.*, 194) has used another symbol which in the text appended to this volume we have taken from the London codex Add. 7201 of Barhebraeus's *Book of Splendours*. Furthermore, the symbol ∇ (ܦܬܚܐ) is just an inverted α and ◌ is the iota. It is not so easy with the remaining symbols, although doubtless the symbol for ē (◌) is somehow

[1] Cf. Merx, *Grammatica Syriaca* (Halle, 1867), 38,48. On ܚܘܪܬܐ see *Bar ʿAlī* (G. Hoffmann, *Syrisch-Arabische Glossen* [Kiel, 1874], 4054). Lee expresses it with a point underneath, Gen 32.26.

[2] This symbol Barhebraeus calls ܥܨܨܐ ܦܬܝܐ.

[3] This symbol is the ܥܨܨܐ ܐܠܝܨܐ in Barhebraeus.

[4] This symbol Barhebraeus omits. On the equivalence of ◌ܘ, see Merx, *Grammatica syriaca*, 38,48.

related to E, ε, for it cannot have come from H on account of itacism.[ix] The nature of the various forms of ŏ,|[52] ū, and ō, of which we have been speaking will become clear further below, where we discuss the order of the classes of the noun.[x]

However, if it turns out that the double-points system or indeed the other system of using Greek vowels, were already well-developed before his day, then we cannot say that this nine-vowel system (with the vowels indicated by Greek letters placed on the line itself) was his own invention. Jacob's explicit purpose in developing his system was merely to explain the morphological canons; he explicitly forbad their general usage. Enough now on this subject.

After speaking about the problem of the vowels, Jacob goes straight on to discuss reading, the difficulty of which is not due (the flow of the text seems to require some such supplement here) to those (Syriac) consonants which the Greeks do not have (ܚ ܛ ܨ ܥ)—for any language will have sounds that others cannot manage—but the difficulty rather lies simply in the lack of written vowels.[xi]

> And as I said above, (the Syrians) are unable to read correctly save by the three systems aforementioned, namely:[1]
>
> 1) by intuition (ܡܪܓܫܐ), because common sense demands a particular reading of a given object however it may have been written (ܩܪܝܢܗ ܕܨܒܘܬܐ ܐܝܢܐ ܕܗܘ ܕܣܝܡ = ἀνάγνωσιν τοῦ πράγματος οὑτινοσοῦν τοῦ κειμένου);
>
> 2) by the tradition of others who have previously tried out the object and its possible readings and were thus able to pronounce the words correctly (?sounds) and hand them on to others. This did not derive from an accurate reading of the letters—for they do not possess such a thing—but rather they (i.e. the first ܡܩܕ̈ܡܝܐ) read according to the tradition of yet others before them;
>
> 3) by careful investigation (ܦܘܚܡܐ), for although they read cursorily and as if the sense of the words were directly obvious, in fact the points help them along and indicate different meanings,[2] so that they who receive (learn) are led to

[1] In Dionysius ἀναγνώσις is dealt with at the very beginning. So also Jacob discusses 'reading' before he gets on to the basics.

[2] The reference here is not to the double points. For when he says here that different senses and meanings of words are distinguished by points, he means merely that ܓܒܪܐ is

> understand not on the basis of the letters but of the sounds which proceed from the lips of the teacher.

I admit that it is not easy to distinguish the third method from the first two and I do not think that I am following him quite right here.

Up to this point he has been talking of the defects of the alphabet. He now moves on to discuss those consonants that are not pronounced, thereby anticipating the later doctrine of the 'hidden letters'. He offers as an example the nun in ܒܢܝܬܐ, which he says was added to distinguish it from ܒܝܬܐ.

|[53] He explains that many people, especially westerners, do not understand what these letters really mean, and they are for this reason unable correctly to read words written in this way. Even the Edessenes themselves have forgotten the pure form of the language and have followed a false reading tradition. This problem is particularly noticeable in foreign loan-words (Hebrew, Greek, Latin, Persian), and he tells us that he has written on this matter already, by which he probably means in his own prolegomena. We saw above that it was for the same reason that many before Jacob had been moved to invent new letters, although Jacob firmly rejected this approach. We can now understand why he was so keen in his letter to George to forbid the use of the letter *h* in R*h*umi, Syn*h*odos, parr*h*esia etc.

Dionysius Thrax, after dealing with the vowels, had spoken about the consonants, and this Jacob also did. He testifies elsewhere[xii] that, in the first book of his *Grammar*, he had discussed those letters which are opposed to each other which cannot be placed next to each other—these incompatibles are the 'thick' (ܥܒܝܬܐ = δασέα), the 'intermediate' (ܡܨܥܝܬܐ = μέσα) and the 'thin' (ܢܩܝܕܬܐ = ψιλά). This whole discussion is borrowed by Jacob Bar Šakko (ܫܟܘ). The nature of the Syriac language does not allow for these originally Greek sequences of consonants (φ χ θ / β γ δ / π κ τ) to be used unaltered, on account of the important and regular sound change regarding sibilants (by which the ܬ that is characteristic of reflexives becomes ܛ after ܨ, and ܕ after ܙ), for which the Greeks had not made any allowance.[xiii] It is no surprise that Jacob followed the Greek system yet further and subsumed the sibilants and the gutturals into the same three classes. He evidently considered himself an astute judge of phonology.

distinguished from ܚܒܪܐ and ܚܒܪܐ by means of a single point. He mentions this at the end of the letter to George. These points were added because the designation of the vowel letters was insufficient to the task.

There can be no doubt that Jacob Bar Šakko (*loc.cit.*) has drawn this same system directly from Jacob, as the next passage in the latter indicates. Jacob therefore arranged the consonants in the following manner:[xiv]

> The 'thick' or ܥܒ̈ܝܬܐ are ܒ ܓ ܕ ܪ ܟ.
> The 'intermediate' or ܡܨ̈ܥܝܬܐ are ܦ ܒ ܬ ܣ ܫ ܚ.
> The 'thin' or ܢܩ̈ܝܦܬܐ are ܝ ܦ ܓ ܨ ܩ.

Jacob of Edessa's rules as extracted from the fragments of his *Grammar* (Wright, ed., p.3a)[xv] are as follows: a thick before an intermediate becomes an intermediate, before a thin it becomes a thin. This is why, when the words ܪܘܓܬܐ, ܚܘܦܬܐ and ܪܘܓܕܬܐ (in which the thicks ܓ, ܕ, and the thin ܦ all precede the intermediate ܬ) are written according to the correct pronunciation, a ܟ will be used in place of the ܓ, a ܛ in place of the ܕ, and a ܟ in place of the ܦ. It seems certain that Jacob must have written these words as ܪܘܟܬܐ, ܚܘܟܬܐ, ܪܘܓܛܬܐ, although only the last of these actually appears in this form here in the manuscript. Either the manuscript has not been copied strictly according |[54] to Jacob's intentions or else it offered the latter reading in a passage which has now been cut out, for the beginning of the whole discussion is missing. What Jacob actually says is: "Because of this [i.e. the law just suggested] I have written the aforementioned words as the pronunciation (ܡܦܩܢܐ ܕܡܠܬܐ, lit. *the issue of the word*[1]) demands, since I have changed each letter into its cognate depending on which letter is placed next to each. Therefore in ܪܘܓܬܐ and ܚܘܦܬܐ, because a ܬ cannot come after a thick ܓ or a thin ܦ, ܬ itself being an intermediate, I have changed both the ܓ and the ܦ into ܟ, which like ܬ is an intermediate. In ܪܘܓܕܬܐ, which is derived from ܪܘܓܕܐ, and which naturally contains the ܕ, since ܬ does not admit a thick, I have changed the ܕ for a ܛ. A similar exchange of letters occurs also in many other words, especially in verbs, which I shall deal with separately later."

By chance the passage of Jacob extant in the fragments concerns only the mutation of the thick consonants. That the intermediates and the thins were discussed in like manner not only follows from common sense but is made clear by Jacob Bar Šakko (as already mentioned, p.ܓܝ). This method is not completely omitted by later grammarians, although in Barhebraeus, who discusses the matter extensively, one seeks in vain for the use of the

---

[1] The Arabs call the place where the required consonant is formed the مخرج (maḫraj; *outcome, articulation*).

terms ܟܪ̈ܝܬܐ, ܢܓܝܪ̈ܬܐ, and ܡܨ̈ܥܝܬܐ. Jacob has retained them, but Barhebraeus was more concerned with the Arabic tradition and so left them out. Barhebraeus reckons at fourteen the number of positions of the mouth from which sounds can be emitted and he identifies seventeen, or at least sixteen, consonant groups.[1] The whole of his grammar, which is marked by the confluence of Greek and Arabic theories, is most especially typified in this description. Those that are traceable to Greek thinking we have translated below into Greek, those that draw on Arabic are expressed in Arabic:

He distinguishes between:

ܡܩܠܝܬܐ = φωνήεντα (*vowels*)

ܠܐ ܡܩܠܝܬܐ = ἄφωνα (*un-vowelled*), or more accurately σύμφωνα (*consonants*).

The Arabic terms follow these Greek distinctions

ܓܓܪ̈ܘܢܝܬܐ (*guttural*) = الحلقية

ܡܫܪ̈ܘܩܝܬܐ (*sibilant*) = حروف الصفير [2]

|55 ܩܫ̈ܝܬܐ (*strong*)

ܡܚ̈ܝܠܬܐ (*weak*). These latter two seem to be the same as the next two.

ܩܫ̈ܝܐ (*strong*) = شديد محض

ܪ̈ܦܝܐ (*weak*) = رخو محض

ܡܨ̈ܥܝܬܐ (*intermediates*) = بين الشديد والرخو

ܚܒ̈ܝܫܬܐ (*closed*) = مطبقة

ܦܬܝܚܬܐ (*open*) = منفتحة

ܥܠ̈ܝܬܐ (*upper*) = مستعلية

ܬܚ̈ܬܝܬܐ (*lower*) = مستفلة

ܡܩܩ̈ܢܝܬܐ (*loud*) = حروف القلقلة

ܫ̈ܠܝܬܐ (*quiet*)

---

[1] I say sixteen because the last two groups, ܪ̈ܚܡܬܐ and ܣ̈ܢܝܬܐ, i.e. the ones that love and the ones that hate, are in reality a single group of compatibles and incompatibles. On Greek orthoepy, see P. Egenolff, *Anonymi Grammaticae Epitoma I* (Berlin, 1877), 7-11.

[2] He shows that these sibilants are made between 'the head of the tongue and the front teeth,' giving as an example the Arabic word اسلية.

ܪ̈ܚܡܬܐ (*allies*) = compatibles
ܣ̈ܢܐܐ (*enemies*) = incompatibles

Barhebraeus's groups, then, agree with the Arabic ones listed by de Sacy,[1] and these are unrelated to the system found in Jacob. Besides, although Barhebraeus relates that Jacob was the first to introduce points for indicating Quššāyā and Rukkāḵā,[2] it is evident that his system was adapted from the Greek to the norms of Syriac. Thus the consonants ܒ݁ ܟ݁ ܕ݁ ܓ݁ ܦ݁ ܬ݁ are not considered the 'thick' forms of the letters ܒ݂ ܟ݂ ܕ݂ ܓ݂ ܦ݂ ܬ݂, but rather as 'thin' while it is the latter group that are termed 'thick', even though the Greeks called χ φ θ δασέα (thick) and never used the term 'thin' for them. He also added the Greek π to the Syriac alphabet, resulting in the following classification according to Jacob:

ܥܒ̈ܝܬܐ (*thicks*) = δασέα: ܒ, ܟ, ܕ, ܐ, ܓ
ܡܨ̈ܥܝܬܐ (*intermediates*) = μέσα: ܦ, ܒ, ܬ, ܣ, ܫ, ܝ
ܢ̈ܩܝܕܐ (*thins*) = ψιλά: π [3], ܨ, ܓ, ܙ, ܗ
ܡܥܫ̈ܢܬܐ (*strongs*) = ܒ݂, ܟ݂, ܕ݂, ܓ݂, ܦ݂, ܬ݂
ܡܪ̈ܟܟܬܐ (*weaks*) = ܒ݁, ܟ݁, ܕ݁, ܓ݁, ܦ݁, ܬ݁

The groups ܐ ܘ ܝ and ܠ ܡ ܢ ܪ are lacking in this system. I would hazard a guess that Jacob called the latter group 'liquids' and the former the 'absorbed letters' (ܐܬܘ̈ܬܐ ܡܬܒ̈ܠܥܢ), which Jacob Bar Šakko also mentions.[4] [xvi]

|[56] After dealing with the letters, Greek grammars moved on to syllables and Jacob appears to follow the same sequence. He calls the syllable ܢܣܒܐ, because [the Greek term] is formed from λαμβάνειν = ܢܣܒ. Later grammarians do not use the word, for the theory of the syllable is very much neglected by the grammarians of Semitic languages. The Arabs have no word for the syllable as such, the term هجا (*haǧa*) meaning to give a

---

[1] S. de Sacy, *Grammaire arabe* (1st ed. Paris, 1810) I, §55 f.

[2] *Gramm.*, 194.

[3] See Merx, *Grammatica Syriaca*, 13.

[4] Bar Šakko, ܟܡ. Even if Jacob somewhat altered the Greek classification according to the characteristics of his own language, he was doing the same thing as the Armenian translator of Dionysius Thrax's Grammar, who organsied the Armenian phones, more numerous than the Greek, according to the Greek groupings. Cf. Cierbied, *Grammaire de Denys de Thrace publiée en Grec, en Arménian et en Français* (Paris 1830), 15.

consonant together with its following vowel; the Syriac ܗܓܝܐ is the means of pronouncing a consonant along with its vowel, while ܡܗܓܝܢܐ is the small line that indicates that a vowel needs to be added to a consonant. The verb ܗܓܝ has the same meaning as ܐܙܝܥ (i.e. *to cause to move*), which corresponds closely to the Arabic حرّك (*ḥarraka*), just as vice versa the term ܫܠܝܐ designates an utterance without a vowel, corresponding to the Arabic سكون (*sukûn*), which means silence. For Jacob himself, ܗܓܝܐ means simply 'pronunciation,' a 'way of pronouncing,' or even just a 'reading'.[1] He says, for example, that the letters of the tetragrammaton in the sacred name are *y* and *h*, ܗܠܝܢ ܕܝܢ ܬܪ̈ܬܝܗܝܢ ܐܚܝܕܢ ܡܬܬܣܝܡܢ ܗܘܝܢ ܟܕ ܗܘܝܢ ܚܕܐ ܒܬܪ ܚܕܐ ܡܫܬܘܬܦܢ ܒܡܦܩܢܗܝܢ ܠܫܡܐ ܗܘ ܡܝܩܪܐ etc. (*when they are both placed together one after the other they combine in their pronunciation [to produce] that majestic name*).[2] In another place ܗܓܝܐ means 'reading' as opposed to 'writing' (ܡܟܬܒܢܘܬ).[3] But if ܗܓܝܐ appears to mean 'syllable' in Barhebraeus, we must compare it with the Arabic حركات, 'movements' or 'vowels', for in reality the shortest syllables (ܦܣ̈ܩܬܐ) are not given the name ܗܓ̈ܝܐ, but rather only those syllables that are marked with written vowels.

As we noted, Jacob takes the word συλλαβή (*syllable*) and renders it in Syriac as ܦܣܩܬܐ, a term that Jacob Bar Šakko also borrows from him.[4] He does not, however, distinguish between the μακράν, βραχεῖαν, and κοινὴν (*long, short, common*) as in the Greek system,[xvii] as these would have no sense in Syriac. Instead he says that the syllable can be either 'simple' (ܦܫܝܛܐ), 'compound' (ܡܪܟܒܐ), or 'double' (ܟܦܝܠܐ). The 'simple' syllable is one that is constituted from a consonant + short vowel; the 'compound' from a consonant + long vowel; the 'double' from consonant + vowel + consonant.[xviii] It makes no difference whether the syllable begins with one consonant or two. In the word ܡܫܘ̇ܚܬܐ the first syllable, ܡܫ̈, is an example of a 'simple' syllable, while the ܘ̇ is a 'compound'; The 'double' is found, for example, in ܣܢܝܬܐ from ܣܢܝ̈ܬܐ, and doubtless also in ܡܒܝ̈ܬܐ.[xix] But why is it that Jacob carefully investigates the notion of the 'syllable' and its various sub-types while this field was ignored by all his successors in Syriac grammar? [xx]

---

[1] Thomas the Deacon (Martin, *Ad Georgium*, p.12) retains the Greek term συλλαβή; where he speaks of ܕܚܘܣܪܢܐ ܗܓ̈ܝܐ (see the penultimate line of p.12) it is the lack of vowels that he is dealing with.

[2] E. Nestle, op.cit., *ZDMG* 32, p.491, l.5.

[3] Lagarde, *Reliquiae iuris ecclesiastici*, 140,19.

[4] Bar Šakko, ܡܘ,11.

The answer to this is to be found in the surviving fragments on |[57] noun inflection. It was impossible to compose a list of these and to describe their inflections without first taking a look at the syllables. The subscription to this section reveals just which text he was following when he defined his list of masculine nouns, for after the 47th type of masculine noun he says: ܫܠܡܘ ܩܢܘܢܐ ܕܫܡܗܐ ܦܫܝܛܐ ܕܕܟܪܐ ܡܬܘܡܝܐ ܐܦ ܕܬܘܪܝܐ ܣܛܪ ܡܢ ܥܠܬܢܝܐ, which expressed in Greek would be: *The end of the canons of the simple masculine nouns, both the primary and the derived, but without the causals.*[xxi] The Syriac version of Dionysius acts as a commentary on this. Where Dionysius discusses the 'shapes' (σχήματα) of the noun, the translator uses the term ܦܫܝܛܐ for ἁπλοῦν (*simple*), and ܡܪܟܒܐ for σύνθετον (*compound*); the two 'species' (εἴδη) of the noun he calls ܛܘܦܣܐ ܩܕܡܝܐ, for πρωτότυπον (*prototype/primary*), and ܕܡܢ ܛܘܦܣܐ ܩܕܡܝܐ ܡܬܠܩܛ, for παραγώγον (*derived*). This explains Jacob's expression ܫܡܗܐ ܩܕܡܝܐ (*basic nouns* or *primary nouns*) and one can easily proceed to equate ܬܘܪܝܐ with the second species, *derived nouns*, even though I cannot find any parallel for this expression elsewhere.[xxii] Now since the ܥܠܬܢܝܐ (i.e. adjectives that end in -ānā and -āyā) are included with the derived nouns in the Syriac Dionysius and are in this passage assigned to the ܬܘܪܝܐ, there can be no doubt that we have understood the word correctly.[1] If this is indeed what is happening, then Jacob must have dealt with all Dionysius's divisions of the noun—genders, species, numbers, and shapes, and although there is no mention of cases, I cannot believe that he would have left this out of his grammar since his successors included it.[2]

After offering this generalised description of the noun according to the Greek system, he lays down the specific forms of nouns by their specific types. The concept of the syllable was a prerequisite for establishing these accurately. In this he follows the lead of Theodosius, who in his distribution of noun forms always has a particular consideration for the system of syllables. If, therefore, we are to understand this matter correctly, we must first take a look at the character of this Theodosian system, which encompassed the whole noun inflection.

---

[1] Rightly then did Barhebraeus add, when he was speaking of 'domestication' (*Gramm.*, 16): "These εἴδη (to which the derivation of the 'domestication' adjectives pertain) the holy Jacob called σχήματα, whereas the σχήματα (i.e. the simple and the compound) he called εἴδη. But there is no need to adhere to the exact words." Barhebraeus thus saw that Jacob had deviated a little from the Greek.

[2] Bar Šakko, p.17,6.

A rational system for classifying all these different forms was the most urgent need. For Theodosius, the threefold notion of gender offered such a system, but since Syriac has no neuter Jacob classified them only into masculines and feminines. After this basic start, Theodosius further subclassified the nouns within each gender according to their final syllable, looking primarily to the penultimate vowel and then to the total number of syllables.

If in the same class, e.g. in the class which included the masculine nouns ending in -ης, he found more syllables in the genitive than in the nominative, then these nouns would come first and be called |[58] περιττοσυλλαβοῦντα (i.e. *having more syllables*), while those that had the same number of syllables in both cases, called ἰσοσυλλαβοῦντα (*iso-syllabic*), would follow afterwards. In this way the first class of masculine nouns is that of Αἴας, Αἴαντος (both *disyllabic* and *having more syllables*). Then came κοχλίας, κοχλίου (both *trisyllabic* and *iso-syllabic*), followed by Λάχης, Λάχητος (*disyllabic* and *having more syllables*); then Χρύσης, Χρύσου (*disyllabic* and *iso-syllabic*); and finally Δημοσθένης, Δημοσθένους (*of more than two syllables* and being *iso-syllabic*).[xxiii]

Following these words in –ας and –ης came the nouns in ις, εις, ευς, υς, ους, ως, in which vowels of the second order are found before the final ς. After this, words in λς and νς, in which consonants precede the final ς. After those in ς come those in ν in the following order: αν, ην, ιν, υν, ων; then the nouns in ξ: αξ, ηξ, ιξ, υξ, ωξ; then those in ρ: ηρ, ωρ; finally those in ψ such as Κύκλωψ.[1] However, Theodosius did not deal in like manner with the monosyllables, although these should theoretically have come first of all. Choeroboscos excuses him on this point, saying: "You should understand that Theodosius said nothing along these same lines concerning the monosyllables, both because the discussion was only meant as prolegomena, and also with an eye to brevity."[2] [xxiv] This omission of Theodosius's was not, then, found acceptable by his successors, and so I think I am justified in positing that Jacob also must have begun with the monosyllabic nouns. What now requires proof is that Jacob composed his own lists according to the Theodosian system in which the number of syllables was the point of greatest significance.

In following Theodosius, Jacob organised nouns into two classes according to gender, dealing with the masculines in 45 types (excepting

[1] It seems that the more obscure Greek classifications have been here omitted.

[2] T. Gaisford, ed., *Georgii Choerobosci Dictata in Theodosii Canones* (Oxford 1842), 15,20-2.

the ܥܠܬܢܝ̈ܐ, or causals) and the feminines in more than 29. There were 83 types of disyllabic noun—hence we can see that he too took syllables into consideration.

Whenever among the fragments we have a lengthy extant sequence of types, their order can be seen to follow that of the vowels,[1] in the same order in which they come in the Greek alphabet: α, ε, ι, ο, ου, ω. The series of types for the feminine nouns makes this point quite clear:

Type 18: ܦܪ̈ܛܐ, ܦܪ̈ܙܐ α.
Type 19: ܡܫܚ̈ܬܐ, ܦܪ̈ܙܐ ε.
Type 20: ܚܟܡ̈ܬܐ, ܕܟ̈ܬܐ ι.
Type 21: ܐܣܢ̈ܝܬܐ, properly ܐܣܢ̈ܛܝܬܐ ι.[2] xxv
|59 Type 22: ܣܦܘܓܐ (σπόγγος) ο.
Type 23: ܕܒܘܬܐ, where ܘ = ου.
Type 24: ܚܪܘܬܐ, where ܘ = ܘ = ō = ω.

The same order crops up again at the very end of the fragments. For after type 28, which is defined by nouns in ‘e’ (such as φλέγμα), appears type 29 containing words formed with long ‘i’ such as ܪܕܝܦܐ, composed of two compound syllables. Even the word ܦܫܝܦܫܐ (*pši-fšā, a bug*)[3] belongs to this type, being as it is composed of two compound syllables. Next—although there may be another type which comes in between—further words are given which are made of two compound syllables of which the first is a

[1] The final ā of the emphatic state is left out. Bar Šakko, ܥܒ,4, calls it the alaph of completion.

[2] This type contains only this word, which is composed of a single syllable compounded with a double syllable (ܥܦܝܦܐ). It is from this that I conclude that by ‘compound syllable’ he means one that is made up of a consonant and a long vowel, and that a ‘double syllable’ is one made from consonant + vowel + consonant. It follows then that the ‘simple syllable’ is one made from a consonant (or two consonants) and a short vowel. Certainly the first syllable in the plural of the word ܡܫܚܬܐ is called ‘simple’ (p.6a, l.8). Now since the plural form is ܡܫܚ̈ܬܐ we see that the matter is confirmed. Syllables with the shortest of all vowels (shewa) are not counted, such that words like ܪܕܝܦܐ should be divided as *rḏī-pā*, *ṭrī-ḏā* etc. The beginning does not count, and *rḏī* and *ṭrī*, with their double consonants, are treated just the same as *pā* and *ḏā*—i.e. as compound syllables.

[3] W. Cureton, ed., *The Third Part of the Ecclesiastical History of John of Ephesus* (Oxford, 1853), 71, l.16.

short ‘o’ as in ܕܠܘܚܝܐ (*dlo-ḥyā*), ܡܣܘܪܩܐ (*mso-rqā*), ܓܠܘܣܩܐ (*glo-sqā*).[1] After this type he provides the feminine nouns that have ܘ̈ = ω, such as ܕܒܘܪܬܐ and ܚܡܘܪܬܐ. So here again he observed the same order: *e, i, ŏ, ō*, i.e. the order of the Greek vowels, which was also, as we saw, the way in which the Greek nouns were ordered.

When we earlier dealt with the vowel symbols and discussed the question of which sounds were represented by each of the three symbols ܘ̇ ܘ̣ ܘ̈ we said that a further reason to believe that ܘ̇ = o, ܘ̣ = ου, and ܘ̈ = ω would be forthcoming later.[xxvi] We can now see this in the agreement of the order of the noun classes. Now that we have seen that the distribution of the classes in Jacob is just the same as that found in Theodosius, and since the symbol ܘ̇ in the word ܣܦܘܓܐ (=σπόγγος) must be o, which is then followed by (Syr) u = (Gk) ου in type 23 and then (Syr) ō = (Gk) ω in type 24, there seems no doubt that we must have been right in matching the symbols with their sounds as we did.

There is one final piece of evidence that demonstrates that Jacob did indeed adopt Theodosius’s method, namely the expression he employs wherever exceptions to his typology are required. In such situations, he usually says: ܪܫܝܡܝܢ or ܪܫܝܡܐ ܠܟ etc., i.e. *let this be noted down*, or *let this be noted by you*. Thus for instance on p.5a (Wright) he explains that feminine nouns of the form ܓܡܠܬܐ, which derive from masculine disyllabic nouns of a simple syllable (with ă) + a compound syllable, such as ܓܡܠܐ, have a plural in the form ܓܡ̈ܠܬܐ; he then continues: ܪܫܝܡܐ ܕܝܢ ܐܠܐ ܠܟ ܦܣܠܬܐ ܦܬ̈ܠܬܐ ܦܣ̈ܠܬܐ ܦܬ̈ܠܬܐ, i.e. *This you should note down* ܦܣܠܬܐ ܦܬ̈ܠܬܐ *etc.* |60 (because according to the type it should be ܦܬ̈ܠܬܐ). The same expression occurs again at p.5b. It is surely a direct translation of the Greek σεσημείωται, which is used in just this sense by both Theodosius and his commentator Choeroboscos.[2] It thus derived from Theodosius as a technical school term.

Of the canons of the masculine nouns only the very last one is extant (namely, the 47th), which includes tetrasyllabic nouns. Since this is the last, we can be sure that he did not have another section on pentasyllabic

---

[1] Bar ʿAlī gives the vocalisation as ܡܘܣܘܪܩܐ (i.e. masorqa). A. Kohut believes that in ܓܠܘܣܩܐ is hidden the Greek κόλλιξ (see his edition of the Lexicon *Sefer ʾArukh ha-shalem* [Israel, 1878-92], s.v. גלוסק). Finally ܕܠܘܚܝܐ was written by the East Syrians with a waw with a point above (ܘ̇).

[2] By way of example, Bekker *Anecdota*, 977,25: σεσημείωται το Πικίας Πικίαντος, which ought to be formed according to the κοχλίας, κοχλίου type, but does not conform to the rule.

masculine nouns. He does, however, separate out from these the ܥܠ̈ܬܢܝܐ, i.e. the qualitative adjectives in *-ānā*, *-āyā*, and *-ānāyā*, and gives different rules for them. They belong to the ܐܬܪ̈ܝܐ, (παράγωγα, *derived nouns*, cf. p.57), which is taken from Dionyius, although the term ܥܠ̈ܬܢܝܐ (*causals*) was invented and used by the Syrians themselves on the reasoning that a basic substantive (e.g. 'earth') is defined as the cause of a secondary one (e.g. 'earthly'). They did not mean that the latter is 'caused' merely on account of that which caused it (e.g. 'earthly' from 'earth'), but rather it is used for certain nouns which derive from (are caused by) such adjectives, as a man can be said to be 'earthly'.[1] This relationship between adjective and prototype noun was called by later authors ܡܬܒܝܬܢܘܬܐ, translated by Amira as 'domestication', which he says is the same thing as 'species' (εἶδος), which is indeed what Dionysius says when speaking of this same relationship.[xxvii] Later on, however, this term ܡܬܒܝܬܢܘܬܐ was understood rather as it is in Arabic grammar, where it is simply the word النِّسْبَة (*denominative noun*) translated into Syriac, and so we owe it to the arabising school of Syriac grammarians. Jacob's doctrine itself filtered down to all the later Syriac grammarians, for whom lengthy digressions on this topic are commonplace.

What we have seen so far of the inner characteristics of this valuable text, in which Jacob became the very first to describe any Semitic language, it has been possible to work almost entirely from the fragments that have been preserved. We can deduce various things beyond this. We learn from a passage on p.3b, where he speaks about the mutation of the mute consonants (thick, intermediate, thin) in verbs, that after finishing the nouns he must have gone on to the subject of the verb, as was the case in the Greek models. The same passage also suggests that Jacob counted three main tenses, according to the Greek norm as worked out by the translator of Dionysius. He recalls that former writers saw the present tense (ܙܒܢܐ ܩܐܡ = ἐνεστώς) as being equivalent to the [Syriac] participle. He even makes a note of the passive (ܡ̈ܠܐ ܚܫܘܫܐ) so he must have maintained a distinction between the active and passive voices.[2] He did, however, depart from the older masters in one respect, for instead of calling verbs ܡܡܠ̈ܠܐ, as the translator of Dionysius had done, he uses the word that became universal later on, namely ܡ̈ܠܐ (cf. above p.9).

---

[1] Jacob of Edessa, *Grammar*, 3b (Wright's page nos., see Appendix)

[2] However, we cannot work out from this evidence whether he also recognised the middle voice. Later grammarians did not use the notion of a passive. Cf. below, ch.9.

|[61] It is much to be regretted that so much of Jacob's work is lost to us. It was so exhaustive that none of his successors dared to deviate from the system he instituted. Both Jacob Bar Šakko and Barhebraeus followed in his footsteps, even where they do not acknowledge his name. This fact can be shown by a few clear examples.

For instance, when Barhebraeus is dealing with the plurals of nouns, he lists them according to the number of syllables while ignoring gender.[1] Not so Jacob, for whom gender was important; but where Jacob's classes can be compared with Barhebraeus's list, one can see that the order is the same in both. Barhebraeus was still taking the material for his own book from Jacob. The following series of feminine nouns puts this point beyond dispute.

Jacob Type 18 ܦܘܪܬܐ, ܚܕܬܬܐ, ܐܦܬܐ = Barhebraeus, *Gramm.*, 31,22; 32,4.
Type 19 ܡܚܝܠܐ = 32,5.
Type 20 ܟܚܡܠܬܐ = 33,14
Type 21 ܐܣܪܬܐ = 33,18.
Type 22 ܣܘܣܠܐ = 33,20.
Type 23 ܕܡܘܬܐ = 33,21.

[1] Barhebraeus treats the nouns according to these Greek categories: i) gender; ii) form; iii) shape; iv) number; 5) quality; 6) case. The 'qualities' which Barhebraeus mentions are the senses of active, passive, and with a possessive—qualities which Amira also included in his grammar (G. Amira, *Grammatica Syriaca sive chaldaica* [Rome, 1596], 115). This theory is taken from the end of Dionysius's treatment of the noun, where we find the following: τοῦ δὲ ὀνόματος διαθέσεις εἰσι δύο, ἐνέργεια (= ܡܥܒܕܢܘܬܐ) καὶ πάθος (= ܚܫܘܫܘܬܐ), ἐνέργεια ὥς κριτὴς ὅ κρίνων, πάθος δὲ, ὡς κριτὸς ὁ κρινόμενος (*There are two 'voices' of the noun, active and passive, active being such as 'the judge judging', passive being such as 'the judge being judged'*). This is clearly done on the analogy of the verb, to which a third διάθεσις ('voice') is added (i.e. the μεσότης, 'middle'). We find this third voice again in Barhebraeus's description of noun types, in which he assigns to it those nouns that signify a 'quality', such as 'intelligence' or 'purity'. This theory of quality is not original. The first inklings of it come from Dionysius, though it became common only in the schools. For instance, we read in the scholia (Bekker, *Anecdota*, 880): εἰ ἄρα τὰ ὀνόματα ἔχουσι διαθέσεις, διὰ τί [μὴ] λέγομεν ἕξ παρέπεσθαι τῷ ὀνόματι, οἷον εἴδη, γένη, σχήματα, ἀριθμοὶ, πτώσεις, διαθέσεις; (*if nouns have voice, surely we should say that the noun has six attributes [not five, as in Dionysius], namely species, gender, shape, number, case, voice?*). Barhebraeus did indeed follow this route (*Gramm.*, p.36,40), in imitation of the Greek schools, and he elsewhere connects it to the Arabic classification.

Type 23a ܙܟܘܬܐ = 33,21.
Type 24 lacking (î in the first syllable) = 33,23 ܗܝܡܢܘܬܐ.
Type 25 lacking (u in the first syllable) = 33,24 ܐܘܪܚܐ.
Type 26 lacking (u in first syllable + fem. ܬ) = 33,25 ܐܘܣܝܬܐ.
Type 27 lacking (a in second syllable + fem. ܬ) = 33,26 ܚܠܡܬܐ.
Type 28 ܦܬܓܡܐ (e in second syllable) = 33,10.
Type 29 ܐܘܪܝܬܐ = 34,1 ܡܕܝܢܬܐ.
Type 30 ܟܠܘܡܣܐ = 34,3 ܟܠܘܡܣܐ.
Type 31 ܕܟܘܪܐ / ܕܟܘܪܬܐ = 34,3 ܡܣܘܟܬܐ / ܡܣܘܢܬܐ and others.

|[62] Wherever we know what Jacob's rules were, we can see that Barhebraeus is following them. Where these rules are not extant, we can still discern Jacob's system in Barhebraeus's lists. It is clearly very unlikely that this should only be the case in places where we are able to make a direct comparison of the two, and so our opinion that the whole structure of Jacob's work was adopted by Barhebraeus cannot be far from the truth.

[i] Some important recent studies of Jacob's *Grammar* must be read alongside Merx, viz. Revell, *Grammar*, and Talmon, *Jacob of Edessa*. Talmon follows Revell in reconstructing the fragments in a different sequence from that in Wright/Merx's edition. The new sequence is adopted in this new edition.

[ii] There has been a great deal of work on the Greek grammatical tradition in recent years. A good entry point to this important field can be found in the relevant articles in chapter XI of S. Auroux et al., eds. *History of the Language Sciences I* (Berlin, 2000); also the various collections co-edited by P. Swiggers and A. Wouters, including *Le Langage dans l'Antiquité* (Leuven, 1990), *Ancient Grammar: Content and Context* (Leuven, 1996), and *Grammatical Theory and Philosophy of Language in Antiquity* (Leuven, 2002).

[iii] The following paragraph (part quotation, part paraphrase) is based upon the first fragments of the text of Jacob's *Grammar*, p.ܟܕ,7 - ܟܘ,10.

[iv] Modern discussions of Jacob's vowel-system include Segal, *Diacritical Point*, 40-44, and Talmon, *Jacob of Edessa*, 164-6.

[v] For the system of double-points, Segal, *Diacritical Point*, 26ff., who finds this system already in place in the seventh century (Merx partly concedes this in the following paragraph). The Greek forms are described by Segal, 44ff., though he does not hazard a guess as to the time of their introduction.

[vi] Nöldeke (Review, 1216) does not dismiss Barhebraeus so lightly here and doubts the wisdom of being precise about long and short vowels.

[vii] Merx says 'ninth' but this must be a mistake.

[viii] On these problems in Barhebraeus, compare the discussion of the same issue in Segal, *Diacritical Points*, p.43, n.1.

[ix] 'Itacism': in the Greek of Jacob's day the letter *H* (eta) was pronounced like an *i*, rather than any variety of *e*. Hence his symbol for an 'e' vowel could not have been derived from the Greek letter eta.

[x] The reconstruction of Jacob's vowel system is especially difficult given the lack of detail in the extant fragments and the errors of interpretation made by Barhebraeus. Merx relies heavily on the supposed debt to the Greek *Canons* of Theodosius. The foregoing section of Merx must be read together with Segal and Talmon, as n.iv above.

[xi] The following quotation is Merx's translation from Jacob's Grammar, p.ܟܗ, l.24.

[xii] Ibid. p.ܟܫ, l.1.

[xiii] See Dionysius Thrax, ch.VI. The point here is that the Greek system organised these nine consonants into these three groups (thick, intermediate, thin) in order to account for sound changes that occur in the Greek language, such as ἐφατ' to ἐφαθ' before a rough breathing. These rules are of course insufficient to explain consonant changes in Syriac.

[xiv] It will be readily seen that Jacob inverts the Greek classification. In the latter the voiced stops (β γ δ) are the 'intermediates,' whereas in Jacob they are 'thicks' and the

---

voiceless stops (π κ τ) become Jacob's intermediates. The phonological reasons for this are explained in Revell, *Grammar*, 367-8, who uses it as evidence for Jacob's independence from his grammatical sources. However, as we shall see also in the case of early Syriac pointing, others prefer to continue following Merx against his revisers, with Talmon, *Jacob of Edessa*, 168-9, suggesting that Revell's reinterpretation of this passage is slightly misguided. Cf. Farina, *La linguistque syriaque*, 181f.

[xv] The page numbering of Wright's edition of Jacob is preserved in the version in the present volume.

[xvi] I have made the English terminology harmonise with that of Gottheil who calls these 'absorbed' in his translation of Elias of Nisibis's *Grammar* , 37. The ܐܬܘ̈ܬܐ ܕܡܬܠܗܡ̈ܢ, on the other hand, are the 'assimilated letters' (*ibid.*, 38).

[xvii] See Dionysius Thrax, chs. VII-X.

[xviii] This interpretation of what Jacob means by the terms 'simple, compound, double' is rejected by Moberg, *Buch der Strahlen*, I,103-4*, and replaced by one in which the terms mean respectively CV, CCV, CCCV, the definition of the syllable thus being that which closes with a vowel. Merx's reading is partly based on a misinterpretation of Jacob's type 21 nouns (see p.58). Moberg still believed it possible that this (revised) interpretation allowed for a Greek borrowing, but Revell, *Grammar*, 366-7, suggests that this is unnecessary. Both Revell, *Grammar*, 366, and Talmon, *Jacob of Edessa*, 169, support Moberg's reinterpretation.

[xix] For how ܐܣܘܬܐ contains a double, see Moberg, *ibid.*, a different reading from Merx's.

[xx] Merx hardly answers his own question of why the concept of the syllable is not discussed after Jacob. Segal attributes it to the new focus on consonants and vowels as separate units (*Diacritical Point*, 24n1).

[xxi] τέλος κανόνων τῶν ἀρσενικῶν ὀνομάτων τῶν ἁπλῶν, τῶν πρωτοτύπων τε καὶ παραγώγων χωρὶς τῶν ܒܒܠܢ̈ܬܐ. In the text of Dionysius Thrax (Uhlig, 24-30, and in the Syriac as given above), there are two 'species' of noun, the Primary and the Derived, or Prototype and Derived-from-the-Prototype.

[xxii] Until, that is, he edited Jacob Bar Šakko—see text in appendix, p.ܘ, note.

[xxiii] In other words, the first criterion is the final vowel (thus ας before ης); the second is the number of syllables in the nominative form; the third is whether or not the genitive has more syllables than the nominative.

[xxiv] ἰστέον δὲ, ὅτι περὶ τῶν εἰς ἂς μονοσυλλάβων οὐδὲν εἶπεν ὁ Θεοδόσιος, ὡς πρὸς εἰσαγομένους τὸν λόγον ποιούμενος καὶ συντομίας φροντίζων.

[xxv] Merx's use of this example to prove his interpretation of Jacob's theory of syllables is based on the assumption that Jacob counted the 'n'. In fact he does not, which is exactly what makes his grammar unusual (Revell, *Grammar*, 369).

[xxvi] Top of p.52.

[xxvii] I.e. George Amira, *Grammatica Syriaca sive Chaldaica*, Rome, 1596, the first really comprehensive Syriac grammar published in Western Europe, discussed in the final chapter.

Chapter 6

JACOB'S IMPROVEMENTS TO THE SYRIAC ACCENTS AND THE RELATIONSHIPS BETWEEN GREEK, SYRIAC, AND HEBREW PUNCTUATION

We would at this point leave Jacob's labours behind and move on, were it not for the fact that we have as yet barely mentioned a matter of the greatest importance—namely the theory of 'pointing' or, as some are used to calling it, 'accentuation'. Jacob Bar Šakko (p. ܠ) expounded Jacob of Edessa's theory of pointing and his text agrees very closely with the discussions that are attributed to Jacob and to Thomas the Deacon. Barhebraeus himself teaches pretty much the same thing, and in this he is again Jacob's disciple.[1]

In the Armenian version of Dionysius Thrax, after the final chapter on conjunctions, there comes an appended treatise on *aṛ-okanouthiun*, a term that corresponds to *προσῳδία* (*prosody*). *Aṛ* is *προς*, *ok-em* is 'to speak', from the root *vac* (whence Latin *vox*). The Armenian word is thus formed in the same manner as the Greek (just as in the Latin word *ac-centus*), which is literally expressed in the word *προσ-ῳδία*. This fact shows for certain that the chapter on accents found in both Bekker's and Uhlig's editions of the *Technē* was already appended to it in the sixth century.[2] The scholiasts differ as to whether this chapter should come at the beginning or at the end of the grammar. One scholion (Bekker, *Anecdota*, 676,9) |[63] argues that the student should commence the study of grammar with accentuation (prosody) and afterwards proceed to understanding the *Technē* itself (*ἡ τῆς τεχνολογίας ἐξήγησις*). However, the text which the Armenian translator of Dionysius followed put the section on accents at the end. Jacob seems to have followed this latter approach, as we can tell from the fact that both Jacob Bar Šakko and Barhebraeus do the same, and we have already amply demonstrated their dependence on Jacob. So we can now turn to an investigation of Jacob's particular concerns regarding accents.

For the purposes of ἀνάγνωσις (*reading*) even the Greeks maintained a basic distinction between the individual parts of pronunciation and the

---

[1] Barhebraeus, *Gramm.*, I, 247.

[2] Bekker, *Anecdota*, 674; Uhlig, 105ff.

business of punctuation—the latter being such things as we would generally call the colon, semicolon, comma etc. They taught that reading should be done καθ' ὑπόκρισιν, κατὰ προσῳδίαν, κατὰ διαστολήν.[i] There are no rules in the grammar regarding the first of these (ὑπόκρισις, *delivery*), but there are in the case of προσῳδία (*prosody*). The parts of prosody were later numbered four: τόνοι, χρόνοι, πνεύματα, πάθη (*accents, quantities, breathings, and other punctuation marks*), but in antiquity only the first three of these were known.[1] In the broadest sense, χρόνος (*quantity*) is to do with separating out the pronunciation of a sentence into its constituent parts usually by means of the στιγμή (*punctuation mark*). According to the theories of the older grammarians, both the logical and the rhetorical approaches to dividing up the sense of an utterance should be considered under the heading of prosody. There is a scholion of Stephanus (early seventh century) on Dionysius Thrax's chapter on the στιγμή which tells us that this is exactly how it was:

> The writer, aiming to write an introductory grammar, left to one side the harder aspects of accentuation, i.e. breathings, quantities and other such marks.... This was so that he might not altogether leave the unintelligent far behind. Like a good nurse, who takes all the meat in hand but gives only a part of it to the child that is being nurtured, thus does he [i.e. Dionysius] encourage us by dealing in summary fashion with the detailed parts of the whole grammar course, and passes onto the issue of punctuation, for this also is very important for reading.

Melampus also wrote in the same vein: "The vital matter of prosody, that is accents, he teaches us in abbreviated form. Matters of punctuation, that is, to do with internal sense-division, he deals with separately, etc."[2] [ii]

---

[1] Bekker, *Anecdota*, 674,11; 703,31; Uhlig, 107 (see apparatus). Choeroboscos added τόνοι μέν εἰσι τρεῖς, ὀξεῖα, βαρεῖα, περισπωμένη· χρόνοι δύο, μακρὰ καὶ βραχεῖα· πνεῦματα δύο δασεῖα καὶ ψιλή (*there are three types of accents: acute, grave and circumflex; and there are two quantities: long and short; and there are two breathings: rough and smooth*). The Byzantines add among the πάθη (*the additional marks*), ἀπόστροφος, ὑφὲν and ὑποδιαστολή (*apostrophe, hyphen and word-divider*), but Choeroboscos, following Herodian, reckons that this has nothing strictly to do with prosody (*Anecdota*, 705,7). The Armenian translator of Dionysius (Uhlig, 107) omits the πάθη.

[2] Bekker, *Anecdota*, 759,26.

When he refers to διαστολή (*internal sense-division*) as being related to στιγμή, he seems to be using a shorthand way of telling us about the original system in which the τελεία στιγμή (*full-point*) was used at the end of a sentence or period, the ὑποστιγμή (*lower-point*) in between a protasis and an apodosis, while the μέση στιγμή (*mid-point*) in those places where the natural divisions in the pronunciation are so far apart that the reader has to take an extra breath.[iii] But Melampus reckons himself rather more precise when he argues that the μέση cannot technically be called a στιγμὴ on account of the fact that not everybody draws breath at the same point and because that which does not work generally for everyone cannot be called a στιγμή.[1]

|[64] An example of the μέση is the point after the word *ἄνακτι* in this verse: ΑΠΟΛΛΩΝΙ ΑΝΑΚΤΙ · ΤΟΝ ΗΥΚΟΜΟΣ ΤΕΚΕ ΛΗΤΩ˙, while an example of a *ὑποστιγμὴ* is found in the point after the word *ἐφιείς* in the verse: ΑΥΤΑΡ ΕΠΕΙΤ ΑΥΤΟΙΣΙ ΒΕΛΟΣ ΕΧΕΠΕΥΚΕΣ ΕΦΙΕΙΣ. ΒΑΛΛΕΝ ·[iv]

If we were to ask how exactly to define the difference between the full-point and the lower-point, they might reply that the difference is one of *duration*, for after a full-point one can be silent as long as one wishes, whereas after the lower-point one must proceed immediately, since the latter is a sign of κρεμαμένης τῆς διανοίας καὶ πρὸς συμπλήρωσιν ὀλίγου δεομένης (*the meaning [of the sentence] hanging in the air, and of something lacking that needs to be made complete*).[2] [v] The position of the full-point is next to the top of the letter (τίθεται ἐπὶ κεφαλῆς τοῦ γράμματος), that of the lower-point being at the base of the letter, while the middle point was half-way up (τίθεται ἡ μέση ἐν τῷ μέσῳ τοῦ γράμματος, ἡ δὲ ὑποστιγμὴ μεθ' ὑποκρίσεως κατωτάτω τοῦ γράμματος).[3]

When considering the meaning of the term 'full-point' we must take care not be prejudiced by our own usage, being accustomed as we are to placing this point at the ends of sentences. The ancients did not think along the same lines as we do when defining where sentences ended. Friedländer has produced an excellent explanation of just how they did think about these things.[4] In fact, the ancients reckoned that even the

---

[1] Ibid., 759,6.

[2] Ibid., 762.

[3] Ibid., 760. L. Friedländer, *Nicanoris περὶ Ἰλιακῆς στιγμῆς reliquiae* (Königsburg, 1850), 591, has explained what lies beneath the term μεθ' ὑποκρίσεως here.

[4] Friedländer, *op. cit.*, 24.

various parts of the longer periods were complete in themselves (αὐτοτελῆ), and they used the full-point where we would not generally do so ourselves. As an example, see Iliad 2.23-5: ΕΥΔΕΙΣ ΑΤΡΕΟΣ ΥΙΕ ΔΑΙΦΡΟΝΟΣ ΙΠΠΟΔΑΜΟΙΟ· ΟΥ ΧΡΗ ΠΑΝΝΥΧΙΟΝ ΕΥΔΕΙΝ ΒΟΥΛΗΦΟΡΟΝ ΑΝΔΡΑ ΩΙ ΛΑΟΙ Τ'ΕΠΙΤΕΤΡΑΦΑΤΑΙ ΚΑΙ ΤΟΣΣΑ ΜΕΜΗΛΕΝ. A full-point has been placed after ἱπποδάμοιο, because the two parts are not connected by any conjunction (ἐπεὶ ἀσύνδετος ὁ λόγος).[1] Where a reproach is expressed, we would use a question mark or an exclamation mark.[vi]

Among these accents which indicate division we must also take note of one that has the opposite effect, namely the hyphen (ὑφέν)—σημεῖον συναφείας συνθέτων λέξεων ἢ σημεῖον ἑνώσεως δύο λέξεων οἷον νικόλᾶος (*A sign that links compounded words or a sign that unites two words, e.g., nikolaos*).[2] It seemed superfluous to the scholiast to use the hyphen in words that were 'derived-from-a-compound' (παρασυνθέτοις),[3] but it was thought necessary in the case of words joined by elision.[vii]

This very old and very straightforward system, which appears to have been developed largely for the accurate reading of Homer, was borrowed by the Syrians. It is the system found in the oldest dated Syriac manuscript, BL Add. 12150, where an upper point is used to close off completed sentences, a middle point is used for separating the inner parts, and a lower point for distinguishing protasis from apodosis. This scribal practice is quite contrary to the later Syriac usage which was to close off completed sentences with a lower point placed upon the line.[viii]

|[65] To take an example, see the following extract from Titus of Bostra II,47:[4] ܐܠܐ ܕܝܢ ܐܢܫ ܢܚܒܐ ܘܡܛܠ ܡܢܐ ܡܬܡܛܠ ܒܗ: ܐܢܫܐ ܠܘܬ ܡܬܐܡܪܐ ܗܘ ܕܪܫܝܐ ܗܘ ܕܡܬܚܫܒܢܘܬܐ ܐܬܐܡܪܐ ܘܡܛܠ ܡܢܐ ܗܟܢܐ ܐܦ ܡܬܐ ܒܗ: ܐܢܫܐ ܕܝܢ ܗܘܐ ܠܐ ܠܬܠܬܐ ܕܫܟܢܐ ܗܘ ܒܪܘܚܐ ܠܥܡܠܐ ܗܘ ܕܟܪܘܗ ܒܟܠܗܘܢ ܪܘܚܗ˙. The protasis of the sentence ܐܠܐ ܕܝܢ ܐܢܫ ܢܚܒܐ is separated from its apodosis by a lower point, which begins with the words ܠܘܬ ܡܬܐܡܪܐ and ends with the final upper point after ܪܘܚܗ. The two intruding questions, which start with ܘܡܛܠ ܡܢܐ, could have been distinguished by a mid-point, but this was not considered necessary.

Another more straightforward example (II,45): ܬܬܒܥ ܗܘܠܐ ܘܬܬܬܟܠ ܒܗܘܢ ܐܣܟܡܐ ܐܦ ܕܝܢ ܡܬܪܥܝܢܘܬܐ ܘܡܕܝܢ ܚܣܝܐ ܘܡܬܬܪܢܝܢ ܒܟܝܢܐ ܗܢܘܢ ܕܡܬܐܡܪܝܢ ܡܬܐܡܪܐ· ܗܘ ܕܐܬܚܙܝ ܕܟܠ ܡܕܡ

[1] Friedländer, *op. cit.*, 47.

[2] Bekker, *Anecdota*, 699.

[3] Ibid., 702.

[4] Citations from P. Lagarde, ed., *Titi Bostri contra Manichæos libri quattuor Syriace.* Abhandlungen der Deutschen Morgenländischen Gesellschaft IX,2 (Berlin, 1859).

ܠܡܚܒܠ܀ ܗܟܢܐ ܓܝܪ ܐܦ ܥܠ ܦܪܙܠܐ ܘܥܠ ܢܘܪܐ ܡܕܓܠ܀ ܘܐܦ ܒܗܘܢ ܕܝܢ ܕܠܩܘܒܠܐ ܥܒܕ ܕܗܘ ܪܓܐ܀ . In Greek the equivalent is: περιγραπτέον τοίνυν τοῦτον τὸν τρόπον καὶ τὴν κατὰ τῶν θανασίμων λεγομένων βοτανῶν κατηγορίαν τῷ μανέντι, πάντα διαβάλλειν ἐσπουδακότι. οὕτω γὰρ καὶ σιδήρου καὶ πυρὸς καταψεύδεται, τοὐναντίον ποιῶν καὶ ἐν τούτοις οὗ βούλεται.[ix] It is clear that the Syriac translator has simplified the Greek periods into individual clauses, and those which he deemed to be complete in themselves according to the norms of his own language he marked out with an upper point, i.e. his equivalent of the τελεία στιγμή [*full-point / upper-point*] of Dionysius.

We have an example of both a full-point and a lower-point at II,54 (p.74,3): ܡܢܝ ܗܟܝܠ ܕܥܒܕ ܠܗ ܐܠܗܐ ܠܫܡܫܐ܀ ܐܝܟ ܕܡܢ ܟܝܢܗ ܗܘ ܛܒ ܕܛܒܐ ܡܣܬܟܠ ܠܗ ܕܢܘܪܢܐ ܢܘܪܐ ܗܘܐ ܕܝܢ ܕܢܥܠܝܘܗܝ ܐܝܟ ܗܟܢܐ ܠܛܒܐ ܡܕܡ ܕܐܝܬܘܗܝ܀ . The Greek is: ὁ τοίνυν Μάνης ἐκθειάζων ὡς τῆς φύσεως ὄντα τοῦ ἀγαθοῦ τὸν ἥλιον, κινδυνεύει πυροειδῆ, μᾶλλον σαφῶς τοιοῦτον δή τινα τὸν ἀγαθὸν εἰσάγειν.[x] The full-point (placed at the top of the letter) at the very end corresponds to the lower-point after ܠܛܒܐ, while the first full-point marks out the sentence ܕܥܒܕ ܠܗ ܐܠܗܐ ܠܫܡܫܐ as being self-contained.

We add here a further example from the Syriac translation of the *Clementine Homilies*[xi] to show that the Syrians (and the Greeks) did not place the points in the same places where we would generally place them: ܗܟܢܐ ܐܦ ܚܛܗܐ ܒܟܝܢܗܘܢ ܠܐܢܫܐ ܕܚܛܐ ܡܘܒܕܝܢ. ܘܐܦ ܟܕ ܠܐ ܝܕܥ ܡܕܡ ܕܠܐ ܘܠܐ ܢܣܥܘܪ܀ ܐܢ ܗܟܝܠ ܥܠ ܡܠܝܢ |66 ܕܠܐ ܫܡܥܝܢ ܡܠܬܐ ܕܝܢܐ ܗܘܐ ܡܬܥܒܕܐ. ܟܡܐ ܝܬܝܪ ܠܐܝܠܝܢ ܕܠܐ ܨܒܘ ܕܢܩܒܠܘܢ ܕܚܠܬܗ ܕܐܠܗܐ ܠܡܫܡܫܘܬܗ. ܐܝܢܐ ܓܝܪ ܕܠܐ ܨܒܐ ܕܢܐܠܦ ܐܝܟ ܡܚܝܒܐ ܘܠܐ ܢܬܚܫܒ ܗܘܐ ܐܝܟ ܝܕܘܥܐ ܡܬܕܝܢ܀ ܝܕܥ ܓܝܪ ܗܘ ܡܕܡ ܕܢܫܡܥ ܠܐ ܪܓܐ܀ ܠܐ ܐܝܬ ܗܟܝܠ ܪܘܚܬܐ ܕܡܦܩ ܒܪܘܚܐ ܠܘܬ ܐܠܗܐ܂ ܝܕܥ ܕܠܒܘܬܐ ܡܛܠ ܗܢܐ... In Greek the extract (from *Hom.* 10,12-13) runs: οὕτως φυσικῶς αἱ ἁμαρτίαι ἀναιροῦσι τὸν ἁμαρτάνοντα, κἂν ἀγνοῶν πράσσῃ ἃ μὴ δεῖ. εἰ δὲ ἐπὶ παρακοῇ λόγων κρίσις γίνεται, πολλῷ μᾶλλον ὁ θεὸς ὀλοθρεύει τοὺς μὴ θελήσαντας τὴν εἰς αὐτὸν θρησκείαν ἀναδέξασθαι. ὁ γὰρ μὴ θέλων μαθεῖν ἵνα μὴ ἔνοχος ᾖ, ἤδη ὡς εἰδὼς κρίνεται. ἔγνω γὰρ ὃ μὴ ἀκοῦσαι θέλει· ὥστε οὐδὲν δύναται πρὸς ἀπολογίαν ἐπίνοια πρὸς καρδιογνώστην θεόν. διὸ κτλ. [xii] The Syriac translator does not place a point where we would expect the period to end, but instead uses an upper point to mark out the self-contained clauses. He uses the mid-point in a manner somewhat similar to our comma. The lower-point after ܐܠܗܐ܂ has the force of a conjunction.[xiii] We shall deal with this further below.

We can discern the same system in Eusebius's *Theophania*, the opening passage of which is pointed as follows: ܗܢܘܢ ܕܐܡܪܝܢ ܥܠ ܠܐܠܗܐ ܕܗܘܐ ܒܗ ܒܟܠܗ....ܘܠܐ ܐܝܬ ܒܗ ܡܘܬܐ ܘܠܐ ܡܬܪܢܝܢܐ܀ ܘܠܐ ܡܢܐ ܗܘ ܘܠܐ ܒܗܝܕܥܬܐ ܘܐܝܟ ܡܬܚܫܒܢܘܬܐ ܘܒܨܝܪܐ ܡܛܠ ܐܝܟ ܕܗܘ ܕܐܬܛܠܡ. ܗܘ ܡܢ ܢܦܫܗ ܡܢ. ܣܥܪܐ ܘܠܐ ܠܗܘ ܡܬܚܙܝܢ ܗܘܘ܀ ܘܡܛܠ ܗܢܐ ܡܢ ܒܢܝܐ ܠܐܠܗܐ ܠܡܪܕܘܬܗ܀

... .[xiv] This explains why it is that the upper point can be written at the end of sections, where most of the time there is no point at all. For example also *Theophania* III,73: ܘܐܦ ܠܐ ܡܬܐܡܪܐ ܡܢ ܦܘܡܗ ܕܟܠ ܡܕܡ ܗܕܐ· ܐܦܠܐ ܕܟܠ ܗܢܐ ܕܢܦܩܘ ܕܡܢ ܦܓܪܐ ܘܢܦܫܐ· ܐܦܠܐ ܠܡܡܬܐ ܦܓܪܐ ܕܐܠܗܐ ܕܡܢ ܒܣܘܒܪܢܘܬܗ ܕܟܠܢܫ ܡܢ ܟܠ. ܡܫܝܚܐ ܡܚܠܡܗ ܕܐܠܗܐ ܠܐܠܗܘܬܗ ܦܪܘܩܢ ܘܐܚܝܐ ܕܡܘܬܐ ܡܚܠܡܗ· .[xv] Here in passing we may note that this system was also transmitted, along with the *Technē*, to the Armenians, who use three points, namely a lower one (sdoragēd), a middle (mitšagēd), and a final, the name of which is 'avardeal ged', 'wertšagēd'. Since the names of the first two clearly indicate what positions are being referred to, the third one mentioned must indeed have been positioned above the line even in antiquity. Today it is usual to end sentences with a double point [:], written in the same way as the Hebrew *Soph Pasuq*, which we shall see later was in fact itself derived originally from the upper point.[1]

|[67] At the end of the fifth century, however, it seems that the professors in the Syriac schools were no longer happy with this system and wanted to revise it. They made some alterations to the existing accents, or rather to the points which distinguish the various parts of speech, and invented some new accents.

Firstly on the matter of the forms: where a lower point was required, they added another positioned upon the line itself. By doing this the simple lower ܬܚܬܝܐ (ܟ̣) developed into the double for .ܟ̣. But then, whenever a protasis was being distinguished from an apodosis by the positioning of this ܬܚܬܝܐ, they designated the individual sub-divisions of protasis and apodosis in a different way.[xvi] Within the protasis, they separated the individual parts by further adding double-points (which are called either ܦܳܩܐ or ܙܘܓܐ), thus .ܟ̣ :ܟ:ܟ In the apodosis, however, the subdivisions were marked by an upper point—its purpose in the ancient system of distinguishing self-sufficient units being now rejected. Onto this new upper point (ܥܠܝܐ) another was then placed upon the line, thereby giving rise to this form for the apodosis .ܟ.ܟ̇.ܟ.ܟ̇. The end of the whole sentence was then marked by a point placed *upon* the line so that the sign which previously had indicated a place for drawing breath (the mid-point) was now being used for closing the clauses and was given the name ܦܣܘܩܐ

[1] Avedichean, *Grammatica Armeniaca* (Venice, 1815), 1309.

(*divider*).[1] Thus the form of the period as a whole would finish up as .ܐ.ܐ̇.ܐ̇.ܐ̣:ܐ:ܐ .

As an example of this, take the following extract from a manuscript written in 688:[2] ܕܗܘܐ ܕܝܢ ܡܛܠ ܕܣܓܝܐܝܢ ܕܡܢ ܩܕܡ ܒܐܘܠܨܢܐ ܘܐܘܠܨܢܐ܆ ܐܦ ܒܡܟܬܒܢܘܬܐ ܡܩܠܐ ܒ ܡܠܐܟܝܢ ܠܐܡܦܘܪܐ ܩܠܘܕܝܘܣ ܡܬܢܢܐ ܘܩܣ̈ܛܐ ܟܕ ܣܗܕܝܢ: ܟܠ ܗܠܝܢ ܐܠܗܐ ܡܫܡܫܢܘܬܐ ܘܟܠܗ ܒܒܠܐ ܕܐܬܪܝܢ ܡܘܟܚܢܐ. ܡܛܠ ܗܘ̣ܐ ܗܘ ܐܬܐܡܪܬ ܘܐܦ ܥܠ ܕܒܠܬ ܫܘܡܠܝܐ ܕܡܫܘܕܥܢܐ. ܐܦ ܐܢܘܢ ܕܡܬܘܬܐ ܘܡܫܝܚܐ ܢܫܐ. ܐܦ ܗܘ ܐܢܫܐ ܡܢ ܟܠ ܢܝܫܐ ܐܚܝܕ ܠܗ ܘܡܫܒܚ ܕܡܫܠܡܐ. ܘܟܠ ܕܐܡܪ ܘܡܬܐ ܐܦ ܕܡܬܘܬܐ ܕܡܫܚ ܕܡܘܣܝܘܢ ܕܡܥܬܝܬܐ ܕܝܠܢܝܬܐ. ܘܐܦ ܗܢܐ ܐܝܟܢܐ ܡܫܬܠܝ.[3] xvii

But the professors, it seems, were still not satisfied. Even though they had managed to distinguish both the form and the composition of the sentence by using these four symbols, they went on to alleviate their pupils' ignorance by deciding that what needed to be learnt was not just a logical system |68 of subdividing the sentence, but rather a rhetorical system for recitation—what the Greeks called ὑπόκρισις (*delivery*). Hence on top of the strictly logical accents (ܦܣܩܐ or ܙܘܓܐ, ܬܚܬܝܐ, ܥܠܝܐ, ܦܣܘܩܐ) they added others that we might call 'rhetorical'. We have already seen (p.28) that Joseph Huzaya was the first to place accents in the Biblical books and that he counted nine of them—of which three (ܙܘܓܐ, ܬܚܬܝܐ, ܥܠܝܐ) should be counted as logical accents; so it is evident that the number of rhetorical accents was initially very much restricted and that the maqreyane gradually added many more later on.[4]

The rhetorical accents as used by Joseph Huzaya were therefore only six in number (the full quotation is given on p.28 above): xviii

ܡܫܐܠܢܐ, denoting a question.

ܦܩܘܕܐ, denoting a command.

ܡܫܟܢܐ, denoting a minor pause.

ܥܨܝܐ, denoting a major pause.

---

[1] We shall see below traces of the older usage in ܡܢܚܬܐ and ܦܣܘܩܐ ܥܠܝܐ, since this mid-point, which was already indistinguishable from ܦܣܘܩܐ, is several times preserved in the manuscripts.

[2] W. Cureton, ed., *The Third Part of the ecclesiastical History of John of Ephesus* (Oxford, 1853), 3.

[3] For the rest, see my *Gramamtica Syriaca*, 90.

[4] Nothing is said in the Joseph Huzaya passage about ܦܣܘܩܐ, which is not included among the nine. It seems, however, unlikely that Joseph did not make use of it and probably it should be added, thereby giving us ten accents. [Cf. Segal, *Diacritical Point*, 67, who concurs on this point—ed.].

ܡܚܣܝܢܐ, by which the reader is advised to speak with a fading voice.[1] [xix]

ܗܘ ܕܡܢܚܬ ܡܢ ܠܘܬ ܪ̈ܘܟܟܢ, which I reckon to be the same as what Jacob calls ܠܘܡܐ ܘܫܐܠܬܐ ܡܫܐܠܢܐ.

It is not apparent from this important passage exactly what signs he used for these points or where they were placed. The author of the passage says that the accents in the scriptures (ܡܟܣܟܣܐ, ܚܝ ܢܟܐ etc.) were written by Joseph according to some definite system and it is quite clear that Joseph's symbols must be the same as those used by the later ܡܩܪ̈ܝܢܐ and are also the same as those which we still use today.

Therefore, they must have been as follows:

1-2) The ܡܫܐܠܢܐ and ܦܩܘܕܐ, indicating respectively a question and a command, were written above the word, as in ܐܝܟܢܐ *how?*; ܙܠ *Go!*.

3) ܦܣܘܩܐ was a point beneath the final letter of a word which required a pause to follow: ܙܕܝ̈ܩܐ ܢܥܡܪܘܢ ܒܐܪܥܐ *the just, they inhabit the earth.*

4) |[69] ܥܠܝܐ is a point above the word (here, ܐܢܐ) which is followed later by a more significant pause, as in: ܗܘ ܗܘܐ ܠܘܩܕܡܟܘܢ، ܘܐܢܐ ܒܬܪܟܘܢ، ܘܐܬܝܬܘܢ ܒܗ ܐܬܝܬܘܢ.

5) ܡܚܣܝܢܐ is as discussed in the above footnote. Its form and usage are the same as for ܡܚܣܝܬܐ.

6) The accent formed with a double ܪܗܛܐ describes its form by its name. If indeed it is the same thing as what Jacob describes as ܠܘܡܐ ܘܫܐܠܬܐ ܡܫܐܠܢܐ then its form is: ܠܐ ܐܡܪܬ ܠܟܘܢ ܠܐ ܬܬܪܗܒܘܢ؛, and its use indicates both a reproach and a question. It could be called 'the sign of reproach'.

The other rhetorical accents are of later date—a fact made seemingly quite probable by the observation that Joseph's accents constitute a complete system on their own. Besides the logical accents, it includes symbols for minor and major pauses, as well as signs for questions, orders, complaints, and reproaches. Such a set of symbols is quite sufficient for designating a wide variety of human emotions and those who later increased the number by a great many recitative symbols only disturbed the simplicity of this system without achieving any real increase in sophistication.

Joseph's system was thus different from both the later one and the older one. It seems to have been the most elegant, being equally distant

[1] This accent is not found in Jacob of Edessa's system, but does seem to be identical with what Jacob calls ܡܚܣܝܬܐ. Its nature is made quite clear by what John Bar Zuʿbi says in BL Add. 25876, f.164: ܡܚܣܝܢܐ ܥܠ ܦܩܘܕ ܦܘܫܐ ܘܡܬܘܚܡܬܐ ܕܡܢ ܦܘܚܠܐ ܡܚܒܘ. ܐܝܟ ܗܘ ܕܐܡܪ ܡܫܝܚܐ ܠܝܗܘܕܝ̈ܐ. ܐܡܪܘ ܠܐܬܘܬܐ ܗܐ ܕܢܣܒܝܢ ܒܒܝܬܟܘܢ. ܐܝܟܢܐ ܗܠܝܢ ܠܡܬܘܡܝܢ ܡܦܝܣܬܐ ܦܘܫܐ ܟܘܠܐ. [again, Segal, *Diacritical Point*, 67, is in agreement—ed.].

both from the excessive fullness of the one and from the meagreness of the other, which he totally surpasses. The older system only made distinctions between the self-sufficient parts of the sentence—between protasis and apodosis—without in any way indicating how the individual parts of protasis and apodosis were related. Joseph's system has a point designed for this very purpose, making clear the internal relations of the period, and making the arrangement of the sentence abundantly clear to the reader.

I am quite certain that this Syriac system of adding vowels and accents was developed principally for the purpose of understanding the Old Testament.

Now in the case of Hebrew, the primary purpose of accents is logical. There is no vestige of rhetorical accents in Hebrew and there were no symbols for such things as commands, complaints, questions etc.[1] Although |[70] they do reflect a certain musical value, in the sense that a particular level of tone is attributed to each individual accent, nevertheless this is secondary, for the tone value of the accents is dependent upon their logical value and not vice versa.

The innate logic of the whole accentuation system, however, did not prevent the development of a parallel system of euphony for chanting—indeed a number of laws for the placement of accents are inexplicable unless we allow that, in selecting their accents, whenever more than one type of accent could theoretically be used, the Hebrew masters would use the one whose melody appeared to be preferable. This holds true at least for the lesser accents. For the major ones, the positioning and the usage is more rule-bound and consistent.

This fact can be readily illustrated by some examples: The Zaqeph qaṭon [◌֔] is preceded by the Pashṭa [◌֙], and the Pashṭa preceded by the Mehuppaẖ [◌֤], as for example in Gen 35.1, וי֤אמר אלהי֙ב אל-יעק֔ב. Where, however, the word to which the Pashṭa belongs is paroxytone, a Yethiv [◌֚] is used, as in Gen 1.12, עֵ֚שׂב מז֤ריע ז֔רע.[xx] If there is absolutely no syllable between the Pashṭa and the Mehuppaẖ, not even a furtive pathach, and if the syllable requiring the Mehuppaẖ is placed immediately before a word

[1] However, the author of the book known as the 'Manuel du lecteur' does note that in selecting musical accents the criterion of the innate rhetoric of the sentence is respected. He writes: ואפשר שיתחלף סדר זה [סדר הטעמים] לפי מלת הפיסוק וגדלו וקטנו אם הוא דרך ספור או יש בו אותיות קריאת או אותיות החמה או אותיות הידיעה לפי ענינו יהיה תוצאותיו ולפי תוצאותיו יהיה סימני טעמיו והמשכילים יבינו (J. Derenbourg, ed., "Manuel du lecteur, d'un auteur inconnu, publié après un manuscript venu de Yémen," *Journal Asiatique* 16 (1870), 309-550, cited from p.415).

with a Pashṭa—with no syllable coming in between—then, in place of a Mehuppaḫ, Merḫa [◌֥] is used. Thus while we have חגתֶם אתו חָג ליהוה (Lev 23.41), and מזרִיע זֶרע למינהו (Gen 1.12), yet where no syllable intervenes, we have היתָה תהו (Gen 1.2) and הכָן לי בזה (Num 23.1). It should be noted that even the furtive pataḥis being counted as a syllable when it is really only an artificial reading aid. This makes it quite certain that we have here a system that is largely designed for musical euphony.

The Tevir [◌֛] is preceded by Darga [◌֧] as long as either two syllables or a syllable with Metheg or Paseq intervenes: שנַיִם מכֹּל (Gen 6.19); תָּם וישָׁר (Job 1.1); וכָר תזבחֻו (Lev 19.5); קנָה יעקֹב (Josh 24.32). But if either a single syllable or no syllable at all intervenes, then Merḫa rather than Darga is used: אלהֵי מצרים (Ex 12.12); עֵץ אֶרז (Num 19.6).[1]

It is clear, then, that these rules which they imposed upon their own usage were designed for euphony as much as for the logical division of the verse—a fact that we shall see holds true also for the later Syriac system. Furthermore, there is no doubt that this highly intricate set of rules for the placing of accents was only gradually refined over time, eventually attaining that level of exhaustiveness that so vexes the minds of students to this day. There is as yet no definite knowledge about the origins of Hebrew accentuation,|[71] save to say that the whole system must have begun with the careful subdivision of the parts of the sentence by means of the greater accents—the ones that some, following Bohlius, have been accustomed to call 'emperors' and 'kings'.[2] Although today there are generally considered to be four of these—Zaqeph, Revia, Segolta, and Ṭiphḥa, it seems to me possible, on the basis of the actual names, that Segolta and Ṭiphḥa were later additions, and that Zaqeph [◌֔] and Revia [◌֗] were in fact the oldest original accents. I believe it very possible to distinguish different periods within the growth of the Masoretic system, as

---

[1] These examples are taken from Derenbourg's edition (cf. previous note), 402, and from the text of Wolfsohn (בן זאב), תלמוד לשון עברי (Vienna, 1830), fol.194. There are more accurate ones in Strack and Baer, ed., *Diqduqe ha'teamim* (Leipzig, 1879), 20. We did say earlier (p.56) that grammarians of Semitic languages did not have any regard for the number of syllables. But note that Judah ben David Ḥayyūǧ counted letters rather than syllables—cf. H. Ewald & L. Dukes, *Beiträge zur Geschichte der altesten Auslegung und Spracherklärung des Alten Testamentes* (Stuttgart, 1844), 194.

[2] These names, unknown to the ancient Hebrew grammarians, were invented by Bohlius in his *Scrutinium Sanct. Scr. ex accentibus* (Rostock, 1636). See W. Gesenius, *Ausführliches grammatisch-kritisches Lehrgebäude der hebräischen Sprache* (Leipzig, 1817), 107.

it cannot all have arisen at once, but we have dealt more fully with this question elsewhere.[1]

There can surely be no doubting that these earliest Hebrew accents are in the main parallel to their Syriac counterparts, reckoning in also the Athnaḥ, which corresponds in both name and usage to the Syriac ܐܬܢܚܬܐ, and the Soph Pasuq (not the Silluq) similarly with the Syriac ܦܣܘܩܐ. Hebrew does differ from the mature usage of the Syrians, however, for the simple upper point (Syriac ܥܠܝܐ = Hebrew Revia) is in Hebrew placed not on the apodosis but rather is used to indicate the *lesser* divisions in both protasis and apodosis equally, while the *greater* divisions (again in both protasis and apodosis) are marked by a double-point, viz. Syriac ܙܘܓܐ or ܪܗܛܐ, Hebrew Zaqeph. The Syrians' careful distinction of apodosis from protasis could be neglected by the Hebrews relatively easily because, for the most part, Hebrew sentences are rather simpler and less intricately formed. So, the Syriac system, and also the oldest Hebrew one, was as follows:

Syriac ܐ:ܐ:ܐ.ܐ̇.ܐ̇.ܐ.

Hebrew אׄ אׄ א֑ אׄ אׄ א:

Or, if the parts require a more precise distribution:

אׄ אׄ אׄ א֑ אׄ אׄ אׄ א:

In the very oldest manuscripts, the Soph pasuq is usually written on top of the line. Since we have already given some Syriac examples of this above, we need now only give some Hebrew ones, taken at random from the Old Testament, excepting the three א״מת books.[xxi] Thus one reads at Gen 14.1:

ויהׄי בימׄי אמרפל מלך שכׄער אריוך מלך אל֑סר כדרלעמר מלך עילׄם ותדעל מלך גוים:
עשו מלחמׄה את ברע מלך סדׄם ואת ברשע מלך עמר֑ה שנאב מלך אדמׄה ושמאבד מלך צביׄים
ומלך בלע חיא צער:

|[72] In this example we can see the basic rule at work, although elsewhere the Revia (i.e. ܥܠܝܐ) alone is used and the Zaqeph omitted, as at Gen 42.27:

ויפתח האחד את שקׄו לתת מספוא לחמרו במל֑ון וירא את כספׄו והנה הוא בפי
אמתחתו:

[1] See my dissertation, "Die Tschufutkaleschen Fragmente, eine Studie zur Geschichte der Masora" in *Verhandlungen des fünften internationalen Orientalisten-Congresses II, Abhandlungen und Vorträge* (Berlin, 1882), 188-225, esp. p.213.

It is quite obvious why this is the case here, for the words לתת etc. do not constitute a self-sufficient part of the sentence and hence do not form a separate proposition; therefore a minor accent is used. We see the same thing at Deut 5.25b: אם יספים אנחנו לשמע את קול יהוה אלהינו עוד ומתנו:, and again at 5.26a: מי יתן והיה לבבם זה להם ליראה אתי ולשמר את כל מצותי כל הימים . See also Neh 9.35.[1]

If Hebrew had such an effective system for indicating the value of the different parts of the sentence, Syriac was in turn more concerned with the type of periods being used, for a very short protasis was separated from a very short apodosis not by the use of ܐܬܢܚܬܐ but by ܡܫܡܥܢܐ, as our text of Jacob Bar Šakko , following Jacob of Edessa, indicates.[2]

We believe these suggestions are sufficient to show not just a similarity but actually a fundamental agreement between the Hebrew and Syriac systems, namely in dividing the sentence using ܐܬܢܚܬܐ (Heb: Athnaḥ) and distributing the separate (grammatical) sections with ܙܩܦܐ (Heb: Zaqeph) and ܪܒܝܥܐ (Heb: Revia). However, the Hebrews were developing their own artificial system and they altered the relationship between ܙܩܦܐ and ܪܒܝܥܐ, such that not only was the former used for the protasis and the latter for the apodosis, but also the ܪܒܝܥܐ (i.e. Revia) was used for distinguishing a section marked with Zaqeph. All this applies only to the logical accents, for there is no trace of there having been any rhetorical accents in Hebrew. They were more concerned with using their symbols for indicating their musical notation—which was always unvarying, very boring and lacking in spirit—than for producing a pronunciation that was convenient and in accord with the nature of the passage.[3] But if the origins of the Hebrew system were, in fact, originally constituted on the model of the Syriac, then it is possible that there are even now, here and there, some rhetorical accents that have been preserved from antiquity, which were conjoined to

---

[1] On the matter of whether the Revia is placed once or twice, consult Luzzatto in S. Baer, *Torat Emet* (Rehelhaim, 1852), 63.

[2] Syriac text, p.33, l.3.

[3] For example, there is always a Silluq at the end of the utterance, i.e. a sort of raising of the voice, which is preceded either by Merḫa or by Ṭiphḥa, such that only two types of utterance-closure occur in the Bible. By endlessly repeating just these, they had no concern as to whether the utterance was a command, a question, or an exclamation. Before an Athnaḥ, either a Munaḥ or a Ṭiphḥa is usually placed, and thus even in the middle part of an utterance the musical tone is always the same—a system of reading that is indeed most tiresome.

musical accents and which themselves do indeed appear to be musical and to indicate musical tone, although originally indicating rhetorical features. Thus Job 21.18 stichometrically:

והיו בהֶבן לפני־רֽוח
וּכמֹץ גנבתֻו סופָה:

|[73] According to the rules, Revia and Revia mugrash are read, but the sense of the utterance is interrogative and the Syriac symbol for the interrogative is an upper point. Thus also at Job 38.18, in the words הַגֵּד אִם־ יָדַעְתָּ כֻלָּהּ:, the Revia mugrash is subdivided from the Silluq, but the sense is an imperative one, and the Syriac ܦܩܘܕܝܐ is an upper point. But this is only in passing.

We see, then, that the basis of the Hebraic system of disjunctive accents is both Greek and Syriac. The usage of the conjunctive accents was also derived from the same source. We cited earlier a scholion (p.64), in which the use of a hyphen (ὑφέν) was required for compound words. There is another scholiast, however, who has a different opinion and who required the hyphen to be placed, 1) in the case of words joined by synaloepha, e.g. κἀγώ; 2) in the case of two words which together express a single idea, e.g. τοξότα λωβητήρ (Il. 11.385), πύκα ποιητοῖο (Il. 18.608), πυλάρταο κρατεροῖο (Il. 13.415), ἄγρων αἰχμητήν.[1] This approach was readily borrowed into Syriac. Very often the Syriac translations of Greek texts use two words for a Greek compound and signify this with a set of two points called ܡܗܝܪܐ, of which one is placed on the last letter of the first word and the other on the first letter of the second word (e.g. πανδύνατος = ܐܚܝܕ ܟܠ). Thomas the Deacon explains this in BL Add. 12178, f.241a, a passage that has been edited by Martin from a Vatican ms which differs somewhat from the London one.[2] In the London ms, it reads as follows: "ܡܗܝܪܐ. Since there are words in the Greek language which, when translated into Syriac, cannot be rendered except by means of two words—such as the negatives [ܐܦܘܦܐܣܝܣ ܡܪܝܡܢܘܬܐ][xxii] ܠܐ ܝܠܝܕܐ (ἀγέννητος) and ܠܐ ܡܫܬܚܠܦܢܐ (ἄτρεπτος)—it seemed to the Holy Fathers and the translators of the Holy Scriptures that one point should be placed below the last letter of the first member, and another point below the first letter of the second member. This indicates that in the Syriac there are two members, but in the Greek only one." Once the London scholion has been compared with the abovementioned Greek text,

---

[1] Bekker, *Anecdota*, 702.

[2] Martin, *Ad Georgium*, 12,16-21; the London ms in Phillips, *Letter*, 73,26-74,10 (tr. 82-3).

it becomes quite clear that this conjunctive accent, which may be called ܢܓܘܕܐ (*dragging*), ܡܚܝܕܢܐ (*uniting*) or ܡܩܦܐ (*interweaving*), is used in exactly the same fashion as the Greek hyphen. We have therefore a conjunctive symbol that was in use in both the Greek and Syriac systems, whose example was followed by the Hebrew masters, who in their turn borrowed it and developed it considerably. We shall see below in discussing ܢܓܘܕܐ and ܡܚܝܕܢܐ that Jacob distinguished these different accents.

The argument by which we are led to this conjecture—namely that the Hebrew accents have a Syriac origin—is as follows: that although |[74] there is some mention of verses (פסוק) in the Talmud (Qiddusim 30a), the Jews were originally forbidden to place points of any sort in their books. This is laid down in the tractate *Sopherim* 3,7 in the following words: "A book which they have divided up into verses and in which the beginnings of the verses are marked out with points, is not to be read."[1] Whoever wrote this was not yet aware of the familiar term used later for a final point, סוף פסוק, for instead he speaks of 'heads of verses', ראשי פסוקים, being indicated by points. Now this tractate *Sopherim* ('On the Scribes') cannot have been written before the sixth century, since it mentions a complete collection of the Talmud[2] that lacked this very tractate, which was then added later as a sort of appendix. It therefore seems certain that the Jews had already at that time begun to divide into verses copies of the sacred books intended for private reading and to mark out these verses with points, but they had not yet settled on the names by which they were later to call them.[3] Add to this that a catalogue of the extraordinary points in the Torah is found in *Sopherim* 6,3, but there is total silence about any other points—both those referring to vowels and those referring to accentuation. The custom of chanting is mentioned, but only such that it would appear that recitation by chanting was not yet applied to the whole text.

---

[1] ספר שפסקו ושנוקד ראשי פסוקים שבו אל יקרא בו:

[2] לעולם הוי רץ למשנה יותר מן הש״ס (*Soph.* 15,6) 'always to follow the Misnah rather than the Torah etc.' Ibid. 15,7: Scripture can be compared to water, the Mishna to wine, the Talmud (הש״ס) to food. The Amoraim are also distinguished from the Tannaim (13,10).

[3] A fact that is all the more remarkable given that they numbered the verses. It was easier to number the words and letters than to number verses which were not yet marked with points. Sopherim has the middle verse of the Torah as being Lev. 8.15, rather than Lev. 8.8 as the Mishna has it—this can be deduced from the fact that *Soph.* 9,3 teaches that the central verse of the Torah begins with the word וישחט.

The word נעימה, which appears several times, can only be explained by reference to chanting. At 14,9, for example, one reads: "The Maphṭir[xxiii] enters, takes up the Torah, and says שמע ישראל by chanting the first verse. The congregation then also responds to him (i.e. in a chant)."[1] Similarly at 14,13, one reads: "Then, lifting up the Torah, he says, 'Our God is one' etc., until he begins the chant, saying, 'The Lord is God, the Lord is his name.' The congregation |[75] then responds to him etc."[2] Thus also the Hallel psalms (Ps 113,114,116-118) are not sung at the Ḥanukka festival, but 'should be recited in a chant'—צריך לקרותן בנעימות.[3]

If we summarise what we have said so far, we may come to the following conclusions:

1) It is certain that in the sixth century, in which the Babylonian Gemara was brought to a close—mention of which is often made in the Tractate *Sopherim*—scribes began to distinguish the individual verses with points, although this was forbidden in books designed for public reading.
2) It is certain that the origin of disjunctive accents, especially the use of the double upper points (Zaqeph = ܙܩܦܐ) is in accord with the Syriac system of punctuation, which was either invented by Joseph Huzaya or at the very least was being used by him at the end of the fifth century / beginning of the sixth.
3) When the Tractate *Sopherim* was composed, the art of cantillation must have been well known, but was not yet used in all reading and, as we can see from the fact that the tractate says nothing

[1] The words are: מיד נכנס המפטיר ואוחז את התורה ואומר שמע ישראל פסוק הראשון בנעימה ואף העם עונין אתו אחרוו:

[2] אה״כ מגביה את התורה ואומר אחד אלהינו וגו׳ ועד מתחיל בנעימה ואומר ה׳ הוא האלהים ה׳ הוא שמו ואחריו עונין אתו העם וגו׳

[3] Soph. 20,9. Thus also does one find the word נעימה as 'chanting' in the 'Manuel du lecteur' (ed. Derenbourg, op.cit.), 415: זה הוא סדורן לפי הנעימה לפי שיש מהן (מהטעמים) דרך גובה ומהן דרך רום ומהם דרך נצב [*This is their arrangement with regard to the chanting according to which some of them (the accents) are the high variety, some are elevated, and others low*]; 383: כל שר או משרת יש לו ניגון ונעימה לבדו [*every king or servant has its own melody and chanting*—ed.]; 416,2 ff.: the fixed movement (הנפה) of the hand and fingers is in agreement with the chanting, and the names of the accents are derived from [this] sound and movement; 398,9: here we see that Zaqeph is a raising of the voice, which name was introduced for ܙܩܦܐ or ܪܘܡܐ. It is the form of the sign, and not the sound, that is described.

about points while dealing extensively with the laws for the writing of scripture, they were not yet indicated with points.

4) The Syrians were also making use of the conjunctive accent ܒܢܘܪܐ, by which they tried to designate the very close connection between two words.

5) The Hebrews, in their selection of conjunctive accents, took account of the euphony of chanting.

From all this it follows that the Hebrews took note of the accents being used in the Syrian schools and then imitated their system, altering it somewhat and adding to the major disjunctive signs. The conjunctive signs, on the other hand, had not been much developed by the Syrians, who only really had the one.[1] This one the Hebrews again made use of and adapted to the customs of their own reading traditions.[2] This process cannot predate the sixth century, because |[76] it was not the older Syriac system that they seem to have borrowed, but rather the one used later by Joseph Huzaya, which included ܦܩܘܕܐ and ܙܘܓܐ.

In seeking a date for this exchange, the *terminus ante quem* can hardly be pushed beyond the middle of the seventh century, since at that time the Syrians again altered their system. We know this because it was then that Jacob of Edessa became, so to speak, the founder of grammar and the true master of accentuation, whose great precepts were followed by all the later scholars. This particular system was first given expression by Thomas the Deacon and much later again by Barhebraeus and Jacob Bar Šakko, after it had been developed and approved by Jacob of Edessa—a fact which Jacob Bar Šakko explains very clearly.[3] If, therefore, the Hebrews did indeed follow the Syrians, what they borrowed was not the developed system of Thomas and Jacob, but rather the older one of Joseph Huzaya. We can firmly conclude, then, that they first began to use accentual marks some time between the eras of Joseph Huzaya and Jacob of Edessa.

[1] From this one ܒܢܘܪܐ, four conjunctive signs were later formed, ܡܚܣܝܢܐ, ܡܫܘܚܠܦ ܡܚܣܝܢܐ, ܒܢܘܪܐ, ܡܫܘܚܠܦ ܒܢܘܪܐ.

[2] Thus one can be certain that the custom of cantillation, i.e. of ornate recitation furnished with definite musical phrases (= ترتيل), is necessarily of greater antiquity than is the business of describing this cantillation once the points had already been depicted in books.

[3] Syriac text, p.37,1.

Now although within the Hebrew system of accents and vowel-signs there was a rule that vowels in pause should be lengthened even if they were not already lengthened by a pausal accent, it is nonetheless important to remember that, from time to time, there was a distinction made between those vowels which the accentual system demanded to be read and those which we find actually marked by symbols—for example the Athnaḥ and Soph Pasuq effect a pause and demand a long vowel, but the short vowel was nevertheless preserved as at Gen 3.6 ויאכַ֣ל: and ותאכַ֖ל, and Isaiah 16.10 השבַ֣תי:. Vice versa, Zaqeph, Segolta, Revia and Ṭarḥa do not effect a pause and do not influence the nature of the vowel, but sometimes a long vowel is still found with Zaqeph, e.g. Gen 12.5 רכָ֔שו, 24.19 אשאָ֔ב, and with Segolta, Lev. 2.13 תמלָ֒ח, and Revia, Lev. 16.4 ילבָ֗ש, Ezek. 22.25 אכָ֗לו, and with Ṭarḥa, Hosea 4.17, אפרָ֖ים.

From these examples we may infer that the vowels and the accents were not added at one and the same time. The major disjunctive accents must have been written in first and then, in accordance with the oral tradition, the vowels. The lesser signs of accentuation were added later and it was by means of these that the previously placed vowels receded a little. For it is out of the question that such a great task, viz., the positioning of all the vowels and accents, could have been both begun and brought to completion all at the same time. Rather we ought to distinguish different periods, of which I believe there to have been three—the ancient period, in which the verses were marked out with the greater points (Soph Pasuq, Athnaḥ, Zaqeph, Revia), the use of which are forbidden in the tractate *Sopherim*; then a middle period, in which the vowels were added; finally, a later period, in which the lesser accents were introduced in order to indicate the cantillation for the vowels,[1] with which they did not always exactly coincide. The older scholars do not always agree with one another about these lesser signs. The whole business began in the sixth century |[77] and was brought to a close in the middle of the seventh[2]—at just that time

[1] It should be noted that the sign at the end of the verse is twofold—the Soph Pasuq, by which the verses are distinguished logically, and the Silluq, by which the modulation of the voice is described such that it ascends by a tone and a half (from an A to a C). Soph Pasuq should be counted amongst the ancient points, Silluq among the later musical ones.

[2] I believe I have published the main reasons for this sufficiently in my article, "Die Tschufutkaleschen Fragmente. Eine Studie zur Geschichte der Masora," in *Verhandlungen des fünften internationalen Orientalisten-Congresses II, Abhandlungen und Vorträge* (Berlin, 1882), 188-225.

when we saw that a new system was being introduced among the Syrians, most likely under the influence of Jacob of Edessa. It is now, therefore, imperative that we deal with the question of what Jacob added to the ancient system, and what he changed.

So to return to the Syriac accents. In addition to the final point, ܦܣܘܩܐ, Joseph Huzaya made use of logical accents: 1 ܙܘܓܐ, 2 ܬܚܬܝܐ, 3 ܥܠܝܐ; and rhetorical accents: 4 ܡܫܐܠܢܐ, 5 ܦܩܘܕܐ, 6 ܫܘܐܠܐ, 7 ܥܨܝܐ, 8 ܡܩܝܡܢܐ, 9 ܗܘ ܕܡܬܩܪܐ ܡܢ ܐܢܫ ܙܘ̈ܓܐ. This last we have suggested is the same as what Jacob called ܐܦܝܐ ܘܬܚܬܝܐ ܡܫܐܠܢܐ, where Jacob's description concerns the sense of this rhetorical accent, Joseph's its visual form.

When we compare those types of accents which Bar Šakko (p.31) ascribes to Jacob of Edessa with these groupings, it at once becomes apparent that the principles of the placement of the logical accents has remained unaltered, while certain new rhetorical accents have been added. In fact what we see is that most of the newly-suggested accents are composed out of two previously existing accents. The list does not merely enumerate the accents, it actually illustrates by examples their being joined together with each other. When we look at the nature and history of the whole system that Jacob developed, it is easy to perceive that there was no absolute logic in their composition. Let us then see what it was he did that was new.

We can see also that he duplicated the number of the primary *logical* accents by adding those which he called their ἀλλοίωσεις (*derivatives*). Thus to the simple accents ܦܫܛܐ (= ܙܘܓܐ), ܥܠܝܐ, ܬܚܬܝܐ, he added ܡܫܚܠܦ ܦܫܛܐ, ܡܫܚܠܦ ܥܠܝܐ, ܡܫܚܠܦ ܬܚܬܝܐ. Phillips noted that the signs of these derivative-accents were the same as those of the primary accents, with this one distinction, that the derivative-accents demand a slightly longer pause than the principal ones. The examples offered by Phillips are the same as those found in Bar Šakko (p.34)—thus ܡܫܚܠܦ ܦܫܛܐ is found in the pronunciation of Gen 6.4, ܓܢܒܪ̈ܐ ܗܘܘ ܒܐܪܥܐ:; while ܡܫܚܠܦ ܬܚܬܝܐ is found at Acts 9.17, ܫܐܘܠ ܐܚܝ.; and ܡܫܚܠܦ ܥܠܝܐ at Jac 1.2, ܟܠ ܚܕܘܐ ܗܘܬ ܠܟܘܢ ܐܚ̈ܝ. If one considers these citations carefully, it becomes clear that the syllables with the accents should indeed be extended just a little to make them fit with natural speech. So what Jacob did was to introduce church-readers to a manner of recitation that was more refined and euphonic than the older system, but without actually altering the signs themselves. The primary and the derivative accents are the same, |[78] but where the nature of the expression demands a longer pause, he would label the accent as a derivative.

As far as the other accents are concerned, the ones that we have been calling 'rhetorical', he did not so much propose new rules as develop existing usage and use different names for the variations. The rhetorical accents, however, are not all of a type; rather they fall into two groups. On the one hand there are those which signify ordering, asking, pleading, or rebuking; and on the other those which indicate a lesser or a greater pause. The first of these two classes of rhetorical accents may be called the *mimetic signs*, or *mimetic accents.*[xxiv] They indicate to the reader how to make his tone of voice reflect emotion—for example soulful sorrow should be expressed by a plangent tone of voice etc. The other class indicates to the reader how much time he ought to allow in between the individual parts of the sentence so as to make the reading pleasant and in accord with the structure of the argument—these we may call *temporal signs*, or *temporal accents*. We can see in this classification traces of a Greek doctrine, since Dionysius Thrax had already said: ἀναγνωστέον δὲ καθ' ὑπόκρισιν, κατὰ προσῳδίαν, κατὰ διαστολήν (*Reading must be in accordance with delivery, prosody, and internal sense-division*). ὑπόκρισιν (*delivery*) must mean the *mimetic* accents, since the scholiast explains the expression καθ' ὑπόκρισιν as κατὰ μίμησιν τῶν προσώπων (*according to the imitation of expressions*); διαστολήν (*sense-division*) then means the *temporal* accents. It is a term variously explained by the scholiasts who nevertheless all agree at least that the term means that one should recite κατὰ στιγμὴν or κατὰ χωρισμὸν τῶν διανοῖων (*according to the punctuation*, or *according to the division of the sense*).[1]

These two classes of accents, then, the mimetic and the temporal, which can already be discerned among the nine accents of Joseph Huzaya, were preserved by Jacob, although in the catalogues of accents that we read today they are all very mixed up and confused. I believe that we can easily untangle this confusion and begin our investigation not with the names of the accents but with the actual signs as such. We shall begin with the mimetic accents, not so much because reading καθ' ὑπόκρισιν holds the primary place in Dionysius Thrax, but more because the system that underlies them is the simplest and most obvious. The whole matter is most

[1] There is no place here for the third law of recitation, namely κατὰ προσῳδίαν (*according to prosody*). For προσῳδία must refer to τόνους, χρόνους, πνεύματα and πάθη, and therefore pertains to individual words only, and not the parts of the whole sentence. Only in the broadest sense does the distribution of the parts indicated by points refer to χρόνον (p.63 above, and Uhlig, 107).

easily set out in accord with the position and number of the points, which I here arrange following George Phillips:[1]

I. One point above the first letter of the word
   1. Ordering, ܦܘܩܕܐ, e.g. ܙܠ (*go!*).
   2. Asking, ܡܫܐܠܢܐ, e.g. ܐܝܟܐ (*where?*)
   3. Praising, ܫܘܒ ܬܘܕܬܐ, e.g. ܬܒܪܟܘܗܝ (*may it be blessed!*)
   4. |[79] Calling, ܡܩܪܝܢܐ, e.g. ܩܪܘ ܠܝ ܢܬܢ (*call me Nathan!*)
   5. Demonstrating, ܡܚܘܝܢܐ, e.g. ܗܐ ܐܡܪܗ ܕܐܠܗܐ (*behold the lamb of God!*)

II. One point below the first letter of the word
   6. Wondering, ܡܬܕܡܪܢܐ, e.g. ܐܝܢܐ.
   7. Desperation, ܡܣܟܝܢܘܬܐ, e.g. ܐܘܝ ܠܝ ܠܡܐ ܐܝܟ ܠܡܐ.
   8. A feeling of unexpected change, ܡܬܦܢܝܢܐ,[2] e.g. ܐܝܬܘܗܝ ܕܝܢ.

III. Two points placed upon the first word
   9. Rebuking, ܐܟܐܐ, e.g. ܐܝܟ ܢܬܦܠܠ.

IV. Two points placed obliquely after the final word of the phrase[3]
   10. Mournful, ܡܥܢܝܢܐ, e.g. ܘܝ ܠܝ:.

V. One point placed upon the first word *and* two points placed obliquely after the final word
   11. Praying, ܡܨܠܝܢܐ, e.g. ܚܘܣ ܫܒܘܩ ܡܪܝܐ:.
   12. Persuading, ܡܦܝܣܢܐ, e.g. ܒܥܐ ܐܢܐ ܡܢܟ ܡܪܝܐ:.

The mimetic accents are simple and straightforward. The point above the letter is a sign of commanding, of questioning, of praising, of calling, of demonstrating, and other such affections as are obviously expressed by means of a slight raising of the voice. The sign of rebuking, the ܐܟܐܐ, which consists in two points over the first letter, is related to these.

In the second group the point placed beneath the first word of the clause indicates to the reader that he should speak with a more relaxed voice, as is appropriate to a sense of admiration, desperation, or in those types of speech which are designated with the ܡܬܦܢܝܢܐ indicating some sort of change made ἐν παρόδῳ [*in mid-sentence*].

There is then the sign for mournful recitation, made by two points placed below the end of the word. When this is combined with the sign of

[1] G. Phillips, 'Syriac Accents,' *Journal of Philology* 9 (1880), 221-229.

[2] Phillips: "It denotes a sudden change of subject." An example is to be found at Rom 3.4, ܐܝܬܘܗܝ ܕܝܢ ܐܠܗܐ ܫܪܝܪܐ—more will be said below about this accent.

[3] Sometimes three points are written, ܘܝ ܠܝ.

commanding or calling, a new sign is created which is used for marking precative phrases or those involving persuasion. This is because both in imprecations and in |[80] expressions where we try to persuade the hearer, there is present both that tone of voice which we generally use in commands and also that which we use in complaining with a mournful voice.

This whole system of mimetic accents was developed from those first ideas which we saw above in the work of Joseph Huzaya.[xxv]

Joseph had only two temporal accents, ܣܡܟܐ and ܥܨܝܐ, indicating the lesser and the greater pauses (p.68 above). This should be borne in mind as we now proceed to set out Jacob's temporal accents, again according to the number and position of the points, which were as follows:

I. One point written above the word
   1. ܡܓܪܪܢܐ *dragging*, e.g. ܟܡܘܪܐ ܕܩܘܪܒܐ ܕܐܠܗܐ, which joins together otherwise separate elements. As we shall see below, the ܡܓܪܪܢܐ should be compared, as also ܡܚܝܕܢܐ, with the conjunctive accents.
II. A point placed high up between two words
   2. ܡܫܚܠܦ ܡܓܪܪܢܐ, *variant of dragging*, e.g. ·ܩܘܫܬܐ ·ܘܫܪܪܐ, which is used wherever the conjunctive ܘ breaks up the separate elements. This accent is also conjunctive.
   3. ܥܨܝܐ, *resistance*, e.g. ܠܐܪܥܐ ܕܐܬܬ ·ܘܒܥܘ ܘܐܬܐܘ ܡܢ ܐܬܘܗܝ.
   4. ܙܘܥܐ, *movement*, e.g. ·ܘܒܪܘܢܐ ·ܘܦܘܠܚܢܐ, which gives half the force (in terms of length) of the accent ܥܠܝܐ.
III. One point placed on the line itself
   5. ܦܫܝܛܐ, *simple*, e.g. ..ܘܡܥܬܐ ܡܢ ܥܠܡ ܠܒܝܬܗ, which sometimes appears at the end of sentences, such as at Joel 2.16. In these cases it is indistinguishable from ܦܣܘܩܐ.
   6. ܡܫܚܠܦ ܡܚܝܕܢܐ, *variant of uniting*, a variant of the accent of conjoining, which we shall see below to be a conjunctive accent. An example is ܡܬܪܘܪܒܝܢ ܒܚܝܠܐ. ܡܬܩܦܝܢ ܘܠܐ ܡܚܠܐ.
IV. A point placed below the line
   7. ܣܡܟܐ, *support*, e.g. .ܙܪܥܐ ܒܪܝܟܐ ܕܐܒܪܗܡ ܘܒܢܝܐ ܕܐܒܪܗܡ ܗܘܘ ܗܘܘ.
   8. ܡܫܚܠܦ ܣܡܟܐ, *variant of support*, e.g. .ܠܐ ܣܡܟܐ. ܘܠܐ ܚܝܠܐ. This indicates a longer pause than ܣܡܟܐ, but not so long as ܬܚܬܝܐ, such that it holds a middle position between the two.
V. Two points placed either above or on the line
   9. ܪܗܛܐ ܕܠܐ ܦܣܩ, *running that does not break off*, e.g. ܠܐ ܬܬܠܘܫܝܢ |[81] ܡܢ ܟܠ ܡܢ ܐܢܫ·· ܘܠܐ ܬܬܪܘܫܝܢ, in which we can see an accent that indicates a very short

pause which does not cause the various elements of the expression to be separated.

10. ܪܗܛܐ ܕܦܣܩ, *running that does break off*, e.g. ܠܐ ܢܗܘܘܢ ܠܟ ܐܠܗܐ ܐܚܪܢܐ.. ܐܬܗܠܟܘ.

The other accents that seem to need listing here (11 ܡܫܚܠܦܢܐ, 12 ܩܘܡܐ, 13 ܡܗܦܟܢܐ) will be dealt with below (p.83).

These points, placed above, upon, and beneath the line, which are meant to define different pausal periods, were developed on the basis of Joseph's fundamental pair, the ܥܨܝܐ and the ܫܡܫܐ, in a way similar to what we saw in the case of the mimetic accents. Jacob split the ancient form of the ܫܡܫܐ into the simple ܫܡܫܐ and the ܡܫܚܟ ܫܡܫܐ and, in the same way, for the ancient ܥܨܝܐ he created two separate names, the ܥܨܝܐ and the ܙܘܓܐ.

However, the ܬܚܬܝܐ and ܡܫܚܟ ܬܚܬܝܐ are quite different sorts of accents. In order to define as accurately as possible what these were, we first have to enquire more closely into the meaning of this term ܡܫܚܟ, and what it contributes to defining the length of the pause. We recall what was said above, that these ܡܫܚܟ accents demand a slightly longer pause that the simple ones. This is what Barhebraeus tells us, viz. that "ܡܫܚܟ ܥܨܝܐ is distinguished from ܥܨܝܐ by the length of its sound...[thus also] ܡܫܚܟ ܐܬܚܬܝܐ from ܐܬܚܬܝܐ...[thus also] ܡܫܚܟ ܦܩܘܕܐ from ܦܩܘܕܐ."[1] The same must be true of ܡܫܚܟ ܫܡܫܐ and ܫܡܫܐ, for as ܫܡܫܐ is half the length of a ܐܬܚܬܝܐ, so the ܡܫܚܟ ܫܡܫܐ is longer than the ܫܡܫܐ but not as long as the ܐܬܚܬܝܐ.[2] The system of these sorts of accents is thus: the major pause is indicated by the point being placed below the line *between* two words; the lesser pause by the point being placed *beneath* the word itself. Hence:

1) Longest pause = ܡܫܚܟ ܐܬܚܬܝܐ
2) Long pause = ܐܬܚܬܝܐ
3) Short pause = ܡܫܚܟ ܫܡܫܐ
4) Shortest pause = ܫܡܫܐ.

Thus where Joseph had had only two types of pause of differing lengths, ܐܬܚܬܝܐ and ܫܡܫܐ, Jacob was able to make use of four, thereby developing a rather more precise system of reading than had previously existed. Again, however, he was not scouting out completely new territory. Jacob has

[1] Phillips, *Letter*, 46-7.

[2] Phillips, *Syriac Accents*, 227-8.

already shown himself to be a follower of the Greeks, and he was their imitator in this matter as well. Thus Friedländer on Nicanor[1]:

> There was a proportional system |[82] used for signifying each of the different periods of time. Nicanor explains that four periods were designated by a final point (ἡ τελεία στιγμὴ δύναται τέσσαρας χρόνους σιωπῆς) [2.23],[xxvi] two by a point above the first (τῇ πρώτῃ ἄνω) [2.52], and one by a point above the second (τῇ δευτέρᾳ ἄνω) [2.132]. From this one can deduce that the ὑποτελεία (*less-than-final point*) must be equal to three periods, a fact confirmed by a corrupt scholion: ἐν τῇ συντάξει ζητοῦμεν εἰ στικτέον ἐπὶ τὸ τηλόθεν ἐκ Λυκίης Ξάνθου ἄπο δινήεντος, ὑποτελὴς γάρ ἐστιν, ἥτις τρίχρονος δύναται εἶναι,[2] which we must emend to read, ὑποτελεία γάρ ἐστιν ἥτις τρεῖς χρόνους δύναται.[xxvii] The ὑποστιγμὴ is said to represent an interval of one period [8.206].

We have, therefore, plentiful evidence that the Greek grammarians categorised the strengths of the different punctuation marks according to how long a pause each represented. On the basis of this, Jacob invented a system in which he tried to establish exactly what each and every point was worth. If ܣܡܟܐ represents two periods, then ܡܘܣܦ ܣܡܟܐ is three, ܐܬܢܚܬܐ four, and ܡܘܣܦ ܐܬܢܚܬܐ five. While the Greek system defined the relations pertaining between the τελεία (ܦܣܘܩܐ) and ὑποτελεία (which would be the ܐܬܢܚܬܐ), the Syriac went further and actually described in an absolute sense the length of each pause—which was applicable to the ܐܬܢܚܬܐ, which to the ܥܠܝܐ etc.

Since this is how the lower point (ܣܡܟܐ, ܐܬܢܚܬܐ) was used, it can scarcely be doubted that the same must hold true of the upper point accents, of which there are four: ܡܘܣܦ ܥܠܝܐ, ܥܠܝܐ, ܥܨܝܐ, ܪܡܙܐ (ܡܘܣܦ ܫܘܪܝܐ and ܫܘܪܝܐ not being included here). It seems that the ܡܘܣܦ ܥܠܝܐ indicated the greatest length of pause, ܪܡܙܐ the shortest. Jacob listed them in order of the lengths of pause they represented. However, what Friedländer said about Nicanor is equally applicable to Jacob, namely that he did not carry out this plan merely in order pedantically to observe fine distinctions; rather, it was designed to alleviate as far as possible the ignorance of his readers. We

[1] L. Friedländer, *Nicanoris περὶ Ἰλιακῆς στιγμῆς reliquiae* (Königsburg, 1850), 119.

[2] J. A. Cramer, *Anecdota Graeca e codd. parisienses* (Oxford, 1839-41), III,8 (B 877).

must also keep in mind, however, the close association of the accents with chanting, among both Syrians and Hebrews (ܢܥܡܐ, נְגִינָה). Barhebraeus is our authority for this—he says that chanting could not be learned save by actually hearing it live,[1] and then shortly afterwards he bemoans the hopeless condition of accentuation.[2] He goes on rather surprisingly to suggest that it was only Syriac and Greek books that were marked up with these musical signs.[3]

|[83] From what we have seen of the character of Jacob's achievement, it does seem that something can be deduced and said also about ܡܫܡܠܝܐ and ܡܘܣܟܦ ܡܫܪܝܐ, those accents which are designated by a point placed upon the line. As Jacob himself said (see p.49), he strove to preserve what was in the ancient manuscripts once the new vowel signs had been introduced, and in these older manuscripts nothing occurs so often as a point upon the line—which is almost the same thing as our modern comma (cf. p.64f.). In the new system, it is not possible to distinguish this sign from the ܦܩܘܕܐ, and when it was preserved in manuscripts copied from ancient exemplars, to which the scribes then added the new points designed to distinguish the sentence-parts, great confusion was bound to arise. For this reason, Jacob's rules for the use of ܡܫܡܠܝܐ, which is not an integral part of the system, are rather intricate. We can scarcely suppose that Jacob's opinion was the same as what we find in Barhebraeus,[4] but it may be possible that the latter was influenced by the former in placing the ܡܫܡܠܝܐ instead of ܚܒܠܐ, ܠܥܠܐ and ܦܘܩܐ and in it not having its own intonation—a fact which is readily explicable

---

[1] *Gramm.*, 247.

[2] Ibid., 248. Phillips, *Letter*, 35.

[3] Ibid., 247. As far as the reference to Greek books is concerned, he can hardly be referring to the points as such, which are very simple and not very common. He is probably speaking about musical notation, of which Christ & Paranikas give some examples in the *Anthologia Graeca*. But did Barhebraeus (the 'son of the Hebrew') really not mention Hebrew chanting? Surely for ܣܦܪ̈ܐ ܣܘܪ̈ܝܝܐ ܘܝܘܢ̈ܝܐ, we should read ܣܦܪ̈ܐ ܥܒܪ̈ܝܐ? We should not, therefore, set too much store by this passage which claims a *Greek* origin for Jacob's accents—I have seen Syriac manuscripts preserved in Dresden library marked up with the Greek musical notation. Wright made note of an Ethiopic manuscript also thus marked (*Catalogue of the Ethiopic mss in the British Museum* [London, 1877], 11a). On the Arabic musical notation, see J. Kosegarten, ed., *Alii Ispahanensis liber cantilenarum magnus* (Greifswald, 1840), 39, and J.P.N. Land, "Recherches sur l'histoire de la gamme arabe," in *Actes du sixième Congrès de Orientalistes* (Leiden, 1885) II, 35-99.

[4] *Gramm*, 254; Phillips, *Letter*, 50.

on the basis of our theory. Phillips is right to add that ܡܫܚܠܐ occurs at the ends of clauses, where it is found instead of ܦܣܘܩܐ.[1] What we said above about the resultant confusion is thus somewhat confirmed.

As for the ܡܗܦܟ ܡܚܝܢܐ, since it is a derivative of the ܡܚܝܢܐ, we shall deal with the pair together (p.84, below). We can move on, then, to discuss those accents that consist of a pair of points, whether placed above the line (ܙܘܓܐ ܕܠܐ ܦܣܩ), upon the line (ܙܘܓܐ ܕܦܣܩ), or below it (ܡܚܝܢܐ). The ܙܘܓܐ ܕܦܣܩ, two points placed upon the line, separates out the parts of a clause but in such a way that it should still all be read continuously, whereas the ܙܘܓܐ ܕܠܐ ܦܣܩ, two points placed above the line, seems rather to bring them closer together, even though they remain separate parts of the clause. This accent can, therefore, be compared with the ܣܡܟܐ, since the latter serves to distinguish the parts of an apodosis which might otherwise appear a self-sufficient and complete unit to which the protasis has been prefixed. There is an example of this ܙܘܓܐ ܕܠܐ ܦܣܩ in James 5.9, ܠܐ ܬܬܐܢܚܘܢ ܚܕ ܥܠ ܚܕ ܐܚ̈ܝ܆ ܕܠܐ ܬܬܕܝܢܘܢ, which makes the idea clear.

The ܡܚܝܢܐ, which joins together two Syriac words which would be one in Greek (such as ܠܐ ܡܝܘܬܐ for ἀθάνατος and ܫܘܐ ܒܐܘܣܝܐ |84 for ὁμοούσιος) is really none other than the Greek ὑφὲν, which we discussed above (p.73). The name, however, is not of ancient usage. In the treatise on the accents by Thomas the Deacon (who may be Thomas of Harkel) it is called ܣܘܪܓܐ, a name which Jacob used for a different accent, as we mentioned above (p.80). We gave earlier (p.73) Thomas's comments on this, which may be repeated in full here:[2]

> ܣܘܪܓܐ ܡܛܠ ܕܐܝܬ ܡ̈ܠܐ ܒܠܫܢܐ ܝܘܢܝܐ: ܕܟܕ ܠܣܘܪܝܝܐ ܡܬܦܫܩ̈ܢ: ܠܐ ܡܫܟܚܐ ܕܢܦܩ̈ܢ ܐܠܐ ܡܢ ܬܪ̈ܬܝܢ
> ܗ̈ܘܝܐ ܠܡܦܩ. ܐܝܟܢܐ ܕܗܠܝܢ ܐܦܘܦܛܝܩܐ ܡܬܦܫܩ̈ܢܐ: ܐܝܟ ܗܘ ܕܠܐ ܡܬܝܠܕ. ܘܠܐ ܡܫܬܚܠܦܢܐ.
> ܘܫܪܟܐ. ܐܬܚܙܝܬ ܠܐܒܗ̈ܬܐ ܩܕ̈ܝܫܐ ܘܡܦܫܩ̈ܢܐ ܕܟܬ̈ܒܐ ܐܠܗ̈ܝܐ: ܕܢܥܒܕܘܢ ܚܕ ܢܚܒܟܘܢ ܠܬܪ̈ܬܝܗܝܢ ܡܢ
> ܐܬܘܬܐ ܐܚܪ̈ܢܝܬܐ ܕܗܘܝܐ ܡܦܩܬܐ: ܘܗܘܝܐ ܐܚܪܢܐ ܠܬܪ̈ܬܝܗܝܢ ܡܢ ܐܬܘܬܐ ܡܦܩܢܝܬܐ ܕܗܘܝܐ ܕܐܝܬ.
> ܕܢܣܩܘܢ ܕܐܦ ܒܠܫܢܐ ܣܘܪܝܝܐ ܕܐܝܬ ܐܢܘܢ ܗܘ̈ܝܐ. ܐܠܐ ܒܚܘܝܐ ܚܕ ܗܘܝܐ ܐܬܝܗܘܢ.
>
> (*ܣܘܪܓܐ: since there are words in the Greek language which, when translated into Syriac, cannot be rendered except by means of two words—such as the negatives ܠܐ ܝܠܝܕܐ (ἀγέννητος) and ܠܐ ܡܫܬܚܠܦܢܐ (ἄτρεπτος) etc.—it seemed to the Holy Fathers and the translators of*

---

[1] "Its mark is the same as that of ܦܣܘܩܐ and is sometimes found at the end of a clause," Phillips, *Accents*, 225.

[2] Cf. Martin, *Ad Georgium*, 12,16-21, and where the same thing is said about the ܚܘܕܪܐ accent. There is a very confused passage about the ܣܘܪܓܐ following this. Also Phillips, *Letter*, 74 (tr. 82-3).

the Holy Scriptures that one point should be placed below the last letter of the first member, and the other point below the first letter of the second member. This indicates that in the Syriac there are two members, but in the Greek only one).

The name ܟܪܘܙܐ is transferred by Jacob to a different accent, but the idea is retained in a somewhat refined manner, for besides the simple ܡܣܒܪܐ, he also has a ܥܘܣܟ ܡܣܒܪܐ (p.80,6), which has a slightly stronger force—as is the case with all the accents called ܥܘܣܟ. The ܥܘܣܟ ܡܣܒܪܐ connects not two words, but rather two parts of the sentence. But since this accent is signified by a single point upon the line, like ܡܣܡܟܐ and ܦܣܘܩܐ, here also we can discern in Jacob a device by which he preserves the simple point from the ancient manuscripts and differentiates them by using different names rather than changing their form or position. For example, in 1 Cor. 15.42, ܡܙܕܪܥ ܒܚܒܠܐ. ܡܩܝܡ ܕܠܐ ܚܒܠܐ, the point in the middle is called ܥܘܣܟ ܡܣܒܪܐ.

We are left now with only the ܡܘܡܐ and ܡܗܘܦܟܐ, accents which were omitted by Bar Šakko (Syriac text, p.34) and which Barhebraeus |[85] merely names without describing.[1] Concerning the latter one he says:

> ܡܗܘܦܟܐ : when I wanted to hear what this accent was from a distinguished elderly Doctor of Melitene,[xxviii] he stated: I neither know about this accent nor have heard about it from my teachers.[xxix] Perhaps the holy man [Jacob] learnt it from the Greeks and called it ܡܩܪܡܬܐ [v.l. ܡܩܪܡܝܬܐ]. And perhaps it was unknown even to those Greeks living in the eastern provinces on account of their different pronunciation."[2] Barhebraeus then distinguishes ܡܘܡܐ from ܦܣܘܩܐ ܗܠܠܐ (the improper ܦܣܘܩܐ) on the basis that the former is attached to a succeeding clause by the copula ܘ. This is why I surmise that ܡܘܡܐ is also the name of a simple point which was distinguished by a special name, just as in the case of the ܥܘܣܟ ܡܣܒܪܐ, in order to maintain the strictly logical system. Since, however, it is apparent that neither Barhebraeus nor his source understood the phenomenon, being of Greek origin, let us see whether something comparable might have existed among the Greek

[1] *Gramm.* 248,6; 258.

[2] Ibid., 258. The quotation is corrupt at the end, something has fallen out which Phillips, 60, does not spot.

grammarians. We shall deal also here with the ܡܚܠܛܐ (left unexplained at p.79 above).

A. ܡܥܦܝܢܐ is an inverting accent, an example of which is given by Barhebraeus (loc. cit.) from Dt 32.1-2, derived in turn from the doctor whose words he cites, which do not fit into Jacob's way of thinking and are quite foreign to his whole system. This 'Doctor of Melitene' distributed the periods such that he would have a ܪܗܛܐ ܕܠܐ ܦܣܩ in the first place, then ܦܣܘܩܐ ܥܠܠܐ, and finally ܐܣܝܟܐ in the following manner (Dt 32.1-2):[1]

ܨܘܬܘ ܫܡܝܐ¨ ܘܐܡܠܠ. ܘܬܫܡܥ ܐܪܥܐ ܡܐܡܪܘܗܝ ܕܦܘܡܝ. ܢܛܘܦ·[2] ܐܝܟ ܡܛܪܐ ܡܠܦܢܘܬܝ. ܘܢܚܘܬ ܐܝܟ ܛܠܐ ܡܐܡܪܝ.

We have here: 1. ܪܗܛܐ ܕܠܐ ܦܣܩ after ܫܡܝܐ.
2. ܦܣܘܩܐ ܥܠܠܐ after ܕܦܘܡܝ.
3. ܐܣܝܟܐ after ܡܠܦܢܘܬܝ.

We can tell from this what the other points mean too, since he tells us what Jacob's method of reading this verse was. Jacob, he says, used 1) ܡܥܦܝܢܐ, then 2) ܡܫܚܠܦ ܡܥܦܝܢܐ ܒܝܕ ܐܬܘܬܐ, and finally 3) ܡܫܚܠܦ ܡܥܦܝܢܐ ܒܝܕ ܣܪܛܘܢܐ. So, if we take out the three abovementioned accents that were inserted by this Doctor of Melitene, then we will be left with Jacob's own arrangement of the verse as follows:

ܨܘܬܘ ܫܡܝܐ(.) ܘܐܡܠܠ. ܘܬܫܡܥ ܐܪܥܐ ܡܐܡܪܘܗܝ ܕܦܘܡܝ. ܢܛܘܦ· ܐܝܟ ܡܛܪܐ ܡܠܦܢܘܬܝ. ܘܢܚܘܬ´[3] ܐܝܟ ܛܠܐ ܡܐܡܪܝ.

The point after ·ܢܛܘܦ must be Jacob's ܡܫܚܠܦ ܡܥܦܝܢܐ ܒܝܕ ܐܬܘܬܐ (*by means of letters*), and thus after ܢܚܘܬ we must assume the ܡܫܚܠܦ ܡܥܦܝܢܐ ܒܝܕ ܣܪܛܘܢܐ (*by means of a small line*); Jacob must have put the ܡܥܦܝܢܐ after ܫܡܝܐ, which was omitted from Barhebraeus's version |[86] because of the ܪܗܛܐ ܕܠܐ ܦܣܩ that is there instead.

The significance of all this may be judged in connection with the rules of Nicanor, as Friedländer decribes them: There are two ὑποστιγμαὶ (*lower-points*), of which one "is placed in complete clauses (ἐν ὀρθαῖς περιόδαις), i.e. in those which are composed of protasis and apodosis such that the latter follows and the former precedes."[4] Such sentences are distinguished by the ὑποστιγμή.

[1] Ibid., 249,10.

[2] Sic Martin. Phillips wrote .ܢܛܘܦ in the English version, but ·ܢܛܘܦ in his Syriac text (Phillips, *Letter*, 60 and ܣܚ).

[3] I have invented this sign on the basis of its name, ܡܢ ܣܪܛܘܢܐ.

[4] L. Friedländer, *Nicanoris περὶ Ἰλιακῆς στιγμῆς reliquiae* (Königsburg, 1850), 59-76.

The other ὑποστιγμή is that "which is placed at the end of parentheses which break up continuous speech," e.g. at Iliad 2.333: Ἀρεῖοι δε μέγ' ἴαχον—ἀμφὶ δὲ νῆες σμερδαλέον κονάβησαν ἀϋσάντων ὑπ' Ἀχαιῶν—μῦθον ἐπαινήσαντες.[xxx] The mark is added to the word Ἀχαιῶν. Nicanor calls this particular ὑποστιγμή, ἀνυπόκριτος (lit. *not in the midst of the sentence*).

B. If one compares this definition of the second type of ὑποστιγμή with what we said before about ܡܥܗܕܢܐ, then it becomes immediately apparent that the two are identical and that ܡܥܗܕܢܐ, the accent of abrogation, is none other than the Syriac translation of the Greek ἀνυπόκριτος, i.e. the ὑπόκρισις (*delivery*) is 'abrogated' by this accent. But this is ἐν παρόδῳ (*in mid-sentence*). For Friedländer believes that the ὑποστιγμή ἀνυπόκριτος is used wherever a certain subordinate clause intervenes into a continuous passage, i.e. that it indicates some sort of the break-up.[1] Exactly the same thing may be illustrated by examples of ܡܥܗܕܢܐ, such as we find in Barhebraeus: ܒܪܫܝܬ [ܦܣܘܩܐ] ܐܝܬܘܗܝ ܗܘܐ ܡܠܬܐ. [ܡܥܗܕܢܐ] ܘܗܘ ܡܠܬܐ ܐܝܬܘܗܝ ܗܘܐ ܠܘܬ ܐܠܗܐ. (Jn 1.1).[2] The words preceding the ܡܥܗܕܢܐ are considered to form an intervening clause. Another example: ܠܐܠܗܐ [ܦܣܘܩܐ] ܠܐ ܚܙܐ ܐܢܫ ܡܡ ܡܬܘܡ. [ܡܥܗܕܢܐ] ܝܚܝܕܝܐ ܐܠܗܐ ܗܘ ܕܐܝܬܘܗܝ ܒܥܘܒܐ ܕܐܒܘܗܝ ܗܘ ܐܫܬܥܝ. (Jn 1.18), where the words 'nobody has ever seen' are marked out as an intervening clause by the ܡܥܗܕܢܐ, because it interrupts the syntax of the sentence. In our own orthography we would mark such interjections with brackets. A further example will illustrate what Nicanor is trying to say (Il 4.210-12):

> ἀλλ' ὅτε δή ῥ' ἵκανον ὅθι ξανθὸς Μενέλαος
> βλήμενος ἦν, περὶ δ' αὐτὸν ἀγηγέραθ' ὅσσοι ἄριστοι
> κυκλόσ', ὃ δ' ἐν μέσσοισι παρίστατο ἰσόθεος φώς.[xxxi]

The apodosis begins from ὃ δ' ἐν μέσσοισι, but the words περὶ δ' αὐτὸν... κυκλόσ' are an insertion. Hence Nicanor says, "ὑποστικτέον εἲς τὸ ἦν καὶ κυκλόσε, ὧν ἡ δευτέρα ἀνυπόκριτος ἐστιν· διὰ μέσου δὲ ταῦτα" (*Both the* ἦν *and the* κυκλόσε *must receive the* ὑποστιγμή, *and the second of these is* ἀνυπόκριτος*—they are in parenthesis*).[xxxii] Therefore, the ὑποστιγμή ἐνυπόκριτος (*lower-point within the flow of the reading*) is the equivalent of the Syriac ܬܚܬܝܐ or ܦܣܘܩܐ, while the ὑποστιγμή ἀνυπόκριτος (*lower-point that breaks up the flow of the reading*) is the Syriac ܡܥܗܕܢܐ.[xxxiii]

---

[1] Ibid., 76.

[2] *Gramm.*, I,260.

|87 The first of these two, which is to be found in straightforward sentences, is the opposite of the βραχεῖα διαστολή (*short sentence-divider*), which is used in inverted sentences (ἀνεστραμμέναις περιόδοις) where the apodosis precedes the protasis. On clauses of this type, Friedländer writes: "Nicanor holds that the order which obtains in nature, i.e. cause preceding effect, is natural also in speaking. Hence if a clause which begins with a causal conjunction (ὅτι, ἐπεί) is placed after the primary clause, then he would call that an inverted sentence."[1]

C. Unless I am mistaken, Jacob's ܡܗܦܟܢܐ (*inverting*) is also to be explained in this way. It is the accent which indicates that a sentence is inverted, that the effect precedes the cause, that in the clause the natural order of things has been reversed. For if we turn again to our earlier example (Dt 32.1), ܨܘܬܘ ܫܡܝܐ. ܘܐܡܠܠ (*Hear, O Heavens, and I shall speak*, or, *that I may speak*; πρόσεχε οὐρανὸς καὶ λαλήσω, or, ἵνα λαλῶ), the speech which he is about to make is really the cause of the hearing; so he should, strictly speaking, have said, "I am about to speak; hear, O Heavens!" This inversion is what the ܡܗܦܟܢܐ indicates. It is equivalent to the βραχεῖα διαστολή which Nicanor deems to be necessary for marking such inverted sentences (περιόδους ἀνεστραμμένας).

D. Finally, the ܡܗܦܟܢܐ ܡܘܣܚܠ (i.e. the slightly stronger ܡܗܦܟܢܐ) can be explained on the basis of the same principle. Jacob again develops the Greek system and makes a distinction where none existed before. Note the examples:

> ܢܪܣܡ· ܐܝܟ ܡܛܪܐ ܡܠܦܢܝ. (may flow like the rain my teaching)
> ܢܚܘܬ ܐܝܟ ܛܠܐ ܡܐܡܪܝ. (may descend like the dew my speech)

We have two similes in which the likeness precedes that with which it is compared.

Nicanor states that only those comparisons in which the thing itself comes first and the likeness second are counted as 'inverted sentences.'[2] The above example from Jacob, in which the likeness comes first, cannot therefore be considered an inverted sentence. However, the logical order has been reversed and Jacob seems to want to indicate this with some sort of accent. He could not use the ܡܗܦܟܢܐ, since this designates a properly

---

[1] Friedländer, *Nicanoris*, p.73.

[2] Ibid.

inverted sentence, and so he invented the ܦܣܘܩܐ ܡܗܦܟܐ as a way of indicating this reversal of the natural order.

E. All that remains now is to say something of the ܩܝܡܐ (a single point upon the line),[1] which, as noted above (p.85), is to be distinguished from the ܦܣܘܩܐ ܥܠܠܐ only insofar as a phrase found after a ܩܝܡܐ should begin with the copula ܘ. Since Barhebraeus, in his catalogue of accents, connects ܩܝܡܐ and ܡܗܦܟܐ in the same way that Nicanor connects περίοδος ὀρθή (*regular sentence*) with περίοδος ἀνεστραμμένη (*inverted sentence*), one might conjecture that ܩܝܡܐ (i.e. *standing*) is a translation of the Greek ὀρθή. But this cannot be so since a copula is placed after a ܩܝܡܐ, and there is not always such a copula in a 'regular sentence'. We should consider instead another Greek punctuation mark, known as the δευτέρα ἄνω, which is |88 usually placed before a καί.[2] An example can be found at Gen 8.14: ܘܝܪܚܐ ܗܘܐ ܐܦ ܐܪܥܐ. [ܩܝܡܐ] ܘܚܡܝܢܐ ܕܐܪܥܐ..ܒܫܒܥܐ ܐܪܥܐ. The point after the first ܐܪܥܐ is the ܩܝܡܐ, just as also after Dan and Naphtali in these words (Gen 35.25): ܘܒܢ̈ܝ ܕܒܠܗܐ ܐܡܬܗ̇ ܕܪܚܝܠ ܕܢ ܘܢܦܬܠܝ. ܘܒܢ̈ܝ ܙܠܦܐ....[3] Nicanor's usage concords with both these examples. He insists that, in the following citation, a δευτέρα ἄνω ought to be placed after πλάζουσι so as to produce a short pause before the καί (Il. 2.132):

> οἵ με μέγα πλάζουσι καὶ οὐκ εἰῶσ' ἐθέλοντα
> Ἰλίου ἐκπέρσαι εὖ ναιόμενον πτολίεθρον.[xxxiv]

Now that we have at last completed the discussion of these points, we can set out in a single table the whole of Jacob's system:

A. Mimetic Accents
   I. A point placed above the word
      1 ܡܙܘܥܐ
      2 ܦܩܘܕܐ
      3 ܡܫܐܠܢܐ
      4 ܡܣܘܚܐ
      5 ܡܢ ܬܘܗܐ
      6 ܡܬܟܫܢܐ

---

[1] But cf. what is said on p.95 in which ܩܝܡܐ is expressed by a pair of points above the line.

[2] Ibid., 57.

[3] Phillips, *Letter*, 60.

II. A point placed beneath the word
    7 ܡܢܚܬܐ
    8 ܦܘܣܩ ܡܢܚܬܐ
    9 ܡܬܪܡܢܢܐ
    10 ܡܥܗܕܢܐ
III. Two oblique points placed above the word
    11 ܐܚܘܐ
IV. Two oblique points placed after the word
    12 ܡܟܟܢܐ
V. The ܡܪܘܚܐ and ܡܟܟܢܐ together make
    13 ܡܙܝܥܢܐ
    14 ܡܦܝܣܢܐ

B. Disjunctive temporal accents
  I. A point placed above the line between two words
    1 ܦܘܣܩ ܥܠܝܐ
    2 ܥܠܝܐ
    3 ܥܙܝܢܐ (the point is placed over the final letter of the word)
    4 ܪܘܚܐ (likewise)
  II. A point placed below the line between two words
    5 ܦܘܣܩ ܬܚܬܝܐ
    6 ܬܚܬܝܐ
    7 ܦܘܣܩ ܫܡܟܐ (the point is placed beneath the final letter of the word)
    8 ܫܡܟܐ (likewise)
  III. Two points placed above the line between two words
    9 ܙܘܓܐ ܘܠܐ ܦܣܩ
  IV. Two points placed upon the line between two words
    10 ܙܘܓܐ ܘܦܣܩ
  V. Two horizontal points
    11 ܦܘܝܐ
    12 ܦܢܝ ܠܥܠܝܬܐ
    13 ܦܘܣܩ ܦܘܝܐ

|89

  VI. A point placed upon the line
    14 ܦܣܘܩܐ
    15 ܫܘܫܠܐ (= ܦܣܘܩܐ ܫܠܡܐ)
    16 ܩܘܩܠܐ
    17 ܡܗܦܟܢܐ

18 ܦܣܘܩ ܡܗܘܦܟܢܐ

C. Conjunctive Temporal Accents

1 ܡܚܝܕܐ, i.e. the Greek hyphen, which Jacob distinguishes from ܫܘܪܐ.

2 ܫܘܪܐ, which the older writers used for the Greek hyphen.

3 ܦܣܘܩ ܡܚܝܕܐ, which joins together the parts of a sentence.

4 ܦܣܘܩ ܫܘܪܐ, which is used in between clauses which are joined together by the copula.

The total therefore becomes thirty six—that is, when we compare Jacob's letter (in both Phillips's and Martin's editions) with the relevant chapters from Barhebraeus and Jacob Bar Šakko. Such a comparative analysis is required since no one author preserved the system wholly intact. The manuscripts are corrupt and Barhebraeus also mixes up Jacob's system with various other teachings.

Now that we have discussed the inner principles and the origins of the system as a whole, we can proceed to set out a reconstruction of all the accents. This will include all the accents which make their appearance in Jacob's letter (using both editions), together with those mentioned in Bar Šakko's grammar. For the latter we have used the punctuation of the London manuscript, with variant readings supplied by Prof. Wright. As soon as one begins to look into the state of the mss themselves one notes that Jacob's actual rules are not to be found as such in any one manuscript, but that if we compare the two textual traditions (i.e. that of Bar Šakko and that of Jacob's letter) then we can reconstruct a text which will exhibit the true original. At the same time we must realise that among the Syrians (who are generally to be lauded for their accurate copying) there are plenty of texts that appear problem-free at first, but which turn out to be so corrupt that the true text cannot be reconstructed without comparing a number of manuscripts. All four manuscripts of Bar Šakko are corrupt, and neither is Jacob's letter preserved clear and intact in any one witness. Readers may thus judge for themselves the state of the text and should compare the editions one with another.

In what follows, the upper line of each pair is the reconstructed text of Jacob's letter (ed. Martin, *Ad Georgium*, p.8ff., with variants from Phillips,

Letter, p.ܣ, l.9 ff); the lower line is the text of Jacob Bar Šakko, as printed at the end of this volume (p.ܟܝ, l.20 ff.).xxxv

ܐܝܠܝܢ ܕܝܢ ܕܐܬܘ̈ܬܐ ܒܩܕܡܝܬܗܘܢ ܗܘܝܐ. ܒܟܠ: ܐܝܬܝܐ.
ܐܬܘ̈ܬܐ ܕܝܢ ܕܒܗܘܢ ܡܫܟܚܢ ܐܢܘܢ

ܩ̈ܠܐ: ܡܘܣܦ ܩ̈ܠܐ: ܐܘܟܝܠ ܡܢܐ ܕܐܣܟܡܐ.
ܐܟܢܐ ܕܡܘܣܦ ܩ̈ܠܐ ܙܘ̈ܓܬܐ ܕܠܐ ܦܣܩ

|90

ܙܘ̈ܓܬܐ ܕܦܣܩ.. ܦܣܘܩܐ. ܡܟܟܢܐ ܐܝܟ ܡܫܡܫܢܐ. ܡܘܣܦ ܒܟܠ:
ܘܙܘ̈ܓܬܐ ܕܦܣܩ ܡܟܟܢܐ ܡܘܣܦ ܓܒܠܐ

ܡܘܣܦ ܠܐܝܬܝܐ. ܦܬܘܪܐ. ܡܣܡܟܐ. ܠܐܦܐ: ܡܬܠܝܢܐ. ܙܘ̈ܓܬܐ܀ ܕܠܐ ܦܣܩ
ܡܘܣܦ ܠܐܝܬܝܐ. ܦܬܘܪܐ. ܡܣܡܟܐ ܠܐܦܐ ܡܬܠܝܢܐ

ܘܕܦܣܩ:·[1] ܠܐܟܐ ܙܘ̈ܓܬܐ.. ܡܡܠܟܢܐ ܐܝܟ ܗܘ ܕܡܬܐܡܪ ܡܛܠܬ
ܠܐܟܐ ܙܘ̈ܓܬܐ ܡܡܠܟܢܐ

ܦܐܪܥܡܘܓܘܢ. ܗܢܘ ܕܝܢ ܕܡܕܡ ܡܫܬܐܠ ܡܢܡܟܐ.[2] ܡܢ ܓܘܐ.
ܡܢ ܓܘܐ.

ܦܬܘܐ. ܡܣܘܝܐ. ܡܪܟܢܐ. ܡܥܡܩܐ. ܡܬܠܝܢܐ. ܡܢܣܒܐ. ܒܟܘܡܪܐ
ܦܬܘܐ. ܡܣܘܝܐ. ܡܪܟܢܐ. ܡܥܡܩܐ. ܡܢܣܒܐ. ܒܟܘܡܪܐ

ܡܢ́ ܡܣ́ ܡܥ́ ܡܣ́ ܦܘ ܕܡܢ ܟܢܝܐ ܢܘܝܐ ܢܩܡ. ܓܪ́ ܡܘܣ́ ܓܪܘܪܐ.
ܡܓܠܝܢܐ. ܡܣܝܒܐ. ܡܘܣܦ ܡܣܝܒܐ. ܓܪܘܪܐ. ܡܘܣܦ ܓܪܘܪܐ.

ܟܪܝܐ. ܪܘܟܐ. ܡܦܟܐ. ܡܘܣܦ ܡܦܟܐ. ܪܘܟܐ ܘܡܦܟܐ. ܡܦܟ́ ܘܡܟܠ́
ܟܪܝܐ. ܪܘܟܐ. ܡܦܟܐ. ܘܡܟܠܝܢܐ.

ܡܬܠܝܢܐ ܘܪܘܟܐ ܘܙܘ̈ܓܬܐ ܕܦܣܩ.. ܪܘܟܐ ܘܙܘ̈ܓܬܐ ܕܠܐ ܦܣܩ܀
ܡܬܠܝܢܐ ܘܪܘܟܐ ܘܙܘ̈ܓܬܐ ܕܦܣܩ. ܪܘܟܐ ܘܙܘ̈ܓܬܐ ܕܠܐ ܦܣܩ

ܘܦܣܘܩܐ. ܦܘܩܐ ܕܟܠ ܐܬܪܐ.[1] ܡܦܩܢܐ ܐܝܟ ܡܡܪܡܢܐ. ܡܘܣܦ

[1] ܕܦܣܩ ܘܠܐ ܦܣܩ Phillips.

[2] ܐܣܪܬܐ Phillips.

ܘܦܣܘܩܐ

ܥܡܗ ܐܬܘܬܐ [ܐܘܟܝܬ ܥܡܗ ܡܘܩܪܐ. ܐܘܟܝܬ ܡܪܗܛܐ.][2] ܠܟܫܐ: ܥܡ
ܠܟܫܐ ܥܡ

ܗܢܘ ܠܥܠܡܐ܀ ܐܠܗܘܗܝ ܕܝܢ
ܗܢܘ ܠܥܠܡܐ. ܘܗܢܐ ܕܐܝܟ ܗܟܢ܀ . . . . ܐܠܗܘܗܝ ܕܝܢ ܒܫܡܝܐ

ܡܘܣܦ ܡܢܗܘܢ ܕܒܢܝܐ ܥܡ ܦܠܓܘܬܐ ܗܘܝܐ
ܡܘܣܦ ܡܢܗܘܢ ܕܒܢܝܐ ܐܘܟܝܬ ܦܘܣܩܐ ܥܡ ܦܠܓܘܬܐ ܗܘܝܐ.

|91

ܒܟܠܐ: ܡܠܟܐ ܕܡܟܬܒܢܘܬܗ ܕܡܘܫܐ ܡܫܝܚܐ
ܒܟܠܐ: ܡܠܟܐ ܕܡܟܬܒܢܘܬܗ ܕܡܦܩܢܘܬܐ:

ܐܫܟܚ. ܡܠܟܐ ܡܕܝܢܐ ܦܠܓܗ ܐܘ ܠܐܘܦܠܐ.
ܐܫܟܚ. ܡܠܟܐ ܡܕܝܢܐ ܦܠܓܗ ܐܘ ܠܐܘܦܠܐ.

ܡܩܝܐ: ܘܚܙܐ ܡܪܢܐ ܕܡܫܝܚܐ ܒܫܡܝܐ ܕܐܢܫܐ ܒܐܪܥܐ:
ܡܩܝܐ: ܘܚܙܐ ܡܪܢܐ ܕܡܫܝܚܐ ܒܫܡܝܐ ܕܐܢܫܐ ܒܐܪܥܐ:

ܡܘܣܦ ܡܩܝܐ: ܒܢܒܝܐ ܕܡܢ ܟܠܗ: ܗܘܐ ܐܠܗܘܢ ܡܪܐ ܕܥܠܡܐ.
ܡܘܣܦ ܡܩܝܐ: ܒܢܒܝܐ ܕܡܢ ܟܠܗ: ܐܠܗܘܢ ܡܪܢܐ ܕܥܠܡܐ

ܡܠܐܟܐ ܡܢܗ ܡܘܬ: ܡܘܬܐ ܠܥܠܡܐ.[3]

ܦܣܘܩܐ. ܟܠ ܪܘܚܐ ܕܡܘܠܕ ܦܠܓܘܬܐ ܐܠܗܘܢ ܦܣܘܩܐ ܗܘ
ܦܣܘܩܐ. ܟܠ ܪܘܚܐ ܕܡܘܠܕ ܦܠܓܘܬܐ ܐܠܗܘܢ ܦܣܘܩܐ ܗܘ

ܡܛܘ. ܡܘܬܪ ܡܢ ܡܫܝܚܐ
ܡܛܘ: ܡܘܬܪ ܡܢ ܡܫܝܚܐ.

ܘܗܟܢܐ ܕܦܣܘܩ.. ܠܐ ܚܡܝܢ ܟܠ ܚܕܬܐ ܐܘܪܚܐ..

1 ܐܬܘܬܐ. Phillips.

2 ܥܡ ܐܬܘܬܐ ܐܘ ܥܡ ܡܪܗܛܐ Phillips.

3 Line omitted, Phillips.

ܙܘܥܬܐ ܕܦܣܘܩ܀ ܠܐ ܠܟܘܢ ܟܠ ܥܒܪ̈ܝ ܐܘܪܚܐ܀

ܡܫܡܥܢܐ ܐܘܟܝܬ ܡܫܡܫܢܐ. ܠܟܘ ܕܐܡܪ ܐܒܪܘܟ. ܠܟܘ ܕܐܡܪ
ܡܫܡܥܢܐ ܠܟܘ ܕܐܡܪ ܐܒܪܘܟ. ܠܟܘ ܕܐܡܪ
ܐܫܡܥ.
ܐܫܡܥ.

ܗܘܝܬ ܒܟܝܐ. ܥܠ ܚܕܐ ܠܗܘܐ ܠܟܘܢ ܐܚܝ܆
ܗܘܝܬ ܒܟܝܐ܆ ܥܠ ܚܕܐ ܠܗܘܐ ܠܟܘܢ ܐܚ̈ܝ܆

ܗܘܝܬ ܠܐܚܝܬܐ. ܫܐܘܠ ܐܚܝ܆
ܗܘܝܬ ܠܐܚܝܬܐ. ܐܚܝ ܫܐܘܠ܆ 92

ܦܩܘܕ ܢܦܘܩ ܚܝܠܐ ܡܢ ܡܕܝܢܬܗ.
ܦܩܘܕ ܢܦܘܩ ܚܝܠܐ ܡܢ ܡܕܝܢܬܗ.

ܚܙܝܬܐ. ܘܥܠܬܐ ܡܢ ܟܠܗ ܥܡܗ.
ܚܙܝܬܐ. ܘܥܠܬܐ ܡܢ ܟܠܗ ܥܡܗ.

ܠܐܦܐ. ܐܝܟ: ܕܐܬܩܛܠ ܒܩܫܝܫܘܗ ܕܡܪܢܐ ܒܥܠ ܘܢܒܝܐ.[xxxvi]
ܠܐܦܐ: ܐܝܟ: ܕܐܬܩܛܠ ܒܩܫܝܫܘܗ ܕܡܪܢܐ ܒܥܠ ܘܢܒܝܐ.

ܠܐܦܐ ܘܦܩܕܐ. ܚܠ ܗܟܢ: ܠܐ ܐܦܩܘܕ ܐܡܪ ܡܪܝܐ:
ܠܐܦܐ: ܘܡܪܝܐ. ܚܠ ܗܟܢ: ܠܐ ܐܦܩܘܕ ܐܡܪ ܡܪܝܐ.

ܠܐܦܐ ܘܡܬܠܟܢܐ. ܠܐ ܐܦܪܐ ܠܟܘܢ: ܘܠܐ ܠܐܬܟܢ܆[ܘܟܢܫܐ ܕܗܘܝܐ:
ܠܐܦܐ: ܘܡܬܠܟܢܐ. ܘܟܢܫܐ ܕܗܘܝܐ: ܠܐ ܠܐܬܪܘܡ ܢܦܫ. ܠܐ ܐܦܪܐ

ܠܐ ܠܐܬܪܘܡ ܢܦܫ:
ܠܟܘܢ ܠܐ ܠܐܬܟܢ.[xxxvii]

ܠܐܦܐ ܘܠܐܚܝܬܐ. ܠܟܘܐ: ܗܘܝܐ ܦܠܚܘ:
ܠܐܦܐ· ܠܐܚܝܬܐ. ܠܟܘܐ: ܗܘܝܐ ܦܠܚܘ:

ܦܫܡܥܢܐ ܐܘܟܝܬ ܡܫܡܫܢܐ. ܡܢ ܠܐܟܡܫ ܐܣܘܪܬܐ: ܡܢ ܠܐܬܟܠܡ
ܡܫܡܥܢܐ. ܡܢ ܠܐܟܡܫ ܐܣܘܪܬܐ:[:.] ܡܢ ܠܐܬܟܠܡ

ܟܠܝܡܬܐ ܕܕܗܘܝܐ:[:.] ܡܢ ܠܐܟܢܝܫ ܟܪܘܒܐ ܟܢܫܢܫ:
ܟܠܝܡܬܐ:[:.] ܡܢ ܠܐܟܢܝܫ ܟܪܘܒܐ ܟܢܫܢܫ:[:.]

ܪ̈ܓܬܐ ܕܠܐ ܦܣܩ ܠܐ ܐܠܨܘܗܝ ܡܢ ܟܠ ܡܢ ܐܢܫ܍ ܘܠܐ ܐܠܦܘܗܝ.
ܪ̈ܓܬܐ ܕܠܐ ܦܣܩ. ܠܐ ܐܠܨܘܗܝ ܡܢ ܟܠ ܡܢ ܐ̈ܢܫ܍ ܘܠܐ ܐܠܦܘܗܝ.

ܪ̈ܓܬܐ ܕܠܐ ܦܣܩ ܘܦܣܩ. ܙܒܢ ܠܟܡ܍ ܘܟܢ ܟܢܫܘܬܐ..
ܪ̈ܓܬܐ ܕܠܐ ܦܣܩ ܘܦܣܩ. ܙܒܢ ܠܟܡ܍ ܘܟܢ ܟܢܘܬܐ:.

ܠܟܠܐ ܪ̈ܓܬܐ ܡܢ ܒܪܝ܍ ܘܡܢ ܒܪ ܒܪܩܐ܍ ܘܡܢ ܒܪ ܢܩ̈ܘܡ܍
ܠܟ̈ܠܐ ܪ̈ܓܬܐ. ܡ̈ܢ ܒܪܝ܍ ܡ̈ܢ ܒܪܩܐ܍ ܡ̈ܢ ܒܪ ܢܩ̈ܘܡ܍. 93

ܡܡܠܠܢܐ ܐܘܟܝܬ ܦܐܪܐܡܘܢܛܝܘܣ ܐܝܟ ܢܘܗܪܐ ܒܗܘܪܐ ܕܐܘܪܚܐ ܡܣܒܪ.
ܡܦܠܠܢܐ. ܒܗܘܪܐ ܕܐܘܪܚܐ ܡܣܒܪ.

ܢܘܢ ܛܘܒܐ. ܛܘܒܘܗܝ ܠܓܒܪܐ ܕܕܚܠ ܡܢ ܡܪܝܐ
ܢܘܢ ܛܘܒܐ܀ ܛܘܒܘܗܝ ܠܓܒܪܐ ܕܕܚܠ ܡܢ ܡܪܝܐ.

ܦܪܘܫܐ. ܦܪܘܩܢ[1] ܠܟ ܟܠܗܝ. ܐܘ [ܟܠܐܢ][2] ܦܠܚܘܢ ܠܐܠܐ.
ܦܪܘܫܐ. ܦܪܘ ܟܠܗܝ ܐܘ܍ ܟܠܐܢ ܦܠܚܘܢ ܠܐܠܐ.

ܡܫܘܚܐ. ܗܘ ܐܡܪܗ ܕܐܠܗܐ ܗܘ ܕܫܒܩ ܣܛܢܐ ܕܟܠܡܐ. ܗܘܘ
ܡܫܘܚܐ. ܗܘ ܐܡܪܗ ܕܐܠܗܐ. ܗܘܘ

ܗܘ ܕܐܡܪܐ ܕܟܠܗܘܢ ܐܠܐ
ܗܘ ܕܐܡܪܐ ܕܟܠܗܘܢ ܐܠܐ.

ܡܪܟܢܐ ܠܟܝ ܫ̈ܠܝܚܝ ܡܟܝܢ ܠܟ ܣܩ̈ܒܠܝ[3] ܡܪܝܐ.
ܡܪܟܢܐ. ܠܟܝ ܫܠ̈ܝܚܝ. ܟܕ ܐܢܐ ܡܟܝܢ ܡܪܝ.

ܡܣܝܡܢܐ. ܟܕ [ܐܢܐ][4] ܡܟܝܢ ܡܪܝ
-

ܡܫܐܠܢܐ. ܐܝܟܢ ܗܘܟܝܠ ܐܚܝܢ
ܡܫܐܠܢܐ. ܐܝܟܢ ܗܘܟܝܠ ܐܚܝܢ

[1] ܦܪܘ Phillips.

[2] Om. Martin.

[3] ܬ̈ܘܠܝܢ [ܠܟ ܣܩ̈ܒܠܝ Phillips.

[4] Om. Martin.

ܡܚܝܠܬܐ. ܐܝ ܐܝܟ ܒܐܒܐ ܐܡܘ ܒܐܒܗ ܘܒܒܝ ܠܗ ܡܢܝܐ.
ܡܒܚܝܠܬܐ. ܐܝ ܐܝܟ ܒܐܒܐ ܐܡܘ ܒܐܒܐ ܘܒܒܝ ܠܗ ܡܢܝܐ

ܡܬܕܡܪܢܐ. ܐܒܝܠܐ ܐܬܒܪܝ ܒܣܘܥܐ ܘܒܟܢܐ ܡܫܡܫܢܘܗܝ. ܐܒܝܠܐ ܗܘܘ
ܡܬܕܡܪܢܐ. ܐܒܝܠܐ ܐܬܒܪܝ ܒܣܘܥܐ ܘܒܟܢܐ ܡܫܡܫܢܘܗܝ. ܐܒܝܠܐ ܕܗܘܘ

ܠܬܗܘܐ ܡܢ ܗܟܢܐ
ܠܬܗܘܐ ܡܢ ܗܟܢܐ.

ܡܒܛܠܐ. ܐܝܬܘܗܝ ܒܪ ܠܐܠܗܐ ܗܪܟܐ.
ܡܒܛܠܐ. ܐܝܬܘܗܝ ܒܪ ܠܐܠܗܐ ܗܪܟܐ.

ܡܚܝܕܐ. ܗܘܐ ܒܐܘܣܝܐ. ܚܣܠܝ ܒܟܠ. ܠܐ ܒܣܘܐܐ 94
ܡܒܝܒܝܕܐ[sic]. ܦܘܐ ܒܐܘܣܝܐ. ܚܣܠܝ ܒܟܠ. ܠܐ ܦܣܘܐܐ.

ܗܘܝܟ ܡܚܝܠܬܐ.[1] ܡܕܘܪܝܢ ܒܢܟܠܐ ܡܚܡܢ ܘܠܐ ܢܟܠܐ.
ܗܘܝܟ ܡܢܝܚܬܐ. ܡܕܘܪܝܢ ܒܢܟܠܐ ܘܡܚܡܢ ܘܠܐ ܢܟܠܐ.

ܒܪܘܪܐ. ܟܡܘܪܐ. ܟܪܘܡܐ. ܟܠܘܬܐ. ܟܐܣܘܪܐ
ܒܪܘܪܐ. ܟܡܘܪܐ. ܟܪܘܡܐ. ܟܠܘܬܐ. ܟܐܣܘܪܐ.

ܗܘܝܟ ܒܪܘܪܐ ܡܘܡܐ ܘܡܪܝܐ ܘܪܟܝܢܐ ܘܡܣܝܢܐ ܢܛܪܝܢ ܐܢܘܢ
ܗܘܝܟ ܒܪܘܪܐ. ܡܘܡܐ. ܘܡܪܝܐ. ܘܪܟܝܢܐ. ܘܡܣܝܢܐ ܢܛܪܝܢ ܐܢܘܢ.

ܟܪܝܗܐ ܒܗܘ ܡܘܡܐ ܠܐܒܪܝܢ ܕܐܢܐ ܒܐܒܝ ܘܐܢܘܢ ܒܗ ܐܢܘܢ
ܟܪܝܗܐ. ܒܗܘ ܡܘܡܐ ܠܐܒܪܝܢ ܕܐܢܐ ܒܐܒܝ ܘܐܢܘܢ ܒܝ ܐܢܘܢ.

ܡܚܝܠܬܐ ܘܟܪܝܗܐ. ܕܐܬܐܡܪ ܡܘܡܢܐ ܒܛܘܪܐ ܗܢܐ ܡܢܝܐ ܚܕܐ
ܡܢܝܚܬܐ ܘܟܪܝܗܐ· ܕܐܬܐܡܪ ܡܘܡܝܐ ܒܛܘܪܐ ܗܢܐ· ܡܢܝܐ ܚܕܐ.

ܙܘܓܐ. ܘܟܪܘܠܐ· ܘܣܩܠܐ
ܙܘܓܐ· ܘܟܪܘܠܐ· ܘܣܩܒܠܐ.

ܦܣܩܐ. ܙܢܝܩܐ ܟܡܪܢ ܒܐܪܟܐ. ܘܣܛܢܐ ܡܬܟܡܪܢ ܡܢܗ.
ܦܣܩܐ. ܙܢܝܩܐ ܟܡܪܢ ܒܐܪܟܐ.

[1] ܡܚܝܕܐ Phillips.

ܗܘܝܟ ܫܡܝܐ. ܠܐ ܡܘܬܐ. ܘܠܐ ܚܝܐ.
ܗܘܝܟ ܫܡܝ̇ܐ. ܠܐ ܡ̇ܘܬܐ. ܘܠܐ ܚܝ̈ܐ.

ܙܘܓܐ ܘܦܫܝܛܐ. ܙܘܓܐ ܡܫܠܡܐ· ܒܚܝܐ ܡܣܬܟܠܐ.
ܙܘܓܐ ܘܦܫܝܛܐ. ܙܘܓܐ· ܡܫܠܡܐ ܒܚܝ̈ܐ ܡܣܬܟܠܐ.

ܫܡܝܐ ܘܡܬܚܙܝܢܐ. ܒܪܫܝܬ ܐܝܬܘܗܝ ܗܘܐ ܡܠܬܐ.
ܫܡ̇ܝܐ ܘܡܬܚܙܝܢܐ. ܒܪܫܝܬ ܐܝܬܘܗܝ ܗܘܐ ܡܠܬܐ܀

ܡܫܡܠܝܢܐ ܘܙܘܓܐ ܘܙܘܓܬܐ ܕܦܫܛ. ܐܢܫܐ ܗܘ ܕܡܫܬܪ ܡܘܬܐ..
ܡܫܡܠܝܢܐ ܘܙܘܓܐ ܘܙܘܓܬܐ ܕܦܫܛ. ܐܢܫܘ ܗܘ ܕܡܫܬܐܪ ܡܘܬܐ:· | 95

ܦܫܘܪ ܘܙܘܓܐ ܘܙܘܓܬܐ ܕܠܐ ܦܫܛ ܘܦܫܘܛܐ. ܙܡܝܢܘ ܕܡܘܬܐ
ܦܫܘܪ ܘܙܘܓܐ ܘܙܘܓܬܐ ܠܐ ܕܦܫܛ ܘܦܫܘܛܐ. ܙܡܝܢܘ ܕܡܘܬܐ

ܕܫܡܥܘ·· ܕܐܘܪܚܐ.
ܕܫܡ̈ܥܘ ܕܐܘܪܚܐ.

ܡܘܡܐ. ܘܚܕܐ ܗܘܐ ܡܢܗ ܐܦܝ ܐܘܪܚܐ. ܘܒܢܝ̈ܗ ܕܟܠܗܘܢ[1] ܕܝ ܘܡܫܬܠܛ
-

ܡܘܦܩܢܐ ܐܘܟܝܬ ܡܬܪܡܝܢܐ. ܕܗܘ ܫܡܝܐ ܘܐܡܠܠ. ܗܘܝܘ ܟܕ
-

ܐܬܐܬ[..]. ܠܫܡܥ ܐܘܪܚܐ ܡܐܡܪܐ ܕܦܘܫܩ. ܐܝܟܢܐ ܟܕ ܡܬܬܪܓܡܢܐ. ܘܒܪܫܡ
-

ܐܝܟ ܡܠܬܐ ܡܬܟܫܦ. ܟܠ ܐܬܐܬܐ ܕܝ ܕܡܢ ܟܠܗܝܢ ܕܕܟܪ. ܡܢ ܟܠܟܠ ܕܝ ܕܪܡܫ.
-

ܠܟܘܠ ܟܡ ܚܪܝ ܠܡܫܡܠܐ. ܟܕ ܠܐ ܐܬܐ: ܘܐܡܫܝܚܘ ܠܐܘܪܚܐ ܠܐܟܝ.
ܠ̇ܟܘܠ ܟܡ ܚܪ̈ܝ ܠ̇ܡܫܡܠܐ. ܟܕ ܠܐ ܐܬ̇ܐ: ܘܐܡ̇ܫܝܚܘ ܠܐܘܪܚܐ ܠܐܟ̇ܝ.

ܡܫܡܠܝܢܐ ܗܟܝܠ ܕܡܬܠܐ ܡܪܡܘܬܐ ܕܕܘܟܬܐ: ܐܘ ܟܡܝܘܬܐ ܦܠܓܘܬܐ:
ܗܟܢ ܐܝܟ ܢܘܩܙܐ ܦܫܝܛܐ ܘܡܬܚܒܠ. ܕܐܝܟ ܟܘܡܪܘܬܐ ܫܘܝܬܐ

[1] ܐܬܠܐܘ. ܕܪܫܝܡ add. Phillips.

ܘܡܫܡܠܝܐ ܕܢܘܩܙܐ ܡܕܡ ܕܚܣܪ ܐܝܟ ܠܦܣܩܐ ܘܡܙܝܥܢܐ ܕܢܘܩܙܐ. ܐܠܐ
ܟܕ ܦܠܓܘܬܐ ܕܡܢ ܡ̈ܠܐ ܐܬܐܟܪܝ܀

ܥܠܘܗܝ ܦܘܪܫܢܐ. ܐܝܟ ܕܐܡܪ ܕܠܐ ܕܢܗܘܐ ܠܦܣܩܐ ܕܡܙܝܥܢܐ. ܕܒܠܚܘܕ:
ܘܙܘܥ ܠܡܥܒܕ ܕܠܦܣܩܐ ܕܒܠܚܘܕ:

ܘܡܫܘܚܬ ܚܕܐ. ܟܕ ܗܘ ܕܝܢ ܦܘܪܫ ܠܡܠܘܐ ܕܬܪܬܝܢ.
ܘܡܫܘܚܬ ܚܕܐ: ܐܝܟ ܕܠܐ ܕܢܗܘܐ. ܟܕ ܗܘ ܕܝܢ ܦܘܪܫ ܠܡܠܘܐ ܕܬܪܬܝܢ.

ܘܐܝܟ ܗܘ ܕܐܡܪ ܕܪܘܚܐ ܕܠܐ ܦܣܩ ܗܢܘܢ ܡܫܘܚܬ ܚܕܐ. ܐܬܐܡܪܬ
ܘܐܝܟ ܗܘ. ܕܐܡܪ ܕܪܘܚܐ ܕܠܐ ܦܣܩ: ܗܢܘܢ ܡܫܘܚܬ ܚܕܐ. ܐܬܐܡܪܬ |96

ܕܝܢ ܡܛܠ ܐܪܒܥܐ ܕܦܠܓܘܬܐ ܗܘ ܕܟܠܗܘܢ ܐܬܐܡܪܬ. ܕܐܬܘܬ ܕܝܢ.
ܕܝܢ ܡܛܠ ܐܪܒܥܐ ܕܦܠܓܘܬܐ ܗܘ ܕܟܠܗܘܢ ܐܬܐܡܪܬ. ܕܐܬܘܬ ܕܝܢ.

ܡܛܠ ܕܬܠܬܐ ܡܕܡ ܗܘ ܕܐܬܐܡܪܘ ܘܐܝܟ ܘܐܬܬܠܬ ܠܡܠ ܚܕܕܐ.
ܡܛܠ ܕܬܠܬܐ ܡܕܡ ܕܐܬܐܡܪܘ ܐܝܟ ܘܐܝܟ ܠܡܠ ܚܕܕܐ܀

ܡܫܘܚܬ ܚܕܐ ܕܝܢ. ܦܣܘܩܐ ܥܡܝܩܐ[1]
ܡܫܘܚܬ ܕܝܢ ܚܕܐ: ܦܣܘܩܐ ܥܡܝܩܐ ܘܬܠܬܘܗ ܥܡܝܩܐ܀

ܘܠܗܘܢ ܐܝܟ ܦܠܓܘܬܐ ܐܬܐܡܪܘ ܠܡܫܡܠܝܘ.[2] ܘܗܟܝܠ ܘܡܫܘܚܬ ܠܐܬܠܬܐ.
ܘܗܟܝܠ ܡܫܘܚܬ ܠܐܬܠܬܐ.

ܦܣܘܩܐ ܘܬܠܬܘܗ ܥܡܝܩܐ ܘܬܠܬܐ ܡܬܬܠܬܝܢ. ܘܚܣܝܐ ܘܡܫܘܚܬ
ܦܣܘܩܐ ܘܬܠܬܘܗ ܥܡܝܩܐ. ܘܬܠܬܐ ܡܬܬܠܬܝܢ. ܘܚܣܝܐ: ܘܡܫܘܚܬ

ܚܣܝܐ ܗܘ[3] ܗܟܢܐ ܡܥܒܪܢ. ܟܕ ܕܚܣܝܐ ܡܡܫܚܢ[4]
ܚܣܝܐ: ܗܘ ܗܟܢܐ ܡܥܒܪܢ. ܟܕ ܕܚܣܝܐ ܡܡܫܚܢ ܐܦ ܗܢܘܢ

ܕܗܘܘ ܗܢܘܢ ܡܬܚܫܒܢ ܠܡܠ ܚܕܕܐ.. ܡܫܘܚܬ ܚܣܝܐ ܕܝܢ ܐܘܟܝܬ ܚܣܝܐ.
ܕܗܘܘ ܡܬܚܫܒܢ ܠܡܠ ܚܕܕܐ. ܡܫܘܚܬ ܚܣܝܐ ܕܝܢ ܐܘܟܝܬ ܚܣܝܐ.[5]

[1] ܗܢܐ ܡܫܘܚܬ ܚܕܐ ܕܝܢ: ܘܦܣܘܩܐ ܘܬܠܬܘܗ ܥܡܝܩܐ Phillips.

[2] ܘܠܗܘܢ...ܠܡܫܡܠܝܘ om. Phillips.

[3] om. Phillips.

[4] ܡܥܒܪܢ...ܡܡܫܚܢ om. Phillips.

[5] The first hand has corrected an original ܚܣܝܐ to ܚܣܝܐ.

ܚܕ ܒܚܘܕ ܐܠܗܘܬܗ ܒܠܡܫܝܚܐ. ܘܡܫܝܚܐ   ܠܒܪܗ. ܘܠܗ ܠܐܠܗܐ.
ܚܕ ܒܚܘܕ ܐܠܗܘܬܗ ܒܠܡܫܝܚܐ. ܘܡܫܝܚܐ ܐܝܟ   ܠܒܪܗ ܘܠܗ ܠܐܠܗܐ܀

ܒܪܝܬܐ ܕܝܢ   ܘܪܘܚܐ ܡܫܡܠܝܢ. ܟܕ ܕܒܪܝܬܐ ܒܫܘܝܐ ܗܘ ܒܡܠܟܘܬܐ.
ܒܪܝܬܐ   ܘܪܘܚܐ ܡܫܡܠܝܢ. ܟܕ ܗܘ ܕܒܪܝܬܐ ܒܫܘܝܐ ܗܘ ܒܡܠܟܘܬܐ.

ܪܘܚܐ ܕܝܢ ܟܠ ܫܡܠܝܐ ܡܠܐܡܪܝܢ. ܠܘܬ ܕܝܢ ܐܝܟ ܐܘ   ܢܘܩܙܐ ܕܪܡܙܝܢ
ܪܘܚܐ ܕܝܢ ܟܠ ܦܫܠܝܐ ܡܠܐܡܪܝܢ. ܠܘܬ ܕܝܢ ܐܝܟ   ܢܘܩܙܐ ܕܪܡܙܝܢ

ܟܣܢܝܐ. ܐܣܟܝܐ. ܡܫܡܫܢܐ. ܡܫܡܠܝܐ. ܘܐܬܟܠܝܐ ܦܢ ܠܐܡܫܘ ܣܢܕܝܢ
ܟܣܢܝܐ. ܐܣܟܝܐ. ܡܫܡܫܢܐ. ܡܫܡܠܝܐ. ܘܐܬܟܠܝܐ ܦܢ ܠܐܡܫܘ ܣܢܕܝܢ 97

ܠܡܫܡܠܝܐ. ܡܫܡܫܢܐ ܕܝܢ ܟܠܐ ܗܘ ܕܪܘܚ ܡܠܐܡܪ. ܕܐܝܟ ܐܡܪ. ܦܠܐ
ܠܡܫܡܠܝܐ. ܡܫܡܫܢܐ ܕܝܢ ܟܠܐ ܗܘ ܕܪܘܚ ܡܠܐܡܪ.

ܐܬܐ ܡܫܝܚ ܡܪܢ ܐܠܘܗܝ ܚܟܡ. ܦܠܐܬܐ ܡܫܡܗܝ ܡܪܝ ܫܠܘ ܠܟܡܠ
-

ܒܟܪܗܘܢ.   ܡܫܡܠܝܐ ܕܝܢ ܟܕ ܡܫܘܐ ܠܫܘܡܠܐ ܐܘ ܠܒܫܟܠܬܐ ܡܫܡܠܐ.
ܡܫܡܠܝܐ ܕܝܢ ܟܕ ܡܫܘܐ ܠܫܘܡܠܐ ܐܘ ܠܒܫܟܠܬܐ ܡܫܡܠܐ܀

Next follows a passage only found in Jacob's letter (Martin, Phillips):

ܐܝܟ ܕܐܡܪ ܒܡܫܡܘܥ ܙܘܥ ܐܬܘ̈ܬܐ. ܠܟܠܗ ܕܐܒ ܐܚܝܢܝ: ܠܟܠܗ ܕܐܒ ܐܡܫܝܚ. ܡܢܐ ܕܐܡܪ ܠܢ: ܗܫܘܡ ܠܙܘܥܐ ܕܐܬܟܬܒܝܢ ܘܐܬܬܢܝ ܠܗ: ܐܝܟ ܡܫܠܡܢܐ. ܡܫܘܚܐ ܦܪܘܫܐ ܦܣܘܩܐ ܡܬܠܚܡܐ ܘܡܢ ܛܘܒܐ. ܘܡܫܠܡܢܐ ܒܠܘ̈ܩܝ ܐܬܘ̈ܬܐ ܡܠܐܡܪ. ܐܘ ܕܢܠܦܘܢ ܗܘ ܕܡܫܡܠܐ ܪܓܫܐ. ܐܘ ܡܢܫܡܫܢܝܬܐ ܡܫܡܠܐ. ܘܕܢܐܦܘܢ ܦܘ ܐܝܟ ܗܘ ܕܡܢ ܠܡܟܬ̈ܒܐ ܟܠܐ ܦܘܩܐ ܐܡܪܐ. ܐܡܠܐ ܗܠܝܢ ܕܘܟ̈ܝ. ܘܐܬܡܫܡܫ ܠܟܠܗܘܢ. ܘܗܐ ܢܘܙܐ ܘܡܬܒܥܐ. ܐܢܘܢ ܐܡܪܐ ܠܟܠܟܠܐ܀ ܕܫܘܚܐ ܕܝܢ ܐܝܟ ܗܘ ܕܡܢ ܡܢܐ ܐܡܪܐ: ܐܡܬܐ ܐܝܟ ܐܘܡ. ܘܐܢܘܢ ܗܟܠܐ ܐܡܪ: ܦܘܢ ܗܘܐ ܕܠܐܒܝܢ. ܡܫܘܚܐ ܕܝܢ ܐܝܟ ܗܘ ܕܒܪܒܟܐ ܡܫܘܐ ܗܘܐ. ܐܝܟ ܗܘ ܕܐܡܪܐ ܕܗܐ ܐܡܪܗ ܕܟܠܗܐ ܗܘ ܕܡܫܡܠܐ ܣܓܝܬܘ ܕܒܠܒܐ. ܘܠܗܘܢ ܗܘ ܗܘ ܕܐܡܪܐ ܕܟܠܗܘܢ ܐܠܐ. ܦܪܘܫܐ ܕܝܢ ܠܗ ܒܬܡܘܡܘܢ ܕܐܒ. ܦܫܘܕܐ ܕܝܢ ܗܘܢܟ ܒܫܘܦ ܟܠܙܐ ܕܦܓܐ ܐܢܐ. ܡܬܠܚܡܐ ܕܝܢ ܐܝܟ ܕܡܢ ܒܩܛܐ ܟܠܐ ܠܟܠܐ ܒܪܟܘܬܐ ܡܠܐܡܪܐ ܢܩܫܐ ܫܘܚܡ ܚܡܫ ܣܓܝܬ̈ܐ. ܗܘܢ ܛܘܒܐ ܕܝܢ ܗܘ ܕܒܗ ܒܡܟܠܬܐ ܛܒܝܢ ܛܘܒܐ. ܛܘܒܘܗܝ ܠܓܒܪܐ. ܐܝܟ ܕܝܢ ܠܐܘ ܠܟܫܐ ܒܡ ܗܢܘܢ ܠܡܫܡܠܝܐ ܗܘܐ. ܒܠܐ ܐܠܐ: ܘܐܡܫܝܢ ܠܙܘܥܐ ܠܠܒܢ. ܘܗܘܘܢ ܕܘܡܪܐ: ܠܟܠܗ ܒܗܢ.

The texts then continue in parallel:

ܡܠܐܘܡܪܢܐ ܕܝܢ ܠܘܬ   ܡܫܡܠܟ ܡܢ ܡܫܡܠܝܐ
ܠܘܬ ܕܝܢ ܡܠܐܘܡܪܢܐ   ܡܫܡܠܟ ܡܢ ܡܫܡܠܝܐ

ܘܡܫܡܠܝܐ ܡܠܐܘܡܪܢܐ   ܡܢ ܟܠ ܟܕ ܚܙܐ ܟܠܐ ܕܟܠܘܗ ܕܒܪܟܐܠ

ܘܡܥܒܕܢܐ ܒܗܘܢ ܕܡܬܦܫܩܢܐ ܐܝܬܘܗܝ: ܡܢ ܕܗܢܐ ܒܟܠ ܕܟܘܬܗ ܕܝܢܐ: 98

ܡܬܐܡܪ ܒܗ ܗܟܢܐ. ܐܝܟܢܐ ܗܘܐ ܠܡܬܡܠܠܘ ܡܢ ܦܘܡܐ. ܐܝܟܢܐ ܐܬܐܡܪ
ܡܬܐܡܪ ܒܗ.
ܒܡܫܘ ܘܒܟܬܒ ܦܬܓܡܘܗܝ. ܡܫܝܚܐ ܕܝܢ ܕܠܐ ܡܢ ܦܘܡ ܢܦܩ ܘܐܬܡܠܠܬ
ܡܫܝܚܐ ܕܝܢ ܕܠܐ ܡܫܬܡܥ ܢܦܩ ܘܐܬܡܠܠܬ

ܢܦܪܐ. ܐܠܐ ܕܡܬܡܠܠܬ ܢܦܪܘܗܝ ܠܦܬܓܡܐ ܗܘ ܕܒܠܒܘܗܝ ܚܫܝܒ
ܢܦܪܐ. ܐܠܐ ܕܡܬܡܠܠܬ ܢܦܪܐ ܠܦܬܓܡܐ ܕܒܠܒܘܗܝ ܚܫܝܒ

ܡܫܝܚܐ. ܡܬܦܫܩܢܐ ܕܝܢ ܫܡܘܫܬܐ ܗܘ ܕܡܠܐ. ܘܒܝܕܗ ܟܠ ܐܝܟܐ
ܡܫܝܚܐ܀ ܡܬܦܫܩܢܐ ܕܝܢ. ܫܡܘܫܬܐ ܗܘ ܕܡܠܐ. ܘܒܝܕܗ ܟܠ ܐܝܟܐ

ܕܡܫܬܟܚ ܕܡܠܐ ܗܘ ܟܕ ܚܫܝܒ ܡܬܦܫܩܢܐ. ܐܘ ܠܫܘܟܠ
ܕܡܫܬܟܚ ܕܡܫܬܟܚ ܕܡܠܐ ܗܘ ܟܕ. ܚܫܝܒ ܡܬܦܫܩܢܐ. ܐܘ ܠܫܘܟܠ

ܡܬܐܟܠܐ ܚܫܝܒ ܠܘܬ ܐܝܟܐ ܕܐܦ ܢܦܩܐ ܠܐܪܥ ܗܢܘܢ ܕܫܘܡܐ ܡܬܐܡܪܝܢ
ܡܬܐܟܠܐ ܚܫܝܒ܀ ܠܘܬ ܐܝܟܐ ܕܐܝܟ ܢܦܩܐ ܠܐܪܥ ܗܢܘܢ ܕܫܘܡܐ ܡܬܐܡܪܝܢ.

ܘܠܫܘܟܠ ܕܡܠܐ ܘܫܡܥܐ ܫܡܝܥ. ܗܘ ܕܝܢ ܕܫܡܥ ܟܠ ܢܦܫܐ
ܘܠܫܘܟܠ ܕܡܠܐ ܘܫܡܥܐ ܫܡܝܥ ܗܘ ܕܫܡܥ ܟܠ ܢܦܫܐ

ܕܐܫܬܡܥܐ: ܟܕ ܕܠܐ ܡܠܐ ܘܠܐ ܫܡܥܐ ܐܡܪܝܢ ܠܦܬܓܡܐ. ܦܫܘܩܐ
ܕܐܫܬܡܥܐ. ܟܕ ܕܠܐ ܕܡܠܐ ܐܠܐ ܕܫܡܥܐ ܐܡܪܝܢ ܠܦܬܓܡܐ܀ ܦܫܘܩܐ

ܕܝܢ ܠܘܬ ܘܡܫܝܚܐ ܡܡܫܠܛܝܢ ܒܗܘܢ ܕܟܠ ܟܠ ܢܦܫܐ ܐܝܟܐ ܠܡܐܡܪ:
ܕܝܢ ܠܘܬ ܘܡܫܝܚܐ ܡܡܫܠܛܝܢ ܒܗܘܢ ܕܟܠ ܟܠ ܢܦܫܐ ܐܝܟܐ ܠܡܐܡܪ.

ܦܫܘܩܐ ܡܬܐܡܪܘ ܗܘ ܕܫܡܥ ܒܫܘܠܡ ܦܬܓܡܐ. ܡܫܝܚܐ ܕܝܢ
ܦܫܘܩܐ ܡܬܐܡܪܘ. ܗܘ ܕܫܡܥ ܒܫܘܠܡ ܦܬܓܡܐ܀ ܡܫܝܚܐ ܕܝܢ:

ܠܒܢܐ ܢܐܡܪ ܒܡܠܬܐ ܠܟܠܗ ܕܒܫܘܪܝܗ ܡܠܝܢ ܡܢ
ܠܒܢܐ ܢܐܡܪ ܒܡܠܬܐ. ܠܟܠܗ ܕܗܘ ܒܫܘܪܝܗ ܡܠܝܢ ܡܢ ܦܘܡܐ ܐܘ

ܢܦܫܐ ܐܚܪܢܐ ܐܝܬܘܗܝ ܒܦܬܓܡܐ: ܗܘ ܕܝܢ ܡܠܝܢ ܡܢ
ܐܝܟܢܐ ܐܘ ܢܦܫܐ ܐܚܪܢܐ ܐܝܬܘܗܝ ܒܦܬܓܡܐ. 99

ܐܝܟܢܐ ܐܘ ܦܘܡܐ ܘܠܫܢܐ. ܠܘܬ ܕܝܢ ܕܥܘܠܐ ܕܦܫܩ ܘܠܐ ܦܫܩ
ܠܘܬ ܕܝܢ ܕܥܘܠܐ ܕܦܫܩ ܘܠܐ ܦܫܩ.

ܘܗܟܢܐ ܐܦ ܥܡܟܘܢ ܐܚܝܢܝ. ܗܘܐ ܕܝܢ ܕܟܠ[1] ܗܘܕܥܐ ܗܘ ܕܝܘܡ ܕܝܢܐ
ܘܗܟܢܐ ܐܦ ܥܡܟܘܢ ܐܚܝܢܝ ܗ ܕܟܠ ܗܘܕܥܐ ܕܝܘܡ ܕܝܢܐ

ܘܐܝܟ ܢܘܪ: ܡܕܢܚܐ܆ ܘܢܦܩ ܒܡܥܪܒܐ. ܘܢܗܪ ܒܟܠ: ܥܠܡܐ.. ܟܠܗ
ܘܐܝܟ ܢܘܪ ܡܕܢܚܐ܆ ܘܢܦܩ ܒܡܥܪܒܐ. ܘܢܗܪ ܒܟܠ ܥܠܡܐ܀ ܘܟܠܗ

Now that we have set forth in detail Jacob's own system and have demonstrated the Greek learning of which he made use, we must finally turn our attention to a third system of pointing, one which occupies a mediate position between the simple earlier system of Joseph Huzaya and the highly developed work of Jacob of Edessa. Once this is done we shall be able to gain a fuller picture of the process of development that allowed the Syriac masters to cultivate the art of pointing their manuscripts and to read with increasing fluency.

This third, intermediate, system is extant in the catalogue of accents composed by one Thomas the Deacon, whom Phillips persuasively identified with Thomas of Harkel.[2] Martin has also edited Thomas's treatise[3] and has furthermore attributed another short anonymous tract (only edited in Phillips)[4] to the same school, albeit not to Thomas himself. This latter work enumerates twenty accents, but the ܡܫܠܡܢܐ, which is found in Thomas's work, is not among them (according to Martin's edition). Hence, argues Martin, the work cannot be Thomas's, as the latter has a total of twenty four accents.[xxxviii]

At the beginning of this anonymous tract,[5] the writer recalls the tradition of the learned masters who devised ten accents. The first of these must surely have been Joseph Huzaya, since we know from elsewhere that nine accents were attributed to Joseph, not including the ܦܩܘܕܐ which, as

[1] ܟܠ Phillips.

[2] Phillips, *Letter*, 90

[3] Martin, *Ad Georgium*, 11-13. See also H. Ewald, "Weitere Erläuterungen der syrischen Punctation, aus syrischen Handschriften," *Zeitschrift für die Kunde des Morgenlandes* 1 (1837), 204-212, at p.205f. [Extracts from this treatise are also found in BL Add. 12178, and edited in Phillips, *Letter*, 83-4—ed.].

[4] Phillips, *Letter*, 68-74 (Appendix I).

[5] Phillips, *Letter*, 68 (trans.75).

we argued earlier (p.68n), must have existed already, thus giving Joseph ten accents in all.

The writer of the tract, therefore, was familiar with Joseph's system, and furthermore Jacob's is dependent both upon this anonymous tract and upon Thomas the Deacon. As a result of this continuous tradition, we can therefore set forth a conspectus of the history of Syriac accents, as follows:

Temporal Accents

	Joseph, c. 500	Thomas, c.616	Jacob, c.670
	ܟܒܝܐ	ܟܒܝܐ	ܟܒܝܐ ܡܘܣܚܦ ܟܒܝܐ
	ܐܫܠܡܐ	ܐܫܠܡܐ	ܐܫܠܡܐ ܡܘܣܚܦ ܐܫܠܡܐ
100	ܙܘܓܐ	ܩܘܐ ܩܪܐ ܕܐܬܡܟܬܐ	ܩܘܐ ܡܘܣܚܦ ܩܘܐ ܩܪܒ ܠܐܬܡܟܬܐ
	ܦܣܘܩܐ	ܦܣܘܩܐ ܡܫܝܚܐ[1]	ܦܣܘܩܐ ܡܫܝܚܐ
	ܟܪܝܗܐ	ܟܪܝܗܐ ܙܘܟܐ ܕܠܐ ܦܣܩ ܙܘܟܐ	ܟܪܝܗܐ ܙܘܟܐ ܕܠܐ ܦܣܩ ܙܘܟܐ
	ܣܡܟܐ	ܣܡܟܐ ܙܘܟܐ ܕܦܣܩ	ܣܡܟܐ ܡܘܣܚܦ ܣܡܟܐ ܙܘܟܐ ܕܦܣܩ
	-	-	ܩܘܡܐ ܡܗܦܟܢܐ ܡܘܣܚܦ ܡܗܦܟܢܐ

[1] Although this accent is lacking in the anonymous tract of Phillips's Appendix I.

Mimetic Accents

ܦܣܘܩܐ	ܦܣܘܩܐ	ܦܣܘܩܐ
ܡܫܐܠܢܐ	ܡܫܐܠܢܐ	ܡܫܐܠܢܐ
-	ܡܚܘܝܢܐ	ܡܚܘܝܢܐ
-	ܪܘܡܐ	ܪܘܡܐ
-	ܡܡܟܟܢܐ (or, ܗܘ ܬܚܬܐ)	ܡܡܟܟܢܐ ܗܘ ܬܚܬܐ
-	ܡܙܥܩܢܐ (or, ܡܬܡܗܡܢܐ)	ܡܙܥܩܢܐ
ܗܘ ܕܡܪܟܒ ܡܢ ܠܘܬ ܐܦ̈ܝܢ	ܡܦܝܣܢܐ ܠܐܒܗܐ	ܡܦܝܣܢܐ ܠܐܒܗܐ
ܡܢܝܚܢܐ	ܡܢܚܬܐ	ܡܢܚܬܐ ܚܘܠܦ ܡܢܚܬܐ
-	ܡܬܕܡܪܢܐ	ܡܬܕܡܪܢܐ
[ܡܙܗܪܢܐ][1]	ܡܟܬܒܢܐ (or, ܡܙܗܪܢܐ)	ܡܟܬܒܢܐ
-	-	ܡܒܥܝܢܐ

Conjunctive Accents

-	ܡܚܣܝܢܐ (or, ܪܡܘܙܐ)	ܡܚܣܝܢܐ ܚܘܠܦ ܡܚܣܝܢܐ
-	ܫܪܘܪܐ	ܫܪܘܪܐ

[1] I.e. *admonitory*, cf. p.86B.

ܦܘܣܚܟ ܚܘܪܐ

|[101] I cannot deny that I have placed some of the accent names in this table a little arbitrarily, e.g. it is possible that two ܪܗܛܐ accents should not be located as they are (the one being placed beside ܚܪܝܢܐ, the other by ܡܫܚܠܐ), and there is also some uncertainty over the accent ܗܘ ܕܡܢܚܬ ܥܡ ܐܙܩܝܦ ܐܘ ܙܩܦܐ, as also with ܦܘܩܐ and ܡܦܘܩܢܐ. However, looking at these tables, there can be little doubt that Jacob's system was developed from Thomas's and Thomas's in its turn from Joseph's. The whole tradition began c.500, was developed by Thomas [of Harkel] c.610, and then given its mature form by Jacob.

Like Jacob, Thomas was influenced by the older Greek teaching, since he discusses oxytones and paroxytones.[1] It was actually he, therefore, who took the first steps on that particular path which Jacob would tread after him. When we compare Jacob's rules with those of Nicanor, as we did earlier, the two are not so close that one could actually posit the former's direct dependence on the latter, but it is enough to prove that Jacob took the basics of his system from a Greek school in which the ancient Alexandrian tradition had been preserved from antiquity.

Just as Barhebraeus follows Jacob's grammar in his list of rules for nouns (p.61), so he does the same in the case of the accents. He adds only a little of his own on the East Syrian accents and on chanting (ܙܡܪܐ), but is in agreement with Jacob on the actual individual signs. Nobody today is qualified to make any judgment on his comments about chanting since we cannot hear the Syrians themselves making their recitations, and it seems very unlikely that they have retained the ancient reading tradition to this day, especially as Barhebraeus himself bore a somewhat unfavourable opinion of the readers of his own time.[2]

This is just about all that can be said about the fragments of Jacob of Edessa as far as grammar is concerned. We have seen him to be a pious, learned and careful man, who directed all his mental effort to the formation of a sound clerical education. He was a man who strove to restore ecclesiastical discipline, the art of singing, the reading of the Scriptures and of the Fathers, and the study of the Greek language. His principal means of achieving this was by taking a particular concern for

---

[1] Martin, *Ad Georgium*, 11-12; Phillips, *Letter*, 83. Thomas's observation about the ܚܘܪܐ is rather obscure and is repeated by Barhebraeus (*Gramm.*, 255, l.4).

[2] *Gramm.*, 248, l.14.

the accurate copying of manuscripts and the proper training of students in the Syriac language. In his role as a bishop of the Syrian church his concern for education went so far as to compose a grammar himself. This grammar was borrowed from the Greek schools and was based on the Greek model, but he effected the task with such diligence and accuracy that every Syriac grammarian who followed him made use of this fundamental text, a point that Barhebraeus makes explicitly a number of times in his *Book of Splendours*. Thus did Jacob become the father of Syriac grammar and the first of Semitic stock to cultivate Semitic grammar, for the Arabic and Hebrew grammarians are without doubt of somewhat later date and the other peoples of the Semitic race left the business of grammar almost entirely untouched.

---

[i] I.e. '*giving due attention to delivery, prosody, and internal division.*' The words come at the very beginning of Dionysius Thrax's *Technē* (Uhlig, 6,14).

[ii] Stephanus: Σκοπὸν ἔχων ὁ τεχνικὸς εἰσαγωγικὴν γράφειν τέχνην, ἀποφεύγει τῶν τόνων τὰ δυσχερῆ, τουτέστι τὸ πνεῦμα, τὸν χρόνον καὶ τὰ πάθη....ἵνα δὲ μὴ παντελῶς ἀνοήτους καταλείπῃ, ὥς πέρ τις καλὸς τροφεὺς ἐκ παντὸς ἐδέσματος λαβὼν μεταδίδωσι παιδὶ τρεφομένῳ [ὑπ'] αὐτῷ οὕτως οὗτος παντὸς τεχνικοῦ διδάγματος τὰ λεπτομερῆ συνάγων ἐντίθησιν ἡμῖν, καὶ μεταβαίνει πάλιν εἰς τὴν στιγμήν, σύμφορος γάρ ἐστι καὶ αὕτη τῇ ἀναγνώσει τῆς γραμματικῆς. Melampus: περὶ του ἀναγκαιοτάτου τῶν προσῳδιῶν, τουτέστι περὶ τοῦ τόνου, διδάξας ἡμᾶς ὡς ἐν συντόμῳ, περὶ τῶν στιγμῶν, τουτέστι περὶ τῆς διαστολῆς διαλαμβάνει κτλ.

[iii] This is the system described in Dionysius Thrax, ch.IV. The *full-point* is sometimes called the *upper point* and is clearly meant to be higher up than the other two varieties.

[iv] The first line is from Illiad 1.36, "*to the Lord Apollo, whom the fair-haired Leto bore.*" The point in Greek marks the natural pause, as in the English. The second is from Iliad 1.51, "*then on the men he let fly his bitter arrow, and struck.*" Here the ὑποστιγμὴ (*minor point*) marks the end of the metrical line and divides the participle from the main verb.

[v] Again, cf. what Dionysius himself says (Uhlig, 7-8).

[vi] Merx appears to mean that we might add an exclamation mark after ἱπποδάμοιο because the statement preceding this is a reproach, not (as with the Greek grammarians) because of the apparently asyndetic nature of the period. The Homeric line means "*You are asleep, son of wise-hearted, horse-taming Atreus! It is not right that a counsellor, to whom the armies are entrusted and upon whom there are so many worries, should sleep all night long.*"

[vii] For words that are derived-from-a-compound, see p.33 above.

[viii] Segal, *Diacritical Point*, 63ff., does not treat the system of pausal accents in Add. 12150 as being fundamentally different from later examples, the only difference being that in this early ms the only commonly found points are the three simplest, viz. ܦܘܣܩܐ, ܥܠܝܐ, and ܬܚܬܝܐ. Where Merx thinks that he sees a 'Greek' full/upper point, Segal sees an early form of the ܥܠܝܐ; where Merx sees a 'Greek' middle-point, Segal assumes a normal ܦܘܣܩܐ (Merx later admits that the ܦܘܣܩܐ did derive from the middle-point as found in this ms.); finally, Merx's 'Greek' lower-point is Segal's ܬܚܬܝܐ. Segal thus integrates Add. 12150 into the development of the accents that one can see in the early biblical mss. and places a question mark against the theory of Greek origins to which Merx was led by his interpretation of the same ms.

However, it seems that here Merx has been more perceptive than Segal and his analysis should be (in part) preferred, on the basis of the observations of F. Stanley Jones, "Early

Syriac Pointing in and behind British Museum Additional Manuscript 12,150" in R. Lavenant, ed., *Symposium Syriacum VII* (Rome, 1998), 429-444. Jones (p.440f.) shows that, once the secondary pointing (which had not before been noted) is accounted for, the system in Add 12150 is fundamentally different from later mss and that Merx's analysis was closer to the mark. What Merx calls the upper point is not actually the highest accentual mark used, but it does mark sentence completion, whereas the point on the line is used for subdivision.

Merx's simplification of the system to three marks explains why his points sometimes look higher than they do in Lagarde's edition from which he took them, e.g. the point on ܡܗܩܐ· is represented in Merx rather higher up than it should be. Jones argues (p.444) that the correspondences Merx used are accurate and that his conclusion of a Greek origin for the accents (*contra* Segal, 63) should stand.

[ix] *We must therefore shut out that madman's habit of ranting about the so-called 'poisonous' plants—eager as he is to slander everything. For he even raves against iron and fire, and in doing this he is really doing the contrary to what is in his interests.*

[x] *Mani therefore deifies the sun as if it were essentially 'good' and is in danger of implying rather that the fiery element is clearly some sort of 'good'.*

[xi] I.e. from the same early ms, BL Add. 12150, dated to AD 411.

[xii] *Thus naturally sins destroy the sinner, even though he does what he ought not in ignorance. But if judgment follows upon disobedience to commands, then much more shall God destroy those who are unwilling to give him their worship. For he who refuses to listen, lest he should be liable, is already judged as if he did know. For he had knowledge of that to which he would not listen—such that this stratagem has no power as a defence in the eyes God who knows the heart. Wherefore etc.*

[xiii] This contradicts what was said at the beginning of this discussion, that, as in the Greek system, the lower-point served to distinguish protasis from apodosis, or as Dionysius says, 'that the thought is not yet complete but is still in need of completion.'

[xiv] Again from the same ms: *Those who say concerning the creation of this whole world...that it has no beginning and no governor, and that there is no Lord and no providence, and that it has arisen by itself randomly, without a reason, and by chance, however this may have happened, they are impious and irrational men. For this reason they are to be kept far from godly men.*

[xv] *And again he who subscribes to the one that alone is over all, the life giving Word of God who is his saviour and death's conqueror, is not moved when he hears about death, or about the dissolution of the soul along with its body, nor does he call death a god.*

[xvi] By 'protasis' and 'apodosis', Merx refers here not to the parts of a conditional sentence as such (as in traditional Greek grammar) but to the Syrian terms ܫܘܪܝܐ and ܦܘܢܝܐ, which refer rather to the two principal subdivisions of the Syriac sentence in general.

[xvii] *Now again, since we see that all of a sudden a ferocious storm has violently and brutally arisen, angered by the violence of its frequent and manifold waves, to fall upon the solid ship of the*

whole orthodox church, because of this we too have been moved to [make] a written version of the recollections, although we shall bring forth only a few of them, even though in every way the times very much hinder and forbid it, and stand as far as possible in the way of us dealing with the record of those ecclesiastical events which have now happened for a second time.

xviii Merx interprets the passage straightforwardly. One must compare Segal's alternative reconstruction of the text (*Diacritical Point*, 66n1). While accepting that the text is problematic as it stands, Segal's reconstruction is quite far-fetched in the number of scribal errors and miscorrections required to achieve it. This especially relates to the sixth item in Merx's list below.

xix Although Merx here suggests the identity of ܡܢܝܚܢܐ and ܡܢܝܚܬܐ, Joseph Bar Malkon later teaches the contrary—see p.124n.

xx The reference to is מזריע, which now has a Yethiv rather than a Pashṭa (both are 'Dukes' among the disjunctive accents).

xxi I.e. Job, Psalms, Proverbs.

xxii Surely the reading of the London ms, ܐܦܘܩܡܢܘܣ ܗܘ ܕܝܢ ܡܬܩܢܝܢܬܐ is preferable to that of the Vatican ms, ܐܦܘܩܡܢܘܣ ܡܬܩܢܝܢܬܐ, since the second term is a translation of the first.

xxiii The reader of the 'dismissal' reading of the Torah in the synagogue service.

xxiv Revell, *Aristotle and the Accents*, 22, rightly prefers to call these 'sense' accents, but we shall keep to Merx's term here.

xxv The development and expansion in the number and nature of the accents, which Merx outlines here in some detail, was almost certainly motivated not purely by internal considerations of recitation, but also by the intrusion of quasi-philosophical theory. The close connection between the study of logic and that of grammar has been remarked upon before (see Introduction). The list of the Aristotelian parts of speech in the anonymous work related to that of Thomas is the same as that in Probus's commentary on the *De Interpretatione* of Aristotle and this list clearly relates to the names of accents. Later grammarians therefore developed the accentual system under the influence of the 'Aristotelian' theory (see Revell, *Aristotle and the Accents*, 22-6). Furthermore, a long list of types of speech found in Paul the Persian's *Elucidation of the De Interpretatione* seems to presage the more elaborate lists of accents which were developed by and after Jacob of Edessa (see Hugonnard-Roche, *Du commentaire à la reconstruction*). Future considerations of the Syriac accentual system must take into account the important influence of theoretical logic. See further discussion in the Introduction, and Daniel King, 'Grammar and Logic in Syriac (and Arabic),' *Journal of Semitic Studies* 58,1 (2013), p.101-120.

xxvi The references in brackets in this quotation are to the Iliad scholia, among which the fragments of Nicanor, grammarian of the 2nd cent. CE, are to be found. The most accessible edition is that of H. Erbse, *Scholia Graeca in Homeri Iliadem (scholia vetera)*, 7 vols. (Berlin: De Gruyter, 1969-1988). A summary of Nicanor's system of eight punctuation

---

marks, which Merx has used to elucidate the Syriac system, may be found in D. Blank, "Remarks on Nicanor, the Stoics and the Ancient Theory of Punctuation," *Glotta* 61 (1983), pp. 48-67.

[xxvii] *In this composition we must ask whether [the sentence], 'from afar out of Lycia, from the eddying Xanthus'* [Il. 2.877] *should be punctuated. For there is a 'second-longest-final point' which has the force of three periods.* This 'corrupt' scholion derives from the **h** group of the A scholia to the Iliad and can be located in the footnotes to the scholia on Iliad 2.877 (Erbse ed.).

[xxviii] Is this doctor from Melitene the ܐܒܕܘܩܘܣ (The Ebdokus of the Berlin mss—see ch.4, endnote xxviii), a priest of Melitene whom Barhebraeus elsewhere mentions as a predecessor of his in writing glossaries of homonyms (Martin, *Œuvres* II,77)?

[xxix] Phillips reads "from my times" (Phillips, *Letter*, ܡܟ).

[xxx] *The Argives shouted aloud—and around them the ships echoed wondrously beneath the shouting of the Achaeans—as they praised the speech.* See Nicanor in Erbse, *Scholia*, sub loc. This was a common example of a parenthesis, cf. also ps.-Trypho in M. L. West, "Tryphon, De Tropis," *Classical Quarterly* 15 (1969), 239.

[xxxi] *But when they had come around where fair-haired Menelaus was, wounded, and around him were gathered all the captains in a circle, the godlike hero came and stood in their midst.*

[xxxii] Erbse, *Scholia*, sub loc.

[xxxiii] See also p.268 where Barhebraeus discusses this accent. Moberg, *Akzentuation*, 89-90, finds this equation particularly weak. Merx does not make use of Jacob's own description of the ܡܗܓܝܢܐ (Phillips, *Letter*, 31-2).

[xxxiv] *Who hinder me greatly and do not allow me to go and sack the well-peopled citadel of Ilium.* Nicanor's note can be found in Erbse, *Scholia*, sub.loc.

[xxxv] In what follows, every effort has been made to follow the positions of the points as presented by Merx. Given the limitations of modern typesetting however, every care must be taken to refer to the original. Even so, Merx makes occasional errors (or approximations) in the positioning of the points, hence reference should also be made to the editions of Martin and Phillips (which do not always anyway agree in the pointing) and to the mss underlying those editions (principally, Vat.Syr. 152 and BL Add. 12178). Phillips, *Letter*, includes an English translation of all of this material.

[xxxvi] Merx's interpretation of the position of the *taksa* varies more than necessary. Vat. Syr. 152, f.189v, shows the *taksa* written as a pair of oblique points more-or-less top left of the final letter of a word. Martin and Phillips do not match in their typographical representation of the ms.

[xxxvii] There is clearly a good deal of corruption in these last two examples. The second half of Jer. 5.9 (which was used for the example of ܬܚܘܬܐ ܘܡܫܪ̈ܝܐ) has been added in both texts

as an extra example of ܐܬܘܬܐ ܘܡܫܐܠܬܐ, but in a different order in each. It does not appear in Phillips's text (save as an editorial addition).

[xxxviii] See discussion about these related texts in the Editor's Introduction. They are certainly very similar indeed and use many of the same biblical passages to illustrate the points. Some passages are identical verbatim, despite the small differences here noted.

Chapter 7

THE EAST SYRIAN GRAMMARIANS ʿENANIŠOʿ AND ḤUNAIN

|[102] Once Jacob had established a whole new approach to language, other learned men followed him by writing similar textbooks, although none of these approach Jacob for depth and subtlety.[i] They were not interested in probing into deeper linguistic matters and merely sought to develop a system which would alleviate as far as possible the difficulty of reading purely consonantal texts. They found two ways of doing this. The simpler approach was to explain difficult words with glosses and keep lists of these glosses, following the order in which these words appeared in the texts; the alternative was to make separate lists of all such words in alphabetical order. This of course leads to the writing of dictionaries. Perhaps the most difficult part of doing this for Syriac was how to deal with those words which were written with the same consonants but pronounced differently according to their meanings in different contexts. These were called ܦܘܫܩ̈ܐ. The first recorded author to have written about these types of words is Joseph Huzaya,[1] but the oldest extant treatise on the subject is the small work by ʿEnanišoʿ, edited by Hoffmann.[2]

Living at about the same time as Jacob of Edessa, ʿEnanišoʿ (650-90) wrote, besides his *Paradise* and a *Book of Philosophical Divisions*, another work entitled ܬܘܪܨܐ ܕܫܡܗ̈ܐ ܘܡ̈ܠܐ ܚܫܘܟ̈ܬܐ ܕܒܟܬܒ̈ܐ ܕܐܒܗ̈ܐ ܕܐܝܬ ܒܦܘܪܫ ܡܫܡܫܢܘܬܐ ܕܒܝܬ ܐܪ̈ܟܐ ܕܥܘܡܪܐ ܗܢܐ ܕܟܠܗܘܢ ܦܘܫܩ̈ܐ ܕܐܚܪ̈ܝܐ ܚܠܦܝܢ ܒܫܪܝܪܘܬܐ. (*A correction*[ii] *of obscure names and words that are in the books of the Fathers, which are in the 'Different Meanings' of the archives of this monastery, and which in truth supersede all the pointings of later [authors]*).[3] This title is given by Thomas of Marga and Hoffmann takes it to mean that ʿEnanišoʿ was making provision for a future time when people would be so far removed from the original teacher that they had to rely

[1] Says Barhebraeus (Martin, *Œuvres*, II,77).

[2] G. Hoffmann, *Opuscula Nestoriana* (Kiel, 1880), 2-49. On ʿEnanišoʿ, see *BO* III,1,145.

[3] Quoted in Hoffmann, *op.cit.*, v. Hoffmann emends the text from ܕܐܝܬ ܒܦܘܪܫ ܡܫܡܫܢܘܬܐ ܕܒܝܬ ܐܪ̈ܟܐ to ܒܦܘܪܫ ܡܫܡܫܢܘܬܐ ܕܐܝܬ ܒܒܝܬ ܐܪ̈ܟܐ (*...by means of a distinction of meanings, which is in the archives of this monastery...*). ܡܫܡܫܢܘܬܐ = χρήσεις / λέξεις, as Hoffmann proves by many examples (p.xiii). But in three of the citations he gives, χρῆσις means simply 'use'. All this is of little moment for our overall thesis here. See ܡܫܡܫܬܐ in Payne-Smith's *Thesaurus*.

entirely on his book for those readings which at an earlier date they would have learned orally. Since the diacritical points were not yet at that time sufficiently developed to differentiate all the vowels, such lists of 'Different Meanings' were used instead. Hoffmann's opinion, then, was that the short text that he was editing was indeed an example of this genre, since the author uses exactly the same pattern six hundred times, writing down first |[103] the ܡܩܪ̈ܝܐ, i.e. the written words, then the ܦܘܪܫ ܡܫ̈ܢܝܬܐ, i.e. the different meanings, and finally the biblical references.

However, Hoffmann missed out on the real meaning of ܦܘܪܫ ܡܫ̈ܢܝܬܐ, because by his transposition of ܕܐܝܬ, (see n.3 below) he made this expression out to be part of the description of ʿEnanišoʿ's own work, rather than the title of a previously existing book. It is not at all certain whether this is really what Thomas of Marga meant. The book that Thomas describes is actually said to be a ܬܘܪܨܐ ܕܡܩܪ̈ܝܐ ܘܡܦܩ̈ܢܬܐ ܚܩ̈ܘܒܬܐ ܕܡ̈ܠܐ ܕܐܒ̈ܗܬܐ. The words that are 'corrected' therein are all words 'in the books of the Fathers', whereas the text he was editing was entirely based on biblical citations. Moreover, Thomas describes the book as a ܬܘܪܨܐ, i.e. a 'correction' or a 'correct form for writing words', and yet there are no such things found in the text Hoffmann edited. One can hardly maintain, therefore, that the two are one and the same. Thomas of Marga's description in fact leads us to the conclusion that what ʿEnanišoʿ wrote was actually more like another extant text (described by Wright), which is called ܡܩܪ̈ܝܐ ܕܦܫܩܐ ܕܒܣܝܠܝܘܣ.[1] In this latter work, the written form of the Greek words, together with their pronunciations, as well as that of the harder Syriac words, are provided in the same order in which they appear in the Syriac version of Basil. It is clearly designed to be used by someone who wants to try to read Basil by themselves. Such a work might accurately be called a ܬܘܪܨܐ ܕܡܩܪ̈ܝܐ ܘܡܦܩ̈ܢܬܐ ܚܩ̈ܘܒܬܐ ܕܡ̈ܠܐ, whereas the sort of text that Hoffmann published would more accurately be called something like *On Homonyms* (ܕܡܝ̈ܢܬܐ).

Let us turn now, therefore, to ʿEnanišoʿ's *On Homonyms,* or *On Similar Words.* The extant form of the work has undergone an expansion by Ḥunain ibn Isḥāq and one other later scholar who has added some Arabic glosses,[2] [iii] such that it is hard now for the reader to be sure whose grammatical theory is being followed at any given moment. The first thing that is really of note is the fact that ʿEnanišoʿ does not make use of the

---

[1] Wright, *Cat.* I,114a (BL Add. 14684).

[2] Part of the text (Hoffmann, *op. cit.*, 68,21ff.) is also to be found in Berlin Sachau 72 and is given in full in the appendix of Gottheil, *Elias*, 61-7.

vowel-names. Such vowel names as do appear (ܦܬܚܐ 18,6; 21,9; ܪܒܨܐ ܟܪܝܐ = *e* 21,16; ܙܩܦܐ = *ā* 18,10) are attributable to Ḥunain, not to ʿEnanišoʿ.[1]

He does not order the various word-forms according to their roots but very exactly in alphabetical order, i.e. participles are found under ܡ, 3rd person masculine imperfects under ܢ, and 2nd person and 3rd person feminine imperfects under ܬ. He does not know any underlying principle for distinguishing Peal from Pael, but very often he finds the meaning of the Pael in something being done repeatedly, whereas the Peal means it is done only once. In fact, none of the Syrians ever understood the derivation of stems and even more recent grammarians—Amira, Sciadrensis, Acurensis, Echellensis, Timothy (Isaac) of Amida, and Assyrus (Petermann 17) in the Book of Inflection (ܦܘܢܝܐ)—have not explained it correctly.[iv]

|104 However, we cannot conclude from this that ʿEnanišoʿ was unsophisticated according to the grammatical standards of his day, nor should we be surprised that he knows the names of the tenses (ܙܒܢܐ ܕܥܒܪ, ܙܒܢܐ ܗܘܐ ܘܕܩܐܡ 14,16 Hoffmann; 14,20) and distinguishes the imperative (ܦܘܩܕܢܝܬܐ 3,15) from the indicative (ܡܫܬܥܝܢܝܬܐ 3,18). He also distinguishes masculine from feminine (ܕܟܪܢܝܬܐ, ܢܩܒܢܝܬܐ 16,15), although he does not manage to separate verbs from adjectives or designate pronouns by the term ܚܠܦ ܫܡܐ, as one can tell from the following comment:[v]

[2] ܒܛܝܢ ܐܦܝܢ. ܘܟܠ ܕܟܘܬܗ ܙܢܐ. ܗ̄. ܕܝܠܢ...ܒܛܝܢ ܐܦܝܢ ܘܟܠ ܕܟܘܬܗ ܙܢܐ. ܗ̄. ܕܐܚܪ̈ܢܐ.

He then gives an example:

[3] ܡܡܠܠ ܡܪܝܐ ܥܡ ܡܘܫܐ ܐܦܝܢ ܠܩܘܒܠ ܐܦܝܢ܀

The point about verbs and adjectives is illustrated by a later comment:

ܣܓܝ. ܗ̄. ܣܘܓܐܐ ܕܩܐܡ ܒܗ ܐܢܫ. ܐܝܟ ܗܘ ܕܣܓܝܘ ܗܘܐ ܩܢܝܢܗ...ܣܓܝ. ܗ̄. ܡܕܡ ܕܙܥܘܪ
[4][vi] ܗܘܐ ܘܩܠܝܠ ܩܠܝܠ ܐܬܪܒܝ. ܐܝܟ ܗܝ ܕܩܠܝܠ ܐܝܬ ܗܘܐ ܠܟ ܩܕܡܝ ܘܣܓܝ ܠܟ.

It is clear from this way of distinguishing ܣܰܓܺܝ from ܣܓܝ that he does not understand very well the difference between an adjective (ἐπίθετον) and a verb (ῥῆμα), and so he can hardly have been well trained in grammatical

[1] Hoffmann, *op. cit.*, xiii.

[2] Ibid., 10,20ff. "*Batain, ʾapain, and everything of this kind, means 'our'...batīn, ʾapīn, and everything of this sort, means 'of others'.*"

[3] *The Lord spoke with Moses face to face* (Ex 33.11).

[4] Ibid., 40,23ff. "*Saggi: that is, the abundance in which a man exists, such as in 'his material wealth was abundant'* (Gen 13.6)*...sgi: that is, that which was small and is bit by bit increased, such as in 'you had little before me, and it was much increased'* (Job 8.7)."

theory. Just how great his confusion in grammatical matters is can be shown from another comment:

ܪܛܢܘ. ܗ̄. ܦܠܝܓܐ. ܐܝܟ ܗܘ ܕܪܛܢܘ ܥܠ ܐܠܗܐ ܘܐܡܪܘ. ܪܛܢ. ܗ̄. ܚܕ ܐܢܫ. ܐܝܟ ܗܘ ܕܪܛܢ ܥܠ ܗܘܐ[1]

The plural and singular usage has been confused with the difference between a Peal and a Pael!

ʿEnanišoʿ uses one particularly unusual term, which I am sure I have never seen used by any other grammarian, namely ܦܘܣܩܢܐ (5,18-20), which he sets in opposition to the imperative, since ܐܬܪܘܒ and ܐܬܪܗܪ are said to be imperatives while ܐܬܪܘܒ and ܐܬܪܗܪ are ܦܘܣܩܢܐ. It is not at all certain just what this is supposed to mean. It cannot be a reference to the perfect tense since he calls this ܙܒܢܐ ܕܥܒܪ (14,16).[2] It might be that it refers to the indicative, which the Syrians lacked a word for, or to the finite verb (ῥῆμα ὁριστικόν), or to the active voice, in which case it would correspond to the Greek ἐνέργεια or ἐνεργητικόν, although the translator of Dionysius Thrax calls this ܡܫܡܫܢܐ ܕܡܥܒܕܢܘܬܐ. However, since Jacob Bar Šakko (Syriac text, p.25) uses the expression ܐܬܘܬܐ ܕܦܘܣܩܢܐ to refer to the pronominal suffixes of the noun, to the alaph of the emphatic state, and to the personal endings on the verb, I would argue that ܦܘܣܩܢܐ means the form of the finite verb (ὁριστικὸν ῥῆμα) and that in this instance it corresponds to the Greek ὅρος, albeit elsewhere it corresponds to ἀποτέλεσμα (*completion*).[vii] If we can see here in Bar Šakko's terminology a particularly ancient tradition |[105] already known to ʿEnanišoʿ, then the same must also be true of the technical terms ܡܛܫܝܐ (*concealed*) and ܡܦܫܩܐ (*open*) which he uses to differentiate the silent *h* from the properly pronounced *h*, terms which surely have their origin among the Syriac masoretes.

At any rate, ʿEnanišoʿ's book has more to do with early Syriac lexicography than Syriac grammar, and furthermore he was the last individual to write on the subject before Jacob of Edessa at the end of the seventh century. After Jacob, nobody dared to write another grammar for more than a hundred years, such was the latter's authority and the volume of the work he accomplished.

---

[1] Ibid., 45,22ff. *"rtan(u), that is, plural, such as in 'they murmured against God and said'* (Ex 17.3 conflated with Mt 20.11)*; ratten* (Pael)*, that is, singular, such as in 'he murmured concerning him'."*

[2] Neither is he thinking of the pluperfect (ὑπερσυντελικόν), which in the version of Dionysius Thrax is ܡܫܡܠܝܐ (see p.17).

The next Syriac grammarians we come to are from the ninth century, but very few indeed of their works have come down to us. The foremost was Išoʿ Bar Nūn (Patriarch of the Church of the East, 824-8) who wrote another work on synonyms (ܦܘܚܡܐ).[viii] He was the teacher of John Masawayh and was on friendly terms with the circles who vigorously pursued the task of translating Greek texts into Arabic at the ʿAbbāsid court.[1] It was with their help that he was elected Patriarch. The most significant of them were Gabriel Boḥtišoʿ and Michael, doctor to the Caliph al-Māʾmūn.[2]

This John Masawayh, who had been taught by the patriarch, was in turn the teacher of none other than Ḥunain ibn Isḥāq, who is said to have been expelled from the school and travelled through Greek-speaking lands where he became highly accomplished in Greek. He was then brought back to al-Maʾmūn's court by Gabriel Boḥtišoʿ, where he was free to spend time in translating both Syriac and Greek books. Besides being a very great master and the teacher of translators, it is said that he also composed twenty five books of his own.[3]

Given the sort of work that Ḥunain engaged in, it was quite impossible for him to ignore grammar. He is said in particular to have been interested in the lexicography of al-Ḫalīli.[ix] His work does not seem to have extended beyond matters of Syriac, Greek, and Arabic vocabulary and it is no surprise, therefore, that a Syriac grammar, entitled ܟܬܒܐ ܕܢܘܩܙܐ, was attributed to him, as well as a compendious lexicon which Bar ʿAlī

[1] On Išoʿ Bar Nun, see *BO*, II,435; III,I,165-6,616, Nr.49; Martin, *Œuvres*, II,77; Wright, *Syriac Literature*, 216-18.

[2] There is nothing known for certain about the lives and times of these doctors since Barhebraeus has quite different information on them from other authors. I refer the reader to G. Weil, *Geschichte der Chalifen* (Mannheim, 1846-1862), II,170,281, since this is not the place to inquire any further into the details of their biographies.

[3] M. Casiri, *Bibliotheca Arabico-Hispana Escurialensis* (Madrid, 1760-70), I,288; Barhebraeus, *Chronicle* (P. Bruns & H. Kirsch, eds., *Barhebraei Chroncion syriacum* [Leipzig, 1789]), 170; id., *Chron. Eccl.* III,198; Ibn Khallikan, *Biographical Dictionary* (MacGuckin de Slane, tr., *Ibn Khallikan's Biographical Dictionary* [London, 1842]) I,478-9; *BO* III,I,164,211,501,511. There is some disagreement over the date of his death, some placing it in AH263 (876/7), others saying that he died on Tuesday 6th Safar 260, which corresponds to 1st Kanun 1185 of the Greeks (AD873).

mentions in the preface to his own lexicon.[1] Barhebraeus also mentions a grammar of his in the *Storehouse of Mysteries*.[2]

Both Casiri and the *Fihrist* state |[106] that Ḥunain wrote a book on the rules of inflection according to the Greek system (كتاب احكلم الاعراب على مذهب اليونانيين مقالتان). However, this surely must have dealt with Arabic grammar rather than Syriac, for اعراب cannot refer to the Syriac language. Elias of Nisibis makes mention of it at a later date. In a disputation on the truth of the Christian religion with Al-Ḥusain Abū l-Qāsim (Vizier Qirwāši, d.AH444), Elias praised a work by Ḥunain ibn Isḥāq entitled في نحو العرب (*On Arabic Grammar*).[3] It was clearly an important piece of ninth century Arabic grammar, composed on the Greek model. Ḥunain also wrote on syntax but whether in this same book or in another I cannot tell.[4]

Later glossographers certainly made use of Ḥunain's glosses, hence their being preserved. He also wrote a short work on homonyms (ܦܘܪܫܢܐ),[5] which is at least partly (if not wholly) extant within the recension of the above-mentioned work by ʿEnanišoʿ. The ultimate aim in composing such a book was to study synonymy, this being what the author is most concerned with. The book teaches one how to distinguish between words of similar meaning and also between words that are written with the same letters but pronounced differently.

In the treatise, Ḥunain uses some technical orthoepic terms that are also found in other grammars: ܡܩܫܝܢܐ, ܡܪܟܟܢܐ, ܪܘܟܟܐ, ܦܬܚܐ, ܣܚܝܦܐ, ܙܩܦ, ܡܪܗܛܢܝܬܐ, ܡܥܒܪܢܝܬܐ;[6] though there are also some other terms not otherwise known. ܩܘܫܝܐ is called ܥܒܝܛ, e.g. when he says ܒ ܥܒܝܛ ܐܝܬ ܠܗ ܟܦ or ܒ ܥܒܝܛܐ ܟܦ, meaning that the letter ܟܦ is pronounced ܩܫܝܐ.[7] The vowel ܦܬܚܐ is described as ܡܫܒܚܬܐ

---

[1] G. Hoffmann, *Syrisch-arabische Glossen* (Kiel, 1874), 2,5. See also Wright, *Syriac Literature*, 212.

[2] Baethgen, *Elias*, 32; G. Hoffmann, "Bibliographische Anzeigen,"*ZDMG* 32 (1878), 738-63, esp p.741.

[3] *BO* III,I,271a.

[4] Baethgen, *Elias*, ch18.

[5] Martin, *Œuvres* II,77.

[6] Hoffmann, *Opuscula Nestoriana*, 32,3.

[7] Ibid. 31,5,6; 20,19,21; 13,10; 6,23 etc. The opposite of ܥܒܝܛ is ܢܩܘܫܐ, a term found also in Išoʿ Bar Nun (via Bar Bahlūl's Lexicon), as well as in Elias of Nisibis (Martin, *Deux dialects*, 459), according to Hoffmann, *op.cit.*, xiv [the reference to Martin seems to be incorrect—ed.].

ܟܠܐ,[1] the ܣܚܪܐ by ܕܡ ܗܘܡܡܝ ܠܘܪܝ ܢܩܘܫܐ ܟܠܡܠܬܐ ܡܢ,[2] and the consonant ܝ with a point beneath (i.e. ī) as ܕܡ ܚܪܐ ܐܝܬ ܟܡܘ.[3 x]

Ḥunain even includes a bizarre discussion of the word ܡܪܝܐ—I hardly know whether to call it Kabbalistic or whether it stems from some etymological fancy of his own. He says that the ܡ stands for ܡܪܘܬܐ (*dominion*), the ܪ for ܪܒܘܬܐ (*majesty*), and the ܝ for ܐܝܬܘܬܐ (*essence*), a theory which recalls that of Caspar Neumann, who believed that the sense of a word was contained within its individual letters and that the meaning of a word could be logically derived from their sequence.[4] |[107] In addition to these works, Ḥunain also wrote a book on points (of which we give a citation below, p.116), which included a special treatment of verbs with gutturals.[5]

But if we have been able to gather only a few small titbits of information about Ḥunain's grammatical studies, of his contemporary John the Stylite we have absolutely nothing save a single small fragment of his grammar (which is mentioned by ʿAbdišoʿ) in John Bar Zuʿbi.[6] Even ʿAbdišoʿ's knowledge of him itself probably derives from the Bar Zuʿbi citation. He numbers him amongst those grammarians who developed Syriac grammar according to the Greek rules.[7 xi]

However, it is not so certain whether this John the Stylite was really a contemporary of Ḥunain, as Assemani claims. He says (BO, *ibid.*) that John lived at the time of Sabrišoʿ, Abraham of Marga, and the patriarch Theodosius. The first of these three died in 836, Theodosius in 868.[8] It is

---

[1] 6,13 [not 16,14—ed.].

[2] 30,22; 31,11; 6,20 etc.

[3] 6,14.

[4] Caspar Neumann, *Clavis domus Heber* (Bratislava, 1712). See also J.D. Michaelis, *Beurtheilung der Mittel, welche man anwendet, die ausgestorbene Hebräische Sprache zu verstehen* (Göttingen, 1757), 94.

[5] Baethgen, *Elias*, 32,15.

[6] BO III,I,256. The fragment can be found at BL Add. 25876, f.65b, in which he argues that all nouns have active and passive senses and that the majority are masculine, an opinion which John Bar Zuʿbi disputes in a lengthy discussion. The fragment runs as follows: ܢܘܣܚ ܕܝܢ ܐܣܛܘܢܐ: ܟܠܙ ܕܐܡܪ: ܕܫܡܗܐ ܟܠܗ ܕܡܫܬܘܕܥܝܢ ܟܠ ܡܥܒܕܢܘܬܐ ܘܚܫܐ ܐܚܝܕܐ ܐܟܠܗܘܢ: ܘܐܟܠܗ ܠܫܡܗܐ ܡܫܡܗܘܢ ܠܕܟܪܘܬܐ. ܐܝܟ ܠܗ ܦܘܪܫܐ. ܕܓܒܪܐ. ܣܘܣܝܐ. ܟܠܒܐ. ܐܡܪ ܕܠܗܘܢ ܠܗ ܫܡܗܐ ܕܡܫܬܘܕܥܝܢ ܡܥܒܕܢܘܬܐ ܘܚܫܐ ܐܚܝܕܐ ܐܝܟ ܕܫܡܗܐ ܕܕܟܪܐ ܐܢܘܢ܀

[7] BL Add. 25876, f.54b.

[8] Barhebraeus, *Chron. Eccl.* III,190,198; BO II,435.

unclear, however, where Assemani gets this information from. Schröter has his doubts about it and prefers to think that this grammarian is identical with the John the Stylite who corresponded with Jacob of Edessa a century earlier.[1]

Schröter's doubts are absolutely justified in this case. But we must also reckon with the comment of John Bar Zuʿbi, who places John the Stylite alongside the likes of Aḥūdemmēh and Joseph Huzaya as a close follower of the Greeks. This can hardly be made to fit with the period *after* Jacob of Edessa, when Syriac grammar had been placed on a firm foundation. Nobody after Jacob was able to escape his shadow, once his work had replaced the role of the Greek summaries. This is why I would not even make John the Stylite a contemporary of Jacob of Edessa, but would prefer to place him before Jacob and to count him among the most ancient of Syriac grammarians.[xii]

In this period, then, Syriac grammar |[108] had hardly developed any further and barely even managed to preserve that state of progress which it owed to Jacob. The primary reason for this problem seems to have been that Jacob's work could not be superseded while the techniques of comparative linguistics had not yet been discovered,[xiii] and because the learned men who followed him were more preoccupied with writing glossaries and lexica than with refining grammatical theories.[2] We can now summarise the state of Syriac grammatical theory at this point.

From all that we have seen so far, one could say that Syriac grammar proceeded from two sources. The first consisted of those masters who taught the correct reading of the Scriptures and established rules for reading and writing. From these rules grew the system of pointing and of vowel marks, the origin of which was entirely native. The second strand derived from those who introduced Greek grammar (Dionysius Thrax and the Theodosian canons) into Syriac. From this new source the Syrians learnt about the parts of speech and the inflection of nouns and verbs. Ḥunain excepted, however, the Syrians never cared for syntax save for the occasional observation about the letters that serve as particles. According

[1] R. Schröter, 'Erster Brief Jakob's von Edessa an Johannes den Styliten,' *ZDMG* 24 (1870), 261-300, esp. p.262.

[2] The order of the glossographers is approximately as follows: 1) Marwazāyā (AD 567); 2) The anonymous sixth century glossary quoted on p.4 above (Wright, *Cat.* II,802b); 3) Gabriel Boḥtišoʿ (before 870); 4) Bar ʿAlī (c.880); 5) Serošewai (900) [see *GSL*, 232]; 6) Bar Bahlūl (c.960).

to ch .18 of Elias of Ṭirhan, Ḥunain did write about predicates and on the protasis and apodosis.

It was Jacob of Edessa who synthesised these two strands—the system of pointing and the theory of parts of speech and inflection—and thereby founded Syriac grammar as such. Until John Bar Zuʿbi in 1210, however, nobody followed in his footsteps and for five centuries grammatical theory barely advanced an inch. Those who came after Jacob did not discuss inflection (or morphology) and none of the Syrians ever understood the nature of the verb! Instead they went on and on about the systems of pointing and accentuation that were taught in the schools. In the next chapter we shall turn our attention to what can be gleaned about this from the grammatical treatises that were written between the end of the ninth century and the age of Bar Zuʿbi.

There are three such texts:

1) The East Syrian Masoretic codex in the British Library dated 899, copied by a certain Babai in the Monastery of Mar Gabriel near Harran, which is similar also to a West Syrian codex of the ninth or tenth century.[1]
2) The ܬܘܪܨ ܡܡܠܠܐ of Elias Bar Šināyā of Nisibis.[2]
3) The ܡܨܝܕܬܐ ܕܢܘܩܙܐ (*Net of points*) of Joseph Bar Malkon, bishop of Mardin, from the same ms.[3]

[1] Wright, *Cat.* I,101,108 (BL Add. 12138 and Add 12178).

[2] Ibid., III,1175 (BL Add. 25876).

[3] Ibid., III,1177-8.

---

[i] The period following Jacob was not quite as dry as Merx believed, for he did not know of Dawidh Bar Paulos, an eighth century West Syrian whose works we possess only in a fragmentary state, but who appears to have built upon Jacob not just in matters of detail but in more general reflections as well (*GSL*, 272, esp. for mss; edition and translation of the main body of extant material by R. J. H. Gottheil, "Dawidh bar Paulos, a Syriac Grammarian," *Journal of the American Oriental Society* 15 (1893), cxi-cxviii). As far as Dawidh's *floruit* is concerned, note that he appears to quote Ḥunain, if the final sentence of his *Grammar* is not a later addition.

[ii] More properly, 'explanation'. The term ܬܘܪܨ in construct expressions such as ܬܘܪܨ ܡܡܠܐ or ܬܘܪܨ ܟܬܒܐ is to be understood as a calque on the Greek terms ὀρθοέπεια and ὀρθογραφία—see Gottheil, *Elias*, 1*. In the absolute form as here it should probably be taken as a shorthand for either or both of these expressions. If this understanding is adopted, then Merx's following argument will need some modification.

[iii] There are further mss of the work (*GSL*, 202n1). Wright, *Syriac Literature*, 176n1, adds that there is another ms in the SPCK collection. Furthermore, Merx's distinction between the *On Homonyms* and the work described by Thomas of Marga seems substantiated by the contents of Notre Dame des Semences 138 (= 291 in Vosté's renumbering) and was accepted by Baumstark (*GSL*, ibid.).

[iv] George Michael Amira, *Grammatica Syriaca, siue Chaldaica* (Rome, 1596); Isaac Sciadrensis, *Grammatica linguae Syriace* (Rome, 1636); Joseph Acurensis, *Grammatica linguae Syriacae* (Rome, 1647); A. Echellensis, *Linguae Syriacae sive Chaldaicae perbrevis institutio* (Rome, 1628); Timothy of Amida (see Wright, *Cat.* III,1180; Sachau, *Verzeichniss*, 700f.); The 'Book of Inflection' seems to refer to the other texts contained in Petermann 17/Berlin Syr. 222 (Sachau, *Verzeichniss*, 700f.) besides the Grammar of Timothy of Amida. A more detailed description is found in the following item in Sachau's Catalogue, Sachau 39/Berlin Syr 223 (Sachau, *Verzeichniss*, 701f.).

[v] The citations below have been taken directly from Hoffmann's text, since Merx offers only paraphrases.

[vi] 'Enanišo''s quotation from Job differs significantly from the Peshiṭta (ܘܬܗܘܐ ܡܣܒܪܬܟ ܘܪܢܝܟ ܘܐܣܝܘܬܟ ܢܦܫܐ ܠܟ).

[vii] See also the discussion of the title of the work by John Bar Penkaye in Ch.VIII (p.136).

[viii] Mosul 109,no. 1; NDS 138, no.6; Seert 108, no.5, a work evidently closely related to that by 'Enaninšo'/Ḥunain.

[ix] The earliest lexicographer of Qur'ānic Arabic. See *GAP*, 123,139.

[x] For a few more comments on the contents of Ḥunain's grammar, see Gottheil, *Elias*, 30*.

[xi] The text was located by Addai Scher in a manuscript in the convent of Notre Dames des Semences and Moberg wrote an article summarising and analysing the text: A. Moberg, "Die syrische grammatik des Johannes Estonaja," *Le monde oriental* 3 (1909), 24-33. Unfortunately, however, he did not publish the text and the ms is at present still in Iraq. Moberg (p.28) also offers a better reading of the words cited by Bar Zuʿbi than those found in Merx.

[xii] Baumsark (*GSL*, 258) asserts, with Schröter, that the grammarian and Jacob's correspondent must be one and the same. The fact that the grammarian used Greek models is hardly sufficient proof against Assemani's suggestion (the Hellenophile Bar Zuʿbi would anyway tend to overemphasise such a characteristic). Thus Moberg sides with the latter, and nobody since Merx has agreed that he must pre-date Jacob. There is much in John the Stylite that was used and developed by Bar Zuʿbi and Bar Šakko, although all his material is itself derivative, partly stemming from Dionysius Thrax, partly from other, unnamed sources. On Jacob's correspondent, see also K. Rignell, *A letter from Jacob of Edessa to John the Stylite of Litarab concerning ecclesiastical canons* (Lund, 1979). The correspondence between Jacob and John has been variously published (see Kruisheer, *Clavis*) and a new edition by J. Van Ginkel is promised.

[xiii] The fact that Jacob's work was largely phonological in nature, which did not sit well with the mindset of subsequent grammarians, may partly explain his lack of successors (Revell, *Grammar*, 368ff.).

|[109] Chapter 8

ELIAS OF NISIBIS, JOSEPH BAR MALKON, AND THE MASORETIC MANUSCRIPTS

Elias Bar Šināyā (or, Elias of Nisibis)[i] was born in 975 in the monastery of Mar Miḫāʾīl near Mosul.[ii] He became a monk under the crippled Abbot John and was consecrated priest by Nathanael, bishop of al-Sin, who afterwards became the Catholicus John V (1001-1011).[iii] After spending some time at the monastery of Simeon opposite al-Sin on the Tigris, Elias was made bishop of Beth Nuhādra in 1002 and raised to the metropolitanate of Nisibis at the end of 1008. He was a friend of the next Catholicus John Bar Nāzūk (1012-18) but quarrelled with Išōʿyabh Bar Ezekiel (1020-25). He outlived the Catholicos Elias I (1028-49) and so died at some time after 1049. Thus does Wright describe his life.[1] Cardahi says that he died in 1056.[2]

ʿAbdišoʿ thought very highly of his abilities and confessed that Elias's Arabic work *On the Division of the Inheritance* (ܥܠ ܦܘܠܓܐ ܕܝܪܬܘܬܐ) formed the basis for his own work on the same subject, which incorporated the whole of Elias's work, translated from Arabic into Syriac.[3] ʿAbdišoʿ's *Nomocanon*, the third tract of which is this aforementioned work on inheritance, has been published by Mai.[4] [iv]

Elias richly deserves the praises heaped upon him by ʿAbdišoʿ, both for what he achieved in church affairs and for his writings. On the basis of the collection of canons that he made we can see that he was not just some ivory-tower researcher of canon law; rather he bravely, albeit in vain, tried to bring the unsavory activities of Išōʿyabh under the rule of law. The latter had sought the favours of the Baghdad court and obtained the patriarchal

---

[1] Wright, *Syriac Literature*, 235-6, basing himself on Rosen and Forshall, *Cat.*, 89,col.2; F. Baethgen, *Fragmente syrischer und arabischer Historiker*, Abhandlungen für die Kunde des Morgenlandes 8.3 (Leipzig, 1884), 101,103,104 = tr.151,2,3; Barhebraeus, *Chron.Eccl.* II, 261,281,283; BO II,444,447, III,I,266,272.

[2] G. Cardahi, *Liber Thesauri de arte poetica Syrorum* (Rome, 1875), 84.

[3] *BO* III,1,268; *GSL*, 288.

[4] A. Mai, *Scriptorum veterum nova collectio* X, 220-31 (Syr.), 54-65 (Lat.).

throne in 1020 by simony, holding it until his death in 1025.[1] Elias also defended the truth of the Christian religion by holding a disputation in seven sessions with Abu'l-Qāsim Al-Ḥusain, one of the most famous men of his day.[2] [v] His care for the Christian flock also extended to penning a commentary on the Nicene creed and an apologetical treatise in which he tried to prove the truth of Christianity by means of logical arguments (كتاب البرهن في تصحيح الامان).[3]

|[110] Finally, he wrote disquisitions on the doctrines of the Trinity and the Unity and an ethical commentary on chastity (في فضيلة العفاف), another on the casting off of sadness (كتاب المعونت علا دفع الهم), and last of all he published some skilfully composed hymns which have been preserved in the East Syrian liturgies.[4]

Throughout his œuvre he showed himself equally capable in both Syriac and Arabic and it seems he should be reckoned among the very first Syrians who wrote in Arabic, a characteristic love of which he shares with his contemporary Elias of Ṭirhan, with whom we deal below. Furthermore, he wrote in Syriac some sermons and a chronicle, some particulars of which were published by the editors of Barhebraeus's ecclesiastical chronicle. Baethgen has published the fragments.[5] [vi] However, when we consider all this we must appreciate that Elias was not some retiring individual who happened to love the minutiae of grammar. He was a hard-working character, keenly involved in real life, who, by writing a grammar, thereby produced a textbook for beginners, for whom Jacob of Edessa's grammar would have proved too detailed. The very reason for his being a bishop was really to provide literature that would assist the clerical schools where the students were now learning Syriac as an ecclesiastical language, since it was gradually ceasing to be spoken in everyday life. We saw earlier that in the ninth century glossaries were being compiled explaining Arabic

---

[1] Elias's letter to the Baghdadians on the ordination of Išōʿyabh is extant in Vat.Syr.129 (Assemani, *Catalogus* III,191). BO III,I,272.

[2] Ibn al-Athīr, *Al Kāmil fi'l-ta'rikh* (C.J. Tornberg, ed., *Ibn El-Athari Chronicon Quod Perfectissimum Inscribitur* [Leiden, 1863]) IX,233,255; BO III,I,270f.

[3] German translation in L. Horst, *Das Metropoliten Elias von Nisibis Buch vom Beweis der Wahrheit und das Glaubens* (Colmar, 1886).

[4] See Cardahi, *op.cit.*, 83. Wright, *Syriac Literature*, 237n3, lists the relevant mss of the latter as follows: Vat. Syr. 90 (Assemani, *Catalogus* II,487), nrs.13,15,17,18; Vat. Syr. 91 (*ibid.*, II,491), Nrs.12,14,16,17; Berlin Sachau I,239.

[5] Baethgen, *op. cit.*

words in Syriac. There can hardly have been any reason for this other than the decline in the use of Syriac, especially among the upper classes who increasingly imitated cultured Arabic literature. Hence it was Elias's project to preserve within his church a knowledge of the national language. This project of his had its end result in Thomas a Novaria's well known glossary published in 1636.[1] [vii] He states this fact himself in the preface to the text, in which he addresses the student as follows: انك التمست ايها الولد العزيز ان اجمع لك كتابا متضمنا معرفة اللغة السريانية بالقول الوجيز فاسعفتك بتاليف هذا واوردت فيه الفاظا يستعان بها على المكاتبة والخطان الخ (*my dear boy, you sought that I should collect a book containing knowledge of the Syriac language in a brief account, so I assisted you with this publication and I furnished therein the information which might be helpful for writing letters and speeches, etc.*). The student was trying to choose a textbook with which to study Syriac and Elias helped him out |[111] by compiling a glossary to assist him in composing letters and speeches. We can see that practicality is uppermost in his mind—for instance, the last chapter consists of a much fuller collection of ܕܡܝ̈ܢܐ, (words that differ in meaning but are visually identical) than all his predecessors had managed;[viii] for example, he places the imperatives of verbs in the place of the perfects (ch. XXVIII) and explains their inflections and aspirations, since they are the most commonly used forms and all other forms can be most easily derived from the imperative.[2] [ix] His grammar is thus made as basic as possible and designed only for students, of which more shortly.

Closely related to Elias's *Grammar* is the *Net of Points* by Joseph Bar Malkon, bishop of Mardin, which often follows Elias word-for-word.[3] It is preserved in BL Add. 25876 and Vat.Syr. 194 (previously Echellensis 27).[4] [x] Virtually the whole of it deals with accents and pointing, as is the case with

---

[1] *Thesaurus Arabico-Syro-Latinus*, Rome, 1636. Recently, Lagarde printed the glossary with the Syriac in Hebrew characters in his *Praetermissorum libri duo* (Göttingen, 1879), 1-96. However, Möller Gotha has shown that Thomas's edition was littered with errors resulting in confusion in the order of the columns (J. H. Möller Gotha, *Über den syrischen Nomenclator des Thomas a Novaria.* Eine Abhandlung der Engelhardt-Reyher'sehen Buch druckerei, 1840).

[2] ينبغى ان تعلم ان...فعل الامر انما اقتصر على ذكره دون باقى الافعال الانواع الاخر لكونه يستعمل كثيرا دون غيره وقد يمكن ان تستنبط منه ذو الفطنة الودعية باقى الافعال الانواع الاخر (*you should know that...it is enough to mention simply the imperative of the verb rather the other verbal forms because it is used more than the others and it is possible for a naturally intelligent person to extract the rest of the verbal forms from it*).

[3] Gottheil, *Elias*, 38.

[4] Wright, *Cat.* III,1177,no.8; BO III,1,308.

Elias as well. Martin believed that Joseph Bar Malkon was identical with Išōʿyabh Bar Malkon,[1] [xi] |[112] among whose works are counted some grammatical investigations.[xii] We do not intend to inquire any further into this question, but can content ourselves at least with the certainty that the *Net of Points*, which is written in verse, was written later than Elias's *Grammar* and at a time when grammarians were beginning to write in verse so that their students might the more easily memorise the contents. Among the Syrians, John Bar Zuʿbi and Barhebraeus both did the same in the thirteenth century, as did Al-Ḥarīrī (d.516H) and Ibn Mālik (d.672H) among the Arabs.[2] [xiii] Since Jacob Bar Šakko also made use of Bar Malkon, we should probably assign the latter to the end of the twelfth or to the thirteenth century.

In treating with the grammar of this period, we shall follow the arrangement of Elias's *Grammar*, so excellently edited by Richard Gottheil.[3] We shall also add a few comments from his other works. After discussing the letters (ch.I), Elias writes in chapter II about the ܐܬܘ̈ܬܐ ܡܬܬܙܝܥܢܝ̈ܬܐ (*vowelled letters*, lit. *letters in motion*), i.e. consonants marked with vowels. He says that

[1] Martin, *De la métrique*, 70. But is Joseph one and the same as Išōʿyabh or did he change his name when he was elevated to the metropolitanate of Nisibis after previously being bishop of Mardin? Assemani does not attribute the *Net of Points* to Išōʿyabh Bar Malkon (*BO* III,1,295), and Martin has not correctly understood the reference in Jacob Bar Šakko. For in all the mss the word is given in the plural: ܕܢܨܝܒܢ̈ܝܐ (even in those mss which have ܕܢܨܝܒܝܢܝܐ, which must be an error on account of the metre). Hence the citation (which can be found in our edition, p.ܟܗ, l.10) cannot be rendered as, "of the Net of Points of the Nisibine" (meaning Bar Malkon himself), but rather as, "of the Net of Points of the Nisibenes" (i.e. of their usage among the Nisibenes). So it is true that Jacob Bar Šakko makes mention of this treatise. Wright (*Syriac Literature*, 257n3) agrees with Martin, mentioning a note in BL Add. 25867 which reads, ܥܠܡ ܡܐܡܪܐ ܕܟܠ ܢܘܩܙܐ. ܕܥܒܝܕ ܠܡܪܝ ܝܫܘܥܝܗܒ ܐܦܝܣܩܘܦܐ ܕܡܪܕܐ. ܡܝܛܪܦܘܠܝܛܐ ܕܝܢ ܕܨܘܒܐ. ܗܘ ܕܗܘܐ ܡܝܛܪܦܘܠܝܛܐ ܕܢܨܝܒܝܢ (*Cat.* III,1178), which must mean that Bar Malkon is the same as Išōʿyabh of Nisibis. Wright thus requires us to read (at the aforementioned reference) ܕܢܨܝܒܝܢܝܐ, i.e. 'bishop of the Nisibenes'. But the metre does not permit it and it is easier to read ܡܕܝܢܬܐ ܕܗܘܐ ܕܢܨܝܒܢ̈ܝܐ, though (as we mentioned) all the mss have the plural marker. Išōʿyabh was ordained bishop of Nisibis in 1190 and died between 1226 and 1256 (Barhebraeus, *Chron. Eccl.* II,370[4], and Wright, *Syriac Literature*, 256-7).

[2] Ḥāǧǧī Ḫalīfa (i.e. Mustafa Kātib Čelebī), *Lexicon bibliographicum et encyclopædicum* (G. Flügel, ed., Leipzig, 1835-58), VI, 110, I, 407.

[3] ܬܘܪܨ ܡܡܠܠܐ ܣܘܪܝܝܐ, *A Treatise on Syriac Grammar by Mar Elia of Sobha* (Berlin, 1887).

among the Arabs there are three types (a, i, u), among the West Syrians five, but among 'us' Easterns there are seven, namely:

1) ܡܬܦܬܚܬܐ, i.e. consonants supplied with *ā* (ܦܬܚܐ), such as the ܐ and the ܕ in ܐܕܡ.
2) ܪ̈ܒܝܨܬܐ, such as the ܝ in ܝܠܕܐ.
3) ܡܬܚܒ̈ܨܬܐ, such as the ܟ in ܟܦܢܐ.
4) ܗܢܝܢ ܕܡܢ ܪ̈ܘܚܬܐ, such as the ܐ in ܐܘ and the ܒ in ܐܪܒܥܐ.
5) ܗܢܝܢ ܕܡܢ ܐܠܝ̈ܨܬܐ, such as the ܢ in ܢܘܪܐ and the ܥ in ܥܘܪܐ.
6) ܗܢܝܢ ܕܡܢ ܡܩܫ̈ܩܬܐ, such as the ܐ in ܐܝܠܝܢ and the ܒ in ܒܝܬ.
7) ܗܢܝܢ ܕܡܢ ܣܚܝ̈ܩܬܐ, such as the ܐ in ܐܝܕܐ and the ܕ in ܕܝܢܐ.

ܐܠܝ̈ܨܬܐ and ܪ̈ܘܚܬܐ pertain to ܘ, while ܡܩܫ̈ܩܬܐ and ܣܚܝ̈ܩܬܐ pertain to ܝ (cf. Elias, p.ܟܒ). The sign of ܦܬܚܐ is called ܚܒܝܒܐ ܚܒܠܐ and the sign of ܪܒܨܐ is called ܚܒܠܐ ܕܟܠܝܠܐ.[1]

|[113] Joseph Bar Malkon's list, however, is not identical to this, since it gives three, rather than two, types of *i* vowel.[2] Joseph therefore has eight vowel signs (ܢ̈ܩܘܙܐ ܕܪܘܚܐ), viz: ܐ̈ܦܬܚܐ, ܙܩ̈ܦܐ, ܪ̈ܒܨܐ, ܪ̈ܒܨܐ ܟܪ̈ܝܐ, ܚܒ̈ܨܐ ܪ̈ܘܝܚܐ, ܚܒ̈ܨܐ ܐ̈ܠܝܨܐ, ܦܩܝܥܐ, ܦܬ̈ܚܐ.

Nothing need be said about ܦܬܚܐ, ܙܩܦܐ, and ܚܒܨܐ (*ī*), nor need we add anything on the ܪܘܚܐ which is *o* (ܘ݁). But for Bar Malkon the ܥܨܨܐ is *u* (ܘ݂), a vowel which Elias calls ܕܡܢ ܐܠܝ̈ܨܬܐ. Therefore (in Bar Malkon), the ܘ in ܟܘܪܝ is a ܥܨܨܐ but the ܘ in ܟܦܘܪ is a ܪܘܚܐ.

Bar Malkon says the following about *i* : if two points are placed horizontally below the letter, this is ܪܒܨܐ ܦܫܝܩܐ, as in ܐܦܪܝܡ, while the ܪܒܨܐ ܕܡܠܝܐ is as found in ܐܦܪܝ (i.e. vertically),[3] and an example of the ܦܩܝܥܐ is ܣܓܝ, the vowel of which is called ܦܩܝܥܬܐ.

The confusion of later scribes, who often failed to distinguish the different sounds of this vowel, is attributable to this lack of grammatical consensus among the experts.[4]

Elias of Nisibis (ch.III) is at pains to make a distinction between radical (ܥܩܪ̈ܢܝܬܐ) and additional/servile consonants (ܡܬܬܘܣܦ̈ܢܝܬܐ). Among the latter, there are some that are added simply out of custom,[xiv] of which he further distinguishes two types, namely those that are generally used by everyone

[1] Ibid., p.ܟ,12 (tr., 28).

[2] BL Add. 25876, f.278a.

[3] The text reads, ܐܦܪܝܡ ܠܘܩܒܠ ܟܠܡܐ ܕܦܫܝܩܘܬܐ ܪܒܨܐ ܦܫܝܩܐ ܗܘ. Then concerning the ܦܩܝܥܐ he says, ܘܠܐ ܟܠܗܘܢ ܦܫܝܩܐ ܗܘ ܐܠܐ ܗܘ ܦܩܝܥܐ ܗܘ. On f.278b he adds, ܘܦܩܝܥܐ ܠܘܬ ܡܕܢܚ̈ܝܐ ܗܢܘ ܕܡܬܩܪܐ ܚܒܨܐ.

[4] See Merx, *Grammatica*, 30,2.

(ܓܘܢܝܬܐ), and those that are specially used only in the scriptures (ܡܫܝܚܝܬܐ).[1] The first of these sub-types concerns only the addition of the ܝ that is logically and traditionally written in words such as ܐܬܠܡܕ, ܐܬܠܡܝ, ܡܣܡܟ, ܙܗܘܘܡ, ܐܬܦܘܡ. Concerning the other type, what he says (according to our transcription from BL Add. 25876, f.7a) is: ܡܬܬܘܣܦܢܝܬܐ ܕܝܢ ܡܫܝܚܝܬܐ ܐܝܠܝܢ ܗܢܝܢ ܐܝܟ
114| 2 ܗܢܝܢ ܕܒܟܬܒܐ ܩܕܝܫܐ ܕܒܠܚܘܕ ܥܠ ܟܠܗܝܢ ܡܬܬܘܣܦܢ. ܐܝܟ ܚܝܬ ܘܢܘܢ ܕܒܚܙܝܢ ܘܪܚܡܝܢ:
3 ܒܥܝܕܐ ܚܒܪܐ ܕܣܘܪܝܝܐ ܦܠܣܛܝܢܝܐ: ܗܢܘܢ ܕܦܫܩܘ ܟܬܒܐ ܩܕܝܫܐ ܠܠܫܢܐ ܥܠ ܟܠܗܘܢ ܡܬܬܩܫܝܢ:
4 ܗܘܘ ܠܚܝܬ ܘܢܘܢ ܕܒܐܝܟ ܗܠܝܢ ܡܠܐ: ܐܝܟ ܕܐܝܬ ܠܡܐܠܦ ܡܢ ܟܬܒܐ ܥܬܝܩܐ ܕܡܠܦܢܐ ܥܒܪܝܐ ܕܐܬܟܬܒܘ
ܘܡܠܠܘ ܘܐܦܠܣܛܝܢܝܐ: ܐܝܟ ܕܟܬܒܐ ܥܒܪܝܐ ܘܦܠܣܛܝܢܝܐ 5 (*servile letters in special use are such as are added only in the Bible—as ḥeth and nun to the words* ܚܙܝܢ *and* ܪܚܝܢ*. Such are used only in the Bible, according to the custom of the Palestinian Syrians who translated the Holy Books into the Syriac language, for they tended to pronounce the ḥeth and nun in such words, as one can learn from the ancient books of the Hebrew [Gottheil has 'old', following a variant reading—ed.] teachers who wrote and spoke in the Syriac and the Palestinian language*). It seems, then, that Elias believed that these Palestinian scholars expounded the scriptures in Syriac, and that, since they not only in general pronounced the ܚ and the ܢ of ܚܝܢ distinctly (this seems to be what ܠܒܝܢ means in this context—see p.106 above where it refers to the hard pronunciation of mute letters),[6] they also wrote these consonants down. He adds that we can be sure of this fact on the basis of the old codices of the Hebrew scholars who both spoke and wrote in Syriac, and in a Palestinian dialect at that. Clearly this is a very important and noteworthy comment! First of all, he offers an opinion on the origin of the Syriac Bible totally unheard of within the rest of the Syriac tradition, which in general held opinions on the matter that were no more than empty legends. He then calls as witness certain ancient codices, and it must indeed be allowed that at the start of the eleventh century there were many more truly ancient codices of the Bible than are extant in our day. But Elias is at least wrong when he claims that ܚܝܢ was only written in full in the Bible, since we find it written this way in the ancient Edessene practice, e.g. in the St. Petersburg ms of Eusebius's *History*, written in 462.

[1] Gottheil, ܠ, l.11.

[2] Gottheil offers ܕܚܙܝܢ ܚܝܢ and ܪܚܡܝܢ ܚܝܢ, to which he adds a third example, ܩܥܡܝܢ ܚܝܢ.

[3] Gottheil ܡܫܩܬܝܢ.

[4] Gottheil ܕܐܬܟܬܒܘ, ܥܒܪ.

[5] Gottheil ܐܝܟ ܗܘܐ ܕܟܬܒܐ ܦܠܣܛܝܢܝܐ, omitting ܥܒܪܝܐ and ܘ.

[6] ܠܒܘ is used also by Bar Šakko when he writes about letters that are pronounced but not necessarily written (p. ܟܛ, l.9).

On the other hand, it is not to be found in the Jerusalem Talmud. Elias is not talking here about the Syro-Palestinian or the Jerusalem dialects, since his reference seems to be to the very oldest translators of the Bible. Perhaps he means the Targumim, of which the Syriac translators of the Old Testament Peshiṭta made such good use.[xv]

After this, Elias mentions that Jacob of Edessa said that one should write ܡܬܡ ܣܡ rather than ܡܢܣܡ in order to distinguish ܡ̈ܢܝܢ |[115] the noun from ܡ̈ܢܝܢ the verb. Bar Šakko repeats this observation.[1] Elias himself seems not to endorse it, however.

The next item in Elias's *Grammar* is a chapter on ܡܩܛܠܐ, *cases*, i.e. the particles ܒܘܟܠ (ch. IV).[2] The vocalisation of these particles and the strength of their aspiration and hardening do seem to have caused some difficulties for the students, since these issues are minutely dealt with in the Masoretic mss.[3] At the end of this long chapter, Elias adds that in the Bible there are some words that do not follow the general rule. These are ܩ̈ܛܠܐ, ܡܗܘܪܐ, ܒܡܥܦܠ,[4] ܡܗ̈ܘܪܝܐ, ܒ̈ܬܝܠܡܐ. The reason why it is only these words that disobey the normal rules is, says Elias, quite obvious. As a result, the following are found: ܒ̈ܬܝܠܡܐ, ܒ̈ܩܛܠܐ, ܒ̈ܩܛܠܐ, ܕ̈ܩܛܠܐ, ܒܡܗ̈ܘܪܝܐ, ܒܡܗ̈ܘܪܝܐ, ܕܡܗ̈ܘܪܝܐ, ܒܡܗܘܪܐ, ܕܡܗܘܪܐ, ܒܡܗܘܪܐ, ܒܡܥܦܠ, ܕܒܡܥܦܠ, ܒ̈ܬܝܠܡܐ, ܒ̈ܬܝܠܡܐ. It is evidence for just how minute such observations could be among the Syrians (rather in the manner of the Rabbis) that Elias adds that there is *just one place* which does not follow this rule, namely Hosea 12.2. To quote him in full: ܦܠܚܝܢ ܠܡܩܛܠܐ ܕܩܕܡ ܕܟܠ [ܕܥܡܐ ܕܬܠܡܐ] ܐܠܐ ܐܢ ܚܕܐ ܕܗܘ: ܕܒܗ ܡܥܡܝܢ [6] ܒܗ ܐܬܐܘ̈ܪܝܐ [5] ܕܗܘܫܥ ܘܐܬܠܘܗܝ ܦܠܚܝܢ ܗܘܐ ܗܘܐ ܘܬܠܡܐ ܠܡܩܛܠܐ ܕܩܕܡ ܕܟܠ. ܘܐܬܠܘܗܝ ܒܪܘܚܐ ܕܐܘܪܚܐ ܘܬܠܡܐ܀ ܥܒܕܗ ܡܢ ܗܟܢܐ ܗܘ ܕܩܕܡ [7]

On seeing such minute precision in a grammar, we should not find it surprising that the official readers and their teachers, the ܡܩܪ̈ܝܢܐ, took such pains to provide strict instructions in the masora on matters such as which letters should not be pronounced (ܡܒܛܠ), which should be vocalised (ܡܬܬܙܝܥ) and which should not (ܐܠܐ ܡܬܙܝܥ).[8]

---

[1] p. ܢܗ, l.8; p. ܢܝ, l.6. Also see above, p.47.

[2] See also Bar Šakko, p. ܠ,6.

[3] Wright, *Cat.* I,105.

[4] With ܩ̈ܛܠܐ, however, he should have added ܠܐ since the vocalisation ܩ̈ܛܠܐܗ is found (Martin, *Tradition karkaphienne*, 247).

[5] Gottheil, ܕܐܘܪܚ.

[6] Gottheil wrongly ܘܦܝܠܡܐ.

[7] Gottheil, ܕܩܕܡ ܕܟܠ ܕܬܝܠܡܐ.

[8] Wright, *Cat.* I,103f.

|[116] Since the vocalisation of the ܒܘܟܠ particles affects the aspiration of following ܒ ܓ, ܕ ܟ ܦ ܬ, Bar Malkon describes their behaviour in the chapter on Rukkāḵā and Quššāyā, but in Elias they have a chapter to themselves (Ch. V), from which the following are the most noteworthy points (f.10a):[1] [xvi]

1. A tau that quiesces in front of ṯ or ḏ becomes t, d when placed after ܒܘܟܠ. Hence, ܠܬܬܘܒܢ, ܠܬܕܘܢ, ܒܬܪܥܐ, ܒܬܬܘܒ. The same examples are used by Bar Šakko (ܟܘ,5). The moveable tau, however, is aspirated, ܘܬܬܩܛܠܘܢ.

2. A relative ܕ placed immediately after the conjunction ܘ, or any other ܒܘܟܠ particle, and then followed by ܕ or ܬ is pronounced quššāyā. Hence, ܘܕܕܡܐ (*wadᵉḏāme*), ܘܕܬܕܥܘܢ (*wadᵉṯedᵉʿon*). Again, the same examples in Bar Šakko (ܟܘ,11).

The exception is that when the first letter of the word is ܕ or ܬ with rukkāḵā, then the preceding relative ܕ will also be rukkāḵā. Hence, ܘܕܬܘܬܐ (*wᵉḏaṯᵉwāṯā*), ܘܕܬܝܒܘܬܐ (*wᵉḏaṯᵉyāḇûṯā*), ܘܕܕܝܨܐ (*wᵉḏaḏᵉyāṣā*) (cf. Bar Šakko, ܟܘ,14).

This rule that Elias describes should actually be applied more generally and need not be restricted to words beginning with *t* or *d*. He does not have in view a complete phonological system.[2]

3. His discussion of the ܬ of the first person is more pointed. The masters differed widely with regard to its aspiration and by religiously following a system of analogy they broke a fundamental law of orthoepy. For Elias says (f.12a) that when the ܬ of the first person masculine (sic!) is placed before an object suffix it is quššāyā, such that one should read ܒܪܟܬܟ (*bareḵtāḵ*) and ܡܫܚܬܗ (*mᵉšaḥteh*); but if there is ī before the ܬ, the latter becomes rukkāḵā, thus reading ܣܢܝܬܟ (*sᵉnîṯāḵ*) and ܣܢܝܬܗ (*sᵉnîṯeh*). He continues (Gottheil, ܟܘ,15): ܣܘܢܩܝܢ ܕܝܢ ܐܦܠܐ ܒܥܠܬܐ ܕܢܘܩܙܐ ܡܢܟ. ܕܒܟܠܗܘܢ ܠܬܐ ܕܗܘܝܐ ܦܘܪܩܢܐ
[3] ܘܒܥܒܪܐ ܕܣܘܥܠܐ ܠܐܘܪܚܐ ܒܗ ܗܘܐ ܡܕܪܟ. ܒܥܘܢ ܕܡܠܐ |[117] ܕܐܡܪܝܢ. ܕܝܕܥܝܢ. [ܦܘܪܩܢܐ] ܡܬܘܪܒܝܢ ܗܢܘܢ ܕܢܬܘܪܒܘܢ.
ܘܦܬܓܡܐ. ܘܦܫܝܩܬܐ ܘܦܫܝܛܬܐ ܡܬܒܥܝܢ ܠܟܠܗ. ܘܗܘ ܕܐܦ ܟܕ ܐܘܫܦܬܐ ܡܬܒܥܝܐ ܠܡܠܬܐ. ܐܡܬܝ ܕܐܦ ܠܗ
[4] ܘܡܠܐ ܕܒܬܪ ܟܠܡܬܗ ܐ̄ܢܫܝܬܐ܀ ܐܟܘܬܐ ܕܝܢ ܕܦܘܪܩܢܐ ܐܢܫܝܐ: ܟܠܗ ܕܡܬܡܠܝܐ ܒ ܡܬܒܥܝܐ ܐ̄ܢܫܝܬܐ: ܘܗܘܝܐ
[6] ܡܕܪܟ ܕܬܬܘܪܒ. ܐܡܬܝ [5] ܠܗ ܕܡܬܡܠܝܐ ܕܒܟܠ ܦܘܪܩܢܐ ܦܘܪܫܐ ܕܢܬܐ. ܘܐܦ ܩܢܘܢܐ ܟܠܗܘܢ ܕܬܬܘܡܠܐ
[7] [1] ܐܝܟ ܗܘ ܕܦܝܟܠܬܐ ܐܝܬܝܗ. ܡܢ ܘܦܝܟܠܬܐ ܕܢܦܫܢ ܠܟܠܗܘܢ ܕܡܬܒܥܝܐ ܗܘܝܢ: ܡܢ ܠܟܠܗܘܢ ܢܩܝܫܬܐ.

---

[1] Equivalent also to Gottheil, *Elias*, ܟܗ,13 (tr., 33).

[2] Merx, *Grammatica*, 70.

[3] Cod., ܢܬܘܪܒܘܢ; Gottheil then wrongly has ܘܒܥܒܪܐ ܣܘܥܠܐ.

[4] Gottheil, ܘܗܘܝܐ ܡܠܐ.

[5] Gottheil wrongly, ܡܬܘܡܠܐ.

[6] Gottheil, ܘܐܦ ܣܘܡܐ.

[7] Cod. ܢܩܝܫܬܐ.

ܘܢܣܒܬܗ ܡܢ ܢܣܒܬܗ. ܘܫܩܠܬܗ ܡܢ ܫܩܠܬܗ. ܘܩܒܠܬܗ ܡܢ ܩܒܠܬܗ. ܗܢܝ.[xvii] It is quite clear from the examples that the forms with quššāyā refer to the first person (ܩܒܠܬܗ *I received him* , ܫܩܠܬܗ *I carried him*, ܢܣܒܬܗ *I took him*) while those with no mark should be rukkāḵā and are third persons in the feminine (ܩܒܠܬܗ *she received him*, ܫܩܠܬܗ *she carried him*, ܢܣܒܬܗ *she took him*). The same state of affairs is to be found in the following verses of Joseph Bar Malkon (f.285b-287) (cf. Gottheil, *Elias*, p.25*,20ff.):

ܘܒܗ ܕܬܠܗ ܕܢܩܫܐ[2] ܠܡܟܠܬܐ ܒܣܪܬܗ ܠܠܟܠܬܐ ܐܢܬܝ܆
ܐܘ[3] ܠܐܬܐ ܗܘ ܕܝܡܟܬܒܘܬܐ (sic) ܘܐܡܪܝܢ ܡܪܕܘܕܝܢ܀
ܐܘ ܒܣܠܦ ܡܫܚܐ[4] ܗܘ ܕܦܪܙܘܦ ܕܠܘܐܡ ܘܥܒܠ ܡܦܩܝܢ܆
ܐܘ ܒܣܠܦ[5] ܡܫܚܐ ܗܘܒ ܕܦܪܙܘܦܐ ܡܒܥܠܐ ܘܐܬܝܗ ܠܘܐܡ܀
118| ܘܐܦ ܠܗܘܐ ܠܗ ܒܣܪܬܐ ܕܡܟܠܬܐ[6] ܡܪܝܗ ܕܬܡܓܬܐ܆
ܘܐܦ ܡܠܡܕܢܐ ܦܩܘܗ ܐܠܐ ܒܬܪ ܦܫܝܛܬܐ܀[7]
ܘܗܟܢ ܐܡܪܐ ܕܢܦܫܟ ܦܪܡܠܘܗܝ ܝܓܒܝܐ ܦܪܘܫܬܗ܆[8]
ܦܬܚܝܬ ܙܘܢܬ ܢܫܒܝܬ ܐܘܝܟܠܬܗ ܡܪܝܬܗ܀[9]

Although a degree of textual confusion remains here (the above text is given exactly as in the manuscript), the rules as a whole are nonetheless clear enough: 1) tau of the 2nd person always has quššāyā; 2) tau of the 3rd person fem. always has rukkāḵā; 3) tau of the 1st person after consonants has rukkāḵā when there is no suffix afterwards, but quššāyā when there is a suffix; 4) tau of the 1st person after ī, and with suffixes (ܥܡ ܡܫܡܫܢܐ), has rukkāḵā. For Bar Šakko's similar treatment of the same subject, see ܟܘ, 5ff.

4. At the end is a warning about the three types of ܦ (Ch.VI).[xviii] The first is ܦ with rukkāḵā as in ܢܦܫܐ, ܢܦܠܬ, ܢܦܩ; the second is "hardened just a little and gently" (ܡܟܝܠ ܡܩܫܝܬܐ ܘܡܫܡܠܝܬ) as in ܦܓܪܐ, ܩܦܘܪܐ, ܦܬܟܪܐ, a type that Bar Malkon calls ܦ ܡܫܡܠܝܐ; the third is the truly "hard" (i.e. plosive) pronunciation, as in ܪܘܦܐ, ܫܦܪܐ,[10] ܦܢܩܐ, although Bar Malkon's examples are

---

[1] In this example the Quššāyā on the tau should be removed. According to the rule as proposed here it should have Rukkāḵā, since it is a 3rd fem.

[2] Gottheil, ܢܩܫܐ, then ܠܟܠܬܐ ܐܢܬܝ, wrongly.

[3] Gottheil omits ܐܘ, then has ܘܐܡܪܝܢܢ for ܘܐܡܪܝܢ.

[4] Gottheil, ܡܫܚܐ ܠܗܘ, but the metre is against it.

[5] Gottheil, ܐܘ ܒܣܠܦ, then ܕܦܪܙܘܦܐ ܦܪܙܘܦܐ which fits the metre.

[6] Gottheil, ܐܝܟ ܠܗܘܐ ܐܚܪܢܐ ܕܡܟܠܬܐ.

[7] That is, after ܝ .

[8] Gottheil reads ܦܪܘܫܬܗ in the ms.

[9] Gottheil, ܦܬܚܝܬ ܙܘܢܬ ܢܫܒܝܬܗ ܐܘ ܟܠܬܗ ܡܪܝܬܗ.

[10] Gottheil, ܫܪܦܐ (i.e. Seraphs), which agrees with Bar Šakko, ܟܝ, l.18.

ܦܘܡܐ, ܦܪܢܣܐ, ܪܘܚܐ, and he calls this type ܡܦܚܬܐ. He adds that experience only, and not a rigid principle, is of any use in distinguishing these different sounds, ܘܟܠܗ ܗܢܐ ܠܗܘܐ ܒܪܡ ܕܝܢ ܢܣܝܘܢܐ ܒܡܫܡܥܐ.[1] He then says the following about this aspiration:

1. ܦ is never rukkāḵā at the beginning or end of a word.
2. Similarly, it is not rukkāḵā after the particles ܒܘܟܠ, save in a very few instances[2] such as Ex 20.25, ܒܦܣܠܬܐ.
3. |[119] Where ܦ is the third radical it is never rukkāḵā before any personal suffix but is always quššāyā in all conjugations.
4. When a vowel is added to it, ܦ is never rukkāḵā, but without a vowel it is rukkāḵā.
5. Every ܦ with a vowel is hard, but this could be either the gentle hardening or the full hardening.

Elias expresses nos. 4 and 5 thus: ܘܟܠܗ ܦܐ ܗܪܟܢ ܠܡܐܡܪ ܕܟܠܗ ܦܐ ܡܙܘܥܬܐ ܐܠܐ ܡܩܫܝܬܐ.[3] ܡܬܢܝܚܢܝܬܐ ܐܠܐ ܡܩܫܝܬܐ ܦܫܝܛܬܐ ܐܘ ܡܫܠܡܢܝܬܐ, which Bar Šakko has copied exactly (p. ܟܝ, l.22), although ܐܘ should be deleted (as in cod.B) following Elias's text. But whereas these grammarians insist on this rule rather severely, the masoretes do not follow it, e.g. against the expression ܚܢܬ ܦܪܝ they have added in the margin ܠܐ ܬܐܡܐ ܦ.[4] So we see just how unsure and even self-contradictory the Masoretic material can be!

Finally in this section he discusses the placing of the point beneath the aspirated ܦ and the hardened ܦ thus: ܘܒܝܬ ܕܦܐ ܗܟܢ ܡܩܫܝܬܐ ܐܬܘܗܝ ܠܬܚܬ ܢܘܩܙܐ ܘܡܬܪܟܟܢܝܬܐ ܠܥܠ ܡܢܗ. These words are echoed in Bar Šakko (*ibid.*) but were by no means used by all since many writers use ܦ̇, ܦ̣, and a ܦ (with a point placed inside). Bar Šakko does this too.

Shortly after distinguishing these three types of ܦ, Bar Malkon summarises the whole matter thus:

ܘܠܐ ܡܪܟܟܝܢ ܠܗ ܐܠܦܐ ܕܒܘܟܠ ܐܝܟ ܕܠܗܠܝܢ: [ܒܟܪܝܟܬܐ]
[5] ܘܗܠܝܢ ܚܕܝܢ܀ ܐܠܐ ܒܦܘܪܢܐ ܐܝܟ ܒܦܣܠܬܐ
[6] ܘܠܐ ܡܩܫܝܢ ܠܗ ܐܠܦܐ ܕܐܝܬ ܒܟܠܗܘܢ ܦܬܓܡܐ:
ܘܠܐ ܡܫܬܠܡܝܢ ܠܗ ܦܪܘܩܐ ܕܡܬܢܝܚܝܢ܀

---

[1] Gottheil, 26*,8, ܗܘܐ ܕܢܣܝܘܢܐ ܒܡܫܡܥܐ.

[2] ܐܠܐ ܐܘ ܒܦܣܝܩܬܐ ܕܚܠܝܢ ms, but ܕܩܠܝܠܬܐ is preferable, as at Gottheil, ܟܗ, l.6.

[3] Gottheil reverses the order, ܡܩܫܝܬܐ ܐܠܐ ܡܬܢܝܚܢܝܬܐ.

[4] Wright, *Cat.* I,104.

[5] Gottheil, ܕܦܣܠܬܐ, which is wrong, cf. Ex 20.25.

[6] On this basis one should read ܐܦܩܘ, ܡܦܩܘ etc. The rule demands ܐܦܪ, for which see Merx, *Grammatica*, I,65.

[1]ܘܦܐ ܡܪܟܒܬܐ ܡܢ ܟܠ ܦܪܘܣ ܠܗܘܐ ܫܟܝܚܬܐ:
ܘܐܦ ܡܬܬܙܝܥܐ ܦܫܝܛܬܐ ܡܬܩܪܝܐ ܐܘ ܩܫܝܬܐ܀

|[120] What he says about ܕܦܣܝܠܬܐ is taken from the masoretic notes to Exod. 20.25, but the pronunciation offered here, which Bar Šakko (ܟܝ, 21) says should be used in a few other places as well, was not universally received, for Barhebraeus recommends the opposite.[2] On the triple ܦ, see also what Jacob said (p.55 above), where the line on ψιλά is the most significant.

If we have here an instance of disagreement among the masoretes on the matter of ܦ, we should point out that some also distinguished three types of ܟ. In the word ܟܐܝܘܣ they required a hard pronunciation to be used which corresponds with the hardest type of ܦ in ܦܢܝܬܐ, i.e. as Caius. But this law is to be found in a West Syrian codex[3] and the usage of one school clearly differed from that of another. Hence we should conclude that minutiae of orthoepy such as these are not natural to Syriac grammar, and that the fastidiousness of the teachers in investigating these matters was so exaggerated that one could not even call the result a systematic theory.

The next chapter in Elias is about letters that are suppressed (Ch. VII),[xix] which also follows the chapter on aspiration in Bar Šakko. The two agree for the most part, save only that Bar Šakko adds some material and is therefore not forced to repeat everything, for anyone who reads Bar Šakko will have already read Elias. The textual corruptions that I have emended in Bar Šakko's text (see p. ܣܗ, notes 3,4) are also found in Elias's version, indicating how poor a state the mss of Bar Šakko are in and that his text cannot be edited without such emendations. The same can be said for Joseph Bar Malkon. I cannot recall there being anything in the latter which is not also found in Bar Šakko. However, there is one thing found in Joseph which should be added by way of confirming Bar Šakko's rule about the lower point indicating the lack of a vowel (p. ܡܟ, l.5), which is as follows:

ܙܢܐ ܠܡܣܝܐ. ܟܠ ܢܘܩܙܐ ܕܫܠܝܢܘܬܐ.
ܗܘ ܕܝܢ ܕܠܫܠܝܢܘܬܐ ܢܦܩ ܒܪ ܘܕܘܟܬܗ ܕܢܩܘܫܐ:
ܠܬܚܬ ܡܢ ܐܬܘܬܐ ܕܠܐ ܡܬܬܙܝܥܢ ܐܝܟ ܗܢܝܢ ܕܡܦܟܝܢ܀

[1] Gottheil, ܗܘܐ ܦܣܝܠܬܐ as the metre demands.

[2] Barhebraeus, *Metrical Grammar*, 335 (Martin, *Œuvres* II, 36). See also Merx, *Grammatica*, 75.

[3] Wright, *Cat.* I,111.

Hence in the midst of the discussion on pointing (f.289r) he digresses a little from the subject at hand and introduces another matter which does not rightly belong,[1] namely:

|[121] "The eighth type, concerning resting points. This [point] which is [meant] for a rest is single and its place is down, underneath vowelless letters, e.g. the ܚ in ܡܫܚܐ."

I have pointed out elsewhere that this usage of the lower point is found in various texts.[2] Those who previously denied this fact may now hear with their ears what they could not see with their eyes, as Herodotus said, ὦτα τυγχάνει ἀνθρώποισι ἀπιστότερα εἶναι ὀφθαλμῶν.[xx]

The next chapter in Elias (Ch.VIII, p. ܟܐ) explains the rules of orthoepy for the silent pronunciation of consonants when they are in certain combinations. Bar Malkon lists exactly the same rules and we can deal here with the rules given by both, which in turn are different from what we found in Jacob of Edessa (p.54):[xxi]

1. Vowelless ܙ before ܟ or ܦ should be pronounced as ܣ, as in ܙܟܐ, ܙܟܘܬܐ, ܙܦܪܐ, ܓܙܦܬܐ (pronounced ܣܦܪܐ etc.).

2. Vowelless ܣ before a consonant which has a vowel and which is Quššāyā should be pronounced as ܙ, as in ܢܣܒ, ܢܣܒܘܢ, ܢܣܒܬܐ, ܢܣܒܝܢ, ܡܢܣܒܐ, ܢܣܒܬ (pronounced ܢܙܒ etc.).

3. Vowelless ܨ before ܛ pronounced as ܙ, e.g. ܨܛܒܬܐ, ܢܨܛܒܐ, ܡܨܛܒܬܐ (pronounced ܙܛܒܬܐ etc.).[3]

4. Vowelless ܦ before a consonant which has a vowel and which is Quššāyā should be pronounced as ܒ, e.g. ܢܦܩ, ܐܦܩܘܗܝ, ܦܘܩܕܢܐ (pronounced ܢܒܩ etc.).

5. |[122] Vowelless hard ܓ before a vowelled ܕ is pronounced as ܟ, e.g. ܦܓܕܐ, ܡܦܓܕܢܐ (pronounced as ܦܟܕܐ etc.)

---

[1] In this section, he treats a number of subjects: 1) 'On the Radical and Servile Letters' (= Elias, ch.III; Bar Šakko, 12,17); 2) 'On Letters Written but not Read', such as the alaph in ܒܬܐ and ܪܝܫܐ, which are called ܡܬܒܠܥܢ (= Elias, ܟܝ, l.6; Bar Šakko, 24,4); 3) 'On Letters that are not Written but are Read', such as the alaph at the beginning of ܝܘܢ and ܡܐ (= Elias, ܟܝ, l.14; Bar Šakko, 24,15); 4) 'On Letters Written but not Pronounced', as the alaph in ܐܢܫܐ and ܡܣܒܐ, which are poorly distinguished from the absorbed letters (ܡܬܒܠܥܢ); 5) 'On Servile Letters' (ܡܫܡܫܢܘܬܐ). After this are some observations on the assimilated letters (ܡܬܚܠܦܢܐ) such as ܣܣ, ܬܕ, ܕܕ, ܬܬ, ܕܬ, ܛܬ, ܢ in ܗܘܢ, ܠ in ܐܙܠ (= Elias, ܟܗ; Bar Šakko, 24,21).

[2] Merx, *Grammatica*, 85.

[3] The Hebrews write הצטדק, but the Syrians ܐܙܕܕܩ, using opposing rules.

6. Vowelless ܓ before the medial ܦ with Quššāyā, such as in ܦܓܪܐ (cf. p.118) is pronounced as ܝ, e.g. ܢܩܦܬܐ ,ܝܣܓܦܬܝ (pronounced ܣܝܦܘܢ etc.).

7. ܘ before a vowelled ܦ is pronounced as ܒ, e.g. ܐܘܦܩܐ ,ܡܦܩܐ ,ܐܬܘܦܝܘ ,ܐܬܘܦܝ, ܝܘܦܘܢ (pronounced ܐܘܒܕܐ etc.).

8. ܗ before ܦ with strong Quššāyā, such as in ܙܦܩܐ, is pronounced as ܙ, e.g. ܗܦܟ ܢܦܩܐ ,ܝܗܦܪܐ (pronounced ܙܦܪܐ etc.). Joseph does not know of this particular usage. In ܘܗܦܟ ܢܦܩܐ and ܒܐܬܗܦܟܬܐ he says that the ܗ should be pronounced rather as ܪ (ܪܦܟ etc.).[1]

9. Vowelless ܟ with Rukkāḵā before ܦ with Quššāyā is pronounced as ܒ, e.g. ܟܦܝܬܐ ,ܟܦܝܦܬܐ (pronounced ܒܦܬܐ etc.).

10. ܫ before a consonant which has a vowel and which is Quššāyā should be pronounced |[123] as the Arabic ج (ܐܝܟ ܓܝܡ ܕܐܪܒܝܐ), e.g. ܝܫܒܘܢ ,ܝܫܟܚܘܢ ,ܝܫܬܘܢ (ܝܓܬܘܢ etc.). Hence a masoretic note is explained that says that the ܫ in the words ܢܫܟܚ and ܐܬܫܟܚܬ should be pronounced as ܟ i.e. ج.[2]

The next two chapters deal respectively with syāmē and some general observations on the association of vowels with consonants (chs. IX,X). There is no need to discuss these here.

In the final chapter (ch. XII) Elias discusses the primary accents ܙܘܓܐ, ܫܘܫܠܐ, ܥܨܝܐ, and ܦܣܘܩܐ, which we need not go over again (see p.71 above). But what he says about ܗܘܝܐ is useful for the light it sheds on how that accent was used (cf. p.80 above):

ܐܝܟ ܗܘܝܐ ܘܦܘܪܫܐ ܡܫܬܚܠܦܝܢ ܠܘܬܗܘܢ ܕܬܪܝܢ: ܐܝܠܝܢ ܕܚܕ ܦܬܓܡܐ ܢܫܠܡܘܢ ܣܟ
ܡܬܬܚܡܝܢ ܒܝܢܬ ܗܘܝܐ ܠܦܘܪܫܐ. ܐܝܟ ܗܢܐ. ܐܕܢܗ ܐܘܚܒ. ܠܐܝܫܝܥ. ܘܐܝܟ ܠܫܠܡܐ ܦܣܘܩܐ[3]
ܗܢܐ. ܘܐܢܬ ܐܬܐܡܪ. ܒܐܩܐ܀ ܐܝܟ ܢܫܠܚܝܢ ܗܘܝܐ ܡܣܬܒܪܐ ܐܡܝܐ ܕܚܕ ܦܬܓܡܐ ܢܫܠܡܘܢ:
ܘܦܘܪܫܐ ܒܬܪܝܢ ܦܬܓܡܐ ܐܘ ܒܬܠܬܐ: ܦܬܓܡܐ ܩܕܡܝܐ ܕܐܬܠܗܘܢ ܗܘܝܐ: ܡܬܦܣܩ
ܒܫܠܡܐ ܘܥܨܝܐ ܕܦܬܓܡܐ ܕܒܬܪܗ ܘܐܬܠܗܘܢ ܦܘܪܫܐ: ܡܬܦܣܩܝܢ ܒܥܠܝܐ. ܘܒܡܘܒܠܐ
ܕܒܗ ܗܘܝܐ ܠܬܚܝܢ ܦܣܘܩܐ. ܐܝܟ ܗܢܐ. ܒܢܝܢܐ. ܕܝܢ ܕܢܩܐ: ܐܫܬܘܝ ܢܒܝܠܐ ܦܠܓܘܬܐ ܡܢ

[1] In the ms of Bar Malkon the examples appear as ܗܦܪܬܐ and ܘܗܦܪܬܐ with ܬ written in each case over the ܪ, implying that the latter be pronounced as a hard tau. There is quite some variation, however, for in Gottheil's text of Elias they are written as ܗܦܪܬܐ ,ܗܦܪܬܝܐ, and ܘܗܦܪܬܐ with ܓ in each case written over the ܬ, although mss B and C omit the ܬ on each occasion. It is thus apparent that the words as printed in Gottheil's edition have resulted from a confusion of the two approaches. For some grammarians wanted to write ܗܦܪܬܐ with ܬ over the ܪ, others preferring to write ܗܦܪܬܐ with a ܓ over the ܪ instead. The scribe has simply pleased everyone by creating the absurd form, ܗܦܪܬܐ, with a ܓ over the joint ܪܬ.

[2] Wright, *Cat.* I,104.

[3] Gottheil ܦܣܘܩܐ .

[1] ܠܡܕܝܢܬܐ ܕܫܡܗ ܢܨܪܬ. ܘܐܝܟ ܗܝ. ܚܢܢܝܐ: ܡܛܠܡܢܐ ܡܠܐ ܣܛܢܐ ܠܒܟ ܕܬܕܓܠ:
ܒܪܘܚܐ ܕܩܘܕܫܐ: ܘܬܛܫܐ ܡܢ ܟܣܦܐ ܕܕܘܡܝ ܩܪܝܬܐ܀

If both protasis and apodosis are short, i.e. if each is constituted of a single clause, then instead of taḥtaya, samka is placed between protasis and apodosis; e.g. 'Abraham begat Isaac' [Mt 1.2]; and 'you shall be called Cephas' [Jn 1.42]. If the protasis be of middling length, such that it is constituted of a single clause, whilst the apodosis is made of two or more, then the first clause [protasis] is divided off [from what follows] by taḥtaya, while the other following clauses, which [together] constitute the apodosis, are [internally] separated by ʿelaya, and then at the end of the whole sentence there is a pasoqa, e.g. 'And in the sixth month the angel Gabriel was sent from before God to Galilee, to the city whose name was Nazareth' [Lk 1.26]; and 'Hanania, why has Satan so filled your heart that you should lie to the Holy Spirit and hide some of the money of the sale of the field?' [Acts 5.3].

At the start of the passage it is clear that the ܣܡܟܐ represents a lesser distinction than the ܬܚܬܝܐ, which divides two-word propositions in both protasis and apodosis, e.g. ܐܘܠܕ. ܠܐܝܣܚܩ or ܬܬܩܪܐ. ܟܐܦܐ. For the most part this agrees with the general rules, albeit not |[124] explained very clearly. Elias of Ṭirhan wrote that the ܣܡܟܐ was said to be ܗܟܢ ܕܐܝܟ ܡܕܡ ܕܡܬܚܫܚ ܠܣܘܡܟܐ ܐܘ ܡܢ ܡܡܠܐ ܕܠܫܢܐ, (f.170b) (*like something that is used for the sake of sustaining [i.e. preserving the continuity] or from the [continuous] pronunciation of the language*).

Neither Elias nor Bar Malkon discuss any other accents. This is what the latter has to say (f.277a):

[2] xxii ܘܐܦ ܕܗܠܝܢ ܡܢ ܗܠܝܢ ܡܬܦܪܫܢ ܢܘ̈ܩܙܐ:
[3] ܘܦܣܝܩܝܢ ܦܘܣܩ̈ܐ܀ ܐܠܐ ܗܠܝܢ ܠܡܢܐ
ܗܢܘ ܕܝܢ ܐܝܟ ܕܗܘܐ ܘܬܚܘܡܐ ܕܡܕܝ̈ܢܬܐ:
ܕܡܣܝܒܪܢܐ ܘܦܫܝܛܐ ܘܫܘܚܠܦܐ ܘܟܪ̈ܝܬܐ܀
ܘܐܦ ܐܚ̈ܪܢܝܬܐ ܘܡܬܟܢܫܢ ܡܢ ܦܣܘܩܐ ܗܠܝܢ:
[4] ܐܬܟܬܒܘ ܥܠ ܟܬܒܝܢ ܘܐܬܢܩܒ ܪܘܫܡܐ ܦܬܓܡܝܢ܀ ܘܠܐ
[1] ܐܝܟ ܩܘܦܐ ܘܡܦܠܓܢܐ ܘܡܬܪܓܡܢܐ:

[1] ܠܓܠܝܠܐ: should have been written. The accent after ܡܘܪܝܐ should then also be restored to ܡܘܪܝܐ:.

[2] This word is used in Neosyriac to mean 'points'. Note then the age of words which are now used by modern Syrians (cf. Gottheil, *Elias*, 40*).

[3] Petermann 9 reads ܠܡܢܐ.

[4] ܘܠܐ] ܕܠܐ, Pet. 9.

[2] ܘܡܒܝܢܬܐ ܠܗܘܢ ܘܡܫܡܠܝܢܬܐ܆ ܘܡܚܝܠܬܐ

Hence with regard to the other accents, even the older Syriac scholars each had his own opinion, no one agreeing with any other. It is hardly surprising that this should happen when we consider the general lack of clarity in these matters, and that each person was free to make up their own minds about them. But we can at least learn from this passage that it is quite hopeless to try to reconstruct a single system of accentuation that was actually in use among the Syrians. The best we can hope for is to reconstruct the system of any one grammarian (as we did above, p.88). Although the codices are often covered in annotations, we generally do not know their origin and we can draw conclusions from them only very cautiously, nor should we attribute them to a given system without good reason, since the usage of the different scholars varies so much. However, it is likely that Jacob's teaching was passed on and used by the West Syrians, and it is indeed likely that the Qarqaphensians adopted them.[3] The same would be true of the other masoretic authorities, Sergius,|[125] Cyril, Philoxenus, ܫܝܠܐ and ܛܘܒܐ.[4]

The Eastern schools, however, should be clearly set apart from this Western tradition, e.g. the school of the monastery of Mār Māri near Seleucia, the schools of Māḥūzā, Aitīlāhā and Kandūqē, and the school that was at Tel Dīnawar in Beth-Nūhadrā, whose ܡܦܩܢܐ and ܡܦܠܚܢܐ were remembered.[5] xxiii The most famous of all was the school of Nisibis. Its teaching may have been preserved by Joseph Bar Malkon, for when Bar Šakko criticises Joseph's *Net of Points of the Nisibenes* (note we showed above, p.111, that it is the teaching preserved by 'the Nisbenes' that is being referred to in all the mss, not that of some particular individual from Nisibis) on the grounds that it is written in poor verse, he is specifically attacking a book that must be reckoned as being from the school of Nisibis

[1] ܘܡܦܪܢܐ Pet. 9.

[2] On p.68 I suggested that ܡܚܝܠܐ and ܡܚܝܠܬܐ were synonymous, but here they seem to refer to different things. They are certainly at least similar.

[3] Martin, *Tradition karkaphienne*, 245,316.

[4] These last two are known to us through the abbreviations ܫ and ܛܘ found in the Masoretic mss. Their identity is discussed by G. Hoffmann, "Zur Geschichte des syrischen Bibeltextes," *Zeitschrift für Alttestamentliche Wissenchaft* I (1881), 159-60. Bar Bahlūl's glosses throw some doubt on them. See also Wright, *Cat.* I,169, and the discussion in Martin, *Tradition Karkaphienne*, 317f.

[5] Wright, *Cat.* I,104,53.

(this is, of course, the very work of Bar Malkon's that we have been quoting).

But even among these schools, the usage of the accents was taught in such a manner that when scriptural examples were selected, the order and layout of the accents would vary greatly according to the special nature of the citation. Their names were not even the same as the ones we saw in Jacob. The East Syrian masoretic codex (Add. 12138) shows this clearly, as we can see from the following combinations of accents:[1] [xxiv]

ܡܛܠܦܣܩܬܐ ܘܙܘܓܐ ܘܐܣܠܐ - ܩܕܡܝܐ ܐܝܟ ܕܠܗ ܐܘܣܡܐܢ ܕܢܒܝܐ ܠܡ:
ܘܐܦ ܐܚܪܢܐ ܦܣܝܩܬܐ ܘܩܫܘܪܐ ܘܐܣܠܐ - ܐܡܪ ܠܗ ܡܠܟܐ· ܐܝܬܝܟ ܡܠܟܢ: ܠܡܥܢܐ ܬܪܘܢܐ ܬܚܬܝܢ
ܐܝܠܝܢ ܗܘ ܕܐܬܝܗܒ:
ܩܫܘܪܐ ܦܣܝܩܬܐ - ܐܫܦܝ ܐܡܪܐ: ܠܝ ܐܝܟ ܕܒܠܐ· ܘܝܗܒ ܠܗܘܢ ܠܒܗ ܘܡܚܠܢܗ
ܘܐܦ ܐܚܪܢܐ ܩܫܘܪܐ ܘܐܣܠܐ - ܠܐ ܬܬܟܠܘܢ ܠܟܘܢ: ܠܐ ܢܫܬܟܚ ܠܗܘܢ: ܠܐܦܝ ܬܚܢܝ ܘܒܗ...
(fol.305a) ܡܪܝܡܢܐ ܙܘܓܐ ܪܒܐ ܘܩܫܘܫܐ - ܠܡܬܚܙܝ ܦܠܛܘܣܝܬ: [126]| ܘܡܬܟܫܦܢܘܬ
ܒܠܒܝܫܗ. ܒܡܠܐ· ܠܗܘܡܐ· ܘܡܒܠ: ܠܟܠܗܘܢ ܢܩܡܘ ܫܡܗܘܢ...ܘܦܡܝܗ ܠܡܕܢܚܐ:
ܘܠܡܥܪܒܐ ܠܒܝܬܗ. ܘܦܠܓ· ܩܛܠܗܘܢ ܠܐܬܘܬܐ ܕܟܬܒܝܢ ܗܘܘ. ܠܡܥܒܕ ܕܡܢ ܡܥܦܢ
ܡܥܝܢܐ: ܘܚܙܘܩܐ ܕܠܗܘܢ
ܘܐܦ ܐܚܪܢܐ ܙܘܓܐ ܪܒܐ ܘܩܫܘܫܐ ܘܐܣܠܐ ܘܐܬܠܘܢ: ܡܪܟܐ ܬܪܥܝܢ. ܘܐܦ ܐܚܪܢܐ ܘܐܬܐ: ܗܟܢܐ· ܕܐܪܥܐ
ܠܐ ܬܪܥܐ.
ܐܣܠܐ ܙܘܓܐ ܡܫܘܚܬܐ ܡܫܘܚܬܐ: ܡܟܝܠ ܒܫܘܠܐ.. ܐܚܪܢ ܐܚܪܢ.

The West Syrian Bar Šakko is not in agreement with the Eastern schools represented here. He maintains total silence on ܣܡܟܐ and ܡܗܓܝܢܐ, accents not used by the Westerns and treated as one and the same by the Easterns. Bar Malkon, on the other hand, does mention them (ܣܡܟܐ is a line above, ܡܗܓܝܢܐ a line below) and explains their usage as follows (f.277b):

1 ܘܙܘܓ ܕܠܘܬ ܕܢܦܩ ܠܥܠ ܠܛܝܒܐ ܕܦܘܣܩܐ:
ܗܘܓܝܐ ܕܡܠܦܢܐ ܬܝܒܘܬܐ ܘܐܣܝܪ ܡܗܓܝܢܐ܀
2 ܘܣܡܟܐ ܗܝܡ ܠܟܠ ܙܘܓܐ ܩܪܝܒ ܡܟܠܝܢܐ ܕܣܢܐܐ:
ܡܐ ܕܢܦܠ ܠܗ ܠܗܘܦܟܐ ܡܦܠܓ ܙܥܐ ܐܣܝܬܐ܀
3 ܠܝ ܠܐ ܠܗܘܐ ܡܟܠܝܢܐ ܕܩܪܝܒ ܠܦܘܣܩܐ ܡܦܣܩܬܐ:
ܐܚܪܢܐ ܕܦܣܩܬܐ ܦܣܝܩܬܐ ܘܙܘܓܐ ܘܙܘܓܐ܀
4 ܘܠܐ ܠܘܬ ܠܗܘܐ ܡܟܠܝܢܐ ܗܘܐ ܡܢܐ ܡܢ ܩܠܐ:
ܕܡܦܣܩܢܘܬܐ ܡܪܝܡܢܐ ܕܙܘܓܐ[2] ܘܡܠܝܐ܀
5 ܘܣܡܟ ܠܝ ܝܗܘܢ ܐܝܟܢ ܕܩܠܝܢ ܬܠܬ ܢܩܝ ܦܣܩܐ:

---

[1] f.304a. See Wright, *Cat.* I,104, item II.

[2] The *Net of Points* is also found in this ms (Petermann 9) and here offers ܕܪܘܚܐ.

ܘܢܕܥ ܒܟܠܐ ܕܡܬܚܒܫ ܒܦܬܓܡܘ ܡܬܦܫܩܐ܀
6 ܘܗܘܢ ܐܝܟ ܕܒܝܬܦܠ ܡܥܒܪܬܐ ܘܐܝܟ[1] ܐܡܪ ܠܗܘܢ܆
ܘܠܟܡ ܐܝܟ ܕܒܘܕܝܗ ܡܥܒܪܬܐ ܘܐܝܟ ܦܬܘܢ ܠܗܘܢ܀
7 |127 ܘܩܢܝܢ[2] ܐܝܟ ܕܒܦܠܓܐ ܡܥܒܪܐ ܘܗܘܢ ܢܥܒܕܘܢ܆
ܘܟܕ ܘܚܕ ܥܡܗܐ ܘܐܦ ܡܢ ܥܡܗܐ ܠܚܕܢܐ ܢܬܪܣܘܢ[3]܀
8 ܡܛܦܝܢܐ ܕܝܢ[4] ܐܝܟܐ ܕܐܦ ܬܟܦܘܬܐ ܙܘܓ܆
ܠܐ ܢܣܒܘܢ ܕܝܢ ܒܪܟܒܘܬܐ ܠܚܪܦܐ ܦܬܝܚ܀

It is not easy to understand this without making use of Bar Zuʿbi's commentary on it. The ܡܛܦܝܢܐ (i.e. *closing off*) has a disjunctive effect. It prevents us from eliding two words that happen to follow one another. Although there is no exact equivalent in the Hebrew masoretic system, the ܢܓܘܕܐ is much the same as the Hebrew Maqqef, i.e. it has a conjunctive effect. The Syrians included these two lines among the other accents, just as was done in Hebrew grammar with the Maqqef.[5] Bar Zuʿbi says that they have opposite effects and that they are among the greater points,[6] which is just what Joseph says in the first line above, "one must know that the line that is called ܢܓܘܕܐ and that which is called ܡܛܦܝܢܐ accompany the greater points."

Now we can look at which were the combinations of syllables to which ܢܓܘܕܐ and ܡܛܦܝܢܐ were applied, according to Bar Zuʿbi:

Ia. If a word, in which the same consonant is repeated [at the beginning of the word], is such that each of the two should be pronounced separately, then it should be joined to a preceding word [ending in a vowel] by ܢܓܘܕܐ, e.g. ܕܠܐ ܡܠܠܐ ܠܐ ¯ܡܦܝܓܝ ܗܘܐ ܠܚܡܘܢ (pronounced *lāmᵉ-mallil*).

Ib. If the same consonant is not repeated then ܡܛܦܝܢܐ is used, e.g. ܘܦܠܠܬܐ ܦܝܠܐ_ ܠܚܡܘܢ (pronounced *pilāṯā / mallil*).

[1] ܘܐܦ (Petermann 9).

[2] ܗܢܝܢ ܘܐܝܟ (Petermann 9).

[3] ܢܥܒܕܘܢ (Petermann 9), with ܢܬܪܣܘܢ written underneath.

[4] ܗܘܠ for ܕܝܢ (Petermann 9).

[5] On these lines, see R. Duval, *Traité de grammaire syriaque* (Paris, 1881), 132, but although Martin had discussed them (*Deux dialectes* , 398), he does not seem to have understood them aright.

[6] This part of Bar Zuʿbi's grammar, on accents, was edited by Martin, *Traité sur l'accentuation chez les Syriens orientaux* (Paris, 1877). I do not always agree with Martin on the meaning of the text but there is no point in enumerating our differences here. Elias of Ṭirhan (ed. Baethgen, *Elias von Tirhan*), ch.28, covers the same ground but only in passing.

|128 IIa. Emphatic states[1] in *ā* followed by the conjunction ܘ are connected to the following word by ܢܝܚܘܪܐ, e.g. ܡܕܝܢ̈ܬܐ¯ܘܡܠܟܐ, ܡܕܝܢ̈ܬܐ¯ܘܟܢܫܐ, ܡܠܟ̈ܘܬܐ¯ܘܥܡܐ, ܓܠ̈ܠܐ¯ܘܡܬܩܠܐ.[2] When the meanings of the words are very closely related, this is best expressed by simply pronouncing the words as if they were one.

IIb. If the first of these word pairs is construct, then ܡܗܓܝܢܐ is used. ܡܕܝܢܬ_ܡܠܟܐ, ܡܕܝܢܬ_ܟܢܫܐ, ܡܠܟܘܬ_ܥܡܐ, ܚܝܠ_ܡܬܩܠܐ. In other words, the disjunctive mark is used here to preserve the distinct pronunciations of each word where they are otherwise closely bound by their form.

IIIa. Prepositions with pronominal suffixes are joined to the following word with ܢܝܚܘܪܐ, e.g. ܥܡܝ¯ܢܗܘܐ ܐܢܬ, ܠܘܬܝ¯ܬܐܬܐ ܐܢܬ. Although this should apply to all suffixes, all the examples given use the first person suffix. Bar Zuʿbi does not give examples, while Barhebraeus offers ܡܢܗܘܢ ܘܢܦܫܗ (cf. VIa below).[3]

IIIb. If the preposition has no suffix and the following word does not begin with a vowel,[4] then ܡܗܓܝܢܐ is used, e.g. ܥܠ_ܓܒܠܐ, ܠܘܬ_ܥܡܡܐ. There are no examples where the second word does begin with a vowel, though in such cases ܢܝܚܘܪܐ would surely be used. According to Martin the Vatican ms omits what the London ms here says about the effect of vowels.

IVa. The particle ܡܢ before words beginning with a vowel or vowelled consonant takes ܢܝܚܘܪܐ, e.g. ܡܢ¯ܓܒܪܐ, ܡܢ¯ܦܓܪܐ, ܡܢ¯ܬܘܕܝܬܐ, ܡܢ¯ܩܕܡ, ܡܢ¯ܐܝܠܝܢ.

IVb. ܡܢ before a consonant with shewa |129 has ܡܗܓܝܢܐ, e.g. ܡܢ_ܫܡܝܐ, ܡܢ_ܡܕܒܪܐ, ܡܢ_ܠܚܒܪܐ ܗܘ, ܗܘ.

Va. The particles ܡܢ, ܐܦ, ܐܘ, ܐܢ require ܢܝܚܘܪܐ before a vowel (ܡܢ is again added here, despite being dealt with in the previous paragraph),[5] e.g. ܡܢ¯ܐܪܥܐ,

[1] Literally, "If the noun consists of two complete [syllables]." See p.18n above for this terminology.

[2] This explains the Neosyriac pronunciation in which the particle ܘ seems to belong to the foregoing word. See Merx, *Neusyrisches Lesebuch* (Breslau, 1872), 57[3].

[3] *Gramm.*, 201.

[4] This seems to be how we should interpret Bar Zuʿbi's exception to the rule: "excepting nouns that begin with ܡܘ ܣܚܪܐ or ܠܒܫ with a vowel." For no word whose first letter is vowelled with *ū* can begin with a waw, since an alaph would be used in such cases. Again wherever I here translate "before a vowel," Bar Zuʿbi speaks of ܡܘ ܣܚܪܐ and ܠܒܫ.

[5] The text of Bar Zuʿbi is corrupt here, as Martin saw. But, since we have seen that ܢܝܚܘܪܐ is a conjunctive line and ܡܗܓܝܢܐ a disjunctive one, we can work out from the examples given just what the rule ought to be. The examples I give are from my own collation of the ms, which is not in all respects identical with Martin's. He made some errors in transcription.

ܐܘ ̄ܠܒܥܠ, ܐܦ ̄ܐܒܥܡܟܠ, ܡܢ ̄ܒܫܬܝܠ, ܡܢ ̄ܒܬܪ,[1] ܐܠܐ ̄ܒܟܦ, ܐܘ ̄ܒܐܢ, ܡܢ ̄ܒܪܗ, ܐܘ ̄ܠܐܣܪ, ܡܢ ̄ܠܐܬܐ, ܐܠܐ ̄ܐܡܫܚ, ܐܠܐ ̄ܠܥܡܐ.

Vb. The same particles before a consonant with either shewa or a full vowel take ܡܗܓܝܢܐ,[2] e.g. ܡܢ_ܒܪܐ, ܡܢ_ܩܥܡܢ, ܐܦ_ܒܥܠ, ܐܘ_ܡܠܟܘ, ܐܘ_ܩܕܡܘ, ܐܠܐ_ܦܟܪܢ, ܐܠܐ_ܩܕܡܢ, ܡܢ_ܩܕܡܐ, ܡܢ_ܦܬܟܪܐ, ܡܢ_ܡܫܝܚܐ, ܡܢ_ܢܚܠܐ, ܐܦ_ܢܚܠܐ, ܐܠܐ_ܡܕܢܚܐ.

VIa. The ܗ suffix on a noun takes ܢܓܘܕܐ if followed by a word beginning with a consonant without a full vowel, e.g. ܒܪܗ ̄ܕܡܠܟܐ, ܪܝܫܗ ̄ܕܐܒܐ.[3] In this example, the upper line |[130] is actually missing in the ms. Presumably, this rule only affects the masculine suffix; the examples given do not tell us whether the feminine is also so treated, but the example given below would suggest this to be the case.

VIb. The same, but before consonants with full vowels, requires ܡܗܓܝܢܐ, e.g. ܒܪܗ_ܕܡܫܝܚܐ, ܪܝܫܗ_ܕܐܠܗܐ, ܡܠܟܬܗ_ܕܫܡܝܐ, ܦܬܟܪܗ_ܕܐܘܪܚܐ. From these we can see that the rule applies also to the feminine suffix.[4]

VIIa. If two vowelless consonants run together at the end of one word and the beginning of the next, then ܢܓܘܕܐ is attached to the penultimate, vowelled consonant of the first word, e.g. ܡܠܟܐ ܐܬܠ ܠܗܘܢ, ܢܬܟܪ ܒܗܘܢ, ܐܡܪ ܠܗܘܢ, ܐܡܪܬ ܡܫܝܚܐ ܠܥܒܕܗ, ܡܢܗܘܢ.[5] This surely reminds one of assimilation in Arabic.[1]

Of the examples given, one is certainly wrong, for ܡܢ ̄ܒܬܪ should not have ܢܓܘܕܐ on the analogy of the other forms. Bar Zuʿbi is self-contradictory with regard to ܡܢ (see IVa).

[1] The example ܡܢ ̄ܒܬܪ is used here as well, though according to these rules it should be in the next section, Vb, with ܡܗܓܝܢܐ (see preceding note).

[2] Bar Zuʿbi subdivides this rule into four parts: 1) ܢܓܘܕܐ in verbs; 2) ܢܓܘܕܐ in nouns; 3) ܡܗܓܝܢܐ in verbs; 4) ܡܗܓܝܢܐ in nouns. In looking at the whole problem from a phonological point of view we have sensibly ignored the distinction between nouns and verbs. This was an unhelpful distinction for the schools to have made and yet a well-worn one, for we see the same thing in the case of the vocalisation of the particles ܒܘܟܠ (cf. p.31), even though there was really nothing in the nature of the topic to warrant it.

[3] The final example, ܪܝܫܗ ̄ܕܐܠܗܐ, does not belong here, and actually appears in the next section since it should take ܡܗܓܝܢܐ.

[4] Bar Zuʿbi adds here that the same rule applies when an alaph is found in place of ܗ. But cf. rule IIa. His addition would suggest that one should write ܒܪܐ_ܕܐܠܗܐ, ܒܪܐ_ܕܡܫܝܚܐ, ܐܒܐ_ܕܟܠܐ, which would not conform to Rule IIa. So one can see how much confusion there was among all these theorists in matters of orthoepy.

[5] Hence we can explain some of the contractions, or rather assimilations, of Neosyriac, e.g. ܐܡܝܪܠܝ (*I have said [cf. Latin 'dictum est mihi']*), ܟܦܝܪܠܝ (*I have ground*), ܩܛܝܠܠܝ (*I have killed*). Bar Zuʿbi does not tell us whether this close connection applies only to certain consonants, as is the case in Arabic. It seems in any case to follow its own rules, as I have demonstrated

I have shown that the same phenomenon also occurs in the Targumic vocalisation (Merx, 'Bemerkungen', as cited below). Such assimilation is therefore common among the Aramaic languages and was also known in Arabic and in Hebrew. From just a small selection of verses ('Bemerkungen', 183) one can see examples of a number of assimilations, *n* and *m*, *n* and *l*, *l* and *m*, *t* and *m*, *l* and *ṣ*, *ḥ* and *l*, *d* and *l*, *b* and *m*, *l* and *l*, *t* and *q*. With the bgdkpt letters we cannot tell when there is assmilation since the Dagesh is added anyway (see ch.X, Appendix II).

VIIb. If a vowelled first consonant in the second word follows a vowelless last consonant in the first word, then ܡܗܓܝܢܐ is needed, e.g. ܚܩܠ_ܕܡܐ. ܢܦܩ_ܟܪܘܙܐ, ܘܗܠܟ_ܠܐܣܘܪܝܐ, ܐܡܪ_ܠܐܠܗܐ, The contraction is found in Neosyriac (see note above).

|[131] VIIIa. Bar Zuʿbi's final observation indicates just how much precision is demanded of the reader. For this tells us that the above rule can be inverted by the accent that goes with it. If words of the type just mentioned (VIIb) are found after the ܙܩܦܐ accent, and there are not more than two of them, then ܢܝܫܐ is used (even though by the rule it should be ܡܗܓܝܢܐ). The vocalisation thus indicated by the ܢܝܫܐ (ܡܬܠܝܢܘܬܗ ܕܢܝܫܐ) creates a single element or word, e.g. ܦܩܘܕܘܢ ܠܡ ܠܗܘܢ ܕܢܗܠܟ ܠܐܣܘܪܝܘܢ. This is the same as the Hebrew use of Maqqef.

But if there were in this example some further element after the ܠܐܣܘܪܝܘܢ, then ܡܗܓܝܢܐ would be found instead: ܦܩܘܕܘܢ ܠܡ ܠܗܘܢ ܕܢܗܠܟ_ܠܐܣܘܪܝܘܢ ܒܡܢܙܚܐ.

VIIIb. He then requires that the same rule applies when using these marks in poetry, ܡܬܘܪܬܐ. ܡܗܓܝܢܐ. ܕܪܘܪܬܐ ܕܒܡ ܢܝܫܘܗܝ.

VIIIc. Finally, it should be noted that Bar Zuʿbi does not enumerate all the conditions under which these marks should be used, but simply offers examples. He usually introduces them with the words ܡܘܕܥܐ ܚܕ, ܡܘܕܥܐ ܐܚܪܢܐ (*one indication, another indication*). This way of expressing himself makes clear that he is only giving us a selection of the indications, or conditions, for the use of these lines, and not all of them.

This throws some new light on the quotation from Joseph Bar Malkon (p.126). His second and third verses correspond to Bar Zuʿbi's seventh rule, save with the further addition that it is not only the ܙܩܦܐ accent that inverts

from the Reuchlian Karlsruhe manuscript that it was done in the same way according to the orthoepy of some of the Hebrew masters—A. Merx, "Bemerkungen über die Vocalization der Targume" in *Verhandlungen des fünften internationalen Orientalisten-Congresses II, Abhandlungen und Vorträge* (Berlin, 1881-2), 142-88, see p. 182.

[1] See S. de Sacy, *Grammaire arabe* (1st ed. Paris, 1810) I, §111-117.

the usage of ܡܦܣܩܢܐ (VIIIa). He says (vs.2) that ܢܓܘܕܐ is placed on the vowel preceding the last vowelless consonant of a word, when a word with a vowelless first consonant follows; (vs.3) this is only the case so long as the vowelless consonant that precedes is not marked with one of these accents: ܦܩܘܕܐ, ܡܙܝܥܢܐ, ܙܘܚܐ, or ܪܗܛܐ; (vs.4) besides, even the final consonant must be other than a waw, yudh or alaph, for these add their own sound (u,i,a) to the foregoing consonant;[1] (vs.5) use ܢܓܘܕܐ if the consonants that lack vowels are of the same category,[2] |[132] but ܡܦܣܩܢܐ where one which runs together without an [interceding] vowel [coalesces] easily.

Vs 6,7 provide examples. ܢܦܩ‾ܡܫܝܚܐ and ܐܡܪ‾ܠܗܘܢ correspond to VIIa; the counter examples ܗܘܘ_ܡܫܝܚܐ and ܡܢܝ_ܠܗܘܢ are excepted from the contraction on account of the final vowel (cf. vs.4).

The next example, ܡܠܟܐ‾ܡܫܝܚܐ, would seem to be related to rules IIa and VIa, even though Bar Zuʿbi is unexpectedly silent on the very close association of this word pair. In ܗܘܘ‾ܢܚܫܘܢ we have assimilation and contraction as in VIIa. I would have thought that assimilation between *ḥ* and *š*, and between *n* and *š* would have occurred in the following examples, ܚܡܫܐ‾ܢܦܫ ܕܝ and ܡܢ‾ܚܡܫܐ‾ܠܟܢܫܐ‾ܢܦܫܗܘܢ, in which the contraction of consonants of the same category should apply also to ܢܦܫ, ܕܝ. On ܚܡܫܐ‾ܠܟܢܫܐ and ܠܟܢܫܐ‾ܢܦܫܗܘܢ, see p.130.[3]

Vs 8: ܡܦܣܩܢܐ (i.e. that which stops, closes, partitions) can be used everywhere, where ܢܓܘܕܐ (i.e. that which attracts, conjoins) would be used but is not needed because the vowelless consonants that run up against each other are easily pronounced (compare this with vs.5). So according to Joseph, all the words in a text should be distinctly pronounced and contraction only used where reading becomes difficult on account of a sequence of vowelless consonants. We can presume that this was the general rule at the School of Nisibis. I cannot tell whether Bar Zuʿbi was wholly in agreement with this.[4]

There is little point in going further into the differences between the different schools in this field and indeed it would anyway be quite

[1] This rule should be understood in the light of the vowelless character of semitic script, e.g. in ܗܘܘ the final ܘ would appear to be a vowelless consonant which transfers its own sound to the foregoing ܘ.

[2] That is, the sounds comes from the same organs, the ܡܦܩܐ is the same as the مخرج (*place of origin*) of Arabic orthoepy. See S. de Sacy, *Grammaire arabe*, §116 (المتجانسون).

[3] See again previous note.

[4] See again the excursus on the Targumic vocalisation (Ch.X, App.II).

impossible to discover exactly what the different usages were since there are no mss available which have been written with the orthoepic signs of a particular school.[1]

*

To return to Elias. The patterns of noun and verb inflection are a mere appendix to the grammar.[xxv] Elias entitles this section ܡܫܘܚܘܬܐ ܕܡܩܕܡܘܬܐ ܡܢ ܙܘܘܓܐ ܕܡ̈ܠܐ, the term ܙܘܘܓܐ here being a translation of συζυγία, i.e. *conjugation* (of the verb). The ignorant scribes of the Bar Šakko manuscript were constantly confused between ܙܘܘܓܐ and ܙܘܓܐ (see the emendation |[133] in our edition, ܠ,7). It is from this usage that the meaning of *to derive* for ܙܘܓ arose, and both Bar Malkon and Bar Zuʿbi use it in this sense. The former says, ܡܢ ܓܠܠ ܘܣܦ̈ ܐܢ ܡܙܕܘܓܝܢ (f.284a, i.e. *if we derive* ܣܦ̈ *from* ܓܠܠ). This follows Elias's theory of ܡ̈ܠܐ ܡܙܕܘܓܬܐ ܘܡܬܥܠܠܢ̈ܝܬܐ (*secondarily derived verbs*, f.108b).[2]

Elias of Nisibis's list of verbal conjugations (Gottheil, *Elias*, ܟ f.) is dependent upon the Greek systems and he lists the forms according to Theodosius's *Canons* of the noun. Joseph Bar Malkon (f.279a), however, aligns the verbal conjugations with the placement of points, thereby following his masters, the ܡܕܢܚܝ̈ܐ. He distinguishes three conjugations:

1) Verbs of two consonants with either *ā* or *ă*, e.g. ܣܡ and ܙܪ (cf. Bar Šakko, ܕ, l.12).

2) Triliteral roots with a silent shewa on the first: a) ܦܩܠ, b) ܗܦܟ, c) ܡܠܐ (cf. Bar Šakko, ܓ, l.1).

3) Triliteral roots with an *a* vowel on the first: a) ܢܓܫ, b) ܙܩܦ, ܬܩܢ, under which he includes also the Aphel forms such as ܐܘܒܠ (cf. Bar Šakko, ܓ, l.13).

The basic criterion of differentiation, then, is the number of consonants. The vowel-type serves to sub-divide according to their Greek ordering, ā ă e i. We argued earlier that the same system was used with respect to the nouns (p.58). The same principle is found in Elias and this surely goes back to Jacob of Edessa. Although there is a certain degree of confusion, the following is Elias's categorisation:

1) ܬܠܐ, ܓܪ, to which he adds ܢܫܒ.

2) ܚܬܐ, ܚܝܐ, ܚܟܡ (which probably should be ܚܟܒ) and ܡܒܐ, which could not be included under the previous group since it retains three consonants.

3) a) ܬܩܢ, ܙܩܦ (invert—it should be ܬܩܢ).
 b) ܐܬܐ, ܐܙܠ.

[1] On the origins of the lines, see Baethgen, *Elias of Ṭirhan*, 48.

[2] When applied to the typology of verbs, ܡܙܕܘܓܐ means σύνθετον (*compound*).

c) ܐܙܠ, ܐܟܠ, ܐܡܪ which should really be categorised with ܝܗܒ and ܢܦܩ.
|134 d) ܐܝܬܝ, which was actually placed after ܐܝܬ and is omitted in ms C.
e) ܝܗܒ, ܝܠܦ, ܝܩܕ (invert).
4) a) ܐܘܟܠ, ܐܘܠܦ (invert—it should be ܐܘܪܒ).
b) ܐܝܠܕ, ܐܝܢܩ etc.

After the verbs, Bar Malkon discusses (f.282a) the pronominal suffix, including the personal terminations on verbs and the derivation of nouns from a verb (ܦܘܫܩܐ ܕܫܡܗܐ ܡܢ ܡ̈ܠܐ). Of the latter he defines four types, 1) ܫܡ ܡܥܒܕܢܘܬܐ, a noun *of acting*; 2) ܕܥܒܘܕܐ , *of an agent*; 3) ܕܥܒܝܕܐ, *of something done*; 4) ܕܚܫܘܫܐ, *of something being experienced*. We find exactly the same order in Bar Šakko (p. ܟܒ), although he omits nos. 1 and 4.

Before moving on to a final assessment of the grammarians dealt with in the present chapter, it remains to enumerate the order in which they arranged their chapters. Elias runs as follows: I, The Alphabet; II, Letters at rest and in motion; III, Radical and Servile letters; IV, Cases (ܒ ܕ ܘ ܠ); V, Quššāyā and Rukkāḵā; VI, Letters that should be secretly absorbed (ܕܡܬܒܠܥܢ); VII, Hidden Letters; VIII, Letters that interchange with each other; IX, The Sign of the Plural; X, On the word ܗܘܠܝܢ; XI, The pointing of the first four accents; XII, List of nouns, together with the inflection of the verb. Such is the contents of Elias of Nisibis's ܬܘܪܨ ܡܡܠܠܐ.

Joseph Bar Malkon's *Net of Points* follows a different procedure. It might be of help here to transcribe his preface, so that readers may realise that Jacob Bar Šakko (p. ܩܗ, l.15) is attacking precisely this short treatise, and not without some justice. Joseph's preface is as follows:

ܒܫܡܗ ܕܐܒܐ ܘܒܪܐ ܘܪܘܚܐ ܩܕܝܫܐ ܠܬܠܬܐ:
ܚܕܐ ܐܘܣܝܐ ܕܚܕ ܐܠܗܐ ܚܕܐ ܐܠܗܘܬܐ܀
ܩܕܝܡ ܥܠ ܩܕܝܡ ܫܘܪܐ ܐܢܐ ܒܡܫܝܚܘܬܐ ܦܓܥܬ.
ܕܠܐ ܐܬܪܚܩ ܡܢ ܦܬܓܡܐ ܕܥܠ ܒܘܪܟܝ܀
ܫܘܒܚܐ ܠܫܡܟ ܡܫܝܚܐ ܗܒܠܢ ܥܠ ܕܗܘ ܠܡܒܥܝܢ:
ܫܪܪܐ ܠܡܫܡܠܝܘ ܘܦܘܪܩܢܐ ܕܒܗ ܠܐ ܢܥܢܝ܀
|135 ܕܡܠܦܢܐ ܐܒܘܗܝ ܕܒܪܡܠܟܘܢܘܬܐ ܢܣܒ:[xxvi]

ܘܢܦܩܘܗܝ ܡܢܝܢܐ ܕܢܘܩܙܐ ܘܡܠܐ ܢܗܝܪܐ ܘܐܡܪ܀
ܕܩܢܘܡܐ ܢܘܩܙܐ ܕܒܟܠܗܘܢ ܡܫܠܡܝܢ:
ܡܫܠܡܝܢ ܐܝܟ ܡܐ ܕܡܫܠܡܐ ܠܡܠܝܐ ܕܐܢܫ܀
ܥܠ ܓܒܪ ܢܘܩܙܐ ܐܘ ܙܒܢܐ ܗ̄ܘ ܘܫܡ ܕܦܘܫܩܐ ܗ̄ܘ.
ܐܘ ܐܝܟܢܐ ܗ̄ܘ ܘܗܘܝܐ ܡܢ ܕܡ̈ܠܐ ܗ̄ܘ ܐܘ ܕܫܡ̈ܗܐ ܗ̄ܘ܀
ܐܘ ܕܦܘܬܐ ܗ̄ܘ ܐܘ ܗܘ ܕܡܬܘܕܥ ܙܒܢ ܘܦܘܫ:

ܐܘ ܗܘ ܕܟܝܡܬܢܘܬܐ (sic) ܗ̄ܘ ܐܘ ܠܢܩ̈ܫܝܢ܀
ܐܘ ܗܘ ܕܠܡܠܘܬܐ ܡܥܒܪ̈ܢܐ ܘܡܠܝܐ ܗܘ ܐܚܪܢ܆
ܘܡܢ ܒܬܪܗ ܕܡܢܗ ܢܒܥ ܢܩܫܐ ܘܢܝܫܘܪ܀

So Joseph's chapters run: I, The four primary accents; II, The points that indicate vowels and, in order to exemplify these, he adds here also the inflections and after these discusses the ܦܘܚܡܐ and ܡܢܘܢܝܐ; III, The plural marker; IV, The points of the canon (ܚܠܦ ܢܩ̈ܙܐ ܕܩܢܘܢܐ), i.e. those points that we call diacritics; V, Rukkāḵā and Quššāyā; VI, The points that indicate the feminine gender, which is here called ܕܢܩܒܘܬܐ—this is what he calls the point at the end of the word ܒܪ̈ܬܗ. After this discussion of the feminine points, he continues:

ܘܐܟܠ ܗ̄ܘ ܕܦܢܝܢ ܒܢܘܢܐ ܡܫܠܡ ܠܢܩ̈ܫܝܢ܆
ܐܚܪ̈ܢܐ ܫܘܠܡ ܘܐܬܘܬܦ ܐܬ̈ܘܢ ܘܗܠܝܢ ܒܠܗܘܢ܀
ܡܠܬܐ ܩܠܐ ܢܩܫܐ ܢܩܫܬܐ ܫܢܝ̈ܬܐ܆
ܢܩܠ ܐܡܬܬܐ ܕܦܪܐ ܒܬܬܐ ܦܟ̈ܗܩܬܐ܀
ܓܪܬܐ ܒܢܬܐ ܦܓܘܪܬܐ ܦܓܘ̈ܪܐ ܦܫܩ̈ܘܬܐ܆
ܡܬ̈ܠ ܢܒܝ̈ܐ ܫܪܪܐ ܠܪܘܚܬܐ ܢܩܡܬܐ܀
136 ܘܝܫܪ̈ܐ ܘܦܠܬܐ ܘܒܗ ܘܠܐ ܒܓܪ ܠܐܪܙ ܡܠܬܐ܆
ܒܫܘܪܒ ܒܪ̈ܢܫ ܢܐܘܪܐ ܕܒܗܘܪܐ ܕܘܡܬܐ܀

Chapter VII, then, is on the ܕܐܬܘܬܐ, ܦܪܘܫܝܐ ܢܘܩܙܐ, i.e. the point that differentiates Dalath from Resh. As a result of some confusion, the subject of the absorbed letters (and others of a similar nature) is also found here. Chapter VIII is on the points of rest (ܕܡܢܝܚܘܬܐ). So it is only here at the very end that he speaks about the hidden letters and the orthoepic variations that we described above (p.121).

So this was the state to which East Syriac grammar had progressed by the time that Bar Zuʿbi, their greatest grammarian, wrote his own work by building on that of his predecessors, whose palm of victory he snatched for himself. Of all that was written by those earlier pioneers, we have now collected together pretty much all that remains—for the rest, there are only names. Among these names, we should probably mention an author of unknown date, John Bar Penkāyē (i.e. son of the potters). According to Barhebraeus's *Ethics*, he was an East Syrian monk, and according to the Book of Pearls he was from Nisibis.[1] His works include ܡܪܕܘܬܐ ܕܛܠܝܐ (*The Education of Boys*), a pedagogical treatise, ܕܪܫ ܡܠܐ ܘܐܓܪ̈ܬܐ (*A Study of Words and Letters*), which presumably dealt with epistolary composition, and ܐܣܪ̈ܐ ܕ

[1] BO III,I,189; II,306.

ܘܦܪܨܘܦܐ, a title of uncertain meaning. I would think that ܐܣܪ̈ܐ here means ‘particles’ and ܦܪܨܘܦܐ refers to the ܐ of the emphatic state, the pronominal suffixes on nouns, and the affixes that indicate persons of verbs (see p.104 above for a discussion of the term ܦܪܨܘܦܐ). So the title would then mean, *On the particles and the emphatic noun and the verb marked with personal affixes.*[xxvii]

Another grammarian mentioned by ʿAbdišoʿ is John Bar Kamis. In Arabic the name is Ibn al-Ḥaddâd, which in Syriac would be ܒܪ ܦܚ̈ܘܡܐ (*son of the ironworkers*). He lived at the time of the patriarch Maḵiḵa (1092-1108) and was the bishop of Thamanūn, near Amid. He was well known for composing hymns, which are still extant in some Vatican mss, but his grammar has disappeared.[1] The last grammarian we need to mention is Išōʿyabh Bar Malkon, consecrated bishop of Nisibis in 1190, whose *Grammatical Problems* is mentioned by ʿAbdišoʿ.[2] Martin has recently argued that he was the author of the *Net of Points* (but see p.111).

We have now dealt with nearly all the East Syrian grammarians and their works. They sought to develop the art of reading, rather than grammar as such, towards a philosophical goal, and they all stood within the Greek|[137] tradition. But there are also plenty of suggestions that from the ninth century onwards the importance of Arabic was gradually on the rise until even the Syriac ecclesiastical schools began to adopt the Arabic system. For instance, we noted (p.123) that ܚ in the middle of a word should be pronounced as Arabic ج. We could also reckon with the fact that vowels are sometimes called ܙܘ̈ܥܐ, which seems to be a calque on the Arabic حركات. We noticed (p.110) that according to the preface to Elias’s glossary, the actual usage of Syriac was already fading away. If at this time the Catholicoi of the Church of the East were seeking the favours of the nobles at the ʿAbbāsid court—who themselves were much attracted by the arts of rhetoric and poetics—it is hardly surprising that the Syrians, like the Arabs, should keenly pursue the study of grammar. After all, grammar was the basis for the whole cultivation of the humanities (ادب) in Arabic. The Syrians, who were well acquainted with the traditions of Arabic grammar, could hardly fail to be affected by it and this is precisely what did happen. From the turn of the eleventh century, Syriac began to be treated according to the pattern of Arabic grammar, and the first to embark on this enterprise was Elias of Ṭirhan.

---

[1] BO III,I,296; Barhebraeus, *Chron. Eccl.*, III,309.

[2] BO III,I,295.

[i] In addition to the literature in *GSL*, 287-8, see K. Samir, "Langue arabe, logique et théologie chez Élie de Nisibe," in *Mélanges de l'Université Saint Joseph* 52 (1991/2), 229-367, and the collection of articles on Elias in id., *Foi et culture en Irak au XIe siècle: Élie de Nisibe et l'Islam*, Variorum Collected Studies 544 (Ashgate, 1996), which have made this figure one of the most studied of Syriac grammarians.

[ii] On Mar Miḫāʾīl, J.M. Fiey, *Assyrie Chrétienne* (Beirut, 1968) II, 660-71.

[iii] On Nathanael, his episcopacy of al-Sin, and ordination of Elias, J.M. Fiey, *Communautés syriaques en Iran et Irak des origines à 1552* (London, 1979) II,192; on the monastery of Simeon, id., *Assyrie Chrétienne* III,100-2.

[iv] Baumstark, *GSL*, 288, separates these two works (the *Nomocanon* and the *On Inheritance*). See now the introduction to the edition by I. Perczel & H. Kaufhold, eds., *The Nomocanon of Abdisho of Nisibis* (Piscataway, NJ, 2009).

[v] Edition (with Russian trans.) in Nikolai N. Seleznyov, *Kitāb al Maǧālis li-Mār Iliyyā muṭrān Nuṣaybīn wa-Risālatuhu ilā l-wazīr al-kāmil Abī l-Qāsim al-Ḥusayn ibn ʿAlī al-Maġribī / Liber sessionum sive disputatio inter Eliam metropolitan Nisibenum et vezirum Abū ʾl-Qāsim al-Ḥusayn ibn ʿAlī alMaġribī et Epistola eiusdem Eliae Nisibeni ad vezirum Abūʾl-Qāsim missa* (Moscow: Grifon, 2017/8). See also K. Samir, "Deux cultures qui s'affrontent: une controverse sur l'iʿrāb au XI siècle entre Élie de Nisibie et le vizir Abū l-Qāsim," in *Foi et culture en Irak* (as n. i), originally published in *Mélanges de l'Université Saint Joseph* 49 (1975/6), 619-49. More recent studies of this important text include David Bertaina, *Christian and Muslim Dialogues: The Religious Uses of a Literary Form in the Early Islamic Middle East*. Gorgias Eastern Christianity Studies 29. Piscataway, NJ: Gorgias Press, 2011; id., "Science, Syntax, and Superiority in Eleventh-Century Christian-Muslim Discussion: Elias of Nisibis on the Arabic and Syriac Languages," *Islam and Christian-Muslim Relations* 22:2 (2011): 197-207.

[vi] There have been various studies on this work, e.g. Witold Witakowski, "Elias Bar Shenaya's Chronicle," in W. van Bekkum et al., *Syriac Polemics: Studies in Honour of Gerrit Jan Reinink*. OLA 170. Leuven: Peeters, 2007, p. 219-237.

[vii] There is a study specifically of Elias's lexicon and its place within the Arabic and Syriac lexicographical traditions by S. Weninger, "Das 'Übersetzungsbuch' des Elias von Nisibis 10./11. Jh. im Zusammenhang der syrischen und arabischen Lexikographie" in W. Hüllen, ed., *The World in a List of Words* (Tübingen, 1994), 55–66, who stresses the close lines of influence between Elias's work and the Arabic lexicography of Abū ʿUbaid over and above the possible Greek influences on either, as had earlier been suggested. The most up-to-date study is Adam McCollum, "Prolegomena to a New Edition of Eliya of Nisibis's Kitāb al-turjumān fī taʿlīm luġat al-suryān," *Journal of Semitic Studies* 58:2 (2013): 297-322. On Thomas a Novaria, see *inter alia*, C. Balzaretti, "Un importante, ma dimenticato orientalista

del sec.xvii, Tommaso Obicini da Novara o.f.m.," *Novarien, Rivista dell'associazione di storia della chiesa novarese* 19 (1989), 49-70.

[viii] McCollum notes (*ibid.*, p.308) that there is a Sinai ms containing a work on homonyms attributed to Elias. This would be of the same general type as those mentioned in the previous chapter, and would complement the work of Elias's lexicon.

[ix] In the footnote For الودعية read الكوذعية (Nöldeke, Review, 1220).

[x] For more mss, *GSL*, 309n13, to which add Mingana Syr. 94, 244a-255a. Baumstark here notes that another metrical grammar is to be found in ms Seert 96 (although Scher's description is so brief that it may in fact be the same text, mistakenly described as seven syllable rather than twelve). Joseph also wrote a prose grammar, found by Scher in a twelfth century ms, together with two later copies (Seert 99,100,101), assuming that is, that Jacob and Išōʿyabh are one (see note x).

[xi] There is nothing metrically objectionable about ܝܠܕܬܐ (Nöldeke, Review, 1219). See also the note to the text of Bar Šakko, 42,8.

[xii] Baumstark (*GSL*, 309n9) reads the Cambridge ms of the *Net of Points* such as to confirm the identity of the two Bar Malkons. Hence the grammatical questions Merx here mentions (from ʿAbdišoʿ, *BO* III,I,295) are to be identified (following Baumstark) with the prose work by Išōʿyabh Bar Malkon discovered by Addai Scher (see note viii).

[xiii] Al-Ḥarīrī's grammatical work, written in the Radjaz metre, is not extant (*EI* III:221a; *GAP*, 226); Ibn Mālik is a rather better known Arab grammarian whose metrical grammar, the *Alfīya*, designed, like that of Elias, for students, and also written in the Radjaz metre, was much commented upon in the later Arabic tradition (*EI* III: 861a; *GAP*, 150).

[xiv] The first sub-group of servile letters are those that 'add a new meaning to the word' i.e. any suffixes, prefixes, or infixes, which are added to the radical consonants. The second group (here described) are really, of course, of the same type and purpose, but Elias is distinguishing those actually pronounced from those that are only written and not spoken.

[xv] Probably little should be made of this passage in terms of genuine historical memory (see Nöldeke, Review, 1217).

[xvi] In discussing Elias's *Grammar*, Merx prefers to use his own transcription of BL Add. 25876, despite the praise he gave to Gottheil's edition which was based on the inferior ms, Berlin Sachau 306. The folio numbers here refer to the former and Gottheil's readings are provided where they differ.

[xvii] "Ḥunayn the Physician teaches in his book on the points, that every *tau* of this (first) person ought really to be pronounced with Rukkākā; and in truth it is certain that this is the correct rule since when we say: ܝܠܕܬ, ܘܦܩܕܬ, ܘܦܩܕܬܟ, and ܘܦܩܕܬܗ, we pronounce the *tau* with Rukkāḵā. It is required also that [the *tau*] should be pronounced with Rukkāḵā when a suffix [has been added]; in like manner as the *tau* of the other persons, as it is

pronounced when it is at the end of the word, so it is pronounced when other [letters] are added. Our ancestral teachers, however, have so regulated it that the *tau* which is spoken for the first person masculine (!) should be spoken with Quššāyā—even though the rule requires that it should be with Rukkāḵā—in order that words in which [this *tau*] is found be distinguished from words which are feminine, e.g. ܩܒܠܬܗ ܐܢܐ (*I have received him*) from ܩܒܠܬܗ ܗܝ (*she has received him*), ܡܩܒܠܬܗ from ܡܩܒܠܬܗ, ܢܩܒܠܬܗ from ܢܩܒܠܬܗ." (Tr. adapted from Gottheil, *Elias*, 36). Merx seems to suggest that the marks of Rukkāḵā have not been added to the second example of each pair here. They are clearly present in Gottheil's text; perhaps the latter added them where the ms was lacking them.

xviii Th. Nöldeke, *Syrische Grammatik* §15. There is a detailed discussion of this phenomenon from the relevant passages of Barhebraeus by R. Voigt, "Das emphatische P des Syrischen," in R. Lavenant, ed., *Symposium Syriacum VII*, Orientalia Christiania Analecta 256 (Rome, 1998), 527-537.

xix Merx here departs from Gottheil's chapter numbering, because he does not count ch.VI (On the letter Pe) as a separate chapter in his table of contents of Elias's *Grammar* (p.134). For convenience, the chapter numbers here are Merx's.

xx "Men trust their ears less than their eyes" (Hdt 1.8).

xxi Cf. Weiss, *Laut- und Akzentlehre*, 11-12.

xxii Apparently a double-ayin form of the root ܕܠܦ (*to drop*)–Nöldeke, Review, 1217. Also p.126.

xxiii These are schools mentioned in the Nestorian masoretic ms (BL Add.12138), save the last which is known from a note in another Nestorian Gospel ms, Add. 14460–see the refs noted, and also A. Becker, *Fear of God and the Beginning of Wisdom* (Univ. Pennsylvania, 2006), 155.

xxiv The reader is referred to Segal, 88-118, for examples of each of these accents separately. For clarity of reading, I have removed all other pointing from these texts, so that the important accents can be seen the more easily. Weiss, *Laut- und Akzentlehre*, 27-64, deals with the patterns of accentuation in the Eastern Masorah.

xxv After discussing Elias's Ch. XI (accents) at great length, we now move onto the final section of Elias's *Grammar*. Merx will later designate this part of Elias as ch.XII (Gottheil, ch.XIII).

xxvi An unusual meaning for this root, equiv. Arabic حرّر.

xxvii John lived at the end of the seventh century and has since become better known as author of the *Riš Melle*, an historical work found in the Mingana collection which includes interesting passages about the early Arab occupation of North Mesopotamia (S.P. Brock, "North Mesopotamia in the Late Seventh Century: Book XV of John Bar Penkāyē's Riš Melle," *Jerusalem Studies in Arabic and Islam* 9 (1987), 51-75; reprinted *Studies in Syriac*

Christianity, II). On the man and his work, T. Jansma, "Projet d'édition du ktaba d-resh melle, de Jean bar Penkaye," *L'Orient Syrien* 8 (1963), 87-106.

Chapter 9

ELIAS OF ṬIRHAN AND THE BEGINNINGS OF THE ARABISING SCHOOL

It would be tempting to believe that the Arabs, who after occupying the land of the Syrians became well acquainted with their literature, also took the art of grammar from the Syrians. Already in Jacob of Edessa's day Christian clerics were debating whether one should teach literature to Muslims—Jacob himself was not against it (p.36). But such a view is quite mistaken. For a start, the pattern of seven parts of speech, which was absolutely fundamental to the Syriac study of grammar, plays no part in the Arabic equivalent. Surely if the Syrians had been their teachers in grammar, they would not have remained content with their three parts of speech. If the Arab grammarians went to Syrian schools, it would be hard to explain why they did not, for instance, make adjectives into a part of speech—or pronouns, or adverbs, prepositions, participles, or the article. Arabic grammar was in fact built on quite a different foundation and has nothing to do with the Syriac. Ḥāğğīm Ḫalīfa already explained that this was the case, in the following words:[1]

> The second prospect, in which it is shown that the highest achievements in science among the Muslims are largely of Persian origin. |[138] Although this might seem surprising it is certainly true. At any rate, most of the Islamic scholars of theology, law, and philosophy, with a very few exceptions, were Persians by language, even when they were Arab by race.[2] Nor was this a matter only of chance. The rural[3] beginnings of the religion of the Prophet necessarily meant that theology and literature were lacking. People retained a memory of the laws by oral tradition and the evidence for them they knew from the

[1] Translated from Ḥāğğī Ḫalīfa (i.e. Mustafa Kātib Čelebī): G. Flügel, ed., *Lexicon bibliographicum et encyclopædicum* (Leipzig, 1835-58) I,97-8.

[2] Known as في نسبته. They were reckoned as Arabs of a sort, rather like freedmen (مولى).

[3] Or, *nomadic*, i.e. Bedouin. The Arabic is لمقتضى احوال البداوة.

Qurʾān and the Sunna. Besides, they had heard the very words of the Prophet, or at least of the Companions of the Prophet. At that time the majority of Arabs were nomads who did not tend towards initiating works of literature or theology; nor, as we said before, was there any need in the slightly later period of the *Tabiun* [the successors of the Companions] for the development of any such arts. Those whose task it was to preserve and propagate the commands used to be called 'readers' (قُرّاء, sing. قَارِئ), readers, that is, of the scriptures and of prophetic utterances that carried authority, as is explained in a number of sources. Once a sufficient amount of time had passed, i.e. from the time of the original tradition down to that of the Caliph Al-Rashid, commentaries on the Qurʾān began to be needed and a fear developed that the Prophet's pronouncements might be lost. It became paramount that such a fate be averted by means of the pen. Then a truer understanding of the authorities became necessary, and an appreciation of what they were saying. Fate, however, brought about a difficult situation, for whereas the majority of the Qurʾān and Sunna stood in need of explanation, the pristine [Bedouin] language was being corrupted. So it became vital that grammatical rules should be established. All the doctrines of the law were made into easy-to-use resources for understanding the commands, so that in every situation the issues might be clear and established by analogy. Since it was things like the writing of Arabic grammar that opened up a pathway into the law, it became thereby almost impossible for the true law to be replaced by any other. It was only the cities that offered some refuge for such ideas and those who dwelt in cities were usually Persians or something similar.[1] The very first writers on grammar, all of Persian origin, were Sībawayhi, Al-Fārisī, and Al-Zağğāğī, who became acquainted with the language through intercourse with the Arab peoples and reduced it to a set of rules for posterity."[2]

---

[1] والحضر هم العجم او من في معناهم.

[2] Almost all of this material is taken from Ibn Ḫaldûn's *Prolegomena*, vol.III, 272, 279, 281f.

|139 This passage shows how grammar was very closely associated with the study of Qurʾān and Ḥadīth, rather as Syriac grammar was studied as part of a preparation for theology. This simple fact explains why it was that the Arabs did not share a grammatical tradition with the rejected Christian religion. But we still need to investigate how Arabic grammar did begin. One cannot simply repeat the list of grammarians from the Fihrist, where there are many names but rather little substance. So we shall skip over the oldest of the grammarians[1] (Abū l-Aswad ad-Duʾalī, ʿĪsā ibn ʿUmar, d.149/766, Al-Ḫalīl, d.170/785, the Yazidis, Quṭrub, d.206/821, Abū ʿUbaid, d.210/825, Al-Aṣmaʿī, d.213/828, Al-Aḫfaš, d.221/835)[i] and take a look at the extant texts themselves, which are the only real source of information on the origins of Arabic grammar. We have Sībawayhi's *Kitāb* (d.177/793), the *Kāmil* of Al-Mubarrad (d.285/897), together with some smaller works by Ibn Duraid (d.321/932). Essentially there are two aspects to these works, first the material itself—expressions and phrases, proverbs, verses, aphorisms, pointed sayings—and then the system by which this material was not so much divided into sections as rather explained on the basis of grammatical theory. It was the work of Arab grammarians, or Persians who had learnt the language, to gather this material; hence we can see from the titles of their books what was their principal concern, namely that the language of Qurʾān and Ḥadīth, of poetry and everyday speech, should be systematised by scholarship. Hence there arose collections with titles such as *Book of Proverbs* (كتاب الامثال), *Book of Unusual Words* (كتاب النوادر), *Book of Words used in Common Dialects* (كتاب اللغات), *Book in which are listed the names of the body-parts of humans, camels, horses, cattle, stars* (كتاب خلق الانسان، الابل، الخيل، الشات، الانوآ). We may also note in the same field books on the plural, the dual, the masculines and feminines, all of which have to do with etymology and usage rather than grammar. We can gain some idea of what sorts of works these were from Ibn Duraid's *On Saddles and Bridles* and *On Clouds and Rain*,[2] in which he uses different methods. In the first he describes and lists the different parts of saddles and bridles and then demonstrates these with further comments; in the other work, he collects descriptions of clouds and rain from the Ḥadīth and from Bedouin oral tradition (or, more likely, he artificially composed them to look like the way the Bedouin would have spoken),

[1] These are all Basrans, as the Kufans were later. The first Kufan grammarian was Arruʿaši, a contemporary of Al-Ḫalīl—G. Flügel, ed., *Kitāb al-Fihrist von Ibn al-Nadim* (Leipzig, 1871) I,66.

[2] W. Wright, *Opuscula Arabica* (Leiden, 1859), 1-46.

embellishes them with unusual words and then explains them. The first method he introduced already in his |140 كتاب الالحان (*Book of Solecisms*).[1] The same method is used in Al-Mubarrad's *Kāmil*, where he tries to include cultured and weighty sayings of every kind, together with examples of everyday speech, also proverbs, warnings, conversations, and letters, and then to add commentary to each. In fact, this is the first complete work in which a commentary follows the texts. Occasionally, chapter headings are given, such as that to chapter 50, *On* لم الاستغاث.

But to comment on this sort of material, one needs grammatical theory, as Al-Mubarrad showed by prefacing his work with a discussion of اعراب (*Arabism*). The grammatical theories that developed in these contexts were thus prolegomena to the exegesis. We will now proceed to discuss this briefly.

One finds already in Sībawayi nearly all the grammatical concepts being used with their technical terms. This shows that the study of grammar was already well advanced by the middle of the eighth century. After all, Sībawayi himself regularly speaks of his own teachers, Al-Ḫalīl (d.170/785), who lived 74 years and so was born c.711, and Yūnus ibn Ḥabīb (d.183/799), who lived 88 years, hence born c. 95/713. These men cultivated the study of grammar in Basra at the turn of the second century AH, but ʿĪsā ibn ʿUmar (d.149/766) had already preceded them. Hence we need to inquire where and how these theories first arose and we may do this by an analysis of grammatical expressions and word-forms.

These grammatical concepts fall into two broad categories—orthoepy and grammar proper. A number of 'grammatical' topics strictly speaking belong with the former, e.g. قلب (*transposition of letters*), وقف (*pausal reading*), ترخيم (*pronunciation with a softer voice*), and تشديد (*stronger pronunciation*). After all, only Arab grammarians themselves could come up with theories about such indigenous subjects. We should also add here theories about the practice of writing, including the contents of, e.g., كتاب النقط والشكل (*The Book of the Points and the Shape*, i.e. *shape of the vowels*)[2] and the works that Abū l-Aswad ad-Duʾalī is supposed to have written at the time of ʿAlī's Caliphate.[3]

---

[1] H. Thorbecke, ed. in the *Festschrift zur XXXVI. Versammlung deutscher Philologen* (Heidelberg, 1882). [See *GAS* VIII,101-5].

[2] Fihrist I, 58, l.6; S. de Sacy, *Chrestomathie arabe* (Paris, 1806) I,234.

[3] S. De Sacy, in *Notices et Extraits des manuscrits de la Bibliothèque nationale* VIII, 306; G. Flügel, *Die grammatischen Schulen der Araber* (Leipzig, 1862), *pref.*

In this book Abū l-Aswad imitated the Syriac script, as the positioning and the naming of the points indicates.[1] [ii]

|[141] Once we have put to one side these books on orthoepy and orthography, everything else falls into the other general category of grammatical theories proper. The sort of theories we are dealing with could only have been developed through the study of *logic*, and this the Arabs could only have received from the Greek schools—since they had no converse with the Syrian ones. Nobody would for a moment believe that—in the short space of time that separates ʿAlī from the earliest grammarians—the Arabs had by themselves discovered without any assistance what the Greek philosophers took more than 200 years (from Plato to the Stoics) to work out. But the Greek logic which the Arabs adopted cannot itself have been transmitted via grammatical texts, inasmuch as the latter always give seven parts of speech, whereas the Arabs seem to know nothing at all of this.[2] If this is the case, then it only remains to ask whether Arabic grammar issued directly from Aristotle. Those Persians who were responsible for the earliest Arabic grammar read Aristotle in the form of a compendium of the commentators. Greek philosophy had flourished amongst the Persians since the time of Khosrau Anushirvan c.570.[3] We have Paul the Persian's book on philosophy that he wrote for that king,[4] [iii] backed up by the testimony of John of Ephesus, who tells us that Khosrau was thoroughly dedicated to philosophy all his life.[5]

It was via compendia of this sort, which the Persians were able to read following the closure of the School of Edessa in 489, that Aristotelian logic found its way to those who became the founders of Arabic grammar. We

---

[1] There is no issue about the fatḥa; and ḍamma (ضمّ = *contraction*) is none other than the Syriac ܥܨܨܐ (*contraction*). But the خفض, which designates the *i* vowel, but not the possessive, is instructive. It means *pressure* and is both an imitation and a translation of the Syriac ܚܒܨܐ, its place later being taken by كسر. Since Abū l-Aswad uses the word كسر in his history, I can only assume that the whole narrative has been invented or altered to fit a later period.

[2] The Arabic grammar of Ḥunain was written according to the Greek pattern (p.106). Could it be that Ḥunain did have seven parts of speech?

[3] See Th. Nöldeke, *Geschichte der Perser und Araber zur Zeit der Sasaniden* (Leiden, 1879), 428.

[4] Land, *Anecdota* IV, 1-30.

[5] W. Cureton (ed.), *The Third Part of the Ecclesiastical History of John Bishop of Ephesus* (London, 1853), 388.

cannot, however, be sure that the latter did not read Aristotle directly, since they do agree in some important matters.[1]

The following are the areas in which the Arabic grammarians made direct use of Aristotelian theories:[iv]

1) They distinguished three parts of speech: اسم (*noun*), فعل (*verb*), and حرف (*particle*), which in Aristotle is σύνδεμος.[2] [v] This categorisation was illustrated by further definitions both in Aristotle and later by the Arabs. But Sībawayhi does not include any such further definitions,[3] from which it follows that the Arabs must have taken this system of division from elsewhere.[vi] |[142] They did not come up with it themselves. Sībawayhi merely gives some examples of nouns, "Man, Horse, Wall (حائط) are nouns." He then suggests that there are many patterns (امثلة) of verbs, which derive from words (لفظة) that are nominal inflections,[4] and these can be formed (بنيات, i.e. built) for the past, the future, and the present. Given that he saw in his own language only two verbal forms, could he really have thought in terms of three tenses and argued that the verb was formed in three ways, to describe that which was, that which is, and that which will be? And note what examples he uses: ذَهَب, سَمِع, مَكُث, جُمِد are all perfects; يَكْتُلُ, يَذهَبُ, يَضرِبُ, يُقتَلُ, يُضرَبُ are futures, or rather, as Sībawayhi says, they are formed for indicating what will be, and has not yet happened; and then he adds the *imperatives* إذهَب, أُقتُل, إضرِب which serve the same purpose and cannot distinguish present (ما هو كائِنٌ لم يَنقَطِع) from future time (ما يكُونُ ولم يَقَع). Note how impossible it is to explain the concept of the present in a language that does not have a separate form for

[1] The following investigation will include only those grammarians from before the age of Al-Ma'mūn; after this Caliph the Arabs had direct access to the text of Aristotle.

[2] Cf. Arist., *Frag.* 126 (Berlin ed., V,1499) [this on the authority of Dionysius of Halicarnassus, *De Compositione Verborum* – ed.].

[3] Ibn Ya'īš, in his commentary on the first book of *Al-Mufaṣṣal*, already made this observation.

[4] Cf. Aristotle, *De int.* 3 (16b) for an explanation of this. Aristotle says, ῥῆμά ἐστι τὸ προσσημαῖνον χρόνον... λέγω δ' ὅτι προσσημαίνει χρόνον, οἷον ὑγίεια μὲν ὄνομα, τὸ δ' ὑγιαίνει ῥῆμα· προσσημαίνει γὰρ τὸ νῦν ὑπάρχειν. καὶ ἀεὶ τῶν ὑπαρχόντων (τῶν καθ'ἑτέρου λεγομένων Merx) σημεῖόν ἐστιν (*A verb is that which indicates time... I will explain [what I mean by saying] that it indicates time. 'Health' is a noun, but 'is healthy' is a verb; for it indicates the present state; and it is always a sign of those things that are [or, are said about something else]*). Just as Aristotle says that ὑγιαίνει derives from ὑγίεια, so Sībawayhi says that verbs derive from nominal inflections, for they call الضرب and القتل inflections, from which the verbs ضَرَب and قتَل derive.

the present tense. This explains why Sībawayhi made use of a system adopted from a foreign language and which he could not possibly have created on the basis of Arabic forms. The source is to be found in the commentators, in such passages as this from Paul the Persian (ch.19), "Since every proposition is spoken according to a tense, and tense is divided into three, past, present, future...." This comes from Ammonius's commentary on the *De Interpretatione*, as Land has shown.[1]

Concerning the third part of speech he says, حرف جاء لمعنى ليس باسم ولا فعل (*a letter or particle, which adds something to the meaning, is neither noun nor verb*). As examples of this he gives ثمّ، سوف, the و of oath taking, لِ of the construct, etc. Here we have a definition which, although essentially negative (it is that which is neither noun nor verb) nonetheless states that these particles do add something to the meaning of an utterance. I doubt whether de Sacy understood the expression جاء لمعنى correctly. He interpreted it to mean "employé pour exprimer un sens" (*used to express meaning*),[2] but Aristotle, from whom the idea of a tripartite division |[143] of the parts of speech was derived, says that the σύνδεσμος is a φωνὴν ἄσημον (*non-indicative word*).[3] The Arabs would appear to be saying the opposite. However, if we accept our own translation (*a particle, that which adds something to the meaning*), this could mean that the particle has no meaning in and of itself but that it affects and modifies the meaning of a whole sentence in some way. This would agree perfectly with what Sībawayhi says, and so too Ammonius:

> But those which are found in neither territory, even if they are added in another way to the propositions and signify that the predicate belongs or does not belong, or when, how, or how often it belongs to the subject, or that they have any other relation to one another, he does not want to call 'parts of the sentence' properly speaking.... So these are not parts of a sentence, but they are parts of speech, of which the sentence itself is also a part.... And you will find that, in certain <passages>, Aristotle seems to relent and call all <the types of

---

[1] Land, *Anecdota*, IV,15,112. The Ammonius passage in Bekker, *Aristotelis Opera*, IV, 113b17 = A. Busse, ed., *Ammonius in Aristotelis de interpretatione commentarius*, Commentaria in Aristotelem Graeca IV.5 (Berlin, 1897), 90,23-5.

[2] De Sacy, *Anthologie*, 361. To obtain de Sacy's meaning for the phrase, it would have to say جاء بمعنى.

[3] *Poetics* 20 (1456b).

> vocal sounds> more generally 'parts of the sentence'. This is why in what follows..."[1] [vii]

There is no doubt that Sībawayhi should be taken to mean, "the particle, which adds something to the meaning, is neither noun nor verb."[viii]

2) إعراب , the noun derived from the verb عَرَبَ, meaning 'to speak with words that conform to the standard Arabic language,' refers simply to pronunciation according to 'Arabism', or what is thought to be pure Arabism. Hence عَرَبَ = ἀραβίζειν, and إعراب = ἀραβισμός, words formed on the analogy of ἑλληνίζειν and ἑλληνισμός (*to Hellenise* and *Hellenism*) as described by Aristotle in the *Rhetoric*, which may be summarised as follows:

"Hellenism consists in five things:[2] 1, the proper use of the words that connect the parts of sentences; 2, the use of appropriate names that match the character of the things being described; 3, the avoidance of ambiguity; 4, the appropriateness of gender distinctions; 5, the correct usage of words relating to number." Hellenism is opposed to 'solecism' (σολοικισμός) and 'to solecize' (σολοικίζειν), i.e. to speak with barbaric [foreign] diction. From this the Arabs calqued the term سَلِيقِيٌّ, which Lane (Lexicon, 1411b) glosses as كلام سليقى, natural or unlearned diction, or diction in which final inflections are not respected. So كلام سليقى is the opposite of 'Arabism', or speech that has been embellished with اعراب. The term occurs in a verse of Az-Zamaḫšarī's *Asās al-balāġa:* ولَسْتُ بنحوى يلوك لسانه ولكن سليقى اقول فاعرب (*I am not a grammarian who massacres his own language, but an uneducated layman who speaks as such even when I use the* اعرب [*Arabism*]). It is possible that this word is derived from the Arabic سليقة (*nature*: Lane, 1411a) and had its own meaning of 'natural'. But I would then question whether the word 'natural' could really have been used in reference to 'Arabism'? If the word's etymology does not require a native derivation, then proof for the opposite lies |[144] in the corresponding pairs ἑλληνισμός / σολοικισμός and اعراب / سليقى. 'Hellenism' means a particular approach to using the Greek language in the light of grammar and logic, and this is just what is meant by اعراب, which was generally restricted to mean the use of final vowel sounds precisely because it was with these sounds that the grammatical and logical connections between the parts of an utterance could be expressed. Using such endings appropriately thus constituted pure 'Arabism'.[ix]

---

[1] Bekker, op.cit., IV,99a = Busse, op.cit., 12,20-24; 12,30-13,1; 15,8-13.

[2] Aristotle, *Rhetoric* III,5.

We can now ask whether it was by chance that there appears to be a relationship between the term اعراب and Aristotle's use of ἑλληνισμός?

3) The grammatical concept of gender is one to which we are very well accustomed. But the fact that we think of gender distinctions as being self-evident, almost 'natural', should not prevent us from seeing the reality—gender distinctions are actually wholly artificial and not at all necessary.[x] It does not result from poetical figures of speech or from the overvivid imagination of people comparing inanimate objects with animals that have natural gender.

Some believe that from the very beginning language was created as a sort of ensouled, rational thing. I fear that they may be attributing a power of systematic reflection into a primitive period in which it was really the imagination that held sway. Quite different was that later philosophical reflection which was necessary for the development of the idea of linguistic gender. It is the essential task of philosophy, and perhaps of grammar too, to gather together all the different forms that exist in a language and then classify and name them. Now if a philosopher decides to classify forms into 'males', 'females' and 'objects', then he is simply using an artificial organising principle which is not inherent to the nature of the language itself. One could just as well call them 'strong' 'weak' and 'middling' or whatever one pleases. In using an analogy based on human family relationships, he is not thereby drawing on nature as such but merely on his own principles.

In fact, Aristotle tells us who the first person was who used this idea of gender distinctions. It was the sophist Protagoras, the one whose basic principle was 'man is the measure of all things' (*Metaphysics* X,1) and it is to him that we owe the idea of comparing the rather dissimilar characteristics of inanimate objects with human relationships. The correct use of these forms that we usually refer to as genders was one of the subjects within Aristotle's discussion of 'hellenism'. This is what he has to say about it: τέταρτον, ὡς Προταγόρας τὰ γένη τῶν ὀνομάτων διῄρει, ἄρρενα καὶ θήλεα καὶ σκευή· δεῖ γὰρ ἀποδιδόναι καὶ ταῦτα ὀρθῶς· ἡ δὲ ἐλθοῖσα καὶ διαλεχθεῖσα ᾤχετο (*A fourth rule is to observe Protagoras's classification of nouns into male, female, and inanimate; for these distinctions also must be correctly given. 'Upon her arrival she had her say and departed'. Rhet.* III,5) . Later on the term οὐδέτερον (*neither*) was substituted for σκευή, thereby introducing the analogy of the sexes which had not even been intended by Protagoras who, because everything was to be measured 'according to the measure of man', divided everything into 'human' and 'object' and the former into 'male' and 'female', and then applied this distinction to inanimate nature. The concept of grammatical gender could only come into play once |[145] the new term οὐδέτερον (*neither*) had come into use, i.e. once the idea of sex-differentiation had become the principle of division. Elsewhere Aristotle identified male, female and in-between (ἄρρενα, θήλεα, τὰ μεταξύ, *Poetics*, 21), but this is really a division into two groups, nouns lacking gender and those with it, the latter being further subdivided into male and female.

Now the Arabs recognised in their own tongue only the masculine and the feminine, there not being any neuter gender in Arabic, and I would argue that they did this on the basis of the Greek theory, since they use what they called the feminine for verbs with broken plurals as their subjects, where the very idea of gender does not really have any relevance. From the fact of this common usage of 'feminines' (which appear to us rather to be 'collectives'), there ought really to have been some other principle by which words more normally called feminine could have been treated. After the Arabs borrowed the idea of the feminine from the Greeks, it was possible to say: every plural is feminine (كُلّ جَمْعٍ مُؤَنَّثٌ),[1] and without the concept they could not have described it is this way. But we can add another reason: the Arabs did not have their own term to describe either sex or grammatical gender,[2] the term جنس being simply the Greek γένος. If they made use of the Greek term for the overall concept, it seems obvious that they must also have borrowed from the same source the specific grammatical concepts of masculine and feminine.

4) ظرف. Among the most notable Arabic grammatical concepts must be included that of the *container*, which is the term used to refer to those words that specify place and time in the accusative. Within المَفْعُولُ فِيهِ (*that in which something happens*) is included the ظرف المكانِ (*the container of place*) and the ظرف الزمانِ (*the container of time*). This is how Sībawayhi describes it,[3] when he says, "The chapter about those words that refer to place and time and use an accusative. This is done because [time and place] are containers, into which things are placed and in which they subsist."

---

[1] W. Wright, ed., *The Kāmil of el-Mubarrad* (Leipzig, 1874-92), 781.

[2] The same observation is true of Syriac, Hebrew, and Ethiopic, in none of which is there any native word meaning 'gender'. The very notion itself is thus clearly foreign to Semitic languages, for they do not generally take any great pleasure in deriving their general concepts from elsewhere.

[3] H. Derenbourg, ed., *Le livre de Sibawaihi : traité de grammaire arabe* (Berlin, 1881-9), 170, l.17-18.

The fact that the ideas of time and place were here brought together—indeed the very fact that the grammatical constructions dealing with time and place were subjected to a single universal law and several different sorts of relationships expressed by a single simple form—betrays the philosophical tradition from which it was derived by the one thinker who was so steeped in that tradition that he decided to use a single technical term to include all the different uses of this accusative. Nor is it difficult to locate the source from which this stream emanated, for whoever devised this syntactical rule had clearly read Aristotle's discussion of time and place (*Physics* IV,1; IV,10). Here he says that, since place can be separated from the thing that it contains (for where there was air there may afterwards be water even though the place remains unchanged), place is neither matter nor form, |[146] for neither of these are separable from the thing itself. For this reason place is also not a part of the thing itself nor its condition, but it is separable from each thing, for place itself seems to be the sort of thing that a container (τὸ ἀγγεῖον) also is. For place is a container which can be changed. Thus place itself is in a place and one can think of there being a place of a place (*Physics* IV,1).

On the question of time he says (Physics IV,12: 221a16-18) that "objects are [in time], just as they are in number; if so, they are surrounded by time, just as the things in number are by number and the things in place by place,"[xi] and then continues (221a28-30), "for this reason, for things to exist in time they must be contained by time, as is the case also with other things that are in something, for instance things that are in a place [must be contained] by place."[xii] At the end he summarizes all this in the words (223a14-15), "it is clear that every change and every movement occurs in time."[xiii]

If in this way both time and place—since it contains everything that is—seem rather like some sort of vessel, then ideas of the local and the temporal could be encompassed by the single conception of the vessel. It hence became possible to speak of the vessel of place, or rather that which is a place, and about the vessel of time, or rather that which is a time. The grammatical theory here under discussion is thus built upon the basis of this philosophical discussion of the nature of time and place and is inconceivable without having such a foundation. Hence we have here grammarians who were followers of Aristotle.

5) Among the technical terms taken from philosophy we must include 'state' (حال), which corresponds to the Greek ἕξις and διάθεσις (*state / condition*). Sībawayhi uses this idea (chs. 82,87,92-7) without defining it, a

fact which proves that its origin lay elsewhere and that it was used in the schools.[1]

In Aristotle, ἕξις and διάθεσις are included among the qualities and are distinguished from each other insofar as ἕξις (*condition*) is a quality that lasts a long time, while διάθεσις (*disposition*) is of short duration only. Conditions are always dispositions but the contrary is not necessarily true (*Categories* 8). In the usage of the later Arabic logicians, حال denotes qualities that quickly pass away such as warmth and coldness, dryness and wetness (see Lane, s.v.)—so we can see that حال is closer to διάθεσις than to ἕξις. The same is true of حال in its grammatical sense.[xiv] However, there was disagreement among the Greek philosophers concerning these two terms. Simplicius discusses them in his commentary on the *Categories*, and compares *Metaphysics* IV,19,20. The grammarians, on the other hand, considered διάθεσις to be an attribute of the verb—active, passive, middle, i.e. voice.[2]

|[147] There is no need to use many examples to show that *disposition* is what is indicated in sentences with حال. The word indicating the *disposition* is not part of the sentence itself but is added into it.[3] It is easy to see the characteristics of حال in all such sentences of the sort, أُدْخُلُوا الْبَابَ سُجَّدًا (*enter the gate prostrating [yourselves]*). The accusative سُجَّدًا denotes a passing *disposition* which adds something to the sense although it is still complete without it.[4]

6) The whole system of thinking of the sentence as construed from فَاعِل (*agent*), فِعل (*action*), and مَفْعُول (*object*), within which there were various subclassifications (although they never used the notion of the subject [ὑποκείμενον],[5] [xv] being satisfied with that of predicate [τὸ

[1] Az-Zamaḫšarī, *Al-Mufaṣṣal*, p.27, says that حال is similar to ظرف. He teaches that the former is used for indicating condition.

[2] Apollonius Dyscolus (F. Portus & F. Silburgius, edd., *Apollonii Alexandrini de syntaxi* [1590]), 242,273,281,297; Dionysius Thrax, above p.17.

[3] Hence the grammarians include حال among the فضلات, i.e. the redundant parts of the sentence. See De Sacy, *Grammaire arabe*, 1st ed., II,336; F. Dieterici, ed., *Ibn ʿAkil's Commentar zur Alfijja des Ibn Malik* (Berlin, 1852), 170-82 [also Wright, *Grammar of the Arabic Language*, 113D].

[4] In other cases, which the Arab grammarians categorised under the حال, De Sacy (*ibid.* II,64) now reckons that other uses of the accusative are in force.

[5] The Greek grammarians did make use of the concept at times, e.g. Apollonius Dyscolus (ed. Sylburg as above note, III,4,199) uses the expression ὑπούσης θηλείας for a feminine subject. Ammonius (Bekker, op.cit, IV,104b42 = Busse, op.cit., 44,21) distinguishes

κατηγορούμενον = الخَبَر] alone) proves clearly that grammar was built upon the foundations of logic. The very idea of خبر could be the cause of some confusion, because it really means something predicated in the logical sense, and all sentences effect some such predication, rather than a predicate in the strict grammatical sense, where there is no such necessity. In the sentence زَيْدٌ حَسَنٌ غُلَامُهُ (*Zaid, his slave is handsome*), the word 'Zaid' is called مُبْتَدَأ (*inchoative*) and the rest is a full sentence consisting of subject (غُلَامُهُ) and grammatical predicate (حَسَنٌ); but the Arabs would refer the thing being predicated (خبر) to the word 'Zaid', although this is not the grammatical subject.

We can see from this example that grammatical structures were less significant than logical ones, which was the more natural approach. The principle lying behind the explanations was not founded on word forms (*signifiant*) but on the content of the sentence (*signifié*), in as far as it was concerned with logic, physics, metaphysics, i.e. philosophy. We can discern in this concept of the *inchoative* (مُبْتَدَأ) a degree of grammatical theorisation, but it is a somewhat confused theorisation, since the inchoative could be either subject or predicate. The category itself was therefore ill-suited for use in constructing grammatical rules. What is quite certain is that the particles (of negation and interrogation), with which |[148] the sentence properly begins, were not dealt with at all, just as was the case with the φωναὶ ἄσημοι = حرف جاء لمعنى (see under no.1 above).

This philosophical approach of taking the sense of the whole utterance rather than just looking at word-forms becomes even clearer when we consider the concepts of فاعِل (*agent*), فِعل (*action*), and مَفْعُول (*object*), which derive from their Greek counterparts ἐνεργεία (*active/agent*) and πάθος (*passive/object*). This conclusion is strengthened by the observation that فِعل is a native Arabic word for ῥῆμα (*verb*)[1] which was added in order to complete the system. Just how far they went in preferring the actual relations of *things* over the structure of *words* we can best gauge from

---

τὸ κατηγορούμενον (*a thing predicated*) from τὸ ὑποκείμενον (*subject*). To the Arabic philosophers, τὸ ὑποκείμενον was المَوْضُوع, not a concept used by grammarians. The closest thing they had was the *inchoative* (مُبْتَدَأ) but the Arabic understanding of this was much confused, firstly because the *inchoative* did not always occupy initial position in the sentence, thus not being a true *inchoative*; also because the predicate (خبر) could sometimes be used in place of the *inchoative*, as in the sentence, أَقَائِمٌ الرِّجَالُ (*do the men stand?*), where أَقَائِمٌ (*do they stand?*) is the *inchoative*.

[1] The Syrians dealt with this in a quite different way (Bar Šakko, p.ܡܐ), but the Greeks did use τὸν ἐνεργῶντα and τὸν ἐνεργούμενον (Apollonius, *op. cit.*, 241, et al.).

Sībawayhi's discussion of the theory of the passive (ch.9). For in the passive sentence يُضْرَبُ زَيدٌ (*Zaid was struck*), the word 'Zaid' is the مَفْعُولٌ, the object. Its verb (فِعْلُهُ) does not apply to it, and the action of the agent (فِعْلُ فَاعِلٍ) does not refer to it.[1] Later grammarians reduced this complex explanation to a rather simpler form, saying that the object (مَفْعُولُ بِهِ) took the place of the agent as its substitute (يَنُوبُ عَن إلفَاعِلِ، قَامَ مَقامَ الفَاعِلِ),[2] which may be a more sensible grammatical explanation, but remains unsound, because the concept of the formal subject had not yet been developed and the grammarians continued to stick to describing *things* rather than the grammatical relations which are encoded in morphology. This is all quite different from what Apollonius Dyscolus says about the intransitive and the passive.[3]

The above remarks should be amply sufficient to demonstrate that the origins of Arabic grammatical theory lie in the study of logic, even in the most fundamental matters such as the distinction of subject and grammatical predicate, and that no better approach was ever discovered. They were unable to do so since they never understood that syntax is an outworking of morphology and needs to be grounded in a right understanding of individual word-forms, whose actual usage in speech can then be defined. However they could not build a syntax on the basis of a sound morphology because their lack of concern with the grammatical nature of nouns and verbs meant that they had no such basis. I am aware that this opinion flies in the face of the very high estimation in which Arabic grammatical theory is generally held by the learned folk of today. |[149] They had to work extraordinarily hard to assimilate all this grammatical theory in the first place and it is human nature to esteem that most which costs the most to attain! There are those, however, whose testimony is not to be ignored and who did not put such a high value on the grammarians' disputes, namely Ibn Chaldun and De Sacy himself. Ibn Chaldun tells us that there were many grammarians who discussed matters of syntax but had not taken the trouble to learn to write good Arabic. His damning verdict on the grammarians was that they had an eye only for the ancient form of the language whilst ignoring contemporary forms, the latter being in no way inferior to the former.[4] Because of this attitude, Ibn Chaldun believed that

[1] His words are: والمفعول الذى لم يتعدّه فعله ولم يتعدّ اليه فعل فاعل كقولك ضُرِبَ زيدٌ ويضرب عمرو

[2] See Dieterici, *Alfijja*, 129; De Sacy, *Grammaire Arabe* II,405,499.

[3] Apollonius, *op. cit.*, III,31.

[4] De Sacy, *Anthologie*, 411: "Be sure to take note of the babbling of some grammarians who are wholly occupied with the syntax of the endings but whose narrow minds cannot raise themselves to the knowledge of reality itself; do not believe them when they tell you

they had turned the science of grammar into a means of teaching dialectic and logic rather than being a way of making it easier to learn the language. What they did instead was to compare and contrast different explanatory theories and adjudge which was to be preferred on the basis of logical reasoning rather than linguistic usage.[1]

De Sacy shares this verdict on Arabic morphological theory and he argues that the Arabs did not understand the nature of verbal forms: "The Arab grammarians do not appear to me to have established clearly any distinction between the modes of their verbs, neither have they explained adequately the nature and purpose of such modes. They only identify three main variables in the verb, of which two concern tense (زمان) and the other is a special mode. This mode is the imperative, which they call امر, i.e. to give a command."[2]

Earlier we saw that this particular morphological analysis was actually of Greek origin. There is no way it could have arisen among the Arabs themselves since there is nothing in the nature of the language that would suggest a threefold division of the verbal forms. When they came across this threefold Greek division, they made use of the Arabic imperative as a way of making up the numbers, but they were never able to agree on how to apply the concept of tense. They could get a grip on the perfect, called ماضٍ (παρεληλυθός),|[150] but whenever they tried to define the meaning of the other verbal form, known as مُضَارِعٌ, the concept of time did not seem quite appropriate since one and the same form was used equally for the indefinite present, definite present, future, future historic, and present historic. Therefore, they did not try to find a name for it which would

that eloquence has all but vanished today and the Arabic language degenerated simply on account of the changes that have come about in relation to the endings, endings whose regular and systematic employment they have made the principal object of their lectures. It was a subject suggested to them by their bias, and by an idea which has taken hold of their minds because of their very limited horizons."

[1] Since this subject is so important, I shall give De Sacy's translation (*ibid.*, 422): "They are content to apply the rules of the syntax of endings to any given example, rather than demonstrating that preference for one explanation over another should be given according to what common sense demands, and not according to the conventions of Arabic language and phraseology. Thus they reduce the art of Arabic grammar, so to speak, to being nothing but a few theoretical rules of dialectic and logic, which is very far indeed from what the language actually does and the way it is used."

[2] De Sacy, *Grammaire* I, §273, and note what we quoted from Sībawayhi, p.142 above.

describe its nature as such, save on the basis of the resemblance between the final inflection and the inflection of nouns. They called this form مُضارِع, i.e. *resembling the noun* or, more charitably, *acting as a noun*.

In their morphological teaching on the verb there are no concepts that are more complicated than this. They make use only of gender, number, and person, but not mood. The situation is similar with regard to the noun where the cases were identified, but the very idea of case itself is absent, there being no single term for it. This is all the more surprising as the cases of the noun and the forms of the imperfect are so very similar to each other that the Aristotelian use of the term πτῶσις (*case*) would seem particularly well suited to describing them, and the later usage of the Greek grammarians (unknown to the Arabs) did not prevent them from following Aristotle. In the latter's usage, the term πτῶσις is not limited to the cases of the noun but is also applied to adverbs derived from adjectives (*Topics* VI,10: 148a10) and even to verbal forms, about which Aristotle says (*Poetics* 20: 1457a18-12), "*Case belongs both to noun and verb, and expresses either the relation 'of' 'to,' or the like; or that of number, whether one or many, as 'man' or 'men'; or it has to do with types of delivery, e.g., a question or a command. 'Did he go?' and 'go' are verbal cases of this kind.*"[xvi] I do not know whether any other language could so easily have made use of this approach. But the fact that the earliest Arab grammarians did not make any use of it suggests that the *Poetics* was unknown to them,[1] [xvii] although other less significant passages, in which the cases of the verb are again discussed, were also not used (e.g. *De Int.* 3,5).

Thus we may draw our discussion of this subject to a close. We have seen that there are no traces in Arabic of either Greek or Syriac syntactical theory, since all the universal laws of Arabism, of gender, of the container, of state, object, subject, action, all these concepts that they used to theorise about syntax were derived from philosophy, not from grammar. It remains only to add a few points on the matter of inflection which will prove that, because the Arabs lacked the basic principles that the Greeks had, they made little progress in the matter of etymology. The above-cited passage from the *Poetics* is preceded by a substantial overview of the parts of speech (λέξεως μέρη). On its own it would have been sufficient to have provided the basic building blocks of grammar, unless it was a text unknown to the Arabs.

[1] On the Arabic interpretation of the Poetics, see F. Lasinio, ed., *Il Commento medio d'Averroe alla Poetica di Aristotele* (Pisa, 1872).

|[151] Aristotle in this passage first distinguishes στοιχεῖα (*letters*), divided into three types: φωνῆεν (*vowels*), ἡμίφωνον (*semivowels*, such as *s* and *r*), and ἄφωνον (*consonants*). The Arabs were aware of none of this, nor do they have anything comparable to the categories of 'roughness' (δασύτης) and 'smoothness' (ψιλότης). They do not even use the concept of the vowel at all.[1] Arabic phonological theories owed nothing to Greek originals but were based wholly on their own observations.

Aristotle next adds the syllable (συλλαβή), which Jacob of Edessa (see p.56) called ܗܓܐ, but again there is no Arabic equivalent. Aristotle's third distinction is that of conjunction, noun, and verb, which, as we have seen (p.141), was derived by the Arabs from logic. The fourth is the article (ἄρθρον), an equivalent of which the Arabs just about had since they called their own version of the article by the name *Alif-Lam*, after the letters of which it was composed. The fifth is case, dealt with above, and the sixth is speech (λόγος) which the Arabs again took from books on logic and called كلامٌ.[2] So we can see that the Arabs did not possess any of these orthoepic principles, especially the most significant of them, the syllable, a fact which proves that they had never read the Greek grammarians. The grammatical principles that they did make use of were drawn from texts about logic, while those of orthoepy they developed on their own account.

But it is in the etymologies that we can show most persuasively that the Arabs were unaware of the traditions of Greek grammar. For nearly all the definitions that the Greeks used were unknown to them. They changed the idea of the verb into that of *action* (فعل), and they made no use of most of its eight attributes—those of mood (ἔγκλισις), of voice (διάθεσις—*active, middle, passive*), of species (εἶδος), shape (σχῆμα), or conjugation (συζυγία). That of tense (χρόνος) was borrowed from logic, leaving only person (πρόσωπον) and number (ἀριθμός), to which they of course added gender, which was not applicable to Greek verbs. It was the same in the case of the noun, where the attributes of species, shape, and case (πτῶσις) were unknown, and they used only gender and number (cases, of course, they did have, but they did not identify the concept as such).

The morphological categories that they did use are therefore person (although they did not use the terms first, second, and third), gender, and

[1] It scarcely needs to be pointed out that the term حركات does not make any difference here. In Hebrew the term was תנועה, in Syriac ܙܘܥܐ.

[2] The definition in *Al-fiyya*, كلامُنَا لَفْظٌ مُفِيدٌ is simply a translation of the Greek ὁ λόγος ἡμῶν λέξις σημαντική.

number. They also added the more general category of inflection (صَرف). The word صَرف I would suggest is a calque on the Greek κλίσις, just as جنس is from γένος, but in the case of number and person the grammarians never seem to have used the names that would be most appropriate, namely عدد and شاخص.[1]

|[152] We still have a few further comments to add about the names of the cases. These are not found in Aristotle as such, but are found in the commentators. Ammonius tells us how there was a disagreement between Peripatetics and Stoics as to whether the nominative was itself a case or not.[2] The Stoics argued that it was, the Peripatetics disagreed because case (πτῶσις) comes from the verb *to fall* (πίπτειν) and the nominative has not fallen/descended from anywhere. The Stoics replied that it had indeed 'fallen' from the basic idea which was held in the mind. Both used the terms εὐθεία and ὀρθή for the nominative, but they gave different reasons for their usage in accordance with their different opinions about the nominative itself. The Peripatetics believed that the other cases were cases properly so called "because they fell from the straight line" (διὰ τὸ πεπτωκέναι ἀπο τῆς εὐθείας) and that the nominative was not therefore really a case at all. This is Ammonius's position. Now if the nominative is the form of the noun from which something 'falls/descends' and which can be described as 'straight', because the other cases are 'oblique' (πλαγίαι πτώσεις), how then did it happen that the Arabs called 'case' رَفْع, which means *elevation*? Is it credible that such a change might have occurred and that the Arabs were indeed following Peripatatic theory, presumably derived from one of the commentators, when they chose the name رَفْع? At any rate it does not yet seem to me certain that رَفْع is a translation of either εὐθεία or ὀρθή, since if it had a Greek background we would expect the names of the other cases also to have Greek origins, and the evidence is very clear that they did not.

---

[1] I say this since these words are not to be found in the indices to either *Al-fiyya* or in Az-Zamaḫšarī's *Al-Mufaṣṣal.* De Sacy, *Grammaire*, 116, does use them but gives no references to original texts. Elsewhere (p.292) he gives a citation from Al-Ḥarīrī, who tries to derive صَرف from صَريف, i.e. from the sound made by a pulley for drawing water. The fact that the root صرف (*he turns*) must translate the Greek κλίνει disproves his theory. But κλίσις is not used by Aristotle, though it does occur in the commentaries (Bekker, op.cit., IV, 104b19 = Busse, *Ammonius de Int.*, 43,18).

[2] Bekker IV, 104a-b = Busse, *Ammonius de Int.*, 42ff.

It is hard, for instance, to form any accurate idea of the origin of the name جَرٌّ for the genitive. The Greek name is γενικὴ πτῶσις (*generic case*) since it has the effect of assigning individuals to their genus.[1] The scholiasts recognised this fact and were followed by the Armenian translator of Dionysius Thrax, who calls the genitive *seṛagan*, *seṛ* being the word for genus. The genitive is used to express the genus to which that noun ought to belong upon which the genitive depends, and so the governing noun's genus is actually determined by the genitive. Thus when we say, 'the tree of the father,' 'the brother of the friend' etc. the genus, to which tree or father pertain, is indicated by the genitive, for "the purpose of genus is to divide an object from things in general."[2] The Arabs were certainly well aware of this concept, which is the same as the إِضَافَةٌ (*construct relation*). In this way of thinking of it, the genitive is called المُضَافُ إِلَيْهِ, literally meaning *the one at whose house lodging is accepted*, i.e. by the governing noun. The governing noun is itself called المُضَافُ, (lit.) *the one who is received into a lodging*. So for the Arabs the genitive expressed the concept under whose control the governing noun |[153] fell, and this agrees closely with the Greek term γενικὴ πτῶσις (*generic case*). In any case, we still need to ask whether the founders of Arabic grammar played free and easy with the Greek formula and made alterations to it so as to replace the philosophical definition with a version of their own that was clearer and more in line with their own particular requirements, or whether they investigated the nature of the genitive closely and were thus able to conclude from their own observations that their notion of it was in close agreement with the Greek. After all, إِضَافَةٌ is not the name for the genitive as such, but rather for the relationship between the two nouns concerned. The name for the genitive proper is جَرٌّ (*dragging*). Sībawayhi (ch.100) says: "A *dragging* is used in the case of every noun, at whose house lodging is accepted (في كلّ اسم مضافٍ اليه),[xviii] and I know that the مضافٌ اليه can be *dragged* (يَنْجَرّ) in three ways, one in which it is neither noun nor container; one in which it is container; one in which it is noun, but not container." To the first of these three groups is assigned the example مررتُ بزيدٍ, i.e. where the particle requires a genitive; to the second class belong particles of place and time, such as خَلْفَ, أَمامَ etc., particles which he goes on to say are actually nouns; and to the third group

[1] See G.F. Schoemann in *Zeitschrift für die Wissenschaft der Sprache* I, 83; H. Hübschmann, *Zur Casuslehre* (München, 1875), 13.

[2] Aristotle, *Topics* VI,3: *The genus ought to divide the object from things in general* (δεῖ γὰρ τὸ μὲν γένος ἀπὸ τῶν ἄλλων χωρίζειν).

belong nouns such as مِثْلٌ, جَيِّرٌ etc. After this he goes on to set out the nature of particles. He says here that what precedes or follows a noun is related (يُضَافُ) to it by means of particles such as ب. Hence in the exclamation يا لَبَكرٍ the word يا is made to refer to بكر by means of the particle ل; in the sentence مَرَرْتُ بزيدٍ the verb is made to refer to زيدٌ by means of the particle ب; and in the sentence انتَ كَعَبْدِ اللهِ the likeness between you and Abdullah is effected by means of the ك. In these examples it is the logical relationship rather than the grammatical one that is of importance. Hence if the Arabs were borrowing the Greek γενικὴ πτῶσις, then they were certainly making a very free use of it. We can see, however, why the word جَرّ was chosen, for it expresses the attraction (lit. dragging) which pulls together the genitive and its governing noun. If this is true, then جَرّ is a term invented by the Arabs themselves rather than adopted from elsewhere.

Similarly, the name used for the accusative نَصبٌ does not seem to bear any resemblance to its Greek equivalent, αἰτιατική. The idea of final cause, which I think is what lies behind the latter term, would be more readily expressed in Arabic with a different word, such as غاية, علة, or سبب. So if we leave the exact meaning of the word نَصبٌ in some doubt (Al-Qāmūs gives it the sense of purpose, end, extremity), then we can at least say that the Arabs were well aware of both the concept and the names of the genitive and accusative cases; yet for this very reason we can be absolutely sure that they never read any of the Greek grammarians. The founders of Arabic grammar knew only of Aristotle, or at least the Aristotelianism developed by the scholiasts. From this source they took the name of the nominative, εὐθεία or ὀρθή, and translated this as رَفْعٌ.

|[154] Let us conclude our findings thus far on the question of the beginnings of Arabic grammar. The Arabs first of all learned from the Syrians how to name and write the vowels; they then recognised the characteristic laws of their own language with the help of some of the categories of Peripatetic philosophy, to which they owed the most useful tools for developing their analysis of syntax. This syntax was then elaborated using a logical approach to language and borrowing new categories, even though they failed to achieve a successful morphology. What they did attain in this field, however, was done on the basis of their own discoveries rather than from borrowings. Lastly, their orthoepy was not all based on Greek principles, because this whole area was built upon تجويد, the art of Qurʾānic recitation.

It was especially significant that this was how things worked out, for Greek grammatical definitions will not work in Semitic languages; indeed those who try to force Semitic grammar into a Greek mould will encounter severe difficulties, as the many examples of this happening in the history of Syriac grammar have amply attested. Hence by proceeding with a fair degree of freedom and unhindered by theories unsuited to their subject matter, the Arabs were the first actually to describe the real characteristics of a Semitic language. The Jewish grammarians later undervalued what was left of them.[1]

Once the construction of Arabic grammar had reached the point at which it was in harmony with the Semitic character of the language, and once the philologists had become accustomed to receiving all the plaudits their culture could offer, it comes as no surprise that the Arabic-speaking Syrians also made use of the Arabic grammatical system for their own language. A struggle then ensued among them between those who were keen to embrace the new approach and those who preferred to keep the old system which had been adopted from the Greek.

The first of the Syrians to follow the new Arabic grammatical tradition was the Catholicos Elias I, who is usually referred to as bishop of Ṭirhan. He was elevated to the patriarchate in 1028 and died 21 years later on May 7th 1049, although he wrote his treatise on grammar before he became Catholicos. Baethgen has edited the work and added a number of noteworthy comments on Elias in his introduction.[2]

Initially Elias focused solely on Syriac literature and discussed Syriac grammatical theory in Arabic. He also made good use of the Aristotelian Organon, concerning which he says that if we want to attain to a full understanding of all things human and divine, then we must be prepared to study both logic and grammar. He then proceeds to an investigation of the Greek grammatical principles |155 that had been adopted into Syriac (at least as much as he could, since he did not himself read Greek) and on this basis believed that he should try to compose a grammatical handbook for students. In this short work he sets out to follow the fully developed Arabic system in such a way as to reveal the hidden depths of the Syriac language.

---

[1] I should add that Judah ben David Ḥayyūǧ expressed the concept of the passive as אשר לא נקרא שם פעלו (H. Ewald & L. Dukes, *Beiträge zur Geschichte der altesten Auslegung und Spracherklärung des Alten Testamentes* [Stuttgart, 1844] III, 148), which is very similar to the description given above (p.148).

[2] F. Baethgen, ed., ܬܘܪܨ ܡܡܠܠܐ ܣܘܪܝܝܐ *oder syrische Grammatik des Mar Elias von Ṭirhan* (Leipzig, 1880). What Baethgen writes in the introduction about Elias of Nisibis should be corrected in light of ch. VIII above.

He was rather affected by the natural tendency to praise one's own tongue, which he fully believed to be in no way inferior to Arabic, but the outcome did not match his laudable intention. He could not avoid using the methods of the earlier grammars, from which he had to take a great deal including much that could not be forced into the Arabic mould (accents, aspiration, the seven parts of speech, cf. ch.30). He was therefore unable to adopt the Arabic system wholesale and the result was a somewhat incomplete and confused work. The definition of grammar itself is the most glaring example of this. It is said to be (p.4,18)ܝܕܥܬܐ ܕܡܬܬܙܝܥܢܘܬܐ ܕܫܡܗܐ ܘܡ̈ܠܐ ܘܦܣܘ̈ܩܝܐ. Since ܡܬܬܙܝܥܢܘܬܐ corresponds to the Arabic حركات (*vocalisations*), Elias must have wanted to say that grammar is "the study of the vocalisations of nouns, verbs, and particles (i.e. ܦܣܘ̈ܩܝܐ must be حَرْف, *particles*)." However, from what follows afterwards it is clear that these vocalisations (ܡܬܬܙܝܥܢܘܬܐ) include logical accents such as ܫܐܠܐ, and so ܦܣܘ̈ܩܝܐ in this context must mean the component parts of a sentence.[1] Hence ܡܬܬܙܝܥܢܘܬܐ becomes the equivalent of Greek prosody (προσῳδία) and sense-division (διαστολή), since Dionysius Thrax (§2) says "*from the prosody we see the art, and from the correct division we see the general sense.*"[xix] The other two terms, then, ܫܡܗܐ ܘܡ̈ܠܐ, must refer to nouns and verbs, from which, according to the Greeks, the τέλειος λόγος (*a complete sentence*) is composed.[2] There is a further confusion in ch.18, where Elias asks why Syriac grammar had not been much developed, saying, "nouns and verbs are unchangeable in Syriac and do not admit ܡܬܬܙܝܥܢܘܬܐ, i.e. different inflections,[xx] neither are they affected by conjunctions or by adverbs of time or place." Other than the fact that this is simply not true, it is contradictory, since if nouns and verbs are not subject to inflection, how can one speak of a grammatical theory of inflection?

Let us close this discussion by adding some further remarks on various specific points that arise. Elias begins by making a distinction between agent and patient (فَاعِلٌ and مَفْعُولٌ), which he translates as ܥܒܘܕܐ and ܡܬܥܒܕܢܐ, or as ܥܒܘܕܐ and ܡܬܥܒܕܢܐ, ignoring the terms that Jacob Bar Šakko and those of the Greek school used, ܥܒܕܘܬܐ and ܚܫܐ. At any rate, what he says in ch.1 is just the same as Bar Šakko.

He next (ch.2) speaks about the indeclinable nature (ܚܬܡܐ, مَبْنِيٌّ) of the nouns. However, he argues that the five or four Greek nominal cases, and

---

[1] In ch.14, he tells us that ܦܣܘ̈ܩܝܐ is equivalent to جملة (*clause*) and he speaks (p.16, l.17) about vocalisations which are found in ܡܐܡܪ̈ܐ and ܦܣܘ̈ܩܝܐ, i.e. in complete sentences and parts of sentences.

[2] Bekker, *Anecdota*, 844.

also the three Arabic ones, are expressed in Syriac by the letters ܠ , ܕ , ܒ, which then causes him some confusion in treating the dative and the ܒܘܚܪܐ, as Baethgen |[156] explains (p.12, n.3). It seems that he has to deal with all this here because فَاعِلٌ and مَفْعُولٌ (*accusative*) are distinguished by their inflections, which could not be the case among indeclinables. While dealing in the third chapter with the passive, he speaks about the مَفْعُولٌ whose subject (فَاعِلٌ) is not mentioned (cf. p.148 above). If he is here referring to the usage of the accusative to indicate time and place, it is not especially obvious. Chapter 4 contains a description of the relation of nouns (i.e. the Arabic إضَافَة).

Chapters 5 and 6 are a greatly confused discussion of جَزم (*apocopation*)and ترخيم (*softening*). He teaches that جَزم should be used 1) on the first radical of the imperfect and imperative of verbs first alaph, yudh, and nun, e.g. ܦܶܠ from ܢܦܶܠ; 2) in the participle (he calls it the 'present') that is formed from the Aphel Perfect, since if ܡܰܚܶܒ derives from ܐܰܚܶܒ, then the alaph must be apocopated; 3) alaph is also lost when a pronoun is added to a participle, e.g. ܦܳܠܚܰܬ from ܐܰܢ̱ܬ ܦܳܠܚܐ; 4) ܘܢ and ܝܢ are apocopated in the 3rd person plural, since ܐܬܘ and ܐܬܝ come from ܐܬܘܢ and ܐܬܝܢ. Finally, he even goes so far as to compare ترخيم, which the Arabs use to mean the shortening of the vocative, with the formation of the construct from the emphatic state, ܡܠܶܟ from ܡܰܠܟܐ etc., and the absolute state in the plural, e.g. ܩܒܝܠܝܢ from ܩܒܝܠܐ. This brings us down to the end of ch. 9.

Ch. 11 concerns definiteness (مَعْرِفَة) and indefiniteness (نَكِرَة), stating that definiteness is always expressed by the addition of a demonstrative pronoun. It is on this basis that he later says (ch.13) that ܪܕܐ = حال, ܡܠܬܐ or ܫܡܠܝܘܬܐ = خبر; and ܡܘܕܥܢܐ = نَعْت. Since these grammatical categories do not exist in Syriac, he writes instead about the accents that serve to clarify how the parts of the sentence interrelate. ܪܕܐ or حال (*state, condition*), which Elias also calls ܐܝܢܝܘܬܐ (*quality*), is expressed by an adverb, such as ܫܒܝܚܐܝܬ (*gloriously*) and ܡܟܝܟܐܝܬ (*humbly*). ܡܘܕܥܢܐ or نعت (*predicate*) is an adjective such as ܟܐܢܐ (*just*) etc. You have a ܡܘܕܥܢܐ ܕܡܘܕܥܢܐ in the sentence ܓܒܪܐ ܣܗܕܐ ܫܪܝܪܐ (*the man is a true witness*). ܡܠܬܐ or خبر (*a report*) is a verb such as ܡܠܠ (*he spoke*). However, this last definition hardly matches the Arabic, where خبر refers to the noun predicate of a nominal sentence, whereas Elias uses a verb. The Arabs would generally call this *action* فِعل, because of the addition of an *agent* (فاعِل). The confusion extends even to the fact that in the sentence ܪܘܚܐ ܗܘ ܓܝܪ ܐܠܗܐ (*God is a Spirit*), the word ܪܘܚܐ is called a ܡܘܕܥܢܐ or نعت, whereas the Arabs would take it as a خبر and not at all as a نعت, or adjective. However, in chapter 19 he denies the existence of nominal sentences, despite the apparent contradiction.

The Arabic grammatical terms for which Elias thought he could locate Syriac equivalents are: فاعِل and مَفْعول, مَبْنِيّ, إضافَة, جزم, ترخيم, مَعْرِفة and نَكِرَة, حال, خبر and نَعْت. In chapter 10 we also have ظروف الزمان والمقام (*adverbs of time and place*).

|[157] The rest of Elias's teaching all derives from the older Syriac grammar or from Aristotelian logic. The chapters on orthoepy and verb formation owe their origin to Syriac theory. He also discusses the bgdkpt consonants (ch.12, with amplification in ch.27),[1] the names of the vowels,[2] the lines ܪܗܘܛܐ, ܡܗܦܟܢܐ, ܡܢܗܪܬܐ and ܡܗܓܝܢܐ (ch.27-28), the accents (ch.29). There is also in chs.24-26 a discussion about verb formation, to which should be added his description of verbal suffixes (ch.15) and the distinction between Imperatives and the Perfect (ch.23).

The rest comes from Aristotle, especially the theory of the five types of sentence, κλητικὴ, ἐρωτηματικὴ, προστακτικὴ, εὐκτικὴ, ἀποφαντικὴ (ch.7),[3] and the arrangement of these types according to the usage of the particles ܠ , ܕ , ܒ. His discussion of cases too derives from the earlier grammarians (chs. 2, 16).

There is no particular system in his ordering of the chapters but rather a series of different issues are dealt with as they arise. In fact, it would be better to describe this short work as a collection of grammatical essays rather than as a 'Grammar' as such. The title that ʿAbdīšōʿ gives to this work, ܡܐܡܪܐ ܬܪܨܡܡܠܠܬܐ,[4] is more appropriate than that used in the Berlin ms, ܬܘܪܨ ܡܡܠܠܐ ܣܘܪܝܝܐ, and the former, I believe, should be used from now on.

The judgment we have passed on Elias may seem rather harsh, but this is because we have focused on what was new in his work. If we looked solely at his ability to reproduce what was available in his day, we would reach a different conclusion. He was the first to attempt a meeting of Arabic and Syriac grammar and it is hardly surprising that he was unable to bring such a difficult task to a successful end, though he certainly did make a start. Even if he failed to achieve what he hoped and left us in some degree of confusion, his failings should nonetheless be excused and he ought to be applauded at least for having pioneered a new path in the quest to uncover what the special characteristics of Syriac really are. It was

---

[1] In ch.30 he also says that *b* is altered after a *u* vowel, and the assimilated letters are also mentioned, p.40, l.10 and p.41, l.20.

[2] The *u* vowel he calls ܥܨܝܪܐ ܘܘ but the *o* is called ܪܒܝܨܐ or ܪܘܝܚܐ ܘܘ (ch.24). Cf. p.112-3 above.

[3] Cf. p.163.

[4] BO III,I,262.

Barhebraeus who brought Elias's planned work to its conclusion. John Bar Zuʿbi and Jacob Bar Šakko, however, completely rejected it.

---

[i] I have given the names of these grammarians as found in *GAP* rather than as Merx gives them. Some of the dates given by Merx differ from those in *GAP*, but Merx's dates have been retained here.

[ii] The fact that some of the early Arabic names for the vowels were calques on the Syriac names (as per Merx's footnote) was used by I. Goldziher, *On the History of Grammar among the Arabs*, 4-9, as evidence for some degree of Syriac influence on Arabic grammar. Also Versteegh, *Arabic Grammar*, 30f.

[iii] On Paul, see D. Gutas, "Paul the Persian on the classification of the parts of Aristotle's philosophy: a milestone between Alexandria and Baghdad," *Der Islam* 60 (1983), 231-267; J. Teixidor, *Aristote en syriaque. Paul le Perse, logician du VIe siècle*, (Paris, 2003); H. Hugonnard-Roche, *La Logique d'Aristote du grec au syriaque : Études sur la Transmission des Textes de l'Organon et leur Interpretation philosophique*, (Paris, 2004), 233-54. Paul's other Aristotelian work, a discussion of the *De interpretatione*, is edited by H. Hugonnard-Roche, "Sur la lecture tardo-antique du Peri Hermeneias d'Aristote," in *Studio graeco-arabica* 3 (2013), 37-104. Also see id., "Du commentaire à la reconstruction: Paul le Perse interprète d'Aristote" in *Interpreting the Bible and Aristotle*, ed. J.W. Watt and J. Lössl, Ashgate, 2011.

[iv] The theory of the Greek origins of Arabic grammar has been hotly debated again in our day. In favour is Versteegh, *Greek Elements* (modified in id., *Arabic Grammar*), Rundgren, *Über den griechischen Einfluss*; against is Elamrani-Jamal, *Logique*. Both works interact with Merx, although one of the latter's weaknesses is that he interacts only with Merx's briefer (French) journal article outlining the theory and not with the material presented in the *Historia artis grammaticae*. See the introduction and King, 'Elements of the Syriac Grammatical Tradition,' for further discussion on the state of the question and research since Merx.

[v] Although (as footnote) Dionysius of Halicarnassus shows us that the division goes back to Aristotle, it is nonetheless found in Paul the Persian, a much closer source for the (Persian) Arab grammarians (see Rundgren, "Über den griechischen Einfluss," 7).

[vi] L. Massignon, "Réflexions sur la structure primitive de l'analyse grammatical en arabe," *Arabica* 1 (1954), 3-16, staunchly defending the right of Arabic grammar to a Semitic heart, asserts that Merx has been disproved in this by the observation that the Arabic tripartite division grew out of an originally bipartite one (p.6).

[vii] Tr. David Blank, *Ammonius On Interpretation 1-8* (London: Bloomsbury, 2013). Greek: ἐν μηδετέρᾳ τούτων χώρᾳ παραλαμβανόμενα, κἂν ἄλλως προσκέωνται ταῖς προτάσεσι, τὸ ὑπάρχειν ἢ μὴ ὑπάρχειν ἢ πότε ἢ πῶς ἢ ποσάκις ὑπάρχει τὸ κατηγορούμενον τῷ ὑποκειμένῳ σημαίνοντα ἤ τινα ἄλλην αὐτῶν πρὸς ἄλληλα σχέσιν, οὐδὲ κυρίως ἀξιοῖ μέρη τοῦ λόγου καλεῖν...λόγου μὲν οὖν ταῦτα οὐ μέρη, λέξεως δὲ μέρη, ἧς καὶ ὁ λόγος αὐτὸς μέρος...εὑρήσεις δὲ ἔν τισι τὸν Ἀριστοτέλην συγχωρεῖν δοκοῦντα καὶ τὰ πάντα κοινότερον μέρη τοῦ λόγου προσαγορεύοντα, διόπερ ἐν τοῖς ἑξῆς ἐρεῖ τινα τῶν μερῶν τοῦ λόγου

σημαντικὰ εἶναι ὡς ὄντων τινῶν καὶ ἀσήμων, εἰ μή τις ἡμῖν φανείη τῆς ῥήσεως ἐκείνης προσεχεστέρα ἐξήγησις οὐδὲν ἐναντίον ἔχουσα τοῖς νῦν εἰρημένοις.

[viii] Versteegh, *Elements*, 43-8, declines from Merx's translation of Sībawayhi's definition of the particle, as did Weiss, "Die arabische Nationalgrammatik und die Lateiner," *Zeitschrift der Deutschen Morgenländischen Gesellschaft* 64 (1910), 349-390. Following Versteegh, Sībawayhi is here differentiating particles that do have their own meanings from others that do not. Versteegh does, however, still locate the origins of the concept in Greek logic but he looks elsewhere than directly to Aristotle.

[ix] Elamrani-Jamal, *Logique*, 34-5, thinks ἑλληνισμός closer in meaning to نحو than to اعراب and so departs from Merx here (although he is again guilty of having read only Merx's shorter version, not the current monograph). Versteegh, *Greek Elements*, 61-3, agrees that the Greek and Arabic terms are organically related but goes further than Merx in explaining how اعراب came to refer only to the inflectional endings by highlighting the development of the term 'hellenism' among later Greek grammarians.

[x] This may be rather less true for English speakers than for Merx's German audience.

[xi] τὰ δὲ πράγματα ὡς ἐν ἀριθμῷ [τῷ χρόνῳ] ἐστίν· εἰ δὲ τοῦτο, περιέχεται ὑπὸ χρόνου ὥσπερ καὶ τὰ ἐν τόπῳ ὑπὸ τόπου. The words *[in time]* are in the mss. but make little sense (E. Hussey, *Aristotle's Physics Books III and IV* [Oxford, 1983], 209). Ross left them in his edition and attempted a defence of the resulting meaning, together with discussion of other conjectural emendations (W.D. Ross, *Aristotle's Physics, A Revised Text with introduction and commentary* [Oxford, 1936], 606).

[xii] διὸ ἀνάγκη πάντα τὰ ἐν χρόνῳ ὄντα περιέχεσθαι ὑπὸ χρόνου, ὥσπερ καὶ τἆλλα ὅσα ἔν τινί ἐστιν, οἷον τὰ ἐν τόπῳ ὑπὸ τοῦ τόπου.

[xiii] φανερὸν ὅτι πᾶσα μεταβολὴ καὶ πᾶσα κίνησις ἐν χρόνῳ ἐστίν.

[xiv] Nöldeke (Review, 1217) distances himself from this particular equivalence between the Greek and the Arabic terms.

[xv] Nöldeke (Review, 1217) suggests المسند اليه.

[xvi] πτῶσις δ' ἐστὶν ὀνόματος ἢ ῥήματος ἡ μὲν κατὰ τὸ τούτου ἢ τούτῳ σημαῖνον καὶ ὅσα τοιαῦτα, ἡ δὲ κατὰ τὸ ἑνὶ ἢ πολλοῖς, οἷον ἄνθρωποι ἢ ἄνθρωπος, ἡ δὲ κατὰ τὰ ὑποκριτικά, οἷον κατ' ἐρώτησιν ἐπίταξιν· τὸ γὰρ ἐβάδισεν; ἢ βάδιζε πτῶσις ῥήματος κατὰ ταῦτα τὰ εἴδη ἐστίν.

[xvii] On the transmission of the *Poetics* in Arabic, see Deborah Black, *Logic and Aristotle's Rhetoric and Poetics in medieval Arabic philosophy* (Leiden, 1990), and Leonardo Tarán and Dimitri Gutas, *Aristotle Poetics: Editio Maior of the Greek Text* (Leiden: Brill, 2012), 77-128.

[xviii] Nöldeke (op. cit.)repudiates the translation of اضاف (IV) by 'to accept lodging'.

[xix] ἐκ τῆς προσῳδίας τὴν τέχνην, ἐκ τῆς διαστολῆς τὸν περιεχόμενον νοῦν ὁρῶμεν.

[xx] Strictly, ܡܬܬܙܝܥܢܘܬܐ refers to the vocalisations of consonants and hence, especially in verbal morphology, to the system of inflecting the verb for persons etc. In the current context it is specifically inflection that grammarian has in mind.

Chapter 10

JOHN BAR ZUʿBI

|158 The greatest of the East Syrian grammarians, Bar Zuʿbi had no interest in joining the arabising school. In one sense he approached the subject from the perspective of euphony and recitation, but it is equally true that he set out to discuss etymology and syntax on the basis of a deep philosophical reflection. We know little about his life, only that he was a monk in the monastery of Sabrišoʿ in Beth Quqe, Arbela, during the catholicate of Sabrišoʿ, who was consecrated in 1226.[1] Jacob Bar Šakko (see next chapter) heard him teach on both logic and grammar. He collected and edited grammatical essays and he also composed a grammatical work in verse, the form which had by then become customary. He also wrote some verse orations, including one on baptism and one on the eucharist.

In his larger grammar, Bar Zuʿbi bases himself wholly on philosophy, though in his metrical grammar he makes a distinction between logic and grammar:[i]

ܘܡܐܡܪܐ ܕܗܘܐ ܒܡܡܠܠܐ:
ܠܐܦ ܠܐ ܕܡܢܝܢ ܠܚܕܕܐ.
ܒܡܡܠܠܐ ܕܡܠܝܠܘܬܐ:
ܘܒܡܡܠܠܐ ܕܓܪܡܛܝܩܘܬܐ.
ܡܡܠܠ ܓܒܪ ܕܡܠܝܠܘܬܐ:
[2] ܡܬܡܠܠ. ܠܘܬ ܦܝܠܣܘܦܐ
ܘܡܡܠܠ ܕܓܪܡܛܝܩܘܬܐ:
ܠܘܬ ܡܠܦܢܘܬܐ ܕܝܠܕܐ.
[3] ܢܡܠܘܢ ܡܡܠܠ ܦܝܠܣܘܦܐ:
ܕܠܐ ܗܝܡܢ ܠܡ ܢܣܒ ܠܘܬܗ.
|159 ܘܠܒܘܟ ܡܡܠܠ ܕܓܪܡܛܝܩܘ:
ܘܝܗܒ ܒܗ ܠܘܬ ܡܘܠܕܐ.

---

[1] See G. Hoffmann, *Auszüge aus syrischen Akten persischer Märtyrer* (Leipzig, 1880), 215, n.1715; BO III,I,307f.; Barhebraeus, *Chron. Eccl.* III,401,410; Wright, *Cat.* III,1175.

[2] ܦܝܠܣܘܦܐ Cod. Petermann 9.

[3] ܡܡܠܠܘ ܕܐܪܣܛܘ Cod. Petermann 9.

ܡܬܐܡܪܐ ܒܪܡܫܝܚܐ.
ܠܡܠܬܐ ܕܬܪܬܐ ܡܬܦܠܓܐ܆ ܘܫܢ.

In the larger grammar, however, he does not follow this rule, but rather wrote: "The Greek grammarians distinguish eight parts of speech. Of these, the Syrian grammarians, by following the Greek theory, found seven in their own language, the article being the one omitted, [while the others are] noun, verb, pronoun, verb of the noun (ܡܠܬܐ ܫܡܐ, i.e. *participle* / μετοχή), adverb, preposition, conjunction. Those, however, who follow the Arabs count only three parts of speech."[1] [ii]

This first section, which follows the Greek pattern, is followed by a second on the vocalisations (ܡܬܚܪܙܢܘܬܐ) which affect the different parts of speech, i.e. accents and aspiration. In this he shows himself to be a faithful follower of the ܡܕܢܚܝܐ and of Joseph Bar Malkon by including the whole of orthoepy and the rhetorical aspects of grammar under this head. This is also a Greek pattern, which we saw in Dionysius Thrax's section on prosody etc. Barhebraeus and Jacob Bar Šakko preserve the same order and are presumably following Jacob of Edessa in this case.

Let us now briefly look more closely at how he goes about this. His definition of the noun is as follows: ܘܫܡܐ ܓܝܪ ܗܟܝܠ ܐܝܬܘܗܝ: ܩܠܐ ܡܫܘܕܥܢܐ ܒܣܝܡܘܬܐ ܕܠܐ ܙܒܢܐ: ܘܗܘ ܕܡܢܘܬܗ ܘܠܐ ܚܕܐ ܐܝܬ ܡܫܘܕܥܢܝܬܐ ܡܢ ܡܬܦܪܫܬܐ. ܘܡܕܡ ܡܬܚܫܒܬܐ. ܡܢ ܟܕ ܗܘ ܕܐܝܬܘܗܝ ܗܘܐ: ܐܘ ܐܝܬܘܗܝ. ܐܘ ܗܘܐ ܐܝܬܘܗܝ. ܡܫܘܕܥ ܫܪܪܐ ܐܘ ܕܓܠܘܬܐ. (*a noun is therefore a word that is, by convention, indicative of something timeless, [and] of which no part is on its own indicative of anything definite, [but] when it is [joined] with something past, present, or future, then it indicates what is true or false*).[2] The first part of this is clearly derived from Aristotle, *De Int.* 16a19-21, "a noun is a word that is indicative according to convention, is without time, and of which no part is indicative on its own."[iii] However, Bar Zuʿbi follows the old Syriac translation of the *De Interpretatione*, known as 'x' in Hoffmann's edition, and used it together with Probus's commentary.[3] For the words ܘܡܕܡ ܡܬܚܫܒܬܐ are taken |[160] directly from Probus,[4] and the rest (ܡܢ ܗܘ...ܐܘ ܕܓܠܘܬܐ) is also similar to Probus.[5] Bar Zuʿbi then goes on, ܘܡܬܚܫܒܐ ܕܐܪܐ: ܠܐ ܚܝܫܐ ܐܝܬܘܗܝ ܐܘ ܐܪܝܐ. ܘܐܡܪܝܢ ܕܚܝܫܐ ܘܐܪܝܐ: ܐܪܝܐ ܕܝܡܐ. ܘܚܝܫܐ ܕܩܠܐ ܡܫܘܕܥܢܐ ܘܚܝܬܐ: ܘܩܠܐ ܡܫܘܕܥܢܐ ܘܐܝܬ ܒܗܘܢ ܣܘܝܡܘܬܐ:

[1] BL Add. 25876, f.35,155.

[2] BL Add. 25876, f.35 (= BL Or. 2314, f.3b).

[3] Hoffmann, *Herm.*, 23,71.

[4] *Ibid.*, 72,11.

[5] *Ibid,*, 72,15-15.

ܐܘܠܨ ܩ̈ܕܡܝܐ ܘܡܬܚܬ̈ܝܐ. (*we must ask whether a sound [φωνὴ] is a genus or a species. We say it is both genus and species; it is species when [it refers only to] a noise [ψόγος]; it is a genus when [it refers to] indicative and physical sounds [φωνὰς σημαντικὰς καὶ φυσικὰς],*[1] *and [to] sounds indicative by convention [συνθήκη], whether spoken or written*). All this again has its parallel is Probus.[2] Bar Zuʿbi follows him in the rest as well: ܘܢܩܫܐ ܐܝܬܘܗܝ. ܡܚܘܬܐ ܕܐܐܪ ܡܬܚܫܢܝܬܐ ܘܡܫܡܥܢܝܬܐ܀ ܩܠܐ ܕܝܢ ܐܝܬܘܗܝ܆ ܢܩܫܐ ܕܡܢܦܫܐ܆ ܐܡܬܝ ܕܗܘܐ ܡܢ ܡܬܚܫܒܢܘܬܐ ܕܢܦܫܐ ܘܪ̈ܐܬܐ. ܟܕ ܡܬܚܒܨ ܐܐܪ ܗܘ ܕܢܦܩ ܡܢ ܢܦܫܐ. ܘܡܬܕܚܐ ܠܥܠ ܐܪܛܪܝܐ ܘܚܟܐ: ܘܢܦܩ ܩܠܐ ܕܡܫܘܕܥ ܟܝܢܐܝܬ: ܐܘ ܕܡܫܘܕܥ ܒܨܒܝܢܐ ܘܡܠܠܝܐܝܬ. ܗܟܝܠ ܬܪܝܨ ܩܪܐ ܠܫܡܐ ܩܠܐ ܡܫܘܕܥܢܐ ܕܡܫܘܕܥ ܠܒܪܢܫܐ ܘܣܘܣܝܐ ܘܟܐܦܐ: ܐܘ ܚܟܡܬܐ ܘܡܪܕܘܬܐ ܘܣܘܟܠܬܢܘܬܐ... (*a noise is a beating of the air perceptible by hearing, and a sound is a noise made by something ensouled, whenever exhaled air, squeezed out of the lungs by a contraction of the chest, is pushed forcefully up the windpipe and the palate or throat,*[3] [iv]*and a sound proceeds that is physically indicative, indicating either by intention or logic; rightly he [Aristotle] therefore calls the noun an indicative sound, which indicates man, horse, stone, or wisdom, discipline, intelligence etc.*).[4]

Further, what Bar Zuʿbi says about ܫܠܡܘܬܐ (συνθήκη, *convention*) proves that he took all this from the Syriac commentaries and not directly from the Greek. For he makes a distinction between ܫܳܠܡܘܬܐ (*agreement, convention*) and ܫܰܠܡܘܬܐ (*completion*) when he writes, "when hearers hear a word that is logically indicative, they agree [ܫܳܠܡܝܢ] to that which is spoken meaningfully," and then goes on to discuss ܫܰܠܡܘܬܐ (*completion*) afterwards. This distinction was the confused invention of some Syriac scribe who did not know what συνθήκη |[161] meant, and so when he read ܫܠܡܘܬܐ, he thought that what was meant was that the parts of the word made no sense.

All this can be gleaned from the initial part of the metrical grammar. I provide the reader with the following as an example of how grammatical theories can be taught mnemonically (Berlin, Petermann 9):[v]

ܢܩ̈ܫܐ ܚܒܛܐ ܕܟܠ ܩܠܝܢ܆
ܬܪܝܨܐܝܬ ܡܬܦܠܓܝܢ܆
ܠܫܠܡܘܬܐ ܐܐܪܝܬܐ܆
ܘܟܝܢܝܬܐ ܘܡܫܡܫܢܝܬܐ..
ܘܠܫܠܡܘܬܐ ܬܘܒ ܡܫܘܕܥܬܐ܆

[1] I.e. the sort of sound that is constituted by the barking of a dog indicating the arrival of visitors.

[2] *Ibid.*, 71,9; 73,29.

[3] Up to this point, Probus is taking his material directly from Ammonius.

[4] *Ibid.*, 71,10; 73,30. For the origin and development of the theories described here, see *ibid.*, 122.

ܪܒܝܥܝܐ ܡܢ ܚܕܐ ܘܬܐܬܐ:
ܘܡܢܗܘܢ ܡܬܐܡܪ ܐܐܪ
ܥܠ ܐܘܪ̈ܗܢܐ ܘܣܓܝܐ..
ܘܟܠ ܐܦ ܗܘ ܡܬܦܠܓ:
ܠܡܫܩܠܐ ܘܥܠܐ ܡܫܩܠܐ.
ܡܫܩܠܐ ܐܝܟ ܗܠܝܢ ܣܬܘܬܐ.
ܘܠܐ ܡܫܩܠܐ ܐܝܟ ܩܠܡܐ.
ܘܡܫܩܠܐ ܬܘܒ ܡܬܦܠܓ:
ܚܝܘܬܐ ܘܕܚܝܘܬܐ.
ܚܝܘܬܐ ܐܝܟ ܗܠܝܢ ܟܠܒܐ.
ܡܫܘܚܬ ܡܬܐܡܪ ܢܦܫܐ..
ܕܚܝܘܬܐ ܠܥܠܡܘܬܐ.
ܐܝܟ ܩܠܐ ܡܬܬܟܬܒܢܐ:
ܘܩܠܐ ܬܘܒ ܡܬܬܟܬܒ̈ܢܐ.
ܠܬܪܝܢ ܐܝܟ ܡܬܦܠܓܝܢ
ܠܡܬܟܠܐ ܕܢܦܩ ܡܢ ܙܢܐ.[162]
ܘܠܡܫܚܠ ܕܪܚܩ ܡܢ ܙܢܐ.

He then distinguishes four types of noun and the five Aristotelian varieties of speech: ...ܦܢܐ ܡܕܒܪܢܐ ܡܬܐܡܪܐ ܦܘܠܐ ܘܗܘ ܫܡܥܝܐ ܕܡܬܐܡܪ ܐܦܘܦܢܛܝܩܘܣ ܕܦܘܣ[vi]

After thus discussing the nature of sounds, words, and sentences, he classifies the different noun groups, but he does not use any system based on grammatical form such as the one Jacob of Edessa made famous. Bar Zuʿbi prefers to follow the philosophers and one can find in his own classification a passage from Paul the Persian.[1] He establishes the following groups, 1) ܟܝ̈ܢܝܐ (*natural*), 2) ܦܪܨܘܦܝܐ (*personal*), 3) ܓܕ̈ܫܝܐ (*accidental*), 4) ܣܘܥܪ̈ܢܝܐ (*designating action*). These are further subdivided as follows:

1. Natural. These indicate the nature of things in the world, both corporeal and incorporeal, such as angels, demons (ܫ̈ܐܕܐ), souls. Corporeal can be animate or inanimate (like the numbers, 'four' etc.). The animate include animals, animals endowed with the nature of plants, plants. Animals can be fliers, swimmers, walkers, and so forth.

2. It would be pointless here to enumerate the category of 'personal nouns' which is ridden with confusion.

3. There are nine subtypes of the 'accidental nouns': 1) quantitative (*short, long* etc.), 2) qualitative (*white, ruddy*), 3) relational (*friend, lord, slaves*), 4) locational (*above, below*), 5) temporal (ܡܚܪ, ܐܬܡܠܝ), 6) positional (ܡܬܟܐ,

[1] *Anec. Syr.* IV, 7,6.

ܦܣܘܩܐ, ܡܒܪܟܐ), 7) essential nouns, or ܐܝܬܘܬܢܐ, which may designate either internal quality (*man is also animal*, ܐܝܬܘܗܝ ܒܪܢܫܐ ܚܝܘܬܐ) or external quality (he has riches, ܐܝܬ ܠܗ ܥܘܬܪܐ), 8) active (ܦܘܥܠܐ), 9) passive (ܚܫܐ).[vii]

4. Those designating action are subdivided into 1) corporeal (ܐܙܠܘܬܐ, ܦܪܚܐ), 2) spiritual (ܚܟܝܡܐ), 3) both corporeal and spiritual (*good, bad, just*), 4) those which accompany the body (ܘܥܡ ܡܣܟܢ ܥܬܝܪܐ) (*poor man, rich man*).

Note how idiosyncratic this system is! He is not even bothered that he reproduces the same list when discussing plurals (f.129a). The accents are set out according to a similar philosophical rationale and, Bar Zuʿbi's other comments aside, herein lies the value of the work. In dealing with the accents in this way, he follows the work of the anonymous writer whose tract may have arisen from the school of Thomas of Harkel.[1]

|[163] He continues (f.56b) with the five varieties of speech. Probus discusses these on the basis of the Aristotelian commentary tradition:[2] ܩܪܝܢܐ (κλητικός), ܡܬܟܫܦܢܐ (εὐκτικός),[3] ܦܘܩܕܢܐ (προστακτικός), ܡܫܐܠܢܐ (ἐρωτηματικός), ܦܣܘܩܐ (ἀποφαντικός). When he explains the characteristics of these types, Probus, who lived not later than the fifth century,[viii] uses biblical examples, showing that he must have worked in the environment of the Christian schools. These examples are of some interest: ܩܪܝܢܐ can be illustrated from the words, ܬܘ ܠܘܬܝ ܟܠܟܘܢ ܠܐܝܐ ܘܫܩܝܠܝ ܡܘܒܠܐ (Mt 11.28); ܡܒܥܝܢܐ (otherwise known as ܡܒܪܟܐ or ܡܬܟܫܦܢܐ) from the words ܒܥܐ ܐܢܐ ܡܢܟ (cf. Lk 8.28, and read ܒܥܐ); ܦܘܩܕܢܐ from the words ܙܠ ܠܩܘܛ ܓܐܪܐ ܘܐܝܬܐ ܠܝ (1 Sam 20.21); ܡܫܐܠܢܐ from the words ܐܝܟܐ ܣܡܬܘܢܝܗܝ (Jn 11.34); the example of ܦܣܘܩܐ is ܐܠܗܐ ܗܘ ܐܝܬܘܗܝ, apparently cited from John's Gospel, while the other example, ܢܦܫܐ ܡܝܘܬܬܐ ܐܝܬܝܗ̇, is non-biblical.

These five species are discussed at some length and he even says: ܩܪܝܢܐ, ܡܬܟܫܦܢܐ, and ܦܘܩܕܢܐ are closely connected and to some extent interchangeable, whereas ܦܣܘܩܐ and ܡܫܐܠܢܐ are used alongside the first three. For a person might begin a speech with an invocation (ܩܪܝܢܐ), an imprecation (ܡܬܟܫܦܢܐ), or a command (ܦܘܩܕܢܐ), and then ask a question, or be asked a question, and this then leads on to a basic assertion (ܡܠܬܐ ܦܣܘܩܐ = λόγος ἀποφαντικός). For instance, one might 'invoke' another person, ܐܘ ܦܠܢ. ܬܐ ܠܟܐ (*O such and such, come here*), and when he has come, ask, ܐܘ ܦܠܢ ܦܠܢ: ܐܝܟܐ ܐܝܬܘܗܝ (*O such and such,*

[1] Phillips, *A Letter of Mar Jacob*, 66ff. (Appendix I).

[2] Hoffmann, *Herm.*, 66 and 115.

[3] Bar Zuʿbi also has ܡܒܪܟܐ instead of ܡܬܟܫܦܢܐ (*ibid.*, 115). Probus himself however calls this type ܡܒܥܝܢܐ. Bazud also, it seems, used the examples found in Probus (*ibid.*, 116). The abovementioned anonymous also calls it ܡܒܥܝܢܐ (Phillips, 68).

is he well?), to which he then answers with a simple assertion, ܐܝܢ ܛܒܐ ܐܝܬܘܗܝ (*Yes, he is well*).

An imprecation or command could take the place of the invocation. He gives an example involving a command—God called and said, ܐܒܪܗܡ ܐܒܪܗܡ܆, and when Abraham had answered, ܗܐ ܐܢܐ, he continued with an assertion ܠܐ ܬܘܫܛ ܐܝܕܟ ܥܠ ܛܠܝܐ. He then shows how this logical distinction of the parts of speech affects the recitation by repeating the same example in five ways: ܠܐ̈ ܦܩܣ ܐܢܬ ܥܡܢ, which could be spoken in the manner of a call, a command, a request, |[164] a question, or a prohibition. It brings naturally to mind that play in which the actor playing the part of the slave ponders how the expression, 'the horses are ready,' which are his only lines in the play, ought to be pronounced!

Bar Zuʿbi next distinguishes three sub-types of 'questions', namely the commanding, the requesting, and the insulting (ܡܨܥܠܢܝܬܐ). The example given for the first is ܡܢܐ ܥܒܕܐ ܐܢܬ ܡܢܝ܆; an insulting question is such as ܗܐ ܕܝܢ ܐܢ̈ܫܐ܆ ܕܥܡܐ ܠܐ ܫܡܥܝܢ܀, from which develops also the ironic question, e.g. ܛܘܒܘܗܝ ܠܥܡܐ܆ ܕܗܟܢܐ ܐܝܬ ܠܗ, which he believes is called ܡܚܣܕܢܝܬܐ (κατ' ὀνειδισμόν). As an example of the requesting type, we have ܡܢܐ ܗܘ ܗܘܐ ܛܒܐ ܗܢܐ܀, and this latter type can shade over into the admiring type, whence the ܡܬܕܡܪܢܐ. The following words then indicate how the other accents all come back to these abovementioned types: ܡܢܐ ܕܝܢ ܕܟܠ ܗܘ ܗܘ ܐܝܬ ܠܗ ܡܫܠܡܢܘܬܐ ܒܣܘܦܐ ܕܦܬܓܡܐ: ܡܬܕܡܪܢܐ ܗܘܐ ܡܐܡܪܐ܀ ܐܡܬܝ ܕܝܢ ܕܟܠ ܗܘ ܗܘ ܡܫܡܫܢܐ ܐܝܬ ܠܗ: ܡܬܟܫܦܢܐ ܗܘܐ ܡܐܡܪܐ. ܐܝܟ ܐܢܫ ܕܐܡܪ. ܡܢܐ ܗܘ ܐܝܟ ܐܝܠܐ ܟܒܪܐ ܗܢܐ܀ (*when* ܡܫܠܡܢܘܬܐ *is joined to a* ܗܘ *at the end of a sentence, the saying is one of admiration; but when a* ܡܫܡܫܢܐ *is joined to a* ܗܘ, *the saying is a request* etc.).

He then proposes a fivefold typology of the basic assertion (ܡܐܡܪܐ ܦܫܝܛܐ):

1) admiring, ܡܬܕܡܪܢܐ, e.g. ܡܢܐ ܛܒ ܗܘܐ ܫܦܝܪ.
2) requesting, ܕܒܥܘܬܐ, e.g. ܬܬܪܚܡܘܢ ܥܠܝܢ.
3) setting down, ܡܬܬܣܝܡܢܐ, e.g. ܬܘܗܐ ܢܦܠܬ ܗܘܬ ܥܠ ܥܡܐ.
4) hypothetical, ܫܘܡܠܐ, e.g. ܐܢ ܐܬܐܬ ܦܠܚ ܐܢܐ ܠܟ.
5) categorical, e.g. ܕܘܝܕ ܢܒܝܐ ܗܘܐ.

Once he has completely exhausted this discussion, he adds, "one ought to know that there are three accents that are used within the categorical type of statement, viz. ܙܘܓܐ, ܥܠܝܐ, ܬܚܬܝܐ. And then there is also ܡܪܗܛܢܐ, ܦܣܘܩܐ and ܬܟܝܠܐ, and also ܡܫܡܫܢܐ. The ܦܣܘܩܐ is like the city governor, the ܬܚܬܝܐ is the city gate, and ܪܗܛܐ the main road leading into the city, and ܥܠܝܐ the main plazas that lead up to the city governor."[1]

|[165] Such is the bond between philosophy and grammar,[2] and such his way of mapping out the accentual system! The division of the sentence into its component parts was the invention of those earlier grammarians who had set aside the even older system (the one we described on p.63) and used just the four basic points (ܥܠܝܐ, ܬܚܬܝܐ, ܪܗܛܐ, ܦܣܘܩܐ) to indicate divisions. To this they went on to add the mimetic, or rhetorical accents, to indicate the type of statement expressed—ܦܩܘܕܐ, ܡܫܐܠܢܐ, ܩܪܝܐ, ܡܬܕܡܪܢܐ (the latter also sometimes called ܡܙܥܩܢܐ or ܡܬܡܗܢܐ). There were nine principal accents in all by the time of Joseph Huazya, or ten if one includes ܦܣܘܩܐ. Different schools then supplemented this system in a variety of ways. We have seen the lists drawn up by Thomas and of Jacob (p.99f.), and in this present chapter we are looking at the Eastern system as expressed by John Bar Zuʿbi and Elias of Ṭirhan, which clearly differs from the aforementioned systems firstly because it uses a different number of accents (30 in the case of Elias of Ṭirhan), and also because the ܙܘܓܐ and ܡܙܝܚܢܐ were also included (p.126f. above), neither of which was ever mentioned by Jacob of Edessa. On the other hand, the Easterns did not have all those variants known as ܦܣܝܩܬܐ, nor did they use ܡܩܝܡܐ (which should not be identified with ܡܩܝܡܢܐ), nor ܡܗܦܟܢܐ, ܐܬܢܚܬܐ, ܡܫܡܥܢܐ, ܣܡܟ ܠܓܘܐ, ܡܢܗܦܟܢܐ or ܡܫܡܥܢܐ, which they called ܪܗܛܐ ܚܕܬܐ.

Bar Zuʿbi gives us his catalogue in this same way, and calls ܪܗܛܐ, ܥܠܝܐ, ܬܚܬܝܐ, and ܦܣܘܩܐ homonyms, each of which includes various sub-types:

ܪܗܛܐ includes seven such sub-types: 1 ܪܗܛܐ ܕܩܕܡܝܐ, 2 ܪܗܛܐ ܕܙܘܓܐ, 3 ܪܗܛܐ ܕܥܠܝܬܐ, 4ܪܗܛܐ ܕܚܪܬܝܐ, 5 ܪܗܛܐ ܕܡܫܡܥܢܐ, 6 ܪܗܛܐ ܕܙܘܓܐ ܕܒܚܪܝܐ, 7 ܪܗܛܐ ܕܦܣܘܩܐ.

ܬܚܬܝܐ has eight: 1 ܬܚܬܝܐ ܕܩܕܡܝܐ, 2 ܬܚܬܝܐ ܕܙܘܓܐ, 3 ܬܚܬܝܐ ܕܦܣܘܩܐ, 4 ܬܚܬܝܐ that is called ܡܬܕܡܪܢܘܬܐ, 5 ܬܚܬܝܐ that is called ܙܘܓܐ ܕܚܪܝܐ, 6 ܬܚܬܝܐ that is called ܦܩܕܐ, 7 ܬܚܬܝܐ that is called ܡܬܢܝܢܐ, 8 ܬܚܬܝܐ from which derives ܐܝܬ ܒܗ ܡܫܐܠܢܘܬܐ.

[1] ܘܗܘ ܕܐܝܟ ܕܐܡܪܢܐ ܦܣܘܩܐ ܠܟܠܗ ܡܫܩܠܐ ܐܝܟ ܒܗ܀ ܪܗܛܐ ܘܥܠܝܐ ܘܬܚܬܝܐ܀ ܘܐܦ ܐܪܒܥܬܗܘܢ. ܡܕܝܢܬܐ܀ ܘܫܘܩܐ ܘܡܠܟܘܬܐ܀ ܘܡܩܡܝܢܐ܀ ܘܗܢܐ ܦܣܘܩܐ: ܠܡܕܝܢܬܐ ܘܫܘܩܐ܀ ܘܬܚܬܝܐ: ܠܫܘܪܐ ܘܡܕܝܢܬܐ܀ ܘܪܗܛܐ ܠܐܘܪܚܐ ܘܡܥܠܐ ܠܡܕܝܢܬܐ ܘܥܠܝܐ ܠܫܘܩܐ ܘܡܕܝܢܬܐ ܘܡܩܪܒܝܢ ܠܗ ܠܫܠܝܛܐ ܕܡܕܝܢܬܐ.

[2] We can now understand why Thomas the Deacon said that the philosophers, especially Aristotle, had examined the ܦܣܘܩܐ (Martin, *Ad Georgium*, 13). Surprisingly, the word ܦܣܘܩܐ is inserted into the Peshiṭta version of the Psalms nine times (37.21, 68.18, 69.19, 78.51, 89.25, 104.18, 105.22, 106.23, 107.21). The word is not found in Barhebraeus's scholia on Ps 68 (J. Knobloch, *Gregorii Bar-Hebræi Scholia in Psalmum LXVIII. e codicibus MSS. syriacis primum edita et annotationibus illustrata* [Bratislava, 1852]). See I. Prager, *De Veteris Testamenti Versione Syriaca quam Peschittho vocant quaestiones criticae* (Göttingen, 1875), 47.

|166 ܥܠܝܐ has six: 1 between the parts of an apodosis, where ܐܬܝܐ precedes, 2 in longer interrogative utterances, 3 where the writer is offering praise to something, such that it is ܡܫܒܚܢܐ, 4 wherever the writer wants to describe something using longer clauses, 5 where the writer wants to summarise in brief what he has already said at length, 6 where a protasis with its apodosis brings a clause to an end and the writer wants to start again from the same protasis.

The ܦܣܘܩܐ is used in twenty different ways, ten of which are found in the Scriptures as follows: 1 the request (ܒܥܘܬܢܐ), 2 ܡܙܘܥܐ, 3 ܦܩܘܕܐ, 4 ܡܬܕܡܪܢܐ, 5 hypothetical (ܣܘܡܟܐ), such as after ܐܢ, 6 set down (ܡܬܬܣܝܡܢܐ), 7 in an oath (ܡܘܡܐ), 8 where there is uncertainty (ܡܬܦܩܥܢܐ), 9 where someone is being persuaded (ܡܦܝܣܢܐ), 10 the true ܦܣܘܩܐ at the end of a sentence.ix

The other ten types pertain to logical or dialectical use: 1 ἀποφαντικός (*basic assertion*), 2 κατάφασις (*positive assertion*), 3 ἀπόφασις (*negative assertion*), 4 πρότασις (*protasis*), 5 ἀξίωμα (*axiom*), 6 thesis (ܡܬܬܣܝܡܢܐ), i.e. opinions held by some but not all, 7 πρόβλημα (*problem*), 8 συμπέρασμα (*conclusion*, cf. *Prior Analytics* 30a29), 9 interrogative, 10 ὅρος (*definition*) = ܐܣܘܡܐ.

To these 'accents' he then adds 1 ܡܣܡܟܢܐ, 2 ܦܠܓܘܬܐ ܡܣܡܟܢܐ, 3 ܡܣܝܟܢܐ, 4 ܢܓܪܐ, 5 ܡܥܕܢܐ ܙܥܐ, 6 ܐܬܝܐ ܕܐܠܟܬܐ, 7 three sorts of ܙܘܚܬܐ, which are ܙܘܚܬܐ ܕܬܪܬܗ, ܙܘܚܬܐ ܕܦܣܘܩ, ܙܘܚܬܐ ܠܚܘܕܘܗܝ, 8 ܡܫܘܚܐ, 9 ܥܨܘܪܐ, 10 ܡܬܕܡܪܢܐ, 11 ܡܬܦܩܥܢܐ.

Elias of Ṭirhan lists the same accents, and Bar Zuʿbi copied this verbatim at the end of his treatise (cf. Appendix I, part 3 to the current chapter). We need not reproduce his examples here since this whole section of Bar Zuʿbi's treatise has been edited by Martin and anyone who wants to examine this whole tiresome mess in greater detail is referred to his book.[1] We should, however, make one important point, viz. that there were four, or perhaps five, different accentual systems which should not be confused with each other. These systems cannot be elicited solely from the grammatical treatises themselves and the manuscripts from which one may be able to derive them still await publication.[2] But such a task would not necessarily be of much use and would surely be tiresome and costly. If someone discovered a text marked up with Joseph Huzaya's accent system, that would certainly be worth publishing, since he is said to have copied

[1] Martin, *Accentuation*.

[2] In just the same way, one cannot discover the Hebrew accentual system solely from reading the oldest Hebrew grammarians, for the latter contain only the names and the order of the accents, together with examples and exceptions.

out Theodore's commentaries using his own pointing and one could then compare these with the extant commentaries of Theodore. We have edited the East Syrian accent system as it is found in the Berlin ms Petermann 9 = Berlin Syr.88 (Appendix |[167] to the present chapter). This consists of three treatises, the first being the oldest Masoretic treatise, the second a more developed Masoretic one, and the third is one which we believe to have been written by Elias of Ṭirhan and which was Bar Zuʿbi's principal source.

But we must return now to the sequence of subjects in Bar Zuʿbi's grammar, for the digression on the five types of sentence was inserted into the middle of the chapter on the noun, and this is why we have also skipped forwards to the end of the grammar and looked at what he says there about accents. He adds into his work a lot of philosophical material, including extracts from Severus Sebokht's *Letter to Jonas the Periodeutes* and from the commentary of Rabban Denḥa (pupil of Catholicos Išoʿ Bar Nun) and from Aristotle's *Analytics*. There is even a discussion of realism and nominalism, in which he examines the question whether the creator or the quality of the creator is primary, and also the creation, the act of creating, or the quality of the creature, and then finally whether ܡܠܟܒܪܐ or ܡܠܟܒܪܘܬܐ is primary (f.66b).

Now that we have done with these rather detailed matters, we can pass on to how he thinks verbs should be classified into groups. To do this, he makes use of the consonant-count and also of the syllable-count while making no reference to the actual form of the root, such that Pʿal, Paʿel, and Afʿel are counted together with other groups of the same verb.[x]

First of all (f.99b) he lists monosyllabic verbs that consist of two or three consonants, followed by disyllabic verbs of three or four consonants. He also considers the vowels on the syllables. This gives rise to the following sequence:

A. 1 ܒܪ, 2 ܒܠܐ, 3 ܒܪܐ.[1]
B. 4 ܦܫ, 5 ܒܣܪ,[2] 6 ܦܪܙ, ܦܢܩ 7 ܐܬܒ, 8 ܢܬܥ, 9 ܐܬܪ.
C. 10 ܐܬܒܠ, 11 ܐܬܦܫ, 12 ܐܬܦܪܩ, 13 ܐܘܬܒ, 14 ܢܦܫ, ܒܠܗܣ, ܠܘܬܫ, 15 ܦܫܪ, ܦܢܩ 16 ܐܬܦܫ.

[1] In what he says about the syllable formed by ܒܪܐ (cf. p.56) we have a trace that takes us back to Jacob of Edessa. In the Greek and Hebraeo-Syriac glossary found in Petermann 9, we find the following: ܗܘܟܢ. ܠܘܬܐ ܐܬܘܬܐ ܐܘ ܠܬܠܬ ܐܬܝܢ ܕܝܢܡ ܠܚܒܘܪܐ. ܕܢܩܫ ܠܬܠܬ. ܕܢ. ܒܐ. ܡܐ. So a single syllable may consist of three consonants.

[2] Thus reads the ms, but this word is out of order and ought to appear as no.4 after ܒܪܐ.

D. Then come the disyllabic verbs of five consonants: 17 ܐܬܕܟܪ and the trisyllables, 18 ܐܬܟܪܙ, ܐܬܬܪܘܡ, ܐܬܬܙܠ, 19 ܐܬܟܣܝ.

E. Then verbs of six consonants written as disyllables: 20 ܐܬܬܟܬܒ, ܐܬܬܪܘܡܡ, and trisyllables, 21 ܐܬܬܘܥܕ, ܐܬܬܣܡܟ, 22 ܐܬܬܟܢܫ, ܐܬܪܘܩ, 23 ܐܬܬܟܣܝ, ܐܬܬܪܘܝ, 24 ܐܬܬܟܬܒܝ, ܐܬܬܚܕܝ, ܐܬܪܘܪܝ.

F. Finally, verbs written with seven consonants, all of which |168 are trisyllabic: 25 ܐܬܦܟܟܡܝ, ܐܬܦܪܢܣ, ܐܬܬܣܪܘܚ, ܐܬܬܡܣܘܚ.[1]

In formulating these groups, the vowel quality is relevant, since *a* precedes *e* and *i*.

We have already seen the principles upon which this categorisation is based in Joseph Bar Malkon (p.133), and Barhebraeus preserves the same again. It would seem to have been devised among the very earliest grammarians, and should probably be attributed to Jacob of Edessa. We also see here the same system being used for classifying the nouns as we noted before (p.58). The same basic principles are used for the verb too, namely the number of syllables and the type of vowel, and there is no use made of the Greek system of simple/compound/derived-from-a-compound, which we saw being applied to Syriac by Aḥūdemmēh and the translator of Dionysius Thrax (p.33,17).[xi]

The next chapter in Bar Zuʿbi (f.111b) is a discussion of the pronoun, the third part of speech. This chapter also has sections on the verbal forms designating the persons, on the suffixes added to the verb, and on the prepositions. This is done in such a way that the feminine forms of the imperative (singular and plural) are considered under the rules relating to pronouns.

The chapter on ܫܡܐ ܡܫܬܠܐ (i.e. the participle, f.127a) also deals with other adjectival forms. It is here that we find the rules about ܫܡܗܐ ܕܢܣܒܬܐ, adjectives derived from nouns by the addition of nun or yudh (e.g. ܪܘܚܐ - ܪܘܚܢܐ - ܪܘܚܢܝܐ), although to designate the relationship between these adjectives and their nouns he does not use the term ܡܬܢܣܒܢܘܬܐ, which is only found for the first time in Barhebraeus, formed on the analogy of the Arabic term نِسْبَةٌ.

The fifth part of speech is the adverb, ܠܘܬ ܡܠܬܐ or ܥܡ ܡܠܬܐ (f.135a). Adverbs can be derived from adjectives, from numbers, from agents, or from verbal nouns, e.g. ܐܪܝܟܐܝܬ from ܐܪܝܟܐ, ܚܕܐܝܬ from ܚܕܐ, ܒܢܝܐܝܬ from ܒܢܝܐ, ܡܘܠܕܐܝܬ from ܡܘܠܕܐ. This also appears to go back to some Greek grammar, for although

[1] He adds that such words, although they do not occur in Scripture, can be formed by analogy. From passives of the type ܐܬܦܠܓ, ܐܬܟܬܒ, ܐܬܐܣܪ one can also create the further forms ܐܬܦܠܓܪ, ܐܬܟܬܒܪ, ܐܬܐܣܪܪ, even though only ܐܬܐܣܪܪ is actually found in Scripture.

Dionysius Thrax (p.20) distinguishes simple adverbs from compound ones, there would still be further need to consider the different types of compounds. Bar Zuʿbi's subcategories of adverbs (of time, place, comparison, assent, negation, amazement, questioning, conjecture [ܕܡܣܬܒܪܢܘܬܐ],[1] choosing, complaining, collecting [ܕܟܢܘܫܝܐ]) also remind one of Dionysius Thrax, although in the latter there were 26 types, not all of which are repeated by Bar Zuʿbi.

The sixth part of speech is the preposition (ܡܩܕܡܘܬܐ ܫܡܗܐ, but in the |169 metrical grammar called ܦܪܘܬܐܣܝܣ). Twenty four of them are listed: ܥܡ ܠܘܬ ܐܝܟ ܡܛܠ ܠܘܬ ܥܠ ܥܡ ܒ ܠ ܕ، ܒܝܬ ܒܡܨܥܬ ܠܘܩܒܠ ܥܠ ܙܒ݂ ܚܕܪ ܩܕܡ ܠܥܠ ܚܠܦ ܩܪܝܒ ܬܚܘܬ ܐܣܬܠ ܒܠܥܕ ܠܥܠ.

The fact that we find ܥܠ, ܐܝܟ, and ܠܥܠ in this list indicates that the Syrians were following the Greek definition of the preposition, "a word placed before all parts of the sentence whether in terms of composition or in grammatical construction."xii Therefore, in the following examples, ܥܠ is indeed being used as a preposition: ܥܠ ܥܠ ܗܕܝܢ ܣܥܪ; ܥܠ ܒܥܠܬܐ; ܡܥܢܝܢ ܡܫܬܠܛܐ; ܥܠ ܙܒܢ ܐܬܝܢܘ ܢܘܪܐ, to which Bar Zuʿbi also adds ܥܠ ܐܣܝܐ; ܒܚܠܡܘܗܝ ܘܡܥܢܝܢܐ ܐܠܗܘܗܝ.

Barhebraeus, in his larger grammar, reproduces the same list of prepositions, though adding a few more types not found here. Barhebraeus, however, omits ܒܥܠܬ, ܚܕܪ, and ܒܠܒܪ (though there is mention of these in the scholia), while adding some that Bar Zuʿbi omits, ܐܬܪ, ܣܚܠ (which is linked with ܐܢܘ), ܡܥܠܝܡ, ܐܣܬܠ with ܐܣܬܠܗ, ܚܣܝܢ, and ܒܠܒܘܗܝ. There is no agreement on the term ܚܕܪ,[2] for which Bar Zuʿbi gives this example, ܥܠ ܚܕܪܝܗ ܡܫܝܚܐ ܐܝܟ ܢܘܗܪܐ. The word ܐܬܪ is illustrated by Jacob Bar Šakko with the gloss ܙܕܘܝ.

The final part of speech is the conjunction (ܐܣܘܪܐ), which also includes the interjection. Bar Zuʿbi makes no use of Barhebraeus's highly artificial distinction between conjunctions that are added for elegance (ܫܘܦܠܝܐ) and those added by necessity (ܐܠܨܢܝܐ). The first group (also called ܣܡܝܟܬܐ) are, ܡܢ, ܕܝܢ, ܓܝܪ ܕܝܢ, ܚܘܕ, ܡܟܝܠ, ܟܐ, ܠܡ.[3] This (following Barhebraeus) was taught by the ܡܠܦܢܐ, which must mean Jacob of Edessa. All the other conjunctions are those added 'by necessity', of which there are nineteen sub-types. Now Jacob taught that the interjections which one uses for elegance form their own group and in this he simply followed Dionysius Thrax again, who says,

---

[1] In Dionysius (above, p.22) this seems to mirror εἰκασμός, just as ܟܢܘܫܝܐ is also for the Greek ἄθροισις.

[2] Barhebraeus, *Gramm.*, 85,17.

[3] *Ibid.*, 157,2.

"expletive conjunctions are those introduced for the sake of the metre or as an embellishment; they comprise..." (see p.24 above).[xiii]

The nineteen other sub-types were constituted, I believe, by Jacob of Edessa and the majority of these originate with the Greek classification of adverbs and prepositions which Jacob borrowed and which is repeated in Barhebraeus. Those that are not Greek he took from the Arabic, to which he owes the following: ܐܬܢܝܐ = حُرُوفُ الاِسْتِثْنَاءِ; ܟܠܘܬܢܝܐ = حروف العَطْفِ; 3 ܦܘܫܩܢܐ = حروف التَّفْسِيرِ; 4 ܡܥܝܪܢܐ = حروف التَّنْبِيهِ. The rest are of Greek origin and were used by Arabs as well as by Syrians, as is proven by the following list:

	|170 Dionysius Thrax[xiv]	Barhebraeus
Adverbs of:	Time	1 ܙܒܢܝܐ
	Middle kind	
	Manner	
	Quantity	
	Number	
	Place	2 ܐܬܪܝܐ
	Wish	10 ܨܒܝܢܝܐ
	Negation	12 ܡܟܦܪܢܝܐ
	Agreement	4 ܫܘܪܪܐ
	Prohibition	
	Analogy	16 ܡܦܚܡܢܐ
	Surprise	13 ܡܬܕܡܪܢܐ
	Supposition	9 ܦܘܫܩܐ
	Order	
	Aggregation	(ܕܟܘܢܫܐ)
	Exhortation	14 ܡܪܘܡܐ
	Comparison	
	Interrogation	5 ܫܘܐܠܐ
	Intensity	17 ܕܫܘܪܬܐ
	Collectivity	
	Denial on oath	
	Assertion on oath	
	Assurance	18 ܗܘܦܘܬܛܝܩܝܐ
	Introducing a debate	
	Religious Ecstasy	

	Lament[1]	15 ܡܪܡܪܢܝܐ
Conjunctions:	Copulative[xv]	
	Disjunctive	
	Synaptic	
	Parasynaptic	
	Purposive	3 ܥܠܠܬܐ
	Expletive	ܡܫܩܠܢܐ (cf. above)
	Adversative	

Fifteen of Barhebraeus's types match the Greek list. Missing are the four abovementioned ones derived |[171] from the Arabic and also ܣܛܘܟܣܝܐ (στοιχειακός), i.e. those particles that consist of only one letter (ܘ ܠ ܕ ܒ) which are elsewhere called 'cases' (πτώσεις), and which the Greeks never mention. It is no surprise that Barhebraeus does not use all the Greek types, for many are very similar and not easily distinguishable in Syriac, e.g. Prohibition with Negation, Analogy with Comparison, Collectivity with Aggregation, and Agreement with Introducing a debate.

Bar Zuʿbi, however, has no interest in this artificial categorisation, although he was certainly aware of it. Rather he lists all the individual conjunctions, together with the interjections, as follows: 1 ܡܢ, 2 ܓܝܪ 3 ܕܝܢ, 4 ܟܕ, 5 ܒܪܡ, 6 ܗܟܝܠ, 7 ܡܟܐ, 8 ܐܠܐ, 9 ܕܝ, 10 ܟܡ, 11 ܗܟܢܐ, 12 ܡܛܠ, 13 ܡܕܝܢ, 14 ܟܝ, 15 ܐܢ, 16 ܐܝܢܘ, 17 ܐܦ , 18 ܒܪ̈, 19 ܐܪܐ, 20 ܟܝ, 21 ܐܬܢܐ, 22 ܟܐܡܬ, 23 ܟܕܘ, 24 ܟܡ, 25 ܟܒܪܢ, 26 ܐܘ, 27 ܡܟܐ, 28 ܟܠܗ, 29 ܕܟܡܐ, 30 ܕܝܡ, 31 ܟܡܐ, 32 ܝܐ, 33 ܐܡܬܝ, 34 ܐܝܟ, 35 ܟܘ, 36 ܗܘܪ, 37 ܒܪ, 38 ܐܦ, 39 ܬܘܒ, 40 ܠܐ, 41 ܡܟܝܢ, 42 ܡܕܡܡܐ , 43 ܟܠ, 44 ܐܡܝܢ, 45 ܗܟܘܬ, 46 ܡܛܘܠ, 47 ܗܐ, 48 ܗܟܢ, 49 ܗܐ, 50 ܐܝܟ, 51 ܗܘ, 52 ܗܝ, 53 ܗܘܡ, 54 ܐܬܢܐ (cf. 21), 55 ܐܘܗ ܐܘܗ, 56 ܗܘܝ.ܗܘܝ, 57 ܗܝ.ܗܝ, 58 ܢܝ (probably read ܝ̈ written without its final alaph), 59 ܝܐ, 60 ܐܘܠܝ, 61 ܘܝ, 62 ܗܢܘ ܕܝܢ, 63 ܘܘ. Forms 55-61 are interjections, ܗܢܘ ܕܝܢ is explicative, ܘ the copula.

He then expatiates in detail on each one. It seems worthwhile here to edit what he says about the particles ܡܛܠ (no.12) and ܐܬܢܐ (no.21) which were not mentioned by Barhebraeus:[xvi]

ܡܛܠ܀ ܡܛܠ ܒܘܝܐ ܚܕ. ܘܡܬܬܣܝܡ: ܣܟܦ ܡܕܝܢ. ܘܡܬܬܦܣ ܒܗ ܒܘܝܐ ܐܦܢܐ: ܦܢܝܬ ܡܬܟܝܠܐ.
ܒܡܠܬܐ ܘܡܬܦܬܘܠܐ ܘܚܕ. ܡܢ ܒܠܬܘ ܟܪܢ ܘܒܝܬ ܡܟܦ ܒܪܘܝܐ ܡܟܠܬܐ ܒܗܘܢ ܠܡܠܬܐܝܢܘܗܝ ܠܡܫܟܠܐ
ܘܡܬܦܘܠܗ: ܐܡܪ ܡܛܠ ܗܕܐ ܠܡ ܪܘܚܐ ܕܡܫܡܫܢܘܬܗܘܢ. ܣܟܦ ܕܐܡܪ ܡܕܝܢ ܗܕܐ |[172] ܠܡ ܪܘܚܐ ܕܡܫܡܫܢܘܬܗܘܢ܀
ܘܡܬܐܡܪ ܠܘܬ ܒܡܫܡܫܢܐ ܘܚܒܪܐ: ܣܟܦ ܐܦ. ܐܝܟ ܕܐܡܪ ܐܝܟ ܡܛܠ ܐܝܟ. ܡܛܠ ܕܣܠܐ ܕܟܠܗܝܢ ܐܬܠܘܬܗܝ ܐܠܐ
ܡܬܟܒܠ ܗܘܐ ܒܗ: ܕܗܘܐ ܡܫܡܠ: ܣܟܦ ܕܐܡܪ. ܘܐܦ ܕܣܠܐ ܕܟܠܗܝܢ ܐܬܠܘܬܗܝ܀

[1] This type is not extant in the Greek of Dionysius, but are in the Armenian version. There the thirteenth type is called "avaghagan: akh, oukh etc.," and the fourteenth is "inghgagan: waj, avagh etc."

This particle is used, for example, by Narsai in his work *On Baptism* (taken from the Vatican ms):

ܟܪܣܐ ܕܡܝܐ ܝܠܕܐ ܐܢܘܢ ܪܘܚܢܐܝܬ
ܘܚܝܠܐ ܕܛܝܒܘܬܗ ܡܠܝܗ ܘܬܪܨ ܣܘܢܩܢܗܘܢ
ܥܝܪܐ ܘܐܢܫܐ ܚܕܝܘ ܐܦ ܚܕܝܢ ܒܛܝܒܘܬܗܘܢ
ܕܢܩܦ ܓܠܐ ܕܒܐܠܠܓܘܪܝܐ ܠܘܬ ܣܘܥܪܢܐ܀

The womb of the waters has begotten them spiritually,
and the power of its grace has filled up and made good their needs.
Angels and men rejoiced and do rejoice in their grace,
that it adheres, to be sure, to the actions allegorically.[xvii]

Bar Zuʿbi continues:

ܐܬܗܐ: ܦܬܓܡܐ ܡܢܒܗܪܢܐ ܗܘ. ܐܝܟ ܗܘ ܕܐܡܪ ܡܪܝ ܐܝܣܚܩ ܠܒܪ ܡܢ ܠܡܚܣܝܘܬܗ. ܕܐܬܗܐ ܓܒܪܐ ܠܫܡܝܐ ܩܪܐ ܐܢܬ: ܘܡܫܬܘܬܐ ܥܡ ܡܫܝܚܐ ܡܫܬܘܕܥ ܠܟ: ܘܕܚܠ ܐܢܬ ܡܢ ܐܘܠܨܢܐ܀. Payne Smith does not include this particle in the *Thesaurus*. Mar Isaac's words are to be translated, "Truly, my man, you are called to heaven and to you is promised a feast with the Messiah! And you fear affliction!"

This should be sufficient to furnish some idea of what Bar Zuʿbi says about particles. He further adds that the following do not appear in Scripture: ܦܘܡ, ܒܠܟ, ܡܟܠܗܘܢ, ܐܬܗܐ, ܐܘܪ, ܛܐܡܟ, ܕܒܝܕܟܘܢ, ܒܥܘܪ, though in fact ܡܛܐ should be added to this list.

There is also a very short tract on the conjunctions (ܐܣܘܪܐ), written in one of the Masoretic schools some time before the end of the tenth century.[1] It is rather meagre and we need only mention its existence here, for it would be serviceable in illustrating the history of the schools, since they wrote a number of little works of this kind.[2]

|[173] While Bar Zuʿbi showed himself a follower of the Greeks throughout this first half of his grammar, which dealt with the seven parts of speech, in the second half he is thoroughly Syrian. In the matter of ܡܫܚܠܦܢܘܬܐ, or the inflections of words, these are organised into two parts, one on the accents (which we dealt with already, p.165), and one on vowels and aspiration.[xviii] The names he uses for the *i* and *u* vowels are as follows: ܪܒܨܐ ܦܫܝܩܐ is two

[1] R.J.H. Gottheil, "A Tract on the Syriac Conjunctions," *Hebraica* 4 (1888), 167-173.

[2] However, the words ܓܪ ܠܬܚܬܝܬܐ ܡܝܬܐ ܠܘܬ ܥܠܝܬܐ (*gēr brings lower propositions to higher ones*) should be interpreted to be about minor and major logical propositions. Similarly, the words ܕܝܢ ܡܦܚܡ ܠܘܬ ܥܠܝܬܐ ܠܬܚܬܝܬܐ ܘܬܚܬܝܬܐ ܠܥܠܝܬܐ means *dēn compares the major with the minor and the minor with the major*, although Gottheil translates it as, *gēr brings that which is below (protasis) to that which is above (apodosis)*, and similarly in the second case.

horizontal points on the line, as in ܐܚܘܪ; ܪܒܨܐ ܥܨܝܐ is a little chain, or ܚܒܨܐ, two oblique points below the letter, as in قيام. The vowel that is expressed by the ܪܒܨܐ ܥܨܝܐ is called ܐܣܩܐ, the vowel written with a yudh and a point beneath it is called ܚܒܨܐ. Hence the three forms of the *i* vowel are:

1. ܪܒܨܐ ܦܫܝܩܐ = ĭ in يحمو.
2. ܪܒܨܐ ܥܨܝܐ = i = ܐܣܩܐ, in بعيرا.
3. ? = î = ܚܒܨܐ, in ܠܐܚܝܢ.

The ܘ in نعمنى is called ܪܘܚܐ, whereas the *u* in تحوله is called ܪܒܨܐ (f.249a). As far as orthography is concerned, he requires that the alaph of afʿel forms before a waw take the vowel ܪܘܚܐ, as in ܐܘܬܒ, ܐܘܪܒ, and similarly in other forms it expresses *au*, e.g. ܪܘܩܕܐ, ܬܘܕܝܬܐ (f.223b). He differs from the rest of the grammatical tradition in stating that the Syriac diminutives that derive from shortened forms of Greek proper nouns should be pronounced with ܦܬܚܐ not with an *e* vowel (as in ܦܘܠܐ from ܦܘܠܘܣ). So ܐܢܝܐ is taken from Anias, ܦܘܠܐ from Paulos and thus also ܐܠܝܘܙܐ, ܐܣܛܦܢܐ, ܦܝܠܝܦܐ, ܡܘܪܝܢܐ.

He puts the discussion about the use of the vowels together with noun formation such that he lists according to their characteristic vowel patterns all those forms that designate nouns of action or agents, or active or passive nouns, from a variety of different roots. It may be useful to offer to the reader those aspects of this chapter that are not shared by |[174] the other grammars and which we can be sure represent reality—i.e. the forms are those in actual use, not figments of the grammarian's imagination.

After nouns of action from geminated roots (ܚܠܠܐ, ܡܠܠܐ, ܡܠܠܢܘܬܐ) he continues (f.218b): "ܦܬܚܐ is placed on the first consonant and ܪܘܚܐ on those immediately preceding the final alaph, e.g. ܡܠܠܐ, ܡܬܩܠܐ, ܡܬܠܠܐ." The next section should be given verbatim: ܦܢܝܢ ܠܘܬ ܡܠܠܐ ܡܢ ܡܠܠܐ: ܗܢܘܢ ܕܗܘܝܢ ܡܠܠܐ: ܚܕܐ ܕܝܢ ܗܝ. ܐܝܟ ܗܘ ܕܡܠܠܘ ܘܡܫܩܠܘ܆ ܘܡܠܠܐ ܕܝܢ: ܡܢܗܘܢ ܕܡܠܠܠ ܡܠܠܠ ܗܘܐ: ܘܠܐܝܢܐ ܠܐܝܢܐ. ܐܝܟ ܗܘ ܕܐܡܢܝܢ. ܡܠܠܢܐ ܪܘܩܕܐ. ܡܠܠܢ ܡܠܠܢܐ܆. The form ܡܠܠܐ is not found in the lexica. It actually appears to be an agentive noun from the secondary verb ܡܠܠ, itself derived from an afʿel participle, which may be the basis for the neosyriac ܡܠܠܐ and yielding ܡܘܠܠܢ, which Stoddard and Nöldeke both take to be derived from the root ܐܠܠ.[xix]

This is what he states about the word ܬܘܕܝܬܐ (pl. ܬܘܕܝܬܐ): ܬܘܕܝܬܐ ܬܘܕܝܬܐ. ܐܝܟ ܡܢܗܘܢ ܠܐܘܪܐ. ܐܝܟ ܡܫܠܡܢܘܬܐ ܕܝܢ: ܬܘܕܝܬܐ ܣܒܪܐ ܬܘܕܝܬܐ ܗܟܢܐ. ܕ ܐܢܐ ܕܝܢ ܡܠܦܢܐ: ܘܡܫܠܡܢ ܗܢܘܢ ܕܬܘܕܝܬܐ ܘܬܘܕܝܬܐ ܠܟܣܢܐ ܐܝܟ ܣܒܪܐ. ܗ ܬܘܕܝܬܐ܆. So the Masoretic tradition had the forms ܬܘܕܝܬܐ and ܬܘܕܝܬܐ, but there was disagreement among the teachers on this. Bar Zuʿbi himself argues for the singular ܬܘܕܝܬܐ, plural ܬܘܕܝܬܐ, for this is what the 'canons' seem to require. In fact, ܬܘܕܝܬܐ is the correct singular form, while ܡܘܡܬܐ is formed on the pattern of ܡܫܟܢܬܐ, the *ay* of which has changed into *ā* (as ܡܢܬܐ from ܡܢܝܬܐ). In the plural, however, both the forms ܡܘܡ̈ܝܬܐ and ܡܘܡ̈ܬܐ are possible, although the first is not attested. In the Targum, the singular is מוֹמָתָא,[1] and in Syriac the syāmē on ܡܘܡܬܐ is false.

A list of nouns then follows (f.241b) from which I here offer a selection of those that might be useful for the future improvement of Syriac lexicons:

1) ܚܨܪܐ (*the lobe of the liver*) is a metaphorical term:[xx] ܡܛܠ ܕܡܟܝܢܐ ܕܡܬܩܪܐ ܕܟܒܕܐ. ܟܠܝܬܐ ܐܘ ܟܒܕܬܐ. Payne-Smith writes ܚܨܪܐ, but Bar ʿAlī |[175] agrees with Bar Zuʿbi and the Babylonian Targum has the construct form חֲצַר. To illustrate the metaphor, it would be useful to add here what Bar Zuʿbi earlier says (f.90a) about the location of the rational and affective faculties after discussing the senses: ܒܡܘܚܐ ܣܘܟܠܐ ܘܦܘܪܫܢܐ ܒܠܒܐ ܘܐܪܓܝܫܘܬܐ ܒܦܠܓܐ ܦܪܘܫܐ: ܘܕܝܢܐ ܒܟܘܠܝ̈ܬܐ ܘܪܓܬܐ ܒܚܨ̈ܐ: ܘܚܕܘܬܐ ܒܛܚܠܐ: ܘܟܡܝܪܘܬܐ ܒܚܨܪܐ ܕܟܒܕܐ: ܘܚܡܬܐ ܒܟܒܕܐ ܘܪܓܬ ܡܐܟܘܠܬܐ ܒܬܪܒܐ ܕܥܠ ܟܘܠܝ̈ܬܐ., i.e. *understanding in the brain, discrimination in the heart, thinking in the discerning part of the diaphragm, judgments in the kidneys, desire in the loins, joy in the spleen, depression in the lobe of the liver, anger in the liver, appetite in the fat around the kidneys.* This reflects an ancient tradition which has expanded over time. In the Old Testament, the heart and kidneys are the loci of understanding and of the affections, to which is added later that the liver (כָּבֵד, generally read now as כָּבוֹד) is the seat of pride (see LXX Gen 49.6, where כְּבֹדִי is rendered as τὰ ἥπατά μου, and Ps 7.6, 16.9 etc. where the modern interpretation by which this word somehow refers to the soul is inappropriate).

2) ܢܒܛܐ. ܐܘ ܠܒܘܫ ܠܒܛܐ. The *Lexicon Syriacum* of Castell and Michaelis has ܠܒܛܐ as meaning the liver, apparently by reading Bar ʿAlī's اللبد (*wool*) as الكبد (*liver*). Elias of Nisibis had it right (*a woollen coat*, see Novaria's *Thesaurus*, 206). In fact, it simply means a garment or covering (نَمَط), and the *n* has turned into *l*.

3) ܟܡܪ̈ܐ ܗ̈ܘ: ܚܩܠ̈ܐ ܕܚܕܪ ܡܕܝܢܬܐ = the plain surrounding a city.

4) ܢܟܝ̈ܐ ܗ̈ܘ: ܡܚܝܠܐ = crippled.

5) ܦܟܟ̈ܐ ܗ̈ܘ: ܙܘܙܐ = coin.

6) ܦܪܛ̈ܐ ܗ̈ܘ: ܦܛܝܣ ܢܚܝܪܐ = flat-nosed.[2] [xxi]

7) ܥܒܝܬܐ ܗܘ: ܙܒܢ ܟܡܘܫܐ = dense

---

[1] Cf. the glossary in my *Chrestomathia Targumica*, Porta Linguarum Orientalium 8 (Berlin, 1888), 211.

[2] From thence the adjective ܦܛܝܣܐ, which is Castell/Michaelis is ܦܛܝܣܐ.

8) ܓܪܓܪܐ ܗܘ: ܓܪܓܠܐ ܘܐܦ ܓܪܓܪܐ ܗܘ: ܐܝܠܢܐ ܪܒܐ = 1 pelvis, 2 a large tree, perhaps the willow.

9) ܦܗܝܐ ܗܘ: ܫܛܝܐ = stupid.[xxii]

10) |[176] ܙܒܪܐ ܐܠܘܐ ܝܠܘܦ = aloe

11) ܣܓܪܝܪܐ ܗܘ: ܝܘܡܐ ܕܡܛܪܐ ܕܒܗ ܡܣܓܪܝܢ ܣܓܝܪܐ. ܡܛܠ ܕܟܠܝܢ ܡܢ ܡܦܩܐ = a rainy day, *lit.* confinement.

12) ܐܪܙܐ. ܐܪܙܘܢܐ. ܘܐܝܟ ܕܐܡܪܝܢ ܐܝܠܐ ܪܒܐ ܕܚܙܐ ܕܬܘܪܐ, although I do not know what animal a ܬܘܪܚܐ is.[xxiii]

13) ܫܓܪܐ. ܐܝܟ ܠܘܙܐ ܘܐܦ ܡܬܩܪܐ ܫܓܪܐ... Something is missing from the gloss, which otherwise says that ܫܓܪܐ is a type of almond called a ܫܓܪܐ!

14) ܫܟܪܐ ܗܘ: ܚܡܪܐ ܕܡܬܥܒܕ ܡܢ ܚܛܐ ܐܘ ܡܢ ܬܡܪܐ ܘܚܙܘܪܐ ܦܩܘܥܐ = wine (or rather beer) made from wheat or from dates and bitter apples. This does not seem to be a gloss on the Hebrew שֵׁכָר, since in the neosyriac glossary I have found the word rendered into English as 'spirit of wine.'

15) ܚܘܪܐ ܗܘ: ܣܘܡܩ ܚܘܪ = whitey-red colour (cf. Payne-Smith, *Thesarus*, 603-4).

16) ܙܪܩܐ ܗܘ: ܦܝܣܬܩܐ. ܐܘ ܦܠܓܘܬܐ ܐܘ ܢܩܡܬܢ ܥܝܢܐ (cf. *ibid.*, 1154). ܫܚܘܡܐ corresponds to الشهل in Bar Bahlūl).

17) ܘܐܘܟܠܐ. ܘܐܦ ܩܘܠܠܐ ܡܬܐܡܪܐ: ܡܐܢܐ ܕܝܗܒܐ ܩܘܠܐ ܗܘ: ܡܐܢܐ ܡܥܒܕܐ ܕܢܚܫܐ. ܐܘ ܕܦܪܙܠܐ ܘܡܫܟܐ ܕܡܫܟܐ[1] ܗܘ ܕܡܫܟܐ ܠܡܫܟܐ = a vessel made of iron or bronze or of leather.

Then, after dealing with the suffixes on numerals, the vocalisation of foreign words (f.246b), and listing the forms of the imperatives with suffixes,[2] he goes on to give a rule about the ܡܗܓܝܢܐ, as follows: ܡܗܓܝܢܐ is found on any verb or noun whose third consonant is vowelless and which is called ܡܫܡܠܝܬܐ ܐܬܘܬܐ, i.e. ܐ ܪ ܗ ܘ ܢ ܝ ܠ ܡ ܥ. One ought therefore to write, ܫܚܪܘܗܝ, ܫܓܠܩܐ, ܫܓܠܓܐ, ܫܓܢܝܬܐ, ܫܪܡܩܬܐ, ܫܪܗܘܢ, ܫܟܢܘܢ, ܐܬܪܡܝܡ, ܐܬܪܡܝܬ. All words, however, |[177] whose [?third] consonant is not one of these, requires ܡܪܗܛܢܐ, as in ܐܬܟܪܝܘ, ܐܬܩܪܝܘ, ܪܘܩܒܐ. However, to these examples he adds ܝܩܦܬܐ, ܓܘܠܬܐ, ܫܒܩܘܗܝ. I cannot tell whether these should have had the ܡܪܗܛܢܐ on the third consonant. He does not fail to point out, however, that sometimes the ܡܪܗܛܢܐ is found in the Masoretic tradition (ܐܝܟ ܡܫܠܡܢܘܬܐ) where this rule ought to specify a ܡܗܓܝܢܐ, e.g. ܫܒܩܬܝܢܝ, ܡܪܢܝܬܐ, ܐܦܪܣܘܗܝ, ܙܪܩܘܗܝ, ܐܬܪܩܘܗܝ etc. But then the usage of the schools does differ on this matter.[3] This brings to a close all that is of real

[1] The ms has ܡܫܟܐ.

[2] The forms he lists are: ܩܪܝܢܝ, ܩܪܝܘܗܝ, ܩܪܝܗ; ܦܩܘܕܝܢܝ, ܦܩܘܕܝܘܗܝ, ܦܩܘܕܝܗ ; ܐܬܦܩܕܝܢܝ, ܐܬܦܩܕܝܘܗܝ, ܐܬܦܩܕܝܗ ; ܐܫܬܠܛܝܢܝ, ܐܫܬܠܛܝܘܗܝ, ܐܫܬܠܛܝܗ ; ܫܡܠܝܢܝ etc.

[3] See Barhebraeus, *Gramm.*, 200.

importance in Bar Zuʿbi, the teacher of Jacob Bar Šakko, to whose work we shall turn next.

---

[i] For mss of the metrical grammar, *GSL*, 311n1.

[ii] For the larger, prose *Grammar*, Merx has made use principally of BL Add. 25876 (Wright, *Cat.* III,1175). There are others extant (*GSL*, 310n12), also Paris Syr 426. A projected edition by Bohas and Contini has not yet been published.

[iii] ὄνομα μὲν οὖν ἐστὶ φωνὴ σηματικὴ κατὰ συνθήκην, ἄνευ χρόνου, ἧς μηδὲν μέρος ἐστὶ σημαντικὸν κεχωρισμένον.

[iv] ψόφος μέν ἐστι πληγὴ ἀέρος αἰσθητὴ ἀκοῇ, φωνὴ δὲ ψόφος ἐμψύχου γινόμενος ὅταν διὰ τῆς συστολῆς τοῦ θώρακος ἐκθλιβόμενος ἀπὸ τοῦ πνεύμονος ὁ εἰσπνευθεὶς ἀὴρ προσπίπτῃ ἀθρόως τῇ τε τραχείᾳ καλουμένῃ ἀρτηρίᾳ καὶ τῇ ὑπερῴᾳ ἤτοι τῷ γαργαρεῶνι. This is the passage taken directly from Ammonius. I have corrected Merx's text according to the more recent edition (Busse, *Ammonius De Int.*, 30,8-11). The second half of the citation is from Probus alone, as referenced.

[v] This important ms for grammatical studies is now numbered as Berlin Syr 88 (Sachau, *Verzeichniss*, 321ff.).

[vi] On the Aristotelian list and its influence on Semitic grammar, see Revell, *Aristotle*.

[vii] These nine are of course taken from the Aristotelian categories, excepting the first, which is not an accident.

[viii] More likely in the sixth century, in fact (Hugonnard-Roche, *La Logique d'Aristote*, 276).

[ix] On the significance of the choice of terms here see H. Hugonnard-Roche, "Du commentaire à la reconstruction: Paul le Perse interprète d'Aristote," in *Interpreting the Bible and Aristotle*, J. W. Watt & J. Lössl eds. (Ashgate, 2011); and following this, D. King, "Grammar and Logic in Syriac (and Arabic)," *Journal of Semitic Studies* 58 (2013), 101-120.

[x] This is an important point. The notion of the root was incorporated into Syriac grammar by Barhebraeus. It has recently been argued that Bar Zuʿbi's approach is perhaps better suited to the characteristics of Syriac—G. Bohas, "Sur l'hypothèse de la racine triconsonantique en syriaque," *Langues et littératures du monde arabe* 5 (2004), 135-158 (see also following endnote).

[xi] There is now an excellent and detailed study (including the texts with translation) of how Bar Zuʿbi has adapted Dionysius's section on the verb to the characteristics of Syriac—G. Bohas, "Les accidents du verbe dans la grammaire de Bar Zoʿbi ou, une adaptation de la *Techne*," *Langues et littératures du monde arabe* 4 (2003), 55-86. In another article, Bohas analyses the way in which Bar Zuʿbi does indeed successfully organise the verbs based on a system of concrete radicals rather than on the notion of the triliteral root (see previous endnote)–"Radical ou racine/schème, l'organisation de la conjugaison syriaque avant l'adoption de la racine," *Le Muséon* 116 (2003), 343-376.

[xii] πρόθεσίς ἐστι λέξις προτιθέμενη πάντων τῶν τοῦ λόγου μερῶν ἔν τε συνθέσει καὶ συντάξει. Dionysius Thrax (Uhlig ed.), 70.

---

xiii παραπληρωματικοὶ δέ εἰσιν, ὅσοι μέτρου ἢ κόσμου ἕνεκεν παραλαμβάνονται. εἰσὶ δὲ οἵδε· δή, ῥά, νύ, ποῦ, τοί, θήν, ἄρ, δῆτα, πέρ, πώ, μήν, ἄν, αὖ, οὖν, κέν, γέ (Uhlig, 96-100).

xiv Dionysius Thrax's adverbial types (which should be compared to those of the Syriac translator of Dionysius given above, ch.2) are: ἐπιρρήματα χρόνου, μεσότητος, ποιότητος, ποσότητος, ἀριθμοῦ, τοπικά, εὐχῆς, [σχετλιαστικά=complaint is missing from Merx's list], ἀρνήσεως,συγκαταθέσεως, ἀπαγορευσεως, παραβολῆς, θαυμαστικά, εἰκασμοῦ, τάξεως, ἀθροίσεως, παρακελεύσεως, συγκρίσεως, ἐρωτήσεως, ἐπιτάσεως, συλλήψεως, ἀπομωτικά, κατομωτικά, θετικά, βεβαιώσεως, θειασμοῦ, planctus (on the last see Merx's footnote).

xv The conjunction types are: συμπλεκτικοί, διαζευκτικοί, συναπτικοί, παρασυναπτικοί, αἰτιολογικοί,

παραπληρωματικοί, ἐναντιωματικοί. The 'questioning' (ἀπορρηματικοί) and 'syllogistic' (συλλογιστικοί) types have been omitted.

xvi I think Merx simply means that Barhebraeus did not transmit the same data about these two particles as Bar Zuʿbi, for he certainly mentions them (*Gram.*, 182,7f.; 183,18), with some interesting remarks. The references in Brockelmann (including Sokoloff's re-edition) are incorrect. See also Nöldeke's remarks about ܐܝܗܐ, meaning 'shame on you' (Review, 1217).

xvii A. Mingana, ed., *Narsai Doctoris Syri Homiliae et Carmina* (Mosul, 1905), I, 348,8-10 (Memra XXI). I have translated the passage as Merx took it—Nöldeke (Review, 1217) reads the word here as ܡܠܝܐ (*flood*); Connolly's translation takes it as ܡ̈ܠܐ (*words*). Bar Bahlūl also mentions this conjunction (1085:21)—see Sokoloff, *A Syriac Lexicon*, sub loc.

xviii Merx only really discusses Bar Zuʿbi's section on the vowels. The theories of aspiration have, however, received an important recent study in G. Bohas, *Les bgdkpt en syriaque* (Toulouse, 2005).

xix Nöldeke (Review, 1219) calls this a strange conjecture. The form is really quite normal.

xx If the East Syrian practice of writing short zqafa for ptaḥa was used, then ܚܙܪ may have been written for ܚܙܪ (as Payne-Smith has it), and from this would have arisen the false form ܚܙܪܐ (Nöldeke, Review, 1217).

xxi Again, Nöldeke (ibid.) suggests ܗܢܡ became ܗܢܡ and hence the false form ܗܢܡܐ.

xxii Perhaps for ܦܗܩܐ by the same procedure (ibid.).

xxiii According to Brockelmann, it is the *capra caucasica* (mountain goat)–cf. Landsberger's *Die Fauna des alten Mesopotamien* (Leipzig, 1934), 94.

Appendix I

THREE TREATISES ON EAST SYRIAN ACCENTUATION

In the foregoing chapters, we have been led to the firm conclusion that Syriac accentuation was invented, or at least developed from the basics, by Joseph Huzaya before being systematised in different ways among the different schools. In places we could see three different Western systems existing side-by-side (p.99), which differed yet again from the East Syrian system. Both Elias of Ṭirhan and the colophon to BL Add. 12138 (dated 899, Wright, *Cat.*, 105b) indicate that among the Easterns there were several differing modes of recitation. We earlier made use of this colophon (p.30) to show that the ancient school differed from that of Rabban Ramišoʿ. But the scribe who wrote the colophon, Babai the deacon, was far from approving of the readings of the older schools, for he used his own critical signs to indicate which of them should be accepted and which rejected. The readings of the ܡܕܪܫܬܐ were used as the fundamental layer and basis for everything else. To these he added further readings marked by colours to indicate whether they were good or bad. In using this particular approach, Babai followed the lead of Ramišoʿ himself, who used to place a red line over his own readings so that these could be readily distinguished from those of the older masters. From the critical signs in this ms we can thus learn what was the scribe's own judgment on the value of the older readings, since he distinguishes readings which are not in the ܡܕܪܫܬܐ but which are still good, from those which *are* in the ܡܕܪܫܬܐ but which are bad. He further adds readings which should be adopted for ease of reading, and he even lists certain alternative readings which are left open to the judgment of the individual reader. What he says at the very end has to do with the curriculum that was developed in the schools and is worth transcribing:

ܟܕ ܕܝܢ ܐܦ ܗܘܐ. ܕܟܠ ܦܣܘܩܐ ܕܦܢܩܝܬܐ ܐܝܟ ܐܝ ܡܕܪܫܬܐ ܘܠܐ ܩܪܝܢܐ [178]| ܘܠܐ ܡܦܫܩܢܐ ܘܠܐ ܪܫܡܐ. ܘܦܫܩܬܐ ܕܟܠ ܦܣܘܩܐ ܕܦܢܩܝܬܐ ܐܝܟ ܐܘܚܕܢܐ ܐܬܪܝܐ. ܘܠܐ ܡܩܪܝܢܘܬܐ ܐܝܟ ܕܕܪܫܢ ܘܡܫܡܥܝܢ ܐܚܪܢ. ܒܩܠܝܬܐ ܕܝܢ ܕܡܕܪܫܬܐ ܟܠܗ ܐܚܪܢ.

ܘܐܠܘ ܟܕ ܕܩܠܝܬܐ ܕܡܕܪܫܬܐ ܗܢܘܢ ܐܢܘܢ ܕܐܬܟܬܒ ܡܢ ܩܕܝܡ ܕܢܗܘܐ [ܢܗܘܘܢ] ܘܕܐܬܪܫܡ ܘܡܫܚ. ܘܟܘܠܗܘܢ ܡܦܪܫ ܒܐܫܟܘܠܐ.

ܘܐܦ ܦܣܩܝܢ ܐܝܬ ܒܟܬܒܐ ܕܡܬܩܪܝܢ ܒܙܘܓܐ ܒܟܠܗܘܢ ܡܩܪܝܢܐ ܡܢܗ. ܐܡܬܝ ܕܝܢ ܕܐܫܬܠܡ ܦܬܐ ܐܝܬ. ܗܘ
ܡܩܪܝܢܐ ܕܫܘܐܠ ܐܬܒܢܝܘܗܝ ܗܘܝܐ ܘܐܦ ܐܝܬ ܢܩܪܐ ܕܐܝܬ ܒܗܘܢ ܫܡܥܐ ܕܐܝܬ ܦܩܘܕܐ ܘܢܩܪܐ. ܡܢܗ ܡܦܩܬܐ ܒܦܩܘܕܐ
ܫܡܥܐ ܒܟܬܒܘܗܝ. ܘܒܕ ܠܐ ܪܒܐ ܐܝܬ: ܕܐܡܪܐ ܦܩܘܕܐ ܐܟܪܙ ܢܩܪܐ ܘܡܢܗ. ܘܟܠ ܐܡܬܝ ܕܐܝܬ ܒܢܩܪܐ[1] ܐܡܪ ܐܘ ܐܡܪ ܐܘ
ܐܡܪܝܢ: ܢܩܪܐ ܗܘ ܒܗ ܡܙܕܩ. ܘܢܬܡܪܐ ܒܟܠܗ ܚܕ.

ܘܗܘܐ ܐܬܬܩܢ ܣܓܝܐ ܕܒܟܬܒܐ ܩܕܡܝܐ ܐܣܟܘܠܝܐ ܡܢܗ ܡܢܗ ܘܠܐ ܠܐܘܡܢܐ ܢܗܘܐ ܗܘ ܚܢܢ ܠܘ ܐܠܦܝܢ ܢܗܘܐ ܒܫܡܥܐ ܡܫܡܗ. ܘܢܣܒܐ ܕܐܬܚܫܒܬܐ ܡܪܟܢܐ. ܘܡܢܐ ܕܐܬܦܣܩܬܐ ܣܦܝܩ. ܘܗܘܐ ܕܒܡܓܪܫܐ ܫܪܟܐ ܡܠܬܢܝܬܐ ܘܡܬܢܪܝܢ.

The first part of this essentially means that all accents and marks that are written in the manuscript in red, including ܡܩܪ̈ܝܢܐ, ܙܘܓܐ, ܡܫܡ̈ܫܢܐ, ܦ̈ܣܩܐ etc., whether they are letters (ܐܬ̈ܘܬܐ) or signs indicating pronunciation (ܡܪ̈ܟܢܬܐ), all these were added by Ramišoʿ and are not found in the books of the older masters, the ܡܦܫ̈ܩܢܐ. These latter were the books written for the instruction of students in the schools from the time of Narsai,[2] Abraham of Beth Rabban, and John of Beth Rabban.

He then goes on to give a few extra rules which are unclear to us since we can never hear the precise intonations; they can be summarised as follows: 1) phrases accented in the book with ܚܪܝܢܐ should be read as ܡܩܪܝܢܐ; 2) where ܬܚܬܝܐ is pronounced, the ܡܩܪܝܢܐ that is marked with a small line should be omitted; |[179] 3) in phrases in which ܢܩܪܐ and ܦܩܘܕܐ appear together: first of all ܫܡܥܐ alone is to be read in the imperative clause and then, if the reader wants to pronounce the ܦܩܘܕܐ (i.e. the phrase marked by the imperative accent), then he must omit the ܢܩܪܐ. But where 'he said', 'he says', 'they say' etc. is found after the ܢܩܪܐ, then the ܢܩܪܐ is correct and should be pronounced according to its own intonation—such is the rule of Ramišoʿ.[3]

He next gives us the famous saying from the schools about accents: "you should read and re-read [it], and not ignore [it], for what has been written is like a light for you, a light that lightens the shadows, a brightness that makes the blackness useful, it is like life hiding in the midst of the elements (i.e. the letters), reason ensnared and caught in a web of notations."

We saw earlier how this system of teaching the art of reading made use of the accents—of the temporal accents for recitation that was 'in time', and mimetic accents for rhetorical recitation (ὑπόκρισις). Such an art could only be learned from the live delivery of a master while a student took notes. The accents themselves had to be chosen in accordance with the

[1] Cf. Treatise II,40. After a verb of speaking, ܢܩܪܐ is needed. ܡܪܝܐ is for κύριον.

[2] The name is erased in the ms, but supplied by Wright.

[3] Cf. Barhebraeus, *Gramm.*, 259.

sense and they had been thus chosen by the masters of old. It was different from how this happened in the case of Hebrew (p.72n above), where the accents simply arose out of musical composition. Hence the Syrians have no absolute rules for the sequence of accents in a sentence, which rather depends upon the particular needs of the passage. This is why the various combinations could not be taught by absolute rules but had to be illustrated by examples.

The older masters began by gathering collections of such examples, and these collections were then altered, expanded, or glossed by commentaries. A late instance of such a commentary was that of Bar Zuʿbi (p.165 above), which attempted to bring the whole subject under the remit of philosophical axioms. We provided another specimen of one earlier (p.125) and the two treatises from the Petermann codex[1] which are reproduced below are of the same type. In the second treatise, each paragraph is marked with an Arabic numeral and these correspond to their equivalents in the first treatise, so that the reader may see how the earlier has been both augmented and repeated in the later. However, there are also some things in the first that are missing in the second, and so Roman numerals have been used to mark those paragraphs in the first treatise which are omitted from the second. Because there was no absolute rule about the sequence of the accents, the writers of the treatises were able to take liberties in their selections. We shall show below that the third treatise is in fact a short work by Elias of Ṭirhan in which he tries to rationalise the system. He numbered the accents at thirty.[2] Since the previous two treatises were only selective and did not |[180] include all thirty, we cannot tell what was the total number of accents in their respective systems. We should similarly conclude that the list of eighteen accents which Ewald published from a Vatican ms is not quite complete.[3]

The following are the accents listed in the two treatises (I have marked with [EW] those which are also found in Ewald's list; simple numerals refer to Elias's catalogue given on p.197-200 above):

---

[1] The ms Berlin Petermann 9 was written in 1571 (Gr.), which is AD1258/9. Our second treatise belongs to this period. The script of the first treatise is in a different hand and is to be dated earlier; the vellum betrays its greater age by its blackness and its brittleness.

[2] Joseph Huzaya devised 10, Thomas the Deacon 24, Jacob of Edessa 36.

[3] H. Ewald, "Weitre Erläuterungen der syrischen Punctation, aus syrischen Handschriften" *Zeitschrift für die Kunde des Morgenlandes* 1 (1837), 204-212.

1) ܒܥܘܬܐ, 3 cf. ܪܗܛܐ ܒܥܘܬܐ I,50.
2) ܪܗܛܐ ܥܠܝܐ 2.
3) ܪܗܛܐ ܢܝܚܐ 3, which is also ܡܦܝܣܢܐ II,22; I,50.[EW]
4) ܡܙܝܥܢܐ 8.[EW]
5) ܡܢܝܚܬܐ 28.
6) ܡܢܝܚܢܐ 27.
7) ܡܫܟܢܐ 29.
8) ܡܩܝܡܢܐ 23.[EW]
9) ܡܥܠܝܢܐ 20.
10) ܡܬܟܫܦܢܘܬܐ II,20.
11) ܡܬܒܝܢܢܐ or ܡܒܝܢܢܐ 26.
12) ܡܬܟܫܦܢܐ II,30; I,XIV.[EW]
13) ܢܩܐ 11; I, XVIII.
14) ܢܩܕܐ 16.[EW]
15) ܣܡܟܐ 12 (ܣܡܟܐ ܕܐܝܟ ܬܚܘܬܐ ܕܥܠܝܐ I,24).[EW]
16) ܥܠܝܐ 5.[EW]
17) ܥܨܝܐ I, IX.
18) ܥܨܝܨܐ 14; I, XXVII, XXII.[EW]
19) ܥܨܝܢ I, VII.
20) ܦܣܘܩܐ 19.[EW]
21) ܙܘܓܐ ܕܦܬܐ 18.
22) ܙܘܓܐ ܕܠܐ ܦܣܘܩ 17.[EW]
23) ܪܘܡܐ 10, which is the same as the ܪܘܚܐ of the Westerns.[1]
24) ܐܬܢܚܬܐ 7.[EW]
25) ܐܬܢܚܬܐ ܕܥܠܬܐ I, VI.

|[181] Beyond these Ewald also has ܢܨܘܪܐ, ܬܚܘܬܐ, ܦ̈ܬܐ, ܕܦܣܘܩ, ܙܘܓܐ, ܐܬܠܐ ܦܣܘܩ, ܥܠܐ: (which our texts seem to call ܪܗܛܐ ܥܠܝܐ), and ܪܗܛܐ ܕܦܣܘܩ:. The last of these uses the same form as the accent that our texts call ܡܩܝܡܢܐ. The ܙܘܓܐ ܕܦܬܐ may lie behind the ܦܬܐ.

Since there are twenty five accents in these treatises, it seems very likely that the system set forth in the third treatise is that of Elias of Ṭirhan. Some of his list of thirty were accidentally never included in the examples, or else they were there originally and were later omitted. We can, however, conclude that this third treatise does definitely belong to Elias of Ṭirhan on the basis of the following citation in Bar Zuʿbi.

At the end of his section on accents (part of which we produced earlier, p.165), Bar Zuʿbi says:

[1] Barhebraeus, *Gramm.*, 258.

ܫܘܝܐ ܡܚܝܠܐ ܠܡܦܪܫܘ ܢܡܘܣܘܗܝ: ܕܦܘܣܩܐ ܕܢܩܙܐ ܙܘܓܐ: ܒܓܒܝܐ[1] ܕܥܡ ܐܢܘܢ ܡܩܝܡܐ ܡܢܗ ܠܟܠܐ ܡܬܘܟܠܐ ܦܝܘܪܘܬܗ. ܟܕ ܠܐ ܡܬܘܣܦܝܢ ܘܠܐ ܡܬܒܨܪܝܢ ܡܕܡ ܒܗܘܢ: ܘܠܡܕܝܢܘ ܐܢܘܢ ܡܢ ܐܬܪܘܬܗܘܢ ܕܒܝܬ ܩܦܘܗ. ܘܐܦ ܠܢ ܗܟܝܠ ܕܢܥܡܐ ܥܩܪܐ ܕܦܘܣܩܐ. ܕܟܠܗܘܢ ܐܬܬܐܡܪܘ ܚܕ ܚܕ ܡܢܗܘܢ ܒܥܩܪܐ ܗܟܢ܆ ܐ ܪܗܛܐ....

If indeed Bar Zuʿbi is copying Elias here, neither adding not omitting anything, then Elias's text must have begun with the words ܘܐܦ ܠܢ ܗܟܝܠ, which are the exact words with which the second part of our third treatise opens (p.197,17 below); and if this second part, which consists of an etymological explanation of nouns, must therefore be attributed to Elias, then presumably the whole of this text as we have it in the Petermann ms is his work, and hence both the works on this subject, one by Elias the master, the other by Bar Zuʿbi the pupil, have been preserved for us. We can see from an example how the latter develops the work of the former. Elias says, ܠ. ܫܘܝܐ ܘܡܕܡܝܢܐ ܙܘܓܐ. ܠܫܒܘܩܐ ܕܪܗܛܐ ܘܬܚܬܝܐ., and Bar Zuʿbi has, ܫܘܝܐ ܘܡܕܡܝܢܐ ܡܢ. ܙܘܓܐ: ܣܚܦ ܪܗܛܐ ܘܬܚܬܝܐ ܡܬܬܐܡܪܝܢ ܐܝܟ ܕܐܡܪ ܡܢܗ ܠܟܠܐ ܡܬܘܟܠܐ. Elias continues, ܡܕܡܝܢܐ. ܙܘܓܐ ܡܬܬܐܡܪܝܢ ܟܕ ܪܚܝܩܝܢ ܠܡܕܝܢܘ ܠܡܬܐܡܪܘ ܐܝܟ ܕܠܡܫܘܕܥܐ ܬܚܬܝܐ, |[182] in which Bar Zuʿbi simply substitutes ܡܬܐܡܪܐ for ܡܬܬܐܡܪܝܢ.[2]

Besides this persistent care with which he treats Elias, he also adds a collection of biblical citations. As we mentioned before, however, there is one big difference between them. Bar Zuʿbi strives to elucidate the accentual system on a philosophical basis and thereby to establish it as a firm science (cf. what he says on ܦܣܘܩܐ, p.166). In so doing he was developing, and attempting to perfect, what Elias had begun. The latter's work, however, was very far from the sort of thoroughgoing and exhaustive treatment that we see in Bar Zuʿbi.[3]

Finally, I must note that the term 'servile accents' (ܡܫܡܫܢܐ), which we know from the writers on Hebrew accentuation, was used also by the Syrians, since it is said that ܙܘܓܐ are the servants of the accents ܪܗܛܐ, ܥܠܝܐ, and ܬܚܬܝܐ (III,ܘ).[4] The phrases ܬܚܬܝܐ ܕܙܘܓܐ̈ (II,43); ܙܘܓܐ ܕܪܗܛܐ (41); ܡܕܡܝܢܐ ܕܙܘܓܐ̈ (19); and ܡܕܡܝܢܐ ܕܪ̈ܗܛܐ (42) have to be understood as 'the ܬܚܬܝܐ that is placed after

---

[1] The ms has ܒܒܓܒܝܐ. Martin, *Accentuation*, 19, emended to ܒܗ ܒܓܒܝܐ, but I would conjecture ܒܓܒܝܘܬܐ.

[2] Cf. Martin, *Accentuation*, 12,16.

[3] Phillips was the first to make a note of Elias's treatise (*Letter*, 85). He believed that Elias had written two such treatises, though we can now see that these are actually two parts of a single work.

[4] As an example I quote from Bar Zuʿbi: ܡܫܡܫ ܡܬܐܡܪܐ ܦܣܘܩܐ ܡܢ ܩܕܡ ܠܟܠܐ ܡܬܐܡܪܐ ܕܙܘܓܐ. ܗ̈: ܪܗܛܐ ܘܬܚܬܝܐ ܘܥܠܝܐ. ܘܩܕܡ ܠܟܠܐ ܡܫܡܫܢܐ ܐܢܘܢ ܕܦܣܘܩܐ. ܘܗܢܘܢ ܡܫܬܡܫܢܐ ܕܡܢܗܘܢ. ܐܝܬ ܠܗ ܗܘ ܠܗܘ ܡܫܡܫܢܐ ܐܚܪܢܐ ܐܝܟ ܡܕܡܝܢܐ ܘܡܩܫܢܐ ܘܙܘܓܐ̈ ܘܡܨܡܨܢܐ (BL Add. 25876, f.156b).

the ܬܚܬܝܐ' ; 'the ܬܚܬܝܐ before the ܙܘܓܐ' etc., such that the ܕ shows that there is some relation between the accents mentioned without defining specifically what that relationship is. For in ܕܬܚܬܝܐ ܥܠܝܐ, the ܥܠܝܐ comes *after* the ܬܚܬܝܐ, but in ܕܙܘܓܐ ܬܚܬܝܐ, the ܬܚܬܝܐ comes *before* the ܙܘܓܐ.

Those accents mentioned by Elias but which do not appear in the two treatises are: 1 ܐ̄. ܙܘܓܐ ܡܫܡܫܢܐ; 2 ܒ̄. ܙܘܓܐ ܕܟܘܡܐ; 3 ܓ̄. ܡܩܪܝܢܐ ܙܥܘܪܐ; 4 ܕ̄. ܫܡܫܢܐ ܕܐܡܪܐ; 5 ܗ̄. ܦܩܘܕܐ; 6 ܘ̄. ܦܩܘܕܐ ܕܐܬܠܐ; 7 ܙ̄. ܦܠܓܘܬܐ ܡܫܡܫܢܐ; 8 ܚ̄. ܡܠܘܐܐ.

In the Petermann ms there are no vowel markings on the names of the accents. I have added them on the basis of the text in BL Add. 25876 just as they were pronounced by Bar Zuʿbi.

|183

There is no need to make a comparison of the East Syrian accentual system with that of the Westerns, since readers can compare the system of the latter which we carefully set out earlier (p.99ff.).[i]

Text I – Catalogue of Accents according to the East Syrian teaching

Berlin Sachau 88 (Petermann 9), f.228b-230a

ܬܘܒ ܒܥܘܕܪܢܐ ܕܡܫܝܚܘܬܗ ܕܐܠܗܐ ܫܪܝܬ ܥܠ ܦܘܫܩ ܐܢܐ. ܦܘܫܩܐ
ܕܐܝܟ ܒܕܘܟܐ ܚܕܐ

1 ܡܦܩܢܐ ܬܚܬܝܐ ܦܣܩܐ ܘܬܪܬܝܢ ܐܚܪܢܐ ܡܢ ܩܕܡ. ܢܝܚܐ ܕܢܕܝܐ.
ܘܡܫܡܫܢܐ ܡܫܡܠܝܢ.

I ܡܙܝܥܢܐ ܘܬܪܬܝܢ ܐܚܪܢܐ ܠܚܣܝܘܬ ܫܘܐܠܐ ܕܫܟܝܚܐ. ܘܡܫܠܡ ܢܛܪܐ
ܡܠܟܐ ܕܪܘܡܐ. ܠܘ ܢܣܬܟܠܘܢ ܘܢܬܪܚܡܘܢ ܚܕ ܡܢ ܚܒܪܐ.

3 ܦܩܘܕܐ ܘܬܚܬܝܐ ܩܠܐ ܩܕܡ ܐܢܬ ܗܘ ܐܠܗܐ. ܩܠܐ ܢܚܬ ܩܕܡܘܗܝ.
ܩܠܐ ܐܢܬ ܗܘܝܬ ܩܕܡ. ܠܦܠܚܝܢ ܐܬܦܩܕ. ܕܩܢܝܐ ܐܢܬ ܒܫܡܝܐ.

6 ܦܩܘܕܐ ܘܡܫܡܫܢܐ ܘܬܪܬܝܢ ܘܐܡܪܝܢ ܥܠܝܗ ܡܢܐ ܠܐܦܐ. ܘܢܐܡܪܘܢ
ܐܦܐ ܗܘ ܚܕܐ. ܘܢܐܡܪܘܢ ܗܘܘ ܠܗ ܠܡܐ ܕܡܛܠ ܠܒܘܗܝ.

4 ܦܩܘܕܐ ܘܡܫܡܫܢܐ. ܩܘܡ ܐܬܩܪܒ ܐܢܐ ܥܡ ܫܠܝܛ. ܩܪܝܬ ܐܢܐ ܠܟܠ
ܫܘܐ. ܩܕܡ ܐܢܬ ܠܦܘܩܕܢ[?]

35 ܬܚܬܝܐ ܘܙܘܓ(1)ܐܦܝܐ ܘܣܒܪ ܐܢܫܝܐ ܥܠܘܗܝ ܘܐܡܪܝܢ. ܘܩܝܡ ܒܪܩܢܐ:
ܘܐܡܪܝܢ. 9a ܐܝܟ ܐܢܫܐ.. ܘܠܐ ܬܬܐܡܪ ܠܟܘܢ ܡܢ (2)ܢܡܘܣܐ.
ܘܟܠܗܘܢ ܒܢܝܐ ܢܬܐܡܪܘܢ.

8 ܬܚܬܝܐ ܦܣܩܐ ܐܝܟ ܡܬܚܙܝܢ ܐܝܟܐ. ܘܟܕ ܐܬܝܠܕ. ܢܩܘܫ ܦܩܘܕ
ܬܘܬܒܐ.

9 ܡܙܝܥܢܐ ܘܬܚܬܝܐ ܕܠܐ ܐܬܐ ܠܡܫܬܐܘܪܘ. ܘܢܦܫ ܘܦܫܩ ܐܪܥܗ. Jes. 28,24.

1) I do not understand this word

2) ܢܡܘܣܐ?

9b ܫܐܠܐ ܥܢܝܢܐ ܕܚܕ ܥܡܐ. ܦܬܚ. ܦܬܚ. ܦܬܚ. ܐܬܪܘܡ. ܝܬܘܪ.

12 ܦܩܘܕܐ ܘܫܐܠܐ ܐܝܟ ܡܬܟܠܢܐ ([1] ܡܪܓܫ ܐܢܬ ܠܗ ܐܝܟ ܩܡܨܐ. ܐܢܬ
ܠܟ ܕܪܥܐ ܐܝܟ ܐܠܗܐ.

13 ܡܬܒܥܝܢܐ ܘܡܪܟܢܐ ܘܫܐܠܐ ܦܬܚܐ ܐܝܟ ܒܠܒܘ ܕܝܫܘܥ
ܕܒܝܬܐ ܠܥܠ.

II ܡܪܟܢܐ ܘܦܩܘܕܐ ܕܡܬܟܠܢܐ ܘܫܐܠܐ. ܐܡܪ ܠܗ ܡܠܟܐ܇ ܐܠܝܬ ܒܥܠܡ.
ܠܥܡܐ ܕܪܚܡ ܒܫܡܝ ܗܘ ܕܐܙܕܩܦ. ܘܐܡܪܝܢ ܐܢܫܝܢ ([2] ܕܐܠܗܐ ܗܢܘܢ
ܐܒܪܗܡ. ܗܕܐ ܡܬܩܪܝܐ ܘܫܐܠܐ. (Cf. 16)

14 ܦܩܘܕܐ ܡܬܩܢܝܢܐ ܘܬܘܟܐ ܐܝܟ ܐܝܕܐ: ܠܝ ܐܝܟ ܒܝܬܐ ܕܒܟܝܢ
ܠܗܘܢ ܒܪܗ ܘܫܒܩܗ.

III ([3] ܡܪܟܢܐ ܘܫܐܠܐ ܐܠܐ ܬܬܒܝܠ ܠܟܘܢ. ܐܠܐ ܬܬܥܠܝܢ ܠܟܘܢ. ܗܘ
ܐܝܟ ܡܪܝܗ ܠܝ. [P. 125 hi accentus ܦܩܘܕܐ ܘܫܐܠܐ dicuntur]

17 ܦܩܘܕܐ ܘܫܐܠܐ ܐܝܟ ܡܬܟܠܢܐ ([4] ܐܝܬܘ ܩܪܒܘ ܕܢܦܫܟ ܐܢܬܘ
ܚܘܪ.

18 ܫܐܠܐ ܕܡܪܟܢܐ ܡܢܘ ܕܝܢ ܗܢܐ ܕܟܐ ܠܗ ܚܘܒ.

20 ܡܬܟܡܠܢܐ ܘܐܡܝܢ܇ ܡܠܟܬܐ܇ ܕܬܝܡܢܐ ܕܫܠܝܡܘܢ. ܩܡܬ ܡܠܟܬܐ
ܚܙܬ ܠܡܠܟܐ܇ ܫܠܝܡܘܢ. ܕܐܬܬ܇ ܡܢ ܥܒܪܘܗܝ ܕܐܪܥܐ܇ ܕܬܫܡܥ
ܚܟܡܬܗ ܕܫܠܝܡܘܢ. [Matth. 12, 42]

1) The examples are taken from Job 39.20; 40.9, just as II,12 ܘܪܓܫ ܐܢܬ ܚܝܠܐ ܐܠܗܐ (Job 40.9), where the Peshiṭta has ܘܪܓܫ.

2) A second hand has used black ink to correct to ܗܘܢ܇ܐ.

3) This accent ܡܪܟܢܐ, when it attaches to the first letter, ought rightly to be placed between the words, hence ܐܠܐ· ܬܬܒܝܠ and ܐܠܐ· ܬܬܥܠܝܢ. Thus also more correctly ܗܘ· rather than ܗܘܐ.

4) The word is hard to read and the reading not certain. In any case, this paragraph has already been given above (no.12) with the same heading but different examples.

ܐܠܐ ܐܝܟܢܐ ܕܚܕ ܡܫܡܠܝܐ. ܒܡܠܬܐ ܗܘ. ܒܫܡܐ ܗܘ. ܘܒܡܠܬܐ ܠܡܢܝܢܐ.

IV ܐܘܟܝܬ ܒܟܠܐ ܘܡܫܡܠܝܐ ܘܡܫܡܠܝܬܐ ܐܝܟ ܒܫܡܐ ܕܡܫܡܠ ܫܡܗܐ ܕܫܡܐ
ܘܫܡܗܘ. ܠܐ ܢܦܩ ܐܠܐ: ܕܒܠܐ ܐܝܬ [1] ܒܫܡܗܘ [2] ܕܐܠܦܝ. ܠܐ ܬܘܚܕ
ܕܫܡܐ ܕܐܠܦܝ ܗܘܝܢ.

V ܡܫܡܠܝܐ ܘܗܘܐ ܒܟܠܐ ܘܡܫܡܠܝܬܐ ܠܐ. ܬܩܢܝܢ ܦܬܓܡܐ ܡܫܡܠܝܢ ܠܡܦܩ:
ܡܛܠ ܐܠܐ. ܡܢ ܒܬܪ ܐܝܢܐ ܕܗܘܐ ܦܬܓܡܐ ܘܢܦܩ ܐܠܐ. ܕܫܡܐ ܒܫܡܐ.
ܠܐ ܢܦܩ ܐܝܬ ܕܐܠܦܐ ܒܗ ܡܬܝܕܥ.

ܐܠܐ ܐܝܟܢܐ ܬܩܢܝܢ ܐܘܟܝܬ ܟܠܗܐ ܘܡܫܡܠܝܐ ܡܢ ܒܬܪ ܕܒܠܝܐ: ܗܘܐ ܠܗ
ܠܡܫܘܠܝܐ: ܘܦܬܓܡ ܡܠܬܐ.

VI ܬܡܢܝܐ ܕܬܠܬܐ. ܫܘܠܫܐ. ܡܠܬܐ ܕܫܘܬܠܦܐ. [Cf. p. 126]

VII ܒܪܢܫܐ ܐܝܟ ܫܘܬܦ ܗܦܟ ܗܘܝܢ: ܘܬܠܚܡ ܡܢܗ ܡܬܕܡܪܢܐ ܕܫܡܐ:
ܐܦܢܐ ܘܦܬܓ ܐܠܐ: ܐܝܟ ܠܟܦ ܬܠܬܐ: [3] ܕܫܘܘܝܢ ܡܫܡܠܝܐ:

VIII ܫܘܘܝܐ ܘܗܘܐ ܒܩܢܐ ܐܘ ܗܘܐ ܬܩܢܘܢܐ: ܕܒܠܐ ܠܠܫܢܐ
ܡܫܡܠܝܐ ܒܫܡܠܝܐ ܘܦܬܓܡܐ ܐܝܟ ܕܢܫܡܥ ܒܐܬܪܐ: ܫܡܥܝܢ ܦܬܓܡܐ:

22 [4] ܐܘܟܝܬ ܦܬܓܡܐ ܕܫܘܫܛܐ ܡܫܡܠܝܐ ܐܝܟ ܢܘܩܢܐ ܠܚܕ ܡܢ ܡܬܚܡܐ
ܕܡܬܐܡܪܐ ܝܬܝܪ: ܘܐܝܟ ܢܘܩܙܐ ܫܘܝܐ ܠܬܪܝܢ ܡܬܐܡܪܢܐ:

1) Illegible. Possibly ܒܫܡܗܘ or ܒܫܡܗܘ
2) Illegible. Possibly ܕܐܠܦܝ.
3) This word, which appears to be ܕܫܘܘܝܢ (or ܫܘܘܝܢ?) was overwritten by the hand of the scribe himself with the word ܡܫܡܠܝܐ.
4) Written thus, without syame.

IX ܡܙܝܥܢܐ ܘܡܪܝܡܢܐ ܣܠܩܢ ܡܢ ܦܩܘܕܐ܆ ܐܘ ܡܠܟܐ܀

23 ܒܟܠܐ ܦܬܐ ܗܘܝܠܐ ܒܐܦ̈ܐ܀

24 ܡܙܝܥܢܐ ܦܘܩܕܢܐ ܕܐܬܡܘܗܝ ܒܚܘܪܐ ܕܝܠܝܐ. ܘܐܟܘܬܗ̇ ܘܐܡܪ ܠܐ
ܢܦܩ ܗܘܐ ܕܢܦܩ ܡܢܐ ܗ̄ܘ܆ ܐܝܟ ܗܘ ܕܒܢ (1 ܕܐܦܝܐ ܡܦܩܢܐ
ܗܘ̇ ܕܐܬܡܢܝ܀ ܘܚܦܝܛܐ ܠܐ ܡܬܚܙܐ ܐܝܟܢ ܡܢ ܗܠܝܢ ܕܡܬܡܢ
(2 ܠܡܬܡܢ̈ܝܢ܀

25 ܡܬܕܡܪܢܐ ܘܒܟܠܐ. ܐܢܫܐ ܗܘܝܐ ܐܝܟܐ ܡܬܢܟܐ ܡܬܡܟܢܟܐ܀

X (3 ܡܬܕܡܪܢܐ ܐܢܫܐ ܢܟܦܝ ܒܥܘܕܪܢܗ ܡܬܢܟܐ ܡܬܚܙܝܐ ܒܬܡܗܐ.
ܐܢܫܐ ܒܪ ܢܟܠܗ ܒܥܡ ܕܐܐ. ܐܢܫܐ ܐܝܟ ܡܢܐ ܒܪܘܚܗ
ܒܒܪܐ ܕܗܘܝ܀

26 ܡܙܝܥܢܐ ܘܪܘܚܐ ܕܠܐ ܦܣܩ ܘܒܟܠܐ. ܡܟܢܟ ܗܘܐ ܕܡܬܡܢ̈ܝܢ
ܠܡܬܡܢܐ܀

Xa ܦܣܘܩܐ ܘܒܟܠܐ ܦܬܚ ܣܘܟܐ ܕܐܟܘܬܐ ܟܠܗ ܩܒܐ܀

28 ܡܬܡܟܢܐ (4 ܘܟܝ ܒܟܠܐ ܕܡܟܠܐ ܗܘܝܐ ܕܢܐ܆ ܘܐܬܡܟܢܐ ܒܟܐ. ܒܗܘ܀

1) ܐܦܝܐ in the ms

2) Since in the ms ܠܡܬܡܢ̈ܝܢ is placed below ܡܬܡܢ, the following arrangement of the points arises.

ܘܚܦܝܛܐ }
ܠܡܬܡܢ̈ܝܢ܀ }

Hence I have written as I have, but I do not know whether I have arranged the accents correctly. Perhaps they should be ܘܚܦܝܛܐ܇ and ܠܡܬܡܢ̈ܝܢ܀.

3) Thus the ms! My conjecture is ܡܬܕܡܪܢܐ ܘܡܬܢܟܐ. Barheb., *Metr.Gram.*, 256, has a weak upper point.

4) Thus the ms. Have the readings ܟܝ and ܕܟܐ been conflated? It is astonishing that this word is missing at p.192,28. I reckon that the word was corrupted already in the earlier copy, because our scribe explains it as far as he can, while others omitted the term, which explains why it is missing at II,28.

XI ܦܣܘܩ ܘܡܫܡܫܢܐ ܦܠܐ ܗܘܟܢܐ ܕܐܡܪ܂ ܡܢ ܘ... ܠܟܘܢ ܦܩ ܕܐܙܠܐ܂
ܘܐܢ ܡܫܡܠܝܢ ܠܗ... ܩܡܝ܂

XII ܡܫܡܠܐ ܘܦܣܘܩܐ ܘܡܫܡܫܢܐ܂ ܡܢܝܢ ܦܠܐ ܒܗܢ ܗܘܟܢܝܢ܂ ܘܐܬܐ ܠܐܟܠܐ
ܐܙܠ ܐܬܐ܂

30 ܡܬܟܬܫܢܐ ܘܡܫܡܫܢܐ ܡܢܝܐ ܦܠܓܗ ܢܟܣܝܢ ܒܟܬܒܝܢ܂

XI ܦܣܘܩܐ ܘܡܫܡܫܢܐ ܕܚܕ ܫܡܐ [1] ܠܦܬܐ

XIII ܡܬܟܬܫܢܐ܂ ܐܟܢ ܕܒܫܡܐ ܢܬܟܬܒ ܫܡܝܢ܂ ܦܠܓܐ ܠܐܠܗܐ ܠܟ ܫܠܡܐ܂

XIV ܡܬܟܬܫܢܐ ܕܒܫܘܠܡܐ ܡܬܦܫܩܝܢ ܫܬܩܘܗ܂ ܐܟܢ ܐܟܢ
ܕܟܬܘ ܕܐܠܗܐ܂

31 ܙܘܓܐ ܐܘܬܠܦܝ ܡܬܟܢܫܐ܂

[2] ܘܙܘܓܐ ܒܡܟܢܫܢܐ܂ ܡܟܢܫ ܠܡܠܬܐ܂ ܠܟܠܗܝܢ ܒܚܬܡܐ܂ ܡܟܢܫܘܗ܂
ܠܟܠܗܘܢ ܐܦܝܐ܂

XV ܦܣܘܩܐ ܘܡܟܢܫܢܐ ܘܙܘܓܐ ܕܒܬܪܐ ܘܡܟܢܫܢܐ ܘܡܫܡܠܐ܂ ܕܡܠܐ
ܘܡܘܩ ܡܢ ܒܗ ܡܬܠܐ ܘܚܙܘ ܠܟ ܡܫܝܚܐ܂ ܘܒܕܘ ܣܘܪܓܝܐ
ܒܬܪ ܕܘܡܝ܂ ܦܢܝܗ ܫܩܝܠ ܡܢܐ܂

XVI ܡܚܝܠܐ ܘܡܫܡܫܢܐ ܐܝܬܝܗ ܡܬܩܪܐ ܘܡܬܩܪܝܢܐ ܒܫܘܡܠܐ ܡܫܝܚܐ܂

XVII ܦܣܘܩܐ ܘܡܫܡܫܢܐ ܣܗܕܐ ܘܡܕܘܪܐ܂

XVIII ܢܫܐ ܕܚܕ ܫܡܐ ܫܠܡܐ܂ ܚܘܒܐ ܒܫܡܫܬܐ܂

1) It is doubtful whether ܡܢܐ here should be read with or without the point. In the other examples ܡܫܡܫܢܐ is written with only the small line.
2) The words marked out with a line are written in the ms in black ink.

40 ܢܩܦܐ (¹ ܘܡܫܡܫܢ ܘܐܩܦ܀

44 ܡܙܝܥܢܐ ܘܢܩܦܐ ܥܠ· ܡܫܡܫ ܘܐܩܦ܀

XIX ܡܙܝܥܢܐ ܘܚܪܝܪܐ ܘܪܗܛܐ· ܒܬܪ ܡܠܬܐ ܒܗ ܒܠܚܘܕ܀

XX ܡܫܡܫܢܐ. (² ܒܪܫܝܬܐ ܐܬܡܘܢ ܗܘܐ ܡܠܬܐ.

XXI ܦܩܘܕܐ ܢܐܙܠ ܡܢ ܟܢܝܘ

XXII ܚܪܝܪܐ ܘܡܙܝܥܢܐ ܘܚܪܝܪܐ ܐܝܟ ܐܝܟ ܘܠܐ ܠܐ. [?ܐܝܟ ܐܝܢ]

50 ܙܘܓܐ ܒܒܘܬܐ ܕܡܫܝܚܐ ܫܠܡ ܗܘܐ ܗܘܟܠ ܛܘܒܐ:

XXIII ܙܘܓܐ ܒܒܠܐ ܘܐܣܬܐ ܘܪܗܛܐ ܬܪܬܐ ܡܫܡܫܢܐ: ܘܡܬܬܒܐ ܒܡܫܡܫܢܘ.

ܐܝܟ ܡܫܡܫܢܐ ܘܡܫܡܫܢܐ ܘܡܙܝܥܢܐ ܘܪܗܛܐ ܕܠܐ ܦܣܩܐ ܕܫܠܡܐ

ܘܡܫܡܫܢܐ ܘܗܘܐ ܒܐܝܟ ܒܥܘܙܐ̈ ܕܐܙܠ

XXIV ܡܬܕܡܪܢܐ ܘܡܫܒܚܢܐ. ܐܝܟ ܐܡܪ ܒܢܘܢ ܘܐܡܪ ܦܬܓܡܝܗܘܢ

XXV ܡܙܝܥܢܐ ܘܪܗܛܐ ܕܠܐ ܦܣܩ ܘܟܕܘ ܒܠܚܘܕ. ܐܝܟ ܗܢ ܐܡܪܢܐ

ܐܝܟ̈ ܘܐܚܝܕ. ܡܢ ܗܘ ܕܚܝ ܕܒܗ ܒܠܥܕ̈ ܕܡܬܚܫܒ

ܒܣܦܪܐ ܕܡܫܠܡ.

XXVI ܦܩܘܕܐ ܦܢܝܢܐ ܒܠ ܫܘܐ ܕܐܬܐ ܕܒܣܝܡ ܕܗܘ ܕܡܬܒܪܟ.

XXVII ܚܪܝܪܐ ܘܡܙܝܥܢܐ ܘܚܪܝܪܐ ܦܠܓ ܐܬܐܡܪ ܘܐܝܟ ܐܬܐܡܪ.

XXVIII ܒܒܘܬܐ ܘܦܩܘܕܐ ܩܘܡ ܩܘܡ ܕܝܢܟܘܢ.

1) Beneath the <he> there are two points, a thick one on top of a thin one. So also beneath ܡܫܡܫ in the next paragraph. There, however, the ink has run and the points have become joined together. This is therefore the form of both ܢܩܦܐ and ܚܪܝܪܐ. On the subject of ܡܫܡܫܢܘܬܐ, ܢܣܒܐ, and ܢܩܦܐ, see ch.12.

2) Doubtful, maybe ܒܪܫܝܬܐ.

XXIX ܦܣܘܩܐ ܘܡܫܡܫܢܐ ܘܡܫܬܠܛܢܐ. ܘܐܬܡܢܝ܃ ܒܪ̈ܘܪܐ ܢܒܝܘ܁ ܘܐܡܢ܃
ܒܪܟܐ̈ ܐܒܘܗ̈ܝ ܚܝ.

XXX ܬܠܝܐ ܕܡܬܒܥܐ ܒܒܠܒܠܐ ܚܝܠܐ̈ ܡܐ ܕܢܦܩ̈ ܒܪܗ ܕܐܠܗܐ̈ ܒܠܐ
ܬܪܘܢܘܣ ܕܡܫܝܚܘ.

14 ܦܣܘܩܐ ܘܡܫܡܫܢܐ ܘܡܬܒܥܢܐ ܘܐܣܝܐ ܘܡܦܝܣܐ ܠܝ ܦܠܛܝܢ
ܡܫܘܬܐ̈ ܒܐܘܡܢܐ̈ ܕܟܬܒܐ.

ܫܠܡ ܢܘܩ̈ܙܐ

ܘܠܡܪܢ ܫܘܒܚܐ ܐܡܝܢ

Text II – Another Catalogue of Accents

Berlin Sachau 88 (Petermann 9), f.22a-27b (exc.f.26), left hand columns olny

ܬܘܒ ܢܝܫܐ ܕܦܘܣ̈ܩܐ

1 ܠܐܣܝܐ ܦܣܝܩܐ. ܐܬܝܐ ܡܢ ܒܪ̈ܒܐ. ܚܙܝܗ ܒܓܙܒܪܐ. ܘܡܫܡ̈ܫܢܐ ܒܡܫܡܫܢܝ.

2 ܠܐܣܝܐ ܕܬܠܬܐ. ܐܝܟܐ ܕܒܠܚܘܕ ܣܡܟܐ ܕܒܫܡܝܐ. ܘܡܫܚܐ ܚܝܠܐ̈
ܡܠܟܐ ܕܐܕܘܡ. ܬܘ ܢܫܬܠܡܘܢ ܘܢܬܒܣܡܘܢ ܒܫܒ ܡܢ ܒܪ̈ܒܐ.

3 ܦܣܘܩܐ ܘܐܣܝܐ. ܦܠܐ ܒܥܐ ܐܝܟ ܕܢܦܠ ܐܠܗܐ. ܦܠܐ ܚܙܝܗ ܒܫܡܘܗ.
ܦܠܐ ܐܝܟ ܕܠܗ ܦܢܝܢ. ܐܠܐ ܐܣܝܐ ܠܒܥܒܕܝܢ (1) ܐܬܥܒܝ. ܦܠܛܝܢ
ܠܒܝܬܐ. ܦܣܠ ܝܠܝܐ. ܢܦܫܐ ܐܝܟ ܒܡܫܒܐ.

4 ܦܣܘܩܐ ܘܡܫܡܫܢܐ ܘܐܣܝܐ. ܦܢܝ ܡܬܦܢܐ ܐܠܐ ܡܢ ܡܫܬܐܒ. ܦܢܝ
ܠܟܢ ܒܟܠ ܦܝܣܐ ܐܠܐ ܐܣܝܐ. ܐܦܢܝܬ ܐܝܟ ܕܢܦܠܗ ܠܗ ܒܪܘܚ ܕܡܫܠܐ
ܒܦܝܣܘ. [?]

1) On the ܒ above the word, cf. the similar examples on p.121,1, also end of ch.12.

5 ܡܫܐܠܢܐ ܘܐܣܟܡܐ ܘܐܟܦ ܦܠܛܐ. ܐܝܟܘܬܐ܇ ܕܐܬܕܟܝܬ ܐܝܟܢ. ܗܟܢܐ܇ ܕܐܬܚܙܝܬ
ܦܬܝܚܝܢ. ܒܡܠܬܐ ܐܝܟܘܬ ܫܢܝ.

6 ܦܩܘܕܐ ܘܡܦܝܣܢܐ ܘܙܩܦܐ. ܘܙܩܦܐ ܐܪܥܐ܇ ܗܒ ܣܒܪܬܐ. ܘܡܦܝܣ
ܕܬܒܥܐ ܠܟ ܒܗܘ ܕܦܩܕ ܠܚܒܪܗ. ܘܡܦܝܣ ܡܦܝܣܢܐ܇ ܡܫܐܠ ܠܐܟܬܐ.

7 ܙܘܓܐ ܘܦܩܘܕܐ ܘܐܣܟܡܐ. ܘܦܩܕܘ ܒܥܕܢܐ܇ ܘܫܕܪ. ܘܒܟܢܘܫܝܐ
ܕܫܡܝܐ܇ ܠܐܡܪܝ.

8 ܐܣܟܡܐ ܫܘܐܠܐ. ܐܝܟ ܕܐܡܪ ܐܣܝܐ. ܘܟܕ ܐܬܦܬܚ. ܡܩܛܠ ܬܫܡܫ
ܬܘܬܒܘܢ.

9 ܫܘܐܠܐ. ܕܠܐ ܐܝܬ ܠܟܠܢܝܫܐ. ܘܐܡܪ ܡܦܩܐ ܐܚܪܢ. ܘܠܐ ܐܬܬܟܝܠ
ܠܟܘܢ ܡܢ ܫܡܝܐ. [ܐܡܫܝܐ. (2 Cf. p. 188] ܐܠܐ ܐܝܟܢܐ ܕܐܝܟ ܫܡܝܐ
ܢܗܘܐ. ܦܪܘܩ. ܡܢܝ.

10 ܦܩܘܕܐ ܘܐܣܟܡܐ. ܦܪܘܩ. ܫܠܡܐ. ܒܫܠܡܐ.

11 ܫܘܐܠܐ ܕܐܝܟ ܫܡܝܐ. ܘܐܡܪ. ܦܪܘܩ ܠܐܒܘܢ. [Hoc est taḥtâyâ šęḥimâ.]

12 ܦܩܘܕܐ ܘܐܣܟܡܐ. ܡܢܐ ܙܕܩ ܠܟܘܢ. ܘܠܟܘܢ ܐܝܬ ܟܠܠ ܐܒܘܗ̄.
ܚܙܐ ܐܝܟ ܒܪ ܐܢܫܐ.

13 ܡܟܝܟܐ ܘܬܚܬܝܐ ܘܐܣܟܡܐ. ܦܪܘܩ ܐܝܟ ܒܟܪܗ ܕܝܘܣܦ ܕܒܥܠܡܐ
ܒܫܡܐ. [Cf. p. 125]

14 ܦܩܘܕܐ ܘܡܦܝܣܢܐ ܘܬܚܬܝܐ ܘܐܣܟܡܐ. ܐܢܬܘܢ ܐܚܝ ܠܝ ܐܝܟ ܕܐܡܪ̈.
ܕܢܗܘܐ ܠܘܬ ܒܥܘ ܡܫܡܠܝܘ. [Cf. p. 125]

15 ܦܩܘܕܐ ܘܐܣܟܡܐ. ܠܐ ܬܬܒܝܫ ܠܟܘܢ. ܠܐ ܬܫܬܠܚ ܠܟܘܢ. ܘܗܘܐ
ܐܝܟ ܡܪܝܡ ܠܟ. [Cf. p. 125]

16 ܡܩܡܨܢܐ ܘܐܚܝܕܐ. ܘܠܐ ܗܘܝܐ ܡܢ ܡܦܩܪ ܐܠܐ ܦܘܫܐ ܗܘ. ܠܐ ܐܬܡܛܝܐ
ܐܢܬܐ ܗܘܝ ܘܡܠܐ ܗܘ.

17 ܦܩܘܕܐ ܘܐܚܝܕܐ ܒܗܠܝܢ ܐܚܪܢܐ. ܐܝܟ ܗܘ ܐܡܪ. ܐܝܟ ܗܘ ܢܚܘܬ
ܕܠܚܘܕ ܕܐܬܝܗ ܡܢ ܝܗܘܕܐ.

18 ܬܚܝܬܐ ܕܡܬܒܥܢܐ. ܗܘ· ܦܘܩ· ܐܩܪܝܒ. ܡܢܝܢ ܕܝܢ ܡܥܠܝ ܠܟܠܐ·
ܟܠܗ ܠܗ.

19 ܡܪܝܡܐ ܕܬܚܬܝܐ. ܘܡܕܐ· ܕܥܒܕ· ܐܬܐ ܠܗܘܢ ܡܢ ܦܓܪܐ. (1 ܘܡܕܐ·
ܠܗܘ ܡܫܡܠܝܐ· ܕܠܐ ܫܡܥ ܐܝܟ ܡܠܟܐ. ܘܠܐ ܡܝܬܪ ܠܗ ܢܟܝܢ ܘܠܐ
ܡܫܠܐ ܡܠܟܐ. ܢܗ

20 ܡܫܠܡܢܘܬܐ. ܢܗܠܟܘܢ ܩܠܐ: ܕܠܗܝܟ ܡܢ ܫܡܝܐ: ܠܐܬܪܐ ܚܝ.

21 ܟܪܝܐ. ܐܝܟ ܡܥܒܕܐ· ܗܘܝ ܕܗܘܝ: ܘܐܬܐ ܠܦܓܪܐ· ܕܗܘ: ܐܦܪܝܡ· ܘܟܠܗ
ܠܗ: ܘܐܬܟܢܟܗ· ܡܫܠܐ· ܡܢܗܘܬܐ· ܕܝܠܗ:

22 ܦܩܘܕܐ ܘܡܪܝܡܐ ܘܙܘܓܐ ܘܦܢܝܢ ܠܗܘ ܡܫܡܥܢܐ. ܘܐܦ ܢܗܘܐ ܠܟܝ
ܡܢ ܦܓܪܐ ܕܡܫܡܠܝܐ· ܢܩܠܐ: ܘܐܦ ܢܗܘܐ· ܦܘܩܐ· ܠܟܠܗ ܡܫܡܠܝܐ:

23 ܟܠܠܐ. ܕܢܗܘܘܢ ܚܕ ܡܢ ܗܘ ܕܐܘܕܥ ܠܗ·. ܚܙܘ ܕܠܐܬܠܬܝܢ
ܢܩܦܐ ܘܕܢܐ·.

24 ܡܪܝܡܐ ܘܦܫܝܛܐ ܘܟܠܠܐ. ܘܐܬܐܘܢ ܘܐܡܪܘ ܠܐ ܢܝܚܝܢ ܗܘܘ ܕܡܢ
ܦܢܐ ܗܘ·. ܘܚܠܐ· ܕܐܝܬܝܗܘܢ ܠܟܠܐ ܐܙܠܐ ܗܘܐ ܠܗ·. ܐܝܟ ܗܘ ܢܟܝܢ·
ܕܐܦܢܐ ܡܫܝܚܐ ܗܘ ܕܐܬܟܢܝܗ·.

25 ܡܫܘܕܥܢܐ ܘܟܠܠܐ. ܐܢܫܐ ܢܦܠܘ ܢܟܪܝܐ· ܐܢܫܐ ܗܘܝܐ ܐܝܟܐ ܡܕܝܢܬܐ·.

1) ܚܕܐ. ms.

26 ܡܠܝܐ ܦܪܘܫܬܐ ܘܡܠܠܐ. ܡܛܠܘ ܗܘܐ ܕܡܫܡܗܝ̈ ܠܡܠܬܐ. ܡܛܠܘ
ܗܘܐ ܕܒܗ ܡܫܡ̈ܗ ܕܡܬܩܪܝܢ ܒܫܡܗ ܘܡܠܬܐ.

27 ܡܢܝܢܐ. ܡܠܠܐ. ܕܐܬܦܫܛܘ ܠܡܢܝܢ ܒܒܢܝ̈ܢ ܦܪ̈ܝܫܝܢ ܘܒܒܢ̈ܝܢ
ܒܒܢܝ̈ܢܐ.

28 ܡܫܡܫܢܐ. ܕܡܠܬܐ ܗܘܐ ܕܒܗ ܘܪܘܫܡܐ ܒܓܘ ܓܒܐ. ܘܐܡܪܢ ܕܐܦ
[1] ܒܡܫܡܫܢ̈ܐ ܘܪܘܫܡܐ ܒܓܒܐ.

29 ܡܐܡܪܐ ܦܝ ܐܡܬܝ ܐܝܟ. ܐܢܗܘ ܗܘܝܘ ܐܝܟܢ.

30 ܡܫܡܫܢܐ ܘܡܬܚܘܝܢܐ ܡܫܡܫܢܐ. ܦܢܝܐ ܦܢܝܐ ܐܝܟܢ. ܦܢܝܐ ܠܡܢܐ
ܠܝ ܡܛܠܐ. ܕܡܢ ܡܫܐ. ܦܢܝܐ ܦܢܝ.

31 ܦܘܪܫܐ. ܐܦܪܘܬܐ ܡܛܠܬܐ. ܡܢܗܠܐ ܕܟܕ ܡܬܐܡܪ ܐܠܐ.

32 ܦܘܪܫܐ ܕܒܝܢܬܐ. ܦܢܝ ܒܝܢ ܐܠܗܐ ܐܢ ܛܒܥܐ ܙܘܢ ܗܦܟܐ.
ܒܡܘܬ ܡܢܚܝ.

33 ܦܘܪܫܐ ܕܦܣܩܐ. ܡܚܐ ܠܝ ܒܡܘܬ. ܦܢܝܐ ܒܡܫܝܚ ܦܢܝܐ.

34 ܦܘܪܫܐ ܕܢܝܚ ܡܛܠܐ. ܒܢܝܐ. ܐܬܝܐ. ܒܡܫܝܚ ܦܓܪܐ.

35 ܦܬܓܡܐ ܕܢܝܚܐ. ܘܐܡܪܝ. ܘܐܡܪ.

36 ܡܫܡܫܐ ܒܢܝܢܐ. ܐܠܐ ܡܦܩܕܐ ܠܡܘܒܠ. [2] ܐܙܠ ܒܠܐ ܟܠܐ ܢܬܐܡܪ.

37 ܦܣܘܩܐ. ܡܪܟܒܐ ܢܚܬܐ ܦܣܘܩܐ

38 ܕܒܡܘܬܐ. ܢܘܟܪܝܐ. ܦܠܓܐ. ܢܝܚܬܐ.

39 ܡܠܝܐ ܦܬܐ. ܡܢܝܢ ܒܗܘ ܡܛܠ ܐܒܘܐ ܗܘ ܦܬܐ. ܒܠܒܐ ܘܒܠܒܐ
ܡܫܠܠܝܢ.

1) In the ms it seems to be ܒܡܫܡܫܬܐ.

2) These two points are doubtful.

40 ܙܥܘܪܐ. ܘܫܡܫܘ ܘܐܟܝܢ. ܘܐܚܪܢ ܘܐܡܝܢ.

41 ܦܩܘܕܐ ܕܪ̈ܥܐ. ܒܠܫܢ ܕܢܫܪܐ ܘܡܫܠܐ܂ ܚܕ ܡܢ ܦܘܫܩܐ܂ ܗ̈ܠܝܢ ܐܚܪ̈ܢܐ܇
ܠܐ ܡܬܝܕܥ ܡܢܐ ܒܠܝ ܕܡܢ ܟܕ ܒܗܝ ܘܐܝܟ ܕܟܠܗ܇ ܠܐ ܡܢ ܡܫܬܘܩ
ܡܬܝܕܥ ܒܡܠܬܐ܇ ܐܝܟ ܕܐܡܪ܃ ܒܟܠܐ ܗܘ ܕܝܢܐ ܒܠܒܘ܇

42 ܡܪܝܡܢܐ ܕܪ̈ܥܐ. ܐܢܐ ܦܪܘܫ ܐܢܐ ܕܡܢ ܐܠܗܝ܆ ܐܠܗܐ܂ ܘܡܠܐ܂ ܦܠܚܝܢ܇
ܠܐ ܡܬܚܫܒܢ ܕܡܢܗ ܕܟܠܗ ܠܫܡܝܐ܂ ܠܒܪܢܫܐ ܗܘ ܐܢܫܐ܇

43 ܐܣܟܡܐ ܕܦܩܘܕܐ. ܗܘܐ ܠܐ ܦܪܝܫ ܩܘܫܝܐ. ܘܐܢܐ܂ ܠܐ ܐܬܚܙܝܬ ܠܗ.

44 ܡܪܝܡܢܐ ܘܙܥܘܪܐ. ܘܫܡܫ ܕܫܘܐ ܘܐܟܝܢ. ܘܟܠܐ܂ ܐܝܟ ܘܐܟܝܢ. ܘܦܝܫ܂
ܠܒܪܐܘ ܘܐܟܝܢ.

45 ܡܪܝܡܢܐ ܫܡܫܢܐ ܘܡܫܡܫܢܐ. ܐܡܠܐ܂ ܚܕܐ ܒܟܠܡܐ ܘܡܫܡܫܢܐ ܗܘܐ.
ܡܠܬܐ܂ ܕܢܩܘܫܐ ܠܐ ܢܬܐܬܐ ܒܠܒܗ. ܐܟܘܬ܂ ܠܟ ܒܟܠܗ̈ܝܢ ܘܠܡܫܒ ܢܐܡܪ.

46 ܫܡܫܢܐ ܘܡܫܡܫܢܐ. ܫܪܝܬܐ ܕܟܠ ܡܫܡܫܝܢ ܐܢܐ.

47 ܐܘܟܝܐ ܕܦܩܘܕܐ ܒܡܚܝܬܐ. ܣܓܝ ܡܢ ܫܒܝܠܐ܂ ܐܘ ܡܠܟܐ܇ ܠܐܠܗܝܢ ܕܐܠܗ܂
ܕܐܠܗܘܬܢ ܘܫܘܒܚܐ܂ ܘܫܘܠܛܢܐ܇

48 ܐܘܟܝܐ ܒܟܠܐ ܘܡܪܝܡܢܐ ܘܐܣܟܡܐ. ܐܝܟ ܕܐܬܟܢܫܘ ܢܩܐ ܩܕܡܝܘܬܐ ܣܒܪܐ
ܘܡܫܬܪܪ̈ܝܢ. ܐܝܟ ܢܬܬܫܝܠ܂ ܒܡܫܝܚܘ ܕܡܪܝܐ ܒܗܘܢ ܘܬܪ̈ܝܢ.
ܡܢܟ [1] ܢܩܘܫ ܕܡܫܡܫܬ ܒܫܡܐ ܟܠ ܡܪܝܐ ܘܡܫܬܒܚ ܒܟܠܐ.

49 ܡܪܝܡܢܐ ܕܐܠܗܐ ܢܘܩܪܐ. ܦܘܩ ܡܪܝܐ ܠܥܠܡܝܢ܆ ܘܡܬܬܪܨ ܒܪ̈ܝܬܐ
ܘܫܪ̈ܝܐ܆ ܒܟܠܗ ܡܪܝܐ ܐܠܗܐ܆

1) Analogy would suggest a ܡܪܝܡܢܐ after ܢܩܘܫ.

50 ܪܘܓܙܐ ܫܒܝܐ. ܒܡܘܡܬܐ ܣܝܦܪ ܡܣܡܝܪ ܘܡܕܝܢ ܢܚܗ: ܠܐ ܠܓܙܐ ܐܝܬܐܐ
ܒܡܬܐܐ ܒܐܦܢ ܠܐܦܐ ܗ̈ܘܝܐ: ܐܘ ܗܦܢܝ ܬܡܬܡܡܢ: ܕܒܠܐ ܒܠܚܘܕܝ
ܡܬܬܠܐ ܒܡܬܠܘܐ ܘܦܝܠܐ ܐܢܝ.

51 ܐܠܐ ܐܝܟܢܐ ܕܐܦ ܒܒܪܝܐ (ܡܬܡܡܪܐ[1]. ܘܬܡܝܢ ܡܬܒܘܬܐ. ܒܬܝܒܘܢ
ܕܦܠܓܢܝ. ܗܢܘ ܡܬܒܐ ܚܕܐ ܠܦܠܓܐ ܦܠܓܢ̈ܝ. ܕܐܬܐ ܡܢ ܒܬܪܗ
ܕܐܦܐ: ܕܬܡܢܐ ܚܒܝܫܘ ܕܦܠܓܢܝ.

52 ܕܝܢ ܡܬܚܬܐ. ܒܡܦܩܐ ܗܘ. ܒܪܟܐ ܗܘ. ܐܠܐ ܐܝܟܢܐ. ܘܠܐ ܕܬܡܪܐ ܐܘ
ܐܝܬܝ ܐܘ ܐܝܬܝ ܕܢܡܝܟ ܒܠܘܬܗ ܐܘ ܡܢܐ ܐܘ ܡܢܐ..

ܫܠܡ.

Text III – A Catalogue of Accents by Elias of Tirhan

Berlin Sachau 88 (Petermann 9), f.17a-21b left hand columns only

ܡܢܝܢܐ ܕܦܘܚܡ̈ܐ ܘܫܘܢܝ ܡܫܪܝܐ ܕܥܠ ܚܕ ܚܕ ܡܢܗܘܢ..

ܐ. ܪܘܓܙܐ ܦܢ̈. ܫܘܝܐ ܕܫܘܚܠܦ ܡܬܩܢ. ܗܘ ܗܘ ܡܬܡܪܐ ܐܪܒܐ.

ܒ. ܬܫܠܡܐ ܕܝܢ ܢܦܩ ܒܪܘܓܙܐ. ܡܢ ܕܦܪܫ ܫܘܚܠܦ ܕܢܦܩܬ.. ܘܡܬܒܠ
ܠܚܘܬܡܐ ܢܣܐ.

ܓ. ܦܩܘܕܐ. ܒܠ ܫܘܡܠܝ ܫܘܚܠܦ ܡܬܩܢ (²ܘ̈ܬ ܡܬܒܠ ܫܪܝ ܠܚܢܐ
ܠܡܬܡܪܐ. ܬܫܠܡܐ ܬܘܒ ܡܬܬܩܢ ܡܬܬܡܥ ܠܚܘܕܬܗ ܒܠܒ ܪܘܓܙܐ.
ܘܡܬܩܪܐ ܠܦܩܘܕܐ ܡܢ ܕܡܬܡܪܐ ܒܪܐ ܠܚܘܬ ܫܘܡܠܝ ܫܘܚܠܦ
ܕܡܬܬܩܢ.

ܕ. ܒܬܪ ܕܝܢ ܕܡܬܚܪܐ ܡܢ ܕܒܦܘܩ ܡܬܡܪܐ ܦܩܕܐ ܡܠܬܐ. ܠܐ ܕܝܢ ܘܡܬܐ

1) ܡܬܡܪܐ ms.
2) Illegible word.

ܘܡܢܗ ܕܢܒܥܐ ܠܗܘܐ ܡܠܬܐ. ܕܒܝܕܗ ܫܡܐ ܡܬܬܫܡܫܐ. ܟܕ ܗܘܢ
ܟܕ ܗܘܝܐ ܕܗܘܐ ܡܠܬܐ. ܐܟܢ ܕܡܬܐܡܪܐ.

ܗ. ܡܐܡܪܐ ܟܡ ܦܠܓ̈ܐ.

ܘ. ܦܠܓ̈ܐ ܟܢܘܫܝܐ ܐܬܦܠܓܘ. ܘܡܫܡܫܢ̈ܐ ܐܝܬ ܕܗܘܢ ܘܡܠܬܐ ܘܐܣܘܪܐ.

ܙ. ܫܡܗܐ ܣܓܝ ܐܝܟܐ ܡܬܬܫܡܫ ܡܐ ܕܡܬܐܡܪܐ ܒܪ̈ܐ ܠܫܘܐ ܫܘܚܠܦܐ.

ܚ. ܫܡܗܐ ܟܠܗ ܗܘ ܫܡܗܐ ܕܐܡܝܪ. ܡܐ ܕܟܠ ܐܡܝܪ ܦܬܐ ܠܗ
ܕܢܫܘܕܥ ܘܡܫܡܫܢܐ ܗܘ ܕܟܠܗ.

ܛ. ܟܪܝܐ ܡܬܬܫܡܫ. ܟܕ ܢܗܘܐ ܒܪܐ ܡܐܡܪܐ ܕܐܬܚܙܝܬ ܡܬܐܡܪܐ.

ܝ. ܟܠܗ ܟܠܗ ܦܫܘܛܐ ܐܬܚܙܝ ܕܢܫܘܕܥ ܕܡܢ ܟܕ ܐܬܐܡܪܐ ܟܠܗܐ.
ܘܡܛܠ ܗܠܝܢ ܚܫܒܘܢܐ ܦܫܝܛܐ.

ܝܐ. ܢܫܐ ܘܡܐܡܪܐ ܦܫܐ. ܠܡܬܩܦܢܐ ܐܝܬ ܕܗܘܐ ܘܕܐܣܝܪܐ[.]

ܝܒ. ܡܐܡܪܐ ܦܫܐ ܡܬܐܡܪ ܟܕ ܙܥܘܪ ܠܡܫܡܥܘ ܠܡܐܡܪܐ ܐܝܟ
ܕܠܫܘܕܥܐ ܡܚܙܐ.

ܝܓ. ܗܘܐ ܦܝ ܕܡܐܡܪ̈ܐ. ܟܕ ܠܗܘܢܝܘܬܐ ܙܥܘܪ ܕܢܫܘܕܥ.

ܝܕ. ܗܘܐ ܕܦܬܓܡܐ. ܟܕ ܗܘܢܝܘܬܐ ܕܡܣܝܢܐ ܡܢ ܗܝ ܕܡܐܡܪܐ.

ܝܗ. ܗܘܐ ܦܫܝܛܐ. ܡܐ ܕܢܗܘܐ ܒܪܐ ܡܫܡܠܝܐ.

ܝܘ. ܗܘܐ ܗܘܐ ܘܐܣܘܪܐ ܦܫܝܛܐ. ܘܗܘܐ ܗܘ ܫܡܫܐ ܦܫܝܛܐ ܟܠܗܝܢ ܡܐܡܪ̈ܐ.

ܝܙ. ܗܘܐ ܟܠܗ ܟܠܗ ܡܫܡܫܢܘܬܐ ܡܟܝܢ ܘܟܝܢܐ. ܘܡܫܡܫܢܘ ܐܬܚܘܝ
ܕܢܦܩ ܟܕ ܘ ܐܘ ܐܝ ܐܘ ܠܐ. ܘܗܘܐ ܟܠܡܐ ܐܘ ܒܪܢܫܐ ܘܟܠܗܝܢ
ܐܝܟ ܠܗ ܐܘ ܟܠܐ ܘܐܣܘܪܐ ܘܡܢ ܦܫܝܛܐ ܠܫܘܕܥܗ.

ܝܚ. ܘܟܠܐ ܡܬܐܡܪܐ ܐܝܟ ܐܬܚܘܝ. ܟܕ ܙܥܘܪ ܠܡܬܚܙܐ ܠܡܐܡܪܐ ܕܢܫܠܐ
ܠܡܫܘܟܠܐ. ܐܘ ܗܘܐ ܡܠܬܐ ܠܦܫܝܛܐ. ܗ̄. ܐܝܟ ܐܘ ܐܬܚܘܝ.
ܘܐܬܚܘܝ ܒܫܠܐ.

ܝܛ. ܡܢܝܢܐ ܚܠܦ ܦܣܘܩܐ ܡܫܝܢܐ. ܘܟܠܗ ܡܫܡܫܢܘܬܐ ܘܢܝܚܘܬܐ
ܦܣܘܩܝܬ.

ܟ. ܡܬܡܬܚܢܐ ܥܠ ܕܦܣܩܐ ܦܣܘܩܝܬ ܘܐܝܟ ܐܡܪ ܕܡܫܡܫܢܘܬܐ ܢܣܒܐ
ܟܡ ܕܦܣܩܐ. [Pro ܢܣܒܐ in codice ܢܣܒܠ exstare videtur.]

ܟܐ. ܡܢܝܚܐ ܥܠ ܦܣܘܩܘܬ ܦܣܩܐ ܡܢܝܚܐ ܘܡܬܕܟܝܢܘܬܐ ܕܡܢ ܦܣܩܬܐ.

ܟܒ. ܡܫܬܐܠܢܐ ܥܠ ܦܢܝܢܘ ܡܫܐܠܬܐ ܐܘ ܡܠܬܐ ܐܘ ܦܣܩܬܐ ܠܡܠܠܬܐ
ܬܐܒܝ ܡܦܣܐ ܘܟܪܝܐ.

ܟܓ. ܐܘܟܝ ܟܪܝܐ ܥܠ ܟܘܠܐ ܟܡܝܐ ܦܣܘܩܝܬ ܘܐܦ ܐܘܟܝܬܐ ܢܣܒܐ
ܠܗ ܐܝܟ ܐܡܪ.

ܟܕ. ܐܘܟܝ ܟܝܢܐ ܥܠ ܫܒܝܐ ܡܟܝܡ.

ܟܗ. ܡܬܡܬܚܢܐ ܢܦܩܡ ܐܡܪ ܕܠܡܠܠܬܐ ܙܟܝܐ ܕܢܦܩܘ (1 ܘܕܢܝܚ
ܦܘܚܠܗ.

ܟܘ. ܢܟܪܐ ܐܝܟ ܦܣܩܬܐ ܠܗܘܢ. ܒܪܒ ܐܝܟ ܐܡܪ ܕܢܦܩ ܓܒܗ
ܡܬܪܐܝܢܘܬܐ ܘܡܘܬܐ ܕܦܘܕܥܐ ܦܦܣܝܩ ܢܟܪܐ.

ܟܙ. ܡܫܬܡܠܝܢܘܬܐ ܠܟܠܬܐ ܐܠܦܝܐ ܘܡܠܗ ܚܠܠ ܕܢܦܐ ܘܐܫܬܐ.

ܟܚ. ܙܘܓܐ ܚܠܦ ܡܬܡܬܚܢܐ ܡܫܝܢܐ ܡܢ ܕܠܐ ܢܗܘܐ ܦܣܩܐ ܕܗܘ ܕܡܬܦܣܩܝܢ
ܓܒܗ ܒܢܫ ܡܠܡܪܐ. ܐܟܙܢܐ ܐܝܟ (2 ܐܪܚܡܢ ܡܪܝܐ" ܚܠܦ ܘܐܝܟ ܐܡܪ
ܐܝܟ ܕܡܫܡܫܢܘܬܐ ܡܬܡܢܝܢܐ.

ܟܛ. ܙܘܓܐ ܕܬܪܬܝܢ ܚܠܦ ܦܣܩܬܐ ܘܡܫܘܪܪܐ ܦܣܘܩܝܬ.

ܠ. ܙܘܓܐ ܦܣܘܩܐ. ܚܠܦ ܦܣܘܩܐ ܡܫܚܐ ܡܫܝܢܐ ܘܡܫܘܪܪܐ
ܦܣܘܩܝܬ .. (3 ܕܬܠܬܐ ܚܠܦ ܬܫܥܐ ܡܫܝܢܐ ܘܡܬܚܡܢܘܬܐ ܘܡܘܡܝܐ
ܕܡܪܢܝܐ ܡܦܦܣܩܐ.

1) Thus ms. Read ܘܕܢܝܚ 2) Read ܐܪܚܡܟ (Ps 18.2) 3) I.e. ܙܘܓܐ ܕܬܠܬܐ.

ܠܐ. ܦܬܓܡ̈ܐ ܡܬܪ̈ܥܝܢܐ ܐܝܬܝܗܘܢ ܡܢ ܦܣܘܩܐ ܘܐܣܛܐ. ܘܥܠ ܫܘܐܠܐ ܕܡܣܬܒܥܝܢ ܒܒܥܘܬܐ ܒܗܝ ܡܫܡܠܝܘܬܐ ܡܟܝܠ.

ܠܒ. ܫܘܫܒܝܢܐ ܡܙܒܒ ܡܢ ܦܣܘܩܐ ܘܚܘܪܐ.

ܠܓ. ܡܫܡܫܢܐ ܣܠܩ ܡܢܚܬܐ ܡܬܐܡܪ. ܘܡܬܩܪܝܐ ܡܟܪܐ. ܘܐܝܟ ܐܝܬܝܗ ܕܣܠܩ ܫܘܫܒܐ ܩ̈ܠܐ ܕܫܘܫܒܠܐ ܗܢܘ ܕܝܚܢ̈ܢ.

ܠܕ. ܦܣܘܩܐ ܥܠ ܦܣܘܩܝܬܐ ܡܬܐܡܪ. ܐܠܐ ܟܕ ܥܠ ܐܝܟܢܐ ܕܦܣܩܝܢ ܡܫܡܫܝܢ ܦ̈ܣܘܩܐ.

ܠܗ. ܦܬܓܡܐ ܡܫܡܫܢܐ ܥܠ ܕܣܡܟܐ ܡܚܝܪܐ.

ܠܘ. ܫܘܫܒܐ ܙܥܘܪܐ. ܗ̄. ܫܘܐܠܐ ܥܠ ܗܘ ܕܠܐ ܪܘܡ ܕܡܣܬܥܩ ܒܦܣܘܩܐ ܡܬܐܡܪܐ ܕܒܫܘܠܡܐ ܟܕ ܒܗ ܒܟܠܐ ܕܥܠ ܫܘܐ ܐܚܪܢܐ ܕܒܬܪܡܪܐ ܘܐܝܟ ܐܝܬܝܗ ܕܫܘܫܒܐ ܣܠܩ Fol. 20a ܡܬܐܡܪ̈ܢܐ ܡܬܝܚܝܕܐ ܗܘܝܐ ܒܦܣܘܩܐ ܡܬܐܡܪ[ܘܢ.] ܘܐܝܟ ܟܕ ܡܫܬܒܚ ܚܕ. ܕܐܦ ܡܬܐܡܪܐ ܡܫܡܫܝܢ ܟܠܗ ܗܘ ܕܡܫܬܟܚ ܐܝܟ ܐܠܗܘܬܐ. ܐܠܐ ܐܝܬ ܐܝܬܝܗ ܕܡܬܪܥܝܢܘܬ ܡܫܡܫܝܢ ܟܪܟܐ ܒܪܘܚܐ? ܐܝܟ ܐܢܫܝܢ ܡܪܢܐ ܣܓܝ̈ܐܐ ܐܘ ܒܒܪܢܫܐ. ܐܝܟ ܐܢܫܝܢ ܡܪܢܐ: ܘܐܝܟ ܐܝܬܝܗ ܕܡܬܚܙܝܢ. ܡܬܩܪ ܐܠܗܘܬ ܘܕܝܢܗ ܠܐܪܥܐ. ܡܚܝܪܐ. ܐܠܗܘܬ ܣܓܕܬ ܐܦܝܢ. ܀

ܠܘܬ ܕܝܢ ܙܘܥ ܒܝ ܕܢܩܘܫ ܡܩܪ̈ܐ ܕܦܣܘܩܐ. ܘܒܟܘܢ ܐܬܟܢܫܘ ܥܠ ܚܕ ܚܕ ܡܢܗܘܢ ܒܦܩܕܐ ܗܟܢ.

ܐ. ܙܘܓܐ ܡܢ ܡܣܒܐ ܕܢܘܩܕܐ ܐܬܡܠܝܘ ܗܘܟܢܐ. ܗ̄ ܕܐܬܐ ܢܘܩܕܐ.
[1]) ܦܣܩܐ ܕܝܢ ܟܘܦ ܕܠܗ ܟܠܗ ܦܣܘܩܐ ܐܚܪܢܐ.

ܒ. ܙܘܓܐ ܕܬܪܝܢ ܐܬܟܢܫ ܟܘܦ ܕܟܠܢ ܗܘ ܡܫܡܫ ܕܢܘܩܕܘܗܝ.

1) There should not be a no. 2 (ܒ) here, so that we end up with 30. If we omit no.19, there are in the end 30 accents, to which the no. 30 (ܠ) was added without referring to any accent (see p.199,200 below).

ܓ. ܐܘܓܐ ܓܡܚܐ ܘܟܦܦܐ ܒܗܘܢ ܕܣܡܝܟ ܗܘ ܒܡܪܡܝܘ ܐܘ ܒܝ ܓܢܒ
ܠܒܪܐ ܡܠܐ ܒܡܪܡܝܐ ܡܠܠܐ.

ܕ. (1 ܐܘܓܐ ܒܪ̈ܝܬܐ ܡܠܬܐ ܕܒܪܐ ܠܡܪܘܡܐ ܒܡܗܡܐ ܕܡܪܡܝܘ.

ܗ. ܒܬ̈ܝܐ ܐܬܡܪ ܒܒܠܒ ܗܘ ܡܡܠܐ ܕܗܘܦܪܗܘܢ.

ܘ. ܡܫܡܫܐ ܕܝܢ ܕܠܗܪ ܠܟܠ ܒܗܘܢ ܕܠܐ (2 ܒܠܗܪ ܦܘܫܩܐ ܐܚܪܢܐ.

ܙ. ܐܬܬܐ ܒܗܘܢ ܕܡܫܡܠܐ ܕܗܘܦܪܗܘܢ ܐܬܬܐ ܗܘ. ܘܡܫܬܡܗ ܒܦܘܫܩܐ
ܕܠܟܐ[.] ܦܫܩܐ ܡܠܬܐ ܕܠܐ ܡܫܬܪܝܐ ܒܦܘܫܩܐ ܐܚܪܢܐ.

ܚ. ܡܙܒܢ̈ܐ ܡܢ ܡܫܬܡܫܢܘܬܐ ܕܠܫܢܐ.

ܛ. ܡܫܡܫܢܐ ܦܠܐ ܒܡܫܝܢ ܡܫܡܠ ܠܡܠܐ ܒܝ ܡܬܡܪܐ.

ܝ. ܦܬܓܡܐ ܡܢ ܦܬܓܡܐ ܕܦܘܫܩܐ ܘܒܗܘܢ ܕܒܪܝܢ ܡܠܠܐ ܡܢ ܡܫܡܫܢܐ ܦܠܐ.

ܝܐ. ܢܒܥܐ ܡܫܡܫܢܐ ܐܬܬܐ ܘܦܬܓܡܐ ܦܘܫܩܐ ܗܘܐ ܐܝܟ ܕܠܦܘܫܩܐ.

ܝܒ. ܦܬܓܡܐ ܐܬܡܪ ܒܗܘܢ ܕܡܠܐ ܠܡܫܡܫ ܕܗܡܝܢ ܠܡܫܡܫܢܐ ܘܡܢ
ܡܫܡܫܐ ܕܫܡܐ. [Cf. p. 124 l. 1.]

ܝܓ. ܦܬܓܡܐ ܕܐܦܪܐ ܘܒܝܬ̈ܐ ܒܗܘܢ ܕܒܩܪ̈ܝܢܘ ܦܫܪ ܗܘ ܘܐܦ ܡܦܫܪܐ
ܗܘ ܘܠܐ ܡܫܬܠܡܐ ܐܠܐ ܒܡܢ ܒܟܠ ܐܡܣܬܪܐ.

ܝܕ. ܒܪܒܪܐ ܡܠܬܐ ܕܒܪܐ ܠܡܠܐ ܒܝ ܡܬܡܪܐ.

ܝܗ. ܡܬܦܫܩܢܐ (3 ܘܡܬܪܓܡܢܐ ܐܝܟ ܦܘܫܩܐ ܕܠܗܘܢ ܒܒܝ ܡܬܦܫܩܝܢ
ܒܗ ܡܬܦܫܩܝܢ ܒܗܘܢ.

ܝܘ. ܢܦܩܐ ܡܠܬܐ ܕܢܦܩ (4 ܠܡܫܚܐ ܒܡܪܝܐ.

1) ܐܘܓܐ has been changed to ܐܘܟܐ in the script of the first hand by erasure.
2) Understand ܠܗܘܪܐ
3) The BL ms of Bar Zoʿbi has ܐܘ ܡܬܪܓܡܢܐ.
4) The BL ms of Bar Zoʿbi has ܠܡܫܚܐ.

ܝܙ. ܙܘܓܐ ܒܗܘ ܕܡܙܘܓ ܠܡܠܐ ܒܡܢܝܢܐ ܘܠܐ ܡܦܠܓ ܐܝܟ ܫܘܪܝܐ
ܘܦܘܣܩܐ.

ܝܚ. ܙܘܓܐ ܕܒܬܪܗ ܒܗܘ ܕܙܕܩ ܡܢܗ ܢܘܩܙܐ ܕܢܠܘܗ ܠܡܢܝܢܐ ܕܒܬܪܗ.
[(¹ ܙܘܓܐ ܦܣܘܩܐ ܡܛܠܐ ܒܡܢ ܦܣܘܩܐ (ܡܠܚܫܐ))]

ܝܛ. ܦܩܘܕܐ ܒܗܘ ܕܐܝܟ ܕܒܦܘܩܕܢܐ ܐܡܝܪ ܘܦܩܝܕܝܢ ܦܩܝܕܝܢ ܠܗ.

ܟ. ܡܬܟܫܦܢܐ ܡܛܠ ܕܐܡܝܪ ܒܛܝܒܘ ܠܡܬܟܫܦܘ ܡܢܗ ܡܦܩܝܢ ܠܗ.

ܟܐ. ܦܩܘܕܐ ܐܘ ܡܫܠܐ ܐܘ ܡܬܟܫܦܢܐ ܒܡܢ ܕܠܘܬܗܘܢ ܦܘܢܝܐ
[..]
(² ܕܒܗܘܢ ܕܩܢܝܢ ܠܡܫܟܚܘ. ܒܡܢ ܡܚܘܐ ܘܡܟܝܠ ܡܩܕܡ ܕܠܘܬܗܘܢ
ܕܒܠܝܢ ܦܘܢܝܐ.

ܟܒ. ܦܩܘܕܐ ܕܠܟܠܐ. [ܕܝܢ] ܡܫܠܐ ܕܢܘܟܪܝܐ ܙܕܩ ܠܗ ܫܡܐ ܗܢܐ.

ܟܓ. ܡܬܟܫܦܢܐ ܒܗܘ ܕܡܬܟܫܦ ܠܡܠܐ ܘܐܝܟ ܗܘ ܕܦܬܚ ܠܗ ܡܢ
ܗܘ ܕܠܥܠ.

ܟܕ. ܦܠܓܘܬܐ ܡܬܟܫܦܢܐ ܒܗܘ ܕܡܬܟܫܦ ܠܡܠܐ ܐܠܐ ܠܗ ܡܫܟܠܠܝܢ.
[ܕܒܗܘ ܦܠܓܘ ܕܡܬܟܫܦܢܐ ܐܬܠܘܗܝ ❖ Cod. Mus. Brit. add.]

ܟܗ. ܢܚܘܬܐ. ܒܗܘ ܕܐܡܝܪ ܕܒܢܚܘܬܐ ܠܡܬܘܚ (³ ܦܩܝܕܝܢ [sic] ܠܗ.

ܟܘ. (⁴ ܡܬܟܫܦܢܐ ܕܝܢ ܕܡܟܫܦ ܐܬܠܘܗܝ ܫܡܗ ܘܟܠܗ ܠܥܠ ܡܬܟܫܦܝܢ ܠܗ.

1) The words in brackets were added in the margin by the same hand as the text. ܡܠܚܫܐ cannot be read. This was done so that the number 19–which belongs with this accent, and by which the actual thing is marked out by Bar Zu'bi –should be transferred to the following accent. That is why we have no.29 at the end instead of no.30, even though there are thirty accents in total. BL ms offers ܙܘܓܐ ܕܦܣܘܩܐ.

2) BL ms: ܓܒܗܘܢ ܕܩܢܝܢ ܠܡܫܟܚܘ. ܒܡܢ ܣܝܘܐ. ܘܟܠ ܗܘܢ ܕܠܘܬܗܘܢ ܘܒܠܝܢ ܦܘܢܝܐ.

3) BL ms: ܦܩܝܕ

4) BL ms: ܡܬܟܫܦܢܐ

ܟܙ. ܡܢܝܚ̈ܬܐ ܐܝܟ ܗܘ ܕܡܢܝܚ ܠܡܫܪܝܐ ܡܢ ܡܫܪܝܐ ܘܡܢ ܫܘܫܒܢܐ

ܕܡܫܬܘܕܝܢ.. [ܡܢ ܡܫܪܝܐ Legas]

ܟܚ. ܡܢܝܚܬܐ ܡܢ [1] ܢܘܚܬܐ ܐܣܛܘܟܣ ܫܡܗ ܒܗܘܢ ܕܡܬܬܠܝܐ ܢܘܚܐ

ܥܠܬ ܠܗܘ ܫܡܐ ܐܚܪܢܐ ܕܢܦܩ ܠܗ.

ܟܛ. ܡܫܡܥܢ̈ܝܬܐ ܫܡܐ ܗܢܐ ܐܬܝܗܒ. ܒܗܘܢ ܕܡܫܡܥܢ ܠܡܫܪܝܐ ܒܒܪܐ ܟܠܐ.

[2] ܠ.

1) BL ms: ܢܘܚ̈ܬܐ. Note how unsure the Syrians were of etymology. Cf. p.125 n5. We now have ܡܢܝܚܐ, ܡܢܝܚܬܐ, and אתנחתא!

2) There is nothing missing. The number 30 is the bottom letter in the second column of f.21b

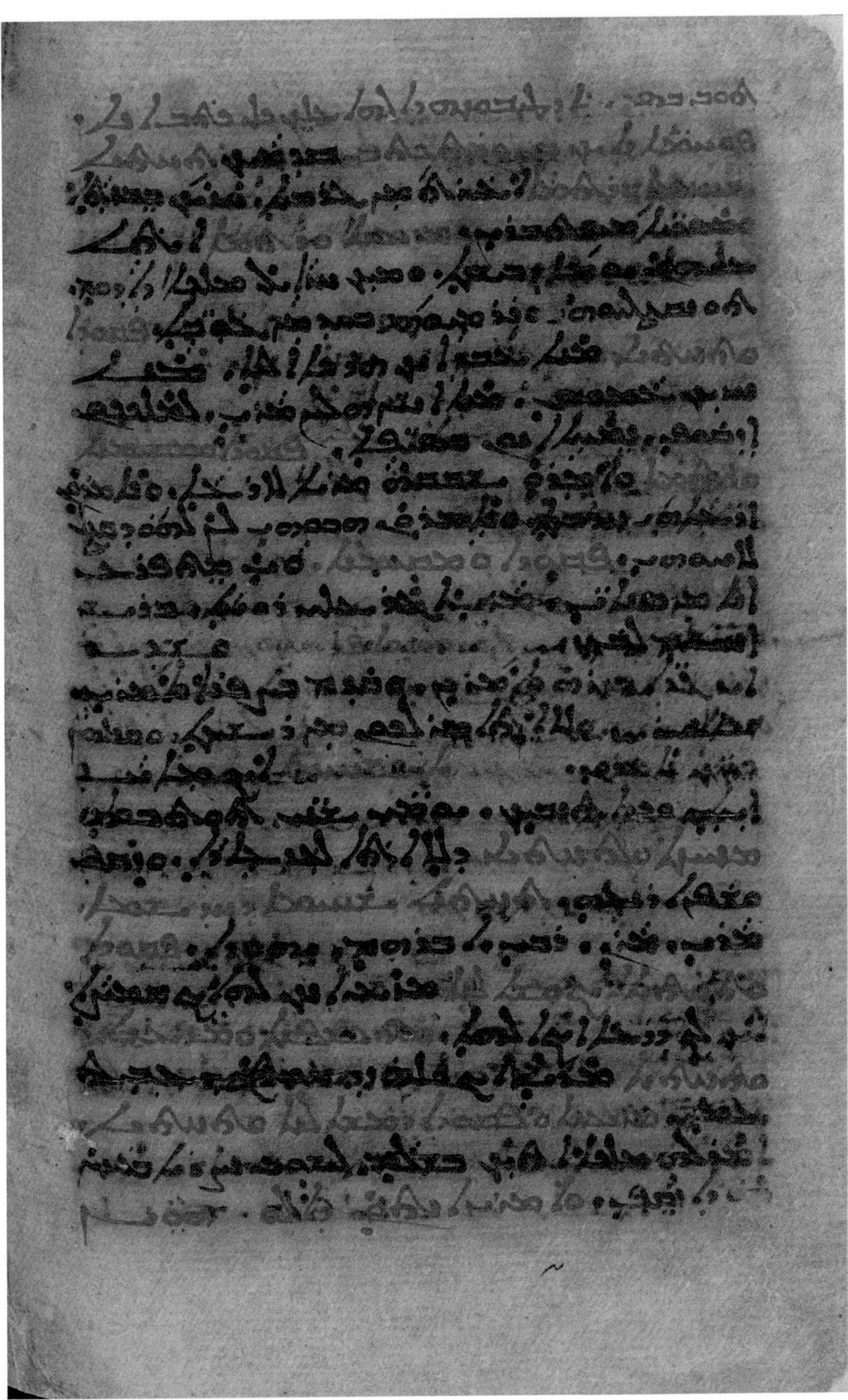

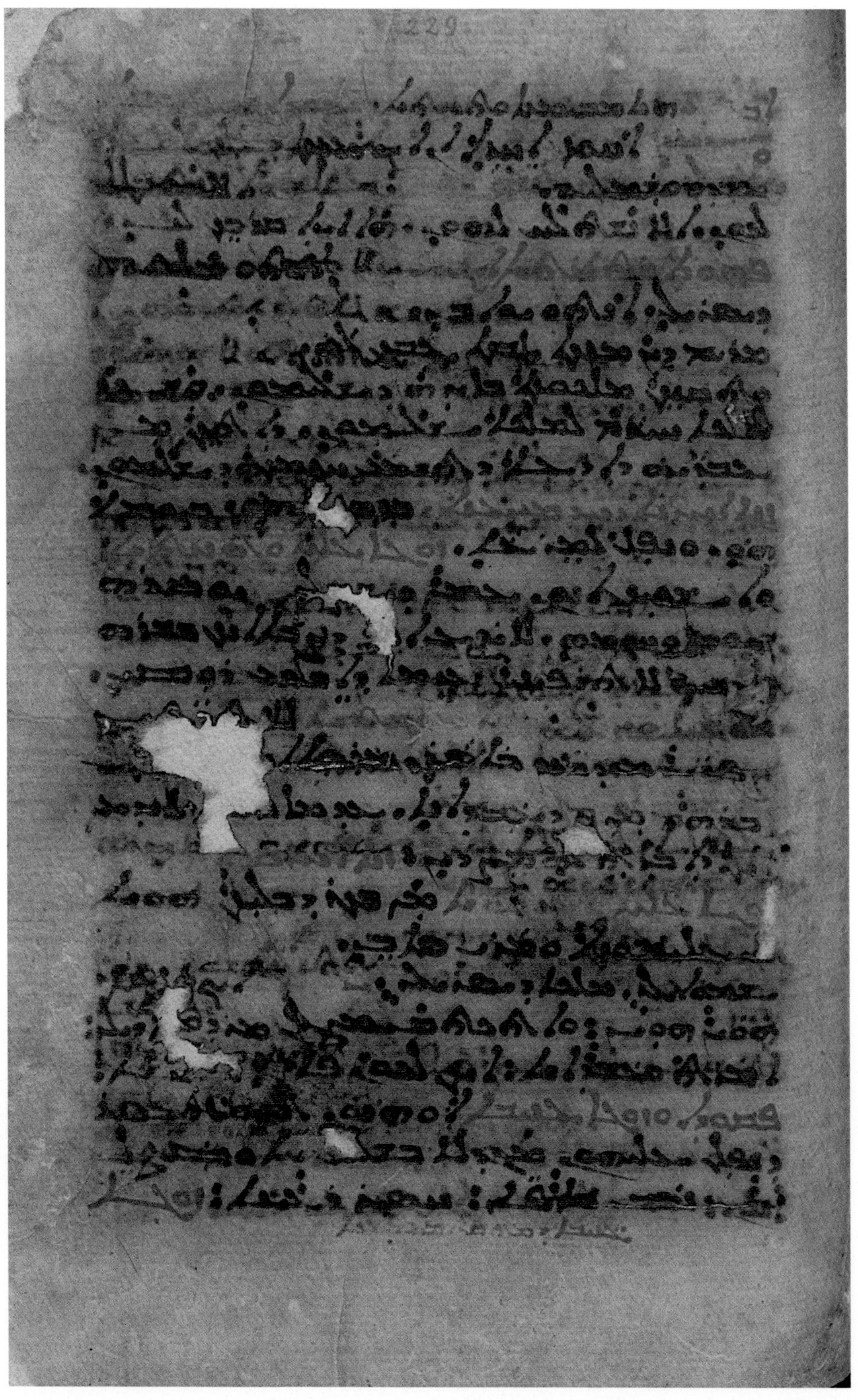

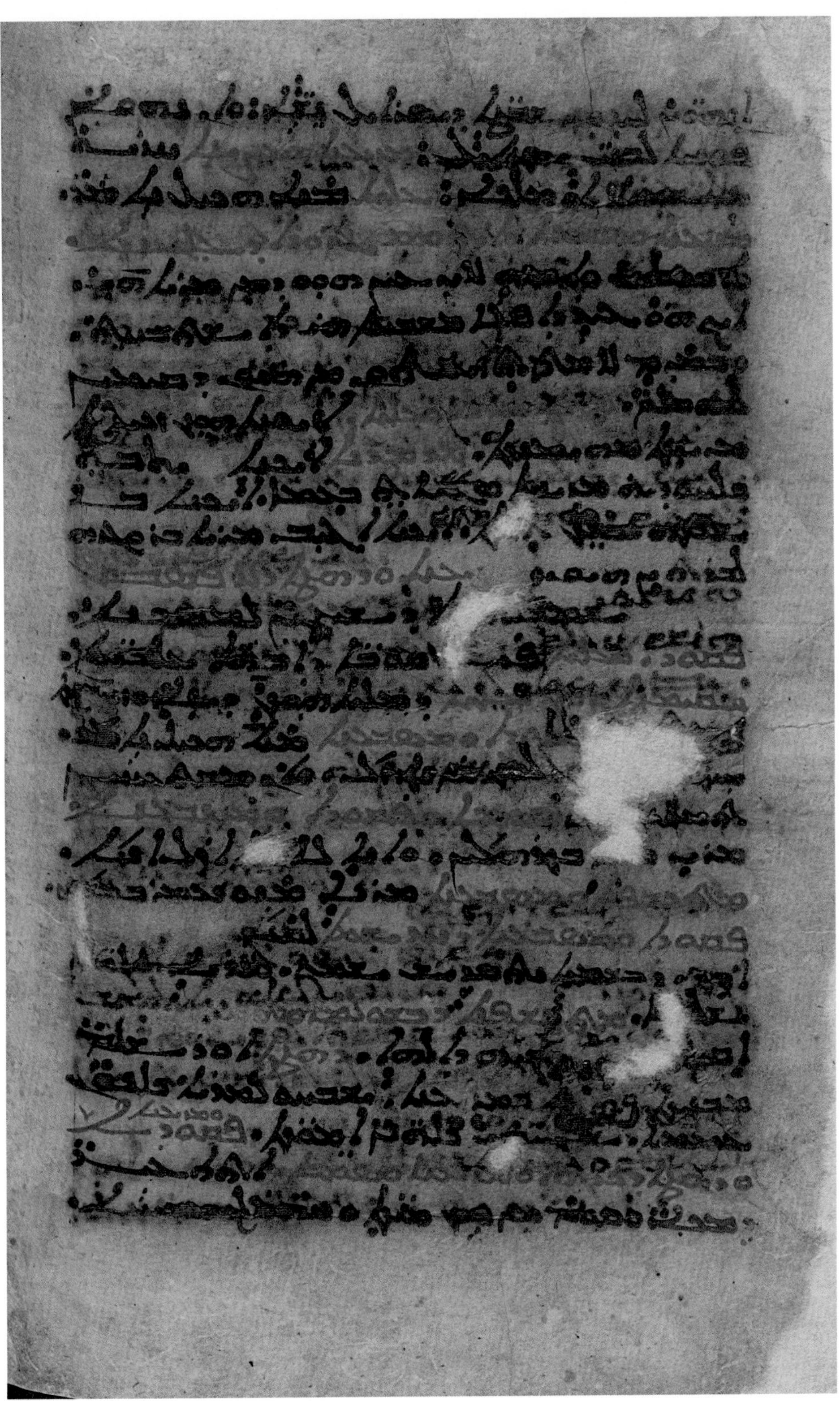

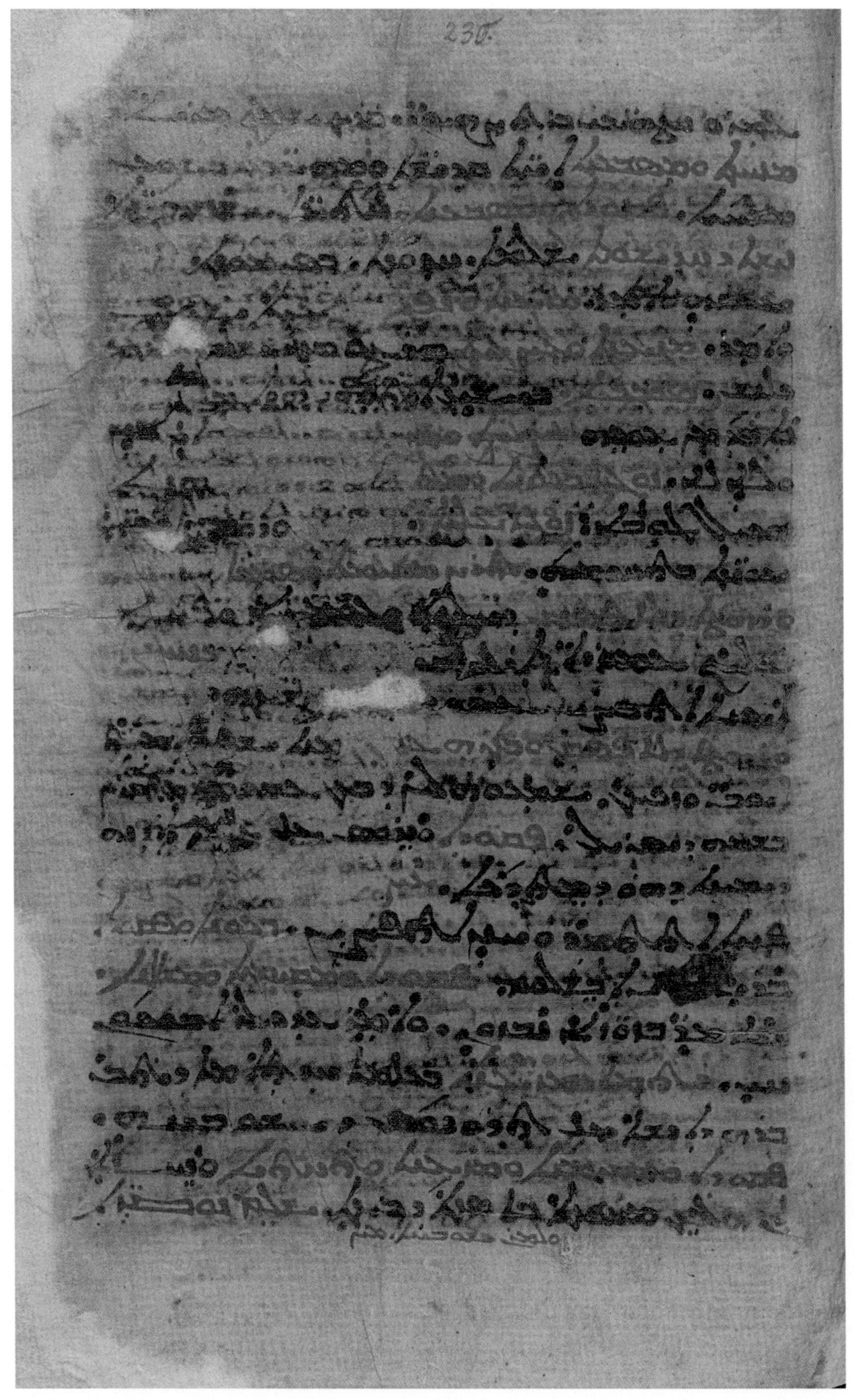

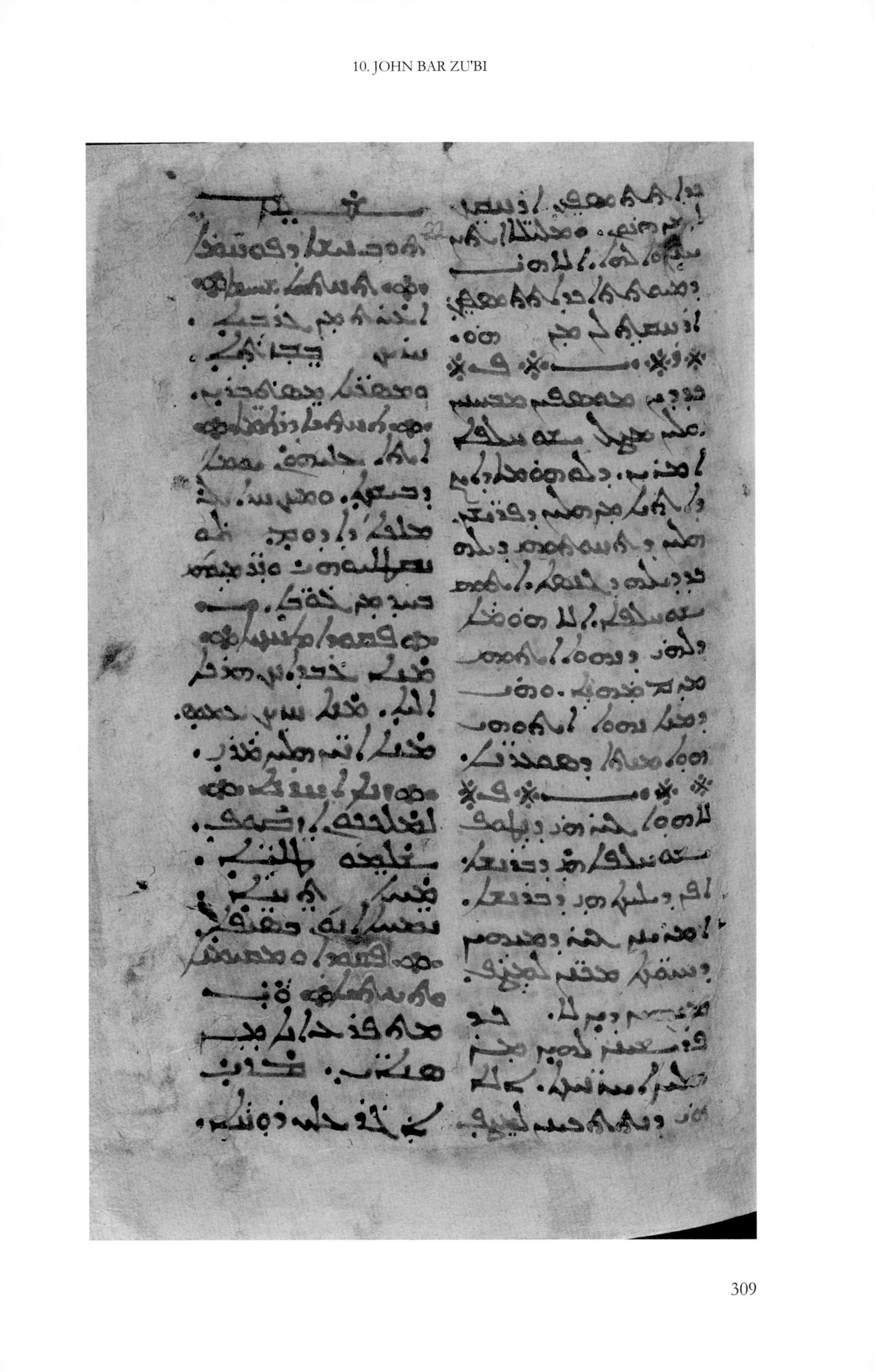

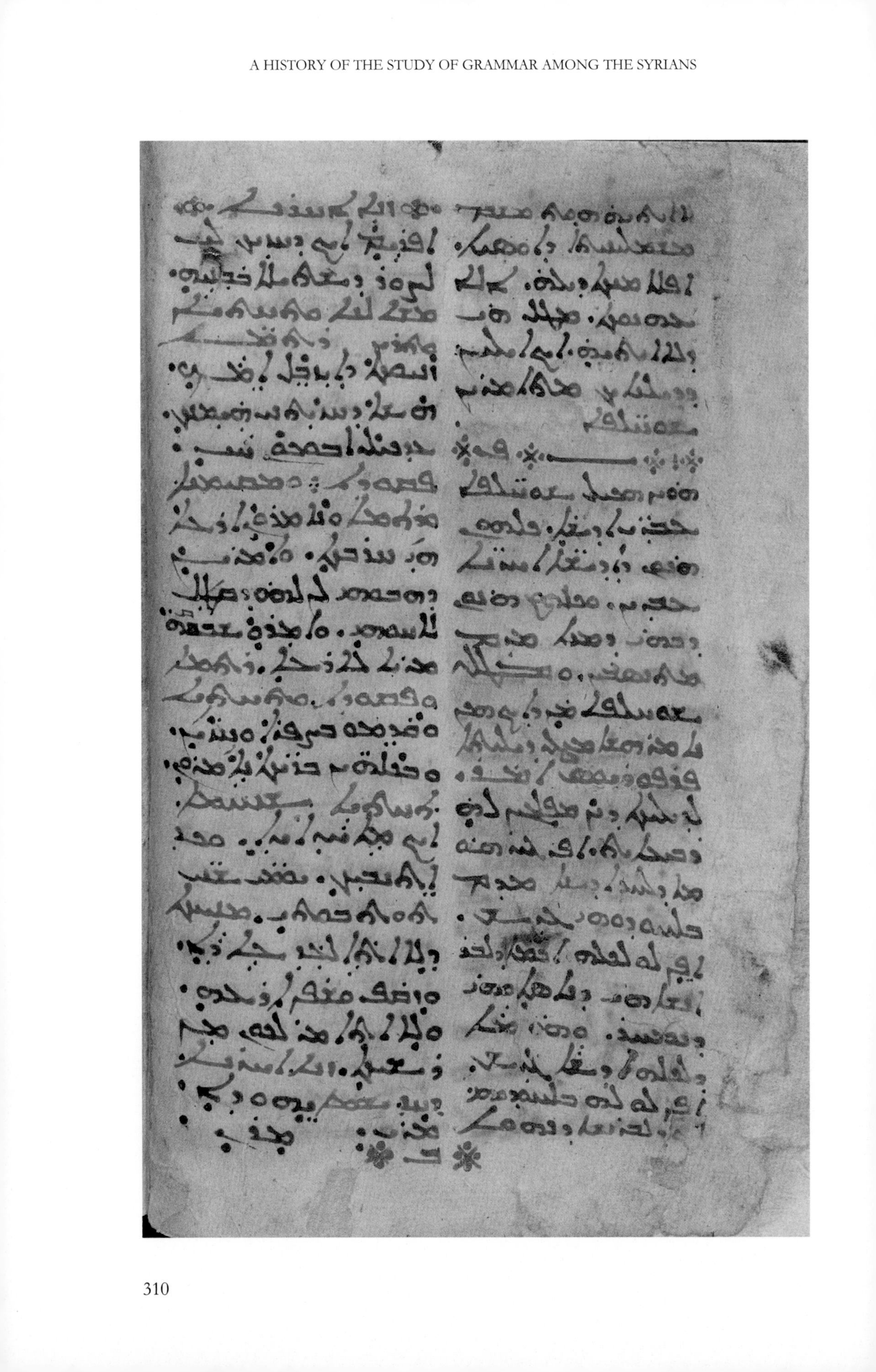

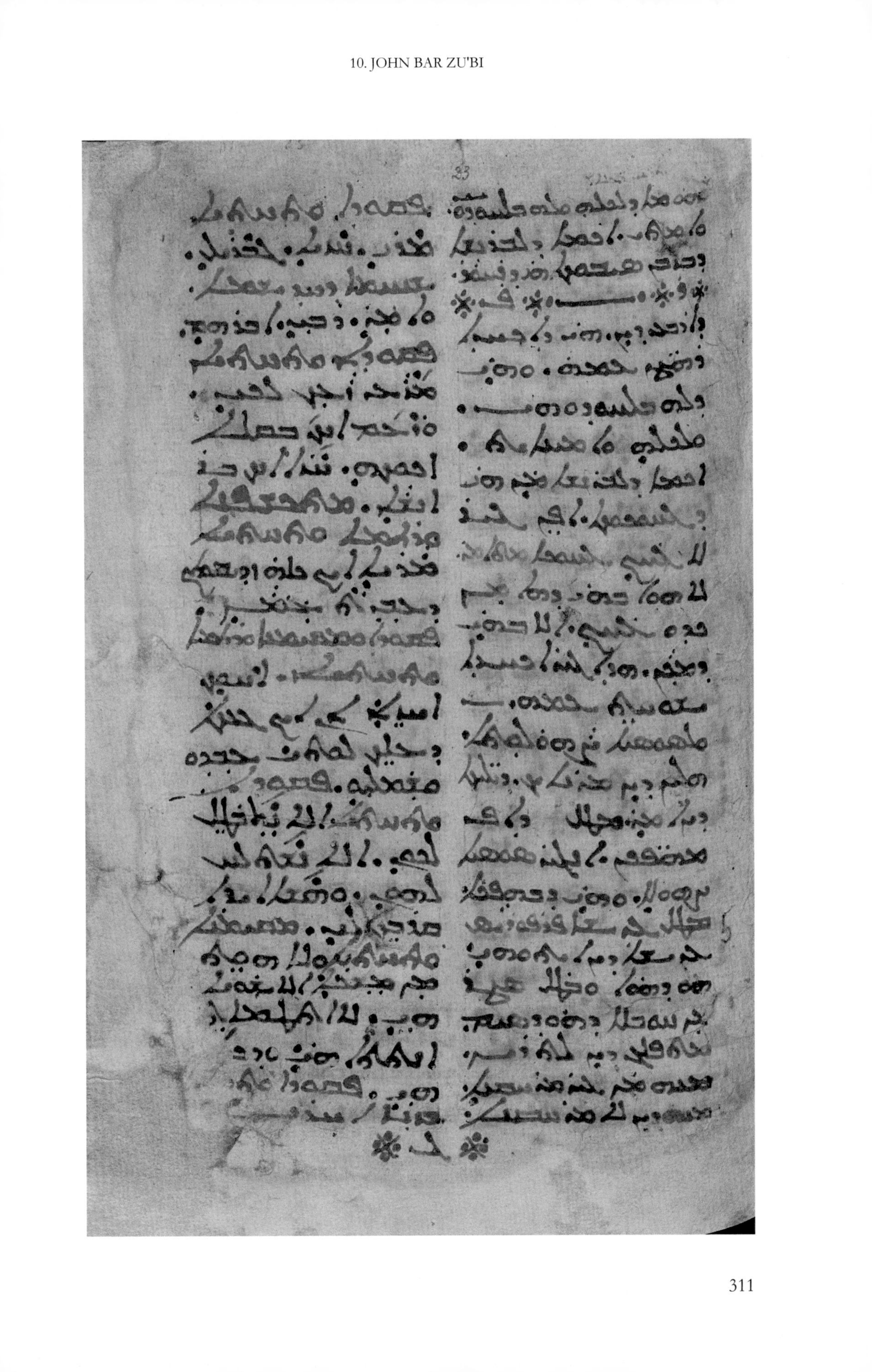

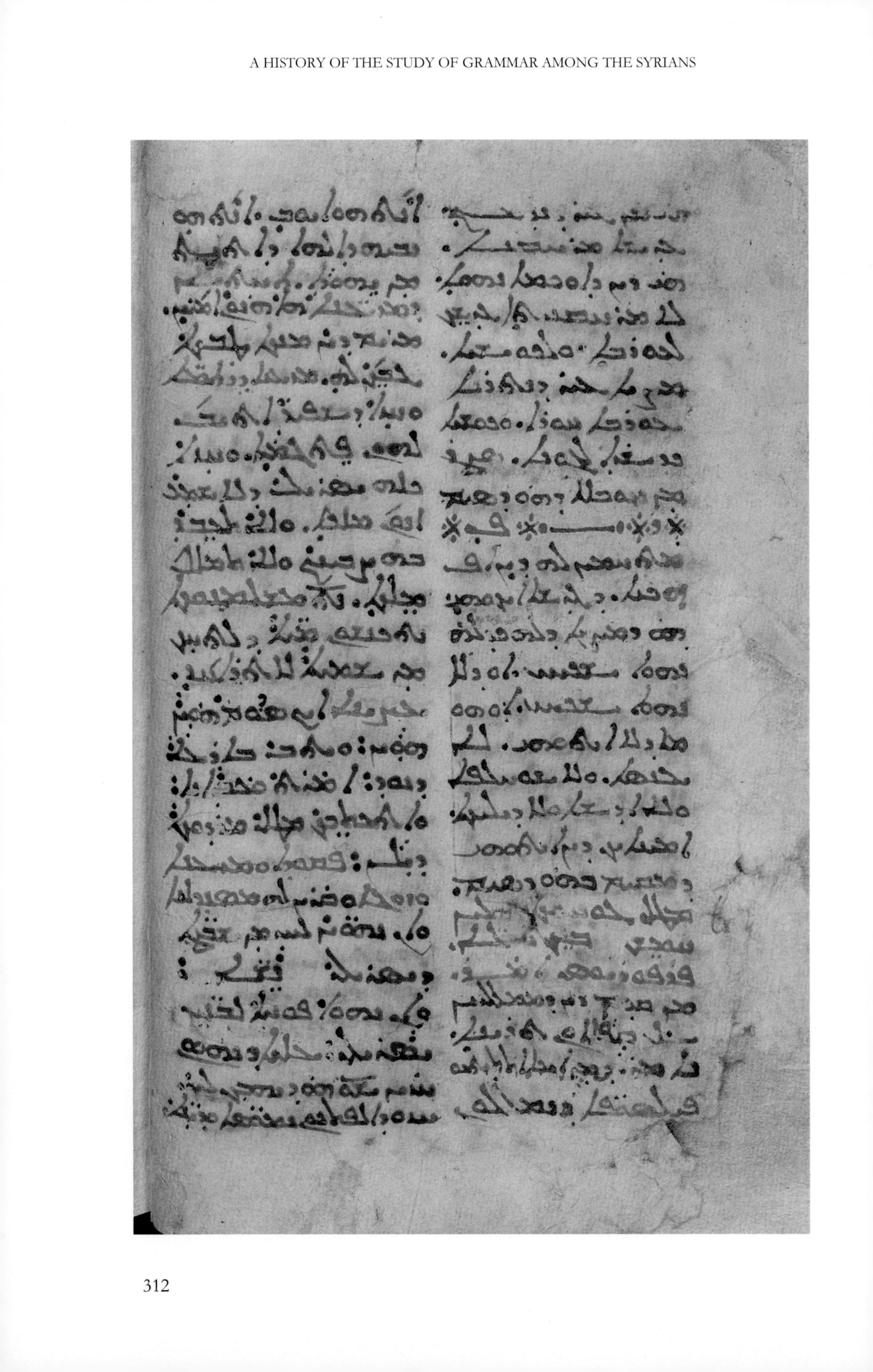

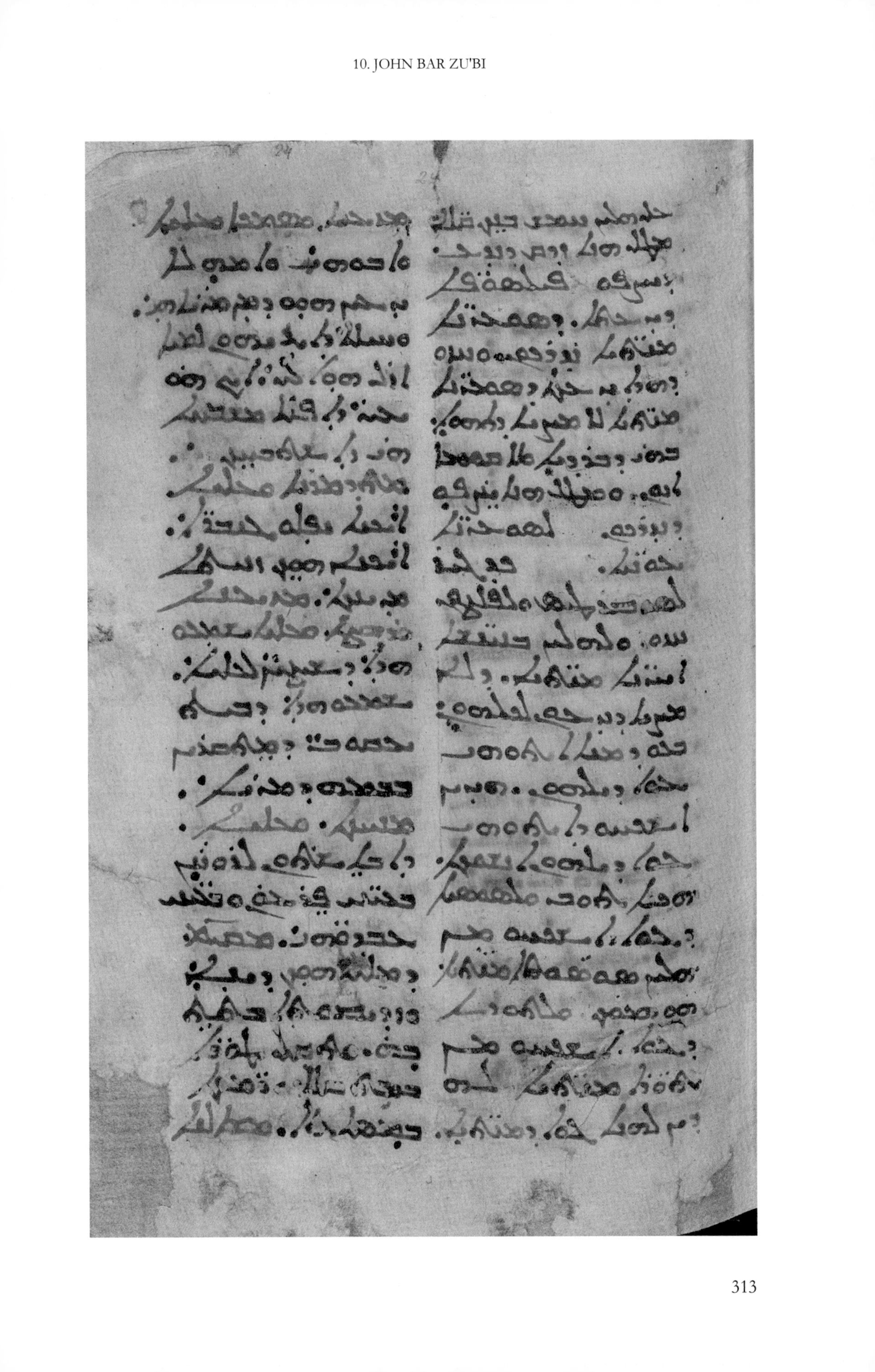

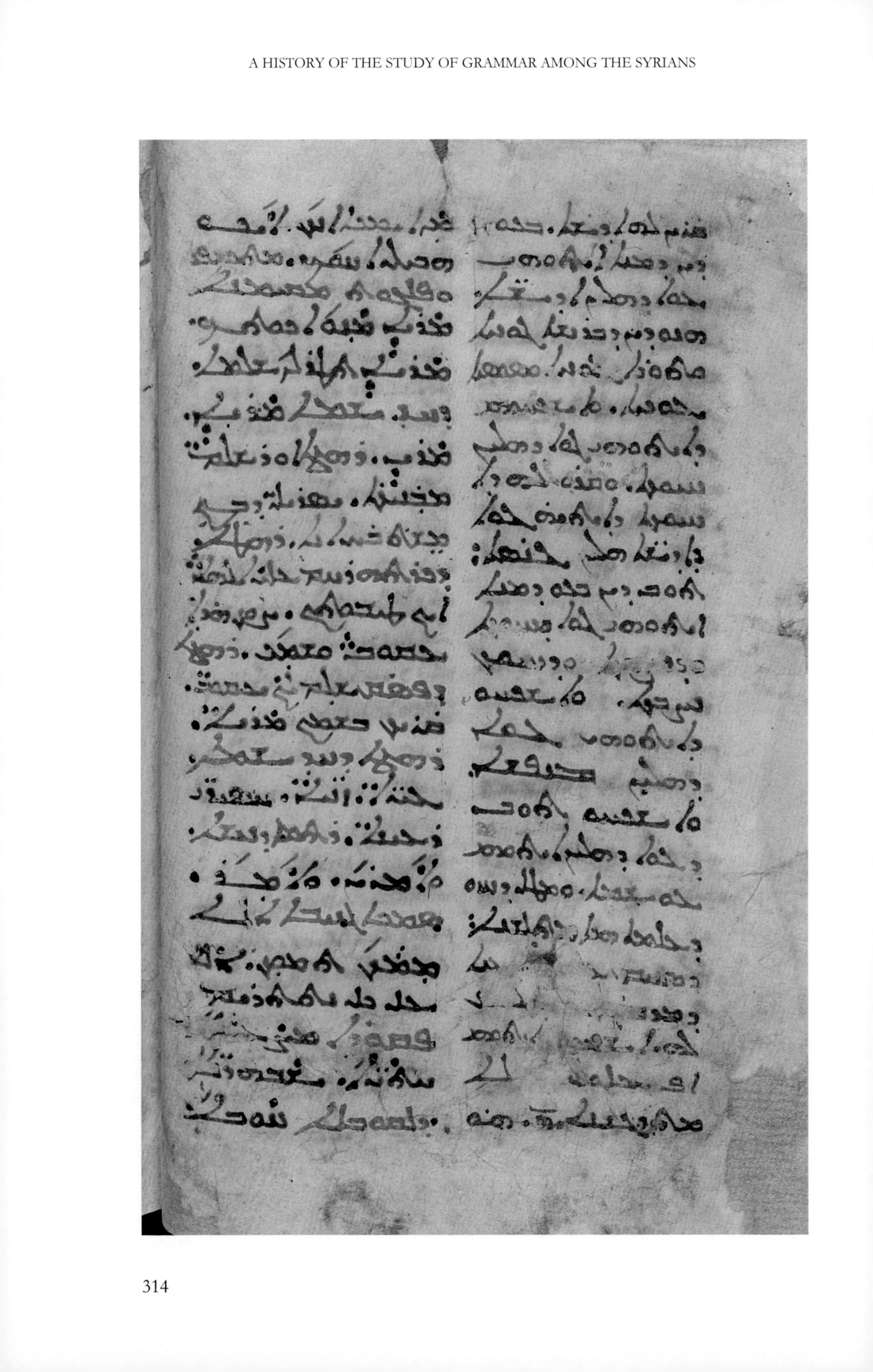

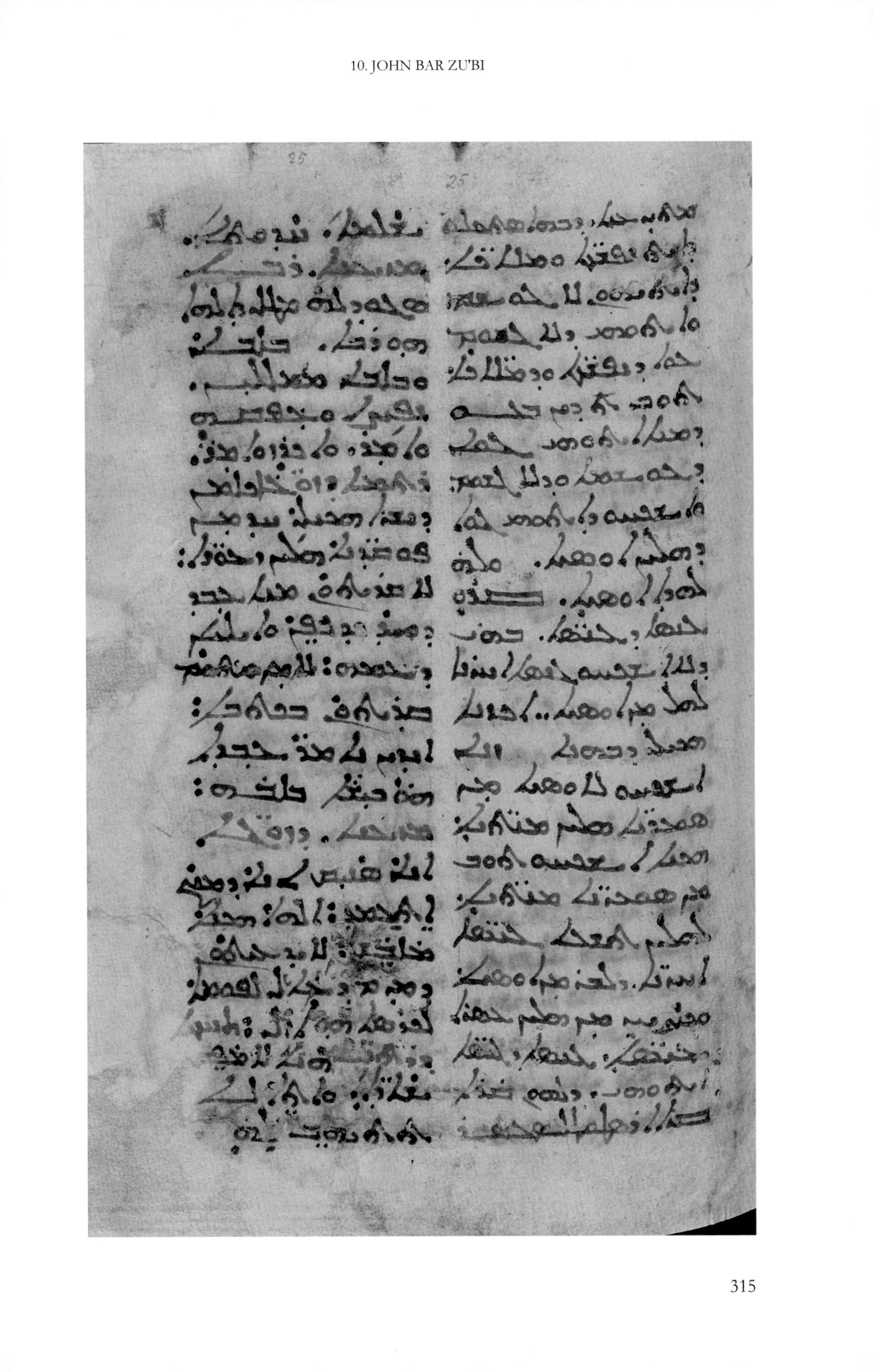

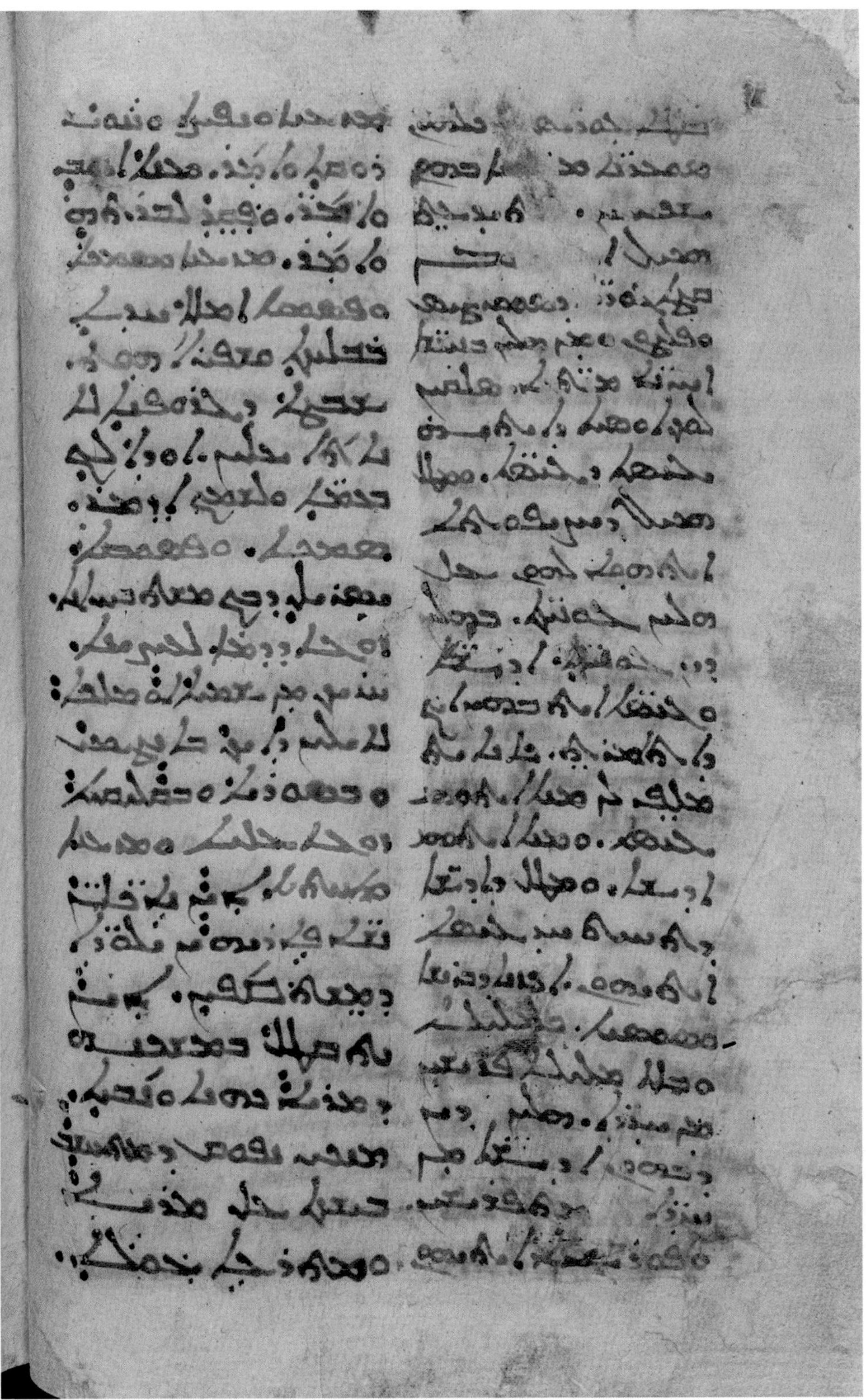

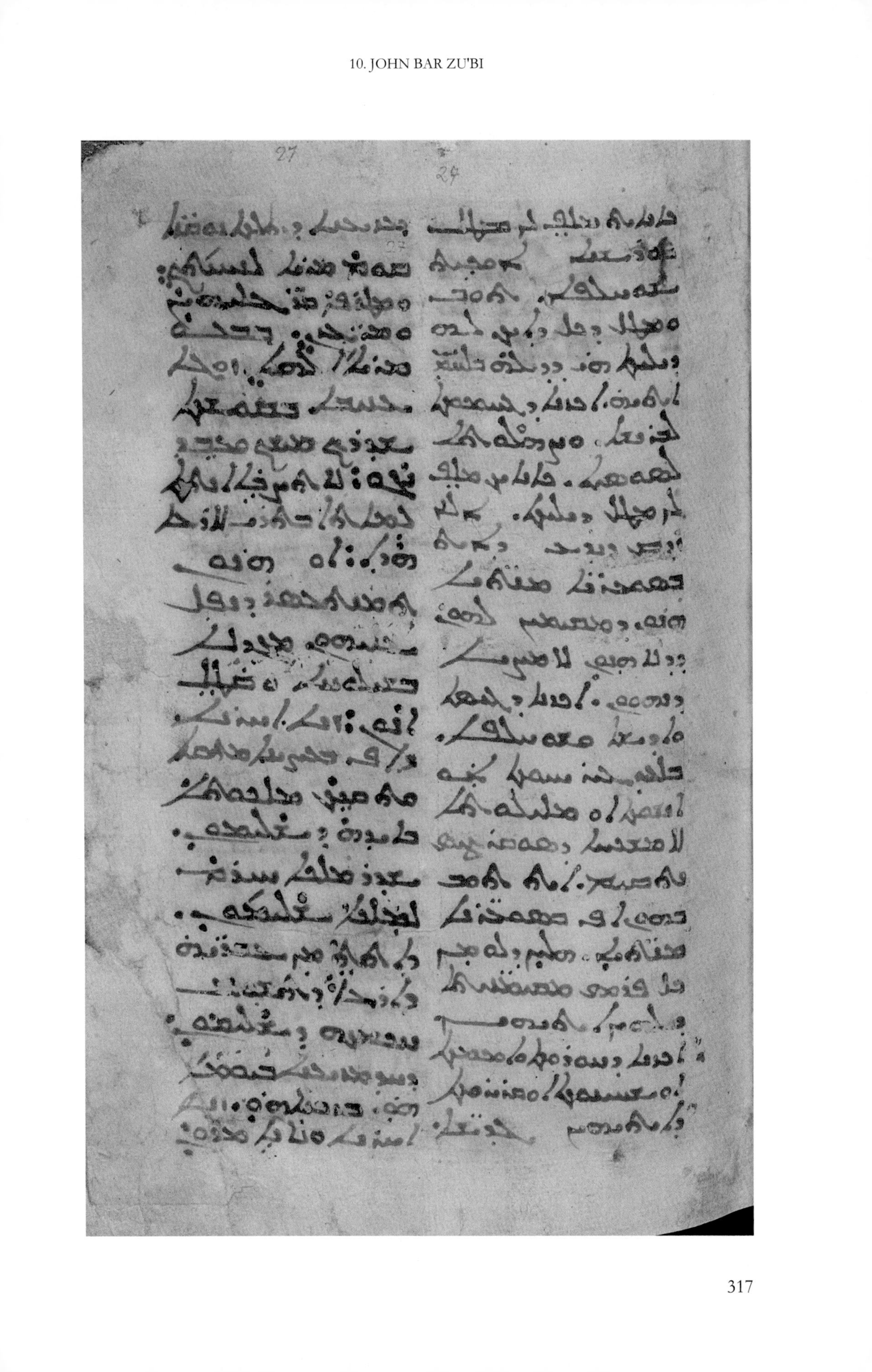

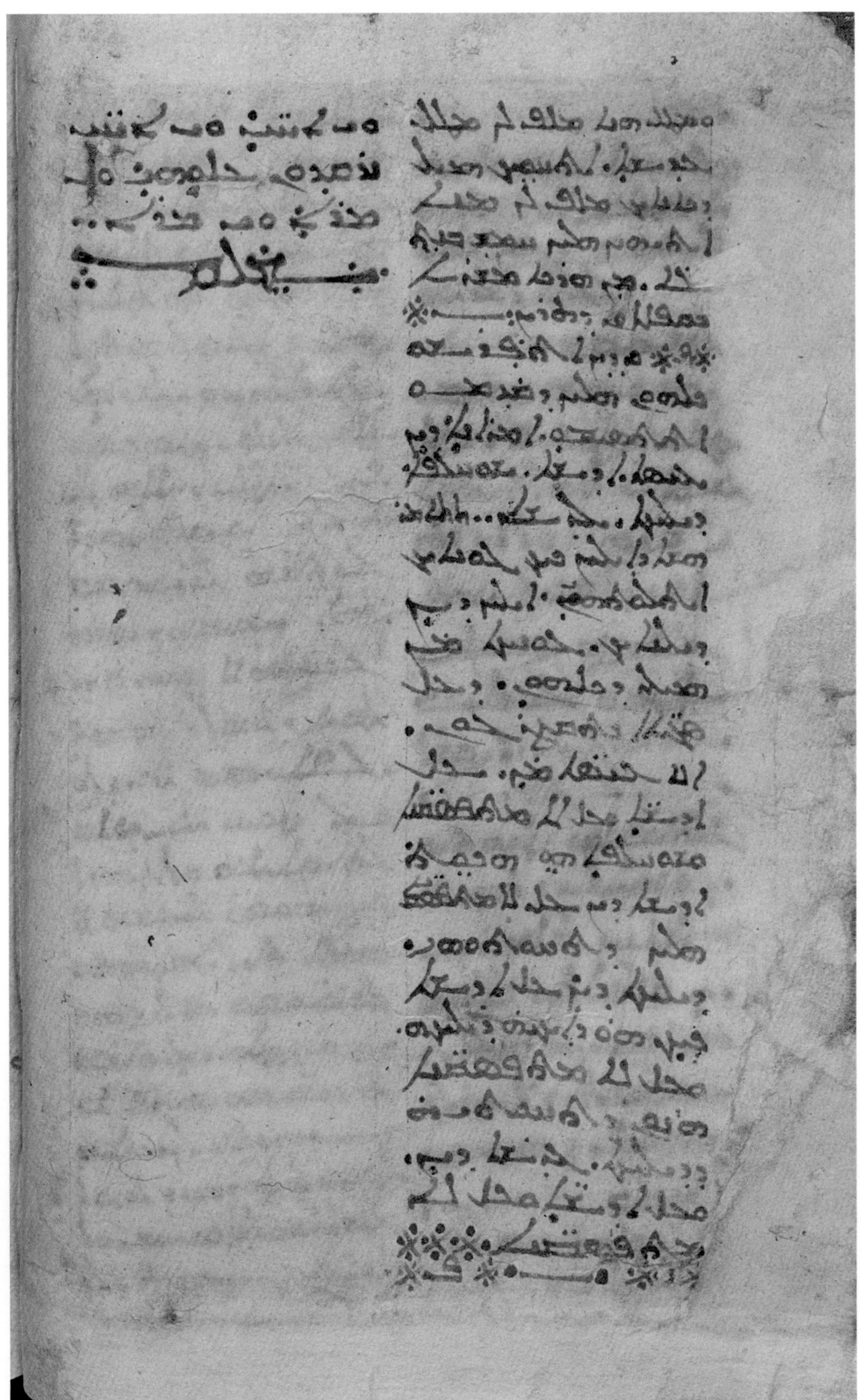

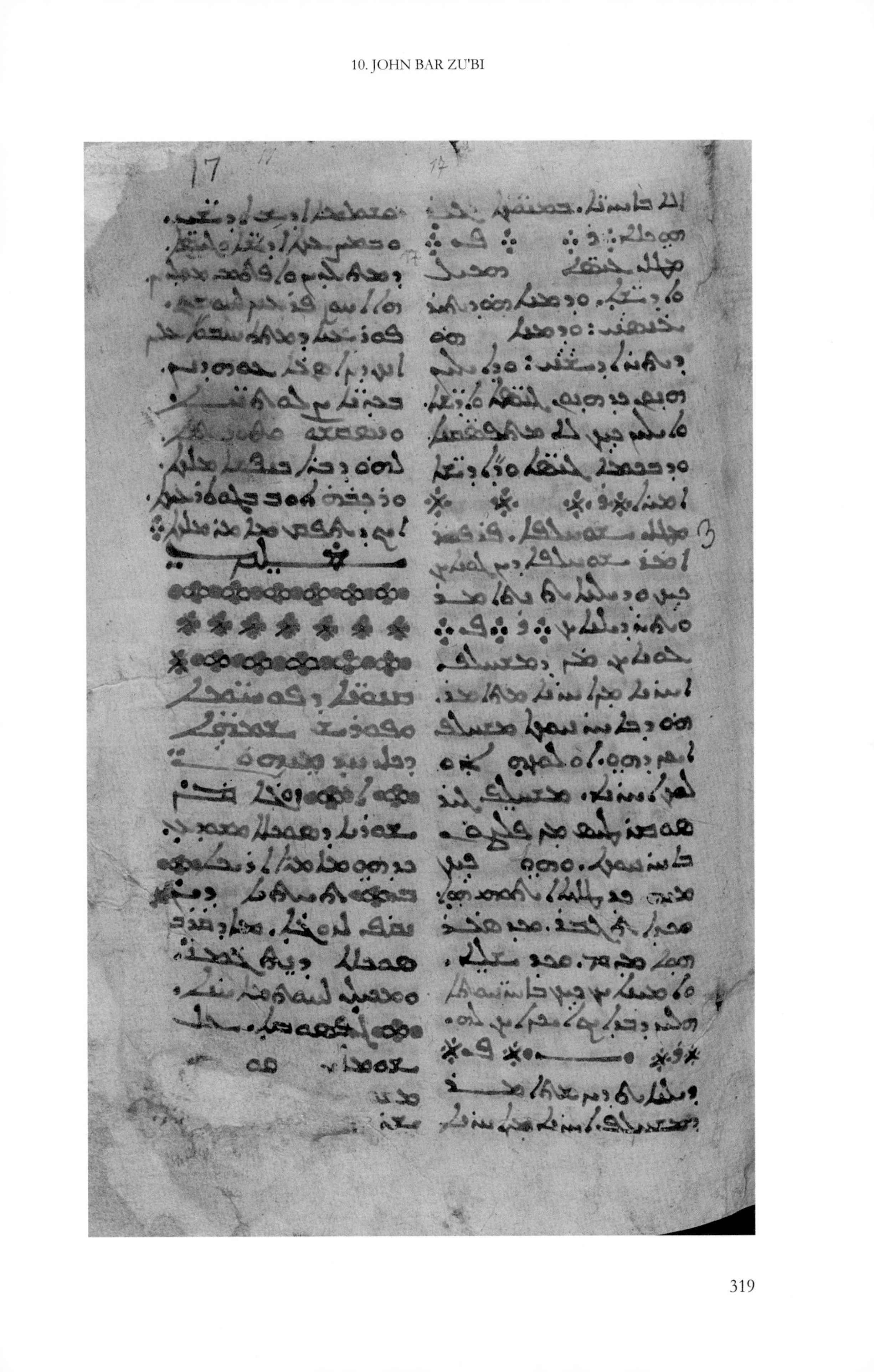

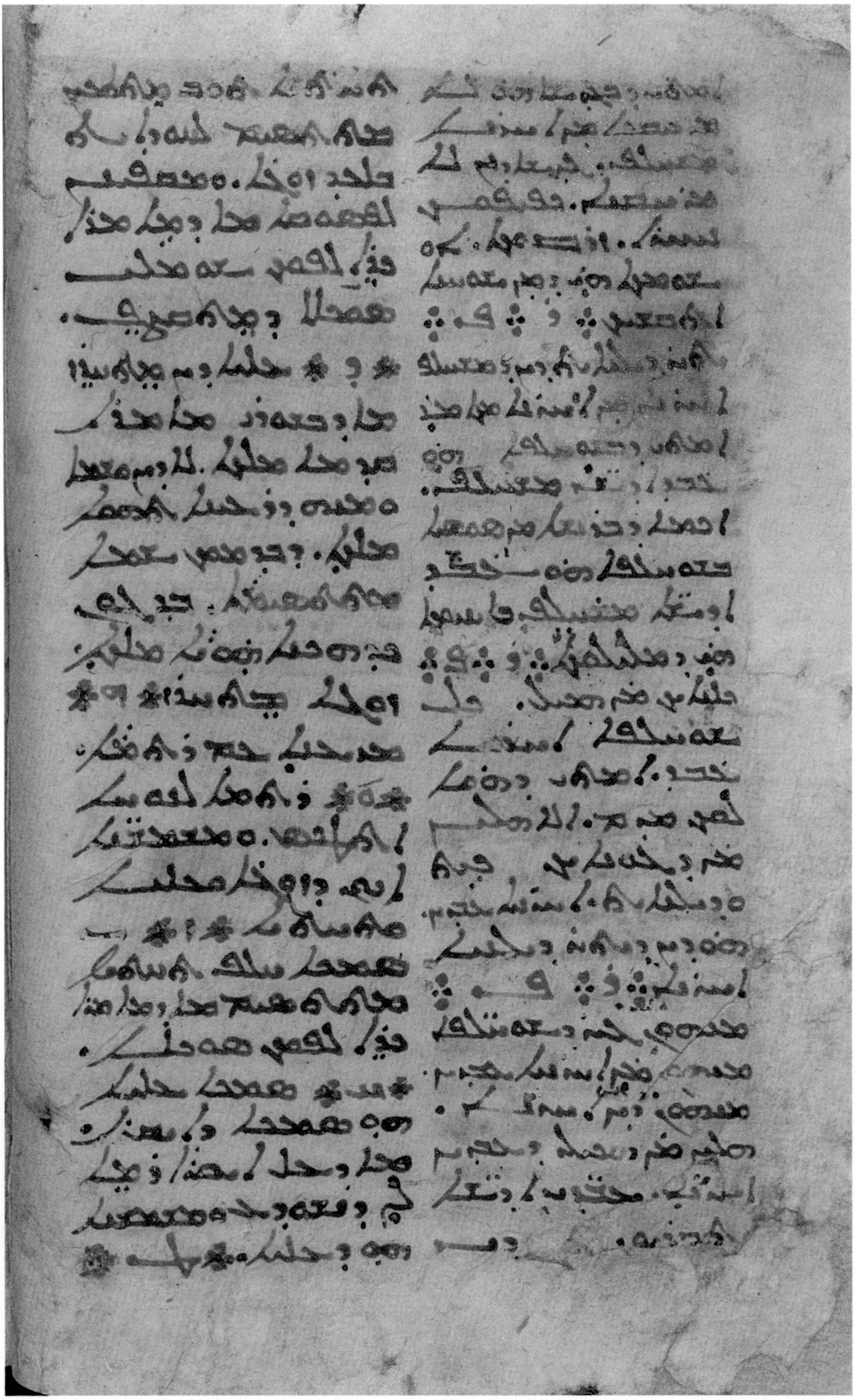

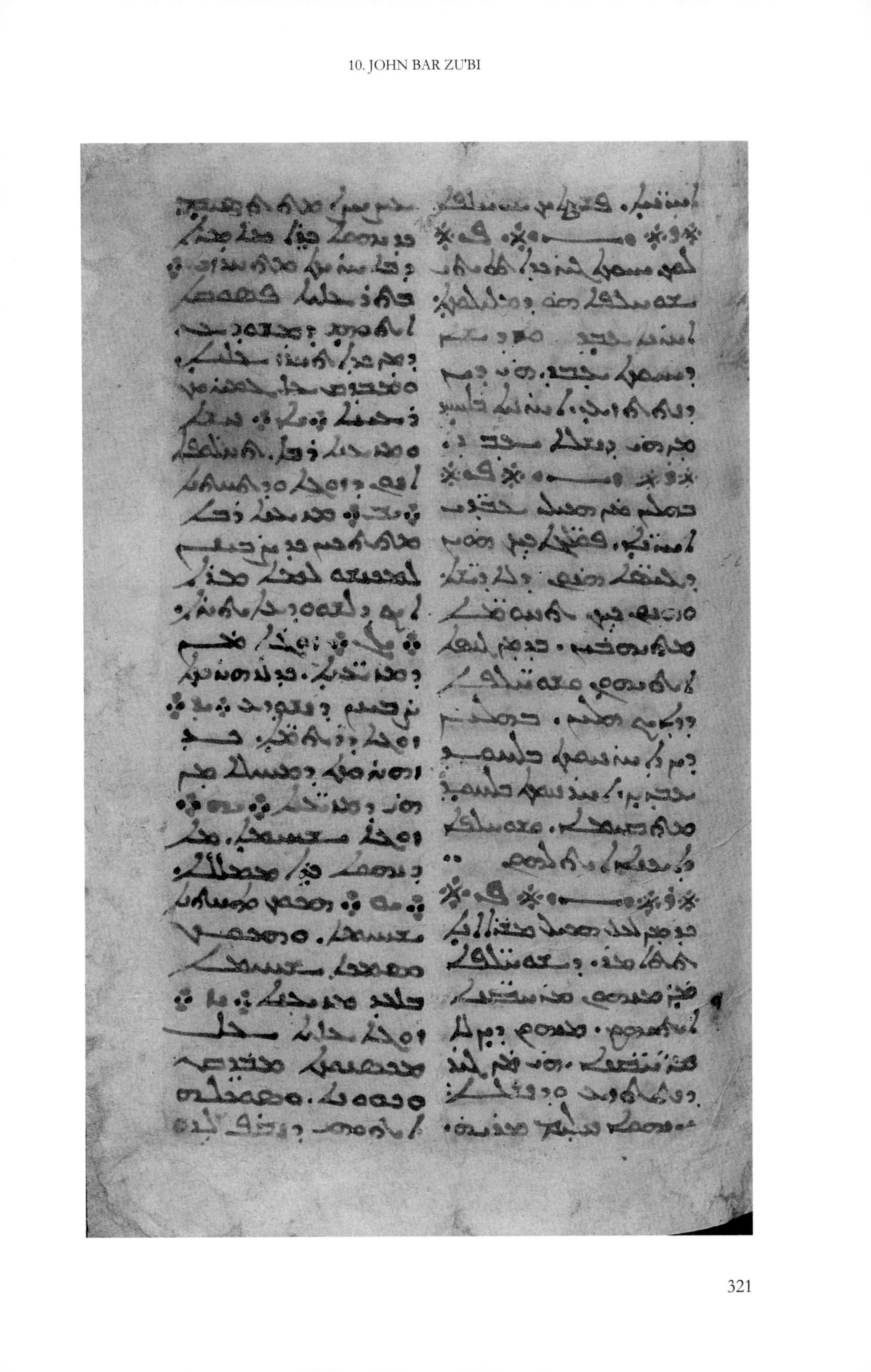

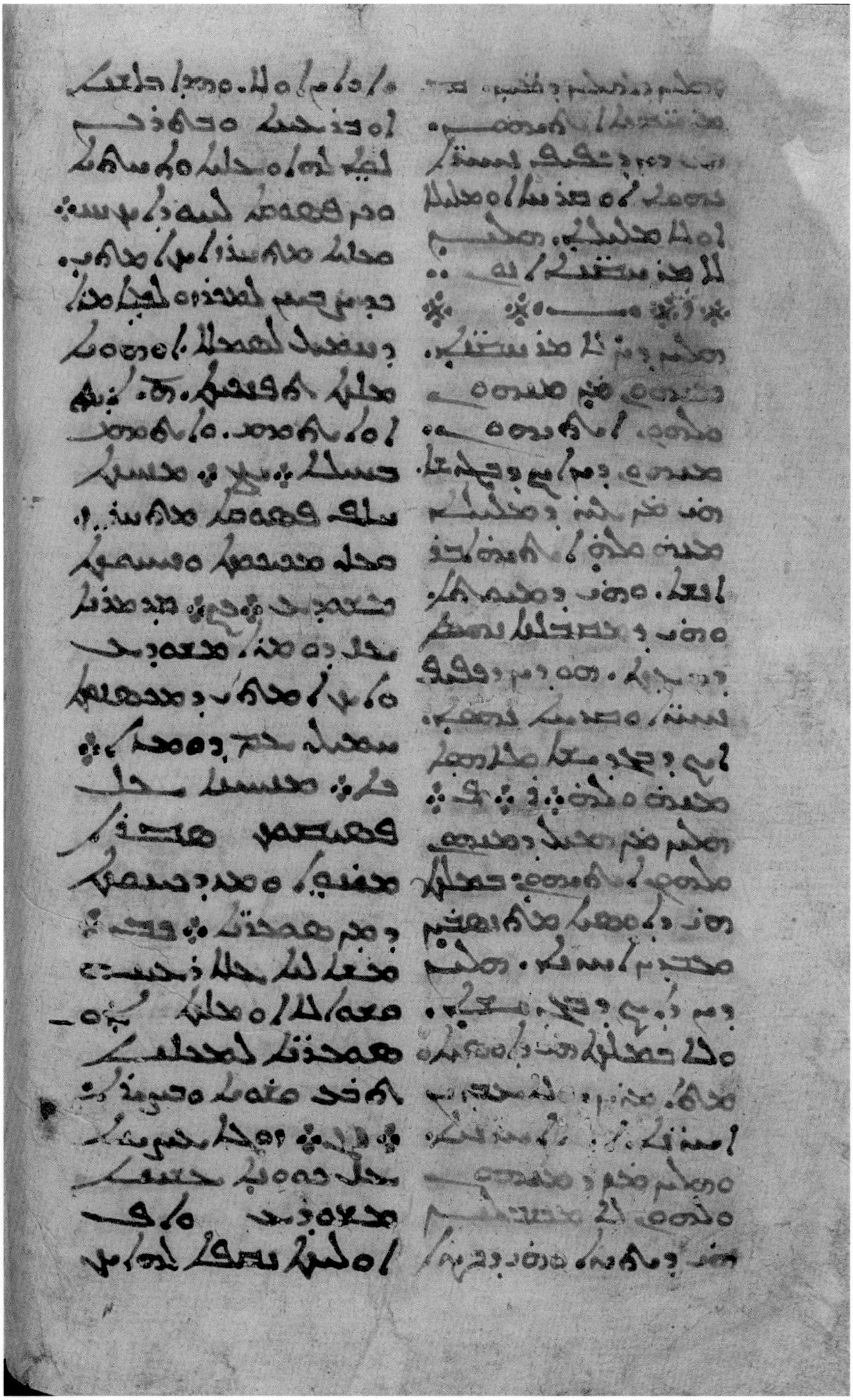

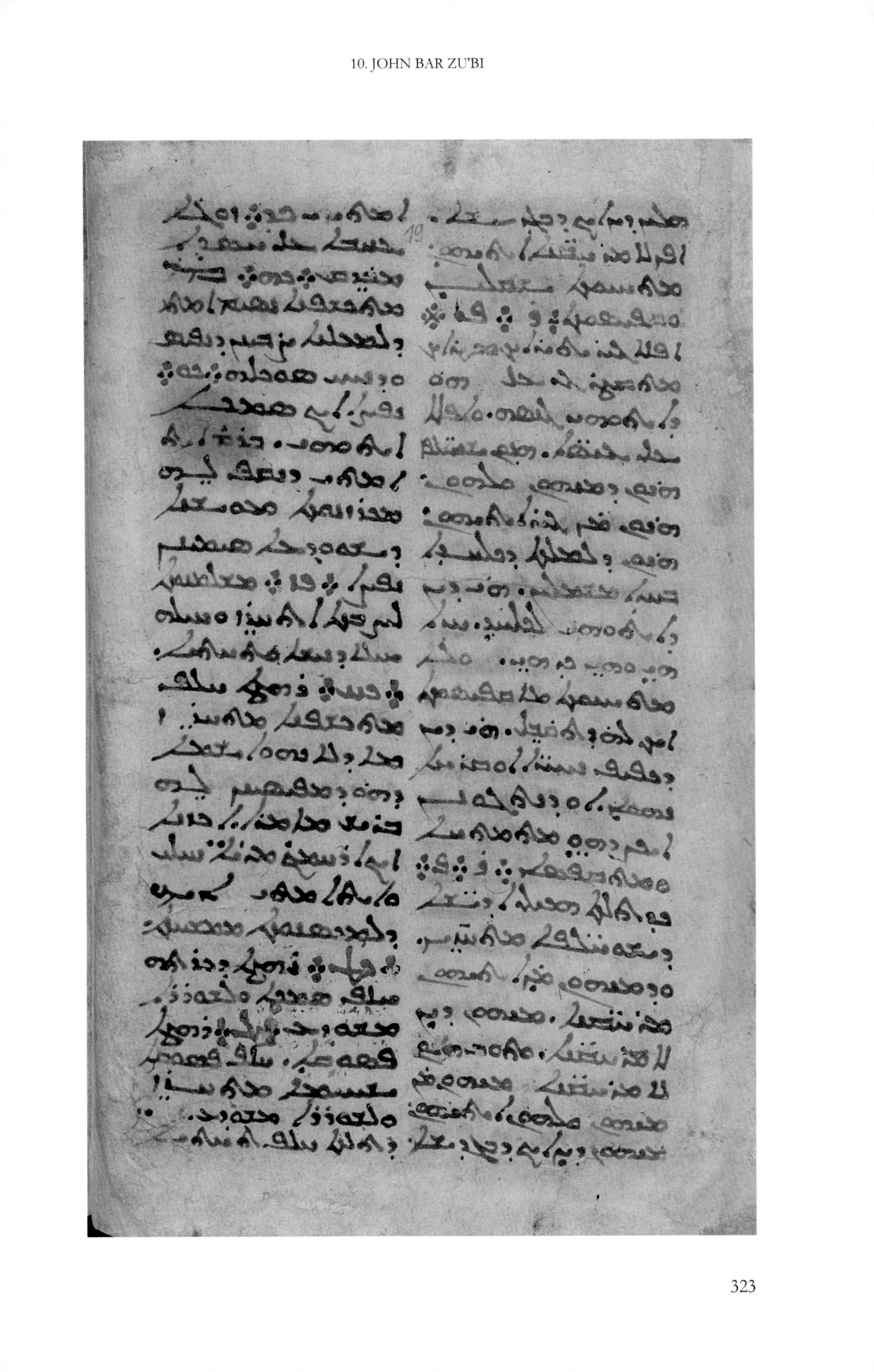

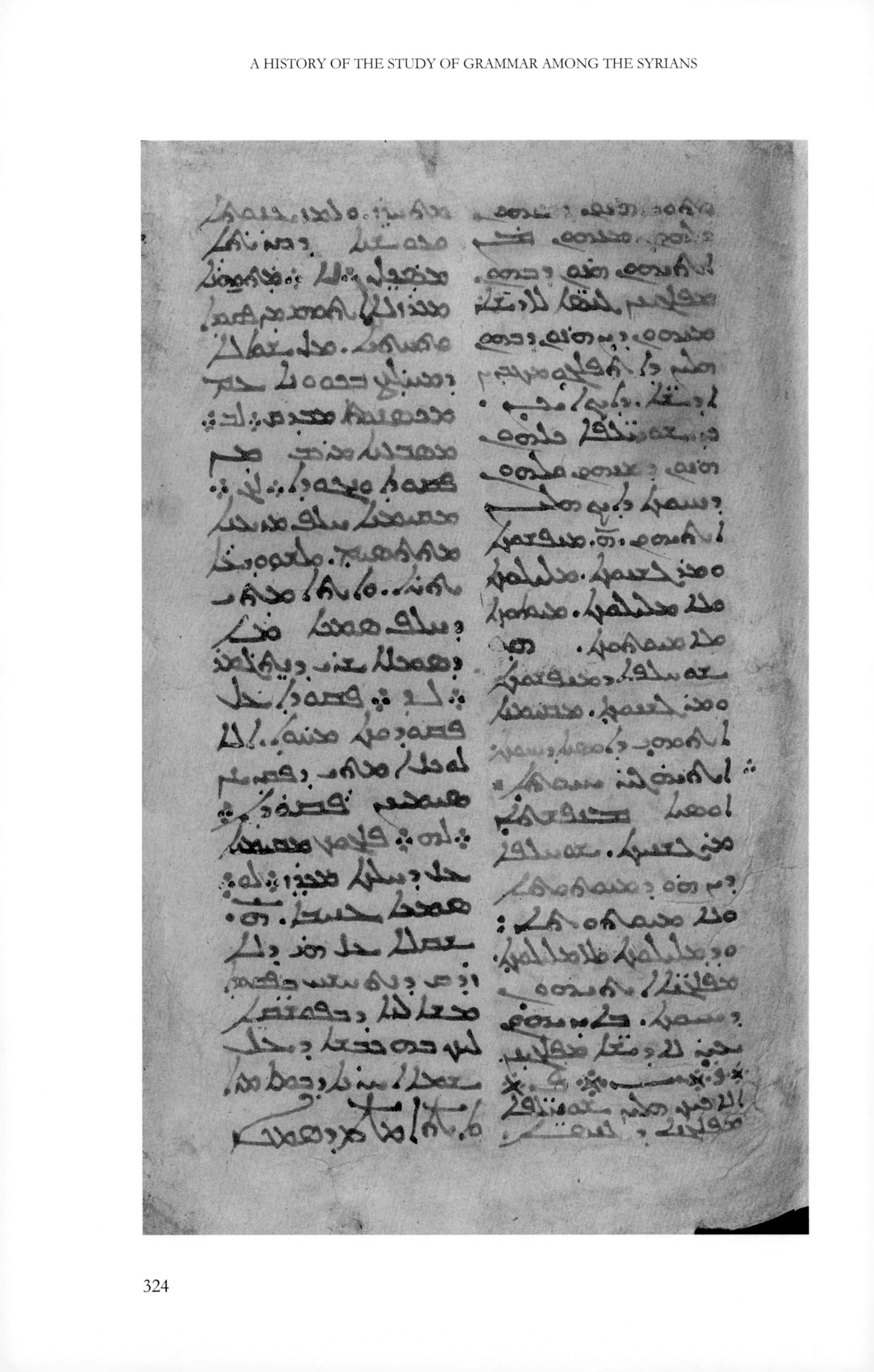

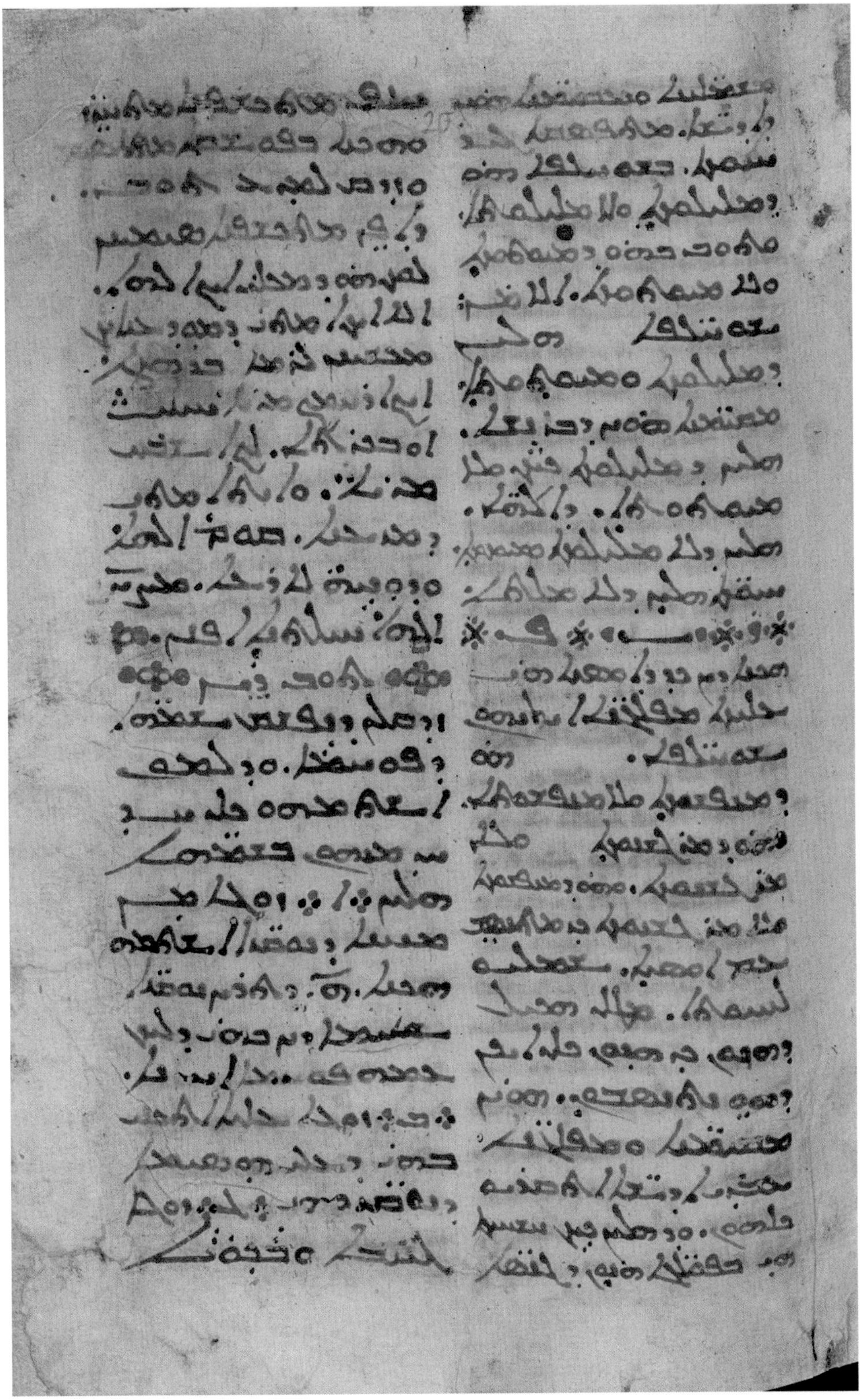

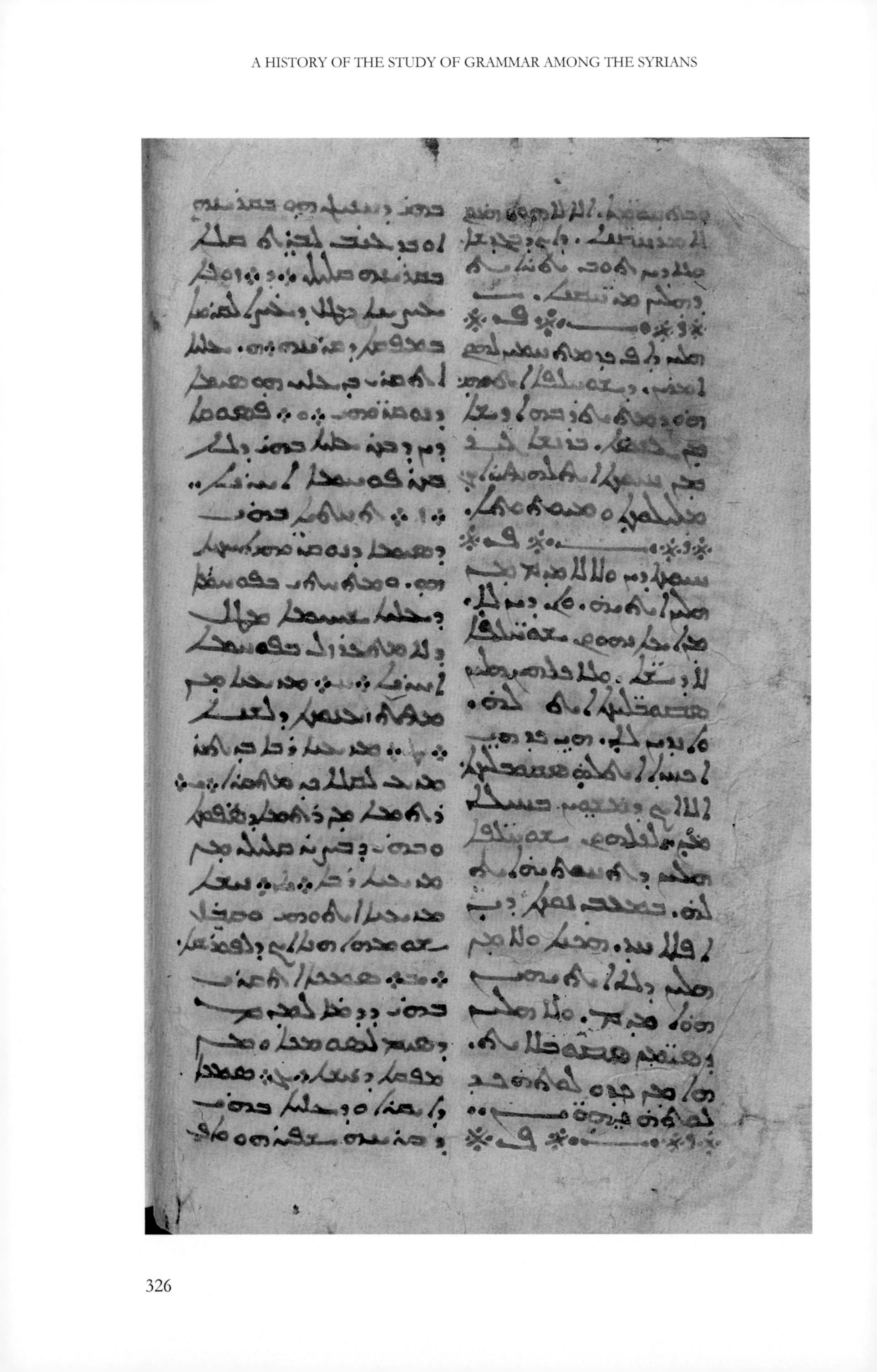

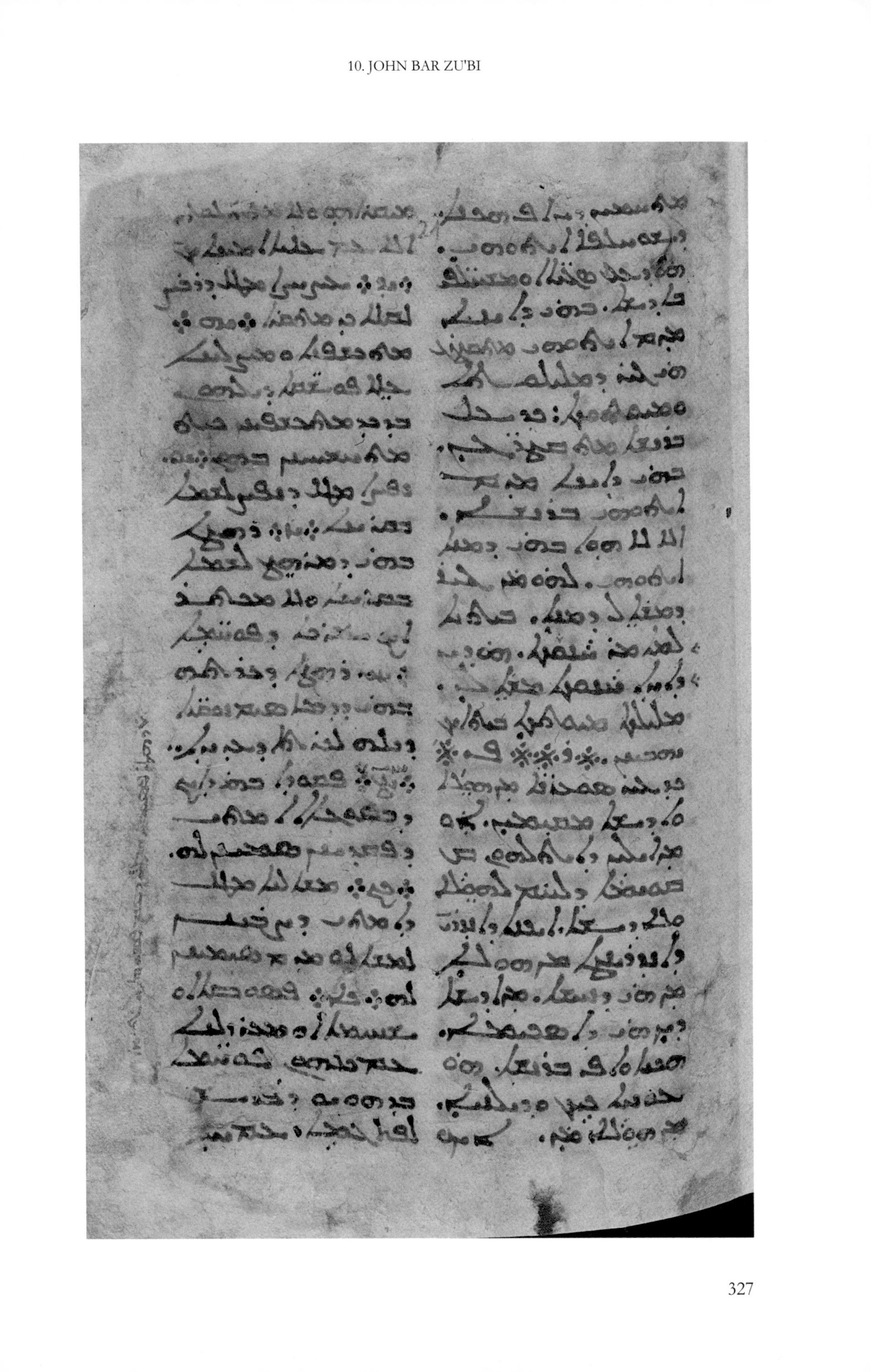

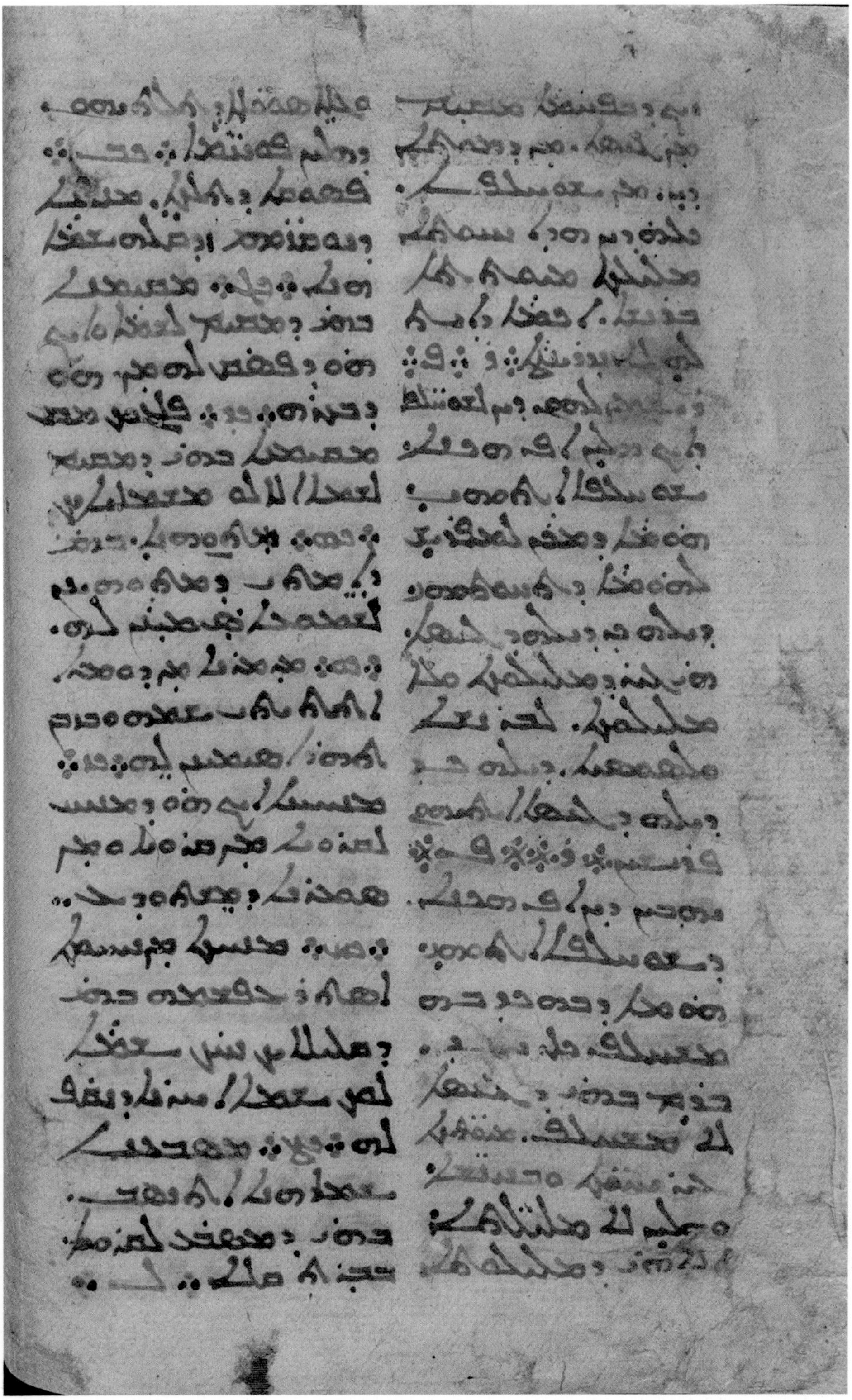

Appendix II

OBSERVATIONS FROM THE REUCHLIAN MANUSCRIPT ON ARAMAIC AND HEBREW ORTHOEPY

The preceding appendix has shown just how precise and accurate the East Syriac grammars could be in their theories of accents. It is clear that they constructed their rules not by whim but for the very practical purpose of encouraging a more elegant recitation. The ears of the great masters would never have been satisfied by any simple or common recitation; instead they strove as hard as they could to express the sense of every individual phrase simply by the modulations of voice and they demanded that just the right tones should be used in just the right places, whether for lamenting, for praying, for ordering, or for persuading. For such people who, to use the Greek term, recited καθ' ὑπόκρισιν (i.e. κατὰ μίμησιν τῶν προσώπων—performing their books like actors on the stage, who strive for the most convincing performance possible), being in any way negligent of the most minute detail concerning individual words or their interconnection was quite out of the question. It is common to praise the Arabs for their beautiful recitations of the Qurʾān, but nothing can be taken away from the Syrians who really achieved just the same level of elegance with their own Scriptures.

A truly refined reading that is καθ' ὑπόκρισιν can be achieved only by using both temporal and mimetic accents. The accents are especially needed for the precise pronunciation of individual words which are sometimes connected with each other very closely, and at other times need to be separated. The East Syrians indicated this by the ܢܓܘܕܐ and ܡܗܓܝܢܐ, which were unknown to the Westerns, and this seems to have been their main contribution to Syriac accentuation. What we have in these particular marks is an attempt to describe a more cultivated pronunciation of Aramaic. Those who read the Scriptures felt |[201] that this could be achieved by bringing some words into a closer phonetic relationship with each other, while driving others further apart. In short, the ܢܓܘܕܐ and ܡܗܓܝܢܐ teach us the best conjunctions and disjunctions to make if we want to read an Aramaic text gracefully—I say 'Aramaic' advisedly, since we can in fact observe the same approach to conjunction and disjunction in the Targums. For when we compare the Syriac usage of these lines with the *conjunctive* and *euphonic* dagesh of the Reuchlian manuscript, the latter becomes more readily comprehensible. On this account, this ms becomes of paramount importance in considering Aramaic orthoepy in general.[ii]

But before we can show how this is the case and illustrate it with examples, we must first of all set out the basic principles in the usage of ܦܘܕܐ and ܡܗܓܝܢܐ among the Syrians, as Bar Zuʿbi's rules (found on p.127) were rather obscure and not at all explicit on many points. Bar Zuʿbi never really understood the fundamental principle that lay behind them, and instead he simply listed certain occasions (ܙܒܢܐ) when one or other of them should be used, without telling us all the conditions under which either should occur (p.131). It will be possible, however, to comprehend the whole affair by using a collation of the Reuchlian codex which is based on natural phonology. Barhebraeus was the first really to introduce such a system.[1]

It is easy enough to understand what happens when the end of a word—whether it be a vowel or a consonant—is joined to the beginning of the next, which might be a vowel, a vowelless consonant, or a vowelled consonant. The different possible combinations are as follows:

I. A vowel follows a final vowel—the Syrians could not have such a form since they reckoned that words could not begin with vowels.
II. A vowelless consonant follows a final vowel.
III. A vowelled consonant follows a final vowel.
IV. A vowel follows a final consonant—initial alaph and yudh count as vowels here (see above p.128n)
V. A vowelless consonant follows a final consonant.
VI. A vowelled consonant follows a final consonant.

I. Bar Zuʿbi does not mention the first case, since as far as he is concerned all words begin with consonants (p.128). So it never even crosses his mind to consider consecutive vowels. The other five options, however, are all mentioned and illustrated by Bar Zuʿbi.

II, III. If a consonant, whether vowelled or not, follows a final vowel, then there is a close conjunction between the words and this is indicated by ܦܘܕܐ (cf. p.128, IIa). For the Syrians, only two such vowels could occur at the end of a word, namely *ā* and *e* (the latter for emphatic masculine plurals), since *au*, *āi*, and *ai* (as in ܡܰܚܟ̈ܬ) |[202] were thought of rather as syllables ending in a consonant which then brings about a following

[1] *Gramm.*, 201.

Quššāyā.[1] So where Bar Zuʿbi speaks about two complete (ܡܫܡܠܝܐ) words (p.128, IIa) he means words that end with *ā* or *e*, or have suffixes added. Once he had done with the latter group (p.128, IIIa), there still remained the words ending in *ā* or *e*. When these come before the relative ܕ (and, by a universal analogy, are positioned before vowelled or vowelless consonants), they form a special case for Bar Zuʿbi and require ܚܘܕܐ to indicate the close conjunction of the words. In Hebrew this sort of conjunction is indicated by a dagesh or by a maqqef, so when the Syrians write ܡܠܟܬܐ¯ܕܫܒܐ and ܡܕܝܢܬܐ¯ܕܡܠܟܐ (i.e. with ܚܘܕܐ), then in the Targums we should expect (if the same phonological rules apply) מַלְכְתָא דִּשְׁבָא and מְדִינְתָּא דְּמַלְכָּא. And indeed this is just what we find, for this appears very frequently in the Reuchlian ms. Examples can be found in my *Chrestomathia Targumica*, 104, where I have edited Habakkuk 3 as it is written in this ms, which includes the following:

1) The dagesh in דְּ, דַּ, and דִּ. E.g. טוּרָא דְּפארן, טוּרָא דְּסיני, מַלְכָּא דִּידוּשְׁלֵם, מַלְכָּא דְּחֶבְרוֹן, נַבְיָא, איכָא דִּיהב, צלוֹתָא דְּצלי, רוּחָא דְּקוּדשׁא, טוּרַיָּא דְּמִלְקַדְמִין, and also before verbs, as in שַׁנַיָא דִּיהבה, שְׁנַיָּא דְּאמרת, דָּרָא דַּעֲברו, דְּצר, and also before particles, e.g. רַשִׁיעַיָּא דְּאִם, עלמָא דִּיליה.

From all these examples we can see that Bar Zuʿbi is incorrect to say that the use of ܚܘܕܐ was restricted to joining two complete nouns, for in fact it can be used wherever a consonant, whether vowelled or not, follows a final *ā*. The state of the noun thus makes no difference, since the conditions for its use are phonetic and can equally well occur before or after particles or between verbs and nouns, in the following way:

2) אישתא מִן, מֵרַשִׁיעַיָּא דַּעבדו, עלמָא לְא־תִפרעָא, איתגלֵיתָא בִּגְבוּרתך, קדישָׁא מִטּוּרָא, נַבְיָא כַּד, שְׁמַיָּא זִיו, שִׁיבְטַיָּא מימרך, תהומַא קַליה, עלמַא גְבורה, להורעָא גְבודתך, כזעתָא טִינָּרִין, הָא כִּשְׁלוֹתא.

In this set of examples *a* is often written for *ā*, although not much should be read into this fact since for some reason the ms often turns the one into the other. E.g. אלָהָא, לָא תָבִי, דינַה[2] דאִיתְּדָנוּ, לאוריתֵא בִּלְבב, רשיעַיָּא מְתִיבא, מְדָרומא,|[203] הודעתַא בְּהוֹן, חמְשַׁח מַלְכִין; the same again in מַא דְּעַבַדְתָּא מִבראשית and in Joshua 1.17, כְּמַא דַּהֲוֵה בְּסַעֲדֵיה דְּמשׁה.[3]

---

[1] See Merx, *Grammatica*, 65.

[2] From the written form אִיתְּדָנוּ, it follows that *d* became *t*. Vice versa, some Syrians used a *d* in ܘܦܝܠܐ, saying ܚܘܒ ܕܠܐ (Wright, *Cat.*, 104), whence the Aramaic orthoepy described in Merx, *Grammatica* I,72, which was taken from Amira, should clearly be augmented in light of the Reuchlian ms.

[3] The Hebrew מַה־זֹּאת is to be explained in the same way. Thus also the different forms of the article הַ / הָ, which I would like to see as being formed according to this phonetic law

What we see happening here after *ā* and *ă* happens in the Targum after all the other vowels as well. This was, of course, impossible in Syriac which had lost all final vowels save for *ā* and *e*. So we see the dagesh:

3) after *ē* : אֲרֵי מלכות, צְוָארֵי סַנְאֵירוֹן, חיילֵי מְרומא, ענני מִיטרא, מֵי נַהרא, יומֵי בְּראשית, מלכֵי מַדי.

after *i* : יקימִינַּנִי לְדדיליה, לִי בְּחֵילא, קדמוֹהִי כְּחוֹבֵיהון, אִיתִי מַבולא, and the *ai* of the construct, which within such a conjunction is resolved into *ayi* : מַלְכָי מִן־קדם, ריגְלָי קְלִילִין (2 Sam 22.34) which can also happen before a vowel, as in לְחַכִּימָיי וּבְאָתָר, where the point in the waw should be taken as a dagesh rather than as expressing the vowel shūreq.

after *u* : נפקוּ, פלחוּ בית, אתפרקוּ טוריא, חַבוּ קֳדָמוהי, חַשִׁיבוּ מַחשבן, קמוּ בִּמְדוריהון, תמהוּ קָמוּ, נַהרין; but it does not occur with ל, e.g. ועָלוּ לבית (Josh 2.1).

after *o* : בְּגוֹ מַשִּׁרְיתא (Josh 1.11); דַהֲווֹ מְהָלְכִין (Judg 5.11).

IV. Bar Zuʿbi gives us examples (under IVa and Va, p.128-9) of the conjunction that occurs when a vowel follows a final consonant. So, for instance, the words ܠܐ, ܟܡ, ܐܦ, ܐܘ, ܡ would all take ܢܩܘܕܐ before vowels. However, although ܡ should take ܢܩܘܕܐ both before a vowel and before a vowelled consonant (IVa), we should note that in the Reuchlian ms we find not only examples such as כַּד־אִתגלי, כַּד־אתגברו, but also כַּד־הָבוּ, and even כַּד־פְּלחו, which break Bar Zuʿbi's rule IVb.

V/VI. A final consonant followed by another consonant, whether vowelled or not, on the following word, was dealt with in Bar Zuʿbi's rules VIIa and VIIb (p.130). According to the Syriac rules, only vowelless consonants (in these contexts) would be contracted, but the Reuchlian ms indicates the contraction of both types. From the third chapter of Habakkuk alone I have collated numerous examples |[204] where we can see that the particles ב ד ו ל are assimilated to the following consonant after being contracted with the vowel of the preceding word into a single syllable. So if it is right to read מִיַּד־מִדְיַנָאֵי as *miyyam-midyanaʾe*, then equally

---

and no longer on the basis of a supposed origin in הל as is argued by some grammarians. Even Kautzsch had his doubts about this phonetic origin of the doubling of the consonant that follows מה or ה, and suggests that it is due to the assimilation of the ה in מה, and of the ל in הל. Even the dagesh after the interrogative ה is in fact purely phonetic. [Tr.– For Kautzsch's statement to this effect, *Gesenius' Hebrew Grammar* (28th ed.), §35l, with further references there given. Not so sure is, e.g., A. Sperber, *A Historical Grammar of Biblical Hebrew* (Leiden, 1966), 19. Summing up the most likely history of the definite article, E. Lipinski, *Semitic Languages: Outline of a Comparative Grammar* (Leuven, 2001), 276-7.]

we should read טוריָא דְמִלְקַדְמִין such that the דמ should on both occasions be contracted to *mm*. Presuming the analogy of reading קדמא as if it were קַמָּא, this word pair is to be pronounced as *turayammiqqammin* (Hab 3.6,7).

This sort of contraction occurs even after a final consonant, which we can see not only in אַרְעָא דְקַיֶּימִית (Josh 1.6), where from *arʿad-qayyemiṯ* we get *arʿaqqayyemiṯ* as indicated by the dagesh in the ק, but even in משירייתהוֹן דְסַגְּאִין (Hab 3.8), the dagesh in the ס shows that *nds* contracts.

On the basis of this sort of contraction we can explain the dagesh in the following examples:

1) After the ו in דִדְחָקוּ ,עַלְעוּלִין וְטַבְעתנון ,שִׁמְשַׁא וְסִיהרא ,מלכַיָא וְשִׁילְטוניא ,חָי־וְקַיָּים, and especially לִמְשִׁיחָךְ וְלִשְׁארא ,אִיתְגְּלִי וְקַדישא ,מלְכִין וּמשירייתהון וְשַׁעְבִידוּ.
2) After the ב in עַמָּךְ בְּמֵימְרָךְ ,תִּדְכַּר בְּמֵיתָן ,יַמָּא בְּמַרכבת.
3) After the ל in עִמָּךְ לְמֵיפְרָק ,באיתגליותָךְ לְמֵתְבָּר ,אִתְגְּלֵיתָא לְמֵיפְרָק.
4) After the ד in היכלָא דְקֻדְשך (Jonah 2.7), אנַא זָעִית דְשַׁבְקָנִי ,צלותא דְצַלִּי.

A more careful study of these examples involving ב ד ו ל would better enable us to categorise the various types of assimilation. The following examples, all taken from Habakkuk 3, will indicate just how far this sort of assimilation extends:

; רנּ , קנּ , פנּ , זנּ , דנּ ; תמּ , שמּ , רמּ , זמּ , למּ , דמּ , חמּ , זמּ , דמּ ; רלּ, נלּ, דלּ, גלּ ; דז ; סב
זתּ ; תשּׁ , זשּׁ , משּׁ , דשּׁ ; רגלַי קַללין in יק especially , זק , לק , דק ; זצּ , לצּ ; זס ,לס.

So long as the Reuchlian ms remains unpublished it will not be possible to draw up a complete list of these but it is already possible to conclude that in the Targums the level of assimilation and conjoining exceeds what was in use in Syriac, since the Reuchlian ms marks a conjunction in places where Bar Zuʿbi requires a disjunction (ܡܦܪܫܐ). The disjunction that should (in Syriac) occur with the construct state and with prepositions and conjunctions before vowelled consonants (rule IIb and IIIb, p.128) is not observed in the Reuchlian ms. Although there is no special sign for disjunction as such in the Reuchlian ms, one can tell where disjunction between two consecutive words should occur by the non-use of dagesh and maqqef. Hence where Bar Zuʿbi says that words after prepositions should be disconnected (IIIb), e.g. |[205] ܠܡܠܟܐ_ܡܫܡܠܐ, the Targums have a connection: מִן צוּרְתָא ,עַל מַלְכִין ,עַל נִּיסא, but I do not know whether the teachers of orthoepy found a dagesh in an initial yodh acceptable. For while a dagesh is found even after a construct state, against the Syriac rule IIb (p.128), such as in מְכוּנַּת־לִיסְטִין (Jdg 5.11), twice in Habakkuk מרכבָת וְקרך is written without the dagesh.

Again, where in Syriac there is a disjunction between a preposition with a suffix and the following noun (rule VIb, p.130), this is not the case in the Targum. So where the Syriac would disjoin ܒܗ̇ܘ_ ܐܠܗܐ, in the Targum we read לדדילֵיה נִצְחנִיך ,תושבחתֵיה מְלְיא ,לֵיה לַחבקק ,(2 Sam 22.3) אל׳ דאתרעי בֶיה קֳרְבָנִי ,עַמֵיה מִנִי, but we seem to be faced with a disjunction in אוריתָך וְלָא.

Finally, the Syriac rules require a disjunction in the case of a vowelled consonant starting a word immediately after a vowelless consonant (rule VIIb, p.130), and the Targum agrees with this, having ישראֵל לְטָעוּתא, לְמֶתְבָר רְשִׁיעי ארעא, but we also have בַבֶל לָא (Hab 3.17).

To this class of assimilations I would add a further example, אַף־בְמֵעְבְדָך (Hab 3.11), where the shewa beneath the maqqef appears to indicate a disjunction. Most likely, by using this unusually positioned sign, the scribe is trying to say that each of the three labials should be pronounced distinctly.

In general, conjunctions are more common in the Targums than are disjunctions, though the latter do have a place in Syriac.[1] This may, however, be clarified on the basis of Joseph Bar Malkon's verse mentioned earlier (p.132), from which we may conclude that the most natural recitation was thought to be one in which each word is pronounced separately. So ܡܗܦܟܢܐ is effectively being used all the time but not necessarily written as such, since it is present by definition. The ܢܝܚܐ, by contrast, is added only where a particular conjunction of words is thought to yield a more graceful flow and so the ܢܝܚܐ is as a result actually written more often than the ܡܗܦܟܢܐ, which is generally superfluous and was not used in Hebrew.

The above observations certainly do not exhaust the available data, nor do they describe every aspect of the topic. They are here simply to encourage others to study Aramaic orthoepy, just as Martin has done up to a point in dealing with the two dialects of Syriac.[2] The dialect of the Targums can now be safely studied alongside this, since the Babylonian mss (from which I extracted my chrestomathy) provide us with data that is free from the rubbish found in later mss. Our own observations have shown that the Reuchlian manuscript, which was the work of a Masoretic school |[206] that did not survive, should also to be compared with these Babylonian witnesses. To bring this chapter to a close, we shall now offer two further

---

[1] See esp. Martin, *Deux dialectes*, 400.

[2] In the article mentioned in the previous note.

notes: one on the subject of the Hebrew dagesh; the other on the inconsistency of the use of ܒܘܕܐ in Syriac.

ON THE NEUTRAL DAGESH IN HEBREW MSS

J. D. Michaelis, followed by Gesenius,[1] gave the name 'neutral dagesh' to a kind of euphonic dagesh forte, which could be seen in certain mss (Erfurt III,IV, Stuttgart, Cassell, Hamburg III,IX). Gesenius rightly spotted that it indicated a conjunction of words and he added examples from Drusius which had been used by Ibn Janaḥ,[2] [iii] who read יתן־לי, אל נמלא, ירוץ צדיק as *jittel-li, en-nemala, jaruṣ-ṣaddīq*. He also notes the dagesh in זטלמנסצקש observed by Lichtenstein in ms Hamburg I. This conjunctive effect is the opposite of that of the dagesh lene after disjunctive accents in the Masoretic system, i.e. where dagesh lene would be used in בגדכפת when they follow disjunctive accents, and a rāphe after conjunctive accents. In effect, therefore, in this official system, the dagesh lene is a sign of disjunction, whereas in the special codices mentioned above (and in the Reuchlian ms too) it is rather a sign of conjuntion.[iv] Michaelis considered the rule in the generally accepted system to be so foundational, that he decided that the positioning of all accents should be judged by it as by a Lydian stone.[3] [v] He relied on it so far as even to distinguish a dagesh lene after disjunctive accents from a dagesh forte in בגדכפת after conjunctive accents, hence at Gen 11.31 the dagesh in אַ֫רְצָה כְּנַ֫עַן he called a dagesh forte whereas that in הִנֵּ֫ה פָּשְׂתָ֫ה (Lev 13.36) is a dagesh lene.[4] So now the dagesh both conjoins and disjoins! Now if this latter disjunctive dagesh occurs only in בגדכפת, where it would be called a dagesh lene, and being placed so as to *remove* aspiration, then the use of one and the same point to indicate two opposite things (conjunction and disjunction) is clearly confused and unhelpful. Neither are the mss in agreement among themselves. For example, the published versions follow this basic rule in printing וִֽירִשְׁ֫תֶּ֫ם גַּם (Josh 1.15) but in the same place the Reuchlian ms has וִֽירִשְׁ֫תֶּ֫ם גַּם (marking the conjunction by the dagesh lene). Similarly, where the Reuchlian has עָתָּ֫ה בֶּן־אָ֫דָם (Ezek 21.11), the editions print בֶן, and again the Reuchlian has וכהתָ֫ה כָּל־רוח, where the

---

[1] W. Gesenius, *Ausführliches grammatisch-kritisches Lehrgebäude der hebräischen Sprache* (Leipzig, 1817), 88.

[2] *Op. cit.*, 81.

[3] J. D. Michaelis, *Anfangsgründe der hebr. Accentuation* (Halle, 1753), §IV.

[4] In id., *Hebräische Grammatik* (1st ed., Halle, 1745).

editions print כָּל (Ezek 21.12). So although the importance of this rule should not be called into question, it was not followed everywhere, the variety being no doubt a result of there being different schools.

Now all this pertains to the neutral dagesh which is used frequently in the Hebrew text of the Reuchlian ms. On this basis we are able to suppose that the conjunction that it indicates was used in Aramaic as well and that it was common to Arabic, Aramaic, and Hebrew.|207 Using the mss in which this dagesh is marked, future orthoepy enthusiasts will have to restore it to all those places where the older editors of the scriptures omitted it or only preserved it rather randomly! However, as I mentioned, the mss are not in harmony with one another, so what can one do?

The reason that the Aramaic texts do not agree with each other, that the Targums differ from the Syriac, and that the Syrians all disagree with each other is simply that it was a matter of such minute detail that was subject to individual whim. A universal consensus was impossible and the course of time would anyway never have preserved any such consensus as might have developed. So while it is possible to reconstruct from the mss the system used by one or other of the schools, one cannot hope to reproduce the system used by all the schools together.

On the inconsistency of Syriac in the use of the conjoining line

The last subject we need to remark upon here is the variety of writing systems that are found among the Syriac schools, since there was as much variety in writing as there was in pronunciation. If the works of Bar Zuʿbi and Bar Malkon were all we had on ܡܘܚܕܐ and ܡܗܓܝܢܐ, then we should believe that the ܡܘܚܕܐ [1] is a small conjoining line always written above the letter, as in ܢܥܒܕ̄ ܗܘܘ. However, BL Add. 12138 proves the opposite, since here we have Gen 39.8 written thus, ܡܪܝ ܠܐ ܝܕܥ_ܥܡܝ_ܡܕܡ ܐܝܟܐ ܒܒܝܬܗ with the marginal note ܥܡܝ ܠ ܘܥܡܝ ܦ, which makes it clear that the line placed lower down indicates a conjoining of the two words, i.e. it is ܡܘܚܕܐ. Similar again is Gen 24.65 where we have the marginal note ܐܩܦ (i.e. *connecting*) next to the words ܘܐܡܪ ܥܒܕܐ ܗܘܝܘ_ܡܪܝ.[2] Martin has gathered other examples from this ms

[1] Ewald attributed to it a restricting, or separating, force, and so called it 'Hemmungsstrich', with which we would not entirely disagree—H. Ewald, "Über das syrische Punctationssystem, nach syrischen Handschriften," *Abhandlungen zur orientalischen und biblischen Literatur* (Göttingen, 1832), 53–129 (p.110).

[2] Wright, *Cat.*, 104. In this example ܡܪܝ is the predicate, *this is my Lord*.

of this lower line joining together a pair of words:[1] ܡܢ ܩܕܡ ܥܒܪ̈ܝܐ_ܗܘ ܗܘܐ, which should be read as *ʿeḇrayeʾu*, ܩܐܡ_ܐܢܬ, read as *qāyimat*, ܡܕܡ_ܕܥܒܕܬ, i.e. *medemdaʿeḇatt*, ܟܠ_ܟܠܗ, ܟܠ_ܥܡܡܐ. Martin gives many more examples from Paris Syr. 15 where the same line is used far more often still: ܢܣܚ_ܡܕܡܕܝܢܐ, ܒܥܘܫܢܐ_ܗܘ ܘܐܠܗܐ, ܘܐܬܐ_ܠܡܐ ܕܡܫܒܚܢܘܬܗ, ܕܒ_ܚܝܐ_ܕܝܢ ܡܥܡܕ, ܡܚܡ_ܒܩܘܒܠ. Martin rightly compares this conjoining line with the Hebrew maqqef, |[208] since in the London ms ܐܩܦ should really be read as meaning *binding* (not just *connecting*). It is not possible, however, to prove for certain from the comment in Add. 12138 whether it was Ramišoʿ who invented it or whether he was just developing existing practice. The comment in question says that all marks in red are from the hand of Ramišoʿ, and those in black belong to the earlier masters (cf. p.177). The red line that Martin says is to be found in ܠܐ ܡܢ_ܟܡܐ_ܡܚܐ ܐܢܬ ܟܡܠܬܗ, ܟܠ_ܥܡܡܐ, and ܟܠ_ܟܠܗ must therefore come from Ramišoʿ, but the same line in black is found in other examples, ܩܐܡ_ܐܢܬ ܟܠܗܘܢ etc., and hence we can see that the older teachers were already using this line in the same way before the time of Ramišoʿ.

If this is how things stand, then this lower line is the older symbol for conjoining two words and was used both by the older teachers and by Ramišoʿ, the scribe of BL Add. 12138 distinguishing the two by colour. At a later date the East Syrians developed the precision of their writing to such a point that they wanted to indicate disjunction as well as conjunction, which they achieved by using both ܢܝܫܐ and ܡܗܓܝܢܐ. But these two lines were of later invention than the single inferior line that indicated conjunction and which we also find in Hebrew. In fact, and for this reason, it must have been received into Syriac at least before 650 (see p.30,75). These symbols have their own histories of development which one can trace by comparing the different mss. We also discover here that not everyone used such conjoining in exactly the same way as was originally the case, whether the differences are over time or between different schools. If we compare the examples given above with the rules given by Bar Zuʿbi, we will at once notice that where the older teachers and Ramišoʿ connect words together, Bar Zuʿbi sometimes separates them. According to his rule VIIb (p.130) a final vowelless consonant is not bound together with a following vowelled consonant but rather has ܡܗܓܝܢܐ, e.g. ܢܗܘܐ_ܕܢܚܐ. The older masters, however, for whom the lower line indicated a conjoining, wanted to say ܢܣܚ_ܡܕܡܕܝܢܐ, which in Bar Zuʿbi's system would be written ܢܣܚ ̄ܡܕܡܕܝܢܐ. The older masters

[1] Martin, *Deux dialectes*, 394.

conjoined ܒ_ܚܐ, but Bar Zuʿbi says the opposite (p.129). There is a similar confusion between the *linea occultans* and the ܡܗܓܝܢܐ.

From our interpretation of the writing systems found in the mss, we can thus conclude that the inferior line was originally a sign of conjunction, but later became a sign of disjunction.

By 899 at the latest (the date when Add. 12138 was written) the ܦܣܘܩܐ and ܡܗܦܟܢܐ, so little used among the earlier writers, were generally introduced. This is evident from the excerpts we gave above (p.126) in which ܦܣܘܩܐ was used frequently. In the end ܦܣܘܩܐ was replaced by the accent ܡܫܒܚܢܐ (p.197, ܠܒ).

[i] On the accents in these lists see also Weiss, *Laut- und Akzentlehre*, 35-6.

[ii] The Codex Reuchlinianus, a twelfth century Hebrew ms of the Prophets together with the Babylonian Targum of ps-Jonathan, has been of great importance in the study of the history of Masoretic vocalisation (both for its Hebrew text, which is non-Tiberian, and for its targum text, which is non-Babylonian). The whole codex was published by A. Sperber, ed., *Codex Reuchlinianus, no. 3 of the Badische Landesbibliothek in Karlsruhe, formerly Durlach no. 55*, Corpus codicum hebraicorum medii aevi, pars 2 (Copenhagen, 1956), replacing Lagarde's older edition, *Prophetae Chaldaice* (Leipzig, 1872), although Merx oddly states here that it had not yet been published in his day. On the Aramaic text, see, e.g., A. Sperber, *The Bible in Aramaic*, vol.IVB (Leiden, 1973), 37-137, together with the introduction to the abovementioned 1956 edition. The critical text is to be found in A. Sperber, ed., *The Bible in Aramaic*, vols. II/III (Leiden, 1959,62)—add the review by R.P. Gordon, "Sperber's edition of the Targum to the Prophets: a critique," *Jewish Quarterly Review* 64 (1973/4), 314-21. On the question of the Hebrew vocalisation, S. Morag, "The Vocalization of Codex Reuchlinianus: is the 'pre-Masoretic' Bible pre-Masoretic?" *Journal of Semitic Studies* 4 (1959), 216-37.

[iii] Drusius: Johannes van den Driesche (1550-1616), Professor of Oriental Languages at Oxford, Leiden, and Franeker. His work here referred to is the *De recta lectione linguae sanctae*, published in *Drusii Opuscula, quae ad grammaticam spectant, omnia* etc. (Franeker, 1609), 1-121. Ibn Janaḥ was a famous Hebrew grammarian (b.c.990 in Cordova).

[iv] Bauer-Leander, *Historische Grammatik der hebräischen Sprache des Alten Testaments* (Halle, 1922), §8b'.

[v] Lydian stone: a type of slate used to test the purity of gold.

Chapter 11

Jacob of Tagrit, otherwise known as Severus Bar Šakko

|209 It is barely four hours on horseback east from Mosul to the renowned monastery of Mar Mattai, built on the mountain known to the Arabs as Jebel Al-Maqlub, and to the Syrians as Alfef. It is a very ancient foundation[1] and held in the highest regard by the Syrian Orthodox, who have buried many of their most famous masters there, including Barhebraeus. The same honour was awarded to Jacob,[2] who was educated in the monastery's school and with whom we shall be dealing in the present chapter.

Also called either Severus bar Šakko (?Shakkako) or Ibn ʿIsa Bar Marqos,[i] Jacob was born in Barṭelli near Mosul[ii] and grew up at Beth Quqa, where his sharp intellect picked up grammar and the first book of logic from the teaching of John Bar Zuʿbi, while the rest of logic and philosophy he took from Arabic books, primarily Kamāl al-Dīn ibn Yūnus, who was at that time the foremost philosopher in Mosul. We can see from Codex Beroeensis 1 that the school of Mar Mattai was well known for having its own curriculum.[3] In this ms, Jacob is called 'a monk by profession, a Mar Mattai man by education (ܒܬܘܠܡܕܐ ܡܬܝܐ), a man of Bartela by birth'. If one could say that he was a 'Mar Mattai man' rather as one might distinguish an Oxford man from a Cambridge one, or an alumnus of Rostok from one of Jena, then we can be quite certain that there was at Mar Mattai a school with its own character and system. Jacob became so well known for all the learned books he wrote that he was summoned by the Patriarch Ignatius II. He became ill on the journey and returned to Mosul, where he died in 1241 (1552 Gr.).[4]

Jacob's works themselves reveal to us what kind of education was available at Mar Mattai, since their contents suggest that they were written for the students there.

---

[1] G. Hoffmann, *Auszüge aus syrischen Acten persischer Märtyrer* (Leipzig 1880), 19,175.

[2] The East Syrian monasteries, in which the patriarchs and catholicoi were buried, were exempt from episcopal jurisdiction and were rather subject in the West to the Patriarch, in the East to the Catholicos (BO III,II,947, from Barhebraeus's *Nomocanon*).

[3] BO II,247.

[4] Barhebraeus, *Chron. Eccl.* III,412; BO II,455,237.

In Rome, in the public schools of the imperial period, grammar was taught first as the basis for all learning, followed by rhetoric and dialectic, the three subjects that constituted the trivium. Among the Greeks, Iamblichus was the first to bring together the subjects that were later called the quadrivium, namely |[210] arithmetic, geometry, music, and spherics, or astronomy. In northern Africa these two curricula were later joined, thereby creating the seven liberal arts which constitute the whole of humanistic training, at least once the highest stage of all has been added—theology. It was at the end of the fifth century with the work of Martianus Capella, and later with Boethius and Cassiodorus, that the approach to education which became standard in succeeding ages was developed. This system of seven liberal arts, made up of trivium and quadrivium, was as well known in the East as in the West, for Tzetzes sets the whole system out in verse thus:

ὁ κύκλος καὶ συμπέρασμα πάντων τῶν μαθημάτων
γραματικῆς, ῥητορικῆς, αὐτῆς φιλοσοφίας,
καὶ τῶν τεσσάρων τε τεχνῶν τῶν ὑπ' αὐτὴν κειμένων,
τῆς ἀριθμούσης, μουσικῆς καὶ τῆς γεωμετρίας
καὶ τῆς οὐρανοβάμανος αὐτῆς ἀστρονομίας.[1] [iii]

Although traces of it are hard to come by, this system was not unknown in Syriac too.[iv] Jacob essentially created a summary of the seven liberal arts as the foundation for theology. This is why I believe that it was at Mar Mattai that this approach to education, which is markedly different from that of the East Syrian schools, was situated.[2] His plan was executed by publishing a book of dialogues which was written at the monastery and which was surely the model for the teaching tradition that was preserved there.

The first dialogue contains the grammar (which I have edited at the back of the present volume as Text 1) in fourteen sections, followed by a metrical grammar, which is not part of the dialogue proper. Of this I have edited only what seemed needful (Text 2).[v] It was the normal custom at that time to write grammars in verse as a mnemonic aid for students, as we showed earlier (p.112).

---

[1] Cf. J. F. Cramer, *Geschichte der Erziehung und das Unterrichts in den Niederlanden* (Stralsund, 1843), 9f.; also see Origen's letter to Gregory Thaumaturgus (ed. P. Koetschau, *Des Gregorios Thaumaturgos Dankrede an Origenes* [Freiburg, 1894], 40-44).

[2] BO III,II,919f.

The next dialogue is that on rhetoric, in twenty eight sections, and then the dialogue on poetics, with twenty one sections, as edited by Martin.[1 vi] A further dialogue is then added to these as a sort of appendix, on the subject of the capacity of the Syriac language. This is essentially a glossary of rare words and synonyms, to which he added also some notes on the dialects of Syriac and testimonia from the scriptures, from Antony of Tagrit, and from the Syriac version of Homer, perhaps that done by Theophilus of Edessa.[2] For example:

ܫܦܝܪܐ. ܫܥܝܥ. ܫܪܝܪ. ܫܦܝܐ. ܦܐܝܐ.|[211] ܡܠܬܐ ܕܝܘܢܝܐ ܠܗܠܝܢ ܡܬܦܫܩܢ ܒܗ. ܘܐܦ ܐܡܝܪܝܢ ܕܦܫܩܘ ܠܡܐܬܪܝܐ. ܫܦܝܪܐ ܗܘ ܐܝܛܘܪ [Hector] ܒܡܟ ܒܡܟ ܘܐܡܪ. ܘܐܝܬܝܟ ܐܡܪ ܥܠ ܫܦܝܪܘܬܗ ܒܣܘܟܐܐ ܠܗ ܫܦܝܪ ܗ̄ ܣܓܝ ܠܓܒܪܐ. ܡܫܦܪܢܐ. ܡܫܒܚܢܐ. ܡܫܒܚܐ ܕܝܢܐ. ܐܡܪ ܡܫܡܠܐ ܡܪܝ ܐܦܪܝܡ ܘܐܦ ܡܢ ܠܓܒܪܐ ܕܡܬܐ. ܡܠܦܢܘܬ ܕܢܦܠ ܒܗ. ܦܚܡܐ. ܡܦܚܡ. ܐܡܪ ܡܪܝ ܐܦܪܝܡ ܕܠܐ ܗܘܫܐ ܡܠܐܟܐ ܠܐ ܦܚܡܝܢ ܦܚܡܐ ܗܘ ܕܐܝܬܐ ܘܕܒܝܢܐ.[3] ܫܡܫܘܬܐ: ܫܡܫܐ. ܐܝܟ ܗܢܐ ܕܡܫܡܫܐ. ܫܡܫ ܘܐܬܪܐ ܠܗ ܠܠ ܫܡܫܘܬܐ. ܘܐܦ ܡܠܬܐ ܕܝܘܢܝܐ ܒܫܡܐ ܗܢܐ. ܡܫܡܫ = ܡܫܡܫ. ܐܡܪ ܐܘܡܝܪܘܣ ܘܫܡܫ ܘܐܬܪܐ ܡܫܡܫ ܗܘܐ.

Payne Smith made good use of the dialogues when compiling his *Thesaurus*, depending upon the Oxford ms Marsh 528, which is why in my edition of the grammar I have added in the margin references to the folio numbers of this ms. But he did not include everything (e.g. ܣܡܠܐ) and so it is to be hoped that Lagarde will as promised bring out a full edition. Once Jacob had dealt with grammar, poetics, and rhetoric in the first book of dialogues, he had essentially summed up the contents of the trivium as it was constituted in the West.

The second book is then on philosophy, which Tzetzes in the verses above placed after rhetoric. Jacob keeps logic separate from philosophy proper, of which it is but the instrument (organon). A special dialogue on logic in fifty two sections is followed by the dialogue on philosophy, subdivided into five parts, 1 on the definitions and parts of philosophy, 2 on ethics, 3 on physics, 4 on the four arts of arithmetic, music, geometry, and astronomy, 5 on metaphysics and theology (ܡܡܠܠܐ ܠܐܠܗܘܬܐ).[vii] If we see this latter part as being a sort of introduction to the higher realms of theology, then it would be certain that, just as Tzetzes required, philosophy is to be closely associated with these four. |[212] But Jacob added poetics to the

[1] Martin, *De la métrique*.

[2] Barhebraeus, *Chronicle* (P. Bruns & H. Kirsch, eds., *Barhebraei Chroncion syriacum* [Leipzig, 1789]), 132.

[3] In the margin ܦܚܡܐ ܠܫܡܫܘܢ is added. Cf. Bar ʿAlī, s.v., and Lane's Arabic Dictionary, under شموس.

trivium and so his system is nothing like that of Tzetzes and nobody has ever located any other Syrian who did the same thing. Martin is right to say that Jacob's work on poetics is unique, at least among texts known from European libraries. But then, if the Syrians never dealt with poetics, and if not even the slightest hint of the Arabic tradition of poetics is to be found in Jacob, then surely we may hazard to suggest that, given he lived at the time of the Crusades, he may have been taught according to the pattern of the Latin schools. After all, the East was at that time full of learned men who had been educated in the Latin system, bishops, priests, teachers, etc. Jacob may have learnt from them and then included poetics in his trivium.[viii]

Jacob treats theology in his other major work, entitled the *Book of Treasures* (ܟܬܒܐ ܕܣܝ̈ܡܬܐ), which Martin compared with Aquinas's *Summa.*[1] But it is outside of our remit to go further into this. Similarly we must pass over his *Exposition of the Offices and Prayers* (ܦܘܫܩܐ ܠܬܫܡܫ̈ܬܐ ܘܨܠܘ̈ܬܐ), and his *On the Creed.*[2] [ix] So let us turn to the grammar which we have here edited.

In the first three sections, Jacob goes over yet again the material from the Greek system on the parts of speech and their characteristics, compressing it into a very brief summary. After this is a section on the six vowels,[3] including a discussion on the changes in vocalisation caused by inflections. The result of this, as we saw in the case of Joseph Bar Malkon, is that the whole inflectional system is dealt with in the section on pronunciation. It also includes the affixes and, since the active and passive senses of the noun are expressed by means of changes of the same sort, this is where we find them. Further, since a description of the consonants that can be affixed to words is a necessary part of this topic, he then deals, in the fifth section, with the radical (ܫܪܫܝ̈ܬܐ) and the servile consonants (ܡܫܬܡܫܢ̈ܝܬܐ). Of the latter, one type is called 'necessary', a second is used for distinguishing words that are written in a similar fashion, and a third has to do with etymology and includes consonants that are hidden in pronunciation or that are assimilated. The relative adjectives (ܫܡܗ̈ܐ ܠܘܬܢ̈ܝܐ) are treated in the same section and I believe he is here following Jacob of Edessa (p.16).

Sections six and seven are about the 'cases', i.e. the particles ܒ ܕ ܘ ܠ which may be prefixed to nouns and verbs. At the same time he speaks

[1] *De la métrique*, 6; BO II,287.

[2] BO II,287.

[3] Jacob only has the six vowels ā,e,a,i,o,u.

about the prefixes of the verb, ܐ ܢ ܡ ܬ, in a section that may be seriously corrupt.

Section eight is all about aspiration and this is followed by the rules for letters that are lost or hidden.

|[213] The tenth part is on the seven letters of completion, namely the alaph of the emphatic state plus the personal affixes of the verb. The mss only number six of these (ܐ ܗ ܝ ܢ ܬ ܘܢ), leaving out ܘ, which is the subject of the next part.

After this, the eleventh section discusses the active and passive sense,[1] or the subject and object of a sentence, which takes the reader partly into the world of syntax. Section twelve is on the passive verbal forms, and after that he tackles sentences of exception (ܫܘܚܠܦܐ) involving the particles ܐܠܐ, ܣܛܪ, and ܒܠܚܘܕ. Compare the Arabic الاستثنا.

The last section is on the accents, the theory being taken from Jacob of Edessa, as we showed above (p.89f.).

Following our edition of the text of this grammar (Text 1, Appendix), we have provided some excerpts (Text 2) from the metrical grammar, which is called 'The Harmony' (ܡܫܠܡܢܘܬܐ). The parts published here are just those that deal with subjects not present in the dialogue. Most of the material in the metrical grammar is the same as that found in the dialogue and there seemed no point editing all these as well.

We have made use of three manuscripts for the main text, those of Oxford, Göttingen, and Berlin (O,G,B), though all three are very poor[2] and have many lacunae, as is indicated in the apparatus.[x]

O and G belong to the same family (p.25, l.22) and the latter appears to have been copied from a ms of which O was the archetype, since six words which are missing in G (p.29, l.18) constitute a single line in O. For the most part G is therefore a recent apograph, some lost pages of which are today made good from an older ms. But the apograph was not copied from those older lost folios which had belonged to the codex before, but is rather based on another copy which is in turn related to O. We can be sure of this because one of the older folio, containing the very end of the grammar, has been preserved, of which we also have extant the version from the subsequent supplement. These two folios from the same ms differ from

[1] Compare the Arabic *fāʿil and mafʿūl.*

[2] Cf. e.g. p.17,n.6,7, where O and G offer ܡܕܝܢܐ and ܪܘܡܐ instead of ܡܕܝܢܬܐ and ܪܘܡܐ. The scribe clearly did not understand the text. Thus also p.20,l.2. The opposite is found at p.20,l.22; p.21,l.1.

each other, the later one being related to O, the earlier to B and a London ms (L) (cf. p.36,n.14; 37,n.1,7,8). I have followed the pointing of G, though I am not sure that it has rewarded my trust in it. Besides, no great importance should be attached to the pointing. I had no desire to give all the pointing from all three mss, for that would merely cause greater confusion than clarity.

Initially deceived by the apparent similarity of the three manuscripts O,G, and L,|[214] I failed to notice how often they offered faulty readings until, while reading the section on geometry in G, I realised that the text was so mutilated that no sense could be made of it, although the section on mathematics had proved no problem to reconstruct. At this point I remembered that I had once seen in one of the Petermann mss in Berlin a similar grammar, attributed to Jacob of Edessa,[1] and I requested Dr Lepsius if he would send the codex to Heidelberg.[xi] This he agreed to do, for which I am most grateful; indeed all his kindness and work on my behalf ought to be commemorated and honoured. The grammar in question turned out, of course, to be that of Jacob Bar Šakko.

This Berlin codex (Petermann 15 = B) was copied in 1826 from an excellent exemplar, although there are many lacunae and almost all the pointing is missing. Without it I would not have been able to reconstruct the text, although I still had to be very critical of its readings. From the apparatus readers will be able to see what I have done with individual readings and to make their own judgment on my success on the basis of the character of the text I have produced. I had already copied out the first few pages before I had to call on the assistance of the Berlin ms and it was too tiresome to start all over again, hence the variants from B for the first few pages of the text are given as a separate list on p.ܡܣ.[xii]

I saw that in Jacob's dialogue on poetics (Martin ed.) the characteristic readings of L were comparable to those of G. It was therefore possible to proceed without the use of L, and then perhaps add in any useful variants it might offer after I had finished the text itself, since at that time I was unable to go to London. Professor Wright therefore compared my finished text with that of the London codex, a labour for which I am indeed most grateful to him, especially since not only was my critical judgment thus subjected to a true test of quality, but my errors could also be corrected. It turned out that L is of the same family as B and, although it belongs to the

[1] Cf. p.48.

thirteenth century (Wright, *Cat.*, III,1165), it is not at all free of the more serious errors found in the others. The resulting stemma is as follows:

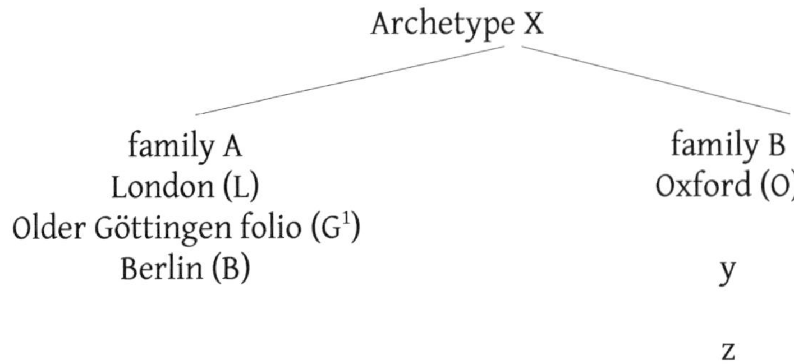

Later Göttingen folios (G)

Now that we have discussed both the ms families and the outline of the text itself, we can offer a final verdict on Jacob. I believe that he |[215] emerged from both a Greek philosophical school and a Syriac reading school, and that he was no follower of John Bar Zuʿbi, even though the latter was his teacher. He does, however, depend on Jacob of Edessa and he brings the latter's teaching together with the method that we saw used by Joseph Bar Malkon.

All that remains now, then, is to provide some annotations to the text, including the variants of L.[xiii] I have not thought it worthwhile to repeat all the punctuation and diacritics that Prof. Wright provided, although if I had had the London ms, I would have placed all the points according to its pattern in the first place. I make no note where L and B agree, since they are of one family, hence the siglum B alone indicates their consensus. However, the lacunae which are found in B and not present in L have been added from the latter.

---

[i] As for this writer's first name, Jacob seems to be both his preferred name and also his episcopal title, Severus being his original name (for this reversal of the usual interpretation, see the evidence of O. J. Schrier, "Name and Function of Jacob Bar Šhakko. Notes on the history of the monastery of Mar Mattai," in *Symposium Syriacum V*, 215-28). Schrier also discusses the alternative of Bar Marqos, but either way Jacob is the name by which he should be called and we have here changed Merx's Severus to Jacob throughout. The patronymic *Bar Šakko* is an abbreviation for Isaac and until recently was still a common name in Barṭelli (J. Vosté, "Deux Manuscrits des Dialogues de Jacques bar Šakko," *Le Muséon* 42 (1929), 157-67, where the pronunciation Shakako is rejected). The identifier 'of Tagrit' is a misnomer for Barṭelli.

[ii] On this important town, its varied history and many churches and monasteries, see J.-M. Fiey, *Assyrie Chrétienne* II,416-39.

[iii] *The cycle and end of learning,*
Grammar, rhetoric, even philosophy,
And the four arts that underlie it,
Arithmetic, music, and geometry,
And astronomy itself that traverses the heavens.

[iv] On this question, see now J.W. Watt, "Grammar, Rhetoric, and the Enkyklios Paideia in Syriac," *Zeitschrift der Deutschen Morgenländischen Gesellschaft* 143 (1993), 45-71.

[v] There is another ms at Mingana Syr. 501, f.61b-79b.

[vi] Martin's edition (which should itself be read alongside the detailed review of Th. Nöldeke, *ZDMG* 34 [1880], 569-78) was continued and completed from the Harvard ms by M. Sprengling, "Severus bar Shakko's Poetics, Part II," *American Journal of Semitic Languages and Literatures* 32,4 (1916), 293-308, who has a rather different appreciation of Jacob's value than that offered by Merx and Martin. Sprengling had already published a long article on Syriac poetics ("Antony Rhetor on Versification," *American Journal of Semitic Languages and Literatures* 32,3 (1916), 145-216) which includes a concordance of passages found in both the Dialogues and in Antony of Tagrit (p.174), a close description of the new Harvard ms of the Dialogues (p.203-5), and a full collation of this latter with Martin's edition (p.205-16). Another and more useful concordance of Jacob with Antony is found in the more recent edition of the latter, J.W. Watt, *The Fifth Book of the Rhetoric of Antony of Tagrit*, CSCO 480 (Leuven, 1986), xix. Extracts from the poetics can also be found in the wider ranging study of D. Margoliouth, *Analecta Orientalia ad Poeticam Aristoteleam* (London, 1887).

[vii] Lagarde never did bring out the promised complete edition. Of Jacob's dialogues, besides the treatises on metrics and grammar already noted, the only part published is the Mathematics by Merx's student Julius Ruska, *Das Quadrivium aus Severus bar Šakkū's Buch der Dialoge* (Leipzig, 1896). In an earlier article, "Studien zur Severus Bar Šakkū's Buch der Dialoge," *Zeitshcrift für Assyriologie* 12 (1897), 145-61, Ruska also studied some fragments

from the philosophical treatises. Baumstark made a further study of the philosophical parts in his *Aristoteles bei den Syrern vom V-VIII Jahrhundert* (Leipzig, 1900), 11-33; 192-210, as later in some detail also did G. Furlani, "La logica nei Dialoghi di Severo bar Shakko," *Atti dell'Istituto Veneto di Scienze, Lettere ed Arti* 86 (1926/7), 289-348. On the Rhetoric (the only part of the first book still unpublished and which, like the section on poetics, is an epitome of Antony of Tagrit), see J. Bendrat, "Der Dialog über die Rhetorik des Jacob bar Shakko," *Paul deLagarde und die syrische Kirchengeschichte* (Göttingen, 1968), 19-26, and J. W. Watt, *Aristotelian Rhetoric in Syriac* (Leiden, 2005), 13-4. Many useful articles on the Syriac tradition of rhetoric generally and of Jacob's place within that tradition may be found in J.W. Watt, *Rhetoric and Philosophy from Greek into Syriac* (Ashgate, 2010). On the psychology, C. Havard, "Jacob bar Shakko, on the faculties of the soul," in *VI Symposium Syriacum* (Rome, 1994), 259-68.

[viii] On the Poetics in Syriac more generally, see Margoliouth, *Analecta Orientalia* (note iv above), and O. Schrier, "The Syriac and Arabic Versions of Aristotle's *Poetics*," in G. Endress and R. Kruk, eds., *The Ancient Tradition in Christian and Islamic Hellenism : studies on the transmission of Greek philosophy and sciences dedicated to H. J. Drossaart Lulofs on his ninetieth birthday* (Leiden, 1997), 259-78. There is important new evidence adduced in V. Berti, *Vita e Studi di Timoteo I Patriarca Cristiano di Baghdad* (Paris, 2009), 325-8 and a general discussion in Tarán, Leonardo and Dimitri Gutas, eds., *Aristotle Poetics: Editio Maior of the Greek Text.* Mnemosyne Supplements 338. Leiden: Brill, 2012, 77-128.

[ix] Details in *GSL*, 311-12.

[x] The mss of the Dialogues mentioned and used by Merx are as follows: Oxford = Marsh 528 (Payne Smith, *Catalogus Codicum Syriacorum*, 642-3); Göttingen = Or.18 (*Verzeichniss der Handschriften im Preußischen Staate 1,3: Die Handschriften in Göttingen* [Berlin, 1894], III, 464-5); Berlin = Petermann 15 / Berlin Syr. 207 (Sachau, *Verzeichniss* II, 684-6); London = BL Add. 21454 (Wright, *Cat.* III, 1165-7). To these must now be added the Harvard ms used by Sprengling (noted above), Urmia 40 (*Catalogue of the Syriac manuscripts...of Oroomiah College* [Oroomiah, 1898], 10) and, the oldest in existence, Notre Dame des Semences 63 (J. Vosté, *Catalogue de la Bibliothèque Syro-Chaldéenne du couvent de Notre-Dame des Semences* [Rome/Paris, 1929], 25, together with a later copy, NDS 64 = Scher 48). NDS 63 is complete and dated 1255 (just fourteen years after Jacob's death). It is described further in Vosté, "Deux manuscrits" (see note i above).

[xi] Karl Richard Lepsius, one of the founding fathers of Egyptology, was head of the Berlin Royal Library from 1873 until 1884, when he died. Merx must have communicated with him on this subject, therefore, a number of years before the publication of the present volume.

[xii] Sic. For the present re-edition, however, all the variants from B have been incorporated into the apparatus itself.

[xiii] These annotations, together with the variants from L (which were provided by Wright) constitute pages 215-229 of Merx's original edition. All this information has now been placed in the apparatus and notes to the text itself, thereby saving the reader the labour of having to keep referring between different parts of the book when reading Bar Šakko's Grammar.

Chapter 12

The Grammar of Barhebraeus

|[229] All that we have presented thus far is really but an introduction to the far more exhaustive and penetrating grammatical work written by a single man, Barhebraeus. His larger grammar, known as the ܟܬܒܐ ܕܨܡܚ̈ܐ, includes within it everything found in the earlier texts; the different and opposing methods of the schools are here amalgamated into a single overarching system.

There is no need to go over yet again the life and works of Barhebraeus. Abbeloos, Lamy and Wright have all contributed to bringing his work to general notice and no student of Syriac is unaware of all this.[i] Nor do we need to repeat the praises heaped upon him by Martin, who is certainly better qualified than anyone to make such a judgment. But Martin's comments, although certainly accurate, really only touch the surface of the matter and nobody has yet been able truly to plumb the depths of Barhebraeus's literary qualities. To achieve such a task would require a knowledge of many more of his works, which yet remain hidden in manuscripts. His historical writings are really just compilations rather than histories of the more developed, modern type, and hence one can hardly base an appreciation of their author's literary character from these alone. At any rate, even the histories have hardly been used to great effect as yet, except perhaps by Victor Langlois who, in the notes to his French translation of the Armenian abbreviation of Michael the Great's Chronicle,[ii] compared Michael's text with that of Barhebraeus. His conclusion was: "What makes Michael's Chronicle so very important for us |[230] is the fact that it was written before Barhebraeus wrote his and that it contains information not found in the latter, most notably everything that Michael writes about the religious controversies following the Council of Chalcedon. Besides details such as this, the two chronicles are of a very similar nature and can be used as controls on each other." The fact that Barhebraeus followed Michael is rather better proved by the fact that the former actually says that it was Michael's Chronicle, written eighty years earlier, that provoked him into composing his own, because nobody had taken up this challenge in the intervening years. Langlois makes one mistake, however, in his comment about Barhebraeus not mentioning the post Chalcedonian controversies. He does in fact deal with this in the second part of the Chronicle, where his opinion is that it was at the time of that council that the churches were divided, the faithful cut off, and true religion rejected.[1]

Again, his *Storehouse of Mysteries* is no easier route to ascertaining the nature of Barhebraeus's literary character. This work is of the same type as the Latin glosses (e.g. the *Glossa Ordinaria* of Walafrid Strabo and the *Glossa Interlinearis* of Rupert of Deutz),[iii] in which the writers' own style and character is completely hidden by the thoroughness of their technique, which is essentially to gather together all the traditions of their predecessors. Barhebraeus is at least somewhat superior to his western colleagues in following such a procedure, since he manages wholly to avoid allegory and seeks rather to illumine the literal sense of the Bible using every assistance he can find.[2] He never wanders off into the swamps of pseudo-mysticism. Nobody has yet made a thorough investigation of Barhebraeus's philosophical or medical works.[3] In his ܣܘܐܕ ܣܘܦܝܐ and ܬܐܓܪܬ ܬܐܓܪܬܐ (which I have prepared for publication)[iv] he sets forth the Aristotelian system in the form of a compendium for teaching students. Although he does not present an original philosophical system of his own here, he nevertheless shows how perceptive an individual he was.

|[231] There remain then only the grammatical works, from which alone can be gleaned the true nature of Barhebraeus's literary merit. We shall now see what this was like.

A writer of a grammar can hardly fail to make use of material that has been collected by his predecessors; Barhebraeus is no exception. He carefully excerpted their works and accepted much of their teaching. He did not do this simply because it was the customary procedure for all writers of his day to amass their material from older authors, but since the very nature of the subject matter left no other course. The strength and originality of a grammarian lies not in the material he uses, but in the

[1] *Chron. Eccl.* I,178.

[2] It begins, ܒ ܡܣܟܢܘ̈ܗܝ ܕܟܝܢܐ ܐܠܗܝܐ: ܡܣܟܢܘ̈ܗܝ ܕܝܢ ܥܣܩܘܬܐ ܠܐܘܪܝܬܐ: ܐܣܝܪܐ ܕܐܝܠܝܢ ܐܠܗܐ: ܘܐܣܝܪܐ ܠܡܟܬܒܢܘܬܗ ܐܝܟ: ܫܒܝܫܘܬܐ ܐܠܝܨܬܐ ܠܢ: ܕܡܥܠܠܐ ܗܘܐ ܘܦܫܠܐ ܕܗܘܐ: ܡܫܩܠܐ ܕܡܠܬܐ ܕܟܬܒܐ ܪܘܚܢܐ ܥܠܗ ܟܐܘܬܗ ܦܪܘܫܘܬܐ ܗܘܐ ܕܒܗܘܢ ܐܢܫ: (G. W. Kirsch & G. H. Bernstein, *Chrestomathia Syriaca cum lexico* [Leipzig, 1832], 144).

[3] Gottheil did edit the list of plant names found in the ܡܢܪܬ ܩܘܕ̈ܫܐ [*Candelabra of the Sanctuaries*] (R.J.H. Gottheil, *A List of Plants and their Properties from the Menarath Kudhshe* (for private circulation, Berlin, 1886). The nature of dioecious plants is especially well described in this text.

method by which he understands, arranges, and describes the characteristics of the language in question; and in this Barhebraeus was both the most masterful and the most original of grammarians. He brought together all that was best from the older books with the most effective theoretical framework available to him.

To put it in a nutshell, Barhebraeus's approach was to take the philosophically-based grammar of the older Syriac authors (which started out from Dionysius Thrax), together with the teachings of Jacob of Edessa (the first to develop etymology and accidence, following the Greek grammarian Theodosius) and import these into a framework of Arabic grammar. The reason he was so successful in this approach was because he did not follow the example of Elias of Ṭirhan and simply make use of some of the Arabic grammatical definitions; rather, he adopted the entire Arabic system while never losing sight of the special characteristics of Syriac as they had been described by Jacob of Edessa. The Arab grammarian whose work he drew on the most was Abu'l Qāsim Maḥmūd ibn ʿUmar Az-Zamaḫšarī, who wrote his Al-Mufaṣṣal in 513/4 AH (AD 1119/20).[v] Just how highly this grammarian's thought was held among the Arabs can be judged from the following verse:

الطويل ولولا التُّقى قلت المفصّل مُعْجِزُ
كآيٍ طِوَالٍ من طِوَالِ المفصّل

Short of committing blasphemy, I would call the Mufaṣṣal a miracle and its verses comparable to those of the Qurʾān.[1] Furthermore, the work was supplemented by a great many commentators in the twelfth and thirteenth centuries. Az-Zamaḫšarī's work was thus the very best that Barhebraeus, who lived 1226-86, could get hold of, and so even in the minute details of the *Book of Splendours* we find him following its authority and example. We can now show this to be the case by giving an outline of the work.[vi]

I. General Arrangement

|[232] He begins the introduction by stating that earlier grammarians had but built on the work of Jacob of Edessa and that he himself, on account of various requests from friends, would take up the task of developing grammatical theory further. He then makes a distinction between the Masoretic and grammatical traditions that were in use among the Syrians—

[1] Ḥāǧǧī Ḫalīfa (i.e. Mustafa Kātib Čelebī), *Lexicon bibliographicum et encyclopædicum* (ed. G. Flügel, Leipzig, 1835-58) VI, 37.

namely the Edessene and the Nisibene, which are obviously interrelated. Being Syrian Orthodox himself, Barhebraeus naturally presumes in general the Western, or Edessene, tradition, although he admits that wherever necessary he has made use of the Nisibene, or Eastern, system.[1] The work is organised into four books and he follows the Arabic system of three parts of speech rather than the traditional Syriac seven (cf. p.159). Hence the titles of the first three books, *On the Noun* (ܫܡܐ, الاسم), *On the Verb* (ܡܠܬܐ, الفعل), and *On Particles* (ܐܣܘܪܐ, الحروف). The fourth book then covers matters concerning all the parts of speech (ܡܫܘܬܦܬܐ), such as orthoepy and pointing (i.e. whatever relates to 'right reading', ὑπόκρισις). One might therefore surmise that in this last book the arrangement of the Greek grammars and that of Jacob of Edessa might have been preserved, but this is not the case. For a start, the excerpts from Jacob that are found in Book 4, Chapter 2 (*Gramm.*, 194) were originally placed in Jacob's introduction, not at the end of his grammar. Furthermore, the very word ܡܫܘܬܦܬܐ implies the opposite, since it is just a translation of المُشْتَرَك, which is what Zamaḫšarī calls his fourth book too. If one doubts the likelihood of this, we may simply compare Barhebraeus's introduction to this fourth book with its parallel in Zamaḫšarī. The former says (*Gramm.*, 193): ܒܬܪ ܕܡܢ ܕܝܠܝܬܐ...ܕܡܠܘܬܐ ܘܡܐܡܪܐ...ܒ...ܕܬܠܬܝܗܘܢ ܗܟܝܠ ܡܐܡܪܐ ܕܐܬܦܪܫܘ ܐܡܠܠܢ: ܒܡܐܡܪܐ ܗܢܐ ܪܒܝܥܝܐ ܠܒܥܘܬܐ ܓܘܢܝܬܐ: ܐܝܟ ܒܥܘܬܐ ܕܐܬܘܬܐ ܫܪܫܢܝܬܐ: ܘܪܘܟܟܐ ܘܩܘܫܝܐ: ܘܙܘܥܐ ܘܩܠܐ: ܘܟܠ ܕܐܝܟ ܗܠܝܢ. ܘܠܟܠ ܡܫܘܬܦܝܢ ܐܘ ܠܬܠܬ: ܡܫܬܘܬܦܢܝܬܐ ܕܒܗܝܢ ܡܢܝܢ: ܡܕܒܪܢܝ. ܕܐܦ ܗܪܟܐ ܡܕܒܪܢܐ ܗܘܐ ܐܠܗܐ ܐܝܟ ܕܒܟܠܗܝܢ. (*after we dealt with the particular aspects of the parts of speech in the former three books, in this fourth book we deal with questions of a general nature* |[233] *such as questions about the basic letters, Rukkāḵā and Quššāyā, the vowels and the sounds, and everything else of this sort, which partake of two or three [of the parts of speech], and here too God is our guide*). This is really nothing but a transposition into the Syriac context of what Zamaḫšarī says: المشترك نحو الامالة والوقف وتخفيف الهمزة والتِقَاء الساكنَين ونظايرها ممّا يتوارد فيه الاضربُ الثلثة او اثنان منها. وانا اورد ذلك في هذا القسم على نحو الترتيب المارّ في القسمَيْن معتصما بحَبْل التوفيق من ربى بريئا من الحول والقوّة الّا به. (*al-muštarak [that which is in common], such as imala, the pause, the softer pronunciation of hamza, the collision of two quiescents, and other like things, means that in which all three [parts of speech], or any two of them, are together concerned; and I introduce this subject in this part in accordance with the aforementioned arrangement in the two parts, being myself sustained by the slender thread of the Lord's help, having neither power nor strength save in Him*). For both these writers, ܡܫܘܬܦܬܐ / المشترك are those aspects of the language which

[1] The most noteworthy examples are found in the discussion of Passive Imperatives (*Gramm.*, 151,2, 152,2, 153,4).

could equally well belong to all three (or any two) of the parts of speech: ما يتوارد فيه الضربُ الثلثة او اثنان منها = ܕܠܟܠ ܡܢܗܘܢ ܐܘ ܠܬܪ̈ܬܝܢ: ܡܫܘܬܦܘܬܐ ܟܕܡ ܡܬܡ. Both writers proceed to conclude their introductions with a pious formula which neither have used in the previous three books. Barhebraeus simply copies Zamaḫšarī and changes his imala, pause, etc., into subjects relating to Syriac orthoepy. We shall see further examples of this close relationship between the two writers, evidence that Barhebraeus often follows the exact wording of Zamaḫšarī.

II. The Noun

Nowhere is the special character of Barhebraeus's grammatical system more clearly visible than in his arrangement of the theory of the noun, in which he brings together the Greek and the Arabic definitions. But before we go further into this, we first need to discuss his definition and organisation of nouns. Here there is a certain amount of interweaving of the different schools. The definition is as follows: ܫܡܐ ܐܝܬܘܗܝ ܩܠܐ ܡܠܐ ܡܡܠܠܝܐ ܦܫܝܛܬ ܣܘܟܠܐ ܕܙܒܢܐ ܠܐ ܩܢܝܐ ܒܟܝܢܗ ܡܕܡ (*the noun is* |234 *a logical sound of simple meaning, which does not have in itself any tense*). In this we can perceive both a Greek and an Arabic origin. When he uses the concept of a *sound* (ܩܠܐ ܡܠܐ) to define the noun, he is basing himself on the theory that we saw in Bar Zuʿbi (p.159). When the question was put as to whether ܡܠܐ was a genus or a species, Bar Zuʿbi (or rather the Aristotelian commentator, Probus) replied that it was a genus whenever it referred to sounds that were indicative of something, or of natural sounds, or of sounds indicative of something by convention [συνθήκη], whether that be spoken or written. They are considered to be indicative either by intention or by logic (ܒܨܒܝܢܝܬ ܘܡܡܠܠܝܬ). So Barhebraeus includes 'noun' as a species under its genus, which is 'word' taken in the logical sense (ܩܠܐ ܡܠܐ ܡܡܠܠܝܐ). He again closely follows the Greek theory when he says that the noun has no tense. The scholion with which he illustrates this point is simply an expansion of Aristotle's ἄνευ χρόνου (*De Int.* 2), upon which Ammonius also commented (see p.159n). However, when he goes on to say that the noun is ܦܫܝܛܬ ܣܘܟܠܐ, he is distinguishing the noun as a species of the genus ܩܠܐ ܡܠܐ (كَلِمَة) from a complete statement (ܡܐܡܪܐ = كلام).[1] This comes straight from Zamaḫšarī, who says, الاسم ما دلّ على معنى في نفسه دلالة مجرَّدة

[1] In the scholion he says, ܩܠܐ ܡܠܐ ܡܡܠܠܝܐ ܕܝ ܓܢܣܐ ܕܫܡܐ ܗܘ ܕܦܫܝܛܬ ܣܘܟܠܐ ܡܢ ܡܐܡܪܐ ܦܪܫܐ ܠܗ (*if 'logical sound' is the genus to which 'noun' belongs, then 'simple meaning' distinguishes it from a statement*). See also the definition of ܩܠܐ ܡܠܐ (*Gramm.*, 2).

عن الاقتران (*the noun is that which itself indicates a meaning in such a way that there is no need for it to have any connection*). Hence we can see Greek and Arabic theories intermingling with each other and spreading throughout every thread and intricacy of Barhebraeus's grammatical work. He is truly a 'Graeco-Arabic' grammarian.

We see this immediately confirmed by his classification of nouns, which is again taken straight from Zamaẖšarī, who says that: nouns can be either |[235] 1) general/appellative (اسم الجنس), which refers both to the thing itself and to everything similar to it, and 2) personal/proper (العلم), used for a single thing only, not including those that are similar to it. Barhebraeus borrows this: "every noun that is a predicate of only one thing is 'personal', e.g. Simon, John; but if it is a predicate for both the one thing and everything similar to it [or, for many similar things], it is 'general' (ܓܢܣܝܐ)."[1] The Arabic term for the latter is اسم الجنس. Just as Zamaẖšarī then goes on to deal with the different forms of the proper noun, so Barhebraeus too places his discussion of the proper nouns at this early stage. This comes as something of a surprise, since no Syriac grammarian had ever organised his discussion of nouns quite like this and he is again mingling Greek and Arabic ideas. This can be easily demonstrated in what follows as we see that within Barhebareus's Syriac-based divisions there are many elements corresponding to the aspects of Greek and Arabic grammatical theory.

III. The Proper Noun

The types are:

1. ܡܕܝܢܝܐ, i.e. κύριον (*Gramm.*, 6; see Dionysius Thrax, 14,1).

2. ܫܠܡܢܐ, i.e. when a name is compounded with another, as in Simon-Peter or Judas-Maccabaeus.

3. ܟܘܢܝܐ, as in ܐܒܐ ܕܥܡ̈ܡܐ (*father of the peoples*) or ܐܒܐ ܕܫܒ̈ܛܐ (*father of the tribes*), Bar-tholomew and Bar-nabas. This is adapted from Zamaẖšarī, او كنية كأَبِي عَمْرٍو وأُمِّ كُلْثُومٍ (*Muf.*, 5,7).

4. ܦܫܝܛܐ as in ܐܒ, and ܡܪܟܒܐ as in ܐܒܪܡ (i.e. *father of the people*), and also ܠܘܬ ܡܪܟܒܐ as in ܐܒܪܗܡ (i.e. *father of many peoples*). This is based on Dionysius Thrax (above, p.12,10), the translator of which used the same examples of the threefold scheme ἁπλοῦν, σύνθετον, παρασύνθετον. When Barhebraeus goes on to subclassify the composite nouns (σύνθετα) into three—those

[1] *Gramm.*, 5.

composed of two complete nouns, e.g. Jeho-Aḥaz, those composed of two defective nouns, e.g. Malki-zedeq, and those composed of a defective and a complete, e.g. Rab-Baita—he is again following Dionysius (p.12). However, these comments on the different forms of proper nouns taken from Dionysius were not enough for Barhebraeus, who went on either to augment them himself or else |[236] to include the following types of composite proper noun, all of which he reckoned to belong to the class of nouns called ܡܪܟܒܐ, which had been added already by his predecessors:

a) Composed of a verb with an unspecified subject and an object suffix. The Syriac is ܡܢ ܡܠܬܐ ܕܐܘܪܡ ܡܫܡܠܝܢ ܠܒܘܪܐ ܟܝܢܐ ܘܣܘܡܟܐ ܣܘܡܟܝܐ, where ܠܒܘܪܐ ܟܝܢܐ is فاعل غايب and ܣܘܡܟܐ ܣܘܡܟܝܐ is مفعول مضمر. The example given is ܢܣܪܘܟ (*Nisrok*) which is clearly derived from ܐܣܪܟ with a 3rd person prefix and a 2nd person suffix.
b) Composed of a particle and a noun, e.g. ܠܐ ܥܡܝ (Hos 1.9).
c) Composed of a particle and a verb, e.g. ܠܐ ܐܬܪܚܡܬ (Hos 1.6)
d) Composed of three nouns, e.g. ܫܡܘܐܠ ܕܢܘܗܝ.
e) Composed of two ܦܠܓܘܬܐ, e.g. ܐܒܝܕ, ܐܣܘܪ, ܫܡܘܐܠ ܒܪ.
f) Composed of nouns or a noun and a particle that form a sentence, e.g. ܥܡܢܘܐܝܠ, ܡܪܝܐ ܙܕܝܩܢ (= יהוה צדקנו, Jer 23.6), ܫܡܘܐܠ ܗܒܢܝ.
g) Composed of a noun and a verb in the perfect tense, again forming a sentence, e.g. ܗܘ ܐܠܗܐ, ܙܟܪܝܐ ܪܒܐ.
h) Composed of a noun and an imperative, e.g. ܨܘܪ ܐܬܠܝ (Ṣudaili).
i) Composed of two verbs, e.g. ܡܣܪܗܒ ܫܠܠ ܚܒ ܒܙܐ (Isa 8.3).

As well as these forms, which derived from the Greek class of composite nouns, he added also two further Arabic types, which he calls ܡܠܬܚܡܐ, i.e. منقول (*customary*), and ܡܬܩܢܬܐ, i.e. مُرْتَجَل, αὐτοσχεδιαστικός (*extemporary / accidental*). In listing all these subtypes of the proper noun he remains close to Zamaḫšarī,[1] but he has to leave out the examples the latter gives from

[1] So that readers may easily compare the two, Zamaḫšarī's classification is as follows. He subdivides the منقول into six parts:

1. منقول عن اسم عين, e.g. ثور, اسد.
2. عن اسم معنى, e.g. فضل, إياس.
3. عن صفة, e.g. حاتم, نأيلة.
4. عن فعل,
    a) Perfect, e.g. شَمَّرَ, نعسبُ.
    b) Imperfect, e.g. تَغْلِبُ, يَشْكُرُ.
    c) Imperative, e.g. اِصْمِتْ.

Arabic tribal usage |[237] and replaces them with the usage of the Syrian Christians, thus...

5.

a) Some ܡܫܬܡܗܢܐ derive from ܫܡܗܐ ܬܚܘܝܝܐ (*basic nouns*, مَصْدَرٌ), which Barhebraeus has in place of Zamaḫšarī's اسم معنى; the examples are ܡܢܝܘܬܐ for a man's name and ܝܡܐ for a woman's (cf. the notes at *Muf.*, 2, on فضيل and إياس).

b) Some derive from ܫܡܗܐ ܐܝܢܝܐ, the qualitative noun (صفة, *Muf.*, 3), e.g. ܫܦܝܪܐ, ܢܨܝܚܬܐ, ܐܚܡܝܢܬܐ (cf. Arabic حاتم, نائلة).

c) Some derive from a verb (*Muf.*, 4), whether Perfect, e.g. ܫܚܐ; Present / Participle, which Barhebraeus carelessly adds to Zamaḫšarī's list, e.g. ܙܒܝܐ; Imperfect, e.g. ܝܚܝܐ; Imperative, e.g. ܟܘܬ, ܚܘܐ (an extraordinary etymology for the name Eve).

d) Some derive from a number of different things, which *Muf.*, 5, introduces in place of a sound (صوت), such that in fact he here introduces those derivations which Zamaḫšarī, under no.1, derived from the noun of substance (عن اسم عين). Since it is here that Barhebraeus outlines the typical Syriac usage in reckoning the proper nouns,[1] it might be of use to reproduce the groups that he enumerates. Proper nouns can be derived from:

   i. the names of heavenly bodies, ܫܡܫܐ, ܣܗܪܐ.
   ii. |[238] the names of places, e.g. ܬܕܡܘܪ, ܟܟܠ are names for men, ܫܘܫܢ, ܫܠܝܡܬ for women.
   iii. the names of animals, ܢܡܪܐ, ܐܪܝܐ (cf. vice versa *Muf.*, 6,11 and no.1 above, اسد, ثور); also of plants, for ܘܪܕܐ (*rose*) is a man's name, and ܪܘܕܝܢ (ῥόδιον, *rose*) a woman's.[2]
   iv. the names of inanimate things, ܟܐܦܐ is a man's name, ܡܘܪܐ a woman's.

---

5. عن صَوْتٍ, e.g. بَبَّة (the name given, as a joke, to Abdallah ibn Al-Ḥāriṯ ibn Naufal because it refers to the sound that a child makes).

6. عن مركّب, which includes composite nouns, whether they create a sentence (as in تأبّط شرا) or not (as in معديكرب and بَعلَبَكّ). It is from this latter subdivision that Barhebraeus creates his list above (4a-f) of additions to the compound nouns of Dionysius.

[1] Zamaḫšarī also explains the Arabic usage (*Muf.*, 6,4) by which the proper names of camels, horses, and sheep were created in line with their characteristics.

[2] When one says ῥόδον in Greek, it cannot really mean a *rose*, but rather what in modern Greek they call ῥόδιον, i.e. the *pomegranate*, which originally derived from ῥόα and then ῥοία (cf. LXX Song of Solomon 4.3).

v. ecclesiastical ranks or church feasts: ܕܝܪܝܐ, ܡܫܝܚܐ, ܣܘܒܪܐ (*annunciation*), ܩܫܝܫܐ, ܢܓܪܐ, ܕܢܚܐ (*epiphany*) are all men's names, while ܩܝܡܬܐ (*resurrection*), ܣܒܪܬܐ (*gospel*) are women's.[1]

vi. the names of days and months: ܚܕ ܒܫܒܐ (neosyr. Ḥošiba, *Sunday*) is a man's name, ܥܪܘܒܬܐ (παρασκευή, *Friday*) is a woman's. ܢܝܣܢ, ܐܕܪ and ܐܝܠܘܠ are all men's names.

vii. names in the plural, e.g. ܩܛܝܠܐ ܡܘܪܝܢܐ.[2] He adds (*Gramm.*, 7,1) to these the diminutives (ܡܙܥܪܢܐ) such as ܡܠܟܘܢܐ (*a little king*) and ܒܝܬܘܢܐ (*a little dwelling*), and then the ܡܠܐ ܢܘܙܢܐ, which comes from the ὑποκοριστικῷ (*diminutives, terms of endearment*) of the Greek grammarians (Dion.Thr., above p.12n), the example he gives is ܐܒܘܢ. One can see just how much detail he has adopted the Greek system.

6. ܡܬܩܢܢܐ or مرتجل,[3] a word that Barhebraeus explains (*Gramm.*, 6,10) as follows: it is the name by which men are called in some arbitrary way when no more accurate likeness can be made with anything else, such as e.g. when a man |[239] is called ܫܡܫܐ (*sun*). There does not have to be any likeness between the person and the name in these cases, for if a woman is called ܡܠܟܬܐ (*queen*) or ܡܪܬܐ (*mistress*), there need be no real likeness involved. In some cases, however, there might be some sort of real likeness, as in when a man who is born in Lent is called Barṣauma (ܒܪܨܘܡܐ, *Son of the Fast*).[4]

Barhebraeus preserves throughout this section the list produced by Zamaḫšarī, adding from time to time elements from the Greek tradition that seemed necessary. The general arrangement is:

Zamaḫšarī (*Muf.*, 5,6)		Barhebraeus (*Gramm.*, 6,4)
Proper Noun	اسم	ܡܪܝܐ (i.e. κύριον, to which he

[1] One can readily compare names from the Romance languages such as Apostolo and Annunziata.

[2] Cf. Zamaḫšarī on plural proper nouns, with which he deals separately (*Muf.*, 8,10), with Barhebraeus (*Gramm.*,7,9).

[3] The Greek term is ἀποσχεδίασμα. A gloss in Arabic explains the Syriac term: الشئ الذى لا يبالى به and على المجاز (see*Thesaurus*, 2245). De Sacy translates المرتجل as *improvisé* (*Grammaire* I,188).

[4] See J. G. Wetzstein, "Ausgewählte griechische und lateinische Inschriften, gesammelt auf Reisen in den Trachonen und um das Haurangebirge," *Abhandlung der Königlichen Akademie der Wissenschaften, Phil.-Hist. Kl.* (1863), 255-368 (esp. p.336f.).

adds ܠܡ̈ܪ)

	كنية	ܟܘܢܝܐ
divided into:		
	مُغْرَد	ܦܫܝܛܐ (plus Dionysius's theory)
	مركّب	ܡܪܟܒܐ (plus the σύνθετα and some others)
	منقول	ܡܬܬܚܒܐ
	مرتجل	ܡܡܫܚܐ

If this were not enough to prove Barhebraeus's dependence upon Zamaḫšarī, then the final paragraph from each should end all such doubts. For at the very end of the chapter on the proper nouns, both writers talk about the indefinite, or universal, noun (ܦܠܢ, فلان) thus:

أسامي	عن	كِناياتٌ	فلانة	وأُمُّ	فلان	وابو	وفلانةُ	-	فلانُ
ܕܩܢܘܡܐ	ܐܢܘܢ	ܟܘܢܝܐ	ܕܦܠܢܝܬ	ܘܐܡܐ	ܕܦܠܢ	ܘܐܒܐ	ܘܦܠܢܝܬ	ܘܦܠܢ	ܦܠܡܘܢܝ
البهأيم ادخلوا	اعلام	عن	كَنَوا	اذا	انهم	ذكروا	وقد	وكُناهم	الأناسِيّ
-	-	-	-	-	-	-	-	-	ܡܢܩܘܡܐ
-	فللدنيت	وهَنةٌ	هَنٌ	واما[1]	-	والفلانة	الفلانُ	فقالوا	اللاَم
-	-	-	ܗ̇ܘܝܐ	-	ܘܐܦܠܢ	-	-	-	-
|240 -	-	-	-	-	-	-	الاجناس	اسماء	عن
-	-	ܐܟܘ	ܐܘܟܝܠܘܢ	ܠܦܠܡܘܢܝ	ܡܡܠܠ	ܚܕ	ܘܐܡܪ	ܘܫܐܠ	ܕܟܝܢܬܐ.
-	-	-	-	-	-	-	-	-	-
-	-	-	-	-	-	-	ܦܠܢ.	ܠܘܬ	ܠܡܕܝܢܬܐ

Barhebraeus omits whatever is of relevance to Arabic alone, he translates literally whatever pertains to both languages, and when something is only relevant to Syriac he illustrates it with Biblical examples (Dan 8.13, Mt 26.18); and there you have his method.

IV. The General Noun

If we were to follow Barhebraeus's own plan and method (as we did when dealing with the proper nouns), then we would need to write a truly enormous commentary. But to do this would be going much further than

[1] But if one compares هَنٌ and يا هَنْ with Syriac ܗܢܐ, it is not ܗ̈ܢܐ that is the word in question, but ܗܢ̄ܐ, rightly written in the ms as ܗ̇ܘܝܐ = ܗ̈ܘܢܐ. This word is found in Bar ʿAlī (3314): ان هذا. ܗܢܐ ܗܘܝܠ. The word ܗܢ̄ܐ should be added to the lexica, where it has been banished through its not being distinguished from ܗ̈ܢܐ.

we originally proposed to do, since we set out merely to locate Barhebraeus's place amongst Syrian grammarians and to outline his literary qualities. In what follows, therefore, we shall be describing rather more briefly how he arranges the subject of the forms of 'general nouns' (اسما الجنس ܫܡܗܐ ܓܢܣܝܐ).

A. Διαθέσεις (*states*).[vii] The first part follows the Greek arrangement, thus γένος = ܓܢܣܐ, εἴδη = ܐܕ̈ܫܐ, σχήματα = ܐܣܟ̈ܡܐ, ἀριθμοὺς = ܡܢ̈ܝܢܐ, διαθέσεις = ܐܝܬܘ̈ܬܐ, and πτώσεις = ܡܦ̈ܠܬܐ. This system is well known to us from Jacob Bar Šakko (p. ܟ, l.18; p. ܕ, l.3) and is reasonably similar to what Jacob of Edessa used. It departs from the Greek example insofar as the *states* (ܐܝܬܘ̈ܬܐ) are included in the section on the noun, which Dionysius did not acknowledge at the relevant place (p.10) and only first mentions at the end of the section on the noun (p.16 = Uhlig, 46), where he writes, 'there are two states of the noun, active and passive.' [viii] But his followers did not necessarily like this, for the scholiast on the above citation writes, 'He is wrong to express it thus; rather he ought to say, 'whenever people see states in nouns, they must be [nouns] that are derived from verbs,''[ix] for the Greeks originally recognised *states* |[241] only in the verb. Barhebraeus now joins this theory about *states* (which was known to both Jacob of Edessa and Jacob Bar Šakko, for whom see p. ܨ, l.15) together with the theory of فاعل and مفعول, as we can see from the way he explains it himself. For when he says,[1] ܒܟܘܪܐ ܡܢ ܐܝܬܘ̈ܬܗ ܥܒܘܕܐ ܘܦܪܘܫܐ ܠܗ ܡܛܠܬܐ ܗܘܘ ܡܠܐ ܕܪܗܛܐ ܠܗ ܐܝܟ ܐܢܐ ܦܘܠܘܣ. ܘܦܘܠܘܣ ܡܩ̈ܒܠ ܠܟܐܦܐ, he is expressing in Syriac the words of Zamaḫšarī: الفَاعِل هو ما كان المُسْنَد اليه مِنْ فِعْلٍ أو شِبْهِهِ مُقَدَّمًا عليه ابدا كقولك ضَرَبَ زَيْدٌ وزَيْدٌ ضَارِبٌ غُلَامُهُ وحَسَنٌ وَجْهُهُ (*Muf.*, 11,7); and when he gives as an example of subject and object ܡܚܝܢܝ ܘܡܚܝܢܐ ܠܝܥܩܘܒ (*Jacob strikes me; I strike Jacob*) he is simply borrowing the equivalent Arabic formula ضَرَبَنِي وَضَرَبْتُ زَيْدًا (*Muf.*, 11,14).

B. Gender. While Barhebraeus takes the Greek theory as his own basis, he equally infuses it with the Arabic, and we can see this happening again in the section on gender. He initially lays out (*Gramm.*, 8) the general criteria for feminines (those with a consonant, those with a vowel, those with one of each, the rules for aspiration) just as Zamaḫšarī gives the general criteria for Arabic feminines (Alif, Tau, and Yā, *Muf.*, 82). He continues to follow him very closely in the matter of the twofold division into natural and metaphorical usages. Zamaḫšarī writes: التانيث على ضربَيْنِ جقيقى كتانيث المراة والناقة ونحوهما مّا بإزأيه ذكر في الحيوان وغير حقيقى كتانبث الظلمة والنعل ونحوهما مّا يتعلق بالوضع والاصطلاح (*the feminine gender is twofold:*

[1] *Gramm.*, 36.

the natural, as is the feminine form of 'woman', 'camel' etc., which are the opposites of the masculine forms of the same animals; and unnatural, such as 'darkness', 'shoe' etc., which are so reckoned according to situation and custom [κατὰ θέσιν and κατὰ συνθήκην]). Barhebraeus says, ܢܩܒܬܐ ܕܝܢ ܟܝܢܝܬܐ ܐܝܬܝܗ̇ ܢܩܒܬܐ ܐܝܠܐ ܕܟܪܐ ܐܝܠܐ ܒܩܘܒܠܗ̇ ܐܝܟ ܐܢܬܬܐ ܣܘܣܝܬܐ ܘܠܐ ܟܝܢܝܬܐ ܐܝܬܝܗ̇ ܢܩܒܬܐ ܐܝܠܐ ܕܒܣܝܡܐ ܘܡܫܡܫܢܘܬܐ ܡܢ ܫܘܪܝܐ ܡܬܢܩܒܐ ܒܡܡܠܠܐ ܐܝܟ ܥܝܢܐ ܘܐܕܢܐ |[242] (*a feminine, which has a masculine corresponding to it, as in 'woman', 'mare', is a natural feminine; unnatural is that feminine which, according to situation and custom [κατὰ θέσιν and κατὰ συνθήκην], was originally feminine in speech, such as 'eye' and 'ear'*). For بإزائه ذكر he has ܕܟܪܐ ܐܝܠܐ ܒܩܘܒܠܗ̇, and for يتعلق بالوضع والاصطلاح he writes ܕܒܣܝܡܐ ܘܡܫܡܫܢܘܬܐ ܡܢ ܫܘܪܝܐ ܡܬܢܩܒܐ. At the end of this section on feminines (*Gramm.*, 16) Barhebraeus copies Zamaḫšarī so closely that he makes a false move. For when, in the discussion on the threefold use of the letter ܬ, he states that ܬ should be used ܐܘ ܡܛܠ ܢܩܒܘܬܐ ܐܘ ܡܛܠ ܪܘܪܒ ܣܘܟܠܐ (*either for the feminine or for strengthening the meaning of a word*) and then also adds ܐܘ ܠܦܘܪܫ ܝܚܝܕܝܐ ܡܢ ܟܢܫܝܐ (*or for distinguishing the particular from the general*, i.e. for creating a singular out of a collective noun, such as ܚܛܬܐ, *a grain of wheat*, from ܚܛܐ, *wheat*), he is thoughtlessly copying Zamaḫšarī (*Muf.*, 82,5). It is clear enough what he means about the ܬ of the feminine, but what he says about this ܪܘܪܒ ܣܘܟܠܐ (i.e. that it strengthens the meanings of words, so that, for example, ܪܘܫܥܬܐ, ܣܟܘܠܬܐ, ܛܘܥܝܬܐ are made stronger words than ܪܘܫܥܐ, ܣܟܠܐ, ܛܘܥܝܐ by the addition of a ܬ) and also about the derivation of singulars from collectives, is taken from the following in Zamaḫšarī: دخولها (التاء)...للفرق بين اسم الجنس والواحد منه كتمرة...وللمبالغة في الوصف كعلاّمة ونسابة وراوية وفروقة وملولة (*the letter 't' is added to distinguish the collective noun from the individual ...and to increase the descriptive force of a word, as in 'very learned', 'an excellent genealogist', 'recitor of many poems', 'very fearful', 'very bored'*). One does not need to consider this for long to realise, however, that the nature of the letter ܬ in forms such as ܣܟܘܠܬܐ is quite different from that in عَلاَّمَةٌ.

C. Species. There is only one matter worth mentioning from what Barhebraeus says about species (εἴδη, ܐܕ̈ܫܐ), in which he has made an alteration to the older |[243] Syriac theory. The Syriac grammarians of the early period had debated the place of the concept of 'species' insofar as it could be used for the forms of the Syriac noun (see above, p.57). The translator of Dionysius included the adjectives in *-aya* and *-ana* among the 'species of the noun' (in accord with the Greek, cf. p.10), while Jacob of Edessa counted these forms under the category of 'shapes'.[x] We can see easily how this came about, for there are two species, πρωτότυπον and παράγωγον (*prototype* and *derived-from-the-prototype*) the examples being γῆ and γαιήϊος, which correspond well to the Syriac pair of ܐܪܥܐ and ܐܪܥܢܐ.

Barhebraeus noted, however, that in Syriac there are really three forms to account for, namely ܐܪܡܐ, ܐܪܡܝܐ, and ܐܪܡܝܝܐ (though this does not happen in the gentilic names, ܪܗܘܡܝܢ, ܪܗܘܡܝܐ). It would therefore seem easier to fit these three forms into the threefold arrangement of the 'shapes', ἁπλοῦν, σύνθετον, παρασύνθετον (*simple, compound, derived-from-a-compound*), but the definition of 'shape' does not allow for this,[1] since the adjectives in question are not 'compound', but are rather 'derivative'. The whole question is made more difficult in Syriac by the fact that ܪܟܝܒ and ܡܪܟܒܐ are equally used for both 'compound' and 'derived'.

While on the basis of the definitions, the Dionysian argument seems the better, Jacob's method has the virtue that it takes into account the threefold 'shapes', which can easily be made to include the three Syriac forms—viz. the two adjectives together with the 'prototype', or basic, noun, which he calls the ܥܠܬܐ (*cause*). Barhebraeus saw this confusion and summed it up thus: ܣܟܡܐ ܠܐܕܫܐ ܩܪܐ [ܐܕܫܐ ܕܬܪܝܨܘܬܐ] ܐܣܟܡܐ ܡܕܝܢ. ܘܠܐܣܟܡܐ ܦܫܝܛܐ ܘܡܪܟܒܐ ܐܕܫܐ. ܘܠܝܬ ܚܣܝܡܘܬܐ ܒܫܡܗܐ (*the holy man [Jacob] calls the species 'shapes', and shapes he calls simple and compound* [correct reading] *species, but there is no restriction on what words can mean*). He himself supported the Dionysian interpretation, as the patronymics could be included amongst the *derived-from-the-prototype* species, e.g. ܥܒܪܝܐ from ܥܒܪ. The latter name is κατὰ τὴν πρώτην θέσιν λεχθέν, or as Jacob puts it, it is the 'cause' (ܥܠܬܐ) lying behind ܥܒܪܝܐ (p.60). Others interpreted this pattern in a philosophical way and used the terms ܛܘܦܣܐ (from Persian تُپك, *idea, image*), both ܛܘܦܣܐ ܩܕܡܝܐ (*first idea*) and |[244] ܛܘܦܣܐ ܬܪܝܢܐ (*second idea*).[2] We can be sure that this way of interpreting it goes back at least as far as the Aristotelian commentator Probus.[3]

Barhebraeus starts out from the formation of these tribal names such as ܥܒܪܝܐ from ܥܒܪ and ܐܒܪܗܡܝܐ from ܐܒܪܗܡ, a subject already exhausted by the translator of Dionysius (p.11) and then disordered by Jacob, and to these he connects the derivation of further adjectives such as ܓܘܫܡܢܐ, ܓܘܫܡܢܝܐ, and ܓܘܫܡܢܐ from ܓܘܫܡܐ. He evidently felt that all these really belonged to the category of patronymics, which he could not fail to compare with the notion of مَنْسُوبٌ and نِسْبَةٌ and نَسَبٌ, i.e. genealogical relationships. The Arabic نِسْبَةٌ is rendered in Syriac as ܒܝܬܝܘܬܐ (*domestication*, as Amira calls it), مَنْسُوبٌ as

[1] This is the definition according to the scholia Erotemata to Dionysius Thrax: σχῆμά ἐστι λέξεων ποσότης ὑφ' ἕνα τόνον καὶ ἓν πνεῦμα ἀδιαστάτως ἀγομένη ἐν ἁπλότητι ἢ συνθέσει (Uhlig, 29).

[2] G. Amira, *Grammatica Syriaca sive chaldaica* (Rome, 1596), 105, and see below, p.251n.

[3] Hoffmann, *Herm.*, index, s.v. ܛܘܦܣܐ.

ܡܬܝܚܣܢܝܬܐ, and نَسَبٌ as ܡܬܝܚܣܢܝܬܐ, which was also sometimes called ܚܠܦܐ and ܐܬܘܒܐ. He stressed that there were simply three stages, ܡܩܕܡܐ, ܬܪܝܢܐ and ܬܠܝܬܝܐ, which agrees with Jacob's nomenclature (p.60). So beginning with the Arabic theory and wanting to make this out to be the same as the older Greek one, he speaks about the species thus (*Gramm.*, 16,29): "the writers of this art [of grammar] called 'species' all those types of relation that refer to nationalities or places (ܫܪܒܬ̈ܐ ܐܘܡܘܬ̈ܐ ܐܘ ܐܬܪ̈ܘܬܐ)." There is no need to go into any detail about all the actual 'species' which he then uses to describe the vocalisation of relative adjectives, as Zamaḫšarī does.

D. Shapes. Whereas he followed the lead of the Arab grammarians in the foregoing matter of species, he turns instead to Jacob of Edessa for categorising the 'shapes'. Shape was earlier (p.20) defined as ܩܠܐ ܡܫܘܕܥܢܐ ܗܘ ܕܡܛܐ ܠܫܡܘܥܐ ܒܝܕ ܡܡܠܠܐ ܕܐܬܘܬ̈ܐ ܟܢܝܫܬܐ (*a phonetic symbol which is brought to the hearer by the pronunciation of a collection of letters*), which agrees neither with the definition found in Dionysius (above, p.12) nor with that offered by his scholoiast, that "'shape' relates to the nature of the signified, for from the 'shape' we know what it is that the word wants to signif y."[1] xi Barhebraeus's definition is rather about the |245 etymologies of words (as I think was the case with Jacob too) and the chapters on this topic deal with the whole system of noun derivation.[2] In doing this, he makes use of Jacob's canons, though he puts them in a different order.

This all suggests that Barhebraeus developed his systems of number and of shape according to the same principle. Initially he lists nouns of three consonants and one vowel, then those of three consonants and two vowels. After this there follow nouns of four consonants and two vowels, then those of four consonants with three vowels, and so on (p.20,19f.). For the vowels, he follows the Greek alphabetical order, resulting in the following list: I, ܢܩܡܐ; II, 1 ܐܘܚܐ, 2 ܕܘܚܐ, 3 ܐܚܐ; III, 1 ܐܘܚܡܐ, 2 ܟܘܚܠܐ, 3 ܐܡܪܐ, 4 ܟܠܘܪܐ, 5 ܢܘܪܐ, 6 ܐܪܚܐ, with ܣܪܚܐ ܕܢܝܐ, 7 ܫܘܚܐ with ܐܘܪܚܐ ܕܢܝܐ, 8 ܢܘܦܐ with ܚܪܝܐ ܕܢܝܐ, 9 ܚܛܒܐ, 10 ܡܠܟܐ, 11 ܡܫܝܚܐ, 12 ܢܝܚܐ; IV, 1 ܦܘܪܢܐ, 2 ܐܘܚܡܢܐ, ܡܟܠܬܐ etc. This is of course also the way that Jacob does it (p.58). According to this arrangement he then (*Gramm.*, 29f.) proceeds to

---

[1] Bekker, *Anecdota*, 859.

[2] If he had accepted the Greek definition we have just cited, he would have grasped the relationship that exists between the meaning of a word and its etymological form. He would then have understood that ܚܒܝܫܐ is active, ܚܒܝܫܐ qualitative and passive, just as he distinguishes (*Gramm.*, 36,38,40) ܚܒܝܫܘܬܐ from ܚܒܝܫܘܬܐ and ܡܫܘܚ ܡܢܐ. Barhebraeus got nowhere near this subtler grammatical principle, but instead used only external criteria to categorise the classes of words, which he called types.

enumerate the plural forms, having no regard for roots but simply mixing together everything that had the same form in the singular. The forms ܐܡܐ, ܕܒܐ, ܐܒܐ etc. he called 'basic types', which is a Greek term,[1] no doubt taken from Jacob, whom Barhebraeus here cites explicitly (*Gramm.*, 20,19). He criticises Jacob's mistake in counting only eight monosyllables, ܦܡܐ, ܫܡܐ, ܕܡܐ, ܦܬܐ, ܐܪܐ, ܚܢܐ, ܒܪܐ, ܠܪܐ, yet the extra ones that he adds himself are really particles and do not belong here at all—ܟܡܐ, ܟܠܐ, ܡܠܐ, ܦܠܐ. On ܒܪܐ, see p.239n.

We saw earlier (p.61) that Barhebraeus followed Jacob's canons when listing the plural forms and from this it follows that we may be able to discern Jacob's work underlying everything that we find here in Barhebraeus. Since the principle underlying the arrangement and order of those canons |[246] (described above, p.59) can be found also in Barhebraeus's chapter on the 'shapes', so it follows that this part of his grammar must also be drawing largely on Jacob's. The latter can thus be recovered from within the *Book of Spendours*. Barhebraeus does, however, make changes to Jacob's order, e.g. not listing the plurals according to gender but mixing them up and thereby doing violence to Jacob's clarity. Jacob's arrangement was the superior one.

V. Categories of Arabic Grammar applied to Syriac

Little more can be added about qualities/states (ܐܝܬܘ̈ܬܐ), which as we saw (p.240) were based on the Greek διαθέσεις, nor about the so-called Syriac cases, for which Barhebraeus simply repeats the old Masoretic rules save only for adding the vocative ܐܘ. Hence all that remains now is to show that the remainder of the section on the noun is taken from Zamaḫšarī. So much is clear from the order in which he deals with the various topics. In the eighth chapter we have the theory of inceptives and predications, ܫܘܪܝܐ ܘܡܠܘܐ, which are the equivalents of the Arabic المبتدأ والخبر (*Muf.*, 12), and in the ninth, the rules about nouns related to the infinitive, ܫܡܗܐ ܢܚܘܬܢܐ, paralleling المصدر (*Muf.*, 16,10). The forms of these nouns are listed at *Gramm.*, 49, and again referred to later at p.96,5.[2] Chapter ten deals with ܐܠܐ (*exceptives*), which correspond to المنصوب على الاستثناء (*Muf.*, 31). In Zamaḫšarī, this belongs here, since it has to do with the rules for the Accusative, but the Syrians had no reason to deal separately with particles of exception (ܐܠܐ, ܣܛܪ, ܒܠܚܘܕ

---

[1] Dionysius Thrax (ed. Uhlig), 26,1,3; 27,6; 28,4.

[2] The Greeks also knew of this topic, for he says (*Gramm.*, 46,3) that a word from which no verb derives is called an ἔτυμον (ܐܛܘܡܘܢ).

etc.) and so Barhebraeus puts it here simply because he is such a close imitator of Zamaḫšarī. Again, the subject of chapter eleven, ܡܣܡܟܢܘܬܐ (*construct relationship*), is nothing but a translation of اضافة, which Zamaḫšarī discusses in his section on the uses of the genitive relationship (*Muf.*, 6f.). Barhebraeus takes the opportunity here to use examples to illustrate the |247 shortened form (ܟܪܝܘܬܐ) of the noun in the construct state (*Gramm.*, 53, to which he returns, 66). The twelfth chapter, ܫܘܪܪܐ is the تاكيد of Zamaḫšarī (*Muf.*, 44), and anyone can see just how far Barhebraeus does depend upon Zamaḫšarī by simply comparing *Muf.*, 44,19, with *Gramm.*, 57,16. The next three chapters closely follow Zamaḫšarī: ܡܛܠ ܦܘܫܩܐ (*Gramm.*, 59) = الصفة (*Muf.*, 46,9); ܡܛܠ ܫܘܚܠܦܐ (*Gramm.*, 61) = البدل (*Muf.*, 48); ܡܛܠ ܟܘܦܦܐ (*Gramm.*, 62) = عطف (*Muf.*, 50).[1] After omitting some chapters which are of no relevance to Syriac, he has one ܡܛܠ ܙܥܘܪܐ, which Zamaḫšarī has under the title المصغر (*Muf.*, 85), and then finally one on numerals, the equivalent of *Muf.*, 93.

Thus throughout the whole of the second half of the section on the noun there is a definite parallel. What follows afterwards owes rather more to the Greek system, which Barhebraeus for some reason has thoroughly mixed up. For he moves on from numerals to treat pronouns, participles (ܡܚܠܛ ܫܡܐ), adverbs (ܠܘܬ ܡܠܬܐ), and prepositions (ܩܕܡ ܣܝܡܐ ܫܡܐ),[2] all of which are thus included in the section on the noun, even though they clearly do not belong there. What has happened is that he has preserved the order of the Greek and older Syriac parts of speech which he ought to have reserved for Book 3, although he does end up dealing with adverbs twice, once on p.82, and then again in Book 3 (*Gramm.*, 166). We can thus see that the plan of weaving the Greek and Arabic systems together did not always work out that well for him.

VI. Pronouns, Participles, Adverbs

We shall make a few remarks on each of these. For the pronoun Barhebraeus adopts the Arabic approach, which Bar Zuʿbi had earlier been compelled to do by the Semitic nature of the language, namely incorporating the suffixal forms in his chapter on the pronoun. Barhebraeus also places his discussion of the personal affixes of the verb (i.e. those that designate the persons) in the chapter on pronouns (*Gramm.*,

[1] He even follows his subdivisions: ܟܘܦܦܐ ܒܐܬܘܬܐ = العطف بالحرف, and ܟܘܦܦܐ ܕܫܘܕܥܐ = عطف البيان.

[2] Dionysius put prepositions first because they relate to nouns, which are the first part of speech; adverbs come after, being concerned with the second part of speech.

74), as was done in the Arabic (*Muf.*, 52).|[248] Since Barhebraeus takes care to keep to the Arabic throughout this chapter, it is all the more surprising that those elements of the Greek theory that remain (*Gramm.*, 79, which are taken from Dionysius, p.18 above), are quite conspicuous.

In the chapter on participles, Barhebraeus shows how little he has understood their real essence, for he fails to distinguish adjectives like ܪܘܡ, agentive nouns such as ܩܛܘܠ, and true participles. He does not see that what makes them different is that they have temporal aspect. He even confuses them with infinitives (p.80, l.5) because of an over-literal interpretation of the expression ܡܠܠܐ ܫܡܐ (*verbal noun*). One could hardly make a parallel between the Syriac infinitives in ܡ and the Arabic مَصْدَر.

Regarding adverbs, he rather pointlessly repeats the Greek division into simple and composite (*Gramm.*, 82,11). If one compares his subclasses of adverbs (ܡܢܝܢܝܬܐ, ܬܚܘܝܢܝܬܐ, ܨܠܘܬܢܝܬܐ, ܫܘܐܠܢܝܬܐ, ܐܘܟܡܝܬܐ, ܟܘܢܫܝܬܐ, ܦܘܚܡܝܬܐ etc.) with those of Dionysius (ἀριθμοῦ δηλωτικά, εὐχῆς, ἐρωτήσεως, σχετλιαστικά,[1] ἀθροίσεως, εἰκάσμου κτλ.), one can readily see where Barhebraeus got his list from. Note also that the same classification of adverbs is given in a different order in Book 3, as we demonstrated above (p.170).

All this should now be sufficient to commend Barhebraeus's excellent judgment in devising a method for composing his grammar.

VII. The Verb

It was not our plan to analyse every aspect of Barhebraeus's grammar in great detail, hence there will be no need to divide up the chapter on the verb into all its constituent elements. It is enough simply to raise some of the most important points as they arise, by which the general approach can best be illustrated.

Barhebraeus extends Zamaḫšarī's definition of the verb. The latter said that الفعل ما دلّ على اقتران حَدَثٍ بزمان (*the verb is that which indicates that an occurrence is combined with tense*), and Barhebraeus comments on this, ܡܚܘܝܢܘܬܐ ܕܥܒܕܐ ܒܫܘܚܠܦ ܦ̈ܘܢܩܐ ܩܢܐ|[249] (*which possesses an indication of action by a change of conjugation*). Then when Zamaḫšarī (*Muf.*, 108) says that it is characteristic of the verb to be preceded by the particle قد, Barhebraeus follows this by saying, ܡܢ ܕܝܠܝܬܐ ܡܬܩܢܝܢܬܐ, ܕܡܠܬܐ ܒܡܥܠܬܐ ܗܐ ܘܐܠܐ (*the addition* [ܒܡܥܠܬܐ = الدخول] *of the particles* ܗܐ

[1] This type is equivalent to those called ܐܘܟܡܝܬܐ (*blackening*), for ܐܘܟܡ means *to blacken*, but metaphorically *to sully, defame*, e.g. ܐܬܐܘܟܡ with this meaning in W. Cureton, *Ancient Syriac Documents* (London, 1864), ܠܗ.

and ܐܡܠܟܢ *are among the particular characteristics of the verb*). For the rest of Zamaḫšarī's rules he substitutes the use of the personal affixes ܬ and ܢ , ܬ of the feminine etc. Immediately, however, he slips into the old Syriac teaching about the prefixes ܐ ܡ ܢ ܬ (cf. Jacob Bar Šakko , p.ܣ, l.3; ܪ, l.10), gender, number, tense, person, state (διαθέσις), species, shape, mood (ἐγκλίσις), which, as can be briefly shown, all derive from Greek sources.

Dionysius gives for the verb eight types of attributes, which the Syriac translation gives as follows: moods (ἐγκλίσεις) = ܡܢ̈ܝܬܐ; states (διαθέσεις) = ܡܬ̈ܡܐ; species (εἴδη) = ܐܕ̈ܫܐ; shapes (σχήματα) = ܐܣܟ̈ܝܡܐ; numbers (ἀριθμοί) = ܡܢ̈ܝܢܐ; persons (πρόσωπα) = ܦܪ̈ܨܘܦܐ; tenses (χρόνοι) = ܙܒ̈ܢܐ; conjugations (συζυγίαι) = ܐܙܘܘܓܐ.[1] The moods (ἐγκλίσεις) are five in number, expressed in Syriac as follows: indicative (ὁριστική) = ܡܚܘܝܢܐ; imperative (προστακτική) = ܦܘܩܕܢ; optative (εὐκτική) = ܡܨܠܝܢܐ; subjunctive (ὑποτακτική) = ܡܣܬܡܟܢܐ; infinitive (ἀπαρέμφατος) = ܡܠܐܡܪܢܘܬܐ ܡܢ ܡܐܡܪܐ.[2]

These Greek distinctions created difficulties for the Syriac grammarians, who did not have moods and who could not distinguish states and species; on the other hand, the Greeks have no gender in verbs. Hence they tried every way they could to make alterations that would allow this classification to |[250] fit their own language. Jacob of Edessa changed the old word for moods,[3] ܡܢ̈ܝܬܐ, to ܙܢ̈ܐ,[4] but Barhebraeus (*Gramm.*, 90,11) instead suggested that there were five species (ܐܕ̈ܫܐ ܚܡܫܐ), by conflating the moods and the species. Instead of the Greek moods, Jacob of Edessa used forms relating to recitation which match the sense of the expressions, hence the imperative mood (ܦܘܩܕܢ), the precative (ܬܟܫܦܬܐ), the interrogative (ܫܐܠܐ), the vocative (ܩܪܝܬܐ), and the definitive (ܦܣܩܐ), also known as the indicative. At first sight it seems that these forms, which either Barhebraeus or Jacob himself (*Gramm.*, 90) introduced in place of the Greek moods, are just the same thing as John Bar Zuʿbi was talking about

---

[1] From ܙܘܘ̈ܓܐ (*marriage* = συζυγία) is then formed ܙܘܥܐ (*motion, vocalisation*). See p.17 above.

[2] Cf. p.17n, where the mss have only ܡܠܐܡܪܢܘܬܐ, again in C on p.28. But this is the equivalent of λέξις (p.9n) so cannot be right here, since ἀπαρέμφατος (*infinitive*) must surely be rendered with its own equivalent. The right reading is preserved, p.28.

[3] The original meaning of this word is explained by the scholiast to Dionysius (Uhlig, 47): βούλησις ψυχῆς διὰ φωνῆς σημαινόμενη (*the will of the soul is indicated by the voice*). From this the Syrians made ܦܘܣܩܢܐ, ܣܥܪܐ.

[4] Amira (G. Amira, *Grammatica Syriaca sive chaldaica* [Rome, 1596], 251) gets his own terms from here, since he says that ܙܢܐ, or mood, is a characteristic of the verb. He also includes ܦܘܩܕܢ, which Jacob used.

when he discussed the five types of speech (p.163 above), which then became the basis of his accentual system. This is the sort of confusion that so easily arose when the Syriac grammarians struggled to find their own equivalents for the Greek moods.[1]

Now that we have taken some note of the sorts of changes that the concept of 'mood' underwent, we may compare more closely the different terminology found in the Syriac Dionysius and in Barhebraeus:

	Dionysius		Barhebraeus
	ܡܢ̈ܬܠܐ	=	ܣܘܡܥܘܬܐ ܐܘܪ̈ܓܐ ܡܐܡ̈ܪܐ (Jacob, ܙܢ̈ܝܐ).[2]
	ܡܬ̈ܡܠܐ	=	ܐܢ̈ܝܫܘܬܐ.
251	ܐܕ̈ܫܐ	=	lacking, since this word is used instead of ܡܢ̈ܬܠܐ.[3]
	ܐܣܟܝ̈ܡܐ	=	ܐܣܟܝ̈ܡܐ.
	ܡܢ̈ܝܢܐ	=	ܡܢ̈ܝܢܐ.
	ܦܪ̈ܨܘܦܐ	=	ܦܪ̈ܨܘܦܐ.
	ܙܒ̈ܢܐ	=	ܙܒ̈ܢܐ.
	ܙܘ̈ܓܐ	=	lacking.
	lacking	=	ܓܢ̈ܣܐ.

Therefore, of the eight attributes of the verb in Greek, two are omitted (species and conjugations) and to the remaining eight is added that of gender, resulting in seven attributes in Barhebraeus. But we shall be disappointed if we think that Barhebraeus will go on to discuss the verb on the basis of the theory as just described. It is really just for show. He does not even make any use of the concept of 'shapes' which would in fact have

[1] Hence it can be explained why the five types of speech designated by accentual points (which are called ܢܘܩ̈ܙܐ, see Phillips, *Letter*, ܝ / 13) are called ܡܢ̈ܬܠܐ. ܢܘܩ̈ܙܐ are the names of the symbols and ܡܢ̈ܬܠܐ the modes of recitation—cf. the subscription to the Paris Karkaphensian ms: ܫܠܡܘ ܢܘܩ̈ܙܐ ܐܘܟܡ̈ܐ ܡܢ̈ܬܠܐ ܘܩܪ̈ܝܢܐ ܡܕܢܚ ܗܐܡܪܐ (Martin, *Tradition karkaphienne*, 283).

[2] If the moods are being here confused with the five types of speech, then we can explain why it is that the accents (which are defined according to these same types of speech) can be called ܢܝ̈ܫܐ ܦܘܪ̈ܫܢܝܐ (*distinguishing points*), for ܢܝܫܐ corresponds to ἔγκλισις, in the sense of an *intention* or *aim*. The scholiast to Dionysius says (Uhlig, 47): προσκλίνεται ἡ ψυχὴ ἢ ὡς ὁριζομένη τὰ παρ' αὐτῆς δρώμενα, οἷον τύπτω, ἢ προστάσσουσα, ἢ εὐχομένη, ἢ διστάζουσα, ἢ οὐδὲν τούτων δηλοῦσα, μόνον δὲ τὸ ὄνομα τοῦ πράγματος προβαλλομένη, οἷον τύπτειν (*the soul inclines/inflects either to define what it has done, e.g. 'I strike', or else to command, or to ask, or to doubt, or to indicate none of these, but merely to state the name of the action, e.g. 'to strike'*).

[3] *Gramm.*, 91,19.

been very suitable for arranging the different classes of verbs under clear formulae. Because he ignores this concept of 'shapes', Barhebraeus only ever touches in passing upon the derivation of stems, or what we sometimes call 'conjugation' (*Gramm.*, 92-4). Furthermore, he fails to apply this concept when he is listing the different types of verbal roots (what we now call first yudh, middle waw etc.).[1] Instead he lists them in the same way |[252] in which we found them in Joseph Bar Malkon (p.133), in Elias of Nisibis, in John Bar Zuʿbi (p.167), and in Jacob Bar Šakko (p. ܪ f.), and which for this reason should surely be attributed back to Jacob of Edessa. The principle of arrangement which Barhebraeus uses results in the following series: ܢܣܒ, ܩܪ (*Gramm.*, 95); ܣܝܒ ܣܒܥܐ (103); ܪܩܕ, ܟܪܟܪ (114); ܐܬܐ, ܐܟܠ, ܝܠܕ (124); ܐܠܐ, ܐܬܐ (126); ܐܘܪ, ܡܘܡܬ, ܐܠܠ (134); ܐܬܩܛܠ etc. (139), which can be compared to the series given before (p.133, above). However, Barhebraeus does surpass his predecessors insofar as he was the first seriously to apply his common sense to the nature of the consonants that make up the verbal roots. Before him nobody took any notice of the weak letters, an omission that left the whole of Semitic etymology in obscurity. Barhebraeus was the first to distinguish the forms of weak roots from the forms of strong roots. The latter consisted of strong letters (ܚܠܝܡܐ = سالم), whilst the former he identified as those roots with ܐ, ܘ, and ܝ, which he named the 'sick' or 'weakened' letters (ܟܪ̈ܝܗܐ = مُعْتَلّ), including also those with ܢ which is |[253] weak in Syriac (*Gramm.*, 119, ܢܦ̈ܩܬܐ) but not in Arabic. This observation of his led him to make further subdistinctions to Jacob's classification, based on the strong or

[1] From the expression ܒܟܘܢܫܐ ܐܣܟܡ̈ܝܗܝܢ ܕܡ̈ܠܐ (*Gramm.*, 101) it follows that he does include the concept of 'shape' in the classification of verbs according to their form. However, it was not only Aḥūdemmēh (p.33, above) who discusses the 'shapes' of verbs, but also Elias (?of Nisibis), who used ܠܐܦ̈ܐ for the 'shapes' of both verbs and nouns: ܐܣܟܡܐ ܦܥܠܝܐ ܘܐܦ̈ܝܢܝܐ ܡܢ [ܐܝܠܝܢ] ܕܒܠܚܘܕ ܡ̈ܠܐ ܕܐܝܬ ܠܗ̇ ܣܘܦܐ. ܕܦܥ̈ܠܐ ܘܐܦ̈ܝܢܐ: ܘܠܐ ܡܬܬܒܥܝܢ ܘܡܫܬܚܠܦܝܢ ܡܢ ܡ̈ܠܐ ܐܚܪ̈ܢܝܬܐ ܐܠܐ ܗܘܝܢ ܐܝܬܝܗܘܢ ܦܥ̈ܠܝܬܐ ܘܐܦ̈ܝܢܝܬܐ. ܘܫܡ̈ܗܬܐ ܕܒܠܚܘܕ ܡ̈ܠܐ. ܒܗܘܢ ܕܥܒܕܝܢ ܡܬܬܢܝܢ ܘܡܫܬܚܠܦܝܢ: ܒܠܚܘܕ ܡ̈ܠܐ ܕܥܒܕܐ ܕܐܝܬܝܗܘܢ ܐܝܟ ܬܠܐܦ ܬܒܐ...ܘܒܠܚܘܕ ܐܝܟ ܡ̈ܠܐ ܦܥ̈ܠܝܬܐ ܘܐܦ̈ܝܢܝܬܐ ܕܡܬܝܢ ܐܝܟ ܐܣܟܡܐ ܦܥܠܝܐ ܘܐܦܝܢܝܐ[.] ܐܣܟܡܐ ܡܫܬܚܠܦܢܐ ܐܝܬܘܗܝ ܒܠܚܘܕ ܡ̈ܠܐ ܕܡܬܬܢܝܢ ܘܡܫܬܚܠܦܝܢ ܡܢ ܐܣܟܡܐ ܦܥܠܝܐ ܘܐܦܝܢܝܐ ܘܐܝܬܝܗܘܢ ܐܝܟ ܡܬܒܪ ܘܡܫܬܒܪ ܡܢ ܬܒܪ...ܡܬܦܩܕ ܡܫܬܦܩܕ ܡܢ ܦܩܕ...ܘܒܠܚܘܕ ܐܝܟ ܡ̈ܠܐ ܡܬܬܢܝܢܐ ܘܡܫܬܚܠܦܢܝܬܐ. ܘܡܬܩܪܝܢ ܐܣܟܡܐ ܠܐܦܝܐ ܘܡܫܬܚܠܦܢܐ. ܡܬܩܪܝܢ ܕܝܢ ܗܠܝܢ ܡ̈ܠܐ ܐܣܟܡܐ ܠܐܦܝܐ ܘܡܫܬܚܠܦܢܐ ܡܛܠ ܠܬܠܬ ܥܠ̈ܠܬܐ. ܚܕܐ ܡܢ ܘܡܫܬܚܠܦܢܐ ܗܘܐ ܗܘ: ܐܦܝܐ ܕܝܢ ܕܐܡܝܪܐ ܕܐܦ ܙܥܘܪܐ ܕܡܬܦܩܕ ܠܐܦܝܐ ܒܫܘܚܠܦܐ. ܘܡܬܐܡܪ ܗܘ ܡܬܦܩܕ ܠܐܦܝܐ: ܘܙܥܘܪܐ ܗܘ ܕܙܥ ܐܝܟ ܡܬܦܩܕ ܠܐܦܝܐ ܡܬܐܡܪ ܡܫܬܚܠܦܢܐ ܕܡܢ ܠܐܦܝܐ: ܗܘܝܐ ܐܦ ܡ̈ܠܐ ܕܟܠܐ ܘܬܠܐ: ܘܟܝܠ...ܡܬܩܪܝܢ ܐܣܟܡܐ ܠܐܦܝܐ: ܚܠܦܝܢ ܡܬܦܩܕ ܠܐܦܝܐ ܕܡܬܬܐ ܘܡ̈ܠܐ ܐܚܪܢ ܕܡܢ ܗܘܝܢ ܡܫܬܚܠܦܢ: ܐܝܟ ܡܬܒܪ ܘܡܫܬܚܠܦ ܡܢ ܚܠܐ ܘܡܟܝܟ ܘܡܫܬܚܠܦ ܡܢ ܚܠܦ ܘܡܬܩܪܝܢ ܐܣܟܡܐ ܡܫܬܚܠܦܢܐ: ܚܠܦܝܢ ܙܥܘܪܘ ܡܫܬܚܠܦܢܐ ܕܙܢ̈ܐ. The second and third causes are described similarly, but there is no need to reproduce them here. This information about Elias comes from Bar Zuʿbi, BL Add. 25876, f.108b.

weak nature of the roots. Hence he introduced into Syriac grammar the Arabic theory of سالِم and مُعْتَلّ (*Muf.*, 127,7), which would have been a fact of great importance had he grasped the *triliteral* nature of the root and made use of it as the basic principle of word derivation. But neither Barhebraeus nor any other Syriac grammarian ever did this. The older grammarians had included the final ܐ of verbs third alaph under the heading of absorbed letters (ܕܡܬܒܠܥܢ) and they never concerned themselves with the real nature of the root.[1] Barhebraeus is to be thus commended for having been the first to have applied his good sense to this phonological feature of the language.[xii]

Another distinction which he took from Arabic grammar and applied to Syriac is that between transitive (ܡܥܒܪܢܝܬܐ), doubly transitive, and intransitive (ܕܟܝܢܝܬܐ) verbs (*Gramm.*, 92-3), which again he takes from Zamaḫšarī (*Muf.*, 115).[2] To the latter is also owed the chapter on the imperative, which he connects closely with the imperfect with the prefixes omitted, a point which no previous Syriac grammarian had made (*Gramm.*, 143; *Muf.*, 114).

VIII. Particles

Because the concept of particles was of special concern to the Arabs, who did not reckon it worthwhile to subdivide them further into prepositions and adverbs as the Greeks so assiduously did, Barhebraeus drew both the concept of the particle and its definition from Zamaḫšarī, |[254] even though the name itself (ܐܣܪܐ) is of Greek origin. This much is clear from the following:

ܐܣܪܐ	ܐܝܠܘ	ܟܪܐ	ܡܠܐ	ܡܡܠܠܐ	ܦܫܝܛܬܐ	ܫܘܛܐ.	ܕܚܘܝܐ	ܐܣܝܪ	ܫܘܘܕܥܐ:[3]
الحرف	-	-	-	-	-	-	ما دلّ	على	معنى في غيره

[1] See Gottheil, *Elias*, ܨܝ / 37-8; and Jacob Bar Šakko , p.ܟܒ, l.10.

[2] Particular note ought to be taken of the theory by which an intransitive verb is made transitive by the addition of a particle or, to put it another way, the agent (فاعل = ܥܒܘܕܐ) is turned object (مفعول به = ܡܥܒܕܐ). An example is ܗܦܟܬ ܨܒܝܢܐ ܠܐܪܥܟ, in which the will (ܨܒܝܢܐ) is directed towards 'your land' by means of the particle ܠ. This comes from Zamaḫšarī's rule, that an intransitive verb becomes a transitive one by the addition of حرف الجرّ, illustrated by the example خَرَجْتُ بِهِ.

[3] Martin suggested ܫܘܘܕܥܐ, but this cannot be right.

ܠܐ ܒܢܝܬܐ. ܘܡܟܠ ܗܘܳܐ ܠܐ ܡܬܦܪܫܐ ܡܢܗ ܕܐܡܪܬ. ܫܡ ܗܘܐ ܗܢܐ: ܐܘ
- - ومن ثَمَّ لم ينفكّ من - اسم - - او

ܡܠܬܐ. ܐܠܐ ܒܕܘܟܝܢ ܕܝܕܝܥܢ.
فعل يصبحه الا في مواضعَ مخصوصة

The Syriac paraphrases the Arabic definition and where it adds that particles are words of simple signification, this is self-contradictory, since if they indicate sense in other words (which Sībawayhi said, جاء لمعنى, p.143), then they cannot carry their own 'simple signification'. Moreover, Barhebraeus diverges from the usual Syriac definition and rightly rejects Jacob's, which was also copied by Jacob Bar Šakko: ܐܡܪܐ ܐܝܟܘ ܡܠܬܐ ܕܡܘܕܥܐ ܡܣܡܟܬܐ (ܘܐܡܪܐ ܠܡܘܕܥܘ ܠܒ ܡܢ̈ܝܐ), which was generally accepted by both East and West Syriac grammarians (*Gramm.*, 156), though he is following Jacob of Edessa when he adds that they do not have gender, species etc. (Cf. Jacob Bar Šakko , p.ܣ l.6).

Because he wove the Greek and Arabic theories about the particle together and yet at the same time wrote a separate chapter on adverbs, Barhebraeus's list of particles is rather confused. However, since we have already discussed this list (p.169), we can pass over it for brevity's sake and leave it to others who may value it more highly. It is not my intention here to explore whether and by what means the Greek list was imported into Arabic, whose subdivisions are closely comparable to the Greek ones.

IX. THE ARRANGEMENT OF THE BOOK ABOUT TOPICS THAT ARE APPLICABLE TO SEVERAL PARTS OF SPEECH AT ONCE

The topics applicable to several parts of speech at once and which form the subject matter of Book 4 generally relate to orthoepy. Although the introduction (ܥܘܠܐܙ) has much in common with that of Zamaḫšarī, the great majority of its contents is taken from the Syriac grammatical tradition and arranged according to the principles of Syriac. Furthermore, the first two chapters, dealing respectively with the defects of Syriac script |[255] and with the method of making good these defects, both derive from Jacob of Edessa's grammar[1] (see above, p.49).[1] The chapter on the positions of the

[1] Barhebraeus does, however, ignore Jacob's observations on ܢܩܙ̈ܐ and ܚܛܛ̈ܐ (Phillips, *Letter*, ܝܚ, and p.53 above).

mouth used to produce different sounds is taken from an Arabic school (see p.54 above). By comparing Zamaḫšarī, *Muf.*, 188,15, with Barhebraeus, *Gramm.*, 195, we can see how much the latter is still depending upon the former.

Orthoepy is the subject of *Gramm.*, 197-210. After consecutive vowelless consonants which have ܡܗܓܝܢܐ and ܪܘܚܐ between them, and after ܡܬܟܢܫܢܝܬܐ (Elias, ܕܝ; Bar Šakko, ܕܡ), ܡܫܚܠܦܢܝܬܐ (Elias, ܠܡ), and ܡܬܬܘܣܦܢܝܬܐ (Bar Šakko, ܕܝ, Elias, ܠ)[2] he has a separate section on ܡܬܒܨܥܢܝܬܐ, i.e. letters that are unwritten but are pronounced in speech, the opposite of the absorbed letters (ܒܠܝܥܬܐ). No other grammarian had used this term before. Among such are the ܘ in ܩܠ and ܡܩܠ; the ܐ in ܒܫܬܐ (*with six*) and ܘܬܘܬܐ (*and letters*) (omitted respectively from ܐܫܬܐ and ܐܬܘܬܐ, *Gramm.*, 204); the ܐ in Greek names, e.g. ܣܛܦܢܘܣ from ܐܣܛܦܢܘܣ etc.; and also the ܐ in words starting in ܢ such as ܢܒܥܬܐ for ܐܢܒܥܬܐ. Elias (ܕܝ) and Bar Šakko (ܕܡ,15) both treat the subject but do not use this term.

The above derives from the Syriac tradition, but the two chapters on hidden letters (ܡܬܟܣܝܢܝܬܐ), a name previously unknown, and on substitutions (ܡܫܚܠܦܢܝܬܐ), have an Arabic source. He goes into such detail on these subjects that one could almost say that he arrives at a coherent phonology for describing the relationships between consonant clusters in which one of the consonants |[256] is affected by the other. Thus the Arabic tradition guided Barhebraeus to the highest point that any Syrian ever attained in understanding the phonological rules of his own language. He follows the principle of distinguishing sounds based on the part of the mouth from which they are produced. The Arabs had sixteen such positions of the mouth (ܡܦܩܢܐ = مخرج), Barhebraeus fourteen, listed on p.54 above. Syriac of course lacked positions for the consonants ض خ ظ ج غ. The basic rule is as follows: 1) when two similar consonants come together without an interceding vowel, the first is absorbed into the second (this is dealt with

[1] Barhebraeus takes from the Syriac school tradition the information he gives about the writing systems of the Romans, Egyptians, and Armenians (p.192, cf. Martin, *Tradition karkaphienne*, 246; also Gottheil, *Elias*, ܘ). From the Fihrist (ed. Flügel, 12) we learn that in the ninth and tenth centuries the difference between the scripts in use among the people and among educated men was considered a serious matter, which they took the trouble to investigate.

[2] Here he deals with the ܘ after *r* in Greek names, as in ܦܪܘܣܐ, with which he confuses the use of ܘ for Greek ε in ܐܪܣܛܘܛܠܝܣ (*Gramm.*, 210).

under the chapter on ܡܫܬܚ̈ܠܦܢܘܬܐ, *Gramm.*, 197)[1]; 2) where two vowelless consonants come together within a word, a helping vowel is added, indicated by ܡܗܓܝܢܐ. It is here, therefore, that he discusses these 'helping syllables' and the different system of using ܡܗܓܝܢܐ in the Nisibene tradition (*Gramm.*, 200); then (p.201) he writes about ܡܛܦܝܢܐ and ܒܝܘܪܐ, which were used only by the East Syrians. In this chapter, the examples he uses show that he is following either Bar Zuʿbi or the latter's teacher, for their examples are identical (see p.128 above), although Barhebraeus omits quite a few that should be necessary for a thorough explanation of the phenomenon.[2]

|[257] X. Orthoepy

At first glance this subject seems to be wholly based on the traditions of the Syrian Masoretic schools. However, when one looks more closely, it becomes clear that the greater part of the orthoepic and phonological material is of Arabic origin and that Barhebraeus couples this together with the laws of the older ܡܩܪ̈ܝܢܐ. This causes him some degree of confusion, in

---

[1] So the first ܠ in ܩܛܠܬܠܗ coalesces with the second, and again in ܒܟܠ ܠܗ. In the latter of these examples, ܡܛܦܝܢܐ would apply.

[2] Since we did not mention Barhebraeus when we showed that ܒܝܘܪܐ was a sign of contraction (p.126), we should note his comments here, on the interpretation of which I disagree with Martin (Martin, *Deux dialectes*, 403). Martin translates the term ܦܫܛܝܢ as *lengthened* in a musical sense, since he believes that ܒܝܘܪܐ was a musical sign that indicated a lengthened note, while ܡܛܦܝܢܐ signified a note made with a lowered voice. In short, Martin includes these marks under the general heading of ܢܥܡܐ, *tone*. However this can hardly be concluded from what Barhebraeus says: ܡܕܢܚܝܐ ܠܐܬܘܬܐ ܠܐܘܠܝܡ ܫܠܝܬܐ ܡܫܚܠܦܬܐ. ܒܡܠܬܐ ܩܕܡܝܬܐ ܕܣܡܝܟܐ ܫܠܝܬܐ. ܕܩܕܡ ܫܠܝܬܐ ܠܘܬ ܡܚܒܠܢܘܬܐ ܕܡܢ ܫܪܝܬܐ ܕܐܬܘܬܐ ܗܢܘ ܕܫܠܝܬܐ ܗܘ ܕܩܘܡܐ ܕܡܝܬܝܢ ܡܨܥܝܐ ܕܡܢ ܐܚܪܢܐ. ܐܝܟ ܕܒܠ...ܠܟܡ ܘܕܘܟܬܐ ܕܡܠܬܐ ܕܡܫܬܡܥܐ ܣܡܝܟܬܐ. ܘܐܝܟ ܕܢܝܐ ܕܐܝܟܢܐ ܠܡܠܬܐ ܡܫܚܠܦܬܐ ܕܒܡܠܬܐ ܕܐܝܟܢܐ. ܒܡܠܬܐ ܡܛܦܝܢܐ ܐܝܟ ܕܝܘܕܐ. ܐܝܟ ܗܢܐ ܕܠܐ ܡܢܝܢ. ܘܡܢܗܘܢ ܗܘܢܐ ܠܘܬܐ ܕܒܝܘܪܐ ܦܫܛܝܢ ܒܡܠܬܐ. ܐܝܟ ܕܐܠܗܐ...ܠܟ ܘܠܐ_ܪܘܚ ܒܫܡܝܐ ܘܠܐ ܕܡܕܒܪܢ_ܗܘܐ. (*for two different consecutive vowelless consonants, the Easterns lengthen the vowelled consonant which is found before the final vowelless consonant on the first word, that is, they extend it and add a horizontal line above it, called* ܒܝܘܪܐ*, as on for instance the* ܠ *of* ܕܝܘܡܐ ܗܠܝܢ*; but when a vowelless consonant at the end of a word meets a vowelled consonant at the start of the next word, they shut out the vowelless one and do not prolong it and they place the line called* ܒܝܘܪܐ *below, as on the* ܐ *of* ܠܐ_ܪܚܡ *and the* ܬ *of* ܡܕܒܪܬ_ܗܘܐ). Barhebraeus opposes ܒܠܗ to ܐܠܗ; in the first example, the alaph in the syllable *la* is ignored and the syllable is extended as far as the dalath of ܕܝܘܡܐ, whereas in the second example, the *la* is closed out before ܪܚܡ and does not extend as far as the initial resh. I can see here no trace of musical notation (cf. p.127 Ib, 128 IIb).

that he sometimes (*Gramm.*, 205) includes subject matter that is really concerned with consonant changes (ܡܫܚܠܦܢܘܬܐ, in Arabic ابدال) under the heading of hidden consonants (ܡܬܛܫܝܢܘܬܐ), since he uses the term ܡܬܛܫܝܢܘܬܐ for what earlier grammarians called ܡܬܛܒܥܢܘܬܐ (*assimilated*).[1] Since Barhebraeus's idea of 'hidden letters' is basically the same as Zamaḫšarī's notion of absorption (ادغام), the chapter on these ܡܬܛܫܝܢܘܬܐ corresponds much of the time to Zamaḫšarī's chapter on absorption, while the chapter on consonant changes (ܡܫܚܠܦܢܘܬܐ) corresponds to Zamaḫšarī's on إبْدَال الحروف. At any rate, everything closely follows the usage of the conjoining dagesh in the Reuchlian codex (see p.200 above) and with the usage of ܡܛܦܣܐ.

Let us give a few of the details. The following are hidden consonants:

1) ܕ disappears into ܛ and vice versa: ܙܒܢܬ ܛܠܝܐ, ܐܚܕܬ ܛܠܝܐ and ܦܠܛ ܬܘܪܐ, ܣܠܛ ܬܠܝܐ (*Gramm.*, 198,8, cf. *Muf.*, 194).

2) ܗ disappears into ܚ whether it precedes or follows: ܩܫܚ ܗܘܐ, ܢܦܩܗ ܣܒܪܗ (*Gramm.*, 198,13)

3) ܥ disappears into ܚ whether it precedes or follows: ܦܬܚ ܥܠܡܐ, ܫܡܥ ܚܒܪܐ.

Both these last two rules originate with Zamaḫšarī: الهاء تُدَّغَمُ في الحاء وقعتْ قبلها او بعدها and العين تدّغم في مثلها وفي الحاء وقعت بعدها او قبلها (*Muf.*, 192).

4) ܢ is hidden when next to ܪ, ܩ, ܟ, ܘ, ܦ, ܦ, ܒ, ܟ, ܛ, ܨ, ܣ, ܪ, ܫ, ܬ. According to Zamaḫšarī (*Muf.*, 194), the letter *nun* is hidden with the letters ترملون, but others say that this happens with fifteen letters, including ج, ك, and ق, and that before ب *nun* turns into م. Barhebraeus does not adhere to this, however.

Just as here the old Syriac theory of the ܡܬܛܒܥܢܘܬܐ has been augmented by the Arabic theory and given a new Arabic-based name, ܡܬܛܫܝܢܘܬܐ, so again in the chapter on ܡܫܚܠܦܢܘܬܐ, he starts with the old Syriac rules, which we earlier followed from Jacob of Edessa (p.53) through Elias of Nisibis and Joseph Bar Malkon (p.124), and tacks on to these some observations based upon the Arabic equivalent. In this latter, a distinction was maintained between the different dialects, the pronunciation of the Ṭayy (لُغَةُ طَيِّئٍ *Muf.*, 174; 176,2) and others (في بعض اللغات, Zam., *Muf.*, 176,7), e.g. the dialects of the Banu Ḥanṭʿal (*Muf.*, 176,9) and the Banu Kalb (*Muf.*, 177,2). Basing himself on this example, Barhebraeus also distinguished between dialects and arranged the different consonant changes accordingly, i.e.:

[1] Barhebraeus's usage is taken from the Arabic إخفاء (*Muf.*, 194,6).

1) |[259] Those that were common amongst all Syrians (*Gramm.*, 205), including those listed by Jacob of Edessa (p.54 above): ܙ is changed into ܣ (as above, p.121,2), ܓ into ܟ (with Quššāyā), and ܒ into ܦ (again , with Quššāyā).[1]

2) Those changes made by the Westerns only, ܠ to ܐ, ܐ to ܝ, ܝ to ܐ, ܗ to ܐ, ܐ to ܘ, ܐ to ܠ (*Gramm.*, 240,7). Much of what is found here has to do with pronunciation, e.g. ܒܘܝܐ (*buyaya*), ܚܒܠܐ with alaph ܐܚܒܠܐ, ܚܙܐܘܗܝ (*hezawuhy*), and these are rightly treated in the chapter on ܡܠܚܠܦܬܐ.[2] True consonant changes include ܦܘܡܐ for ܦܘܡܐ etc. and *ʾuhdānā* for ܥܘܗܕܢܐ.

3) Those changes made by the Easterns in the Scriptures, e.g. the ܠ in ܬܬܥܩܪ (Mt 15.13), being before ܩ, is pronounced as ܢ; the ܙ before ܕ with Quššāyā in ܡܪܘܝܡ (Mt 20.2), and again before ܬ with Quššāyā in ܡܪܐ (Mt 20.13), is pronounced as ܣ. He further adds a number of changes that are not found only in the Scriptures, but which are observed by everyone. These are:

   a. ܦ becomes ܦ when followed by either ܬ or ܫ; hence ܚܦܬܐ and ܐܬܠܦܫܬ should be pronounced as *ḥapeṯa* and *iṯlapešaṯ*. On the other hand, ܦ before ܕ becomes ܒ, e.g. ܩܘܦܕܐ (*an owl*), pronounced as *qubeḏa* (neosyr. ܩܘܒܕܐ). The same happens before ܚ and ܓ, e.g. ܢܦܓܐ and ܡܠܩܦܚܡ.[3]

   b. ܕ followed by ܬ becomes ܬ ; thus ܐܘܚܬܐ, *ʾuḥtta*, and ܫܬܐ, *šitta*. In Mandaean פוכתא from פוכתתא from פוגדתא.

   c. ܓ followed by ܦ becomes ܟ, e.g. ܣܓܦܘܢ.[4]

   d. ܓ followed by ܬ or ܫ becomes ܬ, e.g. ܓܘܓܬܐ, ܢܓܫܐ.[5] Mandaean אטשיא = ܐܓܫܐ!

   e. |[260] ܙ followed by ܓ or by ܟ becomes ܣ, e.g. ܙܓܐ, ܢܣܟܐ.[6]

---

[1] For ܒܥܘ̈ܬܐ ܡܥܡܘܣܬܐ (*Gramm.*, 205,5), read ܒܥܘܬܐ ܡܥܡܘܣܬܐ.

[2] By contrast, the Easterns change ܐ into ܘ in ܝܘܐܝܠ, ܫܡܘܐܝܠ, ܩܡܘܐܝܠ, i.e. they pronounce these as *Yuwil, Šemuwil, Qemuwil* (*Gramm.*, 208).

[3] Th. Nöldeke, *Mandäische Grammatik* (Halle, 1875), 48.

[4] Cf. p.122,6 above.

[5] Cf. p.121,3 above.

[6] Cf. p.121,2 above; Nöldeke, *ibid.*, 45.

f. ܙ followed by ܒ or ܕ becomes ܙ, e.g. ܢܙܕܩܐ, ܣܙܒܐ. The Arabic practice is the same, thus Zamaḫšarī: الصاد الساكنة اذا وقعت قبل الدال جاز إبدالها زايا خالصة في لغة فصحا من العرب ومنه لَمْ يُحْرَمْ مَن فُزْدَ لهُ الاخ.[1] Others did not change ص into ز but pronounced it in a way resembling ز —this was called تضارع. ص with a vowel was not changed into ز, but was pronounced in a similar way. Sībawayhi has this to say about it, المضارعة اكثر واعرب من الابدال والبيان اكثر (*Muf.*, 177,3).[2]

g. ܣ followed by ܒ or ܓ or ܕ becomes ܙ e.g. ܢܣܒܐ, ܚܣܕܐ, ܢܣܓܕ (see p.121,4 above).

h. ܣ followed by ܛ or ܬ becomes ܨ, e.g. ܚܣܛܐ, ܡܣܬܒܐ, ܦܪܣܛܐ. See p.122,7 above for another definition. The Mandaean אכצאליא (root ܚܣܠ) is troubling.[3]

i. ܛ followed by ܪ in words of Greek origin becomes ܨ, e.g. ܐܣܛܪܛܝܘܛ, ܐܣܛܪܛܐ. This explains the Arabic ص in words such as قَصْر (κάστρα), صراط (*strata*), لِصّ (λῃστής, syr. ܠܣܛܐ, and לסטין in the Babylonian Targum). For another definition, see p.122,8.[4] [xiii]

k. In the Greek word ܩܦܕܘܩܐ (*Cappadox*), the ܕ has turned into ܛ (see above, p.122,5). Barhebraeus argued on the contrary that the ܕ here took Rukkāḵā and that the Easterners were wrong to construct this particular rule. His comments are explicable when we consider that they reflect the pronunciation of Greek in the thirteenth century. Nowadays Greeks pronounce τ virtually as a medial consonant, not only when it follows ν (as in μάντις = *mandis*) but even without it (e.g. τέρατα = *derada*).[5] If a Syriac-speaker wanted to render this *d* in his own script,|[261] he would have to use ܕ (i.e. with Quššāyā). So the Greek τ would appear to a Syriac speaker to be simply ܕܠܐ ܡܩܫܝܬܐ. That is why Barhebraeus

[1] فُزْدَ is written here for فُصِدَ. The sense is, "it is not forbidden for your brother to cut your veins [for the purpose of treatment]."

[2] See also Nöldeke, *ibid*.

[3] *Ibid*., 40.

[4] *Ibid*., 45.

[5] The same is true of π, pronounced virtually the same as *b*, for β is *w*, and where they want to transcribe our *b* they use μπ (e.g. μπάγκος = Bank, μπαζάριον = بازار, μπαλκόνιον = Balcony, μπαϊράκια = بيراق etc.). δ before ι cannot be aspirated, hence διά becomes γιά.

says, ܕܠܬ ܡܩܫܝܢܘܬܐ ܝܘܢܝܬܐ: ܛܛ ܡܬܟܬܒܐ ܒܣܘܪܝܝܐ ܐܝܟ ܕܒܦܛܪܘܣ ܘܛܛܘܣ (*the Greek 'd' with Quššāyā is written* ܛ *in Syriac, as in Πέτρος =* ܦܛܪܘܣ*, Τίτος =* ܛܛܘܣ). It follows from this that in Barhebraeus's day the Greeks said *Bedros* and *Didos* as they do now, and so what Barhebraeus means by a "Greek 'd' with Quššāyā" is really a τ, for regular δ would be ܕ, i.e. the medial aspirate ḏ (as in English, *this*). Scholars ignorant of the modern tongue may be able to deduce conclusions about how the ancient Greeks pronounced their own language, but the mediaeval pronunciation of Greek has not as yet been investigated to a similar level of expertise.

l. ܦ before ܒ, ܟ or ܓ becomes ج (cf. p.122,10 and *Muf.*, 177,9).

m. ܛ followed by ܒ, ܟ, or ܟ becomes ܕ, e.g. ܢܛܒܪܘܢ, ܢܛܟܠܘܢ, ܦܛܟܡܐ. In the latter the ܟ has Rukkāḵā.[1]

n. The ܙ in ܚܘܡܙܐ becomes ܨ. The reason is clear, for ܡ assimilates to itself the medial sibilant, and thereby creates an articulated consonant (مطبقة). We shall see the same effect with a guttural (4a).

4) Barhebraeus next mentions the more atrocious mutations (ܫܢܝܐ, which can be compared with the Arabic شاذّ).

a. Among the Westerns, such mutations include changing ܛ with following ܠ into ܛ. For example, they say ܦܘܪܛܢܐ instead of ܦܘܪܛܠܐ (*a flea*, neosyr. ܦܪܛܠܬܐ).[2] Furthermore, for ܛܥܝ they say ܛܥܝ, with a ܛ; for ܛܓܢܐ (τήγανον), ܛܓܢܐ (with a ܠ); for ܓܚܒܐ and ܓܚܟ, they say ܟܚܒܐ and ܟܚܟ (with a ܟ).

b. |[262] Among the Easterns, these include pronouncing ܦ and ܒ as if they were ܘ, e.g. ܐܒܐ ܘܒܪܐ as *awa wawra*, ܢܦܫܐ as *nawša*, ܫܒܩ as *šawiq*. They also change the ܗ of ܗܐ into ܟ, saying ܟܐ ܐܟܠ (*k*ᵉ'*a akil*) instead of ܗܐ ܐܟܠ. They omit the ܟ in ܐܪܟܘܒܬܐ and ܣܘܟܬܐ, dissolving it into the preceding *ū*.[3]

---

[1] Nöldeke, *ibid.*, 42.

[2] This is very important for understanding neosyriac pronunciation. Whenever a guttural is lost in neosyriac, the following syllables are given the pronunciation of the articulated syllables (مطبقة).

[3] See Merx, *Grammatica* I, 6.

5) Besides these mutations used by Westerns and Easterns, there are others in different areas which arose from local habits. He could have enumerated a great number of these had he taken note of the Mandaeans, but in fact he looked only to the Palestinians. These latter pronounced the ṯ in ܐܬܪܐ and ܐܬܐ as ڢ, which is all the more noteworthy in light of the fact that, on the contrary, these people are accustomed to say ك instead of ق.[1] They also change ܩ into ܐ, i.e. they omit it, which is the Egyptian pronunciation that is also found in many Palestinian towns today.[2]

Barhebraeus does not ignore the various dialectal pronunciations (*Gramm.*, 237), but to trace each of these is not our purpose. We shall stick to matters lexicographical and grammatical.[3] We shall also pass over the discussion of aspiration, in which he unwisely separates the nouns from the verbs, making two sections. Those who wish to pursue such matters may read the neosyriac texts published and translated by Prym and Socin.[4]

I have no doubt that anyone who compares this treatise of Barhebraeus on Syriac orthoepy with the rules of the older grammarians will see just how far Barhebraeus has surpassed them; at the same time one cannot deny that he owes his method very much to the Arabic schools to which he remains so close.

XI. Points

Although he followed the Arabic model when discussing orthoepy, when it comes to dealing with the script and its pointing, he is able to rely solely upon the authority of the earlier Syriac grammarians. Most of this derived from the Masoretic schools and included a wide range of different usages.[5]

[1] J.L. Burckhardt, *Travels in Syria and the Holy Land* (London, 1822), 40.

[2] Merx, *Grammatica* I, 8. See the Baedeker *Palästina und Syrien* (compiled by A. Socin), cxxxii: among the Bedouin ق is *g*, but is a hiatus among the city dwellers; those in the countryside and the Bedouin pronounce it almost as *tsch*.

[3] Martin, *Deux dialectes*, has gathered together all of Barhebraeus's notes on this subject.

[4] E. Prym & A. Socin, *Der neu-aramäische Dialekt des Tur-Abdin* (Göttingen, 1881).

[5] I have not made use of Jacob of Edessa's treatise on the pointing of verbs, of their gender, and of vowels, which has been edited by both Martin and Phillips, since it seems to contain only excerpts. Jacob scarcely said ܡܛܠ ܕܫܘܚܠܦܐ ܩܢܝ ܫܘܕܥܐ ܠܡܩܪܝܢܐ, nor can he be reckoned to have connected the word ܐܘܕܐ (*firebrand*) with ܐܘܕܐ and ܐܘܕܐ as if of the third form.

Joseph |263 Bar Malkon divided his grammar into chapters on the basis of eight different pointing systems (cf. p.135), which he named: 1 ܢܘܩܙܐ ܕܦܘܣܩܐ, 2 ܕܙܘܓܐ, 3 ܕܡܫܩܠܐ, 4 ܕܡܘܬܐ, 5 ܕܪܘܒܐ ܘܕܩܘܡܨܐ, 6 ܕܡܫܠܡܢܘܬܐ, 7 ܢܘܩܙܐ ܠܫܡܗܐ ܕܐܬܘܬܐ, 8 ܕܡܠܘܬܐ. Jacob Bar Šakko followed the same course, giving the following names: 1 ܕܦܘܣܩܐ, 2 ܕܡܫܩܠܐ, 3 ܕܡܫܚܠܦܢܐ = Joseph's ܕܙܘܓܐ, 4 ܕܦܘܪܫܢܐ, 5 ܕܪܘܒܐ ܘܕܩܘܡܨܐ, 6 ܕܡܫܠܡܢܘܬܐ, 7 ܠܫܡ̈ܗܐ, 8 ܕܡܠܘܬܐ. John Bar Zuʿbi further divided these eight chapters into two more general groups according to the size of the points, the ܢܘܩܙܐ ܙܥܘܪܐ and the ܢܘܩܙܐ ܪܘܪܒܐ.[1]

Barhebraeus's sharp mind added a third class of point size (ܡܨܥܝܐ ܕܢܘܩܙܐ), though this distinction is rather pedantic. The small points are those designating vowels. The mid-sized points are the syāmē and those designating the persons of the verb, Rukkāḵā and Quššāyā, the dot distinguishing ܪ from ܕ, those designating the feminine and those called ܕܡܠܐ, which signify that an ܗ is to be pronounced as such. The large points, then, are the accents. Hence we see the same basic eight groups, the only difference being that Barhebraeus omits those that are ܕܡܠܘܬܐ (Bar Malkon, p.120 above; Bar Šakko, ܡܚ) and instead has these ܕܡܠܐ, unknown to previous writers. About these he says that the sign of pronunciation (ܡܠܐ) is particular to the letter ܗ; the Westerns place a point of mid-size on the letter after the ܗ[2] to indicate that it should be pronounced, as in ܗܘܐ, ܗܒ, ܗܘܬ; but the Easterns use two small points below for this. If ܗ is to be omitted in pronunciation, the Westerns |264 add no point—hence ܗ without a point need not be pronounced; but the Easterns place a single small point after the ܗ to indicate the same thing. Hence in the phrases ܐܬܠܘܗܝ ܗܘܐ, ܐܬܠܗ ܗܠܝܢ ܗܘܬܠܗ, ܙܕܩܐ ܗܘ ܠܡܣܒܠܗ ܠܡܕܢܚܐ, in all of which the ܗ is not pronounced, the Westerns do not use any points but the Easterns would use single points, as ܐܬܠܘܗܝ ܗܘܐ, ܐܬܠܗ ܗܠܝܢ ܗܘܬܠܗ etc. By contrast, in the phrases ܠܐ ܗܘܝܬ ܐܬܝܐ, ܗܘ ܕܝܡ ܩܕܡ, in which the ܗ *is* pronounced, the pair of points that we have included are placed according to Eastern practice, for Westerns would write ܠܐ ܗܘܝܬ ܐܬܝܐ and ܗܘ ܕܝܡ ܩܕܡ. Finally, both groups place a thicker point above the letter ܗ to indicate the form of the pronoun ܗܘ. Barhebraeus's explanation of all this (*Gramm.*, 242), ignored by grammarians to this day, clears up many problems in the usage of the East Syrian manuscripts, although there is still often room for uncertainty.[3]

---

[1] This text was edited by Martin, *Syriens orientaux et occidentaux* , 422.

[2] I.e. to the left of this letter.

[3] See, for example, p.185,VII above, ܗܘܝܡ ܗܘܝܡ in an East Syrian ms.

Given that we need add nothing further about the other types of points, i.e. syāmē and the points that indicate the persons of the verb, we can move straight on to the final chapter, *On the Accents*. Here Barhebraeus adopts Jacob of Edessa's system (p. 99-100 above), albeit adding foreign elements to it and thereby corrupting it. Once we have identified Jacob's theories and those of the East Syrian schools (p.177), then it may be possible to isolate these foreign elements and to gain insight thereby into Barhebraeus's own contribution. We owe our basic knowledge of Jacob's grammar to the care and attention with which Barhebraeus treated it, although he certainly did not mimic Jacob parrot-fashion. Rather, since he was designing a grammar for practical use, he felt no need to follow Jacob's intentions at every turn. In the introduction he does not speak about the history of the accents, or about Jacob, or the distinctive systems of the East Syrian schools, which he mentions only from time to time when appropriate. The result is that the reader who does not know about the earlier systems is given the impression that the Syrians all used a single homogeneous accentual system. This impression, however, is then overturned by Barhebraeus's own comments, for he says (*Gramm.*, 246f.), "because in the case of every statement, the hearer is able to understand different senses from one and the same phrase (or individual part of a sentence), even without the nouns, verbs, or particles that constitute that phrase being added or subtracted, |[265] but purely by the different modulations of the voice (ܫܘܚܠܦܐ ܕܩܠܐ), so the Syriac scribes, who put in place the precise foundations (ܬܘܪܨܐ ܕܡܠܬܐ) of their language, invented a technique (ܐܬܬܓܪܘ = τέχνην εἰργάσαντο) and made use of the points for indicating the intentions of the pronunciation (ܬܢܝܐ ܦܘܫܩܐ)[1] in such a way

[1] To reach an understanding of what this rather tricky sentence means it is crucial that we realise what the words ܬܢܝܐ ܦܘܫܩܐ refer to. They are clearly different from ܢܘܩܙܐ (*points*) and from ܬܒܐ ܢܘܩܙܐ (*punctuation marks*). Hoffmann, *Herm.*, 201f., argues that ܦܘܫܩܐ is the equivalent of the Greek term *prosody* , which was used in three ways: 1, in music, for the human voice and the sound of pipes; 2, to refer to the accents on individual words, which are thereby either oxytone, paroxytone, or perispomenon; 3, to refer to the system of accents, quantities, and breathings (οἱ τόνοι καὶ οἱ χρόνοι καὶ τὰ πνεύματα), plus also the other signs called the πάθη, which include the sign known as *hypodiastole*, which is "for dividing up the words" (ἡ ὑποδιαστολὴ ἐπὶ διαιρέσει καὶ τομὴ τοῦ λόγου, Bekker, *Anecdota*, 703; 713,20—see also the Supplement to Dionysius Thrax, Uhlig ed., 107). It is worth adding also Herodian's definition, that "prosody is the particular accentual pitch of the appropriate sound in written form as it is pronounced together with one of its

that all those different senses, of which one is the particular sense intended (ܢܝܫܐ, ܕܡܚܫܒܐ), may also be expressed in writing and recognised by the reader looking at a text as easily as they are by a hearer listening to a voice." |266 It is crucial that the positions of these accents which define the correct sense be learnt from seeing examples. For if a reader were to read the sentence ܠܐ ܗܘܐ: ܡܢ ܙܪܥܗ ܕܕܘܝܕ without recognising the accent of rebuke (ܐܟܐܐ) and the accent of the protasis (ܦܩܐ), he might think that it was an apodeictic sentence meaning, 'Christ was not of David's seed.'

So Barhebraeus speaks only of the usefulness and the necessity of the accents without any regard for the history of their development. He then adds that these accents are fitted to certain musical intonations (ܪ̈ܗܛܐ ܢܥܡܬܢ̈ܐ)[1] that can only be taught or learned orally. He lists all the accents

---

companions in a syllable; this may be done either in accordance with the general force of the expression, or in accordance with what is normal in the agreed dialect, or else with the definition and explanation by analogy" (προσῳδία ἐστὶ ποιὰ τάσις ἐγγραμμάτου φωνῆς ὑγιοῦς, κατὰ τὸ ἀπαγγελτικὸν τῆς λέξεως ἐκφερομένη μετά τινος τῶν συνεζευγμένων περὶ μίαν συλλαβήν, ἤτοι κατὰ συνήθειαν διαλέκτου ὁμολογουμένης, ἤτοι κατὰ τὸν ἀναλογικὸν ὅρον καὶ λόγον; Bekker, *Anecdota*, 676,17; 678,11 = A. Lentz, ed., *Grammatici Graeci 3.1* [Leipzig, 1867], 5,1-4). From this it follows that ܦܘܣܩܐ can designate equally the accentuation of individual words or of the whole expression. Now ܢܝܫܐ means *sign, intention, proposal*, and hence the phrase ܢ̈ܝܫܐ ܦܘܣ̈ܩܐ must refer to something other than the points themselves. Therefore, ܢ̈ܝܫܐ ܦܘܣ̈ܩܐ refers to the inner meaning, to the rhetorical character, and especially to the delivery (ὑπόκρισις). It simply means the speaker's intended meaning, which is conveyed to the hearer by means of 'prosody' proper, i.e. by means of a purposeful reading. These 'intended meanings' of the speaker, who ought to make use of the correct reading method by using the signs that could be either temporal or mimetic (p.78), need to be expressed in such a way that the points become signs indicating the exact modulations of the voice. What follows shows that this is indeed how things stood. Jacob Bar Šakko also confirms what we have suggested when he says (p.ܠ, 18) that ܦܘܣܩܐ is divided into two types, one for individual words and the other for the different meanings of whole phrases, which is called ܦܘܣܩܐ in a special sense and which is used for defining the sense of a phrase as precisely as possible (cf. above p.63, 250n, also Bar., *Gramm.*, 247.)

[1] Martin gives an alternative reading (*Gramm.*, 247,16), ܡܢ ܢܩܫܐ, ܪ̈ܗܛܐ ܘܡܩܪ̈ܝܢܐ, (*they have to do with intonations and are recitative*). We noted earlier our uncertainty about the reading of the text at this point (p.82n), since we argued that נעימה is related to the ܪ̈ܗܛܐ ܢܥܡܬܢ̈ܐ (p.74 above). If ܪ̈ܗܛܐ ܢܥܡܬܢ̈ܐ is the correct reading then surely Barhebraeus can scarcely have omitted the Jewish נעימה, but if the variant is right then it is not chanting that is at issue

and gives them their mystical interpretations (which are purely the result of ignorance, *Gramm.*, 248), of which we need speak no more here.[1]

According to him there are forty accents among the Westerns,[2] four basic ones and thirty six derivative. The basic accents are ܦܩܕܐ, ܐܬܢܚܬܐ, ܫܘܐ, ܦܣܘܩܐ. Of the thirty six derivatives, twenty eight are called 'simple', leaving eight as 'composite', although this number cannot be made up from the lists as given in the editions of Martin or Phillips.[3] Among the 'simple' accents some are missing, namely ܡܫܚܠܦ ܡܣܝܡܢܐ,[4] ܩܕܡ ܬܚܘܬܝܐ,[5] ܡܩܝܡܐ, ܡܗܦܟܢܐ, and |267 ܡܫܚܠܦ ܡܗܦܟܢܐ. Further, he includes ܡܫܚܠܦ ܚܪܝܐ which is unknown elsewhere.[6]

We ought also to indicate the elements in Barhebraeus that are taken from the East Syrian system. Barhebraeus notes the ܙܘܩܦܐ ܕܢܬܐ[7] which some people place in the sentence ܐܠܐ ܠܟܘܢ ܟܠ ܫܢܝܢ ܐܘܪܚܐ, even though it is an East Syrian accent, used in place of the ܡܫܡܥܢܐ.[8] In the same way, ܪܗܛܐ is said to be an East Syrian sign which the Westerns did not use,[9] although he does take the opportunity to mention it from time to time, e.g. that the Easterns use it at Proverbs 31.23 instead of ܙܘܩܦܐ.[10] He adds that the Easterns use ܐܬܢܚܬܐ, ܐܠܨܝܬܐ

---

here but the natural intonations of the voice in reading. In the latter case, it is the Greek method of reading that is in view and the Hebrew נעימה has been left out.

[1] This is comparable to the Jewish doctrine of the divine inspiration of the vowel points.

[2] Jacob of Edessa says there are forty seven variations of accents (Phillips, *Letter*, ܡܙ), which are called the 'names of accents' (ܫܡܗ̈ܐ ܕܢܒܓܐ), ܢܒܓܐ referring to the names by which they designate the points, ܢܘܩܙܐ.

[3] See Phillips, *Letter*, ܝܓ / 13.

[4] Jacob Bar Šakko , p.ܥܕ, 13; 94,3 above.

[5] This may be the same as the accent called ܡܫܚܠܦ ܬܩܢܐ (p.89 above). However, Barhebraeus's list is taken from Jacob (p.90 above) where, at least from p.90,l.8, confusion has set in. The order in which the accents are given there (p.90ff.) prove that Barhebraeus used this same list. Furthermore, he read it in much the same condition in which we have it today, for he copies from Jacob the same information on ܡܣܝܡܢܐ which we gave above (p.256; Phillips, ܢܕ / 54).

[6] *Gramm.*, 257, last line; also Phillips, *Letter*, ܢܙ / 57.

[7] *Gramm.*, 253; Phillips, *Letter*, ܡܚ / 48.

[8] See in our list above, 199, ܨܛ; 192,32; 196, ܨܘ.

[9] *Gramm.*, 255,5; Phillips, *Letter*, ܢܓ / 53. For the Westerns, see 180, no.23 above.

[10] *Gramm.*, 260,2; Phillips, *Letter*, ܣܒ / 62.

instead of ܡܦܣܩܢܐ;[1] also, the accent which the Westerns call ܬܚܘܝܐ, the Easterns call ܙܘܓܐ ܡܦܣܩܢܐ and ܫܘܝܐ, while the lesser ܡܦܣܩܢܐ is the ܙܘܓܐ ܕܡܦܣܩܢܐ.[2]

We have said that ܢܝܫܘܪܐ was a sign used only by the East Syrians and wholly unknown to the Westerns. But Barhebraeus says that while ܫܘܪܝܐ is used at 2 Cor. 6.4-6, ܢܝܫܘܪܐ is found on the following words.[3] So here at least he cannot be using Jacob's system. Furthermore, he mentions an accent called ܡܥܡܩܢܘܬܐ, which the teachers in the Persian schools (i.e. following the transfer of the School of Edessa to Nisibis) used. Whenever there were several ܙܘܓܐ followed by a ܬܚܬܝܐ and then a ܦܣܘܩܐ, they would recite the phrase in question, and require it to be recited in a more restrained way (ܐܬ̈ܚܡܨ, var. lect. ܐܬܚܡܨܘ)[4] to achieve a more graceful reading.[5] This accent is only very rarely used, e.g. at Gen 1.9: ܢܬܟܢܫܘܢ ܡܝܐ܆ ܕܠܬܚܬ ܡܢ ܫܡܝܐ܆ ܠܐܬܪܐ܆ ܚܕ܆ ܘܬܬܚܙܐ ܝܒܝܫܬܐ.[6]

|[268] On ܢܝܩܐ, which in Barhebraeus's *Grammar* is written as ܢܝ̈ܩܐ, he says almost exactly the same as what we quoted above (p.178-9) from BL Add. 12138,[7] though he adds the name of Ramišoʿ and thereby provides us with his source for his information about the East Syrian accents.

To finish we ought just to mention that what Barhebraeus says about ܡܦܩܢܐ closely confirms what we said earlier about this particular accent (p.86).[8] He writes as follows:

> ܡܦܩܢܐ ܡܢ ܟܘܠܗ ܢܘܓܐ ܐܝܬܝܐ ܕܡܦܣܩܢܐ܇ ܘܐܝܟ ܢܘܓܐ ܕܠܐ ܐܝܬ ܢܦܫܗ. ܐܝܟ ܠܐ ܠܬܘܪܝܗ܇
> ܘܐܦܪܢܬܐ ܠܟܘ ܕܘܠܐ ܠܟܘܢ ܠܡܬܠܡܢܘ ܡܢ ܕܘܢܫ. ܘܥܘܕܐ ܠܟܪܘܙܬܐ ܢܘܓܐ ܡܦܣܩܢܬܐ. ܕܟܠܗ
> ܘܠܡܠܬܐ ܐܘ ܡܕܡ ܐܚܪܢ ܕܠܐ ܕܒܟܠ ܐܬܬܦܚܡ ܦܘܪܫܢܐ. ܟܠܗ ܕܝܢ ܢܘܓܐ. ܟܘܢ ܕܒܪܢܫܐ
> ܕܡܠܝܢ ܕܡ ܘܡܬܒܠܡ ܘܡܬܟܪܢ ܡܢ ܥܘܕܢܐ ܕܡܫܡܥܢܝܬܐ ܐܬܟܠܠ ܡܟܠܡܘܢ. ܐܝܟ ܕܘܫܐ ܐܬܐܪ ܕܪܓܢܐ
> ܢܡܠܐ ܘܡܥܪܬܐ

---

[1] *Gramm.*, 253; see also 180, no.25 above.

[2] *Gramm.*, 254; Phillips, *Letter*, ܥܒ / 50; also 182 above.

[3] *Gramm.*, 257,14; Phillips, *Letter*, ܦ / 56.

[4] The verb ܚܡܨ means *to constrain, repress* (W. Cureton, ed., *The Third Part of the Ecclesiastical History of John of Ephesus* [London, 1853] 158,240), *to hinder* (G. Bickell, ed., *Isaaci Antiocheni opera omnia* [Giessen, 1873-7] II,204,11; and W. Wright, ed., *The Chronicle of Joshua the Stylite* [Cambridge, 1882], 31,7), or *to provoke* (ἀποστοματίζειν, Lk 11.53).

[5] *Gramm.*, 261; Phillips, *Letter*, ܣܘ / 64-5.

[6] Cf. 191,20; 196, ܦ above, where the Berlin ms has the points horizontally, not obliquely as for ܬܚܘܝܐ. The question is muddled.

[7] *Gramm.*, 259,10; Phillips, *Letter*, ܣܒ / 64-5.

[8] *Gramm.*, 256; Phillips, *Letter*, p.ܠܓ / 55.

> m^ebaṭṭ^elānā means a cessation of motion [=stopping the progress of the speech] where it is thought that there is motion/continuation, but there should not be; as in, 'Do not be amazed that I say to you that you need to be born again.' In this example, the necessity of continuing the speech is thought to be indicated by ܦܚܡܐ or ܐܣܠܐ or some similar accent, since the apodosis is not yet completed; but in fact motion does cease because the protasis is presented to the mind as something profound and elevated, and disconnected from the apodosis, which is more easily understood, as in, 'the spirit blows where it wills etc.'

It is clear at least that ܡܒܛܠܢܐ indicates that the natural progression of the sentence is to be held up. In the Johannine verses, "what is born of flesh is flesh; what is born of the Spirit is spirit; do not be amazed that I say to you that you need to be born again; the Spirit blows where it wills; you hear its voice, but you do not know where it comes from or where it is going; thus it is with the one who is born of the Spirit," it is quite obvious that the ܡܒܛܠܢܐ is added in to break up the démarche, rather as our semi-colons do. Those who take it upon themselves to make editions of the Syriac scriptures should therefore decide what system of accents to use; they should examine the manuscripts, judge between the different schools, and follow one or other of them. For the positioning of the accents constitutes the very exegesis itself.

|269 This is now enough for our brief commentary on Barhebraeus's grammatical goldmine. We set out to describe the method by which the great man attempted to compose a completely new work out of his sources. He never ventured anywhere the Arabs had not preceded him, for example he too failed to distinguish syntax from morphology. This, however, is to be understood on the basis of the purpose for which both Barhebraeus and the Arabs wrote their grammars. They were not writing to help foreigners learn Syriac or Arabic;[xiv] rather they hoped to assist Syrians and Arabs better to understand their own language and therefore better to continue and improve the exegesis of their predecessors. Nothing further need be said about the metrical grammar or the treatise on homonymous words.[xv] In writing the metrical grammar, he follows Joseph Bar Malkon and John Bar Zu'bi, who were surely imitating the practices of the Greeks who

started writing their grammars in verse from the middle of the eleventh century.[1]

[1] V. Egenolff, *Die orthographischen Stücke der byzantinischen Literatur* (Leipzig, 1888), 27f., argues that Nicetas of Serres (Serrhae) was the first to write about grammatical principles in verse [on this writer see Migne, PG 127, col.532—ed.].

[i] For all bibliography and editions of Barhebraeus, H. Takahashi, *Barhebraeus: A Bio-bibliography* (Piscataway NJ, 2005).

[ii] Victor Langlois (tr.), *Chronique de Michel le Grand, patriarche des syriens jacobite* (Venice, 1868).

[iii] Walafrid Strabo was a ninth century pupil of Rabanus Maurus. His *Glossa Ordinaria* was principally a collection of the exegetical traditions taught in the schools and monasteries of Western Europe. Rupert of Deutz was a twelfth century theologian.

[iv] Merx never succeeded in publishing these texts. The first, the *Discourse of Wisdom*, was published by H. F. Janssens, *L'entretien de la sagesse. Introduction aux œuvres philosophiques de Bar-Hebraeus* (Liège, 1937). The second, the *Book of the Pupils of the Eye* was published in id., "Barhebraeus's Book of the Pupils of the Eye," *American Journal of Semitic Languages and Literatures* 47 (1930/1), 26-49,94-134; 48 (1932), 209-63; 52 (1935), 1-21 [reprint, Gorgias Press, 2007]. Much has been done on Barhebraeus'philosophy since Merx's day (though much equally remains unstudied), especially the volumes of the series *Aristoteles Semitico-Latinus*, in which parts of the *Cream of Wisdom* have been edited and analysed. For an overview of the logical works, H. Hugonnard-Roche, "L'oeuvre logique de Barhebraeus," *Parole De L'Orient* 33 (2008), 129-143.

[v] The principal edition of the Mufaṣṣal (which Merx uses throughout) is that of J.P. Broch, ed., *al-Mufassal, opus de re grammatica Arabicum* (Oslo, 1859), hereafter *Muf.* On the work, see *GAP*, 164.

[vi] All Merx's references to Barhebraeus's Grammar are naturally taken from Martin's edition, which has since been much superseded by Moberg's (Moberg, *Livre des Splendeurs*; also his German translation, *Buch der Strahlen*). Fortunately, Moberg's volumes always include Martin's page and line references in the margin, hence the reader may without difficulty use Merx's discussion together with Moberg's edition. Moberg's comments should also naturally be read alongside those of Merx. On the structure of the work, see now R. Voigt, "Die metrische Struktur im *Buch der Strahlen*" in H. Preissler and H. Stern, eds., *Annäherung an das Fremde: XXVI Deutscher Orientalistentag*, ZDMG Suppl. 11 (Stuttgart, 1998), 132-44.

[vii] 'States' is the usual translation of this term in reference to nouns ; in the verb, we usually call them 'voices', i.e. active, passive, middle.

[viii] τοῦ δὲ ὀνόματος διαθέσεις εἰσί δύο, ἐνέργεια καὶ πάθος.

[ix] μεμπτέος ἐστὶν οὕτως ἀποφηνάμενος, ὀφείλων μᾶλλον οὕτως εἰπεῖν· ἔστι δὲ ὅτε καὶ διαθέσεις ὁρῶνται ἐν ὀνόμασι, ῥηματικοῖς οὖσι.

[x] 'Species' and 'shapes' are among the ways in which nouns are divided in Dionysius. Both refer to types of derivation—species are either prototype or derived-from-a-prototype, and shapes are either simple, compound, or derived-from-a-compound. For Jacob's treatment of these, p.57 above.

[xi] σχῆμα εἴρηται παρὰ τὴν σχέσιν τὴν πρὸς τὸ σημαινόμενον· ἀπὸ γὰρ τοῦ σχήματος νοοῦμεν τί ἐστιν ὁ θέλει σημαίνειν ἡ λέξις.

[xii] See the comment at Chapter 10, endnote x. For an indication of how exactly Barhebraeus introduced a different system over that of Bar Zuʿbi, see G. Bohas, "Barhebraeus et la tradition grammaticale syriaque," *Parole d'Orient* 33 (2008), 145-58, esp. p.154 for a reappreciation of Merx's comments here.

[xiii] More instances from Mishna (Erachin. 9,6) and Talmud Yerushalmi (Ned. 4,9) were given by Nöldeke (*ZDMG* 29 [1875], 423 n3), although neither he nor Jeffery (*Foreign Vocabulary of the Qurʾān*, 195-6,240) explains the loan derivation along the lines Merx does.

[xiv] Although in fact, Barhebraeus's *Grammar* did have some impact upon the rise of Syriac in Europe. Moses of Mardin himself brought a copy of the metrical grammar with him on his trip to Rome and it was with the assistance of this 'textbook' that both Masius and Widmanstetter learned their Syriac from Moses. Munich Staatsbibliothek Syr.1 is a manuscript written by Moses, in which Barhebraeus's *Metrical Grammar* is the first item, marked up with Italian annotations in Widmanstetter's own hand (for the identification of which grammar this was, see R. Contini, "Gli inizi della linguistica siriaca nell' Europa rinascimentale" *Rivista di Studi Orientali* 68 [1994], 21 n38). The larger grammar, *The Book of Rays*, was fundamental to the grammatical work of George Amira (*op. cit.*, 24 n59,60). There is thus established some continuity of the grammatical tradition into modern times (see next chapter for further details).

[xv] For further details on these texts (edited in Martin, *Œuvres*, II,1-76 and 77-126, respectively) see Takahashi, *Bio-bibliography*, 358-73.

Conclusion

With the fall of the Caliphate within Barhebraeus's own lifetime, the study of the humanities also came to an end. The Mongols and Turks were hardly promoters of culture. While the study of grammar continued to be strong among the Muslim Arabs, it failed among the Syrian Christians, oppressed as they were by the poverty of their situation. So after Barhebraeus the whole of Syriac literature, including grammar, was given up and for nearly three centuries nobody even wrote a grammar, let alone expanded or advanced the state of the discipline. The future refinement of Syriac grammar belonged elsewhere, removed from Syria to Italy, where the fifteenth century humanistic renaissance produced men eager to learn the languages of the East. It may be that the foremost motivation in this development was the example set by Pico della Mirandola in wanting to open up the Kabbalah, for his followers realised that this could not be done without a knowledge of 'Chaldee'.[1] Among the very first individuals who worked on oriental languages was one Teseo Ambrogio, of the family of the counts of Albonesi and of the palatine counts of Lomello, Doctor *in utroque iure* [i.e. in both canon and civil law], Consul of the College of Lord Judges of Pavia, Canon Regular of the Lateran, and Provost of St Peter's in Ciel d'Oro, Pavia.[i] He was also a good friend of John Potken.[ii] Wanting to make it easier for others to learn the language too, he was burdened with the considerable task of printing books (itself only a recently invented technology), to which end he endeavoured to cut out fonts for oriental languages by means of chalcography.[iii] He was born in 1469,[2] a man of very fertile imagination, well-suited to the comparative study of languages.|[270] He even had a plan to add lines and points onto Latin letters as a way of distinguishing aspirates from non-aspirates (e.g. ܒ݂ from ܒ݁). He thereby became the founder of modern transcription and he explains his main principle in the following verse:

The mute is indicated by a red point above,

---

[1] T. Ambrosius, *Introductio in chaldaicum linguam , syriacam, et armeniacam etc.* (Pavia, 1539), f.19a.

[2] *Op. cit.*, f.193.

The aspirate takes a rosy point beneath.

From the beginning there was a dispute between Ambrogio and Potken about what language the term 'Chaldee' referred to. Potken had used it to mean Ethiopic.[iv] However, at the Fifth Lateran Council (convened by Julius II in 1512, continued by Leo X until 1517) there were both some Ethiopians, who said they had been sent by Prester John, and also some 'Chaldaean Syrians' who were invited to join the mass. Ambrogio learned some Syriac from these latter to add to his basic knowledge of Punic, Hebrew, and Ethiopic. He describes the experience as follows: "some Chaldaean Syrians also joined us in our worship; Joseph a priest, Moses a monk and deacon, and Elias a subdeacon. The priest (Joseph) celebrated the divine liturgy (which we call by the Hebrew name 'Mass' [!]),[v] and he wanted to offer the sacraments to God. But he was not allowed to do this until it was quite clear which rite he was going to follow in performing the hallowed sacraments and what words he would use in accomplishing it. The task then fell to me (at the request of the Reverend Cardinal of Santa Croce, whose hospitality they had received) to translate word-for-word (as the expression goes) the book containing the Chaldaean mass. Lest anyone think that I was trying to escape this assignment, I must say that I considered it a mighty task indeed, even though I had already gained some knowledge of Hebrew and Punic[1] and of the Arabic alphabet...and so I got myself ready to complete the job as soon as possible."[2] He first of all requested the help of a Jew, whose name he does not give but who knew many languages, and then also of Joseph Gallus, the son of Pope Julius II's doctor, who transcribed verbatim in his own language (?French) and in Latin exactly what Elias recited in Chaldee and Arabic, and with this assistance Ambrogio was able to translate the text of the Mass into Latin. This was the very beginning of

[1] 'Punic' was the name at that time given to the language of Melitene (i.e. Armenian). Although this is not the place to discuss other languages, I must just add that Ambrosius gave a particularly good account of Armenian and its condition. He also made some good progress in Coptic, and even some little knowledge of Glagolitic (f.20b). It would be a worthwhile task to investigate and write more about the life of such a well-deserving individual.

[2] This must have been in 1514, for in 1529 he told Widmanstetter that he had first started learning the language about 15 years earlier.

Syriac studies in Europe, which Teseo then tried to promote by writing his *Introduction to Chaldaean, Syriac, Armenian, and ten other languages.*[1] [vi]

It was also Ambrogio who motivated Johann Albrecht Widmanstetter to study Syriac.[2] Widmanstetter became the first editor of a Syriac New Testament and in the preface |[271] to the Vienna edition of 1555 he recalled the story of their meeting: "Ambrogio afterwards spent many years in monastic cells (he was confined by choice in a house of Augustinian canons), developing his inner life such that even the Syrians came to admire his character. However, when I was in the retinue of the Emperor Charles V journeying to Bologna to seek the sacred crown in 1529, my companions from Reggio Emilia and myself happened to be billeted in the monastery where Teseo was living, by then an old man. The following day I went into the church and, happening upon the venerable old man, greeted him. He knew that I had been making enquiries into the monastery's library and its rare book collection. Immediately he took me into a room and pulled off the shelf a copy of the Gospels in Syriac, 'My guest,' he said with a sigh, 'I have applied myself to studying this foreign language for around fifteen years and to this day it has been my foremost love. If only I were to meet some able and eager man who wanted me to teach him this language, sanctified by the very lips of Jesus Christ; for I am now near the end of my days and I need to pass on this knowledge to posterity.'" Ambrogio went on to teach Widmanstetter himself as far as he could and passed on to him many copies of his own works with the solemn promise that it would all be used for the good of the church.

Widmanstetter, as everyone knows, kept the promise.[vii] Four years later he found in the library of Lactantius Ptolomaeus in Siena a copy of the four gospels, together with a selection of the works of Ephrem and Jacob. He was taught Syriac at first by Simeon, bishop of the Syrians of Mount Lebanon, and afterwards with the assistance of Moses of Mardin (or

---

[1] The subscription is as follows: Excudebat Papiae. Ioan. Maria Simoneta Cremonensis. In Canonica Sancti Petri, in Caelo Aureo. Sumptibus et Typis, authoris libri. Anno a virginis Partu 1539 Quinto Kal. April.

[2] Assemani gives a brief report of this in the prologue of *Bibliotheca Orientalis*. A.T. Hoffmann provided an accurate bibliography in his *Grammaticae Syriacae Libri III* (Halle, 1827), 36. See also J.P.N. Land, *Joannes, bischof von Ephesos, der erste syrische kirchenhistoriker* (Leiden, 1856), 25. I do not recall reading anything in the recently edited letters of Masius on the subject.

Antioch)[1] he published the New Testament (1555), which in turn did a great deal to promote the study of Syriac.[viii] The result was that when it was decided to produce a polyglot Bible during the Counter-Reformation, the Syriac part of it was assigned to Andreas Masius, who had availed himself of Moses of Mardin's teaching in Rome[2] and who soon afterwards wrote a grammar and a lexicon which were added to the apparatus of the Antwerp Bible.[ix]

This grammar was the work of a particularly acute intelligence.|[272] In fact, so outstanding was it that, since he treated the verbs according to the example of Hebrew, Masius became the first person correctly to identify the stem system (Pʿal, Paʿel etc.), and equally to classify accurately the different types of weak roots. Here, then, we can see the usefulness of Hebrew grammar in elucidating matters of Syriac. Furthermore, the concept of the 'emphatic state' originated with this grammar. Although the expression is not used as such, it derived from the following observation he makes: "Elias the grammarian, a perceptive man whom I once knew well, wrote that this letter (the alaph at the end of a noun) was an indication of emphasis. Although I would agree this might be the case, I am not easily persuaded that every time a Syriac noun ends in alaph this means that it must be emphatic."[3]

Western Biblical studies brought about significant changes to the way in which Syriac grammar was handled. Taking their lead from Hebrew and Aramaic and being educated themselves in the techniques of Latin grammar, biblical scholars now had to learn and teach a foreign language, as well as to describe its grammar, a task very different from that of the Syrians and Arabs who were working on their native tongue. What naturally happened was that Syriac grammars written for western students were made according to the patterns of Latin grammars with frequent

[1] Moses was sent to Rome by the Patriarch of Antioch, Ignatius, to bring back to Syria a printed version of the Bible (BO I,536).

[2] A. Masius, *Grammaticae linguae syriacae* (in the Antwerp Polyglot, vol.VI, 1571), 4. However, Moses brought a lexicon and a grammar with him from Assyria, which he left at Venice. He gave some copies of these to Widmanstetter, all of whose books were purchased by the Duke of Bavaria. On Moses, see BO I,535. Other than Moses, there was also Sulaca (ܣܘܠܩܐ), the East Syrian Patriarch who was at that time in communion with Rome, also known by his Arabic name of Sʿūd (صعود). Masius made his acquaintance (BO I,523ff.).

[3] Masius, *op. cit.*, 45.

reference to the Targumic dialects and to Hebrew. However, the native Syrians who were based in Rome were rather dissatisfied with this approach, e.g. with the grammars of Masius 1573 and of Tremellius 1569 (the works of Widmanstetter and Mercerus are less significant), and believed that a better job could be done.[x] This was the task that George Amira undertook. He had been accepted in 1583 into the College of Maronites established by Gregory XIII. After returning to Syria in 1595 he was consecrated Bishop of Edessa in the following year and then finally ascended to the patriarchate of the Maronites in 1633, dying in 1644.[1] Being aware of these recent changes in the study of Syriac, he proposed writing his own grammar with a twofold aim.[2] Firstly, he wanted to provide western students of the language, who had hitherto been learning from the abovementioned textbooks, with a grammar that was free of the sorts of mistakes that had arisen as a result of Syriac having been forced into the pattern of Hebrew and Aramaic. Secondly, however, he wanted to write for Syriac-speakers themselves. He writes, "I have come to realise also that this would be of great value to the members of our Maronite College. When they come to Rome from Syria or Cyprus to study, usually as children,|[273] they often struggle to learn Syriac properly, partly because Syriac Grammars are frequently unclear and complicated, but especially because of their generally low quality. This is why, insofar as I myself have some expertise merely on account of having had the chance to study these things since childhood, I have worked hard to make sure I have read every author who has managed to set forth grammar in a lucid and ordered manner. Furthermore, I believe that it would be of great benefit to them if a Grammar could be written in which the technical terms of Syriac grammar were related to their Latin counterparts, the rules of the former being described using the jargon of the latter."

And so the result was that, after both Greek and Arabic theories had been incorporated, and after the first forays into comparative grammar had been tried, it was now the turn of the Latin school to produce a grammar, in which the comparative method was deliberately avoided. All subsequent grammarians based their work ultimately on this, at least until the ancient sources were rediscovered.

---

[1] BO I,552. On the date of his death, J. Acurensis, *Grammatica Linguae Syriacae* (Rome, 1647), pref.

[2] ܓܪܐܡܛܝܩܝ ܣܘܪܝܝܐ ܐܘ ܟܠܕܝܐ ܕܦܝܠܘܣܘܦܐ ܘܬܐܘܠܘܓܘܣ ܓܘܪܓܝܣ ܒܪܗ ܕܡܝܟܐܝܠ ܡܢ ܒܝܬ ܐܡܝܪܐ ܕܒܝܬ ܥܕܢ ܡܢ ܛܘܪܐ ܕܠܒܢܢ ܟܘܡܪܐ ܘܡܠܦܢܐ ܐܘ ܡܦܫܩܢܐ ܕܦܠܓܘܬܗ (Rome, 1596).

Although his treatment of the verb was not very praiseworthy and was far surpassed by Masius's more accurate approach, Amira nonetheless became the master of both eastern and western grammarians. His method and his simple yet precise manner of expression seemed well adapted to the subject, and he was followed in everything save in the theory of verbal roots.[1] He followed Masius in including interjections (**ܡܬܕܡܪܢܘܬܐ ܡܠܬܐ**) and was the first Syriac grammarian systematically to tackle syntax, to which he dedicated thirteen pages.[xi]

Because Amira wanted to teach those who knew no Syriac to begin with, he set out full paradigms both of simple verbs and of verbs with suffixes and arranged them more clearly than Barhebraeus had done. Amira's work, however, was of less use to students of Syrian origin, who still needed to learn Syriac since their mother tongue was now Arabic, but who had not yet had a chance to learn any Latin. It was not long, therefore, before certain learned individuals—Abraham Ecchellensis, Joseph Sciadrensis, and Joseph Acurensis—tried to fill this gap by producing a compendia of Amira's work in Syriac and Arabic.[2] |[274] Abraham has this to say about his project, "I was glad that a task of this kind fell to me, that I might satisfy the wishes of those keen to study Syriac, especially as Amira's grammar was written in Latin. I wanted to create in a single work something to help both teachers and students." Sciadrensis had the same aim as well. He hoped to educate both the Syrian priests and the members of the Maronite College by explaining the divine office, a task in which he was encouraged by Amira himself. Lastly Acurensis, the patriarch of Antioch, followed this trend to the point where he wrote entirely in Arabic,

---

[1] He called the roots 'conjugations' (ܨܒ̈ܬܐ) = اوزان and تصاريف and ܡܘܙܓ̈ܐ. He dealt with the verbs in the following order: I, ܩܛܠ and ܐܬܩܛܠ; II,1 ܩܛܶܠ, ܐܬܩܛܶܠ, 2 ܩܘܼܡ, ܐܬܩܘܼܡ, 3 ܩܲܛܶܠ, ܐܬܩܲܛܶܠ, 4 ܩܛܘܿܠ; III ܐܩܛܶܠ, ܐܬܐܩܛܶܠ; IV,1 ܩܛܘܿܠ, ܐܬܩܛܘܿܠ, ܩܛܘܿܪ, 2 ܐܩܘܼܡ etc. This is the old system in which the passive forms are included.

[2] These grammars are entitled as follows:

I ܒܫܡ ܐܠܗܐ ܚܝܐ ܫܠܝܛܐ ܓܪܡܛܝܩܝ ܐܘܟܝܬ ܐܘܪܚܐ ܠܘܬ ܡܡܠܠܐ ܣܘܪܝܝܐ ܕܥܒܝܕ ܒܦܣܝܩܘܬܐ ܠܡܣܟܢܐ ܐܒܪܗܡ ܒܪ ܕܐܘܪܗܡ ܕܒܝܬ ܚܩܠܢ ܙܕܩ ܡܢ ܩܪܝܬܐ ܡܚܪܘܒܬܐ ܘܩܪܝܬ ܠܡܫܝܚܐ ܢܩܦܐ ܠܬܠܡܝܕܐ ܕܡܪܘܢܝܐ ܘܡܕܪܫܬܐ ܕܪܗܘܡܝ Abraham Ecchellensis..., *linguae syriacae sive chaldaicae perbrevis institutio* (Rome, 1628).

II, ܓܪܡܛܝܩܝ ܕܠܫܢܐ ܣܘܪܝܝܐ ܕܥܒܝܕ ܐܝܣܦ ܫܕܪܝܐ ܡܪܘܢܝܐ ܡܢ ܛܘܪܐ ܕܠܒܢܢ. ܡܬܦܪܫܩܐ ܕܓܪܡܛܝܩܝ ܕܬܪܓܡܢܘܬܐ ܕܣܘܪܝܝܐ ܕܐܣܬܠܩܬ: ܒܪܘܡܝ ܡܕܝܢܬܐ ܒܡܛܒܥܬܐ ܕܡܪܘܢܝܐ ܥܠ ܐܦܝ ܐܦܣܩܘܦܐ ܕܡܫܝܚܝܐ (Rome, 1636). Cf. BO I,552.

III, ܓܪܡܛܝܩܝ ܐܘܟܝܬ ܐܘܪܚܐ ܠܘܬ ܡܡܠܠܐ ܕܠܫܢܐ ܣܘܪܝܝܐ ܕܥܒܝܕ ܝܘܣܦ ܒܥܩܘܪܝܐ ܦܛܪܝܪܟܐ ܕܐܢܛܝܘܟܝܐ ܡܢ ܛܘܪܐ ܕܠܒܢܢ ܕܐܣܬܠܩܬ: ܒܪܘܡܝ ܡܕܝܢܬܐ ܒܡܛܒܥܬܐ ܕܡܫܡܫܢܘܬܐ ܥܠ ܐܦܝ ܡܫܝܚܝܘܬܐ ܘܠܐܠܗܐ ܫܘܒܚܐ:: (Rome, Sacred Congregation of Propaganda, 1647). Cf. BO I,553.

since the students he was aiming at were those actually living in Syria itself. He sent his work to Innocent X in Rome in 1645. On the latter's command it was printed and distributed throughout the Near East, and hence it is difficult to locate copies of it today, though there is one in the Munich Library.[xii]

Concerning the arrangement of these grammars, it is enough to point out that they are organised on the Arabic pattern of nouns, verbs, and particles, with pronouns being included under nouns, participles (ܡܠܬܐ ܡܨܥܝܬܐ) under verbs (following Barhebraeus's mix ups, see p.248 above), and prepositions, adverbs, and interjections all included under particles. All these texts are marked by great clarity and straightforwardness and are especially well-suited to accomplish those particular aims which their writers set out to achieve.

Even if these had been the only grammars to have been officially published it would be wrong to conclude |[275] that there were no others. The education of priests, of which grammar was a central part, had always been the concern of the church hierarchy. Hence, for instance, the Maronites Petrus Metoscita and Gabriel Avodius Hesronita made abridgments of Amira's grammar, and Timothy Isaac, Metropolitan of Amida (d.1622),[1] wrote a Syriac Primer which contained only a set of paradigms based on the Arabic pattern. Copies of the latter are available in BL Add. 21211 and in Petermann 17 in Berlin.[xiii] A final example that should be mentioned is the Grammar of Arsenius (Petermann 18, Berlin) and another anonymous Grammar (Petermann 20) written in Garshuni and including syntax, the author of which follows the Maronite grammatical models.[xiv] These manuscripts offer modern abridgements, mostly rather meagre, written purely as student textbooks.

We have said enough! As I lay aside my pen, with which I have written the story of the study of grammar amongst the Syrians, that line of Virgil comes to mind, 'tantae molis erat Romanam condere gentem' (*what a hard task it was to establish the Roman race*). What hard work it must have been! What sleepless nights! What a lot of mistakes were perpetrated along the way by those in the East who advanced the subject to the point at which our own age could conceive the discipline of Comparative Semitics! But, what dedication to the mother tongue! What love for literature, whose brightness was little by little uncovered and shed abroad to scatter the

---

[1] Rosen and Forshall, *Catalogus codicum manuscriptorum orientalium in Museo Britannico, pars prima* (London, 1838), 89.

clouds darkening men's minds! But, reader, lest you be tempted to belittle the exertions of those who dedicated so much time and effort to the investigation of their language (although even we thought that their books were sometimes a bit trifling), do not forget the words of Aristotle, who after all was the starting point for so much of what we have seen, and who warned us against harbouring any such feeling:

> ὥσπερ γὰρ τὰ τῶν νυκτερίδων ὄμματα πρὸς τὸ φέγγος ἔχει τὸ μεθ' ἡμέραν, οὕτω καὶ τῆς ἡμετέρας ψυχῆς ὁ νοῦς πρὸς τὰ τῇ φύσει φανερώτατα πάντων. οὐ μόνον δὲ χάριν ἔχειν δίκαιον τούτοις ὧν ἄν τις κοινώσαιτο ταῖς δόξαις, ἀλλὰ καὶ τοῖς ἐπιπολαιότερον ἀποφηναμένοις· καὶ γὰρ οὗτοι συνεβάλοντό τι· τὴν γὰρ ἕξιν προήσκησαν ἡμῶν.[1]

[1] Metaphysics 993b: *Just as it is with bats' eyes in respect of daylight, so it is with our mental intelligence in respect of those things which are by nature most obvious. It is only fair to be grateful not only to those whose views we can share, but also to those who have expressed rather superficial opinions. They too have contributed something; they have worked before us to create our starting points* (tr. Tredennick, altered).

[i] For more on Teseo himself, see Levi della Vida's article in the *Dizionario Biografico degli Italiani*, II, 39-43, with further bibliography mentioned. On Teseo's library and his ownership of a copy of the earliest edition of the Qurʾān, see A. Nuovo, "A Lost Arabic Koran Rediscovered," *The Library* (Sixth Series) 12,4 (1990), 273-92 (an article originally published in Italian in 1987 announcing the rediscovery of the earliest printed Qurʾān, which had been owned by Teseo, a fact unknown to Levi Della Vida).

[ii] Potken was the editor of the first printed book in Ethiopic, a Psalter of 1513.

[iii] Description of Ambrogio's founts, together with some images, can now be found in J.F. Coakley, *The Typgraphy of Syriac: A historical catalogue of printing types 1637-1958* (British Library, 2006), 28-30,153-4.

[iv] See the brief note (the promise of further research seems never to have been fulfilled) by M. Goshen-Gottstein, "Ethiopic-Chaldean and the Beginnings of Comparative Semitics in Renaissance Times,' *Atti del Secondo Congresso Internazionale di Linguistica Camito-Semitica* (Florence, 1978), 149.

[v] On the Hebrew etymology of *Missa*, Robert J. Wilkinson, *Orientalism, Aramaic and Kabbalah in the Catholic Reformation: The First Printing of the Syriac New Testament* (Leiden, 2007), 14 n12.

[vi] This first printed book about Syriac was the subject of an article by E. Nestle, "Aus einem sprachwissenschaftlichen Werk von 1539," *ZDMG* 58 (1904), 601-16; and an excellent recent assessment by Robert J. Wilkinson, *op.cit.* (previous note), 20-27, which also includes some specimens from the work (p.xiii).

[vii] The most complete biography is that of M. Müller, *Johann Albrecht V. Widmanstetter. 1506-1557. Sein Leben und Werken* (Bamberg, 1908); again see Wilkinson's assessment, together with further bibliography, *op. cit.*, 137-69.

[viii] One of the principal achievements of Wilkinson's recent work (see notes above) is to show that the 'missing link' between the work of Teseo (published in 1539) and the *editio princeps* of the Syriac Bible published by Widmanstetter in 1555 was the controversial Orientalist Guillaume Postel, who seems to have been making preparations for such an edition already as early as 1537 (see the evidence adduced for this on p.75-6, 80-81, 105-6. To Postel is also owed the kabbalistic ideological background to the *editio princeps* itself (p.176-85). It was the success of Widmanstetter's tendentious narrative of European Syriac studies found in his *Dedication* to the edition that resulted in the ignorance of later scholars (including Merx) with regard to Postel's significance (though his role, and that of the Kabbalah, is to some extent recognised in R. Contini, "Gli inizi della linguistica siriaca nell' Europa rinascimentale," *Rivista di Studi Orientali* 68 (1994), 15-30.

[ix] On these events and their wider significance, see the two articles by A. Van Roey, "Les études syriaques d'Andreas Masius," *Orientalia Lovaniensia Periodica* 9 (1978), 141-58; and "Les débuts des études syriaques et André Masius," *Orientalia Christiana Analecta* 236

(1990), 11-15; also Wilkinson, *op.cit.*, 63-94, and above all its companion volume, Robert J. Wilkinson, *The Kabbalistic Scholars of the Antwerp Polyglot Bible* (Leiden, 2007).

[x] I. Tremellius, *Grammatica Chaldaea et Syra* (Geneva, 1569); J. A. Widmanstadt, *Syriacae linguae...prima elementa* (Vienna, 1556); J. Mercerus, *Tabulae in Grammaticen Linguae Chaldaeae, qui et Syriaca dicitur* (Paris, 1560). On the first of these and his Biblical philology, Robert J. Wilkinson, "Emmanuel Tremellius' 1569 Edition of the Syriac New Testament," *Journal of Ecclesiastical History* 58 (2007), 9-25. Tremellius's grammar is actually an excellent first attempt at an historical description of the known Aramaic dialects and far surpasses the work of Widmanstetter. It also informed his edition of the NT which, however, was attacked as having an anti-Roman (and anti-Kabbalistic!) intention and for ignoring the context of contemporary spoken Syriac (Widmanstetter's work, by contrast, aided as it was by Moses of Mardin and his mission, was partly aimed at a Syriac-speaking readership in the East).

[xi] R. Contini, "Gli inizi" (as noted above) offers an assessment of Amira's linguistic efforts in the light of the earlier Western grammars.

[xii] There is also a copy at the Oriental Institute, Oxford.

[xiii] Petermann 17 = Berlin Syr. 222 (Sachau, *Verzeichniss* II,700); Wright, *Cat.* III, 1180; there is also a copy at Yale, Syriac 12 (see L. Depuydt, "Classical Syriac Manuscripts at Yale University: A Checklist" *Hugoye* 9.2 [2006]), and in Mingana Syr. 74.

[xiv] Petermann 18 = Berlin Syr. 268 (Sachau, *Verzeichniss* II,799); Petermann 20 = Berlin Syr. 267 (Sachau, *Verzeichniss* II,798).

Appended Texts—Notes to the New Edition

Merx edited and appended to his monograph four texts that had been key parts of his research. I have tried to make the arrangement of the texts rather easier to use than was the case in Merx's original. For example, the numerous textual data which were originally found in various places (footnotes, in-text parentheses, lists of corrigenda) have been collected into one set of textual notes and consigned to an apparatus.

Merx's own page and line numberings have been retained in the inner margin so that references from the main text may continue to be used as before. The new page and line numbers given in the outer margins are offered purely as a reference system for the apparatus.

Text I—Jacob Bar Šakko's Grammar: The ms folio numbers referred to in the outer margin are those of the Oxford ms (O). It is missing f.8, and the folio between f.35 and f.36 was not numbered. Merx originally added variants from B on an inserted page (ܡܚܣ), and variants from L were included only in amongst his other annotations (p.215-29). These have now all been brought together in the new apparatus. The other notes that I have placed beneath the apparatus were transposed from the detailed annotations that Merx printed at the end of chapter 11 (p.215-29). All this will hopefully make the text and its apparatus more readily accessible to future readers. See p.213 above for information on the ms relationships.

Text II—Excerpts from Jacob's metrical grammar (see p.213 above).

Text III—The Syriac version of the Technē Grammatikē.

Mss used in this edition:

- A British Library Add. 14620 (ninth century)
- B British Library add. 14658 (seventh century)
- C Berlin Syr. 89 (=Sachau 226, dated 1881)

Merx made a few errors in the collation of B. These have been corrected here from personal inspection of the ms. There is an occasional discrepancy between the text he has printed and the text underlying his translation in ch.2. I have followed whichever seems to have been his preferred reading in each case and made the two consistent with each other.

I have made some minor editorial interventions. Where it seems clear that some of the variants noted in brackets by Merx, especially those of C, are in fact original, I have allowed them into the text.

Other mss containing this text not noted by Merx or otherwise unknown to him:

> *Olim* Mosul 35 (s.xvi/xvii). A. Scher, *Notice sur les manuscrits syriaques...de Mossoul* (Paris, 1907), 15; Kessel and Bamballi, *Field Notes II*, describe this ms in detail, and demonstrate that Merx's **C** (Berlin Syr.89) is an apograph of this ms. Hence the readings of C noted in the present text can for the most part be taken as coming from the "Mosul 35" branch of the tradition. Vööbus, *School of Nisibis*, 102 n17, makes note of the same copy under the alternative shelfmark Baghdad Chaldaean Patriarchate 522.
>
> Vat. Syr. 593. Kessel and Bamballi, op.cit., 25-6, show this to be a copy taken from *olim* Mosul 35.
>
> Mingana Syr. 337/D,E appears to contain at least some extracts from our text, but they may be of no separate value.
>
> According to Gottheil (*JAOS* 15 [1893], cxi), he found an extract from the *Techne* under the name of David bar Pawlos in Berlin Syr. 92 (Sachau 306), but I can find no trace of this, even in Gotheil's own description of the same ms in his edition of the *Syriac Grammar by Mar Elia of Sobha*, p.13-17.

Text IV—Jacob of Edessa's Grammar. Merx's text was a reprint and re-setting of the text in Wright's edition which had been printed only for private circulation. Given that Wright's original publication is easier to read than Merx's handwritten reproduction it has seemed more felicitous here simply to reproduce in facsimile Wright's own work. Note that the fragments should probably be read in the order suggested by Revell, *Grammar of Jacob of Edessa*, 366n2.

Since this is a text that may be of considerable interest, I have appended a translation. The first fragment contains a number of remarkable points of interest. Its contents were carefully analysed both by Merx and by Segal, *Diacritical Point.*

ܡܐܡܪܐ ܥܠ ܟܪܣܛܝܢܘܬܐ ܕܐܝܬܘܗܝ ܡܐܡܪܐ ܩܕܡܝܐ ܕܥܠܬܐ ܕܕܝܠܬ̈ܢܗ
ܕܗܘ ܣܗܕܐ ܩܕܝܫܐ ܕܒܘܡܪܐ ܒܗܝܢܐ ܕܡܪܝ ܡܠܟܝ ܕܐܝܬܘܗܝ ܡܠܦܢܢ
ܠܟܪܣܛܝܢܐ ܗܘ ܕܡܬܩܪܐ ܡܪܝ ܫܐܘܠܐ

ܐܬܠܬ ܠܒܢܝ ܐܝܟ ܣܓܝܐ ܘܫܒܩ ܥܠ ܪ̈ܚܡܐ ܠܒܢ̈ܝܐ ܐܘܠܨܢ̈ܐ ܡܢܗܘܢ ܡܠܦܢܐ ܕܐܬܘܠܕܘ ܒܡܕܝܢܬܐ ܘܕܡܒܕܪܝܢ ܐܬܐܠܡ ܒܡܕܝܢܬܐ ܘܕܡܒܕܪܝܢ ܡܣܝܒܪ ܒܠܒܐ ܥܠ ܐܦ̈ܝ ܡܫܝܚܝܐ

ܠ

ܒܝܕ ܡܥܝܢܐ ܐܠܗܝܐ

ܡܫܪܝܢܢ ܠܡܟܬܒ ܟܬܒܐ ܚܕܐ ܕܡܠܬܐ ܕܕܝܠܗܘܢ ܕܐܡܪܝ ܠܡܪܥܐ ܣܘܪ̈ܝܝܐ ܐܦܝܣܩܘܦܐ ܕܒܘܨܪܐ܀ ܩܕܡ

ܡܐܡܪܐ ܩܕܡ܀ ܠܟܡܐ ܡܢܘ̈ܬܐ ܡܬܦܠܓ ܡܡܠܠܐ ܣܘܪܝܝܐ[1]

ܦܘܠܓܐ ܘܐܫܪܝܢ ܠܡܟܢܘ ܕܐܝܬܝܗܘܢ: ܫܡܐ: ܕܡܠܬܐ: ܚܠܦ ܫܡܐ: ܟܠܠ ܡܒܝܢܐ: ܡܨܥܬ ܫܡܐ: ܦܪܘܫܘܬܐ ܣܘܡܟܐ: ܐܣܘܪܐ:

ܫܘܐܠܐ ܬܘܪܓܡܐ ܦܪܫ ܐܝܟ ܠܗ ܠܡܢܘ̈ܬܐ ܗܠܝܢ

ܦܘܢܝܐ ܫܡܐ ܐܝܬܘܗܝ: ܡܢܬܐ ܦܣܝܩܬܐ ܕܡܡܠܠܐ: ܕܡܫܘܕܥܐ ܓܘܫܡܐ ܡܕܡ: ܐܘ ܫܘܒܕܢܐ: ܐܝܟ ܐܢܫ ܕܐܡܪ ܟܐܦܐ: ܣܘܣܝܐ: ܬܘܪܐ: ܐܘ̈ܡܢܐ: ܨܠܘܬܐ: ܕܚܠܬܐ: ܘܡܫܪܐ ܕܐܝܟ ܗܠܝܢ: ܡܠܬܐ ܐܝܬܝܗ ܡܢܬܐ ܠܐܘܣܝܬܐ ܕܡܡܠܠܐ ܕܡܫܘܕܥܐ ܥܠ ܥܒܕܐ: ܠܗܘ ܡܐ ܕܥܒܕ ܐܢܫ ܐܘ ܚܫܫ: ܐܝܟ ܐܢܫ ܕܐܡܪ: ܟܬܒ: ܩܪܐ: ܦܠܚ: ܚܕܝܢ: ܚܫܝܢ: ܢܕܥܘܢ: ܘܥܒܕܐ ܕܐܝܟ ܗܠܝܢ: ܚܠܦ ܫܡܐ: ܕܝܢ ܐܝܬܘܗܝ: ܟܠܗܘܢ

2a ܚܬܝܟ̈ܐ ܩܠܐ ܕܡܬܬܣܝܡܝܢ ܒܕܘܟܬ ܫܡܗܐ ܘܡܫܘܕܥܝܢ ܐܩܢܘܡܐ: ܠܒܨܘܪܬܐ ܡܕܡ. ܐܘ ܫܘܒܕܢܐ: ܐܝܟ ܕܐܡܪ: ܐܢܐ: ܐܢܬ: ܗܘ: ܐܢܚܢ: ܐܢܬܘܢ: ܗܢܘܢ: ܗ̈ܢܝܢ ܘܡܥܪܬܐ ܕܐܝܟ ܗܠܝܢ: ܟܠܠ ܡܠܬܐ ܕܥܡ ܐܝܬܝܗܘܢ: ܟܠܗܘܢ ܚܬܝܟ ܩܠܐ: ܕܕܐܝܟ ܐܡܝܢܐ ܐܝܬܘܗܝ ܡܕܡ: ܐܘ ܗܟܢ: ܐܘ ܫܠܝܐ ܡܬܒܥܝܢ: ܘܫܘܚܠܦ ܡܢ ܡܠܬܐ ܠܐ ܦܪܝܫܐ ܘܠܐܡܬܝ: ܟܠܠ ܡܠܬܐ ܕܥܡ ܡܬܦܬܚܝܢ: ܡܫܠܠ ܘܐܡܝܢܐܝܬ ܐܘ ܠܡܠܬܐ ܢܦܩܝܢ: ܐܘ ܥܡ ܡܠܬܐ ܡܬܐܡܪܝܢ: ܐܡܝܢܐ ܘܬܐܡܪ: ܫܦܝܪܐܝܬ: ܚܟܝܡܐܝܬ: ܣܓܝܐܐܝܬ: ܐܦ: ܐܡ: ܟܕ. ܬܘܒ. ܗܫܐ: ܐܡܬܝ: ܠܘܬ: ܡܛܠܬܗ: ܟܕܘ: ܡܫܠܠ:

ܘܡܥܪܬܐ ܕܐܝܟ ܗܠܝܢ: ܡܨܥܬ ܫܡܐ:[2] ܕܥܡ ܐܝܬܝܗܘܢ: ܟܠܗܘܢ ܗܠܝܢ ܕܥܡ ܡܠܐܡܬܝ:

7 ܠܐܘܣܝܬܐ] ܕܐܘܣܝ O 14 ܐܢܚܢ ܐܢܬܘܢ] ܐܢܬܘܢ ܐܢܚܢ OG | ܢ̈ܫܝܢ] ܗ̈ܢܝܢ O
17 ܘܠܐܡܬܝ] ܡܠܐܡܬܝ O[first hand] | ܐܘ] om. OG

[1] ܡܡܠܠܐ ܣܘܪܝܝܐ is the γλώσση συριακή of Dionysius Thrax, 9n; ܡܐܡܪܐ is used for λόγος in the expression “the parts of speech” (p.ܢ,12). | [2] ܡܨܥܬ ܫܡܐ = *μετοξή*. By contrast the grammarian Tryphon calls the infinitive *ὄνομα ῥήματος* (H. Steinthal, *Geschichte der Sprachwissenschaft bei den Alten*, 641,575). In Syriac this term referred to adjectives.

ܒܘܣܟ ܫܡܐ ܡܫܡܠܝܢ: ܐܟܘܬ ܕܐܡܪ: ܙܘܓ: ܓܒܠܐ: ܡܬܪܕܩܝܢ: ܚܝܠܐ: ܢܨܚܘܢ:
ܘܡܠܬܐ ܕܐܝܟ ܗܠܝܢ: ܦܘܫܩܐ ܫܪܝܐ ܕܝܢ ܐܬܬܐܡܝܢ: ܒܟܠܗܘܢ ܒܢܝ ܩܠܐ ܕܒܗ ܩܝܡ 2b
ܫܘܟܠܐ ܕܡܬܦܫܩܝܢ: ܐܘ ܩܝܡ ܚܠܦ ܫܡܐ: ܟܪܝܢ ܥܠ ܐܬܬܐܡܝܗܘܢ ܦܪܘܫܘܬܐ
ܘܠܐ ܗܘܐ ܕܡܬܚܠܦ ܢܫܡܘܢ ܐܬܬܐܡܝܢ: ܐܠܐ ܕܡܬܚܠܦ ܐܢܫܐ ܘܐܬܬܐܡܝܗܘܢ ܒܗܠܝܢ: ܟܕ:
ܟܕܝ: ܙܝ: ܒܠܚܘܕ: ܓܪ: ܕܐ: ܠܐ: ܚܠܦ: ܐܝܟ: ܦܢ: ܥܠ: ܠܡܛܠ: ܟܡܐ ܡܛܘ ܩܝܡ
ܘܡܠܬܐ ܕܟܠܗܝܢ ܕܩܝܡܝܢ܀ ܐܝܟܢܐ ܐܡܪܗ: ܡܟܝܠ ܐܪܒܥܐ ܕܡܫܡܠܝܐ: ܘܐܝܟܢܐ ܟܠܗܘܢ
ܟܕ ܡܬܪܐ: ܘܠܐ ܢܣܒܘܢ ܟܠܗ. ܠܐ ܒܫܡܐ: ܘܠܐ ܐܪܥܐ: ܘܠܐ ܡܠܬܐ: ܘܠܐ ܐܝܢܘܬܐ ܘܠܐ
ܗܘ ܚܕܐ ܡܢ ܐܝܠܝܢ ܕܢܦܩܝܢ ܠܒܠܚܘܕ ܡܠܬܐ ܐܢܫܝܬܐ: ܐܬܬܐܡܝܗܘܢ ܕܝܢ ܐܝܬܝܗ
ܗܠܝܢ: ܦܢ: ܕܝܢ: ܓܝܪ: ܟܡܐ: ܟܕ: ܐܦܠܐ: ܡܛܠ ܟܕ:[1] ܐܠܐ ܘܡܠܬܐ ܕܐܝܟ
ܗܠܝܢ: ܘܡܛܠܗ ܡܢ ܕܐܝܟܢܐ ܐܡܪܗ: ܕܠܐ ܢܗܘܐ ܟܪܝܟ ܡܫܡܠܝܐ: ܐܠܐ: ܐܝܟ ܒܟܠܠ
ܟܕ ܫܘܟܠܐ: ܘܙܘܓ ܒܡܬܓܒܐ: ܕܡܢܘܬܐ ܕܐܬܡܠܝܐ: ܫܡܐ ܘܡܠܬܐ ܐܬܬܐܡܝܗܘܢ: ܫܡܐ
ܦܢ ܐܬܬܐܡܝܗܘܢ: ܐܝܟ ܗܝܘܠܐ: ܘܐܝܟ ܗܘ ܕܣܝܡ: ܘܐܝܟ ܓܢܣܐ: ܡܠܬܐ ܕܝܢ: ܐܝܟ 3a
ܦܘܪܫܢܐ: ܘܐܝܟ ܗܘ ܕܡܬܦܠܓ: ܘܐܝܟ ܐܕܫܐ:[2] ܗܠܝܢ ܕܝܢ ܐܬܬܐܡܝܢ: ܡܫܡܠܝܐ
ܘܡܫܘܕܥܢܐ ܡܢ ܫܡܐ ܘܡܠܬܐ ܢܦܩܝܢ: ܘܐܬܬܐܡܝܢ ܐܝܟ ܕܡܫܡܠܝܐ ܘܡܫܬܘܕܥܐ
ܘܡܬܐܡܪ: ܫܡܐ ܕܟܠܗܝܢ ܐܟܚܕܐ: ܡܠܬܐ ܕܝܢ ܟܕ ܐܟܚܕܐ: ܘܫܘܫܠܐ ܗܠܝܢ
ܒܫܘܡܠܝܐ ܕܠܦܪܘܩܐ

ܫܘܠܐ ܠܐܬܬܐܡܐ ܐܝܠܝܢ ܕܢܦܩܝܢ ܒܟܠ ܚܕܐ ܡܢ ܫܡܐ ܘܡܠܬܐ:

ܦܘܠܓܐ ܘܐܫܬܢܝܬ ܕܡܫܡܠܝܐ ܡܢ ܢܦܩܝܢ: ܓܢܣܐ: ܐܕܫܐ: ܐܣܟܡܐ: ܡܢܝܢܐ:
ܐܢܫܘܬܐ: ܡܫܘܚܠܦܘܬܐ: ܘܓܢܣܐ[3] ܦܢ ܕܦܪܨܘܦܐ ܘܡܢܝܢܝܬܐ: ܘܟܠܗܝܢ ܕܝܠܗܘܢ: ܡܢܝܢܐ
ܘܫܘܚܠܦܐ: ܐܟܘܬ ܕܐܡܪ: ܕܟܪܐ: ܢܩܒܬܐ: ܠܘܬܐ: ܦܪܨܘܦܐ: ܦܬܓܡܐ: ܐܬܪܐ:
ܐܬܪܘܬܐ: ܕܬܪܬܐ: ܕܬܪܬܝܬܐ ܘܡܠܬܐ ܕܐܝܟ ܗܠܝܢ: ܘܐܚܪܢܝܬܐ: ܝܚܝܕܐ: ܣܘܓܐܐ:
ܠܬܪܬܐ: ܠܬܪܬܐ: ܚܕܢܝܐ: ܚܕܢܝܐ: ܦܫܝܛܐ: ܦܫܝܛܐ܀ ܐܕܫܐ ܕܝܢ ܠܘܬ: ܦܪܘܣܐ ܘܠܘܬܐ: ܗ̄

4 ܟܠܗܘܢ ܐܬܬܐܡܝܗܘܢ ܐܢܫܐ] ܗܠܝܢ ܐܬܬܐܡܝܗܘܢ ܐܢܫܐ OG 5 ܕܐ] ܕܝ OG txt L 7 ܐܝܢܘܬܐ] sic O | ܘܠܐ...8 ܗܘ] ܘܠܐ ܗܘܝܢ B 8 ܟܠܗܘܢ] ܗܠܝܢ OG | ܐܬܬܐܡܝܗܘܢ] ܐܬܬܐܡܝܢ GBL 9 ܦܢ] ܦܢ L | ܡܛܠ] om. G 10 ܟܪܝܟ] ܟܪܝܟ G 13 ܐܕܫܐ] ܐܕܫܐ G 17 ܢܦܩܝܢ] ܢܦܩܝܢ L 18 ܢܦܩܝܢ] ܢܦܩܝܢ G 20 ܘܫܘܚܠܦܐ] ܘܫܘܚܠܦܐ O 21 ܝܚܝܕܐ] ܘܝܚܝܕܐ O

[1] Compare the list of conjunctions in Dionysius Thrax. | [2] Jacob here describes the noun as ὕλη (*substance*), ὑποκείμενον (*subject*), and γένος (*genus*), and the verb as διαφορά (*differentia*) and εἶδος (*species, forms*). Hence we recognise Aristotle behind this: "The substrate is that of which the rest are predicated, while it is not itself predicated of anything else....In one sense we call the matter the substrate" (τὸ ὑποκείμενον ἐστι καθ' οὗ τὰ ἄλλα λέγεται, ἐκεῖνο δὲ αὐτὸ μηκέτι κατ' ἄλλον...τοιοῦτον δὲ τρόπον μέν τινα ἡ ὕλη λέγεται, Met 1028b36) and "some consider that the one substrate is matter while the contraries are differentiae, i.e. forms" (τὸ μὲν ἓν τὸ ὑποκείμενον ὕλην, τὰ δ'ἐναντία διαφορὰς καὶ εἴδη, Phys. 187a). | [3] On "genus" in Syriac grammar and later in all Semitic grammars as derived from Greek theory, see p.144f.

3b ܥܠܠܐ ܘܥܠܝܠܬܐ:[4] ܥܠܠܐ ܗܘ ܩܕܡܝܐ: ܐܝܠܢܐ ܕܫܡܫܐ: ܐܪܥܐ: ܢܘܪܐ: ܟܘܟܒܐ:
ܥܠܝܠܬܐ: ܕܗܝ ܘܬܪܝܢܐ:[5] ܫܡܝܢܐ: ܐܪܥܢܝܐ: ܢܘܪܢܐ: ܪܘܚܢܐ: ܟܘܟܒܢܝܐ܀ ܐܣ̈ܟܡܐ
ܬܠܬ: ܦܫܝܛܐ: ܘܡܪܟܒܐ:[6] ܦܫܝܛܐ: ܐܝܟ ܕܗܢܘ: ܐܠܗܐ: ܦܛܪܘܣ: ܡܪܟܒܐ:
ܐܝܟ ܕܐܣܝ ܟܠ:

2 ܘܬܪܝܢܐ] ܬܪܝܢܐ OGB

[4] First and second species refer to the protoype noun (πρωτότυπον) and the derived-from-prototype noun (παράγωγον) as in Dionysius (p.10. cf. Amira, *Gramm.*, 105). ܥܠܠܐ and ܥܠܝܠܬܐ are used by Jacob of Edessa for this pair since the former is, as it were, the cause of something's existence, while the latter is the thing caused, just as ܐܕܫܐ refers to a general notion of something, while ܐܕܫܢܐ is what is comprehended by that notion (see p.60). | [5] See p.57,60 for ܬܪܝܢܐ as another name for the derived type in Jacob of Edessa. The clause means "and the caused [type], which is also the second is [such as] heavenly etc." We now have the parallel we sought before (p.57). [6] The third of Dionysius's shapes, the derived-from-a-compound (παρασύνθετον) is omitted.

ܦܣܩ ܒܡܠܐ: ܐܣܘܪ ܘܐܡܪܗ ܘܡܫܪܐ ܕܐܝܟ ܗܠܝܢ܀ ܡܢܝܢܐ ܠܘܬܗ: ܚܕܝܐ
ܘܣܓܝܐ̈ܐ: ܐܝܟܢܐ ܕܐܡܪ: ܦܣܩܐ. ܦ̈ܣܩܐ: ܟܐܦܐ: ܟܐ̈ܦܐ: ܟܬܒܐ: ܟܬ̈ܒܐ܀ ܐܝܬܘܬܐ
ܐܪܒܥ:[1] ܡܥܒܕܢܘܬܐ ܐܝܟܢܐ ܕܐܡܪ: ܦܘܫܩܐ: ܟܬܘܒܐ: ܟܬܘܒܘܬܐ܀ ܚܫܘܫܘܬܐ:
ܩܢܝܢܘܬܐ: ܣܝܡܐ: ܐܒܐ: ܒܥܒܕܐ: ܕܒܝܬܐ: ܩܘܝܐ: ܒܥܒܕܘܬܐ: ܩܢܘܢܘܬܐ:
ܟܝܢܝܘܬܐ: ܡܟܬܒܢܐ: ܡܟܝܠܬܢܐ: ܦܪܘܫܬܐ: ܐܝܟ ܕܐܝܬ ܠܡܐܡܪ: ܙܘܥܐ ܓܘܫܡܐ: ܢܦܫܐ:
ܚܝܐ: ܡܢܝܢܐ: ܦܬܓܡܐ: ܙܘܥܐ ܓܘܫܡܢܝܐ. ܣܘܟܐ܀ ܡܫܘܚܬܐ ܘܦܫܛܐ ܐܝܟܢܐ
ܕܐܡܪ. ܦܫܝܛܐ: ܡܘܫܚܬܐ: ܦܘܫܐ: ܡܥܒܕܐ: ܠܘܬܐ: ܡܬܦܫܛܐ ܕܝܢ ܐܪܒܥ:[2] ܒ: ܕ: ܘ: 4a
ܠ: ܐܝܟܢܐ ܕܐܡܪ: ܒܐܠܗܐ: ܕܐܠܗܐ: ܘܠܐܠܗܐ: ܠܐܠܗܐ:
ܠܡܠܬܐ ܕܝܢ ܢܩܝܦܢ: ܓܢ̈ܣܐ:[3] ܡܢܝܢܐ: ܙܒܢܐ: ܦܪ̈ܨܘܦܐ: ܐܝܬܘܬܐ: ܐܣܟܡܐ܀
ܓܢܣܐ ܕܝܢ ܬܪܝܢ ܐܝܬܝܗܘܢ: ܐܝܟܢܐ ܕܐܡܪ: ܟܬܒ: ܟܬܒܬ: ܟܬܒ: ܟܬܒܢ: ܦܩܕ:
ܦܩܕܬ܀ ܡܢܝܢܐ ܚܕܝܐ ܘܣܓܝܐܐ: ܐܝܟ ܟܬܒ: ܟܬܒܘ: ܫܡܥ: ܫܡܥܘ܀ ܙܒܢܐ
ܕܝܢ ܬܠܬܐ: ܕܥܒܪ: ܘܩܐܡ: ܘܥܬܝܕ:[4] ܕܥܒܪ: ܐܝܟ: ܟܬܒ: ܟܬܒ: ܦܩܕ: ܕܩܐܡ
ܟܬܒ: ܟܬܒ: ܟܬܒ: ܕܥܬܝܕ: ܢܟܬܘܒ: ܢܟܬܘܒ: ܢܟܬܒܘܢ܀ ܦܪ̈ܨܘܦܐ ܕܝܢ ܬܠܬܐ: ܩܕܡܝܐ
ܐܝܟ ܟܬܒܬ ܐܢܐ: ܩܐܡ ܐܢܐ: ܬܪܝܢܐ: ܟܬܒ ܐܢܬ: ܫܡܥ ܐܢܬ: ܩܐܡ ܐܢܬ: ܬܠܝܬܝܐ:
ܟܬܒ: ܩܐܡ: ܫܡܥ: ܐܝܬܘܬܐ ܕܝܢ ܬܪܬܝܢ: ܡܥܒܕܢܘܬܐ: ܐܝܟ: ܦܩܕ: ܦܩܕ:
ܐܬܪ: ܘܚܫܘܫܐ: ܐܝܟ: ܐܬܦܩܕ ܐܬܦܩܕ ܐܬܐܬܪ: ܐܣܟܡܐ ܬܪܝܢ: ܦܫܝܛܐ ܐܝܟ 4b
ܦܩܕ ܐܢܐ ܩܐܡ ܐܢܐ ܐܬܪ ܐܢܐ܀ ܘܡܬܬܪܟܒܢܐ: ܐܝܟ ܡܦܩܕ ܐܢܐ: ܡܦܝܣ ܐܢܐ:
ܡܐܬܪ ܐܢܐ܀[5]
ܠܫܡܐ ܗܝܕܝܢ ܕܝܢ ܢܩܝܦܢ: ܓܢ̈ܣܐ: ܡܢܝܢܐ: ܦܪ̈ܨܘܦܐ: ܐܣܟܡܐ܀[6] ܘܓܢܣܐ ܕܝܢ
ܕܡܬܚܙܝܢ: ܐܝܟ ܐܢܐ: ܐܢܬ: ܗܘ: ܗܝ: ܐܢܬܘܢ: ܗܢܘܢ: ܐܢܬܝܢ: ܗܢܝܢ: ܗܘ ܕܝܢ: ܗܢܘܢ:
ܡܢܝܢܐ ܚܕܝܐ ܘܣܓܝܐܐ ܐܝܟ ܐܢܐ: ܐܢܬ: ܗܘ ܘܗܝ: ܐܢܬܘܢ. ܗܢܘܢ: ܐܢܬܝܢ:

2 ܐܝܬܘܬܐ] ܐܝܬܘܬܐ G 3 ܡܥܒܕܢܘܬܐ] ܡܥܒܕܢܘܬܐ G 6 ܡܫܘܚܬܐ] ܡܫܘܚܬܐ B | ܐܝܟܢܐ]
ܐܝܟ BL 9 ܡܢܝܢܐ ܓܢܣܐ ܢܩܝܦܢ] ܡܢܝܢܐ ܘܓܢܣܐ ܢܩܝܦܢ B 11 ܘܣܓܝܐܐ] ܣܓܝܐܐ G
13 ܟܬܒ] om. OG 16 ܐܬܪ] ܐܬܪ GB | ܦܫܝܛܐ] ܦܫܝܛܐ B ܦܫܝܛܐ L

[1] ܐܝܬܘܬܐ = διαθέσεσι (*states*), of which he enumerates four, namely "active" (ἐνέργεια = ܡܥܒܕܢܘܬܐ), "passive" (πάθος = ܚܫܐ; for these two see Dionysius, p.17), "possessive" (which is one of the species of noun, κτητικῷ = ܩܢܝܢܐ), and "indicators of nature" (ܡܘܕܥܢܘܬܐ ܕܟܝܢܐ = صفة?) which, as the examples show, are in fact names of genera, just as in Greek it is said that "the noun *indicates* either a body or an object" (ὄνομα...σῶμα ἢ πρᾶγμα σημαῖνον). Amira retains these very groupings (p.115) though he describes them in such a way that it is clear that he took them from an ancient and poorly understood source. | [2] On the case, see p.31,13. | [3] In Syriac, gender necessarily had to be added as an attribute of the verb. The Greek "states" (διαθέσεις), which they used also for nouns, they call ܐܝܬܘܬܐ, but they omit "conjugations" (συζυγίας) and "moods" (ἐγκλίσεις), which, however, we come across later on under the rubric of ܡܢܗܓܢܐ (p.ܝ,14). | [4] The parallel Greek terms for the tenses are: ܕܥܒܪ = παρεληλυθώς (*past*), ܕܩܐܡ = ἐνεστώς (*present*); ܕܥܬܝܕ = μέλλων (*future*). | [5] ܦܫܝܛܐ is the "simple" shape (ἁπλοῦν), ܡܬܬܪܟܒܢܐ is the "compound" (σύνθετον). The last, derived-from-a-compound (παρασύνθετον) is omitted. | [6] The attributes of the pronoun do not include case and species. The shapes refers to the difference between the suffixed pronouns (ܢܩܝܦܐ) and the independent pronouns (ܠܚܘܕܝܐ).

ܗܟܢ: ܦܬ̈ܓܡܐ ܕܝܢ ܠܥܠܐ: ܡܕܡܐ: ܐܢܐ: ܚܕܝ: ܠܐܘܪܚܐ: ܐܝܟ: ܐܝܟܢ: ܐܝܟܐ:
ܐܝܟܢ܀ ܠܡܟܠܐ: ܗܘ: ܗܝ: ܗܢܘܢ: ܗܟܢ܀ ܐܣܟܡܐ ܠܘܬ: ܒܡܘܕܝܐ: ܐܝܟ ܐܢܐ:
ܐܢܐ: ܗܘ: ܢܦܫܐ: ܥܒܕ: ܐܘܪ: ܡܠܟܐ: ܒܒܝܬ:

3 ܢܦܫܐ] om. B

ܗ ܠܐܘܪܝ: ܦܠܚܝ: ܚܒܪܗ: ܐܘܪܗ: ܦܠܚܗ: ܚܒܪܟܝ: ܐܘܪܚܟܝ: ܦܠܚܟܝ: ܚܒܪܝܗܘܢ: ܦܠܚܝܗܘܢ: ܘܥܢܕܐ ܕܐܝܟ ܗܠܝܢ܀

ܗܠܝܢ ܕܝܢ ܕܥܠ ܡܠܬܐ:[1] ܡܬܩܪܝܢ ܙܒܢܝܬܐ ܐܝܬܝܗܝܢ: ܐܝܟ ܐܬܡܠ ܗܫܐ: ܗܝܕܝܢ܀ ܡܬܩܪܝܢ ܐܬܪܢܝܬܐ: ܐܝܟ ܐܪܟܐ: ܗܪܟܐ: ܠܗܠ: ܡܬܩܪܝܢ ܠܡܬܚܙܝܢܘܬܐ܀ ܐܘ 5a ܠܡܚܐ ܡܬܩܪܝܢ: ܐܝܟ ܦܣܩܐܝܬ܀ ܡܠܦܦܬܐܝܬ: ܛܒܐܝܬ: ܚܒܝܫܐܝܬ: ܙܗܝܪܐܝܬ܀ ܡܬܩܪܝܢ ܕܐܝܟ ܐܝܟܢܐ ܗܟܢ ܡܢܗ ܡܬܩܪܝܢ ܐܝܟ ܒܪܢܫܐܝܬ: ܛܒܐ: ܐܦ ܠܐ: ܫܦܝܪ ܫܦܝܪ܀ ܡܬܩܪܝܢ ܒܡܢܝܢܘܬܐ ܡܬܩܪܝܢ: ܐܝܟ ܚܕܐ: ܙܒܢ: ܙܒܢܝܢ̈ܬܐ: ܡܠܠܐ ܒܪܢܫܐܝܬ܀ ܡܬܩܪܝܢ ܕܦܘܫܩܐ ܐܝܬܝܗܘܢ ܐܝܟ ܗܟܝܠ: ܟܠܗ ܗܟܝܠ: ܐܟܘܬ: ܗܟܘܬ܀

ܠܡܟܠܒ ܥܡܐ ܕܝܢ ܢܦܩܝܢ: ܒܙܒܢܐ: ܡܢܝܢܐ: ܦܪܨܘܦܐ: ܒܙܒܢܐ ܕܦܪܢܣܐ ܘܢܡܘܣܐ ܐܝܟ ܕܘܟ ܕܘܡܝܐ ܚܘܠܦ ܡܢܝܢܐ ܕܡܢ ܣܪܝܩܐ ܘܦܬܓܡܐ: ܐܝܟ ܚܝܠܐ: ܚܝܠܬܢ: ܢܚܘܬܢ: ܢܚܘܬܝܢ: ܦܪܨܘܦܐ ܕܡܢ ܠܟܠܐ: ܩܕܡܐ: ܕܘܟ ܐܚܪܐ: ܠܘܩܒܠܐ: ܕܘܟ ܐܚܪܐ ܠܐܚܪܢܐ ܕܘܟ ܘܗܠܝܢ ܫܦܩܢ ܐܝܟ ܕܟܬܒܝܢܢ

ܗܘ̈ܠܐ ܕܒܢܝܐ ܥܡܐ ܐܦܝ ܦܘܫܩܐ ܘܡܬܩܪܝܢܘܬܐ ܕܐܝܬ ܠܡܩܪܐ ܘܐܝܟܐ ܒܡܠܬܐ ܗܝ ܡܦܘܪܫܐ

ܦܘܫܐ ܘܐܡܪܝܢ ܕܝܬܝ:[2] ܘܡܬܦܪܫܢ ܗܟܢܐ: ܪܒܨܐ: ܥܨܝܐ: ܦܬܚܐ: ܘܣܩܦܐ: ܘܪܒܘܝ: ܙܩܦܐ: ܘܪܒܨܐ ܦܣܩܐ: ܗܠܝܢ ܗܦܟܐ ܡܬܩܪܝܢܘܬܐ ܐܝܟ ܟܠ ܡܠܬܐ ܘܗܠܐ ܐܫܬܐ: ܥܨܝܐ ܘܡܬܚܬܢ ܘܡܬܚܬܢܐ ܐܚܪܢܐ ܘܠܐ ܐܝܟ ܟܠܗ ܚܕ ܡܢ ܗܠܝܢ ܫܒܥ ܡܬܩܪܝܢܘܬܐ. ܡܠܬܐ ܢܦܩܐ. ܐܬܘܬܐ ܕܝܢ ܐܝܬܝܗܝܢ ܐܝܟ .ܐ. ܘܪ: ܙܩܦܐ: ܘܠܐ: ܗܘ: ܘܦܬܚܐ: ܪܒܨܐ ܕܝܢ ܐܝܬܝܗܝܢ: ܐܝܟ ܝ ܘܝܚܝܕܐ. ܘܚ: ܘܣܩܦܐ: ܦܬܚܐ: ܐܝܟ ܐ ܘܦܬܚܐ: ܗܘ ܘܥܨܝܐ: ܣܩܦܐ: ܐܝܟ ܚ: ܘܪܒܨܐ: ܘܙܩܦܐ: ܥܨܝܐ: ܐܝܟ: ܘ: ܘܐܪܒܘܝ: ܘܡܦܩܢܐ: ܐܝܟ ܘ: ܘܐܒܘܐ ܘܥܨܝܐ ܘܦܬܚܐ ܠܥܠ: ܘܥܨܝܐ ܡܦܩܢܐ: ܠܗܘ ܢܦܩܝܢ: ܣܩܦܐ

2 ܡܬܩܪܝܢ ܕܝܢ [ܡܬܩܪܝܢ L ܚܒܪܗ ܦܠܚܗ ܦܠܚܝܗܘܢ B ܚܒܪܗ ܦܠܚܗ [ܚܒܪܝܗܘܢ ܦܠܚܝܗܘܢ 3 B | ܙܒܢܝܬܐ [ܙܒܢܝܬܐ OG 14 ܡܬܩܪܝܢܘܬܐ [ܘܡܬܩܪܝܢܘܬܐ GB | ܕܐܝܬ [ܠܗ ܕܐܝܬ OG 16 ܕܝܬܝ [ܕܝܬܝ OL 17 ܗܦܟܐ] om. B 18 ܘܡܬܚܬܢ ܘܠܐ [ܘܠܐ ܘܡܬܚܬܢ L 22 ܘܐܪܒܘܝ [ܘܐܪܒܘܝ L(rightly) ܘܐܪܒܘܝ, O | ܘ] om. OG

[1] Compare the adverbial types given here with those in Dionysius (p.21). Barhebraeus's list (p.170) is a little different. Those called here ܦܘܫܩܐ are parallel to the "comparative adverbs" (ἐπιῤῥήματα συγκρίσεως). The ones called "active" and "passive" (ܠܡܬܚܙܝܢܘܬܐ ܐܘ ܚܫܐ, which are usually 'states') are in place of the "middle adverbs". Those described as ܐܝܟ ܐܝܟܢܐ ܗܟܢ, are the adverbs of quality (ποιότης). Those called ܡܢܝܢܘܬܐ are the adverbs of quantity (ποσότης). | [2] For the number of vowels, see David Bar Paulos's theory as explained in Merx, *Grammatica*, 31,38, although he calls o not ܥܨܝܐ, but ܐܣܩܐ. Later in the current text (p.ܟ, 16), these names are confused and require emendation (cf. p.112-3; Barheb., *Gramm.*, 3-4).

ܕܝܢ ܠܚܘܕ܀ ܡܬܦܢܝܢ ܕܝܢ ܗܠܝܢ ܥܠ ܡܬܬܪܝܡܢܘܬܐ: ܒܫܡܗ ܒܗܘ ܡܠܬܐ: ܘܡܬܬܦܝܣܢܘܬܗܘܢ܀ ܐܬܘܬܐ ܕܝܢ ܩܕܡܝܬܐ[1] ܕܫܘܪܝܐ: ܐܠܦ ܐܝܬܝܗܝܢ: ܐ. ܘ:

6a ܝ: ܢܝܟܐ ܕܝܢ ܕܡܢܗܘܢ ܕܦܘܫܚܐ ܐܝܬܝܗܘܢ ܗܟܢܐ܀ ܪܩܝܩܐ: ܐܝܟ ܢܘܩܙܐ ܕܣܝܡܝܢ ܠܟܠ ܡܢ ܬܪܝܢ ܐܝܟ ܝܘܢܐܝܬ: ܠܒܪ ܡܢ ܐܬܘܬܐ ܐܚܪܬܐ ܕܡܬܬܪܡܝܐ ܗܟܢܐ.[2] ܘܬܪܝܢ ܕܝܢ: ܐܝܟ ܢܘܩܙܐ ܕܣܝܡܝܢ ܝܘܢܐܝܬ ܠܟܝܢܐ ܡܢ ܐܬܘܬܐ܀ ܦܬܝܚܐ ܐܘܟܝܬ ܦܽܘܠܽܘܪܳܐ: ܐܝܟ ܢܘܩܙܐ ܕܣܝܡܝܢ ܚܕ ܡܢ ܠܥܠ: ܘܚܕ ܡܢ ܠܬܚܬ܀ ܣܬܝܪܐ ܕܝܢ ܐܝܬܝܗܘܢ ܢܘܩܙܐ ܚܕ ܕܡܬܬܣܝܡ ܠܟܝܢܐ ܡܢ ܠܥܠ. ܚܒܝܫܐ ܕܝܢ ܐܝܬܝܗܘܢ: ܢܘܩܙܐ ܚܕ ܕܡܬܬܣܝܡ ܠܬܚܬ ܡܢ ܗܘ܀ ܠܡܬܚܐ ܐܪܝܟ: ܢܘܩܙܐ ܕܡܬܬܣܝܡ ܠܟܝܢܐ ܡܢ ܗܘ: ܡܬܚܬܝܐ ܕܝܢ: ܬܠܬܐ ܕܝܢ ܢܘܩܙܐ ܦܫܝܛܝܢ ܦܘܫܩܐ ܕܠܐܬܘܬܐ: ܣܛܪ ܢܘܩܙܐ ܗܠܝܢ ܕܫܡܝܢ: ܐܦܝܢ ܠܗ ܠܘܬ ܡܦܩܦܩܝܢ: ܐܒܛܐ ܕܝܢ ܗܘ ܐܦܝܣܛܐ ܘܡܢܗܘܢ ܕܐܬܘܬܐ ܦܫܝܛܐ[3] ܦܫܝܛܝܢ ܠܗܘܢ ܕܝܢ ܟܠ ܡܫܡܥܐ. ܐܝܟ ܗܠܝܢ ܕܒܝܬ ܢܝܬܘܢ: ܠܗܘܢ: ܡܦܝܩܐ ܠܐܘܪܝܟ ܩܛܝܢܬܐ: ܟܠܦ ܦܘܩܕܢܐ: ܗܝܢ ܒܠܚܘܕ

6b ܠܟܠ ܐܬܘܬܐ ܕܢܘܩܙܐ: ܠܐ ܕܝܢ ܗܘܐ: ܗܝܢ ܒܠܚܘܕ ܐܘ ܚܬܐ: ܗܟܢܐ ܘܐܦ ܐܝܟܢܐ: ܗܝܢ ܟܠ ܠܟܠ ܦܘܩܕܢܐ: ܐܝܟ ܐܬܘܬܐ ܕܩܢܝܐ: ܟܠ ܐܒܐ ܕܝܢ ܐܡܗܐ: ܟܠ ܐܒܪܐ ܕܝܢ ܐܒܗ:[4] ܘܗܟܢ ܗܟܢܐ܀

ܠܘܬ ܕܝܢ ܙܘܥ ܠܥܒܕܐ:[5] ܘܗܠܝܢ ܡܬܬܪܓܡܢܘܬܐ: ܐܘ ܢܦܩܝܢ ܡܢ ܫܡܐ: ܐܝܟ ܒ: ܗܘ: ܕܒܥܒܪܐ ܘܐܬܝܗܘܢ ܡܬܦܩܕܬܐ ܡܢ ܦܪܘܫܘܬܐ ܕܫܡܗܝܢ: ܘܐܝܟ: ܗܘ ܕܫܡܗܐ: ܗܘ: ܕܡܠܬܐ: ܘܐܝܬܝܗܘܢ ܕܝܠܝܬܐ ܡܢ ܦܪܘܫܘܬܐ ܕܫܡܗܝܢ. ܘܐܝܟ ܒ: ܕܦܬܐ. ܗܘ ܕܦܬܐ. ܕܦܬܝܚ ܡܢ ܦܪܘܫܘܬܐ ܕܫܡܗܝܢ܀ ܐܘ ܕܟܠ ܫܡܐ ܟܠܗ: ܡܐ ܕܗܘܐ ܡܢ ܡܠܬܐ ܐܘܟܝܬ ܫܘܪܝܐ ܕܡܬܬܪܓܡܝܐ ܒܗ ܕܫܡܐ: ܐܚܪܝܢ: ܕܒ:

1 ܡܬܦܢܝܢ] ܘܡܬܡܣܟܢ BL 2 ܐܠܦ ܐܝܬܝܗܝܢ] ܐܝܬܝܗܘܢ ܐܠܦܐ OGB 3 ܢܝܟܐ] ܡܢܝܟܐ B 4 ܗܟܢܐ] no point OG 5 ܦܘܠܘܪܐ] ܦܘܠܘܪܐ G 7 ܐܝܬܝܗܘܢ] lac. here in OG, supplied by G marg.; om. BL | ܚܕ[2]] om. BL 8 ܢܘܩܙܐ] ܢܘܩܙܐ O 9 ܘܘ] ܘܘ OL 12 ܟܠܦ] ܦܠܟ G 13 ܐܘ ܚܬܐ] ܐܘ ܚܬܐ OBL, read ܐܘ ܚܬܐ (i.e. omicron) 14 ܐܒܐ] ܐܒܐ L 15 ܐܒܗ] ܐܒܗ L | ܘܗܟܢ] ܗܟܢ B 18 ܘܫܡܗܐ] ܫܡܗܐ L | ܘܐܝܬܝܗܘܢ] ܐܝܟ ܐܝܬܝܗܘܢ OG

[1] See also p.ܟܗ,18. This seems to be a unique expression. | [2] The expected example is absent from all mss. | [3] Again, the expected examples are lacking. | [4] Here ܐ is υ and ܘ is ο, making the diphthong ου. Before, ܐ was for ε. | [5] In what follows we can see that for the Syrians the noun, rather than the verb, was the basis of etymology. Compare ܝ,9 and ܠ,3 - question no.12, which attempts to prove that the noun is primary and the verb derivative (see also ܟܚ,15; Bekker, *Anecdota* II,880, III,1024,1271,1275; Steinthal, *Geschichte der Sprachwissenschaft bei den Alten*, 591). There was a dispute between the Arab grammarians of the Kufan school and the Basran on the nature of maṣdar.

ܘܐܝܟ ܕܒܟܬܒܐ. ܘܒܗ ܕܣܝܡܘܬܗ[1] ܐܝܬܘܗܝ ܙܒܢܐ: ܟܕ ܕܝܢ ܐܬܦܪܫ ܒܟܝܢ: ܘܡܫܬܘܕܥ ܥܠ ܡܘܟܟܐ ܕܥܒܘܕܘܬܐ ܘܕܥܒܘܕܐ ܘܕܚܫܐ ܘܕܟܢ: ܗܘܐ ܗܟܝܠ ܗܘ: ܦ̈: ܙܒܢܐ ܕܦܩܕܐ: ܦܠܓܘܬܐ ܕܡܠܬܐ܀ ܗܘܝܐ ܟܕ ܐܡܪ ܐܢܐ. ܡܛܠ ܕܥܒܘܕܐ ܘܠܐ 7a
ܒܥܒܕܐ ܐܬܦܠܓܬ ܕܥܒܘܕܘܬܗ: ܕܟܕ ܕܡܫܬܘܕܥ ܥܠ ܙܒܢܐ ܕܩܐܡ: ܗܘܐ ܒܗ ܗܘ: ܒ. ܒܢܝܢܗ ܕܥܒܕܐ: ܒܗ ܙܒܢܐ ܘܒܟܝܢ: ܕܡܫܬܘܕܥܐ ܥܠ ܙܒܢܐ ܕܥܒܝܪ. ܦ̈. ܐܝܬܘܗ ܕܥܒܕܬܐ܀

ܐܬܦܠܓܬ ܕܝܢ ܡܛܠ ܟܕ ܗܟܢ: ܘܫܡܗܐ ܡܬܬܪܫܝܢ ܒܗܠܝܢ ܡܬܬܪܫܢܘܬܐ ܘܡܬܝܪܝܢ. ܒܗ ܒܐܫܟܢܐ ܘܫܡܗܘܗܝ: ܡܛܠ ܘܐܝܬܘܗܝ ܐܝܟ ܡܬܐܫܬܐ ܠܫܘܚܠܦܐ: ܩܠܐ ܕܝܢ ܐܝܟܢ ܘܡܢܗܘܢ ܘܫܡܗܐ ܐܝܟ ܘܡܬܬܚܘܟܡܢܐ ܡܬܐܡܪܝܢ. ܡܬܐܡܪܝܢ ܠܗ ܒܗ ܟܕ ܒܗ ܕܒܪܐ: ܐܠܐ ܕܡܫܬܢܐ ܘܐܫܬܢܝܐ. ܘܐܝܟ ܐܢܫ܀

ܟ ܟܠ ܦܠܓܘܬܐ ܕܐܝܬܘܗܝ ܠܬܠܬ ܐܬܘܬܐ:[2] ܐܘ ܕܩܕܡ ܗܘܐ: ܐܘ ܦܠܓܐ ܡܢ ܟܠ ܦܪܨܘܦ: ܕܩܕܡ: ܐܝܟ: ܢܦܩ. ܩܡ: ܐܙܠ: ܪܕ: ܩܡ: ܦܠܓܐ ܕܝܢ ܐܝܟ ܒܟܠ: ܐܘܗ. ܚܪ܀ ܠܝ ܘܡܢ ܚܕܪܝܐ ܘܩܐܡ ܐܘ ܕܥܒܝܕ:[3] ܘܡܛܠ ܣܟܠܐ ܠܡܫܬܘܕܥܘ ܡܬܒܥܝܐ: 7b
ܕܦܠܓܝܐ ܚܕܐ ܗܝ ܢܦܫܐ: ܕܩܕܡܐ ܕܝܢ: ܠܬܠܬ ܐܝܟ ܒܟܠ: ܕܐܟܠ: ܐܘܗ ܘܐܘܗܝ. ܚܪ. ܚܪܢ. ܘܐܝܟ ܢܦܩ. ܢܦܩܝܢ: ܩܡ: ܩܡܝܢ: ܐܒܕ: ܐܒܕܝܢ: ܪܕ: ܪܕܝܢ: ܫܩܠ. ܫܩܠܝܢ܀ ܠܘܬ ܕܝܢ ܕܩܕܡܐ ܘܦܠܓܐ: ܒܡܠܬܐ ܡܫܬܚܠܦܐ ܦܫܝܛܘܬܐ: ܡܬܦܪܫܝܢ ܕܦܫܛܐ ܕܡܠܬܗܘܢ ܦܬܓܡܐ: ܕܚܘ̈ܢܝܐ ܘܦܫܝܛܐ: ܘܕܢܝܐ: ܘܡܬܚܠܦܐ: ܘܐܝܟ ܐܢܫ. ܕܐܡܪ: ܡܢ ܩܡ ܩܐܡ: ܩܡܬ: ܩܡܬܐ: ܡܬܡܟܢ: ܐܒܕ ܐܒܕܝܢ: ܐܙܠ: ܐܙܠܐ: ܐܬܐ ܘܡܦܪܫܐ ܘܐܝܟ ܗܟܢ: ܘܡܢ ܒܟܠ: ܕܐܡܪ ܐܟܠ: ܐܟܠܝܢ: ܐܟܠܐ: ܐܟܠܢ: ܐܘܗ. ܐܘܗ: ܐܘܗܝܢ: ܐܘܗܐ: ܐܘܗܢ: ܗܟܢ ܕܝܢ ܕܦܪܫܐ ܒܗܠܝܢ ܬܪܬܝܢ܀ ܘܩܕܡܐ ܒܡܦܪܫ: ܕܟܠ ܡܠܬܐ ܕܝܢ ܡܬܦܠܓܐ ܘܢܦܠ ܒܗ ܠܬܠܬ ܩܢܘܡ: ܐܘ ܠܬܠܬ ܦܪܨܘܦ: ܡܫܬܘܕܥܐ ܥܠ ܕܩܕܡ: ܐܝܟ ܦܩܕܝܢ: ܢܦܩܘܢ: ܢܦܩܝܢ: ܢܣܩܘܢ: ܐܡܪܝܢ: ܢܐܡܪܘܢ: ܬܐܡܪܝܢ: ܢܐܙܠܘܢ: ܘܐܝܟ: ܢܐܙܠܘܢ: ܗܟܢ ܡܫܬܒܚܢܐ ܕܩܕܡܐ

3 ܟܕ] ܘܟܕ L   4 ܕܥܒܘܕܘܬܗ] ܒܥܒܘܕܘܬܐ B | ܗܘܐ] ܗܘܐ ܕܝܢ BL   14 ܣܟܠܐ] om. B | ܠܡܫܬܘܕܥܘ] ܠܡܫܬܘܕܥܘ L   15 ܢܦܫܐ] ܢܦܫܐ GB | ܐܘܗ: ܐܘܗܝ: ܚܪ: ܚܪܢ G   17 ܦܫܝܛܘܬܐ] ܦܫܝܛܘܬܐ L   19 ܡܬܡܟܢ] om. OG | ܐܡܪܐ] ܐܡܪܐ G

[1] ܣܝܡܘܬܐ is almost the correct etymological equivalent for διάθεσις. | [2] On the classification of verbs, see p.133,167. | [3] Something is missing here. The addition of ܗܘܝܐ would suffice.

ܣ ܐܢܘܢ: ܘܟܠ ܕܚܕܐ: ܗ̄ܗ̄: ܘܚܕܐ ܡܢܗ: ܦܬܚܐ ܢ̈ܗܘܐ:[1] ܐܝܟ ܐܟܠܝܢ: ܢܟܠܘܢ: ܬ̈ܐܟܠܝܢ: ܢܐܟܠܢ: ܐܟܘܠ: ܢܟܠܘܢ: ܘܟܠܗܝܢ ܡܫܬܘ̈ܕܥܢܐ ܕܦܬܚܐ ܐܢܘܢ܀[2] ܠܘܬ ܕܝܢ ܕܝܠܗ: ܕܗܠܝܢ ܠܐܪܒܥ ܐܬܘ̈ܬܐ ܕܡܫܬܘܕܥܢ ܐܟܠܐ ܕܥܬܝܕ: ܕܐܬܐܡܪܢ: ܐ: ܢ: ܬ: ܒܗܘܢ ܡܬܚܠܦܐ ܢܩܫܝܢ: ܦܬܚܐ ܕܝܢ ܘܪܒܨܐ: ܕܐܝܟ ܐܢܬ: ܐܬܐܡܪ: ܡܢ ܐܒܕ: ܬܐܒܕ: ܢܐܒܕ: ܡܐܒܕ: ܬܐܒܕܘܢ: ܢܐܒܕܘܢ: ܩܡ: ܬܩܘܡ: ܢܩܘܡ: ܡܩܝܡ: ܢܩܘܡܘܢ: ܬܩܘܡܘܢ: ܘܡܢ ܟܕ ܐܬܐܡܪ: ܢܟܬܘܒ ܐܟܬܘܒ ܢܟܬܒܘܢ ܐܟܬܒܘܢ ܡܟܬܒ: ܟܬܒ: ܢܟܬܒܘܢ: ܬܟܬܒܘܢ: ܡܟܬܒܘ:[3] ܠܡܟܬܒ: ܢܟܬܒܘܢ܀ ܚܢܢ ܕܝܢ ܠܝ ܒܦܪܨܘܦܐ ܠܐܟܬܒܐ ܢܡܠ̈ܠܢ ܡܫܬܘܕܥܢܐ ܡܟܬܒܐ: ܘܦܘܬܚܐ ܕܡܟܬܒܐ ܠܐ ܡܬܡܠܟܐ: ܐܝܟ ܬܫܟܚ: ܬܫܟܚ: ܬܫܟܚ: ܬܪܐ: ܬܫܟܚ: ܦܬܚܐ ܕܝܢ: ܡܬܡܠܟܐ ܦܬܚܗ ܠܬܚܬ: ܐܝܟ ܐܬܐܡܪ: ܡܢ ܢܦܩ ܢܦܩ: ܟܠ: ܢܟܠ: ܟܒ: ܢܟܒ܀

ܗܟܢܐ ܘܗܢܐ ܦܬܚܐ ܢܦܩ ܠܦܪܨܘܦܐ ܡܛܠ ܣܓ̈ܝܐܐ ܕܐܝܟ ܐܢܬ: ܟܒܐ: ܡܢ ܟܒ: ܢܟܒ ܡܢ ܟܠ: ܘܢܦܩܐ ܡܢ ܢܦܩ: ܢܦܩ: ܬܦܩ: ܬܦܩ: ܘܢܦܩ܀

ܠܘܬ ܕܝܢ: ܘܘ: ܕܡܫܬܘܕܥܐ ܠܐܟܠܐ ܕܥܬܝܕ ܘܦܘܩܕ̈ܢܐ: ܒܪܘܫܐ ܒܫܡܐ ܠܗܘܐ: ܘܒܦܬܚܐ ܚܒ̈ܝܫܐ:[4] ܐܝܟ ܢܪܘܙ ܡܢ ܪܙ: ܘܢܩܘܡ: ܘܩܘܡ ܘܢܩܘܡܘܢ: ܘܐܝܟ ܢܪܘܙ ܡܢ ܪܙ ܪܘܙܐ: ܘܪܘܙ: ܘܩܘܠ ܘܢܩܘܠ ܘܩܘܠ܀

ܠܘܬ ܕܝܢ: ܗ̄ܗ̄ ܕܩܕܡ ܬܠ̈ܬ: ܒܩܛܠܐ ܕܡܫܬܘ̈ܕܥܝܢ ܐܟܠܐ ܕܥܬܝܕ ܘܦܩܝܕ̈ܢܝܬܐ: ܒܚܒܝܫܐ ܠܗܘܐ: ܘܬܠܬ: ܕܩܕܡ ܬܠ̈ܬ: ܒܩܛܠܐ ܕܡܫܬܘ̈ܕܥܝܢ ܐܟܠܐ ܕܥܬܝܕ ܘܦܩܝܕ̈ܢܝܬܐ: ܡܚܒܝܫܐ ܠܗܘܐ: ܐܝܟ ܒܚܠܦܝܢ: ܒܟܠܗܘܢ ܢܩܫܘܢ: ܗܕܐ ܕܝܢ: ܐܝܟ ܬܫܟܚ: ܦܩܘܕܘܢ: ܪܡܘܢ: ܢܫܩܘܢ܀

1 ܦܬ̈ܚܐ] ܪ̈ܒܨܐ BL 2 ܕܦܬܚܐ ܐܢܘܢ] ܪ̈ܒܨܐ G 3 ܐܟܠܐ] om. B 4 ܒܪܘܫܐ om. G after ܐܒܕ add ܗܘܒ OG 5 ܬܐܒܕ...ܢܐܒܕܘܢ] twice rpt G | ܡܐܒܕ] ܡܐܒܕ OG 6 ܢܩܘܡ om. B | ܡܩܝܡ] sic | ܬܩܘܡܘܢ om. B 7 ܢܟܬܘܒ...ܡܟܬܒ] ܢܟܬܘܒ ܬܟܬܘܒ ܢܟܬܘܒ ܡܟܬܒ ܢܟܬܒܘܢ ܐܟܬܘܒ ܢܟܬܘܒ G txt L ܬܟܬܒܘܢ ܡܟܬܒ B 8 ܡܟܬܒܘ] corrupt (see note) 16 ܒܫܡܐ...ܚܒ̈ܝܫܐ] ܒܚܒܝܫܐ...ܒܪܘܫܐ OGBL (see note) 17 ܢܪܘܙ] ܢܪܘܙ (without the point) OG | ܘܪܘܙ...18 ܘܩܘܠ] ܘܩܘܠ ܘܢܩܘܠ ܘܩܘܡ ܘܪܘܙ OG 20 ܘܦܩܝܕ̈ܢܝܬܐ] ܦܩܝܕܢܝܬܐ L 21 ܐܟܠܐ] om. B | ܘܦܩܝܕ̈ܢܝܬܐ] ܦܩܝܕܢܝܬܐ L

[1] The folio beginning here is missing in O. | [2] All mss have suffered severe corruption - the section deals with the vowel on the prefix of the imperfect, which is ܪ̈ܒܨܐ. | [3] Both ܡܟܬܒ and ܡܟܬܒܘ are out of place here. It is the future tense that is in question here, hence these examples of the infinitive are inappropriate. I cannot see why ܡ is included among the prefixes of the future. The participle is not in view here, although G twice reads ܡܐܒܕ. | [4] Cf. p.ܗ,17 and the usage of this ܚܒ̈ܝܫܐ at p.ܣ,20 which is correct in the mss, since ܒܪܘܫܐ is u = ܘ, while ܪ̈ܒܨܐ is ܘ. All mss are wrong at this point.

ܓ ܒ ܠܗܘܢ ܕܝܢ ܘܟܠ ܦܠܓܘܬܐ ܕܡܬܢܝܢ ܡܢ ܠܚܕܐ ܐܬܘܬܐ: ܘܡܫܟܚܘܢ ܠܡܬܚܒܪܐ
ܕܚܕ: ܐܘ ܥܡܐ ܐܬܘܬܐ ܡܦܩܬܐ. ܐܘ ܦܬܝܚܐ. ܘܦܫܝܛܐ ܐܘ ܙܩܝܦ ܡܬܥܒܛܐ.
ܐܘ ܦܬܝܚܐ: ܐܝܟ ܢ̈ܓܠܐ: ܩܢ̈ܐ: ܡܩ̈ܛܐ: ܥܡܠܐ: ܚܪܒ: ܗܦܟ: ܐܝܟ ܕܗܘ ܐܘ ܙܩܝܦ
ܡܥܢܝܐ ܡܓܠܝܐ: ܗܘ ܕܒܥܒܪܬܐ[1] ܠܗܘܐ ܠܟܠ ܕܝܢ ܘܚܒܪܬܐ: ܗܘ ܡܢ ܐܝܟ ܝܘܢܣ: 9a
ܡ̈ܠܟ: ܡܩ̈ܛܐ: ܗܘܐ ܕܝܢ: ܐܝܟ ܐܬܐ: ܐܪܥܐ: ܐܡܪ܀ ܠܗܘܢ ܕܝܢ: ܐܬܘܬܐ ܠܙܩܝܦܬܐ:
ܐܡܪܝܢܢ ܐܘ ܙܩܝܦܬܐ ܠܗܘܐ: ܐܘ ܦܬܝܚܬܐ:[2] ܐܝܟ ܐܝܬ ܐܝܟ ܚܠܘܦ ܠܟܠ. ܘܡܬܠܬܐ
ܠܗܘܐ: ܐܝܟ ܕܠܐ ܡܬܐ ܕܝܬܐ ܘܕܚܠܝܢ ܕܫܡܥܝܢ ܡܫܡܥܐ: ܒܗ ܟܠ ܦܪ̈ܘܩܐ
ܘܕܗܘܢ ܡܛܠܡܪܐ: ܗܘ ܡܬܡܠܐ ܘܡܬܡܠܐ ܗܘܐ: ܐܝܟ ܚ̈ܟܝܡ: ܢ̈ܚܬ: ܐܬ̈ܐ: ܚܟ̈ܝܡ:
ܦܬܝܚ: ܚܒܪܐ: ܚܒ̈ܪܐ: ܘܗܠܝܢ ܠܘܬ ܐܬ̈ܘܬܐ ܕܡܫܘܕܥܢ ܡܬܐ ܘܚܠܝܢ: ܗ̄: ܐ:
ܢ: ܠ:[3] ܠܚܠܝܗܝܢ ܙܩܝܦܬܐ ܢܣܒܢ ܒܗ̇ܘ ܒܐܘܡܢܐ: ܒܗ ܟܠ ܦܪ̈ܘܩܐ ܘܕܗܘܢ
ܡܛܠܡܪܐ ܡܠܟܐ: ܐܬܪܐ ܘܐܚܪܢ: ܐܬܪܐ: ܠܐܬܪܐ: ܢܥܦܠ: ܢܫܪܘܢ: ܠܐܬܪܘܢ ܠܐܬܪܘܢ:
ܢܬܟ̈ܫܢ: ܢܟ̈ܢܘܢ: ܢܪ̈ܓܐ: ܘܡܥܢܝܐ ܘܐܝܟ ܗܟܢ: ܘܗܘ ܕܦܬܝܚܐ ܐܘ ܚܒܪ ܠܡܫܡܥ.
ܐܘ ܦܬܝܚܐ: ܐܝܟ ܢܣܒ: ܙ̇ܒܢ: ܫܡܥ: ܣܝܡ: ܦܬܚ: ܒܗܘܢ ܐܢܐ ܐܦ ܡܠܟܐ 9b
ܘܐܢܫ ܐܬܘܬܐ ܘܡܢ ܢܩܦܐ ܒܗܘܢ ܡܬܚܫܒܢ: ܐܝܟ ܠܗܘܐ ܐܬܘܬܐ ܠܙܩܝܦܬܐ ܗ̄ܘ̄:
ܦܬܚ ܒܗܘܢ ܘܡܬܡܠܐ: ܐܝܟ ܡ̈ܠܟ: ܐܘܝܠ[4] ܐܘܕܥ: ܐܘܚܕ: ܐܘܣܦ: ܐܘܥܠ:[5]
ܘܐܝܟ ܒܥܐ: ܦܪܐ: ܣܓܐ: ܒܢܐ: ܟܠܐ:[6] ܘܟܠ ܡܠܟܐ ܘܐܬܘܬܐ ܢܩܦܐ ܡܢ ܐܘܟܝ
ܐܬܘܢ: ܘܡܫܬܢܝܢ ܒܗܘܐ ܠܟܠ ܙܩܝܦܬܐ ܠܗܘܐ ܐܝܟ ܐܬܝܠܕ: ܐܬܟܢܫ: ܐܬܩܘܡ:
ܐܬܬܘܡ: ܘܡܠܟܐ ܕܡܫܘܕܥܢ ܦܪ̈ܘܩܐ ܡܦܩܬܐ: ܐܝܟ ܙܩܝܦ ܡܥܢܝܐ: ܦܪܘܩ
ܐܘ ܒܦܬܝܚܐ: ܐܘ ܒܪܒܝܐ ܘܐܡܪ: ܐܚܘܪ: ܐܬܒܥ: ܐܬܐ: ܐܘܪܐ: ܐܣܝܐ ܘܡܥܢܝܐ ܘܐܝܟ
ܗܠܝܢ: ܐܝܟ ܐܝܬܘܗܝ ܡܠܟܐ ܠܚܠܝܬܐ ܐܬܘܬܐ ܘܚܕܐ ܡܢ ܗܠܝܢ ܐܘܟܝ
ܡܫܬܡܥܐ ܒܫܪܝܬܗ: ܗ̄: ܚ̄: ܟ̄: ܙ̄: ܗܘ ܕܡܫܘܕܥ ܦܬܝܚܬܐ ܠܗܘܐ ܡܢ ܟܠ
ܦܪ̈ܘܩܐ: ܐܠܐ ܠܝ ܒܗܘ̈ܢܝܐ ܕܒܢ̈ܝܬܐ: ܐܝܟ ܟܘܟ̈ܒܐ:[7] ܡܢ ܟܘܟܒܐ: ܘܐܝܟ ܩܘܩܝܣ
ܐܝܟ ܐܝܬ ܩܕܡ ܚܕܐ ܡܢ ܗܠܝܢ ܗܘ ܕܒܥܒܪܬܐ: ܐܘ ܗ̄ ܠܐ ܕܡܬܦܩܬܐ ܐܝܟ ܝܘܢܣ:
ܘܝܩܘܕ:

2 ܐܬܘܬܐ...ܘܦܫܝܛܐ] om. OGB (homoeoteleuton, cf. Barheb., *Gramm.*, 104f.) txt L | ܙܩܝܦ] ܙܩܝܦ B 3 ܚܪܒ] ܚܒܪ B 4 ܗܘ ܕܒܥܒܪܬܐ] ?read ܗܘ ܕܚܒܪܬܐ (see note) 6 ܚܠܘܦ] ܚܠܘܦ G 9 ܚܒܪܐ] ܚܒܪ B | ܠܚܠܝܗܝܢ] om. B 11 ܠܐܬܪܘܢ] om. L 12 ܢܬܟ̈ܫܢ] ܢܬܟܫ B | ܘܦܬܝܚܐ] ܘܦܬܝܚܐ L | ܠܡܫܡܥ] ܠܡܫܡܥ B ܠܡܫܡܥ L 19 ܐܘ om. twice OG | ܐܣܝܐ] ܐܣܝܐ B 22 ܩܘܩܝܣ] ܘܩܘܩܝܣ B

[1] I have not entered my conjecture into the text since the same reading is found elsewhere (p.ܓ,24; ܝ,21; cf. against ܝ,7). The scribe of L preceded me for he has in his margin ܚܒ̈ܪ ܗܘ ܕܚܒܪܬܐ. | [2]An example with an o vowel, such as ܩܘܡ, is missing. | [3] ܢ not here treated as an imperfect prefix (cf. ܝ,3,7). | [5] John Bar Zuʿbi points these Aphel forms with ܙܩܦܐ (see p.173). | [6] This set of examples does not belong here. Either there has been a scribal error or the text has a lacuna. [7] The scribe clearly derives ܟܘܟ̈ܒܐ from the root ܟܘܟܒ, but nouns and verbs are not treated separately.

10a ܗܢܘܢ ܕܝܢ ܐܝܟ ܦܠܚ: ܡܬܦܠܚ: ܦܪܩ: ܡܬܦܪܩ: ܚܒܪ: ܡܬܚܒܪ: ܒܪܗ: ܡܬܒܪܗ. ܘܫܪܟܐ ܕܐܝܟ ܗܠܝܢ܀ ܐܝܟ ܐܝܬ ܒܡܫܠܡܢܘܬܗ ܕܡܠܬܐ: ܐ: ܟܠ ܚܕ: ܕܗܘܐ ܒܗ ܡܬܬܚܡܐ ܘܟܠ ܗܝ ܕܡܫܚܠܦܐ[1] ܠܗܘܐ ܕܐܝܟ ܗܠܝܢ: ܢܦܩܕ: ܢܦܩܕܝ: ܢܦܩܕܘܢ: ܦܩܕ: ܡܬܦܩܕ: ܢܦܩܕ: ܒܪܡ ܒܦܘܩܕܐ ܡܬܐܡܪܐ ܘܐܝܟ ܗܠܝܢ: ܦܩܕ: ܦܩܘܕܘܢ: ܦܩܘܕܝ: ܘܐܝܟ ܗܠܝܢ: ܘܟܠ ܚܕܐ ܕܐܝܬ ܒܫܘܠܡܗ ܠܐܦ: ܘܢܩܦܬ ܒܗ ܟܠܗܘܢ ܐܬܘܬܐ ܗܠܝܢ ܡܢ: ܐ: ܒܟܠ ܚܕ: ܐܘ ܗܘ: ܘܢܦܠܐ ܒܗ: ܡܬܬܒܪܐ[2] ܡܢ ܟܠ ܦܬܓܡ: ܗܠܝܢ ܡܢ ܦܘܩܕܢܐ: ܡܬܠܝܢ ܘܗܘܐ ܦܘܢܐ ܡܬܟܢܫ ܠܗܘ ܕܡܢ ܦܘܩܕܢܐ: ܘܐܝܟ ܐܢܬ: ܐܫܬܡܥ: ܫܡܥܘ: ܫܡܥܘܢ: ܢܫܡܥܘܢ: ܢܫܡܥܘܢܗܝ: ܡܫܬܡܥܝܢ: ܢܫܡܥܢܗ: ܫܡܥܝܢ ܐܢܘܢ: ܡܫܬܥܠ: ܡܫܬܥܠܝܢ: ܡܫܬܥܠܝܢ ܐܢܘܢ: ܢܫܬܥܠܘܢ: ܢܫܬܥܠܘܢ: ܦܘܩܕܢܐ ܠܐܡܪ: ܫܡܥܝܗ ܦܪܘܩܝܗ: ܦܩܘܕܝܗ: ܩܛܘܠܝܗ

10b ܩܛܠܐ ܕܝܢ ܕܦܘܩܕܢܐ ܠܦܪܨܘܦܐ ܚܪܝܢܐ ܡܬܐܡܪܝܢ: ܐܘܟܝܬ ܠܐܬܘܬܐ ܕܡܫܬܘܕܥܐ ܒܪܫܐ ܕܡܠܬܐ: ܘܡܬܐܡܪܝܢ ܕܦܬܝܚ ܦܘܩܕ: ܟܕ ܠܐ ܡܬܕܪܟܐ ܐܝܬ ܙܘܥܐ[3] ܕܡܠܬܐ: ܐܝܟ ܗܠܝܢ: ܫܡܥ ܫܡܥ: ܙܡܪ: ܐܫܬܡܥ܀ ܐܝܟ ܕܒܫܪܝܬܐ ܘܒܡܨܥܬܐ ܒܗ ܚܕܐ ܢܩܫܐ: ܡܠܬܐ ܦܘܩܕܢܐ: ܘܐܝܬ ܒܗ ܗܘ ܕܠܐ ܢܩܫܐ. ܠܐ ܡܬܕܪܟܢܐ ܙܘܥܐ ܕܡܬܬܪܝܨܢܘܬܐ: ܐܝܟ ܗܠܝܢ: ܙܒܢ: ܒܗܠܝܢ: ܫܡܥܘ ܚܕܐ ܘܙܒܢܐ ܒܗܠܝܢ ܫܡܥܘܗ ܫܡܥܬܐܝܬ܀

ܐܝܟ ܐܬܘܬܐ ܕܦܬܝܚܬܐ ܘܡܠܬܐ ܡܫܬܠܡܐ ܐܝܬܝܗ: ܡܫܡܥܢܐ ܡܠܬܐ ܒܡܐܡܪܐ ܦܘܩܕܢܐ: ܐܚܪܢܐ ܕܡܢ ܐܫܬܥܠܝ ܐܫܬܥܠܝ: ܘܡܢ ܐܬܚܕ: ܐܬܚܕܘ: ܐܬܦܪܩ: ܐܬܟܢܫ: ܐܫܬܡܥܘ܀

ܐܝܟ ܠܦܪܨܘܦܐ ܚܪܝܢܐ ܦܬܝܚ ܐܝܬ: ܒܡܠܬܐ ܕܐܝܬ ܒܗ .ܐ. ܦܘܩܕ ܒܗܘ ܒܪܝܬܐ: ܐܟܢ: ܦܩܕ: ܒܥܒܕ: ܙܒܢ: ܚܫܒ܀ ܐܝܟ ܗܘ ܐܝܬ ܒܡܫܠܡܢܘܬܗ ܕܡܠܬܐ: ܦܘܩܕ ܩܠܦ ܘܐܝܬܘܗܝ ܒܠܘ ܕܡܩܒܠܐ: ܐܝܟ ܢܩܫܐ: ܐܬܟܪ܀ ܐܝܟ ܠܫܠܡܐ ܦܘܩܕܐ:

11a ܣܠܩ ܠܘܬ ܚܕ ܒܗ ܡܬܩܛܠܐ ܦܘܩܕ: ܐܟܢ ܢܩܫܘ: ܐܘܗܘ: ܐܝܟ ܠܦܪܨܘܦܐ[4]

1 ܬܒܪ] ܚܒܪ G | ܡܬܚܒܪ] om. B 3 ܡܬܬܚܡܐ] ܡܬܚܡܐ OGBL | ܗܘܐ] ܗܘܝܐ G 4 ܦܩܘܕ] ܦܩܕ L 9 ܡܫܬܥܠܝܢ B; OG om. 10 ܢܫܬܥܠܘܢ] B; OG om. 13 ܕܦܬܝܚ] ܕܦܬܚܝܢ L | ܙܘܥܐ] ܙܘܥܐ B 19 ܦܘܩܕܢܐ] ܦܘܩܕܐ L | ܘܡܢ ܐܫܬܥܠܝ ܐܫܬܥܠܝ] ܘܡܢ ܐܫܬܥܠܝ ܐܫܬܥܠܝ B ܘܡܢ ܐܫܬܥܠܝ L | ܐܬܦܪܩ ܐܬܟܢܫ ܒ ܐܬܟܢܫ ܐܫܬܡܥܘ L 23 ܩܠܦ] ܩܠܦ B and always ܐܫܬܡܥܘ] ܐܫܬܡܥܘܗܝ ܐܬܟܢܫ ܒ L

[1] See ܛ,11; ܟ,4; also Merx, *Grammatica*, 31. | [2] This term applies to waw, just as ܚܪܝܬܐ to yudh (p. ܓ,3). | [3] = ἐγκλίσει, hence the correct reading. | [4] Note the double quššaya on this word (cf. p.118f. on the various pronunciations of the letter ܦ).

ܠ ܫܡܗܐ ܡܫܬܐܠܢܐ ܘܕܝܪܐ ܦܫܝܛܐ: ܐܘܣܦ: ܗܘ: ܗܝ: ܗܢܘܢ: ܗܘ: ܠܗܘܐ ܩܕܡܝܬܐ ܘܬܘܣܦܬܐ:[1] ܐܝܟ ܥܒܕܗ: ܒܝܬܗ: ܢܦܫܗ: ܘܕܡܘܬܗ: ܐܝܟ ܠܦܪܨܘܦܐ ܚܝܘܬܐ ܕܡܬܠܬܢܐ ܬܫܡܫܝ: ܐܘܣܦ ܝܘܕ ܘܠܐ ܢܩܦܐ: ܐܝܟ ܩܘܡܝ: ܪܓܠܝ: ܢܦܫܝ: ܘܕܡܘܬܝ: ܥܒܕܝ: ܐܝܟ ܐܬܘܬܐ ܕܩܕܡ ܝܘܕ ܕܡܫܬܟܚܐ ܬܗܘܐ: ܡܬܬܩܦܐ ܝܘܕ: ܐܝܟ ܩܕܡܢ: ܥܒܕܢ: ܒܝܬܢ: ܡܠܟܢ: ܒܟܢ: ܐܢ: ܕܝܢ: ܐܘܪܢ: ܐܝܟ ܠܡܫܬܐܠܬܐ ܬܗܘܐ ܡܠܬܐ ܡܬܦܠܓܐ ܠܐܦܝܢ: ܐܝܟ ܩܛܠܝܢ: ܒܝܢ: ܒܪܢ: ܥܡܢ: ܐܝܬ ܐܘܪܢ܀ ܠܘܬ ܕܝܢ ܠܦܪܨܘܦܐ ܕܡܬܠܠܐ ܡܫܬܐܠܢܐ: ܡܬܬܘܣܦܐ ܝܘܕ ܒܠܚܘܕ ܒ̄ ܒܬܘܣܦܬܐ ܘܡܬܠܬܐ: ܘܗܘܐ ܡܢ ܩܕܡܘܗ̇ ܙܩܦܐ: ܐܝܟ ܩܘܡܝܢ: ܪܓܠܝܢ: ܢܦܫܬܝܢ: ܘܥܒܕܝ܀ ܘ ܗܘ ܕܝܢ ܕܐܢܬ ܗܘ ܕܫܡܥ ܥܒܕܐ: ܕܦܪܨܘܦܐ ܠܐܚܪܝܢܐ ܘܠܐܚܪܝܢܐ ܘܡܫܬܐܠܢܐ: ܘܬܘܣܦܬܐ ܬܗܘܐ: ܐܝܟ ܠܥܒܕܗ: ܡܪܟܒܗ: ܠܒܝܬܗ: ܡܪܝܗ: ܘܗܝ ܠܘܬ 11b
ܕܫܡܥ ܥܒܕܐ: ܕܢܩܦܐ ܠܥܒܕܐ: ܗܘ ܐܬܘܬܐ ܕܡܬܡܠܝܐ ܦܠܝܓܬܐ ܬܗܘܐ: ܘܠܐ ܡܬܘܪܩܐ ܗܘ: ܐܝܟ ܠܗܘܢ: ܡܢܝ: ܥܒܕܝܢ: ܢܦܫܝܢ: ܘܕܡܘܬܝܢ: ܒܝܬܝܢ: ܡܠܟܝܢ܀ ܟܕ ܠܘܬ ܕܫܡܥ ܥܒܕܐ. ܘܠܦܪܨܘܦܐ ܠܐܚܪܝܢܐ (ܡܫܡܥܢܐ) ܐܚܪܝܢܐ ܐܬܘܬܐ ܘܡܬܡܠܝܐ ܕܝܬܝܪܐ ܬܗܘܐ: ܠܝ ܠܥܒܕܐ: ܘܠܝ ܠܡܠܟܐ: ܐܝܟ ܪܓܠܝ: ܘܢܦܫܝ: ܘܒܝܬܝ: ܘܥܒܕܝ: ܐܒܘܝ: ܥܡܝ: ܫܠܡܝ: ܘܡܠܟܘܬܝ܀ ܗܘ ܕܝܢ ܕܦܪܨܘܦܐ ܡܬܡܠܝܐ ܡܫܬܐܠܢܐ: ܗܘ ܕܡܬܡܠܝܐ ܦܠܝܓܬܐ ܬܗܘܐ: ܐܝܟ ܒܢܝ: ܥܒܕܝ: ܐܒܗܝ: ܐܚܘܗܝ: ܐܚܝ: ܡܠܟܝ: ܐܝܬ ܘܕܝܠܗ ܠܗ܀ ܗܢܐ ܕܡܫܡܥܢܐ ܡܬܬܘܣܦܬܐ: ܗܘ ܘܡܬܡܠܝܐ ܕܝܬܝܪܐ ܬܗܘܐ ܠܥܒܕܐ ܘܡܠܟܐ: ܐܝܟ ܒܝܬܗ: ܢܦܫܗ: ܥܒܕܗ: ܪܓܠܗ: ܡܠܟܗ: ܥܒܕܗ܀
ܘܐܦ ܫܡܐ ܦܫܝܩܐ[2] ܠܝ ܡܢ ܬܠܬ ܐܝܬ ܠܗ ܠܗ ܕܩܢܐ ܕܫܘܦ: ܐܝܟ ܦܠܓܐ ܦܠܘܚ: ܗܘ ܡܢ ܐܝܟ ܕܡܢ ܫܩܠܐ ܫܩܠ: ܘܡܢ ܒܢܝܐ ܒܢܝ. ܗܠܝܢ ܕܝܢ ܐܝܟ ܡܢ 12a
ܟܠܐ ܟܠܝ: ܘܡܢ ܕܡܟܠܠ ܗܡܟܠܠ ܘܡܦܪܫ ܕܐܝܟ ܗܟܢ܀
ܗ ܫܡܗܐ ܕܝܢ ܐܠܝܢ ܕܟܠ ܫܡܗܘܬܐ: ܐܘ ܟܠ ܗܘ ܕܟܐܒ ܐܘ ܟܠ

1 ܡܫܬܐܠܢܐ] om. B   2 ܘܬܘܣܦܬܐ] om. BL   3 ܢܩܦܐ] ܢܩܦܐ G   5 ܒܟܢ] ܒܢܢ L   ܠܡܫܬܐܠܬܐ] ܠܡܫܬܐܠܐ OG   6 ܐܝܬ] om. BL | ܐܘܪܢ] om. OG   9 ܠܐܚܪܝܢܐ] ܠܐܚܪܝܢ L   13 ܡܫܡܥܢܐ] om. OGB   15 ܕܦܪܨܘܦܐ] ܦܪܨܘܦܐ OG   17 ܘܕܝܠܗ] om. OG   ܠܗ] om. BL (ܠܗ corrupted from ܘܕܝܠܗ)   23 ܫܡܗܘܬܐ] ܫܡܗܘܬܐ L

[1] Either ܩܕܡܝܬܐ or ܬܘܣܦܬܐ should be deleted. On the inconsistent usage of these terms, see comments on ܓ,3 and ܝ,3. Here OG have used both words together although it would have sufficed to have written either ܩܕܡܝܬܐ ܠܗܘܐ ܗܘ or ܬܘܣܦܬܐ ܠܗܘܐ ܗܘ (see ܝܒ,4, however). ܗܘ ܬܘܣܦܬܐ is *o*. | [2] "Shortened Noun," i.e. the absolute and construct states of the noun.

ܫܘܫܡܘܬܐ ܡܫܘܚܝܢ: ܡܬܦܪܫܝܢ ܒܗܢܐ ܙܢܐ܀[1] ܐܝܟ ܐܬܘܬܐ ܡܦܫܩܬܐ ܕܡܠܬܐ ܒ
ܡܟܝܠܬܐ ܗܝ: ܫܡܐ ܕܝܢ ܕܡܬܐܡܪ ܡܢܗ ܗܘܐ ܒܗ ܠܘܬܢ ܐܬ̈ܘܬܐ ܕܦܬܝܚܢ ܐܚܝܕܐ:
ܐܝܟ ܕܡܢ ܒܟܪ ܒܟܪܐ: ܘܡܢ ܡܪܐ ܡܪ̈ܝܐ܀ ܗܘ ܕܝܢ ܕܚܒܪ. ܐܝܟ ܚܒܘܪܐ: ܘܦܪܘܫܐ:
ܒܗ ܙܡܝܢܐ ܐܬܘܬܐ ܦܪ̈ܫܬܐ: ܘܗ̈ܘ ܙܘܓܐ: ܐܝܟ ܫܘܩܪܐ: ܠܘܚܐ: ܘܚܡܠܐ: ܡܢ ܗܢܐ
ܦܘܢܐ ܐܬܝܗܘܢ: ܘܐܝܟ ܕܟܬܘܒܝܢ ܒܟܬܒܐ ܡܢ ܒܟܘܪܘܬܐ: ܫܡܘܡܐ ܕܝܢ: ܐܝܟ
ܡ̈ܪܐ: ܒܟܪܐ: ܡܛܠ ܕܐܦܪܝܫ ܡܢ ܒܪ: ܒܪ̈ܐ ܘܒܪܘܪ̈ܐ ܘܒܪܘܪ̈ܐ: ܐܝܟܢ ܕܝܢ ܕܡܢ
12b ܡܢ: ܒܗ ܘܠܐ ܫܡܝܢ ܒܟܝܢܐ ܩܢܐ: ܡܬܪܒܝܢ ܗܟܢܐ: ܐܒܪܐ ܕܡܢ ܦܪܝܫ: ܪܡܙ:
ܫܒܩ: ܡܬܐܡܪ ܡܦܩܐ ܪܡܙܡܐ: ܣܘ̈ܩܬܐ: ܕܡܬܦܪܫ ܕܝܢ ܒܟܘܪܐ ܡܢ ܫܡܘܡܐ:
ܒܗ ܘܐܪܡܙܘܢ ܒܡܕܡ ܡܦܪܫ: ܒܪܡ ܠܫܡܘܡܐ ܕܡܬܐܬܘܬܐ :ܠ: ܐܒܪܐ ܘܐܬܡܪ.
ܡܢ ܦܪܝܫ ܡܦܪ̈ܫܬܐ ܘܡܬܦܪ̈ܫܬܐ: ܘܡܢ ܟܠܗܝܢ ܡܟܠܟ̈ܠܬܐ ܘܡܬܟܠܟ̈ܠܬܐ܀
ܐܝܟ ܡܬܝܕܥܐ ܠܟܠܢ ܕܫܘܫܡܬܐ ܚܕܐ ܡܢ ܗܠܝܢ ܐܪܒܥ ܐܬ̈ܘܬܐ ܡܬܚ̈ܡܝܢܬܐ:
ܘܐܬܝܗܝܢ .ܐ. ܗ. ܢ. ܝ܀ ܗܝ ܠ ܗܘܐ ܠܡܬܝܬܐ: ܘܡܢ: ܝ: ܡܬܚܠܦܐ: ܒܝ:
ܒܡ ܝ ܕܝܢ ܒܡܬܐ: ܐܝܟ ܕܡܫܬܡ̈ܠܝܬܐ: ܕܡܫܬܡܫ̈ܢܝܬܐ: ܡܫܬܡܪ̈ܝܢܐ: ܡܒ̈ܚܢܝܢܐ:
ܡܬܘ̈ܒܠܢܝܬܐ܀ ܒܦܢ̈ܝܬܐ ܕܝܢ ܢܬܚܠܦܐ: ܡܬܚܪܢܐ ܚܘܕ: ܘܐܘ ܡܬܘܒܠܐ[2] ܐܚܪܢܐ
ܕܡܬܐܡܪ ܡܢ ܟܠܗ ܡܟܠܟܠܬܐ ܡܬܟܠܟܠܬܐ ܘܒܪܗ ܠܗܠܝܢ

ܗܘܐܠܐ ܣܡܡܐ ܐܝܟܢ ܐܝܟ ܐܬܘܬܐ ܕܫܘܫܡܬܐ ܘܐܝܟܢ ܕܡܬܐܬܫܡܫܬܐ
13a ܦܘܫܐ ܘܐܝܟܢ ܐܝܟ ܕܐܬܘܬܐ ܕܫܘܫ̈ܡܬܐ ܐܬܝܗܝܢ: ܒܟܠܗܝܢ ܐܝܟܢ ܘܠܐ ܦܬܝܚ
ܡܢܗ ܕܟܬܝܒܢ: ܗܝ ܕܒܗ ܕܡܫܬܡܫ: ܒܟܠܗܘܢ ܐܢܐ ܕܗܘܝܢ ܡܬܐܡܪܐ: ܐܝܟ
ܟܿ: ܒܿ: ܕܿ: ܕܟܒ: ܕܟܬܒܬܘܢ ܐܢܐ ܕܗܘܝܢ ܡܬܐܡܪܐ ܗܘܐ ܕܡܠܬܐ: ܠܐ ܦܬܝܚ
ܡܢܗ: ܐܬܘܬܐ ܕܝܢ ܡܬܐܬܫܡܫܢܝܬܐ ܠܟܠܟܠܐ ܐܢܐ ܕܡܬܦܠܓܢ ܠܡܬܐܬܫܡܫܢܝܬܐ
ܡܦܢܝܢ ܗܘܠܐ ܘܠܡܬܐܬܫܡܫܢܝܬܐ ܕܐܝܟ ܕܟܬܘܒܢܐ: ܘܠܡܬܐܬܫܡܫܢܝܬܐ ܕܡܢ
ܐܬܦܫܛܬ ܒܝܢܐ:

1 ܫܘܫܡܘܬܐ] ܫܡܘܡܘܬܐ L 3 ܦ̈ܪܐ] ܡܪܐ G 8 ܫܡܘܡܐ] ܫܡܘܡܐ G and always
9 ܒܡܕܡ] ܒܡܕܡ OG 10 ܡܟܠܟܠܬܐ ܘܡܬܟܠܟܠܬܐ] ܡܟܠܟܠܐ ܘܡܬܟܠܟܠܐ G
11 ܕܫܘܫܡܬܐ] ܕܫܡܘܡܐ L 12 ܗܝ...ܝ[2]] sic B; OG corrupt | ܠ] ܘܠ L
13 ܡܫܬܡܪ̈ܝܢܐ] ܘܡܫܬܡܪ̈ܝܢܐ 14 ܡܬܘܒܠܐ] ܘܡܬܘܒܠܐ BL(?correct)
15 ܡܬܟܠܟܠܬܐ] ܘܡܬܟܠܟܠܬܐ B 18 ܦܬܝܚ] ܦܬܝܚܝܢ OGB 19 ܕܟܬܝܒܢ]
ܕܟܬܒܢܐ L, ܕܟܬܘܒܝܢ B 21 ܠܡܬܐܬܫܡܫܢܝܬܐ ܡܦܢܝܢ ܗܘܠܐ] om. B

[1] The expected explanation is mising in all mss. | [2] ?correct. One can see how the scribes are copying a text they do not understand.

ܟ

ܘܡܛܠܬܘܣܦܬܐ ܡܦܩܢܬܐ ܫܘܩܠܐ ܕܐܝܬܝܗܘܢ: ܐܝܟ: ܘܘ: ܕܟܬܘܒܐ: ܘܦܫܩܠܐ ܘܢܡܘܣܐ ܕܡܫܘܚܬܐ ܕܟܠ ܡܕܒܪܢܘܬܐ: ܘܗܘ ܕܟܬܒܐ: ܘܚܝܠܐ. ܘܢܗܝܪܐ: ܕܡܫܘܚܬܐ ܕܟܠ ܫܡܝܐ܀ ܘܐܝܟ: ܙܘ: ܕܡܘܣܟܐ ܘܡܫܘܚܬܐ ܘܦܘܪܣܝܬܐ: ܕܡܫܘܚܬܐ ܕܟܠ ܡܕܒܪܢܘܬܐ ܘܢܣܒܐ ܐܚܪܢܐ܀ ܘܐܝܟ: ܡ̄: ܕܡܕܒܪܢܐ: ܘܡܕܝܢܬܐ: ܘܡܫܘܚܬܐ ܕܟܠ ܡܕܒܪܢܘܬܐ ܡܫܘܚܬܐ܀ ܘܐܝܟ ܡ̄: ܘܠ̄ܗ: ܘܡܛܠܦܠܓܘܬܐ: 13b ܘܡܛܠܢܒܥܐ ܘܡܛܠܓܒܪܐ: ܘܟܠ ܢܡܘܣܘܬܐ ܡܬܒܥܐ܀ ܘܐܝܟ: ܢ: ܠܘ: ܘܠܟܠܗܝܢ ܘܡܥܪܒܝܬܐ: ܘܬܝܡܢܝܬܐ: ܘܓܪܒܝܝܬܐ: ܘܗܢܝܢ: ܘܟܠܗ ܕܐܪܥܐ ܘܡܕܢܚܐ܀ ܘܗܢܝܢ: ܘܗܘ: ܘܟܠܗ ܕܐܪܥܐ: ܘܪܘܚܐ: ܘܡܕܢܚܐ܀ ܕܟܠܗܘܢ ܠܡܫܘܚܬܐ ܢܩܦܢ܀ ܘܐܝܟ: ܐ: ܕܐܝܟ ܠܗܠܐ: ܠܐܬܪܘܢ܀ ܘܩܘܡ ܕܐܝܟܢܐ: ܕܥܠܐ: ܕܬܪܘܢ: ܘܠ̄ܗ: ܕܐܝܟܢܐ ܘܢܥܠܐ ܘܠܐܬܪܘܢ: ܘܕܟܠ ܐܝܟܢܐ ܡܕܒܪܢܘܬܐ ܘܪܒܐ ܘܕܟܠ ܡܫܘܚܬܐ: ܘܐܝܟ ܟ̄ܟ̄ܟ̄ ܘܠ̄ܗ ܕܐܬܥܒܝ: ܘܐܬܦܫܛ: ܘܐܬܦܪܫ܀ ܘܡܬܡ ܘܠ̄ܗ ܕܡܬܥܒܝ ܘܡܬܦܫܛ: ܘܡܬܦܪܫ ܕܟܠ ܐܚܪܢܐ ܕܦܐܡ ܡܫܘܚܬܐ: ܘܬܩ̄ܢ ܘܠܗ ܕܢܬܥܒܝ. ܘܢܬܦܫܛ: ܘܢܬܦܪܫ ܕܟܠ ܐܚܪܢܐ ܕܟܠܗ ܡܫܘܚܬܐ܀

ܡܛܠܬܘܣܦܬܐ ܕܡܢ ܕܐܝܟ ܕܡܬܘܪܓܡܐ ܕܬܠܬܝܢ: ܐܝܟܢ ܕܡܬܩܪܝܢ ܟܘܟܒܐ ܘܠܐ ܡܬܚܙܝܢ ܒܫܡܝܐ܀ ܢܗܝܪܐ ܕܡܢ ܦܪܘܛܘܡܐ ܩܕܡܝ ܐܝܟ ܘܩܕܡܝ ܐܝܟ ܓܒܪܐ: ܘܐܝܬܘܗܝ ܠܬܠܬܝܢ: ܐܚܪܢܐ ܕܢܦܩܘܢ ܠܗܘܢ ܠܟܘܟܒܐ ܕܡܫܘܚܬܐ 14a ܓܒܪܐ ܡܫܘܚܬܐ ܒܫܘܒܚܐ܀ ܕܬܠܬܝܢ ܕܡܢ ܬܪܬܐ ܕܦܘܪܫܐ ܠܩܕܡܐ: ܐ̄: ܒ̄: ܓ̄: ܕ̄: ܗ̄: ܘ̄: ܙ̄: ܚ̄: ܐ ܕܬܠܬܝܢ ܗܢܘܢ ܕܡܛܠܬܘܣܦܬܐ ܕܦܪܘܫܬܐ ܘܡܫܘܚܬܐ ܐܝܟ ܕܟܠܗ ܕܪܘܚܬܐ: ܘܫܡܝܐ: ܘܡܝܐ: ܘܐܪܥܐ: ܘܢܘܪܐ: ܕܢܦܩܘܢ ܒܗܘܢ ܪܘܚܐ: ܒܫܡܝܐ: ܘܫܡܝܐ ܠܫܡܝܐ ܘܡܝܐ ܡܢܗܘܢ: ܟܠܗ ܠܗ ܘܡܢ ܫܡܝܐ: ܘܐܪܥܐ ܢܘܪܐ: ܓܒܪܐ ܕܡܫܘܚܬܐ: ܘܠܗܘܢ ܕܟܠܗ ܘܢܩܘܡ ܡܢܗ ܫܡܝܐ܀ ܒ̄ ܐܝܟ ܐܚܪܢܐ ܦܐܪܐ: ܕܢܦܩܘܢ ܡܢ ܐܚܪܢܐ ܕܟܠܗ: ܠܗ ܐܚܪܢܐ ܡܢ ܟܘܟܒܐ܀ ܙ̄ ܐܝܟ ܗܘ ܕܟܬܒܐ. ܕܬܠܬܝܢ ܒܫܘܒܚܐ: ܕܢܦܩܘܢ

1 ܘܡܛܠܬܘܣܦܬܐ] ܕܡܛܠܬܘܣܦܬܐ OG 2 ܘܗܘ] ܘܗܘܘ OG 3 ܫܡܝܐ] ܫܡܝܐܬܐ B 6 ܠܘ] ܠ OG | ܘܠܟܠܗܝܢ...7 ܘܡܥܪܒܝܬܐ] ܡܥܪܒܐ ܘܠܟܠ B 7 ܘܟܠܗ] om. B 8 ܘܟܠܗ] om. B | ܢܩܦܢ] ܢܩܦܢ O 10 ܕܐܝܬܘܗܝ ܘܐܬܦܫܛ] ܠܐܝܬܘܗܝ ܐܬܦܫܛ B 14 ܕܬܠܬܝܢ] ܕܬܠܬܐ L 15 ܘܠܐ ܡܬܚܙܝܢ] ܘܡܬܚܙܝܢ O 17 ܓܒܪܐ] ܕܬܠܬܝܢ (pl.) B 18 ܟܠܗ] om. B 19 ܕܪܘܚܬܐ] ܪܘܚܐ B 21 ܐܝܟ] om. OG; lacuna in B

ܡܢ ܓ̈ܠܐ: ܘܐܝܟ ܢܝܒܬܐ: ܕܢܦܩܘܢ ܡܢ ܬܠܬ ܐܬܘ̈ܬܐ܀ ܗ ܕܟܦܠܘܬܗܘܢ ܕܢܦܩܘܢ ܝ
ܡܢ ܦܘܡܐ ܐܝܟ: ܘܗܢܘܢ ܕܒܙܘܥܗܘܢ ܕܢܦܩܘܢ ܡܢ ܙܘܥܐ܀ ܒ̈ ܐܝܟ ܗܢܘܢ ܕܦܫܝܩ
14b ܠܡܠܐ ܠܚܝܠܐ ܗܠܝܢ ܕܡܫܬܡܥܢ ܡܢ ܚܢܟܐ. ܘܟܢܦܐ: ܘܢܝܒܐ: ܘܟܢܦܐ: ܕܐܬܝܗܝܢ:
ܟ̈ܢܦܐ: ܘܟ̈ܢܦܐ: ܘܢܝ̈ܒܐ: ܘܟ̈ܢܦܐ: ܟܕ ܕܝܢ ܒܟܠܗ ܡܫܡܥܢܘܬܐ ܚܠܦ ܚܡܫܐ
ܗܠܝܢ: ܟܠܗܝܢ ܡܫܬܡܥܢ ܠܐܠܦ ܐܬܘܬܐ ܡܢܩܫܢܝܬܐ[1] ܘܚܡܫܐ ܐܝܟ ܚܢܝܢܐ:
ܘܐܫܬܟܚ ܠܗܘܢ ܗܘ: ܐܣܝܪܐ: ܒܪܡ ܕܝܢ ܐܬܦܠܓܘ ܩ̈ܠܐ ܗܠܝܢ ܠܬܪܬܝܢ ܣܕܪ̈ܐ:
ܐܚܪܢܐ ܕܡܬܦܬܚܝܢ ܡܢ ܩ̈ܠܐ ܕܡܫܬܡܥܐ: ܐܝܟ ܓܒܝܬܐ ܕܐܬܝܗ ܡܢ ܓܒܐ ܡܢ ܓܒܝ
ܘܐܬܝܗܘܢ ܡܢ ܓܒܐ ܕܐܝܟ: ܘܢܝܒܐ ܡܢ ܚܕ ܘܦܢܝܬܐ܀ ܘܒܗ ܓܒܠܐ ܐܬܬܫܡܫܬ
ܗܘ ܟܝܢܐ ܦܓܪܢܝܐ ܐܣܬܐ: ܠܟܘܪܗܢܐ ܕܡܢ ܚ̈ܢܐ ܕܢܫܡܬܐ ܡܢ ܓܘܫܡܐ: ܘܚܕ ܡܢ
ܦܢܝܬܐ ܠܐ: ܐܝܟ ܗܢܘܢ ܕܒܡܬܒܥܠܐ ܐܬܬܫܡܫܬ ܡܟܠ ܠܐܘܪܚܐ: ܚܕܐ ܓܝܪ: ܐܝܟ
ܕܐܬܦܪܘܛܘܓܪܐܦܝܛܐ: ܒܗܘ ܕܡܠܬܐ ܡܢ ܡܬܚܫܠܐ: ܘܬܘܪܐ ܟܡܝܪܐ ܐܬܝܗܘܢ
ܒܗ ܬܬܝܢܬܐ: ܘܐܚܪܬܐ ܐܝܟ ܕܠܫܘܪܝܐ ܘܡܢ ܡܦܩܢܐ ܠܟܠܐ܀ ܡܬܬܠܝܢ ܠܫܘܪܝܐ
15a ܘܡܢ ܡܬܬܠܝܢ ܠܟܠܗܝܢ: ܘܓܒ̈ܠܐ: ܠܫܘܪܝܐ ܘܡܢ ܓ̈ܠܐ ܕܣܘܪ̈ܐ: ܘܓܒ̈ܠܐ ܕܬܠܬܐ
ܘܐܬܝܗܘܢ ܢܓܪܐ. ܘܓ̈ܠܐ ܕܢܗܘܐ܀ ܗܝ: ܐܝܟ ܕܠܡܦܢܐ: ܕܡܬܦܢܝܢ ܡܢ ܩ̈ܢܐ ܡܟܬܐ
ܡܬܦܠܓܢܝܬܐ: ܘܓܒ̈ܢܐ ܠܫܘܪܝܐ ܘܡܢ ܓܒܪܐ: ܘܦܝܠܬܐ ܡܢ ܫܠ̈ܬܐ ܘܐܬܝܗܘܢ
ܡܫܝܢܐ܀ ܗ ܐܝܟ ܗܢܘܢ ܕܡܬܦܫܩܝܢ: ܡܟܠܐ ܘܐܬܝܗܝܢ ܡܢ ܦܘܩ̈ܕܐ: ܐܝܟ
ܕܐܬܦܪܘܛܘܓܪܐܦܝܛܐ: ܘܐܢܫܐ ܕܡܬܦܢܝܢ ܡܢ ܦܩܦܩܐ ܘܐܬܝܗܝܢ ܡܢ ܦܩܦܩܐ܀ ܠܗܘܢ
ܕܝܢ ܐܣܪܢܝܬܐ ܚܡܫ ܦܘܫܩܐ ܕܐܬܘ̈ܬܐ: ܡܬܦܪܫܝܢ ܚܡܫܐ ܕܡܢܗܝܢ: ܚܝܘܬܐ ܡܢ
ܗܠܝܢ: ܐܝܟ ܚܡܫܐ ܗܠܝܢ: ܩ̈ܠܬܐ: ܦܬ̈ܐ: ܐܘ̈ܬܐ: ܐܝܕܐ: ܓܝܣܐ: ܘܚܘܪܐ ܕܐܝܟ
ܗܠܝܢ: ܡܠܬܐ ܕܟܠܗܝܢ: ܡܢ ܦܫܝܛܐ ܗܘ ܘܐܦܢ: ܩܕܡܐ ܡܕܝܢܐ: ܘܡܢ ܡܬܟܠܐ ܕܡܘܐܠܐ
ܘܩ̈ܠܐ ܚܒܝ ܐܠܦ܀ ܡܕܐ: ܦܬܐ: ܦܬܚܐ: ܦܬܚܐ: ܦܬܚܐ: ܗܠܝܢ ܕܡܬܦܢܝܢ ܦܬܚܐ ܕܝܢ
ܗܠܝܢ ܕܒܬܪܐ ܘܡܬܪܟܢܐ: ܘܗܠܝܢ ܕܡܬܢܟܝܢ ܘܐܬܝܗܝܢ ܚܝܘ̈ܬܐ܀

1 ܕܟܦܠܘܬܗܘܢ] ܕܟܦܢܘܬܗܘܢ B ܕܟܦܠܘܪܗܘܢ G 2 ܙܘܥܐ] ܙܘܥܐ GB | ܐܝܟ ܗܢܘܢ] ܐܝܟ ܗܘ ܡܫܡܥܢܘܬܐ] ܘ om. B | ܘܦܫܝܩ] ܘܦܠܝܩ G 4 ܘܟܢܦܐ ܘܢܝܒܐ ܘܟܢܦܐ] ܘ om. B | ܗܢܘܢ L ܚܠܦ ܗܠܝܢ ܚܡܫܐ OG ܚܠܦ ܚܡܫܐ] ܚܠܦ ܚܡܫܐ ܗܠܝܢ | ܡܫܡܥܢܘܬܐ OG 5 ܡܢܩܫܢܝܬܐ] ܡܩܫܢܝܬܐ B 7 ܡܢ[2] ܡܢ B | ܓܒܐ ܡܢ ܓܒܝ ܘܐܬܝܗܘܢ] om. OG txt BL (B ܡܢ) 8 ܡܢ[1]] om. B | ܚܕ B ܚܕ G ܚܕ O 12 ܠܟܠܗܝܢ...13 ܘܓܒ̈ܠܐ] om. OGB (OG have ܕܣܘܪ̈ܐ ܘܓܒ̈ܠܐ) txt L 15 ܡܢ] ܘܡܢ L | ܫܠ̈ܬܐ] ܐܫܠܬܐ OG 20 ܘܐܦܢ] ܘܐܦܢ OGB 21 ܦܬܚܐ[2]] B corrupt 22 ܘܡܬܪܟܢܐ] G adds ܡܬܢܐ in marg., hence ܗܠܝܢ also om.

[1] Note the name of this alaph which is elsewhere called ܐܠܦ ܕܡܫܡܥܢܐ (cf. ܩܘ,2; 128n).

ܗ ܐܝܟ ܐܝܟܐ: ܗܠܝܢ ܕܒܢܝܢܫܐ: ܘܕܒܥܝܪܐ: ܐܝܟܢܐ ܕܝܢ ܗܠܝܢ ܕܡܬܐ ܘܩܘܪܝܐ ܦܪ̈ܫܐ
ܠܟܠܗܘܢ܀ ܐܝܟ ܐܝܠܝܢ ܕܒܢܝܢܫܐ ܐܢܬܘܬܐ[1] ܕܝܢ: ܕܡܘܬܐ ܗܠܝܢ ܠܥܢܒܬܐ ܕܒܓܠܠܐ 15b
ܡܬܡܢܝܢ: ܐܘ ܒܪܘܚܐ ܐܘ ܒܩܛܠܐ ܕܢܦܫܐ: ܐܘ ܠܗܘܩܫܐ ܗܢܘܢ ܕܐܬܝܗܒܘ ܠܒܢܝܐ
ܠܡܬܒܥܠܢܘܬܐ: ܢܦܠܐ ܢܦܠܐ: ܩܕܡܐ ܚܪܘܬܐ ܕܒܢܝܢܫܐ ܘܕܒܥܝܪܐ ܚܝܘܬܐ: ܒܢܝܐ ܕܝܢ
ܗܠܝܢ ܕܡܛܠ: ܘܒܗܘܢ ܦܘܠܚܢ܀ ܢܦܠܐ ܚܕ: ܚܘܫܐ ܡܫܬܢܐ: ܐܠܐ ܢܦܠܐ ܢܦ̈ܠܐ ܐܬܝܠܕܘܢ
ܒܢ̈ܝܐ ܕܥܘܠܐ ܘܕܢܟܝܢ ܒܦܘܩܕܢܗܘܢ: ܢܦܠܐ ܒܢ̈ܝܬܐ: ܐܬܝܠܕܘ ܩܘܫ̈ܒܬܐ ܘܕܚܘܪܐ:
ܐܚܝܢܐ ܡܢ ܡܢܬܐ ܕܦܫܝܛܬܐ: ܘܫܒܝܠܬܐ ܘܐܝܟ ܗܠܝܢ܀
ܘܡܬܦܫܩܢܘܬܐ ܕܐܝܟ ܡܢ ܐܦܣܦܠܘܓܝܐ ܐܬܝܠܕܘ: ܐܝܠܝܢ ܕܡܬܬܩܢܢ
ܒܩܕܡܝܐ ܘܒܬܪܗ: ܟܕ ܒܥܘܡܐ ܠܐ ܡܬܚܫܚܝܢ: ܒܢܝܢ ܕܝܢ ܬܠܬܝ̈ܬܐ ܐܬܝܠܕܘ: ܡܛܠ
ܕܟܕ ܡܬܦܠܓܝܢ ܗܘ ܚܕܐ ܐܘ ܡܛܠܬܐ: ܡܬܬܚܝܢ ܗܠܝܢ ܐܬܘܬܐ ܕܢܦܩܝܢ ܒܥܘܡܐ:
ܘܡܛܠ ܕܡܠܝܬܐ ܐܬܝܠܕܘ: ܒܗܘ ܕܡܢ ܩܕܡܝܐ ܐܝܟܢ ܕܡܬܒܥܝܢ ܐܬܐܡܪܬ
ܫܘܪܝܐ ܐܬܝܢ ܝܘܡܝܢ ܩܠܝܠ: ܦܣܘ ܝܘܡܝܢ ܐܬܘܬܐ ܐܝܟ ܕܐܬܦܫܩܬ: ܡܬܚܒܪܝܢ 16a
ܕܝܢ ܥܡܘܕܐ: ܐܘ ܡܬܚܦܝܢ ܡܢ ܒܟܠ ܡܬܐܡܪܢܘܬܐ ܕܢܦܩܝܢ ܒܚܕܐ ܕܡܛܠ:
ܘܒܗܠܝܢ ܕܟܠܗ: ܘܕܘܟܝܐ ܘܡܘܕܥܢܐ ܕܫܪܟܐ: ܗܠܝܢ ܐܬܘܬܐ܀ ܐܬܝܠܕܘ ܕܝܢ ܐܝܟ
ܗܠܝܢ܀ ܩܕܡܝܐ ܕܝܢ: ܐܝܟ: ܕ: ܕܒܡܕܝܢܬܐ: ܒܒܝܬܐ: ܒܥܠܐ: ܝܢܩܬܐ: ܝܢܩܘܬܐ
ܘܢܦܝܠܘܬܐ: ܗܠܝܢ ܕܟܕ ܡܬܝܠܕܝܢ ܡܬܐܡܪܝܢ: ܠܐ ܢܦܫܐ ܕܟܠܗ̇ ܚܝ̈ܘܬܐ: ܡܛܠ ܕܝܢ
ܕܫܘܚܠܦܐ ܡܬܐܡܪܝܢ: ܡܬܐܡܪܐ: ܕ: ܐܝܟ ܡܕܝܢܬܐ: ܒܚܝܘܬܐ: ܚܝܘܬܐ: ܘܐܝܟ
ܚܝܘܬܐ܀ ܠܘܬ ܕܝܢ ܬܘܢ ܡܬܚܫܚܢܐ ܒܥܡܢܘܬܐ: ܘܝܩܢܘܬܐ: ܘܪܓܠܬܐ: ܘܫܒܝܠܬܐ
ܒܗ ܢܦܠܐ: ܒܗܘ ܕܐܬܡܪ: ܡܬܝܠܕܐ: ܘܥܢܝܐ: ܘܪܓܠܬܐ: ܘܫܒܝܠܐ܀ ܗ̄ܗ̄ ܕܝܢ
ܡܬܚܫܚܐ: ܒܥܘܒܕܐ ܘܥܒܘܕܐ ܘܫܠܝ: ܡܛܠ ܕܟܠ ܡܬܝܠܕܐ ܕܡܬܐܡܪܐ
ܐܬܒܪܟܬܗ: ܘܐܝܟ ܒܡܬܚܫܚܢܘ: ܗܗ: ܐܬܘܬܐ ܐܡܪܢ ܕܗܘܝܐ ܥܡܐ ܢܦܠܝܢ ܒܗ 16b
ܐܬܪܝܢ ܗܘܐ: ܐܢܫܐ ܘܐܬܡܪܝܢ ܒܡܢ ܐܬܝܠܕܘ: ܥܘܪܢܐ: ܐܬܝܠܕܘ ܥܘܒܕܐ:
ܐܬܚܙܝ: ܒܗܘ̈ܢܐ: ܐܬܝܠܕܘ ܥܘܒܕܐ: ܐܬܦܪܝ ܘܢܛܪ: ܐܬܝܠܕܘ: ܥܘܒܕܐ܀
ܐܝܟ ܢܦܠܐ ܗ̄ܗ̄ ܒܡܠܬܐ

2 ܐܢܬܘܬܐ] in marg. B add. ܠܕܡܠܓܝ (الد مالغ)   4 ܩܕܡܐ ܚܪܘܬܐ] ܩܕܡܐ ܚܪܘܬܐ L
5 ܘܒܗܘܢ] ܒܗܘܢ OG | ܐܠܐ] om. OG   6 ܘܕܢܟܝܢ] ܕܢܟܝܢ OG   9 ܡܬܚܫܚܝܢ] ܡܬܬܚܝܢ L   10 ܕܢܦܩܝܢ] ܢܦܩܝܢ OGB   12 ܐܬܝܢ] ܐܬܝܢ O ܐܬܝܢ B read ܐܬܝܢ or ܐܬܝܢ
14 ܗܠܝܢ] ܗܠܝܢ L | ܐܬܘܬܐ] no point in mss   16 ܘܢܦܝܠܘܬܐ] ܢܦܝܠܘܬܐ OG
19 ܘܥܢܝܐ ܘܪܓܠܬܐ ܘܫܒܝܠܐ] ܘ om. x3 L

[1] B has a marginal gloss, ܠܕܡܠܓܝ, in error for الدماج, pl. of دُمْلُج, meaning an arm-band or bracelet from which an amulet is hung. This has little to do with the text, unless perhaps he was thinking of the expression relating to idolatry at Isa 57.8, יד חזית (*you saw his hand*, a euphemism for nakedness)?

ܗ ܐܬܡܬܚܘܬܐ: ܡܛܠ ܕܗܘܐ ܡܫܚܐ ܚܕܐ ܗܿܘ: ܢܦܠܐ ܒܗ: ܐܝܟ ܐܬܦܠܓܘ ܡܢܘܬܐ: ܐܬܦܪܫ ܣܘܡ̈ܟܐ: ܐܬܦܠܓ ܒܘܪ̈ܟܐ: ܐܬܦܪܫ ܣܘܟ̈ܠܐ: ܘܡ̈ܢܐ ܕܐܝܟ ܗܠܝܢ܀ ܡ̈ܠܐ ܕܝܢ: ܐܝܟ ܠܐ ܕܡܬܡܠܠܢ: ܘܡܬܦܠܓܢ: ܘܡܬܓܠܝܢ܀ ܕܐܬܡܢܝܢ ܗܿܢ ܦܡ: ܡܢ ܦܘܟ̈ܠܐ: ܗܿܢ ܕܝܢ ܡܢ ܡܬܚܫܚܢܘܬܐ: ܗܘܐ ܕܝܢ ܡܢ ܕܘܟ̈ܠܐ: ܘܐܝܟ ܐܪ̈ܓܠܐ: ܐܪ̈ܓܠܐ: ܐܪ̈ܠܐ: ܐܪ̈ܓܠ: ܒܐܪܓܠܝ: ܒܐܪ̈ܓܠܗܿ: ܘܒܐܪ̈ܓܠܝ ܘܒܐܪ̈ܓܠ: ܗܟܢ ܕܝܢ ܐܡܪܝܢ ܐܪ̈ܓܠܬܗܿ ܐܪܓܠܝܢ: ܘܐܪ̈ܓܠܝܢ: ܘܐܪܓܠ: ܘܒܐܪܓܠ: ܠܐܪܓܠܐ: ܟܠ܀ ܘܐܝܟ ܗ: ܕܡܬܦܩܦܩܝܢ: ܘܐܬܡܢܝܘ ܡܢ ܦܘܩ̈ܕܐ܀ ܘܐܝܟ: ܙ: ܕܣܢܘܪܗ ܘܣܢܘܪܗܿ: ܘܡܣܢܪܘܢ ܘܐܬܡܢܝܢ ܡܢ ܣܘܪ̈ܕܐ: ܘܐܝܟ

17a ܗܘ: ܕܡܬܚܡܠ ܘܐܬܡܢܝܗ ܡܢ ܚܝܠܐ܀ ܘܐܝܟ: ܫ: ܘܝܢ: ܚܦܪܝܢ ܚܝܢ: ܘܙܪܥܝܢ ܚܝܢ: ܘܟܠܝܢ ܚܝܢ: ܕܡܬܦܘܪܐ ܥܠ ܦܪ̈ܘܩܐ ܡܩܕܡܐ ܗܣܬܝܢܐ: ܘܐܝܟ ܕܠܦܘܪܫܐ ܕܡܢ ܦܪ̈ܝܢ ܘܙܪ̈ܝܢ: ܘܟܠܝܢ: ܠܗ ܡܢ ܕܡ̈ܫܚܬܐ: ܦܪ̈ܝܢ: ܙܪ̈ܝܢ: ܟܠ̈ܝܢ: ܘܡܬܪܐ ܕܐܝܟ ܗܠܝܢ܀

ܐܠܐ ܕܝܢ ܐܦ ܐܬܘܬܐ ܐܚ̈ܪܢܝܬܐ ܕܡܬܬܘܣܦܢ ܥܠ ܡܠ̈ܬܐ: ܘܡ̈ܢܝܢ ܠܗܘܢ ܐܚܪܢܝܬܐ ܠܘܬ ܐܝܠܝܢ ܕܡܢܗܘܢ ܐܬܐܝܬܝܗ܀ ܐܝܟ ܗܿܘ: ܘܗܿܝ ܕܡܬܬܘܣܦܢ ܥܠ ܡܠܬܐ ܐܚ̈ܪܢܝܬܐ ܘܡ̈ܢܝܢ ܠܗܘܢ ܐܚܪܢܝܬܐ ܕܠܘܬ ܕܝܢ ܐܚ̈ܪܢܐ. ܐܝܟ ܦܝܢܬܐ ܘܦܠܓܘܬܐ܀ ܠܐܡܪ ܦܝܠ̈ܓܬܐ ܘܦܠܓܘ̈ܬܐ܀ ܘܐܝܟ ܐܬܘܪܐ ܘܦܪ̈ܗܛܐ: ܦܪ̈ܗܛܐ ܗܕܘܡܐ ܕ̈ܟܝܐ ܕܡ̈ܪܝܐ: ܘܐܝܟ ܐܪܒܥܐ ܘܦܪ̈ܝܐ ܘܚܡܫܐ: ܡܬܘܡܝܬ: ܘܐܬܘܪܐ ܘܦܬܗܘܐ ܘܡܬܚܫܚܢܐ ܗܟܢܐܝܬ: ܗܝ ܐܝܟ ܦܪܝܐ ܘܦܪ̈ܝܐ: ܘܪܘܚܐ: ܘܡܫܝܚܐ܀ ܘܦܪܝܫܐ

17b ܗܘ ܡܢ ܗܝ: ܗܟܢ ܕܗܝ: ܡܬܦܘܪܐ ܥܠ ܐܚܪܢܝܬܐ ܗܿܢ ܐܘܣܝܬܐ ܢܬܝܬܐ: ܗܘ ܕܝܢ ܥܠ ܐܚܪܢܝܬܐ ܩܘܡܝܬܐ. ܐܝܟ ܩܢܘܡܐ ܐܬܘܪܐ܀ ܘܐܬܘܒ ܗܿܘ ܕܒܗ ܕܗܘ ܢܦܩ ܠܗ ܗܿܘ: ܐܝܟ ܠܟܝܢܐ: ܘܡܦܪܫܐ ܘܡܫܪܝܐ: ܗܘ ܕܝܢ ܠܐ ܢܦܩ ܠܗ: ܠܗ: ܚ ܩܘ. ܘܥܠܘܗܝ ܦܝܢܝܢ܀ ܐܠܐ ܕܝܢ ܠܣܘܦܐ ܐܦ: ܩ: ܕܡܬܬܢܝܚ ܥܠ ܠܡܠܬܐ ܢܩܝܐ: ܐܝܟ ܦܠܝܛܘܢܝܩܘܬܐ: ܐܪܣܛܘܛܠܝܩܘܬܐ: ܓܐܘܡܛܪܝܩܘܬܐ ܘܗܠܝܢ ܓܒܪ ܡܠܬܐ ܦܠܚܝܢ ܐܝܟ ܕܒܐܣܟܘܠܐ: ܠܘܬ ܐܪܣܛܘܛܠܝܣ. ܘܦܠܛܘܢ:

2 ܣܘܡ̈ܟܐ] ܣܘܡܟܐ L   3 ܠܐ] om. OG   5 ܒܐܪܓܠܗܿ] om. all mss (O has *linea occultans*) | ܐܪܓܠܬܗܿ...6 ܐܪܓܠܝܢ] ܐܪܓܠܘܢ ܐܪܓܠܝܢ B   7 ܡܢ] om. B   8 ܚܦܪܝܢ] ܘܚܦܪܝܢ OG   10 ܘܙܪ̈ܝܢ] ܙܪܝܢ add. G   15 ܘܦܪ̈ܗܛܐ] ܦܪܗܛܐ L | ܗܕܘܡܐ] om. OG   16 ܕ̈ܟܝܐ all mss; leg. ܟܠܟܝܐ (Payne-Smith ܕܟܠܟܝܐ) | ܕܡ̈ܪܝܐ] ܕܡܪܝܐ L   17 ܘܡܬܚܫܚܢܐ] ܟܚܫܚܐ OG   18 ܢܬܝܬܐ] ܘܡܬܝܬܐ BL   19 ܗܘ] om. B   23 ܦܠܚܝܢ] om. B

ܢ ܘܒܐܘܡܢܘܬܐ܀ ܐܝܟ ܕܒܗܘܢ[1] ܕܝܢ ܐܦ. ܪ: ܕܪܫ ܠܗ ܦܫܛ ܡܬܦܫܩ ܒܢܗ:
ܐܝܟ ܣܦ̈ܬܐ ܕܢܦܩܢ ܡܢ ܣܦܬܐ܀ ܐܝܟ ܕܒܗܘܢ ܕܝܢ ܐܦ ܠܐܘܬܝܢ ܐܬܘ̈ܬܐ ܡܬܪܒܝܢܐ:
ܘܐܝܟܢܘܢ. ܩ: ܟ̄: ܓ̄ ܕܝܢ ܡܬܐܡܪ̈ܢ ܒܚܢܟܐ: ܘܟܠܗܝܢ ܐܝܟ ܕܒܐܘܦܩܐ ܢܘܪ̈ܝܢ
ܠܗܘܢ ܐ̱ܣܛܘܟܣܐ ܕܒܗܘܢ ܡܫܬܟ̈ܚܢ ܕܒܗܘܢ ܐܬܬܝܗܒ: ܐܝܟ ܐܚܘܕܝܘܬܐ: ܡܢ
ܐܚܘܬܐ: ܘܐܘܟܠܫܝܐ: ܡܢ ܐܘܟܠܝܗܘܢ: ܘܗܟܢ ܗܘܐ ܒܩܘܡ
ܗܘܐܠܐ ܥܠܬܐ ܡܢܐ ܐܝܟܢܘܢ[2] ܡܩܦܠܬܐ: ܘܐܢܢ ܢܩܦܢ: ܦܘܡ ܥܩܪܐ܀ 18a
ܦܘܫܐ ܘܐܡܪܝܢ ܕܡܩܦܠܬܐ ܐܝܟܢܘܢ ܐܬܘ̈ܬܐ ܕܢܩܦܢ ܦܘܡ ܥܩܪܐ ܘܡܬܪ̈ܦܝܢ[3]
ܠܐܬܘܬܐ ܦܩܘܕܝܬܐ ܕܥܡܪܐ: ܕܝ ܗܘܝܐ ܕܝܢ ܐܬܘ̈ܬܐ ܕܬܪ̈ܝܢ ܙܘܥ̈ܐ. ܐܝܟܢܘܢ ܕܝܢ
ܐܪܒܥ: ܒ̄: ܕ̄: ܘ̄: ܠ̄: ܕܡܬܩܕ̈ܡܢ ܒܫܘܪܝܗ ܕܡ̈ܠܐ: ܢܩܦܢ ܕܝܢ ܦܘܡ ܥܩܪܐ
ܗܘܝܐ܀ ܐܘ ܚܕܐ ܕܒܗܘܢ ܢܦܠܐ: ܐܝܟ ܐ̱ܢܫ ܕܐܡܪ ܒܠܒܐ: ܕܠܒܐ: ܘܠܒܐ: ܠܠܒܐ܀
ܐܘ ܬܪܬܝܢ: ܐܝܟ ܐ̱ܢܫ ܕܐܡܪ: ܒܕܠܒܐ: ܘܒܠܒܐ: ܘܕܠܒܐ: ܒܘܠܒܐ܀ ܐܘ ܬܠܬ:
ܐܝܟ ܐ̱ܢܫ ܕܐܡܪ ܒܕܠܒܐ. ܒܕܘܠܒܐ: ܘܒܕܠܒܐ. ܘܕܒܠܒܐ܀ ܐܘ ܐܪܒܥܬܝܗܘܢ
ܐܟܚܕܐ. ܐܝܟ ܐ̱ܢܫ ܕܐܡܪ ܘܒܕܘܠܒܐ. ܘܒܕܠܠܒܐ܀ ܘܪܘܚ ܒܚܒܘܬ: ܘܟܠ ܐܢܫܐ
ܕܢܦܠ ܚܕܐ ܡܢ ܡܩܦܠܬܐ ܩܕܡ ܒܫܡܗ: ܘܐܬܘܬܗ ܦܘܡܝܬܐ ܕܡܬܐܪܟܢܝܬܐ 18b
ܦܬܚܐ ܕܡܬܦܬܚܐ ܗܘ ܦܩܘܕܬܐ ܐܠܐ ܐܢ ܢܗܘܐ ܐܬܘܬܐ ܦܘܡܝܬܐ ܕܒܫܡܗ: ܐ:
ܕܡܬܐܡܪܢܐ ܕܡܬܐܪܟܢܝܢ ܠܦܩܘܕܬܐ ܐܢ ܚܕܐ ܐܝܟܢܐ ܗܝ ܦܩܘܕܬܐ ܐܘ ܬܠܬ:
ܐܝܟ ܕܠܒܐ: ܠܠܒܐ ܘܡܢܪܐ܀ ܘܐܢ ܢܦܠ ܚܕܐ ܕܡܢ ܦܩܘܕܬܐ ܩܕܡ ܒܫܡܗ
ܘܐܬܘܬܗ ܦܘܡܝܬܐ ܥܩܝܡܬܐ. ܡܬܦܬܚܐ ܗܝ ܡܩܦܠܬܐ: ܐܠܐ ܐܢ ܢܗܘܐ ܐܬܘܬܐ
ܦܘܡܝܬܐ ܕܒܫܡܗ: ܡܬܪ̈ܦܝܢ ܠܦܘܡܝܬܐ: ܐܝܟ: ܐ: ܘܐ̱ܢܫܐ: ܘܡܦܬܚܐ ܠܗ
ܠܦܩܘܕܬܐ ܕܡܢ ܩܕܡܘܗܝ܀ ܘܐܢ ܢܩܦܢ ܬܪܬܝܢ ܡܩܦܠܬܐ ܩܕܡ ܒܫܡܗ ܘܐܬܘܬܗ
ܦܘܡܝܬܐ ܕܡܬܐܪܟܢܝܬܐ: ܡܬܦܬܚܢ̈ ܦܩܘ̈ܕܬܐ ܦܘܡܝ̈ܬܐ: ܘܡܬܪܟܢܐ ܬܪܬܝܢܬܐ:
ܐܝܟ ܐ̱ܢܫ ܕܐܡܪ: ܒܕܒܝܬܐ: ܘܒܕܒܝܬܐ ܒܒܝܬܐ.

2 ܐܬܘ̈ܬܐ ܠܐܘܬܝܢ] ܠܐܘܬܝܢ ܐܬܘ̈ܬܐ B 3 ܡܬܐܡܪ̈ܢ] ܡܬܐܡܪܝܢ BL 4 ܕܒܗܘܢ] ܕܒܗ OG 5 ܘܗܟܢ ܗܘܐ ܒܩܘܡ] ܡܢ ܒܦܘ ܗܘܐ OG 7 ܦܘܫܐ] om. OG | ܘܡܬܪ̈ܦܝܢ] ܡܬܪ̈ܦܝܢ OG 8 ܘܙܘܥܐ] ܙܘܥܐ OG 9 ܥܩܪܐ] ܥܩܪܐ L 11 ܕܒܠܒܐ] ܘܕܒܠܒܐ B 12 ܕܒܐܠܒܐ...13 ܘܕܠܒܐ] om. B (homoeoteleuton) 15 ܦܬܚܐ] om. B | ܘܒܫܡܗ...ܐܬܘܬܐ] ܐܬܘܬܐ ܕܒܫܡܗ ܦܘܡ OG 16 ܡܢ...17 ܦܩܘܕܬܐ] om. B (homoe.) 17 ܒܫܡܗ] ܒܫܡܗ OG and often elsewhere 18 ܡܬܦܬܚܐ] om. B 20 ܐܬܘܬܐ, OG 22 ܒܒܝܬܐ] ܒܒܝܬܐ OGB

[1] Here begins the older part of L, the previous nine folios being a later addition. | [2] Poorly transmitted and expressed such that it appears to be masculine. | [3] Another instance of the scribes not understanding their text.

ܣ

ܒܡܬܒܥܝܢܐ܀ ܘܐܦ ܐܝܟܢܐ ܐܬܘܬܐ ܦܘܩܕܢܝ̈ܬܐ ܕܒܗܝܢ ܡܬܒܥܝܐ: ܡܡܠܠܢܐ
ܦܘܩܕܢܐ ܡܢ ܡܡܠܠܐ ܘܡܬܦܠܓܐ ܠܬܪ̈ܬܝܢܝܬܐ: ܐܝܟ ܐ̱ܢܫ ܕܐܡܪ: ܒܡ̈ܫܝܚܢܐ:
19a ܘܒܡ̈ܫܝܚܢܐ: ܕܒܡ̈ܫܝܚܢܐ ܠܡ̈ܫܝܚܢܐ܀ ܘܐܦ ܢܦܠܝܢ ܐܪܒܥ ܦܘܩܕܢܝ̈ܬܐ ܩܕܡ
ܟܫܡܗ: ܕܐܬܘܬܗ ܦܘܩܕܢܝܬܐ ܡܬܐܡܪܝܢܝܬܐ: ܡܡܠܠܢܐ ܦܘܩܕܢܐ ܦܘܩܕܢܝܬܐ
ܘܠܡܠܟܘܬܐ: ܘܡܬܦܠܓܢܐ ܠܬܪ̈ܬܝܢܝܬܐ: ܐܝܟ ܐ̱ܢܫ ܕܐܡܪ: ܘܒܦܘ̈ܩܕܢܐ: ܘܒܦܘܩܕܢ
ܘܕܒܝܬܐ܀ ܘܐܦ ܐܝܟܢܐ ܐܬܘܬܐ ܦܘܩܕܢܝܬܐ ܕܒܗܝܢ ܡܬܒܥܝܐ: ܡܬܦܠܓܐ
ܦܘܩܕܢܐ ܦܘܩܕܢܝܬܐ ܘܠܡܠܟܘܬܐ: ܘܡܡܠܠܢܐ ܠܐܘܟܠܐ: ܐܝܟ ܐ̱ܢܫ ܕܐܡܪ:
ܒܒܡ̈ܫܝܚܢܐ. ܘܕܒܡ̈ܫܝܚܢܐ: ܒܒܡ̈ܫܝܚܢܐ܀ ܘܐܦ ܢܦܠܝܢ ܐܪܒܥ ܦܘܩܕܢܝ̈ܬܐ ܩܕܡ
ܟܫܡܗ: ܘܐܝܟܢܐ ܐܬܘܬܐ ܦܘܩܕܢܝܬܐ ܡܬܐܡܪܝܢܝܬܐ: ܡܬܦܠܓܢܐ ܦܘܩܕܢܐ
ܦܘܩܕܢܝܬܐ ܘܠܡܠܟܘܬܐ: ܘܡܡܠܠܢܐ ܠܬܪ̈ܬܝܢܝܬܐ ܘܕܡܫܝܚܬܐ ܐܝܟ ܐ̱ܢܫ ܕܐܡܪ:
ܘܟܪ̈ܡܐ: ܘܟܒܝܬܐ. ܘܐܝܟ ܫܡܗܐ ܗܠܝܢ ܕܒܝܬܐ ܕܫܡܗܘܬܐ: ܘܟܒܝܬܐܠܗܘ
ܘܟܒܝܬܡܘܬܐ ܘܟܒܝܬܡܠܟܘܬܐ ܘܟܒܝܬܐܠܗܐ ܘܟܒܝܬܫܡܫܐ܀[1] ܘܐܦ ܐܝܟܢܐ
19b ܐܬܘܬܐ ܡܢܡܠܠܐ ܕܒܗܝܢ ܡܬܒܥܝܐ. ܡܡܠܠܢܐ ܦܘܩܕܢܐ ܦܘܩܕܢܝܬܐ ܘܠܡܠܟܘܬܐ
ܘܡܬܦܠܓܢܐ ܠܐܘܟܠܐ ܘܕܡܫܝܚܬܐ ܐܝܟ ܐ̱ܢܫ ܕܐܡܪ ܘܒܒܡ̈ܫܝܚܢܐ: ܘܒܒܝܬܐ
ܘܒܒܝ̈ܬܐ܀ ܡܫܠܡܢܐ ܕܝܢ ܐܦ ܗܢܐ ܠܡܕܥ ܕܟܠ ܦܘܩܕܢܐ ܕܢܦܠ ܩܕܡ ܟܫܡܗ:
ܐܘ ܒ ܡܠܐ ܡܬܦܢܝܐ: ܐܘ ܒ ܦܬܚܐ: ܐܠܐ ܐܢ ܢܗܘܐ ܦܘܩܕܢܐ ܕܒܗܝܢ: ܐ:
ܘܡܛܠ ܠܗ ܠܡܬܐܡܪܢܘܬܗ ܐܘ ܠܡܠܟܘܬܗ: ܠܦܘܩܕܢܐ ܗܘ ܕܡܢܡܠܠܗ܀[2]
ܘܐܘܪܚ ܡܩܕܡܐ ܩܕܡܝܐ. ܐܘ ܦܬܚܐ ܗܢܘ ܡܢܘܬܐ ܠܐ ܡܬܦܢܝܢ: ܗܠܝܢ ܐܝܟ
ܐܘܟܠ ܦܘܩܕܢܐ ܕܢܦܠܝܢ ܩܕܡ ܡܠܬܐ܀ ܩܕܡ ܟܠܐ ܕܝܢ: ܠܐܘܪܚ ܡܢܗܘܢ ܢܦܠܝܢ: ܕ:
ܗܗ: ܐܝܟ ܐܝܬ ܕܐܡܪ: ܕܢܚܬ. ܘܢܚܬܐ ܘܗܠܝܢ ܫܩܠܝܢ ܠܦܫܝܩܬܐ܀
ܗܘܠܐ ܡܫܡܗܐ ܐܢܫ ܐܝܟ ܦܘܩܕܢܐ ܕܢܦܠܝܢ ܩܕܡ ܡܠܐ܀[3]
ܦܘܠܐ ܘܐܡܪܢܢ ܕܐܝܬܝܗܘܢ ܗܠܝܢ ܐܘܟܠ: ܐ: ܩ: ܕ: ܠ: ܕܡܬܩܪܝܢ ܩܢܘܡܝܐ
20a ܐܡܬܐ. ܘܡܩܛܥܝܢ ܠܡܬܒܥܝܢܐ ܕܡܬܢܗܪܐ ܟܠܗܘܢ: ܘܡܡܫܩܪܝܢ ܠܗܘܢ ܪܒܝܐ
ܘܦܘܪܩܢܐ܀[4] ܩܪܘܢ ܐ ܗܘܐ ܠܦܘܪܩܢܐ ܡܢܡܠܐ ܐܝܟ ܠܐܡܪ: ܩܦܘܡ ܐܬܘܡ܀
ܩܕܡ ܕܝܢ ܗܘܐ ܠܦܘܪܩܢܐ ܠܐܘܟܠܐ: ܐܝܟ ܡܦܝܡ܀ ܘܩܪܐ ܗܘܐ ܩܢܘܡܝܐ

1 ܡܡܠܠܢܐ] ܘܡܡܠܠܢܐ BL 4 ܐܬܘܬܐ, OG | ܦܘܩܕܢܝܬܐ...ܡܬܐܡܪܝܢܝܬܐ] om. BL (homoe.) 6 ܘܐܦ] ܐܦ L 8 ܒܒܡܫܝܚܢܐ] ܘܒܡܫܝܚܢܐ OGL ܘܒܡܫܝܚܢܐ B ܘܐܦ] ܐܦ B 10 ܐܝܟ] om. L 11 ܗܠܝܢ] om. L | ܕܫܡܗܘܬܐ] ܕܫܡܗܘܬܐ (without vowel) L 12 ܘܟܒܝܬܫܡܫܐ] ܘܒܝܬܫܡܫܐ L 13 ܕܒܗܝܢ...ܦܘܩܕܢܐ] om. OG(homoe.) 16 ܢܗܘܐ ܦܘܩܕܢܐ] ܢܗܘܐ ܐܬܘܬܐ ܡܢܡܠܠܐ L | ܕܒܗܝܢ] ܕܒܗܝܢ OG 17 ܘܡܛܠ] ܡܛܠ OGB 22 ܩܢܘܡܝܐ] om. B 24 ܗܘܐ ܐ] ܗܘܐ B ܐ ܗܘܐ G 25 ܐܝܟ...21,1 ܡܦܝܡ] om. B(homoe.)

[1] 1 Sam 30.28-9, hence Gottheil's ? is unecessary (*Elias*, 19*). | [2] This sentence (ܡܫܠܡܢܐ...ܕܡܢܡܠܠܗ) means, *finally it must be known that every case (i.e. b d w l) that occurs in front of a word is to be read as either vowelless or with pathach, unless the first letter of the word be alaph, inasmuch as this causes the vowel or the shewa of the preceding particle to disappear.* | [3] I have not seen the prefixes of the imperfect and infinitive called "cases" as here. See p.150. | [4] Note the quššāyā, though elsewhere with rukkāḵā, ܣ,23, ܣܐ,17.

ܡܗ ܠܦܪܘܩܐ ܕܟܠܗܝܢ ܚܝܪ̈ܬܐ ܘܫܘܚܠ̈ܦܬܐ: ܐܝܟ ܠܡܫ̈ܬܐܐ ܢܦܫܗ̇܀ ܘܟܝܢܝܐ ܕܪܚܝܩ ܢܦܫܗ̇܀ ܐ̄ ܗ̇ܘܐ ܠܦܪܘܩܐ ܕܐܘܚܐ ܕܟܪܝܐ ܐܝܟ ܠܢܦܫܗ̇܀ ܘܠܦܪܘܩܐ ܕܟܠܗܝܢ ܕܡܬܐܠܝܢ ܐܝܟ ܠܢܦܫܗ̇ ܗ̇ܘ܀ ܡܦܩ̈ܢܝܢ ܕܝܢ ܠܡܬܒܥܢܘܬܐ: ܐܟܘܬ ܕܗܝ ܕܐܡܪ ܒܡܠܬܐ: ܕܟܐ: ܗܟܝ: ܦܠܗ: ܗܠܝ: ܗܘܪ: ܕܘܪ: ܡܟܪ: ܗܓܪ. ܦܓܠ: ܒ݁ ܒܬܠܬ ܡܢ ܗ̇ܠܝܢ ܐܘܚܕ̈ܐ ܐܬܘ̈ܬܐ: ܟܠ ܟܠ ܚܕܐ ܡܢ ܗ̇ܠܝܢ ܡ̈ܠܐ ܡܬܡܢܝܐ ܠܬܠܬ ܕܟܠܗܝܢ ܡܬܒܥܢܘܬܐ ܘܐܝܟ ܕܟܝܠ: ܐܟܘܬ ܕܐܡܪ ܐܬܪܟܐ: ܐܬܪܟܝ: ܐܬܗܦܟܝ: ܐܦܠܛ: ܐܬܦܠܓܘ: ܐܬܕܘܕ: ܐܬܪܟܘ: ܐܬܟܠܠܘ: ܐܬܟܠܝ܀ ܟܗ ܟܕܐ ܟܢ ܙܩܝܦܐ ܘܡܬܘܕܐ ܟܗ ܒܝܬܠܐ ܦܬܘ̈ܪܐ: ܐܬܪܟܐ ܡܬܪ̈ܟܐ ܝܪ̈ܟܐ: ܐܝܪܟܐ: ܐܬܪܟܝ: ܡܬܪܟܝ: 20b
ܢܪܟܝ: ܐܬܪܟܝ: ܐܬܟܠܝ ܡܬܟܠܝ: ܢܬܟܠܝ: ܐܬܟܠܝ: ܐܬܗܦܟܘ: ܡܬܗܦܟܝ: ܢܬܗܦܟܘ: ܐܬܗܦܟܘ܀ ܟܕ ܗܘܐ ܙܢܐ ܦܝܣ ܫܪܒܐ ܕܡ̈ܠܐ ܡܬܦܩܕܢܝܬܐ ܟܠ ܗܦܟܬܐ܀ ܗ̇ܠܝܢ ܐܝܟ ܡܬܦܩܕܢܐ ܕܢܦܠܢ ܟܠ ܡ̈ܠܐ: ܘܐܦ ܦܘ̈: ܪ̈: ܕܡܠܟܢ ܟܠ ܦܩܕܐ: ܡܠܟܢ ܠܗܘܢ ܟܠ ܡ̈ܠܐ ܐܝܟ ܕܟܝܐ ܘܟܢܝܐ: ܕܟܐ: ܘܟܐ: ܕܢܟܐ: ܘܢܟܐ. ܦ̄: ܕܝܢ ܘܟܠ ܠܐ ܡܠܟܢ ܟܠ ܡ̈ܠܐ܀

ܗܘܐܠܐ ܠܡܩܝܡܐ ܐܡܟܢ ܐܝܟ ܐܬܘ̈ܬܐ ܕܬܪܬܝܢ ܙܘܓܐ ܘܡܘܡ̈ܢܐ: ܟܕ ܦܝܫܬܘܬܐ ܗܢܫܐ ܘܐܝܟ ܠܗܘܢ ܗܘܝܐ ܘܐܦܢܝܢ ܕܝܠܗ ܐܬܝܗܘܢ ܐܬܘ̈ܬܐ ܡܫܬܚܠܦܢܝ̈ܬܐ ܘܪܟܝܢ ܡܬܪ̈ܟܟܝܢ ܘܩܫܝܢ ܡܬܩܫ̈ܝܢ: ܒ: ܓ: ܕ: ܟ: ܦ: ܬ܀ ܦܘܓ̈ܝ ܗ̇ܠܝܢ ܥܠ ܐܘ ܩܘܫܝܐ ܡܬܪܟܟܝܢ ܘܡܬܩܫܝܢ: ܐܘ ܒܙܢܐ ܩܢܘܢܝܐ: ܩܘܫܝܐ ܩܡ: ܗ̇ܠܝܢ ܘܡܬܪܟܟܝܢ ܡܢ ܢܛܝܪܝܢ ܘܠܐ ܦܝܫܬܘܬܐ ܗܢܫܐ: ܡܛܠ ܕܝܩܢܘܢܐ ܕܝܢ: ܗ̇ܠܝܢ 21a
ܘܡܬܪܟܟܝܢ ܟܕ ܦܝܫܬܘܬܐ ܗܢܫܐ ܐܘܟܝܬ ܐܬܘ̈ܬܐ܀ ܗ̇ܠܝܢ ܩܡ ܐܝܟ ܐܬܐ: ܡܕܢܚܐ: ܩ݁ܕܡܝܬܐ ܐܓܪܐ: ܟܘܪܬܐ: ܡܕܒܚܐ: ܡܝܬܒܠܐ: ܠܘܟܬܐ:[1] ܗ̇ܠܝܢ ܕܝܢ ܢܛܝܪܝܢ ܡܬܪܟܟܝܢ܀ ܐܝܟ ܟܬܒܐ: ܢܘܟܪܝܐ ܗܫܐ: ܙܟܬܐ: ܟܕܘ: ܣܟܡܐ: ܓܒܪܐ: ܙܘܟܬܐ: ܗܦܟܬܐ: ܘܗ̇ܠܝܢ ܡܬܐܠܝܢ ܡܬܩܫܝܢ܀ ܐܝܟ ܕܝܢ ܕܡܬܪܟܟܝܢ ܒܩܢܘܢܐ: ܟܕ ܐܘܚܕ ܡܩܒܠܬܐ ܕܡܠܟܢ ܟܠ ܦܩܕܐ ܡܬܪܟܟܝܢ: ܐܟܘܬ ܕܐܡܪ ܟܬܒܐ ܕܟܬܒܐ: ܠܟܬܒܐ:[2] ܟܬܒܐ: ܠܟܬܒܐ: ܘܟܬܒܐ: ܕܟܬܒܐ: ܟܬܝܒܐ: ܕܟܬܝܒܐ: ܘܟܬܝܒܐ: ܠܟܬܝܒܐ

2 ܗ̇ܘ] ...3 ܘܠܦܪܘܩܐ om. BL (homoe.) 5 ܗ̇ܠܝܢ...ܐܘܚܕ²] om. B(homoe.) | ܐܬܘ̈ܬܐ] ܐܬܘ̈ܬܐ O 6 ܘܐܝܟ ܕܟܝܠ] ܘܐܝܟܢ, OG | ܐܬܪܟܐ] points confused in all mss 10 ܡܬܦܩܕܢܝܬܐ] ܡܬܦܩܕܢܝܢ B 11 ܘܐܦ] G corrupt 16 ܕܝܠܗ...ܡܫܬܚܠܦܢܝ̈ܬܐ] ܕܝܠܗ ܐܬܘ̈ܬܐ ܐܝܠܝܢ ܡܫܬܚܠܦܢܝܬܐ B 20 ܗ̇ܠܝܢ] erasure mark L | ܐܝܟ] om. G 21 ܗ̇ܠܝܢ] om. B 22 ܓܒܪܐ] ܓܒܪܐ B 25 ܟܬܒܐ] ܟܬܒܐ L | L adds ܟܬܒܐ after ܕܟܬܒܐ | ܠܟܬܒܐ] om. B

[1] See Merx, *Grammatica*, 71. | [2] See Merx, *Grammatica*, 69,VII.

ܨܘ

ܒ̈ܬܐ: ܕܒ̈ܬܐ: ܘܒ̈ܬܐ: ܠܒ̈ܬܐ: ܒܬܫܡܫܬܐ: ܕܬܫܡܫܬܐ: ܘܬܫܡܫܬܐ: ܠܬܫܡܫܬܐ܀ ܦ:
ܐܝܟ ܗܠܝܢ ܙ̈ܢܐ ܕܡܫ̈ܚܠܦܢ ܘܕܘܟܝܬܗ ܠܡܠܬܐ ܘܗܠܝܢ ܢܩܝܦܢ܀[1] ܐܝܟ ܡܬܚܫܒܢܐ
ܐܬܘܬܐ ܦܬܝܚܬܐ ܕܟܬܒܝܢ: ܠ̄: ܫܒܝܠܐ: ܘܒܬܪܗ: ܪ̄: ܐܘ: ܠ̄: ܡܬܒܥܝܢܬܐ

21b ܡܬܐܡܪܢܝܬܐ: ܘܒܬܪ ܡܢ ܩܕܡܝܗ ܚܕܐ ܡܢ ܡܫܩܠܬܐ: ܠܐ ܡܬܬܚܒܐ ܗܝ: ܠ̄:
ܘܚܢܢ ܠܟܬܒܝܢ: ܐܠܐ ܡܦܩܢܝܬܐ ܕܬܫܪܝܬܐ: ܐܝܟ ܗܝ ܕܦܬܚܝܢ ܘܠܘܗܝ ܚܒܘܫܝܬܐ:
ܘܬܘܪܝ ܐܘܚܐ: ܘܒܬܘܪܐ[2] ܕܐܣܩܘܕ: ܘܬܬܘܒ: ܘ̈ܐܘܗܝ ܘܬܬܘܒܘܢ܀ ܐܝܟ ܗܘܐ:
ܠ̄: ܕܚܢܢ ܠܟܬܒܝܢ ܡܬܐܡܪܢܝܬܐ ܡܬܬܚܒܐ: ܐܝܟ ܗܝ ܕܐܡܪܝܢ: ܒܬܫܡܫܬܐ:
ܘܬܫܡܫܬܐ ܠܬܫܡܫܬܐ. ܕܬܫܡܫܬܐ܀ ܘܠܝ ܡܬܚܙܝܢ ܐܬܘܬܐ ܦܬܝܚܬܐ ܕܟܬܒ:
ܪ̄: ܐܘ: ܠ̄: ܡܬܐܡܪܢܝܬܐ: ܘܒܬܪ ܡܢ ܩܕܡܝܗ: ܪ̄: ܡܫܩܠܬܐ: ܘܡܢ ܒܬܪܗ
ܡܫܩܠܬܐ ܚܒܝܫܬܐ ܡܦܩܢܝܬܐ ܕܬܫܪܝܬܐ: ܪ̄: ܗܝ ܕܐܝܬܝܗ ܡܫܩܠܬܐ ܕܡܢ ܐܬܘܬܐ
ܦܬܝܚܬܐ ܕܟܬܒܝܢ: ܐܝܟ ܗܝ ܕܐܡܪܝܢ: ܘܪܘܡܐ ܘܪܘܝ: ܘܐܬܪܘܡܘܢ ܘܪܘܡܬܐ܀
ܐܝܟ ܗܘܐ ܐܬܘܬܐ ܦܬܝܚܬܐ ܕܟܬܒܝܢ ܫܒܝܠܐ. ܡܬܦܬܚܢܐ: ܪ̄: ܡܫܩܠܬܐ:

22a ܘܡܬܬܚܒܐ ܗܝ ܐܬܘܬܐ ܦܬܝܚܬܐ ܕܢܩܫ ܟܬܒܝܢ: ܐܝܟ ܗܝ ܕܐܡܪܝܢ: ܘܪ̈ܘܡܐ:
ܘܪ̈ܘܡܬܐ: ܘܪ̈ܘܡܬܐ܀ ܐܝܟ ܡܬܚܫܒܢܬܐ ܚܕܐ ܡܢ ܗ̈ܠܝܢ ܢܩܝܦܢ: ܟܡܝܢܬܐ
ܫܡܫܬܐ ܕܡܠܬܐ ܘܕܡܬܚܠܦܢܐ ܡܢ ܗܘܠܐ: ܟܕ ܗܘ ܕܡܬܐܡܪ ܚܕ ܫܡܐ:
ܘܟܕ ܐܘ ܕܡܬܬܢܝܬܐ: ܚܕܢܝܬܐ ܐܘ ܬܪ̈ܝܢܝܬܐ: ܐܘ ܣܓܝܐܢܝܬܐ: ܟܕ ܗܘ
ܡܬܐܡܪܐ ܒܙܒܢ̈ܐ ܬܠܬܐ ܘܒܫܘܚܠܦܐ ܕܦܪ̈ܨܘܦܐ ܡܬܐܡܪ. ܟܠܢܫ ܡܢ ܗܠܝܢ ܬܠܬܐ:
ܐܝܟ ܕܟܬܒܐ: ܟܬܒܬ: ܐܡܪܝܢ: ܟܬܒܬ: ܟܬܒܬܝ: ܟܬܒܬܘܢ: ܟ̄ ܚܢܢ ܠܐ
ܡܫܬܟܚܐ ܙܘܓܐ ܒܟܠܗܘܢ ܦܪ̈ܨܘܦܐ: ܘܟܠ ܗܠܝܢ ܐܝܟ ܦܫܛ ܒܟܠܗܘܢ ܦܪ̈ܨܘܦܐ
ܘܩܠܐ ܕܟܠܗܘܢ ܡܬܐܡܪ ܟܠܢܫ ܚܕ ܡܢ ܗܠܝܢ ܬܠܬܐ: ܐܠܐ ܠܝ ܒܙܒܢ̈ܐ ܕܒܬܪܟܢ܀
ܠܝ ܕܝܢ ܒܡܬܚܠܦ ܒܫܡܗ̈ܐ ܘܡܠܬܐ ܡܬܚܫܒܐ ܚܕܐ ܡܠܟܐ: ܐܝܟ ܕܡܬܐܡܪܐ
ܚܕ ܡܢ ܙܘܓܐ ܕܡܠܬܐ: ܡܫܬܘܕܥ ܡܢ ܙܟܝܐ: ܗܟܢܐ ܕܡܬܐܡܪܐ ܒܟܠܗܘܢ ܩܠܐ

22b ܒܬܪ ܗܘ ܙܘܓܐ[3] ܘܡܫܬܘܕܥ ܗܘ ܦܪܨܘܦܐ ܘܙܒܢܐ: ܘܒܗ ܒܟܠܗܘܢ ܦܪ̈ܨܘܦܐ

1 ܠܬܫܡܫܬܐ] B corrupt in the preceding 2 ܘܕܘܟܝܬܗ G | ܐܝܟ] ܘܐܝܟ L 6 ܘܬܬܘܒܘܢ] ܘܬܬܘܒܘܢ L 8 ܘܬܫܡܫܬܐ ܠܬܫܡܫܬܐ ܕܬܫܡܫܬܐ] ܘܬܫ ܠܬܫ ܕܬܫ L | ܘܠܝ] B corrupt 9 ܪ̄¹] om. L 11 ܕܟܬܒܝܢ] ܟܬܒܝܢ L | ܐܝܟ ܗܝ] ܐܝܟ L | ܘܪܘܡܬܐ] om. B 14 ܗܠܝܢ] om. BL | ܟܡܝܢܬܐ] ܟܡܝܢ L 17 ܡܬܐܡܪܐ] ܡܬܐܡܪ ܟܠܢܫ OGB 18 ܟܬܒܬܝ] ܡܢ ܟܬܒܬܝ B 19 ܡܫܬܟܚܐ] ܡܫܬܟܚ L | ...ܦܫܛ 20 ܦܫܛ ܒܟܠܗܘܢ ܦܪ̈ܨܘܦܐ ܩܠܐ OGB ܦܫܛ ܒܟܠܗܘܢ ܦܪ̈ܨܘܦܐ L 22 ܙܘܓܐ] ܙܘܓܐ ܘܟܠܗܘܢ] ܒܟܠܗܘܢ OGBL | ܡܫܬܘܕܥ G 23 ܙܘܓܐ] ܙܘܓܐ OGBL | ܡܫܬܘܕܥ G | ܘܒܗ] ܘܒܗ OG

[1] On the ܦ, see ܨܗ,15, also p.118. | [2] This belongs here since Jacob is not speaking only of ܘ and ܝ, (cf. ܟܛ,15). Merx, *Grammatica*, 70, should be supplemented accordingly. When he writes ܘܪ̈ܘܡܬܐ (l.14), he does not contradict this rule but is rather following another grammatical law (see p.116). | [3] From ܛ,12,21, it is evident that he is dealing with conjugation, i.e. ܙܘܓܐ = συζυγίᾳ.

ܠܐ ܕܟܠܗܘܢ ܟܠܗ ܡ̈ܠܐ ܕܗܘ ܙܒܢܐ ܗܘܘ ܐܝܟܢܐ܀ ܐܠܐ ܐܢ ܬܗܘܐ ܡܠܬܐ. ܘܡܦܩܘܕܢܐ
ܐܝܟܐ ܕܟܠܗܝܢ: ܗܠܝܢ ܕܒܥܘܬܪܗ ܕܡܠܬܐ: ܐܝܟ ܢܦܩܘܕ: ܢܩܛܠ: ܢܐܡܪ: ܢܦܠܘܚ: ܢܐܠܦ:
ܘܐܝܟ ܢܒܥܐ: ܢܚܙܐ: ܢܗܘܐ: ܢܐܬܐ܀ ܟܠܗܘܢ ܟܡܐ ܡ̈ܠܐ ܕܐܝܟ ܗܠܝܢ: ܡܢ
ܡܬܐܡܪ̈ܢ ܟܠ ܦܪ̈ܨܘܦܐ ܩܕܡܝܐ: ܡܢ ܬܠܬܐ ܠܘܬ ܬܪ̈ܝܢ. ܐ̄. ܘܫܪܟܐ ܡܬܦܥܠܐ
ܐܬܬܐ ܠܘܬ ܢܩ̈ܒܬܐ ܕܟܠܗܘܢ[1] ܐܝܟ ܐܬܦܩܕ: ܐܬܩܛܠ. ܐܬܐܡܪ: ܐܬܦܠܚ: ܐܬܐܠܦ: ܘܫܪܟܐ ܕܐܝܟ
ܗܠܝܢ܀[2] ܐܝܟ ܕܒܟܘܠܗܘܢ ܠܟܠܗܘܢ ܕܡܬܦܥܠܐ ܚܕܐ ܡܢ ܗܠܝܢ ܢܩܒܠ ܘܬܗܘܐ
ܐܬܬܐ ܕܡܢ ܩܕܡܘܗܝ ܡܟܝܠܐ: ܗܘ ܕܡܢ ܩܕܡ ܡܟܝܠܐ: ܐܘ ܕܡܬܟܠܐ: ܐܘ ܕܚܒܪܬܐ:
ܐܘ ܦܠܓܘܬܐ: ܡܦܩܬܢܝܬܐ ܕܡܬܦܥܠܢܐ ܐܬܬܐ ܕܒܟܠܗܘܢ ܠܟܠܗܘܢ. ܐܝܟ ܡܦܩܕ:
ܢܟܬܐ: ܡܩܛܠ: ܐܬܠ: ܟܬܠ: ܟܬܝܠ: ܐܬܩܛܠ: ܐܬܦܩܕ[3]: ܐܝܟ ܬܗܘܐ ܐܬܬܐ 23a
ܕܡܢ ܩܕܡܘܗܝ ܘܐܬܬܐ ܡܬܐܡܪܢܝܬܐ ܐܘ ܗ̄ܗ̄ ܫܪܟܐ: ܐܘ ܗܘ ܕܒܟܠܗܘܢ: ܐܘ: ܬ:
ܫܪܟܐ ܡܦܩܕܢܝܬܐ ܡܬܦܥܠܢܐ ܐܬܬܐ ܗܘ ܐܬܦܥܠܬܐ:[4] ܐܝܟ ܬܫܬܐ ܢܟܬ: ܢܐܡܪ: ܘܐܝܟ
ܢܦܩܕ. ܘܢܩܛܠ: ܘܐܝܟ ܡܢܬ ܘܐܬܠ܀ ܐܝܟ ܬܗܘܐ ܡܟܝܠܐ ܗܘ ܠܟܠܗܘܢ: ܘܟܠ
ܐܝܟܐ ܕܟܠ ܡܦܩܘܕܢܐ: ܬܗܘܐ ܒܪ̈ܘܟܐ ܟܬܒ: ܐܘ ܩܛܠ: ܐܘ ܐܬܚܝ: ܐܘ ܐܬܟܬܒ:
ܡܢ ܟܠ ܦܪ̈ܨܘܦܐ ܚܝܐ ܘܒܪܝܐ ܐܘ ܢܩܒܬܐ: ܩܪܝܒܐ ܐܘ ܠܟܠܗܝܢ ܡܬܐܡܪܐ:
ܘܟܠܗܘܢ ܒܟܠܗܘܢ ܐܬܬܐ ܐܬܪܬܝܬܐ ܘܐܬܦܥܠܬܐ ܚܕܬܐ ܦܪ̈ܨܘܦܐ ܢܩ̈ܦܐ:
ܡܬܦܥܠܐ ܐܬܬܐ ܐܬܦܥܠܐ: ܒܫܪܟܢܐ ܕܗܘ ܡܟܝܠܐ: ܡܢ ܗܘܐ ܗܘ ܐܬܬܐ
ܡܬܐܡܪܢܝܬܐ: ܘܗܘ ܕܡܢ ܩܕܡܘܗܝ ܡܟܝܠܐ: ܐܝܟ ܐܬܟ ܕܐܡܪ: ܟܬܒܬ ܟܬܒܬ:
ܟܬܒܬܝ: ܟܬܒܬܘܢ: ܟܬܒܬܝܢ: ܩܛܠܬ: ܩܛܠܬ: ܐܬܩܛܠܬ: ܐܬܟܬܒܬܘܢ ܐܬܟܬܒܬ܀
ܐܝܟ ܗܘܐ ܐܬܬܐ ܐܬܦܥܠܬܐ ܕܒܫܪܟܢܐ ܡܟܝܠܐ. ܘܗܘ ܕܡܢ ܩܕܡܘܗܝ
ܡܬܐܡܪܢܝܬܐ: ܐܘ ܠܐܬܘܗܝ ܡܬܐܡܪ̈ܢܝܬܐ ܕܡܬܦܥܠܐ: ܐܝܟ ܐܬܟ ܕܐܡܪ: ܟܬܒܬ: 23b
ܩܛܠܬ: ܐܬܩܛܠܬ:[5] ܟܬܒܬܘܢ: ܩܛܠܬܘܢ܀ ܐܝܟ ܬܗܘܐ ܡܟܝܠܐ ܡܦܩܘܕܢܐ ܐܝܟܐ
ܕܩܐܡ: ܗܘ ܕܝܢ ܡܬܦܥܠܐ ܘܡܬܦܥܠܐ. ܟܕ ܬܗܘܐ ܡܢ ܟܬܒ ܙܒܢܐ ܕܟܬܒ. ܐܘ
ܐܬܟ: ܐܘ ܡܬܟܬܒ܀ ܘܐܢ ܬܗܘܐ ܡܦܩܘܕܢܐ ܐܝܟܐ ܕܩܐܡ: ܗܘ ܕܝܢ ܗܘܝܐ
ܡܬܦܥܠܐ ܘܡܬܦܥܠܐ ܟܕ ܬܗܘܐ ܡܢ ܩܛܠ ܙܒܢܐ: ܕܐܬܟܬܒ: ܐܘ ܢܬܟܬܒ: ܐܘ
ܢܬܟܬܒ܀ ܘܐܢ ܬܗܘܐ ܡܟܝܠܐ

1 ܟܠܗ] om. OGBL | ܙܒܢܐ] ܙܘܢܐ OGBL 2 ܢܩܛܠ] ܢܩܛܠ B 5 ܘܟܠܗܘܢ] ܘܟܠܗܝܢ OGB | ܐܬܩܛܠ] ܐܬܩܛܠ B 7 ܕܡܢ[1]] ܡܢ B 8 ܡܦܩܕ] ܡܦܩܕ B 9 ܐܬܦܩܕ] ܐܬܦܩܕ B 13 ܡܦܩܘܕܢܐ...ܟܬܒ] om. B(homoe.) 15 ܐܬܪܬܝܬܐ] ܐܬܪܬܝܬܐ OG ܦܪ̈ܨܘܦܐ] ܦܪܨܘܦܐ L 17 ܟܬܒܬ] om. B 18 ܩܛܠܬ] ܩܛܠܬ OGBL 19 ܡܬܐܡܪܢܝܬܐ B 20 ܟܬܒܬ] ܟܬܒܬ OG 21 ܐܝܟ ܬܗܘܐ ܡܟܝܠܐ] ܐܢ ܬܗܘܐ OG 22 ܡܬܦܥܠܐ ܘܡܬܦܥܠܐ] ܡܬܦܥܠܐ ܘܡܬܦܥܠܐ L | ܙܒܢܐ] ܙܘܢܐ GB ܙܘܢܐ L 23 ܐܬܟ] om. L

[1] Merx, *Grammatica*, 65. | [2] Merx, *Gramamtica*, 66,3; 63, IV. | [3] On the imperative of the Ethpeal, Merx, *Grammatica*, 80,II. | [4] Merx, *Grammatica*, 68,1. | [5] On the concurrence of *d* and *t*, Merx, *Grammatica*, 72,X.

ܦܣܘܩܬܐ ܡܪܕܘܬܐ ܡܬܦܪܫܐ ܐܬܘܬܐ ܐ̱ܚܪܢܝܬܐ ܕܒܫܘ̈ܠܡܗ: ܐܠܐ ܐܢ ܬܗܘܐ ܡܫܬܐ ܟܗ
ܘܡܦܩܘܕܬܐ ܦܪܨܘܦܐ ܡܫܡܠܝܐ ܐܘ ܟܬܒܘܐ: ܘܠܗܘܐ ܐܬܘܬܐ ܕܡܢ ܩܕܡܗ̇ ܕܐ̱ܚܪܢܝܬܐ
ܗܟܒܢܬܐ: ܘܡܢ ܩܕܡܗ̇ ܕܗܘ ܗܟܒܢܬܐ:[1] ܘܘ: ܟܕܢܝܬܐ: ܟܠܢܐ ܟܢ ܕܐܝܟ ܗܢܐ:
ܡܬܦܫܩܐ ܐ̱ܚܪܢܝܬܐ ܕܒܫܘ̈ܠܡܐ ܐܝܟ ܒܦܓܘܕܘܗܝ. ܘܒܥܒܕܘܗܝ ܘܐܬܥܘܕܒܘܗܝ
ܘܐܣܝܪܘܗܝ ܘܐܣܝܪܘܬܗܘܢ܀ ܘܢܘܗ ܠܟܝܢܐ: ܕܝ̄: ܕܟܠܐ ܟܠܐ ܒܫܘ̈ܠܡܐ
24a ܘܡܟܠܬܐ: ܘܐܝܬܘܗ̇ ܥܡܐ ܕܦܪܨܘܦܐ ܩܕܡܝܐ ܕܬܪܝܢܐ ܘܬܠܬܗ ܚܕܐ ܐܬܘܬܐ: ܐܘ ܬܪܬܝܢ
ܐܘ ܬܠܬ: ܕܡܬܦܫܩܐ ܗܘ: ܠ: ܐܝܟ ܐ̱ܢܫ ܕܐܡܪ: ܟܬܒܬܝ ܐܢܐ: ܫܡܥܬܝ: ܒܪܟܬܗ̇:
ܚܒܝܬܗ̇: ܡܫܟܚܬܗ̇: ܩܒܠܬܗ̇. ܦܬܚܬܗ̇܀ ܐܝܟ ܠܗܘܐ ܐ̈ܬܘܬܐ ܕܡܢ ܩܕܡ: ܠ̄: ܬ̄:
ܣܒܝܪܬܐ ܡܬܐܘܕܝܐ: ܠ: ܐܝܟ ܗܢܝܬܝ ܘܗܢܝܬܗ̇: ܘܩܪܝܬܝ: ܘܟܪܝܬܝ:
ܘܟܪܝܬܗ̇܀ ܘܐܦ ܕܝ: ܕܠܐ ܡܕܡ ܕܡܬܐܡܪ ܒܠܐ ܦܪܨܘܦܐ ܩܕܡܝܐ: ܘܐܝܬ
ܒܗ̇: ܬ̄: ܣܒܝܪܬܐ ܙ̈ܘܓܝ: ܐܝܟ ܡܣܝܬܗ̇: ܐܫܩܝܬܗ̇: ܐܚܝܬܗ̇. ܐܫܩܝܬܘܢ.
ܐܘܡܝܬܘܢ܀ ܐܝܟ ܐܝܬ ܒܗ̇: ܝ: ܠܐ ܬܐܙܠܝ ܗܟܝ: ܐܝܟ ܐܫܟܚܬܝ ܢܣܒܬܗ̇.
ܒܥܠܬܝ ܒܪܬܝ: ܐܦܩܬܝܘܢ: ܐܘܣܠܬܘܢ܀ ܐܝܟ ܒܠܐ ܦܪܨܘܦܐ ܕܐܣܝܪܐ
ܡܬܐܡܪ: ܠܐ ܬܐܙܠܝ ܐܢ ܐܝܬ ܒܗ̇: ܝ: ܣܒܝܪܬܐ: ܘܐܢ ܒܠܬ ܒܗ̇: ܐܝܟ ܐܝܬܝܬܘܢ:
ܐܫܟܚܬܘܢ: ܐܟܠܬܘܢ܀ ܗܟܢܐ ܬܘܒ ܘܐܢ ܬܗܘܐ ܒܡܬܚ̈ܬܝܬܐ ܐܝܬܝܬܗ̇:
24b ܐܘܒܠܬܗ̇: ܐܫܟܚܬܗ̇܀[2] ܐ̱ܚܪܢܐ ܕܝܢ ܐܡܪܝܢ ܕܙܘܓ ܕܬܐܦܫܩ: ܠ: ܕܡܦܩܕܬܐ ܕܒܘܟ
ܦܪܨܘܦܐ ܩܕܡܝܐ ܕܚܕܢܐ: ܠܬܐܘܕܝܘܢ ܕܝܢ: ܠ: ܕܡܬܡܟܟܐ ܘܒܟܠ ܦܪܨܘܦܐ ܠܐܟܝܠܬܐ

1 ܡܪܕܘܬܐ] ܡܪܕܘܬܗ B 2 ܐܘ] om. B 3 ܘܡܢ²...ܗܟܒܢܬܐ] om. L (homoe.) ܗܟܒܢܬܐ²] ܐܬܘܬܐ ܗܟܒܢܬܐ L 4 ܒܦܓܘܕܘܗܝ] ܒܦܘ̈ܓܕܘܗܝ B ܒܦܓܘܕܘܗܝ OG txt L ܘܐܬܥܘܕܒܘܗܝ] ܐܬܥܘܕܒܘܗܝ | ܘܒܥ̈ܒܕܘܗܝ] ܘܒܥܒܕܘܗܝ GB 6 ܘܐܝܬܘܗ̇] ܘܐܝܬܘܗ̇ L 7 ܗܘ] ܗܝ L 12 ܐܝܟ] om. OG | ܐܫܟܚܬܝ] ܐܫܟܚܬܗ̇ OGL 16 ܕܝܢ] om. L 17 ܠܬܐܘܕܝܘܢ] ܠܬܐܘܕܝܘܢ G ܠܬܐܘܕܝ BL

[1] The omission is found in L but not B, indicating that the latter is independent of the former. | [2] Only here in Jacob (or rather his scholiast) have I seen quššāyā required in ܐܝܬܝܬܘܢ, ܐܫܟܚܬܘܢ and the like; hence I suggest that the ܠܐ of l.13 should be omitted (although even L reads it), unless the way the examples are formed forbids this [Nöldeke (Review, 1219) has no problem with the form in the text, however-ed.]. Even if others do want to write ܬ with quššāyā only in the first person after a long *i*, while using rukkāḵā in the third person feminine (so that the two forms can be distinguished correctly), such a usage would still be an invention of the theorists rather than a true reflection of how it was actually pronounced. The analogy from strong verbs requires quššāyā in the first person, which is then carried over also in verbs 3rd-yudh. A similarly old usage is now known from Ḥunayn, although there too it is an artificial way of reading, since the first person is given rukkāḵā ܐܪܡܝܬܗ̇, while the second is given quššāyā, ܐܪܡܝܬܗ̇ (Hoffmann, *Opuscula* , 10). The confusion was as follows: a) some placed rukkāḵā on the *t* after the ܝ of the first person (e.g. Ḥunayn, Bar Šakko, Joseph Bar Malkon - for the last named, see p.118 above); 2) others placed quššāyā in the same case; 3) some placed quššāyā on the *t* after ܝ of the fem.sing. and in the second person both singular and plural; 4) there were others who required rukkāḵā in ܩܒܠܬܗ̇ (*she received it*). It is clear then that the problem was solved differently in the different schools. See p.116f. above and Gottheil, *Elias*, 30*.

ܒܡܠܐܝܢܐ: ܐܢܫܝܐ ܕܢܦܩܝܢ ܠܚܡܫܐ ܕܬܢܝܢܐ ܡܢ ܢܩܠܝܢܐ: ܐܝܟ ܗܘ ܘܩܛܠܬܗ ܐܢܬ ܡܢ ܩܛܠܬ̈ܗ ܗܘ ܘܡܩܛܠܬܗ ܐܢܬ: ܡܢ ܡܩܛܠܬܗ ܗܘ ܘܢܫܩܬܗ ܐܢܬ ܡܢ ܢܫܩܬܗ ܐܝܟ ܚܠܦ ܦܪ̈ܘܫܐ ܠܐܪܒܥܐ ܕܬܪܝܢܐ ܗܘܝܢ ܗܘܝ: ܠ: ܡܬܦܩܕܝܢ ܡܬܦܩܕܢܐ: ܐܝܟ ܚܒܝܒܬܟ: ܘܚܒܝܒܬܟܝܢ: ܚܒܝܒܬܗ: ܘܡܚܒܒܬܗ܀ ܘܐܦ ܚܠܦ ܗܢܐ[3] ܦܪ̈ܘܫܐ ܒܡܠܝܢܐ ܗܘܝ: ܡܬܦܩܕܝܢ ܡܬܦܩܕܢܐ ܐܝܟ ܐܝܬ ܢܐܡܪ: ܚܒܝܒܬܟ: ܡܚܒܒܬܟ ܪܚܡܬܟ ܚܒܝܒܬܝ: ܡܚܒܒܬܝ ܪܚܡܬܝ: ܚܒܝܒܬܗ: ܡܚܒܒܬܗ ܪܚܡܬܗ܀ ܠܗܘܢ

1 ܐܢܫܝܐ] ܐܢܫܐ L 2 ܩܛܠܬ̈ܗ] vowels as in mss (here and following) ܗܘ[2]] om. G 4 ܘܚܒܝܒܬܟܝܢ ܘܚܒܝܒܬܗ L 5 ܚܠܦ ܗܢܐ] ܗܢܐ OGBL ܡܬܦܩܕܢܐ...ܐܝܟ] om. OG | ܢܐܡܪ] ܐܝܟ ܢܐܡܪ OGB 6 ܚ̈ܒܝܒܬܟ ܡ̈ܚܒܒܬܟ ܪ̈ܚܡܬܟ L ܚܒܝܒܬܝ ܡܚܒܒܬܝ ܪܚܡܬܝ om. BL | ܚܒܝܒܬܗ ܡܚܒܒܬܗ ܪܚܡܬܗ] ܚ̈ܒܝܒܬܗ ܪ̈ܚܡܬܗ ܡ̈ܚܒܒܬܟ B ܚ̈ܒܝܒܬܗ ܡ̈ܚܒܒܬܗ ܪ̈ܚܡܬܗ L

[3] Although all mss read ܗܢܐ, the pronoun is here meant, since he uses this term to define the ending of the third person feminine.

ܕܡܢ ܘܟܠ ܫܡܐ ܡܫܡܠܝܐ ܕܐܝܬ ܠܗ: ܚ: ܘܡܬܚܫܒܢ ܐܬܘܬܐ ܦܬܝܚܬܐ: ܘܐܝܬ
ܠܗ: ܐܝܟ: ܡܬܦܫܩܐ ܗܘ ܐܝܟ: ܡܫܬܝܗܘܢ:[1] ܦܬܝܚܬܗܘܢ: ܢܝܚܬܗܘܢ ܚܕܝܬܗܘܢ:
25a ܘܣܛܪܐ ܕܬ̈ܪܬܝܢ܀ ܠܘܬ ܕܡܢ ܠܝ ܐܝܬ ܠܗ ܒܫܡܫܐ: ܚ: ܣܓܝܐܐ ܘܢܘܟܪܝܐ ܠܗ ܚܕܐ
ܡܢ ܐܬܘ̈ܬܐ ܕܡܬܬܘܚܝܢ: ܘܗܘܝܐ ܐܘ ܙܡܝܩܬܐ: ܐܘ ܦܬܝܚܬܐ: ܡܬܬܘܚܐ ܗܝ
ܐܬܘܬܐ: ܐܝܟ ܡܪܝܡܐ: ܦܠܓܘܬܐ: ܚܟܝܡܐ: ܪܡܚܐ: ܡܪܝܡܬܐ ܪܡܬܐ ܢܗܝܪܐ. ܡܪܝܡܐ.
ܦܠܓܘܬܐ܀ ܐܝܟܢ ܗܘܐ ܐܬܘܬܐ ܕܩܪܝܬ: ܚ: ܦܬܝܚܬܐ: ܡܬܬܩܢܐ ܐܬܘܬܐ ܕܒܬܪ: ܬ:
ܐܝܟ ܒ̈ܪܝܬܐ ܡܟܝܠܬܐ: ܒܘܬ̈ܩܝܬܐ܀ ܐܝܟܢ ܣܠܩ ܗܘܐ: ܬ: ܘܘ: ܒܪܝܢܬܐ ܐܘ ܒܥܒܝܐ:
ܗܝ ܠ̄: ܕܬܬܪܗ ܡܬܬܪܒܝܐ: ܐܒܝܠܐ ܕܐܬܡܪ. ܙܒ̈ܢܬܐ: ܒܪ̈ܢܬܐ ܒܪ̈ܘܬܐ:[2] ܗܘܝܘ̈ܬܐ:
ܡܚܘܬܐ: ܗܝܒܘܬܐ: ܫܪ̈ܘܬܐ: ܘܕܬ̈ܪܬܝܢ ܠܗܠܝܢ܀ ܠܘܬ ܕܡܢ ܡܠܬܐ ܕܡܬܩܪܝܐ
ܠܐܚܪܝܐ ܕܒܬܪ ܗܘܝܐ ܐܬܘܬܐ ܐܝܬܝܬܐ ܡܬܪܟܒܬܐ: ܗܘܝ ܕܡܬܚܫܒܐ ܫܠܡܬܐ ܡܢ
ܐܬܚܪܝܗ ܟܠ ܐܚܪܢܐ ܕܩܐܡ ܫܡܝܐܝܬ: ܦܫܛ ܠܐܬܘܬܐ ܡܪܟܒܬܐ ܐܝܟ ܒܪܘ ܒܬ̈ܪܝܢ:
25b ܒܢܟ: ܒܢ̈ܝܢ: ܒܥܝ: ܒܥ̈ܝܢ: ܚܙܝ ܚ̈ܙܝܢ: ܦܫ: ܦܫܝܢ: ܫܡܥ ܫ̈ܡܥܝܢ: ܢܣܒ
ܢܣܒܝܢ܀[3] ܐܝܟܢ ܗܘܐ ܐܬܘܬܐ ܩܪܝܬܐ ܦܬܝܚܬܐ: ܠܐ ܡܬܬܦܬܚܐ ܐܬܘܬܐ
ܡܪܟܒܬܐ: ܐܢܝ ܢܦܩ: ܡܢܦܩܝܢ: ܒܪܘ ܡܒܪܝܢ: ܦܪܩ ܡܦܪ̈ܩܝܢ܀
ܗܠܝܢ ܐܢܝ ܦܘܫܩܐ ܕܙܘܥ̈ܬܐ ܘܡܦܫ̈ܩܬܐ: ܕܗܠܝܢ ܢܦܩܢ ܐܬܘ̈ܬܐ: ܦ:[4] ܕܡܢ: ܒܡܠܬܐ
ܕܬ̈ܠܬ ܡܬܬܪܝܡܐ: ܡܪܟܒܬܐ: ܐܝܟ: ܦ: ܕܢܦܠ. ܘܢܦܠ ܘܢܦܠܝܢ: ܘܢܦܠܬܝܢ:
ܘܦܬܟܠ ܡܦܫܩܬܐ ܘܦܫܩܬܐ: ܐܝܟ ܩ̈: ܕܦܩܕܐ: ܘܦܬܘܪܐ ܘܦܠܚܐ: ܘܐܦ̈ܩܐ܀
ܘܫܦܝܪ ܡܦܫܩܬܐ: ܐܝܟ: ܦ: ܕܦܪܝܡܐ: ܘܫܦ̈ܪܐ: ܘܙܘܦܐ[5] ܦܪ̈ܘܩܘ: ܦܘܠܘܣ.
ܦܠܓܐ: ܘܡܪܟܒܬܐ ܠܐ ܡܬܬܚܠܦܐ ܒܚܡܫ: ܚܡܫ ܒܚܡܫܐ ܘܐܦܠܐ ܒܚܘܠܡܐ:
ܘܡܐ ܕܡܬܚܠܦܐ ܚܕܐ ܡܢ ܡܬܩܠܬܐ ܩܕܝܡ ܒܚܡܫܐ ܕܐܬܘܬܐ ܩܪܝܬܐ: ܦ: ܠܐ
ܡܪܟܒܐ ܠܗ ܐܝܟ ܕܠܗܠܝܢ ܐܬܪܘܟܬܐ܀ ܐܠܐ ܠܝ ܒܪܘܚܬܐ ܕܟܠܡܬܐ ܐܝܟ ܗܝ:
ܕܪܘܚܐ ܕܐܪܥܢ ܕܡܫܡܫܐ: ܘܠܐ ܢܬܦܝܣܘܢ ܒܦܫܝܛܬܐ܀ ܘܙܘܦ ܠܚܝܒܐ ܕܟܠܗ:
26a ܦ: ܡܪܟܒܬܐ ܐܠܐ ܠܝ ܡܟܠܬܐ: ܘܠܐ: ܦ: ܡܬܐܪܟܒܬܐ ܐܠܐ ܡܦܫܩܬܐ܀ ܘܢܦܠܐ
ܕܙܘܥܐ

1 ܘܟܠ] om. OG 2 ܡܬܦܫܩܐ] ܐܝܟ ܡܬܦܫܩܐ L | ܢܝܚܬܗܘܢ] ܫ̈ܢܝܚܬܗܘܢ B 3 ܘܢܘܟܪܝܐ] ܘܢܘܟܪ L 6 ܦܬܝܚܬܐ] all mss, for ܙܡܝܩܬܐ 7 ܐܝܟܢ] ܘܐܝܟܢ B | ܒܥܒܝܐ] ܕܒܥܒܝܐ L 8 ܒܪ̈ܘܬܐ] ܒܪ̈ܢܬܐ OGL ܒܪܢܬܗ B 11 ܐܬܚܪܝܗ] ܐܬܚܪܝܢܗ OG | ܕܩܐܡ] ܕܩܐܡ OGBL 14 ܐܢܝ] om. B 16 ܘܢܦܠ] ܘܢܦܠ OG | ܘܢܦܠܝܢ] ܘܢܦܠܝܢ OGB 17 ܘܐܦ̈ܩܐ] ܘܐܬܦܩܐ L 18 ܘܙܘܦܐ] ܘܙܘܘܦܐ B 19 ܡܬܬܚܠܦܐ] ܡܬܦܠܓܐ O 20 ܘܡܪܟܒܬܐ] ܡܪܟܒܬܐ OG | ܒܚܡܫܐ ܕܐܬܘܬܐ] ܒܚܡܫ ܕܐܬܘܬܗ L 21 ܗܝ] ܗ OG om. B 22 ܒܦܫܝܛܬܐ] ܒܦܫܝܛܬܐ L | ܘܙܘܦ] ܘܙܘܦܐ B 23 ܠܝ] om. B ܡܦܫܩܬܐ] ܕܦܫܩܐ B

[1] This is a dubious form - it should be ܡܫ̈ܬܝܗܘܢ in line with ܡ̈ܝܘܗܝ (*his water*) and ܡ̈ܫܬܝܗ (Barheb., *Carmina*, ed.Scebak, 143,4) [Nöldeke (Review, 1219), upholds the text, however-ed.]. | [2] ܒܪ̈ܘܬܐ should be read here since the ܒܪ̈ܢܬܐ of the mss is not relevant. The waw ܒܪ̈ܝܬܐ is found in ܙܒ̈ܢܬܐ and ܒ̈ܢܝܬܐ (i.e. the noun denoting the actor of the root ܒܢܐ) and ܒܪ̈ܘܬܐ (*fir tree*). The other examples have waw ܕܚܘܒܐ. | [3] See Merx, *Grammatica*, 68; 63,IV; 66,3. | [4] See Merx, *Grammatica*, 73, and p.118 above. | [5] O distinguishes three classes of pe, the points being placed below, above, and within the letter.

ܒ ܐܬܘ̈ܬܐ: ܢܘܩܙܐ ܕܡܬܐܡܪ ܒܥܠܡܐ ܡܢ ܐܬܘܬܐ: ܕܡܦܩܢܐ ܕܝܢ ܢܘܩܙܐ ܕܡܬܐܡܪ ܒܒܠܠ ܡܢ ܐܬܘܬܐ܀ ܘܗܟܢ ܡܬܠ ܙܘܥܐ ܘܩܘܫܐ ܕܬܢܐܡ ܗܟܢ ܦܬܚܐ ܐܬܘܬܐ ܦܣܩ ܒܦܣܝܩܬܐ܀

ܗܘ̈ܠܐ ܠܫܡܗܐ ܐܝܟܢ ܐܝܟ ܐܬܘܬܐ ܕܡܬܟܬܒܢ ܘܡܬܩܪܝܢ: ܘܚܕܝܐ ܐܝܠ: ܘܕܐܝܟ ܐܡܝܐ: ܘܡܬܠ ܡܝܐ܀

ܦܘܫܐ ܘܐܡܪܝܢ ܡܕܡܟܐ ܕܐܬܘܬܐ ܐܘ ܡܬܟܬܒܢ ܡܬܟܬܒܢ: ܐܘ ܡܬܚܫܒܢ ܡ̈ܬܚܫܒܢ܀ ܘܗܟܢ ܕܝܢ ܕܡܬܟܬܒܢ ܐܝܬܝܗܝܢ ܠܟܠܗ: ܐ: ܘ: ܝ: ܘܟܠ ܚܕܐ ܡܢܗܝܢ ܟܕ ܒܡܢ ܠܟܠܐ ܐܬܪܐ ܕܡܬܟܬܒܐ܀ ܐܘ ܟܕ ܡܢ ܟܠܡܐ ܘܡܪܝܐ ܡܬܟܬܒܐ܀ ܐܘ ܕܡܬܟܬܒܐ ܡܢ ܟܠܡܐ ܘܡܬܐܡܪܐ ܒܦܪܝܫܐ܀ ܐܘ ܡܬܦܪܫܐ ܒܟܠ̈ܡܐ ܘܡܬܟܬܒܐ ܒܦܪܝܫܐ܀ ܘܐܝܟܢ ܕܡܬܟܬܒܢ ܒܟܠܡܐ ܘܦܘܫܐ ܐܟܚܕܐ: ܐܝܬܝܗܝܢ ܐܝܟ: ܐ: ܕ̈ܟܝܐ: ܕܫܪܐ: ܕܡܬܐ: ܕܡܬܟܬܒܢ ܡܐ ܕܐܡܪܝܢ: ܟܢܗ ܕܝܠܗ: 26b
ܕܡܢܗ: ܘܟܠܝ: ܘܫܪܝ: ܕܩܢܝ܀ ܙܪܩ ܗܘܐ ܟܕ ܕܐܬܦܐܝ ܘܘ: ܐܘ ܝ: ܟܬܪ: ܐ: ܕܩܛܐ ܗܟܢ: ܡܐ ܕܐܡܪܝܢ ܗܘܘ: ܟܢܗ: ܘܫܪܗ: ܘܡܢܗ: ܟܠܝ: ܘܫܪܝ: ܕܩܢܝ: ܐܝܟ ܕܬܐܟ ܟܬܪ: ܠ: ܕܥܡܠܗ: ܘܥܡܠܝ: ܘܟܬܪ ܡ: ܕܦܠܚܗ: ܘܦܠܚܝ: ܘܟܬܪ: ܕ: ܕܟܪܗ ܘܟܪܝܗ܀ ܐܝܟܢ ܕܡܬܟܬܒܢ ܡܢ ܟܠ̈ܡܐ ܘܡܬܐܡܪܢ ܒܦܪܝܫܐ: ܐܝܟ: ܐ: ܕܐܒܩܐ ܘܐܢܫܐ ܘܐܝܟܢ: ܘܐܒܝܕ: ܘܐܝܟ ܗ̄ܗ̄: ܕܟܠ: ܘܡܬܠ: ܘܐܝܟܢ ܕܡܬܦܪܫܢ ܒܟܠܡܐ: ܘܡܬܟܬܒܢ ܒܦܪܝܫܐ. ܐܝܬܝܗܝܢ: ܐܝܟ: ܐ: ܡܕܡܟܐ ܕܐܢܫܐ: ܘܐܚܪܢܐ: ܕܐܢܫܐ: ܘܐܚܪܢܐ: ܘܐܝܟ: ܐ: ܕܩܛܐ ܘܩܛܐ: ܘܗܟܢܐ: ܘܐܝܟ: ܗܘ: ܕܡܠܗ: ܘܦܠܚܗ: ܘܥܒܕܗ: ܘܐܝܟ: ܝ: ܕܟܠܝ ܘܥܡܠܝ ܘܥܒܕܝ ܘܕܥܒܕܝܢ ܘܥܡܠܝܢ ܘܦܠܚܝܢ: ܘܥܡܠܝܢ ܘܦܠܚܝܢ܀ ܘܝܕܥܬܐ ܕܟܠ ܚܕܐ ܡܢ ܗܟܢ: ܠܦܬܓܡܐ ܟܬܒܐ܀

ܐܝܟܢ ܕܝܢ ܕܡܬܚܫܒܢ ܐܝܬܝܗܝܢ ܗܟܢ: ܒ̄: ܓ̄: ܕ̄: ܟ̄: ܦ̄: ܬ̄ܩ̄: ܪ̄: ܠ̄: 27a
ܡܬܚܫܒܢ ܕܝܢ ܗܟܢܐ: ܟܠ ܐܬܘܬܐ ܕܒܠܫܢܐ ܒܦܬܓܡܐ ܒܡܫܠܡܢܘܬܐ ܠܟܣܐ ܘܦܘܪܫܢܐ ܫܠܡܐ ܘܬܪܝܨܘܬܐ ܕܡܬܐܡܪܢܘܬܐ: ܕܡܬܚܫܒܐ ܡܕܡܟܐ ܕܐܬܘܬܐ ܫܠܡܬܐ: ܐܝܟ ܦ̄ ܕܦܬܓܡܐ: ܘܦܬܓܡܐ: ܘܦܬܓܡܐ: ܘܐܝܟ ܒ: ܕܐܒܝܕܐ: ܘܗܘ

2 ܗܟܢ...ܡܬܠ] om. OG(homoe.) | ܕܬܢܐܡ] ܬܢܝܢ B   7 ܘܗܟܢ] ܗܟܢ OG
ܐܝܬܝܗܝܢ ܕܝܢ] ܐܝܬܝܗܝܢ OG   11 ܐ] om. OGBL   12 ܕܐܬܦܐܝ] ܠܚܘܠ L
13 ܘܫܪܗ] om. OGB | ܟܢܗ] ܘܟܢܗ L   15 ܘܡܬܐܡܪܢ] ܡܬܐܡܪܢ G   16 ܕܐܒܩܐ
ܘܐܝܟܢ ܘܐܒܝܕ] ܡܬܠ ܡܠܐ ܐܘ ܡܐ ܡܐ OGBL | ܕܟܠ ܘܡܬܠ] ?read ܡܬܠ ܒܟܠ
20 ܘܥܡܠܝܢ ܘܦܠܚܝܢ] om. L   24 ܘܬܪܝܨܘܬܐ] ܠܬܘܩܢܐ L

ܕܦܫܝܛܐ: ܘܟܠ ܕܡܬܓܠܠܢ: ܘܦܫܡܬܐ ܘܡܦܬܠܠܢ ܘܡܬܩܠܠܢ: ܘܡܬܠܠܢ ܘܬܓܠܠܐ: ܗܘ
ܘܩ: ܕܡܬܦܩܦܩܝܢ ܘܡܬܩܡܩܡܝܢ: ܘܙ: ܕܡܙܘܙܗ ܘܡܙܘܙܝ ܘܡܬܙܘܙܝܢ ܘܡܬܙܘܙܝ. ܘܐܝܟ: ܠ̄:
ܕܐܬܬܪܒ: ܘܐܬܬܗܝܡ ܘܐܬܬܦܢ: ܘܐܬܬܝܒܣ ܘܐܬܬܠܒ: ܘܐܝܟ ܕܐܦܪܝܡ ܘܫܠܡܘܢ
ܘܡܬܦܫܩܢܐ ܘܡܬܦܫܩܢܐ: ܘܡܬܦܫܦܫܢܐ: ܘܕܝܢܟܪܐ ܘܦܪܥܐ: ܕܐܝܟ ܗܠܝܢ܀[1]
ܘܟܠ ܐܡܬܐ ܕܐܝܬ: ܠ: ܡܦܫܡܬܐ ܥܒܕܬܐ: ܘܒܠܐܘܗ: ܕ: ܡܦܫܡܬܐ: ܡܬܦܥܠܢܐ
ܗܝ ܠ: ܐܝܟ ܕܐܬܪܒ: ܐܬܬܪܒ: ܐܬܪܟܝ: ܐܬܪܟܝ: ܐܬܪܟܢ܀ ܘܟܠ ܐܡܬܐ ܕܐܝܬ: ܕ:
27b ܥܒܕܬܐ ܘܦܠܐܘܗ: ܠ: ܡܦܫܡܬܐ: ܡܬܬܐܡܪܢܝܬܐ: ܡܬܦܥܠܢܐ ܗܝ ܕ: ܐܝܟ ܡܕܝܢܬܐ
ܚܒܝܒܬܐ ܢܩܝܒܬܐ܀[2] ܘܟܠ ܐܡܬܐ ܕܐܝܬ: ܠ̄: ܥܒܕܬܐ ܘܦܠܐܘܗ: ܬ: ܕܡܬܦܥܠܢܐ ܗܝ:
ܠ: ܐܝܟ: ܐܬܦܪܥ ܐܬܦܪܥ: ܐܬܦܪܥܝ ܘܐܬܦܪܥܬ܀ ܘܟܠ ܐܡܬܐ ܕܐܝܬ: ܬ̄: ܥܒܕܬܐ:
ܘܦܠܐܘܗ: ܠ̄: ܡܦܫܡܬܐ ܕܡܬܬܐܡܪܢܝܬܐ: ܡܬܦܥܠܢܐ ܗܝ: ܬ: ܐܝܟ ܐܬܦܪܦܪܗܘܢ
ܐܬܦܪܦܪܬ: ܕܐܬܦܪܦܪܬܘ: ܘܬܦܪܦܪܗܘܢ܀ ܘܟܠ ܐܡܬܐ ܕܐܝܬ: ܕ: ܡܬܦܪܥܬܐ
ܥܒܕܬܐ: ܘܦܠܐܘܗ: ܠ̄: ܡܬܦܪܥܬܐ ܕܡܬܬܐܡܪܢܝܬܐ ܡܬܦܥܠܢܐ ܗܝ: ܕ: ܐܝܟ ܣܒܬܐ:
ܣܒܬܐܝܬ: ܣܒܬܘܬܐ܀ ܘܟܠ ܐܡܬܐ ܕܐܝܬ: ܢܘܢ: ܥܒܕܬܐ: ܘܡܢ ܩܕܡܘܗ: ܝ:
ܣܡܝܟܬܐ ܘܡܢ ܒܬܪܗ: ܠ: ܡܦܫܡܬܐ ܕܡܬܦܥܠܢܐ ܗܝ: ܢܘܢ ܐܝܟ ܡܕܝܢܬܐ ܫܦܝܪܬܐ
ܕܩܝܪܬܐ܀ ܘܗܘܝܐ ܠܝ ܐܝܟ ܩܕܡܘܗ ܕܢܘܢ ܐܬܘܬܐ ܦܠܓܬܐ: ܐܝܟ ܕܟܝܬܐ ܘܦܝܫܬܐ:
28a ܘܟܠ ܐܡܠܐ ܕܗܘܝܐ: ܠ: ܡܬܬܐܡܪܢܝܬܐ: ܗܘ: ܕܡܢ ܩܕܡܘܗ ܥܒܕܬܐ:
ܡܬܦܢܝܐ ܡܬܬܐܡܪܢܘܬܐ ܕܠ: ܟܝ: ܘܡܬܦܥܠܢܐ ܗܘ: ܠ: ܐܝܟ ܗܝ ܕܐܦܪܝܡ:
ܐܬܟܠ: ܢܬܟܠ: ܬܬܟܠ: ܐܬܟܠܢ ܬܬܟܠܢ: ܢܬܟܠܢ: ܢܬܟܠܢܝ:[3] ܐܝܟ ܗܘܝܐ: ܪ̄:
ܡܬܬܐܡܪܢܝܬܐ ܦܢܝܬܐ: ܘܠ: ܥܒܕܬܐ: ܐܘ ܢܬܦܠܓܘܢ ܡܬܬܐܡܪܢܝܬܐ: ܡܬܦܠܓܬܐ:[4]
ܠ: ܐܝܟ ܐܬܟܠܗ. ܘܐܬܟܠܢ ܘܐܬܟܠܢ܀ ܘܩܝܠ ܠܟܠܗܝܢ ܕܟܠܗ ܐܬܘܬܐ
ܕܡܬܦܪܥܬܐ ܦܝܩܢܬܐ ܐܘ ܡܬܦܥܠܢܐ: ܐܠܐ ܐܢ ܐܬܝܢ ܥܒܕܬܐ: ܗܟܢ ܦܝܠܐ
ܐܬܘܬܐ ܕܡܬܦܪܥܬܐ ܘܡܬܦܥܠܢܐ ܐܝܟ ܕܟܠܐ ܕܦܘܫܩܬܐ܀
ܗܘܐܠܐ ܠܡܫܠܡܘ ܐܡܪܝܢ ܐܝܟ ܐܬܘܬܐ ܕܫܘܡܠܝܐ܀ ܦܘܫܩܐ ܘܐܦܪܝܡ ܕܐܬܘܬܐ
ܕܫܘܡܠܝܐ ܐܬܬܐܡܪܘ: ܐܡܪܝܢ ܕܗܐ ܕܒܬܪ ܦܘܫܩܐ ܩܕܡܝ ܠܦܘܫܩܐ ܦܫܝܩܐ:

[ܘܦܫܡܬܐ...ܘܡܬܩܠܠܢ | L ܕܡܦܠܠܝܢ ܘܡܬܡܠܠܝܢ ܘܡܬܦܠܠܝܢ ܘܡܬܠܠܝܢ [ܕܡܬܓܠܠܢ...ܘܡܬܩܠܠܢ 1 om. B 4 ܘܡܬܦܫܩܢܐ] om. BL | ܘܡܬܦܫܦܫܢܐ] ܘܡܬܡܫܡܫܢܐ L 5 ܡܦܫܡܬܐ[1]] sic mss; read ܡܬܦܪܥܬܐ 6 ܐܬܪܟܝ] ܐܬܬܪܟܝ O ܐܬܬܪܟܝ G | ܐܬܪܟܝ ܐܬܪܟܢ] ܐܬܪܟܢ ܐܬܪܟܢ L 7 ܕ...8 ܗܝ] om. BL(homoe.) 9 ܐܝܟ] om. OG | ܐܬܦܪܥ] ܐܬܦܪܥ B ܡܬܦܪܥܬܐ ܝ ܣܡܝܟܬܐ 13 B ܬܦܪܦܪܗ] ܘܬܦܪܦܪܗܘܢ 11 L ܐܬܦܪܥܬܐ G ܐܬܦܪܥܬ] ܘܐܬܦܪܥܬܐ ܘܡܢ] om. OG(homoe.) 15 ܘܗܘܝܐ] ܘܗܘܝܐ OG | ܘܢܘܢ] ܢܘܢ OG 16 ܗܘ] ܗܘ ܝ B ܗܘ OG 17 ܡܬܬܐܡܪܢܘܬܐ] ܡܬܬܐܡܪܢܝܬܐ OG 23 ܐܡܪܝܢ...ܘܫܘܡܠܝܐ] twice OG 24 ܦܫܝܩܐ] ܦܫܝܩܬܐ L

[1] See Merx, *Grammatica*, 109,IIa. | [2] See Merx, *Grammatica*, 109,IIb. | [3] On ܐܬܟܠ see Merx, *Grammatica*, 350. | [4] On ܡܬܦܠܓܬܐ see p.106,25 above.

ܗ ܘܡܠܦܢܝܢ ܐܬܘܬܐ ܡܢܩܫܢܝܬܐ ܘܡܢܩܝܬܐ: ܐܝܬܝܗܝܢ ܕܝܢ ܚܡܫ: ܐ̄: ܗ̄: ܢ̄: ܝ̄: ܬ̄:
ܬܘ:[1] ܗܟܘܬܗܘܢ ܕܝܢ ܕܡܥܒܕܐ ܣܝܡܬܐ ܘܦܫܝܛܬܐ: ܕܢܬܝܬܐ: ܘܡܬܠܬܝܬܐ: 28b
ܬܐܟܦ ܦܥܠܝܢ ܡܫܡܗܐ؛ ܟܕ ܐܡܪ: ܢܩܐ: ܐܩܪܐ: ܬܟܢܐ: ܡܟܐ: ܟܬܒܬܐ:
ܬܟܬܒܬܐ: ܟܬܒܬܐ: ܡܬܟܬܒܬܐ: ܡܬܟܬܒܐ: ܦܬܚܐ: ܩܛܠܐ: ܢܦܩܐ: ܢܦܠܐ:
ܡܐܟܠܬܐ ܢܦܩܬܐ: ܗܟܢܐ ܗܟܝܠ ܘܡܬܐ ܘܠܐ ܡܢܝܢ ܬܐܟܦ ܦܥܠܝܢ ܡܫܡܗܐ؛
ܟܕ ܕܝܢ ܬܗܐ ܐܝܟ ܕܢܦܪܘܫ ܠܟܠܗܝܢ ܐܬܘܬܐ ܕܡܫܡܗܐ: ܡܬܝܕܥܢ ܗܟܢܐ: ܦܬܓܡܐ
ܡܬܪܬܝܢ: ܟܬܒ: ܡܫܬܟܚܝܢ ܟܪܢܐ ܗܢܐ؛ ܢܟܬܘܒ: ܐܟܬܘܒ: ܬܟܬܘܒ: ܢܟܬܘܒ
ܐܟܠܘ: ܐܬܠܘ: ܟܠܟܘ ܡܟܬܘܒ: ܢܟܬܘܒ: ܢܟܬܒܘ: ܘܢܟܬܒܘܢ؛ ܦܬܓܡܐ ܕܝܢ
ܢܩܒܝܬܐ ܟܗܢܘ: ܢܟܬܒܢ: ܐܬܟܬܒܢ: ܢܟܬܒܢ: ܟܬܒܢ: ܬܟܬܒܢ: ܐܟܬܒܢ؛[2]
ܦܬܓܡܐ ܕܝܢ ܕܬܪܝܢ: ܬ: ܡܫܡܗܐ ܒܗ: ܢܟܬܒ: ܐܬܟܬܒ: ܐܟܬܒܐ: ܬܟܬܒ:
ܢܟܬܒ: ܘܢܟܬܒ: ܟܬܒܬ؛ ܡܟܬܒܐ ܕܝܢ ܕܡܫܬܘܕܥܐ ܕܟܝܐ ܕܟܕ ܟܬܒܬܘܢ ܢܫܬܡܫ: 29a
ܒܗ ܒܐ̄ ܦܥܠܐ ܡܫܡܗܐ: ܢܟܬܒ ܬܟܬܒ: ܩܛܠ ܓܒܪܐ: ܐܟܬܒ ܗܘܐ: ܢܟܬܒ
ܗܘܝ: ܟܬܒ ܩܪܝܐ: ܡܬܟܬܒ ܩܛܠ: ܐܬܩܪܝܬ ܦܪܐ؛ ܗܟܢ ܕܝܢ ܐܬܘܬܐ
ܕܡܫܡܗܐ ܒܬܚܘܡܗܘܢ ܕܟܝܐ ܡܬܩܪܝܢ: ܡܬܦܢܝܢ ܕܝܢ ܐܦ ܦܬܓܡܐ ܕܗܢܘܢ:
ܕܬܠܬܝܗܘܢ ܐܬܘܗ ܡܬܟܬܒܐ؛ ܐܡܪܬ ܕܡܫܬܡܠܝܢ ܦܬܓܡܐ ܢܟܬܒܐ ܐܘܟ ܐܝܟ
ܡܟܬܒܐ: ܟ ܢܗܘܐ ܗܟܢܐ ܟܬܘܒܬܗ ܢܟܬܘܒ ܢܟܬܒ: ܐܘܟ: ܐܟܬܒܬ ܕܝܢ
ܘܡܬܝܕܥܐ ܐܝܟ ܡܢ ܦܬܓܡܐ ܕܢܩܒܬܐ ܢܫܬܡܫܐ: ܬ: ܦܬܓܡܐ ܗܟܢܐ ܟܬܘܒ: ܢܟܬܒܬ:
ܢܟܬܒ: ܐܘܟ ܢܟܬܒ؛ ܘܗܟܢܐ ܐܦ ܦܬܓܡܐ ܕܬܪܝܢ ܒܗ ܒܗܘܢ: ܬ. ܦܬܓܡܐ
ܡܫܡܗܐ: ܒܢܩܒܐ ܕܝܢ ܒܟܝܢܗ ܡܬܦܪܫܝܢ ܣܓܝ ܐܬܘܬܐ ܡܟܬܒܬܐ:[3] ܘܒܢܘܢܐ
ܘܡܟܬܒܐ. ܢܦܠܬ ܟܘܟܒܐ ܡܢ ܫܡܝܐ ܕܨܦܪܐ: ܐܬܬܥܝܪܝ ܩܘܡܝ ܐܘܪܫܠܡ: ܘܢܟܬܒ:
ܐܬܬܥܝܪܬ: ܘܡܟܬܒ؛ ܗܟܢܐ ܐܦ ܦܬܓܡܐ ܕܗܘ ܕܡܫܬܡܠܐ: ܒܢܩܒܐ ܒܟܝܢܗ 29b
ܡܬܦܪܫ: ܘܒܗܠܝܢ ܕܐܝܬ ܣܓܝܐܐ ܡܬܦܪܫܝܢ ܡܫܟܚܐ ܐܡܪܬ ܐܢܐ. ܐܬܒܝܬ
ܐܢܐ: ܐܡܪܬ ܗܝ:[4] ܐܟܬܒ: ܐܬܟܬܒ: ܐܟܬܒ: ܢܟܬܒ: ܢܟܬܒ: ܢܟܬܒ؛ ܘܗܟܢܐ
ܐܫܬܟܚ ܠܩܢܝܐ ܘܩܠܐ ܕܡܫܬܡܫܝܢ؛ ܐܦ ܡܟܬܒܐ ܗܝ ܕܠܫܡܐ ܐܝܟ. ܐܘ
ܟܠ ܐܝܟ: ܐܘ ܟܠ ܫܡܐ ܡܠܐܡܪ: ܒܥܠܡܐ ܕܦܬܓܡܐ: ܐܘ ܢܟܬܒܢܬܐ
ܡܕܡ: ܐܘ ܚܝܐ: ܐܘ ܫܘܟܢܐ

1 ܡܢܩܫܢܝܬܐ] ܡܫܘܚܬܐ B ܡܢܩܫܢܝܬܐ L | ܗ̄] ܗ̄ ܘ̄ L 2 ܣܝܡܬܐ ܘܦܫܝܛܬܐ] ܣܝܡܐ OG ܘܦܫܝܛܬܐ 6 ܬܗܐ] om. BL | ܐܝܟ] ܟܪܢܐ OG 10 ܕܬܪܝܢ] ܕܬܪܝܢ OG ܡܫܡܗܐ] ܡܟܬܒܬܐ B txt L ?read ܡܫܡܗܐ 13 ܩܛܠ] ܩܛܠ B | ܦܪܐ] ܗܘܐ L | ܗܟܢ] om. B 14 ܡܬܦܢܝܢ...30,3 ܝܗܒܘ om. B | ܦܬܓܡܐ] ܦܬܓܡܐ L 16 ܟܬܘܒܬܗ] ܟܬܘܒܬܗ L 19 ܡܟܬܒܬܐ] ܡܟܬܒܬܐ O ܡܟܬܒܬܐ G 21 ܒܢܩܒܐ] ܒܢܩܒܐ L 22 ܐܢܐ] om. L 23 ܐܢܐ] om. L | ܗܝ] om. L

[1] L’s addition of ܘ makes the number up to seven. See p.27,9 above. | [2] On this type of ܢ see Merx, *Grammatica*, 118,II. | [3] I.e. the ܬ of the second person masculine is the same as that of the third person feminine, the two being distinguished by points instead of vowel letters. The scriptural citations given are Isa 14.12; 51.17; Ps 3.6. | [4] In these laste examples, the pronouns are written in superscript above the verbs, but are omitted in L.

ܡܕܡ܀[1] ܟܗܘܐ ܠܟܠ ܐܬ̈ܘܬܐ ܫܩܠܝܢ ܣܘܡܟܢܐ: ܟܠܗܘܢ ܡܩܕܡܬܐ: ܟܝ: ܗ. ܢܝ. ܒ
ܠܘܬܝ: ܣܩܘܒܠܝ: ܩܕܡܝ. ܒܣܬܪܝ: ܥܠܝ: ܡܛܠܬܝ: ܠܘܬܗ ܕܦܠܢ: ܣܩܘܒܠܗ: ܘܗܟܢ
ܬܚܘܬܗ ܒܣܬܪܗ: ܠܘܬܗܘܢ: ܬܚܘܬܗܘܢ ܘܥܡܗܘܢ: ܩܕܡܝܗܘܢ: ܐܢܬܝܗܝܢ:
ܒܩܕܡܝܗܝܢ: ܒܬܪܝܗܝܢ: ܘܗܠܝܢ ܕܣܟܐ܀ ܗܠܝܢ ܗܟܝܠ ܐܬ̈ܘܬܐ: ܟܠ ܐܡܬܝ
ܕܬܐܬܝܢ ܠܘܬ ܫܡܐ ܒܓܒܝ ܠܐܘܣܦܐ ܒܡܘܡܐ: ܡܫܬܚܠܦܝܢ ܠܗ ܠܡܘܡܐ ܘܪܟܢܐ
30a ܐ̱ܚܪܢܐ: ܘܡܫܬܠܡܝܢ ܠܗ ܠܦܪܨܘܦܐ ܐܚܪܢܐ: ܒܡܠܬܐ ܕܝܢ ܗܕܐ܀ ܟܠܗܘܢ ܒܪܐ ܟܡ
ܐܚܬܡ: ܘܐܘܣܦ ܠܟܠܗܘܢ ܘܗܠܝܢ ܐ̱ܚܪܢܐ ܡܩܕܡܬܐ: ܗܠܝܢ ܕܝܢ ܐܬ̈ܘܬܐ ܫܒܥ ܐܢܝܢ:
ܐ: ܡܦܠܓܢܝܬܐ ܕܫܘܡܐ: ܘܡܥܡܪ ܐܝܬ ܒܓܒܝܐ ܕܣܘܦ ܠܐܘܣܦܐ ܕܡܢܝܢܐ:
ܘܡܛܠ ܕܡܬܐܡܪ ܒܐܢܝܢ ܟܠ ܐܝܟ: ܗܐ ܩܛܝܠ ܠܐܘܣܦܐ ܕܐܬ̈ܘܬܐ
ܗܘܩܡܬܐ܀[2] ܒܪܟܘ ܢܒܪܗ ܒܪܟܬܗ ܒܪܗ ܢܟܒܪ ܟܠܟܬܝ ܒܪܟܡ ܒܪܗ ܡܟܒܪܬ ܒܟܠܟ
ܒܪܟܟ ܒܪܬܐ ܢܒܪܐ ܟܠܟܘܢ. ܒܪܟܢ ܒܪܝ ܢܟܒܪܘ ܟܠܟܢ ܒܪܟܗ ܒܪܟܢ ܢܒܪܗ
ܟܠܟܝ܀ ܗܠܝܢ ܕܒܪܟܘܬܐ ܐܝܟ ܐܦܐ ܫܡܥܐ ܠܡܫܬܡܥܢܘܬܐ: ܘܡܢܗܘܢ ܠܟܠܗܘܢ
ܠܡܠܘܬܗܘܢ܀[3]

30b ܗܘܬܠܐ ܐܫܟܚܢܢ ܟܕ ܐܡܬܝ ܡܩܘܪܒܐ ܕܡܫܬܡܠܝܢ ܠܟܬܒܐ ܡܢ ܣܘܦܐ܀[4]
ܦܘܠܐ ܘܐܡܪܝܢ ܡܢ ܠܘܬܐ ܡܩܘܪܒܐ ܐ ܡܢ ܣܛܪܐ ܐܘܟܝܬ ܡܬܒܘܥܬܐ ܕܟܬܒܐ
ܘܣܘܦܐ ܒ ܡܢ ܟܠܐ: ܕܠܐ: ܐܘܪܚܝܢ ܕܟܠ ܫܡܥܐ ܐ ܡܢ ܫܘܪܝܐ ܘܦܘܢܩܐ
ܕܡܩܕܡܐ: ܗ: ܡܦܝܣܢܐ ܟܬܒܐ ܟܠ ܫܡܥܐ܀ ܘܐܝܟ ܠܡܐܡܪ ܕܟܬܒܐ ܐܚܬܗ

1 ܟܗܘܐ] ܟܗܘܢ L; ?read ܘܟ 2 ܠܘܬܗ...ܣܩܘܒܠܗ] ܠܘܬܗ ܣܩܘܒܠܗ ܕܦܠܢ 4 ܟܠ] ܕܟܠ B 5 ܫܡܐ] ܡܩܕܡܐ OG | ܒܡܘܡܐ] ܡܘܡܐ OGBL 6 ܘܡܫܬܠܡܝܢ] ܘܡܫܬܠܡܝܢ OG ܐ̱ܚܪܢܐ...ܘܡܫܬܠܡܝܢ] om. BL (homoe.) | ܒܡܠܬܐ] ܡܠܬܐ B | ܒܪܐ] ܒ BL (see note) 7 ܠܟܠܗܘܢ] om. BL | ܐ̱ܚܪܢܐ] ܐܬ̈ܘܬܐ L 8 ܡܦܠܓܢܝܬܐ] read ܡܦܠܓܢܘܬܐ 10 Before ܢܒܪܗ B adds ܒܪܐ 12 ܐܦܐ] ܐܦ B 16 ܘܦܘܢܩܐ] ܘܡܦܢܩܐ L

[1] On this classification, see the comments to the current text on p.3,l.19; p.4,l.10. | [2] Those letters marked in red ink in the ms are here given with a line above the letter. | [3] In L the paradigm is given as follows:

ܒܪܟܘ	ܒܪܐ	ܢܒܪܗ	ܟܠܗ	ܗܠܝܢ ܕܒܪܟܘܬܐ
ܒܪܟܬܗ	ܒܪܗ	ܢܟܒܪ	ܟܠܟܬܝ	ܐܝܟ ܐܦܐ ܫܡܥܐ
ܒܪܟܡ	ܒܪܗ	ܡܟܒܪܬ	ܒܟܠܟ	ܠܡܫܬܡܥܐ
ܒܪܟܟ	ܒܪܬܐ	ܢܒܪܐ	ܟܠܟܘܢ	ܘܡܢܗܘܢ
ܒܪܟܢ	ܒܪܝ	ܢܟܒܪܘ	ܟܠܟܢ	ܠܟܠܗܘܢ
ܒܪܟܗ	ܒܪܟܢ	ܢܒܪܗ	ܟܠܟܝ	ܠܡܠܘܬܗܘܢ

It follows that l.6 should read ܟܠܗܘܢ ܒܪܐ ܟܡ ܐܚܬܡ. In the paradigm the first form should then appear as ܒܪܟܘ, with the the root letter kaf not needing to be in red - if, that is, the scribe had understood what he was writing. I am sure, however, that originally it read ܟܠܗܘܢ ܒܪܐ ܒܪ ܟܠ ܟܡ ܐܚܬܡ such that the ܒ in LB arose from ܒܪ, and the ܒܪܐ from ܒܪܐ. If this is not the case, then the other three paradigms (those of ܒܪ ܒܪ ܟܠ) were added later than Jacob's original, a suggestion made more probable by the fact that the verbal and particle forms of ܟܠ have been confused. There are six letters suffixed to the form ܒܪܐ; if we add the alaph of the emphatic state (see l.7), then this becomes seven, which is what Jacob says at ܟܗ,1. | [4] Perhaps we see here some influence from Arabic grammar, since this has to do with فاعِل and مَفْعُول (see De Sacy, *Grammaire* II,387).

ܗܘ ܕܩܕܡ ܠܫܘܚܠܦܐ ܡܕܡ: ܫܘܪܝܐ ܕܝܢ: ܗܘ ܡܐ ܕܡܫܬܡܠܐ ܡܢ ܥܒܘܕܐ: ܐܚܪܢܐ ܕܐܡܪ ܡܠܟܐ: ܐܝܟܠܐ ܕܗܘ ܠܒܪܐ: ܐܬܝܠܕܘ ܥܠܬܐ ܗܘܐ: ܥܒܘܕܐ ܘܥܒܘܕܘܬܐ ܘܫܘܚܠܦܐ: ܒܟܠ ܕܐܝܟܠܐ ܥܒܘܕܘܬܐ ܐܬܝܠܕ: ܕܗܘ ܕܡܢ ܥܒܘܕܐ: ܘܠܫܡܐ ܫܘܪܝܐ܀ ܘܒܟܠܡܐ ܗܘܕܝܐ ܦܪܝܐ ܕܠܦܢܝܢ ܫܘܪܝܐ ܒܟܠ ܥܒܘܕܐ ܒܡܐܡܪܐ: ܐܝܟ ܗܢܘ ܕܐܡܪ ܒܠܒܐ ܡܫܠܠܐ ܕܗܘ: ܘܠܫܡܐ ܕܦܠܘܪܐ ܕܡܪܢܐ ܐܝܟܠܐ: ܘܗܘܗܦ

2 ܐܬܝܠܕܘ] ܐܬܝܠܕ OGL   5 ܗܢܘ] om. L | ܕܦܠܘܪܐ] ܕܦܠܘܪܘ L

ܐܣܠܘܗܝ ܡܕܝܢܬܐ ܠܡܕܒܪܐ܀ ܒܕܝܠܗ ܡܢ ܢܬܠ ܡܫܬܘܕܝܢ ܠܚܕܘܬܐ: ܐܝܟܢܐ ܣܐ
31a ܘܐܦܪܝܥ ܡܘܣܝܢ ܐܝܟ ܠܡܕܒܪܐ: ܦܘܠܘܣ ܐܡܪ ܡܢܬܐ: ܠܒܝ ܡܘܫܐ ܡܐܬܘܬܐ܀
ܡܢ ܝܟܠܐ ܕܝܢ ܕܩ̈ܠܐ: ܐܪܐܪܘܗܝ: ܡܫܬܒܚܝܢ ܠܡܘܠܕܐ: ܐܝܟܢܐ ܕܐܦܪܝܥ:
ܘܗܘܝܘ ܐܘܚܕ ܠܐܦܪܝܥ: ܘܪܝܫ ܐܝܣܘܪ ܠܝܫܘܥ: ܘܐܡܪ ܡܠܦܢ ܠܡܫܝܚܐ:
ܡܢ ܩ̈ܠܐ: ܐܪܐܪܘܗܝ:[1] ܐܬܦܪܝܥ ܘܐܝܟܐ ܐܝܬܘܗܝ ܚܕܘܬܐ: ܘܐܝܟܐ ܫܘܒܚܐ:
ܡܢ ܛܘܒܐ ܗܢܐ ܘܦܪܝܫܘܬܐ ܕܡܫܝܚܐ: ܗܟܝܠ ܗܢܐ ܐܫܬܒܩܬ ܠܚܕܘܬܐ
ܒܦܪܝܫܬܐ ܘܫܘܒܚܐ ܒܐܪܥܐ: ܐܝܟ ܕܐ ܘܐܡܪ ܕܗܘ ܡܪܝܐ ܥܡܡܐ ܠܒܝ ܗ̄
ܠܡܫܒܚ: ܘܗܢܐ ܡܫܡܫܝܢ ܒܛܠܐ ܠܡܪܝܐ ܘܥܡܐ ܘܐܝܟ ܗܠܝܢ܀ ܒܕܝܠܗ ܒ
ܡܢܗ ܡܦܩܩܢܐ ܠܗܘ ܦܠܓܡܐ ܕܐܘܪܫܠܡ: ܠܐܠܗܐ ܠܐ ܚܙܐ ܐܢܫ ܡܡܠܠܝܢ:
ܡܢ ܐܠܗܐ ܗܢܐ ܕܗܘܕܝܐ. ܐܫܬܒܚܘ ܠܚܕܘܬܐ ܘܠܫܘܒܚܐ܀ ܗܢܐ ܐܦ
ܠܗܘ ܦܠܓܡܐ: ܠܗܢܐ ܗܢܐ ܐܢܐ ܚܙܝܬ ܠܐܠܗܐ: ܠܐܘܪܫܠܡ ܐܫܬܒܚܘܗܝ: ܐܝܟܢ
31b ܕܝܢ: ܘܐܢܐ ܡܢ ܠܒܝ ܠܒܪܐ ܠܐܠܗܐ: ܗܘܐ ܕܝܢܐ ܕܝܠܗ ܠܐ ܬܫܒܘܚܬܐ ܘܡܫܝܚܐ
ܗܠܝܢ: ܐܢܐ ܐܝܬܘܗܝ ܚܕܘܬܐ: ܘܐܝܟܐ ܫܘܒܚܐ܀ ܘܐܝܟܢܐ ܕܐܡܪ ܠܒܘܫܐ: ܡܛܠ
ܕܗܕܐ ܕܝܠܗ ܘܢܛܠܘܢ ܠܡܫܝܚܐ ܕܡܘܠܕܐ: ܐܝܟܢ ܕܚܝܢ ܡܦܩܝܢ ܒܗܘܢ:
ܐܫܬܒܚܘ ܡܢ ܦܪܝܫܘܬܐ ܕܗܕܐ: ܘܡܢ ܚܢܢܐ ܕܡܘܠܕܐ: ܕܠܡܫܝܚܐ ܠܐ
ܦܠܓܝܢ: ܕܢܐܡܪ ܕܚܕܘܬܐ. ܗܕܐ ܐܝܟ ܠܡܫܝܚܐ ܕܝܢ ܫܘܒܚܐ: ܘܡܛܠ ܐܡܪ
ܗܘܐ ܠܡܫܝܚܐ: ܡܛܠ ܕܡܠܟܐ ܗܘܐ ܕܝܢܐ ܠܗܘ ܕܡܠܟܘܬܐ ܚܕܘܬܐ: ܡܢ
ܡܕܒܪܐ ܡܕܝܢܬܐ ܘܦܠܚܬܐ: ܐܘ ܕܪܢܝܬܐ ܐܘ ܡܕܒܪܝܬܐ: ܘܐܝܟ ܐܢܝܢ: ܐܝܟܢܐ
ܘܐܡܪ ܡܫܝܚܐ: ܘܦܪܝܥܝܢ ܐܡܘܬܐ ܚܕܬܐ: ܐܫܬܒܚܘ ܕܚܕܬܐ ܐܝܟ ܕܦܪܝܥܝܢ ܗ̄
ܚܕܝܢ: ܐܡܘܬܐ ܢܐܡܢ: ܡܛܠ ܕܠܗ ܐܡܘܬܐ ܡܫܒܚܝܢ ܗܘܝ: ܦܪܝܫܝܢ ܐܡܪ
32a ܗܘܐ: ܘܐܝܟ ܗܘ ܘܐܡܪ ܕܗܘ:[2] ܡܕܒܪܐ ܠܗܘܐ ܚܙܘ: ܗ̄ ܚܙܘ ܐܝܬܘܗܝ ܫܘܒܚܐ.
ܡܕܒܪܐ ܕܝܢ ܚܕܘܬܐ: ܘܐܝ ܠܗ ܗܘ ܐܝܬܘܗܝ:

1 ܡܢ] om. BL | ܡܫܬܘܕܝܢ] ܡܫܬܘܕܝܢܘܬܐ B ܡܫܬܘܕܝ̈ܢ L   2 ܦܘܠܘܣ] ܦܐܘܠܘܣ L | ܠܒܝ ܡܘܫܐ] ܡܘܫܐ ܠܒܝ L   6 ܗܢܐ[1]] ?om.   7 ܐܝܟ ܕܐ] ܐܝܟܢܐ B   11 ܠܐܠܗܐ] accent om. L | ܐܝܟܢ] ܐܝܟ B   12 ܡܢ] om. B | ܠܐܠܗܐ] ܕܐܠܗܐ OG | ܘܡܫܝܚܐ] ܘܒܡܫܝܚܐ L   16 ܫܘܒܚܐ...ܐܡܪ] ܫܘܒܚܐ ܘܡܛܠ ܐܡܪ L   19 ܐܫܬܒܚܘ] ܐܫܬܒܚܘܢ L   20 ܡܛܠ...ܗܘܝ] B corrupt (dittography)   21 ܚܙܘ ܗ̄ ܚܙܘ ܐܝܬܘܗܝ ܫܘܒܚܐ] text as O (according to marginal correction) ܚܙܘ ܗ̄ G ܗ̄ ܐܘ ܫܘܒܚܐ ܐܝܬܘܗܝ B ܠܗܘܐ ܫܘܒܚܐ

[1] L explains this word with a marginal gloss, واصله. | [2] In fact, Isaiah 42:11.

ܕܗܘܘ̈ܢ ܐܡܪ ܗܘܐ. ܘܟܕ ܠܗܘܐ: ܘܐܢܫܐ ܕܐܡܪ ܡܫܝܚܐ ܡܢܒ̈ܚܠܡ ܠܡܪ ܩܕ̈ܝܫܐ ܕܫܬܡܫܐ ܡܘܪ̈ܝܬܐ ܕܬܡܠܬܐ: ܗ̄ ܡܘܪ̈ܝܬܐ ܡܢܒ̈ܚܠܡ ܠܩܕ̈ܝܫܐ: ܘܡܝܚܐ ܡܢ ܡܢܒ̈ܚܠܡ ܕܟܠ ܝܡܚ̈ܠܬܢܘܬܐ ܡܫܘܕܥܐ ܩܕܝܫܐ ܕܡܢ ܕܢܝܐܝܠ ܐܝܟ: ܐܘܐ ܕܗܘܝܘ ܣܐܡܝܢ܀ ܘܡܢ ܡܚܒܘܬܐ ܕܫܘܕܬܐ ܡܠܐܟܝܐ ܗܘܐ ܢܛܪܐܝܬ: ܐܚܡܠ ܕܢܗܘܝܢ ܡܢ ܠܟܠ܀ ܠܘܬ ܕܡܢ ܗܘ ܕܒ ܡܠܐܡܝܢ ܠܓܘܕܐ: ܘܠܐ ܫܒܩ ܠܗܘܢ ܫܘܡܠܐ ܠܟܠ: ܠܐ: ܐܘܐܘܗܝ ܐܬܢܐ ܕܡܢܝܢ ܠܐܘܪܚܐ: ܘܚܒܨܬܗ ܪܓܠܗ ܕܒܠܥܡ ܠܐܣܘܪܐ:[1] ܗ̄ ܐ̄ܬܐ ܣܓܪܬܗ ܠܪܓܠܗ: ܘܐܚܕܐ ܕܡܢܝܡ ܠܐܘܣܛܠܛܘܢ ܕܡܢܗܘܢ ܘܐܬܠܟ ܦܣܩܘܗ ܪܫܗ ܕܦܣܝܩ[2] ܗܘ ܕܡܢ ܐܣܦܘܩܠܛܪܐ ܠܪܫܗ: ܕܦܣܝܩ ܓܙܪ ܦܣܩ. ܪܫܗ ܕܦܣܝܩ[3] ܗ̄ ܗܪܘܕܝܣ: ܘܐܦ ܒܦܐܘܠܘܣ ܦܢܝܢ: ܕܡܢܝܫܟܪܘܢ: ܒܗܘܘ ܠܠܚܡܐ 32b

ܘܡܫܠܡܝܢ ܗܘܐ ܢܣܒ ܗܘܐ ܠܚܡܐ ܘܒܪܟ ܘܩܨܐ: ܐܦ ܟܣܐ ܗܟܢ ܘܐܡܪ܀ ܠܘܬ ܟܠ ܐܡܬܝ ܕܐܟܠܝܢ ܐܢܬܘܢ ܠܚܡܐ ܗܢܐ: ܘܫܬܝܢ ܐܢܬܘܢ ܟܣܐ ܗܢܐ܀[4] ܐܬܓܒܠ ܐܝܟܐ ܠܟܠܗܘܢ ܡܦܩܝܢ ܠܐܠܗܐ: ܘܟܠ: ܠܐ ܦܓܠܟ ܠܟܠ ܣܘܡܠܐ: ܒܠܐ ܡܢ ܠܚܡܐ ܕܐܬܐܟܠ ܠܐ ܕܢܬܐܟܠ܀ ܗܟܢܐ ܐܦ ܦܬܟܪܐ ܗܘ ܕܦܪܝܡ ܒܥܝ̈ܢܝܗܘܢ ܢܟܦܘܬܐ ܘܫܕܝܬܗ ܥܦܪܗ ܠܢܚܠܐ ܕܢܚܬ ܡܢ ܛܘܪܐ ܗ̄ ܠܥܦܪܗ܀[5]

ܠܘܬ ܕܡܢ ܕܝ ܕܐܦ ܚܢܝܐ ܐܝܟ ܓܒܠܬܐ: ܕܦܩܝܕ ܠܓܘܕܐ: ܘܫܒܝܩ: ܠܐ: ܠܟܠ ܫܘܡܠܐ. ܐܝܟܢܐ ܕܢܛܪ ܢܛܘܪܘܬܐ ܘܝܠܝܕ ܗܘ ܗܘܡܢܝܐ܀ ܐܚܪܢܐ ܕܐܡܪ. ܘܡܫܝܚܐ ܘܡܢ ܠܟܢܫܘܗܝ. ܘܡܪܐ ܐܫܬܡܥ ܠܥܡܘܕܘܗܝ ܘܓܙܪܗ: ܘܐܦ: ܗ: ܕܣܓܦ ܗܘܡܠܐ ܗܘ ܕܫܡܝܐ ܒܐܢܫܝܢ ܡܩܕܫܐ ܘܩܛܠܐ ܕܐܬܦܪܩܘܗܝ: ܠܝ ܠܐܘܪܫܠܡ: ܢܛܪ ܦܫܐ ܡܫܠܡܬܐ ܕܫܠܡܐ ܘܠܝ ܠܘܬܘܢ ܐܘܬܘܢ: ܟܠ: ܠܟܠ ܫܘܡܠܐ: ܕܐܝܟ ܐܡܝܢ. ܡܥܢܝܬܗ ܠܥܦܪܗ: 33a

ܦܣܩܘܗ ܠܪܫܗ: ܒܝ ܠܐܘܪܫܠܡ. ܗ: ܠܐܡܪ: ܓܙܪ ܦܣܩ ܪܫܗ. ܘܡܥܢܝܬ ܒܥܦܪܗ ܘܚܒܨܬܗ ܪܓܠܗ. ܗܟܢܐ ܘܐܦ ܗܘ ܦܬܟܪܐ ܕܐܝܟ ܠܐܘܣܛܠܛܘܢ ܕܟܠܗܘܢ: ܗܘܐ ܕܡ ܗܘ ܡܢ ܕܒܓܠܟ ܠܐ ܫܒܩ ܪܓܠܗ ܠܡܬܢܥܡܘ. ܗ ܠܐ ܫܒܩ ܡܢ ܕܐܬܢܝܚܘ ܪܓܠܗ ܘܗܘܝܐ ܡܢ ܡܚܒܘܬܐ ܕܫܘܕܬܐ: ܡܠܐܡܝܢ ܠܓܘܕܐ ܘܫܘܡܠܐ: ܘܟܕܝܢܐ ܗܘܐ ܦܢܝܡ

1 ܠܡܪ] om. B   2 ܠܩܕܝܫܐ] ܩܕܝܫܐ L   3 ܝܡܚܠܬܢܘܬܐ] ܢܡܚܠܢܘܬܐ B | ܕܢܝܐܝܠ] Thus all mss   4 ܣܐܡܝܢ] ܣܐܡܝܢ L | ܡܠܐܟܝܐ] ܘܡܠܐܟܐ OG   5 ܡܠܐܡܝܢ...ܠܟܠ] ܠܓܘܕܐ ܠܐ ܫܒܩ ܠܟܠ ܫܘܡܠܐ ܠܟܠ B | ܘܠܐ] ܠܐ L   6 ܗ̄] om. B   8 ܐܣܦܘܩܠܛܪܐ] ܐܣܦܘܩܠܛܘܪܐ L | ܕܦܣܝܩ[2]] ܘܦܣܝܩ L   10 ܘܡܫܠܡܝܢ] ܘܗܘ ܡܫܠܡܝܢ | ܗܘܐ[1]] om. OG | ܐܦ] ܘܐܦ L | ܠܘܬ] ܘܠܘܬ L   11 ܕܐܟܠܝܢ ܐܢܬܘܢ] ܕܐܟܠܝܢܘܢ OGB   13 ܦܬܟܪܐ] ܠܦܬܟܪܐ L   17 ܠܥܡܘܕܘܗܝ] ܠܥܡܘܕܝ L   18 ܠܝ...19 ܕܫܠܡܐ] om. G   19 ܐܘܬܘܢ] om. B | ܠܥܦܪܗ] ܠܥܦܪܐ Lcorr   22 ܠܐ[2]] om. O txt GB | ܕܐܬܢܝܚܘ] ܕܐܬܢܝܚ L   23 ܘܗܘܝܐ] ܗܘܝܐ L | ܘܟܕܝܢܐ] ܕܟܝܢܐ B

[1] Num 22.25 | [2] Mk 6.27 | [3] Mt 14.10 | [4] 1 Cor 11.23-6 | [5] Deut 9.21

ܐܬܥܝܪ ܡܢ ܗܘܦܟܐ ܕܦܨܚܐ ܠܦܢܝܐ: ܗܘܝ ܐܦ ܗܘ ܕܐܡܝܪܐ ܠܗܘܢ. ܘܢܩܦܬ ܐܝܟ ܠܥܡܗ. ܘܗܠܝܢ ܗܘܝ ܠܢܘܗܪ܀

ܫܘܐܠܐ ܠܐܘܣܒܝܘܣ ܐܝܟܢ ܐܝܬ ܐܬܠܬܐ ܕܦܪܨܘܦܐ ܫܘܫܛܬܐ: ܒܩܛܠܐ ܕܡܢ ܡܬܝܬܝܢ ܡܢ ܫܡܝܐ ܘܕܐܝܟ ܐܢܫܐ

ܦܘܫܩܐ[1] ܐܘܟܝܢ ܐܬܝܗܘܢ ܐܬܠܬܐ ܕܡܢ ܬܠܬܝܢ ܥܠ ܩܠܐ ܕܟܝܢ ܠܗܘܢ ܠܗܠ
33b ܫܘܫܛܬܐ: ܘܢܩܦܘܢ ܠܗܘܢ ܝܘܡܐ ܕܡܬܚܙܝܢܘܬܐ: ܐ: ܕ: ܝ. ܠ. ܘܦܠܚܝܢ ܡܚܝܘܢ ܬܠܬܐ ܫܘܫܛܝܢ ܠܟܠ ܥܡܐ ܕܢܚܘܢ ܠܗ. ܐ. ܐܚܪܢܐ ܕܬܐܡܪ ܡܢ ܕܘܟܬܐ ܐܘܪܚ. ܡܕܐ ܐܡܪܬ. ܓܒܪܐ ܐܚܪܢ. ܘܡܕܐ܀ ܒ̄ ܢܦܩܐ ܠܐܚܐ ܕܫܘܫܛܬܐ ܠܟܠܗ ܥܡܐ ܕܐܝܟ ܠܒܝܬܗ. ܓ̄. ܐܚܪܢܐ ܕܬܐܡܪ ܕܢܚܐ ܡܕܝܢܚ. ܝܪܚܐ ܡܕܝܢܚ. ܕܗܘܐ ܡܕܝܢܚܐ. ܪܚܡܬܐ ܡܕܝܢܚܐ. ܪܩܝܥܐ ܡܕܝܢܚ. ܕܟܪܟܐ ܡܕܝܢܚܝܢ. ܝܘܡܐ ܡܕܝܢܚ ܘܡܕܐ ܕ̄ ܠܗܘܢ ܬܠܬܐ ܠܟܠ ܥܡܐ ܕܫܘܪܝܗ. ܗ̄. ܘܕܟܪܐ ܠܗ ܠܗܠ ܫܘܫܛܬܐ. ܐܚܪܢܐ ܕܟܕܡܐ ܐܬܚܠܠ. ܕܟܝܢܐ ܐܬܚܙܝ. ܕܬܐܢܐ ܐܬܚܙܝ. ܕܡܕܢܐ ܐܬܚܙܝ ܕܟܠܐ ܐܬܚܙܝܐ܀ ܘ̄: ܠܗܘܢ ܬܠܬܐ ܟܪܝܐ ܘܐܝܟ ܗܢܐ. ܕܡܕܢܐ ܐܬܡܪ. ܣܘܦܐ ܐܬܝܪ ܫܘܟܢܐ ܐܢܟܠܝܢ. ܠܗܘܪܐ ܐܬܬܘܕܝ܀ ܐܦ. ܙ̄. ܐܦ. ܚ̄. ܒܢܘܢ ܠܗ ܫܩܒ. ܛ̄. ܫܡ ܡܬܐܘܣܐ ܒܢܝܫܬܐ ܕܥܡܐ. ܐܝܟ ܕܡܢ ܬܘܪܐ ܐܬܐܬܐ. ܒܘܪܐ ܐܬܚܙܝ. ܥܪܒܐ ܐܬܚܙܝ. ܘܡܕܐ. ܘܗܘܐ ܒܟܠܗ ܥܡܐ ܕܐܝܟ ܠܗ. ܝ̄.
34a ܢܛܝܪܬܐ. ܝ̄ܐ. ܕܝܢ: ܐܚܪܢܐ ܕܡܢ ܫܡܝܢܐ ܢܫܬܒܩ.[2] ܒܚܝܠ ܕܐܡܪ ܒܐܪܥܐ. ܡܢ ܢܘܡܐ ܩܕܡܝܐ ܠܦܛܝܪܘܬܗܘܢ ܫܡܝܢܐ ܡܢ ܒܬܝܟܘܢ. ܒܚܝܠ ܕܟܠ ܕܢܐܟܘܠ ܢܫܬܒܩ ܘܡܕܐ

ܫܘܐܠܐ ܠܐܘܣܒܝܘܣ ܡܛܠ ܐܝܟܢܐ ܢܫܬܒܩܘܢ ܠܗܘܢ ܚܛܗܝܗܘܢ ܘܐܝܟܢ ܒܢܝ ܩܠܐ ܗܘܐ

ܦܘܫܩܐ ܘܐܡܪܝܢ: ܕܢܫܬܒܩܘܢ ܐܝܟܢܐ: ܕܐܝܬ ܡܬܚܙܝܐ ܡܢ ܩܘܠܐ. ܐܘ ܕܐܬܝܠ ܡܢܝܬܐ ܒܩܘܠܐ. ܗܘܐ ܕܝܢ ܗܘܐ: ܠܥܠܡ ܒܢܝ ܩܠܐ. ܘܐܝܟܢܐ ܗܟܢ. ܐܠܐ. ܘܗܢܝܢ. ܘܒܢܣܘܪ܀ ܐܠܐ ܡܛܠ ܐܡܪ ܒܡܫܬܥܝܢ ܘܡܬܦܩܦܩܝܢ. ܡܛܘܠ ܕܡܬܐܡܪܐ ܡܫܬܥܝܢܐ ܕܡܛܠ ܐܡܪ. ܗܘܐ ܢܫܬܒܩܘܢ ܒܚܪܬܐ ܡܠܐ ܡܕܪܢܫܝܬܐ: ܗܘ ܕܐܝܟܢܐ. ܠܐ. ܐܝܟ ܗܘ ܕܐܡܝܪܐ. ܐܝܠܝܢ ܕܡܢ ܩܕܡܝܢ ܕܚܛܝ ܐܝܠܝܢ: ܐܠܐ ܠܐ ܠܥܠܡ

1 ܕܦܨܚܐ] ܗܦܨܚܐ B   2 ܗܘܪܐ] om. OG   7 ܐ] om. OG   11 ܥܡܐ] om. OGB   12 ܠܗܘܢ] om. B   13 ܐܦ] om. B   15 ܐܬܐܬܐ] ܐܬܐܬ L   17 ܕܢܐܟܘܠ] ܢܐܟܘܠ OG   23 ܡܛܠ ܐܡܪ] ܡܛܠ ܐܡܪ L | ܘܡܬܐܡܪܐ] ܘܡܛܠ ܐܡܪ B

[1] A later hand begins here (up to ܝܒ,19). | [2] Note the mindless confusion of ܫܡܝܢܐ and ܚܡܝܪܐ (Ex 12.15)

ܠܐ ܐܦ ܓܒܪ ܡܢ ܡܬܐܡܪܐ ܦܣܘܩܐ ܡܦܛܦܛܢܐ. ܗܘ ܡܐ ܕܐܟܠ ܒܗ. ܒܥܐ ܕܐܡܪ
ܐܠܐ ܠܐ ܟܠܒܦܝ܀ ܘܒܡܬܐܡܪܐ ܐܦܘܦܛܝܩܐ ܗܘܐ ܢܫܒܘܚܬܐ ܒܒܪܬܐ ܡܠܐ ܫܘܐܠܬܐ. 34b
ܗܝ ܕܐܡܠܬܗ ܠܝ. ܐܝܟ ܗܝ ܕܐܡܝܪܐ. ܘܟܕ ܐܬܐ ܠܟܠ ܝܬܐ: ܠܐ ܐܫܟܚ ܒܗ ܡܕܡ:
ܐܠܐ ܐܢ ܝܬܝܪܐ ܒܟܠܗܘܢ ܐܟܠ ܗܘܟܠ ܒܡܬܐܡܪܐ ܦܣܘܩܐ. ܗܘ ܡܐ ܕܐܦ ܡܢܗ.
ܒܥܐ ܕܐܡܪ. ܐܠܐ ܐܢ ܝܬܝܪܐ ܒܟܠܗܘܢ܀ ܘܠܗܘ ܐܡܝܪܐ. ܘܠܐ ܡܫܟܚ ܠܐܢܫ ܕܢܟܦܠ
ܒܡܕܡ: ܐܠܐ ܐܢ ܠܡܡܠܠܘ ܘܠܡܦܣܩ. ܘܐܪܡܗ ܒܫܬܩܘܗܝ ܘܠܐܢܫ ܠܐ ܝܗܒ. ܐܠܐ
ܠܡܦܩ ܒܠܫܢܘܗܝ. ܘܐܝܟ ܡܫܬܥܝ ܠܐ ܐܟܪ ܐܠܐ ܒܪܗ ܕܐܟܘܠܐ܀ ܘܪܘܦ ܠܡܦܩ
ܕܠܘܬܗ ܐܦܘܦܐܛܝܩܐ ܒܟܬܒܐ ܣܓܝ ܡܬܚܙܝܢ. ܗ̄. ܠܐ ܠܐ. ܒܟܬܒܝ ܐܡܪ܀ ܩܗ̈ܢ. ܐܝܟ
ܗܝ ܕܐܡܝܪܐ. ܗܢܘܢ ܕܝܢ ܕܐܟܠܗ: ܗܘܝܢ ܗܘܘ ܐܪܒܥܐ ܠܐܦ̈ܝ ܓܒܪ̈ܐ. ܫܡܥ ܡܢ
ܒܢ̈ܐ ܘܫܒ̈ܐ. ܐܪܝܡܬ ܐܝܕܝ ܠܘܬ ܐܠܗܐ ܕܩܢܝܢܗ ܫܡܝܐ ܘܐܪܥܐ:[1] ܘܠܐ ܐܣܒ ܡܢ
ܟܠܡܕܡ ܕܐܝܬ ܠܟ. ܫܡܥ ܡܢ ܡܕܡ ܕܐܡܠܗ ܬܠܡܝܕܐ܀ ܬ̈ܠܡܝܕܘܗܝ. ܐܟܘܬ. 35a
ܘܠܡܫܝܚܐ ܘܟܠܟܠ ܕܐܝܬ ܒܗ ܐܘܡܢ ܒܒܘܪܐ: ܒܠܫܢܗ ܕܒܝܬܐ ܘܠܚܡܐܬܐ
ܘܒܨܒܘܬܐ ܕܢܦܫܐ ܘܕܪܓܬܐ ܐܝܟ ܠܚܡܠܟ ܓܒܪܗ ܕܡܪܝܐ. ܘܢܪܟܢ ܒܢ̈ܝ
ܐܢܫܐܝܬ ܠܟܠܗܘܢ ܟܡܐܘܬܗ ܕܟܝ. ܒܠܫܢܗ ܒܡܬܐ ܘܒܠܐ ܘܡܫܝܚܐ. ܗܝ
ܒܪܗ ܒܗܘܢ: ܘܬܗܘܐ ܡܫܝܚܐ ܘܟܠ ܕܒܗ ܣܢܝܐ ܠܡܪܝܐ. ܒܠܫܢܗ ܠܪܚܡ
ܕܢܬܐ ܐܝܟ. ܘܡܪܐ ܕܐܝܟ ܗܟܢ܀

ܗܘܐܠܐ ܐܘܟܠܟܣ: ܐܝܟܢ ܐܝܬܝ ܢܩܙܐ ܒܫܡܝܐ ܕܦܣܘܩܐ ܘܟܡܐ ܐܝܬܝ ܦܘܣܩܐ
ܘܐܡܪܝܢ ܕܦܣܘܩܐ ܠܐܘܪ ܐܢܬܝ ܐܡܠܬ̄. ܐܘ ܟܠ ܦܣܘܩܐ ܕܒܬܪ ܩܠܐ: ܫܩܘܠܐ ܒܟܠ
ܘܩܠܐ: ܕܟܠܗܘܢ ܡܢ ܟܟܠ ܦܠܣܢ ܐܘ ܟܠ ܫܘܐܠܐ ܡܩܛܝܢܐ ܗܟܢ
ܘܡܟܬܒܐ ܡܬܐܡܪܢ ܦܣܘܩܐ ܘܟܢܒܝܬܐ ܕܙܘܓܐ ܐܬܬܫܝܡܘ ܢܩܙܐ ܕܡܢ
ܒܬܫܝܬܐ ܕܦܣܘܩܐ ܐܝܟܘܢ ܐܘܟܐ ܘܐܝܟܘܢ ܐܝܟ ܕܬܫܐ ܠܢܩܙܐ ܫܩܠܐ: 35b
ܘܐܫܠܐ. ܘܟܠܐ: ܘܦܣܘܩܐ[2]
ܘܫܩܠܐ ܦܬ ܠܡܘܪܐ ܫܘܛܐ ܡܫܡܘܥ. ܘܟܬܝܒ ܗܪܡܐ ܕܡܬܐܡܪܐ ܡܬܬܐܫܡ ܒܝ
ܗܘܐ ܡܬܐܡܪܐ ܐܘܟܐ. ܐܝܟ ܗܝ ܕܬܐܘܦܝܠܘܣ: ܒܪ ܕܝܢ ܐܬܟܒ ܫܡܥܘܢ

3 ܠܝ] ܐܢ OGBL (but ܗܘܦܘܬܛܝܩܐ = ὑποθετικός / hypothetical)   6 ܐܠܐ[2]] ܐܠܐ ܐܢ. ܘ] ܐܢܘ 10 L ܡܬܗܦܟܝܢ] ܡܬܚܙܝܢ | L ܐܦܘܦܗܝܩܐ] ܐܦܘܦܐܣܝܩܐ 8 L ܠܝ OG ܐܢܐ. B 12 ܐܪܝܡ] ?read ܐܪܝܡܬ (Josh 6.22)   14 ܘܡܫܝܚܐ ܗܝ ܒܪܗ] L ܘܡܫܝܚܐ ܗܝ ܒ̇ܪܗ 15 ܒܪܗ] ܒܪ OGB   18 ܐܘܟܠܟܣ] ܐܘܟܠܟܣܢܐ L 19 ܐܢܬܝ] ܐܢܝ OG   20 ܦܠܣܢ] ܦܠܣܢ OG   21 ܦܣܘܩܐ] ܦܣܘܩܐ OG 22 ܟܬܫܐ] ܟܬܫܐ B | ܫܩܠܐ...23 ܘܦܣܘܩܐ] see note

[1] Gen 14.22 | [2] L has the accents correctly, i.e. ܦܣܘܩܐ. ܫܩܠܐ: ܟܠܐ:. See p.89 above for how this passage can assist in understanding Jacob of Edessa's system.

ܟܒ ܒܒܒܠ ܠܒܢܝܢ ܕܗܘܘ̈ܐ: ܒܡܘܩܒ ܐܪܘܕܝܣ ܡܠܟܐ ܘܟܠܟܡ ܕܢܦܫܐ ܗܝܟܠ ܠܒܢܝ ܡܢ ܦܘܩܕܢܐ ܕܟܘܪܫ ܕܟܘܪܐ: ܘܢܒܥ ܗܘܐ ܠܒܢܝܢܐ. ܡܛܠ ܕܝܢ ܕܐܘܪܫܠܡ ܐܬܟܒܫ ܗܘ ܡܐܡܪܐ: ܠܐܬܚܒܫܘ ܥܩܐ ܒܡܪܟܒܬܗ. ܗ̄ ܒܬܪ ܥܡܐ ܕܗܘܘ̈ܐ ܚܝܐ ܦܡ: ܡܛܠ ܢܥܡܬܐ ܘܠܐ ܢܬܐܟܪ ܦܪܘܐ. ܡܛܠ ܐܪܥܘܬܐ ܦܠܓܡܐ. ܘܐܣܪܝܬ ܡܛܠ ܕܒܬܪ ܗܘܘ̈ܐ ܢܬܐܪ ܒܢܝܢ ܗܢܡܝܗ ܡܢ ܕܒܗܘܢ ܐܣܪܝܢ.

ܐܣܬܐܡܐ ܕܝܢ ܐܝܬ ܐܡܬܝ ܕܢܦܩ ܒܥܩܐ ܡܐ ܕܦܪܝܒ ܗܘܠܐ ܕܬܠܓܡܪ ܘܒܥܘܒܕܐ ܕܡܐܡܪܐ ܚܪܐ ܘܒܣܘܐܡܐ. ܘܐܝܬ ܐܡܬܝ ܕܡܬܐܬܗܝܡ ܡܐ ܕܡܐܡܪܐ ܦܠܡ. ܦܘܪܥܢܐ ܡܚܡܠ ܢܦܩ. ܐܝܟ ܗܝ. ܒܝ ܕܝܢ ܐܬܐ ܢܥܘܕ ܠܐܬܘܪܐ ܘܦܣܪܐ ܘܦܠܠܢܩܘܣ. ܡܥܐܠ ܗܘܐ ܠܐܠܟܡܢܝܘܗܝ ܘܐܡܪ. ܘܐܝܟ ܗܝ ܕܢܒܟܘܢ ܡܢ ܡܟܡܘܬܗ ܒܟܘܢ ܡܚܩܘܠܐ. ܘܟܠܗܘܢ ܚܬܝܢ ܚܘܠܐ. ܘܗܘܐ ܐܟܠ ܘܫܬܐ ܒܡ ܬܘܐ ܡܛܠ ܕܝܢ ܕܥܘܒܕܐ ܕܡܐܡܪܐ ܐܬܟܒܫ: ܙܘܡܐܠ ܐܬܐܬܗܝܡ ܐܣܬܐܡܐ ܒܐܣܪܝܬ ܡܐܡܪܐ ܐܡܝܢܐ ܕܢܬܝܕܥ ܕܒܟܡ ܗܘܠܐ ܘܡܥܪܐ ܡܚܡܠ ܦܘܪܥܢܐ. ܐܝܟ ܗܝ ܕܡܥܠܠ ܗܘܐ ܠܐܠܟܡܢܝܘܗܝ ܘܐܡܪ܀

ܒܒܬܐ ܕܝܢ ܡܬܐܬܗܝܡ ܚܝܠܐ ܗܘܪܡܐ ܕܡܐܡܪܐ ܘܦܘܪܥܢܐ ܒܝ ܡܥܐܠܝܢ ܗܘ ܗܘ ܡܐܡܪܐ ܐܦܩܬ ܦܘܪܥܢܐ ܐܘܡܬܐ. ܐܝܟ ܗܝ ܗܘܐ ܕܝܢ ܦܠܢ ܕܗܘܐ ܕܢܬܦܠܐ ܡܕܝܢ ܘܐܬܐܡܪ ܡܢ ܡܪܝܐ ܒܝܕ ܢܒܝܐ ܕܗܘܐ ܒܬܘܟܠܐ ܐܬܚܝܒ ܘܐܬܟܪܝ ܒܙܐ ܘܢܦܪܘܢ ܥܡܗ ܒܥܒܘܐܡܠ. ܘܐܝܟ ܗܝ ܕܒܬܟܐ ܕܢܚܒܘܬܗ ܕܥܡܘܢ ܡܥܡܝܢܐ ܒܪܗ ܕܕܘܝܕ ܒܪܗ ܕܐܒܪܗܡ܀

ܦܥܘܡܐ ܕܝܢ ܒܟܠ ܥܘܡܪܢ ܗܘܠܐ ܡܦܩܘܕ ܘܟܠ ܒܡܫܪܘܬܐ ܙܒܢܐ ܡܚܒܘܩ ܘܐܝܬ ܐܡܬܝ ܘܠܐ ܦܠܝ ܦܬܪ ܒܒܬܐ. ܡܬܐܬܗܝܡ ܕܝܢ ܡܐ ܕܒܟܠܗ ܗܘܠܐ ܐܬܡܥܠ ܐܝܟ ܗܝ ܕܗܘܐ ܙܒܢܐ ܘܗܘܐ ܙܦܪܐ ܢܘܡܐ ܚܝ. ܘܐܝܟ ܗܝ ܕܢܘܡܐ ܚܒܫ ܠܗܘܐ ܒܦܪܘܫܘܬܐ. ܐܝܢ ܐܝܬ ܕܡܥܠܝܢ ܥܘܘܕܐ ܕܒܡܐܡܪܐ ܒܪܐ ܐܡܝܢܐ ܕܚܝܢ ܦܠܓܡܐ ܢܬܐܡܪ. ܠܐ ܡܬܐܬܗܝܡ ܒܗ ܥܩܐ ܐܠܐ

1 ܗܘܚܠ] om. B 2 ܘܢܒܥ] ܢܐܦܠ L 3 ܗܘ] ܒܗ L 4 ܢܥܡܬܐ] ܢܥܘܕ B 5 ܘܐܣܪܝܬ] ܘܐܣܪܬ: L 5 ܗܘܘ̈ܐ] om. BL 6 ܕܦܪܝܒ] ܕܦܪܝܒ OG 8 ܘܦܣܪܐ...9 ܘܦܠܠܢܩܘܣ] ܘܦܠܠܢܩܘܣ ܘܡܕܝܢܐ ܘܦܣܪܐ L 10 ܡܢ...11 ܬܘܐ] ܬܘܐ ܡܢ L 11 ܡܛܠ ܕܝܢ] ܕܝܢ ܡܛܠ B | ܕܝܢ] ܕܝܢ L | ܐܬܐܬܗܝܡ] ܐܬܐܬܗܝܡܘ B 12 ܐܡܝܢܐ] om. L ܡܐܡܪܐ...ܐܦܩܬ] om. B 15 ܕܗܘܐ...ܡܕܝܢ] om. B 16 ܗܘܐ] ܗܝ OG | ܒܪܐ] ܒܪܐ: L 17 ܡܥܡܝܢܐ] ܡܥܡܝܢܐ: L 20 ܦܠܝ] ܦܠ OG 23 ܒܗ ܥܩܐ ܐܠܐ ܡܬܐܬܗܝܡ] om. BL (homoe.)

ܠܝ

ܡܬܐܡܪܝܢ ܒܡܘܠܟܗܘܢ ܠܫܡܐ. ܘܩܪܝܢ ܢܩܦ ܦܘܢܝܐ. ܐܝܟ ܗܘ ܕܟܕ ܒܟܠ ܠܐܦܘܠܓܝܐ. ܐܬܐܡܪܬ ܥܠܘܗܝ ܡܕܝܢܬܐ. ܘܐܝܟ ܗܘ ܕܟܘܡܪܐ ܘܐܟܠܬܐ. ܗܘܬ ܕܡܬܚܘܝܐ ܒܦܠܚܝܐ ܡܕܝܢܬܐ ܕܒܒܠ܀ ܐܝܟ ܗܟܘܬ ܘܦܘܠܚܢܐ ܕܡܬܚܫܒܝܢ ܐܘܪܚܗܘܢ ܟܠܗ. ܐܢܫܐ ܕܝܢ ܦܠܚܐ ܢܬܚܫܒܘܢ ܥܠܘ ܒܫܡܐ ܗܟܢܐ ܡܬܐܡܪܝܢ ܥܠܝܗ ܗܟܘܬ ܠܦܘܠܚܢܐ. ܐܝܟ ܗܘ ܕܐܚܪܢܐ ܐܡܪ ܠܐܒܘܗܝ. ܘܐܝܟ 36a
ܗܘ ܕܥܠ ܠܐܝܡܪܐ ܕܐܦܐ܀ ܐܝܟ ܡܬܚܫܒ ܗܟܘܬ ܡܬܡܪܚܐ. ܐܢܫܐ ܕܝܢ ܦܠܚܐ ܢܬܚܫܒ: ܘܦܘܠܚܢܐ ܟܠܗܘܢ ܦܠ̈ܚܐ ܐܘ ܟܢܫܝܢ. ܦܠܚܐ ܡܢܗܘܢ ܘܐܝܬܝܗܘܢ ܗܟܘܬ ܕܡܬܐܡܪܝܢ ܒܫܡܐ܀ ܘܡܥܪܐ ܘܦܠ̈ܚܐ ܕܟܠܗܘܢ ܘܐܡܪܘܢ ܦܘܠܚܢܐ. ܕܡܬܦܫܩܝܢ ܒܟ̈ܬܒܐ ܘܒܡܘܠܟܢܐ ܕܟܠܗ ܗܘ ܟܠܐ. ܡܬܐܡܪܝܢ ܦܫܝܛܐ. ܐܝܟ ܗܘ ܒܢܝܢܐ ܕܡܢ ܕܥܬܐ. ܐܡܬܝ ܕܬܪܝܨܐܝܬ ܡܬܐܡܪܐ ܡܢ ܟܠܗ ܠܟܠܗܘܢ: ܠܡܕܝܢܬܐ ܘܥܩܪܗ ܬܪܘܐ: ܘܐܝܟ ܗܘ ܡܫܝܚܐ ܦܪܩܗ ܘܗܘܝܐ ܦܠܐ ܗܟܝܠ ܠܟܘ: ܘܐܘܟܠ ܒܪܘܚܐ ܕܩܘܕܫܐ: ܘܐܬܩܢܐ. ܡܢ ܦܫܩܐ ܕܘܩܕܡܗ ܕܡܪܝܐ܀ ܐܡܬܝ ܕܡܢ ܕܗܘܘܐ ܘܦܘܠܚܢܐ ܠܐܘܪܚܗܘܢ ܕܡܬܚܫܒܝܢ ܐܘܪܚܐ: ܡܢ ܐܢܫ ܙܘܥ ܕܡܬܦܫܩ ܗܟܘܬ ܕܫܘܩܐ: ܘܒܡܘܠܟܗܘܢ ܕܡܬܐܡܪܝܢ ܠܫܡܐ܀ ܘܡܬܦܫܩ ܦܘܠܚܢܐ ܕܟܠܗ. ܘܒܡܘܠܟܢܐ ܕܡܬܐܡܪܝܢ ܦܫܝܛܐ. ܐܝܟ ܗܘ. ܘܗܘܐ
ܕܟܕ ܫܡܥܝܢ ܕܡܫܬܘܣ ܓܘܫܐ ܘܩܪܝܢ ܐܚܪܐ ܠܡܠܬܐ: ܟܕ ܒܢܐ ܘܐܡܬܝ: ܗܘܐ 36b
ܟܪܐ ܡܢ ܡܟܝܢܐ ܘܡܢ ܟܝܢܗ ܐܡܪܗ: ܡܬܚܫܒܝܢ ܗܘܘ ܐܝܟܐ ܐܢܫܝܢ ܕܡܬܦܫܩ ܗܘܘ ܫܡܥܝܢ ܠܗ ܒܠܒܐ ܕܡܠܬܐ ܘܡܬܐܡܪܐ ܦܫܝܛܐ܀ ܗܟܢ ܐܝܟ ܐܘܪܚܐ ܢܘܩܪܐ ܕܬܗܝܪܐ ܘܦܘܬܚܐ:

ܐܘܟܠܐ ܕܡܢ ܕܒܗܘܢ ܫܡܥܝܢ ܐܢܘܢ: ܐܟܪܐ ܕܡܬܡܗܢܐ ܥܠܝܐ: ܙܘܓܐ ܕܠܐ ܦܣܘܩ: ܘܙܘܓܐ: ܕܦܣܘܩ: ܡܦܩܕܢܐ: ܗܘܦܟ ܓܒܝܐ: ܗܘܦܟ ܠܫܡܐ ܦܣܘܩܐ ܡܫܐܠܢܐ: ܠܦܩܐ: ܡܩܝܡܢܐ: ܠܥܠܝܐ ܙܘܓܐ: ܡܡܠܠܢܐ: ܢܗܘܪ ܥܘܠܐ: ܦܪܘܩܐ: ܡܢܚܬܢܐ: ܡܪܟܢܐ: ܡܦܣܩܢܐ: ܡܥܠܝܐ: ܡܬܪܗܛܢܐ: ܡܬܒܥܢܐ: ܡܢܚܬܢܬܐ: ܗܘܦܟ ܡܣܒܪܢܐ: ܟܪܘܙܐ: ܗܘܦܟ ܟܪܘܙܐ: ܟܪܝܗܐ: ܙܘܓܐ:[1] ܫܡܥܐ ܘܡܬܚܫܒܬܐ: ܡܬܐܡܪܐ ܘܙܘܓܐ ܘܪܒܬܐ ܕܦܫܩ. ܙܘܓܐ ܘܪܒܬܐ ܕܠܐ

2 ܘܐܟܠܬܐ] ܘܐܟܠܬܐ (no point) L 3 ܕܡܬܚܘܝܐ] ܡܬܚܘܝܐ. L 9 ܟܬ̈ܒܐ] ܟܬܒܐ L 10 ܕܥܬܐ] ܕܥܬܐ. ܘܐܩܝܡ 11 ܠܟܠܗܘܢ] ܠܟܠܗܘܢ. L | ܗܘ ܡܫܝܚܐ] ܗܘ ܡܫܝܚܐ. L 12 ܠܟܘ] ܠܟܘ: L | ܕܩܘܕܫܐ] ܕܩܘܕܫܐ: L | ܘܐܬܩܢܐ] ܘܐܬܩܢܐ (no point) L 13 ܕܘܩܕܡܗ] ܕܘܩܕܡܗ ܟܠܗ: L | ܐܡܬܝ] ܐܡܬܝ OG 14 ܒܡܬܐܡܪܝܢ] ܡܬܐܡܪܝܢ B 16 ܠܡܠܬܐ...ܘܐܡܬܝ] ܠܡܠܬܐ: B | ܐܡܬܝ] ܐܡܬܝ OG 17 ܐܡܪܗ] ܐܡܪܗ. L | ܐܝܟܐ] ܐܝܟܐ OG 18 ܐܝܟ] ܐܝܟ ܟܕ ܒܢܐ ܘܐܬܡܠܠ ܘܐܡܬܝ: L 21 ܦܣܘܩ] ܦܣܘܩ OG ܦܣܘܩ. L 23 ܡܢܚܬܢܬܐ] read ܡܣܒܪܢܐ and ܗܘܦܟ ܡܣܒܪܢܬܐ. 24 ܙܘܓܐ] see note

[1] There appears to be something missing here. Comparison with Barhebraeus (*Gramm.*, 247) suggests perhaps ܙܘܓܐ. ܫܡܥܐ. ܗܘܦܟ ܫܡܥܐ. ܙܘܓܐ ܘܫܡܥܐ ܘܡܬܚܫܒܬܐ. ܡܬܐܡܪܐ (cf. p. ܠܝ,18 below).

37a ܦܣܩ ܘܦܣܘܩܐ: ܠܐܟܐ[1] ܟܕ ܩܪܝ ܠܡܟܠܬܐ: ܘܩܪܐ ܕܐܝܟ ܗܟܢ܀ ܚܢܢ ܕܝܢ ܓ
ܟܠ ܟܠܚܕ ܚܕ ܡܢܗܘܢ ܦܠܓܘܬܐ ܡܢ ܟܠܗܝܢ ܦܣܘܩܝܢ. ܐܬܐܡܪܘܢ ܕܝܢ
ܒܥܠܬܐ ܡܘܚܠܦ ܡܥܢܝܐ ܘܩܠܐ ܐܘܟܝܬ ܦܘܣܩܐ ܟܕ ܦܠܓܘܬܐ ܗܘܝܐ.
ܟܠܝܐ: ܟܠܝܐ ܘܟܠܝܘܬܗ ܘܡܫܟܚܢܝܬܐ:
ܐܣܝܪܐ. ܟܠܐ ܡܪܟܢܐ ܢܛܠܒ ܐܘ ܠܐܘܦܝܠܐ
ܥܩܐ: ܘܚܕܐ ܡܪܢܐ ܕܫܒܩܬ ܒܡܠܬܐ ܕܐܝܬ ܒܐܘܪܚܐ:
ܗܘܣܟ ܥܩܐ: ܟܬܪܐ ܕܡܢ ܒܬܪ:
ܐܬܐ ܥܘܪ̈ܐ ܕܠܡܟܠܬܐ ܘܦܣܘܩܐ. ܟܠ ܢܘܩܙܐ ܕܟܬܒܝܢ ܦܠܓܘܬܐ ܐܬܐ
ܦܣܘܩܐ ܗܘ ܗܟܢܐ: ܫܩܝܠ ܡܢ ܚܫܒܬܐ.
ܙܘܓܐ ܕܦܣܩ ܠܐ ܟܒܫ ܟܠ ܟܬܒ ܐܘܪܚܐ
ܡܟܒܢܝܐ: ܠܟܘܠ ܕܐܝܟ ܐܒܪܗܡ ܠܟܘܠ ܕܐܝܟ ܐܝܣܚܩ
ܗܘܣܟ ܟܟܒܐ: ܟܠ ܚܕܐ ܠܗܘܐ ܟܟܘܢ ܐܝܟ:
ܗܘܣܟ ܐܣܝܪܐ ܐܝܟ ܫܐܘܠ
ܦܩܘܕܐ. ܢܩܘܫ ܚܢܢܐ ܡܢ ܦܩܘܕܗ.
ܡܫܒܩܢܐ. ܘܟܠܬܐ ܡܢ ܟܠ ܟܘܬܗ
37b ܠܦܩܐ: ܐܡܪ: ܢܬܦܫܠ ܟܢܫܝܗ ܕܡܪܝܐ ܟܘܠܐ ܘܟܠܐ
ܠܐܟܐ ܘܩܪܝܐ: ܟܠ ܗܟܢ: ܠܐ ܐܦܩܘܢ ܐܝܟ ܡܪܝܐ
ܠܐܟܐ: ܘܡܫܐܠܢܐ. ܘܟܠܡܐ ܕܗܘܝܐ: ܠܐ ܬܬܒܩܫ ܢܦܫܝ ܠܐ ܐܡܪܬ ܟܠܦܝ ܘܠܐ
ܬܬܪܟܝ
ܠܐܟܐ: ܘܐܣܝܪܐ. ܗܘܝܐ ܡܟܠܝܢ
ܡܟܠܝܢܐ. ܟܕ ܬܬܒܥܘܢ ܐܘܪܚܬܐ: ܟܕ ܬܬܥܠܡܘܢ ܟܬܪܒܘܬܐ: ܟܕ ܬܦܫܟܘܢ ܦܪ̈ܝܫܬܐ
ܦܬܝܚܝܢ܀[2]
ܙܘܓܐ ܕܠܐ ܦܣܩ. ܠܐ ܬܬܐܣܦ ܚܕ ܟܠ ܚܕ ܐܚܝ: ܘܠܐ ܬܬܪܝܫܘܢ
ܙܘܓܐ ܕܠܐ ܦܣܩ ܘܦܣܩ. ܙܘܬ ܟܠܡ ܘܟܢܫ ܟܢܫܬܐ

1 ܘܦܣܘܩܐ] G om. the preceding; ܘܡܫܟܚܐ ܡܟܬܒܐ B 2 ܟܠ] om. OG 3 ܒܥܠܬܐ] ܒܥܠܬܐ L 4 ܟܠܝܐ] ܟܟܠܐ: L | ܘܡܫܟܚܢܝܬܐ: L 5 ܠܐܘܦܝܠܐ] ܠܐܘܦܝܐ. L 6 ܥܩܐ] om. B 8 ܕܦܣܘܩܐ] ܦܣܘܩܐ BL | ܢܘܩܙܐ] ܢܘܩܙܐ B 10 ܕܦܣܩ] ܕܦܣܩ̈ L | ܟܠ] om. OG | ܐܘܪܚܐ] ܐܘܪ̈ܚܐ L 12 ܟܟܒܐ] ܟܟܒܐ: L | ܐܝܟ] ܐܝܟ: L 13 ܫܐܘܠ] ܫܐܘܠ. L 14 ܦܩܘܕܗ.] ܦܩܘܕܗ. L 17 ܠܐܟܐ ܘܩܪܝܐ] ܠܐܟܐ.ܘܩܪܝܐ. L ܡܪܝܐ] ܡܪܝܐ. L 18 ܬܬܒܩܫ] ܬܬܒܩܫ L | ܠܐ ܐܡܪܬ] om. O | ܟܠܦܝ] ܟܠܦܝ: L 20 ܗܘܝܐ] ܗܘܝܐ ܐܠܗܐ O ܐܠܗܐ ܗܘܝܐ: L | ܡܟܠܝܢ] ܡܟܠܝܢ. L 21 ܐܘܪܚܬܐ] ܐܘܪܚܬܐ. L | ܟܬܪܒܘܬܐ] ܟܬܪܒܘܬܐ. L 22 ܦܬܝܚܝܢ] ܦܬܝܚܝܢ. L 23 ܐܚܝ̈ L 24 ܙܘܬ ܟܠܡ] ܟܠ B | ܟܠܡ̈ ܘܟܢܫ ܟܢܫܬܐ.. L

[1] After ܠܐܟܐ Barhebraeus adds [ܘܟܠ ܐܬܘܬܐ] ܡܘܡܐ. ܡܘܦܩܐ. ܡܘܣܟ ܡܘܦܩܐ | [2] Evidently the ܡܟܠܝܢܐ can be written in a variety of ways.

ܬܠܬܐ ܙܘܓܝܢ. ܬܪ ܒܪܝ ܬܪ ܒܪ ܒܪܗܫ ܬܪ ܒܪ ܢܒܝܫ[1] ܠܗ
ܡܡܠܠܢܐ. ܠܥܘܠܐ ܕܐܘܠܐ ܢܗܘܐ.
ܢܘܚ ܛܘܒܐ܆ ܛܘܒܘܗܝ ܠܓܒܪܐ ܕܕܚܠ ܡܢ ܡܪܝܐ܀
ܦܩܘܕܐ ܡܪܘ ܠܘܬܝ. ܬܘ ܠܘܬܝ ܟܠܟܘܢ ܠܐܝܐ..[2]
ܡܢܝܚܢܐ. ܗܐ ܐܡܪܗ ܕܐܠܗܐ. ܗܢܘ ܗܘ ܕܐܡܪܢܐ ܕܫܠܘܬ ܐܬܐ[3]
ܡܪܟܢܐ. ܟܫܝܒ ܣܛܘܡܝ. ܟܠܐ ܐܒܐ ܡܫܝܚ ܡܪܝ܀
ܡܫܐܠܢܐ. ܐܝܟܘ ܗܒܝܠ ܐܚܘܟ 38a
ܡܢܝܚܬܐ. ܠܝ ܐܝܟ ܛܐܠܝܐ ܕܥܒܪ ܠܗ ܡܪܝܐ܀
ܡܫܬܪܝܢܢܐ. ܐܝܟܢܐ ܐܬܒܨܝ ܥܣܘ ܘܒܥܝܢ ܡܛܫܝܬܐ ܐܝܟܢܐ ܗܘܘ ܠܡܬܒܥܘ ܡܢ ܥܒܕܐ܀[4]
ܡܩܒܠܢܐ. ܐܠܗܘܗܝ ܥܡܢ ܠܫܠܡܐ ܩܪܝܒܐ܀
ܡܢܝܚܢܐ[5] ܡܘܬ ܠܐܘܟܡܐ ܢܣܒܠܝ ܥܒܠ. ܠܐ ܡܟܘܬܐ܀[6]
ܗܘܦܟ ܡܢܝܚܬܐ. ܕܡܕܪܟܝܢ ܩܕܝܫܐ ܘܡܫܡܫܝܢ ܕܠܐ ܠܐܝܐ܀
ܟܪܘܙܐ. ܚܒܘܫܐ. ܚܙܘܩܐ. ܨܠܘܬܐ. ܚܐܘܪܬܐ܀
ܗܘܦܟ ܟܪܘܙܐ ܢܘܡܐ ܘܢܝܚܐ ܘܪܟܝܟܐ ܘܡܫܝܢܐ ܢܛܪܝܢ ܐܠܗܘܗܝ܀
ܣܝܢܝܐ ܒܟܘ ܢܘܡܐ ܐܬܒܪܟܝ ܕܐܢܐ ܐܝܬܝ ܘܐܠܗܝ ܥܡ ܐܠܗܝ܀
ܡܢܝܚܬܐ ܘܡܪܟܢܐ܆ ܕܐܬܐܡܪ ܢܘܡܐ ܠܥܘܪܐ ܗܢܐ ܡܪܝܐ ܚܝܐ܀
ܙܘܓܐ ܘܒܪܘܠܐ ܘܡܫܩܠܐ܀
ܦܩܕܐ. ܕܪܘܚܐ ܟܡܪܝܢ ܓܐܘܟܐ܀
ܗܘܦܟ ܦܩܕܐ. ܠܐ ܡܟܘܬܐ. ܘܠܐ ܣܟܠܐ܀
ܙܘܓܐ ܘܦܩܕܐ. ܪܘܚܐ ܩܕܝܫܬܐ ܒܟܠܐ ܡܫܒܚܬܐ܀
ܦܩܕܐ ܘܡܫܩܠܢܐ. ܒܪܫܝܬ ܐܠܗܘܗܝ ܗܘܐ ܡܠܬܐ܀
ܡܫܐܠܢܐ ܘܙܘܓܐ ܘܙܘܓܢܐ ܕܦܣܩ ܐܝܟܢܐ ܗܢܝ ܙܕܩܝܢ ܡܛܘܬܐ܀ 38b
ܦܣܘܩ ܘܙܘܓܐ ܘܙܘܓܢܐ ܕܠܐ ܦܣܩ ܘܦܣܘܩܐ. ܘܣܝܡܗ ܕܡܫܘܬܐ ܕܡܢܝܢ ܘܐܘܟܐ
ܬܟܣܐ ܟܠܗ ܚܢܝܢ ܒܡܫܡܫܢܬܐ. ܟܠܠܐ ܓܠܐ ܘܐܦܣܩܗ ܠܙܘܓܐ ܠܐ ܟܢܝ܀

L ܡܪܗ ܠܘܬܝ ܬܘ ܠܘܬܝ ܟܠܟܘܢ ܠܐܝܐ. 4 L ܬܪ ܒܪܝ̈ ܬܪ ܒܪܗܫ̈ ܬܪ ܒܪ ܢܒܝܫ̈. 1 ܗܢܘ ܐܡܪܗ [ܐܝܟܘ ܗܒܝܠ ܐܚܘܟ 7 ܡܪܝ. [ܡܪܝ 6 L ܗܢܘ [ܗܢܘ 5 B ܟܠܟܘܢ [ܟܠܟܘܢ ܡܫܩܠ ܗܒܝܠ ܐܚܘܟ B | [ܐܚܘܟ om. OG 9 ܐܬܒܨܝ [ܐܬܒܨܝ L | ܘܒܥܝܢ [ܘܒܥܝܢ BL ܡܫܬܪܝܢܢܐ [ܡܢܝܚܢܐ 12 L ܩܪܝܒܐ. [ܩܪܝܒܐ 11 L ܥܒܕܐ· 10 L ܡܛܫܝܬܗ [ܡܛܫܝܬܐ L | ܡܟܘܬܐ. L 14 ܚܒܘܫܐ [ܚܒܘܫܐ B 17 ܘܡܪܟܢܐ· [ܘܡܪܟܢܐ L | ܕܐܬܐܡܪ [ܕܐܬܐܡܪ L ܗܘ [ܗܘ 23 L ܒܪܫܝܬ [ܒܪܫܝܬ L | ܘܡܫܩܠܢܐ [ܘܡܫܩܠܢܐ 22 L ܚܝܐ. [ܚܝܐ ܠܐ ܟܢܝ [ܠܐ ܟܢܝ 25 L ܡܟܘܬܐ·: [ܡܟܘܬܐ OG

[1] From L’s reading it appears that ܬܠܬܐ ܙܘܓܝܢ is simply ܙܘܓܐ ܘܠܐ ܦܣܩ repeated three times. | [2] L’s ܡܪܗ on ܠܘܬܝ is unlikely, and ܟܠܟܘܢ is surely wrong - Mt 11.28. | [3] L removes the accent in question here and neither does it have an accent on ܗܐ . | [4] The mss are all corrupt here - Obad 6. | [5] Neither reading is right. L has conflated the incorrect ܡܫܬܪܝܢܢܐ (which I emended at ܠܒ,23) with the name of this accent, ܡܢܝܚܢܐ. Not even the accent names can be transmitted correctly! | [6] L finishes all these sentences in this fashion (instead of a ܀) - this can be assumed hereafter without being noted in each case. For this accent and the Greek words that underlie these Syriac terms (ὁμοούσιος, πανδύνατος, ἀθάνατος), see p.73 above.

ܠܗ ܘܚܠܡ ܐܢܘܢ ܢܘܩܪܐ ܦܩܝܕܬܐ ܘܡܬܪܬܐ. ܘܐܝܟ ܕܠܒܝܫܝܢܘܬܐ ܡܫܒܠܬܐ ܚܕ ܦܠܓܘܬܐ ܘܡܢ ܟܠܗܝܢ ܐܬܐܡܪ̈ܝ܀ ܘܙܘܥ ܠܡܕܝܢ ܕܝܗܝܐ ܕܟܠܗ ܘܕܡܘܣܝܩܝ ܚܟܡܐ: ܚܕ ܗܠܐ ܕܢܒܘܐ. ܒܬܪ ܕܝܢ ܦܢܝܢ ܠܬܪܝܢ ܐܢܫܐ. ܘܚܕ ܦܢ: ܕܫܠܦ ܙܘܥܐ ܕܠܐ ܦܫܩ. ܡܫܚܘ ܡܘܣܝܩܝ ܚܟܡܐ. ܐܬܐܡܪܝܢ ܕܝܢ ܡܢܗ̈ܠܝ ܐܪܒܥܐ ܦܠܓܘܬܐ ܗܘ ܕܒܟܠܗܘܢ ܐܬܐܡܪܝܢ. ܕܬܪܝܢ ܕܝܢ: ܡܢܗ̈ܠܝ ܕܫܡܝܐ ܦܢܝܐ ܕܐܬܐܡܪܝܢܗܝܢ ܚܕ ܘܬܪܝܢ ܚܠܦ ܚܒܪܐ܀ ܡܘܣܝܩܝ ܕܡܢ ܚܟܡܐ: ܡܬܩܪܝܐ ܚܘܫܒܐ ܘܚܠܦܘܗܝ ܚܘܫܒܐ܀ ܘܗܘܝܐ ܡܘܣܝܩܝ
39a ܐܣܛܘܐ. ܡܬܩܪܝܐ ܘܚܠܦܘܗܝ ܚܘܫܒܐ. ܘܡܬܡܪܐ ܡܬܐܠܝܐ܀ ܘܩܠܐ: ܘܡܘܣܝܩܝ ܩܠܐ: ܗܘ ܗܘܝܐ ܡܦܣܩܝܢ. ܗܢܘ ܕܩܠܐ ܡܬܦܫܩܝܢ ܐܝܟ ܗܢܘܢ ܕܢܗܘܘܢ ܫܘܚܠܦܐ ܚܠܦ ܚܒܪܐ. ܡܘܣܝܩܝ ܩܠܐ ܕܡܢ ܐܘܪܓܢ ܡܬܩܪܝܐ. ܚܕ ܒܢܘܪ. ܐܣܠܐܘ̄ ܒܬܘܡܒܐ. ܘܚܘܫܒܐ ܐܝܟ ܚܠܦܘܗܝ ܘܠܗ ܐܣܛܘ̈ܐ܀

ܒܪܢܫܐ ܘܪܘܚܐ ܡܦܣܩܝܢ. ܗܢܘ ܕܒܪܢܫܐ ܠܡܘܕܥܐ ܗܘ ܕܒܦܠܓܘܬܐ. ܘܗܘܐ ܕܡܢ ܠܗܘܢ ܫܡܥܐ ܡܬܐܡܪܝܢ܀

ܠܗܒ ܕܝܢ ܐܝܟ ܢܘܩܪܐ ܕܦܫܝܢ ܠܚܒܪܐ. ܐܣܛܘܐ. ܡܦܫܩܬܐ. ܡܬܒܥܝܐ. ܘܐܬܐܠܝܢ ܦܢ ܒܐܦܝܢܘܬ ܚܒܪܝܢ ܠܒܬܘܡܒܐ. ܡܦܫܩܬܐ ܕܝܢ ܠܒܠ ܗܘ ܕܒܗ ܡܬܐܡܪ. ܡܬܒܥܝܐ ܕܝܢ ܒܗ ܡܢܝܢܐ ܒܩܘܡܐ ܐܘ ܠܡܬܠܝܐ ܡܬܒܥܝܐ܀

ܠܗܒ ܕܝܢ ܡܬܩܪܝܢܐ ܡܘܣܝܩܝ ܡܢ ܡܢܝܢܐ ܘܡܬܒܥܝܐ. ܗܢܘ ܕܡܬܩܪܝܢܐ ܐܣܠܐܘ̄: ܡܐ ܕܫܠܘ ܠܒܠ ܘܠܗܠܝܢ ܕܪ̈ܒܘܬܐ: ܡܬܩܪܝܢ ܠܗ. ܡܢܝܢܐ ܕܝܢ ܕܠܐ ܡܬܩܠܝ ܢܦܫ ܘܡܬܦܪܫܐ ܢܦܫ. ܐܠܐ ܕܡܬܐܡܪܐ ܢܦܫ ܠܦܠܓܘܬܐ ܕܒܟܠܗܘܢ ܫܒܝܩ ܡܢܝܢܐ܀

39b ܡܬܒܥܝܐ ܕܝܢ. ܒܫܘܚܠܦܐ ܗܘ ܕܗܘܐ ܘܒܟܠܗܘܢ ܦܠܓ ܐܝܟܐ ܕܡܬܩܠܝܢ ܘܡܫܬܟܚ ܕܗܘܐ ܗܘ ܚܕܐ. ܫܒܝܩ ܡܬܒܥܝܐ. ܐܘ ܠܡܬܠܝܐ ܡܬܐܠܝܐ ܫܒܝܩ܀

ܠܗܒ ܐܡܐ ܘܐܝܟ ܢܘܩܪܐ ܠܬܪܝܢ ܗܢܘܢ ܕܢܦܫܐ ܡܬܐܡܪܝܢ ܘܠܡܬܠܝܐ ܗܘܐ ܘܫܡܥܐ ܫܡܥܝܢ ܗ̄ ܕܢܦܫ ܟܠܗ ܢܦܫ ܕܐܬܡܟܢ. ܟܕ ܕܠܐ ܗܘܐ ܐܝܠܐ ܕܫܡܥܐ

1 ܐܢܘܢ] om. OGB   2 ܘܙܘܥ] ܙܘܥ B | ܕܝܗܝܐ] ܝܗܝܐ OG | ܚܟܡܐ] ܚܟܡܐ: L   3 ܘܠܐ ܦܫܩ.] ܕܠܐ ܦܫܩ L   5 ܕܫܡܝܐ...6 ܚܟܡܐ] om. OG (homoe.)   6 ܚܟܡܐ] ܚܟܡܐ. L | ܚܘܫܒܐ...7 ܘܗܘܝܐ] om. OG (homoe.)   7 ܡܬܐܠܝܐ] ܡܬܐܠܝܬܐ L   9 ܚܠܦ] ܩܠܐ BL[corr.] | ܐܘܪܓܢ] ܘܚܠܦ L   10 ܐܝܟ] om. OG | ܘܠܗ] ܘܠܗܘܢ OG   14 ܠܒܠ] om. OG   17 ܠܒܠ] ܠܒܠ OG   18 ܡܬܩܠܝ] ܡܬܩܠܝܢ L   20 ܘܒܟܠܗܘܢ] ܒܟܠܗܘܢ G1 | ܘܡܫܬܟܚ] ܡܫܬܟܚ G1   22 ܘܐܝܟ] ܘܐܦ G1 | ܕܢܦܫܐ] ܕܢܦܫܬܐ L   23 ܗ̄] ܗܘܐ G1 | ܕܠܐ] ܠܐ OG

ܠ ܐܡܪܝܢ ܒܦܠܓܘܬܐ܀ ܦܣܘܩܐ ܕܝܢ ܗܢܐ ܘܡܫܝܚܐ ܡܫܬܟܚܝܢ ܒܗܘܢ ܕܒܟܠ ܟܠ ܢܘܡܘܣܐ ܐܝܬܝܗ ܒܡܐܡܪܐ. ܦܣܘܩܐ ܡܫܬܡܠܝܐ. ܗܘ ܕܫܠܝܡ ܒܫܘܠܡ ܦܠܓܘܬܐ܀ ܫܠܝܡܐ ܕܝܢ: ܒܗܘܐ ܕܐܡܪ ܒܡܠܬܐ. ܒܗܘ ܕܗܘ ܒܫܘܠܡܗܘܢ ܫܩܠ ܡܢ ܒܒܬܐ ܐܘ ܠܐܬܠܬܐ. ܐܘ ܢܘܡܘܣܐ ܐ̱ܚܪܢܐ ܐܝܬܘܗܝ ܒܦܠܓܘܬܐ. ܗܢܐ ܕܝܢ ܙܘܥܬܐ ܕܦܣܘܩ ܘܠܐ ܦܣܩ: ܙܘܓܐ ܐܝܬ ܐܝܟ ܒܚܕܐ ܐܡܬܝܬܐ. ܗ̄ ܒܟܠ ܗܕܡܐ ܕܡܢܝܢ ܙܘܥܬܐ. ܘܐܝܟ ܐܢܫ ܚܕ ܡܢܝܢܐ ܘܣܓܝ ܫܘܚܠܦܐ. ܙܢܝܢ ܒܒܢܝ ܡܢܝܢܐ܀

ܒܝܕܐ ܒܗܘܢܐ ܠܐܘܡܢ ܡܟܬܒܬܐ ܘܡܫܠܡ ܦܣܩܘܬܐ ܕܢܘܢܐ. ܐܘܚܕܬ ܢܘܩܙܐ ܘܦܘܢܩܐ. ܐܝܟ ܡܟܬܒܢܘܬܐ ܕܡܕܝܢܬܐ ܡܢܝܢ ܡܬܚܫܒ ܘܐܬܪ̈ܘܗܝ. ܫܘܬܦܐ ܕܫܘܪܢܐ. ܘܐܬܪܐ ܘܐܬܚܝܕ ܓܪܡܛܝܩܝ܀ ܘܗܘܝܐ ܢܫܡܥ ܫܠܐ ܒܡܐܡܪܐ ܒܡܢܝܢܐ ܘܡܕܡܐ ܕܦܪܓܡܛܝܐ ܗܘܐ ܡܕܡܝܬܐ ܘܪܘܡܡܐ ܦܬܚܐ ܕܐܬܠܬܘܗܝ ܒܟܠ ܐܘܡܢܘܬܐ ܕܦܪܓܡܛܝܩܘܬܐ: ܒܟܠܬܐ ܕܠܗ ܕܕܝܐܠܩܛܝܩܐ ܕܐܦܘܕܝܩܛܝܩܐ ܫܩ̈ܠܐ ܐܫܟܚܝ. ܐܝܟ ܠܒܟܠܬܐ ܕܐܫܟܚܝ. ܐܝܬ ܕܝܢ ܒܝ ܒܗܘܢ ܐܝܟ ܚܠܐ ܠܬܠܬܐ: ܒܚܘܬܐ ܦܪܫ ܚܠܦ ܘܡܘܬܗ ܐܢܐ ܒܪܢܐ ܕܦܫܛܐ: ܘܚܠܦ ܢܦܫܐ ܕܒܪܝ. ܒܗܘ ܕܐܬܒܝ ܒܚܝܠܐ ܗܘܒܐ ܘܙܘܕܐ. ܐܡܬܝ ܕܢܐܬܐ ܒܚܘܠܡܢܗ ܕܢܦܫ ܘܒܟܠ ܕܒܟܠ ܒܚܘܠܡܢܗ ܕܗܘܐ ܫܡܝܢܬܐ ܙܘܥܬܐ. ܠܡܣܘܟܬܐ ܒܫܘܡ ܡܠܐܟܐ. ܕܒܗ ܫܘܟܠܐ ܠܒܠܥܡܝܢ ܐܡܝܢ܀

ܫܠܡ ܡܐܡܪܐ ܩܕܡܝܐ ܕܟܠܗ

ܕܕܝܠܩܛܝܩܐ ܕܦܪܓܡܛܝܩܘܬܐ

ܕܥܡ ܫܡܐ ܡܫܡܗ

2 ܐܝܬܝܐ G1B ܐܝܬ OG 3 ܒܡܠܬܐ ܕܐܡܪ [ܕܐܡܪ ܒܡܠܬܐ G1 5 [ܗ̄ ܒܟܠ ܗܕܡܐ L ܡܢܝܢ̈ [ܡܢܝܢܐ[1] 6 L ܗܘ̇ܕܡܐ [ܗܕܡܐ | B ܗ̄ ܒܟܠ ܗܘ̇ܕܡܐ G1 ܗܘܡܐ:ܒܟܠ ܗܕܡܐ ܗܘ [ܘܦܬܚܐ | G1 ܘܡܕܡܝܬܐ [ܡܕܡܝܬܐ 10 ܒܡܢܝܢܐ] om. BL 9 L ܒܒܢܝ [ܒܒܢܝ L ܕܕܝܠܩܛܝܩܐ [ܕܕܝܠܩܛܝܩܐ 11 O ܘܐܬܠܬܘܗܝ ܐܝܟ [ܘܐܬܠܬܘܗܝ ܒܟܠ | L ܘܦܬܚܐ· L ܒܗܘܢ: [ܒܗܘܢ 12 L ܕܫܩ̈ܠܐܘܬܐ ܐܦܘܕܝܩܛܝܩܐ: OG ܕܫܩ̈ܠܐ ܐܦܘܕܝܩܛܝܩܐ: [ܘܡܘܬܗ 13 L ܘܡܘܬܗ OG ܢܦ̈ܫܬܗ L txt G1 | [ܐܢܐ...ܕܒܪܝ] om. L 14 [ܘܙܘܕܐ L ܡܠܐܟܐ ܘܠܐ ܢܫܡܥ ܫܡܝܢܬܐ ܒܚܘܠܡܢܗ 15 [ܙܘܥܬܐ] om. L 15...ܘܒܟܠ | L ܘܙܘܕܐ 18 [ܫܠܡ] Subscription in B reads ܫܠܡ ܘܐܫܠܡܢ ܟܠܗ ܗܢܐ ܕܐܬܠܬܘܗܝ ܡܐܡ̈ܪܐ ܕܡܢ ܘܡܠܟܐ ܕܐܡܪ ܠܡܕܝܢܬܐ ܗܘܐ ܒܡܟܬܒܢܐ ܠܐܝܠܐ ܡܢܝܢ ܡܫܡܗ ܐܘܪܚܐ ܕܐܒܝܢ ܐܝܟ ܢܦ̈ܫܢ ܡܢ ܟܠ ܒܫܢܐ ܒܫܡ ܡܫܝܚܐ ܗ̄ ܠܐܦܝܦܢܘܢ ܒܢܝܢ ܐܚܪ ܫܢܬ ܒܫܢܬ ܢܘܗܪܐ ܘܒܗܘ ܕܡܫܝܚܐ܀ L has ܫܠܡ ܡܐܡܪܐ ܡܕܡܝܐ ܫܒܠܬܐ ܩܕܡܝܐ ܕܕܝܠܩܛܝܩܐ.

ܟܣ

ܠܘܬ ܕܒܢ̈ܝܐ ܡܕܡ ܕܡܬܚܫܒܝܢ ܡܢ
ܟܠܐ ܕܝܠܗ ܕܡܬܟܬܒܐ ܕܩܕܡ ܡܢܗ
ܐܪܡܝܐ ܒܡܫܚܠܦܘܬܐ

ܘܐܦ ܦܘܫܩܐ ܘܦܘܪܫܢܐ ܗܢܘܢ ܘܠܐ ܡܢܝܢ ܐܘܪܚܐ 50b
ܐܡܝܢܐ[1] ܟܠܗ ܕܒܟܠܗܝܢ ܚܕ ܢܬܦܪܫܘܢ:
ܣܟܐ ܐܢܫܐ ܢܬܠܡܕ ܦܫܝܩܐ ܒܦܘܪܫ ܠܩܪܝܘܗܝ܀
ܘܡܫܘܚܬܐ ܠܘܬ ܕܣܝܡܐ ܠܗ ܡܬܐܡܪ: 51b
ܘܥܠ ܣܝ̈ܡܐ[2] ܡܢܝܢ ܦܘܪܫܐ ܗܢܐ ܕܡܫܬܟܚܝܢ
ܐܝܟܘ ܕܒܟܬܒ ܠܐ ܡܬܐܡܪ ܚܕܐ ܐܚܪܢܐ
ܢܣܒ ܠܫܡܗܐ ܐܝܟ ܪ̈ܚܡܐ ܪ̈ܓܠܐ ܟ̈ܪܟܐ
ܘܐܦ ܡܬܐܡܪ ܚܕܐ ܐܚܪܢܐ ܠܐ ܢܣܒ ܢܩܘܕܐ.
ܐܝܟ ܝܫܐ ܒܦܬܐ ܫܒܝܠܐ ܢܬܡܪ ܒܬܪܐ܀
ܕܪ̈ܘܟܟܐ ܕܝܢ ܘܩܘܫ̈ܝܐ ܠܘܬ ܐܝܟ ܢܩܦܝܢ: 56b
ܕܪܘܟܟ[3] ܒܗ ܒܟܠܗ ܘܩܘܫܝ ܒܗ ܒܟܠܗ ܠܗ ܡܬܬܚܫܒܢ܀
ܚܡܫ ܐܬܘ̈ܬܐ ܕܫܡܥܢ ܗܘܝ ܒܗܝܢ ܦܠܘܣܘܦܘܣ:
ܒ. ܓܡ. ܟ. ܕ. ܟܦ. ܦ. ܬ. ܡܢܗ ܘܒܚܫ܀
ܡܬܪ̈ܟܟܢ ܟܕ ܐܘ ܒܪܝܫܗ ܐܝܟ ܐܒܐ:
ܐܒܐ ܓ̈ܒܪܐ ܡܝܬܝܐ ܣܓܝܐܬܐ ܦܘܫܬܐ ܦܬܟܪܐ܀
ܘܟܕ ܒܪܫܐ ܒܟܠܗ ܐܬܘܬܗ ܕܐܘܪܚܐ ܐܬܘܬܐ:[4]
ܒ. ܕ. ܟܦ. ܘܘ ܟܦ. ܠ ܕܒܪܘܟ ܒܬܪܗ܀
ܐܝܟ ܒܟܠܬܐ ܒܒܪܐ ܒܒܪܐ ܒܒܝܫܬܐ ܒܐܪܥܐ:

19 ܫܘܒܚܐ] ܫܘܚܠܐ B   20 ܘܟܕ] ܐܘ ܟܕ L

[1] A section on the ܡܫܘܚܬܐ. | [2] A section on the mark of the plural. | [3] A section on the marks of rukkāḵā and quššāyā. | [4] In what follows, where rukkāḵā and quššāyā are not noted they ahve been omitted.

ܕܒܡܠܬܐ ܕܒܬܪܐ ܕܕܘܟܐ ܕܒܐܝܐ ܕܝܬܝܪܬܐ ܢܩܒܬܐ
ܘܒܝܬܐ ܘܒܢܝܐ ܘܕܒܪܐ ܘܒܪܘܟܐ ܘܐܬܟܘܟܬܐ:
57a ܠܒܡܠܬܐ ܠܒܝܬܐ ܠܒܪܐ ܠܒܫܝܐ ܘܠܡܬܘܪܟܬܐ܀
ܘܦ ܕܐܫܬܪܪ ܠܐ ܡܬܦܪܫܐ ܒܟܢܘܫܝܐ:
ܘܢܩܙܐ ܠܠܒܬܐ ܘܡܬܩܪܝܐ ܒܗܘܢ ܒܗܕ ܫܡܝܐ܀
ܡܦܩܕܢܝܬܐ ܒܗ ܐܦ ܡܫܐܠܢܝܬܐ ܘܡܬܟܫܦܢܝܬܐ:
ܡܦܩܕܢܝܬܐ ܒܗ ܐܝܟ. ܦ. ܕܦܩܘܕܐ ܦܩܕ ܦܘܩܕܢܐ܀
ܡܫܐܠܢܝܬܐ ܕܝܢ ܐܝܟ ܫܐܠܐ ܐܦ ܦܘܫܩܐ:
ܘܡܬܟܫܦܢܝܬܐ ܐܝܟ ܕܒܥܐ ܙܟܝܐ ܢܨܝܚܐ܀
ܘܐܝܟ ܡܬܦܠܓ ܒܝܢܬ ܦܠܓܘܬܐ ܕܐܝܟ ܣܥܝܬܐ.
ܘܐ. ܐܦ. ܕ. ܐܬܐ ܦܬܓܡܐ ܒܢܩܝܦܘܬܐ
ܘܩܕܡܝ ܙܘܓܐ ܘܕܪܘܦܐ ܘܢܩܫܬܐ.
ܘܦܬܟܐ ܡܬܩܪܐ ܚܕܐ ܦܘܣܩܐ ܕܗܝ ܦܣܝܩܬܐ
ܠܐ ܡܬܦܪܫܐ ܗܘ. ܠ. ܕܒܝܢ ܠܒܫܡܐ ܫܡܝܐ:
ܐܝܟ ܘܐܡܪ ܘܐܡܪܝܢ ܐܪܥܐ ܘܐܦ ܒܐܪܥܐ܀
ܘܐܝܟ ܗܘܐ. ܠ. ܕܒܝܢ ܠܫܡܫܐ ܢܦܠ ܙܘܥܐ:
ܡܬܦܪܫܐ ܒܗ ܐܝܟ ܕܐܬܡܘܬܐ ܐܦ ܘܐܬܡܘܬܐ܀
57b ܘܐܝܟ ܐܬܘܬܐ ܕܒܝܢ ܠܒܫܡܐ ܗܘܐ. ܕ.
ܘܗܝ ܡܬܩܪܐ ܡܦܩܬܐ ܐܣܬܐ ܦܫܛ ܠܒܝܬܐ
ܐܬܪܘܗܝ ܕܐܬܪܗ ܕܒܝܢ ܠܫܡܫ ܡܢܗ ܕܠܐ ܕܗܘܐ:
ܐܝܟ ܘܕܘܟܐ ܘܕܐܬܪܗܘܢ ܠܗ ܬܘܒ ܘܕܘܩܝܢ܀
ܘܐܝܟ ܐܬܘܬܐ ܕܒܝܢ ܠܫܡܫܐ ܗܘܐ ܡܬܒܬܐ
ܦܢܐ ܠܒܝܬܐ ܘܪܟܢ ܡܬܒܬܐ ܐܝܟ ܘܕܘܪܩܐ܀[1]
ܘܐܝܟ ܡܩܕܡܬܐ ܕܒܝܢ ܠܫܡܫ. ܠ. ܐܦ. ܕ.

---

3 ܠܒܡܠܬܐ] written twice L | ܠܒܪܐ ܠܒܝܬܐ L(against the metre) 8 ܦܘܪܥܢܐ L
10 ܐܝܟܐ] ܟܐ G 13 ܚܕܐ] ܚܕ O 14 ܕܒܝܢ] ܕܒܢܝܢ L (and generally below) 19 ܘܗܝ OGL(against the metre with ܐܣܬܐ) | ܐܣܬܐ] om. OG 23 ܠܒܝܬ L | ܘܕܘܪܩܐ L

---

[1] There is no quššāyā on second dalath, which was placed contrary to the rule.

ܓ ܘܢܦܠ ܒܟܠܗܘܢ ܗܘ ܦܚܕ ܒܟܠܗ ܐܝܟ ܘܙܘܥܐ܀
ܠܘܬ ܗܟܝܠ ܘܬܗܪܬܐ ܘܬܬܕܡܪܘܬܐ܆
ܘܬܫܒܘܚܬܐ ܘܫܪܟܐ ܕܡܫܡܫܢܘܗܝ ܒܬܫܒܘܚܬܐ܀
ܘܟܠ ܠܒܢܝܢܐ ܕܡܬܐܡܪ ܠܗ ܡܬܦܠܠܐܝܬ܆
ܘܗܘ ܐܬܘܬܐ ܕܢܦܫ ܦܠܓܘܬܐ ܠܐܝܐ ܫܡܠܝܐܝܬ.
ܘܐܬܘܬܐ ܬܘܒ ܕܫܪܪܗ ܬܗܘܐ ܡܪܟܒܐܝܬ܆
ܡܐ ܕܡܬܦܠܓܝ ܗܡܐ ܠܪܘܟܒܐ ܡܢܗ ܡܦܫܡܐܝܬ܀
ܐܝܟ ܒܢ̈ܝ ܟܪܟܐ ܘܒܪܒܝܬܐ ܘܒܝܬ ܟܢܟܡ܆ 58a
ܘܒܒܝ ܟܒܝܢܐ ܘܣܪܝ ܣܪܝܢܐ ܘܥܡܪܝ ܥܡܪܢܐ܀
ܘܐܦ ܐܬܘܬܐ ܕܢܝܫ ܦܠܓܘܬܐ ܦܠܝܓܘܬܐ ܬܗܘܐ܆
ܡܐ ܕܡܬܦܠܓܝ ܗܘ ܕܪܘܟܒܐ ܠܐ ܡܫܬܟܚܐ܀
ܐܝܟܢܐ ܕܐܬܐܡܪ ܢܦܝܩ ܡܢܦܩܝܢ ܢܦܩ̈ܬܐ ܢܦܝ̈ܩܬܐ܆
ܦܪܝܫ ܡܦܪܫܝܢ ܦܪܫܬܐ ܡܦܪܫܬܐ ܦܪܝܫ ܦܪܫܬܐ܀
ܗܟܢܐ ܫܘܡܠܝܐ ܐܦ ܒܡܫܠܡܘܬܗ ܐܠܐ ܗܘ ܚܪܝܬܐ܆[1]
ܘܟܠܗܘܢ ܚܕ ܒܗܘܢ ܗܘܟܡ ܣܘܟܠ ܡܪܟܒܘ ܡܪܟܒܬܐ܀
ܐܝܟ ܗܘܝܐ ܢܗܝܪܐ. ܟܪܝܬܐ ܡܪܝܪܬܐ ܡܪܝܪܐ܆
ܒܪܝܬܐ ܕܥܡܝܩܬܐ ܡܪܝܪܐ ܦܣܝܩܬܐ ܗܪܝܪܐ܀
ܘܐܦ ܐܬܘܬܐ ܕܒܫܘܪ̈ܝ ܗܡܐ ܘܗܘ ܕܡܢ ܡܢܘ܆
ܬܗܘܐ ܦܠܝܓܬܐ ܗܣܟܦ ܦܚܕ ܠܗܘܢ ܕܟܠܗ. ܢ܀
ܐܝܟ ܒܪ̈ܝܬܐ ܐܦ ܐܘܣܝܬܐ ܘܐܘܒ ܡܟܝܠܬܐ܆
ܟܠܗ ܗܝ ܚܕܐ ܦܢܝܢ ܘܟܢܝ ܐܝܟ ܡܠܐܟܘܬܐ܀
ܘܐܦ ܣܟܦ ܗܘܐ. ܢ. ܬܗܘܐ ܗܘ ܣܚܪܝܬܐ ܐܘ ܡܪܟܒܬܐ܆ 58b
ܒܠܗ ܕܢܦܫܐ ܕܗܝ ܐܝܟ ܥܠܝܬܐ ܒܪܘܬܐ܀
ܘܒܗ ܡܬܒܢܝܐ ܒܪܫ ܦܠܓܘܬܐ ܐܬܘ ܕܪܘܬܐ܆
ܒܗܘ ܕܢܦܫܐ ܦܚܕ ܘܡܢܗ ܕܠܐ ܙܘܒܢܐ܀

---

2 ܘܬܬܕܡܪܘܬܐ] ܘܬܬܕܡܪܬܐ mss 3 ܘܫܪܟܐ] ܘܕܫܪܟܐ B 4 ܟܠ ܘܠܘܬ OGB (against the metre) 9 ܟܒܝܢܐ] ܟܒܝܢܐ mss 13 ܡܦܪܫܝܢ] ܡܦܪܫܝܢ etc. mss 15 ܚܕ ܡܢ ܣܘܟܠ ܡܪܟܒܬܐ L 22 ܣܚܪܝܬܐ] ܚܪܝܬܐ L (cf.fn on l.14)

---

[1] L^{corr} has changed ܚܪܝܬܐ here to ܣܚܪܝܬܐ - cf. note to ܠ,1.

ܡܐ ܐܝܟ ܕܒܫܝܡ ܐܘ ܐܟܘܡ. ܐܘ ܐܪܝܟ
ܐܟܢܐ ܠܗܘܢ ܐܟܘܪ ܐܘܟ ܐܘ ܐܬܟܪ.
ܐܝܟ ܟܝܢܐ ܒܡܘܠܕܗ ܠܒܫܗ ܚܕܐ ܡܢ ܗܠܝܢ:
ܢܦܫܗ ܐܢܬܝ ܘܗܘܝ ܕܡܬܚܫܚ ܠܗܘܐ ܡܠܝܠܐ
ܘܕܝܢ ܡܠܝܠܐ ܕܢܦܫܐ ܐܝܬܝܗ ܐܘ ܠܡ ܕܡܝܬܐ
ܐܘ ܠܗܘܢ ܦܠܚܘܬܐ ܠܟܢ̈ܫܬܐ ܡܢܗ ܡܦܩܢܘܬܐ.
ܐܟܢܐ ܕܐܡܪ ܡܦܩܢ ܡܠܟܐ ܘܚܝܠܬܐ ܘܐܝܟ ܘܟܡܐ ܘܟܠܗܝܢ
ܘܐܝܟܢ ܘܐܣܛܪܛܝܓ ܘܐܬܪ̈ܘܢ ܘܡܪ̈ܕܘܬܐ ܕܪ̈ܘܚܝܢ ܠܟܘܢܐ.
ܘܐܝ ܐܬܪܐ ܕܡܢ ܦܘܡ ܐܢܫܐ ܢܦܩܐ ܗܘܐ.
ܐܘ ܗܘ ܕܢܘܚܠܐ ܗܘ ܐܘ ܠܟܡܪܐ ܐܘ ܡܘܬ ܕܦܫܝܩܐ.
ܐܘ ܠܗܘܢ ܣܓܝܐܬܐ ܡܢܗ ܡܬܟܬܒܢ ܠܟܢܫܐ:
ܣܓܝ ܣܓܝ ܘܢܦܩ ܝܘܡ ܢܗܘܘܢ ܡܢܗ
59a ܐܝܟ ܡܠܟܐ ܕܗܘܐ ܐܠܗܘܬܗ ܗܘ ܦܠܚܘܬܐ.
ܡܫܩܘܠܐ ܠܟܠܐ ܕܟܪ ܒܡܫܩܠܐ ܕܨܒܝܢܐ.
ܘܒܙܘܢ ܒܟܝ ܐܘ ܩܕܡ ܘܐܝܟ ܘܐܬܟܪܡ ܠܗܘܐ:
ܒܡܠܟܐܡܪܐ ܟܠ ܦܘܪܣܐ ܗܘ ܠܟܠܗܘܢ.
ܕܟܪܝܐ ܘܚܝܠܐ ܘܐܟܠܝܢ ܒܚܕܘ:
ܐܝܟ ܕܐܢܬܝܢ ܐܘܟܠܐ ܡܩܪܒܐ ܢܩܝܦܐ.
ܦܨܢ ܕܐܢܫܐ ܕܟܫܝܢܐ ܕܗܘ ܦܠܚܘܬܐ:
ܡܐ ܕܡܠܟܘܬܐ ܗܘܐ ܕܡܬܚܫܚ ܠܗܘܐ ܡܠܟܬܐ.
ܐܝܟ ܟܪܝܐ ܟܪܝܐ ܟܪܝܐ ܐܘ ܐܟܪܝܐ:
ܟܪܝܘܗܝ ܟܪܝܘܗܝ ܐܚܪܢܐ ܐܚܪܢܐ ܫܟܝܚܐ ܫܟܝܚܐ.
ܠܗܘܢ ܠܗ ܕܐܠܐ ܟܠܪ ܒܚܝ̈ܠܬܐ ܕܡܠܟܐ:
ܘܟܠ ܦܘܪܣܐ ܩܕܡܝܐ ܡܫܡܫܐ ܕܟܪܝܐ.
ܘܐܟܠܝܢ ܟܠܗܘܢ ܚܕܐ ܐܘ ܠܐܚܪܢ ܐܘ ܠܟܠ ܐܢܫ:

---

1 ܐܟܘܡ] ܐܟܝܪ B 2 ܐܟܘܪ] ܐܟܘܝ B 6 ܡܢܗ] ܡܢܗ G 12 ܐܝܟ ܣܓܝ L 14 ܕܨܒܝܢܐ] ܠܨܒܝܢܐ OG 15 ܩܕܡ] ܩܕܡ G

ܦܫܛ ܠܗܘܢ ܐܦܢ ܠܒ̈ܢܝ ܡܠ̈ܬܐ ܡܫܝܚܝܬܐ܀
ܐܘ ܐܬܘ̈ܬܐ ܕܦܘܡ. ܐ̄. ܬܗܘ. ܚ. ܦܫܝܛܬܐ:
ܙܩܘ ܠܗܘܢ. ܐ̄ܘ. ܘܣܢܝܩ ܣܢܝܩܝ ܣܢܝܩܬܗ ܠܥܢܝܢܬܗ܀
. . . .
ܘܗܘܝܐ[1] ܕܦܘܩܕܢ ܥܠ ܚܒܘܫܝܐ ܚܕ ܗܘ ܡܢܝܚܐ.
ܟܒܝܫܐ ܡܢ ܐܬܘ̈ܬܝ ܘܠܐ ܡܬܬܪܝܡ ܐܝܟ ܕܒܦܬܓܡܐ܀
. . . .
ܠܡܫܘܡܕܝܬܐ[2] ܕܢܝܚܐ[3] ܠܐ ܡܬܟܬܒܢ:
ܐܘ ܢܩܒܬܐ ܘܠܐ ܐܫܬܟܚܘ ܠܒܢܝ ܣܘܪ̈ܝܝܐ܀
ܣܡܘ ܦܘܩܕܐ ܠܡܬܬܪ̈ܨܘܢ ܠܟܬܝܒܬܐ: 62a
ܐܝܟ. ܚ. ܕܬܬܡܠܠ ܘܬܬܟܬܒ ܘܡܢ ܢܝܫܐ ܘܠܐ ܩܢܘ ܟܠܒܬܐ܀
ܘܠܡܬܝܒܘܬܐ ܐܚܪܢܐ ܘܚܝܠ ܕܟܦܝܦ ܚܝܠ:
ܘܕܪܝܫ ܚܝܠ ܘܟܦܝܦ ܚܝܠ ܘܟܬܒܐ ܢܣܩܘܢ܀
ܘܟܠܟܠܬܐ ܡܢܗ ܗܘܘ ܦܠܣܛܝܢ̈ܝܐ ܘܠܐ ܐܬܘܪ̈ܝܐ:
ܕܢܝ ܦܠܣܛܝܢ[4] ܗܢܘܢ ܣܡܘ ܗܘܘ ܠܦܘܩܕܘܬܐ܀
ܘܟܢܫܐ ܙܥܘܪܐ ܘܠܗ ܩܢܘܢܐ ܐܝܟ ܗܘܐ ܠܗܘܢ:
ܘܗܘ ܕܢܩܘܫ ܘܢܬܦܠܓܢ ܟܠܠ ܡܢܗܝܢ܀
ܠܗ ܡܩܕܡܝܬܐ[5] ܘܐܝܟ ܕܡܢ ܟܢܫܐ ܘܠܐ ܩܢܘܢܐ.
ܐܬܬܘܩܦܘ ܗܠܝܢ ܗܢܘܢ ܐܬ̈ܘܬܐ ܘܠܐ ܠܥܘܡܪܐ܀
ܐܠܐ ܒܬܪܗ ܩܢܘܢܐ ܐܬܬܘܣܦܘ:
ܘܐܬܦܫܛܘ ܠܟܠܗ ܡܢܗܘܢ ܦܠܓܘܬܗܘܢ܀
ܗܘ ܕܡܢ ܢܝܫܐ ܥܠ ܕܡܢ ܢܝܫܐ ܗܘ ܘܐܬܦܫܛ:
ܩܢܝ ܘܫܡܗ ܗܘ ܕܡܬܝܚܐ ܗܘ ܗܘܐ ܘܙܩܘܦ܀
ܘܗܘ ܕܐܝܟ ܕܬܬܩܪܐ ܘܐܬܟܬܒ ܘܐܬܡܠܠ ܡܬܝܚܬܐ ܗܘ:

3 ܟܬܢܝܗܝ L   8 ܕܢܝܚܬܐ L   10 ܠܟܬܝܒܬܐ] ܠܟܬܝܒܬܐ L   12 ܘܠܡܬܝܒܘܬܐ] ܘܠܡܣܝܒܘܬܐ L ܘܠܡܬܝܒܘܬܐ B, but the plural of ܫܡܐ should be restored, so read ܫܡ̈ܗܝܬܐ [but cf. Nöldeke, Review, 1219].   13 ܢܣܩܘܢ] ܢܣܩܘܢ L(against the metre) 14 ܘܟܠܟܠܬܐ] ܟܠܟܠܬܐ L | ܐܬܘܪ̈ܝܐ] ܐܬܘܪܝܐ O   15 ܦܠܣܛܝܢ] ܦܠܣܛܝܢ L   18 ܠܗ ܡܩܕܡܝܬܐ ܘܐܝܟ ܕܡܢ ܟܢܫܐ L   19 ܐܬ̈ܘܬܐ ܗܢܝܢ L   23 ܘܙܩܘܦ] ܙܩܘܦ L

[1] f.59b concerns the lower point that indicates the absence of a vowel. | [2] f.61b concerns letters that are not pronoucned. | [3] L's reading breaks the metre - see discussion on p.111n. | [4] See p.114 above (from Elias of Nisibis) on these Palestinians. Jacob seems to have taken his information from Elias. | [5] See p.238,6.

ܟܠ ܡܠܬܐ ܓܝܪ ܘܐܬܘܬܐ ܫܡܗܝܗܘܢ ܐܝܬܝܗܘܢ܀
62b ܘܚܕ ܕܦܘܫܩܐ ܟܠ ܦܪܝܫ ܘܒܢܝܢ ܦܫܝܩܢ:
ܕܒܦܪܨܘܦܐ ܡܫܡܠܝܐ ܦܝܐ ܡܣܘܪܗܘܢ܀
ܗܐ ܓܝܪ ܘܒܣܡ ܐܝܬ ܡܬܠܬܘܫܐ ܕܐܬܘܬܐ ܐܝܣܡ:
ܐܘܟܝܬ ܐܝܬ ܕܒܗ ܦܪܨܘܦܐ ܢܫܒܚ ܡܫܡܘܕܝܢ܀
ܢܗܘܐ ܕܐܘܪܗܝ ܠܡܠܬܐ ܫܐܡ ܕܢܦܘܩ ܦܬܝܚ:
ܡܢ ܙܒܢܝܢ ܐܦ ܦܪܝܫ ܘܡܠܬܐ ܙܒܢܝܢ܀
ܘܗܘܐ ܡܢ ܙܘܥܗ ܐܦ ܫܘܚܠܦܗ ܘܦܘܪܫܢܐ
ܡܢܗܘܢ ܕܠܐ ܚܣܝܪ ܠܗܘܢ ܠܡܠܐ ܐܽܘܪܚܐ:
ܡܛܠ ܕܐܝܬ ܒܐܬܘܬܐ ܗܘܝ ܕܡܫܬܠܛܢ ܕܦܫܝܛܐ ܒܡܠܬܐ
ܢܩܫܬܐ ܐܬܡܢܝܢ ܠܗ ܘܐܬܡܢܝܢ ܠܗܘܬܐ܀[1]

. . . . .

ܘܐܝܬ[2] ܐܬܘܬܐ ܕܫܘܥܒܕܝܢ ܒܡܠܬܐ:
ܘܠܐ ܗܘ ܡܫܥܒܕܝܢ ܒܠܚܘܕ ܚܕܐ ܢܩܫܬܐ܀
ܥܒܝܬܐ ܓܝܪ ܘܡܨܥܝܬܐ ܐܦ ܢܩܝܕܬܐ
ܫܘܥܒܕܝܢ ܘܢܬܠܘܢ ܠܗܝܢ ܒܥܠܬܐ܀
ܥܒܝܬܐ ܓܝܪ. ܒ. ܓܡ. ܟ. ܕ. ܐ. ܛ
ܘܡܨܥܝܬܐ ܕܝܢ. ܦ. ܓܕ. ܬ. ܫ. ܫ. ܣ.
63a ܢܩܝܕܬܐ ܕܝܢ ܗܠܝܢ ܐܝܢ. ܦ. ܟ. ܪ. ܗ:
ܐܝܟ ܗܕܐ ܘܫܘܥܒܕܗܘܢ ܦܪܘܩ ܒܡܠܬܐ܀
ܥܒܝܬܐ ܓܝܪ ܠܡܨܥܝܬܐ ܘܠܢܩܝܕܬܐ:
ܫܥܒܕܝܢ ܘܒܗܝܢ ܒ ܗܝ ܐܦ ܢܩܝܕܬܐ
ܘܡܨܥܝܬܐ ܠܘܬ ܠܥܒܝܬܐ ܘܠܢܩܝܕܬܐ:
ܫܥܒܕܝܢ ܘܠܐ ܗܘ ܡܫܥܒܕܝܢ ܒܢܩܝܕܬܐ܀
ܣ. ܡܨܥܝܬܐ ܗܝ. ܘܟ. ܠܥܒܝܬܐ ܘܫܥܒܕܝܢ:

4 ܐܝܬ] ܠܝ L | ܐܝܣܡ] ܣܡ ܠܝ B ܐܣܡ (no point) L 9 ܠܡܠܐ] ܠܒܢܝ OG 11 ܐܬܡܢܝܢ ܠܗ] ܐܬܡܠܝܢ ܠܗ OG | ܠܗܘܬܐ] ܠܗܘܐ B 17 ܕ] om. B 18 ܦ] om. B 19 ܐܝܢ] ܐܢܝܢ L 20 ܘܫܘܥܒܕܗܘܢ] ܘܫܥܒܕܗܘܢ G (against metre)B

[1] I have added the vowels. | [2] For this section on heavy, intermediate, and smooth letters, see Dionysius Thrax §6.

ܡܢ ܘܗܟܢܐ ܕܡܬܢܩܦܝܢ ܡܫܬܠܡܝܢ ܠܟܢܫܐ ܕܡܠܠܘܬܗܘܢ
ܘܐܢܫܐ ܕܪ̈ܥܝܐ ܣܓܝܐܬܗ ܠܟܠܗ ܢܓܠܐ[1] ܠܡܘܟܝܢ:
ܐܟܝ ܣܓܝܐܐ ܪ̈ܓܠܐ ܪ̈ܓܫܐ ܦܘܪܥܢܐ:
ܦܘܪܥܢܐ ܡܢ ܥܡܐ ܕܗܘܟܐ ܘܟܕ ܦ̈ܬܝܟܐ ܗܘܝ܀
ܘܠܐ ܦܓܥܬ ܐܢܬ ܓܡܘܪܐ. ܗ. ܠܡܕܪܫ:
ܐܝܟ ܦܫܝܩ ܠܫܘܠܡܐ ܘܓܘܡܪܐ
ܕܗܘ ܡܢ ܦܓܥܐ ܘܗܘ ܡܢ ܠܡܟܐ ܘܦܪ̈ܘܣ ܠܗܘܢܐ:
ܘܟܠ ܥܡܐ ܘܡܠܟܐ ܕܗܦܟ ܐܝܟܢܐ ܣܘܪ ܠܐܬ̈ܘܬܐ܀
ܘܡܢ ܥܘܠܠܐ ܕܫܡܥܠܘܬܗܘܢ ܠܘܝ ܠܡܠܐ:
ܘܗܟܢܐ ܠܡܐܡܪ ܕܟܠ ܐܬܘܬܐ ܕܡܬܡܠܠܢܐ: 63b
ܥܡܠܐ ܐܝܟܢܐ ܗܘ ܡܫܘܚܐ ܡܢܝ ܘܠܐ ܚܝܘܬܐ܀

. . . .

ܐܬܐ[2] ܠܐ ܠܡܐܪ ܐܝܟ ܒ̈ܝܫܡܝܐ ܘܐܬܘܪܝܐ.
ܘܐܟܘܬܐ ܬܐܒ ܡܢ ܗܘܪܝܐ ܕܠܒܝܬܐ ܗܘܐ
ܡܬܦܓܥܐ ܠܗܘܢ ܗܘ ܡܬܬܪܢܡ ܗܘ ܐܦ ܒܦܠܡ:
ܡܦܩܝܢ ܠܗܘ ܘܠܐ ܡܫܘܚܐ ܘܠܐ ܒܘܬܡ܀
ܐܟܝ ܐܟܐ ܘܐܟܘܬܐ ܘܐܦ ܒܦܩܠܐ:
ܢܦܫܐ ܕܟܢܐ ܦܘ̈ܦ ܓܒܠ ܟܒܝ ܢܦܠܐ܀
ܣܓܝ ܠܐ ܡܓܥܒܝܢ[3] ܠܗܘܢ ܐܬ̈ܘܬܐ ܒܦܠܐܬܐ:
ܡܢ ܢܬܡܪܘ ܡܕܝܢ ܫܝܡܝܢ ܢܦܬ[4]ܐܬܐ܀
ܐܬܐ ܕܝ ܠܡܐܪ ܪ̈ܟܝ ܘܡܠܡܝܢ[5] ܠܒܝܬܐ ܘܟܠܐ.
ܘܐܝܟ ܐܟܘܪܝܐ ܘܐܝܟ ܒܒܟܝܐ ܦܘܡܗܘܢ ܠܚܠܠܐ܀
ܘܡܕܝ ܘܣܓܝ ܕܟܠ ܐܬ̈ܘܬܐ ܕܦܬܝܢ ܥܘܣܟܦ:
ܦ̈ܬܟܐ ܐܝܟ ܘܠܐ ܗܘ ܦܬܝܢ ܘܟܠ ܟܝ ܦܦ܀
ܘܗܠܝܢ ܐܢܝܢ ܘܠܐ ܡܫܘܚܐ ܡܠܠܝܢ: ܒܦ. ܘܒ:

3 ܐܟܝ] om. OG 6 ܐܝܟ] ܗܝܟ L | after ܘܓܘܡܪܐ add. ܘܠܐ ܠܐ ܬ ܘܠܐ ܗܘ OG 7 ܘܗܘ] ܗܘ B 9 ܘܡܢ] ܡܢ L | ܕܫܡܥܠܘܬܗܘܢ] ܕܫܡܥܠܘܬܗܘܢ mss (against the metre, cf. 20,ܡܠܠ) 10 ܕܟܠ] ܟܠ G 13 ܒ̈ܝܫܡܝܐ] ܒ̈ܝܫܡܐܝܬ B 16 ܡܦܩܝܢ] ܡܦܩܝܢܐ OG 19 ܡܓܥܒܝܢ] ܡܓܥܒܝܢ L 20 ܡܕܝܢ ܫܝܡܝܢ] ܫܝܡܝܢ ܡܕܝܢ L 21 ܘܡܠܡܝܢ] ܗܠܡܝܢ BL 25 ܐܢܝܢ] om. L (against metre)

[1] Not a word found in the lexica. Elsewhere Jacob glosses it with ܣܚܦ (to drag). I take it as a gloss. It could be emended to ܢܓܕܐ but this would not suit the meaning. | [2] A section on the correct pronunciation of the labials. | [3] The reading is rather uncertain (cf. note on l.21 below) | [4] I.e. "easily," see Barheb, *Gramm.*, 16,12. | [5] Cf. l.19 - both B and L offer ܗܠܡܝܢ for ܠܡܝܢ. However, since ܗܠܡܝܢ and ܡܠܡܝܢ could easily result from ܘܠܡܝܢ and ܡܠܡܝܢ respectively, whereas ܗܠܡܝܢ could not readily be corrupted into ܘܠܡܝܢ (a very rare term), Jacob's original must have read ܡܠܡܝܢ and ܘܠܡܝܢ. In this case the verb in question must mean "to pronounce accurately."

ܒ ܡܬܬܪ̈ܓܡܝܢ ܠܗܘܢ ܐܬܘ̈ܬܐ ܠܐ ܠܡܬܒܥܝܐ܀

. . . .

63a ܟܠ ܡܒܠܝܢ[1] ܫܡܐ ܡܢܝܢܐ ܕܡܫܡܠܐ ܗܘܐ ܢܕܥܝܢ

ܟܠ ܡܒܠܝܢ ܫܡܐ ܗܘܝܢ ܡܕܪܫܝܢ ܕܐܬܠܡܕ ܒܝܬܗ܇

ܗܘ̇ ܕܡܫܡܠܝܐ ܕܗܘܝܐ ܫܠܡܘܬܐ ܘܟܠܐ ܡܦܩܘܢ܀

ܐܝܟܢܐ ܕܐܝܟ ܦܠܓ ܡܛܝܡܝܢ ܚܕܝܢ ܒܝܠܐ ܫܡܗܘܢ܇

ܘܐܡܪܝܢ ܕܡܫܡܠܝܗܝ ܐܘ̄ ܦܠܦܬܐ ܒܠܒܘܫ ܒܗ ܠܘܬܝ܀

ܘܠܗܘܢ ܡܢܝܢܐ ܢܦܩܝܢ ܒ̈ܢܝܐ ܐܘ ܡܬܝܠܕܐ.

ܒܢ ܦܪ̈ܘܦܐ ܘܚܠܝܢ ܡܢܗܘܢ ܒܗ ܒܢ ܥܒܕܐ܀

ܘܒ̈ܢܝܐ ܒܢ ܠܘܬ ܒܡܫܠܐ ܕܝܢ ܐܘ ܕܝܢܐ.

ܘܡܫܡ̈ܠܝܐ ܠܘܬ ܚܝܠܐ ܣܓܝܢ ܬ̈ܘܪܝܢ ܡܢܗ ܘܠܐ ܥܡܠܐ܀

ܘܦܪ̈ܘܦܐ ܠܐܚܝ ܠܐܚܪܐ ܒܝܬܗ ܐܝܟ ܕܐܝܟ ܐܢܐ

ܕܐܝܟ ܐܢܐ ܒܢ ܘܕܐܝܟ ܚܕܐ ܘܐܢܐ ܠܘܬܝ ܐܢܐ܀

. . . .

63b ܘܦܫܘܠܐ[2] ܕܡܫܚ̈ܬܐ ܕܢܩܝܢ ܡܘܨܠܝܐ.[3]

ܒܡܫܘܚܘܬܐ ܐܚܪܐ ܕܡܛܠ ܒܫܘܠܡ ܡܫܡܠܐ

ܠܐ ܬܬܦܠܐ ܕܦܠܓ ܦܪܝܫܘ ܠܡܠܬܐ ܘܐܢܐ܇

ܘܠܫܘܪܝܐ ܘܠܫܡܝܫܘܬܗ ܗܘܐ ܡܫܡܫܢܐ܀

ܘܐܦ ܡܫܡܠܐ ܡܢ ܬ̈ܠܬܐ ܐ̱ܬܪ̈ܝܢ ܒܫܡܐ

ܘܕ̈ܢܒ ܕܫܠܐ ܕܦܫܡܐ ܡܫܬܠܛܐ ܘܠܐ ܬܫܒܘܚܐ.

ܫܡܥ ܦܫܘܠܐ ܕܫܡܫܗ ܡܦܩܕܐ ܒܪ̈ܡܫܬܗ܇

ܘܐܝܟ ܕܫܦܝܪ ܠܗ ܦܪܝܫ ܦܠܓܝ ܘܫܡܥ ܘܠܐ ܡܕܪܘܗ܀

ܫܡܐ ܒܢ ܡܠܬܐ ܘܐܘ ܐܡܪܐ ܘܐܪܦܐ ܠܡܪܝܐ.

ܘܠܫܘܪܝܐ ܒܝܢ ܠܟܠܗܘܢ ܒܪܒܘ ܪܘܚܐ.

ܒܡܫܚ̈ܬܐ ܠܐ ܐܫܬܘܝ ܘܦܫܘܠܗܘܢ܇

4 ܟܠ] om. L (against metre) 9 ܒܗ ܒܢ] ܒܗܘܢ B 10 ܘܡܫܡ̈ܠܝܐ ܐܘ ܕܝܢܐ ܕܝܢ ܒܡܫܠܐ ... ܠܘܬ] om. O (homoe.) 11 ܚܝܠܐ] om. L (against metre) | ܬ̈ܘܪܝܢ] ܬܘܪܝܢ L 13 ܐܢܐ] om. B 15 ܡܘܨܠܝܐ B ܡܘܨܠܐ L 18 ܘܠܫܡܝܫܘܬܗ] txt B ܘܫܡܫܘܬܗ OGL Martin 19 ܘܐܦ] ܐܦ BL Martin | ܡܫܡܠܐ L 21 ܦܫܘܠܐ] ܦܫܘܠܐ G 22 ܦܠܓܝ] ܘܦܠܓܝ G 23 ܘܐܘ ܐܡܪܐ] ܐܘ ܐܡܪܐ OL

[1] A section on adjectives. | [2] A section on the errors made by other grammarians. This section was also edited in Martin, *La Métrique*, 68. | [3] The “man from Mosul” in question is probably Elias of Ṭirhan, the first to use a system of three parts of speech.

ܐܝܟܐ ܡܡܠܠܐ ܗܘ ܫܘܪܝܐ ܩܝܐ ܗܘܐ ܗܘܝܘܡ܀
ܒܢܡܘܣܗ ܗܘ ܦܘܫܩܐ ܗܘܝ ܡܫܘܚܘܬܗ:
ܛܘܪܬܐ ܡܡܠܠܐ ܘܐܘܪܝܬܐ ܕܟܠܗܝܢ ܠܗ ܫܡܥܝ
ܘܟܒܠܐ ܒܝܕ ܫܡܝܢܘܬܐ ܡܓܠܬܐ ܒܪܩ ܡܠܬܐ.
ܐܘܟܠܐ ܘܢܣܓ ܡܡܠܠܐ ܒܡܠܬܐ ܕܓܠܬܐ܀[1]
ܒܗ ܒܪܢܐ ܒܟܝ ܐܦ ܒܪ ܐܝܫܘܥ ܒܪ ܐܠܗܐ:
ܕܦܠܓ ܒܡܡܠܠܐ ܐܘܪܚܐ ܕܠܐ ܛܘܥܝܬܐ.
ܒܗܢ ܒܠܚܘܕܝܗܘܢ ܘܐܝܟ ܫܘܪܝܐ ܫܘܪܝܐ ܗܘܝ: 64b
ܘܒܫܡܝܢܘܬܐ ܘܡܠܟܘܬܐ ܘܦܬܓܡܐ ܦܢܝ܀
ܡܕܝܢܬܐ ܘܢܩܘܫܐ ܘܕܪ̈ܟܐ[2] ܒܗܢ ܒܡܫܘܚܬܗ:
ܢܒܥܠ ܫܩܠܐ ܘܢܩܫܬܐ ܒܗܝ ܙܘܒܢܗ:
ܠܐ ܐܫܬܟܚ ܒܗܘܠܐ ܘܐܝܟܐ ܘܠܡܫܘܚܬܗ:
ܘܡܫܘܚܬܐ ܒܗ ܡܛܠ ܐܠܐ ܘܟܠܟܠ ܘܐܪܦ܀
ܛܥܢ ܛܘܢܗ ܗܢܘܢ ܒܡܫܘܚܬܗ ܒܡܐܡܪܐ ܕܪܒ
ܫܡܐ ܕܝܢ ܒܠܫܢܗ ܫܩܠܐ ܘܫܒܪܐ ܚܒܠ ܘܢܦܠ.
ܚܙܐ ܒܙܒܢܗ ܕܗܘܐ ܡܫܘܚܬܐ ܘܟܪܝ ܫܩܠܝܗ:
ܘܡܠܘܗܝ ܐܝܟ ܐܢܐ ܕܡܠܗ ܒܗ ܫܩܠܝܗ܀
ܗܒ ܡܫܝܚܐ ܐܘܪܚܐ ܘܢܦܩ ܓ̄ ܐܘܚܕܢܐ:
ܘܡܠܡܕ ܠܗ ܐܝܟܐ ܛܘܪܐ ܕܗܘܐ ܡܫܘܚܬܐ:
ܡܦܩܬܗ ܕܝܢ ܠܗܘܢ ܐܦ ܡܫܬܟܚܐ ܐܢܫܐ ܐܘܪܚܐ:
ܐܢ ܦܠܐ ܐܝܟ ܦܘܡܝܗ ܠܡܗܘܐ ܟܠܗ ܫܪܪܐ܀
ܠܟܠܟܠܗ ܗܒ ܙܒܢܗ ܠܗܘܢ ܐܘܪܚܬܗܘܢ.
ܒܗ ܙܒܢܐ ܘܡܫܝܚܐ ܫܡܥܘ ܠܟܠ ܕܟܝܢ
ܒܢܝܐ ܕܐܡܪܬ ܐܦ ܒܡܕܝܢܬܐ ܘܒܫܘܚܠܦܐ. 65a
ܘܗܘܐ ܐܬܥܘܕܪ ܫܘܚܠܦ ܐܪܥܐ ܕܥܡܐ ܗܘܐ܀

2 ܒܢܡܘܣܗ] ܒܢ̈ܡܘܣܗ B | ܡܫܘܚܘܬܗ] ܡܫܘܚܬܗ GB 4 ܘܟܒܠܐ] ܠܐ ܟܒ BL Martin 5 ܘܢܣܓ] ܘܣܓ O(seemingly) ܘܣܓ GL ܢܣܓ B 6 ܐܝܫܘܥ] ܐܫܘܥ L (Wright's reading) 7 ܛܘܥܝܬܐ] ܛܘܥܝ̈ܬܐ G ܛܥܝ̈ܬܐ B 8 ܫܘܪܝܐ 2] ܫܘܪܝܐ G 9 ܘܦܬܓܡܐ] ܦܬܓܡܐ ܦܬܓܡܐ OG 10 ܘܕܪ̈ܟܐ] ܕܪ̈ܟܐ GL | ܒܡܫܘܚܬܗ] ܒܡܫܘܚܬܗ BL (ref. ܡܕܝܢܬܐ) 13 ܡܛܠ ܐܠܐ ܘܟܠܟܠ] ܡܛܠ L ܐܠܐ ܡܛܠ ܘܟܠܟܠ om. OG 14 ܛܘܢܗ] ܛܘܢܗܘܢ OGL ܠܗܘܢ B 15 ܘܢܦܠ] ܘܟܠܟܠ L 18 ܡܫܝܚܐ] ܡܫܝܚܐ L 19 ܠܗ] om. L (against metre) 21 ܦܠܐ] ܦܠ G 23 ܙܒܢܐ] ܙܒܢܗ G | ܫܡܥܘ] ܘܫܡܥܘ G

[1] On ܢ̈ܣܓ (i.e. he aborted the speech with a deceitful word), cf. Jacob of Edessa (Schröter): ܘܫܡܝ ܠܗ ܕܠܐ ܕܚܠܬܐ ܒܝܢܝ ܡܐܡܪ̈ܐ ܗܠܝܢ ܕܢܣܓ ܗܘܐ ܐܢܘܢ (he fearlessly placed his own verses into those memre, which he thereby made "abortive") - i.e. he edited it under a false name and composed it in double metre etc. ܢ̈ܣܓ is not possible next to ܒܡܠܬܐ, it is rather a corruption of ܢ̈ܣܓ [Nöldeke (Review, 1219) reads ܢܣܝܓ, however, with the meaning "to sew together"-ed.]. | [2] See p.111 above.

ܠܗܘܢ ܗܟܝܠ ܫܡ̈ܗܐ ܘܐܪ̈ܒܥܐ ܘܗܘܝܢ ܠܬܠܬܐ:
ܘܒܡܫܘܚܬܗ ܕܝܠܐ ܐܣܝܪܐ ܚܙܝܐ ܡܒܟܬܐ*
ܢܣܠܦ ܒܪܝܐ ܘܗܒܝܢ ܠܗܘܢ ܒܪܫܐ ܫܩ̈ܠܐ ܐܪ̈ܒܥܐ.
ܘܐܦ ܠܬܠܬܐ ܘܗܘܝܢ ܫܡ̈ܗܐ ܘܗܒܝܢ ܐܝܟ ܢܒܥܐ*
ܘܐܢ ܙܒܢܐ ܐܝܬ ܐܘܣܦ ܐܣܝܪܐ ܕܝܠܐ ܒܟܠ ܗܠܝܢ:
ܫܡ̈ܗܐ ܘܫܩ̈ܠܐ ܘܐܪܒܥ ܐܠܐ ܦܣܩܢ ܦ̇ܟܒܝܢ
ܗܟܢ ܐܢܘ ܙܢ̈ܝܢ ܕܡܫܘܚܬܐ ܠܐܪܒܥܝܢܝܬܐ.
ܘܠܐ ܚܣܪ ܡܢܗܘܢ ܙܥܪ ܒܪ ܡܢܟܘܢ ܒܢܡܘܣܬܐ*
ܡܢܝ ܡܟܦܦܢ ܕܝܢ ܗܘ ܗܢܘܢܝܐ ܗܘ ܦܒܢ ܟܡ:
ܒܗܕܐ ܡܫܘܚܬܐ ܘܡܬܩܪܝܢ ܛܝܪ ܐܪܒܥܐ ܕܢܒܘܝܢ*
ܘܐܝܬ ܒܗ ܠܙܒܢܐ ܕܟܠ ܡܬܩܫܚܬܐ ܠܗܘܡ ܦܬܐܬܐ:
ܘܠܬܩܠܬܐ ܕܐܘܡ ܠܐܒܕ ܦܘܐܝܬܐ*
ܘܐܦ ܡܬܩܪܐ ܕܩܛܠܐ ܠܛܝܪ ܗܢܘܢܐܝܬ:
ܒܬܠܬܝܗܝܢ ܕܝܠܢ ܦܪܡܐ ܡܢܝ ܒܛܝܠܬܐ*
65b ܗܐ ܟܘ ܗܘܐ ܐܪܡܦܝܠܐ ܗܘ ܦܪܡܟܬܐ.
ܘܦܫܘܬ ܐܝܬ ܒܗ ܗܝ ܕܠܐܪܒܥܬܐ ܒܢܡܘܣܬܐ*
ܒܗܘܬ ܡܐ ܕܦܓܪܐ ܗ̱ܘܘ̈ ܩ̈ܛܝܠܐ ܒܝܡܛܝܗܘܢ:
ܢ̇ܦܩ ܡܒܟܬܐ ܒܣܠܐ ܘܡܢܝܐ ܒܟܠ ܠܗܝܢܗܝܢ*
ܡܢܝ ܕܠܐ ܕܗܘܘ ܘܐܫܬܪܝ ܙܒܘܬܐ ܒܡܫܡܫ ܕܝܠܐ
ܘܗܘ ܛܠܘܡܝܐ ܕܒ ܠܐ ܚܦܐ ܡܝܬ ܒܣܩܡܐ*
ܘܒܟܢ ܢܣܦ ܘܒܫܘܪܝܐ ܘܒܫܘܠܡܐ
ܫܘܒܚܐ ܘܬܘܕܝܬܐ ܠܐܒܐ ܘܠܒܪܐ ܘܠܪܘܚܩܘܕܫܐ*
ܫܠܡ ܒܥܘܕܪܢ ܐܠܗܐ*[1]

3 ܐܪ̈ܒܥܐ] om. G 6 ܦ̇ܟܒܝܢ] ܡܟܒܝܢ B 8 ܒܢܡܘܣܬܐ] ܒܢܡܘܣܬܐ L 10 ܘܡܬܩܪܝܢ ܛܝܪ] ܡܬܩܪܝܢ ܕܛܝܪ G 11 ܡܬܩܫܚܬܐ] ܡܫܘܚܬܐ O 14 ܒܬܠܬܝܗܝܢ] ܒܬܠܝܗܝܢ L 16 ܘܠܐܪܒܥܬܐ] ܘܠܐܪ̈ܒܥܐ G 20 ܕܒ ܠܐ ܚܦܐ ܡܝܬ ܒܣܩܡܐ] ܕܒ ܚܦܐ ܒܗܘܢ ܣܗܡܘܬܐ* ܢܗܘܐ ܡܢܝܢܐ ܒܗܘܢ ܘܡܥܒܕܘܬܐ ܒܟܠ ܡܢܝ ܡܫܘܚ ܣܝ ܥܡ ܠܟܠܡܘܬܐ B 22 ܘܠܪܘܚܩܘܕܫܐ] ܒܪܡܝܕܘܬܐ ܐܡܝܢ add. B

[1] The subscription in G reads ܫܠܡ ܡܐܡܪܐ ܩܕܡܝܐ ܒܥܘܕܪܢ ܡܪܢ, but the metrical grammar really has nothing to do with the Dialogues, from which they are clearly distinguished (l.14 above). This subscription is therefore inappropriate. That of B is as follows: ܘܐܬܕܪܢ ܠܗܘܢ ܒܟܬܒܐ ܡܫܝܚܐ ܡܠܐ ܡܫܘܚܬܐ ܘܐܬܠܗܘܢ ܒܗܝ ܟܬܒܐ ܡܫܡܫ ܦܘܪܢܣܘܬܐ. ܘܢܫܡܘܥ ܠܗ ܡܪܢܐ ܡܬܩܢܘܗܝ ܒܫܘܠܡܐ ܘܫܘܒܚܘܗܝ ܠܥܠܡܝܢ ܥܡ ܩܕ̈ܝܫܐ ܐܒܗ̈ܬܐ ܠܥܠܡܥܠܡܝܢ ܐܡܝܢ*

ܓܪܡܛܝܩܘܣ ܕܕܝܘܢܘܣܝܘܣ ܬܪܩܐ

ܬܘܒ ܡܐܡܪܐ ܕܓܪܡܛܝܩܐ ܕܥܠ ܦ̈ܠܓܘܬܗ ܕܡܠܬܐ

ܐܡܪܝܢ ܗܟܝܠ ܬ̈ܚܘܡܝܗܘܢ ܕܗܘܝܐ. ܕܡܠܬܐܡܪܢܘܬܐ ܐܝܬܝܗ̇. ܡܠܬܐ ܕܥܘܪܬܐ ܕܝܘܩܢܐ ܕܡܠܬܐ. ܡܠܬܐ ܕܝܢ ܐܝܬܝܗ̇. ܙܥܘܪܐ ܕܝܘܩܢܐ ܕܡܠܬܐܡܪܢܘܬܐ ܕܡܬܘܕܥܐ ܙܒܢܐ ܡܫܠܡܢܐ. ܦ̈ܠܓܘܬܗ ܕܝܢ ܕܡܠܬܐ ܐܝܬܝܗܝܢ ܬܡܢܐ. ܗܢܘ ܕܝܢ. ܫܡܐ. ܡܐܡܪܐ. ܕܫܘܬܦܘܬܐ ܫܪܒܬܐ. ܚܠܦ ܫܡܐ. ܡܩܕܡܘܬܐ ܩܛܪܐ. ܥܠ ܡܐܡܪܐ. ܐܣܪܐ. ܕܐܝܬܝܗܘܢ ܒܝܘܢܝܐ ܗܟܢ. ܐܘܢܘܡܐ ܪܝܡܐ ܡܛܐܘܟܝ. ܐܪܬܪܐ. ܐܢܛܘܢܘܡܝܐ ܦܪܘܬܐܣܝܣ ܐܦܝܪܝܡܐ. ܣܘܢܕܐܣܡܘܣ

ΟΝΟΜΑ. ΡΙΜΑ. ΜΕΤΩΧΗ. ΑΡΘΡΑ. ΑΝΤΟΝΥΜΙΑ.
ΠΡΟΘΕΣΙΣ. ΕΠΙΡΙΜΑ. ΣΥΝΔΕΣΜΟΣ. ܒ

ܦܠܝܓܐ ܒܗܘܢ ܕܝܢ ܐܝܟ ܕܐܡܪܝܢ ܐܝܟ ܐܪܒܥܐ ܐܝܬܝܗܘܢ ܠܐܣܟܝܡܐ ܫܡܐ ܢܦܠ.

ܥܠ ܫܡܐ

ܫܡܐ ܗܟܝܠ ܐܝܟ ܕܐܡܪܝܢ. ܐܝܬܘܗܝ. ܦܠܓܐ ܕܡܠܬܐ ܕܡܬܘܕܥܐ. ܐܘ ܓܘܫܡܐ ܐܘ ܨܒܘܬܐ. ܓܘܫܡܐ ܓܝܪ. ܟܐܦܐ. ܩܝܣܐ. ܣܝܦܐ. ܨܒܘܬܐ ܕܝܢ. ܡܪܕܘܬܐ. ܚܟܡܬܐ. ܫܘܕܥܢܘܬܐ. ܡܛܠ ܕܐܡܪ p.10
ܓܘܢܝܐ ܘܚܕܝܐܝܬ. ܓܘܢܝܐ ܓܝܪ. ܟܐܦܐ. ܩܝܣܐ. ܣܝܦܐ. ܚܕܝܐܝܬ ܕܝܢ. ܦܘܠܘܣ. ܐܪܝܣܛܛܠܝܣ. ܣܘܩܪܛܝܣ.

ܢܦܩܝܢ ܕܝܢ ܠܫܡܐ. ܗܠܝܢ ܚܡܫܐ. ܓܢܣܐ.. ܐܕ̈ܫܐ. ܐܣܟܝܡܐ ܡܢܝܢܐ ܡܦܠܬܐ.

ܓܢܣܐ ܗܟܝܠ ܐܝܬܝܗܘܢ ܬܠܬܐ ܦܝܢ ܗܢܝܐ ܠܡܠܬܐ. ܕܟܪܐ ܘܢܩܒܬܐ. ܘܐܚܪܢܐ ܠܟܪ ܡܢ ܗܠܝܢ: ܗܘ ܕܠܐ ܕܟܪܐ ܘܠܐ ܢܩܒܬܐ ܐܝܬܘܗܝ. ܐܝܟ ܕܡܬܠܗܘ ܕܠܗܝܐ ܢܘܝܐ. ܒܟܬܒܐ ܕܝܢ ܣܘܪܝܝܐ ܓܢܣܐ ܐܝܬܝܗܘܢ ܬܪܝܢ. ܕܟܪܐ ܘܢܩܒܬܐ. ܐܢܫܝܢ ܕܝܢ ܡܘܣܦܝܢ ܥܠ ܗܠܝܢ ܬܪܝܢ ܐܚܪܢܝܢ. ܘܟܠܚܕ ܦܝܢ ܦܪܝܫ ܫܡܐ ܓܘܢܝܐ. ܠܗܘ ܕܝܢ ܐܚܪܢܐ ܥܠ ܓܘܢܝܐ. ܫܡܐ ܗܟܝܠ ܓܘܢܝܐ ܐܝܬܘܗܝ. ܐܝܟ ܗܘ ܕܓܡܠܐ ܢܫܪܐ. ܕܟܪܐ ܕܝܢ ܘܢܩܒܬܐ ܕܬܪܝܗܝܢ ܦܝܢ. ܥܠ ܓܘܢܝܐ ܕܝܢ ܐܝܬܘܗܝ. ܗܘ ܕܫܘܬܦܢܝܬܐ. ܘܟܬܝܒܐ. ܘܐܝܟܢ ܕܕܡܝܢ
ܠܗܠܝܢ. ܕܟܪܐ ܓܝܪ ܘܢܩܒܬܐ ܢܦܠܬ ܡܫܬܡܫܝܢ. ܓ

ܐܕ̈ܫܐ ܕܝܢ ܐܝܬܝܗܘܢ ܬܪܝܢ. ܩܕܡܝܐ ܘܫܘܪܝܐܝܬ. ܛܘܦܣܐ ܦܫܝܛܐ. ܘܗܘ ܕܡܢ ܛܘܦܣܐ ܦܫܝܛܐ ܡܬܝܠܕ. ܛܘܦܣܐ ܦܝܢ ܦܫܝܛܐ ܐܝܬܘܗܝ. ܗܘ ܕܟܗܢܐ ܦܝܢ ܦܫܝܛܐ ܡܬܐܡܪ. ܐܝܟ ܗܘ̇ ܕܫܡܫܐ ܐܪܥܐ ܘܢܘܪܐ ܘܐܐܪ. ܗܘ ܕܝܢ ܕܡܢ ܛܘܦܣܐ ܦܫܝܛܐ ܡܬܝܠܕ ܘܡܬܐܡܪ. ܐܝܟ ܗܘ̇ ܕܫܡܫܢܝܐ ܐܪܥܢܐ ܢܘܪܢܐ.

3 Tit: ܬܘܒ ܡܐܡܪܐ ܕܫܘܝܐ ܘܡܫܠܡܐ ܒܟܠ ܙܒܢ ܡܢܝܢ ܣܘܦܐ ܗܘܝܐ ܕܥܠ ܫܡܐ B ܬܘܒ ܡܡܠܠܐ ܦܝܠܘܣܘܦܐ | 6 ܕܥܘܪܬܐ] ܕܥܘܪܬܗ̇ BC | ܐܝܬܝܗ̇] ܡܢ C | ܕܡܠܬܐ] ܕܡܠܬܐܡܪܢܘܬܐ B 5 ܕܓܪܡܛܝܩܘܬܐ C | ܡܫܠܡܢܐ. ܦܠܓܐ B | ܘ om. C | ܘܫܘܬܦܘܬܐ] 7 C ܡܬܘܕܥܐ ܡܫܠܡܐ | C ܕܥܘܪܬܐ ܕܡܠܬܗ̇ B ܕܥܘܪܬܗ̇ ܕܡܠܬܐ | C ܡܩܕܡܘܬܐ ܩܛܪܐ 8 ܕܐܝܬܝܗܘܢ...ΣΥΝΔΕΣΜΟΣ om. BC 12 ܒܗܘܢ] om. AB | ܐܝܟ[2] om. C ܕܗܘܝܢ ܐܡܪܝܢ C | ܕܐܡܪܝܢ] 14 om. AB ܫܡܐ ܥܠ] 13 om. AB ܢܦܠ] | C ܕܐܣܟܝܡ | C ܐܪܒܥܐ ܡܢܝܢ | C ܡܬܘܕܥܐ] ܕܡܬܘܕܥܐ C 15 ܐܝܟ ܐܢܫ ܕܐܡܪ ante ܓܘܫܡܐ add. C | ܫܘܕܥܢܘܬܐ + ܚܟܡܬܐ A | ܡܛܠ ܕܐܡܪ] ܦܘܠܘܣ. ܐܪܝܣܛܛܠܝܣ ܣܘܩܪܛܝܣ. ܓܘܢܝܐ ܘܚܕܝܐܝܬ] om. C 16 C ܘܡܛܠ ܕܐܡܪ B ܡܛܠ ܕܐܡܪ ܕܝܢ ܐܣܟܝܡܐ BC | ܐܢܫܐ C | ܢܦܩܝܢ ܠܗ 18 C ܦܛܪܘܣ. ܦܘܠܘܣ. ܝܘܚܢܢ. B ܦܛܪܘܣ. ܝܘܚܢܢ. ܐܝܬܝܗܘܢ ܠܐܝܟ[1] 21 C ܕܬܠܬܐ 20 ܡܢ] om. A | C ܐܝܟ ܕܠܗܝܐ 19 B ܓܢܣܐ | BC ܡܬܘܕܥܐ ܘܢܩܒܬܐ | BC ܕܟܪܐ 23 B ܘܢܩܒܐ | C ܐܝܟ ܐܢܫ ܕܐܡܪ ܓܡܠܐ ܢܫܪܐ] ܐܝܟ ܗܘ 22 C ܠܟܪ ܡܢ | C ܗܘ ܕܫܘܬܦܢܝܬܐ. ܘܐܝܟܢ [ܠܗܠܝܢ ܕܕܡܝܢ ܘܐܝܟܢ ܕܟܬܝܒܐ ܗܘ | C ܗܝܟܠ + ܦܝܢ | C ܕܕܪܐܝܬ | BC ܕܟܪܐ ܕܝܢ [ܡܫܬܡܫܝܢ ܢܦܠܬ ܘܢܩܒܬܐ ܓܢܣ ܕܟܪܐ 25 C ܐܝܟ ܕܟܬܝܒܐ ܘܐܝܟܢ ܕܠܗܠܝܢ ܕܕܡܝܢ B ܕܐܝܟ ܗܟܢ ܛܘܦܣܐ[1] 26 C ܕܟܪܐ ܕܝܢ ܘܢܩܒܬܐ ܕܬܪܝܗܝܢ ܢܦܠܬ ܡܬܚܫܒܝܢ ܠܡܫܬܡܫܘ B ܘܢܩܒܬܐ ܢܦܠܬ ܡܫܬܡܫܝܢ ܘܫܘܪܝܐ | BC ܗܘ [ܦܝܢ | BC ܘܫܘܪܝܐ 28 ܘܐܐܪ] om. BC | ܕܟܗܢܐ C | ܦܝܢ] ܗܘ BC 27 C ܡܢ B ܘܢܘܪܐ

ܘܐ̈ܪܒܥܐ ܗܠܝܢ ܕܡܢ ܛܘܦܣܐ ܦܫܝܛܐ ܚܒܝܫ ܩܘܡܗ ܐܝܬܝܗܘܢ ܡܟܝܠ. ܘܡܬܡܠܝܢ. ܡܢ ܐܟܘܐ. ܘܡܢ ܡܝܐ ܘܡܢ ܦܫܡܐ. ܘܡܢ ܫܡܝܐ ܘܡܢ ܡܬܦܪܫܘܬܐ. ܘܡܢ ܠܒܪ ܡܢ ܫܡܝܐ. ܘܡܢ ܡܬܡܪܐ.

p.11 ܡܢ ܫܡܝܐ ܗܟܢܐ ܕܐ̈ܣܘܬܐ ܐܝܬܝܗܘܢ. ܗܘ ܕܡܬܢܛܠ ܡܢ ܫܡܝܐ ܕܐ̈ܣܘܬܐ ܡܬܐܬܝܢ. ܐܝܟ ܗܘ ܕܒܗ. ܡܗܘܪܐ. ܬܐܬܝܐ ܕܝܢ. ܐܦ ܡܢ ܐܣ̈ܘܬܗܘܢ ܕܐ̈ܣܘܬܐ. ܐܝܟ ܗܘ ܕܡܫܬܟܚܐ. ܒܚܘܒܢܐ. ܐܘܣܝܐ. ܡܬܢܛܠ ܕܝܢ ܗܘܐ ܠܟܠܗ ܛܘܦܣܐ ܚܝܐ. ܫܘܪܝܬܐ ܕܝܢ ܚܕ ܐܝܟ ܗܘ ܕܡܗܘܐ ܒܟܠܟܠܐ. ܡܪܘܢܐ. ܗܟܘܬ ܕܝܢ ܐܦ ܫܡܝܐ ܕܢܡܘܬܐ ܡܬܢܛܠ ܩܕܡ ܠܟܠܗ ܛܘܦܣܐ ܚܝܐ. ܫܘܪܝܬܐ ܕܝܢ ܚܕ. ܒܟܠܗܘܢ. ܐܝܟ ܗܘ ܕܡܫܪܟܠܐ

ܟ ܡܗܘܕܝܬܐ. ܒܪܢܝܬܐ ܡܢ ܫܡ̈ܗܐ ܕܝܢ ܕܢܩܒܠܬܐ. ܠܐ ܡܬܐܡܪ ܗܘܐ ܫܡܐ.

ܡܢ ܗܘܐ ܕܚܝܐ ܡܬܬܡܛܐ ܠܐܝܠܝܢ ܗܘ ܕܐܝܬܝܗ ܦܬܘܐ ܢܦܠ ܘܢܚܡ ܠܚܝܐ ܠܚܝܐ. ܐܝܟ ܗܘ ܕܒܬܪܗ ܕܝܘܚܢ. ܘܢܛܪܗ ܕܐܕܡ. ܘܫܝܬ ܕܚܢܘܟ.

ܡܢ ܦܘܫܡܐ ܕܝܢ ܐܝܬܝܗܘܢ ܐܝܟܢ ܕܚܕ ܒܪ ܚܕ ܒܢܝܢܐ ܡܬܝܠܕܝܢ. ܐܝܟ ܗܘ ܕܗܘܐ ܕܐܬܐ ܡܢ ܡܫܝܚܐ ܗܘܢܐ. ܐܘ ܚܕ ܒܪ ܫܪܒܬܐ. ܠܒܪ ܡܢ ܒܢܝܢܐ. ܐܝܟ ܗܘ ܕܡܫܝܚܐ ܢܣܒ ܗܘܐ ܩܕܡ ܐܬܐ ܡܢ ܒܬܘܠܬܐ ܚܬܢ ܡܚܝܠܐ. ܛܘܦܣܐ ܕܝܢ ܕܦܘܫܡܐ ܕܡܬܢܛܠ ܘܫܘܪܝܬܐ ܠܟܠܗ ܐܝܬܝܗܘܢ. ܐܝܟ ܗܘ ܕܐܬܐ ܡܢ ܦܠܡ. ܛܒ ܡܢ ܦܠܡ ܡܬܐܬܐ ܡܢ ܟܠ.

ܫܡܝܐ ܕܝܢ ܐܝܬܝܗܘܢ. ܐܝܟܢ ܕܚܕ ܩܕܡ ܡܬܐܡܪܝܢ ܘܠܡ ܡܥܢܝ̈ܢܐ ܡܬܐܡܪܝܢ. ܛܘܦܣܗܘܢ ܕܝܢ ܐܝܬܝܗܘܢ ܠܐܕܡ. ܡܬܢܛܠ ܘܫܘܪܝܬܐ. ܚܕ ܐܝܟ ܗܘ ܕܗܒܠ ܘܩܝܢ ܘܫܝܬ ܫܡܥܘܢ. ܐܚܪܢܐ ܐܝܟ ܗܘ ܕܒܪܐ ܕܒܪܐ. ܘܡܫܝܚܐ ܕܡܫܝܚܐ.

p.12 ܘܡܬܦܪܫܢܘܬܐ ܕܝܢ ܐܝܬܝܗ. ܐܝܟܢ ܕܠܦܪܘܫܘܬܐ ܕܛܘܦܣܐ ܦܫܝܛܐ. ܫܦܝܪ ܡܢ ܦܘܫܡܐ ܕܠܡ ܐܚܪܢܐ ܡܬܘܕܥ. ܐܝܟ ܗܘ ܕܛܒܘܬܐ ܘܒܪܝܘܬܐ.

ܠܒܪ ܡܢ ܫܡܝܐ ܕܝܢ. ܐܝܬܝܗܘܢ ܐܝܟ ܗܘ ܕܡܗܘܐ ܡܫܡܫ. ܘܐܦܛܪܘܦܘܣ. ܐܦܝܣܩܘܦܘܣ.

ܒ ܡܢ ܡܬܡܪܐ ܕܝܢ ܐܝܬܝܗܘܢ. ܗܘ ܕܡܢ ܡܫܡܠܝܐ ܢܗܪ ܫܘܡܗܐ ܐܝܟ ܗܘ ܕܫܘܟܠܠܐ ܘܡܫܝܚܐ ܘܢܚܫܐ.

ܐܩܡܝܐ ܕܝܢ ܕܫܡ̈ܗܐ ܐܝܬܝܗܘܢ ܠܟܠܐ. ܦܫܝܛܐ. ܡܪܟܒܐ. ܘܠܒܪ ܡܢ ܡܪܟܒܐ. ܦܫܝܛܐ ܐܝܬܝܗܘܢ. ܐܝܟ. ܡܪܟܒܐ ܐܚܪܢ. ܘܠܒܪ ܡܢ ܡܪܟܒܐ ܕܝܢ. ܐܝܟ ܗܘ ܕܐܚܪܢ ܫܘܟܠܐ ܕܝܢ ܕܡܪܟܒܐ ܐܝܬܝܗܘܢ

1 ܘܐ̈ܪܒܥܐ] ܐܪ̈ܒܥܐ ܕܝܢ B ܐܪ̈ܒܥܐ C | ܗܠܝܢ] ܕܗܠܝܢ BC | ܦܫܝܛܐ] ܦܫܝ̈ܛܐ C | ܚܒܝܫ] ܦܒܝܫ B ܚܒܝܫ C 2 ܡܝܐ] ܘܐ̈ܣܘܬܐ ܫܡܝܐ ܡܢ | ܫܡ̈ܝܐ C 3 ܫܡܝܐ¹] ܡܬܦܪܫܢܘܬܐ C ܡܬܦܪܫܢܘܬܐ B ܡܬܦܪܫܘܬܐ] | ܫܡܝܐ C ܫܡܝܐ] | ܡܝܐ A ܕܒܗ] ܕܒܗ ܡܗܘܪܐ 4 ܡܬܐܬܝܢ] read ܡܬܬܚܡܝܢ | ܡܢ ܫܡܝܐ ܡܢ ܐ̈ܣܘܬܐ ܡܕܝܢ C ܡܢ ܫܡܝܐ ܡܢ ܐ̈ܣܘܬܐ B ܐܘܣܝܐ ܒܚܘܒܢܐ] | ܕܡܫܬܟܚܐ C ܕܐܡܫܬܟܚܐ B ܕܡܫܬܟܚܐ ܗܘ] ܗܘ | ܐܦ ܡܢ] ܐܝܟ ܕܡܢ B | ܡܗܘܕܝܬܐ BC transp. ܒܟܠܟܠܐ ܕܡܗܘܝܢ | ܗܘ] ܗܘ C | ܚܕ] ܚܕ ܒܟܠܗܘܢ C | ܗܘܐ ܫܡܐ C ܗܘܐ ܫܡܐ B ܗܘܐ ܫܡܐ] 5 ܗܘ] | ܡܗܘܫܐ C ܛܘܦܣܐ] | ܕܢܡܬܐ BC ܕܢܡܘܬܐ] | ܕܝܢ¹] om. C 6 ܡܪܘܢܐ] ܡܪܘܢܐ ܒܟܠܟܠ̈ܐ ܕܡܗܘܝܢ C ܫܡܐ ܘܚܝܐ] B ܗܘ BC 7 ܕܡܫܪܟܠܐ] ܕܐܫܪܟܠܐ B ܒܟܠܟܠܐ add. C 8 ܒܪܢܝܬܐ] om. B 9 ܘܚܝܐ] ܘܚܝܐ ܫܡܐ B ܠܚܝܐ ܠܚܝܐ] ܠܚܝܐ ܘܠܚܝܐ B ܠܗ | ܘܢܚܡ] ܘܠܐ ܢܚܡ A | ܐܝܠܝܢ] om. BC | ܘܚܝܐ ܕܝܢ ܫܡܘܗܝ | ܡܬܐܡܪ ܘܐܝܬܘܗܝ] ܐܝܬܘܗܝ BC | ܗܘ] ܗܘ BC 10 ܕܝܘܚܢ] om. A 11 ܦܘܫܡܐ] ܦܫܡܐ BC | ܩܕܡ] om. BC | ܗܘ] ܗܘ B | ܗܘܢܐ] ܐܝܟ ܗܘܢܐ C | ܗܘ] ܗܘ B 12 ܒܢܝܢܐ] ܒܢ̈ܝܢܐ C | ܫܘܪܝܬܐ ܘܡܬܢܛܠ] ܡܬܢܛܠ ܫܘܪܝܬܐ B ܐܦ | ܕܦܘܫܡܐ] ܦܘܫܡܐ BC | ܛܘܦܣܐ] ܛܘܦܣܐ B 13 ܦܠܡ²] ܕܦܠܡ BC 14 ܗܘ] ܗܘ B | ܫܘܪܝܬܐ C | ܡܬܐܡܪܝܢ ܘܠܡ] ܡܬܐܡܪܝܢ ܠܡ | ܩܕܡ] om. B 15 ܡܥܢܝ̈ܢܐ] | ܗܘ¹] ܗܘ BC | ܚܕ] ܚܕ ܩܕܡ C | ܡܬܢܛܠ] ܘܡܬܢܛܠ C 16 ܛܘܦܣܗܘܢ] ܛܘܦܣܐ B | ܫܡܥܘܢ] ܫܡܥܘܢ B | ܗܘ²] ܗܘ BC 17 ܐܝܟ²] om. C | ܐܚܪܢܐ] ܐܚܪܢܐ C | ܫܡܥܘܢ BC ܘܡܫܝܚܐ ܕܡܫܝܚܐ] ܘܡܫܝܚܐ ܕܡܫܝܚܐ C 18 ܘܡܬܦܪܫܢܘܬܐ] ܘܡܬܦܪܫܢܘܬܐ BC | ܐܝܬܝܗ] ܐܝܬܝܗܘܢ ܫܡܐ C | ܕܠܦܪܘܫܘܬܐ] ܕܠܦܪܘܫܘܬܐ C ܕܠܦܪܘܫܘܬܗ B | ܕܛܘܦܣܐ] ܛܘܦܣܐ C | ܡܬܘܕܥ] ܡܬܘܕܥ ܠܦܘܫܡܐ C 19 ܐܚܪܢܐ ܕܠܡ] ܘܐܚܪܢܐ B | ܦܘܫܡܐ] ܦܫܡܐ B 20 ܗܘ] ܗܘ B | ܘܐܦܛܪܘܦܘܣ] ܐܦܛܪܘܦܘܣ B | ܐܦܝܣܩܘܦܘܣ] ܐܦܝܣܩܘܦܘܣ C ܐܦܝܣܩܘܦܘܣ B 21 ܡܬܡܪܐ] ܡܬܠܐ B | ܗܘ] ܗܘ BC | ܫܘܡܗܐ ܢܗܪ] ܢܗܪ ܫܘܡܗܐ C | ܡܫܡܠܝܐ] ܡܬܡܪܐ ܡܢ C 23 ܐܩܡܝܐ] ܐܩܝܡܐ B | ܐܝܬܝܗܘܢ ܠܟܠܐ] ܠܟܠܐ ܐܝܬܝܗܘܢ C ܠܟܠܐ ܐܝܬܝܗܘܢ B | ܘܠܒܪ] ܠܒܪ C | ܦܫܝܛܐ ܐܝܬܝܗܘܢ | ܐܩܝܡܐ C ܦܫܝܛܐ ܩܕܡ ܐܝܟ ܗܘ ܘܐܟ ܡܪܟܒܐ ܕܝܢ ܐܝܟ ܗܘ ܘܐܚܪܢ ܡܪܟܒܐ ܕܝܢ ܐܝܟ ܗܘ ܘܐܚܪܢ] ܐܚܪܢ ܡܪܟܒܐ ܐܚܪܢ B ܦܫܝܛܐ ܩܕܡ | ܕܡܪܟܒܐ] ܡܪܟܒܐ BC | ܗܘ] ܗܘ BC | ܘܠܒܪ] ܠܒܪ BC | ܐܚܪܢ] ܐܚܪܢܘܢ A 24 ܐܚܪܢ] ܘܐܚܪܢ ܗܘ C

ܠܥܠܐ. ܡܢܗܘܢ ܦܢ ܐܝܬܝܗܘܢ ܡܢ ܠܬܪܝܢ ܡܬܦܫܩܝܢ. ܐܝܟ ܗܘ ܕܗܘܐ ܚܕ. ܡܢܗܘܢ ܕܝܢ ܐܝܬܝܗܘܢ ܡܢ ܠܬܪܝܢ ܡܠܐ ܫܡܗܢܝܬܐ. ܐܝܟ ܗܘ ܕܩܕܝܫ. ܡܢܗܘܢ ܕܝܢ ܐܝܬܝܗܘܢ. ܡܢ ܡܠܬܐ ܚܕܐ ܫܡܗܢܝܬܐ ܘܡܢ ܡܬܦܫܩܢܝܬܐ. ܐܝܟ ܗܘ ܕܡܠܟ ܡܠܟ̈ܐ. ܡܢܗܘܢ ܕܝܢ ܡܬܪܟܒܝܢ. ܡܢ ܡܠܬܐ ܚܕܐ ܡܬܦܫܩܢܝܬܐ ܘܡܢ ܐܚܪܬܐ ܫܡܗܢܝܬܐ. ܐܝܟ ܗܘ ܕܒܪܙܕܘܬܐ.

ܡܢܝܢܐ ܕܝܢ ܕܟܠܗܝܢ ܗܠܝܢ ܐܝܬܝܗܘܢ ܠܥܠܐ ܚܝܠܬܐ ܘܐܘܚܕܢܬܐ ܘܫܘܠܛܢܬܐ. ܒܟܠܗܝܢ ܕܝܢ ܫܘܪܝܐ p.13
ܐܝܬܝܗܘܢ ܠܬܪܝܢ ܚܝܠܬܐ ܘܫܘܠܛܢܬܐ ܐܝܟ ܕܒܢܝܢܫܐ ܘܟܝܢ ܐܢܫܐ. ܐܝܬܝܗܘܢ ܕܝܢ ܐܦ ܫܡܗ̈ܬܐ ܐܚܪ̈ܢܐ ܐܝܟܢ ܕܐܚܪ̈ܢܐ ܡܢ ܐܝܬܝܗܘܢ. ܘܟܠ ܫܡܗ̈ܬܐ ܡܬܩܪܝܢ ܐܝܟ ܗܘ ܕܥܡܐ. ܚܝܠܐ. ܓܘܕܐ. ܠܘܬ ܕܝܢ ܐܝܬܝܗܘܢ ܫܡܗ̈ܬܐ ܐܚܪ̈ܢܐ. ܐܝܟܢ ܕܫܘܠܛܢܬܐ ܦܢ ܡܬܐܡܪܝܢ. ܟܠ ܚܕ ܕܝܢ ܐܘ ܟܠ ܠܬܪܝܢ ܡܬܩܪܝܢ ܐܝܟ ܗܘ ܕܫܡܗ̈ܐ ܘܡܬ̈ܐ ܘܬܪ̈ܥܐ.. ܠܘܬ ܕܝܢ ܐܝܬܝܗܘܢ ܫܡܗ̈ܬܐ ܐܚܪ̈ܢܐ ܐܝܟܢ ܕܚܝܠܬܐ ܦܢ ܡܬܐܡܪܝܢ. ܘܟܠ ܠܬܪܝܢ ܡܬܩܪܝܢ ܐܝܟ ܗܘ ܕܐܘܪܚܐ: ܘܦܬܐ.

ܝܘ ܡܦܠܓܬܐ ܕܝܢ ܕܫܡܗ̈ܐ ܐܝܟ ܕܟܢܫܐ ܗܠܝܢ ܚܡܫ ܐܝܬܝܗܘܢ. ܗܘ ܕܝܢ. ܠܐܘܪܚܐ. ܓܢܣܢܝܬܐ. ܡܬܐܡܪܢܝܬܐ. ܟܠܠܢܝܬܐ. ܡܬܦܪܫܢܝܬܐ. ܠܐܘܪܚܐ ܡܢ ܐܝܬܘܗܝ. ܡܦܠܓ ܗܢܐ ܐܝܟ ܐܢܫ ܕܐܡܪ ܓܢܣܐ. ܓܢܣܢܝܬܐ ܐܝܬܘܗܝ. ܡܬܐܡܪܢܐ ܘܐܕܫܐ. ܗܘ ܕܝܢ ܕܓܢܣܐ. ܘܫܘܫܠܐ. ܡܬܐܡܪܢܝܬܐ ܕܝܢ ܐܝܬܘܗܝ ܡܬܐܡܪܢܐ ܗܘ ܕܝܢ ܠܓܢܣܐ. ܟܠܠܢܝܬܐ ܕܝܢ ܐܝܬܘܗܝ ܟܠܠܝܐ ܗܘ ܕܝܢ ܒܓܢܣܐ. ܡܬܦܪܫܢܝܬܐ ܕܝܢ ܐܝܬܘܗܝ ܡܬܦܪܫܢܐ. ܐܝܟ ܗܘ ܕܐܘ ܓܢܣܐ. ܫܘܪܝܐ ܕܝܢ ܗܘܐ ܐܕܫܐ ܡܬܦܠܓܐ. ܘܠܐ ܡܬܦܪܫ.

ܡܬܦܠܓܝܢ ܕܝܢ ܠܚܡܫܐ ܗܠܝܢ. ܐܝܟܢ ܕܐܦ ܐܕܫܐ ܡܬܐܡܪܝܢ. ܡܪܢܐ. ܡܬܐܡܪܢܐ. ܡܬܚܫܒܢܐ. ܕܟܠ ܡܢܝܢ. ܐܝܟ ܕܟܠ ܡܢܝܢ. ܫܡܘܠܐ ܫܡܗܐ. ܕܩܝܡ ܫܡܗܐ. ܡܬܓܠܐ ܫܡܗܐ. ܠܬܝܢ ܫܡܗܐ. p.14
ܟܠ ܫܡܐ. ܟܠ ܟܡܐ. ܡܬܡܠܠܐ. ܠܐ ܡܬܚܡܫܢܐ. ܗܘ ܕܐܦ ܡܬܡܢܝܢܐ. ܡܬܦܪܥܢܐ ܘܡܫܘܚܬܐ ܐܝܬܘܗܝ. ܡܡܫܚܢܐ. ܡܬܦܩܕܢܐ. ܡܬܟܬܒܢܐ. ܓܢܣܐ. ܚܫܝܒܐ. ܡܬܓܠܝܢܐ ܡܬܡܫܚܢܐ ܫܪܝܐ.

ܝܙ ܡܪܢܐ ܕܝܢ ܐܝܬܘܗܝ. ܗܘ ܕܠܐܕܫܐ ܕܟܠܗ ܡܬܝܗܒ. ܐܝܟ ܗܘ ܕܝܘܣܦ. ܕܒܢܝܡܝܢ ܕܝܥܩܘܒ. ܡܬܐܡܪܢܐ ܕܝܢ ܐܝܬܘܗܝ. ܗܘ ܕܠܐܕܫܐ ܕܓܘܐ ܡܬܝܗܒ. ܐܝܟ ܗܘ ܕܒܢܝܢܫܐ ܫܘܫܠܐ. ܠܗܘܐ

1 ܡܬܦܫܩܝܢ] ܡܬܦܫܩ̈ܢܐ BC | ܐܝܟ ܗܘ ܕܗܘܐ ܚܕ] ܚܕ ܕܗܘܘ ܐܝܟ B ܚܕ ܕܗܘܐ ܗܘ ܐܝܟ C 2 ܐܝܟ ܗܘ ܕܩܕܝܫ ܡܬܦܫܩܢܝܬܐ] 3 ܗܘ] ܗܘ C | ܗܘ...ܐܝܟ] om. A | ܡܢܗܘܢ ܕܝܢ ܐܝܬܝܗܘܢ ܡܢ ܡܠܬܐ ܚܕܐ ܫܡܗܢܝܬܐ ܘܡܢ ܡܬܦܫܩܢܝܬܐ ܐܝܟ ܗܘ 4 ܐܚܪܬܐ] ܘܐܚܪܬܐ B ܐܘ ܡܢ ܐܚܪܬܐ C | ܗܘ] ܗܘ C | ܕܒܪܙܕܘܬܐ] ܕܒܪܙܕܘ AC 5 ܡܢܝܢܐ[1]] ܡܬܦܫܩܢܝܬܐ BC | ܚܝܠܬܐ ܘܐܘܚܕܢܬܐ ܘܫܘܠܛܢܬܐ] ܐܘܚܕܢܬܐ ܫܘܠܛܢܬܐ C | ܡܘܬܐ...ܕܝܢ] om. A | ܡܘܬܐ] ܡܢ ܡܘܬܐ C | ܕܟܢܫܐ] ܕܟܢܫܐ B | ܐܢܫܐ ܘܟܝܢ] BC | ܕܒܢܝܢܫܐ] ܗܘ ܕܒܢܝܢܫܐ BC | ܘܫܘܠܛܢܬܐ ܚܝܠܬܐ] om. B | ܠܬܪܝܢ ܐܝܬܝܗܘܢ] ܠܬܪܝܢ ܐܝܬܝܗܘܢ C 6 ܗܘ] C | ܡܬܩܪܝܢ] ܡܬܩܪܝܢ C | ܘܟܠ] ܟܠ ܟܠ C | ܐܝܟܢ] om. B 7 ܐܚܪ̈ܢܐ] ܐܚܪ̈ܢܐ B | ܘܐܚܪ̈ܢܐ BC ܟܠ ܚܕ ܟܠܗܘܢ] ܕܝܢ ܚܕ ܟܠ | ܘܫܘܠܛܢܬܐ] ܐܝܟ ܫܘܠܛܢܐ C | ܐܦ ܐܝܬ C ܐܝܬ B | ܐܦ] ܐܝܬܝܗܘܢ 8 ܗܘ BC ܟܠ ܠܬܪܝܢ ܕܝܢ] ܠܬܪܝܢ ܘܟܠ 10 ܘܬܪ̈ܥܐ B | ܘܬܪ̈ܥܐ] ܗܘ BC | ܗܘ] 9 ܡܬܩܪܝܢ C | ܡܬܩܪܝܢ] ܡܬܩܪܝܢ C | ܘܟܠ ܡܢ] ܡܢ 12 ܐܝܬܝܗܘܢ ܚܡܫ BC | ܚܡܫ] ܐܝܬܝܗܘܢ ܚܡܫ 11 ܗܘ BC | ܗܘ] ܡܬܩܪܝܢ C | ܡܬܩܪܝܢ] ܓܢܣܢܝܬܐ ܕܝܢ C | ܓܢܣܢܝܬܐ] 13 ܠܐܘܪܚܐ B | ܕܝܢܐ] ܕܝܢܐ B | ܐܝܟ ܡܬܐܡܪܢܝܬܐ C | ܡܬܐܡܪܢܝܬܐ] ܗܢܐ ܡܦܠܓ ܗܢܐ ܡܦܠܓ before ܫܘܫܠܐ there is an erasure in A | ܕܓܢܣܐ] ܓܢܣܐ B | ܘܐܕܫܐ] ܐܕܫܐ B | before ܡܬܐܡܪܢܐ there is an erasure in A 14 ܡܬܐܡܪܢܐ] ܡܬܐܡܪܢܐ ܗܘ C | ܒܓܢܣܐ] ܐܝܟ ܕܐܡܪ ܒܓܢܣܐ BC | ܟܠܠܢܝܬܐ] ܐܘܚܕܢܐ] ܐܘܚܕܢܐ ܘܡܬܦܠܓܐ ܕܫܘܪܝܐ C | ܡܬܦܪܫܢܝܬܐ] 15 ܡܬܦܪܫܢܐ ܗܘ C | ܗܘ ܕܝܢ ܐܝܟ ܐܝܟ ܕܐܡܪ C | ܗܘ ܟܠܠܢܝܬܐ C | ܗܘ ܟܠ ܟܠ ܫܘܪܝܐ C adds another title after ܡܬܦܪܫ | C ܡܬܦܠܓܐ ܡܬܦܠܓܐ] ܡܬܦܠܓܐ | C 16 ܡܬܦܠܓܝܢ] ܡܬܦܠܓܝܢ C | ܠܚܡܫܐ] ܠܚܡܫܐ B | ܐܝܟܢ] om. C | ܫܡܗܐ ܐܚܪ̈ܢܐ ܗܠܝܢ C | ܡܬܚܫܒܢܐ] om. C | ܡܬܐܡܪܢܐ] ܡܬܐܡܪܢܐ B | ܡܪܢܐ] ܡܪܢܐ B | ܡܬܚܫܒܢܐ] ܡܬܚܫܒܢܐ C | ܡܬܐܡܪܝܢ] ܡܬܐܡܪܝܢ C ܡܬܚܫܒܢܐ] ܕܟܠ ܡܢܝܢ ܐܘ ܕܟܠ] add. C in marg. ܫܡܗܐ ܫܡܗܐ] 17 ܡܬܚܡܫܢܐ C ܡܬܚܡܫܢܐ B 18 ܫܡܐ A ܫܡܐ] ܟܡܐ A ܟܡܐ B ܟܠ C | ܕܩܝܡ ܫܡܗܐ] ܘܫܡܗܐ C | ܘܩܝܡ] ܟܠ ܐܘ ܟܠ ܫܡܝܢ ܫܡܗ ܫܡܘܠܐ] ܡܫܘܚܬܐ B | ܘܡܫܘܚܬܐ] ܡܫܘܚܬܐ C | ܡܬܦܪܥܢܐ] ܡܬܦܪܥܢܐ C | ܠܐ ܡܬܚܡܫܢܐ] ܠܐ ܡܬܚܡܫܢܐ B | ܕܟܠ BC 19 ܡܬܓܠܝܢܐ] ܡܬܓܠܝܢܐ C | ܓܢܣܐ] ܓܢܣܐ B | ܡܬܟܬܒܢܐ] ܡܬܟܬܒܢܐ C 20 ܕܝܢ] ܕܝܢ ܐܝܬܘܗܝ BC ܡܢ ܕܝܢ ܕܝܥܩܘܒ ܕܒܢܝܡܝܢ ܘܝܘܣܦ ܗܘ ܐܝܟ] ܗܘ ܕܠܐܕܫܐ ܕܟܠܗ ܡܬܝܗܒ | C ܗܘ ܗܘ] ܗܘ ܕܠܐܕܫܐ ܕܟܠܗ C | ܕܝܥܩܘܒ ܡܬܝܗܒ ܗܘ...ܡܬܝܗܒ] om. C | ܐܝܬܘܗܝ] om. C | ܡܬܐܡܪܢܐ] ܡܬܐܡܪܢܐ C 21 ܐܝܟ ܗܘ ܕܝܘܣܦ ܕܒܢܝܡܝܢ ܕܝܥܩܘܒ BC | ܗܘ] ܗܘ B | ܕܒܢܝܢܫܐ...ܠܗܘܐ] ܕܒܢܝܢܫܐ ܫܘܫܠܐ B

ܡܬܬܫܡܥܢܐ ܕܝܢ ܐܝܬܘܗܝ. ܗܘ ܕܟܠ ܫܡܐ ܡܢܝܐ ܘܡܬܬܚܝܢܐ ܡܬܬܫܝܡ. ܘܡܬܘܕܥ ܐܘ ܘܡܬܚܫܐ ܐܘ ܚܘܝܐ. ܡܬܝܗܒ ܕܝܢ ܐܬܚܬܐܝܬ. ܐܘ ܡܢ ܢܦܫܐ ܐܘ ܡܢ ܦܓܪܐ. ܐܘ ܡܢ ܗܠܝܢ ܕܡܢ ܠܒܪ. ܡܢ ܢܦܫܐ ܗܟܢܐ ܕܐܝܟ ܗܘ ܕܢܚܦܐ ܐܘ ܗܠܠܐ. ܡܢ ܦܓܪܐ ܕܝܢ. ܐܝܟ ܗܘ ܕܡܩܦܪܐ ܐܘ ܡܫܚܠܐ. ܡܢ ܐܝܠܝܢ ܕܡܢ ܠܒܪ ܕܝܢ ܐܝܟ ܗܘ ܕܬܐܡܪܐ ܐܘ ܡܫܚܠܐ.

ܗܘ ܕܝܢ ܕܟܘܬ ܡܢܝܢ ܐܝܬܘܗܝ. ܐܝܟ ܗܘ ܕܐܬܐ ܟܘܬ ܚܕܐ. ܘܢܦܫܐ ܟܘܬ ܢܦܫܐ. ܘܡܫܝܚܐ ܟܘܬ ܫܡܫܐ.

ܗܘ ܕܝܢ ܕܐܝܟ ܕܟܘܬ ܡܢܝܢ ܐܝܬܘܗܝ. ܐܝܟ ܗܘ ܕܠܟܠܐ ܘܐܡܫܡܫܐ.

ܫܘܬܦ ܫܡܐ ܕܝܢ ܐܝܬܘܗܝ. ܐܢܐ ܕܟܠ ܫܡ̈ܗܐ ܫܘܬܦܐܝܬ ܡܬܬܫܝܡ. ܐܝܟ ܗܘ ܕܝܘܣܦ ܒܪ ܝܥܩܘܒ. ܘܝܘܣܦ ܒܪ ܚܠܗ. ܘܝܘܣܦ ܕܡܢ ܪܡܬܐ. ܫܘܬܦ ܫܡܐ ܕܝܢ ܐܝܬܘܗܝ. ܐܝܟ ܟܠܒܐ ܕܝܡܐ ܘܟܠܒܐ ܕܐܪܥܐ.

ܣܓ̈ܝܐܐ ܫܡ̈ܗܐ ܕܝܢ ܐܝܬܝܗܘܢ: ܐܝܠܝܢ ܕܒܫ̈ܡܗܐ ܡܢ ܡܫܚܠܦܝܢ. ܒܟܝܢܗܘܢ ܕܝܢ ܚܕ ܒܟܝܢܗܘܢ ܕܟܝܢܐ ܡܬܘܕܥܝܢ ܐܝܟ ܗܘ ܕܣܦܣܪܐ. ܣܝܦܐ. ܚܪܒܐ.

ܦܠ̈ܝܓܝ ܫܡ̈ܗܐ ܕܝܢ ܐܝܬܝܗܘܢ: ܐܝܟ ܗܘ ܕܡܢ ܐܝܠܝܢ ܕܫܪ̈ܝܢ ܡܬܬܫܡܝܢ ܫܡ̈ܗܐ ܐܝܟ ܗܘ ܕܚܝܡܝܢ ܘܢܘܟܪ̈ܝ.

ܢܓ̈ܝܕܝ ܫܡ̈ܗܐ ܕܝܢ ܐܝܬܝܗܘܢ ܐܝܟܢܐ ܕܐܝܟ ܫܡ̈ܗܐ ܡܬܬܫܡܗܝܢ. ܡܢܓܕܐܝܬ ܠܟܠ ܚܕ. ܐܝܟ ܗܘ ܕܓܒܪܐ ܘܟܢܘܫܐ ܗܘܐ ܕܝܢ ܫܡܐ. ܠܐ ܢܦܩ ܟܠܠ ܢܦܫܗ. ܠܗ ܕܝܢ ܟܠܠ ܡܢ ܕܟܢܘܫܐ ܡܬܐܡܪܐ. ܐܦ ܓܒܪܐ ܐܝܬܘܗܝ.

p.15

ܟܠ ܫܡܐ ܕܝܢ ܐܝܬܘܗܝ ܗܘ ܕܟܠ ܫܡܐ ܐܚܪܢܐ ܡܢܐܝܬ ܡܬܐܡܪ ܐܝܟ ܗܘ ܕܟܠ ܚܕ ܫܡܐ ܕܐܢܫܐ ܦܓܪܗ ܘܡܕܪܝܐ ܐܬܐܡܪܬ.

ܫܡܐ ܕܝܢ ܕܟܠ ܚܕܐ ܐܝܬܘܗܝ. ܗܘ ܕܟܠ ܚܕܐ ܡܬܘܕܥ ܐܝܟ ܕܚܝ̈ܘܬܐ ܘܦܬ̈ܘܪܐ ܘܡܬܘܫܡܐ.

ܡܫܡܠܝܐ ܕܝܢ ܐܝܬܘܗܝ. ܗܘ ܕܡܫܡܠܝܐܝܬ ܡܬܐܡܪ. ܐܝܟ ܗܘ ܕܦܢܘܗ ܐܢܫܐ. ܐܢܫܐ. ܚܡܪܐ. ܐܝܟ ܚܡܪܐ.

ܠܐ ܡܬܬܫܡܥܢܐ ܕܝܢ ܐܝܬܘܗܝ ܗܘ ܕܠܘܩܒܠ ܡܫܡܠܝܐ ܡܬܐܡܪ. ܐܝܟ ܗܘ ܕܡܢ ܕܘܝܕ. ܐܢܐ ܕܘܝܕ ܥܒܕܐ ܕܘܝܕ ܐܡܪ ܕܘܝܕ.

1 ܘܡܬܬܚܝܢܐ] ܡܢܝ ܡܬܬܚܝܢܐ ܟܠ ܐܘ C | ܘܡܬܘܕܥ] ܘܡܬܘܕܥ ܡܢܝܢ ܫܡܥܐ ܗܘܐ ܗܘܘ C | ܐܘ] om. B 2 ܐܘ[4]...ܠܒܪ] om. B 3 after ܠܒܪ C adds ܟܠܗܘܢ ܡܬܬܫܡܫܝܢ | ܗܠܠܐ] ܦܡ ܗܠܠܐ C | ܕܐܝܟ] ܐܝܟ ܡܢ ܐܝܠܝܢ ܕܝܢ] ܕܝܢ ܠܒܪ ܕܡܢ ܐܝܠܝܢ ܡܢ 4 BC ܡܫܚܠܐ] ܡܫܚܠܐ B | ܐܝܟ ܕܡܩܦܪܐ B | ܗܘ[1] ܗܘ ܫܡܐ C | BC ܫܡܐ ܕܝܢ ܗܘ ܕܟܘܬ ܡܢܝܢ] ܡܢܝܢ ܕܟܘܬ ܕܝܢ ܗܘ 5 BC ܗܘ] ܗܘ | C ܡܢ ܗܠܝܢ ܕܝܢ ܕܡܢ ܠܒܪ B ܕܡܢ ܠܒܪ ܕܐܝܟ] om. B 7 ܕܐܬܐ ܟܘܬ ܚܕܐ] ܚܕܐ ܟܘܬ ܕܐܬܐ B | BC ܗܘ] ܗܘ | B ܐܝܟ] ܐܝܟ C | ܡܟܝܢܝܢ ܠܟܡܢܐ C ܫܡܐ ܐܢܐ ܕܟܠ ܫܘܬܦܐ ܫܘܬܦܐܝܬ...ܡܬܬܫܝܡ] ܫܘܬܦ B | ܘܐܡܚܡܠܐ] ܘܐܡܚܡܠܐ C 8 ܫܘܬܦ] ܫܘܬܦ B | ܗܘ] ܗܘ ܐܝܟ ܝܘܣܦ[1] 9 BC ܗܘ] ܗܘ | C ܫܡܐ ܕܟܠ ܦܪ̈ܨܘܦܐ ܫܘܬܦܐܝܬ ܡܬܬܫܝܡ B, whence ܡܬܬܫܝܡ ܕܟܠ | C ܫܘܬܦܘܗܝ] ܫܡܐ om. B | ܝܥܩܘܒ...ܕܐܪܥܐ] repeated B | ܕܡܢ] ܝܘܣܦ C | ܝܘܣܦ[2] B | ܘܟܠܒܐ ܕܝܡܐ ܘܟܠܒܐ] ܘܟܠܒܐ ܕܝܡܐ ܟܠܒܐ ܕܝܡܐ C 10 ܕܐܪܥܐ] ܕܐܪܥܐ C 11 ܕܒܫ̈ܡܗܐ] ܫܡ̈ܗܐ B 12 ܕܟܝܢܐ] ܣܦܣܪܐ ܣܝܦܐ ܘܣܦܣܪܐ] ܣܦܣܪܐ B | ܘܣܦܣܪܐ] ܣܦܣܪܐ B | ܡܬܘܕܥܝܢ] ܡܬܝܕܥܝܢ C | om. B C ܘܣܦܣܪܐ ܗܘ[2] om. B C ܫܡ̈ܗܐ ܣܓ̈ܝܐܐ | ܣܓ̈ܝܐܐ] C ܗܠܝܢ | om. B ܗܠܝܢ] ܗܢܘܢ C 13 ܗܘ[1] ܚܪܒܐ C ܐܝܬܝܗܘܢ ܫܡܐ] ܐܝܬܝܗܘܢ C | BC 14 after ܘܢܘܟܪ̈ܝ A adds ܘܡܢܝܢ 15 ܢܓ̈ܝܕܝ] ܢܓܝܕ A ܢܓܝܕܝ B ܢܓܝܕ C | om. B 16 ܘܟܢܘܫܐ] ܟܢܘܫܐ ܓܒܪܐ B | ܠܐ ܢܦܩ ܟܠܠ ܢܦܫܗ] ܠܐ ܢܦܩ ܟܠܠ ܢܦܫܗ C | ܠܗ ܕܝܢ] ܠܗ B ܕܝܢ ܠܗ ܟܠܠ ܡܢ ܕܟܢܘܫܐ ܡܬܐܡܪܐ B ܐܦ ܓܒܪܐ ܐܝܬܘܗܝ] ܐܝܬܘܗܝ ܓܒܪܐ ܐܦ ܡܬܐܡܪܐ ܘܟܢܘܫܐ ܡܢ ܟܠܠ | C ܠܒܪ ܡܬܐܡܪ] ܐܝܬܘܗܝ 18 C ܗܘܐ ܐܦ ܓܒܪܐ ܐܝܬܘܗܝ ܘܐܦܠܐ ܟܠܗܘܢ ܕܟܢܘܫܐ ܡܬܐܡܪܐ ܡܢ ܦܓܪܐ ܘܐܦ ܓܒܪܐ ܐܝܬܘܗܝ ܡܢܝ] ܡܬܐܡܪ | BC ܡܢܝܐ] ܡܢܐܝܬ | C ܕܟܠ[1] ܕܟܠ | C ܫܡܐ ܗܘ] ܗܘ[1] om. B | C ܘܐܝܬܘܗܝ ܐܝܟ] | C ܫܡܐ ܐܚܪܢܐ ܗܘܐ ܗܘܘ C ܟܠ ܫܡܐ] ܫܡܐ ܘܟܠ BC | ܟܠ ܚܕ[1] 20 ܗܘ C | ܗܘ[2] C ܡܬܐܡܪ ܗܘ ܕܡܫܡܠܝܐ] ܫܡܐ ܐܝܟ ܐܢܫܐ ܐܢܫܐ ܕܦܢܘܗ ܗܘ ܐܝܟ ܡܬܐܡܪ ܘܡܫܡܠܝܐܝܬ ܗܘ | C ܫܡܐ ܗܘ] ܗܘ 21 B ܕܟܠ ܐܢܫܐ] ܐܢܫ C | ܐܢܫܐ] ܗܘ C | ܡܬܐܡܪ] ܡܬܐܡܪ ܡܢܝ C | B ܐܝܟ ܗܘ ܕܦܢܘܗ ܐܢܫܐ ܚܡܪܐ ܐܝܟ ܚܡܪܐ ܡܢܝ] ܡܬܐܡܪ om. C 23 ܡܬܬܫܡܥܢܐ] ܡܬܬܫܡܥܢܐ B | ܗܘ[1] ܗܘ ܫܡܐ C | ܡܫܡܠܝܐ] ܡܫܡܠܝܐ ܫܡܐ C | ܡܬܐܡܪ C | ܕܘܝܕ[1] ܕܘܝܕ B (cf. p.263f.) | ܕܘܝܕ[2] ܕܘܝܕ B 24 ܕܘܝܕ[1] ܕܘܝܕ B | ܕܘܝܕ[2] ܕܘܝܕ B

ܡܩܪܝܢܐ ܕܝܢ ܐܬܩܪܝ. ܐܝܟܐ ܕܐܦ ܡܬܦܪܫܐ ܡܠܐܡܪܐ. ܘܡܩܘܝܐ ܥܠ ܕܩܘܡܐ ܡܕܡ. ܐܝܟ ܗܘ ܕܐܝܟ ܗܘܐ. ܘܐܝܟ ܗܘܐ ܘܕܐܝܟ ܗܘܐ ܟܠܗ. ܚ

ܡܗܝܡܢܐ ܕܝܢ ܐܬܩܪܝ ܐܝܟ ܗܘ ܕܟܡܐ. ܟܢܫܐ. ܟܘܪܐ.

ܡܬܦܢܝܢܐ ܕܝܢ ܐܬܩܪܝ. ܗܘ ܕܡܢ ܬܪܝܢ ܐܘ ܡܢ ܣܓܝܐܐ ܦܝܐ ܡܫܡܫܐ ܥܠ ܚܕ. ܐܝܟ ܡܢ ܬܪܝܗܘܢ ܚܕ. ܐܘ ܡܢ ܥܠ ܚܕ ܡܢܗܘܢ.

ܡܩܥܝܢܐ ܕܝܢ ܐܬܩܪܝ. ܗܘ ܕܚܕܐ ܦܣܘܩܐ ܠܥܕܡ ܕܡܫܬܠܡܐ ܒܗ. ܐܝܟ ܗܝ ܕܒܬܘܟܠܬܐ ܘܐܪܡܠܘܬܐ. p.16

ܡܬܟܫܦܢܐ ܕܝܢ ܐܬܩܪܝ. ܗܘ ܕܡܢ ܕܢܬܟܫܦܘܢ ܕܒܢܝ ܟܠܐ ܡܬܐܡܪ ܡܬܟܫܦܢܐܝܬ. ܐܝܟ ܗܝ ܕܢܗܘܐ ܕܡܐ ܘܥܠܝܢ ܕܐܪܚܐ.

ܟܢܫܐ ܕܝܢ ܐܬܩܪܝ. ܗܘ ܕܠܐܪܥܐ ܡܬܬܢܐ ܡܬܦܠܓ. ܐܝܟ ܗܘ ܕܢܣܒܬ. ܘܐܬܟܠܬ.

ܡܣܝܒܐ ܕܝܢ ܐܬܩܪܝ. ܗܘ ܕܡܢ ܟܢܫܐ ܡܬܦܠܓ. ܐܝܟ ܗܘ ܕܐܬܐ. ܘܫܘܫܐ ܘܐܪܥܐ. ܘܥܒܕܐ. ܘܐܬܠܐ.

ܡܬܬܝܚܢܐ ܕܝܢ ܐܬܩܪܝ. ܗܘ ܕܬܝܚܐ ܡܩܘܝܐ ܐܝܟ ܗܘ ܕܦܩܕܐ. ܠܫܢܐ. ܠܒܠܒܐ.

ܡܬܡܗܝܢܐ ܕܝܢ ܐܬܩܪܝ ܗܘ ܕܥܠ ܡܗܝܢܐ ܡܩܘܝܐ. ܐܝܟ ܗܘ ܕܚܝ ܠܒܟ. ܠܟܠܐ. ܛ

ܦܩܘܕܐ ܕܝܢ ܐܬܩܪܝ. ܐܝܟ ܗܘ ܕܠܟܘܠ ܡܠܟܐ.

ܩܪܝܐ ܕܝܢ ܕܡܫܠܡܐ ܐܬܩܪܝܘ ܬܪܝܢ. ܡܬܡܢܝܢܘܬܐ ܘܫܠܡ܀ ܡܬܡܢܝܢܘܬܐ ܦܠܓ ܐܬܩܪܝܬ. ܐܝܟ ܗܝ ܕܙܢܝܐ ܕܙܢܝ. ܫܠܡ ܕܝܢ ܐܬܩܪܝ. ܐܝܟ ܡܬܬܙܝܥܢܐ ܕܡܬܙܝܥ.

ܘܗܠܝܢ ܦܘ ܬܬܐܡܪ ܥܠ ܗܟܢܐ ܕܐܬܩܪܝ ܡܢܐ ܦܪܝܫܐ ܕܡܠܬܐ. ܢܐܡܪ ܕܝܢ ܡܟܝܠ ܐܦ ܥܠ ܡܐܡܪܐ ܕܐܬܩܪܝ ܡܢܝܢܐ ܕܬܪܝܢ ܕܡܠܬܐ.

ܥܠ ܡܐܡܪܐ

ܡܐܡܪܐ ܕܝܢ ܐܬܩܪܝ. ܡܬܐܡܪܢܘܬܐ ܕܠܐ ܡܫܘܚܠܦܬܐ ܡܡܠܠܐ ܕܝܢ ܕܪܝܫܐ ܘܦܬܓܡܐ ܘܡܠܬܢܝܐ. ܘܡܫܡܫܢܐ ܘܡܬܡܢܝܢܘܬܐ ܘܫܠܡ.. ܢܦܩܝܢ ܕܝܢ ܠܡܐܡܪܐ. ܠܡܠܐ.. ܦܬܓܡܐ.. ܦܬܓܡܐ. ܠܪܫܐ. ܠܡܫܬܡܥܢܐ. p.17 ܡܢܝܢܐ. ܦܬܓܡܐ. ܪܟܢܐ ܪܥܠܐ.. ܐܝܟ ܕܒܟܬܒܐ ܗܘܝܐ ܠܡܠܐ ܗܘܝܢ. ܒܟܬܒܐ ܕܝܢ ܡܘܪܝܐ. ܗܟܢܐ ܐܬܩܪܝܘ..

ܦܬܓܡܐ ܗܟܠ ܫܡܗ ܐܬܩܪܝ.. ܡܬܫܡܫܢܐ. ܦܘܕܐ. ܡܪܟܢܐ.

ܡܩܕܡܢܐ. ܡܬܐܡܪܢܘܬܐ ܡܢ ܡܐܡܪܐ. ܦ

1 ܡܩܪܝܢܐ] ܡܩܪܝܢܐ B ܡܩܪܝܢܝܬ C | ܐܝܟܐ] ܐܝܟܐ ܗܟܢܐ C | ܡܠܐܡܪܐ] ܡܠܐܡܪܐ ܡܢ ܣܬܡܐ C ܐܬܩܪܝ B ܐܝܟ ܗܘ ܕܟܡܐ ܟܡܐ ܟܢܫܐ ܟܘܪܐ] ܟܘܪܐ ܟܢܫܐ ܕܟܡܐ ܗܘ ܐܝܟ | C ܗܟܢܐ ܐܝܟ] ܐܝܟ 3 B ܘܐܝܟ] ܘܕܐܝܟ 2 ܡܢ ܐܘ 5 BC ܕܡܢ] ܡܢ[2] | B ܦܝܐ ܡܬܦܫܡܫܐ] ܡܫܡܫܐ ܦܝܐ | B ܬܪܝܢ ܐܬܩܪܝ] ܬܪܝܢ | C ܗܟܢܐ ܗܘ] ܗܘ 4 ܡܩܥܝܢܐ ܕܝܢ] ܡܩܥܝܢܐ...ܘܐܪܡܠܘܬܐ 6 C ܐܘ ܡܢ ܥܠ ܚܕ ܡܢܗܘܢ B ܘܐܘ ܡܢ ܚܕ ܡܢܗܘܢ] ܡܢܗܘܢ ܚܕ ܥܠ ܗܝ ܐܝܟ | C ܐܬܩܪܝ ܗܟܢܐ ܗܘ ܕܚܕܐ ܦܣܘܩܐ ܡܫܬܠܡܐ ܐܦ ܠܥܕܡ ܕܒܗ ܡܫܬܠܡܐ ܐܝܟ ܗܘ ܕܒܬܘܟܠܬܐ ܘܐܪܡܠܘܬܐ C ܡܬܟܫܦܢܐܝܬ ܡܬܐܡܪ] ܘܐܪܡܠܘܬܐ ܘܒܬܘܟܠܬܐ] ܘܐܪܡܠܘܬܐ ܕܒܬܘܟܠܬܐ ܗܘ ܐܝܟ B 8 ܗܘ] ܗܘ ܗܟܢܐ C | ܡܬܐܡܪ ܡܬܟܫܦܢܐܝܬ C ܗܘ[1] | BC ܟܢܫܐ] ܟܢܫܐ 10 C ܟܢܫܐ | C ܘܟܘܫܠܗ B ܕܗܘܘ ܕܐܝܢ] ܕܐܝܢ ܘܐܝܢ ܕܢܗܘܐ 9 BC ܗܘ] ܗܝ C adds ܐܝܟ after ܡܬܦܠܓ | C ܗܟܢܐ ܗܘ] ܗܘ[1] 11 C ܡܬܦܠܓ ܡܢܗ] ܡܬܦܠܓ | C ܗܟܢܐ ܗܘ B ܐܝܟ ܠܐܪܥܐ ܘܫܘܫܐ ܘܥܒܕܐ ܘܐܬܠܐ] ܘܐܬܠܐ ܘܥܒܕܐ ܘܐܪܥܐ ܘܫܘܫܐ ܕܐܬܐ ܗܘ ܐܝܟ | ܠܫܘܡܠܐ ܘܗܟܢܐ ܣܬܡܐ ܡܩܘܝܐ] ܡܩܘܝܐ ܡܢ | BC ܕܥܠ ܬܝܚܐ] ܕܬܝܚܐ | C ܗܟܢܐ ܗܘ] ܗܘ[1] | B ܡܬܬܝܚܢܐ C ܡܬܬܚܫܢܐ] ܡܬܬܝܚܢܐ 13 ܠܟܠܐ] | B ܚܝ] ܕܚܝ | C ܡܢ ܡܩܘܝܐ] ܡܩܘܝܐ | C ܗܟܢܐ ܗܘ] ܗܘ[1] 14 C ܠܪܫܐ] ܠܫܢܐ | C ܡܩܘܝܐ ܘܠܟܠܐ C 15 ܗܘ] ܗܘ ܐܝܟ C ܗܟܢܐ ܗܘ 16 ܕܡܫܠܡܐ] ܕܡܫܠܡܐ BC | ܐܬܩܪܝ] om. B | ܘܫܠܡ ܡܬܡܢܝܢܘܬܐ] is red in C as if chapter heading | ܗܝ ܐܝܟ] om. B ܗܘ ܐܝܟ ܗܟܢܐ C 17 ܫܠܡ] ܘܫܠܡ B | ܐܝܟ] ܗܟܢܐ ܐܝܟ C | ܐܝܟ ܡܬܬܙܝܥܢܐ] ܡܬܬܙܝܥܢܐ ܐܝܟ ܗܘ ܡܬܬܙܝܥܢܐ C ܐܝܟ B 18 ܬܬܐܡܪ] ܕܬܬܐܡܪ ܡܢܝ ܗܘܐ C | ܕܡܠܬܐ] om. C 19 after ܕܡܠܬܐ comes the subscription of B: ܫܠܡ ܡܐܡܪܐ ܦܪܝܫܐ. After this point, only AC 22 ܡܡܠܠܐ] ܡܡܠܠܐ ܕܪܝܫܐ C 23 A lacks the points after ܠܡܠܐ 24 ܪܥܠܐ] ܪܥܠܐ AC | ܗܘܝܢ ܠܡܠܐ] om. C | ܒܟܬܒܐ ܕܝܢ ܗܟܢܐ ܐܬܩܪܝܘ] ܐܬܩܪܝܘ ܗܟܢܐ ܒܟܬܒܐ ܕܝܢ ܡܘܪܝܐ C 26 ܫܡܗ ܐܬܩܪܝ] ܐܬܩܪܝܘ ܫܡܗ C 27 ܡܩܕܡܢܐ] ܡܩܕܡܢܐ C | ܡܬܐܡܪܢܘܬܐ ܡܢ ܡܐܡܪܐ] ܡܬܐܡܪܢܘܬܐ ܡܢ ܡܐܡܪܐ C ܡܬܐܡܪܢܘܬܐ ܡܐܡܪܐ A

ܦܬܓܡܐ ܕܝܢ ܐܝܬܝܗܘܢ ܠܬܠܬܐ. ܒܥܒܕܢܘܬܐ. ܘܚܫܐ. ܘܡܨܥܝܘܬܐ.. ܡܥܒܕܢܘܬܐ ܕܝܢ ܐܝܬܝܗ. ܐܝܟ ܗܝ ܕܦܠܚ ܐܢܐ. ܥܒܕ ܐܢܐ. ܟܬܒ ܐܢܐ.. ܚܫܐ ܕܝܢ ܐܝܬܘܗܝ. ܐܝܟ ܗܘ ܕܡܬܦܠܚ ܐܢܐ ܡܬܥܒܕ ܐܢܐ. ܡܬܟܬܒ ܐܢܐ.. ܡܨܥܝܘܬܐ ܕܝܢ ܐܝܬܝܗ. ܗܝ ܕܒܝܬ ܡܢ ܡܥܒܕܢܘܬܐ ܡܬܐܡܪܐ. ܟܕ ܕܝܢ ܡܢ ܚܫܐ.. ܐܝܟ ܗܝ ܕܙܕܩܬ. ܗܦܟܬ. ܡܠܟܬ. ܪܘܚܬ. ܚܫܒܬ..

ܐܕܫܐ ܕܝܢ ܐܝܬܝܗܘܢ ܠܬܪܝܢ. ܛܘܦܣܐ ܩܕܡܝܐ. ܘܗܘ ܕܡܢ ܛܘܦܣܐ ܩܕܡܝܐ ܡܬܝܠܕ. ܛܘܦܣܐ ܡܢ ܩܕܡܝܐ ܐܝܬܘܗܝ. ܐܝܟ ܗܝ ܕܚܫܒܬ.. ܗܘ ܕܝܢ ܕܡܢ ܛܘܦܣܐ ܩܕܡܝܐ ܡܬܝܠܕ ܐܝܬܘܗܝ. ܐܝܟ ܗܘ ܕܡܬܚܫܒ ܐܢܐ..

ܐܣܟܡܐ ܕܝܢ ܠܬܠܬܐ ܐܝܬܝܗܘܢ.. ܦܫܝܛܐ ܘܡܪܟܒܐ ܘܕܡܢ ܡܪܟܒܐ.. ܦܫܝܛܐ ܗܟܝܠ ܐܝܬܘܗܝ. ܐܝܟ ܗܝ ܕܙܘܓܬ ܐܢܐ.. ܡܪܟܒܐ ܕܝܢ ܐܝܬܘܗܝ. ܐܝܟ ܗܝ ܕܡܬܙܘܓܬ ܐܢܐ.. ܕܡܢ ܡܢ ܡܪܟܒܐ ܕܝܢ: ܐܝܟ ܗܝ ܕܡܬܙܘܓܢܘ ܡܬܙܘܓܬ ܐܢܐ..

ܡܢܝܢܐ ܡܢ ܐܝܬܝܗܘܢ ܐܝܟ ܕܒܫܡܐ ܢܝܫܐ. ܠܬܠܬܐ.. ܗܢܘ ܕܝܢ. ܚܕܝܘܬܐ. ܬܪܝܢܘܬܐ. ܣܓܝܐܘܬܐ.. ܐܝܟ ܕܒܫܡܐ ܕܝܢ ܗܕܡܝܐ. ܬܪܝܢ. ܚܕܝܘܬܐ ܘܣܓܝܐܘܬܐ. ܘܚܕܝܘܬܐ ܡܢ ܐܝܬܝܗ. ܐܝܟ ܗܝ ܕܦܫܠ ܐܢܐ ܥܒܕ ܐܢܐ.. ܣܓܝܐܘܬܐ ܕܝܢ ܐܝܬܝܗ. ܐܝܟ ܗܝ ܕܦܫܠܝܢܢ. ܥܒܕܝܢܢ. ܦܠܚܝܢܢ..

ܦܪܨܘܦܐ ܕܝܢ ܐܝܬܝܗܘܢ ܠܬܠܬܐ. ܩܕܡܝܐ. ܐܢܫܐ ܠܬܠܝܬܝܐ.. ܩܕܡܝܐ ܗܘ ܐܝܬܘܗܝ. ܗܘ ܕܡܡܠܠ ܐܝܬܘܗܝ ܡܡܠܠܐ. ܐܢܫܐ ܕܝܢ ܐܝܬܘܗܝ ܗܘ ܕܠܘܬܗ ܐܝܬܘܗܝ ܡܡܠܠܐ.. . ܠܬܠܝܬܝܐ ܕܝܢ ܐܝܬܘܗܝ. ܗܘ ܕܥܠܘܗܝ ܗܘܐ ܡܡܠܠܐ..

ܗܐ ܙܒܢܐ ܕܝܢ ܐܝܬܝܗܘܢ ܠܬܠܬܐ.. ܗܘܐ ܕܩܐܡ ܘܗܘ ܕܥܒܪ ܘܗܘ ܕܥܬܝܕ.. ܗܘ ܕܩܐܡ ܕܒܗ ܐܝܬܘܗܝ ܦܠܚܐ ܡܪܝܐ.. ܘܡܬܩܢܐ ܕܥܡܠܐ. ܩܪܝܐ. ܡܬܩܢܝܢܐ. ܠܐ ܡܬܩܢܝܐ.. ܐܚܪܐ ܕܝܢ «ܠܐ ܡܬܩܢܝܐ» p.18 ܐܝܬܝܗܘܢ ܠܬܠܬܐ.. ܗܘܐ ܕܩܕܡ ܥܒܕ ܗܘ ܕܥܡܠܐ. ܘܗܘ ܩܪܝܐ ܥܒܕ ܗܘ ܕܡܢ ܒܬܪ ܥܒܕ ܘܗܘ ܠܐ ܡܬܩܢܝܐ ܥܒܕ ܗܘ ܕܥܬܝܕ.. ܘܗܟܢ ܠܐܡܪ. ܐܦ ܥܠ ܡܢܝܢܐ ܠܬܠܬܐ ܕܡܠܬܐ..

ܥܠ ܫܘܬܦܘܬܐ

ܫܘܬܦܘܬܐ ܕܝܢ ܐܝܬܝܗ. ܡܬܐܡܪܢܘܬܐ ܕܡܬܐܡܪܐ ܡܢ ܕܡܠܬܗܘܢ ܕܡܐܡܪܐ ܘܫܩܠܘܬܐ.. ܢܣܒ ܐܦ ܠܗ. ܐܝܟܢ ܕܢܣܒ ܠܡܐܡܪܐ ܘܠܫܩܠܘܬܐ. ܘܫܪܝ ܡܢ ܦܪܨܘܦܐ ܘܦܬܓܡܐ..

ܥܠ ܫܪܓܐ

ܫܪܓܐ ܕܝܢ ܐܝܬܝܗ. ܡܠܬܐ ܙܥܘܪܬܐ ܕܡܠܬܐ.. ܗܝ ܕܡܬܐܡܪܐ ܡܬܬܫܡܫܐ. ܡܢ ܩܕܡ ܦܬܓܡܐ ܕܫܩܠܘܬܐ. ܘܒܢܝܢܐ ܗܝ ܡܬܬܫܡܫܐ ܐܝܟ ܕܒܫܡܐ ܢܝܫܐ. ܒܫܘܠܡܐ ܕܝܢ ܕܒܫܡܐ ܫܘܪܝܐ. ܐܝܟ ܗܝ ܕܒܢܦܫܐ. ܒܢܦܫܐ. ܒܫܪܝܪܘܬܐ ܕܒܢܦܫܐ.. ܡܒܬܠܐ ܕܝܢ ܐܝܬܝܗܘܢ ܠܬܠܬܐ ܦܪܝܫܬܐ ܘܫܪܝܐ.. ܦܪܝܫܬܐ ܡܢ ܐܝܟ ܕܠܡܐܡܪ ܐܝܟ. ܫܪܝܐ ܕܝܢ ܐܦܩܐ.. ܡܫܩܠܬܐ ܕܝܢ ܐܘ ܫܘܬܦܘܬܐ ܐܝܟ ܕܒܫܡܐ ܫܘܪܝܐ ܐܝܟ ܕܒܫܘܪܝܐ ܐܝܬܝܗ ܒܫܡܐ ܕܝܢ ܢܝܫܐ ܡܫܬܚܠܦܐ

1 ܘܣܟܠ ܘܡܪܟܒܘܬܐ] ܣܟܠ ܡܪܟܒܘܬܐ C 2 ܐܢܐ ܥܒܕ ܐܢܐ ܟܬܒ ܐܢܐ ܚܫܐ ܕܝܢ ܐܝܬܘܗܝ ܐܝܟ ܗܘ ܕܡܬܦܠܚ ܐܢܐ ܡܬܥܒܕ ܐܢܐ ܡܬܟܬܒ] om. C 3 ܡܪܟܒܘܬܐ] ܡܪܟܒܘܬܐ C | ܡܢ ܡܥܒܕܢܘܬܐ ܡܬܐܡܪܐ] ܡܢ...ܡܬܐܡܪܐ C 4 ܪܘܚܬ ܡܠܟܬ] ܪܘܚܬ ܚܫܒܬ ܡܠܟܬ C ܡܠܟܬ ܪܘܚܬ ܚܫܒܬ A ܚܫܒܬ] ܚܫܒܬ 5 ܘܗܘ] ܘܗܘ C 6 ܗܘ[2] ܗܝ C 7 ܐܢܐ ܘܡܬܚܫܒ] ܡܬܚܫܒ ܐܢܐ C 8 ܐܝܬܝܗܘܢ ܠܬܠܬܐ] ܐܝܬܝܗܘܢ ܠܬܠܬܐ C | ܘܡܪܟܒܐ] ܡܪܟܒܐ C 9 ܐܝܟ ܗܝ[3] ܐܝܟ ܗܝ ܐܝܬܘܗܝ C 11 ܘܣܓܝܐܘܬܐ] ܣܓܝܐܬܐ C 12 ܣܓܝܐܘܬܐ] ܣܓܝܐܬܐ C | ܘܣܓܝܐܘܬܐ] ܘܣܓܝܐܬܐ C 14 ܠܐܢܫܐ] ܠܬܪܝܢܐ C 15 ܠܐܢܫܐ] ܠܬܪܝܢܐ C 16 after ܡܡܠܠܐ C repeats ܠܬܠܝܬܝܐ ܐܝܬܘܗܝ ܗܘ ܕܥܠ 18 ܕܥܡܠܐ] ܕܥܡܠܐ C | ܐܚܪܐ] ܐܚܪܢܐ C | ܠܐ ܡܬܩܢܝܐ[2] AC (where it is a marginal gloss to correct an error below; it does not belong here) 19 ܒܬܪ] ܗܘܐ ܡܢ ܒܬܪ C | ܠܐ ܡܬܩܢܝܐ] ܡܬܩܢܝܐ AC (corrected in marg as noted above) 20 ܘܗܟܢ...ܕܡܠܬܐ] ܘܗܟܢ ܠܐܡܪ ܡܢܝܢ ܐܦ ܥܠ ܡܐܡܪܐ ܕܐܡܪ ܕܝܢ ܡܬܠܠ ܐܦ ܥܠ ܫܘܬܦܘܬܐ ܕܡܠܬܐ ܠܬܠܬܐ ܡܢܝܢܐ ܕܝܢ ܐܘ ܘܐܝܬܝܗ C 23 ܐܦ] ܕܝܢ ܐܦ C 25 ܡܢ] om. C 26 ܡܫܩܠܬܐ] ܡܫܩܠܬܐ A ܡܢ ܫܘܪܝܐ ܘܐܘ ܒܫܘܠܡܐ ܕܝܢ ܕܒܫܡܐ ܢܝܫܐ ܘܐܘ [ܕܒܢܦܫܐ ܒܫܪܝܪܘܬܐ ܒܢܦܫܐ ܕܒܢܦܫܐ ܗܝ ܐܝܟ ܫܘܪܝܐ ܕܒܫܡܐ ܕܝܢ ܒܫܘܠܡܐ ܕܫܘܪܝܐ ܕܝܢ ܠܟܠ ܢܣܒ ܠܗ ܕܝܢ ܫܪܓܐ ܡܬܬܫܡܫܐ ܡܬܬܫܡܫܐ܀ ܫܪܓܐ ܡܢ ܐܝܬܝܗܘܢ: ܐܝܟ ܗܘ ܕܒܢܦܫܐ: ܒܫܡܐ ܒܢܦܫܐ܀ C (a corrupt text that seems to discuss nouns with initial mem and taw and the aleph of the determinate state) | ܫܘܪܝܐ] ܢܝܫܐ A 27 ܡܒܬܠܐ ܕܝܢ] ܘܡܫܬܚܠܦܐ ܦܪܝܫܬܐ ܠܬܠܬܐ ܐܝܬܝܗܘܢ ܕܝܢ ܡܒܬܠܐ C 28 ܡܫܩܠܬܐ] ܡܫܩܠܬܐ C | ܕܒܫܡܐ] ܒܫܡܐ C 29 ܕܝܢ] ܫܪܝ C ܐܝܬܝܗܘܢ ܫܪܝܐ ܗܝ

ܐܝܬܘܗܝ.. ܐܦ ܗܢܐ ܕܝܢ ܥܠ ܫܪܒܐ. ܐܝܟ ܕܒܪܝܐ ܗܘܐ ܠܡܬܐܡܪܘ.. ܢܐܡܪ ܕܝܢ ܐܦ ܚܠܦ ܫܡܐ. ܗܒ
ܘܐܝܬܘܗܝ ܡܢܟܐ ܫܡܝܫܬܐ ܘܡܠܟܬܐ..

ܚܠܦ ܫܡܐ

ܚܠܦ ܫܡܐ ܕܝܢ ܐܝܬܘܗܝ ܗܟܝܠ. ܡܠܬܐ ܡܬܐܡܪܢܘܬܐ ܡܕܡ ܕܡܬܚܫܚܐ ܚܠܦ ܫܡܐ. ܘܐܝܬܘܗܝ ܡܫܘܕܥܢܘܬܐ ܕܦܪܨܘܦܐ ܡܬܚܙܝܐ.. ܢܣܩܝܢ ܠܗ ܕܝܢ ܗܠܝܢ. ܦܪܨܘܦܐ. ܓܢܣܐ. ܡܢܝܢܐ. ܡܫܘܚܬܐ ܙܒܢܐ. ܐܙܠܐ.. p.19

ܦܪܨܘܦܐ ܡܢ ܕܦܪܨܘܦܐ ܩܕܡܝܐ ܐܝܬܝܗܘܢ ܗܠܝܢ.. ܐܢܐ. ܐܢܬ. ܗܘ.. ܗܢܘܢ ܕܝܢ ܕܡܢ ܦܪܨܘܦܐ ܩܕܡܝܐ ܐܝܬܝܗܘܢ ܗܠܝܢ.. ܕܝܠܝ ܕܝܠܟ ܕܝܠܗ..

ܓܢܣܐ ܡܩܒܠ. ܟܕ ܒܢܐ ܡܠܐ ܦܡ: ܠܐ ܗܘܐ ܟܠܗܘܢ ܡܬܦܪܫܝܢ. ܟܕ ܒܠܥܒܕܐ ܕܝܢ ܡܬܦܪܫܝܢ ܐܝܟ ܗܢ ܕܐܢܬ ܘܐܢܬܝ.. ܡܛܠ ܕܝܢ ܘܟܕ ܒܢܐ ܡܠܐ ܘܟܕ ܒܠܥܒܕܐ. ܐܝܟ ܕܒܟܠܗܝܢ ܫܘܪܝܐ ܡܬܦܪܫܝܢ.. ܐܝܟ ܗܢ ܕܠܟ ܠܟܝ ܠܟܘܢ. ܗܘ ܕܝܢ ܠܗ ܠܗ ܘܐܠܗܝܢ ܕܠܗܘܢ ܕܩܕܡ.. ܗܢܘܢ ܕܝܢ ܕܡܢ ܦܪܨܘܦܐ ܩܕܡܝܐ ܡܬܐܡܪܝܢ ܐܝܬܝܗܘܢ: ܐܝܟ ܠܗ. ܗܘ ܕܠܗ. ܗܘ ܕܠܗ..

ܡܢܝܢܐ ܕܝܢ ܦܪܨܘܦܐ ܩܕܡܝܐ ܐܝܬܝܗܘܢ: ܚܕܢܝܬܐ ܦܡ: ܐܢܐ. ܐܢܬ ܗܘ.. ܣܓܝܐܝܬܐ ܕܝܢ: ܚܢܢ: ܐܢܬܘܢ. ܗܢܘܢ. ܕܝܢ ܕܡܢ ܦܪܨܘܦܐ ܩܕܡܝܐ ܡܬܐܡܪܝܢ ܐܝܬܝܗܘܢ: ܚܕܢܝܬܐ ܦܡ: ܕܝܠܝ. ܘܕܝܠܟ ܕܝܠܗ ܣܓܝܐܝܬܐ ܕܝܢ: ܕܝܠܢ. ܕܝܠܟܘܢ. ܕܝܠܗܘܢ..

ܡܫܘܚܬܐ ܐܘ ܙܒܢܐ ܕܦܪܨܘܦܐ ܩܕܡܝܐ ܐܝܬܝܗܘܢ: ܠܦܪܘܫܘ ܦܡ: ܐܢܐ ܐܢܬ ܗܘ.. ܒܡܫܘܚܬܐ ܕܝܢ ܕܕܝܠܟ ܕܕܝܠܗ ܕܕܝܠܗ..

ܡܬܐܡܪܢܘܬܐ ܕܝܢ: ܠܟ ܠܗ ܠܟܘܢ.. ܒܢܒܝܘܬܐ ܕܝܢ: ܚܢ ܚܘ ܚܢܘܢ.. ܗܢܘܢ ܕܝܢ ܕܡܢ ܦܪܨܘܦܐ ܩܕܡܝܐ ܡܬܐܡܪܝܢ ܐܝܬܝܗܘܢ: ܕܠܟ ܕܠܗ ܕܠܗ. ܠܟ ܠܗܘܢ. ܚܢ ܚܘ. ܚܢܘܢ.. ܗܓ

ܐܫܬܡܥܐ ܦܡ ܦܠܓܐ ܐܝܬܘܗܝ: ܕܠܟ ܕܠܗ ܕܠܗ.. ܡܢܝܢܐ ܕܝܢ ܐܝܬܘܗܝ. ܕܠܟ ܕܢܦܫܟ ܕܠܗ ܕܢܦܫܗ ܕܠܗ ܕܢܦܫܗ..

ܐܙܠܐ ܕܝܢ: ܡܢܗܘܢ ܦܡ ܐܝܬܝܗܘܢ ܦܪܨܘܦܐ ܩܕܡܝܐ. ܐܝܟ ܗܘ ܕܐܢܐ ܐܢܬ ܗܘ.. ܡܢܗܘܢ ܕܝܢ ܐܝܬܝܗܘܢ: ܐܝܟ ܗܢ ܕܡܬܐܡܪ ܡܢ ܦܪܨܘܦܐ ܐܝܟ ܠܟܘܢ ܐܝܟܢ ܕܡܫܡܠܝܬܐ ܐܠܦܝܢ ܐܘ ܐܝܟܢ ܕܐܦ ܕܠܘܬ ܦܪܨܘܦܐ ܡܬܐܡܪܝܢ. ܐܝܬܝܗܘܢ ܕܝܢ ܐܢܫܝܐ. ܐܝܟܢ ܕܠܚܕ ܡܠܐ ܡܫܘܕܥܝܢ: ܐܝܟ ܗܢ ܕܠܗܘܢ. ܡܫܡܠܝܐ ܕܝܢ ܐܝܬܝܗܘܢ: ܕܠܗܘܢ ܠܐܢܫܐ. ܡܢܗܘܢ ܦܡ ܐܝܬܝܗܘܢ: ܐܝܟ ܗܢ. ܕܕܠܟ ܕܕܠܗ ܕܕܠܗ ܣܓܝܐܝܬܐ ܦܡ: ܐܝܟ ܕܡܢ ܣܓܝܐܐ. ܐܝܟ ܗܢ ܕܣܢܝ. ܕܠܗ.. ܡܢܗܘܢ ܕܚܠܦ ܫܡܐ ܐܝܬܝܗܘܢ ܥܡ ܫܪܒܐ.. ܡܢܗܘܢ ܕܝܢ ܕܠܐ ܫܪܒܐ.. ܘܥܡ ܫܪܒܐ ܥܡ ܐܝܬܝܗܘܢ. ܐܝܟ ܗܘ ܕܗܘ ܕܠܗ ܗܘ ܕܗܘ ܕܠܗ.. ܘܠܐ ܫܪܒܐ ܕܝܢ ܐܝܬܝܗܘܢ: ܐܝܟ ܗܘ ܕܐܢܐ. ܐܢܬ. ܗܘ.. ܘܗܟܢ ܠܐܡܪܝܢ ܥܠ ܚܠܦ ܫܡܐ.. ܢܐܡܪ ܕܝܢ ܐܦ ܥܠ ܡܫܡܫܢܘܬܐ ܫܡܝܫܐ ܘܐܝܬܘܗܝ ܡܢܟܐ ܡܠܬܐ ܘܡܠܟܬܐ.. p.20

[ܕܝܢ...ܫܡܐ 4 C ܡܟܝܠ ܐܦ ܥܠ ܗܢ ܕܡܬܐܡܪ ܡܢ ܣܓܝܐܐ [2ܐܦ | C ܗܟܢ ܠܐܡܪ ܡܢܝܢ ܗܘܐ [ܕܝܢ ܗܢܐ ܐܦ 1
C ܡܩܒܠܬܐ [ܡܩܘܒܠܬܐ 5 C ܘܐܦ ܗܠܐ ܗܢܐ ܕܚܠܦ ܫܡܐ ܐܝܬܘܗܝ ܡܬܐܡܪܢܘܬܐ ܡܕܡ ܕܚܠܦ ܫܡܐ ܡܬܚܫܚܐ
ܓܢܣܐ ܕܝܢ ܕܡܢ A ܓܢܣܐ ܕܦܪܨܘܦܐ [ܓܢܣܐ 9 C ܡܬܐܡܪܝܢ ܐܝܬܝܗܘܢ 8 C ܗܘ [ܗܘܐ 7 C ܙܒܢܐ [ܙܒܢܐ 6
ܚܘ ܠܗ [ܠܗ ܠܗ | C ܗܘ ܗܘܐ [ܗܘܐ ܗܘ 11 C .om [ܕܝܢ | A ܘܐܢܬ ܘܐܢܬ [ܘܐܢܬܝ ܘܐܢܬ 10 C ܦܪܨܘܦܐ
ܐܝܟ [ܘܠܟܘܢ ܗܘ ܠܟ ܐܝܟ | C ܦܪܨܘܦܐ ܩܕܡܝܐ [ܩܕܡܝܐ ܦܪܨܘܦܐ | C .om [ܕܝܢ 12 C ܠܗܘܢ [ܘܠܗܘܢ | C
C ܘܗܢܘܢ [ܗܢܘܢ 14 C ܗܘ [ܗܘܐ | C ܕܦܪܨܘܦܐ ܩܕܡܝܐ [ܩܕܡܝܐ ܦܪܨܘܦܐ 13 C ܗܢ ܕܗܘ ܕܠܗ ܘܕܠܗ
ܡܩܘܒܠܬܐ [ܡܩܒܠܬܐ 16 C ܕܗܘ A ܗܘ [ܕܗܘܐ | C ܡܬܐܡܪܝܢ [ܡܬܐܡܪܝܢ | C ܦܪܨܘܦܐ ܩܕܡܝܐ [ܩܕܡܝܐ ܦܪܨܘܦܐ
ܚܢ ܚܘ 19 C ܕܠܗ ܕܠܗ ܕܗܘ | A ܕܕܠܗ [ܕܕܠܗ 17 C ܗܘ [ܗܘܐ | C ܩܕܡܝܐ [ܩܕܡܝܐ | C ܦܡ
C ܐܝܟ ܡܬܐܡܪܝܢ ܡܢ ܦܪܨܘܦܐ 23 C ܗܘ [ܗܘܐ | C ܗܢ [ܗܘ | C ܕܦܪܨܘܦܐ [ܦܪܨܘܦܐ 22 C ܠܗܘܢ
ܘܐܦ ܡܢ ܠܘܬ A ܘܐܦ ܠܘܬ ܦܪܨܘܦܐ ܡܬܐܡܪܝܢ [ܡܬܐܡܪܝܢ ܦܪܨܘܦܐ ܕܠܘܬ ܘܐܦ 24 transp. C [ܐܠܦܝܢ ܕܡܫܡܠܝܬܐ
C ܦܪܨܘܦܐ ܡܬܐܡܪܝܢ | C ܐܢܐ ܦܡ ܕܝܢ [ܕܝܢ ܐܝܬܝܗܘܢ | C ...ܐܝܬܝܗܘܢ26 [ܕܝܢ see comment in translation. C
reads: ܐܝܬܝܗܘܢ ܕܠܗܘܢ ܡܢܗܐ ܡܫܘܕܥܝܢ ܐܝܟ ܗܢ ܕܕܠܟ ܕܕܠܗ ܕܗܘ ܡܢ ܣܓܝܐܐ ܕܝܢ ܐܝܟ ܗܢ ܕܣܢܝ ܕܠܗ
C ܫܪܒܐ [2ܫܪܒܐ | C ܠܐ ܫܪܒܐ [ܫܪܒܐ ܘܠܐ | C ܫܪܒܐ [1ܫܪܒܐ 27 C ܡܢ ܗܘܢ ܗܟܢܐ ܕܟܠܐ [ܡܢܗܘܢ 26
C ܗܢ [ܗܘ | C ܫܪܒܐ [ܫܪܒܐ | A ܗܘ ܕܠܗ [ܕܠܗ ܕܗܘ ܗܘ | C ܗܘ [ܕܗܘ ܗܘ 28 C ܗܢ [ܗܘ
C ܫܡܝܫܐ [ܫܡܝܫܐ 29 C ܥܠ ܗܠܐ ܗܘ ܕܡܬܐܡܪ [ܥܠ | C ܠܐܡܪ ܐܦ [ܠܐܡܪܝܢ | C ܘܗܟܢ ܡܢ [ܘܗܟܢ

ܥܠ ܡܦܩܬܐ ܫܡܗܐ..

ܡܦܩܬܐ ܫܡܗܐ ܕܝܢ ܐܝܬܝܗ̇ ܡܬܬܪܢܘܬܐ ܡܢܗ̇ ܗ̇ܝ ܕܡܬܦܩܐ ܡܬܬܫܡܗܐ: ܒܪܝܫ ܟܠܗܝܢ ܡܢܘܬܐ ܕܡܠܬܐ:

ܘܒܪܘܒܟܠܗܝܢ ܘܠܦܠܓܘܬܗܝܢ. ܐܝܬܝܗܝܢ ܕܝܢ ܟܠܗܝܢ ܐܝܟ ܕܒܟܬܒܐ ܢܘܗܪܐ. ܠܡܦܪܫܘ ܦܢܝܬܐ ܡܢ ܗ̇ܠ ܗܒ
ܡܬܒܥܐ ܕܝܢ ܠܘܬܗܝܢ.. ܒܟܬܒܐ ܕܝܢ ܗܘܢܝܐ. ܠܐ ܡܕܡ ܕܠܒܪ ܠܓܘܫܡܐ. ܘܡܬܟܬܒܐ ܡܬܟܬܒܢ. ܘܡܬܟܬܒܐ ܐܝܟ ܒܟܬܐ ܕܡܥܒܕ ܐܢܐ ܗܫܐ ܐܢܐ ܒܗܘܢ: ܕܠܐܝܬ ܕܟܝܢܗܘܢ ܒܦܪܘܫܐ.. ܦܫܝܛܐܝܬ ܘܥܠ ܐܝܬܝܗܝܢ ܘܟܠܗܝܢ. ܡܢ. ܟܠܗ. ܟܠ. ܡܕܡ. ܟܘܠ. ܐܝܟ ܕܒܡܐܡܪ. ܡܢ ܒܡܠܬܐ܀ ܟܠܗ ܒܡܠܬܐ܀ ܒܢ ܒܡܠܬܐ ܡܢ ܒܡܠܬܐ܀ ܟܠܗ ܒܡܠܬܐ. ܘܟܠܗܝܢ ܗ̇ܢܝܢ ܠܐ ܘܦܩܢ ܥܠ ܢܦܫܗܘܢ܀ ܡܬܒܥܐ ܕܝܢ ܐܝܬܝܗܘܢ ܘܟܠܗܝܢ. ܟܠܗܝ. ܟܠܝܗ. ܟܗ. ܟܡܐ ܟܡܐ. ܣܓܝ. ܟܠ. ܟܠܗܘܢ. ܟܝܘܡ. ܠܐܝܬ. ܐܝܬ. ܡܢܐ.. ܐܦ ܥܠ ܘܟܠܗܝܢ ܠܐܝܬ ܟܡܐ ܕܡܕܡ. ܢܐܡܪ ܕܝܢ ܐܦ ܥܠ ܥܠ ܡܐܡܪܐ ܘܐܝܬܘܗܝ ܡܢܝܢܐ ܡܫܡܫܢܐ ܕܡܠܬܐ..

ܥܠ ܥܠ ܡܐܡܪܐ

ܥܠ ܡܐܡܪܐ ܕܝܢ ܐܦܢܝܢ ܣܓܝܐܐ. ܘܐܝܬܘܗܝ ܡܢܝܢܐ ܕܡܠܬܐ ܠܐ ܡܬܦܠܓܢܐ ܕܡܬܐܡܪܐ ܥܠ ܡܐܡܪܐ ܐܘ ܒܟܠܗܘܢ ܕܡܐܡܪܐ.. ܡܢܗܝܢ ܕܥܠ ܡܐܡܪܐ ܐܝܬܝܗܝܢ ܦܢܝܬܐ. ܡܢܗܝܢ ܕܝܢ ܡܬܒܥܝܢܐ. ܘܡܢܗܝܢ ܡܬܦܩܢܘܬܐ ܐܝܟ ܟܠܗܝܢ.. ܦܢܝܬܐ ܗܝ ܐܝܬܝܗܝܢ ܐܝܟ ܗ̇ܝ ܕܒܥܠܡܐ. ܡܬܒܥܝܢܐ ܕܝܢ ܐܝܟ ܗ̇ܝ p.21
ܕܒܥܠܡܐ ܥܠܡܝܢܐ ܘܡܢܗܘܢ ܡܢ ܐܝܬܝܗܝܢ ܡܫܘܕܥܢܝܬܐ ܕܐܢܫܐ.. ܐܝܟ ܗ̇ܘ ܕܐܬܐ. ܗ̇ܪܟܐ. ܗܪܟܐ.. ܠܗܠܝܢ ܕܝܢ ܐܝܟ ܐܬܪܐ ܢܗܝܪ ܐܢܫ ܠܐܬܪܐ ܐܚܪܢܐ. ܡܫܬܡܫܢܝܬܐ ܕܐܚܪܢܐ ܩܕܡ.. ܐܝܟ ܗ̇ܝ ܕܩܕܡܝܐ. ܠܥܠܡ.

ܠܥܠܡ ܡܢܝ. ܐܬܡܠܝ ܡܢ ܐܬܡܠܝ.. ܠܡܢܗܝܢ ܕܝܢ ܡܬܦܩܢܘܬܐ. ܐܝܟ ܗ̇ܝ ܕܐܬܐܡܪܬ. ܢܘܗܪܐܝܬ. ܘܗܘ
ܡܬܡܠܝܐ.. ܠܡܢܗܝܢ ܕܝܢ ܕܒܩܘܕܡܝܐ. ܐܝܟ ܡܦܩ. ܒܫܢܬ. ܫܒܥܠܐܝܬ ܒܫܢܝܐܝܬ ܒܝܬܝܬܐ..
ܠܡܢܗܝܢ ܕܝܢ ܕܒܡܦܩܢܘܬܐ. ܐܝܟ ܗ̇ܝ ܕܫܒܥܐܝܬ ܒܟܘܪܝܬܐ..
ܡܢܗܘܢ ܕܝܢ: ܡܫܘܕܥܢܐ ܐܝܬܝܗܘܢ ܕܩܢܘܡܐ ܘܡܬܢܝܢܐ. ܐܝܟ ܗ̇ܝ ܕܚܕ. ܬܪܝܢ. ܬܠܬܐ..
ܡܢܗܘܢ ܕܝܢ ܡܫܘܕܥܢܐ ܕܐܬܪܘܬܐ. ܐܝܟ ܗ̇ܝ ܕܒܐܬܪܐ ܠܐܬܪܐ.. ܡܢܗܘܢ ܕܝܢ ܐܬܪܢܝܐ ܐܝܬܝܗܘܢ ܐܝܟ ܗ̇ܝ ܕܥܠ. ܒܐܝܟܐ.. ܗܘܝܘ ܕܒܫܘܠܡܗܘܢ ܐܝܬܝܗܘܢ ܠܐܬܪܐ.. ܐܝܟ ܗ̇ܘ ܠܐܬܪܐ ܒܐܬܪܐ. ܡܢ ܐܬܪܐ.. ܐܝܟ ܗ̇ܝ ܕܒܐܬܪܐ. ܒܟܠܐ ܡܢ ܒܟܠܐ.
ܡܢܗܘܢ ܕܝܢ ܡܫܘܕܥܢܐ ܐܢܘܢ ܕܙܒܢܐ.. ܐܝܟ ܗ̇ܝ ܕܝܘܡܢܐ. ܒܝܡܡܐ. ܒܠܠܝܐ.
ܡܢܗܘܢ ܕܝܢ ܡܚܘܝܢܐ ܐܢܘܢ ܕܦܘܩܕܢܐ ܐܝܟ ܗ̇ܝ ܕܐܙܠ. ܬܐ..
ܡܢܗܘܢ ܕܝܢ ܡܬܡܪܢܐ ܐܝܬܝܗܘܢ. ܐܝܟ ܗ̇ܝ ܕܚܒܢ..
ܡܢܗܘܢ ܕܝܢ ܡܫܘܕܥܢܐ ܐܢܘܢ ܕܫܘܐܠܐ ܐܘ ܕܟܦܪܢܐ. ܐܝܟ ܗ̇ܝ ܕܠܐ. ܠܘ. ܠܐ ܗܘܐ ܠܐ ܕܝܢ ܠܐ ܟܠ ܟܠܗ..

C ܡܬܬܫܡܗܐ] ܡܬܬܫܡܗܐ C | ܗ̇ܝ] ܒܗ̇ܝ C | ܡܬܬܪܢܘܬܐ] ܡܬܬܪܢܘܬܐ ܘܡܬܬܫܡܗܐ C 2 ܥܠ] ܕܥܠ C 1 ܟܠܗܝܢ] ܒܟܠܗܝܢ C | ܐܝܬܝܗܘܢ] ܐܝܬܝܗܝܢ C | ܘܠܦܠܓܘܬܗܝܢ] ܠܦܠܓܘܬܗܝܢ C 4 ܡܢܘܬܐ ܕܡܠܬܐ] ܡܢܘܬܗܝܢ ܕܡܠܬܐ C 3 ܘܡܬܟܬܒܐ 6 ܡܬܟܬܒܢ] ܘܡܬܟܬܒܐ ܡܬܟܬܒܢ C ܠܐ 5 ܗ̇ܠ] ܗ̇ܠܝܢ C | ܗܠ] ܠܡܦܪܫܘ ܒܗܢܐ C | ܠܡܦܪܫܘ] C | ܐܝܟ ܒܟܬܐ ܕܡܥܒܕ ܐܢܐ] ܐܝܟ ܕܒܟܬܐ ܐܦ ܐܢܐ ܘܡܬܟܬܒܐ C 7 ܡܢ[1]...9 ܘܟܠܗܝܢ] om. A 8 after ܢܦܫܗܘܢ] C adds ܐܝܟ ܕܒܟܬܐ ܒܝܬ ܐܝܟ AC ܥܠ ܡܐܡܪܐ] ܥܠ ܥܠ ܡܐܡܪܐ | C ܢܐܡܪ] ܢܐܡܪ C | ܡܕܡ ܐܝܟ ܕܡܕܡ] ܕܡܕܡ 10 ܐܝܟ ܒܟܬܐ ܢܘܗܪܐ ܡܢܗܘܢ ܘܥܠ ܘܒܬܪ ܩܠܐ [ܡܢܗܝܢ[1] 14 om. A [ܡܐܡܪܐ[2] ܥܠ 13 AC ܥܠ ܡܐܡܪܐ] ܡܐܡܪܐ ܥܠ ܥܠ 12 ܗ̇ܝ ܐܝܟ | om. C [ܠܗܘܢ ܐܝܟ ܡܬܦܩܢܘܬܐ ܘܡܢܗܝܢ 15 C ܡܢܗܘܢ [ܡܢܗܝܢ[2] | C ܐܝܬܝܗܘܢ [ܐܝܬܝܗܝܢ] C | ܗܪܟܐ 16 om. A (homoeoteleuton) [ܐܝܬܝܗܝܢ ܡܢ ܘܡܢܗܘܢ ܥܠܡܝܢܐ ܘܒܥܠܡܐ ܗ̇ܝ ܐܝܟ ܕܝܢ ܡܬܒܥܝܢܐ ܕܒܥܠܡܐ] [ܡܢܝ ܠܥܠܡ 19 C ܕܝܢ ܕܐܚܪܢܐ [ܩܕܡ ܕܐܚܪܢܐ] | om. A [ܐܬܪܐ] | om. C [ܐܝܟ[1] 17 C ܗܪܟܐ ܗܪܟܐ [ܗܪܟܐ] ܡܢܗܝܢ ܕܝܢ ܕܐܬܡܠܝܬ [ܕܒܩܘܕܡܝܐ] ܕܝܢ ܠܡܢܗܝܢ 20 C ܡܢܗܝܢ ܕܝܢ ܡܬܦܩܢܘܬܐ [ܡܬܦܩܢܘܬܐ ܕܝܢ ܠܡܢܗܝܢ] | C ܥܠܡ ܡܢܝ C ܒܟܘܪܝܬܐ [ܒܟܘܪܝܬܐ] 21 C ܒܝܬܝܬܐ ܒܫܢܝܐܝܬ [ܒܝܬܝܬܐ ܒܫܢܝܐܝܬ] | C ܘܡܦܩ ܒܫܢܬ [ܒܫܢܬ ܡܦܩ] | C ܡܢܗܘܢ [ܐܝܬܝܗܘܢ ܐܬܪܘܬܐ ܕܝܢ ܡܢܗܘܢ ܠܐܬܪܐ ܘܒܐܬܪܐ ܗ̇ܝ ܐܝܟ ܘܐܬܪܘܬܐ ܡܫܘܕܥܢܐ ܕܝܢ ܡܢܗܘܢ 23 om. C [ܕܩܢܘܡܐ] 22 C ܘܒܝܡܡܐ [ܒܝܡܡܐ] C ܗ̇ܝ ܘܠܐܬܪܐ [ܠܐܬܪܐ ܗ̇ܘ] 24 (ܐܬܪܢܝܐ error for ܐܬܪܢܝܐ) C ܕܝܢ ܐܬܪܢܝܐ ܐܝܬܝܗܘܢ C ܘܐܙܠ ܗ̇ܝ [ܬܐ ܘܐܙܠ] | C ܡܚܘܝܢܐ ܐܢܘܢ ܕܦܘܩܕܢܐ [ܕܦܘܩܕܢܐ ܐܢܘܢ ܡܚܘܝܢܐ] 27 om. C [ܒܠܠܝܐ ܒܝܡܡܐ] 28 ܘܚܒܢ] C adds ܡܢܐ 29 ܐܢܘܢ] ܐܝܬܝܗܘܢ C | ܘܟܦܪܢܐ] ܘܕܟܦܪܢܐ C | ܗܘܐ] ܗܘܐ C | ܠܐ[3]] om. AC

ܡܢܗܘܢ ܕܝܢ ܡܫܘܕܥܢܐ ܐܢܘܢ ܕܐܘܪܚܐ. ܕܦܠܚܘܬܐ. ܐܝܟ ܗܢܘ ܕܐܢ. ܐܝܢ. ܐܝܟܢܐ. ܐܝܟܢ..
ܡܢܗܘܢ ܕܝܢ ܡܚܒܪܢܐ ܐܢܘܢ ܘܠܐ ܡܫܬܘܬܦܢܘܬܐ. ܐܝܟ ܗܢܘ ܕܠܚܘܕ. ܗܘ..
p.22 ܡܢܗܘܢ ܕܝܢ ܐܝܟ ܕܙܒܢܐ ܘܫܐܠܬܐ ܐܝܬܝܗܘܢ. ܐܝܟ ܗܢܘ. ܕܐܡܬܝ. ܐܡܬܝ ܓܝܪ. ܐܡܬܝ ܕܝܢ..
ܡܢܗܘܢ ܡܫܪܪܢܘܬܐ ܐܝܟ ܗܢܘ ܕܫܪܝܪ. ܫܪ. ܟܡܐ ܐܚܪܢܝܢ..
ܗܗ ܡܢܗܘܢ ܕܝܢ ܡܫܘܕܥܢܐ ܐܢܘܢ ܕܡܢܝܢܐ ܡܕܡ. ܐܝܟ ܗܢܘ ܕܙܒܢܝܢ. ܐܚܕܐ. ܡܚܕܐ ܐܚܪܢ..
ܡܢܗܘܢ ܕܝܢ ܡܫܘܕܥܢܐ ܐܢܘܢ ܕܛܘܟܣܐ ܐܝܟ ܗܢܘ ܕܒܬܪܟܢ. ܡܢܗ ܘܠܗܠ. ܘܡܢܗ ܘܠܥܠ..
ܡܢܗܘܢ ܕܝܢ ܦܩܘܕܐ ܐܢܘܢ. ܐܝܟ ܗܢܘ ܕܐܘܦܐ. ܐܘܟܠ. ܐܝܬܐ. ܗܠܐ. ܬܐ. ܗܒ..
ܡܢܗܘܢ ܕܝܢ ܡܕܡܝܢܐ ܐܝܬܝܗܘܢ. ܐܝܟ ܗܢܘ ܕܡܠܟܐܝܬ ܟܪܝܐܝܬ..
ܡܢܗܘܢ ܕܝܢ ܡܫܐܠܢܐ ܐܝܬܝܗܘܢ. ܐܝܟ ܗܢܘ ܕܐܝܡܟܐ. ܐܝܟܢ. ܐܝܟܘ. ܐܝܡܐ. ܐܝܡܬܝ..
ܡܢܗܘܢ ܕܝܢ ܡܬܒܥܝܢܐ ܐܝܬܝܗܘܢ ܕܨܠܘܬܐ. ܐܝܟ ܗܢܘ ܕܒܥܝܢ ܠܟ. ܡܛܠ ܠܟ..
ܡܢܗܘܢ ܕܝܢ ܥܠ ܡܬܘܡܝܘܬܐ ܡܫܘܕܥܝܢ. ܐܝܟ ܗܢܐ ܕܐܝܡ ܕܐܦܠܡ..
ܡܢܗܘܢ ܕܝܢ ܡܬܚܫܚܢܐ ܐܢܘܢ ܕܡܬܘܡܝܘܬܐ. ܐܝܟ ܗܢܐ ܕܠܐ ܐܦܠܡ
ܡܢܗܘܢ ܡܫܪܪܢܐ ܐܢܘܢ. ܐܝܟ ܗܢܘ ܕܒܫܠܡܐ ܗܘ. ܚܝܡܐ ܗܘ..
ܡܢܗܘܢ ܕܝܢ ܕܐܘܣܟܬܐ ܐܝܟ ܗܢܘ ܕܢܗܘܐ. ܢܗܘܐ..
ܡܢܗܘܢ ܕܝܢ ܥܘܕܪܐ ܕܡܘܟܟܐ ܡܢܝܢ. ܐܝܟ ܗܢܐ ܕܥܡܝܢܐܝܬ ܘܗܘܕܝܐܝܬ. ܠܐܡܗܐܝܬ..

ܐܦ ܗܕܐ ܡܢܝܐ ܥܡܝܡܝܬܐ ܕܡܠܬܐ. ܐܝܟ ܕܡܫܬܡܥܐ ܠܐܡܪ ܡܢܝܢ.. ܢܐܡܪ ܕܝܢ ܐܦ ܥܠ ܐܣܪܐ. ܘܐܠܘ ܗܢܝܢ ܡܢܝܐ ܠܡܨܥܬܐ ܕܡܠܬܐ. ܘܚܣܝܢ ܠܡܠܬܐ. ܘܠܐ ܢܦܘܩ ܠܒܪ ܡܢ ܡܫܘܚܬܐ ܕܐܪܓܬܐ: ܘܢܩܘܡ ܫܪܝܛ ܠܫܪܒܐ..

ܗܪ

ܥܠ ܐܣܪܐ

p.23 ܐܣܪܐ ܗܟܝܠ ܐܝܬܘܗܝ. ܡܬܐܡܪܢܘܬܐ ܡܕܡ. ܕܐܣܪܐ ܠܪܚܝܩܐ ܥܡ ܩܪܝܒܐ. ܘܫܘܝܐ ܠܐܫܘܝܘܬܐ ܘܡܫܬܥܒܕܢܘܬܐ ܕܡܠܬܐ ܕܦܘܫܩܐ.. ܡܢܗܘܢ ܕܝܢ ܕܐܣܪܐ ܐܝܬܝܗܘܢ ܡܣܬܝܪܐ. ܡܢܗܘܢ ܕܝܢ ܡܦܪܫܢܐ. ܡܢܗܘܢ ܕܝܢ ܡܩܦܝܢܐ. ܡܢܗܘܢ ܕܝܢ ܡܛܠ ܡܩܦܝܢܐ. ܡܢܗܘܢ ܕܝܢ ܥܠܠܝܬܐ. ܡܢܗܘܢ ܕܝܢ ܡܬܐܡܪܢܐ. ܡܢܗܘܢ ܕܝܢ ܣܘܩܒܠܐ. ܡܢܗܘܢ ܕܝܢ ܡܫܡܠܝܢܐ ܐܝܬܝܗܘܢ܀

ܡܣܬܝܪܐ ܗܟܝܠ ܐܝܬܝܗܘܢ: ܐܝܠܝܢ ܕܠܦܘܩܕܐ ܕܡܫܒܪܝܢ ܠܒܪ ܡܢ ܡܫܘܚܬܐ ܡܫܢܝܢ ܘܡܣܝܒܪܝܢ ܠܗܘܢ. ܐܝܟ ܗܢܘ ܕܦܘܡ. ܕܝܢ. ܐܦ. ܐܠܐ. ܐܘ ܦܘܡ. ܐܘ ܕܝܢ. ܐܘ ܐܝܟܢ..

ܡܦܪܫܢܐܝܬ ܕܝܢ ܐܝܬܝܗܘܢ ܐܝܠܝܢ ܕܠܡܫܡܠܝܘ ܦܬܓܡ ܥܡ ܚܒܪܗ: ܘܡܦܪܫܝܢ ܡܢ ܣܘܟܠܐ ܠܣܘܟܠܐ. ܐܝܟ ܗܢܘ ܕܐܘ. ܐܘܟܝ. ܐܘܟܝܬ. ܐܘ ܐܢ..

ܡܩܦܝܢܐ ܕܝܢ ܐܝܬܝܗܘܢ ܠܟܠܗܘܢ ܐܝܠܝܢ ܕܥܠ ܗܘܝܐ ܡܕܡ ܡܫܘܕܥܝܢ: ܥܠ ܢܦܩܘܬܐ ܕܝܢ ܡܣܩܝܢ. ܐܝܟ ܗܢܘ ܕܐܢ. ܐܢܗܘ. ܐܢܝܢ. ܐܢܝܢ ܗܘܝ܀

1 ܕܦܠܚܘܬܐ] C ܘܕܦܠܚܘܬܐ | ܐܢ…ܐܝܟܢ] C ܐܢ ܐܝܢ ܟܢ 3 ܘܫܐܠܬܐ] C ܘܫܐܠܬܐ 4 ܡܫܪܪܢܘܬܐ] C ܡܢܗܘܢ ܕܝܢ ܡܫܪܪܢܘܬܐ
ܐܚܪܢ ܡܚܕܐ] C ܡܚܕܐܝܬ ܐܚܪܢ | ܕܙܒܢܝܢ] C ܕܙܒܢܐ | ܡܫܘܕܥܢܐ] C ܡܘܕܥܢܐ 5 ܕܒܬܪ] A ܕܒܬܪ | C ܡܘܕܥܝܢ
6 ܕܒܬܪܟܢ] C ܕܒܬܪܟ | ܘܠܗܠ] om. C 9 ܐܝܬܝܗܘܢ] C ܐܢܘܢ | ܕܐܝܡܟܐ] C ܐܝܟܐ 11 ܕܐܝܡ ܕܐܦܠܡ] C
14 ܕܐܘܣܟܬܐ] C adds ܡܢܗܘܢ ܕܝܢ ܡܬܚܫܚܢܐ ܐܢܘܢ ܕܡܬܘܡܝܘܬܐ. ܐܝܟ ܗܢܐ ܕܠܐ ܐܦܠܡ [ ] after | C ܐܝܡ ܕܐܦܠܡ
ܠܐܡܗܐܝܬ] | C ܥܘܕܪܐ] C ܥܘܕܪܐ 15 Nöldeke [Review, 1216] C ܢܗܘܐ [ܢܗܘܐ] | C ܘܐܠܘܗܝ
ܐܦ ܥܠ ܗܕܐ ܡܢܝܐ ܥܡܝܡܝܬܐ C adds ܡܢܝܢ after | C ܗܟܢ ܡܢ [ܗܕܐ…ܕܡܠܬܐ] 16 C ܠܥܡܗܐܝܬ ܗܘܕܝܐܝܬ
ܘܐܠܘ [ܫܪܝܛ ܘܢܩܘܡ] 18 C ܘܚܣܝܢ ܠܡܠܬܐ [ܠܡܠܬܐ ܘܚܣܝܢ] 17 C ܢܐܡܪ ܕܝܢ ܐܝܟ ܕܡܫܬܡܥܐ | ܕܡܠܬܐ
ܡܩܦܝܢܐ ܕܝܢ ܡܢܗܘܢ ܡܦܪܫܢܐ ܕܝܢ ܡܢܗܘܢ | C ܘܡܫܬܥܒܕܢܘܬܐ [ܘܡܫܬܥܒܕܢܘܬܐ] 21 C ܘܡܬܐܡܪܢܐ [ܘܫܘܝܐ] 20 C ܥܡܝܡܝܬܐ
ܐܝܬܝܗܘܢ] om. A ܡܢܗܘܢ ܕܝܢ ܡܫܡܠܝܢܐ ܡܢܗܘܢ ܕܝܢ ܣܘܩܒܠܐ ܡܢܗܘܢ 23 om. A [ܡܩܦܝܢܐ ܡܛܠ ܕܝܢ ܡܢܗܘܢ
ܡܦܪܫܢܐܝܬ] 26 C ܐܠܐ ܐܘ ܦܘܡ ܐܘ ܕܝܢ ܐܘ ܐܢ A ܐܠܐ ܐܘ ܦܘܡ ܕܝܢ ܐܘ ܐܝܟܢ [ܐܠܐ…ܐܝܟܢ] 25 C ܡܣܝܒܪܝܢ [ܘܡܣܝܒܪܝܢ] 24
ܗܘܝܐ] | Nöldeke [Review, 1216] C ܡܩܦܝܢܐ [ܡܩܦܝܢܐ] 28 C ܠܟܠܗܘܢ ܐܝܠܝܢ [ܐܝܠܝܢ] | C ܡܦܪܫܢܐ
ܐܢ] C om. ܐܢ | om. A ܐܢ] 29 C ܦܘܡ ܠܐ ܡܫܘܕܥܝܢ [ܡܫܘܕܥܝܢ] | C ܐܝܬܘܬܐ A ܐܝܬܘܬܐ

ܡܠܐܢ ܡܥܒܕܢܐ ܕܝܢ ܐܝܬܝܗܘܢ. ܟܠܗܘܢ ܐܝܠܝܢ ܕܒܗܝܢ ܗܘܝܘܬܐ ܐܦ ܛܒܥܐ ܡܬܝܕܥܝܢ. ܐܝܟ ܗܢܐ ܕܟܠܐ. ܕܟܠܐ ܟܠܐ. ܕܗܘ. ܟܠܐ ܕܝܢ. ܟܠܐ ܟܠܐ ܕܝܢ ܕܗܘ.

ܗܣ
p.24 | ܒܟܠܡܬܐ ܕܝܢ ܐܝܬܝܗܘܢ: ܐܝܠܝܢ ܕܟܠ ܦܘܪܫܢܐ ܡܠܬܐ ܚܝܠܬܐ ܡܬܝܕܥܝܢ. ܘܡܠܬܐ ܗܝ ܒܟܠܡܬܐ ܡܬܬܚܡܝܢ. ܐܝܟ ܗܢܐ ܕܐܡܪ. ܐܡܝܢ.

ܡܬܐܡܪܢܐ ܕܝܢ ܐܝܬܝܗܘܢ: ܗܢܘܢ ܕܒܗ ܡܬܦܫܩܝܢ ܗܦܟܬܐ ܡܬܕܡܝܢ ܠܡܦܫܩ ܐܢܘܢ

ܡܬܐܡܪܢܐ ܕܝܢ ܐܝܬܝܗܘܢ ܟܠܗܘܢ ܐܝܠܝܢ ܕܠܘܩܒܠ ܣܓܝܐ ܘܡܘܬܪܐ ܘܐܣܩܘܠܐ ܡܫܡܫܝܢ. ܐܝܟ ܗܢܐ ܕܐܘܐ.. ܐܠܐ ܐܝܬ ܦܡ

ܡܩܒܠܢܐ ܕܝܢ ܐܝܬܝܗܘܢ: ܟܠܗܘܢ ܐܝܠܝܢ ܕܡܠܬܐ ܡܫܘܚܠܦܬܐ ܐܘ ܙܒܢܐ ܡܬܚܫܒܝܢ. ܐܝܟ ܗܢܐ ܐܝܢ. ܐܘܐ. ܐܝܟ ܕܝܢ. ܐܝܟ ܠܐ ܦܡ. ܐܝܟ ܡܢ ܐܝܟ ܟܡܐ

ܠܘܬ ܐܢܫܝܢ ܕܡܘܫܚܝܢ ܟܠܗܘܢ ܐܦ ܗܢܘܢ ܕܠܡܘܬܒܐ. ܕܟܪܘ.. ܟܪܘ ܕܝܢ. ܐܦ ܗܟܢ ܐܬܐܡܪ ܡܢ ܟܠܐ ܐܚܪܢܐ..

ܗܘ
| p.25 ܟܠܐ ܡܕܡ ܐܢܫ ܠܐ ܐܫܟܚܬ ܟܠܗܝܢ. ܠܐܝܠܝܢ ܕܝܢ ܕܐܫܟܚܬ ܐܝܟ ܕܡܨܐ ܐܢܐ. ܡܟܬܒܬ ܫܡܥܬ ܐܝܟ ܕܒܦܘܪܫܢܐ ܘܒܡܫܘܕܥܢܘܬܐ ܕܐܝܠܝܢ ܕܟܬܝܒܝܢ ܠܟܬܒܐ..※

A only ܐܝܟ ܕܒܣܘܟܠܐ ܕܝܢ ܡܠܬܐ ܦܠܚ ܐܢܐ ܠܗ ܠܟܬܒܐ ܚܕܐ ܡܬܬܪܓܡܢܘܬܐ. ܘܗܘܝܬ ܐܢܐ ܒܟܬܒܐ ܠܐܝܠܝܢ ܕܣܝܡܝܢ ܣܘܟܠܝܗܘܢ. ܕܒ ܢܫܟܚܘܢ ܡܕܡ ܒܟܬܒܐ ܐܝܟ ܣܟܠܘܬܝ: ܠܐܝܬܝ ܢܬܪܥܘܢ ܘܠܐ ܢܫܟܚܘ. ܕܐܝܠܝܢ ܕܒܫܡܥܬ ܡܬܬܒܝܢ ܕܢ ܡܫܡܫܢܘܬܗܘܢ ܢܬܪܘܢ. ܘܢܦܪܩܘܢ ܠܡܬܝܒܘܬܗܘܢ ܐܓܪܐ ܕܒܥܡܠܗܘܢ.. ܘܡܢܐ ܢܫܟܚܘܢ ܠܚܘܒܐ ܕܡܫܝܚܐ. ܘܢܬܟܠܘܢ ܠܚܘܒܗ ܘܢܥܕܘܢ ܠܫܘܒܚܗ ܠܥܠܡܐ ܕܥܠܡܝܢ ܡܢ ܥܡ ܐܒܐ ܘܪܘܚܐ ܩܕܝܫܐ. ܕܗܘ ܒܗ ܐܬܓܠܝܬ ܐܠܗܘܬܐ❖❖❖

C only ܚܪܡ ܕܝܢ ܐܝܟ ܕܗܘܐ ܢܗܘܐ ܡܠܐܢ ܗܘܠܐ ܡܢ ܦܪܘܫ: ܦܠܚܢܐ ܠܗ ܠܟܬܒܐ ܚܕܐ ܡܬܬܪܓܡܢܘܬܐ ܘܐܦ ܠܗ ܢܘܗܪܐ ܡܠܬܐ ܠܐܝܠܝܢ ܕܣܝܡܝܢ ܣܘܟܠܝܗܘܢ ܘܡܢܐ ܒܡܫܟܚܘܢ ܠܗܘܢ ܠܟܬܒܐ. ܡܢ ܕܝܠܗܘܢ ܢܗܘܘܢ ܠܟܠܗܘܢ. ܘܟܠܗܘܢ ܕܫܘܦܪܐ ܦܡ ܢܫܟܚܘܢ. ܘܟܠܗܘܢ ܕܠܐ ܫܟܝܚܝܢ ܠܗܘܢ ܠܐܝܬܝ ܢܬܪܥܘܢ ܘܠܐ ܣܦܩ. ܠܗܠܝܢ ܕܝܢ ܕܒܫܡܥܬ ܡܬܬܒܝܢ: ܕܢ ܡܫܡܫܢܘܬܗܘܢ ܢܬܪܘܢ. ܘܠܡܬܝܒܘܬܗܘܢ ܢܦܪܩܘܢ ܐܓܪܐ ܕܥܡܠܗܘܢ ܡܫܬܒܚܐ:

ܡܬܦܫܩ ܐܢܐ ܗܟܝܠ ܘܦܠܚ ܐ̄ܢܐ ܐܦ ܗܘܟܐ: ܡܠܬܐ ܗܝ ܕܡܠܬܐ ܐܝܟ ܕܐܬܬܪܓܡ. ܘܐܦ ܕܝܢ ܠܗܘܐ ܐܝܟ ܐܦܘܬܐ ܕܡܬܦܪܫܐ ܠܗ ܠܐܚܝܐ: ܕܟܠܗܘܢ ܐܝܠܝܢ ܕܟܬܝܒܝܢ ܠܣܦܪܐ

1 ܡܥܒܕܢܐ] ܡܩܒܠܢܐ C Nöldeke [Review, 1216] | ܗܘܝܘܬܐ] ܐܝܘܬܐ A Nöldeke [Review, 1216] ܐܝܬܘܬܐ | ܛܒܥܐ] ܛܒܥܐ ܡܕܡ C | ܐܝܟ ܗܢܐ ܕܟܠܐ...ܕܗܘ[2] ܟܠܐ ܟܠܐ ܕܗܘ ܟܠܐ ܕܝܢ ܟܠܐ ܕܝܢ ܕܗܘ A ܐܝܟ ܗܢܐ ܕܟܠܐ C ܟܠܐ ܕܗܘ ܟܠܐ ܕܝܢ ܟܠܐ ܕܝܢ ܕܗܘ 3 ܒܟܠܡܬܐ] ܒܟܠܡܬܐ C | ܚܝܠܬܐ] ܡܬܚܝܠܬܐ C 4 after ܐܡܝܢ C adds ܡܠܬܐ. ܡܬܚܠܬܐ. ܡܠܬܐ ܗܘܐ. ܡܠܬܐ ܕܝܢ. ܡܠܬܐ ܗܘ. ܡܠܬܐ ܗܢ ܕܝܢ. ܡܠܬܐ ܗܘܐ ܕܝܢ. ܡܠܬܐ ܗܘܐ ܕܝܢ❖ 5 ܡܬܐܡܪܢܐ] om. A | ܡܬܦܫܩܝܢ] ܡܬܐ ܡ A txt C | ܗܦܟܬܐ] ܗܦܟܬܐ C | after ܐܢܘܢ] C adds ܟܠܗܘܢ. ܐܝܟ ܗܢܐ ܕܐܘܐ. 6 ܡܬܐܡܪܢܐ] ܣܘܥܪܢܐ C | ܡܫܡܫܝܢ] ܡܫܡܫܝܢ C 7 ܐܝܬ] ܟܠܐ. ܕܟܠܐ. ܟܠܐ ܟܢ. ܕܟܠܐ ܟܢ. ܐܘܐ ܟܢ. ܡܕܡ❖ om. C; either delete ܐܝܬ or emend to ܐܝܬܝܗܘܢ | after ܦܡ] C adds ܗܘܐ ܗܟܠܐ. ܗܘܐ ܟܡܐ ܗܟܠܐ ܐܝܟ ܗܢܐ. ܕܝܢ. ܐܘܐ. ܠܐ. [ܐܝܟ...ܟܡܐ] | C ܡܠܬܐ ܙܒܢܐ] ܙܒܢܐ | A om. [ܐܝܠܝܢ ܟܠܗܘܢ ܐܝܬܝܗܘܢ ܕܝܢ ܡܩܒܠܢܐ 8 ܕܝܢ [ܕܡܘܫܚܝܢ 10 A ܘܐܠܐ ܗܟܢܘ [ܐܘܐ] 9 A ܗܘܝܢ [ܐܝܢ ܗܢܐ] | C ܗܟܢܘ. ܐܝܟ ܕܝܢ. ܐܝܟ ܦܡ. ܐܝܟ ܟܡܐ❖ C ܗܟܢ [ܠܐܝܠܝܢ] | C ܒܟܬܒܐ ܫܘܪܢܐ [ܒܟܬܒܐ] | C ܘܡܕܡ [ܡܕܡ] 12 C ܐܦ ܟܠܐ [ܟܠܐ] 11 C ܡܘܫܚܝܢ | C ܡܟܬܒܬ [ܡܟܬܒܬ] 13 C ܠܟܬܒܐ ܗܘܝܢ [ܠܟܬܒܐ] | C ܘܡܬܦܪܫܢܐ [ܐܢܐ ܕܦܠܚ] 14 A ܦܠ [ܦܠܚ] (or read ܦܠܚܬ) 16 A ܡܬܬܒܝܢ [ܡܬܬܒܝܢ] C ܡܬܬܒܝܢ 20 ܡܫܬܒܚܐ] ܡܫܬܒܚܬ usually for ܡܫܬܒܚܬ in A ܒܫܡܥܬܗܘܢ] read ܒܫܡܥܬܗܘܢ

24 ܘܐܬܬܪܓܡ ܐܝܟ ܕܡܠܬܐ] This shows that C is a recension made by a later scribe, since ܡܠܬܐ here is ῥῆμα for which the older translator used ܡܬܐܡܪܢܐ. The words in the older subscription (above) ܡܬܬܪܓܡܢܘܬܐ ܚܕܐ ܠܟܬܒܐ have been altered here to ܐܝܟ ܕܐܬܬܪܓܡ ܠܡܠܬܐ, and the former should be taken to imply that the older scribe intended to set forth the verbal paradigm, which, however, is quite different from the geenral sense of the older subscription. So a later grammarian who was well-educated in Greek emended, amplified and improved the older translation by making a fresh collation of the Greek text.

ܠܝܠܘܦܐ ܗܘܐ. ܐܝܟܢܐ ܕܡܢ ܦܘܠܚܐ ܕܚܕܐ ܡܠܬܐ. ܢܬܕܪܟܘܢ ܒܡܬܚܫܚܘ ܐܦ ܒܫܪܟܐ ܕܡܢܘܬܐ
ܐܚܪܢܝܬܐ ܕܗܝ ܕܡܠܬܐ: ܗܠܝܢ ܕܒܗܘܢ ܡܬܩܝܡܐ ܟܠܗ ܐܘܡܢܘܬܐ ܕܡܠܠܘܬܐ: ܘܡܘܦܪܐ ܟܠܗ
ܕܡܡܠܠܐ ܕܗܘܝܐ. ܡܬܦܪܫܐ ܕܝܢ: ܕܐܦ ܢܟܠܐ ܡܩܒܠܐ ܒܡܡܠܠܐ ܥܘܢܝܐ. ܐܝܟ ܥܘܢܝܐ ܐܘܡܝܐ ܘܠܐ
ܡܪܩܘ ܕܗܘܐ ܙܘܒܢܐ ܐܝܟ ܡܐ ܕܐܠܐ: ܘܐܝܟ ܕܡܬܚܫܚܝܢ ܗܘܘ ܒܡܐܪܦ. ܩܐܡ ܐ̄ܢܐ ܕܝܢ ܕܐܡܪܬ ܡܠܬܐ ܚܕܐ
ܐܝܟ ܕܡܢܐ ܒܩܘܪܒܐ ܢܘܡܪܐ ܘܫܩܠܐ ܠܡܪܐ. ܗܢܘ ܕܝܢ ܗܘ ܕܡܬܐܡܪܐ ܡܢ ܣܓܝܐܐ ܡܐܡܪܐ܀

p.26 A ܡܐܡܪܐ ܡܬܬܣܝܡܐ ܡܫܘܕܥܢܐ ܕܐܝܟܢܐ ܐܝܬܘܗܝ ܘܡܢܝܢܐ ܕܡܠܬܐ -
C ܡܐܡܪܐ ܡܬܬܣܝܡܢܐ ܡܫܘܕܥܢܐ ܕܐܝܟܢܐ ܘܡܢܝܢܐ ܕܡܠܬܐ ܦܪܨܘܦܐ ܘܡܫܘܕܥܢܘܬܐ
A ܕܩܐܡ ܚܕܝܐ. ܦܬܚ ܐܢܐ. ܦܬܚ ܐܢܬ.
C ܕܚܣܪ ܡܬܚܫܚܢܘܬܐ ܕܦܪܨܘܦܐ ܠܡܠܬܐ ܕܐܝܟܢܐ ܕܩܐܡ. ܚܕܝܐ: ܦܬܚ ܐ̄ܢܐ. ܦܬܚ ܐ̄ܢܬ.
A ܕܥܒܪ ܫܡܠܝܐ - ܦܬܚܬ. ܦܬܚܬܘܢ ܦܬܚܢ.. ܕܡܬܚܫܚܢܘܬܐ - ܕܐܝܟܢܐ ܕܥܒܪ.
C ܦܬܚ: ܫܡܠܝܐ ܕܝܢ: ܦܬܚܬ. ܦܬܚܬܘܢ. ܦܬܚܢ܀ ܡܬܚܫܚܢܘܬܐ ܕܝܢ ܕܐܝܟܢܐ ܕܥܒܪ
A - ܚܕܝܐ. - - - ܦܬܚ ܕܗܘܐ. ܩ̄ ܗܘܝܬ. ܩ̄ ܗܘܐ.. ܗܢ̈ܝ ܦܬܚܢ
C ܡܛܠܐܡܪ: ܚܕܝܐ. ܒܗܘ ܕܐܝܟ ܗܘܐ. ܦܬܚܬ. ܦܬܚܬ ܦܬܚܐ. ܫܡܠܝܐ. ܦܬܚܢ.
A ܦܬܚܢ ܗܘܝܬܘܢ: ܩ̄ ܗܘܘ.. ܕܡܬܚܫܚܢܘܬܐ ܕܐܝܟܢܐ ܕܥܬܝܕ. ܚܕܝܐ. ܐܦܬܚ. ܬܦܬܚ.
C ܦܬܚܬܘܢ. ܦܬܚܘ܀ ܘܡܬܚܫܚܢܘܬܐ ܕܐܝܟܢܐ ܕܥܬܝܕ: ܚܕܝܐ: ܐܦܬܚ. ܬܦܬܚ.
A ܢܦܬܚ.. ܫܡܠܝܐ - ܬܦܬܚܘܢ ܢܦܬܚܘܢ܀܀
C ܢܦܬܚ. ܫܡܠܝܐ: ܢܦܬܚ. ܬܦܬܚܘܢ. ܢܦܬܚܘܢ܀
p.27 A ܡܐܡܪܐ ܡܫܘܕܥܢܐ ܕܫܘܐ ܕܦܪܨܘܦܐ ܠܡܠܬܐ. ܕܐܝܟܢܐ ܕܩܕܡ ܚܕܝܐ܀ ܐܬܦܬܚܬ.
C ܡܐܡܪܐ ܡܫܘܕܥܢܐ ܕܫܘܐ ܕܦܪܨܘܦܐ ܠܡܠܬܐ. ܕܐܝܟܢܐ ܕܩܐܡ܀ ܚܕܝܐ: ܐܬܦܬܚܬ.
A ܐܬܦܬܚܬ. ܐܬܦܬܚ.. - - - - - - -
C ܐܬܦܬܚܬ. ܐܬܦܬܚ. ܫܡܠܝܐ ܕܝܢ: ܐܬܦܬܚܢ. ܐܬܦܬܚܬܘܢ. ܐܬܦܬܚܘ. ܕܐܝܟܢܐ ܕܥܒܪ:
A ܫܡܠܝܐ ܐܬܦܬܚܢ ܗܘܝܢ.
C ܚܕܝܐ. ܐܬܦܬܚܬ ܗܘܝܬ. ܐܬܦܬܚܬ ܗܘܝܬ. ܐܬܦܬܚ ܗܘܐ. ܫܡܠܝܐ. ܐܬܦܬܚܢ ܗܘܝܢ.
A ܐܬܦܬܚܘ ܗܘܘ. ܐܬܦܬܚܘ ܗܘܝܬܘܢ.. ܕܐܝܟܢܐ ܕܥܬܝܕ ܚܕܝܐ. ܐܬܦܬܚ.
C ܐܬܦܬܚܬܘܢ ܗ̈ܘܝܬܘܢ. ܐܬܦܬܚܘ ܗ̈ܘܘ. ܕܐܝܟܢܐ ܕܥܬܝܕ ܚܕܝܐ: ܐܬܦܬܚ.
A ܬܬܦܬܚ. ܢܬܦܬܚ: ܫܡܠܝܐ: ܢܬܦܬܚܘܢ. ܬܬܦܬܚܘܢ.
C ܬܬܦܬܚ. ܢܬܦܬܚ: ܫܡܠܝܐ: ܢܬܦܬܚܘܢ. ܬܬܦܬܚܘܢ. ܐܬܦܬܚܘ
A ܡܐܡܪܐ ܠܐ ܡܬܬܣܝܡܢܐ ܕܐܝܟܢܐ ܠܐ ܡܬܬܣܝܡܐ ܡܫܘܕܥܢܐ ܕܡܬܚܫܚܢܘܬܐ ܚܕܝܐ
C ܡܐܡܪܐ ܠܐ ܡܬܬܣܝܡܐ ܕܐܝܟܢܐ ܠܐ ܡܬܬܣܝܡܐ: ܘܡܫܘܕܥܢܐ ܕܡܬܚܫܚܢܘܬܐ: ܚܕܝܐ
A ܕܡܦܬܚ ܡܦܬܚ ܐܢܐ. ܕܡܦܬܚ ܦܬܚ ܐܢܬ. ܡܦܬܚܐ ܡܦܬܚܐ܀ ܫܡܠܝܐ. - ܡܦܬܚܐ
C ܡܦܬܚܐ ܦܬܚ ܐ̄ܢܐ. ܡܦܬܚܐ ܦܬܚ ܐ̄ܢܬ. ܡܦܬܚܐ ܦܬܚ ܫܡܠܝܐ ܕܝܢ: ܡܦܬܚܐ
A ܦܬܚܢ. ܡܦܬܚܐ ܦܬܚܢ ܐܢܬܘܢ. ܡܦܬܚܐ ܦܬܚܝܢ..
C ܦܬܚܢ. ܡܦܬܚܐ ܦܬܚܬܘܢ. ܡܦܬܚܐ ܦܬܚܝܢ.

3 ܡܦܬܚܐ] sic! 20 ܕܩܐܡ] ܐܬܦܬܚܬ is not present tense (ܕܩܐܡ), hence the reading is wrong
34 ܡܦܬܚܝܢ] sic! Read ܦܬܚܝܢ (ܡܐܡܪܐ ܠܐ ܡܬܬܣܝܡܐ is for ῥῆμα ἀόριστον)

---

1 ܕܡܠܬܐ ܕܗܝ ܐܚܪܢܝܬܐ ܕܡܢܘܬܐ ܒܫܪܟܐ ܐܦ ܒܡܬܚܫܚܘ ܢܬܕܪܟܘܢ ܡܠܬܐ ܕܚܕܐ ܦܘܠܚܐ ܕܡܢ] "that by the conjugation of a single verb, they may progress to make use also of the rest of the other parts of the same verb." The meaning is absurd and makes no sense - one can either take ܡܠܬܐ (= ῥῆμα) as being equivalent to "verb" or else to a "word" (λόγος). 5 ܡܐܡܪܐ] The older text can here be easily distinguished from the later recension. 13 ܦܬܚ ܕܗܘܐ] Earlier the imperfect was called the "opposite" tense (ܕܠܩܘܒܠܐ)! A follows Dionysius, while C follows Syriac grammar. 27 ܐܬܦܬܚܘ] The first person form is lacking. 28 ܐܬܦܬܚܘ] This item does not belong.

A ܡܬܐܡܪܐ ܠܐ ܡܬܠܫܡܐ ܡܘܗܒܬܐ ܕܫܡܐ ܚܕܬܐ.. ܡܫܒܚܐ ܡܚܒܐ ܐܢܐ. ܡܫܡܫܐ
C ܡܬܐܡܪܐ ܠܐ ܡܬܠܫܡܐ. ܡܘܗܒܬܐ ܕܫܡܐ܀ ܚܕܬܐ: ܡܫܡܫܐ ܡܫܐ ܐܢܐ. ܡܫܡܫܐ
p.28 A ܡܫܐ ܐܢܬ.. ـ ـ ܣܓܝܐܬ. ܦܫܡܫܝܢ. ܡܫܡܫܐ ܡܫܒܚ ܐܠܗܝ. ܡܫܡܫܐ
C ܡܫܐ ܐܢ̄ܬ. ܡܫܡܫܐ ܡܫܐ. ܣܓܝܐܬ. ܡܫܡܫܐ ܡܫܝܢ. ܡܫܡܫܐ ܡܫܝܢ - -
A ܡܫܒܚܝܢ܀܀܀
C ـ
A ܡܛܠ ܡܪܢܝܬܐ ܕܝܢ ܕܡܢ ܡܬܐܡܪܐ. ܠܐ ܡܘܗܒܬܐ ܠܐ ܒܪ̈ܢܫܐ ܘܠܐ ܒܦܪ̈ܨܘܦܐ. ܘܠܐ ܒܡܫܝ̈ܚܐ ܘܠܐ
C ܡܛܠ ܡܪܢܝܬܐ ܕܝܢ ܕܡܢ ܡܬܐܡܪܐ ܠܐ ܡܘܗܒܬܐ. ܠܐ ܐܢ̈ܫܐ ܘܠܐ ܦܪ̈ܨܘܦܐ ܘܠܐ ܡܫܝ̈ܚܐ. ܘܠܐ
A ܒܡܟܒܝܢܘܬܐ. ܘܠܐ ܒܫܡܐ. ܐܠܐ ܥܠܝܗ̇ ܡܛܠ ܡܬܐܡܪܐ ܦܘܫܐ܀ ܒܡܫܒܚܐ
C ܡܟܒܝܢ̈ܘܬܐ ܘܠܐ ܫܡ̈ܐ. ܐܠܐ ܥܠܝܗ̇ ܡܛܠ ܡܬܐܡܪܐ ܒܪܐ ܕܐܝܟ ܗܘܐ. ܒܡܫܡܫܐ.
ܚܒ A ـ ܒܡܒܢܝ. ܒܡܫܠܡ. ـ ܒܓܘܪܐ. ܘܐܬܠܝܢ ܕܒܗܠܝܢ ܕܩܫܝܢ:
C ܒܡܬܡܪ: ܒܡܒܢܝ: ܒܡܫܠܡ: ܒܡܪܘܡ. ܒܓܘܪܐ. ܘܐܝܟܢ ܕܒܗܠܝܢ ܕܩܫܝܢ܀
A ܡܫܡܫ ܗܘܐ ܒܫܡܗ.. ܥܠܝܬ ܐܒܪܐ ܕܒܝܬ ܡܫܝܚܐ܀
C ܡܫܡܫ ܗܘ̈ܐ ܒܫܡܗ ܣܓܝܐܬܐ ܐܣܬܝܬܐ ܕܐܝܟ ܗܟܢ. ܘܒܡܦܠܚܢܐ ܒܥܕܬܐ ܡܦܠܚܝܢ.
ܒܪܡ ܕܝܢ ܐܝܟ ܕܠܐ ܢܐܦ. ܥܪܒܐ ܒܝܬ ܡܛܥܝܐ. ܐܬܝܐ ܡܢ ܒܥܠܐ ܡܢܪܐ ܘܕܠܐ ܡܬܐܦ. ܙܪ̈ܥܬܐ ܒܗܢ
ܘܐܝܟ ܗܟܢ ܒܟܠ ܦܘܠܚܐ ܡܢܪܐ ܠܐ ܥܒܝܕܝܢ. ܐܠܐ ܐܝܟ ܕܡܠܝܐ ܕܫܦܝܪܐ ܡܛܠܬܐ ܣܓܝ ܐܘ ܠܬܐܡܝܢ:
ܒܝܘܡ̈ܝ ܐܦ ܐܢܐ ܒܥܕܬܐ ܐܝܟ ܗܘܠܛܐ ܒܥܕܬܐ: ܘܡܫܡܫ ܐ̄ܢܐ ܒܗ ܒܥܪܒܐ. ܒܝ ܒܥܢܐ ܡܢ
ܐܒܘܬܗܘܢ ܕܒܗܘܢ ܐܝܠܝܢ ܗܪܐ ܘܐܬܬܣܝܡ ܒܗܠܝܢ ܕܛܥܝܢ ܘܐܢ ܗܘ ܕܡܬܚܙܝܐ ܒܗܘܢ ܕܫܩܝܢ
ܘܐܦ ܒܡܫܡܫܢܘܬܐ ܕܐܣܝܪܐ ܒܛܥܝܢ ܐܘ ܕܠܐ ܒܛܥܝܢ: ܗܕܐ ܒܡܘܫܚܬܗܘܢ ܡܬܠܝܐ ܐܬܘܬܗ܀
C ܥܠܝܢ ܡܫܡܫܐ ܕܟܠ ܐܣܪܘܬܐ ܡܫܠܡܐ ܕܒܝܬ ܡܫܝܚܐ. ܕܒܗܝ ܒܪܡ ܡܢ ܢܣܟ ܗܘܬ.
ܡܫܪܝܐ ܕܒܗ̇ ܙܒܢ ܡܢ ܢܣܟ ܡܫܡܫܢܐ ܘܒܗܢ ܣܦܘܢܐ ܘܒܣܝܡܐ ܨ̈ܠܘܬܐ ܕܫܪܐ ܚܝܘܬܐ ܣܓܝܐ
ܒܗܠܝܢ ܕܒܗ ܕܚܝܠܐ ܐ̄ܠܗܝܢ܀

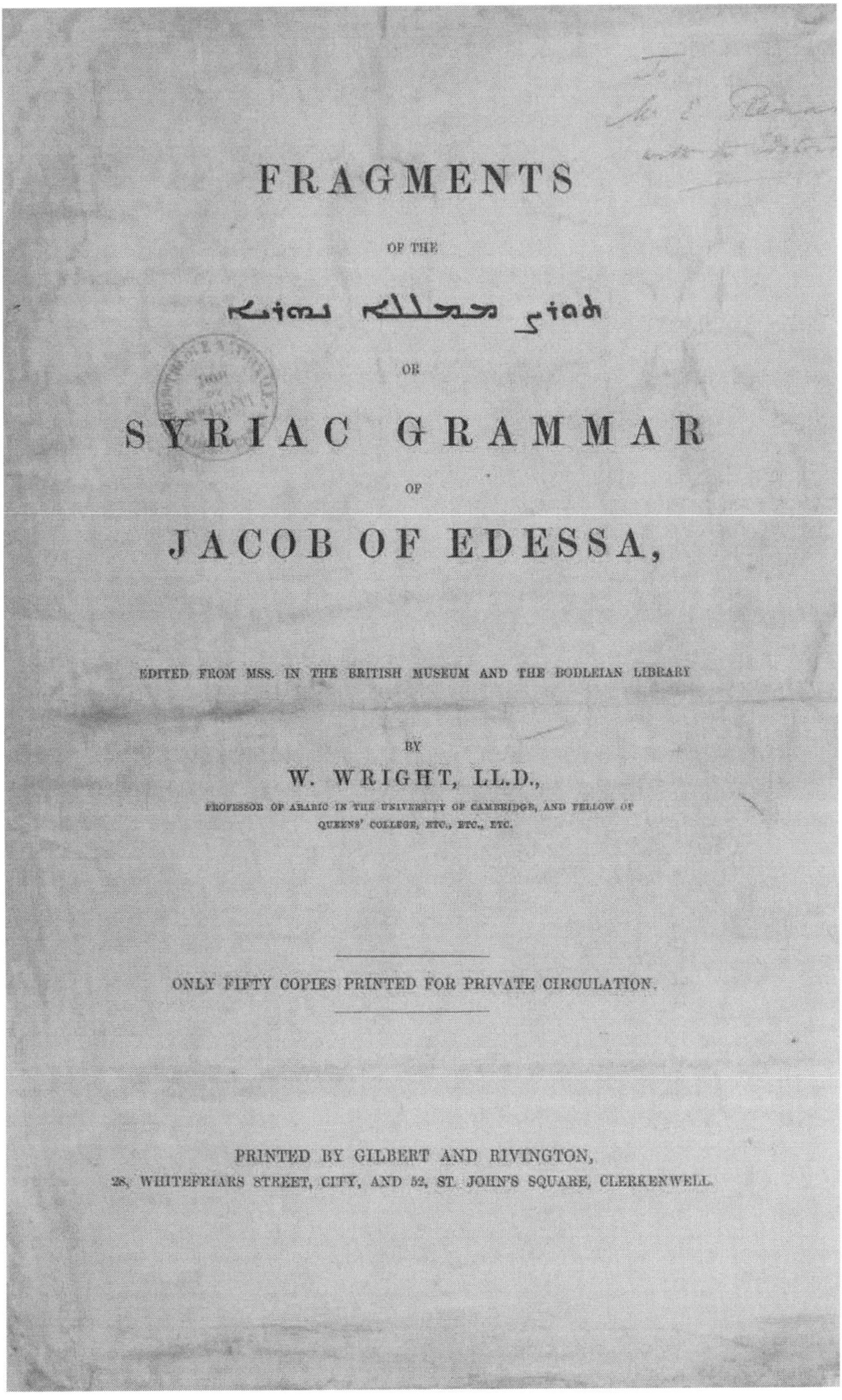

FRAGMENTS

OF THE

ܬܘܪܨ ܡܡܠܠܐ ܣܘܪܝܝܐ

OR

SYRIAC GRAMMAR

OF

JACOB OF EDESSA,

EDITED FROM MSS. IN THE BRITISH MUSEUM AND THE BODLEIAN LIBRARY

BY

W. WRIGHT, LL.D.,
PROFESSOR OF ARABIC IN THE UNIVERSITY OF CAMBRIDGE, AND FELLOW OF QUEENS' COLLEGE, ETC., ETC., ETC.

ONLY FIFTY COPIES PRINTED FOR PRIVATE CIRCULATION.

PRINTED BY GILBERT AND RIVINGTON,
28, WHITEFRIARS STREET, CITY, AND 52, ST. JOHN'S SQUARE, CLERKENWELL.

In an article entitled "Jacques d'Édesse et les Voyelles Syriennes," which appeared in the Journal Asiatique for Mai-Juin, 1869, p. 447, M. l'Abbé Martin remarks, p. 453: "On le considère généralement comme l'auteur de la première grammaire, non pas qu'il n'ait eu aucun prédécesseur, mais en ce sens qu'il les a tous éclipsés et qu'il a fait tomber leurs ouvrages dans un entier oubli. C'est à ce livre qu'il doit, sans aucun doute, d'être regardé comme le restaurateur de la langue syriaque. Malheureusement, cette grammaire, qui portait le titre de *correction du langage*, n'est point parvenue jusqu' à nous, et il devient par suite plus difficile de préciser en quoi consista cette réforme si célèbre dans les annales syriennes." In the same article, pp. 457—9, he quotes a passage from the ܟܬܒܐ ܕܨܡ̈ܚܐ, or larger Grammar, of Gregory bar Hebræus, in which that writer speaks of and reproduces the vowel-signs invented by Jacob. In Add. 7201, fol. 195 *a*, this passage runs as follows:—

ܟܡܝܢܐ ܕܠܐ ܚܝܠ ܡܛܠ ܢܩܫܝܢ ܬܘܪܝܬ
ܐܬܘ̈ܬܐ ܦܘܪܫܢܝܬܐ. ܟܝ ܦܘܪ̈ܬܐ ܕܡܢ ܕܝܠܗ
ܐܬܚܠܦ ܢܩܫܝܢܐ ܢܩܒ. ܠܡ̈ܠܝܬܐ ܡܢ ܥܒܕ.
ܘܠܩܪܐ ܢܩܘܫܝܬܐ ܚܕܐ. ܘܠܐܬ̈ܘܬܐ ܡܥܒ̈ܕܢܝܬܐ
ܒܢ̈ܩܘܪܐ ܕܩܘܫܬ ܘܠܡܥ̈ܪܬܐ ܕܡܬܬܩ̈ܒܫܢ ܦܪܫ.
ܘܦܬܓܡܐ ܡܢ ܙܪ ܠܦܘܫܩܐ ܐ ܘܠܙܩܦܐ ܐܪܒܥܐ
ܟ ܘܠܙܩ̈ܦܐ ܬܪܝܢ ܒ ܘܠܫܡ̈ܐ ܐܪܒܥܐ ܠ
ܘܠܫܡ̈ܐ ܬܪܝܢ. ܥ ܘܠܗܒ̈ܐ ܐܪܒܥܐ ܦ
ܘܠܗ̈ܒܐ ܬܪܝܢ ܕ ܘܠܩ̄ܘ ܫܘܝܬܐ ܕ ܘܡܬܦܪܫܢ
ܡܡܪ̈ܢܐ ܢܗܡ̈ܐ ܕܠܐ ܫܘܝܢ ܟܠ ܚܕ ܡܢ
ܠܦ̈ܐܬܐ ܐܬܠܬܐ ܕܡܥܝܢܢ ܫܒܥܐ. ܒܠܚܘܕ ܦ
ܡܥܫܢ ܐܘܪ̈ܣܐ، ܟܕ ܠܐ ܕܥܒܕ̄ܘܬ ܚܢܝܦ
ܘܫܡܥ ܐܢܬܘܢ، ܢ̈ܡܘ.

Till I had read M. Martin's article, I believed, like himself, that the work of Jacob was wholly lost to us, unless, perchance, it still lurked, like the ܡܠܟܐ ܡܫܝܚܐ, in the recesses of some library in the East. But the perusal of his essay opened my eyes, and I saw what I had not seen before.

In the volume of Syriac fragments marked Mus. Brit. Add. 17,217, I had observed two leaves, foll. 37 and 38, apparently belonging to a grammatical treatise of considerable antiquity, for the writing was of the ix[th] or x[th] cent. However, they had been washed, in order that they might be used as palimpsest, and so but little of the contents was legible, and that little not very intelligible, because of the strange signs that appeared here and there. The passage of Bar Hebræus, however, made everything clear; the permission of the Trustees of the British Museum was obtained for the application of a chemical reagent; and I was soon in possession of the text of two portions of the lost ܬܘܪܨ ܡܡܠܠܐ. Another fragment of the same manuscript was also found by me in Add. 14,665, fol. 28, which had shared the fate of its fellows, and was besides covered in part with rude Arabic writing, so that it could only be deciphered with difficulty.

About this time my friend Dr. Neubauer wrote to me from Oxford that he had discovered two leaves of an ancient grammatical work in Syriac, which had been overlooked by Dr. Payne Smith (the present Dean of Canterbury), and did not, therefore, appear in his Catalogue of the Syriac MSS. in the Bodleian Library. These, which are bound, with other miscellaneous fragments, in the volume numbered Bodl. 159, I found to be portions of the introduction of the ܬܘܪܨ ܡܡܠܠܐ, from a manuscript also of the ix[th] or x[th] cent.; and by the kindness of Dr. Neubauer, and the liberality of the Curators and Principal Librarian of the Bodleian, I am able to print them with the others.

The oldest system of vowel-punctuation used by the Syrians was, as is well-known, that by means of small points or dots above and below the consonants (ܐ̤, ܐ̇, etc.), which has been retained by the Nestorians. Subsequently, about the time of Jacob of Edessa, the Greek vowels were introduced in the same positions (ܐ or ܐ, ܐ or ܐ, etc.)—whether by himself or by others, is not perfectly clear,—and were gradually extensively adopted by the Jacobites. The earliest examples of their use in the Nitrian manuscripts are in Add. 17,134, fol. 83 (dating from about A.D. 675, and perhaps autograph of Jacob), and Add. 14,429 (dated A.D. 719).* Jacob planned, however, a further reformation, namely, the introduction of a series of vowel-signs which could be written, like the Greek vowels, on a level with and between the consonants; and it was partly with the view of recommending this system to his countrymen that he composed the ܬܘܪܨ ܡܡܠܠܐ ܢܗܪܝܐ. That he should have failed is perhaps a matter of regret, but certainly not of surprise.

The proposed vowel-system, as exhibited by Bar Hebræus, was:—

ܦܬܚܐ ă as in } ܟܬܒ (ܟܬܒ).
ܪܒܨܐ ܐܪܝܟܐ ē as in }

ܪܒܨܐ ܟܪܝܐ ĕ as in ܬܫܡܫܝܢ (ܬܫܡܫܝܢ).
ܚܒܨܐ ܐܪܝܟܐ ī as in ܚܒܝܒ (ܚܒܝܒ).
ܚܒܨܐ ܟܪܝܐ ĭ as in ܬܫܡܫܝܢ (ܬܫܡܫܝܢ).
ܥܨܨܐ ܐܪܝܟܐ ū as in ܚܒܝܒ (ܚܒܝܒ).
ܥܨܨܐ ܟܪܝܐ ŭ as in ܐܘܪܗܝ (ܐܘܪܗܝ).

He should have added that ܐ takes the place of ܙܩܦܐ, ā†, as in ܐܘܪܗܝ (ܐܘܪܗܝ), ܟܬܒܬܐ (ܟܬܒܬܐ).

These vowel-signs seem to be akin to the ܬܘܣܦܬܐ ܕܐܠܦ ܒܝܬ ܢܗܪܝܬܐ, or "Additions to the Mesopotamian Alphabet," given in Add. 14,620, fol. 13 *b* (see Land in the Zeitschrift der Deutschen Morgenländischen Gesellschaft, Bd. xxii., p. 550, and Martin, "Jacques d'Édesse et les Voyelles Syriennes," pp. 459, 460); viz.—

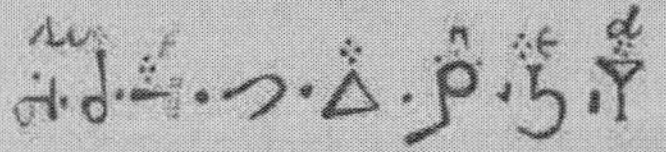

[Syriac vowel signs]

It should be observed that the fragments of the ܬܘܪܨ ܡܡܠܠܐ, which I now publish, do not exhibit the vowel ܚܒܨܐ ܟܪܝܐ, ĭ, ܥ, as in ܬܫܡܫܝܢ (ܬܫܡܫܝܢ), but furnish us with *three* figures for *u*, viz. ܘ, as in ܡܫܘܚܐ (ܡܫܘܚܐ), ܐܘܪܚܐ (ܐܘܪܚܐ); ܘ, as in ܟܬܘܒܬܐ (ܟܬܘܒܬܐ), ܕܘܒܪܬܐ (ܕܘܒܪܬܐ); and ܘ, as in ܒܪܘܟܬܐ (ܒܪܘܟܬܐ), ܓܘܠܬܐ (ܓܘܠܬܐ).

W. WRIGHT.

August 24th, 1871.

* See my Catalogue, nos. CCCCXXI. and LX.

† Pronounced in Jacob's time, and even earlier, by the Western Syrians as *ō*. This is evident from the selection of the Greek *o mikron* (ο) to represent the sound, and from such spellings as ܬܘܡܘܣܐ for ܬܐܡܘܣܐ in Add. 17,202 (see, for example, my Catalogue of Syriac MSS. in the Brit. Mus., p. 1048, 2nd col., line 21), and ܩܘܪܘܣܐ for ܩܪܘܣܐ in Add. 14,660 (in my Catalogue, p. 1161, 2nd col., line 20).

ܕܬܗܘܐ ܘܬܫܟܚ (fol. 1 *a*, col. 1) ܫܘܒܩܢܐ.
ܐܟܪܙܘܬܐ ܕܝܢ ܕܒܫܡܗܘܢ ܡܫܘܚܐ ܡܬܬܪܓܡܢܐ
ܠܡܫܡܠܝܐ ܗܘܝܐ. ܒܬܪ ܕܝܢ ܬܘܕܝܬܐ ܕܐܝܬܘܬܐ
ܩ̈ܢܘܡܐ ܗܠܝܢ ܕܫܡܗ̈ܝܢ ܡܢ ܗܦܟܐ ܗܘܝܐ.
ܕܟܐܢܘܬܗܘܢ ܡܥܒܕܐ ܐܢܫ ܠܚܘܒܐ ܘܣܥܘܪܘܬܗܘܢ
ܕܠܗܘܢ ܕܩܢܘܡܐ. ܘܬܘܪܓܡܐ ܕܫܡܗ̈ܐ
ܘܕܡ̈ܠܐ ܕܢܗܘܢ. ܘܒܪ ܡܢ ܬܪ̈ܬܝܗܘܢ ܐܕܪܟܬ:
ܡܢ ܐܠܗܘܬܗ ܘܡܢ ܡܢܝܢܘܬܐ ܕܐܒܐܢܐ
ܕܒܬܪܟܐ: ܗܘ ܕܐܝܬ ܠܗܘܢ ܕܡܢ ܡܘܡܢ.
ܗܕܐ ܐܬܬܣܒܪܬ. ܕܒܪ ܡܛܠ ܗܘܢܐ ܘܬܘܡܢܐ
ܕܠܗܘܢ ܕܩܢܘܢܐ ܟܠܗܘܢ ܕܡܬܬܩܢܝܢ ܐܬܬ̈ܐ:
ܠܗܘܬ ܗܘ ܕܢܫܘܢ ܥܡܠܐ ܘܚܘܫܒܐ ܕܠܗܘܢ
ܕܩܢܬ ܩܠܐ: ܘܠܐ ܗܘܐ ܡܛܠ ܥܡܠܢܐ
ܘܬܘܡܢܐ ܕܠܗ ܕܗܦܟܐ. ܐܥܡܠܢܐ ܠܝ
ܥܠܝܬܝ. (sic) ܡܛܠ ܣܘܟܐ ܗܘ ܕܬܥܒܕ
ܗܕܐ: ܘܡܛܠ ܗܘ ܕܐܡܪܢܐ. § ܕܕܥܒܕ ܛܒܬܐ
ܘܠܐ ܥܒܕ ܠܗ ܚܛܝܬܐ ܗܘܬ ܠܗ. ܕܒܗ ܕܝܢ ܐܦ
ܗܕܐ ܐܣܪܬܐ. ܕܫܘܚܠܦܐ ...... ܘܡܠܐ
ܐܝܬ ܟܠ ...... ܕܡܫܬܟܚܝܢ ܕܕܠ ....
ܐܝܬܝܗܘܢ ܡܢ .... (col. 2) ܗܘ ܒܗܬ
.... ܘܢܒܝܐ. ܐܦ ...... ܐܡܪܝܢܐ
ܐ .... ܗܢܘܢ .... ܝ ܗܠܝܢ ܕܠܗܘܢ
ܕܬܫܡܫܬܐ ܘ ... ܐܡܪܝܢܐ ܕܝܢ ܐܠܐ ܘ ...
ܗܠܝܢ ܕܥܕܬܐ: ܐܦ ... ܗܢܐ ܫܡܥܐ
ܕܗܦܟܐ ... ܫܡ̈ܗܐ ܒܪ̈ܝܬܐ ..... ܟܠܗܐ
ܟܪ ܟܪܙ[ܐ] .... ܐ ܐܝܬܘ[ܗܝ] .... ‖

§ See the Epistle of S. James, ch. iv. 17.

‖ Seventeen or eighteen lines wanting.

Bodl. 159.

(fol. 1 *b*, col. 1) ..... [ܒܪ]ܬ ܩܠܐ ...... ܐ
ܐܦ ܗܠܝܢ ...... ܐܡܪܬ، ܕܢܩ̈ܪܒܘܢ ....
..... ܒܐܬܘ̈ܬܐ ܘܡܣܪܚܬܐ .... ܒܫܬ
ܢܨܪܚܬܐ. ܐܬܟܠܘ .... ܘܦܬܚܘ ܡܢ ܗܕܐ
.... ܙܒܢܬܐ: ܠܐ ܢܗܒ ܐܢܐ ....
ܒܫܡܗܘܢ: ܐܘ ܗܕ[ܘܢ] ..... ܥܡܗܘܢ: ܐܘ
ܒܗ ܐܣܝܪܐ .... ܢܘܢ. ܡܛܠ ܕܣܝܡ
.... ܡܬܠܐܐ .... *
(col. 2) ܒܗܢ ܐܦ ܗܢܘܢ ܡܩ̈ܢܝܐ. ܐܝܟ ܒܪ
ܐܡܪܬ ܐܦ ܡܢ ܟܪ̈ܣܛܝܢܘ ܕܠܗܘܢ. ܐܦ ܠܐ
ܠܗܘܢ ܐܝܬ ܗܘܐ ܡܦܪܫܐ ܡܫܡܠܝܐ. ܠܐ
ܒܪ ܚܝܢ ܗܘܘ ܐܠܗܐ ܐ̄ܬ ܐܬܘ̈ܬܐ ܒܠܫܢܐ.
ܐܠܐ ܘܐܦ ܒܗ ܐܬܬ̈ܩܫܝ.† ܠܘ ܐܚܪܢܐ
ܐܬܬ̈ܘܩܫܝ.† ܐܠܐ ܗܘ ܗܘ ܒܗܢܐ ܕܒܗܢܐ
ܘܐܦܢܐ ܕܡܐ ܐܘ ܒ̄. ܐܚܪ̈ܢܐ ܕܝܢ ܒܪ̈ܝܢܐ
ܐܚܪ̈ܢܐ ܘܐܦܣܘ ܐܚܪ̈ܢܝܬܐ. ܒܗܟܢܐ ܕܦܘ̈ܫ
ܒ̄. ܒܡܫܝܚܐ. ܘܐܬܬܦܝܣ ܡܦܪܫܐ ܡܫܡܠܝܐ.
ܐܢܐ ܕܝܢ ܒܗ ܡܢܚ ܐܢܐ ܠܓܠܝܬܐ ܗܘ، ܕܓܠܝܬ
ܐܢܘܢ ܠܗܘܢ ܕܢܦܫܗܘܢ ܐܬܘ̈ܬܐ: ܐܡܪ̈ܢܐ
ܕܝܢ ܗܘ، ܕܠܐ ܢܦܫܐ ܐܚܪܢܐ ܕܠܗܘܢ ܒܬܪܟܐ
ܕܬܘܒܝܢ ܒܗܟܢܐ ܠܡܫܐ: ‡ ܒܦܫܪܐ ܗܢܐ ܠܐ
ܡܫܡܠܝܐ ܕܠܫܢܐ ܢܫܪܐ. ܘܢܣܒ ܐܢܐ ܟܠ
ܒܡܠܐ ܕܦܘܠ ܕܡܢ ܡܘܡܢ ..... [ܐ]ܬܬܦܣܬ
ܒܗܟܢܐ ..... ܥܠܝܬܝ. ܗܘ، ...... ܐ

* Seventeen or eighteen lines wanting.

† Originally ܐܬܬ̈ܩܫܝܢ.

‡ With what follows compare M. Martin's article in the Journal Asiatique for 1869, Mai-Juin, p. 456.

(fol. 2 a, col. 1) ܫܢܬ̄ ܐܘ ܒܐ̄ ܐܘ ܓܕܐ̄ ܐܘ ܥܡ̄. ܐܘ ܥܒܕܐ ܡܕܡ ܕܐܝܬ ܒܗ ܚܕܐ ܡܢ ܗܠܝܢ: ܡܛܠ ܕܐܦܠܐ ܒܟܠܗ ܠܒܢܝܗܘܢ ܡܥܬܩܝܢ. ܡܛܠ ܗܕܐ. ܐܦܠܐ ܡܩܒܠܝܢ ܟܠ ܢܥܣܬܗܘܢ. ܗܘ ܕܡܘܬ ܐܦ ܠܠܫ̈ܢܐ ܐܚܪ̈ܢܐ ܐܝܬ ܐܬܘ̈ܬܐ ܡܕܡ ܡܕܡ. ܕܠܘ ܟܠܗܘܢ ܗܢܘܢ ܠܥܡ̈ܐ ܕܥܒܕܐ ܡܥܒܕܝܢ ܕܢܡܘܣܐ ܐܝܬ ܒܕܪ̈ܐ ܗܠܝܢ. ܗܘܝܢܐ ܗܟܢܐ: ܐܡܪ ܐܢܐ ܕܝܢ ܡܡܠܠܐ ܗܢܐ ܐܡܪܘܗܝ. ܠܐ ܗܘܐ ܠܒܢܝܗܘܢ ܦܪܫܬ ܠܗܘܢ: ܐܠܐ ܡܦܩܐ ܗܢܐ ܕܠܗܘܢ. ܡܛܠ ܠܐ ܡܫܠܛܘܬܗ ܘܢܡܘܣܝܘܬ ܐܬܘ̈ܬܐ ܐܠܗ̈ܬܐ ܕܟܠ. ܘܐܝܟ ܕܦܩܕܬ ܐܚܪܢܝܬ. ܠܐ ܡܫܟܚܝܢ ܠܡܥܒܪܐ. ܦܪܝܫܐܝܬ ܡܕܡ. ܡܟܝܠ ܡܢ ܗܠܝܢ. ܟ̄ ܕܩܕܡ ܐܬܬܚܡܝܢ ܡܢ ܠܥܠ: ܐܡܪܢܐ ܕܝܢ ܐܘ ܒܡܕܢܚܐ. ܡܛܠ ܠܡܚܘܬܐ ܘܗܘܢܐ ܕܬܐܒ ܗܘ ܡܢܗ ܕܥܒܕܐ ܐܢܫܐ ܗܘ ܕܫܒܩ. ܐܘ ܡܢ ܡܫܠܛܢܘܬܐ ܕܐܚܪ̈ܢܐ. ܐܝܠܝܢ ܕܡܕܝܢܝܢ ܡܫܟܚܝܢ ܒܗ ܒܥܒܕܐ ܘܡܦܪܢܬܐ ܕܒܗ: (col. 2) ܘܡܫܟܚܝܢ ܐܡܪܝܢ ܠܗܘܢ ܠܒ̈ܢܬ ܩ̈ܠܐ ܦܪܝܫܐܝܬ ܘܡܫܠܡܝܢ ܠܗܘܢ ܠܐܚܪ̈ܢܐ. ܠܐ ܗܘܐ ܡܢ ܦܪܝܫܘܬܐ ܕܡܪܝܐ ܕܐܬܘ̈ܬܐ. ܠܐ ܓܝܪ ܐܝܬ ܠܗܘܢ ܗܕܐ. ܐܠܐ ܐܦ ܗܢܘܢ ܡܢ ܡܫܠܛܢܘܬܐ ܕܐܚܪ̈ܢܐ. ܐܘ ܡܢ ܦܘܠܚܢܐ ܗܟܢܐ. ܒܪ ܡܦܪܣܝܬ ܫܪܝܪ. ܘܐܝܟ ܕܠܡܐܡܪ ܐܝܟ ܗܘ ܕܐܬܝܢ ܠܗܘܢ ܗܢܘܢ ܦܪ̈ܝܫܐ ܦܠܫܝܢ ܟܠܗܘܢ. ܒܪ ܐܦ ܙܘܒܢܐ ܡܕܡ ܡܕܡ ܕܡܢ ܢܘܩܐ ܐܝܬ ܠܗܘܢ ܡܬܕܪ̈ܝܢ. ܘܡܫܬܘܕܥܢܐ ܕܗܘܩܢܐ ܡܕܡ ܡܕܡ. ܐܝܟܢܐ ܕܐܦ ܗܢܘܢ ܕܡܫܬܥܠܝܢ: ܠܐ ܗܘܐ ܡܢ ܐܬܘ̈ܬܐ ܡܫܬܡܠܝܢ. ܐܠܐ ܡܢܗܘܢ ܕܩ̈ܠܐ ܢܩ̈ܘܫܐ ܕܟܝܢܐ ܦ̈ܓܘܬܐ ܕܗܘ ܕܡܩܒܠ. ܐܝܬ ܕܝܢ ܐܡܬܝ. ܕܐܦ ܐܬܘ̈ܬܐ ܫܪ̈ܝܬܐ ܡܫܒܚ ܒܗܘܢ ܒܥܡ̈ܡܐ ܒܪ ܒܬܪܝܢ ܠܗܘܢ ܡܕܝܢ̈ܬܐ. ܡܛܠ ܦܘܪܥܢܐ ܕܥܡ̈ܡܐ ܐܚܪ̈ܢܐ. ܐܝܠܝܢ ܕܗܒܝܢ ܗܒܝܢ ܒܪ ܗܒܝܢ ܐܬܘ̈ܬܐ ܕܠܐ ܘܠܐ ܐܒܕܬܗܘܢ.

ܐܝܟ (fol. 2 b, col. 1) ܕܢܐ ܐܡܪܢܐ ܕܗܘ ܕܓܒܪܐ ܘܕܓܒܪ̈ܐ. ܕܠܐ ܗܘܐ ܡܛܠ ܕܡܒܠܐ ܠܗ̇ ܠܗ̇، ܢܘ̄ ܐܬܬܚܡܬ ܒܗ̇. ܠܐ ܓܝܪ ܡܩܒܠ ܗܘܐ ܒܠܗ̇. ܐܦܠܐ ܒܒܪܬ ܩܠܐ ܢܦܫܐ. ܐܠܐ ܡܛܠ ܦܘܪܥܢܐ ܕܥܡ̈ܡܐ ܕܗܘܘ ܕܓܒܪ̈ܐ. ܕܗܒܝܢ ܒܪ ܗܒܝܢ ܐܬܘ̈ܬܐ ܕܠܐ ܘܠܐ ܐܝܬ ܠܗ ܐܝܟ ܗܘ ܕܓܒܪܐ. ܡܫܟܚܐ ܕܝܢ ܡܢ ܒܬܪ ܡ ܒܪ ܚܕ ܠܗܕܐ ܢܘ̄ ܕܬܬܒܥܐ: ܘܠܐܚܪ̈ܢܝܬܐ ܐܬܘ̈ܬܐ ܕܒܗ̇ ܒܕܝܩܘܬܐ ܡܛܠܠܬܗ̇ ܕܠܒܬܐ ܣܩ̈ܝܡ ܒܥܩܒܐ: ܐܡܪܢܐ ܕܝܢ ܕܒܠܗܘܢ ܡܚܪ̈ܒܢܐ: ܘܐܚܪ̈ܢܐ ܕܒܘܩܝܬܐ ܐܚܪ̈ܢܝܬܐ ܒܓܪܡ: ܘܠܐ ܡܡܠܠܝܢ ܦܪܝܫܐܝܬ ܒܠܫܢܐ ܗܢܐ ܐܡܪܘܗܝ. ܒܪ ܠܐ ܐܫܬܟܠܘ ܠܚܠܬܐ ܕܡܛܠܬܗ̇ ܐܬܬܫܡܫܬ ܒܗ ܒܥܒܕܐ: ܘܠܗܠܝܢ ܐܚܪ̈ܢܝܬܐ ܒܗ̇ ܒܕܝܩܘܬܐ. ܐܦ ܒܒܪܬ ܩܠܐ ܢ̈ܦܫܬܐ ܢܝܫ. ܘܠܐ ܒܠܫܢܐ ܗܢܘܢ ܒܓܒܪܐ ܗܘܐ ܡܢ ܒܬܪܡ ܒܪ ܐܬܟܬܒܬ. ܐܠܐ ܐܦ ܐܢܫܝܢ ܡܢܗܘܢ ܕܐܡܪܘܗܝ. ܐܘ ܒܢܬ ܡܢ ܗܢܘܢ ܕܡܡܠܠܝܢ ܦܪܝܫܐܝܬ ܒܡܡܠܠܐ ܗܢܐ (col. 2) ܢܗܪܐ. ܘܠܐ ܒܠܫܢܐ ܬܢܢ ܩ̈ܠܐ ܢܡܘܣܝܬܐ ܘܠܒܪ ܡܢ ܡܡܠܠܗܘܢ ܕܡܫܬܚܫܚܝܢ ܒܗܘܢ: ܠܐ ܡܫܟܚܝܢ ܠܡܥܒܪܐ ܦܪܝܫܐܝܬ. ܐܠܐ ܐܦܠܐ ܗܠܝܢ ܒܬܪ̈ܝܬܐ. ܡܫܟܚܐ ܓܝܪ ܐܝܬ ܠܗܘܢ ܕܢܫܬܡ ܒܬܘܩܦܗܘܢ. ܘܡܢ ܡܡܠܠܐ ܚܕܪܝܢ. ܘܡܢ ܠܥܡܐ ܡܢܢܐ. ܬܫܡܫܬܐ ܕܐܝܬ ܠܗܘܢ ܒܡܡܠܠܝ. ܐܦ ܡܢ ܠܥܡܐ ܙܘܡܚܢܐ. ܡܛܠ ܐܘܣܝܢܐ ܕܗܘܐ ܠܡܠܟܘܬܐ ܕܙܘ̈ܡܢܐ ܒܐܬܪܐ ܗܢܐ. ܗܘ ܕܡܘܬ ܐܦ ܡܢ ܠܥܡܐ ܦܪܣܝܐ. ܘܐܝܟ ܕܦܩܕܬ ܐܚܪܢܝܬ. ܘܠܐ ܚܕܐ ܡܚܫܚܝܢ ܐܡܪܝܢ ܦܪܝܫܐܝܬ ܐܘ ܦܓܪ̈. ܡܛܠ ܫܘܠܛܢܐ ܕܐܬܘ̈ܬܐ. ܘܡܛܠܠܬܗ̇ ܕܗܕܐ. ܩܛܠܬܐ ܡܢ ܙ̈ܢܝܐ ܚܒܠܐ ܕܗܘܘ ܒܠܫܢܐ ܗܢܐ. ܘܒܝܘ ܒܫܡܫܐ ܡܪܝܐ ܕܗܪܝܢܐ. ܢܓܕ ܠܡܦܩܘܬܐ ܐܬܘ̈ܬܐ. ܗܠܝܢ ܕܗܝܢ̈ܐ ܡܢ ܡܓܪܐ ܗܢܐ. ܠܚܘܕ ܡܫܝܚܘܬܐ

ܕܡܫܝܚܘܬܗ ܕܠܒܢܝܢܐ ܗܘܝܐ. ܘܠܘܬ ܗܿܝ ܕܢܦܩܐ
ܬܪܝܨܘܬ ܘܕܠܐ ܚܒܠܐ: . . . .
. . . .
. . . .

BRIT. MUS. ADD. 17,217.

(fol. 37 *a*) ܡܕܡ. ܐܚܪ̈ܢܐ ܕܝܢ. ܕܡ̈ܬܬܠܝܢܐ
ܐܝܬܝܗܘܢ ܗܢܘܢ. ܐܦ ܠܒܪ ܢܦܩܝܢ
ܡܫܒܚܘܬܐ ܗܕܐ. ܒܪܡ ܐܝܟ ܕܗܘ ܐܢ
ܐܝܬܝܗܘܢ ܠܡܣܟܢܐ ܕܟܠܗܐ ܢܦ̈ܫܢ ܀܀
ܕܐܬܚܠܠܬܐܢܐ. ܕܐܬܚܠܠܬܐܢܢ.
ܚܐܬܚܫܬܐܢܐ. ܚܐܬܚܫܬܐܢܢ.
ܫܐܬܠܫܬܐܢܢ. ܫܐܬܦܪܬܐܢܢ.
ܪܐܬܚܠܬܐܢܢ. ܠܐܬܚܫܬܐܢܢ.
ܪܐܬܠܫܬܐܢܢ. ܪܐܬܠܚܬܐܢܢ.
ܚܐܬܠܡܬܐܢܢ. ܠܐܬܚܫܪܬܐܢܐ.
ܠܐܬܚܫܪܬܐܢܢ. ܒܗܝܕ ܐܝܬ ܗܘܒܠ
ܐܘ ܡܘܢܐ ܐܢܫ ܒܥܠܡ. ܕܡܬܐܡܪܐ
ܗܘ ܡܬܒܢܝܢܐ ܐܚܪ̈ܢܬܐ. ܕܡܬܝܗܒܝܢ
ܕܡ̈ܠܘܬܐ. ܘܡܫܬܡܠܝܢ ܠܫܘܪܝܐ. ܘܠܐ ܡܫܬܠܡ
ܐܘ ܕܡܫܬܬܩܢܝܢ (sic) ܡܕܡ ܫܘܪܝܐ. ܐܘ
ܕܡܬܐܡܪܝܢ ܒܬܪ ܫܘܪܝܐ. ܗܢܘ ܕܝܢ ܒܢܝܢܬܐ
ܠܡܫܝܚܘܬܐ ܘܠܩܘܪܒܐ. ܘܡܫܝܚܘܬܐ ܠܒܢܝܢܬܐ
ܘܠܩܘܪܒܐ. ܘܩܘܪܒܐ ܗܿܘ ܕܡܬܝܒܘܬܐ ܠܒܢܝܢܬܐ
ܘܠܡܫܝܚܘܬܐ. ܘܐܦ ܗܘ ܕܡܬܬܩܦܠ ܐܝܬܘܬܐ
ܒܢܝܢܬܐ ܡܕܡ ܡܫܝܚܘܬܐ ܐܘ ܡܕܡ ܩܘܪܒܐ.
ܡܫܬܠܡܢܐ ܐܝܟ ܗܿܝ. ܘܗܢܘܢܐ ܐܘ ܡܫܝܚܘܬܐ
ܐܘ ܩܘܪܒܐ: ܘܡܛܠ ܗܕܐ ܐܝܟ ܒܫ̈ܡܗܐ ܗܠܝܢ
ܕܦܪܫܘ ܐܝܬܘܬܗܘܢ ܗܟܢܐ: ܗܢܘ ܕܝܢ ܪܗܛܘܬܐ.
ܒܗܘܢܬܐ. ܪܗܛܘܬܐ. ܐܝܟ ܕܬܕܥܘܢ. ܗܘܐ ܗܘ
ܡܫܡܗܐ ܕܒܪܬ ܡܠܐ ܚܬܝܬܐ. ܟܕ ܢܦܩܬ ܡ̈ܢܝܢ
ܠܐܬܘܬܐ. ܠܚܝܘܬܐ ܠܒܪܬ ܚܫܡܗ. ܠܗܘܝܬ ܐܬܘܬܐ
ܗܝ ܕܡܫܬܐܝܠܐ ܗܘܬ ܒܬܪ ܚܕܐ ܚܕܐ ܡܫܡܗܐ.
ܪܗܛܘܬܐ ܒܬܪ ܘܡܫܡܗܘܬܐ: ܡܛܠ ܕܠܐ
ܡܦܩܠܐ ܬܿ ܕܐܬܝܬܐ ܒܬܪ ܠܿ ܕܐܝܬܝܗ̇

ܒܝܬܐ: ܐܘ ܒܬܪ ܦ̄ ܕܐܝܬܝܗ̇ ܢܩܕܬܐ: ܟܕ
ܐܝܬܝܗ̇ ܗܝ ܡܫܝܚܬܐ. ܠܡܫܝܚܘܬܐ ܕܐܟܘܬܗ̇
ܦ̄ ܥܒܝܕܐ ܠܬܪ̈ܬܝܗܝܢ. ܒܪ̈ܘܚܬܐ ܕܝܢ
ܕܐܝܬܝܗ̇ ܡܢ ܫܡܐ ܕܪܘܚܐ: ܘܡܫܝܚܐ ܐܝܬ ܐܝܬ
ܗܘܐ ܠܗ ܒܗ ܪ̇. ܒܕܠܐ ܡܫܒܠܐ ܠܡܫܝܚܘܬܗ̇.
ܠܘܬ ܦ̄ ܕܐܝܬܝܗ̇ ܐܦ ܗܝ ܡܫܝܚܬܐ.
ܥܒܝܕܐ ܠܗܕܐ. ܒܗ̇ ܒܡܫܝܚܘܬܐ ܠܗܠܝܢ. ܐܦ
ܒܡܘ̈ܫܚܬܐ ܩܘ̈ܠܐ ܘܡܫܚܢ ܐܝܬ ܕܢܘ̈ܚܐ. ܗܘ
ܗܢܐ ܫܘܠܦܐ ܕܬܘܬܒܐ. ܐܡܝܢܐ ܕܡܫܬܥܠܐ
ܬܘܬܒܐ: ܐܝܟܢܐ ܕܐܦ ܕܠܝܢܐ ܐܝܬ ܡܬܠܠܗ
ܡܠܬܐ ܒܒܪ ܐܢܫܐ. ܓ̇ܠܡ.

ܘܗܢܐ ܕܐܪ̈ܒܥܝܢ ܘܥܣ̈ܪܐ ܕܫܡ̈ܗܐ ܕܟܢܘܢܐ
ܦܩ̈ܘܕܐ. ܡܬܦܪܣܢܐ. ܡܬܡܚܠܢܐ.. ܗܠܝܢ
ܗܟܝܠ ܡܢ ܡ̈ܠܐ ܫܩ̈ܝܠܬܐ ܕܢܟܢܐ ܕܗܟܢ
ܡܬܦܫܩܝܢ. ܘܗܕܐ ܕܠܝܬܐ ܐܝܬ ܠܗܘܢ
ܠܟܠܗܘܢ. ܕܢܦܩܘܢ ܡܢ ܦ̄ ܐܬܘܬܐ ܕܠܐ
ܡܠܝܢ. ܐܝܟ ܗܢܐ ܕܐܦ ܠܗܘܢ ܠܡ̈ܠܐ ܫܩ̈ܝܠܬܐ
ܗܠܝܢ ܕܡܬܚܙ̈ܝܢ ܠܗܘܢ. ܐܠܐ ܗܢܐ ܡܬܡܫܚܢܐ
ܚܘܝܬܐ. ܗܢܐ ܕܣܝܡܝܢ ܡ̈ܠܐ ܡ̈ܬܚܫܒܢ ܀
ܦܠܓܢܐܝܬ ܕܝܢ ܗܘ ܗܘܟܡܐ ܡܬܐܡܪܝܢ܀
ܒܡܘ̈ܠܕܐ ܒܠܚܘܕ ܕܗܿܝ ܩ̄ ܕܒܝܬܠܗܘܢ ܀
(fol. 37 *b*) ܡܬܦܪܣܢܐ. ܡܬܡܚܠܢܐ.
ܡܬܦܪ̈ܣܢܐ. ܡܬܡܚܠܢܢ.
ܡܬܚܫܠܢܐ. ܡܬܡܚܠܢܐ. ܡܬܫ̈ܠܢܐ.

ܡܬܡܚܠܢܢ. ܫܠܡܘ ܩܘܢܐ ܕܫܡ̈ܗܐ

ܦܩ̈ܘܕܐ ܕܡܫ̈ܠܢܐ ܩܘܕܡܝܐ ܐܦ ܕܬܪ̈ܝܢܐ: ܗܠܝܢ
ܡܢ ܫ̈ܠܝܚܐ ܀

ܡܛܠ ܫܘ̈ܡܗܐ ܫ̈ܠܝܚܐ ܀ ܫܘ̈ܡܗܐ ܫ̈ܠܝܚܐ
ܟܕ ܐܝܬ ܠܗܘܢ ܒܗܘܢ ܠܟܠܗ ܒܢ̈ܬ ܩܠܐ
ܕܗܢܘܢ ܡܬܩ̈ܢܐ ܕܐܝܬܝܗܘܢ ܓܠܝܬܐ.
ܡܡܠܠܝܢ ܬܘܦܣܬܐ ܗܿܝ ܡܡ̈ܠܠܢܝܬܐ ܕܠܗܘܢ.
ܘܡܫܢܐ ܗܘܝܢ ܬܪ̈ܝܢܐ ܡ̈ܬܬܦܫܩܢܐ.
ܘܡܬܦܠܓܝܢ ܒܠ ܗܘܢ ܡܬ̈ܩܢܐ. ܟܕ ܠܘ ܒܠ

ܡܕܒܪܢܐ ܗܘ̇ ܕܡܦܩܐ ܠܗ ܒܥܠܬܐ ܘܡܕܒܪܗ
ܡܬܐܡܪ̈ܢ. ܘܡܬܬܦܝܣ ܚܕ ܚܕ ܡܢܗܘܢ ܐܘ
ܡܬܦܠܓܢ. ܐܠܐ ܐܚܪ̈ܢܐ ܥܠ ܡܕܒܪܢܐ
ܐܚܪܢܐ. ܘܗܘ ܕܡܢ ܗܢܐ ܥܠ ܐܚܪܢܐ.
ܘܗܘ ܕܡܢ ܐܚܪܢܐ ܥܠ ܗܢܐ. ܠܗܘܢ ܬܠ̈ܬܐ
ܕܬܩ̈ܢܝܢ ܒܝܘܢܝܘܬܗ ܕܬܠܝܬܝܘܬܐ. ܐܠܐ ܡܢ ܡܕܡ
ܕܢܦܩ ܐܝܟ ܠܗܘܢ ܠܥܡ̈ܡܐ ܗ̇ܘܝܘ
ܬ̈ܠܝܬܝܐ ܘܠܡܘܢܝܘܗܝ. ܠܗܝܢ ܠܬܘܩܦܬܐ
ܗܠܝܢ ܕܡܬܚܡܝܢ ܠܗܘܢ ܕܢܐܡܪ ܕܗܘ. ܕܡܢܗ̇
ܘܕܐܝܠܝܢ ܐܝܬܝܗܝܢ. ܘܕܗ ܗܠܝܢ ܕܠܬܪ̈ܝܢ. ܗܟܢܐ
ܢܦܫ ܠܥܡ̈ܡܐ ܡܫ̈ܡܠܝܢܘܬܗܘܢ. ܬܠܬ ܗ̇ܢ ܗܟܝܠ
ܡܢ̈ܝܢ ܠܝ ܬܘܩܦܬܐ ܗܠܝܢ ܕܡܩ̈ܝܡܝܢ ܠܗܘܢ
ܠܥܡ̈ܡܐ ܗ̇ܘܢ ܬܠܝܬܝܐ ܒܡܫܡܠܝܐ ܗܢܐ
ܢܐܡܪ. ܐܝܟܢܐ ܕܐܦ ܒܡܟܣܪܐ ܗܘ ܡܕܒܪܢܐ
ܦܘܬ. ܐܝܬܝܗܘܢ ܕܝܢ ܬܠ̈ܬ ܗܢܝ̈ܢ. ܗܢ̇ܝ ܕܡܢ
ܬܪ̈ܝܬܝܗܘܢ ܗܠܝܢ ܡܬܐܡܪܐ ܗܘܐ ܕܝܢ ܬܠܐ. ܕܐܝܟ
ܐܡܝܢ. ܡܢ ܥܠܡܐ ܥܠܡܝܢܝ. ܘܡܢ ܐܪܒܥܐ
ܐܪ̈ܒܥܝܢ. ܘܡܢ ܐܠܗܐ ܐܠܗܝܢ. ܘܡܢ ܐܢܫܐ
ܐܢܫܐ. ܘܡܢ ܪܘܚܐ ܪܘܚܢܝ. ܘܬܘܒ ܪܘܚܢܝܐ
ܒܝܕ ܬܪ̈ܝܢܘܬܗ ܬܘܩܦܬܐ. ܘܡܢ ܠܡܥܡܕܢܐ
ܠܡܥܡܕܢܝ. ܘܬܘܒ ܠܡܥܡܕܢܝܐ. ܘܦܓܪܢܐ
ܘܦܓܪܢܝ. ܘܡܠܐܟܐ ܘܐܐܪܢܝ. ܘܢܘܪܢܐ
ܘܢܘܪܢܐ. ܘܡܫܝܢܐ ܡܫܝܢܝ. ܘܐܦ ܐܪܥܢܐ
ܡܢ ܐܪܥܢܐ. ܘܗܘ ܗܘܕܝܢ ܐܦ ܠܗܘܢ
ܗ̇ܘ ܐܚܪܢܐ ܕܡܢ ܥܠܬܐ ܐܚܪ̈ܢܝܐ ܕܩܪܒܘܬܐ
ܗܠܝܢ ܡܕܡ̈ܝܢܬܐ ܐܝܬ ܠܗܘܢ ܒܟܝܢܐ. ܠܗܠܝܢ
ܦܪܝܫܝܢ ܥܡ̈ܡܐ ܬܠܝܬܝܐ. ܘܬܪ̈ܝܢܝܐ
ܘܡܬܬܩܢܝܢܐ. ܬܠܝܬܝܐ ܡܢ: ܥܠ ܕܡܢ ܐܚܪ̈ܢܐ
ܐܝܬ ܠܗܘܢ ܦܪܝܫܘܬܐ. ܕܗܘܝܘ ܗܘܘ ܠܗܘܢ
ܥܠܬܐ. ܬܪ̈ܝܢܐ ܕܝܢ. ܥܠ ܕܡܠܦܢܘܬܐ ܬܪ̈ܝܢܐ
ܘܡܬܬܝܕܥܝܢ ܒܡܫܡܠܝܐ. ܬܠܝܬܝܘܬܐ ܕܝܢ.
ܡܛܠ ܕܥܠ ܗܠܝܢ ܡܕܡ̈ܝܢܐ ܕܡܬܬܣܝܡܝܢ
ܘܡܬܦܠܓܝܢ. ܗܠܝܢ ܘܕܐܝܟ ܗܠܝܢ ܐܝܬܝܗܘܢ
ܥܡ̈ܡܐ ܬܠܝܬܝ̈ܐ. ܗܠܝܢ ܕܡܢ ܐܚܪ̈ܢܐ ܐܝܬ
ܠܗܘܢ ܥܠܬܐ ܕܡܬܝܢܘܗ̇. ܗܘܝܘ ܕܐܦ

ܗ̇ܘܝܘ ܒܕܡܘܬܐ ܕܟܠܗܘܢ ܬ̈ܟܣܐ ܕܡܥܠܠܐ
ܗܢܐ ܢܘܗܪܐ. ܟܕ ܢܛܪܝܢ ܠܗ ܠܡܘܢܝܐ ܗܘ
ܕܠܘܬ ܕܠܥܠ. ܒܫܘܠܡܐ. . . . .
. . . .
. . . .
(fol. 38 *a*) ܠܗܠܝܢ ܕܫܡܝܐ ܢܦܩ. ܐܝܟ ܕܚܢܢܐ
ܐܝܬܝܗܘܢ.. ܗܘܠܝܐܗܘܢ ܗܟܝܠ ܕܥܡ̈ܡܐ ܗܠܝܢ
ܕܡܘܢܝܐ ܗܢܐ. ܬ̈ܠܝܬܝܐ ܡܬܬܩܢܝܢ ܀ ܒܗ̇
ܒܕܡܘܬܐ ܐܦ ܗ̇ܘܝܘ ܕܠܘܬ ܒܗܘܢ ܦ̄.
ܐܝܟ ܡܘܢܝܐ ܗܘ ܠܓܘܢܐ ܡܬܐܡܪܝܢ
ܦܠܢܐܝܬ *. ܕܐܡܪܐ. ܕܐܡܪܝ. ܣܕ. ܝ̄.
ܦܐܡܐ. ܦܐܪܐ. ܚܠܟܐ. ܗܠܝܢ ܐܝܟ ܡܘܢܝܐ
ܗܘ ܠܓܘܢܐ. ܒܫܘܠܡܐ ܒܠܫܘܢ ܕܐ̄ ܗ̇ܝ
ܕܡܫܠܡܘܬܗܘܢ ܠܓ̄. ܗ̇ܝ ܕܚܢܢܐ. ܡܬܐܡܪܝܢ
ܦܠܢܐܝܬ. ܕܐܝܟ ܐܡܝܢ. ܦܐܟܐ. ܦܐܪܐ. ܦܐܪܝ.
ܦܐܪ̈ܐ. ܦܐܪ̈ܝ. ܚܠܐܟܐ. ܚܠܐܟܝ. ܪܫܡܐ
ܕܝܢ ܢܗܘܐ ܒܡܘܢܝܐ ܗܢܐ ܚܕ ܐܬܬܐ: ܐܝܟ ܡܢ
ܡܘܢܝܐ ܐܚܪܢܐ ܐܝܬܝܗܘܢ. [ܘ]ܬܦܐܢܐ.
ܬܦܐܘܬܐ. ܀. ܦ̄. ܟ̄. ܡܓܘܢܐ. ܦܐܪܐ.
ܥܒܕܬܐ. ܒܝܫܬܐ. ܐܦ ܗܠܝܢ ܐܝܟ ܐܝܬ ܒܗܘܢ
ܦ̄. ܐܝܟ ܠܝܬ ܒܗܘܢ. ܐܝܟ ܡܘܢܝܐ ܗܘ
ܠܓܘܢܐ ܡܬܐܡܪܝܢ ܦܠܢܐܝܬ. ܕܐܝܟ
ܐܡܝܢ. ܡܠܟܐ. ܡܠܟܝ. ܦܪܟܐ.
ܦܪܟܝ. ܗܕܟܐ. ܗܕܟܝ. ܓܪܟܐ.
ܓܪܟܝ. ܥܕܟܬܐ. ܥܕܟܬܝ. ܒܗܟܬܐ.
ܒܗܟܬܝ. ܪ̈ܫܡܐ ܕܝܢ. ܒܓܟܬܐ ܡܛܠ ܕܡܢ
ܒܓܟܢܬܐ ܦܫܝܛܐ. ܘܡܢ ܟܕ ܚܕܪܐ ܥܒܕ
ܥܒܕܐ. ܘܡܛܠ ܗܕܐ ܠܥܒܕܢܐ ܐܚܪ̈ܢܝܢ
ܦܠܢܐܝܬ. ܠܒܟܬܐ ܡܢ ܠܒܟܢܬܐ
ܠܟܒܝ. ܒܟܦܬܐ (sic) ܡܢ ܒܟܦܢܬܐ

* Margin, ܗܕܒܐ.

ܠܐܟܘܪ ܀ ܒ. ܠ̈. ܠܐܒܝܬܐ. ܕܐܒܝܬܐ. ܫܘ̈ܚܐ
ܕܡܘܢܐ ܗܘܐ ܕܒܝܬ ܠ̈ ܐܬܘܬܐ ܘܠܘܝܬܐ.
ܡܢ ܫܘ̈ܚܐ ܕܙܘ̈ܓܐ ܫ̈ܒܝܢܐ ܗ̇ܢܘܢ ܕܒܝܬ ܛ̈
ܕܡܢ ܫܘܠܐ ܒܫܘܪܐ ܘܫܘܠܐ ܡܪܟܒܐ ܘܐܕܪܐܝܬ
ܗܘܘ ܒ̈ ܡܬܦܠܣܝܢ ܒܗ ܡܬܬܘܣܦ ܠܗܘܢ
ܒܫܘܠܡܗܘܢ ܐܬ̈ܐ܃ ܫܘܠܐ ܐܣܝܪܐ ܘܗܘܘ
ܬܠܬܝܢ ܫ̈ܘܠܐ. ܒܗ ܡܬܐܡܪܝܢ ܦܫܝܛܐܝܬ.
ܕܐܡܝܢ ܐܡܝܢ. ܒܒܠܬܐ. ܠܐܒܝܐ.
ܠܐܒܝܬܐ. ܕܒܠܬܐ. ܕܐܒܝܐ. ܕܐܒܝܬܐ.
ܫܘܠܬܐ. ܫܐܦܝܐ. ܫܐܦܝܬܐ. ܠܦܘܬ
ܡܘܢܐ ܗܘܐ ܐܡܪܝܢ ܡ̈ܠܝܢ ܐܦ ܦܪܠܬܐ.
ܡܐܪܝܬܐ. ܘܠܐ ܒܕܝܠܝ. ܗ̇ܢܘܢ ܕܝܢ
ܕܐܡܪܝܢ ܡܘܪܝܐ. ܠܦܘܬ ܡܘܢܐ ܕܫܘ̈ܚܐ
ܡܢܝܢܐ ܐܡܪܝܢ. ܘܠܐ ܠܫܡܥܐܝܬ.. ܐܝܟܢ ܐܦ
ܕܬܐܡܪܘܢ ܒܡܘܢܐ ܗܘܐ: ܫܘ̈ܚܐ
ܕܡܬܬܢܐ ܕܠܝܬ ܒܗܘܢ ܦ̇. ܐܦ ܗܠܝܢ ܐܡܝܢ
ܡܘܢܐ ܗ̇ܘ ܕܠܒܐ ܡܬܐܡܪܝܢ ܡܫܬܡܗܢܘܬ.
ܦܠܬܐ. ܦܠܬܝ. ܡܦܠܬܐ. ܡܦܠܬܝ܀
ܒܦܠܬܐ ܕܝܢ ܠܘ ܝܫܘ ܚܠܝܫ ܡܬܐܡܪܢܐ
ܒܡܘܢܐ ܡܫܬܡܗܢܐ. ܡܛܠ ܚܝܠ ܕܫܘܘܕܥܐ
ܡܫܬܡܗܢܐ ܡܢܝܢ. ܐܦ ܒܗ ܡܬܐܡܪܢܐ
ܣܕܝܩܬ ܀ ܙܘܓܐ ܕܝܢ ܐܝܬ ܠܝ. ܦܠܬܐ.
ܦܓܥܬܐ. ܒܬܠܬܐ. ܒܓܘܢܝܬܐ. ܘܙܦ
ܗܘܐ ܕܝܢ ܐܡܝܢ ܡܘܢܐ ܕܡܬܐܡܪ. ܒܬܠܬܐ.
ܠܦܪܝܬܐ. ܐܝܟܢܐ ܕܢܩܘܫ ܦܘܫ ܡܢ ܫܘܚܐ
ܗ̇ܘ ܕܒܓܘܢܝܬܐ ܕܡܥܘܒܕ ܫܘܫܐ.
ܕܡܬܐܡܪ ܐܦ ܗܘ (fol. 38 b) ܡܫܬܡܗܢܘܬ
ܒܓܘܢܝܬܐ ܀ ܒܐ. ܝ̈. ܐܣܝܪܬܐ. ܒܗܘܢܐ
ܡܘܢܐ ܕܡܢ ܫܘܠܐ ܒܫܘܪܐ ܘܫܘܠܐ ܦܫܝܛܐ.
ܠܐ ܐܫܬܟܚܘ ܫܘ̈ܚܐ ܒܡܫܡܠܝܐ ܗܘܐ. ܐܦ
ܗܘܐ ܕܝܢ ܚܕ ܕܐܫܬܟܚ. ܦܫܘܛܐ ܐܝܬܘܗܝ.
ܘܡܘܢܐ ܗ̇ܘ ܕܡܢ ܬܪܝܢ ܫ̈ܘܠܐ ܡܪܟܒܐ
ܘܙܦ ܕܡܬܬܗܦܟ. ܕܐܡܝܢ ܐܡܝܢ. ܣܪܝܩܬܐ.
ܣܪܝܩܬܐ. ܡܘܢܐ ܗ̇ܘ ܗܘܒܐ. ܗܘܟܢܐ

ܬܠܬܐ ܗܘܐ ܕܡܬܬܦܫܛ. ܡܢ ܚܢܢܐ ܕܝܢ
ܕܡܫܡܠܝܐ ܢܗܘܪܐ. ܠܐ ܗܘܐ ܚܕ ܝ̈
ܐܬܘܬܐ ܘܠܘܝܬܐ ܡܬܐܡܪܢ ܡܫܬܡܗܢܘܬ.
ܐܠܐ ܚܕ ܛ. ܣܪܝܩܬܐ ܠܒܪ ܐܡܪܝܢ ܐܘܪܗܝܐ
ܣܕܝܩܬ. ܣܪܝܩܬܐ ܕܝܢ ܡܫܬܡܗܢܘܬ.
ܠܬܐܒܐ ܕܝܢ ܒܚܝܠܐ ܡܛܠ ܦܘܪܫܢܐ ܕܠܘܬ
ܫܘܚܐ ܗ̇ܘ ܕܣܪܝܩܬ ܐܦ ܐ̈ ܐܘܣܦ (sic) ܠܗ̇
ܒܫܘܪܗ ܒܗ ܡܬܬܬܒܐ ܦ̇. ܠܐ ܕܝܢ ܢܦܩܐ
ܒܫܠܐ ܘܡܫܬܡܗܢܐ ܀ ܒܗ. ܦ̈. ܦܘܫܠܐ.
ܦܘܪܠܐ. ܣܘܠܠܐ. ܦܪܘܠܐ. ܗܠܝܢ ܕܠܘܬ
ܐܫܟܚ ܒܡܘܢܐ ܗܘܐ. ܘܒܠܗܘܢ ܡܫܬܡܗܢܝܢ
ܕܢܘܚܪܐ ܐܝܬܝܗܘܢ ܕܠܫܢܐ ܢܗܪܝܐ. ܐܝܟ
ܥܠܝܡ ܠܡܘܢܐ ܗ̇ܘ ܠܦܘܢܐ. ܗ̇ܘ ܦ̇ܢ ܠܒܪ
ܕܦܘܪܠܐ ܘܗ̇ܘ ܕܣܠܘܠܝ ܡܩܢܐ ܐܝܬܝܗܘܢ.
ܗ̇ܘ ܕܝܢ ܕܦܪܘܠܝ ܒܚܪܬܐ. ܘܗ̇ܘ ܕܣܠܘܠܝ
ܫܒܩܐ ܕܩܘܫܝܬܐ ܐܝܬ ܘܠܐ ܡܬܐܡܪ
ܡܫܬܡܗܢܘܬ ܀ ܦܘܠܠܐ. ܦܘܠܠܝ.
ܦܪܘܠܐ. ܦܪܘܠܝ. ܦܪܘܠܠܐ. ܦܪܘܠܠܝ܀
ܡܬܐܡܪܝܢ ܕܝܢ ܗܠܝܢ ܒܚܒܪܐ ܠܘܬ ܐܢܫܝܢ.
ܐܦ ܕܚܢܢܐܝܬ ܀ ܚܒ. ܠ̈. ܝ̈. ܝܥܘܬܐ.
ܕܝܥܘܬܐ. ܒܥܘܪܐ. ܗܠܝܢ ܫܘ̈ܚܐ ܕܡܘܢܐ
ܗܢܝ. ܐ̈ ܢ̈ ܦ̇ܢ ܐܝܬ ܒܗܘܢ ܦ̇. ܒܗ ܗܘܝܢ
ܬܠܬܝܗܝܢ ܫܘ̈ܠܐ ܒܗ ܟ̈ ܐܬܘܬܐ ܘܠܘܝܬܐ.
ܘܒܗ ܒ̈ ܐ̈: ܢܦܫܝ ܡܫܬܡܗܢܘܬ. ܕܐܡܝܢ
ܐܡܝܢ. ܝܥܘܬܐ. ܝܥܘܟܒܘܬܐ. ܕܝܥܘܬܐ.
ܕܝܥܘܟܒܘܬܐ ܀ ܐܝܢܝܢ ܠܝܬ ܒܗܘܢ ܦ̇.
ܒܡܘܢܐ ܗ̇ܘ ܠܦܘܢܐ ܡܬܐܡܪܝܢ ܡܫܬܡܗܢܘܬ.
ܒܥܘܪܐ. ܒܥܘܪܝ ܀ ܗܘ ܗܕܡܘܬ. ܐܦ
ܐܚܝܢܐ ܐܝܟܘ ܕܡܫܬܟܚܝܢ ܀ ܩ̈ܕܝܫܐ ܕܝܢ
ܗܢܝܢܬܐ. ܒܢܝܢܬܐ. ܕܠܐ ܐܝܬ ܠܗܘܢ
ܕܬܐܡܪܘܢ ܡܫܬܡܗܢܘܬ. ܚܒ. ܝ̈. *ܒܪܘܬܐ.

* Marg. ܗܪܟܐ ܡܫܠܡܐ ܕܝܢ ܡܘܢܐ ܒܗ ܗܢ ܐܘܪܗܝܐ.

ܓܠܘܬܐ . ܚܘܪܬܐ . ܐܦ ܗܠܝܢ ܕܒ ܗܘܡ
ܬܠܬܝܢ ܩ̈ܠܐ . ܟܕ ܦ̄ܘ . ܘܟܕ ܐܬܪ̈ܝܢ ܐ̄
ܡܬܐܡܪܝܢ ܦܓܝܢܐܝܬ (sic) . ܕܐܝܟ ܐܡܪ .
ܒܪܣܬܐ . ܒܪܘܣܐܬܐ . (sic) ܓܡܠܬܐ .
ܓܠܘܣܐܬܐ . ܚܪܣܬܐ . ܚܪܘܣܐܬܐ . ܙܢܝܬܐ
ܕܐܝܟ ܐܝܬ ܠܝ . ܡܢܘܬܐ . ܫܢܘܬܐ . ܫܢܝܘܬܐ .
ܙܢܘܬܐ . ܒܢܘܬܐ . ܡܢ ܗܠܝܢ ܡܢܘܬܐ ܗ̄ܝ .
ܟܕ ܒܪ̈ܝ ܠܗ ܦܫܝܩܐ ܠܚܒܠܐ ܗܘ ܡܬܚܙܝܐ .
ܢܦܩ ܦܓܝܢܐܝܬ . ܟܕ ܚܕܐ ܐ̄ ܐܬܘܬܐ
ܡܠܝܬܐ . ܘܬܪܬܝܢ ܐ̄ . ܕܐܝܟ ܐܡܪ ....

. . . .

Brit. Mus. Add. 14,665.

ܘܐܦ ܗܠܝܢ ܕܡܘܢܐ ܗܢܐ (fol. 28 *a*, col. 1)
ܕܟܕ ܟ̄ ܐܬܘܬܐ ܡܠܝܬܐ ܕܡܢ ܬܪܝܢ ܩ̈ܠܐ
ܡܬܝܕܥܝܢ . ܐܝܟ ܕܡܫܬܡܥܝܢ ܒܗ ܐܦ
ܐܚ̈ܪܢܝܢ . ܟܠܗܘܢ ܢܦܪܫ ܡܢܢܐ . ܠܐ ܓܝܪ
ܗܟܢ ܐܝܟ ܕܡܫܬܡܥ ܒܗ ܩܠܝܠܐܝܬ .
ܒܪܟܡܐ . ܒܪܟܡܘܗܝ . ܦܠܟܘܢܐ .
ܦܠܟܘܢ . ܦܠܟܘܢܐ ܐܝܟ ܫܡܐ ܡܢܢܐ
ܐܬܘܗܝ . ܘܫܘܠܡܐ ܡܫܬܡܥ* ܇ ܦ̄ܠ ܡܢܢܐ
ܕܟܣܪܝܢ .... ܠ ....†
ܒܗܢܐ ܡܢܢܐ ܠܐ ܐܫܬܡܥܘ ܬ̈ܫܡܫܐ
ܕܚ̈ܝܢܐ . ܠܐ ܓܝܪ ܠܟܠ ܗܢܐ ܙܘܒܢܐ
ܕܡܢ ܬܪܝܢ ܩ̈ܠܐ ܡܬܝ̈ܕܥܐ ܠܫ̈ܡܗܐ

. . . .

(2nd col.) ܡܫܝܚ ܠܗ ܠܡܢܝܢܐ ܗܢܐ ܕܐܝܟ ܐܡܪ .
ܙܘܓܐ . ܙܘܓܬܐ . ܦܪܕܐ . ܦܪܕܬܐ . ܫܘܒܐ .
ܫܘܒܬܐ . ܙܢܓܠܐ ܙܢܓܠܬܐ . ܦܪܓܠܐ .
ܦܪܓܠܬܐ . ܫܓܠܐ . ܫܓܠܬܐ . ܦܓܠܐ .
ܦܓܠܬܐ . ܡܢ ܗܠܝܢ ܡܟܝܠ ܐܬܡܚ̈ܝܢ .
ܕܡܢܝܢܐ ܗܢܐ ܕܡܢ (?) ܬܪܝܢ ܥܩ̈ܠܐ ܡܬܝ̈ܕܥܐ

* Margin, ΦΛΕΓΜΑ. ΦΛΕΓΜΑΤΑ, in small, neat characters.

† Illegible rubric. The marginal letters ܦ̄ܠ are very uncertain.

ܠܓ̈ܢܣܐ ܢܩܒܬܢܝܐ ܠܫܡ . ܘܠܐ ܗܘܐ ܠܕܟܪܢܐ .
ܚܕ ܕܝܢ ܫܡܐ ܐܫܬܟܚ ܒܗ . ܘܗܘܐ ܢܦܩ
ܠܡܢܝܢܐ ܗܘ ܕܡܢܐ ܕܡܬܡܠܐ ܗܘܐ ܢܩܒ̈ܝܐ .
ܘܡܫܠܡܐ ܕܐ̄ ܗ̇ܝ ܕܡܫܡܠܝܐ ܠܗ . ܡܬܦܢܝܢ
ܦܓܝܢܐܝܬ . ܕܐܝܟ ܐܡܪ . ܦܠܓܡܐ .
ܦܠܓܡܛܐ . ܥܠܝܗ̇ ܡܢܝܢܐ ܕܟܣܪܝܢ ܘ[ܬܘܒ] ܇

. . . .

(verso, 1st col.) ܦܘܪܘܣܐ . ܓܠܘܣܘܣܐ .
ܡܠܘܟܠܐ . ܡܫܘܪܐ ܇ ܘܬܘܒ ܫܘܒܗܐ
ܬܠܬܝܢܐ ܕܡܟܟܝܘܬܐ ܘܕܝܫܐ . ܕܠܘܝܫܐ .
ܦܘܪܝܐ . ܦܘܪܝܐ . ܟܠܘܢܐ . ܟܠܘܢܐ ܇ ܟܠܗܘܢ
ܗܢܠ ܫܡ̈ܗܐ ܬܪ̈ܝܢܐ ܦܫܝܩܐ ܕܒ̈ܪܢܐ ܕܟܕ
ܩ̄ ܐܬܘܬܐ ܡܠܝܬܐ ܕܡܢ ܬܪܝܢ ܥܩ̈ܠܐ
ܡܬܝܕܥܐ : ܘܟܠܗܘܢ ܗ̇ܢܘܢ ܬܘܒ ܬܠܬܝܢܐ
ܕܐܝܬ ܠܗܘܢ ܒ̄ ܒ̈ܥܠܐ ܗ̇ܘ ܐܚܪܢܐ ܡܢܢ ܐ̄
ܗ̇ܝ ܕܡܫܡܠܝܐ ܠܗܘܢ : ܒܗ̇ ܒܡܢܝܢܐ ܠܟܠܗܘܢ
ܡ̈ܢܝܢܐ ܡܬܐܡܪܝܢ ܦܓܝܢܐܝܬ . ܕܐܝܟ ܐܡܪ .
ܦܠܦܪܐ . ܦܠܦܪܘܢ . ܟܠܦܣܐ .
ܟܠܦܣܘܢ . ܟܠܦܠܐ (sic) . ܡܠܦܠܝܢ .
ܡܣܦܪܐ . . . .

. . . .

(2nd col.) . . . . . . ܕܟܕ ܬ̄ ܕܡܢ . . . . . .*
ܐܦ ܗܢܐ ܬܘܒ ܠܫ̈ܡܗܐ ܢܩܒܬܢܝܐ
ܠܫܡ ܘܠܐ ܡܫܬܟܚܝܢ ܒܗ ܕܟܪ̈ܢܐ ܐܝܟ
ܕܐܬܝܐ ܇ ܡܬܝܕܥܐ ܗܪܟܐ . ܐܝܟ ܕܠܫܡܐ
ܗ̇ܘ ܕܒܚܘܪܐ ܘܗ̇ܘ ܕܒܥܘܪܐ ܕܡܬܕܥܘ
ܐܬܬܗܝܒܘ ܒܗ̇ܘ ܕܟܣܪܝܢ ܘܫܡܫܐ .
ܬܓܒܘ ܢܩܒܬܢܐܝܬ . ܕܐܝܟ ܐܡܪ .
ܐܘܪܬܐ . ܒܘܪܬܐ . ܐܓܪܬܐ . ܒܒܪܬܐ .
† . . . .
ܒܬܪ ܗܠܝܢ ܡܟܝܠ ܇ ܩ̄ܠ ܩܘܢܝܐ ܕܥܠ̈ܡܐ
ܬܪܝܢ ܩ̈ܠܐ ܐܘ ܬܠܬܐ ܒܚܠܝ . ܕܡܢ . . . . .

. . . .

* The greater part of this rubric is illegible.

† Illegible rubric.

JACOB OF EDESSA, *GRAMMAR*

There follows a translation of the fragments of Jacob's *Grammar* as reconstructed in Wright's edition which was reproduced in the foregoing pages. For ease of reference, we have preserved the order of the fragments as Wright presented them. However, it seems likely that they should be read in the order 1-3-4-2.

Note that Fragment 1 had not been included in Payne Smith's catalogue of the Syriac mss in the Bodleian since it was Wright who first identified it as part of Jacob's work (see comments in his introduction). Martin believed Fragment 1 to derive from a different treatise.

Fragment 1: Bodleian Syr.159, additional folios

(fol.1b, col.1) Expressions...also these...when they are found...in Syriac letters...Mesopotamian, forbidden... and remained from this.... I do not know....of them. Or th[ese]...or since others....Because they saw...many.... [17 or 18 lines missing]

(col.2) One of their grammarians states that originally even the Greeks did not have a complete script, for they possessed only 17 letters. Moreover, even when other [letters] were added [to their alphabet], they were not added all at once, but rather one person added one or two at a certain time, and then others added other [letters] at other times, until there were 24 in number, and [hence] a complete script was established. But since I know the reason that prevented [my predecessors] from adding further letters, viz. so that all the books that had been written up to the present time in this imperfect script of the Mesopotamian language would not be lost, and since I [also] respect the labour of my predecessors ...it was difficult until...your request.... ...... would become and would assume *(fol.1a, col.1)* completion, viz. that there should be established accurate paradigms (i.e. morphological patterns) for this language without actually adding the vowel letters that the script lacks, by means of which [vowels] one can demonstrate the application of the paradigms, and the orthography of the nouns and verbs that are [established] by them. And being as I am constrained [on one side] by your request, and [on the other] by the threat that [all previous] books might become lost (i.e. become obsolete)–which is just what motivated those former [grammarians]–I think that I shall fulfil your request by adding letters purely for the sake of the ?sense [of words] and the establishing of paradigms, the goal being to demonstrate the

variations and pronunciations[1] of the sounds themselves, and not for the sake of perfecting the arrangement of the script. [So I shall fulfil your request] because it is [your] affection that seeks it, and on account of the saying that it is a sin for one to know the good but not carry it out (James 4:17). Know, then, also this other thing, that the nouns......and verbs are......that they were supposed......and are from........(col.2) thus......Greek. ......spoken......those ones......of the books themselves and......viz. [the letter] alaph......and the rest, and also......this name of the script......Hebrew nouns......for in the Hebrew language......is......[17 or 18 lines missing].

(fol.2a, col.1)... ...[the letters] ḥet or ʿayin or ṣade or šin, or any word containing any of them, because these are not present anywhere in their language. Because of this they also have no need to make use of them. In just the same way other languages also have various other letters, which no other languages are able to pronounce in their language. The Syrians, then, viz. [the speakers of] this Edessene dialect,[2] are hindered not by their language but by this script of theirs, since it is incomplete and lacks vowels; and, as I said before, they are unable to read anything accurately apart from these three [methods] that were previously established above, viz. either:

1) by intuition, because of the appropriate sense that the reading of any given piece is tending towards.

2) or else by tradition [passed on from] others, who had previously had experience of the text and its readings, *(col.2)* and who were capable of pronouncing the sounds accurately and passing them on to others – not on the basis of an accurate [system of] notation of the letters, for they do not have that, but rather they also [received it] from the tradition of others.

3) By much practice, for although [readers] quickly pass over and fly across the readings as if they had learned them by rote, there are in fact a variety of symbols among the points that assist them and that indicate to them the various senses [of the sentences], such that those who receive [i.e. learn these readings], understand not on the basis of the letters but of the sounds which are pronounced by the lips of the tradent.

But there was a time when even the former [experts] placed additional letters in the nouns when writing them so as to differentiate [them] from other nouns having the very same letters but not the same sound. *(fol.2b, col.1)* Let me offer by way of example [the words] gabrā and ganbārā, where it is not because it [really] has the nūn that [the nūn] is placed in it. For it didn't need it and it isn't even pronounced in the word. Rather [it is written there] to differentiate this noun gabrā, which has the very same letters but not the same sound as [the word] ganbārā. Later on when many people saw this written nūn and other letters of the same sort which had been placed in nouns for this [same] reason–I mean by this all the Westerners and inhabitants of other areas, who don't speak this Edessene dialect accurately–since they did not understand the reason why [that nūn] had been placed in the noun [ganbārā], and those other [letters] of the same sort, they actually pronounced them in the word.

And it was not only they who later knowingly did this, but even some Edessenes, i.e. those who speak this *(col.2)* Mesopotamian dialect accurately, are unable to read accurately not just unusual sounds [that have come] from outside of their dialect and which they are used to, but even familiar [sounds]. For they have many such that have been set down in their books from Hebrew and Greek, while there are even a few from the Roman language as a result of the power of the Roman Empire in that region.[3] The same goes for Persian, and as I said before they do not say or read any of them accurately as a result of the lack of letters. For just this reason there were many lovers of labour in this language who saw the difficulty that the Syrians had in reading and who wanted to add to the letters those that were lacking from the script, according to the needs of linguistic usage. And with regard to this matter of reading accurately and easily.......

Fragment 2: BL Add. 17217, f.37 *(but note: should probably be placed as fragment 4)*[4]

(fol.37a)...some. But others establish them as causal [adjectives],[5] for they also give this opinion, but they in any case follow the common rule: daḥūltānā > daḥūltānē; ḥayūstānā > ḥayūstānē; šagūštānē; šapūrtānē; rayūgtānē; laḥkūštānē; ragūštānē; ragūstānē; ʿayūqtānē; naḥšērtānā > naḥšērtānē.

So remember, O reader who loves work, how in the previous discourse I spoke of those letters that are opposed to one another and which do not permit of being placed either in front of or after each other, i.e. the thicks [cannot be placed next] to the intermediates and the thins; the intermediates [cannot be placed next] to the thicks and the thins; and the thins likewise [cannot be placed next] to the thicks and the intermediates.[6] And if a thick letter should come up before an intermediate or before a thin, then it will change and become [respectively] either an intermediate or a thin. Because of this I have written the aforementioned nouns, i.e. rayūgtānā, ʿayūqtānā, and ragūztānā , as the pronunciation demands, since I have changed each letter into its cognate depending on which letter comes immediately after each.[7] For in rayūgtānā and ʿayūqtānā, because a /t/ cannot come after a thick /g/ or a thin /q/, since it is itself an intermediate, I have changed both of them into an equivalent intermediate /k/. In the case of ragūztānā, being derived from the noun ragūztā and [hence] naturally containing /z/, since [the /t/] does not allow its thickness, I have changed it into /s/, which is also intermediate. You will find that this exchange of letters occurs likewise in many other places, especially in verbs, which I am dealing with separately [in the section] on the verb. The end.

Paradigm 47 of simple masculine nouns[8]

metragšānā, metḥablānā

These are constituted from passive verbs of the present tense [i.e. participles], and they all have this property, that they start with the consonantal letter /m/, as also do those passive verbs that give rise to them.[9] But this will be understood more precisely when we examine these verbs. However, the plurals are pronounced as follows, with only the /a/ at the end being changed: *(fol.37b)*

metragšānā > metragšānē; metḥablānā > metḥablānē[10]

The paradigms of the simple masculine nouns, both the primary and the derived, are at an end, save only for the causals.

Concerning causal nouns [i.e. adjectives]:

Causal nouns [i.e. adjectives], while they all individually have the [same] sounds as the primary [nouns] which are their causes, take their own productive affix;[11] and in this way they become derived [*lit:* secondary] adjectives, and are predicated of the primary [nouns], although [in fact] each one is attributed or predicated not of that primary [noun] which was [its] cause and from which it was derived, but rather any one [such adjective] is [predicated] of a different primary [noun], and the [adjective] that [derives] from this [primary noun] [is predicated] of some other [primary noun], and [the adjective from the other one is predicated] of this one,[12] according to the requirements of the arrangement of speech.[13]

But before we establish those causal nouns [i.e. adjectives] and their paradigms, we must explain the affixes that form them, how many and which they are, and, by understanding these we shall establish their abstract nouns. So then there are three affixes known to us that form causal [adjectives] in this Mesopotamian dialect, as I also established in the former discourse. These are /nā/ and /yā/, and the compound of the two of them, namely /nāyā/. For example:

šmayyā > šmayyānā; arʿā > arʿānāyā; allāhā > allāhāyā; nāšā > nāšāyā; rūḥā > rūḥānā, and also > rūḥānāyā, by [adding] two affixes; and also gūšmā > gūšmānā, and also > gūšmānāyā; pagrānā and pagrānāyā; mallākāyā; āarrāyā; nūrānā and nūrānāyā; mayyānāyā; medrānāyā; also arʿānāyā with arʿānā.

Likewise also we call all those various [nouns] that take their designation[14] from other nouns for primary things "causal nouns [i.e. adjectives]," "derived" [*lit:* secondary], and "adjectives." [We call them] causal because they have a reading [i.e. an inflectional form] that [comes] from other [nouns] such that the latter are the "cause" of them; [we call them] "derived" because of their being brought into the language by a second order; [we call them] "adjectives" because they are "subjected" and predicated of these primary [nouns]. These and those like them are causal nouns, the cause of whose natures [derives] from other things. These too are just the same as all the other nouns of this Mesopotamian dialect, since they keep the rule of the language in altering........

Fragment 3: BL Add. 17217, f.38 *(should be read as fragment 2)*

[Paradigm 17 /ā/ ܐ][15]

(fol.38a)...pronounce these marks, even if it is masculine. Therefore the majority of the nouns that are in this paradigm are found to be verbal nouns.[16] In the same way those that do not have a /t/ are pronounced[17] in the plural in accordance with the general rule, [e.g.] krāʿā > krāʿē.

[Paradigm] 18 /a/ ܒ

prakkā; prazzā; klakkā

These are pronounced in the plural in accordance with the general rule only by altering the /ā/ that is on the end of them into /ē/ in the usual way, e.g.

prakkā > prakkē　　prazzā > prazzē　　klakkā > klakkē

Note that ḥadtātā is in this paradigm, even though it is also part of another paradigm. [Also] tpayyā > tpawwātā.

[Paradigm] 19 /e/ ܶ

mgennā; preddā; šbettā; ksettā

These also, whether or not they have the /t/,[18] are pronounced in the plural in accordance with the general rule, e.g.

mgennā > mgennē　　preddā > preddē　　šbettā > šbettē

sʿeddā > sʿeddē　　greddā > greddē　　ksettā > ksettē

Note that gbettā is an abbreviation of gbentā and is a noun loaned from Hebrew,[19] and for this reason its plural is pronounced gubnē

lbettā [likewise] from lbentā, [whose plural is] lebnē

gpettā[20] [likewise] from gpentā, [whose plural is] gupnē

[Paradigm] 20 /i/ ܺ

gbittā; dkittā

Nouns of this paradigm, which are formed with the vowel letter /i/ from masculine singular nouns which are [themselves made] of a simple syllable and a compound syllable [joined by] /a/, and which have a yodh in them, become trisyllabic when another syllable /tā/ is added to their endings, being pronounced in the plural as:

gbittā [from] gabyā [gives the plural] gabyātā[21]

dkittā [from] dakyā [gives the plural] dakyātā

špittā [from] šapyā [gives the plural] šapyātā

Some people pronounce qrittā according to this paradigm, [viz.] qaryātā, and they aren't wrong. But people who pronounce it as quryas, according to the form of Greek nouns, are not right, even though feminine nouns without a /t/ are also to be found in this paradigm. The following are pronounced in the plural according to the common rule:

pʿirrā > pʿirrē   sʿirrā > sʿirrē

Nobody, however, pronounces bʿirrā in the plural form because it possesses a plural meaning even when it is pronounced in the singular.[22] You should note, however, that [in the case of] pnittā > penyātā [and] brittā > beryātā, it ought according to the aforementioned rule be brittā > baryātā, so as to be distinguished from the noun berittā which means a market, which is also pronounced *(fol.38b)* in the plural [as] beryātā.[23]

[Paradigm] 21 /ē/   ܶ

ʾḥrētā

The language has no nouns in this paradigm, which [is formed] from one doubly-compound syllable [ʾḥri] and one simple syllable. However, even this one that does exist, is really an abbreviation and ought to be formed within the paradigm of [nouns] of two compound syllables, viz. ḥrē-ntā > ḥrēnyātā. That is how the paradigm requires that it should be formed, but ordinarily in the Mesopotamian dialect the plural is not pronounced with the vowel letter /ē/, but with an /a/. For the Edessenes pronounce it as ḥrētā in the singular, ḥranyātā in the plural. However, so as to distinguish [it] from the noun ḥartā, older books also used to add an alaph to the beginning [of the word]- when it is written, but not when it is pronounced in reading and listening.

[Paradigm] 22 /o/   ܘ

spoggā; sroggā; ḥloggā; ṭroggā[24]

Only these words are found in this paradigm and all of them are considered foreign to the Mesopotamian dialect, even though they follow the common rule, for spoggā and sroggā [25] are Greek, while ṭroggā is Hebrew.[26] Ḥloggā is a place-name and hence has no plural.

spoggā > spoggē   sroggā > sroggē   ṭroggā > ṭroggē

Some people, out of custom, pronounce these words in the masculine as well.

[Paradigm] 23 /ū/   ܽ

ṣbūtā; dmūtā; ʿbūtā

The nouns of this paradigm, if they have the /t/ [of the feminine], are pronounced in the plural as trisyllables by means of the vowel letter /e/ and two alaphs, e.g.

ṣbūtā > ṣebwātā dmūtā > demwātā

But if there is no /t/ [of the feminine] the plurals are pronounced by the common rule:

ʿbūrā > ʿbūrē

Thus also any others that might occur, though one should note especially snūtā and brūtā, which are not pronounced in the plural.

[Paradigm] 23 /ō/[27]

brōtā; ṣlōtā; ḥrōtā

These also are pronounced in the plural as trisyllabic by [adding] /wā/ and then two alaphs as in:

brōtā > bārawwātā ṣlōtā > ṣlawwātā ḥrōtā > ḥrawwātā

But you should note also mḥōtā; šiyyōtā; šʿōtā; diyyōtā; kbōtā. Of these, mḥōtā, since it makes that first syllable simple, its plural is pronounced by means of a single vowel letter /a/ and two alaphs, as in.......

Fragment 4: BL Add. 14665, f.28 *(should be read as fragment 3)*

(fol.28a, col.1) [Paradigm 28 /e/]

...and also the [nouns] in this paradigm, formed of the vowel letter /e/ with two compound syllables, even if there are other [nouns] in it as well, all keep the rule, for I do not think that many are found in [this paradigm]: kreqsā > kreqsē; plegmā > plegmē. But plegmā is a Greek noun and means an inflammation.

Paradigm 29 /i/

......in this paradigm there are no masculine nouns, for this composition that [consists] of two compound syllables is not appropriate for nouns.......

(col.2)......it constitutes this paradigm as in, e.g.: rdīpā > rdīptā; ṭrīdā > ṭrīdtā; šbīqā > šbīqtā.[28] rdīpā > rdīptā; ṭrīdā > ṭrīdtā; šbīqā > šbīqtā; psīqā > psīqtā.[29] Therefore from these it is understood that this paradigm [consisting of nouns] of two compound syllables is appropriate to the feminine gender and not to the masculine. But there is one noun in [this paradigm] and this [one noun] keeps the common rule of this Mespotamian dialect, and is pronounced in the plural by changing the /ā/ into /ē/. As in pšīpšā > pšīpšē. The end of the 29th paradigm.

[Paradigm 30 /o/ ܘ]

(fol.28b, col.1).........pʿormā, glosqā, qṭoblā, msorqā, and also verbal nouns both active and passive, [e.g.] dloḥya, krokya, ʿroqya, ʿlobya. All these are simple, masculine singular nouns with the vowel letter /o/ and two compound syllables. Moreover all of those verbal [nouns] which have the /y/ in the last syllable before a long /ā/ at the end are pronounced in the plural in the same way as in all the paradigms, as in pʿormā > pʿormē; glosqā > glosqē; qṭoblā > qṭoblē; msorqā > [msorqē]........

......

[Paradigm 31 /ō/ ܳ]

(fol.28b, col.2)...by means of /ō/ of ......this also is again appropriate to feminine nouns and it so happens that there are no masculine [nouns] in it. This would be understood even if you made those nouns zʿorā and bkōrā, which were located earlier in the 25th [paradigm], feminine, as in zʿortā; bkōrtā.[30]......

...after these, therefore, 83 paradigms of disyllabic nouns, o lover-of-work, which......

---

1 ܫܘܚܠܦܐ ܘܬܘܪܨܐ – Merx takes these terms to mean respectively *inflection* and *phonology*. More accurately, "morphology and phonology."

2 ܡܡܠܠܐ I have rendered variously as speech, language or dialect according to the contextual sense.

3 "Romans" refers to Byzantines, but Jacob has already mentioned the Greek language, and we know (as Jacob surely did) that there were a number of Latin loans in Syriac; hence he may well mean Latin rather than Byzantine Greek.

4 Revell, *Grammar of Jacob*, 366, and note 2, argues that *Frag 2* should be placed as the last of our extant fragments, viz. after *Fr 3-4*, since it concerns two paradigms of the type CV+C(C)V+CCV+CV, which appear to have been numbered 46 and 47. He assumes that Jacob is following Theodosius's system at least insofar as he is proceeding from simpler forms towards more complex ones.

5 See Merx p.60 for discussion of the category of "causal" adjectives.

6 Revell, op.cit., calls them "heavy, medium, clear."

7 The ms does not bear this out – only one of the nouns listed above has been written phonetically in this way. It is possible that a scribe did not understand what Jacob had written and spelt the words according to the customary system.

8 Or perhaps, "paradigm of 47 simple masculine nouns."

9 I.e. the participles themselves from which these adjectival forms are derived.

10 The words are written again both with and without the vowel letters.

11 Lit: capable, or receptive. A ܫܡܐ ܡܩܒܠܢܐ would be an abstract noun, but it is not clear what an affix thus specified would be.

12 Jacob seems to be pointing out that a derived adjective cannot work together with its own primary noun, i.e. one cannot say "heaven is heavenly" or "earth is earthly," but only that "earth is heavenly," etc.

13 ܡܠܠܘܬܐ, in Jacob seems to be synonymous with ܡܡܠܠܐ. See also Moberg, 56* (Rede).

14 ܟܘܢܝܐ (*lit:* appellation). Talmon (p.178) suggests "status"; Moberg (p.51*), "Benennung".

15 Our extant fragment of Jacob's grammar begin *in medias res*, in the middle of paradigm number 17. Jacob is listing paradigms of nouns consisting of [in his system] a compound syllable + a simple syllable. These paradigms are listed in order of the first vowel, such that paradigm number 17 is nouns of shape CCV+CV and with /ā/ as their first vowel; then paradigm 18 is nouns CCV+CV with /a/; paradigm 19 is nouns CCV+CV with /e/ and so forth. Likely at paradigm 26 began the paradigms of nouns having the shape CCV+CCV (compound + compound), again going through each vowel in turn. *Frag* 4 (to be placed as 3) contains parts of paradigms 28-31. *Frag* 2 (to be placed as 4) contains parts of paradigms 46 and 47, treating of tetrasyllabic nouns

16 Or, *infinitives.* In Dionysius Thrax, the infinitive is called ἀπαρέμφατος, whereas other influential grammarians such as Apollonius called it ὄνομα ῥήματος. This terminology appears in some of the scholia to Dionysius Thrax and seems to have already influenced the Syriac translator of Dionysius, who called it ܡܠܬܐ, ܡܬܐܡܪܢܘܬܐ. Jacob's expression ܫܡܐ ܡܠܬܢܝܐ appears to be a more precise rendering of the same Greek terminology, and testifies both to Jacob's close knowledge of the Greek grammatical tradition and to his attempt to convert it to Syriac use. Further on, however, Jacob uses the same expression to refer to verbal nouns that are clearly not infinitives (see fragment 4).

17 It is not without significance that Jacob uses this expression "is spoken" rather than some other term, since his grammar is based on the spoken pronunciations of the language rather than being simply an analysis of its written or abstract form.

18 "Having a /t/" means of course feminine nouns.

19 In fact a common Semitic root, but Jacob knew of it for a Hebrew word as well.

[20] Ms reads geptā, a scribal error.
[21] These are all emphatic forms of passive participles.
[22] I.e. the collective term for domestic animals, as in "sheep".
[23] Syriac knows both beryātā and baryātā as plurals of brittā (creature); Jacob wants to instil usage of the latter in order to avoid the homophonous word for markets. Although Jacob's grammar benefits from the virtue of being grounded in the spoken form of the language, it remains prescriptive and an attempt to force the language into well-organised patterns.
[24] The precise quality and quantity of the /o/ vowel here intended is not absolutely clear. We shall simply use /o/.
[25] Ms has sroggā and ḥloggā. The latter, however, does not appear to be a loan, unlike spoggā (Gk *spongos* = sponge) and sroggā (Gk *surigx* = gateway). The latter is a conjectural emendation made by Merx, ad loc.
[26] In fact, Persian.
[27] It is not clear why there are two paradigms numbered 23. From a phonological point of view, this paradigm could be assimilated into no.22, but perhaps Jacob considered that brōtā and ṣlōtā had a slightly different vowel quality to spoggā and sroggā - we have signified this by using ō for this paradigm as a convenience only.
[28] The same three are repeated first without the special vowel symbols, and then with them added.
[29] The forms that belong in this paradigm are the feminines rdīptā etc. In the above list, Jacob is merely demonstrating their derivation from the masculine forms.
[30] These nouns are written both without, and then with, Jacob's /ō/ letter *in place of* the regular Syriac waw.

I. Index nominum et rerum.

II. Index syriacus, arabicus, hebraicus.

III. Index graecus.

19*